ear	Gross Domestic Product in 1987 Dollars (billions)	Personal Consumption Expenditures in 1987 Dollars (billions)	Government Purchases in 1987 Dollars (billions)	Gross Private Domestic Investment in 1987 Dollars (billions)	Exports in 1987 Dollars (billions)	Imports in 1987 Dollars (billions)	Treasury Bill Interest Rate	U.S. Dollar (1973 = 100)	Federal Budget Surplus (+) or Deficit (−) (billions)	Money Supply (December) (billions) M_1	M_2
959	1,931.3	1,178.9	477.8	296.4	73.8	95.6	3.405	—	−2.6	140.0	297.8
960	1,973.2	1,210.8	479.2	290.8	88.4	96.1	2.928	—	3.5	140.7	312.4
961	2,025.6	1,238.4	503.3	289.4	89.9	95.3	2.378	—	−2.6	145.2	335.5
962	2,129.8	1,293.3	525.9	321.2	95.0	105.5	2.778	—	−3.4	147.9	362.7
963	2,218.0	1,341.9	538.7	343.3	101.8	107.7	3.157	—	1.1	153.4	393.3
964	2,343.3	1,417.2	551.7	371.8	115.4	112.9	3.549	—	−2.6	160.4	424.8
965	2,473.5	1,497.0	569.9	413.0	118.1	124.5	3.954	—	1.3	167.9	459.4
966	2,622.3	1,573.8	628.5	438.0	125.7	143.7	4.881	—	−1.4	172.1	480.0
967	2,690.3	1,622.4	673.0	418.6	130.0	153.7	4.321	120.0	−12.7	183.3	524.4
968	2,801.0	1,707.5	691.0	440.1	140.2	177.7	5.339	122.1	−4.7	197.5	566.4
969	2,877.1	1,771.2	686.1	461.3	147.8	189.2	6.677	122.4	8.5	204.0	589.6
970	2,875.8	1,813.5	667.8	429.7	161.3	196.4	6.458	121.1	−13.3	214.5	628.1
971	2,965.1	1,873.7	655.8	481.5	161.9	207.8	4.348	117.8	−21.7	228.4	712.7
972	3,107.1	1,978.4	653.0	532.2	173.7	230.2	4.071	109.1	−17.3	249.3	805.2
973	3,268.6	2,066.7	644.2	591.7	210.3	244.4	7.041	99.1	−6.6	262.9	861.0
974	3,248.1	2,053.8	655.4	543.0	234.4	238.4	7.886	101.4	−11.6	274.4	908.6
975	3,221.7	2,097.5	663.5	437.6	232.9	209.8	5.838	98.5	−69.4	287.6	1,023.3
976	3,380.8	2,207.3	659.2	520.6	243.4	249.7	4.989	105.7	−52.9	306.4	1,163.7
977	3,533.2	2,296.6	664.1	600.4	246.9	274.7	5.265	103.4	−42.4	331.3	1,286.7
978	3,703.5	2,391.8	677.0	664.6	270.2	300.1	7.221	92.4	−28.1	358.4	1,389.0
979	3,796.8	2,448.4	689.3	669.7	293.5	304.1	10.041	88.1	−15.7	382.8	1,497.1
980	3,776.3	2,447.1	704.2	594.4	320.5	289.9	11.506	87.4	−60.1	408.8	1,629.8
981	3,843.1	2,476.9	713.2	631.1	326.1	304.1	14.029	103.4	−58.8	436.4	1,793.3
982	3,760.3	2,503.7	723.6	540.5	296.7	304.1	10.686	116.6	−135.5	474.4	1,952.9
983	3,906.6	2,619.4	743.8	599.5	285.9	342.1	8.63	125.3	−180.1	521.2	2,186.3
984	4,148.5	2,746.1	766.9	757.5	305.7	427.7	9.58	138.2	−166.9	552.2	2,374.7
985	4,279.8	2,865.8	813.4	745.9	309.2	454.6	7.48	143.0	−181.4	619.9	2,569.7
986	4,404.5	2,969.1	855.4	735.1	329.6	484.7	5.98	112.2	−201.0	724.3	2,811.6
987	4,540.0	3,052.2	881.5	749.3	364.0	507.1	5.82	96.9	−151.8	749.7	2,910.1
988	4,718.6	3,162.4	886.8	773.4	421.6	525.7	6.69	92.7	−136.6	786.4	3,069.9
989	4,836.9	3,223.1	900.4	789.2	469.2	544.9	8.12	98.6	−124.2	793.6	3,223.1
990	4,884.9	3,262.6	929.1	744.5	505.7	557.0	7.51	89.1	−165.3	825.4	3,327.8
991	4,848.4	3,256.7	936.7	672.6	539.6	557.2	5.42	89.8	−200.7	896.7	3,425.4

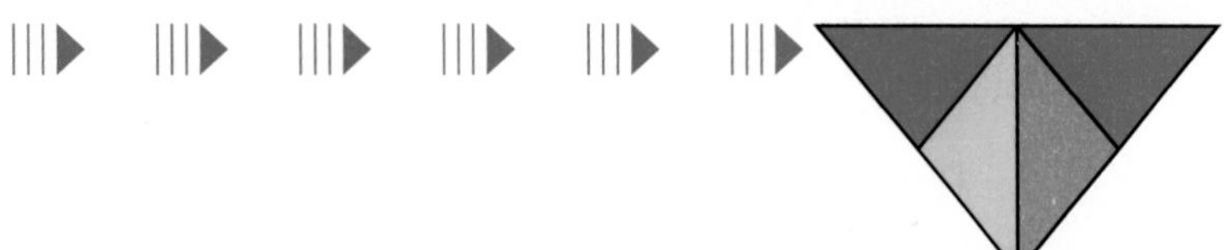

DETAILED CONTENTS

PART II Macroeconomic Theory 98

CHAPTER 6 Macroeconomic Concepts 100

CHAPTER 7 Measuring Gross Domestic Product 119

CHAPTER 14 Money, Prices, and Interest 241

CHAPTER 15 Commercial Banking and the Federal Reserve 257

CHAPTER 16 Monetary Policy 277

CHAPTER 20 Stabilizing the Business Cycle 357

CHAPTER 21 Rational Expectations 378

PART III The World Economy 394

CHAPTER 22 Productivity, Growth, and Development 396

CHAPTER 23 International Trade and Comparative Advantage 416

CHAPTER 24 Protection and Free Trade 431

CHAPTER 25 The International Monetary System 450

PART IV Product Markets 472

CHAPTER 26 Elasticity of Demand and Supply 474

CHAPTER 27 Demand and Utility 494

APPENDIX 27A Indifference Curves 508

CHAPTER 28 Business Organization, Corporate Finance, and Financial Markets 516

CHAPTER 34 Antitrust Law and Regulation 651

CHAPTER 35 The Economics of Information 671

PART V Factor Markets 692

CHAPTER 36 Factor Markets 694

CHAPTER 37 Labor Markets 712

CHAPTER 38 Labor Unions 733

CHAPTER 39 Interest, Rent, and Profit 752

CHAPTER 40 Income Distribution and Poverty 771

PART VI Microeconomic Issues 794

CHAPTER 41 Market Failure, the Environment, and Exhaustible Resources 796

TO THE INSTRUCTOR

This fifth edition of *Principles of Economics* preserves the best qualities of the previous editions while adding new material that reflects the dynamic changes in the field of economics. From the first edition, we have adhered to two ideas: first, that the exciting topics of modern economics—rational expectations, information economics, search theory, real business cycles—belong in an introductory course in economics, and second, that economics is about the real world and, therefore, economic principles are best illustrated using real-world examples. The real-world approach that we introduced has since become an integral part of all successful principles texts. In the fifth edition, we have added over 140 new real-world examples.

This fifth edition is the most significant revision ever of *Principles of Economics*. Why was it necessary to make such extensive changes? First, the collapse of socialism and the subsequent painful transition of the former socialist economies to market economies have significant implications for an increasingly interdependent world economy. Second, it is critical that the text reflect the continuing search for consensus in macroeconomics. In the 1990s the level of consensus is greater than it was throughout the 1980s. The acceptance of the natural rate of unemployment as the value for Keynes's full employment; the importance of search theory as one explanation for unemployment; and the realization of inflationary expectations are all examples of this growing consensus. Third, the increasing reliance on microeconomic analysis to explain macroeconomic behavior has been the most significant development in macroeconomics. A fourth change has been the shift in the focus of Keynesian economics from depression economics to the rigidities and imperfections that deflect modern economies from full employment.

New to This Edition

With the coverage of such crucial developments, the fifth edition of *Principles of Economics* continues to be the most modern and up-to-date text on the market. We discuss both traditional and modern topics at a level accessible to the reader. New to the fifth edition are:

Macroeconomics

- A new macroeconomics sequence. We begin by introducing the business cycle, unemployment, inflation, and growth—the four major issues of modern macroeconomics. We then introduce aggregate supply and aggregate demand before examining Keynes's income/expenditure model and multiplier analysis. This sequence provides flexibility, enabling instructors to teach the macro core to fit their own syllabus, omitting coverage of multipliers and the income/expenditure model if desired.
- An entirely new chapter (8) on the microeconomic foundations of macroeconomics: the factors that cause people to spend and to save, why people hold money, and how businesses invest. This chapter shows clearly that to understand modern macroeconomics we must first understand the behavior of individuals and firms in the marketplace.
- Chapter 7 on national income accounting captures the U.S. government's historic decision to change its measure of total output from gross national product to gross domestic product. GDP is used throughout the text.
- Updated analysis of bank reform and the cause of recent bank failures in Chapter 15.

- Exploration of the policy problems caused by the 1990–1992 recession, including analysis of recent changes in Fed behavior (in Chapter 16) and the impact of the recession on the 1992 presidential campaign (in Chapter 12).
- Separate chapters on fiscal policy and public debt. The fiscal policy chapter (12) discusses fiscal policy and economic growth and presents the case against fine tuning. The chapter on public debt (13) covers the Ricardian Equivalence Theorem, the twin deficits, and the latest material on deficit reduction.
- The most modern coverage of unemployment theory, including search theory and implicit contracting, in Chapter 18.
- Discussion of real business cycle theory and examination of major questions about the measurement of GDP fluctuations (Chapter 20).
- The most modern coverage of rational expectations (Chapter 21), with market-clearing models and a discussion of the public's ability to predict inflation and macroeconomic policy.
- A more current discussion of classical economics in Chapter 10, broadening the view to include economic growth, amplification of Say's Law, and a more realistic version of the simple quantity theory of money.

Microeconomics

- A new chapter (4) discussing the collapse of socialism and why capitalism has outperformed socialism. The chapter describes the Soviet administrative-command economy, its internal contradictions, and the painful transition from a socialist economy to a market economy.
- An updated chapter (35) on the economics of information. Information theory is applied to problems of unemployment, the savings and loan crisis, and the health care crisis.
- Updated discussion of monopoly rent seeking in Chapter 32, based upon the most recent research. New examples on predatory pricing, collusive behavior, and other forms of strategic behavior.
- Inclusion of the latest research on environmental issues such as global warming, recycling, acid rain, and nonrenewable resources (Chapter 41).
- Coverage of the price system and frictions—the teachings of 1991 Nobel Laureate Ronald Coase in Chapter 3.
- New information on actual demand and supply elasticities (Chapter 26).
- Discussion of production functions before cost curves in Chapter 29 to provide a more logical introduction to cost curves.
- Leveraged buyouts as an example of the "greed" of the 1980s (Chapter 28).
- The growth of world capital markets (Chapter 28).
- An updated evaluation of deregulation in Chapter 34.
- The latest information on changes in the U.S. distribution of income and international comparisons of income distributions in Chapter 40.
- Chapter 43 on public choice summarizes the views of modern public-choice theorists in an easy-to-understand format.
- The introduction of Cournot oligopoly at a simple level (Chapter 33).

The Global Economy. This fifth edition of *Principles of Economics* clearly reflects the globalization of the world economy. Many economic experiences are common to all countries, and many economic conditions describe fundamental human behavior irrespective of international boundaries. We must also remember, however, that there is considerable diversity in world economic experience.

Principles of Economics deals with the world economy in a number of ways. First, a new chapter (4) explores the economics of capitalism and socialism and the reasons for the apparent failure of the socialist economic system. Second, the text makes extensive use of examples from other countries to illustrate the economic theories and principles imparted in each chapter. We make a special effort to show when the U.S. experience is common to other countries and when it differs. Third, we devote three separate chapters to the global economy (23–25)—to the fundamental forces that cause economies to trade, to the welfare losses caused by artificial restrictions on the global economy, and to the financial arrangements required for conducting international trade. The growing internationalization of the world economy is further reflected in "international perspective" sections throughout the text. We wish to emphasize that this is not a text on the U.S. economy; it is a text on the global economy. The following is a partial list of examples that cover the global economy:

- The Unannounced Reform: China's Dying State Sector. (Chapter 4)
- Popular Attitudes Towards Free Markets: Are Americans and Soviets Different? (Chapter 4)
- The German Approach to Economic Policy. (Chapter 10)
- Creating a Commercial Banking System: Russian Banks. (Chapter 15)
- Canada: Multiple Expansion and Banking Concentration. (Chapter 15)
- Unemployment and Jobless Benefits in Europe. (Chapter 18)
- Productivity as a Source of Growth: World Experience. (Chapter 22)
- The German Telephone Monopoly. (Chapter 34)
- Labor Versus Leisure in Germany and Japan. (Chapter 37)

Use of Color. The fifth edition introduces the use of four colors to the text. Color is used strategically to enhance the many tables, charts, and graphs, and to highlight the various pedagogical devices designed to aid student understanding. For example, in graphs, supply curves are always orange and demand curves are always blue. This use of color helps students to identify key terms and concepts and facilitates accurate interpretation of data.

Organization

Principles of Economics is divided into six parts. Part I (Chapters 1–5) introduces the basic concepts of economics that must be learned before one can proceed to macroeconomics or microeconomics proper. Four of the five chapters contain the standard topics of economic methodology, scarcity, opportunity costs, the production possibilities frontier, the law of diminishing returns, the law of comparative advantage, the workings of the price system, and the laws of supply and demand. The student is also introduced to the concepts of relative prices and marginal decision making, which are critical topics in both microeconomics and macroeconomics. An appendix to Chapter 1 explains how to read graphs and avoid distortion pitfalls. A fifth chapter, devoted to the collapse of communism and the transition to market economies, explores recent developments in the alternative to the market model, so that students can understand what might be expected in these "economic laboratories" and can immediately apply the basic concepts. From Part I, the instructor can move either to macroeconomics (Chapters 6–25) or to microeconomics (Chapters 26–43).

The development of macroeconomic theory begins in Part II with a discussion of the basic concepts of inflation, unemployment, and the business cycle (Chapter 6) and the basic principles of national income accounting (Chapter 7). Chapter 8 then introduces macroeconomic behavior—investment, consumption, and saving.

Chapter 9 introduces aggregate supply and aggregate demand, the basic analytical tools of modern macroeconomics. This early introduction provides flexibility for instructors who do not want to cover in great detail the ensuing Keynesian material. Chapter 10 contrasts the Keynesian and classical views of macroeconomics. Chapter 11 presents Keynes's income/expenditure model and multipliers. Chapters 12 and 13 focus on fiscal policy and national debt.

The next three chapters consider the role of money in the economy. Chapter 14 discusses the relationship between money, prices, and interest rates. Chapter 15 considers the definition of money and the determinants of the money supply. Chapter 16 discusses monetary policy—how the Federal Reserve Board can control the supply of money.

Chapters 17, 18, and 19 discuss the problems of inflation, unemployment, and stagflation (the combination of high inflation and high unemployment). These chapters use modern theories of monetary economics, job search, and inflationary expectations to explain these occurrences.

Chapter 20 discusses stabilization and raises the fundamental issue of whether government authorities can or should control the business cycle. The chapter covers real business cycle theory and presents the cases for and against policy activism.

Chapter 21 discusses rational expectations, or the new classical macroeconomics. It shows how attempts to anticipate macroeconomic policy can make it difficult for policymakers to control the business cycle.

Part III examines the world economy by first analyzing the determinants of economic growth and the problems of economic development (Chapter 22) and then moving to the discussion of international economics in Chapters 23–25. Chapter 23 shows how the law of comparative advantage applies on an international scale. Chapter 24 looks at the pros and cons of protection. Chapter 25 examines international monetary mechanisms and the balance of payments.

Part IV begins the microeconomics core with 10 chapters on the product market (Chapters 26–35). Chapter 26 covers price elasticities of demand and supply as well as income and cross-price elasticities of demand. Chapter 27 deals with demand and utility (with an appendix on indifference curves). Business organization, corporate finance, and financial markets are discussed in Chapter 28, and short-run and long-run costs are explained in Chapter 29 (with an appendix on equal-output curves, or isoquants). The standard market models of perfect competition, monpoly and monopolistic competition, and oligopoly, are covered in Chapters 30–33, with a special chapter (32) devoted to a comparison of monopoly and competition. Chapter 34 discusses relations between government and business, particularly government regulation and antitrust law, and Chapter 35 introduces the role of information costs.

Factor markets are taught as a five-chapter unit in Part V (Chapters 36–40). Chapter 36 gives a theoretical overview of the workings of factor markets, and Chapters 37 and 39 focus on specific factor markets. Chapter 38 considers the role of labor unions in an economy, and Chapter 40 examines the determinants of income distribution and poverty.

Microeconomic issues are the focus of Part VI (Chapters 41–43). Chapter 41 explains the economics of exhaustible resources and of market failure (public goods and externalities). Chapter 42 focuses on public finance, in particular of issues of taxation. Chapter 43 discusses modern theories of public choice.

Suggestions for Course Planning

This book is intended for the two-semester sequence in microeconomics and macroeconomics that is traditionally taught as a first- or second-year college course. The book is available in both a combined hardbound volume and micro/macro split softbound volumes. The combined volume can also be used for an intensive one-semester course that covers both microeconomics and macroeconomics by selecting only core chapters (as suggested below). Because the book was written with the micro/macro splits in mind, even the instructor who is using the combined volume can teach either macro or micro first. Instructors who choose to drop the Keynesian income/expenditure model and use only aggregate supply and demand need only drop Chapter 11.

Suggested Outline for an Intensive One-Semester Course (32 chapters)

Introduction:

1. The Nature of Economics
2. The Economic Problem
3. The Price System
5. Supply and Demand

Macroeconomics:

6. Macroeconomic Concepts
7. Measuring Gross Domestic Product
8. Macroeconomic Behavior
9. Aggregate Demand and Supply
10. Classical and Keynesian Macroeconomics
11. Keynesian Economics: The Multiplier
12. Fiscal Policy
14. Money, Prices, and Interest

15. Commercial Banking and the Federal Reserve
16. Monetary Policy
17. Inflation
18. Unemployment
19. The Phillips Curve: Inflation and Unemployment
20. Stabilizing the Business Cycle

Microeconomics:

26. Elasticity of Demand and Supply
27. Demand and Utility
28. Business Organization, Corporate Finance, and Financial Markets
29. Productivity and Costs
30. Perfect Competition
31. Monopoly and Monopolistic Competition
33. Oligopoly
34. Antitrust Law and Regulation
35. The Economics of Information
36. Factor Markets
37. Labor Markets
39. Interest, Rent, and Profit
40. Income Distribution and Poverty
41. Market Failure, the Environment, and Exhaustible Resources

Suggested Outline for an Intensive One-Quarter Course (22 chapters)

Introduction:

1. The Nature of Economics
2. The Economic Problem
3. The Price System
5. Supply and Demand

Macroeconomics:

6. Macroeconomic Concepts
8. Macroeconomic Behavior
9. Aggregate Demand and Supply
10. Classical and Keynesian Macroeconomics
12. Fiscal Policy
14. Money, Prices, and Interest
15. Commercial Banking and the Federal Reserve
16. Monetary Policy
19. The Phillips Curve: Inflation and Unemployment
20. Stabilizing the Business Cycle

Microeconomics:

26. Elasticity of Demand and Supply
27. Demand and Utility
28. Business Organization, Corporate Finance, and Financial Markets
29. Productivity and Costs
30. Perfect Competition
36. Factor Markets
37. Labor Markets
39. Interest, Rent, and Profit

Instructors who want a course with a focus on growth and development should incorporate Chapter 22 on productivity, growth, and development. Instructors who want a course with a greater focus on international economics should incorporate Chapter 4 on capitalism and socialism and Chapters 23–25 on international trade and comparative advantage, protection and free trade, and the international monetary system.

Instructors who want a one-semester course that has a heavier microeconomic emphasis can include the core macro chapters in the Quarter Course list and the micro chapters from the Semester Course list. Those who desire a course with a heavier macroeconomic emphasis can include the micro chapters from the Quarter Course list and the macro chapters from the Semester Course list.

Supplements

This book has a complete package of supplements, which includes an *Instructor's Manual, Study Guide,* computer software, *Test Bank, Four-Color Transparencies,* computerized *Test Bank,* the *HarperCollins Economics Laser Disc,* and the *HarperCollins Economics Videos.*

The *Instructor's Manual* was revised by Henry Thompson of Auburn University. It supplies the instructor with many teaching tools, including additional numerical examples and real-world illustrations not contained in the text. A chapter outline gives a brief overview of the material in the chapter to assist the instructor in preparing lecture outlines and in seeing the logical development of the chapter. Special-approaches sections tell the instructor how this chapter is different from corresponding chapters in other textbooks and explain why a topic was treated differently in this text or why an entirely new topic not covered by other texts was introduced in this chapter. Optional-material sections give the instructor a ranking of priorities for the topics in the chapter and enable the instructor to trim the size of each chapter (if necessary). Each chapter also includes key points to learn, teaching hints, special projects, bad habits to unlearn, additional essay questions, answers to the end-of-chapter "Questions and Problems," and answers to the "Review Quizzes" that are given in the *Study Guide.*

The *Study Guide* was written by Jeffrey Parker of Reed College and John Vahaly of the University of Louisville. The analytical nature of the *Study Guide* should challenge the student and help him or her to better prepare for exams. The *Study Guide* supplements the text by providing summaries of critical concepts and by taking the student step by step through a review of each key graph and equation presented in the text. It contains multiple-choice and true/false questions and, unlike other study guides, not only lists the answers but also gives *explanations for the answers.* In addition to objective questions, each chapter of the *Study Guide* also contains analytical problems and essay questions. Again, the *Study Guide* provides not only the answers to the questions, but also the step-by-step process for arriving at the answers. At the back of the *Study Guide* are "Review Quizzes" that contain multiple-choice questions for each chapter; answers are found in the *Instructor's Manual,* so that these quizzes can be used by the instructor as homework or as chapter quizzes.

TARGET computer software, written by Jeffrey Parker and available on floppy disks for the IBM-PC, is an interactive tutorial. It breaks key concepts into building blocks, provides graphs and numerous questions, and contains a diagnostic final exam for each key concept covered.

The *Test Bank,* prepared by Brandt Stevens of B. K. Stevens Consulting, contains 3000 new and revised multiple-choice questions, most of which have already been class tested. For each chapter in the text, the *Test Bank* contains 4 different tests (coded A, B, C, or D). Whether the instructor is trying to compose a one-chapter quiz or a 23-chapter final exam, that instructor can choose from among the questions in the *Test Bank,* the questions in the "Review Quizzes" at the back of the *Study Guide,* or the additional essay questions in the *Instructor's Manual.* The *Test Bank* is available on perforated paper in book form and on the TestMaster computerized testing system.

Four-Color Transparencies are available for 103 key figures and tables.

The *HarperCollins Economics Laser Disc* allows students to call up nearly a thousand images at the touch of a button. It provides video clips and many animated graphics (e.g., shifting demand and supply curves) to highlight economic principles.

The *HarperCollins Economics Videos* are 5–15 minute lecture starters arranged by economic topic. They include special topics pertinent to key regions of the United States.

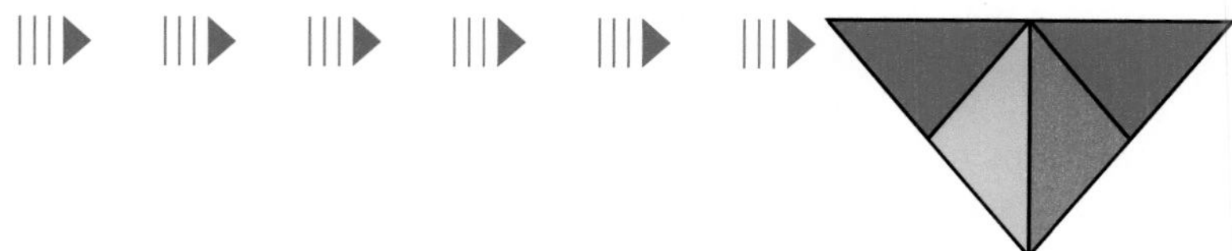

TO THE STUDENT

Recent national and world events demonstrate that an understanding of economics is necessary as we move into the twenty-first century. The recession of the early 1990s has taught us again that the economy remains subject to the ups and downs of the business cycle. These very fluctuations determine whether a good job awaits you after graduation or whether your future includes unemployment benefits or settling for a position that is less desirable than the one you had hoped for. The collapse of the communist economic system has altered the world in a fundamental and irreversible way. The global economy has taught us that our economic lives and fortunes are intertwined with those of people around the world. Higher interest rates in Germany can affect the number of jobs in the United States. Corporate decisions made in board rooms in Japan, Korea, and Brazil determine which nations are on the economic rise.

This text teaches you what you need to know about modern economics. It presents the latest findings of prominent economists, and it teaches you how to "think like an economist." Economics is not an easy subject; there is too much to learn and too little time in which to learn it. Therefore, we would like to present some guidelines for using this text.

Economics cannot be mastered through memorization. Economics relies on economic theories to explain real-world occurrences—for instance, why people tend to buy less when prices rise or why increased government spending may reduce unemployment. An economic theory is a logical explanation of why the facts fit together in a particular way. If the theory were not logical, or if the theory failed to be confirmed by real-world facts, it would be readily discarded by economists.

The successful student will learn that economics is built upon a number of fairly simple and easy-to-understand propositions. These propositions and assumptions—that businesses seek to maximize profits or that consumers base their expenditure decisions on disposable income, for example—form the building blocks upon which economics is based. These propositions are typically little more than common sense and should not intimidate the student. If a major building block is missing, however, the whole structure can fall apart. To prevent the student from overlooking or forgetting a critical building block, we frequently engage in pedagogical review. In other words, when a new proposition is added to a theoretical structure, the underlying propositions are briefly reviewed.

Another factor that can make economics difficult for the student is that economics—like other academic disciplines—has its own specific vocabulary. Unlike the physical sciences, however, where the student may encounter a certain term for the first time, much of the vocabulary of economics—terms such as *efficiency, capital, stock,* and *unemployment*—has a common usage that is already familiar to the student. Economists, however, use the vocabulary of economics in a very exact way, so that the economic usage of a term often differs from the common usage. In this book, each key term appears in boldface type when it is first discussed. Immediately following the paragraph where the term first appears in boldface type, the economic definition of the term is set off in a blue-shaded box. At the end of each chapter is a list of all the key terms that have been boldfaced and formally defined in that chapter; a glossary at the end of the book contains all the definitions of key terms and gives the number of the chapter in which each term was defined.

What we call the modern developments of economics are simply new attempts to explain in a logical manner how the facts bind together. Modern developments have occurred because of the realization that established theories were not doing a good job of explaining the world around us. Fortunately, the major building blocks of modern theory—that people attempt to anticipate the future, that rising prices motivate wealth holders to spend less, that people and businesses gather information and make decisions in a rational manner—rely on common-sense logic.

Economics is valuable only if it explains the real world. Economics should be able to answer very specific questions such as: Why are there three major domestic producers of automobiles and hundreds or even thousands of producers of textiles? Why is there a positive association between the growth of the money supply and inflation? Why does the United States export computer software and corn to the rest of the world? Why do restaurants rope off space during less busy hours? If Iowa land is the best land for growing corn, why is corn also grown in Texas while some land stands idle in Iowa? Why do interest rates rise when people expect the inflation rate to increase? What is the impact of the well-publicized government deficit? Why does a rise in interest rates in Germany affect employment in the United States? The successful student will be able to apply the knowledge he or she gains of real-world economic behavior to explain any number of events that have already occurred or are yet to occur.

In writing this book, we have made a conscious effort to present arguments and evidence on both sides of every economic controversy. We attempt to make a case for each distinct viewpoint, even if it would be more interesting and less complicated to come out strongly in one camp. Although we are aware of our own free-market bias, we believe it is best to allow the student to keep an open mind at this very early stage in the study of economics.

This book contains a number of important learning aids.

1. The *Chapter Insight* that precedes each chapter provides a brief overview of the important points to be learned in that chapter.
2. *Definitions* are set off in blue-shaded boxes following the paragraphs in which key terms are introduced.
3. *Key Ideas*—important economic principles or conclusions—are set off in blue-shaded boxes.
4. *Boxed Examples* allow the student to appreciate how economic concepts apply in real-world settings without disrupting the flow of the text. They supplement the numerous examples already found in the text discussions.
5. A *Summary* of the main points of each chapter is found at the end of each chapter.
6. *Key Terms* that were defined in the chapter are listed at the end of each chapter.
7. *Questions and Problems* that test the reader's understanding of the chapter follow each chapter.
8. *Suggested Readings* are listed for each chapter for the student who wishes to pursue an interesting topic even further.
9. A *Glossary*—containing definitions of all key terms defined in blue-shaded boxes in chapters and listed in chapter "Key Terms" sections—appears at the end of the book. Each entry contains the complete economic definition as well as the number of the chapter where the term was first defined.
10. A thorough *Index* catalogs the names, concepts, terms, and topics covered in the book.
11. Statistical data on the major economic variables are found on the front and back inside covers for easy reference.

In addition to these text learning aids, there are several nontext aids to make this course easier. The *Study Guide* provides extensive review of key concepts and an abundance of drill questions and challenging problems. The *Target* computer software provides interactive review with diagnostic features to pinpoint trouble spots.

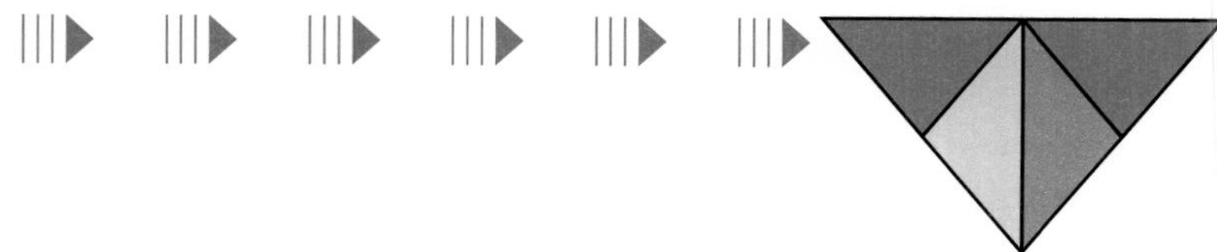

ACKNOWLEDGMENTS

We are deeply indebted to our colleagues at the University of Houston who had to bear with us in the writing of this book. John Antel, Richard Bean, Joel Sailors, Thomas DeGregori, Gerald Dwyer, Paul Evans, Louis Stern, Thomas Mayor, Irwin Collier, Janet Kohlhase, and David Papell gave their time freely on an incredible number of pedagogical points in the teaching of elementary economics. Thanks are also extended to Daniel Y. Lee of Shippensburg University, Steven Rappaport of DeAnza College, Bill Reid of the University of Richmond, and Ed Coen (the Director of Undergraduate Studies at the University of Minnesota) for their valuable comments. To Gary Smith of Pomona College, Calvin Siebert of the University of Iowa, and Allan Meltzer of Carnegie-Mellon University, we are particularly grateful for sharing with us their vast knowledge of macroeconomic issues.

It is impossible to express the depth of our appreciation for the suggestions and contributions of numerous colleagues across the country who reviewed this and previous editions:

David Abel	Mankato State University
Jack Adams	University of Arkansas (Little Rock)
Mark Aldrich	Smith College
Ken Alexander	Michigan Technical University
Susan Alexander	College of St. Thomas
Richard G. Anderson	Ohio State University
Richard K. Anderson	Texas A & M University
Ian Bain	University of Minnesota
King Banaian	St. Cloud State University
A. K. Barakeh	University of South Alabama
George Bittlingmayer	University of Michigan
Robert Borengasser	St. Mary's College
Ronald Brandolini	Valencia Community College
Wallace Broome	Rhode Island Junior College
Pamela J. Brown	California State University, Northridge
James Burnell	College of Wooster
Louis Cain	Loyola University of Chicago
Anthony Campolo	Columbus Technical Institute
Than Van Cao	Eastern Montana College
Kathleen A. Carroll	University of Maryland, Baltimore County
Shirley Cassing	University of Pittsburgh
Harold Christenson	Centenary College of Louisiana
Robert E. Christiansen	Colby College
Richard Clarke	University of Wisconsin, Madison
John Conant	Indiana State University
Barbara J. Craig	Oberlin College
Jim Davis	Golden Gate University
Larry De Brock	University of Illinois, Urbana

David Denslow	University of Florida
John Devereux	University of Miami (Florida)
Tim Deyak	Louisiana State University, Baton Rouge
James Dunlevy	University of Miami (of Ohio)
Mary E. Edwards	St. Cloud State University
Anne Eicke	Illinois State University (Normal)
Charles J. Ellard	The University of Texas, Pan American
Herb Elliott	Allan Hancock College
Randy Ellis	Boston University
Andrew W. Foshee	McNeese State University
Ralph Fowler	Diablo Valley College
Dan Friedman	University of California, Los Angeles (UCLA)
Joe Fuhrig	Golden Gate University
Janet Furman	Tulane University
Charles Gallagher	Virginia Commonwealth University
Dan Gallagher	St. Cloud State University
Eugene Gendel	Lafayette College
Kathie Gilbert	Mississippi State University
Lynn Gillette	Northeast Missouri State University
J. Robert Gillette	Texas A & M University
Debra Glassman	University of Washington
Philip Grossman	Wayne State University
Ronald Gunderson	Northern Arizona University
David R. Hakes	University of Missouri, St. Louis
Barbara Haney Martinez	University of Alaska, Fairbanks
Charles E. Hegji	Auburn University at Montgomery
Ann Hendricks	Tufts University
David J. Hoaas	Centenary College of Louisiana
Thomas K. Holmstrom	Northern Michigan University
Edward Howe	Siena College
Todd L. Idson	University of Miami (Florida)
S. Hussain Ali Jafri	Tarleton State University
James Johannes	Michigan State University
James Kahn	State University of New York, Binghamton
Yoonbai Kim	Southern Illinois University
Chris Klisz	Wayne State University
Byung Lee	Howard University
Daniel Y. Lee	Shippensburg University
Jim Lee	Fort Hays State University
Richard Lotspeich	Indiana State University
Robert Lucas	University of Chicago
Ron Luchessi	American River College
Roger Mack	DeAnza College
Michael Magura	University of Toledo
Allan Mandelstamm	Virginia Polytechnic Institute
Don Mar	San Francisco State University
Jay Marchand	University of Mississippi
Ben Matta	New Mexico State University
James F. McCarley	Albion College
Jerome L. McElroy	St. Mary's College
Jim McKinsey	Northeastern University

Larry T. McRae	Appalachian State University
Michael Meurer	Duke University
Robert Milbrath	Catholic University of America
Masoud Moghaddam	St. Cloud State University
W. Douglas Morgan	University of California, Santa Barbara
Kathryn A. Nantz	Fairfield University
Clark Nardinelli	Clemson University
Norman Obst	Michigan State University
John Pisciotta	Baylor University
Dennis Placone	Clemson University
John Pomery	Purdue University
Marin Pond	Purdue University
Hollis F. Price, Jr.	University of Miami (Florida)
Henry J. Raimondo	University of Massachusetts, Boston
Betsy Rankin	Centenary College of Louisiana
Stanley S. Reynolds	University of Arizona
Dan Richards	Tufts University
Jennifer Roback	Yale University
Malcolm Robinson	University of Cincinnati
Mark Rush	University of Florida
Elizabeth Savoca	Smith College
Robert Schmitz	Indiana University
Steven Soderlind	St. Olaf College
David Spencer	Washington State University
Mark A. Stephens	Tennessee Technological University
Brandt K. Stevens	Illinois State University
Alan Stockman	University of Rochester
Don Tailby	University of New Mexico
Michael Tannen	University of the District of Columbia
Helen Tauchen	University of North Carolina
Robert Thomas	Iowa State University
Roger Trenary	Kansas State University
George Uhimchuk	Clemson University
James M. Walker	Indiana University
Richard J. Ward	Southeastern Massachusetts University
M. Daniel Westbrook	Georgetown University
John B. White	Old Dominion University
Roberton Williams	Williams College
F. Scott Wilson	Canisius College
Laura Wolff	Southern Illinois University, Edwardsville
Gary Young	Delta State University (Mississippi)

It was again a pleasure to work with John Vahaly and Jeffrey Parker, who, in addition to preparing the *Study Guide,* contributed insightful comments on the text. Dr. Willard W. Radell provided valuable help reviewing the art program.

At HarperCollins, we are grateful for the continued support of Jack Greenman, and the encouragement and creativity of Bruce Kaplan, our sponsoring editor. We appreciate the skillful editing of Arlene Bessenoff, our developmental editor. It has been a great pleasure to work with these professionals.

Roy J. Ruffin
Paul R. Gregory

1

Basic Economic Issues

1 The Nature of Economics

CHAPTER INSIGHT

As individuals, producers, and voters in a democratic society, we must understand economics to sort out the sense from the nonsense in our economic affairs. The larger issues that economists study are important to us as well. How do economies work? Why do some perform better than others? Societies need such knowledge to choose the type of economy in which their citizens live and work, and individuals need it to make decisions affecting their livelihoods and those of their children.

Economics doesn't supply magic formulas that will help you "get rich quick," but it does teach you why some people and businesses are successful while others fail and why our economic future is difficult to predict. Economics explains why gasoline prices rise or fall, why airlines merge, why interest rates rise with inflation, why you earn more than your neighbor.

Some parts of our economic knowledge are fairly certain and other parts are uncertain. Many areas of economics are changing and remain controversial. This book will explain our present understanding of economics—both what we know and what we don't know.

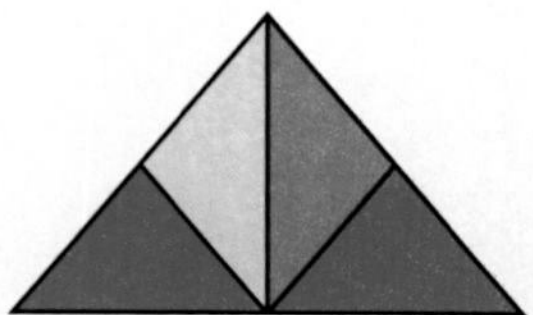

ECONOMICS: THE BASIC THEMES

The evidence of economic concerns surrounds us. Newspaper editorials fret about the value of the dollar abroad and the dangers of rising imports and trade deficits. Politicians and pundits warn of ruinous federal deficits.

Sometimes change within an economy is gradual and scarcely noticeable. At other times, it is dramatic. The past two decades are shaping up as an era of momentous change. In 1980, some one-third of the world's population lived in communist countries. By the end of the twentieth century, far fewer people will live in such economies. Events have shown that economies of the type pioneered in the former Soviet Union operate less efficiently and provide lower standards of living than their capitalist counterparts. As the communist societies came to recognize this fact, they began the difficult process of changing the way their economies work. The Berlin Wall was torn down, and the communist East German economy was integrated into that of a united Germany. The nations of Eastern Europe and what was once the Soviet Union moved away from public ownership and government dictation of economic actions to private ownership and private decision making.

Although the collapse of Communism captured the headlines of the 1980s and 1990s, changes in other economic spheres have been no less striking. The remaining trade barriers within Europe were removed in 1992, and goods can now move from the Netherlands to France as easily as they move from Illinois to Washington. Decisive steps have been taken to unite Canada, the United States, and Mexico in a common market. Overall, we live in a world economy in which goods, people, and capital flow freely across national borders. The car you drive might be built in Korea; your neighbor might work for British Petroleum; and your business loan could be from a Canadian bank.

People everywhere strive to improve their standard of living; they worry about inflation, unemployment, and poverty as they go about the ordinary business of earning a living and making ends meet. They are confronted with difficult choices: when to buy a home, whether to change jobs, whether to attend college, whether to buy stocks or bonds. The study of economics offers help in dealing with these questions and concerns.

> **Economics** studies how people choose to use their limited resources (land, labor, and capital goods) to produce, exchange, and consume goods and services.

This definition of economics touches on the basic themes of economic science.

Scarcity

If there were no scarcity, there would be no need to study economics. Scarcity is present when the virtually unlimited wants of a society are greater than its economy can meet. We will define this concept more formally in Chapter 2. The existence of scarcity does not imply that most people are poor or that their basic needs are not being met. Scarcity exists simply because it is human nature for people to want more than they can have. If what we want to buy exceeds our income, we must make choices.

Choice

Choice and scarcity go together. Everyone must make *trade-offs*. To have more of one thing, we must have less of another. An individual must choose between taking a job and pursuing a college education, between saving and consuming, between going to a movie and eating out. Businesses must decide where to purchase supplies, which products to offer on the market, how much labor to hire, and whether to build new plants. Nations must choose between more defense and more spending for public education; they must decide whether to grant tax reductions to businesses or individuals; and they must decide how much freedom their citizens should have to buy or sell goods in foreign countries.

Specialization

Specialization is the tendency of participants in the economy (people, businesses, countries) to focus their activity on tasks to which they are particularly suited: Some people specialize in medicine, others in law. Saudi Arabia specializes in oil production, General Motors in automobile production, Lockheed in military hardware, the economics professor in teaching economics.

The principal message of Adam Smith, the founder of modern economics, in his 1776 mas-

EXAMPLE 1 Specialization and the Pin Factory

Economic science seeks to explain the facts of economic life. Perhaps the most basic question is why some people and countries are rich while others are poor. Adam Smith's key insight was that people and countries that effectively specialize will be wealthy.

In his classic *Wealth of Nations,* Adam Smith used the pin factory to illustrate the benefits of specialization. In his day (the late eighteenth century), pins were manufactured through a large number of separate operations. Then (and now) pin making consisted of (1) drawing wire, (2) straightening, (3) pointing, (4) twisting, (5) cutting heads and heading the wire, (6) tinning and whitening, and (7) papering and packaging. The major advantages of specialization were achieved by separating pin production into many operations: One set of workers would do the straightening, another the pointing, another the twisting, another the cutting of heads, and so on.

According to Adam Smith's calculations, the average specialized worker could produce 5000 pins a day (the number of pins per day divided by the number of workers in the pin factory). If each person worked alone, only a few pins would be produced per worker. The specialized worker, in this case, could produce almost 1000 times more wealth than the unspecialized worker.

Source: Clifford Pratten, "The Manufacture of Pins," *Journal of Economic Literature* 18, 1(March 1980): 93–96.

terpiece, *The Wealth of Nations,* was that specialization creates wealth. Without specialization, we could not enjoy the high living standards that many of us take for granted. In Smith's words, "The greatest improvement in the productive powers of labor... seems to have been the effects of the division of labor."[1] *Division of labor* was Adam Smith's expression for specialization. (See Example 1.)

Exchange

Exchange complements specialization by permitting individuals to trade the goods in which they specialize for those that others produce. In Smith's words, specialization "is the necessary... consequence of a certain propensity in human nature: the propensity to truck, barter and exchange one thing for another."[2] Without exchange, specialization would be of no benefit because specialized producers cannot meet their own consumption needs from their own production.

Exchange is all around us. We exchange our specialized labor services for money; then we exchange money for a huge variety of goods. America exchanges its wheat for TV sets made in Japan. Within a business, different departments exchange skills in engineering, purchasing, and marketing to produce and sell the firm's output. A travel agency exchanges its ability to market group tours for discounted airline tickets. A foreign-car manufacturer agrees to supply fuel-efficient engines to an American auto manufacturer in return for marketing and repair outlets.

MARGINAL ANALYSIS

The economy is just people making decisions about the ordinary business of making a living and spending their money. Economists study how these decisions are made and analyze their implications. Because individuals are the main actors of economics, the student of economics has an enormous advantage over the struggling physics student, who cannot ask, "What would I do if I were a molecule?" The student

[1] Adam Smith, *The Wealth of Nations,* ed. Edwin Cannan (New York: Modern Library, 1937), chapter 1.

[2] Smith, *Wealth of Nations,* chapter 13.

EXAMPLE 2 Economics Majors and Molecules: Are Economists Different?

The economist has a presumed advantage over the physicist. The physicist cannot ask, "How would I behave if I were a molecule?" The economist, however, can ask, "How would I behave if I were a buyer or a seller? If I were looking for a job?" But are economists typical "molecules," or do they think and act differently from others?

An experiment was conducted at a northeastern university to test whether economists are indeed different. Economics majors were asked to play a simple bargaining game in a laboratory setting with majors from other disciplines. The object was to divide $10 between two players. One student would propose a division (such as I get $9 and you get $1), and the other student could either accept or reject the proposal. If the proposal were rejected, each player would receive $0.

Economics presumes that individuals are rational: They try to do the best for themselves given the constraints they face. Rational players would propose a large amount for themselves (say $9), knowing that their opponents would prefer the small amount offered to nothing. The rational player should be willing to accept a small amount offered by the other player.

The experiment showed that economists are indeed different from others. The average economist accepted a minimum of $1.70 and proposed to keep $6.15, whereas the average noneconomist accepted a minimum of $2.44 and proposed to keep $5.44. Economists behaved more rationally than did noneconomists.

Source: John R. Carter and Michael D. Irons, "Are Economists Different, and If So, Why?" *Journal of Economic Perspectives* 5, 2 (Spring 1991): 171–77.

of economics *is* one of the "molecules" economists study. (See Example 2.)

Crucial to individual behavior are the incentives—the carrots and sticks—that face people in any given situation. The "carrots" are the benefits that people receive from engaging in an economic activity; the "sticks" are the costs of the activity. Individuals are guided in their economic decisions by costs and benefits.

The most important tool used by economists to study economic decision making is the comparison of costs and benefits, or **marginal analysis.**

> **Marginal analysis** aids decision making by examining the consequences of making relatively small changes from the current state of affairs.

Marginal analysis explains how you might go about deciding how much studying is "enough." First, you would examine the benefits of a slight (marginal) increase in your present amount of studying. If you were to increase your studying time by, say, 1 hour per day, you would probably earn higher grades, the respect of your fellow students, and a better job upon graduation. Although you wouldn't be able to measure these results exactly, you would have a general idea of the benefits that additional study might yield. Next, you would examine the costs of 1 more hour of studying per day. You might have to sacrifice earnings from a part-time job; you might have to give up leisure activities that you value highly (dating, your favorite soap opera, an extra hour of sleep).

Whether you are studying enough depends upon whether you feel that the benefits of the extra studying would outweigh the additional costs. If so, you would conclude that you are not studying enough, and you would study more. If the extra costs would be greater than the extra benefits, you would conclude that you should not increase your study time.

Businesses make choices in a similar fashion. Consider the local Burger Bonanza fast-food restaurant. Its owners must decide if its current hours of operation (11 A.M. to midnight) are "enough."

EXAMPLE 3 The Rent Gradient and Marginal Analysis

Economics teaches that people make decisions using marginal analysis, weighing costs and benefits at the margin. Consider the choices of housing locations in cities like Atlanta, Houston, or Los Angeles where people commute to work on congested freeways. Houses and apartments located closer to the city center offer benefits in the form of shorter commuting times. Thus, the closer the location to the city center, the higher the price or the rent. In cities like Houston, for example, housing prices drop by $5000 for each additional mile from the city center.

Along with additional factors like schools and other amenities, marginal analysis says that people weigh the extra costs of more centrally located homes against the extra benefits of shorter commuting times. People tend to balance the marginal costs and benefits, typically choosing that location where they perceive the extra benefits of shorter commuting times to roughly equal the extra costs in the form of higher prices or rents.

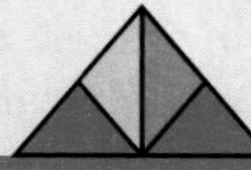

Before taking action, Burger Bonanza's owners would have to make a decision *at the margin.* They would estimate how much extra revenue would be gained by opening for breakfast. They would also estimate the extra costs of opening earlier (the extra supplies, larger payroll, higher utility bills, more advertising dollars). If the extra benefits from opening earlier (the additional revenue) exceeded the extra costs, the owners would decide to open early for breakfast. If the extra benefits fell short of the extra costs, they would not change their hours of operation. People and businesses make all kinds of economic decisions by comparing the extra costs with the extra benefits associated with making small changes. (See Example 3.)

> To make decisions at the margin, a decision maker must consider the extra (or marginal) costs and benefits of an increase or decrease in a particular activity. If the marginal benefits outweigh the marginal costs, the extra activity is undertaken.

MICRO AND MACRO

Microeconomics

Economics is divided into two main branches called *microeconomics* and *macroeconomics.* These branches deal with economic decision making from different vantage points.

> **Microeconomics** studies the economic decision making of firms and individuals in a market setting; it is the study of the economy on a small scale.

Microeconomics focuses on the individual participants in the economy: the producers, workers, employers, and consumers. In everyday economic life, things are bought and sold, and people decide where and how many hours to work. Business managers decide what to produce and how to organize production. These activities result in *transactions* that take place in markets where buyers and sellers come together. People engaging in transactions are motivated to do the best they can for themselves with the limited resources at their disposal; they make their decisions by marginal analysis.

Microeconomics studies how businesses operate under different competitive conditions and how the combined actions of buyers and sellers determine prices in specific markets. Microeconomics studies the distribution of income by focusing on households as earners of wages, interest, rent, and profit.

Microeconomics assumes that the individual economic actors are *rational.* Households spend their limited income to gain maximum satisfaction; they decide where to work and how much to work in the same fashion. Businesses choose the type and quantity of products and the manner of production in order to obtain maximum profits (the difference between earnings from sales and costs of production).

Because microeconomics studies the way people weigh the costs and benefits of actions at the margin, it has expanded into areas outside the traditional realm of economics. Microeconomics is used to deal with environmental problems; to explain how voters and public officials make their political decisions (whether to vote or stay home, whether or not to support a water project that benefits only a small group of voters); and to analyze marriage, divorce, fertility, crime, and even suicide patterns. Microeconomic analysis is also used by the courts to determine legal settlements and compensation for personal injuries. The expansion of microeconomics into a wide variety of other fields has led social scientists to call it an "imperialist" discipline.

Macroeconomics

Macroeconomics studies the production of the entire economy: the *general* price level (rather than individual prices), the national employment rate, government spending, government deficits, trade deficits, interest rates, and the nation's money supply.

> **Macroeconomics** is the study of the economy as a whole, rather than individual markets, consumers, and producers.

Macroeconomic studies rely on measures called *aggregates,* which add together (or aggregate) individual microeconomic components. These aggregates include such measures as gross domestic product (GDP), the consumer price index (CPI), the unemployment rate, and the government surplus and deficit. Just as microeconomics studies the relationships between individual participants in the economy, macroeconomics studies relationships between such aggregate measures. What are the determinants of inflation? What is the relationship between inflation and interest rates? Is it necessary to have higher unemployment to achieve lower inflation? What are the effects of government deficits on prices and interest rates? What is the relationship between the money supply and inflation?

The Convergence of Micro and Macro

When the science of economics was born more than 200 years ago, there was no distinction between micro- and macroeconomics. Early economic thinkers felt that it was necessary only to study the behavior of consumers and producers in the marketplace to understand the economy as a whole. After all, the macroeconomy is nothing more than the sum total of individual decisions on what to buy, what to produce, and where and how long to work. These early pioneers did not realize what modern economists have long recognized: that generalizing from the part to the whole can lead to mistakes (the fallacy of composition discussed later in this chapter).

Macroeconomics was born in the 1930s as a consequence of the Great Depression. Economic thinkers of this period needed new approaches to explain the aggregate behavior of the economy. Why should an economy suddenly produce much less output and supply many fewer jobs?

Since then, however, modern economics has reemphasized the importance of understanding individual behavior as a basis for understanding the behavior of the economy as a whole. As a result, a close relationship has developed between microeconomics and macroeconomics. Macroeconomists apply microeconomic analysis to macroeconomic questions because the economy is made up of individuals; and how individuals behave can help to explain how the economy as a whole behaves.

The behavior of persons and individual businesses sheds light on a number of key macroeconomic issues. How does inflation affect the output decisions of businesses and the job-search strategies of the unemployed? How are private saving decisions affected by government debt? How do people form expectations of inflation? How do households space their saving and spending decisions over their lifetimes?

> Microeconomics and macroeconomics have converged because macroeconomic relationships cannot be analyzed without understanding the behavior of the individuals who make up the economy.

METHODOLOGY IN ECONOMICS

Economists use theories to explain how the economy works. Why not let the facts speak for themselves? The American economy includes millions of households and firms and thousands of separate federal, state, and local governments. All these entities make decisions about producing vast numbers of goods and services using complex combinations of resources. Gathering information about so many economic choices is an incredibly complex and unmanageable task. Making sense of these millions of facts is even more difficult. Logical theories explain how the economy works by showing how the facts fit together in a coherent manner.

Theories and Hypotheses

A **theory** is simply a plausible and coherent explanation of the relationship among certain facts. It typically consists of at least one **hypothesis,** or logical assumption, about a particular aspect of this relationship. Normally, but not always, theories contain some hypotheses in the form of "if A, then B." Two examples of hypotheses are, "If a good's price falls, people will want to buy more of it," and "If income rises, people will consume more."

> A **theory** is an explanation of the relationship among factors that may be crucial determinants of a phenomenon.
>
> A **hypothesis** is a tentative assumption about a particular aspect of the relationship among several events or factors.

Economic theories focus on the most important systematic factors that determine economic behavior. The process of zeroing in on these factors is called *abstraction.*

Imagine trying to explain the number of cars sold in Sunshine County each year. Many factors are obviously irrelevant, such as the eye color of county residents or the average temperature in Tokyo. Other factors could conceivably be relevant, but their effect, if any, would be trivial. These factors might include the number of sunny days, a larger than average number of weddings, or a decline in the number of honor-student graduates. Economic theory would *not* focus on these factors but would rather try to zero in on the *most important* factors that systematically affect the phenomenon being studied (car sales). Theory may suggest, for example, that whether cars were particularly cheap or expensive in a given year would affect their annual sales. It could also suggest that whether Sunshine County incomes were rising or falling would significantly affect car sales.

Although thousands of factors could affect car sales, theory cannot afford to look at all of them. Many are insignificant; many do not affect the phenomenon in a systematic fashion. Theory should search only for important and systematic factors that explain the phenomenon being studied.

Testing Theories: The Scientific Method

Because theories are abstracted from the real world, it is necessary to test them. For example, suppose we theorize that higher gasoline prices induce people to buy less gasoline and that lower gasoline prices induce them to buy more. This theory makes sense. But is it true? Data on gasoline prices and purchases are shown in Table 1. Do people really buy less gas when the price rises?

As the price of gasoline rose by 30 percent from the early 1970s to the early 1980s (after adjustment for inflation), per capita consumption of gasoline fell—from 344 gallons to 316 gallons per year. As

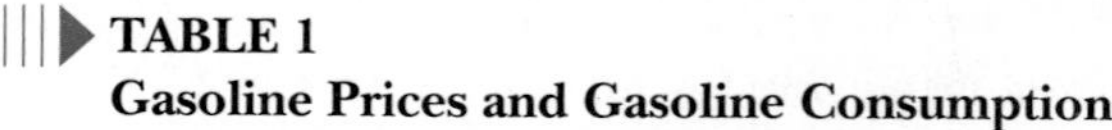

TABLE 1
Gasoline Prices and Gasoline Consumption

Years	Price per Gallon (constant 1986 dollars)	Per Capita Fuel Consumption of Automobiles (gallons per year)
1970–1973	$1.18	334
1980–1982	$1.53	316
1985–1986	$1.07	350

Source: *Statistical Abstract of the United States* (selected years). Department of Energy, Energy Information Administration, *Monthly Energy Statistics* (selected issues).

TABLE 2
Egg Prices and Egg Consumption

Years	Price per Dozen (1986 dollars)	Yearly per Capita Consumption (number of eggs)
1974–1976	$1.31	280
1977–1979	$1.05	274
1980–1983	$0.89	266
1984–1987	$0.81	253

Source: *Statistical Abstract of the United States* (various years).

gasoline prices declined between the early and mid-1980s, per capita gasoline consumption rose from 316 gallons to 350 gallons per year. The data in both these instances are consistent with the theory but, while they fail to refute it, they have not proved it beyond any doubt. Should contradictory data arise, the theory would have to be reformulated or revised.

The data on egg prices and consumption do in fact appear to contradict the theory that higher prices induce people to consume less. As Table 2 shows, egg prices fell substantially after 1974, yet egg consumption per capita declined. Clearly, we must either say that the theory does not hold for eggs or we must revise the theory to explain the behavior we observe. In this case, factors other than price influenced consumption. During the 1970s and 1980s, the egg lost some of its popularity because of allegations that cholesterol contributes to heart disease. Concern that eggs are unhealthful depressed egg consumption despite falling prices.

The theory can therefore be reformulated as follows: The higher the price of an item, the less of it people will want to buy, holding other factors (like unfavorable publicity, in this case) constant. We will examine this theory more closely in Chapter 5.

The previous examples illustrate how the scientific method can be applied to a simple economic theory:

1. A theory was formulated.
2. Relevant facts were gathered (Tables 1 and 2), and irrelevant facts were discarded.
3. The theory was evaluated in light of the facts.
4. When the facts failed to confirm the theory (Table 2), the theory was reformulated.

The **scientific method** helps people to evaluate their beliefs in light of the facts and formulate their beliefs in a way that can be tested by others. It thus raises human thought above the level of the individual, separating the idea from the person as much as possible. Claude Bernard, nineteenth-century writer, summarized the orientation of scientific subjects in comparison to artistic ones: "Art is I; science is we."

> The process of formulating theories, collecting data, testing theories, and revising theories is called the **scientific method.**

The Uses of Economic Theories

Economic theories allow us to make sense of an extremely complicated world. They enable us to understand economic relationships, make sense of past events, and even predict the consequences of actions yet to be taken. For example, economists have used well-tested theories of the relationship between product prices and quantities purchased to predict the effects of changes in energy prices. The United States entered uncharted territory when energy prices skyrocketed in the 1970s, and it was comforting at the time to have a scientifically tested theory as a guide. As we saw in the previous discussion, these predictions proved accurate, as did predictions of increased gasoline use in response to lowered prices in the mid-1980s.

> Theory can say something about facts that have yet to be collected and about events that have yet to occur; that is, theory can be used to make *predictions.*

The scientific method says that a theory that does not work in practice cannot be a good theory. If an economic theory does not work in practice (if it is not supported by the facts), it must be discarded and a new theory put in its place.

THE *CETERIS PARIBUS* PROBLEM

Ceteris paribus is a Latin term meaning "other things being equal." Any attempt to establish the relationship between two factors must hold constant the effects of other factors to avoid confusing the relationship; otherwise, the ***ceteris paribus* problem** will occur.

> The ***ceteris paribus* problem** occurs when the effect of one factor on another is masked by changes in other factors.

Cause-and-effect relationships rarely involve only two factors. The real world is complex; many factors explain real-world phenomena. In the egg example, at least two factors affected consumer purchases. Far more variables are involved in such complex areas as heart disease and cancer research. Public health officials have devoted decades of research to understanding the effects of factors like smoking or diet on health.

To understand how one factor affects another, we must be able to sort out the effects of all other relevant factors. Does egg consumption fall as a result of increasing egg prices or growing fear of cholesterol? Does heart disease decrease as a result of the decreased incidence of smoking, improved diet, or some other factor? Figuring out these effects is not a simple matter. In fact, an entire branch of economics, *econometrics,* combines economic theory and statistics in an effort to deal with the *ceteris paribus* problem.

COMMON FALLACIES IN ECONOMICS

False economic propositions often appear reasonable. Logical economic fallacies can be found routinely in newspapers, statements of public figures, and even in the writings of professional economists. The two most common logical fallacies that plague economic thinking are the *false-cause fallacy* and the *fallacy of composition.*

The False-Cause Fallacy

The fact that event A occurs with or precedes event B does not mean that A has caused B. One well-known example of the **false-cause fallacy** is the so-called Super Bowl phenomenon. In 19 of the last 21 years, the stock market rose when the National Football Conference team won the Super Bowl and fell when it lost. To conclude that the one event (the NFC team winning the Super Bowl) caused the other event (higher stock market prices) would be a false-cause fallacy. Believe it or not, there are people who buy or sell in the stock market on the basis of which team wins the Super Bowl!

> The **false-cause fallacy** is the assumption that because two events occur together, one event has caused the other.

Determining whether variables that are statistically correlated are involved in a cause-and-effect relationship is one of the most difficult problems of science. Economic theory attempts to establish in a scientific manner whether such a relationship exists. Since there is no logical reason to expect that the outcome of a football game will affect the stock market, we must reject a cause-and-effect relationship between the two events. On the other hand, experts in economics offer a number of logical theories that specify cause-and-effect relationships between variables (such as the overall state of the economy, interest rates, expectations of inflation) and the stock market.

> A statistical correlation between two variables does not prove that one has caused the other or that the variables have anything to do with each other. For causation to be established, there must be a logical theory explaining the effect of one variable on the other.

The Fallacy of Composition

A classic example of the **fallacy of composition** would be the assertion that the best way to escape a fire in a crowded movie theater is to run to the exit. If *one* person runs to the exit, he or she will escape unharmed. If *all* people run to the nearest exit, few will escape unharmed.

> The **fallacy of composition** is the assumption that what is true for each part taken separately is also true for the whole or, in reverse, that what is true for the whole is true for each part considered separately.

To illustrate the fallacy of composition with an economic example, consider what would happen if the government were to print $10,000 and give it away to one person. Clearly, this action would make that individual better off. With the extra $10,000, the person could buy a car, invest in the stock market, or finance a college education. But if the government were to give everyone $10,000, increased consumer spending might push up prices, and $10,000 would buy less than it would have bought before the extra money went into circulation. Society as a whole would not end up any better off. What is true for each part taken separately—namely, that receiving money makes one person better off—would not necessarily be true for the whole.

WHY ECONOMISTS DISAGREE

Economists have the unfair reputation of being unable to agree on anything. People joke about getting "six different answers from only five economists"; they say, "If all the world's economists were laid end to end, they would never be able to reach a conclusion."

The image of widespread disagreement among economists is distorted. The results of a survey of 100 professional American economists, reported in Table 3, confirm that there is considerable agreement among economists about *what can be done.*[3] More than 80 percent of the economists agree on propositions involving judgments of this nature. However, there is more disagreement over what ought to be done: Should we equalize the distribution of income? Should we increase defense spending? Such questions require moral and political value judgments about which individuals naturally disagree. An international survey confirms these findings: Economists tend to agree on *what can be done,* while disagreeing on *what ought to be done.*[4]

[3] J.R. Kearl, C. L. Pope, G. T. Whiting, and L. T. Wimmer, "A Confusion of Economists," *American Economic Review* 69, 2 (May 1979): 28.

[4] Bruno S. Frey, Werner Pommerehne, Friedrich Schneider, and Guy Gilbert, "Consensus and Dissension among Economists: An Empirical Inquiry," *American Economic Review* 74, 2 (December 1984): 986–94

Positive Economics

Positive economics explains how the economy works.

> **Positive economics** is the study of *what is* in the economy.

Economists generally agree about the microeconomic relationships that prevail in an economy, but not about the macroeconomic relationships.

Microeconomic relationships are easy matters on which to achieve agreement. (For instance, virtually all economists would agree that a freeze in Florida will raise citrus prices.) Thus there is consensus among economists that rising prices reduce consumption (*ceteris paribus*), that rising income will have differential but predictable effects on consumer products, that wage and price controls cause shortages, that tariffs and quotas raise prices to consumers, that rent controls reduce the quantity and quality of housing, and that minimum-wage laws increase unemployment among youth and unskilled workers.

Economists have studied macroeconomics for a shorter time than microeconomics and thus tend to disagree about it more. The points of disagreement include such questions as, What are the causes of inflation and unemployment? What is the relationship between deficits and interest rates? Can we combine low unemployment and low inflation? Can government policy be used to achieve employment and inflation goals?

Why has economics still to resolve these vital issues? The basic answer is that the economy is an unbelievably complex organism composed of millions of individuals; hundreds of thousands of business firms; a myriad of local, state, and federal government offices. The economy is us, and our collective economic actions are difficult to analyze because emotions are volatile, expectations can change overnight, relationships that held last year no longer hold today, and it is costly and difficult to collect up-to-date economic facts. Unlike the physical sciences, economics is denied a controlled laboratory setting. Many economic events are random and unpredictable. Bad weather can cause poor harvests; armed conflicts can occur without warning in different parts of the globe; oil-producing countries can form a price-fixing alliance; consumer spending can shift in response to changing expectations.

TABLE 3
Do Economists Disagree?

Propositions	Agreement (percent)
1. Tariffs and import quotas reduce general economic welfare.	97
2. The government should be an employer of last resort and initiate a guaranteed job program.	53
3. The money supply is a more important target for monetary policy than interest rates.	71
4. Cash payments are superior to transfers-in-kind.	92
5. Flexible exchange rates offer an effective international monetary arrangement.	95
6. A minimum wage increases unemployment among young and unskilled workers.	90
7. The government should index the income tax rate structure for inflation.	68
8. Fiscal policy has a significant stimulative impact on a less than fully employed economy.	92
9. The distribution of income in the United States should be more equal.	71
10. National defense expenditures should be reduced from the present level.	66
11. Antitrust laws should be used vigorously to reduce monopoly power from its current level.	85
12. Inflation is primarily a monetary phenomenon.	57
13. The government should restructure the welfare system along lines of a "negative income tax."	92
14. Wage-price controls should be used to control inflation.	28
15. A ceiling on rents reduces the quantity and quality of housing available.	98
16. The Fed should be instructed to increase the money supply at a fixed rate.	39
17. Effluent taxes represent a better approach to pollution control than imposition of pollution ceilings.	81
18. The level of government spending should be reduced (disregarding expenditures for stabilization).	57
19. The Fed has the capacity to achieve a constant growth of the money supply if it so desires.	66
20. Reducing the regulatory power of federal commissions would improve the efficiency of the U.S. economy.	78
21. The federal budget should be balanced over the business cycle rather than yearly.	83
22. The fundamental cause of the rise in oil prices in the mid-1970s was the monopoly power of the large oil companies.	25
23. The redistribution of income is a legitimate role for government in the context of the U.S. economy.	81
24. In the short run, unemployment can be reduced by increasing the rate of inflation.	64
25. The ceiling on interest paid on savings deposits should be removed.	94
26. "Consumer protection" laws generally reduce economic efficiency.	52
27. The economic power of labor unions should be significantly curtailed.	70

Source: Adapted from J. R. Kearl, C. L. Pope, G. T. Whiting, and L. T. Wimmer, "A Confusion of Economists?" *American Economic Review* 69, 2 (May 1979): 30.

Normative Economics

Economists also disagree—often strongly—about **normative economics.**

> **Normative economics** is the study of *what ought to be* in the economy.

Economists disagree on whether we should have more unemployment or more inflation; whether income taxes should be lowered for the middle class, the rich, or the poor; whether we should have job programs for the poor or government-subsidized health programs. These disagreements are only partly over "what is." Opponents in a debate may agree on what will happen if program A is chosen over program B, but they may disagree sharply over their personal evaluation of the desirability of those consequences. (See Example 4.)

Normative economics always involves some concern over an economic problem—perhaps people

EXAMPLE 4 Positive and Normative Science: Rainforests and Birds

Virtually all sciences can be broken down into positive and normative components. A positive biologist may study the empirical trade-offs involved in rainforest destruction. For every acre of rainforest destroyed, the positive biologist can calculate the trade-off between how many people can have new homes made of wood and how many fewer species of birds there will be. But the positive biologist becomes a normative biologist when he or she concludes that the loss of bird species resulting from rainforest destruction is "bad," and that the gain of homes made of wood is insufficient compensation.

Economists focus more on the normative-positive distinction than other scientists because their subjects are human agents who tend to complain when they suffer from inflation or unemployment. Other scientists deal primarily with nonhuman subjects that do not "argue back."

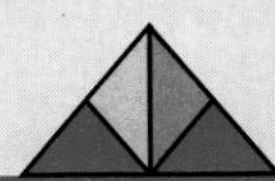

think that there is too much inflation, too much poverty, too much unemployment, or inadequate medical care. In democracies, there is usually some pressure to pass a piece of legislation designed to correct the problem, but economic problems are not easy to solve. Normative economists must pay attention to the **principle of unintended consequences,** according to which the ultimate effects of economic or social policies may be different from the apparent or intended effects. Indeed, the "cure" can sometimes be worse than the "disease."

> The **principle of unintended consequences** holds that policies may have ultimate or actual effects that differ from the intended or apparent effects.

A simple noneconomic example would be the treatment of bats. Because bats cause diseases and destroy crops, they have been poisoned, dynamited, and buried alive by the millions in their caves. As a result, bats are disappearing. But it turns out that these animals are vital to hundreds of economically important plants and trees: Almost 500 products, from bananas to medicine, rely on them. Eliminating bats can thus have ultimate side effects that are even more serious than the problems caused by the bats themselves.

Numerous economic policies can have similar negative consequences. Rent control can cause housing shortages; unemployment benefits can increase unemployment; raises in the minimum wage can hurt the poor by eliminating jobs; welfare checks given to poor mothers can break up families; free housing for the homeless can hurt other poor people; taxing the goods rich people buy also taxes those who serve the rich; equal pay for men and women can result in fewer jobs for women; bank deposit insurance to protect consumers can encourage bankers to act irresponsibly; medical insurance for some can lead to an explosion of medical costs for everyone; safety legislation for workers can lower their wages; and making cigarette advertising illegal can raise the profits of cigarette producers.

The principle of unintended consequences is not a counsel for despair. Rather, the principle tells us that the challenge is to develop good economic policies, not to pose superficial solutions to difficult problems. In economics, as in medicine, recognizing a problem does not mean knowing its solution. At one time, doctors made their patients worse off by bleeding them; they recognized the illness but did not know the cure. Economic policy makers have not done much better.

Economists can make important contributions to sound economic policy. For example, they have suggested that we deal with pollution by setting up a market for pollution rights. Likewise, economic solutions to such problems as poverty and the lack of adequate medical care require a careful balancing of all the costs and benefits involved. But such solutions are elusive. They are the source of many honest disagreements about the possible ultimate effects of any policy.

The Visibility of Economic Disputes

Although there are strong disagreements in other sciences, they are less visible to the public eye than economic disagreements. Theoretical physicists have disagreed about the physical nature of the universe since the foundation of physics, but this controversy is understood by only a few theoretical physicists.

It does not require much disagreement to bring economic disputes to public attention. Everyone is interested in economic questions: Will inflation accelerate? Will I lose my job? When will interest rates fall? Why is the price of gasoline rising so fast? Why are home mortgages so hard to come by? Economists do disagree, particularly on some big macroeconomic issues. But often what the public perceives as disagreements over questions of "what is" (positive economics) are really disagreements over what ought to be. In general, there is more agreement than disagreement among economists.

The next chapter will begin to use the tools of the scientific method to explain how economic choices are made in a world of scarce resources. What are the costs of making choices? What arrangements are used to resolve the problem of choice? Graphical analysis makes these questions easier to answer. The appendix to this chapter reviews the guidelines for working with graphs.

SUMMARY

1. Increased knowledge improves the quality of each person's decision making as an individual, a voter, a member of society. The four themes of economics are scarcity, choice, specialization, and exchange.
2. Marginal analysis aids economic decision making by examining the consequences of making relatively small changes in the current state of affairs.
3. Microeconomics studies the economic decision making of firms and individuals in a market setting; it is the study of the economy on a small scale. Macroeconomics studies the economy as a whole and deals with issues of inflation, unemployment, money supply, and the government budget; it is the study of the economy on a large scale. Modern macroeconomics uses microeconomic analysis to study inflation, unemployment, and saving.
4. Theory allows us to make sense of the real world and to learn how the facts fit together. There is no conflict between good theory and good practice. Economic theories are based upon the scientific method of hypothesis formulation, collection of relevant data, and testing of theories. Economic theory makes it possible to predict the consequences of actions that have yet to be taken and about facts not yet known.
5. The *ceteris paribus* problem occurs when it is difficult to determine relationships between two factors because of the effects of other factors.
6. Two logical fallacies plague economic analysis: the false-cause fallacy (assuming that event A has caused event B because A is associated with B) and the fallacy of composition (assuming that what is true for each part taken separately is true for the whole or, conversely, assuming that what is true for the whole is also true for each part).
7. Economists tend to agree on positive economic issues (what is) while disagreeing on normative issues (what ought to be). The major unresolved issues of positive economics tend to be concentrated in macroeconomics, an evolving field in economics. Disagreements among economists are more visible to the public eye than disagreements in other scientific professions.

KEY TERMS

economics
marginal analysis
microeconomics
macroeconomics
theory
hypothesis
scientific method
ceteris paribus problem
false-cause fallacy
fallacy of composition
positive economics
normative economics
principle of unintended consequences

QUESTIONS AND PROBLEMS

1. Why do people have to make economic choices?
2. The state of California is considering transporting water from mountain watersheds to Los Angeles. It calculates that the extra cost of an acre-foot of water shipped is $150 and the extra

benefit of an acre-foot of water shipped is $200. Using these numbers, what would an economic analyst recommend to legislators voting on this project?

3. Using the example of study time, assume that two days before an exam your professor announces that it will account for 100 percent of your grade. How would this announcement affect your study time? Explain your answer using the logic of marginal analysis. From this answer, try to construct a general rule about changing costs and benefits and economic decision making.
4. Which of the following topics would fall under macroeconomics? Which under microeconomics? Explain why in each case.

   a. The price of fish
   b. The interest rate
   c. Employment in the computer industry
   d. The general price level
   e. The national unemployment rate
   f. Unemployment in Oklahoma
   g. The number of new homes built in the United States

5. We concluded that the data in Table 1 "fails to refute" the theory that higher prices reduce gasoline consumption. Why didn't we say that the data in Table 1 "prove the theory?
6. Explain how you would use the scientific method to determine what factors cause the grade point averages of students in your class to differ. Explain why you must use abstraction.
7. "If I try to drive faster on the freeway, I will get home quicker." Explain under what conditions this statement is true and under what conditions it is a logical fallacy. Also explain which logical fallacy is involved.
8. "The price of corn is low today because people are now watching too much TV." This statement is a potential example of which logical fallacy (or fallacies)?
9. Economists would be more likely to agree on the answers to which of the following questions? Why?

   a. Should tax rates be lowered for the rich?
   b. How would lowering tax rates for the rich affect economic output?
   c. How would an increase in the price of VCRs affect purchases of VCRs?
   d. Should government defense expenditures be reduced?
   e. How would an increase in military spending affect employment?

10. "The severe heat and drought of the summer of 1988 substantially reduced revenue from wheat and corn crops in the Midwest. The incomes of all wheat and corn farmers therefore fell in 1988." Which logical fallacy may be involved in this statement and why?
11. Use the data in Table A to devise some simple theories and to test them against "the facts."

TABLE A

	1980	1986
Price of chicken (per lb.)	$0.72	$0.84
Per capita consumption of chicken (lbs.)	50.1	59.1
New passenger cars (millions sold)	6.4	7.5
New car prices (1980 = 100)	100	125
Personal income (billions of dollars)	$2156	$3534

12. Identify which of the following statements are hypotheses.

    a. The U.S. population rose more rapidly in the 1950s than in the 1980s.
    b. People who get severly sunburned are more likely to develop skin cancer.
    c. An increase in income causes people to buy more consumer goods.
    d. The United States and Western Europe have the highest incomes among the world's nations.
    e. Cats can see better in the dark than dogs.
    f. If people believe that a product is hazardous to their health, they will consume less of it.

SUGGESTED READINGS

Boulding, Kenneth. *Economics as a Science.* Boston: University Press of America, 1988.

Buchanan, James. *Cost and Choice: An Inquiry in Economic Theory.* Chicago: University of Chicago Press, 1979.

Friedman, Milton. *Essays in Positive Economics.* Chicago: University of Chicago Press, 1966.

Hausman, Daniel, ed. *The Philosophy of Economics, An Anthology.* New York: Cambridge University Press, 1984.

Jevons, Marshall. *The Fatal Equilibrium.* New York: Ballantine, 1986.

Kohler, Heinz. *Scarcity and Freedom.* Lexington, Mass.: D.C. Heath, 1977, part 1.

Mundell, Robert A. *Man and Economics.* New York: McGraw-Hill, 1968, chap.1.

Stigler, George. *The Economist as Preacher.* Chicago: University of Chicago Press, 1982.

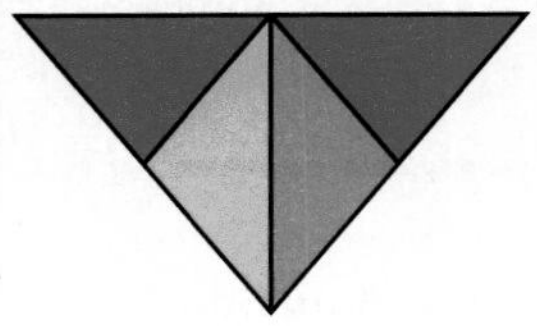

APPENDIX 1A

Reading Graphs

APPENDIX INSIGHT

Understanding how to use graphs is essential to learning modern economics. This appendix teaches graph construction, positive and negative relationships, dependent and independent variables, and the concept of slope for both linear and curvilinear relationships. It shows how slopes can be used to find the maximum and minimum values of a relationship, and it explains how to calculate the areas of rectangles and triangles. Finally, it describes three common pitfalls of using graphs: the ambiguity of slope, the improper measurement of data, and the use of unrepresentative data.

Economics makes extensive use of graphs. A graph is simply a visual scheme for picturing the quantitative relationship between two variables. This book contains graphs dealing with many different economic relationships in both microeconomics and macroeconomics. These graphs are used to present factual data and to provide support for various economic theories.

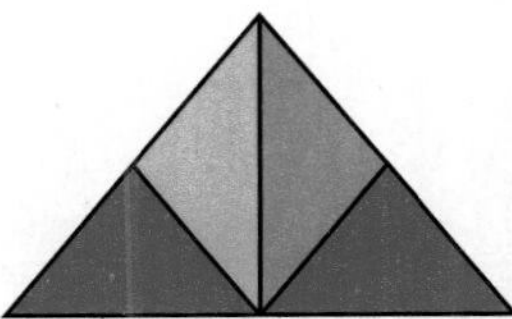

THE USE OF GRAPHS IN ECONOMICS

Graphs can efficiently describe quantitative relationships. As the Chinese proverb says, "a picture is worth a thousand words." It is easier both to understand and to remember a graph than the several hundred or perhaps thousands of numbers that the graph represents.

Positive and Negative Relationships

The first important characteristic of a graph is the **positive (direct)** or **negative (inverse) relationship** between the two variables.

> A **positive (direct) relationship** exists between two variables if an increase in the value of one variable is associated with an *increase* in the value of the other variable.
>
> A **negative (inverse) relationship** exists between two variables if an increase in the value of one variable is associated with a *reduction* in the value of the other variable.

For example, an increase in the horsepower of a car's engine will increase the maximum speed of the automobile (holding other factors such as the weight of the car, constant). Panel *a* of Figure 1 depicts this relationship in a graph. The *vertical axis* measures the maximum speed of the car from the 0 point (called the *origin*); the *horizontal axis* measures the horsepower of the engine. When horsepower is 0 (the engine is stopped), the maximum speed the car can attain is obviously 0; when horsepower is 300, the maximum speed is 100 miles per hour. Intermediate values of horsepower (between 0 and 300) are graphed. When a line is drawn through all these points, the resulting curved line describes the effect of horsepower on maximum speed. Since the picture is a line that goes from low to high speeds as horsepower increases, it is an example of an *upward-sloping curve.*

> When two variables are positively related, the graph of the relationship is an upward-sloping curve.

FIGURE 1
Graphing Positive and Negative Relationships

(*a*) A Positive Relationship

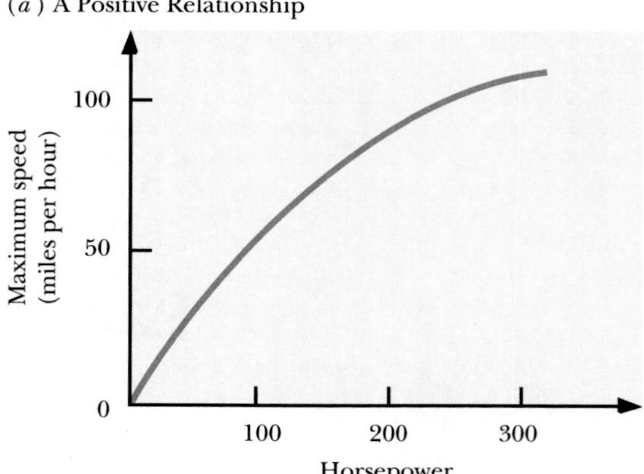

(*b*) A Negative Relationship

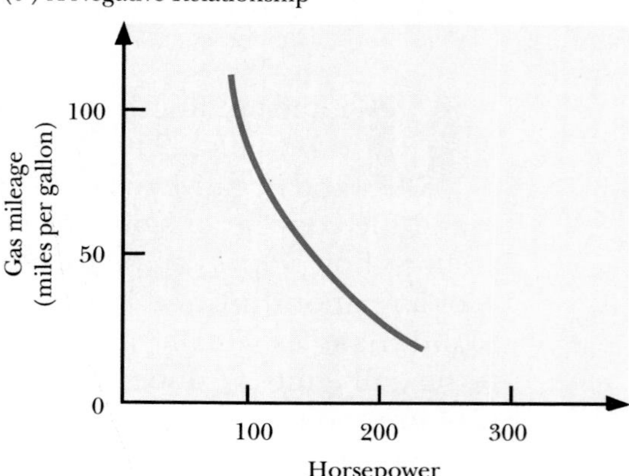

Panel *a* shows a positive relationship. As the horizontal variable (horsepower) increases, the value of the vertical variable (maximum speed) increases. The curve rises from left to right. Panel *b* shows a negative relationship. As the horizontal variable (horsepower) increases, the vertical variable (mileage) decreases. The curve falls from left to right.

Now let's consider an example of a negative (inverse) relationship. As the horsepower of the automobile increases, the gas mileage will fall (again, other things being equal). In panel *b* of Figure 1, horsepower is still measured on the horizontal axis, but gas mileage is now measured on the vertical axis. Since the picture is a curve going from high to low values of gas mileage as horsepower increases, it is an example of a *downward-sloping curve.*

When two variables are negatively related, the graph of the relationship is a downward-sloping curve.

Dependent and Independent Variables

In relationships involving two variables, one variable is the **dependent variable** and the other is the **independent variable.**

The **dependent variable**—denoted by *Y*—changes as a result of a change in the value of another variable.

The **independent variable**—denoted by *X*—causes the change in the value of the dependent variable.

An increase in engine horsepower *causes* an increase in the maximum speed of the automobile in panel *a* of Figure 1. A horsepower increase *causes* a reduction in gas mileage in panel *b*. In both examples, horsepower is the independent variable. The other two variables are said to depend upon horsepower because the changes in horsepower bring about changes in speed and gas mileage. Maximum speed and gas mileage are dependent variables.

One goal of economic analysis is to find the independent variable(s) that explain certain dependent variables. What independent variables explain changes in inflation rates, unemployment, consumer spending, housing construction, and so on? In many cases, it is not possible to determine which variable is dependent and which is independent. Some variables are interdependent (they affect each other), and some have no cause-and-effect relationship.

ADVANTAGES OF GRAPHS

We can tell at a glance whether a curve is positively or negatively sloped. We have to work harder to read all the information that a graph contains. The data for a sample graph are given in Table 1. The numbers in this table describe the quantitative relationship between minutes of typing and number of pages typed. Let us assume that the quantitative relationship between minutes and pages is known: Every 5 minutes of typing will produce 1 page of manuscript. Thus 5 minutes produce 1 page, 15 minutes produce 3 pages, and so on. Zero minutes will, of course, produce 0 pages. The data are graphed in Figure 2.

TABLE 1
The Relatioship between Minutes of Typing and Number of Pages Typed

	Minutes of Typing (*X* axis)	Number of Pages Typed (*Y* axis)
	0	0
a	5	1
b	10	2
c	15	3
d	20	4
e	25	5

Points *a, b, c, d,* and *e* completely describe the data in Table 1. Indeed, a graph of the data acts as a substitute for the table from which it was constructed.

FIGURE 2
Constructing a Graph

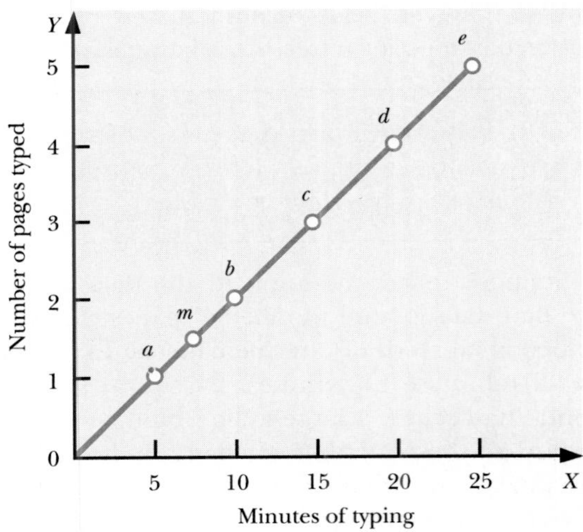

This graph reproduces the data in Table 1. Point *a* shows the 5 minutes of typing produce 1 page of typing; *b* shows that 10 minutes produce 2 pages, and so on. The upward-sloping line drawn through *a, b, c, d,* and *e* shows that the relationship between minutes of typing and number of pages typed is positive. The points between *a, b, c, d,* and *e* (such as *m*) show the number of pages typed for amounts of typing time between the 5-minute intervals.

TABLE 2
The Relationship between Minutes of Typing and Number of Pages Typed (data rearranged)

	Minutes of Typing (*X* axis)	Number of Pages Typed (*Y* axis)
b	10	2
a	5	1
	0	0
e	25	5
c	15	3
d	20	4

This is the first advantage of graphs over tables: They provide an immediate visual understanding of the quantitative relationship between the two variables just by the plots of points. Since the points in this case move upward from left to right, we know that there is a *positive relationship* between the variables. (See Example 1.)

This may not seem to be a great advantage for this simple and obvious case. However, suppose the data had been arranged as in Table 2.

After lengthy inspection of the data, it becomes clear that there is a positive relationship between *X* and *Y;* however, it is not immediately obvious. A graph makes it easier to see the relationship.

> The first advantage of graphs over tables is that it is easier to see the relationship between two variables in a graph than in a table.

Suppose that in addition to the data in Table 1, we had data for the number of pages that could be typed at all kinds of intermediate values of typing time: 6 minutes, 13 minutes, 24 minutes and 25 seconds, and so on. A large table would be required to report all these numbers. In a graph, however, all these intermediate values can be represented simply by connecting points *a, b, c, d,* and *e* with a line. Thus a second advantage of graphs is that large quantities of data can be represented more efficiently in a graph than in a table.

> The second advantage of graphs over tables is that large quantities of data can be represented efficiently in a graph.

FIGURE 3
Shifts in Relationships

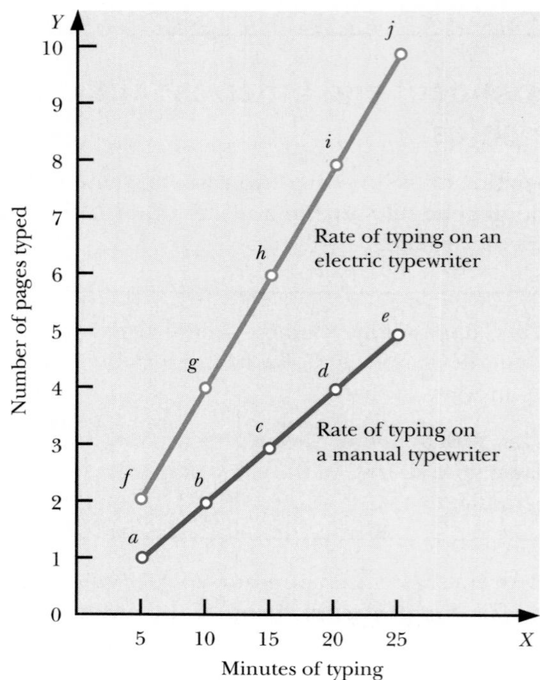

The curve *abcde* graphs the data in Table 1 that show the relationship between minutes and pages using a manual typewriter. The new (higher) curve *fghij* shows the relationship between minutes and pages with an electric typewriter. As a consequence of the change from the manual to the electric typewriter, the relationship has shifted upward. Any given *X* is now associated with a higher *Y* value.

The data in Tables 1 and 2 reveal the relationship between minutes of typing and number of pages typed (Figure 2). The relationship can change, however, if other factors that affect typing speed change. Assume that Table 1 shows minutes and pages typed on a manual typewriter. If the typist works with an electric typewriter, a different relationship will prevail. With an electric typewriter, the typist can type 2 pages instead of 1 every 5 minutes. Both relationships are graphed in Figure 3. Thus, if factors that affect speed of typing (for example, the quality of the typewriter) change, the relationship between minutes and pages can shift. Economists frequently work with relationships that shift, so it is important to understand shifts in graphs.

EXAMPLE 1 Graphical Presentation: Could the Challenger Disaster Have Been Prevented?

One picture is worth a thousand words, if the picture is drawn properly. The chart on the left was prepared by the manufacturer of the Challenger space shuttle solid-fuel rocket boosters. It relates the damage to the boosters to the temperature at launch time on shuttle flights prior to the Challenger disaster. The design of the chart, arranged by date rather than temperature, does not clearly show the danger the rocket boosters faced during launches at low temperatures. The chart on the right directly relates booster damage (on the vertical axis) to launch temperature (on the horizontal axis) and extrapolates the expected damage at very low launch temperatures (the Challenger was launched at a temperature of 31 degrees).

On the day of the Challenger disaster, the chart on the right lay buried in NASA files. If the data had been presented in that format, NASA officials might have ordered a postponement of the flight, thereby saving the lives of the astronauts.

Source: Phil Patton, "Up from the Flatland," *New York Times Magazine,* January 19, 1992, 30.

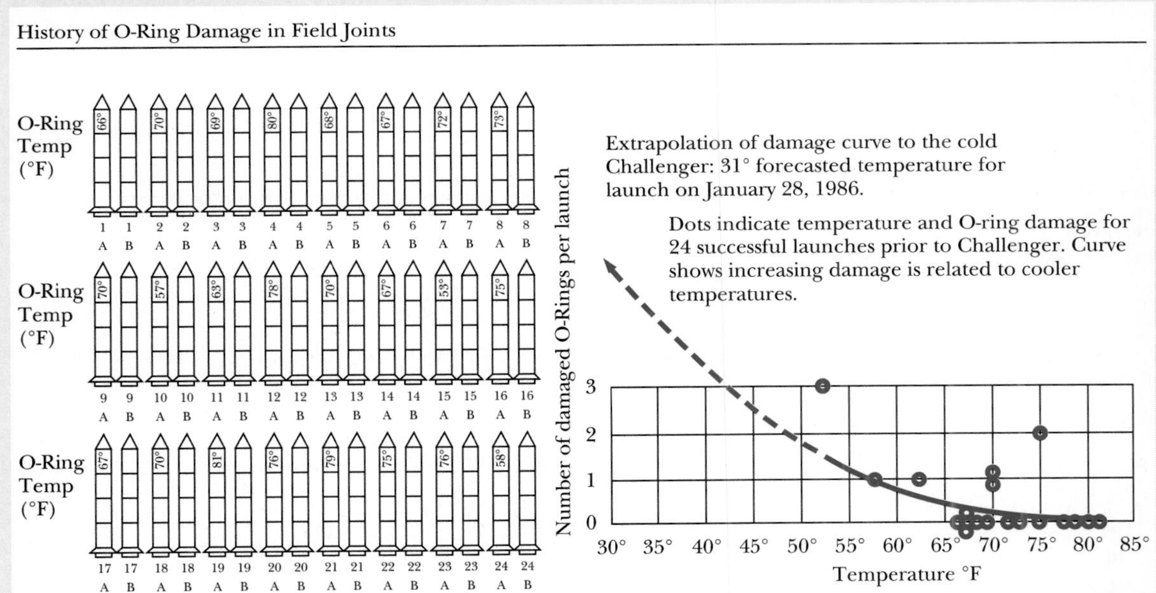

Source: Phil Patton, "Up from the Flatland," *New York Times Magazine,* January 19, 1992, 30.

UNDERSTANDING SLOPE

The magnitude of the reaction of a dependent variable (Y) to a change in an independent variable (X) is represented by the *slope* of the curve depicting their relationship. Many central concepts of economics require an understanding of slope.

The **slope** of a curve reflects the response of one variable to changes in another. Consider the typing example. Every 5 minutes of typing on a manual typewriter produce 1 page; equivalently, every minute of typing produces $1/5$ of a page. As we shall demonstrate, the slope of the line *abcde* is $1/5$ of a page of typing per minute.

> The **slope** *of a straight line* is the ratio of the rise (or fall) in Y over the run in X.

To understand slope more precisely, consider the straight-line relationship between the two variables X and Y in panel *a* of Figure 4. When $X = 5$, $Y = 3$; when $X = 7$, $Y = 6$. Suppose now that variable X is allowed to *run* (to change horizontally) from 5 units to 7 units. When this happens, variable Y rises (increases vertically) from 3 units to 6 units.

The slope of the line in panel *a* is

$$\frac{\text{Rise in } Y}{\text{Run in } X} = \frac{3}{2} = 1.5$$

A *positive value of the slope* signifies a *positive relationship* between the two variables.

This formula works for negative relationships as well. In panel *b* of Figure 4, when X runs from 5 to 7, Y falls from 4 units to 1 unit, or rises by -3 units. Thus, the slope is:

$$\frac{\text{Rise in } Y}{\text{Run in } X} = \frac{-3}{2} = -1.5$$

A *negative* value of the slope signifies a *negative relationship* between the two variables.

If ΔY (delta Y) stands for the change in the value of Y and ΔX (delta X) stands for the change in the value of X,

$$\text{Slope} = \frac{\Delta Y}{\Delta X}$$

FIGURE 4
Positive and Negative Slope

(*a*) Positive Slope

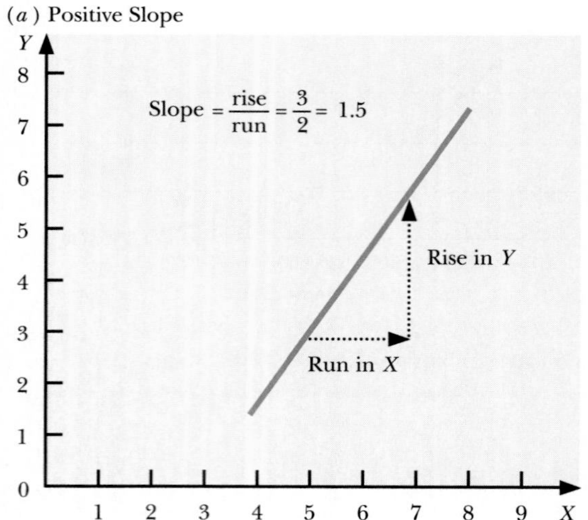

(*b*) Negative Slope

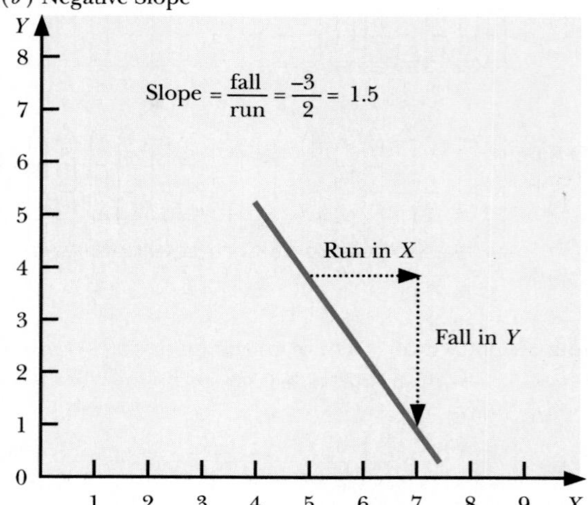

Positive slope is measured by the ratio of the rise in Y over the run in X. In panel *a*, Y rises by 3 and X runs by 2, and the slope is 1.5. Negative slope is measured by the ratio of the fall in Y over the run in X. In panel *b*, the fall in Y is -3, the run in X is 2, and the slope is -1.5.

FIGURE 5
Calculating Slopes of Curvilinear Relationships

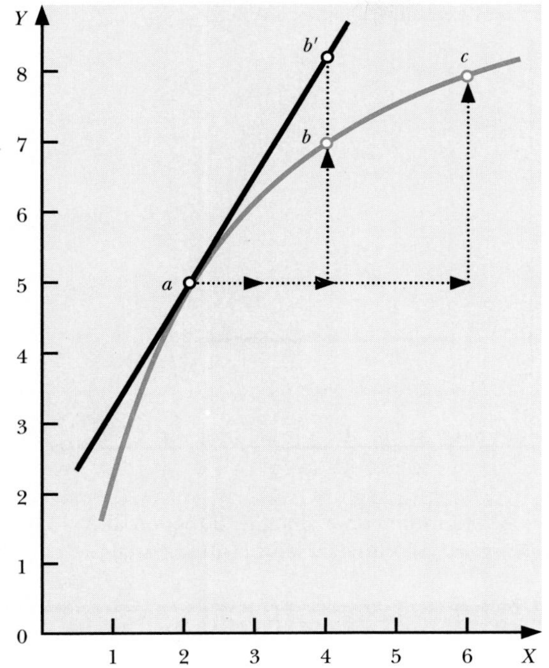

The ratio of the rise over the run yields a slope of 1 from *a* to *b* but a slope of 3/4 from *a* to *c*. From *b* to *c*, the slope is 1/2. To compute the slope at point *a*, the slope of the tangent to *a* is calculated. The value of the slope of the tangent is 3/2 since between *a* and *b*′, $\Delta Y = 3$ and $\Delta X = 2$.

This formula holds for positive or negative relationships.

Let us return to the typing example. What slope expresses the relationship between minutes of typing and number of pages? When minutes increase by 5 units ($\Delta X = 5$), pages increase by 1 unit ($\Delta Y = 1$). The slope is therefore $\Delta Y/\Delta X = 1/5$. In Figures 2, 3, and 4, the points are connected by straight lines. Such relationships are called *linear relationships*.

Figure 5 shows how the slope is measured when the relationship between *X* and *Y* is curvilinear. When *X* runs from 2 units to 4 units ($\Delta X = 2$), *Y* rises by 2 units ($\Delta Y = 2$); thus the slope between *a* and *b* is $2/2 = 1$. Between *a* and *c*, however, *X* runs from 2 to 6 ($\Delta X = 4$), *Y* rises by 3 units ($\Delta Y = 3$), and the slope is 3/4. In the curvilinear case, the value of the slope depends on how far *X* is allowed to run. Between *b* and *c*, the slope is 1/2. Thus the slope changes as one moves along a curve. In the linear case, the value of the slope will *not* depend on how far *X* runs, because the slope is constant and does not change as one moves from point to point.

There is no single slope of a curvilinear relationship and no single method of measuring slopes. An individual slope can be measured between two points (say, between *a* and *b* or between *b* and *c*) or at a particular point (say, at point *a*). Insofar as the measurement of the slope between points depends upon the length of the run, a uniform standard must be adopted to avoid confusion. This standard requires that *tangents* be used to determine the slope at any single point on a curve.

To calculate the slope at *a*, let the run of *X* be "infinitesimally small" rather than a discrete number of units such as 1/2, 2, or 4. An infinitesimally small change is difficult to conceptualize, but the graphical result of such a change can be captured simply by drawing a **tangent** to point *a*.

> A **tangent** is a straight line that touches the curve at only one point.

If the curve is really curved at *a*, there is only one straight line that just barely touches *a* and only *a*. Any other line (a magnifying glass may be required to verify this) will cut the curve at two points or none. The tangent to *a* is drawn as a straight black line in Figure 5.

The **slope** of a curvilinear-relationship at a particular point is measured by means of the tangent to that point:

> The **slope** *of a curvilinear relationship* at a particular point is the slope of the straight-line tangent to the curve at that point.

The slope of the tangent at *a* is measured by dividing the rise by the run. Because the tangent is a straight line, the length of the run does not matter. For a run from 2 to 4 ($\Delta X = 2$), the rise (ΔY) equals 3 (from 5 to 8). Thus the slope of the tangent is 3/2 or 1.5.

FIGURE 6
Maximum and Minimum Points

(*a*) *Y* is Maximized When Slope Is Zero

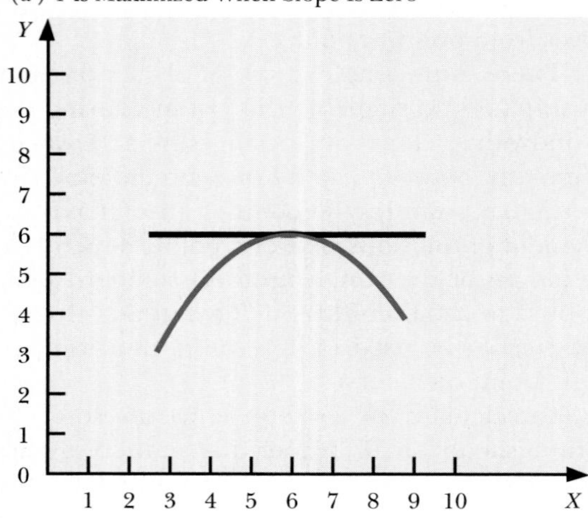

(*b*) *Y* is Minimized When Slope Is Zero

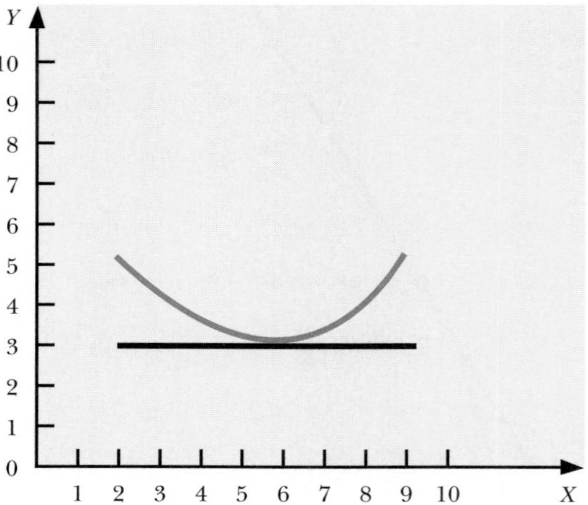

Some curvilinear relationships change directions. Notice that in panel *a*, when the curve changes direction at $X = 6$, the corresponding value of *Y* is *maximized.* In panel *b*, when $X = 6$, *Y* is *minimized.* In either case, the slope equals zero at the maximum or minimum value.

MAXIMUM AND MINIMUM VALUES

Figure 6 shows two curvilinear relationships that have distinct high points or low points. In panel *a*, the relationship between *X* and *Y* is positive for values of *X* less than 6 units and negative for values of *X* more than 6 units. The exact opposite holds for panel *b*. The relationship is negative for values of *X* less than 6 and positive for *X* greater than 6. Notice that at the point where the slope changes from positive to negative (or vice versa), the slope of the curve will be exactly 0; the tangent at point $X = 6$ for both curves is a horizontal straight line that neither rises nor falls as *X* changes.

> When a curvilinear relationship has a zero slope, the value of *Y* reaches either a high point (a maximum)—as in panel *a*—or a low point (a minimum)—as in panel *b*—at the *X* value where slope is zero.

Maximum and minimum values of relationships are important in economics. Suppose, for example, that *X* in panel *a* of Figure 6 represents the production of automobiles by General Motors (in units of 1 million) and that *Y* represents GM's profits from automobile production (in billions of dollars). According to this diagram, GM should settle on $X =$ 6 million units of automobile production because its profits would be higher at this output than at any other production level.

Suppose that in panel *b*, *Y* measures GM's costs of producing an automobile, and *X* still measures automobile production. Production costs per automobile are at a minimum at $X = 6$. In other words, GM will produce cars at the lowest cost per car if it produces 6 million cars.

SCATTER DIAGRAMS

The **scatter diagram** (see Figure 7) is a statistical tool frequently used to examine whether a positive or negative relationship exists between two variables. Statisticians have more powerful and exact tools to measure relationships, but the scatter diagram is a convenient analytical instrument.

FIGURE 7
A Scatter Diagram of Mortgage Rates and Housing Starts, 1970–1990

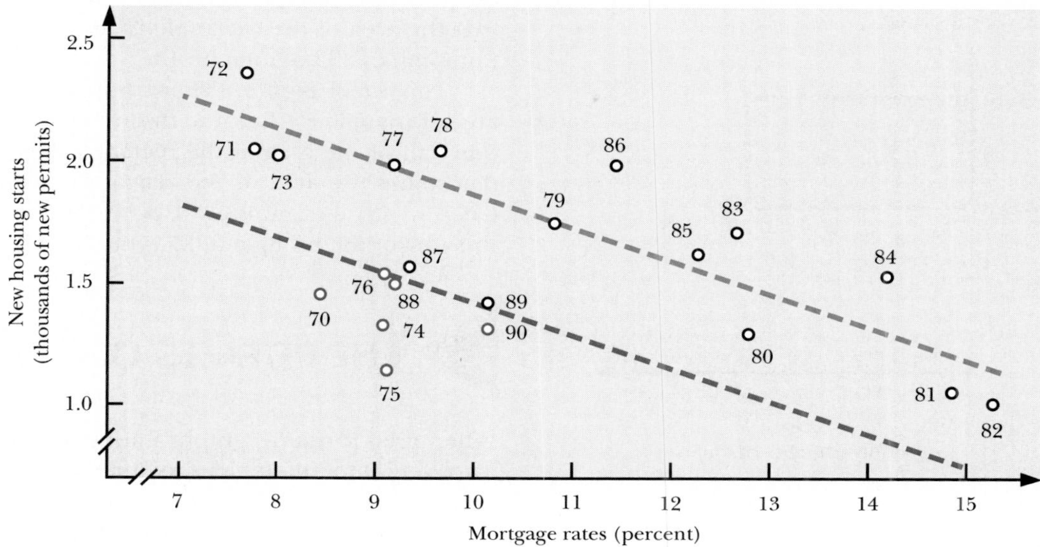

The generally falling pattern of dots suggests that there is a negative relationship between these two variables. The fact that not all dots lie on a single line suggests that other factors besides the independent variable (mortgage rates) affect the dependent variable (housing starts).

Source: *Economic Report of the President.*

A **scatter diagram** consists of a number of separate points, each plotting the value of one variable (measured along the horizontal axis) against a value of another variable (measured along the vertical axis) for a specific time interval.

In Figure 7, mortgage interest rates are measured along the horizontal axis, and new housing starts (the number of new homes on which construction has started) are measured along the vertical axis. Each of the 21 dots on the scatter diagram shows the combination of mortgage rate and number of housing starts for a particular year from 1970 to 1990. The pattern of dots provides convenient visual information about the relationship between the two variables. If the dots show a pattern of low mortgage rates accompanying high housing starts and high mortgage rates accompanying low housing starts, the scatter diagram suggests a *negative relationship,* indicated by a generally declining pattern of dots from left to right. A generally rising pattern of dots from left to right shows a positive relationship. If there were no relationship, the dots would be distributed randomly.

Figure 7 shows a negative relationship between mortgage rates and housing starts. The broad, negatively sloped band traces out the general pattern of declining dots. Such a pattern makes sense: Most people would expect the number of houses being built to drop when the cost of borrowing to buy a home rises.

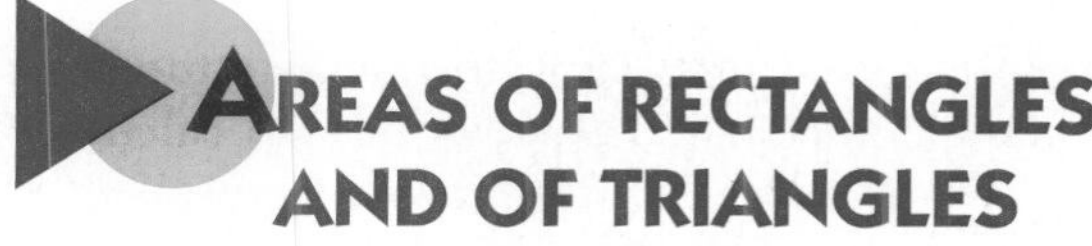

AREAS OF RECTANGLES AND OF TRIANGLES

In economics, it is important to understand how areas of rectangles and of triangles are calculated.

FIGURE 8
Calculating Areas of Rectangles and Triangles

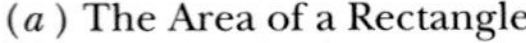

(*a*) The Area of a Rectangle

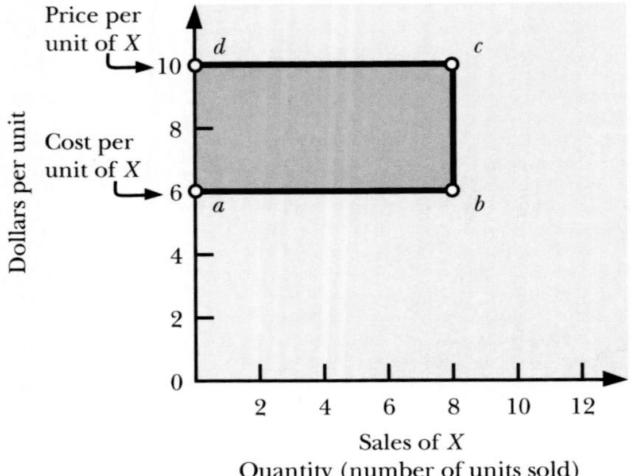

(*b*) The Area of a Triangle

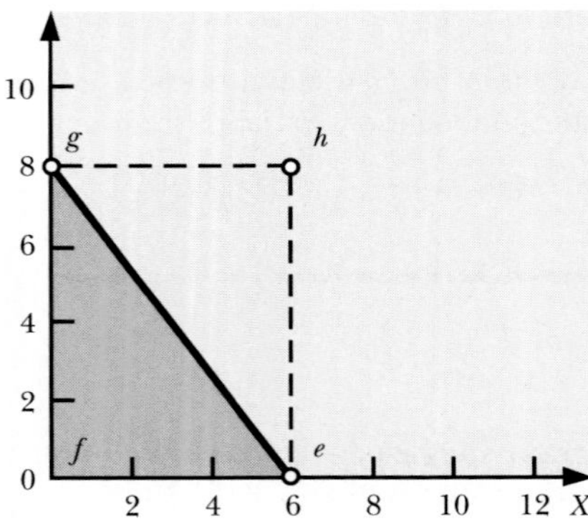

The area of the rectangle *abcd* in panel *a* is calculated by multiplying its height (*ad,* or equivalently, *bc*) by its width (*ab,* or equivalently, *dc*). The height equals $4, and the width equals 8 units; therefore, the area of the rectangle equals $32. As the text explains, $32 is the amount of this firm's profits. The area of the triangle *efg* in panel *b* is one-half of the area of the corresponding rectangle *efgh.* The area of the rectangle is 8 × 6 = 48. The area of the triangle *efg* is therefore 0.5 × 48 = 24.

Panel *a* of Figure 8 shows how to calculate the area of a rectangle, and panel *b* shows how to calculate the area of a triangle. Panel *a* shows a firm selling 8 units of its product for a price of $10, and it costs $6 per unit to produce the product. How much profit is the firm earning? The firm's profit is the area of the rectangle *abcd.* To calculate the area of a rectangle, the height of the rectangle (*ad* or *bc,* or $10 − $6 = $4 per unit) must be multiplied by the width of the rectangle (*ab* or *dc,* or 8 units). Multiplication shows that the area of the rectangle is $4 per unit times 8 units equals $32 of total profit.

Panel *b* of Figure 8 shows how to calculate the area of triangle *efg.* Because this triangle accounts for one half of the area of the rectangle *efgh,* one must determine the area of the rectangle (which equals 8 × 6 = 48) and multiply it by ½. In this example, the area of the triangle is 0.5 × 48 = 24.

THE PITFALLS OF GRAPHS

When used properly, graphs illuminate the world in a convenient and efficient manner. They may, however, be used to confuse or even misinform. Factions in political contests, advertisers of competing products, or rivals in lawsuits can take the same set of data, apply the standard rules of graph construction, and yet offer graphs that support their own positions. This misuse of graphs is especially apparent in national political campaigns, where the incumbent seeks to demonstrate how well the country's economy has been managed while the opposition shows how badly the nation's economic affairs have been bungled.

It is important to be able to form an independent judgment of what graphs say about the real world. This section warns the graph consumer about three of the many pitfalls of using graphs: (1) the ambiguity of slope, (2) the improper measurement of data, and (3) the use of unrepresentative data.

The Ambiguity of Slope

The steepness of the rise or fall of a graphed curve can be an ambiguous guide to the strength of the relationship between the two variables. The graphed slope is affected by the scale used to mark the axes, and the slope's numerical value depends upon the unit of measure.

In Figure 9, panel *a* provides an example of the *ambiguity of slope.* If you look carefully, you will see that both the right-hand and left-hand graphs plot exactly the same numbers: the sales of domestically produced cars for the years 1978 to 1986. In the left-hand graph (because each unit on the vertical axis represents 1 million cars), the decline in sales appears to be rather small. In the right-hand graph (because each unit now measures a half-million cars), the decline appears to be quite steep. The impression one gets of the magnitude of the decline in auto sales is affected by the choice of units on the vertical axis even though both graphs provide identical information about the sales of U.S.-produced cars.

Improper Measurement

A second pitfall in reading and evaluating graphs is *improper measurement*. This is not simply an incorrect count of a variable (counting 20 chickens instead of 15). A variable may give the appearance of measuring one thing while in reality it measures another. Improper measurement is thus often subtle and difficult to detect.

In economics, two common types of improper measurement are (1) inflation-distorted measures and (2) growth-distorted measures. These are most often encountered in *time-series graphs,* in which the horizontal *X* axis measures time (in months, quarters, years, decades, etc.) and the vertical *Y* axis measures a second variable whose behavior is plotted over time.

Panel *b* of Figure 9 gives an example of the importance of **inflation distortion** by graphing the per capita national debt (the average person's share of the national debt) before and after adjustment for inflation. *Inflation* occurs when prices, on the average, rise. Per capita national debt (without adjustment for inflation) increased more than five times between 1950 and 1990. We can make this rise appear as steep or as flat as we wish by changing the scale on the vertical axis, but that is not the point here. The dashed line shows the per capita national debt adjusted for inflation. The rather surprising result is that, after the effects of inflation are removed, the per capita national debt actually decreased over the 30-year period from 1950 to 1980. From 1980 to 1990, per capita debt rose sharply after adjustment for inflation. If we look at the entire 40-year period, per capita debt in 1990 was only moderately above that of 1950 after adjustment for inflation.

Inflation distortion is the measurement of the dollar value of a variable over time without adjustment for inflation over that period.

Generally speaking, economic measures of output, employment, and the like tend to rise over time even after adjustment for inflation. They rise because population grows, the labor force expands, the number of plants increases, and the technology of production improves. To look at the growth of a particular index without taking into account the overall expansion can lead to **growth distortion.** People who want to demonstrate alarming increases in alcohol consumption or crime can point to increases in gallons of alcohol consumed or crimes reported without noting that population may be increasing at a rate that is as fast or faster. Panel *c* of Figure 9 shows the problem of growth distortion. The left-hand graph shows the inflation-adjusted output of the 100 largest manufacturing concerns from 1954 to 1977. By looking at this graph, one might conclude that the dominance of American manufacturing by giant concerns is on the rise, because the output of these concerns has risen by a considerable amount. However, by looking at the output *share* of the 100 largest manufacturing companies (the right-hand chart), we find that the output of these companies has just been keeping up with manufacturing output in general.

Growth distortion is the measurement of changes in a variable over time that does not reflect the concurrent change in other relevant variables with which the variable should be compared, such as population size.

Misinterpretations of time-series graphs can be avoided by (1) maintaining a careful distinction between graphs that do and do not account for inflation and (2) using per capita figures where appropriate or expressing graphs as percentages or as shares of some total.

Unrepresentative Data

A final pitfall in the use of graphs is the problem of *unrepresentative* or *incomplete data.* The direction of a graphed relationship may depend upon the selection of the time period. For example, Soviet grain harvests fluctuated dramatically in the final years of that nation's existence, with disastrous harvests following good harvests. If a good harvest year is chosen as the first year of a graph and a bad harvest year as the last, the assessment of Soviet agricultural performance will be more unfavorable. It will be less unfavorable if the graph starts with a bad harvest year

FIGURE 9
Examples of Pitfalls in the Use of Graphs

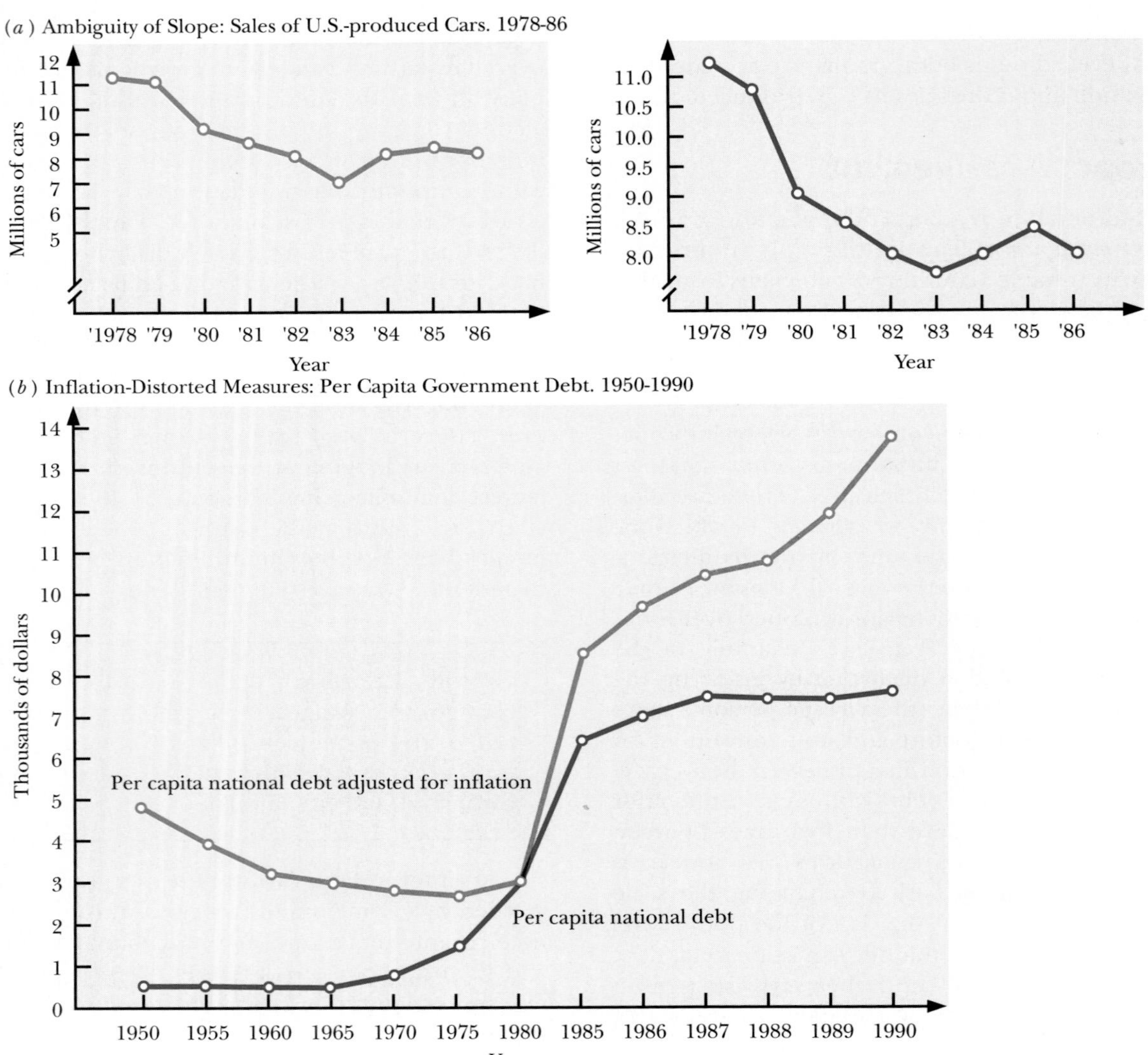

In panel *a*, the choice of units on the vertical axis determines the steepness of slope. Although both figures plot the same data, the graph on the right appears to yield a steeper decline in domestic auto sales. In panel *b*, the graph of per capita government debt (not adjusted for inflation) shows a steady rise in per capita debt. After the inflation distortion is removed (the orange line), we find that per capita debt actually declined over the 30-year period from 1950 to 1980. From 1980

and ends with a good one. Because the graphical relationship depends upon the choice of years covered by the graph, biased observers have the opportunity to present their particular version of the facts.

The problem of unrepresentative data also applies to comparisons across states, regions, or countries. The outcome can be manipulated by deliberate selection of the states or countries to include in the figure. Panel *d* of Figure 9 shows how unemployment data can be manipulated. Suppose your goal is to demonstrate that the 1982 U.S. unemployment rate was not much different from the rates of

FIGURE 9 (CONTINUED)

(*c*) Growth-Distorted Measures: Output of 100 Largest Manufacturing Companies

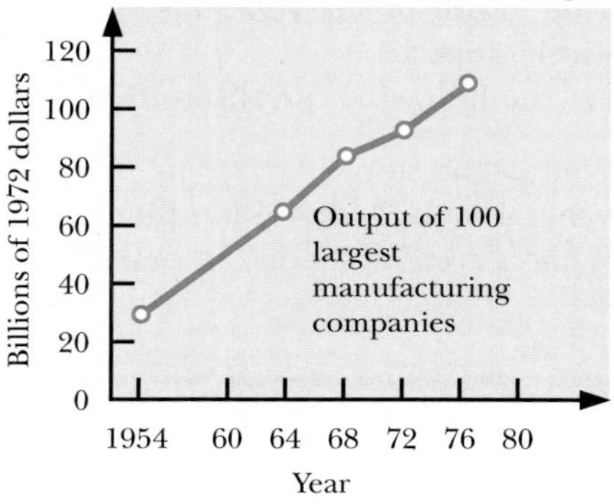

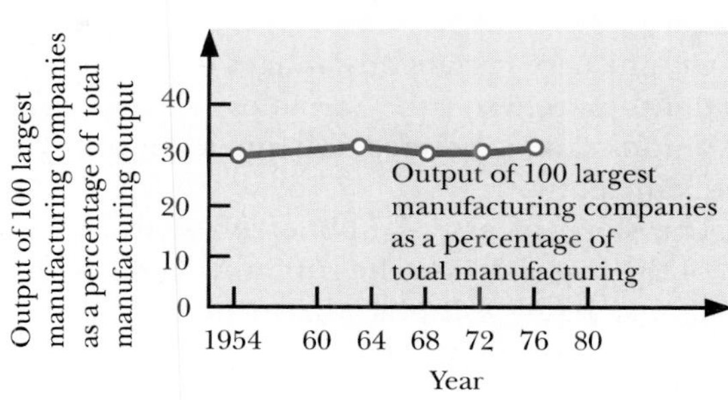

(*d*) Unrepresentative Sample: U.S. Employment in International Perspective

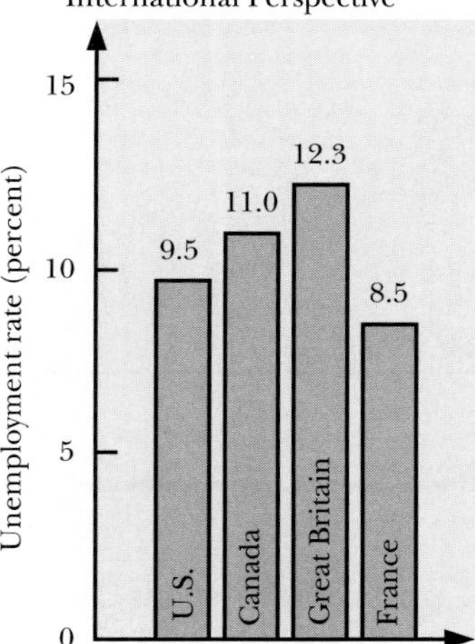

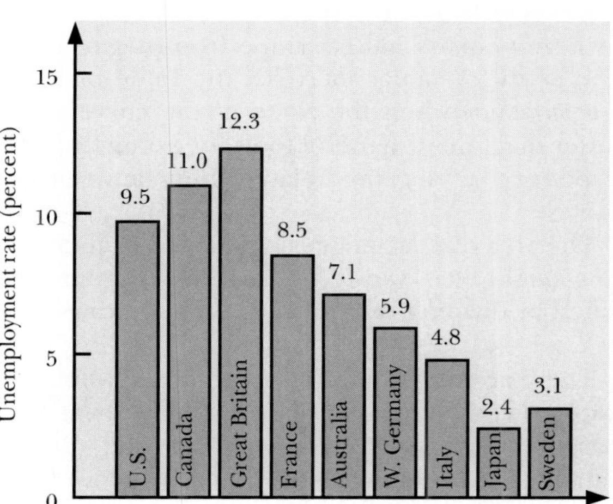

to 1988, per capita debt rose prior to and after adjustment for inflation. In panel *c*, the left-hand graph shows that the output of the 100 largest manufacturing firms has been increasing since 1954 by substantial amounts. This graph, however, fails to reflect the overall growth of the economy, including the growth in total manufacturing. The right-hand graph adjusts for growth distortion and shows that the share of output of the 100 largest manufacturing firms has barely changed since 1954. In panel *d*, when the sample is limited to four high-unemployment countries (the left-hand side), the U.S. unemployment rate does not appear to be high by international standards. When a broader and more representative sample is taken of nine countries (as shown in the right-hand graph), the U.S. unemployment rate does appear to be high by international standards.

other countries. The left-hand chart, comparing U.S. unemployment with that of three other countries, suggests that U.S. unemployment is not different. However, in the right-hand chart of eight industrialized countries, the U.S. unemployment rate appears relatively high.

SUMMARY

1. Graphs are useful for presenting positive and negative relationships between two variables. A positive relationship exists between two variables if

an increase in one is associated with an *increase* in the other; a negative relationship exists between two variables if an increase in one is associated with a *decrease* in the other. In a graphical relationship, one variable may be an independent variable and the other may be a dependent variable. In some relationships, it is not clear which variable is dependent and which is independent.

2. Graphs have certain advantages over tables: The relationship between the variables is easier to see, and graphs can accommodate large amounts of data more efficiently.

3. The slope of a straight-line relationship is the ratio of the rise in Y over the run in X. The slope of a curvilinear relationship at a particular point is the slope of a straight-line tangent to the curve at that point. When a curve changes slope from positive to negative as the X values increase, the value of Y reaches a *maximum* when the slope of the curve is zero; when a curve changes slope from negative to positive as the X values increase, the value of Y reaches a *minimum* when the slope of the curve is zero. Scatter diagrams are useful tools for examining data for positive or negative relationships between two variables.

4. The area of a rectangle is calculated by multiplying its height by its width. The area of a triangle is calculated by dividing the product of height times width by 2.

5. There are three pitfalls to be aware of when using graphs: (1) the choice of *units* and *scale* affects the apparent steepness or flatness of a curve; (2) the variables may be inflation distorted or growth distorted; and (3) omitted data or incomplete data may result in an erroneous interpretation of the relationship between two variables.

KEY TERMS

positive (direct) relationship
negative (inverse) relationship
independent variable
dependent variable
slope
tangent
scatter diagram
inflation distortion
growth distortion

QUESTIONS AND PROBLEMS

1. Graph the following data:

X:	0	1	2	3
Y:	10	20	30	40

What is the slope?

2. As income falls, people spend less on cars. Is the graph of this relationship positively or negatively sloped?
3. As the price of a good falls, people buy more of it. Is the graph of the relationship positively or negatively sloped?
4. Answer the following questions using Figure A.
   a. What is the slope?
   b. What is area A (shaded in blue)?
   c. What is area B (shaded in orange)?

FIGURE A

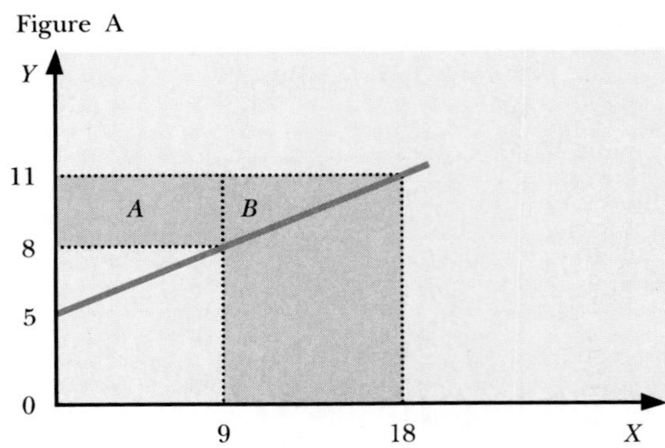

5. The federal government spent $96 billion in 1970 and almost $1 trillion in 1992 on goods and services. What types of distortions affect this kind of comparison?
6. Prepare two scatter diagrams (A and B) from the data in Table A. In your opinion, do these diagrams reveal any positive or negative relationships?
7. During a 1992 U.S. presidential debate, suppose the incumbent faces an increase in unemployment last year of 240,000 workers, or approximately 0.1 percent. Which figure will the incumbent mention in his public statements? To which will his opponent refer?
8. Suppose thefts in a small town rise from a total of 1 to 2 cases in a given year. A sheriff running for reelection will refer to which change in her public speeches—the absolute change ("only" 1 additional break-in last year) or the percentage change (a 100 percent increase)?

TABLE A

	Diagram A		Diagram B	
	Unemployment Rate	Inflation Rate	Interest Rate	Inflation Rate
1970	4.8	5.2	8.0	5.2
1971	5.8	4.8	7.4	4.8
1972	5.5	4.0	7.2	4.0
1973	4.8	6.0	7.4	6.0
1974	5.5	9.4	8.6	9.4
1975	8.3	9.1	8.8	9.1
1976	7.6	5.8	8.4	5.8
1977	6.9	6.3	8.0	6.3
1978	6.0	7.8	8.7	7.8
1979	5.8	9.5	9.6	9.5
1980	7.0	9.8	11.9	9.8
1981	7.5	9.3	14.2	9.3
1982	9.5	6.2	13.8	6.2
1983	9.5	4.1	12.0	4.1
1984	7.4	4.0	12.7	4.0
1985	7.1	3.6	11.4	3.6
1986	6.9	2.7	9.0	2.7
1987	6.1	3.4	9.4	3.4
1988	5.5	3.3	8.9	3.3
1989	5.3	4.1	8.5	4.1
1990	5.5	4.2	8.6	4.2
1991	6.8	2.9	7.5	2.9

Source: *Economic Report of the President.*

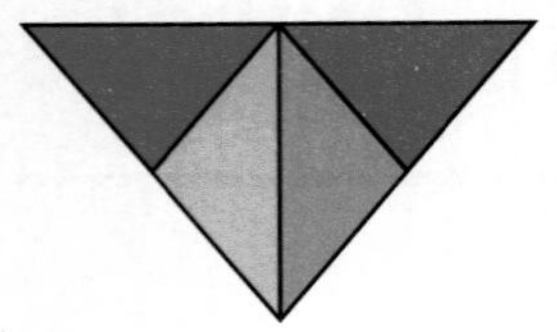

2 The Economic Problem

CHAPTER INSIGHT

People always seem to want more than they can possibly have. One person might want a luxury car for each day of the week, a 10-bedroom home in the best part of town, a 15-room ski lodge in Colorado, a staff of 25 servants, 100 pounds of Maine lobster per month, a different 20-carat diamond ring for each day of the year—the list could go on and on. The only limits are time, imagination, and appetite. If we added together the wish lists of everyone in the United States, the total number of luxury cars desired might equal 100 million per year, the total weight of Maine lobster wanted might be 100 tons per week, and so on.

Obviously no economy can meet all these wants. There are not enough skilled engineers and craftspersons to build the millions of luxury autos, the waters off Maine will not yield the desired tonnage of lobsters per week, and Colorado ski country is not big enough for everyone to have a lodge.

How shall we use our scarce resources? That is the economic problem. Because we can't produce enough to meet our virtually unlimited wants, we must choose among alternatives, and we must make these hard choices in an orderly fashion.

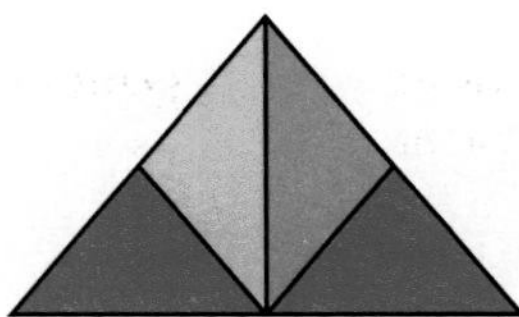

UNLIMITED WANTS, SCARCE RESOURCES

We live in what John Kenneth Galbraith has called "the affluent society."[1] Although many people are poor by American standards, the standard of living of most American families is high by world standards. Is it appropriate to speak of scarcity in an affluent society? This question underscores the importance of attaching exact meanings to economic terms. The economic definition of scarcity is different from the dictionary definition. In economics, scarcity is defined not by the ability to attain a particular standard of living or purchase the necessities of life, but by the ability to satisfy wants; and although our economy can produce goods and services worth trillions of dollars, people's wants dwarf this production capability.

Suppose a committee were appointed to allocate the goods and services that can be produced with available resources among all the people who want them. The task would not be easy. Those in charge would have to make hard choices. Allocations could be made at random (perhaps through lotteries) or according to rules. One rule might be to meet the wants of those who offer something in return. Another might involve determining which people have the best claims on the basis of their social behavior. Alternatively, all goods could be divided equally.

The imbalance between what people want and what they are able to acquire illustrates the most basic facts of economic life: *scarcity* and *choice*. The economy cannot fulfill everyone's wants; therefore, someone or something must decide which wants will be met.

> The most important fact of economics is the law of scarcity: There will never be enough resources to meet everyone's wants.

THE DEFINITION OF ECONOMICS

Briefly stated, **economics** can be defined as the study of how *scarce resources* are *allocated* among *competing ends*. To understand this definition, however, we must understand the exact economic meanings of *scarcity*, *resources*, *allocation*, and *competing ends*.

Scarcity

In Houston, Texas, a now-defunct airline announced that any tickets not sold 10 minutes before departure on its Houston-to-Dallas/Fort Worth flights would be given away free of charge. Crowds of people gathered at the departure gate in the hope of getting one of the few available free tickets, but many travelers had to return home disappointed. In economic terms, the "free" tickets were not a **free good;** they were a **scarce good.**

> An item is a **scarce good** if the amount available (offered to users) is less than the amount people would want if it were given away free of charge.
>
> An item is a **free good** if the amount available is greater than the amount people want at a zero price.

Scarce goods usually command a price, even though it may not be obvious at first glance. Indeed, a good may be scarce—and costly—in one place or under one set of circumstances and free in another, as the following examples will show. (See Example 1.)

Tumbleweeds. Along an Idaho highway stands a delightful sign: "Tumbleweeds are free, take one." Like the "free" airline ticket, tumbleweeds have a price of zero, but unlike the ticket, tumbleweeds in Idaho are a free good. Tourists may want to take one home as a souvenir, but the number of tumbleweeds available far exceeds the number people want, even at no cost. In Alaska, however, tumbleweeds may be such a rarity that the number people want exceeds the number available. Exotic orchids can be freely picked in some remote Hawaiian islands, but they command a high price in New York City. Mesquite used to be a worthless bush to Texas ranchers until fine restaurants started paying $1 or more per pound for mesquite chips.

Landing and Takeoff Slots. Congested airports like New York's LaGuardia, Washington's National, and Chicago's O'Hare can handle only a limited number of takeoffs and landings per day. More planes wish

[1]John Kenneth Galbraith. *The Affluent Society* (Boston: Houghton Mifflin, 1957).

EXAMPLE 1 Rides in the Space Shuttle Are Not a Free Good

Every year, the National Aeronautics and Space Administration (NASA) receives thousands of requests from persons who wish to ride the shuttle (even after the tragic *Challenger* disaster). Some wish to do so for scientific reasons; others wish to do so for personal satisfaction or even for financial gain. One singer-composer has petitioned NASA to allow him to ride on the space shuttle in order to get inspiration for new songs.

There are five or six seats available on each shuttle flight, yet thousands wish to fly each flight. Because the number of seats available is only a small fraction of the number of people wishing to fly each flight, rides on the space shuttle are not a free good.

What type of allocation system does NASA use to decide who gets this scarce good? It has rigorous selection programs for its professional astronauts based upon scientific knowledge, piloting skills, dedication, and so on. It has allowed influential congressional representatives to fly in the space shuttle.

Eventually, as space flight becomes more frequent and safe, rides into space will be allocated on the basis of price. Those willing and able to pay the price will get a ride into space.

People have virtually unlimited wants. When goods and services are offered free, people's desires are limited only by their imaginations. Just as NASA cannot meet the demand for rides in the space shuttle (at a zero price), the resources of society are no match for people's wants.

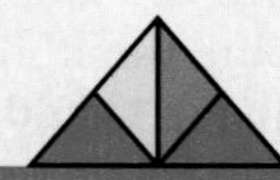

to use these airports than can be accommodated. Committees of government officials and airline management determine how to allot takeoff and landing slots, and competing airlines engage in intense negotiations to obtain them. Even though the airlines do not pay for them, landing slots are a scarce commodity at major airports. At uncongested airports, on the other hand, landing slots are a free good because there are more slots than the airlines want.

Los Angeles Air. The early residents of Los Angeles did not have to worry about clean air; before the automobile age and the mass migration to southern California, clean air was not scarce. Although no one is charged outright for clean (or cleaner) air, it has become a scarce good. Residents pay to obtain it when they purchase homes in distant suburbs where smog is less severe, when they commute a long way to work, and when they buy air filtration systems for their homes.

> Goods may be scarce even if they are free, and goods may be free at one time and place and scarce in another time and place.

Resources

Resources, also known as **factors of production,** include the natural resources (land, mineral deposits, oxygen), the capital equipment (plants, machinery, inventories), and the human resources (workers with different skills, qualifications, ambitions, managerial talents) that are used as *inputs* to produce scarce goods and services. These resources represent the economic wealth of society because they determine how much output the economy can produce. The limitation of resources is the fundamental source of scarcity.

> The **factors of production,** or **resources**, are the inputs used to produce goods and services. They can be divided into three categories: land, labor, and capital.

Land includes all natural resources—unimproved and unaltered by labor or capital—that contribute to production. Desert land that has been irrigated would not be considered "land" by this definition because labor and capital were used to alter its natural condition. Other items that we would not ordinarily call "land"—such as air and water—do fall into this category, as long as they are in their natural state.

Land is a catchall term that covers all of nature's bounty—minerals, forests, land, water resources, oxygen, and so on.

Capital is not one of nature's gifts; it includes equipment, buildings, and inventories created by the factors of production. *Plant and equipment capital* is long-lived: When it is used to produce output, it is not *consumed* (used up) immediately; it is consumed gradually in the process of time. An assembly plant may have a life of 40 years, a computer a life of 5 years, and a lathe a life of 10 years. In 1992, the total value of all U.S. capital was approximately $28 trillion.[2]

Capital is the equipment, plants, buildings, and inventories that are available to society.

When economists speak of capital, they mean physical capital goods—buildings, computers, trucks, plants—rather than *financial capital,* which represents ownership claims to physical capital. AT&T shareholders own financial capital, but their shares really represent ownership of AT&T's physical capital.

Economists also make a distinction between the *stock* of physical capital and *additions* to that stock. The stock of capital consists of all the capital (plants, equipment, inventories, buildings) that exist *at a given time.* This stock usually grows. New plants are built, new equipment is manufactured, additions are made to inventories. Through **investment** society adds to its stock of capital.

Investment is addition to the stock of capital.

Labor resources consist of the people in the work force, with their various skills, education, and natural ability, who contribute to production in various ways. The ditchdigger contributes muscle power; the computer engineer contributes mental abilities; the airline pilot contributes physical coordination and mental talents. In the United States today, the labor force consists of more than 120 million individuals.

Labor is the combination of physical and mental talents that human beings contribute to production.

Capital investment can add to the stock of **human capital** just as it adds to the stock of physical capital.

Human capital is the accumulation of past investments in schooling, training, and health that raise the productive capacity of people.

In 1992, the stock of human capital was valued at approximately $10 trillion.[3] Investment in the training and education of people raises the wealth of society because, like investment in physical capital, it increases production capacity.

Entrepreneurs can be considered a separate factor of production. The term *labor,* however, can be stretched to mean entrepreneurial labor as well.

An **entrepreneur** organizes, manages, and assumes the risks for an enterprise.

Entrepreneurs organize the factors of production to produce output, seek out and exploit new business opportunities, and introduce new technologies and inventions. The entrepreneur takes the risk and bears the responsibility if the venture fails.

Allocation

Society cannot function without a satisfactory way to **allocate** scarce resources.

[2]OECD (Organization for Economic Cooperation and Development), Department of Economics and Statistics, *Flows and Stocks of Fixed Capital* (Paris: OECD, 1983), p. 9. Figures updated by the authors.

[3]Calculated from John W. Kendrick, *The Formation and Stocks of Total Capital* (New York: Columbia University Press, 1976), Appendix B. Figures updated by the authors.

Allocation is the apportionment of scarce resources to specific productive uses or to particular persons or groups.

Consider what would happen without organized allocation. People would have to fight with one another for scarce resources. The timid would not compete effectively; the elderly or weak would be left out. Such free-for-all allocation was common in the Dark Ages, but it is rare in modern societies. It reappears when social order breaks down. That is why martial law must sometimes be declared to prevent looting and violent competition for scarce goods during floods, natural disasters, and wars. Societies cannot function unless the allocation problem is resolved in a satisfactory manner.

Market Allocation. Most economies allocate scarce resources through the **market.**

The **market** is an arrangement by which buyers and sellers exchange goods or services.

Here is how *market allocation* works. Commodities such as TV sets are scarce because the number desired at a zero price exceeds the number offered. Raising the price of TV sets encourages production and discourages consumption. Market allocation uses higher prices to restrict the number of buyers to the supply available. The market uses prices to equate the number of TV sets offered for sale to the number buyers are prepared to purchase. Most goods and services are allocated by the market in our society. Market allocation and the price system are discussed in Chapter 3.

Government Allocation. Although market allocation is accepted without reservation in most cases, its use is sometimes controversial. When market allocation is unacceptable, society turns to **government allocation.**

Government allocation occurs when government authorities determine who gets scarce goods.

Under such a system, access to the scarce resource is determined not by willingness to pay, but by administrative authority.

In the United States, the government allocates resources to national defense, diplomacy, and law enforcement; grants licenses for television and radio stations; and even uses lotteries to allocate scarce resources. The Federal Communications Commission allocates cellular-phone franchises by lottery, and the Immigration Service has used lotteries to allocate green cards to emigrants.

Government allocation does not eliminate the need to make hard choices. In Great Britain, the government's National Health Service allocates the bulk of England's medical-care resources. Because the number of doctors, nurses, dialysis machines, organ donors, and hospital beds cannot meet all wants for "free" medical care, the National Health Service allocates public medical-care resources by a system of rules. Patients who want elective surgery must wait weeks and months to see a specialist; elderly patients are denied transplants and other costly procedures. A private medical market supplements the British system of public allocation.

There is endless controversy about which allocation system (or combination of systems) is best. (See Example 2.)

Competing Ends

Whatever allocation system is used, it must somehow allocate scarce resources among **competing ends.**

Competing ends are the different purposes for which resources can be used.

Individuals compete for resources: Which families will have a greater claim on scarce resources? Who will be rich? Who will be poor? The private sector (individuals and businesses) and the government compete for resources. Even current and future consumption compete for resources: When scarce resources are invested in physical and human capital to produce more goods and services in the future, these same resources cannot be used in the present.

Finally, society must choose between competing national goals when allocating resources. What is most important: price stability, full employment, elimination of poverty, or economic growth?

EXAMPLE 2 Rationing Health Care: The Oregon Plan

Oregon's public health officials have created a panel of experts to develop rules for allocating the state's scarce public health resources. As mandated by Oregon's Basic Health Services Act, the panel must compile a list of 800 illnesses and then draw a line between those that do and do not qualify for assistance. People who qualify for Medicaid can be treated for illnesses above the line but not for those below the line.

How are Oregon officials ranking illnesses that qualify for treatment? The aim is to rank treatments in the order that people value them. Treatments for dangerous but curable diseases like appendicitis rank high as do preventive measures such as prenatal care. Illnesses that defy treatment such as AIDS, or trivial illnesses like viral warts, are at the bottom of the list. Pain killers for cancer patients rank high, along with bone marrow transplants.

When resources are scarce, an allocation system must be used. As an Oregon official stated, "Everyone cannot have everything." Although it seems cruel to deny some people treatment, a rational method must be found for determining who gets what.

Source: "Health Care: Rational Choice," *The Economist*, March 23, 1991, p. 32.

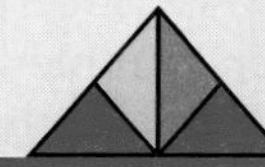

THE ECONOMIC PROBLEM

The economic problem of how to allocate scarce resources among competing ends raises three questions: *What* products will be produced? *How* will they be produced? *For whom* will they be produced?

What?

Should society devote its limited resources to producing civilian or military goods, luxuries or necessities, goods for immediate consumption or goods that increase the wealth of society (capital goods)? Should small or large cars be produced? Should buses and subways be produced instead of cars? Should the military concentrate on strategic or conventional forces?

How?

What combinations of the factors of production will be used to produce the goods that people want? Will coal, petroleum, or nuclear power be used to produce electricity? Will bulldozers or workers with shovels build dams? Should automobile tires be made from natural or synthetic rubber? Should Diet Coke be sweetened with saccharin or another sugar substitute? Should tried-and-true methods of production be replaced by new technology?

For Whom?

Will society's output be divided equally or unequally? Will differences in wealth be allowed to pass from one generation to the next? What role will government play in determining allocation? Should government change the way the economy distributes its output?

OPPORTUNITY COSTS

Whenever people have to choose what will be produced, how it will be produced, and for whom it will be produced, they must sacrifice some valuable alternatives. The cost of such a sacrifice is called an **opportunity cost.**

> The **opportunity cost** of a particular action is the loss of the next best alternative.

If a person buys a new car, the opportunity cost of doing so might be a European trip, an investment in the stock market, or enrollment in a university. To find the true cost of the car we must therefore factor in the cost of losing the next best alternative. If the government increases defense spending, the opportunity cost is the next best alternative that had to be sacrificed (public education, tax reduction) to make the funds available.

The notion of opportunity cost supplies a shortcut method of differentiating free goods from scarce goods.

> Free goods have an opportunity cost of zero. Scarce goods have a positive opportunity cost.

Why does the Idaho tumbleweed have no opportunity cost? If one tumbleweed is taken, the amount available is still greater than the amount wanted. Nobody has to go without a tumbleweed because someone else took one.

The opportunity cost of an action can involve the sacrifice of time as well as goods. To gather the free tumbleweed, the traveler must sacrifice time (although the time cost may be very small). Consider the opportunity cost of attending a football game with a free ticket. The three hours spent at the game could have been devoted to alternative activities such as studying. If a major exam were scheduled for the next day, the opportunity cost of the game could be quite high. The notion of sacrificed time as an opportunity cost is an important ingredient of modern economics.

Economic decisions are based on opportunity costs. In committing its resources to a particular action (such as producing cars), a business must consider the opportunities it forgoes by not committing these resources to another activity (such as producing trucks). Before signing a contract to work for Ford Motors, workers must consider the other employment opportunities that they are passing up. People with savings to invest must weigh the various alternatives before they commit their funds to a particular investment. (See Example 3.)

> Every choice involved in the allocation of scarce resources has opportunity costs.

EXAMPLE 3 The Pacific Yew and Ovarian Cancer: Scarcity, Allocation, and Opportunity Costs

The Pacific yew, a shrublike tree native to the Pacific West Coast, was long regarded as a weed, which loggers would burn. So uninteresting was this tree that no one kept inventories on the number in existence. It was a free good . . . until recently.

Studies by the National Cancer Institute have revealed that taxol, a substance that comes from the Pacific yew, is effective in treating advanced cases of ovarian and lung cancer. However, it takes six 100-year-old trees to treat a single cancer patient, and most of the mature Pacific yews have been destroyed; they can be found on 1 in every 20 acres of Oregon's forests.

Scientists expect that it will take two to three years of research to produce synthetic taxol. Until then, there will not be enough to treat all patients who need it. Taxol and the Pacific yew are now scarce goods. People want more than is available. Its scarcity means that an allocation system must be used to distribute the available taxol. Currently, the National Cancer Institute determines which patients will receive the drug.

The case of the Pacific yew and taxol shows that goods can quickly change from free to scarce. In fact, environmental groups are now worried that the Pacific yew will disappear because of the demand for taxol. As the good becomes scarce, its opportunity cost is apparent. To save lives, the Pacific yew may have to disappear.

Source: "Tree Yields a Cancer Treatment, but Ecological Costs May Be High," *New York Times,* May 13, 1991.

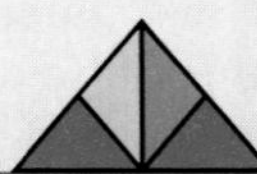

PRODUCTION POSSIBILITIES

Economists use the concept of the **production possibilities frontier (PPF)** to illustrate the function of scarcity, choice, and opportunity costs.

> The **production possibilities frontier (PPF)** shows the combinations of goods that can be produced when the factors of production are used to their full potential.

When this concept is presented graphically, the *production possibilities curve,* which represents the PPF, reveals the economic choices open to society. An economy can produce any combination of outputs on or inside the PPF.

Suppose an economy produces only two types of goods: tanks and wheat. Table 1 gives the amounts of wheat and tanks that this hypothetical economy can produce with its limited factors of production and technical knowledge. Figure 1 provides a graphic representation of this information, plotted along a production possibilities curve.

Suppose further that this economy has resources that can be used for either wheat or tanks. Land may be better suited for wheat; tank production may require more capital. If our hypothetical economy chose to be at point *a* on Figure 1, it would be producing no tanks and the *maximum* of 18 tons of wheat from the factors of production available. At point *f*, the economy would be producing no wheat and the *maximum* of 5000 tanks. At point *c*, 2000 tanks are produced; the maximum number of tons of wheat that can be produced is therefore 15. Each intermediate point on the production possibilities frontier (PPF) between *a* and *f* represents a different combination of wheat and tanks that could be produced using the same resources and technology.

Although our hypothetical economy is capable of producing output combinations *a* through *f*, it cannot produce output combination *g* (17 tons of wheat and 3000 tanks) because *g* uses more resources than the economy has. It can, on the other hand, produce the output combination at point *h*, which is

FIGURE 1
The Production Possibilities Frontier (PPF)

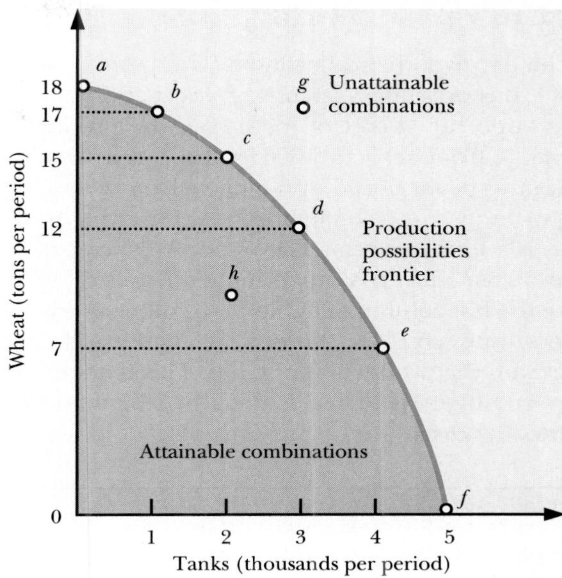

The PPF shows the combinations of outputs of two goods that can be produced from society's resources when these resources are used to their maximum potential. Point *a* shows that if 18 tons of wheat are produced, no tank production is possible. Point *f* shows that if no wheat is produced, a maximum of 5000 tanks can be produced. Point *d* shows that if 3000 tanks are produced, a maximum of 12 tons of wheat can be produced. Point *g* is above society's PPF. With its available resources, the economy cannot produce 17 tons of wheat and 3000 tanks. Points like *h* inside the PPF and therefore attainable, represent an inefficient use of the society's resources.

TABLE 1
Production Possibilities Schedule

Combination	Tanks (thousands)	Wheat (tons)	Opportunity Cost of Tanks (in tons of wheat)
a	0	18	0
b	1	17	1
c	2	15	2
d	3	12	3
e	4	7	5
f	5	0	7

inside the frontier because it requires fewer resources than the economy has.

The Law of Increasing Costs

When our hypothetical economy is at point *a* on Figure 1, it is producing 18 tons of wheat and no tanks. The opportunity cost of increasing the production of tanks from zero to 1000 is the 1 ton of wheat that must be sacrificed in the move from *a* to *b*. The opportunity cost of 1000 more tanks (moving from *b* to *c*) is 2 tons of wheat. The opportunity cost of the move from *e* to *f* is a much higher 7 tons of wheat. (See the last column of Table 1.) In other words, the opportunity cost per thousand of tank production rises with the production of tanks. This tendency for opportunity costs to rise is described by the **law of increasing costs.**

> The **law of increasing costs** states that as more of a particular commodity is produced, its opportunity cost per unit increases.

The bowed-out shape used to represent the production possibilities frontier reflects the law of increasing costs. Suppose our hypothetical economy were at peace, producing only wheat and no tanks (at *a* on the PPF). Its archenemy declares war, and the economy must suddenly increase its production of tanks. The amount of resources available to the economy is not altered by the declaration of war, so the increased tank production must be at the expense of wheat production. The economy *must move along its PPF* in the direction of more tank production.

As tank production increases, the opportunity cost of a unit of tank production will not remain the same. At low levels of tank production, the opportunity cost of a unit of tank production will be relatively low. Some factors of production will be suited to producing both wheat and tanks; they can be shifted from wheat to tank production without raising opportunity cost. As tank production increases further, resources suited to wheat production but ill-suited to tank production (experienced farmers make inexperienced factory workers, agricultural equipment is poorly adapted to tank factories) must be diverted into tank production. Ever-increasing amounts of these resources must be shifted from wheat production to keep tank production expanding at a constant rate. The opportunity cost of a unit of tank production (the amount of wheat sacrificed) will rise, reflecting the law of increasing costs.

The Law of Diminishing Returns

Underlying the law of increasing costs is the **law of diminishing returns.** Suppose that wheat is produced by means of land, labor, and tractors. The law of diminishing returns states that if labor is increased in equal increments, holding land and tractors constant, the corresponding increases in wheat production will be smaller and smaller.

> The **law of diminishing returns** states that when the amount of one input is increased in equal increments, holding all other inputs constant, the result is ever smaller increases in output.

The law of diminishing returns recognizes that output is produced by combinations of resources. Wheat is produced by labor, farm machinery, and chemical fertilizers. Tanks are produced by skilled labor, unskilled labor, assembly-line equipment, and managerial talent. The law of diminishing returns applies when one or more factors are fixed. Under those circumstances, output must be expanded by an increase in the factors that can be varied. As more and more of the variable factors are used, there will eventually be too much of the variable factor relative to the fixed factors. Accordingly, the amount of extra output produced by additional inputs of the variable factor will decline.

Suppose a farm has a fixed amount of land (1000 acres) and a fixed amount of capital (10 tractors). Initially, 10 farm workers are employed, which means that each would have 100 acres to farm and that each would have 1 tractor. If the number of farm workers increases to 20, each worker would have 50 acres to farm and 2 workers would have to share 1 tractor. If the number of farm workers increases to 1000, each worker would farm 1 acre and 100 workers would share each tractor. Obviously, each worker would be less productive if each had only an acre to farm and had to wait for 99 other workers to use the tractor.

Efficiency

The ability of an economy to operate on its production-possibilities frontier depends upon its ability to use its resources with maximum **efficiency.**

In Figure 1, if the economy produces output combinations that lie on the PPF, the economy is said to be efficient. When an economy is operating on its PPF, it cannot increase the production of one good without reducing the production of another good. If the economy operates at points inside the PPF, such as *h*, it is said to be *inefficient* because more wheat could be produced without cutting back on the other good.

Efficiency occurs when the economy is using its resources so well that producing more of one good results in less of other goods: resources are neither misallocated nor unemployed.

If workers are unemployed or if productive machines stand idle, the economy is not operating on its PPF because available resources are not being employed. If these idle resources were used, more of one good could be produced without reducing the production of other goods. Misallocated resources are those that are not used to their best advantage. If a surgeon works as a ditchdigger, if cotton is planted on Iowa corn land, or if supersonic jets are manufactured in Trinidad, resources are misallocated. If resource misallocations are removed, more of one good could be produced without sacrificing the production of other goods.

FIGURE 2
The Effect of Increasing the Stock of Capital on the PPF

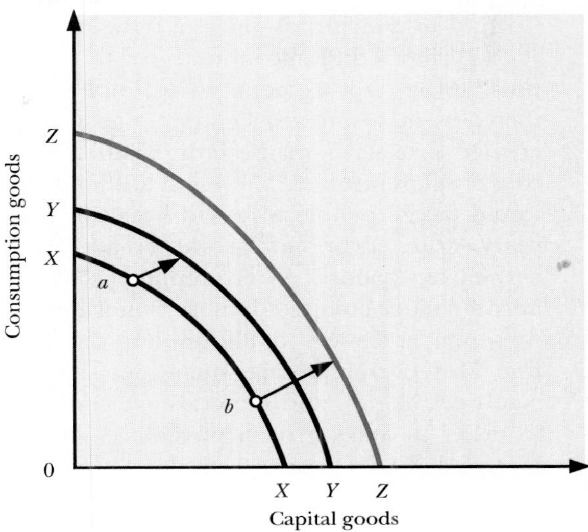

Suppose the current PPF is curve *XX*. If the economy chooses point *a*, allocating most resources to the production of consumption goods and few to the production of new capital goods, the PPF in the future will shift out to curve *YY*. But if the economy chooses point *b*, with comparatively little consumption and comparatively high production of new capital goods, the future PPF will shift out further to *ZZ*.

Economic Growth

Economic growth occurs when the production possibilities frontier, as represented in Figure 1, expands outward and to the right. One source of economic growth is the expansion of capital.

Capital Accumulation. Deciding where to locate on the PPF may represent a choice between capital goods and consumer goods. Capital goods are the equipment, plants, and inventories added to society's stock of capital. These goods can be used to satisfy wants in the future. Consumer goods are items like food, clothing, medicine, and transportation that satisfy consumer wants in the present. The choice between capital goods and consumer goods is shown in Figure 2.

In this figure, the economy with the PPF labeled *XX* must choose among the combinations of consumer goods and capital goods located on *XX*. What are the implications of selecting *a* or *b*? If *a* is chosen, more consumer wants are satisfied today, but additions to the stock of capital are smaller. If *b* is selected, fewer wants are satisfied today, but additions to the stock of capital are greater. Since capital is productive, a larger stock today means more production in the future. The society that selects *b* will therefore experience a greater outward shift of the PPF and will be able to satisfy more wants in the future.

The society that selects *a* will satisfy more wants today but will not be in as good a position to satisfy future wants. If society chooses *a*, the PPF expands from *XX* now to *YY* in the future. If it locates at *b*, the PPF expands more: from *XX* now to *ZZ* in the future. At *ZZ*, the economy will be able to satisfy more wants than at *YY*.

There are limits to the rule that less consumption today means more consumption tomorrow. If all resources were devoted to capital goods, the labor force would starve. If too large a share of resources is put into capital goods, worker incentives might be low and efficiency might be reduced. (See Example 4.)

EXAMPLE 4 To Grow or Not to Grow?

This chapter presents economic growth in a technical way as a rightward shift in the PPF. Economic growth is made possible by improvements in technology and increases in resources. Economic growth has created prosperity in the industrialized countries and has resulted in levels of affluence that would dazzle people who had lived 50 to 100 years earlier. Economic growth creates "bads" as well as "goods." As economies grow, they become more congested; there is more smoke, noise, air and water pollution, and deforestation. Moreover, increasing quantities of natural resources like oil and minerals are consumed in order to make growth possible. Some critics feel that economic growth does more harm than good, and they argue for zero growth or for much slower growth.

Economists use marginal analysis to gauge the costs and benefits of economic growth. They recognize that economic growth provides us with more material goods and services, but that economic growth has costs in the form of greater pollution and resource use. More economists, however, reject the notion that society would be better off with no economic growth. Societies accustomed to rising material living standards would find it difficult to adjust to zero growth. Economists argue that the growth of material output need not be synonymous with the growth of pollution. If society devotes resources to pollution abatement, it can grow without increasing pollution. Finally, economists argue that economic growth does not necessarily lead to the depletion of scarce resources. As resources are used up, their value will be bid up, and people will use less of the resource, thus preserving it for future generations.

Source: Mancur Olsen and Hans H. Landsberg (eds.), *The No-Growth Society* (New York: W.W. Norton, 1973).

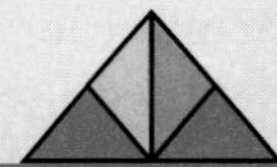

> Societies must choose between consumption today and consumption tomorrow. The society that devotes a greater share of its resources to producing capital sacrifices consumption now but enlarges its supply of capital and will thus have a higher rate of economic growth.

Shifts in the PPF. The position of the production possibilities frontier is based on the size and productivity of the resource base. Capital accumulation is only one reason for the PPF to shift. Increases in labor or land or discoveries of natural resources will also shift the PPF outward. Technical progress occurs when society learns how to get more outputs from the same inputs. Thus, technical progress, or advances in productivity, also shift the PPF outward.

Technical progress and accumulation of productive factors like land, labor, and capital have different effects on the PPF. Technical progress may affect only one industry or sector—whereas labor, capital, and land can be used across all sectors. Figure 3 illustrates a technical advance in wheat production without a corresponding change in the productivity of resources devoted to tank production. Accordingly, the PPF shifts from *af* to *bf*. Here the PPF shifts upward but not rightward.

Production Possibilities and the Economic Questions. All societies must solve the economic questions of *what, how* and *for whom*. This book will concentrate on how market economies solve the economic questions.

In market economies, the *what* problem is solved when consumers decide what they want to buy and how much they are willing to pay and when voters cast their ballots for or against public spending programs. The *how* problem is solved when producers determine how to combine resources to their best advantage. Because people are paid according to the resources they own, the *for whom* decision depends on how the ownership of the economy's land, labor, and capital is distributed.

FIGURE 3
Technical Progress in Wheat Production

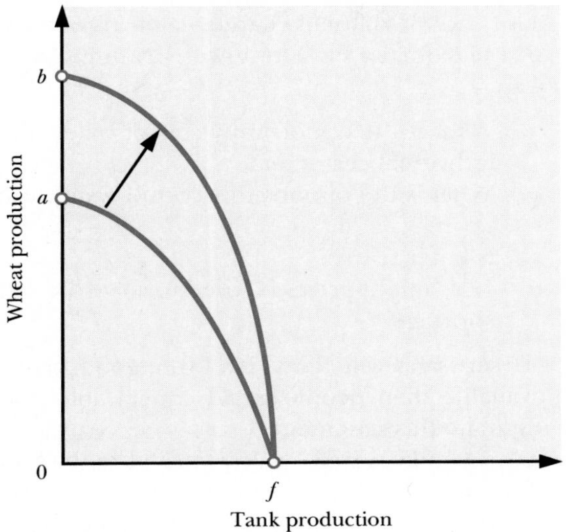

If a higher-yielding strain of wheat is discovered , a larger quantity could be produced with the same resources. Since this increase in wheat production would not influence tank production, the PPF would rotate from *af* to *bf*.

One solution to the *what, how,* and *for whom* problems is shown in Figure 4. The *what* problem is nothing more than the choice of location on the PPF. In this diagram, society chooses point *a*. The *how* problem is solved behind the scenes by decisions on how the factors of production are to be combined. The success with which the *how* problem is solved can be read directly from the PPF diagram. If the economy is operating on its PPF, such as at *a*, it is solving the *how* problem with maximum efficiency. If it is operating inside the PPF, at *b*, for example, it is not solving the *how* problem with maximum efficiency. The outcome of the *for whom* problem is shown on the PPF diagram. The orange rectangles show how the consumer goods (necessities and luxury goods) are distributed among the members of society (the rich, the middle class, and the poor). The rich receive most of the luxury goods, the middle class receives some luxury goods, the poor receive negligible luxury goods.

The next chapter explains how the price system solves the *what, how,* and *for whom* problems, how it facilitates specialization and exchange, and how it provides for the future.

FIGURE 4
The Economic Problem: *What? How? For Whom?*

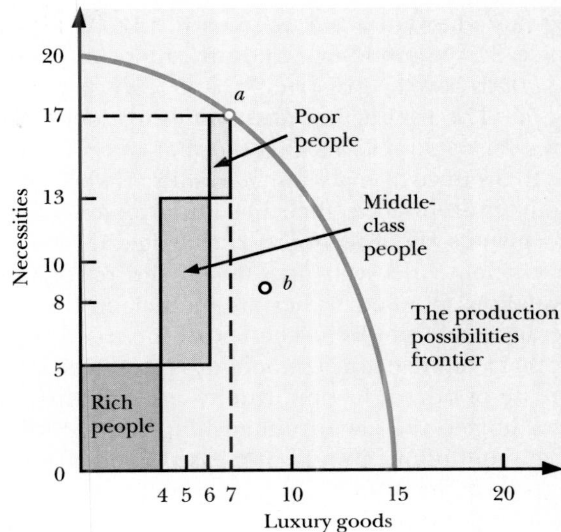

The PPF reveals the choices open to society. The *what* question is solved by the choice of where to locate on the PPF. Here society chooses *a*, of 7 units of luxuries and 17 units of necessities. The *how* question is solved when society decides how to combine resources to produce these outputs. Society can solve this problem efficiently and operate on the frontier (at *a*) or inefficiently and operate inside the frontier (at *b*). The *for whom* question is the division of society's output among the members of society. In this diagram, the rich get 4 units of luxuries and 5 units of necessities; the middle class gets 2 units of luxuries and 8 units of necessities; the poor get 1 unit of luxuries and 4 units of necessities.

SUMMARY

1. Wants are unlimited; there will never be enough resources to meet unlimited wants.
2. Economics is the study of how scarce resources are allocated among competing ends. A good is *scarce* if the amount available is less than the amount people would want if it were given away free. A good is *free* if the amount people want is less than the amount available at a zero price. The ultimate source of scarcity is the limited supply of resources. The resources that are factors of production are land, labor, and capital. Because scarcity exists, some system of allocating goods among those who want them is necessary. The two major allocation systems are market allocation and government allocation.

3. Economics is the study of how societies solve the economic problems of *what* to produce, *how* to produce, and *for whom* to produce.

4. The opportunity cost of any choice is the next best alternative that was sacrificed to make the choice. Scarce goods have a positive opportunity cost; free goods have an opportunity cost of zero.

5. The production possibilities frontier (PPF) shows the combinations of goods that an economy is able to produce from its limited resources when these resources are used to their maximum potential and for a given state of technical knowledge. If societies are efficient, they will operate on the production possibilities frontier. If they are inefficient, they will operate inside the PPF. The law of increasing costs says that as more of one commodity is produced at the expense of others, its opportunity cost will increase. According to the law of diminishing returns, when the amount of one input is increased in equal increments, holding all other inputs constant, successive increases in output become smaller. The two sources of economic inefficiency are unemployed resources and misallocated resources. Economic growth occurs because the factors of production expand in either quantity or quality, or because technological progress raises productivity. The choice of consumer goods over capital goods affects economic growth. Generally, the greater the share of resources devoted to capital goods, the better is the economy's ability to meet wants in the future. The choice of consumer goods over capital goods is really a choice between meeting wants now and meeting them in the future.

KEY TERMS

economics	allocation
scarce good	market
free good	government allocation
resources	competing ends
factors of production	opportunity cost
land	production possibilities frontier (PPF)
capital	law of increasing costs
investment	law of diminishing returns
labor	efficiency
human capital	
entrepreneur	

QUESTIONS AND PROBLEMS

1. In the early nineteenth century, land in the western United States was given away free to settlers. Was this land a free good or a scarce good, according to the economic definition? Explain your answer. Explain why land in the United States is no longer given away free.
2. The town of Hatfield charges each customer $75 per year for water. The town is running out of water.
   a. What is the opportunity cost of water to the individual customer?
   b. What is the opportunity cost of water to the town?
   c. Is water scarce?
   d. How might prices be used to solve the water shortage?
3. "Desert sand will always be a free good. More is available than people could conceivably want." Evaluate this statement.
4. A local millionaire buys 1000 tickets to the Super Bowl and gives them away to 1000 Boy Scouts. Are these tickets free goods? Why or why not?
5. In the American West, irrigation has turned desert land into farmland. Does this example demonstrate that nature's free gifts are not fixed in supply?
6. Determine in which factor-of-production category—land, labor, or capital—each of the following items belongs.
   a. A new office building
   b. A deposit of coal
   c. The inventory of auto supplies in an auto supply store
   d. Land reclaimed from the sea in Holland
   e. A trained mechanic
   f. An automated computer system
7. Draw two production possibilities curves for tank production as opposed to wheat production, like the one in Figure 1. In the first, show what would happen if the technology of tank production improved while the technology of wheat production remained the same. In the second, show what would happen if the technologies of tank and wheat production improved simultaneously.
8. Consider an economy that has the choice of producing either bricks or bread. There are exactly 100 workers available. Each worker can produce one brick or one loaf of bread. There is no law of diminishing returns. What is the economy's production possibilities curve?
9. By purchasing a new color TV set, I have passed up the opportunity to buy a personal computer,

to take a vacation trip, to paint my home, and to earn interest on the money paid for the TV. What is the opportunity cost of the color TV? How would the opportunity cost be determined?

10. How does the production possibilities curve illustrate the choices available to an economy?
11. If widgets were given away free, people would want to have 5 million per month. When would widgets be free goods and when would they be scarce goods? Under what conditions would the opportunity cost to society of widgets be positive?
12. Look at the data in Table A for a hypothetical corn farm. It shows how much corn would be produced by different numbers of farm hands (each working an 8-hour day). Explain whether these data illustrate the law of diminishing returns.

TABLE A

Number of Farmhands	Output of Corn (thousands of bushels)
1	50
2	100
3	140
4	160
5	170

13. Consider the data in Table B on a hypothetical economy's production possibilities frontier (PPF).

    a. Graph the PPF.
    b. Does the PPF have the expected shape?
    c. Calculate the opportunity cost of guns in terms of butter. Calculate the opportunity cost of butter in terms of guns. Do your results illustrate the law of increasing costs?
    d. If this economy produced 700 guns and 3 tons of butter, would it be solving the *how* problem efficiently?
    e. If at some later date this economy produced 700 guns and 12 tons of butter, what would you conclude has happened?

TABLE B

Hundreds of Guns	Tons of Butter
8	0
7	4
5	10
3	14
1	16
0	16.25

SUGGESTED READINGS

Franklin, Raymond S. *American Capitalism: Two Visions*. New York: Random House, 1977, chap. 1.

Gregory, Paul, and Robert Stuart. *Comparative Economic Systems,* 4th ed. Boston: Houghton Mifflin, 1992, chaps. 1 and 2.

Heilbroner, Robert L. *The Making of Economic Society*. Englewood Cliffs, NJ: Prentice Hall, 1962, chap. 1.

Mundell, Robert A. *Man and Economics*. New York: McGraw-Hill, 1968, chaps. 1 and 2.

North, Douglas C., and Roger LeRoy Miller. "The Economics of Clamming and Other 'Free' Goods." In *The Economics of Public Issues,* 5th ed. New York: Harper and Row, 1980, 152–56.

Olson, Mancur, and Hans H. Landsberg. *The No-Growth Society*. New York: W. W. Norton & Company, 1974.

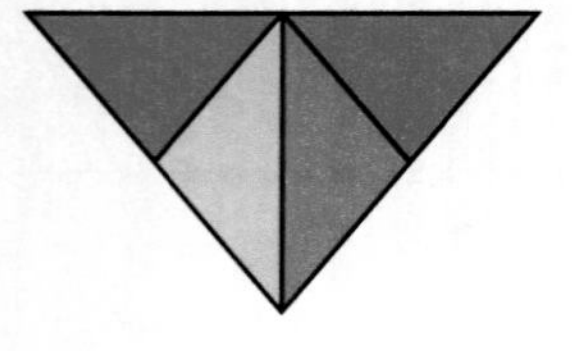

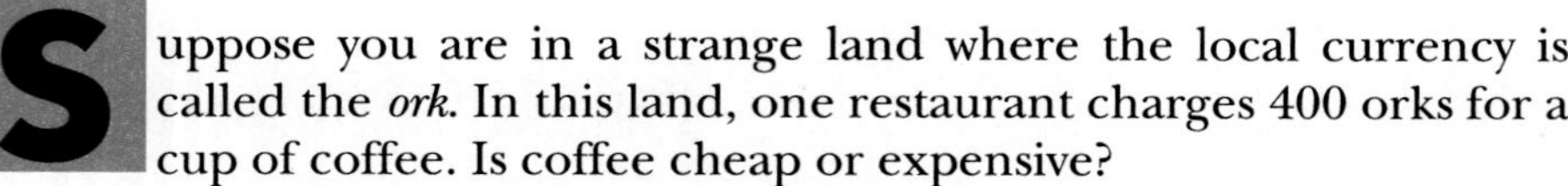

3 The Price System

CHAPTER INSIGHT

Suppose you are in a strange land where the local currency is called the *ork*. In this land, one restaurant charges 400 orks for a cup of coffee. Is coffee cheap or expensive?

To determine whether this price is high or low, you must gather more information. The menu lists the price of a soft drink as 1200 orks, and another customer tells you that the typical worker earns 24,000 orks per hour. You decide that coffee is cheap: "Back home I pay $0.40 for a cup of coffee and $0.40 for a soft drink, and I earn $10.00 an hour. At home, an hour's work will purchase 25 soft drinks or 25 cups of coffee. Here an hour of work will purchase 20 soft drinks and 60 cups of coffee." This story illustrates that a money price in isolation from other money prices is meaningless. What is important is how a particular money price stands relative to other money prices.

The concepts of money prices and relative prices are important components of the price system that coordinates market economy. The prices people pay for goods and services affect the decisions of thousands of producers and millions of consumers. As Adam Smith noted more than two centuries ago, the selfish private decisions of individuals can become a social virtue for the entire economy. (See Example 1.)

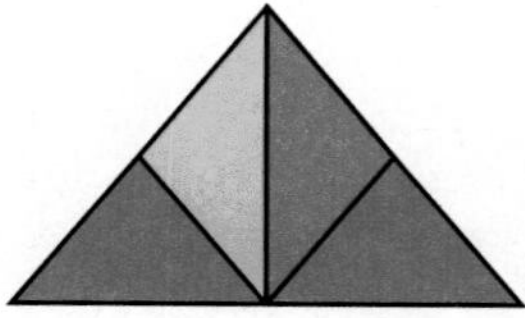

EXAMPLE 1 Adam Smith, Prices, and the Invisible Hand

Adam Smith (1723–1790), the founder of modern economics, was born in Kirkaldy, Scotland, in 1723. He became professor of moral philosophy at the University of Edinburgh in 1753. He was the prototype of the absent-minded professor—he was so engrossed in his thoughts that he sometimes forgot where he was. Smith lectured on ethics and published *The Theory of Moral Sentiments* in 1759—a book that brought him much fame but little fortune. The book argued that morals were the result of sympathy rather than self-interest.

In 1764 Smith devoted time to developing his thoughts on economics. During this time, governments were active in granting monopolies and controlling foreign trade. Because of Smith's reputation, he received an appointment as the tutor of a young duke. He spent the next three years in France, where he discussed economic issues with leading French intellectuals and began a book on economics. Finally, in 1776, he published *An Inquiry into the Nature and Causes of the Wealth of Nations,* usually called *The Wealth of Nations.* One of the greatest books ever written, it brought Smith lasting fame.

Smith's great idea was that private greed may be a public virtue. He wrote:

> It is not from the benevolence of the butcher, the brewer, or the baker, that we expect our dinner, but from their regard to their own interest. We address ourselves, not to their humanity but to their self-love, and never talk to them of our own necessities but of their advantages.

The self-interest of individuals leads them to specialize in those activities that maximize their own gain, as we have already seen in Smith's example of the pin factory in Chapter 1. In so doing, the nation as a whole experiences the greatest improvement in the productive powers of its labor force. The degree of specialization—or what Smith called the division of labor—is the result of our inclination to engage in bargaining and exchange of one good or service for another. Smith argued that a system of free enterprise can solve the economic problems of society better than government monopolies and regulations.

THE CIRCULAR FLOW OF ECONOMIC ACTIVITY

Economic activity is circular. Consumers buy goods with the incomes they earn by furnishing labor, land, and capital to the business firms that produce the goods they buy. (See Example 2.)

The **circular-flow diagram** illustrates how output and input decisions involving millions of consumers, hundreds of thousands of producers, and millions of resource owners fit together.

> The **circular-flow diagram** summarizes the flows of goods and services from producers to households and the flows of the factors of production from households to business firms.

As Figure 1 illustrates, the flows from households to firms and from firms to households are handled by two markets: the market for goods and services and the market for the factors of production. The circular-flow diagram consists of two circles. The outer circle shows the *physical flows* of goods and services and

EXAMPLE 2 The Size of the Circular Flow

The amount of activity in the circular flow of economic activity is staggering. There are more than 20 million business firms in the U.S. economy, interacting with 80 million households. Business firms employ 120 million persons. The value of capital resources in the circular flow is more than $20 trillion. The annual value of goods and services that flow from business firms (including government) to households is over $7 trillion. We cannot even count the millions of distinct goods and services the economy produces. The field of economics called *national income accounting* explains how economists measure the total flow of goods and services from businesses to households and the flow of factor resources from households to businesses.

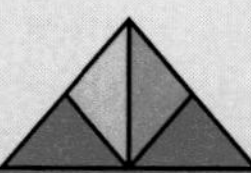

FIGURE 1
The Circular Flow of Economic Activity

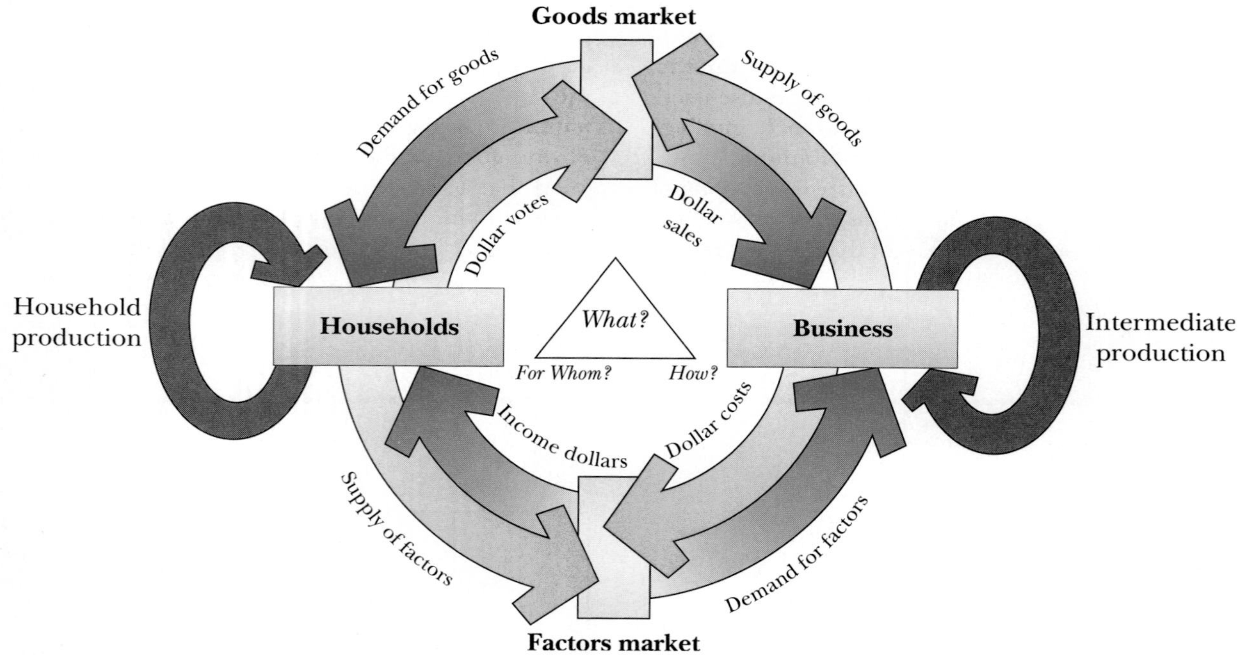

Economic activity is circular. The outside circle describes the flow of physical goods and services and productive factors through the system: business furnishes goods to households who furnish land, labor, and capital to business. The inside circle describes the flow of dollars: households provide dollar sales to business, whose costs become incomes to households. These two circles flow in opposite directions. The triangle gives a pictorial representation of the relationship of the circular flow to the solution to the *what, how,* and *for whom* questions. The circular-flow diagram shows that flows of intermediate goods remain entirely within the business sector and do not enter the circular flow. It also shows that because household-production services are produced and consumed within the family, they do not enter the circular flow.

of productive factors. The inner circle shows the *flows of money expenditures* on goods and services and on productive factors. The physical flows and money flows go in opposite directions. When households buy goods and services, goods flow to the households, but the sales receipts flow to businesses. When workers supply labor to business firms, productive factors flow to businesses, but the wage income flows to households.

For almost every physical flow in the economy, there is a corresponding financial transaction. To obtain goods, the consumer must pay for them. When firms sell products, they receive sales revenues. When businesses hire labor or rent land, they must pay for them. When individuals supply labor, they receive wages.

Two types of goods and services do not enter the circular flow. *Intermediate goods* (discussed later in the chapter) are goods that businesses sell to other businesses. For example, the steel industry supplies steel to the automobile industry, which produces the automobiles that enter the circular flow. The other goods and services that do not enter the circular flow are those produced and used within the household. For example, the cooking, cleaning, transportation, and other services provided by one family member to another are not part of the circular economic flow.

RELATIVE PRICES AND MONEY PRICES

A **relative price** indicates how one price stands in relation to other prices. A relative price is quite different from a **money price**. In the ork example, coffee sells for 400 orks and soft drinks for 1200 orks. Three cups of coffee is the relative price of a soft drink (relative to coffee), and one-third of a soft drink is the relative price of coffee (relative to a soft drink). If coffee and soft drinks had both sold for 400 orks, then the relative price of a soft drink would have been one cup of coffee.

> A **relative price** is a price expressed in terms of other related commodities.
>
> A **money price** is a price expressed in monetary units (such as dollars, francs, etc.).

Money prices are most meaningful when they are compared to prices of *related* goods. For example, it makes sense to compare the price of electricity to natural gas because commercial and residential users make choices between natural gas and electricity. Should we heat and air condition our homes with electricity or natural gas? Should manufacturers use electricity or natural gas as fuel? The money prices of natural gas and electricity, shown in Figure 2*a*, rose substantially over the last 20 years. However, the relative price of electricity (the price of electricity divided by the price of natural gas) fell during this same period. (See Figure 2*b*.) In 1970, a BTU of electricity cost 7.37 times as much as a BTU of natural gas. By 1990, a BTU of electricity cost less than 4 times a BTU of natural gas.

> The money price of a commodity can rise while its relative price falls. The money price can fall while its relative price rises. Money prices and relative prices need not move together.

Relative prices play a prominent role in answering the economic questions of *what, how,* and *for whom.* Money prices do not. Relative prices signal to buyers and sellers what goods are cheap or expensive. *Buying and selling decisions are based on relative prices.* If the relative price of one good rises, buyers substitute other goods whose relative prices are lower. For example, the change in the relative price of electricity, as cited in Figure 2*b*, will encourage consumers to use electricity rather than natural gas.

The emphasis on relative prices does not mean that money prices are unimportant. Money prices, or the price level, are important in macroeconomics. *Inflation* is a general increase in money prices. Elections are won or lost on the basis of inflation; the living standards of people on fixed incomes can be damaged by inflation. People worry that inflation drives up interest rates. But even in the case of inflation, money prices are not considered in isolation. Instead, the level of money prices today is compared to the level of money prices yesterday. Ultimately, this is also a form of relative price.

> In microeconomics there is greater interest in relative prices than in money prices. In macroeconomics, there is greater interest in the level of money prices than in relative prices.

FIGURE 2
Money Prices and Relative Prices of Natural Gas and Electricity

(*a*) Money Prices

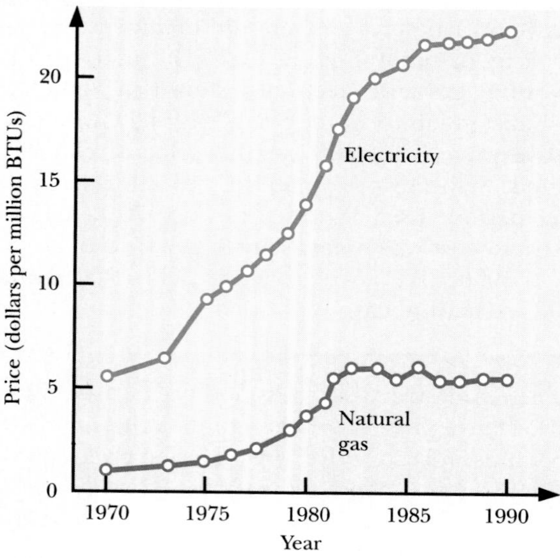

(*b*) Relative Prices

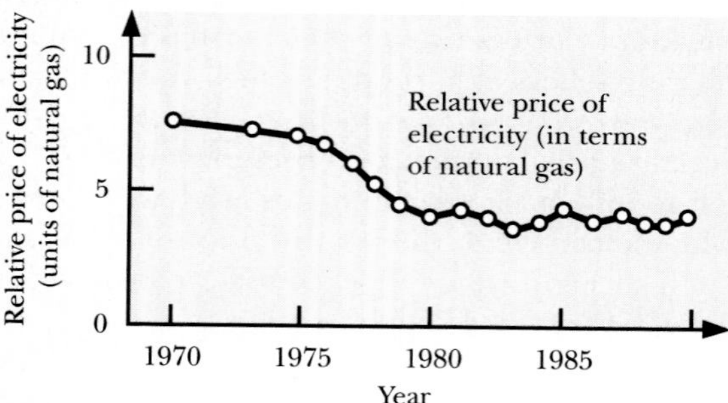

Figure 2*a* shows that the price of both electricity and natural gas rose from 1970 to 1990. Electricity prices tripled, but gas prices rose sevenfold. Figure 2*b* shows that the price of electricity *in terms of natural gas* actually fell.

Source: Department of Energy, *Monthly Energy Review,* Energy Information Administration.

THE PRINCIPLE OF SUBSTITUTION

Relative prices are important because of the **principle of substitution.**

The **principle of substitution** states that practically no good is irreplaceable. Users are able to substitute one product for another when relative prices change.

Virtually no good is fully protected from the competition of substitutes. Aluminum competes with steel, coal with oil, electricity with natural gas, labor with machines, movies with TV, one brand of toothpaste with another, and so on. The only goods for which there are no substitutes are minimal quantities of water, salt, or food and certain life-saving medications, such as insulin.

To say that there is a substitute for every good does not mean that there is an *equally good* substitute for every good. One mouthwash may be a close substitute for another; a television show may be a good substitute for a movie; apartments may be good substitutes for private homes. However, carrier pigeons are a poor substitute for telephone service; public transportation may be a poor substitute for the private car in sprawling cities; steel is a poor substitute for aluminum in the production of jet aircraft.

Increases in relative prices provide signals for consumers to evaluate possible substitutes. When the relative price of crude oil rises, utilities switch from oil to coal. When the relative price of coffee increases, people consume more tea. When the relative price of beef rises, people buy more poultry and fish. There is no single recipe for producing a cake, a bushel of wheat, a car, comfort, recreation, or happiness. Increases in relative prices motivate consumers and firms to search out substitutes. (See Example 3.)

THE PRICE SYSTEM AS A COORDINATING MECHANISM

An economy is made up of millions of consumers and hundreds of thousands of enterprises, and millions of resource owners. Each participant makes economic decisions to promote his or her self-interest. How are the decisions of all these people and businesses coordinated? What prevents the economy from collapsing when all these decisions clash? Is it necessary to have someone or something in charge?

EXAMPLE 3 You Can't Shake Hands with a Fax

In 1991 the airlines raised fares for business travelers. Typically, business travelers, who are unable to plan their trips well in advance or stay over a weekend, are charged unrestricted fares that are double or triple those paid by the leisure traveler. The round trip unrestricted fare from Chicago to Los Angeles went up from $778 to $1079. One travel agent remarked, "People call and it's embarrassing to tell them the fares."

The increase in business air fares has caused business travelers to seek out substitutes. With the advent of the telefax machine, it is now possible to exchange documents instantaneously. Also, the telephone companies offer teleconferencing as an alternative to air travel. Business travelers simply switched from air travel to the now-cheaper substitutes. Travel agencies were so hard hit by "customer resistance" that they had to switch to a four-day work week.

Shortly after the increase in air fares, one major airline began running an ad to convince reluctant business travelers that the fax machine was a poor substitute for air travel. "You can't shake hands via fax," said the ad.

Source: "Climbing Air Fares Are Scaring Off Air Travelers," *Wall Street Journal*, Oct. 17, 1991.

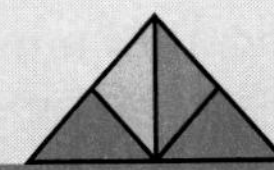

The Invisible Hand

Adam Smith (writing in 1776) described how the price system solves the economic problem efficiently without conscious direction:

> Every individual endeavors to employ his capital so that its produce may be of greatest value. He generally neither intends to promote the public interest, nor knows how much he is promoting it. He intends only his own security, only his own gain. And he is led by an *invisible hand* to promote an end which was no part of his intention. By pursuing his own interest he frequently promotes that of society more effectively than when he really intends to promote it.[1]

Smith's "invisible hand" works through the **price system**. A modern economy produces millions of commodities and services, each of which has a money price. These millions of money prices form millions of relative prices that inform buyers and sellers as to what goods are abundant and what goods are in short supply. Relative prices reflect the scarcity of each good.

[1]Adam Smith, *The Wealth of Nations*, ed. Edwin Cannan (New York: Modern Library, 1937), 423.

> The **price system** coordinates economic decisions by allowing resource owners to trade freely, buying and selling at whatever relative prices emerge in the marketplace.

Equilibrium

Each economic agent (household or business firm) makes buying and selling decisions on the basis of relative prices. The family decides how to spend its income; the worker decides where and how much to work; the factory manager decides what inputs to use and what outputs to produce. Insofar as these decisions are made individually, what guarantees that there will be enough steel, bananas, foreign cars, domestic help, steel workers, copper, and lumber for homes? What ensures that there will not be too much of one good and too little of another? Is Adam Smith's invisible hand powerful enough to prevent shortage and surplus?

If automobile producers decided to produce more cars than buyers want to buy *at the price asked by the automobile producers,* there would be many unsold cars. Since dealers must pay their bills and earn a liv-

EXAMPLE 4 Pencils: The Price System at Work

It is remarkable that not a single person knows how to make a pencil from start to finish. If one thinks about what it takes to make a pencil—the trees that produce the wood, the saws that fell the trees, the steel that makes the saws, the engines that run the saws, the hemp that makes the ropes that are necessary to tie down the logs, the training of loggers, the mining of graphite in Sri Lanka for the lead, the mining of zinc and copper for making the bit of metal holding the eraser, and the rape seed oil from the Dutch East Indies that is used in the eraser—it is clear that no one single person knows how to make a pencil. The decisions of the thousands upon thousands of people involved are coordinated through the price system without centralized direction. That all these activities have made it possible for you to go to the bookstore and buy a pencil for, say, a mere 25 cents, boggles the mind.

Source: Milton and Rose Friedman, *Free To Choose* (Orlando, FL: Harcourt, Brace, Jovanovich, 1980).

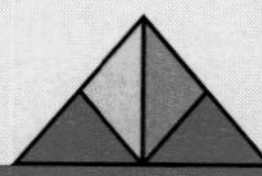

ing, they must sell cars at lower prices. As the money price of cars falls, the relative price tends to fall, and customers begin to substitute automobiles for European vacations, home computers, or remodeled kitchens. The decline in the relative price of automobiles signals automobile manufacturers to produce fewer cars. Eventually, a balance between the number of cars people are prepared to buy (the demand) and the number offered for sale (the supply) will be struck, and the corresponding price is called an **equilibrium price**.

> The **equilibrium price** of a good or service is that price at which the amount of the good people are prepared to buy (demand) equals the amount offered for sale (supply).

Equilibrium prices provide information to participants in the economy. Each participant will specialize in information that is personally relevant. The economy itself requires enormous information about how to produce different goods, product qualities, product prices, worker efficiencies, and so forth. The price system allows people to make decisions by knowing only the relative prices that are important to them. (See Example 4.) People buy more of a good that has become relatively cheap; people economize on goods that have become relatively expensive. They need not know why the good has become cheap or expensive. Frederick Hayek (1899–1992), a Nobel Prize winner in economics, once described the workings of the price system as follows:

> The marvel is that in a case like that of a scarcity of one raw material, without an order being issued, without more than perhaps a handful of people knowing the cause, tens of thousands of people whose identity could not be ascertained by months of investigation, are made to use the material or its products more sparingly: i.e., they move in the right direction.

Just as checks and balances in an ecological system prevent one species of plant or animal from overrunning an entire area and, in the end, extinguishing itself, relative prices provide the checks and balances in the economic system. If one product is in oversupply, its relative price will fall; more will be purchased and less will be offered for sale. If one product is in short supply, its relative price will rise; less will be purchased and more will be offered for sale.

Markets

The price system works through markets. If a company needs a letter typed, it can hire a temporary secretary for the job. If Boeing Corporation needs jet engines for its new-generation aircraft, it can search the market for a subcontractor. Such markets can provide an efficient solution to the economic problem.

According to Nobel Prize winner Ronald Coase, businesses will work through markets as long as it is more efficient than doing the work within the business. Is it easier to hire a typist for each typing job through the market or to employ a permanent typist? Is it better for Boeing Corporation to research and develop its own jet engines rather than to acquire those engines through market contracts with other firms?

Of course, there are costs associated with using markets. Information about prices and product qualities is not free. Time and resources must be devoted to determining the best price or best quality in the market. There are professionals devoted to finding the best deals, bringing buyers and sellers together, and determining demands for products that are to be introduced. On a larger scale, corporations use marketing departments, comparative sales departments, and procurement departments to compile and process information on prices and qualities. In some cases, businesses find the costs of using markets to be so high that they decide to do the job "in-house."

What, How, and For Whom

The price system solves the *what, how,* and *for whom* problems without conscious direction. No single participant in the economy needs to see the big picture; each participant need only know the relative prices of the goods and services of immediate interest to that person. The millions of individual economic decisions made daily are coordinated by the price system.

Consider an economy in which all property is privately owned. Resource owners are free to set prices without government intervention. Each individual owns certain quantities of resources—land, labor, capital—that are sold or rented to business firms that produce the goods and services people want. Everything is sold at a price agreeable to the buyer and seller.

What is produced is determined by *dollar votes* cast by consumers for different goods and services and by the dollar costs of producing these goods and services. When consumers choose to buy a particular good or service, they are casting a dollar vote for that good or service. Their dollar votes determine what will be produced. If no dollar votes are cast for a particular product, it will not be produced. If enough dollar votes are cast for a product relative to its cost of production, it will be produced. The quantities that will be produced will be determined by prices. A higher price signals to firms that greater profits can be made by increasing production of that product. If consumers want more wheat, they will bid up wheat prices. In turn, the higher wheat prices will encourage farmers to grow more wheat.

How goods are produced is determined by business firms that seek to utilize land, labor, and capital resources as economically as possible. Business firms produce those outputs that receive high dollar votes by combining resources in the least costly way. Business firms follow the principle of substitution. If the relative price of business travel rises, businesspeople travel less and make more long-distance telephone calls. If the relative price of land is increased, farmers use less land and more tractors and labor to work the land more intensively. If business firms fail to reduce their costs through the use of the best available techniques and the best combination of the factors of production, other firms may drive them out of business.

For whom is determined by the dollar values the market assigns to resources owned by households. People who own large quantities of land or capital will have a large claim on the goods and services produced by the economy; those who are fortunate enough to provide high-priced labor services (doctors, lawyers, gifted athletes) will similarly receive a large share of the total output.

SPECIALIZATION

In a market economy, the price system does more than balance supply and demand. It also encourages specialization, which raises efficiency and allows economies to produce ever larger outputs from their available inputs.

Productivity and Exchange

Suppose a sailor were stranded on an uninhabited island—a modern Robinson Crusoe. The sailor would have to make decisions about whether to make fish nets or fish hooks or whether to sleep or break coconuts. The sailor would not be *specialized;* he would have to be a jack-of-all-trades. Solving the *for whom* problem would be easy—everything he produced would be for himself—the problems of *what* and *how* could be solved without explicit relative prices, property rights, or markets.

In the modern economy, a jack-of-all-trades is rare; a specialist is commonplace. A typical household consumes thousands of articles; yet one member of the household may specialize in aligning suspension components on an automobile production line. Everyone in our economy (except hermits) is dependent on the efforts of others. We produce one or two things; we consume many things.

Specialization gives rise to exchange. If people consumed only those things that they produced, there would be no trade and there would be no need for money. Money, trade, and specialization are all characteristics of a modern economy.

> When people are specialized, they produce more of particular goods than they consume. These surpluses will be exchanged for other goods that they want.

Specialization raises productivity. Increased productivity was defined in Chapter 2 as the production of more output from the same amount of resources. As Adam Smith noted in *The Wealth of Nations,* specialization is a basic source of productivity advances. It raises the productivity of the economy and raises incomes in two ways. First, specialization allows resources, which have different characteristics, to be allocated to their best use. Second, by concentrating certain resources in specific tasks, economies can produce outputs in large-scale production runs. In many industries, production costs per unit drop when goods are produced on a large scale.

The Law of Comparative Advantage

Specialization makes possible higher productivity and higher incomes. People, land, and capital come in different varieties. Some people are agile seven-footers; others are small and slow. Some land is moist; other land is dry. Some machines can move large quantities of earth; others can perform precision metal work.

Because the factors of production have different characteristics and qualities, specialization offers opportunities for productivity advances. Economists refer to the best employment of a resource as its *comparative advantage.* The agile seven-footer has a comparative advantage in basketball. Land with high moisture content is best used in corn production; land with a relatively low moisture content is best used in wheat production. Earth-moving machinery can be used in road building; precision tools can be used in aircraft manufacturing. Each resource has some comparative advantage.

The agile seven-footer will earn a larger income playing professional basketball than professional soccer. The Kansas farmer will make more profits by growing wheat; the Iowa farmer will make more profits growing corn. The owner of the earth-moving equipment will make more income using it in road building than in home building. If all resources are used to make the most income possible, specialization will follow naturally.

A comparative advantage is not the same thing as an *absolute advantage.* One resource has an absolute advantage over another when it can produce a particular output at a higher level of productivity. A single resource may hold an absolute advantage in the production of several outputs. The agile seven-footer may also be the fastest typist around. Some farmland is suited to growing both wheat and corn. Conversely, a resource might not hold an absolute advantage for any output. Some people are less efficient than other people at every task they try. How are comparative advantages determined in these cases? (See Example 5.)

In 1817, the English economist, David Ricardo, formulated the **law of comparative advantage**.

> The **law of comparative advantage** states that it is better for people to specialize in those activities in which their advantages over other people are greatest or in which their disadvantages compared to others are the smallest.

Suppose you can do any and every job better than anyone else. What would you, as such a superior person, do? You would not want to be a jack-of-all trades because your *margin* of superiority will be greater in one occupation than in another. The job in which your margin of superiority over others is the *greatest* is the job you will do because it will give you the highest income.

At the other extreme, suppose there is no person in the community to whom you are superior in any job. What would you do in such an unfortunate situation? The job in which your disadvantage compared to others is the *smallest* would be the job that maximizes your income.

Example 6 shows the relationship between the law of comparative advantage and opportunity costs, concluding that people specialize in those tasks in which their opportunity costs are lower.

EXAMPLE 5 Comparative Advantage and Hawaiian Pineapples

The law of comparative advantage states that people and, by extension, countries specialize in those activities that they perform relatively better than others do. What matters is comparative, not absolute, advantage.

For more than 60 years, the Hawaiian island of Lanai had a comparative advantage in growing pineapples. Lanai soil, climate, and workers produced pineapples for world markets at prices that yielded large profits for the Dole Company, owner of more than 90 percent of the island.

Even though Lanai workers remain the world's most productive pickers of pineapple, 1991 was the last year that a pineapple crop was planted on Lanai. Why? Lanai pineapple pickers earn $8.23 per hour; those in Thailand, however, earn less than $.90 per hour. Lanai workers therefore had to be almost nine times more productive than Thai workers for their pineapples to remain competitive. Even though Lanai pickers are more productive than Thai workers in absolute terms, they lack a sufficient margin to offset lower Thai wages.

It might appear that Lanai pineapple pickers are losers from changing comparative advantage. In fact, Hawaii has a greater absolute advantage in tourism than in pineapples. Lovely beaches, friendly people, and a warm climate attract visitors from all over the world. Thus, the development of tourism, an activity in which Lanai has comparative advantage, raised wages throughout the island to such an extent that the Dole Company could no longer operate a profitable pineapple business. As Lanai's comparative advantage shifted from pineapples to tourism, pineapple pickers became bartenders, hotel maids, and concierges. It was the profitability of tourism that made growing pineapples unprofitable!

Source: "After a Long Affair, Pineapple Jilts Hawaii for Asian Suitors," *New York Times,* December 26, 1991.

Thus, a mediocre computer programmer could possibly be the best clerk in the local supermarket. The clerks in the local supermarket may not be able to stock shelves and work a cash register as well as the computer programmer, but they have a comparative advantage in that occupation. An attorney may be the fastest typist in town, yet the attorney is better off preparing deeds than typing them. An engineering major may have verbal skills that exceed those of an English major, but his or her comparative advantage is in engineering.

> The law of comparative advantage is nothing more than the principle that people should engage in those activities where their opportunity costs are lower than other people's. The price system encourages the factors of production to work according to their comparative advantage.

Comparative Advantage and International Trade

The law of comparative advantage applies to people and countries. Just as one person cannot transfer his or her talents to another, one country cannot transfer its people, climate, or natural resources to another country.

Each person has certain intrinsic "resources," such as intelligence, looks, manual dexterity, verbal skills, mathematical skills, and so forth. So, too, does a country. Each country can be defined in terms of its resources: land, labor, and capital. The resource profile of the United States is quite different from Japan or South Korea. The United States is rich in capital and scientific personnel. South Korea has an industrious work force. A country's resources are best committed to those activities for which its advantages are the largest or its disadvantages are the smallest.

EXAMPLE 6 The Comparative Advantage of Lawn Mowing versus Typing

A simple numerical example of comparative advantage will illustrate the principle in a more concrete fashion. Both Jack and Jill can mow lawns and type, and neither cares whether they type or mow lawns. As the accompanying table shows, Jack can type 20 pages a day or mow 2 lawns a day. Jill, on the other hand, can type 50 pages a day or mow 8 lawns a day. Jill is clearly more efficient in absolute terms at both tasks than Jack; she can type 250 percent (50 ÷ 20) as fast and can mow lawns 400 percent (8 ÷ 2) as fast as Jack.

Now what should Jack and Jill do? We must first determine the (relative) prices of mowing lawns and typing. Suppose typing earns $2 a page and mowing lawns pays $16 per lawn. If Jack mows lawns all day, his income would be $32 ($16 × 2 lawns) per day; typing would earn Jack $40 ($2 × 20 pages) per day. Thus, Jack would wish to type. Jill, on the other hand, could earn $128 mowing lawns ($16 × 8 lawns) or $100 typing ($2 × 50 pages). Thus, Jill would prefer to mow lawns.

Jill has a comparative advantage in mowing lawns; Jack has a comparative advantage in typing. Although Jill is better than Jack in all activities, her *greatest* advantage over Jack is in mowing lawns (she is 4 times as fast). In typing, Jill is only 2.5 times as fast. Jack's *least* disadvantage is in typing; thus, Jack prefers to be a typist.

Notice that Jill will earn $128 daily mowing lawns and Jack will earn $40 a day typing. Jill's superior productivity is reflected in higher earnings. Notice that Jack in effect competes with Jill in typing by charging a lower price per unit of his time. If there are 8 hours to the work day, Jill is earning a wage of $16 per hour ($16 = $128 ÷ 8 hours) and Jack is earning only $5 an hour ($5 = $40 ÷ 8 hours). Thus, Jill's hourly wage is slightly more than 3 times Jack's hourly wage. Jack's lower rate allows him to compete with Jill in typing: she is 2.5 times as efficient as a typist, but her wage is more than 3 times as high—which in the marketplace offsets her absolute advantage in typing.

To mow 1 lawn, Jack must sacrifice 10 pages of typing. Jack's opportunity cost of lawns equals 10 pages of typing. To mow 1 lawn, Jill must sacrifice 6.25 pages (50 ÷ 8). Jill mows lawns because her opportunity cost of lawn mowing is lower than Jack's.

	Lawns per Day (1)	Pages per Day (2)	Opportunity Cost of Lawn Mowing (pages) (3) = (2) ÷ (1)
Jack	2	20	10
Jill	8	50	6.25

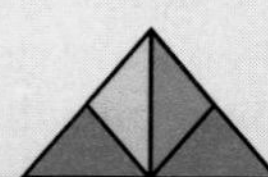

America's largest advantages are in the production of high-technology goods, such as airplanes. South Korea's least disadvantages are in the production of such goods as TV sets and clothing; it exports these goods even though the United States has a higher absolute productivity.

Economies of Large-Scale Production

If all people were the same, if all land were identical, and if all capital were the same, would there still be specialization? Even if all people in an automobile manufacturing plant had identical skills, it would still be better to have one person install the engine, another bolt down the engine, and so on in an assembly line. Individuals who focus on one task can learn their jobs better and don't waste time switching from job to job. The per-unit costs of production are frequently lower at large volumes of output. Modern mass-production techniques require numerous specialized tasks to be carried out. Even if all agricultural land were identical, the economies of large-scale production would still make it better to plant one farm with corn, another with wheat, and so on, than to plant smaller strips of corn and wheat on single farms.

> Specialization raises productivity not only through the lowering of opportunity costs through comparative advantage but also by allowing economies of large-scale production.

The Need for Money

Money is useful in an *exchange economy*—that is, an economy where people are specialized—because it reduces the cost of transacting with others. Money enables any person to trade with anyone else, unlike a **barter** system in which you must trade with someone who wants what you specialize in.

> **Barter** is a system of exchange where products are traded for other products rather than for money.

In barter, for example, it would be necessary for barefoot bakers to exchange goods with hungry shoemakers. A successful barter deal requires that the two traders have matching wants. Money is useful precisely because such coincidences of wants are rare.

Money may take many forms. In simple societies, fishhooks, sharks' teeth, beads, or cows have been used as money. In modern societies, money is issued and regulated by government, and money may (gold coins) or may not (paper money) have an intrinsic value of its own.

> **Money** is anything that is widely accepted in exchange for goods and services.

If one form of money were abolished (by law), another form would replace it. The costs of barter are so high that societies must have something to serve as money.

HOW THE PRICE SYSTEM PROVIDES FOR THE FUTURE

The price system provides checks and balances and promotes efficiency through specialization and exchange. It also uses interest rates to provide for the future.

Roundabout Production

The shipwrecked sailor in our earlier example shares a problem that is common in modern economies: how to provide for the future. The sailor would be confronted with a clear choice of eating more today versus eating more tomorrow. If the water were clear, he could wade out and, with patient effort, catch fish with his bare hands. He may be successful in catching enough fish to survive. However, if the sailor were to devote a few days to making a fishing net from vines, he would be able to increase his catch and reduce his effort—but at the sacrifice of having less to eat for three days. Making a net to catch the fish is an example of **roundabout production.**

> **Roundabout production** is the production of goods that do not immediately meet consumption needs but may be used to produce more goods.

With roundabout production, producers are dependent on things produced in the past for the things that are produced today. The wheat harvested today requires a harvesting machine produced in the past; the bread produced today is baked in ovens that were produced in the past; the shirt produced today is manufactured on a sewing machine produced in the past.

The price system is responsible for producing the capital goods that enable society to produce more in the future. Households and businesses set aside some of their income in the form of savings. Households save today so that they can consume more tomorrow. They accumulate funds in savings accounts and retirement programs; they buy stocks, bonds, and life insurance. These funds are used by businesses to produce more capital goods. Businesses also save from their profits, borrow from financial institutions, sell bonds, and issue stock. They use the proceeds to build plants, to buy capital equipment, and to build up their inventories.

Interest Rates

The stock of capital goods is one generation's legacy to the next. The modern interstate highway system will be enjoyed not only by the generation that built it, but by future generations. Likewise, the ultimate benefits of the investment in space exploration will be enjoyed by future generations. Households must sacrifice consumption today to save; however, by saving, the household will increase its consumption in the future. The sacrifice of current consumption is the cost of saving. The benefit of saving is that **interest** will be earned. Future consumption will increase by more than the sacrifice of current consumption because a dollar sacrificed today yields more than a dollar tomorrow. The higher the interest rate, the greater the inducement to save.

> **Interest** is the price of credit, usually the annual amount as a percentage of the amount borrowed.

The rate of interest acts not only as an inducement to save, it also signals to businesses whether they should borrow for investment. Like any other price, the interest rate provides a *balance*—in this case, balancing the amount people are willing to save with the amount businesses want to borrow for investment. If the interest rate is low, businesses will clamor for the savings of individuals because they find it cheap to add to their capital stock. However, at a low interest rate few people will be willing to save. The reverse is true at high interest rates: few businesses will want to invest, but households will be quite willing to save.

> The interest rate balances the amount of saving offered by households with the amount of investment businesses wish to undertake. The price system, operating through the interest rate, solves the problem of allocating resources between present and future consumption.

LIMITS OF THE INVISIBLE HAND

The price system solves the problems of *what, how,* and *for whom;* it balances the actions of millions of consumers and thousands of producers; it even solves the difficult problem of providing for the future. The price system has great strength, but it has weaknesses as well. These weaknesses must be examined to determine the costs and benefits of interfering with the price system.

Income Distribution

There is no guarantee that resource allocation through the price system will solve the *for whom* problem in a way that will satisfy everyone. Some people believe that income should be distributed evenly; others believe that the gap between rich and poor should be large. Many believe that it is unfair for people to be rich just because they were lucky enough to inherit wealth or intelligence.

Economics cannot determine what is a "good" or "fair" solution to the *for whom* problem. Such judgments about income distribution are in the realm of normative economics. Although positive economics can say what may happen to efficiency or economic growth if the income distribution is changed, it cannot make scientific statements about the desirability of the change.

Public Goods

Another weakness of the price system is that it cannot supply *public goods,* such as a national defense system and a legal system, which are necessary to society. In the case of private goods, there is an intimate link between costs and benefits: The person who buys a car enjoys the benefits of the car; the person who buys a loaf of bread eats that loaf. Public goods, on the other hand, are financed not by the dollar votes of consumers but by taxes. In most cases, the benefits each individual derives from public goods will not be known. Moreover, it is difficult to prevent nonpayers (called *free riders*) from enjoying the benefits of public goods. Even if someone does not pay taxes, the national defense establishment protects that person from enemy attack just as well as it protects the payers.

If private individuals were left with the choice of buying and selling public goods, few public goods would be produced. Yet society must have public goods to survive. The price system, therefore, is inadequate for providing public goods.

Monopoly

Adam Smith's "invisible hand" works so well because individual buyers and sellers compete with one another. The invisible hand will not function as well in a *monopoly*—that is when a single seller can hold back the amount of goods, drive up the price, and enjoy large profits. While the monopolist would benefit from such actions, the buyer would not. Monopoly threatens the smooth functioning of the invisible hand.

Macroeconomic Instability

The invisible hand may solve the economic problem of scarcity but may provide an unstable level of overall economic activity. It is a historical fact that economies are subject to fluctuations in output, employment, and prices—called *business cycles*—and that these fluctuations have been costly.

The study of the causes of the instability of capitalism was pioneered by John Maynard Keynes during the Great Depression of the 1930s, and this theme remains a principal concern of macroeconomics.

This chapter has described how scarce resources are allocated by the price system. Equilibrium prices are like an invisible hand that coordinates the decisions of many different persons. The next chapter examines capitalism and socialism as alternate ways to organize the economy.

SUMMARY

1. The circular-flow diagram summarizes the flows of goods and services from producers to households and the flows of factors of production from households to producers.

2. Relative prices guide the economic decisions of individuals and businesses. They signal to buyers and sellers what substitutions to make.

3. The principle of substitution states that no single good is irreplaceable. Users substitute one good for another in response to changes in relative prices.

4. The "invisible hand" analogy of Adam Smith describes how a capitalist system allows individuals to pursue their self-interest and yet provides an orderly, efficient economic system that functions without centralized direction. If too much of a product is produced, its relative price will fall. If too little of a product is produced, its relative price will rise. The balance of supply and demand is called an equilibrium. The *what* problem is solved by dollar votes. The *how* problem is solved by competition among producers that encourages them to combine resource inputs efficiently. The solution of the *for whom* problem is determined by: (a) who owns productive resources and (b) what the relative prices of resources are.

5. Specialization increases productivity. It occurs because of the differences among people, land, and capital and because of the economies of large-scale production. The law of comparative advantage states that the factors of production will specialize in those activities in which their advantages are greatest or in which their disadvantages are smallest.

6. The price system provides for the future by allowing people to compare costs now with benefits that will accrue in the future. The interest rate balances the amount of saving offered with the amount of investment businesses wish to undertake.

7. The price system cannot solve the problems of income distribution, public goods, monopoly, or macroeconomic instability.

KEY TERMS

circular-flow diagram
relative price
money price
principle of substitution
price system
equilibrium price
law of comparative advantage
barter
money
roundabout production
interest

QUESTIONS AND PROBLEMS

1. Why does the circular-flow diagram show physical quantities moving in one direction and dollar quantities moving in another direction?

2. "The principle of substitution states that virtually all goods have substitutes, but we all know that there are no substitutes for telephone service." Comment on this statement.
3. Explain why you can usually find the items you want at a grocery store without having ordered the goods in advance.
4. In 1963 an average car cost about $2000; in 1991 an average car cost about $17,000. But on the average, what cost $100 in 1963 cost about $390 in 1991. Did the relative price of a car increase or fall compared to most goods and services?
5. Not every product has a good substitute. Which of the following pairs of products are good substitutes? Which are poor substitutes? Explain the general principles you used in coming up with your answers.

   a. Coffee and tea
   b. Compact Chevrolets and compact Fords
   c. Cars and city buses
   d. Electricity and natural gas
   e. Telephones and express mail

6. Computer manufacturers want to sell more personal computers than customers want to buy at the current price. Explain why the equilibrium price could be higher or lower than the current price.
7. You own a three-carat diamond ring that you no longer like. In fact, you would like to have a new color television set. How would you get the television set in a barter economy? Discuss the efficiency of exchange in a barter economy versus a monetary economy.
8. "Specialization takes place only when people are different. If all people were identical, there would be no specialization." Evaluate this statement.
9. Assume that while shopping, you see long lines of people waiting to buy bread while fresh meat is spoiling in butcher shops. What does this tell you about prevailing prices? What is your prediction about what will happen to the relative price of bread?
10. Bill can prepare 50 hamburgers per hour or wait on 25 tables per hour. Mike can prepare 20 hamburgers per hour or wait on 15 tables per hour. If Bill and Mike were to open a hamburger stand, who would be the cook? Who would be the waiter? Would Bill do both?
11. Why would private industry find it difficult to organize national defense? How would private industry charge each citizen for national defense?
12. In an hour's time, Jill can lay 100 tiles or can mortar 50 bricks. Tom can lay 10 tiles or 20 bricks in an hour's time. What is Jill's opportunity cost of mortaring bricks compared to Tom's opportunity cost of mortaring bricks? According to the law of comparative advantage, in which activity should each specialize? Explain why it is that Jill should not do both activities and let Tom rest simply because Jill is better at both activities.
13. Which of the following transactions would enter the circular flow and which would not?

    a. U.S. Steel sells steel to General Motors.
    b. General Motors sells a car to Jones.
    c. Jones takes a job from General Motors and receives $100 in wages.
    d. Jones has his suit cleaned at the local dry cleaner and pays $5.
    e. Jones washes his dress shirt.

14. Explain how an increase in the interest rate alters society's provision for the future.
15. An acre of land in California produces more tobacco than an acre of land in New England—a cold region poorly suited to agriculture. Tobacco production flourishes where the climate is warm. Yet, New England produces tobacco and California does not. Why?
16. What is the opportunity cost of saving? What is the benefit?

SUGGESTED READINGS

Hayek, Frederick A. "The Price System as a Mechanism for Using Knowledge." *American Economic Review* 35, no. 4 (September 1945): 519–28. Reprinted in *Comparative Economic Systems: Models and Cases,* 5th ed., edited by Morris Bornstein, 49–60. Homewood, Ill.: Richard D. Irwin, 1985.

McKenzie, Richard, and G. Tullock. *Modern Political Economy.* New York: McGraw-Hill, 1978.

Neuberger, Egon. "Comparative Economic System." In *Perspectives in Economics: Economists Look at Their Field of Study,* edited by Alan A. Brown, et al., 252–66. New York: McGraw-Hill, 1971.

Radford, R. A. "The Economic Organization of a P.O.W. Camp." In *Economica* 12 (November 1945): 189–201.

Smith, Adam. *The Wealth of Nations,* ed. Edwin Cannan. New York: Modern Library, 1937, book 1.

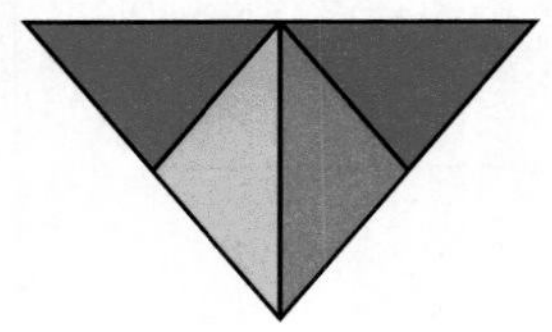

4

Capitalism and Socialism

CHAPTER INSIGHT

Imagine you are Ivan Ivanov, an engineer employed by the AZLK Automobile Works of Moscow in 1991. Your monthly pay is 400 rubles. Your wife works in a research institute as a chemist and earns 300 rubles. You pay 10 rubles a month for a two-room apartment that is owned by the Auto Works and that you share with your elderly parents. Your basic foodstuffs are handed out once a week at the factory. (The factory supplies two cars per year to a large state-owned farm). Other groceries are obtained either by patient hours waiting in line at state food stores, where prices are low, or in private markets, where one lemon costs 10 rubles.

You see that your socialist system is on the verge of change. There is a newly formed parliament, and, for the first time, you voted in the Russian presidential election. There is talk at the factory of increased freedom from government directives; some of your fellow workers have left to form their own small companies. Although you hear that economic life is better in the capitalist system, you fear the changes the reformers suggest. What if this new life is worse?

This chapter compares socialism and capitalism and explores the difficulties faced by socialist countries determined to make the transition to capitalism.

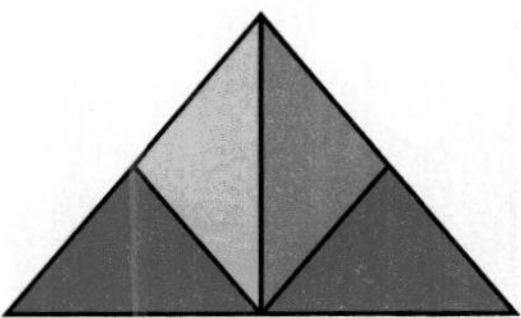

ECONOMIC SYSTEMS

In times of scarcity, societies must find orderly ways of allocating resources. Each society uses an **economic system** to solve allocation problems and to maintain order.

> An **economic system** is the set of property rights, resource allocation arrangements, and incentives that a society uses to solve the economic problem.

Economic systems are differentiated according to the specific institutions they establish for each of these three attributes.

1. *Property Rights.* The factors of production may be owned primarily by society (or by a government that is supposed to represent society), by private individuals, or by a combination of the two. The person or body that holds property rights has the right to determine how the resource is used and to receive the income the resource generates.
2. *Allocation Arrangements.* Resources can be allocated by the price system or by government planners. In economic systems in which resources are allocated by price, individual firms decide what and how to produce; in systems in which allocation is determined by the government, officials give orders about production to enterprises. When the price system allocates resources, decision making is *decentralized.* When planners make allocations, decision making is centralized.
3. *Incentive Systems.* An economic system must motivate its participants (workers, managers, entrepreneurs) to carry out their economic tasks. *Economic incentives* can be used to motivate people. Alternatively, *moral incentives* (medals, public praise) or even *threats* may induce individuals to produce.

The two major economic systems are **capitalism** and **socialism**.

> **Capitalism** is an economic system characterized by private ownership of the factors of production, market allocation of resources, and the use of economic incentives.

> **Socialism** is an economic system characterized by state ownership of the factors of production, the use of moral as well as economic incentives, resource allocation by economic plan, and centralized decision making.

No real-world economy fits exactly into one of these two molds. In all economies, there is a mixture of private and public ownership, administrative and market allocation, economic and moral incentives, and centralized and decentralized decision making. However, in most economies, the major traits of one particular economic system will dominate.

Property Rights

In a capitalist economy, **property rights** are taken for granted. It is assumed that goods (e.g., a quart of milk), services (e.g., a shoe shine), and assets (e.g., a piece of land or a share of stock) can be bought or sold.

> **Property rights** are the rights of an owner to buy, sell, or use and exchange property (i.e., goods, services and assets).

Prevailing property rights are a key determinant of the nature of the economic system.

Property Rights in a Capitalist System. In a capitalist society, most property is owned by private individuals. As discussed in Chapter 3, Adam Smith argued that if individuals are allowed to own property and to pursue their own economic self-interest, an "invisible hand" will cause them to act in the public interest. By pursuing private profits, they will produce the goods and services that people want and will offer them at prices that are reasonable compared to costs of production.

Private owners of property are motivated by self-interest to obtain the best deal possible for themselves. The legal system protects private property from theft, damage, and unauthorized use and defines where property rights reside. This legal protection ensures that owners will reap the benefits of decisions that are in their self-interest and will suffer the consequences of decisions that are not in their self-interest.

EXAMPLE 1 The Unannounced Reform: China's Dying State Sector

When China began the restructuring of its economy in the 1980s, state enterprises accounted for most of China's industrial production. In 1992 China marked an important milestone: more output was produced by private and cooperative companies than state enterprises. Although China's communist leaders were aghast, they saw no alternative but to accept the growth of the private sector as a way to create jobs and income.

An examination of how China's state enterprises run explains why they cannot compete with the private sector. The Shanghai No. 2 Cotton Mill has a payroll of 10,600 people, less than one-half of whom are actually engaged in production. The others prepare party slogans and do odd jobs. The manager does not have the right (nor the incentive) to fire such workers. The mill must produce what the government orders and must deliver to customers at prices set by the state. Other state enterprises often refuse to pay their debts to the Shanghai Mill. Some state enterprises must resort to innovative measures to collect debt, like sending sick and disabled workers to plead for repayment of debts.

The managers of Shanghai No. 2 Cotton Mill are most interested in maximizing the incomes and benefits of their workers—their most important constituency. They would not think of laying off workers, despite rising losses. In fact, nearly 40 percent of China's state enterprises are losing money, and those that are profitable cover the losses of other enterprises.

Although the Chinese leadership continues to speak in favor of state enterprises, private enterprises are quietly driving state enterprises from the scene. The "dinosaur" state enterprises are fading away.

Source: "As China's Economy Thrives, the Public Sector Flounders," *New York Times*, Dec. 18, 1991.

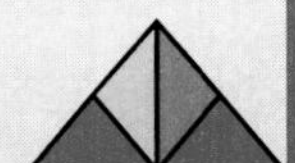

Property Rights in a Socialist System. In a socialist society, most property is owned by the state, and the state has rights to use and exchange that property. Individual ownership of property has been limited to a few head of livestock, a private home in some circumstances, a private car, a TV, and so on. However, the emphasis on state ownership is changing, although at a slow pace. (See Example 1.)

Allocation Arrangements

Resources can be allocated either by market or by plan. Capitalism is characterized by market resource allocation. Socialism is characterized by resource allocation through government decree.

Market Allocation. Market allocation is the use of relative prices to determine what, how, and for whom to produce. Private ownership and market allocation are intertwined.

An owner of private property has the right to use the property to the owner's best advantage and to sell the property at the best price possible. The actions of the owners of private property will be guided by relative prices. For example, the farmer will look at the relative prices of corn and soybeans to decide how much of each crop to plant; the private owner of an oil refinery will use the relative prices of gasoline, fuel oils, and kerosene to determine how much of each petroleum product to refine. The private owner of labor (that is, the individual worker) will look at the relative wage rates in different occupations to help determine where to seek employment.

Allocation by Plan. In planned resource allocation systems, the decisions concerning what, how, and for whom to produce are made by the government. A central authority determines output targets and makes the basic investment decisions. Industrial ministries issue output targets to enterprises and tell them what materials to use. Although planners cannot decide exactly for whom the output is produced, they play a significant role in determining who will get the scarce automobiles, apartments, and vacations.

Incentive Systems

Any economic system must provide incentives for people to work hard and to take economic risks.

Incentives in a Capitalist System. A capitalist system uses economic incentives to motivate employees. Higher salaries, bonuses, and stock options are rewards for tasks that are well done. Entrepreneurs are rewarded by having the value of their businesses grow.

Incentives in a Socialist System. A socialist system relies more heavily on moral incentives, although no economic system can afford to rely on moral incentives alone. In socialist systems, there is greater emphasis on "working for the good of society." Medals, honorary positions, and other noneconomic incentives are used to motivate workers.

KARL MARX

Karl Marx was the prophet of state ownership and government resource allocation. (See Example 2.) In Marx's judgment, economies based on private ownership and market allocation would ultimately collapse to be replaced by a new type of economy. Marx argued that Adam Smith's system was unfair to workers, who were exploited by the factory owners, and that it was unstable. The exploited workers, living near subsistence, would be unable to buy goods spewed out by the prolific factories; the factory owners would increase their exploitation of workers; and large-scale economic crises would result. Eventually, the workers of the world would unite against the factory owners in a revolutionary movement that would demand a new economy based on social ownership and government command.

Marx argued that this new economy would prove superior to Adam Smith's "invisible hand." Workers would prosper; income would be fairly distributed; and work would cease to be a chore. Everyone would relish working for the public good. Scarcity would disappear; the economic problem would cease to exist.

EXAMPLE 2 Karl Marx: The Father of Socialism

Karl Marx (1818–1883) remains the most prominent critic of capitalism. As a newspaper editor, his calls for radical reforms led to his suppression and flight to Paris in 1843. In 1847, Marx joined the Communist League, and in 1848 he wrote the famous *Communist Manifesto,* calling for a socialist revolution based upon a united worker class. Exiled from the continent, Marx lived in poverty in London. He was plagued by chronic illnesses, and several of his children died. He worked as a correspondent for the *New York Times* and received a small pension from benefactors. In 1864 he formed the International Working Men's Association (The First International), an organization that promoted international socialism and socialist revolution. Marx's views on economics and revolution are summarized in his four-volume *Das Kapital,* three volumes of which were published after his death.

Although Marx was the prophet of socialism, he said remarkably little about socialism as an economic system. He did write that a transitional period would follow the overthrow of capitalism. During this phase, called socialism, scarcity would prevail, individuals would be paid according to their contribution to production, and a strong state (the dictatorship of the proletariat) would direct the economy. As the productive capacity of the economy grew, eventually a second stage of absolute abundance, called communism, would be reached. Class conflicts would disappear; people would work for pleasure; and distribution would be according to need.

THE RISE AND FALL OF COMMUNIST SOCIALISM

Two historic events appeared to lend credence to Marx's predictions: the Russian Revolution in 1917 and the Great Depression. During much of the nineteenth century Russia was a hotbed of anarchistic ideas. Vladimir Lenin and then Joseph Stalin used an oppressive one-party dictatorship to eliminate private ownership and to destroy market allocation. Government planners and ministry officials replaced market allocation. Rigid labor codes dictated hours of work and pay. The price system ceased to play a real role in the economy. Prices were set arbitrarily by government officials.

During the Great Depression (starting in England and Europe in the mid-1920s and spreading to the United States with the stock market crash of 1929), aggregate output plummeted and unemployment soared. At its worst point, one out of four American workers was unemployed and output had fallen by one-third. The Great Depression appeared to substantiate Marx's claim that Adam Smith's system was unstable. Workers began to look to the radical alternatives proposed by Marx, while politicians looked for solutions to preserve the existing order.

The Soviet propaganda machine provided a vivid contrast to the despair of the Great Depression. Smiling workers were shown enthusiastically building the world's largest hydroelectric dam; cheerful farmers were shown bringing in bumper crops. Soviet statisticians published reports of astonishing successes both in industry and in agriculture.

As the world divided into political blocs at the end of World War II, the Soviet system was installed in Eastern Europe and China. The one-party propaganda systems of these countries immediately began to herald astonishing economic successes. European democracies allowed the Communist party to compete freely with other parties in the political arena. In 1957 the Soviet launching of the first manned space vehicle, *Sputnik,* added considerable weight to Nikita Khrushchev's threat to bury the West economically.

Thirty years later, it was evident that Khrushchev's faith in socialism had been misplaced. Living standards in the Soviet Union and Eastern Europe had fallen to a small fraction of their potential. (See Figure 1.) Consumers were no longer content to stand in long lines for shoddy products. China had failed to keep up with its capitalist neighbors. The technology gap between the capitalist and socialist countries had become enormous. Growth rates, which had been acceptable in the 1950s and 1960s, declined steadily in the 1970s and 1980s. (See Example 3.)

FIGURE 1
Relative Efficiency:
The Former Soviet Union and USA

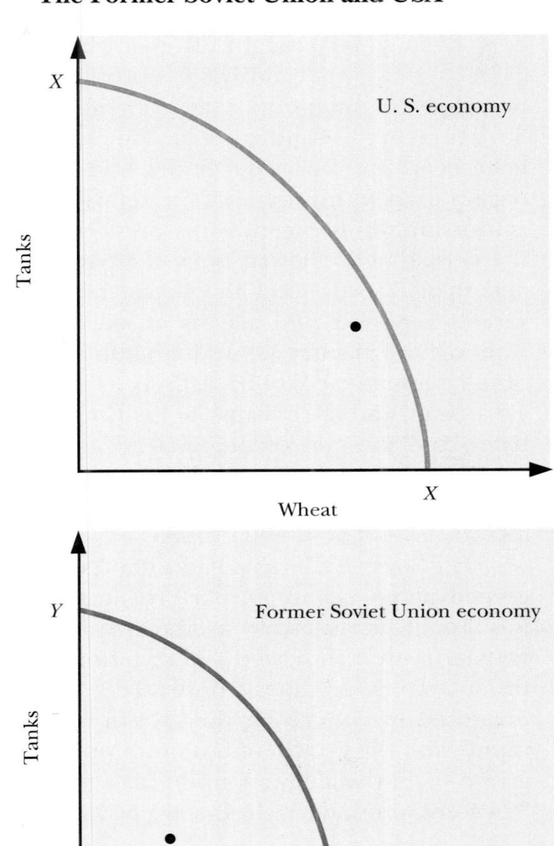

It is impossible to determine just how close an economy is to operating on its production possibilities frontier (PPF). Most evidence suggests, however, that the economy of the former Soviet Union operates well below its PPF, while the U.S. economy operates close to its PPF. (Note: The U.S. economy has been drawn to have a larger resource base due to its more advanced technology.)

EXAMPLE 3 Soviet Productivity and the Origins of Perestroika

Long-term observers of the Soviet economy were caught off guard in March 1985 when Mikhail Gorbachev announced his intent to radically reform the Soviet economy. Although such comments had been heard from previous Soviet leaders, Gorbachev carried through with the reforms. Press censorship was reduced; a free press emerged; the people were allowed to elect a parliament and then directly elect the presidents of the various republics and mayors of major cities. Although Gorbachev was undoubtedly unaware of the consequences of his actions (the August 1991 coup, and the collapse of the Communist party, and the end of the Soviet Union), he set into motion a process that cannot be reversed. Why was Gorbachev willing to take such a dramatic and bold step in 1985?

The Soviet leadership had always been concerned about economic performance, which was broadly measured by productivity. Productivity growth is indicated by expansion of the production possibilities frontier (PPF) and is measured by comparing the growth of factor inputs with the growth of output. If output has grown by 10 percent and inputs have grown by 3 percent, productivity has grown by 7 percent.

The accompanying table shows the dismal record of Soviet productivity growth from 1966 to 1985. In 1976 Soviet output began to grow less rapidly than factor inputs. From 1976 to 1980, output grew at an annual rate of 2.2 percent while factor inputs grew at 3.9 percent annually. In effect, the Soviet PPF was shrinking.

Gorbachev referred to the period from 1970 to 1985 as the "period of stagnation." The productivity growth during this period indicated there was a drastic need for restructuring. An economy that produces far below its PPF cannot survive. Everyone becomes aware of its gross inefficiences.

Soviet Productivity Growth (annual rates of growth)

Years	Output	Factor Inputs	Productivity
1966–70	6.0	5.6	0.4
1971–75	5.3	5.0	0.3
1976–80	2.2	3.9	−1.7
1981–85	1.9	3.0	−1.1

Source: *Handbook of Economic Statistics,* 1990, p. 66.

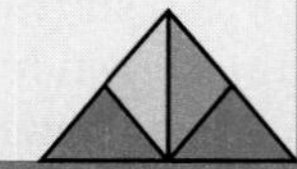

In 1985 Mikhail Gorbachev, dissatisfied with the socialist system, announced his desire to restructure the Soviet economy. The economic, political, and social reforms that Gorbachev initiated permitted Eastern Europe to emerge from Soviet dominance. Democratic forces in those countries overthrew the communist political system and enacted their own dramatic economic and political reforms, which culminated with the dismantling of the Berlin Wall and the subsequent reunification of Germany. The failed coup of Soviet hard-liners in August 1991 triggered the disintegration of the Soviet Union into independent countries. Almost without exception, these new countries vowed to replace their socialist economies with a market system. By the end of the year, only a few countries, such as Cuba, North Korea, and China, had leaders in favor of keeping the socialist system.

To understand the reasons for the collapse of socialism in the former Soviet Union and Eastern Europe, we must understand the characteristics of Soviet socialism and its inherent weaknesses.

THE SOVIET ADMINISTRATIVE-COMMAND ECONOMY

The *administrative-command economy* was a specific variant of socialism. Its basic principles were:

1. Overall direction of economic activity by the Communist party
2. Public ownership of capital
3. Dictation of outputs by a state planning apparatus
4. Balancing of supplies and demands by administrative methods
5. Managerial rewards based upon output target fulfillment

The **administrative-command economy** is an economic system in which the Communist party provides overall direction, a state planning apparatus determines the uses of resources, capital is owned by the state, and managerial rewards are based upon fulfillment of output targets.

In the administrative-command economy, individuals were not allowed to own capital—that is, factories, plants, and equipment—they could own only "nonproductive" assets such as automobiles, apartments, and homes. Although some assets could be owned collectively, such as collective farms, collective owners could not exercise normal property rights, such as the right to sell their shares of the assets. Restrictions on private ownership related to large-scale industry and small-scale retail and service activities. Physicians and artisans could only legally practice their trades through publicly owned and operated facilities. All the steel, automobile, machinery, shoe, and watch factories were state owned.

In the Soviet administrative-command economy, the Communist party set priorities on what was to be produced, how it was to be produced, and for whom. The party issued general instructions to a planning apparatus of state officials and bureaucrats, whose job it was to implement the party's directives. State planning officials and industrial ministries prepared detailed plans for enterprises that told them what to produce, what inputs to use, and what capital investments to make. The planning bureaucracy made adjustments in these instructions in the course of plan fulfillment. Steel plants were told how much and what types of steel to produce and to whom it must be delivered. Shoe factories were told how many pairs of different types of shoes to produce, to whom to deliver, and what prices to charge.

Operating instructions replaced the price system as an instrument of resource allocation. Relative prices were not used in decision making. The supplies and demands for the various resources were balanced administratively.

In the Soviet **administrative-command economy,** enterprise managers were judged according to how close they came to fulfilling the output targets assigned by the state. A shoe factory met its target if it produced the planned number of shoes, even if they were all the same size and color.

Incentives and Information

For an economy to operate on its PPF, its participants must be properly motivated and informed. If they lack motivation or information, they will be unable to use their resources to best advantage. The failure of the administrative-command economy can be traced to motivation and information problems.

The Incentive of Property. In a capitalist economy, the private owners of capital seek out the best profit opportunities for their capital and economize on their use of resources. If they need to hire a professional staff of managers, they can devise a reward system that encourages efficient use of resources. In an administrative-command economy, capital is owned by the state—by everyone and hence by no one. If no one owns the capital resources, there is no incentive for the state enterprise manager to innovate or increase productivity.

Managerial Rewards. In administrative-command economies, rewards must be determined according to objective standards. The manager must be rewarded on the basis of how well he or she meets the enterprise "plan." Because the plan is made up of a large number of tasks—how much to produce, what assortments, what costs, what new equipment, and so on—planners must focus on one or two measurable targets. Usually those are targets that are important to the planners themselves, such as the volume of output. Enterprise managers, therefore, have typically been rewarded on the basis of how close they come to fulfilling the state's output targets.

Basing managerial rewards on output leads to two important incentive problems. First, managers can more easily fulfill output targets by sacrificing quality or assortment. The shoe manufacturer will mass produce only one type of shoe style because the enterprise has been told to produce 10,000 pairs of shoes per month. The construction firm will rely on gravity in place of mortar, thereby producing apartments that collapse during earthquakes. The oil well-drilling company, instructed to drill 10 wells per month, will select easy drilling terrain even though it will yield no oil.

Second, enterprise managers will also be tempted to conceal capacity from their superiors. The managers' lives are easy when their output targets can be fulfilled using 60 percent of the enterprise's capacity. Hence the manager will try to persuade superiors that the enterprise can only produce a maximum of 10,000 pairs of shoes per month instead of the 15,000 pairs it can realistically produce. The manager knows that if the enterprise overfulfills the plan (and reveals its true capacity), it may gain temporary bonuses, but the enterprise will be subject to more ambitious plan targets in the future.

Information Problems. The price system provides invaluable information on opportunity costs. In market economies, such costs are the basis for resource allocation decisions. When the price system indicates that a previously used material has become too expensive relative to new materials, the manufacturer will seek out substitutions. A shoe manufacturer will switch from one shoe fashion to another when the old brand can only be sold at a substantial discount.

The administrative-command economy does not use the price system to make allocation decisions. If there is "too little" of one resource, its relative price does not rise. Rather, an administration official calls users of the resource to make sure they use less.

The early critics of socialism argued that the lack of information on opportunity costs would prove fatal. (See Example 4.) Without markets to deter-

EXAMPLE 4 The Austrian Critics of Socialism

Ludwig von Mises and Frederick Hayek, a Nobel laureate, founded a school of economic thought now called the *Austrian School.* Both economists praised the efficiency with which market economies process and utilize information on relative prices. Hayek wrote that the principal problem of economics is "how to secure the best use of resources known to any member of society, for ends whose relative importance only these individuals know."

How is the economy to utilize knowledge about product prices, qualities, and location that is not available to any one person or institution in its entirety? Hayek and Mises' answer is that the specialization in information about the price system enables each individual to participate effectively in the economy, acquiring knowledge only about those things that he or she needs to know. Hayek writes of the "marvel" of the price system: "The marvel is that in a case like that of a scarcity of one raw material, without an order being issued, without more than perhaps a handful of people knowing the cause, tens of thousands of people whose identity could not be ascertained by months of investigation, are made to use the material or its products more sparingly; i.e., they move in the right direction."

Mises was an early critic of socialism. In his classic article "Economic Calculation in the Socialist Commonwealth," published in 1922, Mises anticipated most of the modern-day problems of the socialist economies, arguing that socialist economies would lack market exchange and would hence lack the vital information provided by the price system. Without relative prices, socialist managers would lack the information to make rational economic decisions. Moreover, lacking property rights, socialist managers would not behave in an economically rational manner, but would overdemand and waste scarce resources.

Source: Frederick A. Hayek, "The Price System as a Mechanism for Using Knowledge," *American Economic Review* 35, no. 4 (September 1945): 519–528.

mine relative prices, no one in the economy knows what things are worth. If the manager does not know whether aluminum, composite plastics, or ceramics are "cheap," that manager cannot make a rational decision on what material to use. If the manager does not know what goods buyers want (as reflected in a high price), the manager cannot produce those goods.

Moreover, planners do not have as much information about local production conditions as managers do. The enterprise managers may even gain by concealing information from their superiors or by providing them with false information. Therefore, planned socialism often operates on the basis of inadequate or even false information.

Inherent Shortage. The planned socialist economies are plagued with shortages: people stand in line for goods; enterprise managers cannot find the materials they need. Although it may appear that these shortages are a result of planners ordering incorrectly, such shortages may be inherent in these economies.

The Hungarian economist Janos Kornai has argued that the administrative-command economy automatically generates shortages because enterprises lack the incentive to use resources economically. Enterprises are judged on their ability to produce outputs, not on their ability to make a profit. Planners, reluctant to let their enterprises fail even when they are losing money, do not hesitate to use subsidies to bail them out. This lack of budget discipline, which Kornai calls "soft budget constraint," leaves enterprises unrestrained in their demands for resources. This drive to stockpile resources causes all goods to be in short supply. Everyone is chasing resources, but few succeed in getting what they want.

Transition to a Market Economy

Restructuring the administrative-command economy will not be easy. There is no precedent for dismantling a socialist economy. (See Example 5.)

Immense economic and political problems must be solved if the transition to a market economy is to be successful. The administrative-command economy created large enterprises and whole industries that have been operated inefficiently and that have produced products that no one wants. These enterprises cannot survive in a market environment, yet a large proportion of the work force is employed in such industries. For example, Russian enterprises that produce low-quality, reinforced concrete will not survive in a market economy; however, the demise of such enterprises have a high price in terms of jobs, with such industries employing more than 100,000 workers.

Defininng property rights is another problem that must be solved before the transition to a market economy can be made. In the administrative-command economy, the slogan was, "Property belongs to everyone and hence to no one." A market economy cannot operate under this assumption. Property rights must be defined, but it will be an extremely difficult economic and political task. How it is done determines who will be rich and who will be poor.

Market economies developed their economic laws, customs, and institutions over centuries. The administrative-command economies have operated for over 60 years without laws and institutions that are supportive of market allocation. To make the transition, new laws must be put in place and modern economic institutions (such as a modern banking system) must be established. These things will not be accomplished quickly.

In those countries that have opted for a quick transition from socialism to capitalism—a shock therapy treatment—the costs of transition have been high. Inflation has soared, output has fallen, and unemployment has risen. There is evidence, however, from the Polish experience with shock therapy that inflation stabilizes rather quickly and that stores fill up with goods. The major problem has been dealing with inefficient state enterprises that account for most of the employment. It is considered too costly to close them down. Countries that have opted for a slow transition, such as the Soviet Union prior to the August 1991 coup, faced growing stagnation as they were caught in a no-man's-land between planned socialism and market resource allocation. Inflationary pressures grew, output stagnated, consumers and workers became more disenchanted, and corruption grew. (See Example 6.) Russian President Boris Yeltsin's January 1992 decision to emulate Poland's "shock therapy" approach was a further indication that the "go-slow" approach was ineffective.

These are only a few of the problems that Eastern Europe and the Soviet Union are encountering in their quest for transition. The outcome is still uncertain.

EXAMPLE 5 Speed of Transition

History offers little guidance for transforming a centrally planned economy into a market economy. There is no experience to guide a change that most countries in transition today experience simultaneously with the creation of a new political order. There is relatively little disagreement that such transitions are necessary, but there is much controversy about the timing, scope, speed, and sequencing of reforms. The World Bank issued

The Phasing of Reform (as suggested by the World Bank)

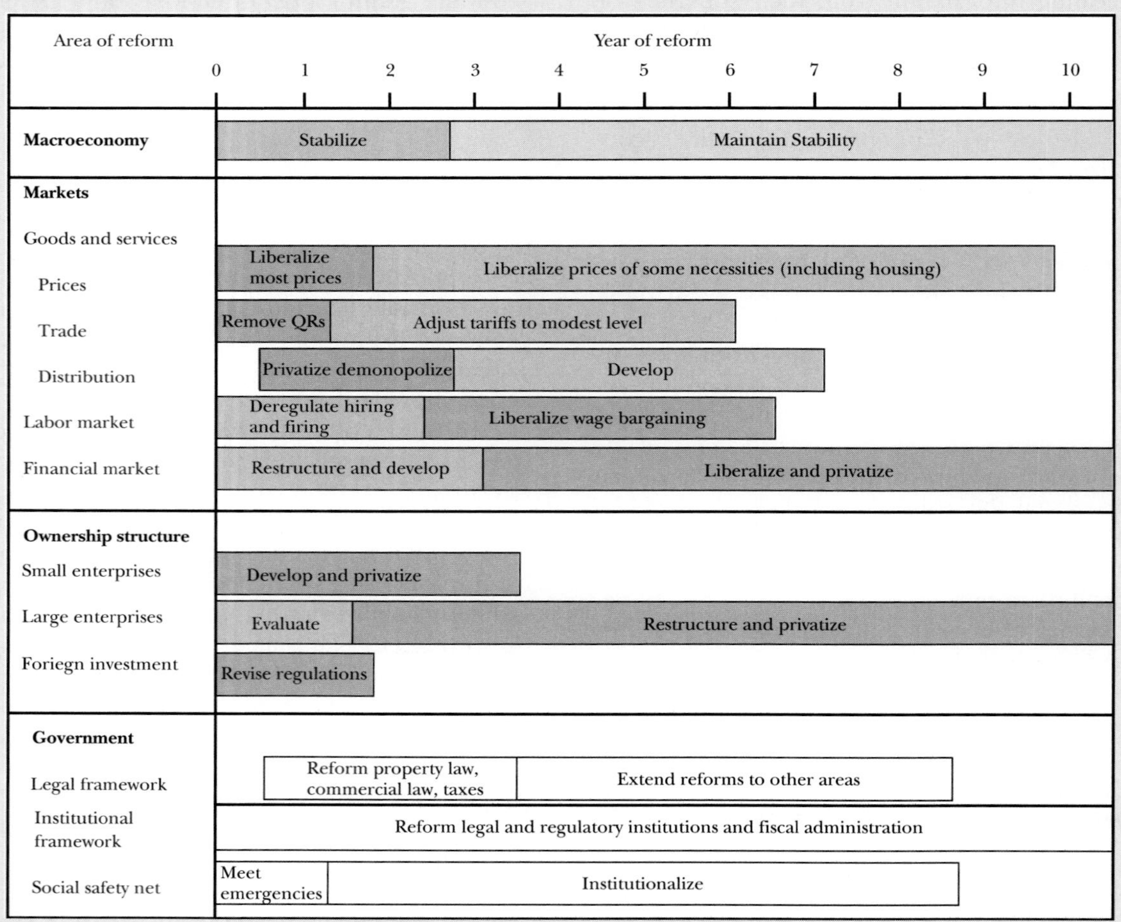

Note: Dark shading indicates intensive action. QRs, quantitative restrictions.

a report in 1991 analyzing several perspectives regarding the transition problem.

One school of reform proposes instituting changes in the nature of ownership before or together with changes that address macroeconomic stability and markets. Early privatization, it claims, reduces the risk that the economy will remain state-controlled and increases the pressure for complementary market-oriented reforms. But another school of thought calls for initial macroeconomic and market-building reforms, leaving privatization—at least for large state enterprises—to a second stage. (Under both proposals some agricultural, retail, and residential assets would be privatized early.) This theory is based on the belief that without an infrastructure of financial institutions, experience, and expertise, rapid privatization could lead to widespread corruption and economic and political chaos.

No single reform sequence is suitable for every transitional economy. Hungary has had more than two decades of experience with decentralized economic decisions. Macroeconomic conditions range from great instability (the former Soviet Union) to relative stability (Czechoslovakia). Private sector activity has been relatively higher in predominantly agricultural countries such as China and Viet Nam, but negligible in more industrialized nations.

A preferred sequencing (see attached figure) would include early steps to stabilize the macroeconomy and deregulate domestic- and external-sector prices to give clear, accurate signals for economic activity and for the valuation of enterprises. These steps would be accompanied and followed by intense efforts to rationalize enterprises, improve economic decision making, reform trade policy, and build managerial skills and a strong financial sector. Privatization of large state enterprises would become the next priority. Protection would be cut and the economy would be opened to foreign competition on a firm, preannounced schedule. Institution building would be a basic theme throughout. The legal contractual system, the structure of ownership, and the roles of key organizations in the economy would require reform and restructuring.

Large-scale privatization would not be at the head of this sequence, but there would be early legal commitments (the distribution of shares) that would guarantee private ownership within a reasonable time. This program would advance as rapidly as the development of institutional capacities permits. However, a three-to-five-year time span seems optimistic in light of the fitful progress achieved in the transitional economies by the early 1990s.

Reforms will surely involve painful adjustments. Inflation and unemployment will worsen as price controls are removed and the real economic losses of some activities are revealed. Political opposition may mount with these developments and with the rise in income inequality that comes after radical change in the incentive structure. But progress in exports and the availability of consumer goods could soon follow. And, given the relatively strong human resource endowments in these countries, prospects for growth could be excellent.

Source: The World Bank, *World Development Report 1991: The Challenge of Development* (Oxford: Oxford University Press, 1991), 145–46.

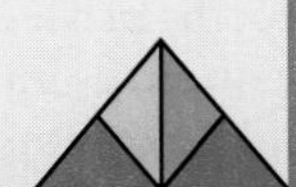

EXAMPLE 6 Popular Attitudes Toward Free Markets: Are Americans and Soviets Different?

Soviet citizens had lived in a planned economy for over 60 years. At the time of its demise, only the most elderly citizens had recollections of living under a market economy. This lack of experience with market economies is often given as a reason for the difficulty faced by the citizens of the former Soviet Union in making the transition from socialism to capitalism. In particular, antagonistic attitudes of the Soviet people towards market allocation has been suggested as an obstacle to the acceptance of capitalism.

In May 1990 a joint Soviet-American team of researchers conducted random telephone interviews of Moscow and New York residents to compare their attitudes toward free markets. Questions were asked about the fairness of price increases, income distribution, the importance of incentives, resistance to exchange of money, and attitudes toward business. To the surprise of the research team, the responses of Moscow and New York residents were very similar.

The research team writes,

> Indeed we have found that Soviets are concerned with fair prices and with income inequality, so that these concerns might help prevent change to a market economy. However, at the same time, these concerns appear to be little different among Americans. Perhaps Americans would resist perestroika with as much vigor if they inherited the Soviet political and institutional system.

Source: Robert Schiller, Maxim Boyko, and Vladimir Korobov, "Popular Attitudes Toward Free Markets: The Soviet Union and the United States Compared," *American Economic Review*, vol. 82 (June 1991): 385–400.

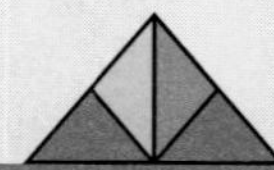

The next chapter will look more closely at the process of market resource allocation—at how supply and demand combine to determine prices and quantities in the marketplace.

SUMMARY

1. Economic systems are characterized by property rights arrangements, resource allocation methods, and incentive systems. Capitalism is characterized by private property rights, market allocation, and economic incentives. Socialism is characterized by public ownership, government allocation, and moral incentives.

2. Marx argued that capitalism had fatal flaws and that a new and superior type of economy, called socialism, would inevitably replace it.

3. The Soviet administrative-command economy used a one-party system, a state planning system, state ownership of capital, and managerial rewards based upon plan fulfillment. The inefficiencies of the administrative-command economy related to property and incentive problems, a faulty system of managerial rewards, and information problems. The administrative-command economy also appeared to generate shortages.

4. The inefficiency of the administrative-command economy has prompted a search for ways to transform it into a market economy. No one knows the best way to convert an administrative-command economy into a market economy.

KEY TERMS

economic system
capitalism
socialism
property rights
administrative-command economy

QUESTIONS AND PROBLEMS

1. Imagine first that you are the owner of a small business, and then, in contrast, that you are the manager of a state-owned enterprise. Would you behave differently in these two situations? Why?
2. You are the manager of a state-owned factory that produces light bulbs. You are judged on the basis of how close you come to fulfilling the state's target for light bulb production. Explain how you might ensure that you can fulfill your light bulb production quota.
3. Explain why the Soviet administrative-command economy operated well below its potential as defined by its resource base.
4. Economists argue that property rights and incentives are closely related. Explain why this relationship exists.
5. In administrative-command economies, a common complaint is: "Everyone owns capital and no one owns capital." Explain what this means and how this might affect economic activity.
6. The previous chapter explained how the price system provides valuable information to participants in the economic system. Consider how the lack of price information in the administrative-command economy may complicate economic decision making.
7. Explain why a lack of budget discipline at the enterprise level can lead to persistent shortages in the administrative-command economy.

SUGGESTED READINGS

Bergson, Abram. *Productivity and the Social System: The USSR and the West.* Cambridge, MA: Harvard University Press, 1978.

Gregory, Paul R., and Robert Stuart. *Soviet Economic Structure and Performance,* 4th ed. New York: HarperCollins, 1990.

Hayek, Frederick A. "The Price System as a Mechanism For Using Knowledge," *American Economic Review* 35, no. 4 (September 1945): 519–28.

Heilbroner, Robert. "Analysis and Vision in the History of Modern Economic Thought," *Journal of Economic Literature* 18, no. 3 (September 1990): 1097–1114.

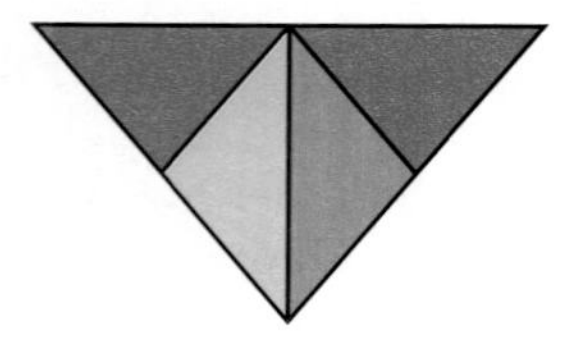

5 Supply and Demand

CHAPTER INSIGHT

Supply-and-demand analysis can solve puzzles whose solutions are not readily apparent. Consider the curious fact that fresh Hawaiian-grown pineapples sell for more in Hawaii than on the West Coast—even though shippers must pay transportation costs to the mainland. Why should a Hawaiian-grown pineapple cost more in Hawaii? Here is another puzzle: Nurses are currently being offered cash bonuses of $1000 to $2000 for signing employment contracts with major hospitals. Why do nurses receive sign-on bonuses when other professionals do not?

This chapter uses supply-and-demand analysis to answer these and other questions. It shows how supply and demand interact to set prices in competitive markets that equate quantity demanded with quantity supplied. It also shows the shortages and gluts that arise when prices are not allowed to adjust to equate supply and demand.

It has been said that if you teach a parrot the phrase "supply and demand," you will create a learned economist. This quip does not do justice to the complexity of supply-and-demand analysis. An economist needs to know more than the parrot, just as the physician must know more than the prescription, "Take two aspirin and call me in the morning."

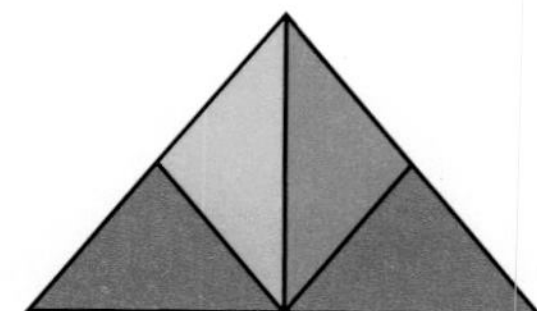

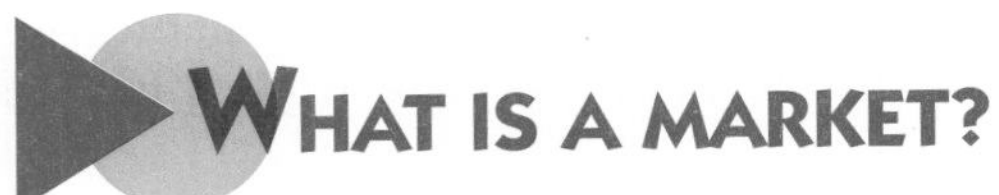

WHAT IS A MARKET?

To understand supply and demand, we must focus on how a *single market* works. In each **market,** buyers and sellers base their decisions on price.

> A **market** is an established arrangement that brings buyers and sellers together to exchange particular goods or services.

Types of Markets

Retail stores; gas stations; farmers' markets; real estate firms, the New York Stock Exchange (where stocks are bought and sold); Chicago commodity markets (where livestock, grains, and metals are traded); auctions of works of art, gold markets in London, Frankfurt, and Zurich; labor exchanges; university placement offices; and thousands of other specialized arrangements are all markets. A market is an arrangement for bringing together buyers and sellers of a particular good or service. The New York Stock Exchange uses modern telecommunications to bring together the buyers and sellers of corporate stock. The university placement office brings university graduates together with potential employers. The gas station brings together the buyers and sellers of gasoline. In some markets, the buyers and sellers confront one another face-to-face (as they do in roadside farm markets). In other markets, the buyer never sees the seller (the Chicago commodity markets).

The actual form a particular market takes depends on the type of good or service being sold and the costs of transporting the good. Some markets are local, others are national, others are international. Residential real estate is usually bought and sold in local markets; houses cannot be shipped from one place to another (except at great expense). College textbooks are usually exchanged in a national market. The New York Stock Exchange, the various gold exchanges, and the Chicago commodity exchanges bring together buyers and sellers from around the world. (See Example 1.)

Perfectly Competitive Markets

Markets exist in almost infinite variety. This chapter deals with a special type of market called a **perfectly competitive market.**

EXAMPLE 1 L.A.'s Grand Central Market

Los Angeles's Grand Central Market lies in the geographic intersection of the four-county metropolitan area. On weekdays, an average of 20,000 customers shop in the market. On weekends, the number swells to 50,000. The Grand Central Market pulsates with activity as people look for deals and hard-to-find goods, such as pork-tongue enchiladas, skullcaps, slippery elm, 20 brands of pepper, and squaw vine. Grand Central carries parts of animals not sold at supermarkets—lambs heads, beef lips, eyes, ears, and snouts. The booths are owned and operated by people of 17 different nationalities, many of them trading in four languages. Says one frequent customer, "If it's food and it's not here, you can't buy it anywhere."

A market is anything that brings buyers and sellers together for the purpose of making transactions. L.A.'s Grand Central Market has accomplished this function for over 80 years. It offers buyers and sellers of common and exotic food products a convenient way to come together to make deals.

Source: "L.A.'s Grand Central Market," *The Christian Science Monitor,* November 23, 1990.

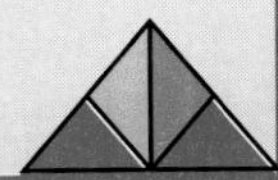

In a **perfectly competitive market,** (1) The product's price is uniform; (2) buyers and sellers have perfect information about price and product quality; (3) there are large numbers of buyers and sellers; (4) no single buyer or seller purchases or sells enough to change the price.

The principal characteristic of a perfectly competitive market is that buyers and sellers face so much competition that no person or group has any control over the price.

Stocks and bonds and commodities such as wheat, foreign currencies, pork bellies, lumber, cotton, cattle, and platinum are bought and sold in perfectly competitive markets. However, the markets where most people buy and sell goods are not perfectly competitive. Buyers and sellers may not be perfectly informed about prices and qualities. Two people pay different prices in adjacent grocery stores for the same brand of cookies. Houses that are virtually identical sell at different prices. Chemically equivalent brand-name and generic drugs sell at different prices. AT&T and General Motors exercise some control over the prices they charge. Large buyers (like Coca-Cola, the world's largest sugar buyer) exercise some control over the prices they pay.

Nonetheless, the concept of the perfectly competitive market serves as a useful guide to the way many real-world markets function. Although markets like the local grocery store, the college placement office, or the roadside stand are not perfectly competitive, many of them function as if they were. And for many questions (such as what happens to price if supply or demand increases?), the markets for such major goods as steel, aluminum, and cars also behave as if they were perfectly competitive.

DEMAND

As we have seen in earlier discussions, people tend to want more than the economy can provide. But the goods and services that we *want*—those that we would claim if they were given away free—are quite different from the goods and services we **demand.**

The **demand** for a good or service is the amount people are prepared to buy under specific circumstances during the specified time period.

What we are actually prepared to buy depends on price and various other factors to be studied in this chapter.

The Law of Demand

The most important factor affecting the demand for a good is the price. People buy more if the price of a good falls; they buy less if the price rises, holding other factors constant (*ceteris paribus*). This idea constitutes a fundamental law of economics, the **law of demand.**

The **law of demand** states that there is a negative (or inverse) relationship between the price of a good and the quantity demanded, holding other factors constant.

The demand for a good or service also depends on other factors like the prices of related goods (for example, the demand for tea depends on the price of coffee), income, and tastes. These other factors will be studied later. For the moment, we want to concentrate on the price of the good or service itself.

The main reason that the law of demand holds true is that people tend to substitute other, cheaper goods or services as the price of any good or service goes up. If the price of gasoline rises, drivers will cut back on less essential driving, and more people will take the bus, walk, or ride their bicycles to work. If the price of tea rises, more people will drink coffee or soft drinks, or heavy tea drinkers may cut back one or two cups a day. In other words, the **quantity demanded** is negatively related to the price of a good or service. (See Example 2.)

The **quantity demanded** is the amount of a good or service consumers are prepared to buy at a given price (during a specified time period), holding other factors constant.

When a price rises enough, some people may even stop buying the good altogether. Thus, as the price rises, the number of actual buyers may fall as some people switch entirely to other goods.

As the price of a good goes up people also tend to buy less because they feel poorer. If a person buys a new car every year for $15,000 (after trade-in), and the price rises to $19,000, the person would need

EXAMPLE 2 M&Ms and the Law of Demand

The law of demand states that the quantity demanded will increase as the price is lowered, as long as other factors that affect demand do not change. In the real world, factors that affect the demand for a particular product change frequently. Tastes change, income rises, and prices of substitutes and complements change. In 1984, the makers of M&M candy conducted an experiment that illustrates the law of demand. Over a 12-month test period, the price of M&Ms was held constant in 150 stores, and the content weight of the candy was increased. When the price is held constant and the weight increased, the price per ounce is lowered. In the stores where the price per ounce was dropped, sales rose by 20 to 30 percent almost overnight, according to the director of sales development for M&Ms. As predicted by the law of demand, a reduction in price causes the quantity demanded to rise, *ceteris paribus*.

Source: "Why Do Hot Dogs Come in Packs of 10 and Buns in 8s and 12s?" *Wall Street Journal,* September 21, 1984.

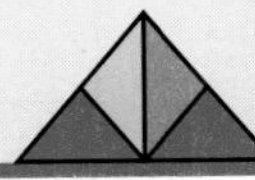

an extra $4000 yearly income to maintain the old standard of living. The $4000 increase in the price of the car is like a cut in income of $4000.

The law of demand shows why the concept of *need* is not very useful in economics. A "need" implies the inability to do without something. But when the price changes, the law of demand says that the quantity demanded will change. For example, a person's "need" for a daily shower would likely disappear if it cost $50 to take one! Since the word *need* implies absolute necessity, this word is avoided in discussions of demand.

The negative (or inverse) relationship between quantity demanded and price is called the *demand curve* or the *demand schedule*. To avoid confusion, we shall henceforth talk about the *demand schedule* when the relationship is in tabular form and the *demand curve* when the relationship is in graphical form.

The Demand Schedule

Table 1 shows a hypothetical demand schedule for corn. Buyers in the marketplace demand 20 million bushels of corn per month at the price of $5 per bushel. At a lower price—say, $4 per bushel—the quantity demanded is higher. In this case, the quantity demanded at the lower price of $4 is 25 million bushels. By continuing to decrease the price, it is possible to induce buyers to purchase more and more corn. As Table 1 shows, at the price of $1, quantity demanded is 50 million bushels.[1]

The Demand Curve

The demand schedule of Table 1 can be portrayed graphically (Figure 1) as the demand curve. For demand curves, price is on the vertical axis and

TABLE 1
Demand Schedule for Corn

	Price (dollars per bushel)	Quantity Demanded (millions of bushels per month)
a	5	20
b	4	25
c	3	30
d	2	40
e	1	50

[1]Notice that it is important to state the units of measurement for both price and quantity. In this example, price is in dollars per bushel, and quantity is in millions of bushels per month. The time period, whether it be a minute, a day, a week, a month, or a year, must be specified to make the demand schedule meaningful.

FIGURE 1
The Demand Curve for Corn

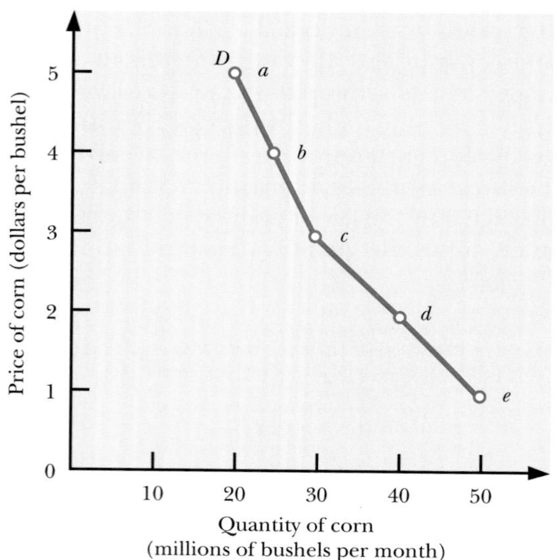

Table 1 describes how the quantity of corn demanded responds to the prices of corn, holding all other factors constant. At *a,* when the price of corn is $5 per bushel, the quantity demanded is 20 million bushels per month. At *e,* when the price of corn is $1, the quantity demanded is 50 million bushels. The downward-sloping curve (*D*) drawn through these points is the demand curve for corn. Graphically, it shows the amounts of corn consumers would be willing to buy at different prices in the specified time period.

quantity demanded is on the horizontal axis. In this demand curve, prices are in dollars per bushel and quantities are in millions of bushels per month. When price is $5, quantity demanded is 20 million bushels (point *a* in Figure 1). Point *b* corresponds to a price of $4 and a quantity of 25 million bushels. When price falls from $5 to $4, quantity demanded rises by 5 million bushels from 20 million to 25 million bushels. The remaining prices and quantities in Table 1 are also graphed.

The curve drawn through points *a* through *e* is the demand curve *D.* It shows how quantity demanded responds to changes in price. Along the demand curve *D,* price and quantity are *negatively* related. This means the curve is downward sloping.

The demand curve shows that as larger quantities of corn are put on the market, lower prices are required to clear the market (to sell that quantity). The price needed to sell 25 million bushels of corn is $4 per bushel. To sell a larger quantity of corn (say, 30 million bushels), a lower price ($3) is required.

This book uses two types of demand curves: (1) the demand curves of individuals (households) and (2) the **market demand curve.** Just as one must state the units of measurement for prices and quantities of the demand curve, one must also specify which demand curve is being used. Normally, this book will use a market demand curve.

> The **market demand curve** is the demand of all persons participating in the market for a particular product.

To illustrate, the demand curve for corn in Figure 1 refers to all buyers in the corn market, an international market that brings together all buyers (American and foreign) of corn. The demand curve for Hawaiian real estate brings together all buyers of Hawaiian real estate; the demand curve for U.S. automobiles brings together all private, corporate, and governmental buyers of U.S.-produced automobiles.

Shifts in the Demand Curve

A demand curve assumes that all other factors are held constant: It shows what would happen to the quantity demanded if *only the good's own price* were to change. In the real world, however, other factors play an important role.

A change in the product's own price will cause a movement along a demand curve. A change in another factor affecting demand will alter the relationship between price and quantity demanded, thereby causing the entire demand curve to shift.

> A leftward shift of the demand curve means that people wish to buy smaller quantities of the good at each price: It signifies a *decrease in demand.* A rightward shift of the demand curve means that people wish to buy larger quantities of the good at each price: It signifies an *increase in demand.*

The factors that can shift the demand curve include: (1) the prices of related goods, (2) consumer income, (3) consumer preferences, (4) the number of potential buyers, and (5) expectations. (See Example 3.)

EXAMPLE 3 Factors That Cause a Demand Curve to Shift

Factor	Example
Change in price of substitutes	Increase in price of coffee shifts demand curve for tea to right.
Change in price of complements	Increase in price of coffee shifts demand curve for sugar to left.
Change in income	Increase in income shifts demand curve for automobiles to right.
Change in preference	Judgment that cigarettes are hazardous to health shifts demand curve for cigarettes to left.
Change in number of buyers	Increase in population of City X shifts demand curve for houses in City X to right.
Change in expectations of future prices	Expectation that prices of canned goods will increase substantially over the next year shifts demand curve for canned goods to right.

The Prices of Related Goods. Goods can be related to each other as either substitutes or complements. Two goods are **substitutes** if the demand for one rises when the price of the other rises (or if the demand for one falls when the price of the other falls). Examples of substitutes are coffee and tea, two brands of soft drinks, stocks and bonds, bacon and sausage, oats and corn, foreign and domestic cars, natural gas and electricity. Some goods are very close substitutes (two different brands of fluoride toothpaste), and others are very distant substitutes (Toyota cars and MD-80 aircraft).

> Two goods are **substitutes** if the demand for one rises when the price of the other rises (or if the demand for one falls when the price of the other falls.).

Two goods are **complements** if the demand for one falls when the price of the other increases. Examples of complements are automobiles and gasoline, food and drink, dress shirts and neckties, skirts and blouses. Complements tend to be used jointly (for example, automobiles plus gasoline equals transportation). An increase in the price of one of the goods effectively increases the price of the joint product of the two goods. (See Example 4.)

> Two goods are **complements** if the demand for one falls when the price of the other rises (or if the demand for one rises when the price of the other falls).

Income. It is easy to understand how income influences demand. As people's incomes rise, they spend more on **normal goods** and services. But as income increases, people also spend less on **inferior goods.**

> A **normal good** is one for which demand increases when income increases, holding all prices constant.
>
> An **inferior good** is one for which demand falls as income increases, holding all prices constant.

Lard, day-old bread, and secondhand clothing are examples of inferior goods. For some people, inferior goods might be hamburgers, margarine, bus rides, or black-and-white TV sets. But most goods—from automobiles to water—are normal goods.

Preferences. *Preferences* are what people like and dislike without regard to budgetary considerations. One may *prefer* a 10-bedroom mansion with servants but may only be able to afford a 3-bedroom bun-

EXAMPLE 4 The Pineapple Paradox Explained

The chapter introduction asked why Hawaiian-grown pineapples sell for more in Hawaii than on the mainland, despite the fact that shippers must pay transportation costs to the mainland.

This chapter teaches that the demand for a particular good depends upon the price of the substitutes. If the price of substitutes is high, the demand for the product will increase, thereby driving up its price. Fresh fruits must be air freighted to Hawaii at considerable expense. They are offered at prices 20 to 30 percent above mainland prices. High-priced fresh fruits substitute for fresh Hawaiian pineapples; with the high prices of substitutes, the demand for pineapples is pushed up, raising the price in Hawaii above the price paid on the mainland.

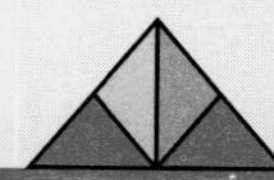

galow. One may prefer a Mercedes-Benz but may drive a Volkswagen. Preferences plus budgetary considerations (price and income) determine demand. As preferences change, demand changes. If people learn that eating oat bran muffins lowers weight and cholesterol, the demand for oat bran muffins will increase. Business firms try to influence preferences by advertising. The goal of advertising is to shift the demand curve for the advertised product to the right. (See Example 5.)

The Number of Potential Buyers. If more buyers enter a market, demand will rise. The number of buyers in a market can increase for many reasons. Relaxed immigration barriers or a baby boom may lead to a larger population. The migration of people from one region to another changes the number of buyers in each region. The relaxation of trade barriers between two countries may increase the number of foreign buyers. If Japanese restrictions on imports of U.S. meat products were removed, the number of buyers of U.S. meat products would increase. Lowering the legal drinking age would increase the number of buyers of beer.

Expectations. If people believe that the price of coffee will rise substantially in the future, they may decide to stock up on coffee today. During inflationary times, people often start buying up durable goods, such as cars and refrigerators. The mere expectation of an increase in a good's price can induce people to buy more of it. Similarly, people can postpone the

EXAMPLE 5 The Greasy Look and the Demand for Shampoo

Fashion consultants say the greasy look is in and shampooing is out. Ever since the Hollywood Harley-Davidson set and French male designer models began sporting a greasy look, the demand for shampoo has threatened to decline. Dirty hair is not for everyone; it works best for men with thick, wavy hair with a short to mid-length cut. One Swedish hairdresser, who has not shampooed his hair for seven years, declared, "I had Proctor & Gamble (the company that owns Vidal Sassoon) come down on me like a ton of bricks."

The reason shampoo companies dislike the greasy look is obvious. If a large percentage of the male population stops shampooing and accepts the greasy look, the demand for shampoo will drop, and shampoo prices will have to fall.

Source: "Those Who Itch to Be Ultra-Trendy Now Shun Shampoo," *Wall Street Journal,* November 20, 1990.

purchase of things that are expected to get cheaper. During the 1980s and 1990s, as home computers grew cheaper and cheaper, some buyers deliberately postponed their purchases on the expectation of even lower prices in the future.

How The Demand Shift Works. Figure 2 shows the demand curve for white dress shirts. This curve, *D*, is based on a $5 price for neckties (a complement), a $10 price for sport shirts (a substitute), a certain income, given preferences, and a fixed number of buyers.

An increase in the price of neckties (a complement for white shirts) from $5 to $7.50 shifts the entire demand curve for white shirts to the left from *D* to *D*′ in panel *a*. White dress shirts are usually worn with neckties. If neckties increase in price, consumers will buy fewer of them and will substitute less formal shirts for shirts that require neckties. As a result, the demand for white dress shirts will decrease, shifting left.

An increase in the price of sport shirts (a substitute for white dress shirts) from $10 to $15 shifts the demand curve for white shirts to the right of *D* to *D*″ in panel *b*. When the price of sport shirts increases, consumers substitute white dress shirts for sport shirts. As a result of this substitution, the demand for white dress shirts will increase, shifting right.

If consumer income increases and if white dress shirts are a normal good, demand will increase (*D* will shift to the right). If preferences change and white dress shirts fall out of fashion, demand will decrease (*D* will shift to the left). If buyers expect prices of white dress shirts to rise substantially in the future, demand today will increase.

FIGURE 2
Shifts in the Demand Curve: Changes in Demand

(*a*) Decrease in Demand

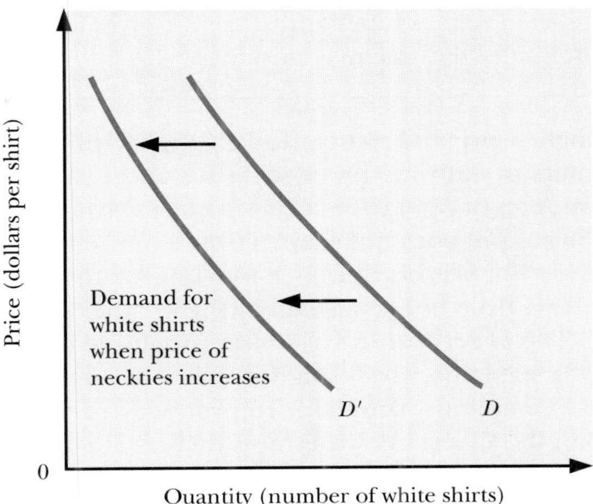

(*b*) Increase in Demand

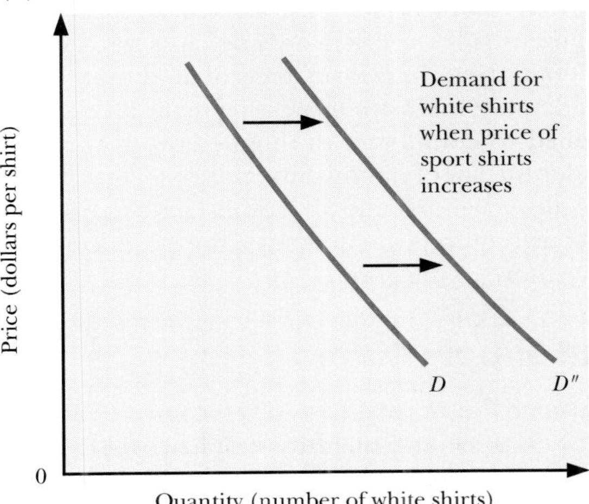

The demand curve for white dress shirts depends on the price of neckties and the price of sport shirts. When the price of neckties is $5 and the price of sport shirts is $10, the demand curve for white shirts is *D*. In panel *a*, if the price of neckties rises to $7.50, holding the price of sport shirts at $10, then at each price for white dress shirts the demand falls. The demand curve shifts to the left from *D* to *D*′. In panel *b*, keeping the price of neckties at $5 and raising the price of sport shirts to $15 will raise the demand for white shirts. The demand curve will shift rightward to *D*″. A rightward shift depicts an increase in demand, and a leftward shift illustrates a decrease in demand.

SUPPLY

The amounts of goods and services that firms are prepared to **supply** to the market depend on price and a variety of other factors.

> The **supply** of a good or service is the amount that firms are prepared to sell under specified circumstances during a specified time period.

The **quantity supplied** of a good should change when the price of the good changes.

> The **quantity supplied** of a good or service is the amount offered for sale at a given price, holding other factors constant.

A higher price for corn, for example, will induce farmers to cultivate fewer soybeans and plant more corn. A higher price for corn will make farmers more willing to put out a little extra effort to make sure that corn is not wasted during harvesting or to prevent the crop from being harmed by the weather or pests.

The *law of diminishing returns* (discussed in Chapter 2) explains why a higher price is required to increase quantity supplied. To produce a larger output in the short run, firms must increase their use of factors of production that are not fixed in supply. But the factors of production that are fixed in supply will eventually limit the extra output that each additional unit of the expanding input can produce.

The corn farmer with a fixed amount of land will eventually experience rising costs for each extra unit of output. Inferior parcels of land must be cultivated; more intensive harvesting techniques must be applied to counteract the higher production costs. Under the law of diminishing returns, greater output encounters more and more obstacles, so a higher price is required to encourage the producer to produce more of the good.

The Supply Curve

Consider the normal case of a positive relationship between price and quantity supplied. Table 2 shows a hypothetical supply schedule for corn, which is graphed in Figure 3. When the price of corn is $5 per bushel, farmers are prepared to supply 40 million bushels per month (point *a*). As the price falls to $4, the quantity supplied falls to 35 million bushels (point *b*). Finally, when the price is $1, farmers are prepared to sell only 10 million bushels (point *e*).

The smooth curve drawn through points *a* through *e* is the supply curve, *S*. It shows how quantity supplied responds to price, *ceteris paribus*—in other words, how much farmers are prepared to offer for sale at each price. Along the supply curve, the price and supply of corn are positively related: A higher price is needed to induce farmers to offer a larger quantity of corn on the market.

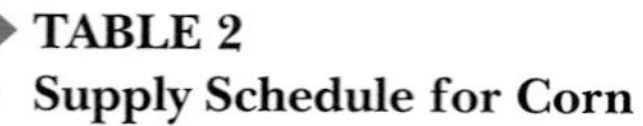

TABLE 2
Supply Schedule for Corn

	Price (dollars per bushel)	Quantity Supplied (millions of bushels per month)
a	5	40
b	4	35
c	3	30
d	2	20
e	1	10

FIGURE 3
The Supply Curve for Corn

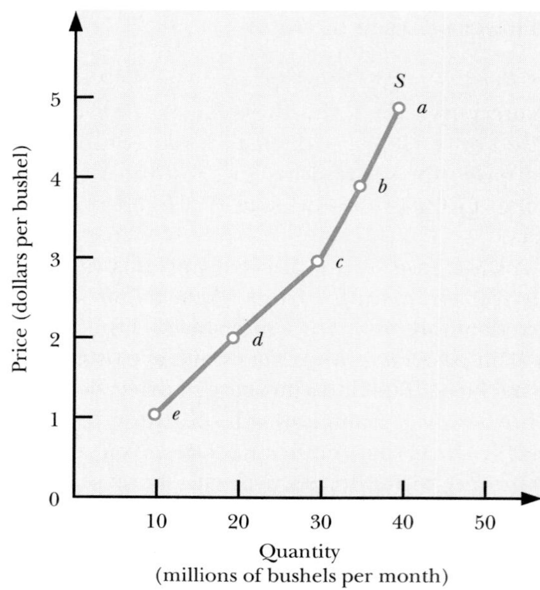

This graph depicts how the quantity of corn supplied responds to the price of corn. In situation *a*, when the price of corn is $5 per bushel, the quantity supplied by farmers is 40 million bushels per month. In the last situation, *e*, when the price is $1 per bushel, the quantity supplied is only 10 million bushels per month. The upward-sloping curve (*S*) drawn through these points is the supply curve of corn.

Shifts in the Supply Curve

Factors other than a good's own price can change the relationship between price and quantity supplied, causing the supply curve to shift. These other factors include (1) the prices of other goods, (2) the prices of relevant resources, (3) technology, (4) the number of sellers, and (5) expectations.

Prices of Other Goods. The resources used to produce any particular good can almost always be used elsewhere. Farmland can be used for corn or soybeans; engineers can work on cars or trucks; unskilled workers can pick strawberries or cotton; trains can move coal or cars. As the price of a good rises, resources are naturally attracted away from other goods that use those resources. Hence the supply of corn will fall if the price of soybeans rises; if the price of cotton rises, the supply of strawberries may fall. If the price of trucks rises, the supply of cars may fall. If the price of fuel oil rises, less kerosene may be produced.

The Prices of Relevant Resources. As resource prices rise, firms are no longer willing to supply the same quantities of goods produced with those resources at the same price. An increase in the price of coffee beans will increase the costs of producing coffee and decrease the amount that coffee companies are prepared to sell at each price; an increase in the price of corn land, tractors, harvesters, or irrigation will reduce the supply of corn; an increase in the price of cotton will decrease the supply of cotton dresses; an increase in the price of jet fuel will decrease the supply of commercial aviation at each price.

Technology. *Technology* is knowledge about how different goods can be produced. If technology improves, more goods can be produced from the same resources. For example, if a new and cheaper feed allows Maine lobster farmers to lower their costs of production, the quantity of lobsters supplied at each price will increase. If an assembly line can be speeded up by rearranging the order of assembly, the supply of the good will tend to increase. Technological advances in genetic engineering can increase the supply of medicines and even milk.

The Number of Sellers. If the number of sellers of a good increases, the supply of the good will increase. For example, the lowering of trade barriers (such as licensing requirements for foreign firms) may allow foreign sellers easier entry into the market, increasing the number of sellers.

Expectations. It takes a long time to produce many goods and services. When a farmer plants corn or

EXAMPLE 6 Expected Oil Prices, the Supply of Oil, and Wildcat Drilling

Government officials and the public complain about reliance on foreign oil. Both would like to see more domestic oil exploration. In late 1990, despite the fact that crude oil was selling at a high $40 per barrel, the number of drilling permits was declining. Why was exploration and drilling declining when oil prices were at their highest level since 1981? Does this fact suggest that the supply curve for oil is not upward sloping?

The Kuwait crisis and the ensuing Gulf War caused the price of oil to shoot up as world crude oil supplies shrank. However, new domestic exploration projects take three to five years to bear fruit. Hence oil companies base their exploration decisions on what they think the price of oil will be over the long run. Those who expected the Gulf War to end quickly and push the price of oil down to $12 per barrel, were not willing to invest. Those who expected the long-run price to settle around $19 per barrel, made investments in exploration projects.

This example demonstrates that the current quantity of crude oil supplied depends upon past expectations of the current price of oil. If oil prices are expected to fall below a certain level (in this case, $19), exploration and new drilling will cease.

Source: "Oil Firms Wary of US Drilling," *The Christian Science Monitor*, October 15, 1990.

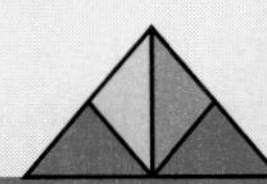

wheat or soybeans, the prices that are expected to prevail at harvest time are actually more important than the current price. A college student who reads that there are likely to be too few engineers four years hence may decide to major in engineering in expectation of a high income. When a business firm decides to establish a plant that takes five years to build, expectations of future business conditions are crucial to that investment decision.

Expectations can affect supply in different directions. If oil prices are expected to rise in the future, oil producers may produce less oil today to have more available for the future. In other cases, more investment will be undertaken if high prices are expected in the future. This greater investment will cause supply to increase. (See Example 6.)

How the Supply Shift Works. Figure 4 shows the supply curve, *S*, for corn. The supply curve is based on a $10-per-bushel price of soybeans and a $2000 yearly rental on an acre of corn land. If the price of soybeans rises to, say, $15 a bushel, the supply curve for corn will shift leftward to *S′* in panel *a* because some land used for corn will be shifted to soybeans. If the rental price of an acre of corn land goes down from $2000 to $1000, the supply curve will shift to the right—to, say, *S″* in panel *b*. The reduction in the land rental price lowers the costs of producing corn and makes the corn producer willing to supply more corn at the same price as before.

> A leftward shift of the supply curve means producers are prepared to sell smaller quantities of the good at each price: It indicates a *decrease in supply*. A rightward shift of the supply curve means that producers are prepared to sell larger quantities at each price: It indicates an *increase in supply*.

Example 7 summarizes the factors that cause supply curves to shift.

FIGURE 4
Shifts in the Supply Curve: Changes in Supply

(*a*) Decrease in Supply

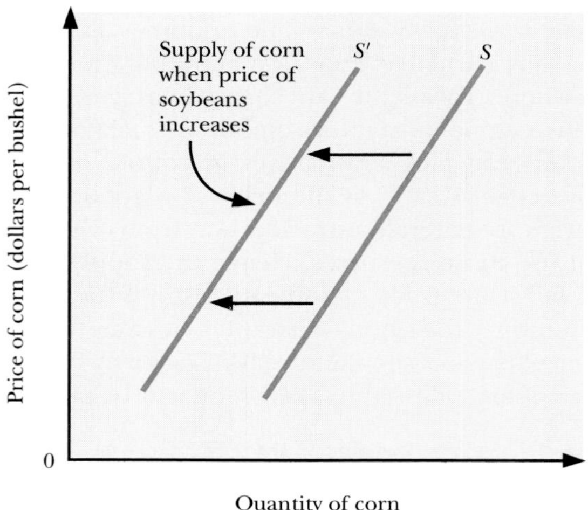

(*b*) Increase in Supply

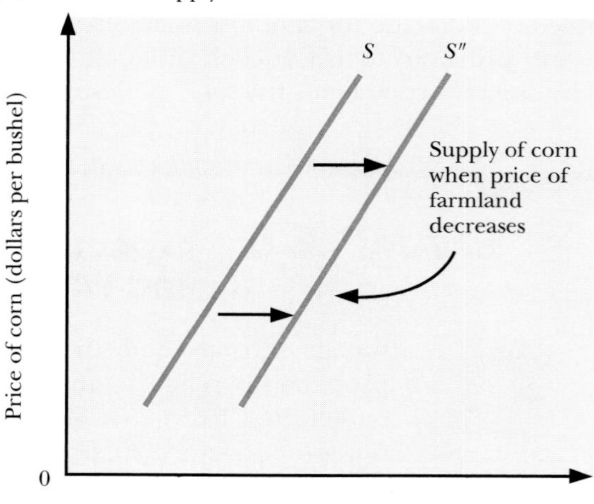

The supply curve of corn depends on the price of soybeans and the price of farmland. When farmland is $2000 an acre per year and soybeans are $10 per bushel, *S* is the supply curve for corn. Panel *a* shows that if farmland stays at $2000 per acre per year but soybeans fetch $15 instead of $10, profit-seeking farmers will switch farmland from corn to soybeans and cause the supply curve for corn to shift to the left from *S* to *S′* (a decrease in supply). On the other hand, panel *b* shows that if soybeans remain at $10 per bushel and farmland falls from $2000 to $1000 per acre, the supply curve for corn will shift to the right from *S* to *S″* (an increase in supply).

EQUILIBRIUM OF SUPPLY AND DEMAND

Along a given demand curve, such as the one in Figure 1, there are many price/quantity combinations from which to choose. Along a given supply curve, there are also many different price/quantity combi-

EXAMPLE 7 Factors That Cause a Supply Curve to Shift

Factor	Example
Change in price of another good	Increase in price of corn shifts supply curve of wheat to left.
Change in price of resource	Decrease in wage rate of autoworkers shifts supply curve of autos to right.
Change in technology	Higher corn yields due to genetic engineering shift supply curve of corn to right.
Change in number of sellers	New sellers entering profitable field shift supply curve of product to right.
Change in expectations	Expectation of a much higher price of oil next year shifts supply curve of oil today to left; expectation of higher ball-bearing prices in future causes more investment, shifting supply curve to right.

nations. Neither the demand curve nor the supply curve is sufficient by itself to determine the *market* price/quantity combinations.

Figure 5 puts the demand curve of Figure 1 and the supply curve of Figure 3 together on the same diagram. Remember that the demand curve indicates what consumers are prepared to buy at different prices; the supply curve indicates what producers are prepared to sell at different prices. These groups of economic decision makers are (for the most part) entirely different. How much will be produced? How much will be purchased? How are the decisions of consumers and producers coordinated?

Suppose that the price of corn happened to be \$2 per bushel. Figure 5 tells us the same thing that Figures 1 and 3 tell us separately: At a \$2 price, consumers want to buy 40 million bushels and producers want to sell only 20 million bushels. This discrepancy means that at \$2 there is a **shortage** of 20 million bushels.

> A **shortage** results if at the current price the quantity demanded exceeds the quantity supplied; the price is too low to equate the quantity demanded with the quantity supplied.

At a \$2 price, 20 million bushels will be traded. Consumers, who wish to buy 40 million will be able to buy only the 20 million bushels corn producers are willing to sell. At a price of \$2 per bushel, some people who are willing to buy corn cannot find a willing seller. The demand curve shows that a number of consumers are willing to pay more than \$2 per bushel. Such buyers will try to outbid one another for the available supply. With free competition, the price of corn will be bid up if there is a shortage of corn.

The increase in the price of corn in response to the shortage will have two main effects. On the one hand, the higher price will discourage consumption. On the other hand, the higher price will encourage production. Thus the increase in the price of corn, through the actions of independent buyers and sellers, will lead both buyers and sellers to make decisions that will reduce the shortage of corn.

What would happen if the price were \$4 per bushel? At that price, consumers want to buy 25 million bushels and producers want to sell 35 million bushels. Thus, at \$4 there is a **surplus** of 10 million bushels on the market.

> A **surplus** results if at the current price the quantity supplied exceeds the quantity demanded: The price is too high to equate the quantity demanded with quantity supplied.

FIGURE 5
Market Equilibrium

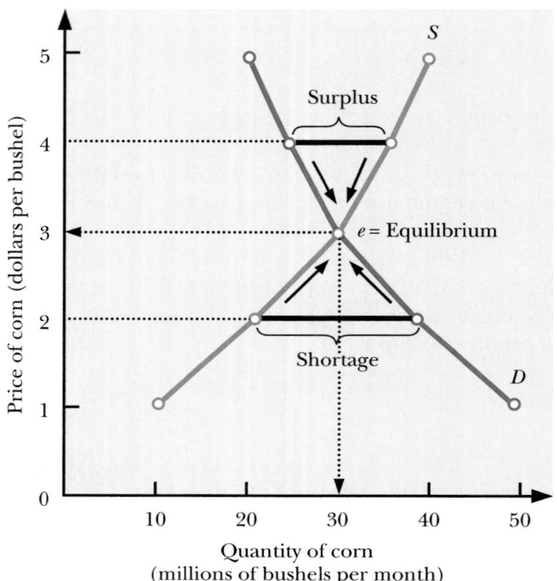

This figure shows how market equilibrium is reached. On the same diagram are drawn both the demand curve for corn (from Figure 1) and the supply curve for corn (from Figure 3). When the price of corn is $2, the quantity demanded is 40 million bushels, but the quantity supplied is only 20 million bushels. The result is a shortage of 20 million bushels of corn. Unsatisfied buyers will bid the price up.

Raising the price will reduce the shortage. When the price of corn is raised to $4 per bushel, the quantity supplied is 35 million bushels. The result is a surplus of 10 million bushels of corn. This surplus will cause the price of corn to fall as unsatisfied sellers bid the price down to get rid of excess inventories of corn. As the price falls, the surplus will diminish. The equilibrium price is $3 because the quantity demanded equals the quantity supplied at that price. The equilibrium quantity is 30 million bushels.

At a $4 price, 25 million bushels will be traded. Although producers are willing to sell 35 million bushels, they can find buyers for only 25 million bushels. With a surplus some sellers will be disappointed as corn inventories pile up. Willing sellers of corn will not be able to find buyers. The competition among sellers will lead them to cut the price if there is a surplus of corn.

This fall in the price of corn will simultaneously encourage consumption and discourage production. Through the corrective fall in the price of corn, *the surplus of corn will therefore disappear.*

According to the demand and supply curves portrayed in Figure 5, when the price of corn reaches $3 per bushel, the shortage (or surplus) of corn disappears completely. At this **equilibrium (market-clearing) price,** consumers want to buy 30 million bushels and producers want to sell 30 million bushels.

> The **equilibrium (market-clearing) price** is the price at which the quantity demanded by consumers equals the quantity supplied by producers.

There is no other price/quantity combination at which quantity demanded equals quantity supplied—any other price brings about a shortage or a surplus of corn. The arrows in Figure 5 indicate the pressures on prices above or below $3 and show how the amount of shortage or surplus—the size of the brackets—gets smaller as the price adjusts. (See Example 8).

The equilibrium of supply and demand is stationary in the sense that once the equilibrium price is reached, it tends to remain the same as long as neither supply nor demand shifts. Movements away from the equilibrium price will be restored by the bidding of frustrated buyers or frustrated sellers in the marketplace. The equilibrium price is like a rocking chair in the rest position; give it a gentle push and the original position will be restored.

What the Market Accomplishes

The market coordinates the actions of a large number of independent buyers and sellers through equilibrium prices. An equilibrium price does two things. First, it *rations* the scarce supply of the good among all the people who would like to have it if it were given away free. Some people must be left out if the good is scarce. The price determines who will be excluded by restraining consumption.

Second, the system of equilibrium prices *economizes on the information required to match supplies and*

EXAMPLE 8 Equilibrium Prices and Lunch with Princess Di

In the fall of 1990, Princess Di, the wife of Prince Charles, scheduled a charity luncheon in Washington, D.C. The price: $3000 for regular attendees and $4000 for attendees who would also be invited to a private reception with Princess Di. Much to the chagrin of the organizers, only half the seats to the charity luncheon were purchased. Although a good number of celebrities were in attendance, the empty seats proved an embarrassment.

What happened? A prominent social hostess noted that in Washington, D.C., charity events like this one are typically priced at $1500 or less. The $3000 to $4000 price was simply too high for this type of market. If Princess Di wished to have all the seats filled, the price would have had to be lowered by $1500.

This example shows that even the demand curve for prominent charity events is downward sloping. If the price is too high, the quantity supplied will exceed the quantity demanded. If the price is lowered, however, an equilibrium of quantity demanded and supplied can be achieved.

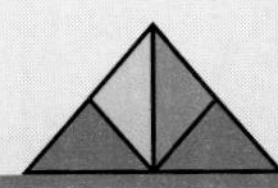

demands. Buyers do not have to know how to produce a good, and sellers do not need to know why people use the good. Buyers and sellers need only be concerned with small bits of information, such as price, or small portions of the technological methods of production. The market accomplishes its actions without any one participant's knowing all the details. Recall the pencil example in Chapter 3: Pencils get produced even though no single individual knows *all* the details for producing a pencil.

The same is true of the corn market. Sellers of corn do not need to know the motivations of the buyers of corn and vice versa. The price buyers pay tells sellers what they need to know, and the price sellers ask for tells buyers what they need to know. When the price settles at equilibrium, the actions of buyers and sellers are harmonized.

Disequilibrium Prices

To understand the rationing function of equilibrium prices, consider what happens when prices are not allowed to rise to equilibrium. For many years, the price of natural gas shipped interstate was held below equilibrium by the Federal Power Commission. During the Arab oil embargo in the summer of 1974, gasoline prices were held below market-clearing levels by government regulations. Prices of consumer goods in the former Soviet Union were held below equilibrium for a long time by government pricing policies. In such cases, shortages and long lines resulted.

Rent controls reveal the effects of disequilibrium pricing. Municipal governments, under pressure from renters, can *freeze* rents (that is, prevent rents from rising). Figure 6 shows the market for rental housing in Windy City. As usual, the supply curve is upward sloping; the demand curve is downward sloping. In a free (unregulated) market, the rent would settle at $500 per month for a standard rental unit. But suppose a price ceiling of $300 is established by the Windy City council. As long as landlords are free to supply the number of apartments they wish, a lower price will mean a correspondingly smaller number of units offered for rent. Figure 6 shows that 6000 units are supplied at a price of $300 and 8000 units at a price of $500. The quantity demanded rises to 11,000 units as the price falls from $500 to $300. Accordingly, the price ceiling results in a shortage of 5000 units. If the price could rise from $300 to $500, there would be no shortage.

Windy City residents who already have apartments will be pleased by the $300 ceiling (although they may wonder why the apartment house is deteriorating). Residents looking for apartments without success will be unhappy. A number of them would gladly pay more to have an apartment.

FIGURE 6
The Effect of Rent Ceilings on the Market for Rental Housing

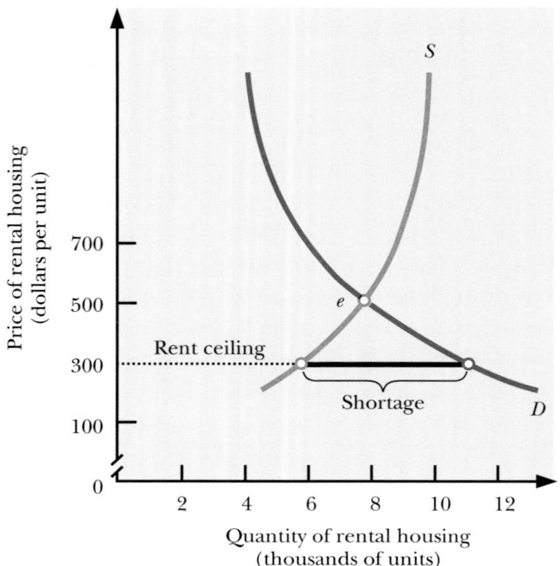

If the equilibrium price/quantity combination for the rental market is $500 per unit and 8000 units (point *e*), a rent ceiling of $300 per month on a standard housing unit would lower the quantity supplied to 6000 units and raise the quantity demanded to 11,000 units, creating a shortage of 5000 units of rental housing.

Understanding Shortage and Surplus

The terms *shortage* and *surplus* (glut) are often misused. One often hears inaccurate references to "shortages" of sugar or other commodities, as in the following statement that might appear in a typical newspaper:

> Projections of supplies and demands reveal that there will be a large surplus of medical doctors by the end of the 1990s. The supply of M.D.s will exceed demand generally, but surpluses will be greatest in particular specialities.

In economics, a shortage occurs when the price is not allowed to *rise* to its equilibrium level. A surplus occurs when the price is not allowed to *fall* to its equilibrium level. If there are no impediments to these price adjustments, shortages and surpluses will disappear as prices adjust. A surplus of doctors is not the same as a surplus of corn. By a "surplus of doctors," writers actually mean that supply and demand conditions push *down* the relative price of physicians' services, not that there will be doctors with no patients. A sugar shortage is not a shortage in the same sense as a shortage of rent-controlled apartments. By a "sugar shortage," writers really mean that supply and demand conditions are pushing *up* the price of sugar. (See Example 9.)

EXAMPLE 9 Why Nurses Receive Sign-on Bonuses

In 1991, major U.S. hospitals were advertising $1000 to $2000 cash bonuses to trained nurses who were willing to sign employment contracts. Why do nurses receive sign-on bonuses and other professions do not?

In the 1980s, enrollment in nursing colleges dropped, largely as a consequence of the relatively low pay of nurses. For potential nurses, compensation opportunities appeared better in alternative professions—teaching, word processing, computer programming, and management trainee programs. In the late 1980s and early 1990s, a "nursing shortage" became apparent. The number of nurses hospitals wished to hire at prevailing wages far exceeded the number available at those wages.

This chapter teaches that whenever a good is in short supply, its price tends to rise. Because of the complexity of changing union wage scales and public employee salaries, hospitals—struggling with understaffed nursing departments—raised salaries by offering sign-on bonuses.

CHANGES IN THE EQUILIBRIUM PRICE

Prices change. Sometimes they go up, and sometimes they go down. Because they do not change at the same rate, relative prices also change. This section will investigate the reasons for price changes. Thus far we have seen that the equilibrium price is determined by the intersection of the demand and supply curves. The only way for the price to change is for the demand or supply curves themselves to shift, and this shift can occur only if one or more of the factors that affect supply and demand *besides the good's own price* changes.

Change in Demand (or Supply) versus Change in Quantity Demanded (or Supplied)

We make a careful distinction between movements along a demand curve and shifts in the entire curve. A change in the good's own price—as from p_2 to p_1 in panel *a* of Figure 7—causes a movement along the demand curve and is referred to as a **change in quantity demanded.** When a change in a factor other than the good's price shifts the entire curve to the left or to the right (as in panel *b*), we call that a **change in demand.**

> A **change in quantity demanded** is a movement along the demand curve because of a change in the good's price.
>
> A **change in demand** is a shift in the entire demand curve because of a change in a factor other than the good's price.

Similarly, panel *a* of Figure 8 shows that a rise in the price of a good (from p_2 to p_1) causes a **change in quantity supplied** but does not change the location of the supply curve. A **change in supply,** shown in panel *b,* occurs when a factor other than the good's own price changes, shifting the entire supply curve to the left or to the right.

FIGURE 7
Change in Demand versus Change in Quantity Demanded

(*a*) Change in Quantity Demanded

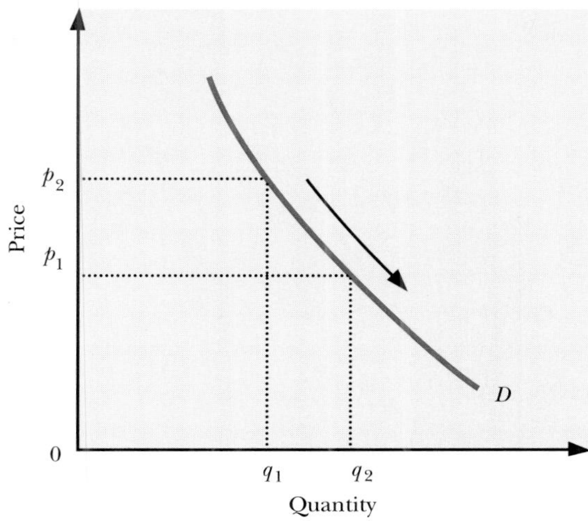

(*b*) Change in Demand

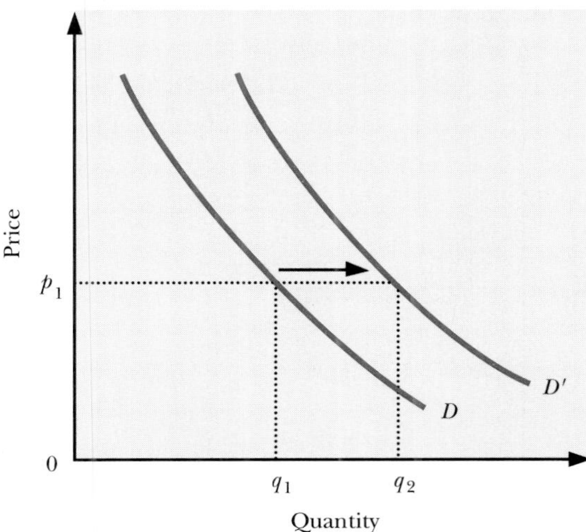

In panel *a,* the increase in quantity demanded (from q_1 to q_2) is the result of the drop in price (from p_2 to p_1). The change in price causes the movement along the demand curve (D). In panel *b,* the increase in quantity (from q_1 to q_2) is the result of a shift in the demand curve (an increase in demand) to D', holding price constant. When demand increases, the whole demand curve shifts as the result of some change that leads consumers to buy more of the product at each price.

FIGURE 8
Change in Supply versus Change in Quantity Supplied

(*a*) Change in Quantity Supplied

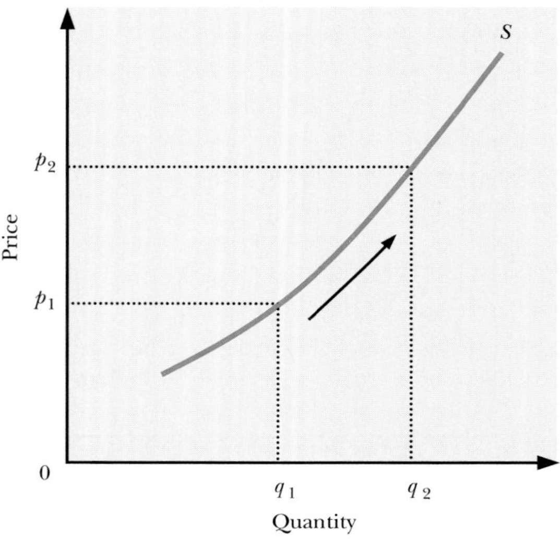

(*b*) Change in Supply

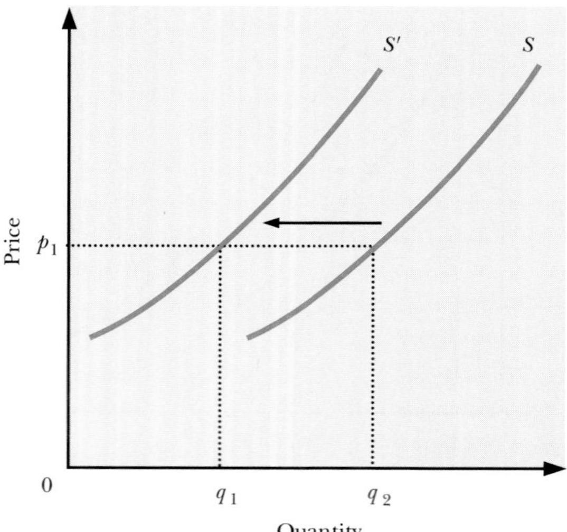

In panel *a*, the increase in quantity supplied (from q_1 to q_2) is the result of a rise in price (from p_1 to p_2). The change in price causes a movement along the supply curve (*S*). In panel *b*, the decrease in supply (from q_2 to q_1) is the result of the shift in the supply curve (decrease in supply) from *S* to *S*′, holding price constant. Firms wish to sell less at the same price.

A **change in quantity supplied** is a movement along the supply curve because of a change in the good's price.

A **change in supply** is a shift in the entire supply curve because of a change in a factor other than the good's price.

The Effects of a Change in Supply

Changes in supply or demand influence equilibrium prices and quantities in given markets.

Consider a natural disaster, such as severe flooding, that affects the supply of wheat, as illustrated in Figure 9. The initial demand curve, *D,* and the initial supply curve, *S,* are based on conditions before the natural disaster. Suddenly, and without warning, torrential rains hit the wheat fields prior to harvest, ruining about one-half of the potential wheat crop. Now, instead of offering 50 million bushels at $5 per bushel, farmers offer only 25 million at this price. They offer smaller quantities of wheat at all other prices. The supply curve for wheat has shifted left to *S*′ (the supply of wheat has decreased). Will this supply reduction affect the demand curve?

When the supply curve changes for a single good—like wheat—the demand curve normally does not change. The factors influencing the supply of wheat *other than its own price* have little or no influence on demand. In our example, the severe rains will not shift the demand curve. Thus we can usually assume that the demand and supply curves are independent in the analysis of a single market.

The supply curve has shifted to the left (supply has decreased); the demand curve remains unchanged. What will happen to the equilibrium price? Before the flood, the price that equated quantity supplied with quantity demanded was $5. After the flood, the quantity supplied at a $5 price is 25 million bushels and the quantity demanded is 50 million bushels. At the old price, there would be a shortage of wheat. Therefore, the price of wheat will be bid up until a new equilibrium price is attained (at $10), at which quantity demanded and quantity supplied are equal at 30 million bushels. As the price rises from the old equilibrium price ($5) to the new equilibrium price ($10), there is a movement up the new supply curve (*S*′). Even with a flood, a higher price will coax out more wheat.

FIGURE 9
The Effects of a Natural Disaster on the Price of Wheat

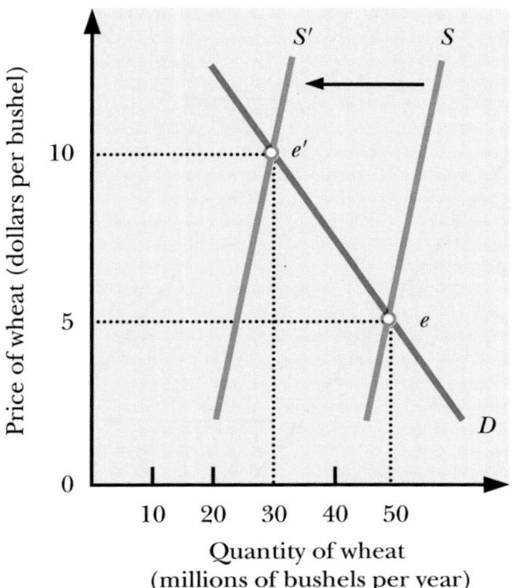

In this graph, a natural disaster shifts the supply curve of wheat from *S* to *S'*. Where \$5 formerly brought forth 50 million bushels of wheat (on *S*), the same price now brings forth only 25 million bushels of wheat (on *S'*). This decrease in supply raises the equilibrium price from \$5 to \$10. The movement from *e* to *e'* is a movement along the demand curve. Although the demand curve does not change, quantity demanded decreases from 50 million to 30 million bushels as the price rises from \$5 to \$10 per bushel.

> A decrease in supply without a change in demand causes the price to rise and the quantity demanded to fall. An increase in supply without a change in demand causes the price to fall and the quantity demanded to rise.

The following example of a typical newspaper report illustrates the danger of confusing changes in quantity demanded (or supplied) with changes in demand (or supply).

> The state agriculture office reports that warm weather and sufficient moisture have produced a plentiful supply of lettuce this year. However, lettuce prices are not expected to drop because consumers usually increase their demand for lettuce when prices fall. The demand increase will offset the supply increase.

The good weather reported by the agriculture office shifts the supply curve to the right and causes a movement along the demand curve. Thus, the increase in supply does not cause an increase in demand but an increase in *quantity demanded.*

The conclusion of the newspaper report (that prices will not drop) is incorrect given the stated facts. As supply increases (as the supply curve shifts to the right), the price falls. As the price falls, there is a movement down the demand curve as consumers increase their quantity demanded in response to lower prices. When supply increases, the price will fall if the demand curve remains unchanged.

The Effects of a Change in Demand

A change in demand for wheat is illustrated in Figure 10. The initial situation is depicted by the demand

FIGURE 10
The Effects of an Increased Preference for Bread on the Price of Wheat

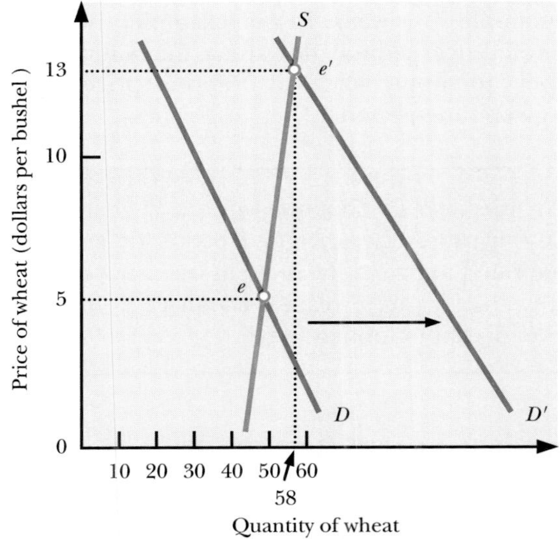

If for some reason people want to eat more bread as the result of a change in preferences, the demand curve for wheat will shift to the right. The shift in the demand curve from *D* to *D'* depicts an increase in demand. This increase in demand drives up the equilibrium price from \$5 per bushel to \$13 per bushel. As price rises from \$5 to \$13, quantity supplied increases from 50 million to 58 million bushels resulting in movement along the supply curve, *S*.

curve, D, and the supply curve, S. The equilibrium wheat price is \$5, and the equilibrium quantity is 50 million bushels. Hence D and S are the same curves as in Figure 9. Now imagine a change on the demand side. Say, for example, that new medical evidence shows that eating wheat will increase one's lifespan. This news would shift the demand curve for wheat sharply to the right (from D to D'). This massive increase in demand for wheat would drive the price of wheat up to \$13 per bushel (from e to e'). When the price rises, the quantity supplied rises from 50 million to 58 million bushels. *There has been no increase in supply, only an increase in quantity supplied* in response to the higher price.

Notice that when the demand curve shifts as a result of some change in demand factors other than the good's price, there is no shift in the supply curve—the supply curve remains the same. As we have seen, these curves should be considered independent in a single market. If a market is small enough relative to the entire economy, the link between the factors that shift demand curves (summarized in Example 3) and those that shift supply curves (summarized in Example 7) is weak. In our example, the change in preferences should not affect the willingness of farmers to supply wheat at different prices during any given time period.

> An increase in demand without a change in supply causes the price to rise and the quantity supplied to rise. A decrease in demand without a change in supply causes the price to fall and the quantity supplied to fall.

FIGURE 11

The Effects of an Increase in Demand and a Decrease in Supply on the Price of Wheat

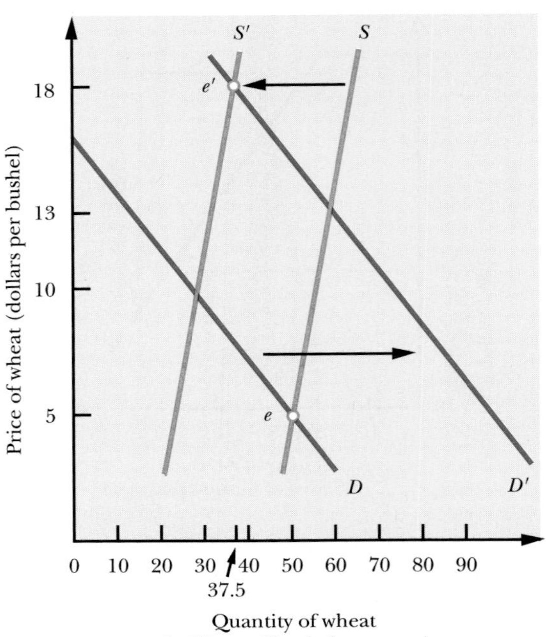

This graph combines the supply change in Figure 9 and the demand change of Figure 10. The original equilibrium was at a price of \$5 and a quantity of 50 million bushels. After the shift in supply (from S to S') and the shift in demand (from D to D'), there is a shortage at the old price (quantity supplied equals 25 million bushels, and quantity demanded equals 90 million bushels). The equilibrium price rises to \$18, and the equilibrium quantity falls to 37.5 million bushels.

Simultaneous Changes in Supply and Demand

Figure 11 combines the two previous cases and illustrates what happens to price and quantity if the two events (the flood and the change in preferences) occur together. The supply curve shifts to the left from S to S' (supply falls), and the demand curve shifts to the right from D to D' (demand increases).

Prior to these changes, equilibrium price was \$5, and equilibrium quantity was 50 million bushels. The shifts in supply and demand disrupt this equilibrium. Now at a price of \$5, the quantity supplied equals 25 million bushels and the quantity demanded equals 90 million bushels—an enormous shortage. The new equilibrium occurs at a price of \$18 and a quantity of 37.5 million bushels. The two shifts magnify each other's effects. As we have shown, if there had been only the supply change, price would have risen to \$9. If there had been only the demand change, price would have risen to \$13. The combined effects cause the price to rise to \$18. In this case, the causes of the changes in supply and demand are independent.

Figure 12 shows the effects of all possible combinations of shifts in supply curves and demand curves.

FIGURE 12
Summary of the Effects of Shifts in Supply Curves and Demand Curves

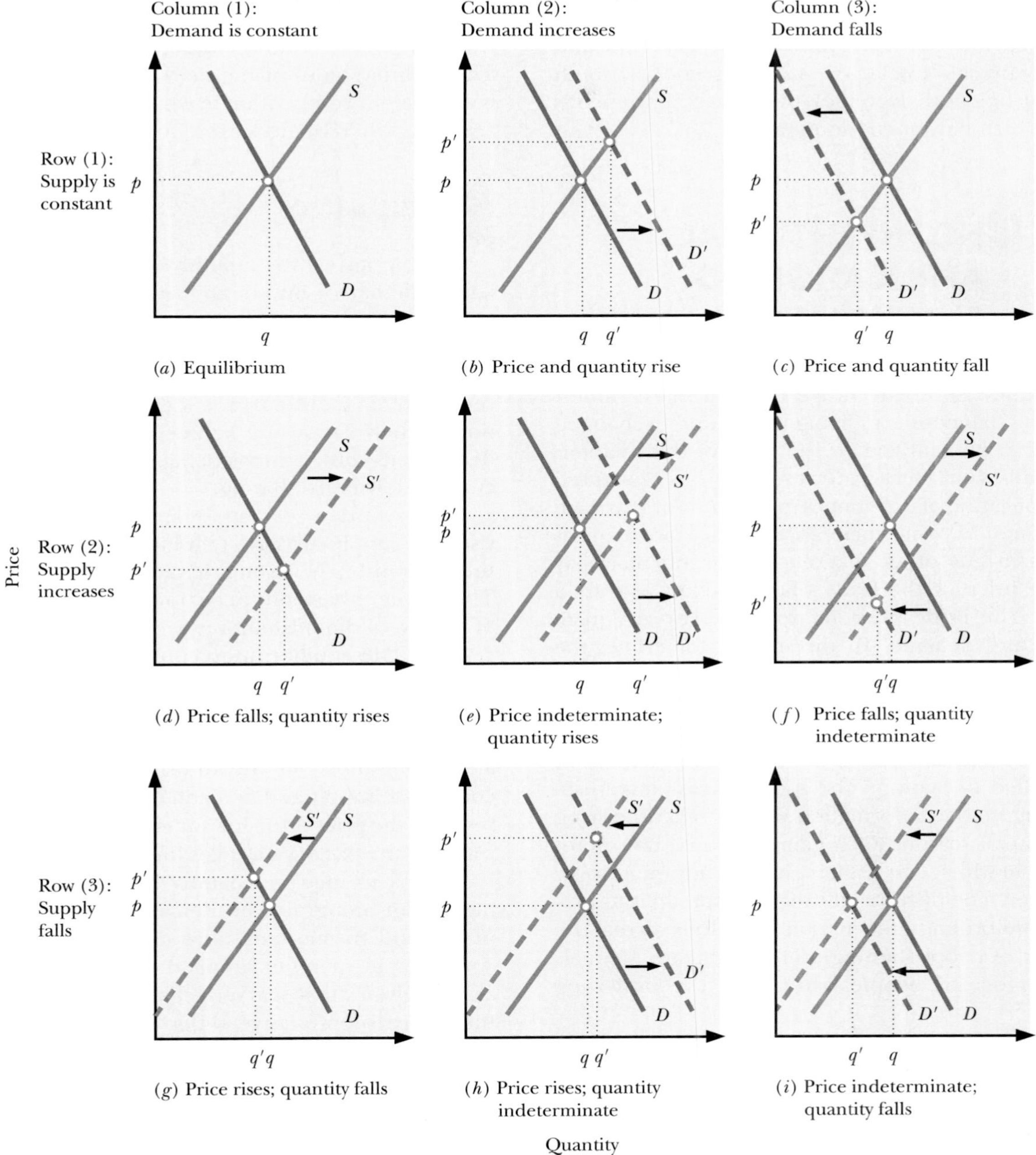

This figure gives the results of all possible combinations of shifts in supply curves and demand curves. To read it, match the rows and columns. For example, the figure in panel *e*, at the intersection of row 2 and column 2 shows what happens when supply and demand increase simultaneously. The figure in panel *i*, at the intersection of row 3 and column 3, shows what happens when both supply and demand fall.

As panels *e, f, h,* and *i* demonstrate, the effects of simultaneous changes in supply and demand are sometimes indeterminate. If supply increases (shifts right) and demand decreases (shifts left), the price will fall. If supply decreases and demand increases, the price will rise. If, however, both demand and supply curves move in the same direction (if both increase or if both decrease), the price effect depends upon which movement dominates.

UNCONVENTIONAL APPLICATIONS OF SUPPLY AND DEMAND

The concepts of supply, demand, and equilibrium price apply to a wide range of exchanges. Almost anything that admits to being priced and exchanged freely can be analyzed by the tools of this chapter. Economist Gary Becker, for example, has pioneered the application of economics to the study of marriage and crime. In some societies, marriage proceeds as it does in any other market—the groom may pay a bride price or the bride's family might provide a dowry. The bride price or dowry serves to equate supply and demand. In the market for crime, the price of crime is the punishment that criminals expect to receive; they balance this punishment against the amount they expect to earn from mugging, robbing, or burglarizing. Demand and supply can even be applied to betting. The sports pages contain interesting market information every weekend during the football season. Each game has a certain point spread, in which one team is given an advantage over the other. The purpose of the point spread is to provide equilibrium in the market for betting so that the number of people betting on favored team A equals the number of people betting on the underdog team B.[2]

These first five chapters focused on how economies allocate resources. The tools of supply-and-demand analysis show how equilibrium prices are established in market economies and how and why prices change. Relative prices signal to buyers what to purchase and signal to firms what and how to produce. The economic problems of *what, how,* and *for whom* are solved by the invisible hand of the market allocation system, which directs the circular flow of resources among households and businesses. The invisible hand of the market works best under conditions of competition in which no buyer or seller (or group thereof) can exercise control over prices.

[2]See Richard A. Zuber, John M. Gandar, and B. D. Bowers, "Beating the Spread: Testing the Efficiency of the Gambling Market for National Football League Games," *Journal of Political Economy* 93, 4 (August 1985): 800–806.

SUMMARY

1. A perfectly competitive market consists of a large number of buyers and sellers, each of whom accepts the market price as given.
2. The law of demand states that quantity demanded falls as price goes up, *ceteris paribus,* and vice versa; the demand curve is a graphical representation of the relationship between price and quantity demanded—other things being equal. The demand curve is downward sloping.
3. As price goes up, quantity supplied usually rises; the supply curve is a graphical representation of the relationship between price and quantity supplied. The supply curve tends to be upward sloping because of the law of diminishing returns.
4. The equilibrium combination of price and quantity occurs where the demand curve intersects the supply curve or where quantity demanded equals quantity supplied. Competitive pricing rations goods and economizes on the information necessary to coordinate supply and demand decisions. A shortage results if the price is too low for equilibrium; a surplus results if the price is too high for equilibrium.
5. A change in quantity demanded means a movement along a given demand curve; a change in demand means the entire demand curve shifts. A change in quantity supplied means a movement along a given supply curve; a change in supply means the entire supply curve shifts. The demand curve will shift if a change occurs in the price of a related good (substitute or complement), in income, in preferences, in the number of buyers, or in the expectation of future prices. The supply curve will shift if a change occurs in the price of another good, in the price of a resource, in technology, in the number of sellers, or in the expectation of future prices. A change in the equilibrium price/quantity combination requires a change in one of the factors held

constant along the demand or supply curves. Supply-and-demand analysis allows one to predict what will happen to prices and quantities when supply or demand schedules shift.

6. The concepts of supply, demand, and equilibrium price can be applied to a wide range of exchanges.

KEY TERMS

market
perfectly competitive market
demand
law of demand
quantity demanded
market demand curve
substitutes
complements
normal goods
inferior goods
supply
quantity supplied
shortage
surplus
equilibrium (market-clearing) price
change in quantity demanded
change in demand
change in quantity supplied
change in supply

QUESTIONS AND PROBLEMS

1. List the four characteristics of a perfectly competitive market. If any of the four conditions are not met, explain why the principal characteristic of a perfectly competitive market (no person or group can control price) may not be met.
2. "People need bread. If the price rises, people will not buy less of it." Evaluate this statement in terms of the reasons demand curves are downward sloping.
3. Plot the supply and demand schedules for the hypothetical product in Table A as supply and demand curves.

TABLE A

Price (dollars)	Quantity Demanded (units)	Quantity Supplied (units)
10	5	25
8	10	20
6	15	15
2	20	10
0	25	5

a. What equilibrium price would this market establish?
b. If the state were to pass a law that the price could not be more than $2, how would you describe the market response?
c. If the state were to pass a law that the price could not be less than $8, how would you describe the market response?
d. If preferences changed and people wanted to buy twice as much as before at each price, what will the equilibrium price be?
e. If, in addition to the above change in preferences, there is an improvement in technology that allows firms to produce this product at lower cost than before, what will happen to the equilibrium price?

4. American baseball bats do not sell well in Japan because they do not meet the specifications of Japanese baseball officials. If the Japanese change their specifications to accommodate American-made bats, what will happen to the price of American bats?
5. "The poor are the ones who suffer from high gas and electricity bills. We should pass a law that gas and electricity rates cannot increase by more than 1 percent annually." Evaluate this statement in terms of supply-and-demand analysis, assuming that equilibrium prices rise faster than 1 percent annually.
6. Much of the automobile rental business in the United States is done at airports. How do you think a reduction in airfares would affect automobile rental rates?
7. If both the supply and demand for coffee increase, what would happen to coffee prices? If the supply increased and the demand fell, what would happen to coffee prices?
8. Which of the following statements uses incorrect terminology? Explain.

a. "The recent fare war among the major airlines has increased the demand for air travel."
b. "The recession of 1990–1992 has caused the demand for air travel to fall."

9. What factors are held constant along the demand curve? Explain how each can shift the demand curve to the right. Explain how each can shift the demand curve to the left.

10. What factors are held constant along the supply curve? Explain how each factor can shift the supply curve to the right. Explain how each factor can shift the supply curve to the left.
11. Why is the demand curve downward sloping?
12. Why is the supply curve normally upward sloping? Can you think of any exceptions?
13. What is the effect of each of the following events on the equilibrium price and quantity of hamburgers?

    a. The price of steak (a substitute for hamburgers) increases.
    b. The price of french fries (a complement) increases.
    c. The population becomes older.
    d. The government requires that all the ingredients of hamburgers be absolutely fresh (that is, nothing can be frozen).
    e. Beef becomes more expensive.
    f. More firms enter the hamburger business.

14. "As a general rule, if *both* supply and demand increase or decrease, the change in price will be indeterminate." Is this statement true or false? Illustrate with a diagram.
15. "As a general rule, if demand increases and supply decreases, or vice versa, the change in quantity will be indeterminate." Is this statement true or false? Illustrate with a diagram.
16. The number of compact discs sold in markets has more than quadrupled over the past three years. The average price of a compact disc, however, has fallen. Use supply-and-demand analysis to explain this phenomenon.

SUGGESTED READINGS

Kohler, Heinz. *Intermediate Microeconomics: Theory and Applications,* 3rd ed. New York: HarperCollins, 1990.

Leftwich, Richard H., and Ansel M. Sharp. *Economics of Social Issues,* 3rd ed. Dallas: Business Publications, Inc., 1978, chapter 2.

Manne, Henry G. "The Parable of the Parking Lots." *The Public Interest* 23 (Spring 1971): 10–15.

North, Douglas C., and Roger LeRoy Miller. *The Economics of Public Issues,* 8th ed. New York: HarperCollins, 1990, chapter 1.

Stigler, George. *The Theory of Price,* 4th ed. New York: Macmillan, 1987, chapters 1 and 3.

Macroeconomics

II

Macroeconomic Theory

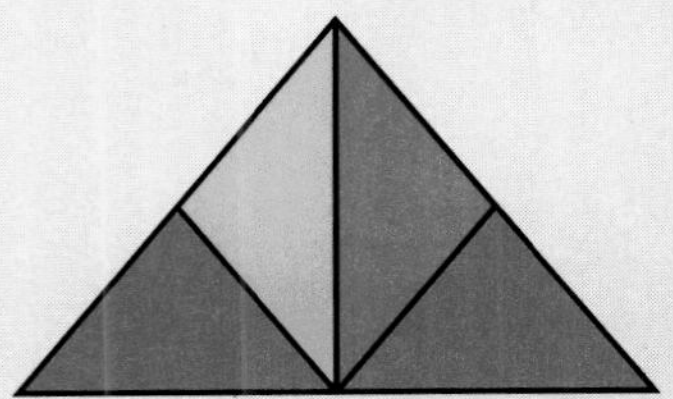

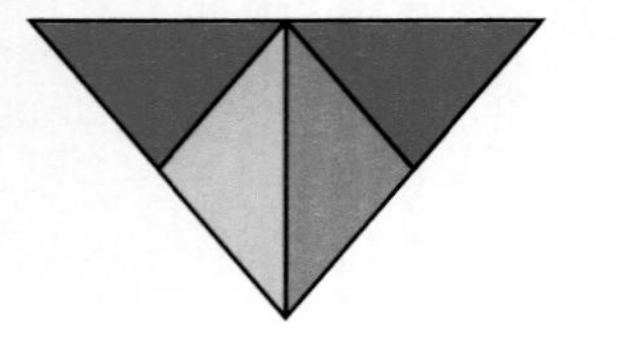

6 Macroeconomic Concepts

CHAPTER INSIGHT

Microeconomics studies the economy "in the small." It explains the behavior of firms and households in the marketplace using the basic analytical tools of supply and demand.

In contrast, *macroeconomics* studies the economy "in the large." Its basic analytical tools are aggregate demand and aggregate supply. Macroeconomics explains how the economy as a whole behaves: why unemployment rises or falls, why inflation accelerates or slows down, why the total output of goods and services fluctuates, why interest rates rise or fall, and what policies can be pursued to reduce inflation or to limit unemployment.

Families and businesses know that macroeconomic conditions affect their lives. At times business activity is strong. Jobs are plentiful, incomes are rising, and the output of goods and services is expanding at a healthy pace. People are optimistic about the future. At other times, business activity is weak. There are many job seekers but few jobs. The output of goods and services ceases to expand and may even contract.

Macroeconomics studies the "big issues" in economics: inflation, unemployment, interest rates, and deficits. (See Example 1). In this chapter and the chapters that follow, we examine these issues and try to explain their causes and their relationships to each other.

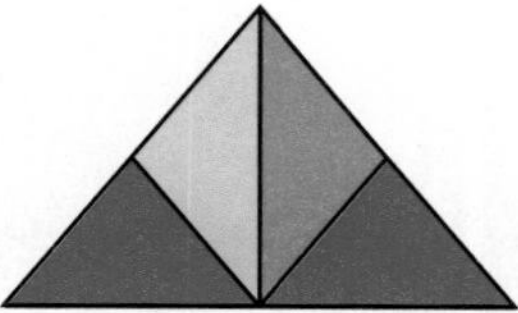

BUSINESS CYCLES

It is clear to most people that macroeconomic events have a significant impact on their lives. Thus, there is ongoing concern about when and why such events occur. As we noted in the Chapter Insight, macroeconomic activity moves in cycles. These cycles resemble the patterns of such natural phenomena as sunspots, droughts, epidemics, and animal reproduction. Over the very long run, economies tend to increase output through the process of economic growth. The labor force grows as population expands; capital accumulation increases the economy's capital stock; technological improvements raise productivity. The American economy of 1992 produced a volume of output more than 20 times that of 1892. This increase translates into an annual rate of growth of about 3.3 percent.

Many distinguished economists—such as Nobel laureate Simon Kuznets, Wesley Clair Mitchell, Joseph Schumpeter, Gottfried Haberler, N. D. Kondratieff, and Arthur Burns—have studied trends and movements in the level of business activity around the generally rising, long-run trend in output. These trends outline the **business cycle.**

> The **business cycle** is the pattern of upward and downward movements in the general level of real business activity.

Business cycles represent an area of controversy in modern economics. Economists continue to debate their causes and inevitability, as well as the government's role in dealing with them.

Recessions and Depressions

The terms **recession** and **depression** are used to describe business cycles.

> As a general rule, a **recession** occurs when real output declines for a period of 6 months or more.
>
> A **depression** is a very severe downturn in economic activity that lasts for several years. Real output declines during this period by a significant amount, and unemployment rises to very high levels.

EXAMPLE 1 The Economy as a National Concern

People living in modern societies have a lot to worry about—drugs, crime, the threat of nuclear war, and so on. Regular polls tell us how the American population's concerns about the health of the economy stack up against their other worries. The economy is consistently one of the public's major worries. Concern over the economy becomes increasingly acute during recessions. In late 1990, as the American economy was about to enter a recession, the top concern was drugs. As the recession continued, the economy began to overshadow drugs as a subject of concern. Even when the eyes of the world were shifted to the Persian Gulf in August 1990 (with Iraq's invasion of Kuwait), the American public rated the economy as a concern equal to that of the Mideast. As the recession deepened in early 1991, concern over the economy was four to five times greater than any other concern, including drugs, the poor and homeless, and the Mideast.

Source: "What's the No. 1 Problem?" *New York Times*, October 20, 1991.

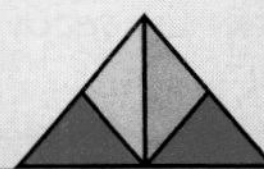

The National Bureau of Economic Research (NBER) is a nonprofit, private research organization that is accepted as an authority for deciding when a recession begins and ends. The 6-month declining output rule is not ironclad. If an economic downturn is especially severe, it may be classified as a recession even if it lasts less than 6 months. A depression is a very severe and extended recession. Fortunately, although we have had a number of recessions since the turn of the century, we have had only one severe depression—the Great Depression of the 1930s.

As the old joke says, "A recession is when my neighbor is out of work. A depression is when I am out of work!" This perspective illustrates why a major depression can leave a lasting imprint on a nation's way of thinking about the economy. (See Example 2.)

The Four Phases of the Business Cycle

Business cycles are divided into four phases, irrespective of their severity and duration. As Figure 1 shows, the four phases of the business cycle are

1. Downturn or recession (or depression if the decline in activity is prolonged and severe)
2. Trough
3. Expansion (or recovery)
4. Peak

During the *recession* phase, the level of business activity is in general decline. The various indexes of business activity (building permits, total output, employment, business formation, new orders) indicate that the economy is producing a declining rate of output. The unemployment rate rises, and the

FIGURE 1
The Phases of the Business Cycle

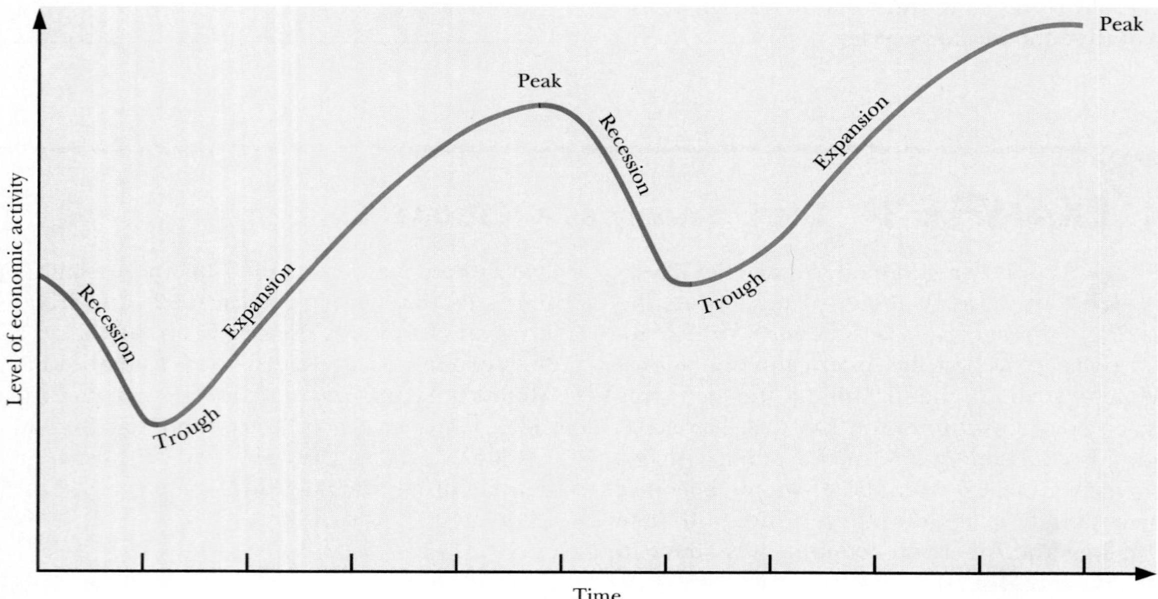

This figure illustrates the four phases of the business cycle. Since 1924, the average recession has lasted 1 year, and the average recovery has lasted 4 years. Each peak in the figure is higher than the previous one because of the long-term growth of output.

EXAMPLE 2 Trying to Track the Business Cycle

Businesses, common people, stock market investors, international bankers, and financiers try to foresee the economic future, asking questions like, "Are we coming out of the recession? Will inflation heat up? Will interest rates rise?" Shrewd individuals who can correctly answer these questions succeed in their economic lives. The accompanying figures illustrate information that people use to chart the course of the economy. Each week a slew of similar economic statistics are released. Prior to their release, professional forecasters have attempted to predict what the figures will actually be. On the basis of these forecasts, economic agents may have already formed their views of the future of the economy. In later chapters, we will discuss why events that differ from such forecasts seem to have a greater effect on economic actions than do events that occur as predicted.

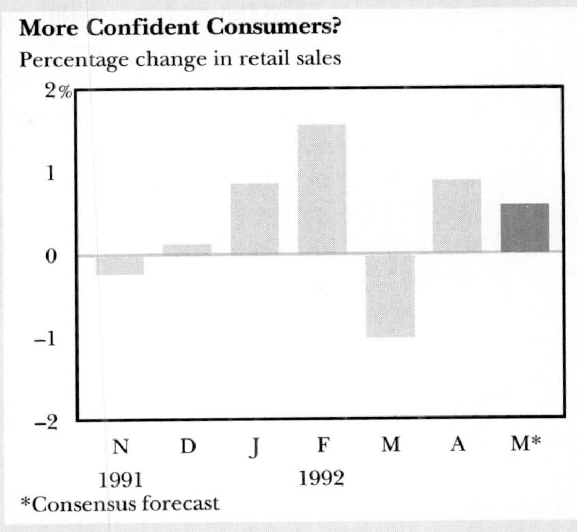

Source: "Tracking the Economy," *Wall Street Journal,* June 8, 1992, A2.

Statistics to Be Released This Week

Economic Indicator	Period	Release Date	Previous Actual	Technical Data Consensus Forecast
Consumer Credit	April	June 9	−$1.61 billion	**No change**
Retail Sales	May	June 11	+0.9%	**+0.6%**
Producer Prices	May	June 11	+0.2%	**+0.3%**
Initial Jobless Claims	Week to May 30	June 11	407,000	**400,000**
Money Supply: M1	Week to June 1	June 11	−$3.0 billion	**+$5.0 billion**
Money Supply: M2	Week to June 1	June 11	−$10.7 billion	**+$4.0 billion**
Money Supply: M3	Week to June 1	June 11	−$6.7 billion	**−$7.4 billion**
Consumer Prices	May	June 12	+0.2%	**+0.3%**
Business Inventories	April	June 12	+0.4%	**No change**

Statistics Released Last Week

Personal Income (ann. rate)	**$4,990.3 billion**	**New-Home Sales** (annual rate)	**530,000**
April	+0.1%	April	+1.3%
Personal Spending (ann. rate)	**$4,043.7 billion**	**Factory Orders**	**$243.85 billion**
April	+0.3%	April	+1.0%
Constr. Spending (ann. rate)	**$418.8 billion**	**New-Car Sales**	**1,151,331**
April	−0.3%	May	+3.6%*
Purchasing Mgrs. Survey	**56.3%**	**Unemployment Rate**	**7.5%**
May	+5.0	May	+0.3
Leading Indicators Index	**148.9**	**Nonfarm Payrolls**	**108,450,000**
April	+0.4%	May	+68,000

* Change from May 1991.

Source: "Tracking the Economy," *Wall Street Journal,* June 8, 1992, A2.

number of people employed declines (or the growth of employment slows). The *trough* (or lowest point) occurs when the various indicators of business activity stop falling. The economy reaches a low point from which recovery begins.

During the *recovery* stage of the business cycle, the various output indicators point to expanding output. The final stage occurs when the business cycle reaches its *peak,* the point at which the various indicators of production and employment fail to yield further increases. When the next stage—recession—begins, the economy enters another business cycle.

Length of Cycles

The duration of the business cycle is the length of time it takes to move through one complete cycle. The length of the business cycle can be measured either as the number of months between the peak of the cycle and the next peak or as the time it takes to move from trough to trough. No two business cycles are identical. Government studies of the business cycle from 1924 to the present (see Table 1) show that the average duration is almost 5 years. The recession phase lasts, on the average, slightly less than 1 year.

TABLE 1
American Business Cycles, 1924–1992

Trough	Peak	Length of Cycle, Peak to Peak (months)
July 1924	October 1926	41
November 1927	August 1929	34
March 1933	May 1937	93
June 1938	February 1945	93
October 1945	November 1948	45
October 1949	July 1953	56
May 1954	August 1957	49
April 1958	April 1960	32
February 1961	December 1969	116
November 1970	November 1973	47
March 1975	January 1980	62
July 1980	July 1981	12
November 1982	July 1990	118
July 1991	—	—

Source: U.S. Department of Commerce, *Handbook of Cyclical Indicators,* a supplement to *Business Conditions Digest.*

The expansion phase lasts, on the average, about 4 years.

Magnitude of Cycles

There is a big difference between small cyclical swings in which the economy stays near full employment and large swings from boom to depression. During the Great Depression, total output fell in 1933 to 70 percent of its 1929 level. The unemployment rate rose from 3 percent in 1929 to 25 percent in 1933. The recession of 1982, regarded as severe, saw a 2 percent fall in output and a rise in the unemployment rate from 7.5 percent to 9.5 percent. The milder recession from 1990 to 1991 saw real output declining at negative annualized rates of 2.5 percent in the fourth quarter of 1990 and the first quarter of 1991, after which growth resumed but at a slow rate. The unemployment rate rose from 5.5 percent to slightly over 7 percent.

Business cycles affect various industries, occupations, and regions differently. Some industries, such as the auto, steel, and machine-building industries, are hit harder by economic downturns than others. In the 1990–1991 recession, for example, automobiles and retailing were especially hard hit.

Business Cycles and the World Economy

The ups and downs of major industrial economies create ripple effects throughout the world economy. National economies do not exist in isolation. They trade goods and services with one another. Their credit markets are interrelated, with multinational firms borrowing dollars in New York, London, Zurich, Tokyo, or even Hong Kong. A country that experiences rapid economic growth will increase its purchases (imports) from other countries. High interest rates in one country will raise interest rates throughout world credit markets. Economies are interrelated through flows of goods and services and through flows of credit. Therefore, it is not surprising that business cycles tend to spread from country to country.

There is a saying among experts that, "When the industrial economies catch cold, the developing economies of Asia, Africa, and Latin America catch pneumonia." Recessions, which mean the loss of a relatively small amount of employment and output in the industrialized countries, cause severe losses of output and employment in poorer countries. True to form, the U.S. recession from 1990 to 1991 spread first to western Europe and then to the developing countries with increasingly stronger repercussions.

Figure 2 shows that the world's economies share common periods of rapid or slow growth. Industrial countries experience common inflation and unemployment trends. Interest rates rise and fall together. Business cycles do not move together in perfect harmony among countries. There are leads and lags, but over the long run, a common general trend is evident.

Inflation, Unemployment, Interest Rates, and Deficits

The business cycle measures changes in the level of real business activity. This level affects, or even determines, two key macroeconomic variables: *inflation* and *unemployment.* The general relationship between real business activity and unemployment is obvious. When real business activity expands, business firms offer more positions, employment expands, and the number of people without jobs declines. Although the relationship between employment and unemployment is complex, for the purposes of this discussion we can assume that there is an inverse relationship between the level of business activity and unemployment.

Macroeconomics also studies the relationship between the level of business activity and inflation. Inflation is an upward movement in the general price level. The complex relationship among inflation, unemployment, and the level of business activity is one of the most important issues in modern macroeconomics. In general, it can be said that when business activity is expanding and employment opportunities are ample, the general level of wages and prices tends to rise. When business activity is weak and employment opportunities are scarce, there is less pressure on wages and prices, and inflationary pressures tend to moderate.

The business cycle is also related to *interest rates* and *government deficits,* as we shall see in subsequent chapters. During a contraction in business activity, businesses cut back on their expansion plans, so the demand for credit is weak. As a result, interest rates tend to fall during recessions. With the strong growth of business activity, credit demand surges, pushing up interest rates. By contrast, government deficits tend to rise during recessions. As business activity declines, government tax revenues fall, but government must increase its spending on unemployment insurance and welfare programs. During expansions, tax revenues increase, and fewer people require welfare assistance and unemployment benefits. The relationships between interest rates, government deficits, and the business cycle are complex and require a great deal of study and explanation. We can, however, say that, more often than not, interest rates and government deficits are symptoms of the business cycle rather than causes.

In a world with an ideal level of business activity, all able-bodied persons wishing to work would have satisfactory jobs. Prices would be stable, and living standards would rise steadily. In such a world, the economy would avoid both *busts* (sharp downward movements in economic activity) and *booms* (sharp upward movements in economic activity). Progress would be steady and secure both at home and abroad. This ideal world would not experience sudden external shocks, such as world-wide crop failures or sharp increases in energy or raw-material prices. Businesses and consumers could be confident of a bright and predictable future.

Economic reality is usually not like the ideal macroeconomic world. In one period, economic activity expands; in the following period, economic activity contracts. During a boom period, jobs are easy to find, but prices are rising. During a bust period, jobs are scarce, but prices are stable or even falling. During some periods, prices rise at a rapid pace. At other times, they rise at a moderate rate. On rare occasions, prices even fall throughout the economy. In some cases, prices increase so rapidly that the economy as a whole is paralyzed.

Although economics rarely achieves the ideal level of business activity, policymakers should at least strive toward ample jobs, stable prices, and steadily rising living standards. If we can satisfactorily understand the causes of rising prices, unemployment, and changes in the level of business activity, we will be in a better position to achieve macroeconomic goals.

UNEMPLOYMENT

Unemployment and inflation are the central issues of macroeconomics. The U.S. government is committed by the Employment Act of 1946 to create

FIGURE 2
The International Business Cycle

(*a*) Industrial Production

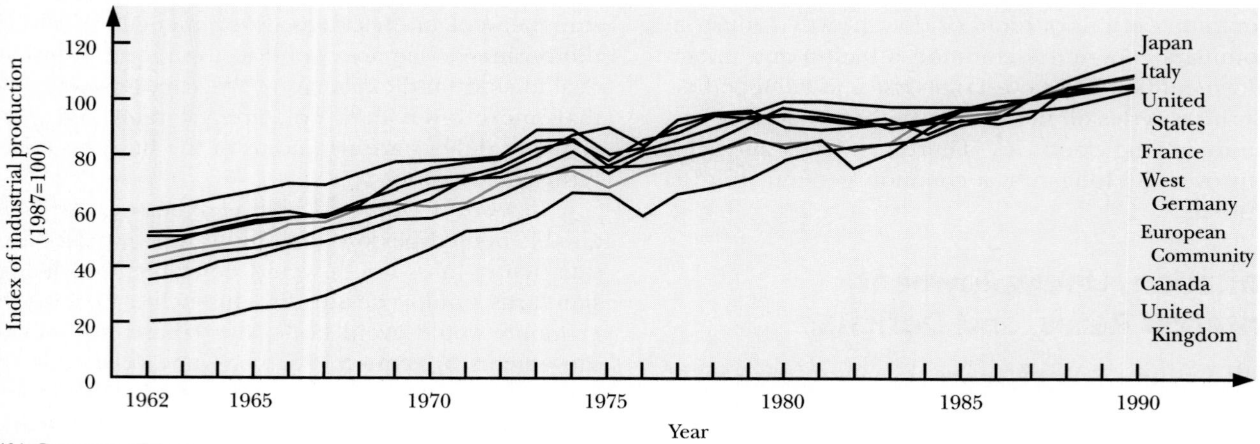

(*b*) Consumer Prices

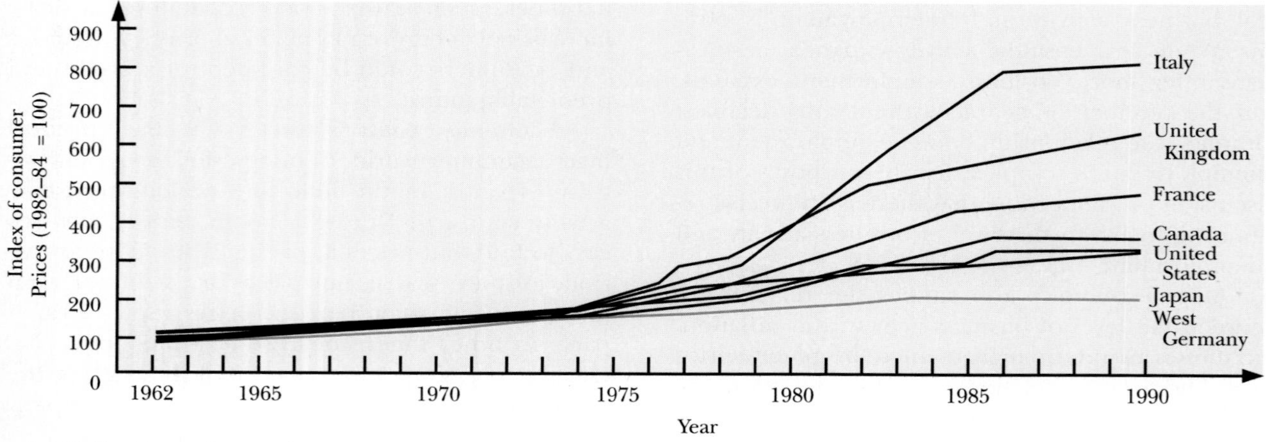

(*c*) Civilian Unemployment Rate

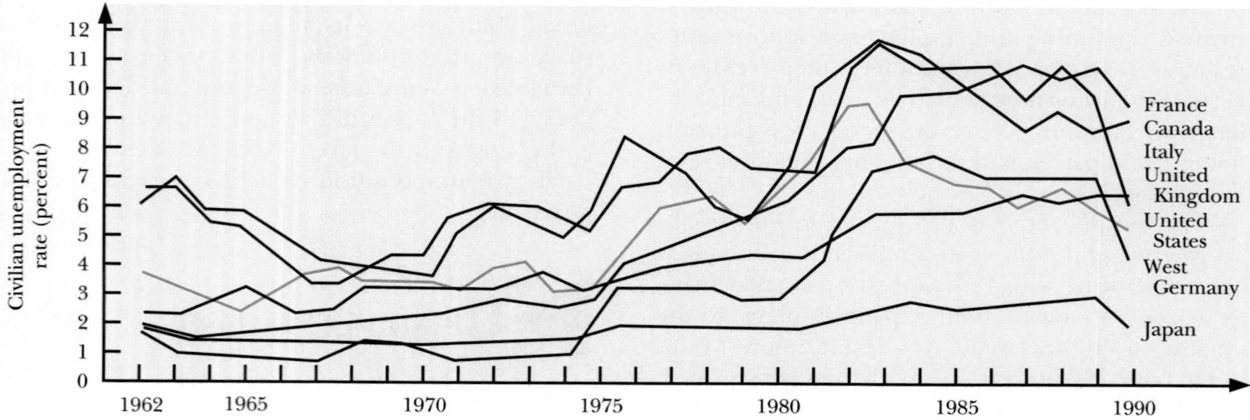

Source: *Economic Report of the President.*

and maintain "useful employment opportunities... for those able, willing, and seeking to work." Thus, unemployment is and continues to be an important factor in macroeconomic policy.

The Unemployment Rate

Each person 16 years or older can be classified in one of three labor market categories:

1. Employed
2. Unemployed
3. Not in the labor force

A person who currently has a job, whether full- or part-time, is *employed.* Even persons who want to have full-time jobs but are able to find only part-time work are counted as employed. Employment is an either/or state; either you have a job or you don't.

A person is classified as *unemployed* if he or she (1) did not work at all during the preceding week, (2) actively looked for work during the previous four weeks, and (3) is currently available for work. Persons laid off from jobs or waiting to report to a new job within 30 days are also classified as unemployed.

Persons without jobs who do not meet the three conditions of unemployment are classified as *not in the labor force.* The **labor force** consists of all persons either currently working or unemployed.

> The **labor force** equals the number of persons employed plus the number unemployed.

A person is not in the labor force either by choice (as in the case of full-time students) or because an appropriate job cannot be found.

The number of persons unemployed does not show the relative magnitude of unemployment. The **unemployment rate** relates the number unemployed to the size of the labor force.

> The **unemployment rate** is the number of persons unemployed divided by the number in the labor force.

Historical Trends in Unemployment

Figure 3 shows long-term trends in unemployment. Since 1900, the unemployment rate has varied from lows of near 1 percent to a high of 25 percent during the Great Depression of the 1930s. The massive unemployment of the 1930s is the principal reason we refer to this period as the Great Depression. A 25 percent unemployment rate means that one out of every four persons seeking work is out of a job. It is no wonder that the Great Depression had a tremendous effect on economic thinking and that many Americans who experienced the Great Depression firsthand harbor a deep fear of mass unemployment.

Between 1900 and 1947, no distinct trends in the unemployment rate are apparent. However, since World War II, the unemployment rate has moved generally upward. During the period between World War II and 1960, the unemployment rate ranged from 2.5 percent to 5.5 percent, whereas after 1960, unemployment rates of 5 to 9 percent became commonplace. In the 1960s, the unemployment rate ranged from 3.4 percent to 6.5 percent. In the 1970s, the unemployment rate ranged from 4.8 percent to 8.3 percent. In the first half of the 1980s, the range was from 7 percent to 9.5 percent. In the second half of the 1980s and the early 1990s, the unemployment rate was between 6 percent and 7 percent.

A comparison of Figure 3 and Table 1 shows the clear positive relationship between the unemployment rate and recessions (depressions). During each recession, the unemployment rate has increased (including the 1990–1991 recession.)

Trends in Employment, Unemployment, and the Unemployment Rate Compared

The unemployment rate rises when unemployment increases faster than the labor force grows. Hence, a rising unemployment rate can be caused by relatively rapid growth of unemployment, relatively slow growth of the labor force, or by a combination of the two.

The relationships between employment, unemployment, and the unemployment rate are complex. Panel *a* in Figure 4 shows trends in the labor force broken down into the number of persons employed, unemployed, and not in the labor force. Panel *b* graphs the unemployment rate.

Figure 4 demonstrates that in the long run, both employment *and* unemployment have risen as the U.S. economy has grown. In 1950, employment was 60 million and unemployment was 3.3 million. In

FIGURE 3
The Unemployment Rate, 1900–1992

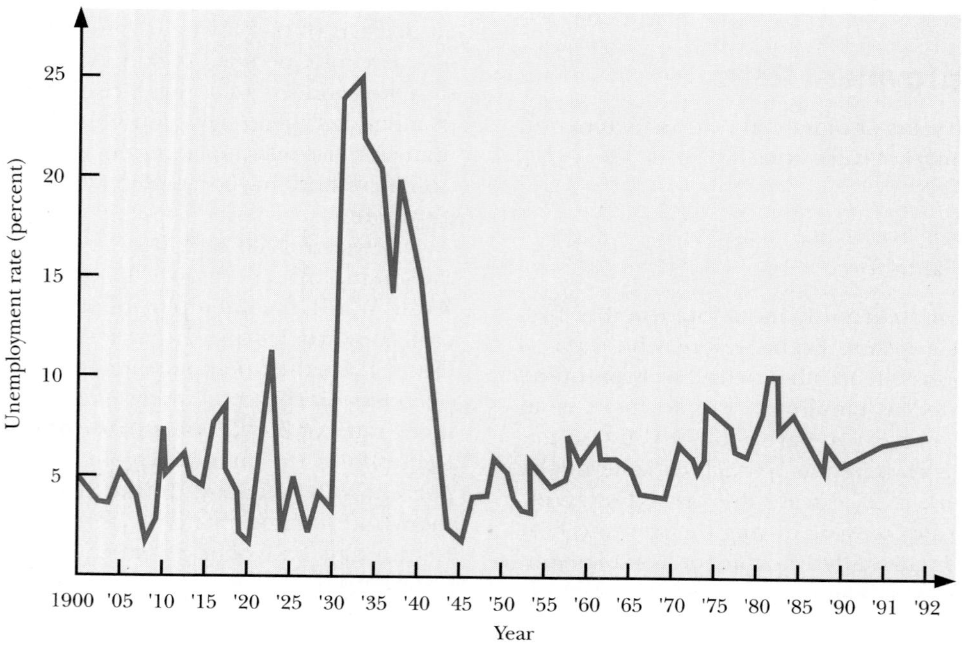

The unemployment rate has been rising in recent years, but it is far from reaching the level experienced during the Great Depression of the 1930s.

Source: *Historical Statistics of the United States; Economic Report of the President.*

early 1992, employment was 118 million and unemployment was 7.7 million.

In the shorter run, employment and unemployment can move together (such as during the early 1970s and the early 1980s) or in opposite directions (such as during most of the 1960s, the mid-1970s, and the mid-1980s). The 1960s experienced low and declining unemployment, whereas the 1970s saw high and generally rising unemployment. Surprisingly, the rate of increase in *employment* was lower in the 1960s than in the 1970s! The higher unemployment *rates* of the 1970s were caused not by slow employment growth but by unemployment rising faster than the increase in the labor force.

Figure 4 shows the effect of the business cycle on employment, unemployment, and the number of people not in the labor force. During recessions, (vertical gold bars) unemployment rises, employment falls, or slows its rate of increase, and the number of people not in the labor force rises. The unemployment rate rises during recessions because unemployment rises at a faster pace than people leave the labor force.

The unemployment *rate* does not necessarily move in tandem with unemployment. From 1971 to 1973, there was a sharp drop in the unemployment rate even though the number of unemployed remained stable. The unemployment rate fell because employment rose sharply while the number unemployed held steady. The same pattern occurred during the substantial expansion of employment from 1975 to 1979.

Full Employment

Full employment does not require that everyone actively looking and available for work currently have a job. If there were absolutely no unemployment, the economy would lack the movement among jobs necessary to any changing economy. Full employment

FIGURE 4
Employment, Unemployment, and the Unemployment Rate

(*a*) The Employment Status of Workers

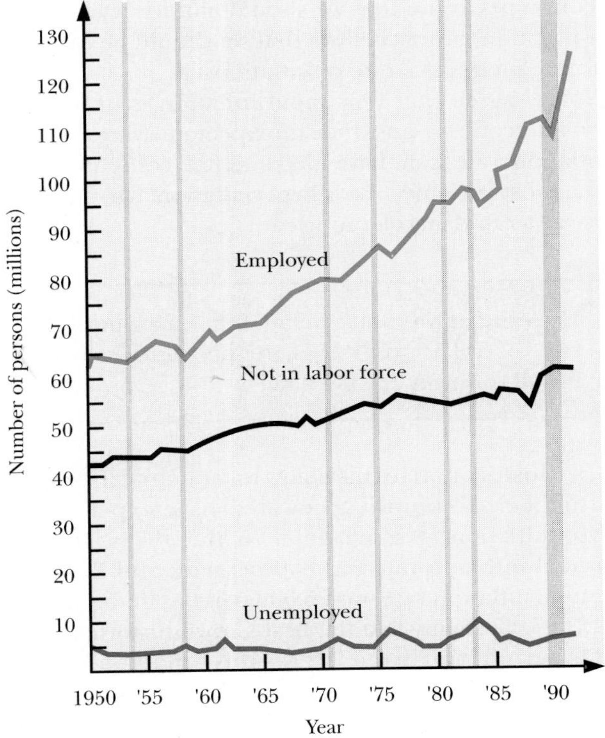

(*b*) The Unemployment Rate

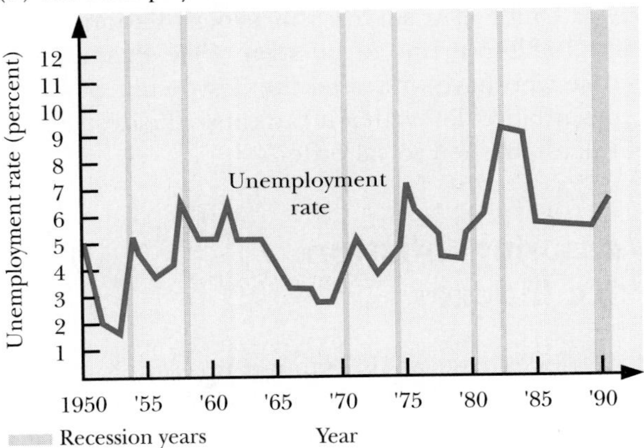

Employment often increases, though its rate slows, during periods of rising unemployment. However, in the case of major recessions, as in 1975 or 1983, employment decreased.

Source: *Survey of Current Business.*

occurs when the ever-shifting labor market is in balance. In a dynamic economy, jobs are created while other jobs disappear. Some people enter or reenter the labor force while others withdraw or retire. In some professions, there are more job applicants than jobs. In other professions, there are more jobs than applicants. The labor market is in approximate balance when the number of jobs being created roughly equals the number of qualified applicants available to fill those jobs. As new jobs are created or as people leave jobs, individuals with the appropriate qualifications enter the labor force or move from other jobs to fill those vacancies. There may be imbalances within particular occupations or industries, but on the average there can be a balance between the number of unfilled jobs and the number of qualified job seekers. The unemployment rate at which this balance is attained is called the **natural rate of unemployment.**

> The **natural rate of unemployment** is that unemployment rate at which there is an approximate balance between the number of unfilled jobs and the number of qualified job seekers.

The economy is at full employment when it is operating at the natural rate of unemployment. The perception of what constitutes full employment at the natural rate has been changing. In the early 1960s, economists felt that full employment was at an unemployment rate of around 4 percent. In the late 1970s, the figure was 5 percent to 5.5 percent. During the 1980s and early 1990s, the natural rate of unemployment was considered to be in the 5.5 to slightly over 6 percent range.

As the chapter on inflation and unemployment will explain, inflationary pressures remain the same when labor markets are in balance. When an economy is at the natural rate of unemployment, the prevailing rate of inflation should continue. The relationship between inflation and unemployment is one of the most important relationships of macroeconomics.

INFLATION

People fear **inflation** for a number of reasons—some justified, others not. Some nations have experienced runaway inflation that has paralyzed their economies and caused political upheavals. In the United States, the rapid inflation of the 1970s and early 1980s left a deep imprint on the American consciousness. During this period, people regarded inflation as the nation's number one problem and even despaired of finding a solution.

> **Inflation** is a general increase in prices.

Inflation occurs when prices in the entire economy are rising on average. Some prices rise faster than the average increase, and some rise slower. Some prices even fall. For example, the prices of pocket calculators, home computers, and silicon chips fell throughout the inflationary 1970s and early 1980s. On the other hand, crude oil prices rose five times faster than the average price increase between 1972 and 1981. The average rate of inflation is measured by price indexes, as will be explained later.

Whether inflation is perceived as moderate or rapid is relative to its time and place. In the mid-1950s, when prices in the United States were rising 2 percent per year or less, an inflation rate of 5 percent would have been viewed with concern. In fact, the "alarming" 1966 inflation rate of 3.3 percent motivated government authorities to impose strict anti-inflationary measures. After several years of near double-digit inflation in the late 1970s and early 1980s, the 3 percent to 4.5 percent inflation rates of the rest of the 1980s were taken as signs that inflation was under control. In some Latin American countries or the former Soviet Union, where prices double or quadruple (or worse) annually, the double-digit inflation rates of the late 1970s would be the object of envy. The rate of inflation—just like any other measure of prices—must be evaluated in relative terms.

The opposite of inflation, **deflation,** has been rare in modern times.

> **Deflation** is a general decline in prices.

The economy experienced substantial deflation during the Great Depression of the 1930s. Since the mid 1930s, inflation has been the rule and deflation the exception. The year 1955 was the last year in which a general decline in prices was recorded.

Magnitude of Inflation

There is general agreement that it is desirable for the economy to operate at the natural rate of unemployment (full employment). There is less agreement on what constitutes an optimal rate of inflation. Some economists argue that we should aim for a zero rate of inflation; others believe that we should be content with a "moderate" rate of inflation.

All agree that very rapid inflation is unhealthy for an economy and that unexpected swings in the inflation rate can have detrimental consequences. The most extreme case is **hyperinflation,** when prices rise at a rapid, accelerating rate.

> **Hyperinflation** is a very rapid and accelerating rate of inflation. Prices might double every month or even double daily or hourly.

Most economies have slow to moderate inflation. A number of countries, however, have experienced hyperinflation at some time. In the 1980s, Israel's annual inflation rate was 800 percent, and Bolivia's annual inflation rate was 25,000 percent in the spring of 1985. Germany had the best-known historical case of hyperinflation in the 1920s—this condition helped bring Hitler to power. The American South experienced hyperinflation during the Civil War. Whether the new governments of the republics of the former Soviet Union can survive the hyperinflation of the early 1990s remains to be seen. (See Example 3.) People who have witnessed the destructive power of hyperinflation know that it can cause the destruction of the established social order.

Measuring Inflation: Price Indexes

If all prices rose at the same rate—say, 3 percent per year—there would be no problem measuring inflation. The inflation rate would obviously be 3 percent per annum. As we noted earlier, however, all prices do not rise at the same rate during a period of inflation; some rise more rapidly than others, and some even fall. The different rates of price increase must be combined in a **price index** that measures the general increase in prices.

EXAMPLE 3 Conditions During the German Hyperinflation

One of the best documented cases of hyperinflation is that of Germany following World War I. The Treaty of Versailles required that the German government pay war reparations to France and Great Britain. In order to make these payments, the German government began printing money. From August 1922 to November 1923, the German government increased the supply of paper money by 314 percent per month. Within 15 months, the price level rose more than 10 billion times its starting level. Prices rose 322 percent per month.

Hyperinflation reduces economic efficiency by forcing people to devote most of their efforts to avoiding the inflation tax. Workers paid in the morning had to be given time off to rush off and spend their wages before they became worthless. People could be seen carrying cash around in wheelbarrows. Firms paid their workers three times a day—after breakfast, lunch, and dinner. As matters worsened, people refused to accept money at all. Instead, they demanded foreign currency, precious metals, or real goods. The economic chaos created by the hyperinflation helped bring Hitler to power and explains why the Germans, even to this day, have a deep-seated fear of inflation.

A **price index** shows the cost of buying a given market basket of goods in different years as a percentage of the cost of the same market basket in some base year.

A *market basket* is the combination of goods and services consumed by a typical family. Price indexes measure the changing cost of purchasing the same market basket of goods in different years. If the typical market basket of goods costs $200 per week in 1990, $220 per week in 1991, and $230 per week in 1992, the price index in 1990 is 100 (the base year), 110 in 1991 ($220/$200 × 100), and 115 in 1992 ($230/$200 × 100). This price index shows that the typical market basket cost 10 percent more in 1991 than in 1990 and 15 percent more in 1992 than in 1990.

Economists and government officials compile different indexes to measure the general change in prices. The most widely known price index in the United States is the consumer price index, or CPI.

The **CPI** measures changes in consumer prices paid by households.

The media report monthly changes in the CPI that are closely followed by business, the public, and government officials. Many government pensions, including 38 million Social Security pensions and more than 3 million military pensions, and the wages of 8.5 million union workers and government employees are tied to the CPI; if the CPI rises, these pensions and wages are adjusted to reflect the higher cost of living. Since 1985, federal income tax rates have been adjusted to reflect changes in the CPI. For these reasons, it is important that the CPI accurately gauge the rate of increase in consumer prices.

The CPI measures changes in the prices of only those goods and services that families purchase for consumption. It does not measure the prices of the other goods and services that the economy produces. In the early 1990s, 65 percent of the total output of the economy was devoted to personal consumption. The remaining 35 percent went to business investment, government services, and exports and imports. The CPI, therefore, is not the most general measure of the rate of inflation. A more general measure is the **GDP deflator.**

The **GDP deflator** measures the change in the prices of all final goods and services (consumer goods, investment goods, and government) produced by the economy.

FIGURE 5
The U.S. Price Level, 1800–1992

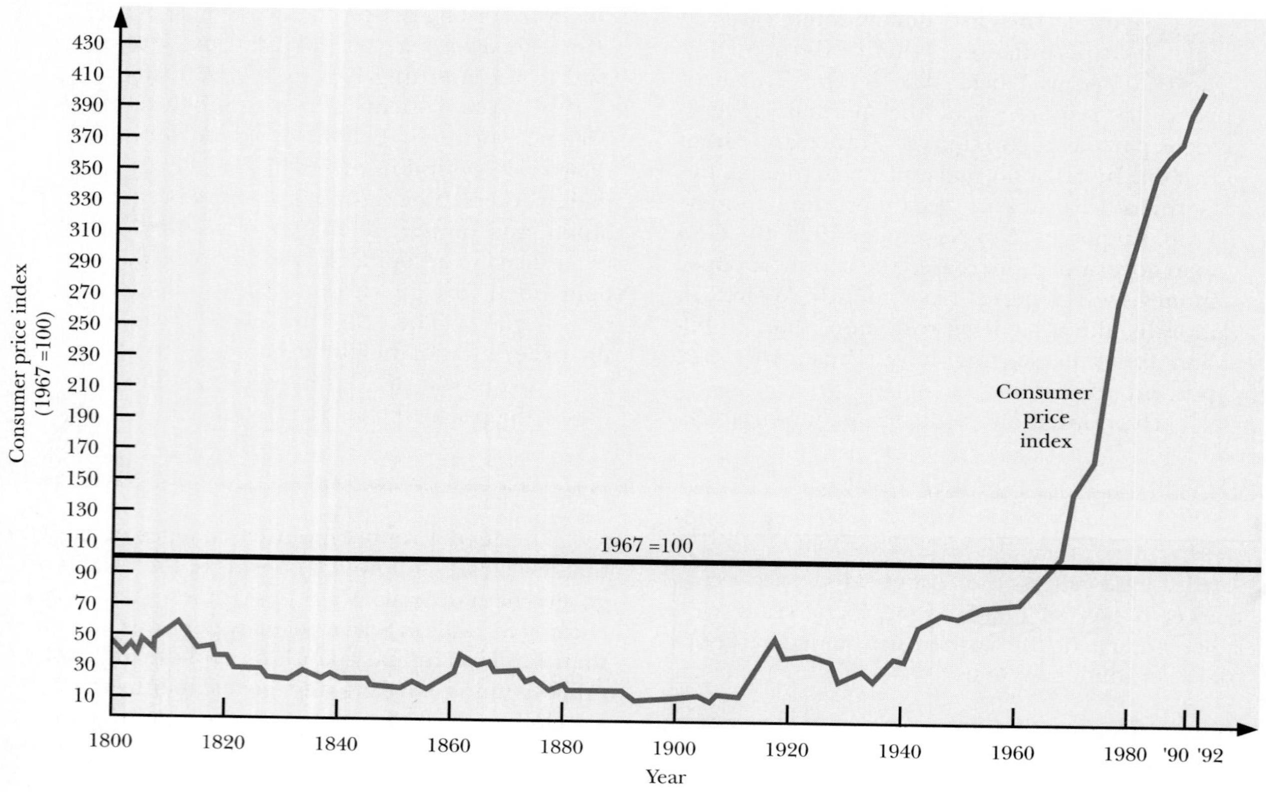

The price level has continuously risen since World War II, deviating from the pattern of the preceding 140 years.

Source: *Historical Statistics of the United States: Economic Report of the President.*

The GDP deflator measures the change in the prices of machinery and construction, government, exports and imports, as well as consumer prices. Because the GDP deflator is a more general measure of inflation, most of the inflation figures subsequently cited in this book use the GDP deflator.

Historical Trends in Inflation

Trends in inflation over the past two centuries (Figure 5) reveal that the sustained inflation of the past half-century is a fairly new phenomenon. Until 1930, prices were as likely to fall as to rise. Prior to World War II, *deflation* was just as common as *inflation*. The unusual feature of the post-World War II period has been the notable absence of deflation. Unlike earlier times when periods of inflation tended to balance periods of deflation, the postwar era has been one of continuous increases in prices, albeit at varying rates.

Historically speaking, inflation is not inevitable, even though it may appear so to the current generation. Figure 6 shows why most readers have come to think of rising prices as one of the constants of life along with death and taxes: the CPI has shown a price decrease in only one of the last 40 years (1955). Moreover, the inflation rate tended to rise from 1960 to the early 1980s. The mid-1980s, however, witnessed a retreat from the high inflation rates of the late 1970s and early 1980s. Between 1982 and 1989, the average annual inflation rate was 4.0 percent. In 1990 and 1991, the annual inflation rate was between 3 percent and 4 percent.

FIGURE 6
Inflation Measures: The Consumer Price Index and the GDP Deflator, 1951–1991

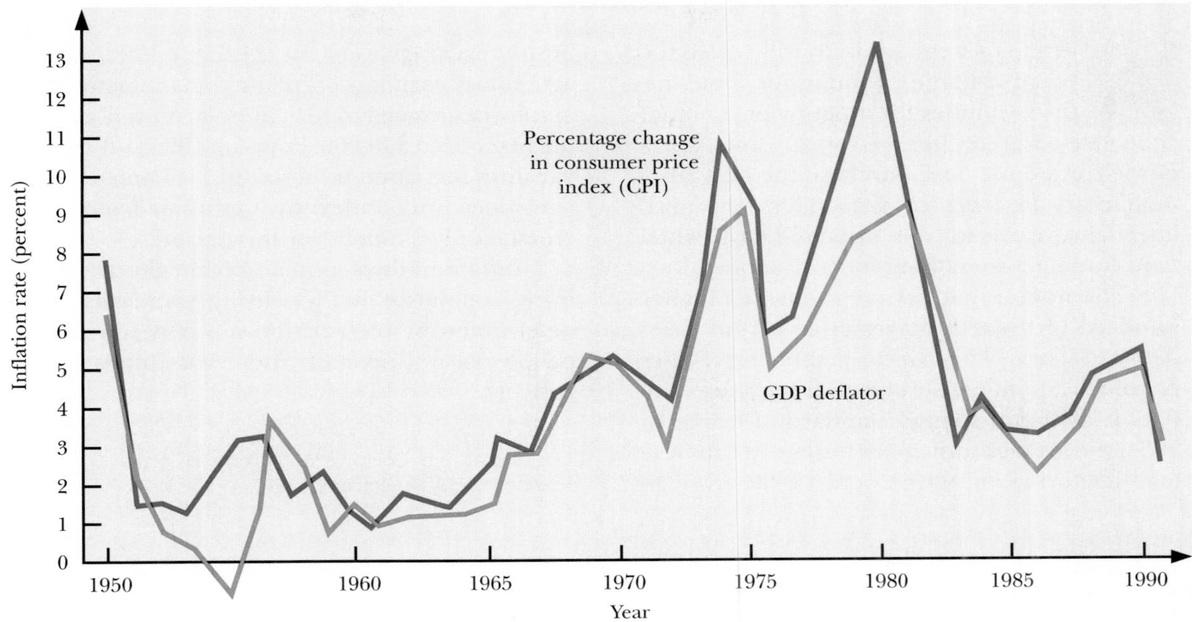

The rate of inflation as measured by the CPI and GDP deflator accelerated sharply from the early 1960s to 1981. After 1981, the inflation rate slowed down.

Source: *Statistical Abstract of the United States: Economic Report of the President.*

Effects of Inflation

People fear that rising prices will automatically lower their standard of living. Alarming increases in housing prices or food prices are taken as proof that living standards are falling. This confusion is a classic example of the *ceteris paribus* fallacy discussed in Chapter 1. During inflation, prices of outputs and inputs, wages, rents, and interest rates all tend to rise. Yet, as the prices of the things we buy rise, so do the prices of the things we sell (such as labor). Living standards are determined by the relationship between income and prices. If income is rising faster than prices, living standards are rising; if income is rising slower than prices, living standards are falling. (See Example 4.)

To illustrate the logical fallacy of equating rising prices with falling living standards or falling prices with rising living standards, consider the Great Depression of the 1930s. Between 1929 and 1933, prices dropped by 25 percent while people's incomes fell by 45 percent. Falling prices did not result in rising living standards. Because incomes declined more than prices between 1929 and 1933, living standards dropped.

Inflation Redistributes Income. People more correctly fear inflation because it redistributes income by causing income to increase faster than prices for some people and slower than prices for others. Inflation, however, does not automatically redistribute income from creditors to debtors or from the old to the young. Generally speaking, inflation redistributes income away from those who have underestimated its magnitude.

When people enter into multiyear money contracts (such as employment or loan contracts), they try to anticipate what the rate of inflation will be over the life of the contract. When Bradford lends Taylor money to be repaid at some future date, both must attempt to anticipate inflation. Errors can be costly.

EXAMPLE 4 A Whole Cent to Spend! Prices, Income, and Living Standards

A newspaper columnist fondly recalls the year 1924, when a youngster could buy three candies for a penny or a box of chocolate-covered cherries for 29 cents, see a movie for a dime, and purchase the best automobile on the road for $255. This columnist, like many, yearns for the "good old days" when "you could get something for your money."

The notion that low prices mean a higher standard of living is an example of the *ceteris paribus* fallacy. This kind of thinking causes people to automatically equate rising prices (inflation) with a declining standard of living. In 1924, the average annual earnings of a full-time manufacturing employee were $1400. Average hourly earnings were 50 cents. In 1992, average hourly earnings of full-time manufacturing employees exceeded $13; average annual earnings exceeded $40,000. Between 1924 and 1992, earnings increased by more than 25 times. The consumer price index, on the other hand, increased only 8 times over this period.

Inflation does not automatically reduce living standards. Rather, living standards are determined by the relationship between what people earn (income) and what things cost (prices).

Source: John Gould, "A Whole Penny to Spend!" *Christian Science Monitor,* November 23, 1990.

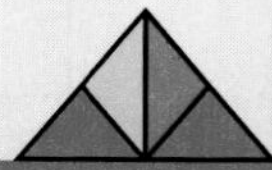

Suppose Bradford lends Taylor $10,000 for 5 years at an annual interest rate of 5 percent (Bradford expects a relatively low rate of inflation), but the actual inflation rate turns out to be 10 percent per year over the 5-year period. The $500 interest payment Bradford receives each year does not compensate for the loss in purchasing power suffered each year. When Taylor repays the $10,000 principal at the end of the 5 years, Bradford receives dollars that will each buy only $0.62 worth of goods and services compared to 5 years earlier. Clearly, inflation has redistributed income from the lender (Bradford) to the borrower (Taylor). If the loan had been negotiated differently (say, at a 20 percent interest rate), income would have been redistributed from the borrower to the lender. The $2000 annual interest payment would have handsomely compensated Bradford for the payment of interest and principal in cheaper dollars.

Similarly, multiyear wage contracts can redistribute income from employee to employer, or vice versa. If a union negotiates a 3-year wage contract calling for annual pay increases of 5 percent, and the annual inflation rate over this period turns out to be 10 percent, income will have been redistributed from employee to employer. If the contract had called for a 20 percent annual pay increase, on the other hand, income would have been redistributed from the employer to the employee.

As these two examples show, the income redistribution effects of inflation depend upon the ability to anticipate inflation. The lender who anticipates inflation correctly will demand an interest rate that will compensate for inflation's erosion of the value of interest and principal payments. Union negotiators generally will refuse to accept wage increases that do not compensate for inflation. (See Example 5.)

It is clearly in the interests of all who enter into contracts involving money payments over time to anticipate inflation correctly. Some people succeed; others fail. For the economy as a whole, inflation can be lower or higher than generally expected. When actual inflation differs from the previously anticipated inflation, income is redistributed.

Economists do not know exactly how to anticipate inflation. Later chapters will discuss various views of how inflationary expectations should be formed.

Inflation Creates Inefficiencies. When inflation is rapid and erratic, it becomes very important to predict it accurately. If business decision makers believe

EXAMPLE 5 Inflation, Interest Rates, Stocks, and the Dollar

Inflation affects interest rates, stock prices, and dollar exchange rates. This influence raises fear in some people and causes the investment community to pay much attention to inflation.

Higher inflation means higher interest rates. As inflation increases, people are less willing to save at prevailing interest rates because rising prices reduce the purchasing power of tomorrow's income. Borrowers, who will be able to repay loans in cheaper dollars, are more anxious to borrow. These two forces drive up interest rates as the rate of inflation increases.

Higher interest rates typically depress the value of stocks. Persons with funds to invest have a choice of stocks or bonds. Higher interest rates mean higher returns on bonds and hence draw funds from stocks to bonds. The flow of funds from stocks to bonds depresses stock prices.

Inflation typically drives down the dollar exchange rate (the rate at which the U.S. dollar can be exchanged for pounds or marks or yen). A high rate of inflation in the United States (combined with lower inflation abroad) means that U.S. goods become more expensive than foreign goods. U.S. consumers spend more on foreign imports and foreigners buy fewer U.S. goods, thereby driving down the dollar exchange rate.

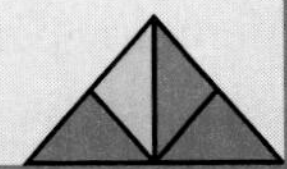

that the inflation rate will be 10 percent during the coming year, and the actual rate is 30 percent, they will lose money.

The presence of rapid, erratic inflation creates two types of inefficiencies. First, business decision makers become more concerned with anticipating inflation than seeking out profitable business opportunities. Creative efforts are diverted from innovation and risk taking to anticipating inflation. Second, inflation leads to speculative practices that do not add to the economy's productive capacity. Those who try to outwit everyone else because they expect greater inflation will speculate in real estate, foreign currencies, gold, and art objects. Such speculative investments are made *in place of* productive investments in plants, equipment, and inventories.

The negative effects of inflation on economic efficiency are most pronounced during hyperinflation. Workers become reluctant to accept their wages in money (preferring to be paid in terms of products), and money is spent immediately. Businesses refuse to enter into fixed contracts, and most transactions involve barter exchanges of goods and services. In other words, hyperinflation results in the loss of the efficiency of money transactions. Most efforts during hyperinflation aim at keeping up with inflation rather than at productive economic activities.

Inflation Contributes to Business Cycles. Inflation's effect on the level of business activity is one of the most important issues of macroeconomics. Does inflation cause more output to be produced *ceteris paribus?* Subsequent chapters will be devoted to this complex question. Some economists believe that inflation (whether anticipated or unanticipated) has a negligible effect on output and employment. Others say that inflation, especially when it is unanticipated, can significantly and positively affect output and employment.

If rising inflation can raise output and employment, then slowing inflation can lower output and employment. Any contribution inflation makes to the ups and downs of general business activity gives people another reason to be concerned about inflation.

STAGFLATION

During periods of high unemployment, we would expect inflation to be low. Low unemployment would be expected to accompany high inflation. Such was the case in the United States and Europe prior to the mid 1960s. Both the unemployment and the inflation rate showed upward trends in the United States from the late 1960s to the early 1980s (see Figure 7), resulting in **stagflation.**

> **Stagflation** is the combination of high unemployment rates and high inflation over a period of time.

The stagflation of the 1970s and early 1980s spawned new theories to explain why high unemployment did not drive down inflation. Economists and policy makers began to grumble that "the economy doesn't work the way it is supposed to." The stagflation of the 1970s and early 1980s seemed to confirm individuals' worst fears: that high inflation could be combined with high unemployment. Stagflation will be discussed in detail in the chapter on inflation and unemployment.

ECONOMIC GROWTH: THE LONG-RUN PERSPECTIVE

Although inflation, unemployment, and the business cycle dominate public discussion, they reflect the short-term ups and downs of the economy. **Economic growth** determines the long-term health of the economy and the level of living standards.

> **Economic growth** is the expansion of the real output of the economy, or the increase of the real output of goods and services.

When economic growth occurs, particularly if it outpaces the growth of population, the volume of goods and services available to the population

FIGURE 7
The Stagflation of the 1970s and 1980s

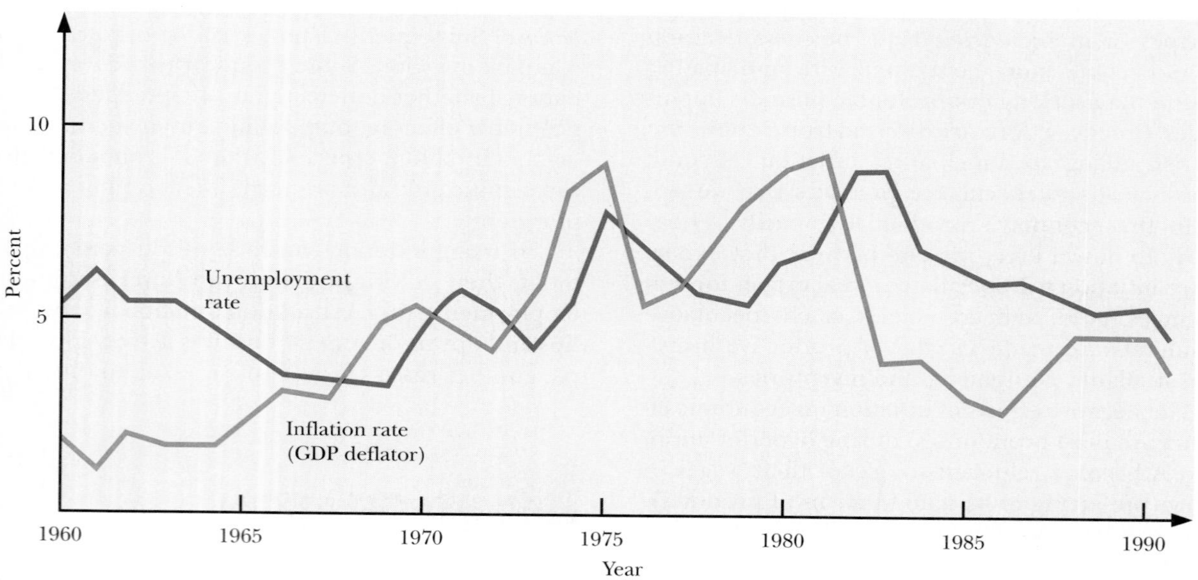

Inflation and unemployment both showed upward trends from the late 1960s to the early 1980s. The combination of high inflation and high unemployment is stagflation.

Source: *Economic Report of the President.*

expands and living standards rise. Countries that are considered to be rich today have experienced long periods of economic growth. The wealth of North America, Western Europe, and Japan is rooted in a long legacy of economic growth. India and Niger are poor today because they have failed to experience economic growth over an extended period.

Economic theory must explain not only the ups and downs of economic activity, including the accompanying factors of inflation, unemployment, government deficits, and fluctuations of interest rates, but also economic growth. What are the causes of economic growth? Why has long-term economic growth occurred in only an extremely limited number of countries?

This chapter has discussed the macroeconomic concepts of the business cycle, unemployment, and inflation. The next chapter will examine how to define and measure total output (gross domestic product) and its various components.

SUMMARY

1. Macroeconomics is the study of the economy as a whole. Macroeconomists study such topics as inflation, unemployment, and the business cycle.

2. The business cycle is the pattern of upward and downward movements in the level of business activity. A recession is a decline in real output that lasts 6 months or more. A depression is a very severe recession, lasting several years. The four phases of the business cycle are: recession, trough, recovery, and peak. The world economy appears to share common business cycles.

3. A person is unemployed if he or she is not working, is currently available for work, and is actively seeking a job. Full employment is reached at the natural rate of unemployment.

4. Individuals are classified into three labor market categories: employed, unemployed, or not in the labor force. The labor force is the sum of the employed and unemployed. The unemployment rate is the number unemployed divided by the labor force.

5. Since the 1950s, there has been an upward movement in the unemployment rate. Unemployment, employment, and the number not in the labor force are affected by the business cycle in a complex fashion.

6. Inflation is a general increase in prices. It is measured by price indexes that determine the changing cost of buying a standard market basket of goods. The most important price indexes are the consumer price index (the CPI) and the GDP deflator. Prior to the 1930s, deflation was just as common as inflation. There has been a clear inflationary trend since the mid-1930s.

7. People fear inflation because it redistributes income, creates economic inefficiency, and contributes to the fluctuations of business cycle.

8. Both the inflation rate and the unemployment rate experienced upward trends from the late 1960s to the early 1980s. Modern macroeconomics is seeking to explain the combination of high unemployment and high inflation, which is called stagflation.

9. Long-term economic growth determines a country's wealth and living standard.

KEY TERMS

business cycle
recession
depression
labor force
unemployment rate
natural rate of unemployment
inflation
deflation
hyperinflation
price index
CPI
GDP deflator
stagflation
economic growth

QUESTIONS AND PROBLEMS

1. How would each of the following people be classified according to the definition of unemployment?
   a. A high-school student casually looking for an after-school job.
   b. A person who quits his or her job to become a full-time homemaker.
   c. A laid-off auto worker waiting to be recalled to his or her previous job.
   d. A person who has quit his or her job to search for a better job.
2. Describe the relevant criteria by which government statisticians determine whether a person is "unemployed" or "not in the labor force."

3. In 1982, a typical market basket costs $500. In 1988, the same market basket costs $800. What is the price index for 1988, using 1982 as the base year?
4. Explain how inflation can redistribute wealth from lenders to borrowers.
5. Explain how and why hyperinflation reduces economic efficiency.
6. Jones lends $100 to Smith for 1 year. During this year, the inflation rate is 5 percent. How much interest and principal would Jones have to receive to be able to buy the same physical quantities of goods and services when the loan is repaid as when the loan was made?
7. Does the relative duration of expansions and recessions help explain the fact that long-term economic growth has been positive?
8. Do you think that an economy that is in a recession is operating at the natural rate of unemployment?
9. Evaluate the validity of the following statement: "Inflation is as inevitable as death and taxes."
10. Explain why the stagflation of the 1970s and early 1980s was an unexpected phenomenon.
11. Explain why the unemployment rate does not always rise when unemployment rises.
12. What are the apparent effects of the business cycle on employment, unemployment, and the number of individuals not in the labor force?
13. If recoveries last four times longer than recessions, what would you expect the long-term trend in real business activity to be?
14. Explain why the GDP deflator may be a better measure of inflation than the CPI.

SUGGESTED READINGS

Bresciani-Turroni, Costanino. *The Economics of Inflation.* London: Allen & Unwin, 1937.

Bureau of Labor Statistics. *Handbook of Labor Statistics.* U.S. Department of Labor, June 1985.

Economic Report of the President (annual report).

Friedman, Milton. *Dollars and Deficits.* Englewood Cliffs, NJ: Prentice Hall, 1968.

Gavin, William T., and Alan C. Stockton. "The Case For Zero Inflation." *Economic Commentary.* Federal Reserve Bank of Cleveland, September 1988.

Gordon, Robert J. "The Consumer Price Index: Measuring Inflation and Causing It." *Public Interest* 59 (Spring 1981): 112–34.

Triplett, Jack E. "The Measurement of Inflation: A Survey of Research on the Accuracy of Price Indexes." In *Analysis of Inflation,* edited by Paul H. Earl. Lexington, MA: Lexington Books, 1975, chap. 2.

"Watching For Recovery," *The Margin* (Fall 1991).

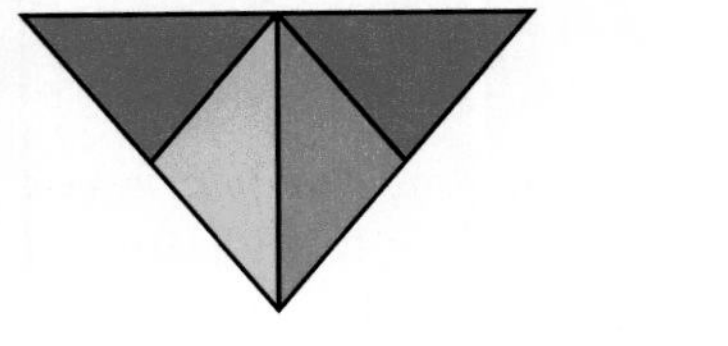

7

Measuring Gross Domestic Product

CHAPTER INSIGHT

Each year both individuals and companies must sort through many receipts and records to determine how much income to report to the IRS. Some individuals perform their own calculations; others seek the assistance of professional accountants. In large corporations, a whole department may be devoted to tracking such information. For an entire economy, consisting of more than two hundred million persons and several million firms, the enormity of this task is staggering. Yet, it is necessary to keep track of how much an economy produces. The total output of the economy, or gross domestic product (GDP), indicates the path of the business cycle. The ups and downs of GDP explain the ups and downs of employment and unemployment, as well as changes in inflationary pressures.

This chapter will explain how to measure GDP; it will also explain the relationships between an economy's total output and total income, saving and income, and saving and investment. It shows the various ways to measure the total output of the economy, explains the difference between real and nominal output, and discusses the items that are not included in the measure of total output.

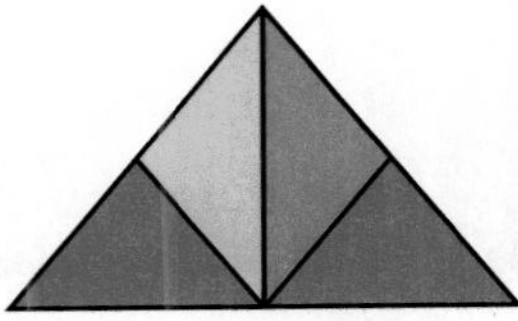

NATIONAL INCOME ACCOUNTING

Statisticians, government officials, and private economists puzzled for many years about how to measure the total output of an economy. After World War II, agreement was reached on a method of **national income accounting.** (See Example 1.)

> **National income accounting** defines and measures the total output of an economy and distinguishes the components of the total output.

The Circular Flow

The circular-flow diagram introduced in Chapter 3 illustrates the most important principle of national income accounting: *The value of total output equals the value of total income.* According to this identity, if the economy produces a total output of $500 billion, then a total income of $500 billion will automatically be created in the process. Let's consider why.

In producing output, costs are incurred. Workers and capital costs must be paid, and land must be rented. The business owners receive any profits that remain after all costs are met. The act of producing goods and services, therefore, creates income for those supplying the factors of production. The presence of this income prevents the value of output from exceeding or falling short of the sum of factor payments. If $500 billion worth of output is produced and sold but only $450 billion is paid to (or earned by) the factors of production, the $50 billion remaining is profit for the owners of business firms; profits are income, just like wages, rents, and interest. If $500 billion worth of output is produced and sold but $550 billion is paid to the factors of production, the $50 billion difference falls on business owners as losses, thereby reducing their income.

EXAMPLE 1 Simon Kuznets, the Father of National Income Accounting

Simon Kuznets is called the father of national income accounting. The methodologies that Kuznets worked out for measuring the total output of the economy, supported by his own studies of U.S. national output and the U.S. business cycle, were adopted by the Department of Commerce and later by the United Nations. Virtually all countries (except the communist countries) use common accounting procedures to determine their GDPs, thanks in large part to Kuznets. In 1971, he was awarded the Nobel Prize in economics for his pioneering work in national income accounting.

Born in Russia, Kuznets headed a statistical office in the Ukraine during the early years of Soviet rule. He later emigrated to the United States and received his Ph.D. from Columbia in 1926. Kuznets was a member of the research staff of the influential National Bureau of Economic Research. During World War II, he was associate director for Planning and Statistics of the U.S. War Production Board. He served as president of the American Economic Association and the American Statistical Association. After teaching at the University of Pennsylvania and John Hopkins, Kuznets joined the Harvard faculty in 1960 and remained there until he retired. Kuznets died in 1985.

Colleagues say that Kuznets was happiest spending many hours bent over a calculator. In a field long devoted to deductive reasoning, Kuznets insisted on facts and measurement. These facts and measurements are particularly important to macroeconomics, which focuses on explaining aggregate output, employment, and the business cycle. Without accurate measure of output, modern macroeconomics would lack a factual foundation.

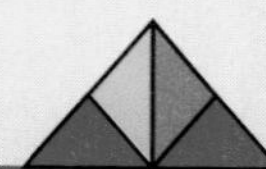

A Simple Example

Consider a simple hypothetical economy consisting of five industries, whose annual sales are shown in panel *a* of Figure 1. In this economy, steel is made from ore and coal (in addition to land, labor, and capital), autos are made from steel, and clothing is made from cotton. Goods used to produce other goods (such as the coal and ore used to produce steel) are **intermediate goods.** Goods used by final consumers are **final goods.**

> **Intermediate goods** are goods used to produce other goods, such as wheat for making flour or flour for making bread.
>
> **Final goods** are goods that are destined for final use by consumers or firms, such as bread or investment goods.

In this example, the value of final goods is the sum of the value of automobile sales and of clothing sales. There are no capital goods (such as plant and equipment) produced by this simple economy.

The circular-flow diagram for this simple economy is given in panel *b* of Figure 1. The upper part of the circle shows the flows of goods and services from businesses to households. This stream contains only the final goods—cars and clothing. The intermediate goods—ore, coal, steel, and cotton—flow from one firm to another but do not flow to households. As the cars and clothing flow to households, money payments for these final goods flow from households to businesses.

In addition to buying intermediate goods, firms must also hire factors of production—land, labor, and capital—owned by households. The bottom part of the circle in the circular-flow diagram shows the flows of the factors of production from households to businesses and the reciprocal factor payments made by businesses to households. The dollar flow of payments for goods and services in the upper half of the diagram exactly equals the dollar flow of factor payments in the bottom half.

The circular-flow diagram provides a starting point for understanding the meaning of the total output of an economy. The diagram includes only final goods in the flow of output from firms to households. Intermediate goods are not considered part of total output because they remain entirely within the business sector. Cotton is an intermediate good because it is used to produce another good, clothing. Automobiles are a final good because they are consumed by households and do not reenter the production process to produce other goods. The prices of final goods include the value of the intermediate goods used in their production.

The table in panel *a* of Figure 1 is divided into three parts. Column 1 lists intermediate goods used within the business sector; column two shows the final goods that are produced. Intermediate goods are not important in their own right; they are a means to an end. Material well-being is determined by the final goods and services that the economy produces. Column 3 will be discussed later.

Gross Domestic Product: Definition

The most comprehensive measure of the total output of the economy is **gross domestic product (GDP).**

> **Gross domestic product (GDP)** is the market value of all final goods and services produced by the factors of production located in the country during a period of one year.

A *good* is a tangible object, such as a can of peaches or an automobile, that has economic value. A *service* is an intangible product (such as a movie or an airline trip) that has economic value. In our simple economy that produces only cars and clothing for final use, GDP equals the value of the automobiles and clothing produced by the economy in one year's time. The value of automobile production during one year is $200 billion, and the value of clothing manufacture during one year is $90 billion. GDP is, therefore, $290 billion.

GDP does not include the value of intermediate goods because some products would be counted two times or more. Including them in our example results in a total of $460 billion (= $20 + $100 + $50 + $200 + $90 billion). The value of ore and coal is already counted in the value of steel, and the value of steel is already counted in the value of autos. The value of cotton is already counted in the value of clothing. The measure of total output should not count products more than once.

FIGURE 1
A Simple Example of GDP

(a) Annual Sales, Value Added, and GDP

	Value of Intermediate Goods (billions of dollars of annual sales)		Value of Final Goods (billions of dollars of annual sales)	Value Added of Each Industry (billions of dollars)
Ore, coal	20		—	20
Steel		100	—	80
Autos			200	100
Cotton	50		—	50
Clothing			90	40
Total (GDP)			290	290

(b) The Circular Flow

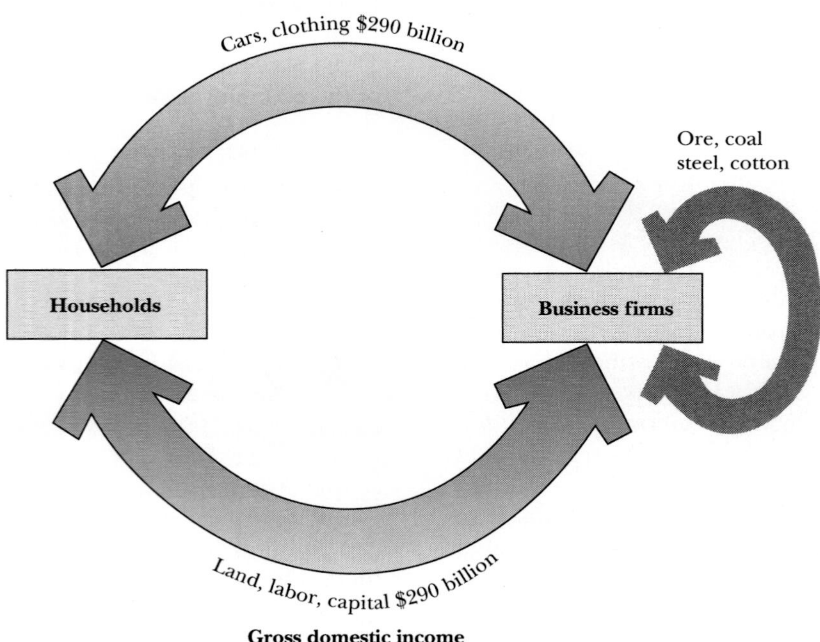

The first column of panel *a* shows the intermediate goods used to produce final goods. The arrows show the flow of intermediate goods through the production process. The second column shows the value of the final goods produced from intermediate goods and from the factors of production. GDP is the value of final goods, or $290 billion. The third column shows the value added of each industry—the value of sales minus purchases from other industries. Ore and coal and cotton are raw material industries that do not purchase materials from other industries. The value added of each industry equals its factor payments. The sum of value added ($290 billion) equals the value of final sales.

Panel *b* shows the circular flow of this economy. The upper part of the circle shows the flow of final products (automobiles and clothing) from businesses to consumers, whose personal consumption expenditures pay for the final products. The lower part of the circle shows the flow of factor services from households to businesses. Households receive payments for their factor services to equal the payments for final products in the top circle. Intermediate goods (ore and coal for making steel, cotton for making clothing) remain within the business sector and are not counted in GDP.

GDP includes only final goods. If intermediate goods were included, they would be counted more than once.

GROSS DOMESTIC PRODUCT: THE SUM OF OUTPUT OR INCOME

Because the total output of the economy equals the total income of the economy, GDP can be calculated either by summing the value of all final goods and services produced in one year or by summing all factor incomes earned in one year. Both approaches yield the same outcome. (See Example 2.)

The Sum of Final Expenditures

In Figure 1, GDP is the sum of the sales of the two final products—clothing and automobiles—produced by the hypothetical economy. In this simplified example, only one type of final product is produced: goods for final consumption by households. In the real world, there are four types of final expenditures that are summed to calculate GDP:

1. Personal consumption expenditures, C
2. Federal, state, and local government purchases of goods and services, G
3. Investment expenditures, I
4. Net exports, $X - M$

Personal consumption expenditures are purchases of food, clothing, TVs, stereos, movie tickets, plane tickets, and auto repairs. These are all expenditures on final products that are destined for use by households rather than reused to produce other goods.

Federal, state, and local government purchases of goods and services are counted as final expenditures. Governments spend money to run the legal system, to provide for the national defense, and to run the schools. Although some government expenditures strongly resemble intermediate expenditures—such as government regulation of business or agricultural extension services—by convention, almost all government expenditures for goods and services are counted as final goods and services. Because they are typically not sold to the final consumer, there is no market valuation for government services. Unlike other items that enter into GDP, government services are usually valued at the *cost of supplying* them. For example, the value of public education is taken to be

EXAMPLE 2 How GDP Is Estimated

The Department of Commerce uses two teams of economists and statisticians to estimate GDP. Each team works independently, and then the two teams meet to reconcile their estimates. As this chapter shows, GDP can be estimated by calculating either the value of final output or the total of income. One Department of Commerce team uses Census Bureau surveys of firms to estimate the total output of consumption and investment goods. To these figures are added government purchases of goods and services and net exports. The second team uses census surveys of household income and business profits to which are added depreciation and indirect business taxes.

The national income accounting identity says that the two figures should conceptually add up to the same number. In earlier years, the two teams would meet 3 days before the GDP estimate was due to reconcile differences, but with growing concern over the security of the GDP figures, now they meet only 1 day before the deadline. Although it would appear that estimating GDP is a technical business that only requires adding up numbers, in reality a great deal of human judgment must be used, especially when the estimates of the two teams disagree.

Source: Timothy Tregarthen. "Estimating GNP: A Leakproof Lockup?" *The Margin* (September/October 1988): 12.

the sum of public expenditures on education; the value of national defense is the sum of expenditures on national defense. Only government *purchases of goods and services* are counted in GDP. **Transfer payments** are not included.

> **Transfer payments** are payments to recipients who have not supplied current goods or services in exchange for these payments.

Transfer payments, as the name implies, are transfers of income from one person or organization to another. Transfer payments are made by both private and governmental organizations. An industrial corporation may contribute to a worthy charity; government may transfer income from taxpayers to poor people through welfare programs. The largest transfer payments are handled by the Social Security Administration, which transfers incomes from those currently working to retired or disabled workers and their dependents. Government interest payments are considered as transfer payments.

Investments are expenditures that add to (or replace) the economy's stock of *capital* (plants, equipment, industrial and residential structures, and inventories). Unlike intermediate goods, which are used up entirely in the process of making other goods (steel is used up to make autos, cotton is used up to make clothing), capital is only *partially* depleted in making other goods. A steel mill may have a useful life of 40 years. In producing steel in any one year, only a small portion (say, 1/40th) of the mill is consumed. The ore and coking coal, on the other hand, are entirely consumed in producing steel. A computer's working life may be seven years (before it becomes obsolete). The bank using the computer to manage its accounts uses up only a portion (say, 1/7th) of the computer in producing one year's banking services. The using up of capital is called **depreciation.** Depreciation is a business cost, just like labor costs or material costs.

> **Depreciation** is the value of the existing capital stock that has been consumed or used up in the process of producing output.

Investment is classified as either **inventory investment** or **fixed investment.** Both types increase the economy's productive capacity.

> **Inventory investment** is the increase (or decrease) in the value of the stocks of inventories that businesses have on hand.
>
> **Fixed investment** is investment in plant, structures, and equipment.

If business inventories are $200 billion at the beginning of the year and $250 billion at the year's end, inventory investment is $50 billion. Inventory investment can be either positive or negative, representing year-end inventories that are either larger or smaller than inventories at the beginning of the year.

All the final expenditures by households, businesses, and government added together do not equal the total output of the economy because some of the items purchased are produced by other countries (imported from abroad); these goods and services must be subtracted from total purchases. On the other hand, some of the domestic economy's output is exported to other countries; these goods and services must be added to total purchases. The total output of the economy is therefore the sum of final expenditures *plus* exports *minus* imports. The subtraction of imports from exports yields the *net exports* of goods and services ($X - M$).

> GDP is the sum of personal consumption expenditures, government purchases of goods and services, investment expenditures, and net exports.
>
> $$\text{GDP} = C + G + I + X - M$$

Table 1 gives U.S. GDP by final expenditure categories.

GDP as the Sum of Incomes

As noted above, the total output of the economy can be calculated either as the value of final output or as the total income created in producing that output. As the circular-flow diagram shows, the value of final goods and services produced by an economy (GDP) exactly equals **gross domestic income (GDI).**

> **Gross domestic income (GDI)** is approximately the sum of all income earned by the factors of production.

TABLE 1
GDP by Final Expenditure, 1991

Expenditure Category	Amount (billions of dollars)		Percentage of Total
Personal consumption expenditures		**3887**	**69**
Durable goods	445		
Nondurable goods	1250		
Services	2192		
Government purchases of goods and services		**1087**	**19**
Federal government	445		
State and local government	642		
Gross private domestic investment		**726**	**13**
Nonresidential structures	175		
Equipment	376		
Residential structures	195		
Inventory investment	−20		
Net exports		**−27**	**−1**
GDP		**5673**	**100**

GDI *approximately* equals GDP because GDI includes depreciation and sales and excise taxes that are not exactly payments to the factors of production.

With GDP = GDI, GDP can be calculated either by adding up the incomes earned by the factors of production located in the country or by summing the incomes paid out by producing enterprises. Both methods yield the same total. In the example of a hypothetical economy in Figure 1, the contribution to GDP produced by any one industry—by ore and coal, by steel, by automobiles, by cotton, or by clothing—does not equal each industry's sales because of double counting. The automobile industry's share would be overstated by this method because the dollar value of its sales includes the dollar value of the steel that it uses to produce cars. Instead, each industry's contribution to GDP is determined by calculating each industry's **net output,** or **value added.**

The **net output,** or **value added,** of a firm is the value of its output minus the value of its purchases from other firms. Accordingly, the net output, or value added, of an industry is the output of that industry minus its purchases from other industries.

Column 3 of panel *a* in Figure 1 shows that the value added of the automobile industry is the sales of automobiles ($200 billion) minus purchases from the steel industry ($100 billion). Its value added, therefore, is $100 billion. The value added of steel is the output of steel ($100 billion) minus its purchases from the ore and coal industries ($20 billion), or $80 billion. The value added of ore and coal equals its production ($20 billion) because in this example, ore and coal make no purchases from other industries. The value of industry output minus the purchases from other industries equals the payments to labor, capital, land, and entrepreneurship. Panel *a* shows that the sum of industry value added ($290 billion) is the same as the sum of the value of final products ($290 billion).

GDP can be calculated either as the value of final output minus the purchases from other industries or as the sum of incomes.

U.S. GDP is calculated as the sum of incomes in Table 2 and as the sum of industry value added in Table 3.

TABLE 2
Gross Domestic Product by Type of Income, 1991

Type of Income	Amount (billions of dollars)	Percentage
Compensation of employees	3388	60
Proprietors' income	380	7
Rental income of persons	42	insig.
Corporate profits	324	7
Net interest	481	8
Depreciation, indirect business taxes, net payments to rest of world, and other adjustments	1057	18
GDP = GDI	**5672**	**100**

REAL GDP

Because GDP is measured in dollar values, the GDP of an economy can rise either because the *quantities* of goods and services produced increase or because the *prices* of these goods and services rise. The concepts of nominal and real GDP serve to distinguish quantity changes from price changes.

GDP that is measured in current prices is **nominal GDP, or GDP in current dollars.**

> **Nominal GDP, or GDP in current dollars** is the value of final goods and services produced in a given year in that year's prevailing prices.

When nominal GDP rises, it is not immediately apparent whether the increase is a result of rising prices or increasing outputs of real goods and services. The distinction is significant because the material well-being of society is improved by increasing the output of goods and services but not when prices rise and the quantities of real goods and services remain constant. Thus, in order to compare GDP levels over a period of time, economists eliminate the effect of rising prices by measuring **real GDP,** or **GDP in constant dollars.**

> **Real GDP,** or **GDP in constant dollars,** measures the volume of real goods and services by removing the effects of rising prices on nominal GDP.

Between 1982 and 1991, nominal GDP rose from \$3.2 trillion to \$5.7 trillion, while real GDP rose from \$3.2 trillion to \$4.3 trillion (in the constant prices

TABLE 3
Gross Domestic Product by Net Output (value added), 1991

Industry	Value Added (billions of dollars)	Percentage
Agriculture, forestry, fisheries	113	2.0
Mining	45	0.8
Construction	272	4.8
Manufacturing	1032	18.2
Trasportation and utilities	408	7.2
Wholesale and retail trade	822	14.5
Finance, insurance, real estate	856	15.1
Services	1236	21.8
Government and government enterprises	877	15.3
Rest of the world	11	0.2
GDP	**5672**	**100.0**

Source: *Survey of Current Business.*

FIGURE 2
Gross Domestic Product (GDP) in Current and Constant Dollars

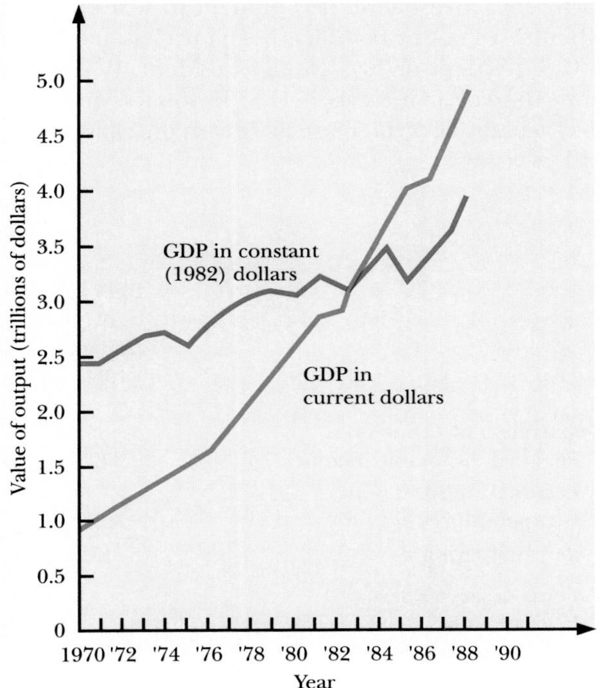

Source: U.S. Bureau of the Census.

of 1982). Nominal GDP increased 78 percent; real GDP increased 34 percent. The difference was due to rising prices. Figure 2 shows U.S. real GDP and nominal GDP over the past two decades.

Real GDP shows movements in the level of real economic activity. The amount of employment (and unemployment) in the economy is related to real GDP. Recessions occur when real GDP declines; booms occur when real GDP expands rapidly. For these reasons, macroeconomists are more interested in real GDP than in nominal GDP.

FROM GDP TO DISPOSABLE INCOME

Gross domestic product is the broadest measure of the economy's total output. (See Example 3.) GDP includes items that do not represent new production, such as depreciation, and items that do not represent income for individuals or businesses, such as indirect taxes. Moreover, GDP does not show the amount of income flowing to households because it omits transfer payments and includes items that households do not receive, such as social security payroll taxes.

Table 4 shows the step-by-step process for determining how much of gross domestic income households are actually free to spend and to save.

1. **Gross National Product (GNP).** Both GDP and GNP are defined in terms of goods and services produced, but different criteria are used to determine which goods and services to include in the calculations for each. GDP covers the goods and services produced by labor and property located in

TABLE 4
From GDP to Personal Disposable Income, 1991

Item	Amount (billions of dollars)
Gross Domestic Product (GDP) = GDI	**5672**
Factor income receipts from foreigners	135
Factor income payments to foreigners	−122
Gross national product (GNP) = GNI	**5685**
Depreciation (capital consumption)	−623
1. Net national product (NNP)	**5062**
Indirect business taxes*	−519
2. National income	**4543**
Corporate taxes, undistributed corporate profit, Social Security contributions	−1314
Transfer payments and government interest	+1607
3. Personal income	**4836**
Personal taxes	−618
4. Personal disposable income	**4218**

*Minor items, such as business payments and government subsidies, are also subtracted here.

Source: Department of Commerce, Bureau of Economic Analysis.

EXAMPLE 3 Two Ways to Measure Personal Saving

Personal saving is what remains of personal disposable income after personal consumption spending. Savers automatically increase their personal assets by the amount of their saving. If $500 is saved by a person who has no debts, and a savings account of $1000, it will show up automatically as a $500 increase in the savings account.

Government statisticians produce two measures of personal saving. The Department of Commerce calculates personal saving as what is left over from personal disposable income. The Federal Reserve Board calculates personal saving by the increase in personal net assets. The accompanying table shows that the Federal Reserve estimated 1989 personal saving at $257 billion, whereas the Department of Commerce estimated it at $172 billion, for a difference of $85 billion.

Did American families save $257 or $172 billion in 1989? Why do the methods not yield the same answer? Unreported income will not appear in the estimate of personal disposable income. By subtracting personal consumption from personal disposable income (which does not include unreported earnings), the amount of saving is understated. Unreported earnings could explain the lower $172 billion figure. The higher $257 billion figure could be the consequence of attributing too little of the $595 billion increase in financial assets to U.S. savers rather than to foreigners. With a large influx of foreign investment, it is difficult to sort out whether a stock or bond has been purchased by a U.S. resident or by a foreign resident. What appears to be an increase in U.S. personal saving may actually be an increase in foreign purchases of U.S. assets.

Measures	Billions of Dollars, 1989
Department of Commerce	
Personal disposable income	3725
Personal consumption expenditures	−3553
Personal saving	172
Federal Reserve Board	
Increase in financial assets (bank accounts, bonds, stocks, mutual funds, life insurance)	595
Investment in tangible assets (real estate, cars)	256
Net increase in debt	−594
Personal saving	257

Source: Federal Reserve System, *Flow of Funds Accounts.*

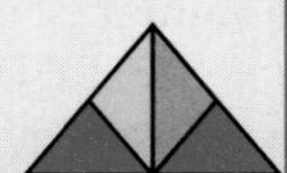

the United States. As long as the labor and property are located in the United States, the suppliers (that is, the workers and, for property, the owners) may be residents of either the United States or other countries. GNP covers the goods and services produced by labor and property supplied by U.S. residents. As long as the labor and property are supplied by U.S. residents, they may be located either in the United States or abroad.

To move from GDP to GNP one must add factor income receipts from foreigners, which represent the goods and services produced abroad using the labor and property supplied by U.S. residents, and subtract factor income payments to foreigners, which represent the goods and services produced in the United States using the labor and property supplied by foreigners. Factor incomes are measured as compensation of employees, corporate profits (dividends, earnings of unincorporated affiliates, and reinvested earnings of incorporated affiliates), and net interest. GDP measures the production taking place in that country, not the production produced by the factors of production owned by the country's citizens. Hence, GDP is regarded as a better measure of total production. (See Example 4.)

2. **Net national product (NNP).** GNP includes depreciation, the value of the capital used up in producing output. If GNP is $2500 billion and depreciation is $250 billion, then 10 percent of output simply replaces the capital that has been consumed. Net national product (NNP) measures the total value of *new* goods and services available to an economy in a given year.

Net national product (NNP) equals GNP minus depreciation.

3. **National income.** Included in NNP are a variety of sales and excise taxes—called *indirect business taxes*—that do not actually represent a payment to the factors of production. Although they augment the revenues of government, sales and excise taxes do not generate income for individuals. When indirect business taxes are subtracted from NNP, national income—or the total payments to the factors of production in the economy—remains.

National income equals net national product minus indirect business taxes. National income equals the sum of all factor payments made to the factors of production in the economy.

4. **Personal income.** Not all national income is actually received by persons as income. Corporate profits that are retained by the corporation, corporate income taxes, and social insurance contributions are not received by persons. Personal income does include transfer payments and interest payments that individuals receive from government (which, remember, are not included in GNP).

Personal income equals national income *minus* retained corporate profits, corporate income taxes, and social insurance contributions *plus* transfer payments and government interest payments.

5. **Personal disposable income.** Individuals must pay federal, state, and local income taxes. In order to determine potential spending power, income taxes must be subtracted from personal income to yield personal disposable income.

EXAMPLE 4 Gross Domestic Product as a Substitute for Gross National Product

In December 1991, the U.S. Department of Commerce announced that it would start using an alternative measure of the total output of the economy, gross domestic product (GDP). The difference between GNP and GDP is as follows: GNP measures the total output produced by American factors of production (land, labor, and capital) whether they are used in the U.S. or in other countries. GDP measures the total output produced by factors of production used in the United States, be they owned by U.S. residents or by foreign residents. For example, the salary of a Canadian hockey star playing for a U.S. team is included in U.S. GDP but not in U.S. GNP (the salary is part of Canada's GNP). The profits of an American-owned computer plant located in Taiwan are part of U.S. GNP but not part of U.S. GDP.

In the case of the U.S. economy, the difference between GNP and GDP is not great. In 1990, GDP was $5423 billion and GNP was $5465 billion. The rates of growth of real GNP and of real GDP also are very close. (See ac-

(*continued*)

EXAMPLE 4 *(Continued)*

companying figure). For other countries that have a significant number of foreign workers and a significant amount of foreign ownership, there can be large differences between GNP and GDP.

Why feature GDP? GDP refers to production taking place in the United States. It is, therefore, the appropriate measure for much of the short-term monitoring and analysis of the U.S. economy. In particular, GDP is consistent in coverage with indicators such as employment, productivity, industry output, and investment in equipment and structures.

In addition, the use of GDP facilitates comparisons of economic activity in the United States with that in other countries. GDP is the primary measure of production in the System of National Accounts, the set of international guidelines for economic accounting that the U.S. economic accounts will be moving toward in the mid-1990s. GNP, however, will continue to be used in historical statistics.

Source: "Gross Domestic Product as a Measure of U.S. Production," *Survey of Current Business,* August 1991.

New Measure of Growth

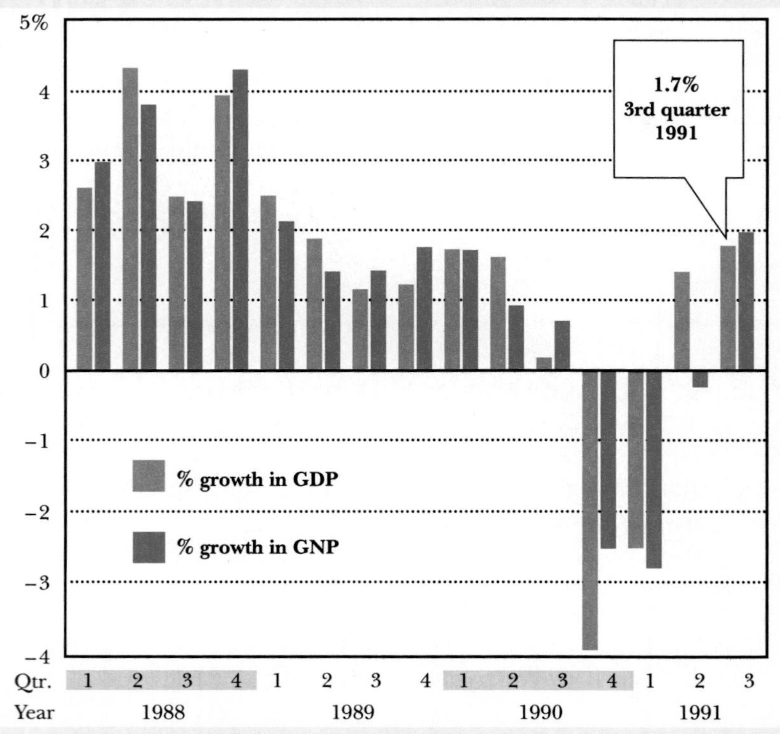

Source: U.S. Department of Commerce.

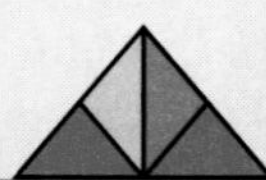

Personal disposable income equals personal income minus income tax payments.

6. **Personal saving.** Personal disposable income is the sum that persons actually have at their disposal. They can either spend it on personal consumption expenditures or they can save it.

Personal saving equals personal disposable income minus personal consumption expenditures.

Personal saving is what remains of personal disposable income after personal consumption expenditures (Remember, income tax payments are already subtracted from personal income to get disposable income). Individuals save by refraining from consumption. When individuals save, they add to their assets by increasing funds in savings accounts, buying bonds, stocks, or precious metals. Accordingly, the amount of personal savings in the economy can be determined either by subtracting personal consumption from personal disposable income or by calculating the increase in the value of personal assets.

Personal saving is achieved by refraining from consumption.

SAVING EQUALS INVESTMENT

Saving is necessary in order to carry out capital investment. Businesses invest in plant, equipment, and inventories by using their depreciation funds or retained earnings or by borrowing. At the economy-wide level, saving and investment will be equal. The equality of investment and saving does not mean that the amount savers want to save always equals the amount businesses want to invest. What it means is that forces in the economy cause the two to be equated.

Not all private saving in the economy is the personal saving of individuals. Businesses save by retaining profits that are not distributed to owners as dividends and by setting aside funds to replace capital that is depreciating. The sum of personal saving and business saving is **private saving.**

Private saving is the sum of the personal saving of individuals and of business savings (in the form of retained profits and depreciation).

Just as individuals save by not spending all their personal disposable income, so do economies save by not spending all their income. Personal saving is what is left over after consumption and income taxes. Private saving (S) equals the amount of income not spent on consumption (C) or used for taxes (T), or

$$S = \text{GDI} - C - T \qquad \textbf{(1)}$$

GDP equals the sum of final expenditures (we take the case where net exports are zero), or

$$\text{GDP} = C + I + G \qquad \textbf{(2)}$$

Because GDP = GDI, the right-hand side of equation 2 can be substituted for GDI in equation 1.

$$S = C + I + G - C - T \qquad \textbf{(3)}$$

From equation 3, one can see that investment equals the sum of private saving (S) and the government surplus (or deficit) ($T - G$).

$$I = S + (T - G) \qquad \textbf{(4)}$$

The government surplus (or deficit) ($T - G$) is *public saving*. Government is like a household (although government does not have to pay taxes). The government saves if its income (T) exceeds its expenditures (G). When this happens the government is running a surplus. The government dissaves if its income is less than its expenditures. When this happens, it is running a deficit. Deficits require government to increase its debt by borrowing.

Equation 4 shows that investment equals the sum of private and public saving (or dissaving). If investment in the economy is $200 billion, then the sum of public and private saving must also be $200 billion. If investment is $200 billion, and the government deficit is $50 billion, then private saving must equal $250 billion.

Investment can be financed through the private saving of persons and businesses and through government saving (or dissaving). A third source of investment finance—foreign saving (or dissaving)—is discussed in Example 5.

EXAMPLE 5 Foreign Saving as a Source of Investment Finance

The equality of saving and investment still holds in an economy with net exports, but **foreign saving** must be included in the calculations.

> **Foreign saving** equals imports minus exports.

Private saving (S) equals the amount of income not spent on consumption (C) or used for taxes (T), or

$$S = \text{GDI} - C - T \qquad (1)$$

GDP equals the sum of final expenditures, or

$$\text{GDP} = C + I + G + (X - M) \qquad (2)$$

Because GDP = GDI, the right-hand side of equation (2) can be substituted for GDI in equation (1).

$$S = [C + I + G + (X - M)] - C - T \qquad (3)$$

Simplifying equation (3) and solving for I, investment equals the sum of private saving (S), public saving ($T - G$), and foreign saving ($M - X$).

$$I = S + (T - G) + (M - X) \qquad (4)$$

In equation (4), ($T - G$) is *government saving* (or dissaving if a negative number). Imports minus exports ($M - X$) measures (approximately) the amount of foreign saving (if a positive number) or dissaving (if a negative number) in the domestic economy. When imports exceed exports, the country's earnings from the rest of the world (exports) are less than its expenditures (imports). The difference must be financed by a transfer of savings (mainly in the form of loans) from the rest of the world to the domestic economy.

Thus, domestic investment has three sources of financing: private saving, government saving (or dissaving), or foreign saving. As the accompanying table shows, 11 percent of U.S. domestic investment in 1990 was financed from foreign saving in the domestic economy. Federal government dissaving subtracted \$140 billion from the saving pool, while foreign saving added \$84 billion back in. Foreign saving allowed the U.S. economy to raise the amount of domestic investment by 11 percent. In effect, foreign saving allows an economy to consume more than it produces.

Categories in 1990 U.S. Saving and Investment Account	Billions of Dollars		Proportion of Investment Financed by Form of Saving	
Gross saving (including foreign saving)	795		100	
Personal saving	206		26	
Business saving (including capital-accumulation allowances)	644		81	
Government dissaving	−140		−17	
Federal dissaving		−165		−20
State and local saving		25		3
Net foreign saving from abroad	84		11	
Gross private domestic investment	705		—	

Source: Department of Commerce, *Survey of Current Business.*

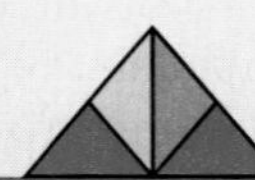

When net exports are zero, investment equals the sum of private and public saving.

OMISSIONS FROM GDP

The definition of GDP leaves several gray areas. National income economists must consider what to do with nonmarketed goods and services, including household production, illegal activities, leisure, and economic "bads."

Nonmarketed Goods and Services

Many final goods and services are not acquired through regular market transactions. Vegetables can be grown in the backyard instead of bought at the grocery store. A leaky faucet can be repaired by the homeowner instead of by the plumber. These are examples of *nonmarketed goods and services* that have been consumed without using organized markets. In most cases, GDP includes only those transactions that take place through markets. Barter transactions and production within the household are not included.

The exclusion of nonmarketed goods and services can have a substantial effect on the size of GDP. Life insurance companies advise families to carry life insurance on homemakers because it would cost the family tens of thousands of dollars per year to replace the homemaker. If services performed by homemakers were purchased—if dirty clothes were taken to the laundry or if babysitters were hired—these services would enter GDP. The inclusion of homemakers' services would raise GDP dramatically. There are currently more than 29 million homemakers in the United States. If each produces household services worth, say, $30,000 per year, then the total value of their services would equal $870 billion, or 15 percent of 1991 GDP. The less-developed countries (LDCs) of Africa and Asia tend to have a larger proportion of transactions outside of organized markets. Accordingly, GDP measures tend to understate the total output of LDC economies.

Illegal Activities

GDP typically does not include illegal goods and services—such as illegal gambling, murder for hire, prostitution, and illegal drugs—even though they *otherwise* meet all the requirements for inclusion in GDP: they are final products, and they are purchased in market transactions. Moonlighting activities—such as an electrician working for cash after hours—also belong to this category according to some definitions.

No one knows the exact dollar volume of illegal market activities. The available estimates of the size of the American underground economy vary considerably.

The Internal Revenue Service estimates its volume at between 6 percent and 8 percent of legal GDP; private economists estimate a range from .33 percent to 4 percent of legal GDP. Although the American underground economy is large in absolute size, it is much smaller in relative terms than in other countries, such as France and Italy, where it may reach 25 percent of legal GDP.

Should illegal activities be included in GDP? If GDP is to measure the level of economic activity, illegal economic activities would need to be included. Official GDP could show slackening production and employment when in reality activity has simply shifted from the legal to the underground economy. Government economic policies are based upon measured GDP and measured unemployment. If illegal activities are omitted, a false impression of economic activity, unemployment, and income may be obtained.

There are two basic arguments for not including illegal activities in GDP. First, it is impossible to obtain reliable statistics on the underground economy. Second, because most underground activities are illegal, legislators, at least, do not believe they raise the material well-being of society. In fact, according to prevailing legislation, such activities lower material well-being.

The Value of Leisure

The number of hours the average American works per year has declined dramatically over the past 50 years. In effect, our society has chosen to produce a smaller flow of goods and services in return for more leisure. Should GDP reflect this voluntary choice of leisure? After all, voluntary increases in leisure raise material well-being just as increases in goods and services do.

GDP would increase dramatically if the value of leisure were included. In 1900, workers in manufacturing worked, on average, a 60-hour week. By 1991, this figure had fallen to 40 hours per week. If American workers worked the same number of hours now as they did in 1900, personal income would be much larger than it actually is. The choice of leisure over higher money incomes indicates that people value leisure more than the extra earnings sacrificed.

Leisure is not included in GDP because GDP is narrowly defined to encompass only goods and services. It does not include intangibles such as the value individuals place on leisure.

Economic "Bads" and Measures of Economic Welfare

GDP measures only the final goods and services that an economy produces; it is not a measure of well-being. What if these goods and services are not economic goods but *economic "bads"*? Many "bads" are already excluded because they are illegal, but what about legal "bads" such as air, water, and noise pollution? What about the prison camps common in totalitarian countries or the cures sold by medical quacks? Economic "bads" such as pollution are particularly troublesome. Economists have long recognized that polluters, whether they be individuals or firms, do not bear the full costs of their polluting activities. Society must pay some of these costs.

Economic "bads" have caused some economists to argue for a different measure of total output, called the *measure of economic welfare.* The measure of economic welfare would subtract the value of economic "bads" from the value of economic goods. An accepted method of calculation, however, does not yet exist. How does one know whether something enters the measure of economic welfare as a plus or a minus and what its numerical value should be?

GDP IN INTERNATIONAL PERSPECTIVE

How large is American GDP relative to that of other economies? To make this comparison, the GDPs of the United States and of other countries must be calculated in a common set of prices, such as U.S. dollars. There are two approaches to such a calculation. The first is to take the other country's GDP and convert it into dollars using the current exchange rate (the number of dollars it takes to buy the other country's currency). The second and preferred approach is to convert the other country's GDP into dollars using *purchasing power parity rates.* A purchasing power parity rate shows how much real goods and service one U.S. dollar can buy in the U.S. compared to what one unit of the foreign currency can buy in that country. To give a simple example, if $1 buys four loaves of bread and 1 German mark buys two loaves, then the purchasing power rate is $1 = 2 German marks. Purchasing power comparisons can be quite different from exchange rate calculations (see Example 6).

Table 5 (which uses purchasing power parity) shows that the U.S. economy produces more output than any other economy (more than double that of Japan).

The figures in Table 5 illustrate an important point: Country size is a prime determinant of relative GDP. Thus, U.S. GDP is many times that of Switzerland because the U.S. population is 250 million and Switzerland's population is less than 7 million. Another useful measure, therefore, is **GDP per capita.**

> **GDP per capita** is a country's GDP divided by its population.

GDP per capita is a better comparative measure of a country's productivity, prosperity, and wealth.

TABLE 5
Comparisons of GDP and per Capita GDP, 1990

	GDP (billion 1990 U.S. dollars)	GDP per Capita (1990 dollars)
United States	5465	21,840
Australia	254	14,941
Canada	517	19,885
Japan	2115	17,056
Sweden	138	16,235
Switzerland	126	18,806
France	874	15,607
Germany (West)	1016	16,655
United Kingdom	858	15,053

Source: *Handbook of Economic Statistics 1991,* 34.

EXAMPLE 6 Is the United States Still the World's Richest Country?

The text described two ways of computing relative GDP. One method uses exchange rates to convert foreign GDP into U.S. dollars. The other method uses purchasing power parity rates to convert foreign GDP into U.S. dollars. The two approaches can yield quite different results when exchange rates do not reflect purchasing power. In the early 1990s, the U.S. dollar was "undervalued" in foreign exchange markets; that is, the market exchange rates at which foreign currencies exchanged for dollars were below the dollar's purchasing power. For example, one U.S. dollar exchanged for 1.6 German marks even though one dollar could buy more goods and service in the United States than 1.6 German marks could buy in Germany.

The accompanying table shows that the United States remained the world's "richest" country on the basis of purchasing power parity calculations of per capita GDP in 1990. However, using exchange rates, the United States fell below a number of countries. Most economists, however, believe that purchasing power parity better reflects relative output.

	Exchange Rate	Purchasing Power
U.S.	100	100
Belgium	90	80
Denmark	117	74
France	97	83
Germany	109	87
Italy	87	67
Japan	107	87
Netherlands	84	72
United Kingdom	79	67

Source: *Handbook of Economic Statistics, 1991,* 56.

It shows how much output is available, on average, for each man, woman, and child in the country. On a per capita basis, the United States is still the world's richest country, followed closely by Canada and Switzerland.

This chapter explained how the economy's total output is measured and described its components. The next chapter will examine macroeconomic behavior.

SUMMARY

1. National income accounting measures the total output of the economy. The value of total output equals the value of total income because the act of producing output automatically creates an equivalent amount of income. Gross domestic product (GDP) is the broadest measure of the total output of the economy. GDP is the dollar value of all final goods and services produced by an economy during a one-year period. Only final goods and services are included, in order to avoid the double counting of products.

2. GDP can be calculated by measuring the total value of final products or by measuring the total value of income. The total value of income can be calculated as the sum of factor payments or as the sum of the value added by all industries. Therefore, the three methods for computing GDP are

a. GDP = Personal consumption expenditures + Government expenditures for goods and services + Investment + Net exports.

b. GDP = Compensation of employees + Proprietors' income + Rental income + Corporate profits + Interest + Depreciation + Indirect business taxes.

c. GDP = The sum of the value added of all industries. Value added equals the value of output minus purchases from other sectors. Value added also equals the sum of factor payments made by the sector.

3. Nominal GDP is the value of final goods and services in current market prices. Either increasing output or rising prices can cause nominal GDP to rise. Real GDP measures the volume of real output by removing the effects of changing prices.

4. Gross national product (GNP) measures the output produced by factors of production owned by a country's citizens, whether these factors are used at home or abroad. Net national product (NNP) equals GNP minus depreciation. National income equals NNP minus indirect business taxes. Personal income equals national income *minus* factor payments not received by individuals and social insurance contributions *plus* transfer payments. Personal disposable income equals personal income minus personal taxes.

5. Saving and investment are equal by definition. Investment is the addition to the economy's stock of capital. Saving is that portion of income that is not spent on consumption and taxes. Saving equals the sum of private saving and government saving (or dissaving).

6. Nonmarketed goods, illegal goods, and the value of leisure are not included in GDP. Some economists argue that the appropriate measure of total output is the measure of economic welfare, which equals GDP minus the cost of economic "bads."

7. The United States is the world's largest economy and has the world's highest per capita income.

KEY TERMS

national income accounting
intermediate goods
final goods
gross domestic product (GDP)
transfer payments
depreciation
inventory investment
fixed investment
gross domestic income (GDI)
net output
value added
nominal GDP
real GDP
gross national product (GNP)
net national product (NNP)
national income
personal income
personal disposable income
personal saving
private saving
foreign saving
GDP per capita

QUESTIONS AND PROBLEMS

1. The economy produces final goods and services valued at $500 billion in 1 year's time but sells only $450 billion worth. Does this result mean that the value of final output does not equal the value of income?
2. Discuss the implications (in Figure 1) of $5 billion worth of coal being purchased directly by households to heat their homes. Assume nothing else in Figure 1 changes. How and why will this change affect GDP? Will it affect value added?
3. An industry spends $6 million on the factors of production that it uses (including entrepreneurship). It sells $10 million worth of output. How much value added has this industry created, and how much has this industry purchased from other industries?
4. Explain why investment is regarded as a final product even though it is used as a factor of production to produce other goods.
5. A large corporation gives a grant to a classical musician to allow her to train her skills in Europe. How will this payment enter into GDP? Into personal income? Will this payment differ from one made to an engineer employed by the corporation?
6. Which of the following investment categories can be negative: inventory investment, fixed investment, or net fixed investment (gross investment minus depreciation)? Explain your answer.
7. Explain why GDP measures may tend to overstate the GDP of rich countries relative to poor countries.
8. Personal disposable income is $100 billion, personal consumption expenditures are $80 billion, taxes are $40 billion, and government expenditures for goods and services are $50 billion. Net exports equal $0, and there is no business saving. How much total saving is there in the economy? How much is private saving?
9. In an economy, $300 billion worth of final goods and services are purchased. Explain under what conditions GDP will be more or less than $300 billion.
10. Calculate GDP, net national product, and national income from the following data: consumption equals $100 billion; investment plus

government spending equals \$50 billion; net exports equal \$0; depreciation equals \$10 billion; indirect business taxes equal \$5 billion.

11. In year 1, nominal GDP was \$200 billion. In year 2, nominal GDP was \$300 billion. In year 1, the general price index was 100. In year 2, the general price index was 125.
    a. Express year 2 GDP in the prices of year 1.
    b. Calculate the growth of real GDP.
12. What happens to measured GDP when a person marries his or her housekeeper?
13. Explain why illegal goods are not counted in GDP.
14. In Nevada gambling is legal, whereas in most other states it is illegal. If one were to measure Nevada's final output, would it be necessary to include the net income produced by the gambling industry? What would happen to measured U.S. GDP if gambling were legalized in all states?
15. A corporation earns a profit of \$10 million. It distributes \$4 million of this profit to its shareholders. It also sets aside in its depreciation accounts a sum of \$6 million to replace depreciating capital. How much money has this corporation saved?
16. In 1992, the federal government spent more than it took in as revenues. The revenues of state and local governments, however, exceeded their expenditures. Which government units were saving and which were dissaving? How would total government saving or dissaving be calculated?

SUGGESTED READINGS

Adams, F. G. *National Accounts and the Structure of the U.S. Economy*. New York: General Learning Press, 1973.

Kuznets, Simon. *Modern Economic Growth*. New Haven, CT: Yale University Press, 1966, chap. 1.

Ruggles, Richard, and Nancy D. Ruggles. "Integrated Economic Accounts for the United States, 1947–1980." *Survey of Current Business* 62 (May 1982): 1–12.

Tanzi, Vito. "Underground Economy Built on Illicit Pursuits Is Growing Concern of Economic Policymakers." *International Monetary Fund Survey*, February 4, 1980.

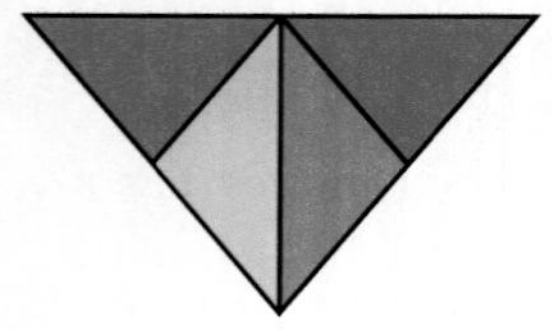

8 Macroeconomic Behavior

CHAPTER INSIGHT

It is said that the world revolves around money. This chapter is about the money people spend and the money people hold. How people and firms behave with respect to spending and holding money is a crucial factor in determining the behavior of the macroeconomy.

The last chapter examined the composition of GDP. About 80 percent of GDP consists of consumption and investment expenditures. The rest mainly represents government expenditures. Understanding the basic patterns of consumption and investment behavior, therefore, is important in understanding the entire macroeconomy. This chapter will focus on the various factors that can cause consumption and investment to change. Government spending will be studied in Chapter 12.

This chapter will also take a first look at the subject of money, that which people spend. We shall see that the main link between money and spending is the rate of interest. Later chapters will discuss how the amount of money in the economy is determined.

This chapter contains many of the ideas developed by John Maynard Keynes (1883–1946), whose 1936 book, *The General Theory of Employment, Interest, and Money* forced economists to begin thinking in terms of aggregates like GDP, consumption, investment, money, and the rate of interest.[1]

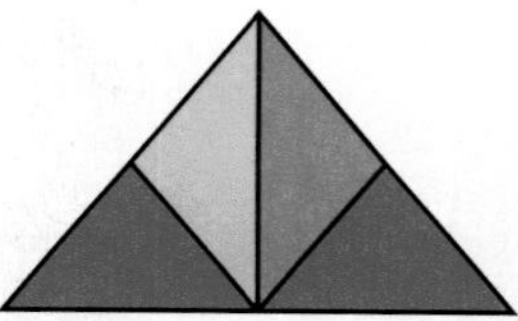

CONSUMPTION, INCOME, AND SAVING

Of every dollar of disposable income in the U.S. economy, an average of $0.93 is spent on personal consumption—on purchases of food, clothing, shelter, services, and durable goods such as cars, TV sets, and refrigerators. Two facts characterize consumption and income. First, as income increases, people increase their consumption. If your income goes up by $1000, you are likely to increase your consumption spending. What is true for individuals is true for the economy. As aggregate income increases, so does aggregate consumption. Second, for the economy as a whole (but perhaps not for a particular individual) consumption does not increase as much as income. If your income goes up by $1000, your consumption will likely increase by less than the full $1000. Part of the increase in income will find its way into an increase in saving. The same is true for the economy as a whole. An increase in income will cause consumption to increase by less than the increase in income.

These two facts are illustrated in Table 1, which provides data on GDP (Y), consumption spending (C), and saving (S), for a hypothetical economy with no government spending, no taxes, and zero net exports. (Later on, we show what happens when there is government spending, taxes, and net exports.) *All variables are in real terms.* Because there are no taxes, every dollar earned is available as disposable income for either consumption or saving. In this special case, GDP equals disposable income.

Consumption varies with income. When income is $100 billion, then consumption is $125 billion, and saving is −$25 billion. At this level of income, households are borrowing or drawing down their financial assets (savings accounts, stocks, bonds). When income rises from $100 billion to $200 billion, consumption rises by $75 billion, to a total of $200 billion. At this income level, households are

TABLE 1
The Consumption/Income and Saving/Income Schedules

Output = Income, Y (1)	Consumption, C (2)	Saving, S (3)
100	125	−25
200	200	0
300	275	25
400	350	50
500	425	75
600	500	100

Columns 1 and 2 show the consumption/income schedule in billions of dollars. There are no taxes, so income and disposable income are the same. The marginal propensity to consume (MPC) is 0.75; the marginal propensity to save (MPS) is 0.25. The average propensity to consume (APC) varies: it is 1 when Y = 100 and 0.85 when Y = 500. The data in the three columns are graphed in Figure 1. Panel *a* graphs the consumption/income schedule; panel *b* graphs the saving/income schedule.

just breaking even. A further increase in income from $200 billion to $300 billion raises consumption spending to $275 billion. Households are now more than breaking even; they have unspent income left over for saving. At $300 billion, saving is a positive $25 billion.

The schedules displayed in Table 1 are the **consumption/income schedule** and the **saving/income schedule**.

> The **consumption/income schedule** shows the amount of desired consumption at different levels of income.
>
> The **saving/income schedule** shows the amount of desired saving at different levels of income.

These schedules typically show consumption and saving out of *disposable income.*

The Average Propensity to Consume

To fully understand the consumption/income relationship we must distinguish between the average amount of income devoted to consumption and the

[1]Keynes was one of the intellectual giants of the twentieth century, making contributions to mathematics, philosophy, and economics. He was a shrewd investor, sponsored the arts, advised governments, helped manage banks and insurance companies, edited a major economics journal, helped set up the International Monetary Fund, wrote a syndicated newspaper column, and, in the meantime, revolutionized the study of economics.

extra amount of additional income devoted to consumption. The **average propensity to consume (APC)** is simply consumption as a fraction of income, or C/Y. In Table 1, when income is \$100 billion, consumption is \$125 billion, and APC = 125/100 = 1.25. When income is \$400 billion, consumption is \$350 billion, and APC = 350/400 = .875. Notice that as income rises, APC falls. This reflects the basic economic fact that the richer people are, the smaller the fraction of their income they devote to consumption.

> The **average propensity to consume (APC)** is consumption divided by income, or C/Y.

The Marginal Propensity to Consume

The average propensity to consume describes consumer behavior at a given moment in time, but it gives us no clue about what consumers will do if their income increases or decreases. In the consumption/income schedule in columns 1 and 2 of Table 1, whenever income increases by \$100 billion, consumption increases by \$75 billion. Hence, in this hypothetical economy, every additional \$1 of income increases desired consumption by \$0.75. The fraction of additional income that is spent on consumption is called the **marginal propensity to consume (MPC)**.

> The **marginal propensity to consume (MPC)** is the change in desired consumption (C) per \$1 change in income (Y).
>
> $$\text{MPC} = \frac{\Delta C}{\Delta Y}$$

The Greek delta symbol (Δ) placed before a variable is simply shorthand for "the change in" that variable.

At the beginning of this chapter, we noted that the average propensity to consume in the American economy is around 0.93. What is the marginal propensity to consume? The answer depends on whether we are concerned about the short run (one year) or the long run (5 to 10 years). If there is an increase in income this year, the effect on consumption will be smaller than if there is an increase in income that is expected to be maintained for the next 10 years. Thus, the long-run MPC should exceed the short-run MPC. The best estimates are that the long-run MPC is about 0.92 (close to the APC), whereas the short-run MPC is about 0.72. Thus, the hypothetical example in Table 1 should be regarded as approximating the short-run consumption/income schedule.

The Marginal Propensity to Save

In the hypothetical economy of Table 1, whenever income increases, saving increases as well. The saving/income schedule given by columns 1 and 3 shows that saving increases by \$25 billion for every \$100 billion increase in income. Every extra \$1 of income increases desired saving by \$0.25. The fraction of the increase in income that is saved is called the **marginal propensity to save (MPS)**. (See Example 1.)

> The **marginal propensity to save (MPS)** is the change in desired saving (S) per \$1 change in income (Y)
>
> $$\text{MPS} = \frac{\Delta S}{\Delta Y}$$

When there are no taxes in the economy (as in this hypothetical example), an additional dollar of income is either consumed or saved. Hence,

$$\text{MPC} + \text{MPS} = 1$$

When some income is spent on taxes, income and disposable income are no longer one and the same. It is, therefore, useful to refer to the marginal propensity to consume *out of disposable income* and the marginal propensity to save *out of disposable income.* If MPC and MPS are defined in relation to disposable income, then it is always true that MPC + MPS = 1.

The consumption/income and saving/income schedules of Table 1 are graphed in Figure 1. Consider first the consumption/income schedule in panel *a* of Figure 1. The slope of the consumption/income curve equals the MPC. For example, when Y increases from 200 to 300, C increases from 200 to 275, for an MPC of 0.75 (75/100). The steeper the slope, the higher the MPC. The 45-degree line from the origin has the property that any point on it is the same distance from both axes. For example, the vertical line drawn from an income of \$600 billion on the horizontal axis to the 45-degree line is the same length as a horizontal line drawn from a consumption spending level of \$600 billion on the vertical axis to the 45-degree line. If the consumption/income curve coincided with the 45-degree line, all income would be spent on consumption at every level of income. The vertical distance between the C curve and the 45-degree line measures saving, which is the difference between income and consumption. By comparing the 45-degree reference line with the consumption/income curve, the amount of saving at each level of income can be read directly from the diagram. For example, at an income level of \$600 billion, saving is \$600 billion (Y) minus \$500 billion (C), or \$100 billion (S).

The intersection of the 45-degree reference line and the consumption/income curve (point a) is a very useful reference point. To the right of point a, saving is positive because consumption is below income. For example, when income is \$400 billion, consumption is \$350 billion, and saving is \$50 billion. To the left of point a, the economy is **dissaving** (saving is negative) because income is less than consumption spending. For example, when income is \$100 billion, consumption is \$125 billion, and saving is −\$25 billion.

> The economy is **dissaving**—total saving is negative—when consumption spending exceeds disposable income. The economy is either increasing its indebtedness or financing consumption by drawing down its savings.

At point a, the economy is neither saving nor dissaving; saving equals zero. In our example, the intersection occurs at an income level of \$200 billion. At this income, the vertical distance to the 45-degree line is the same height as the vertical line to the consumption/income curve. Income and consumption are the same; no income is left over for saving.

The corresponding relationship between saving and income is graphed in panel b. The saving/income curve shows the amount of saving at different levels of income. The slope of the saving/income curve shows the MPS. Saving is zero when income is \$200 billion. For income greater than \$200 billion, saving is positive; for income less than \$200 billion, saving is negative (there is dissaving). Like the consumption/income curve, the saving/income curve is positively sloped.

EXAMPLE 1 Marginal Propensities to Save in International Perspective

Keynesian economics uses the marginal propensity to consume and the marginal propensity to save as cornerstones of aggregate expenditure analysis. What do the marginal propensities of different countries look like? The accompanying table shows the marginal propensities to save that have been calculated from national family budget studies of a number of countries. The table shows a wide range of MPSs for different countries. There appears to be no apparent country pattern. A wealthy country like Switzerland has the same MPS as a poor country like India.

Country	MPS
Belgium	.46
Israel	.42
India	.15
Canada	.35
Germany	.17
Switzerland	.15
United Kingdom	.12–.27
United States	.20–.41
U.S.S.R.	.33

Source: Paul Gregory and M. Mokhtari, "Soviet Household Saving Under Quantity Constraints," *SIP Working Paper*, November 1988. The figures cited are from Moulaert and Canniere; Sadan and Tropp; Ramanthan, Agarwala and Drinkwater; Mayer, Perry and Husby.

FIGURE 1
The Consumption/Income and Saving/Income Curves

(*a*) The Consumption/Income Curve

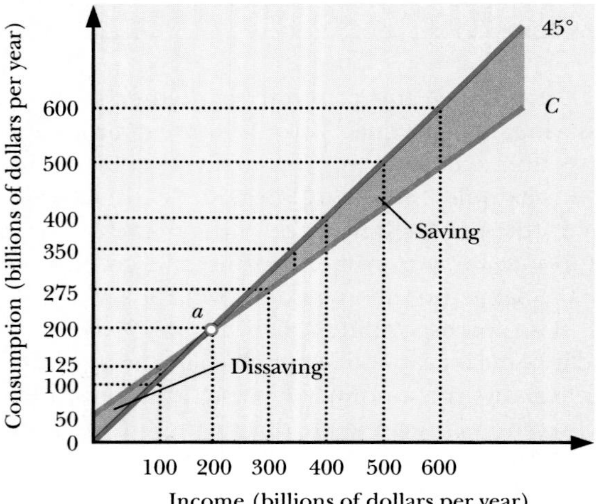

(*b*) The Saving/Income Curve

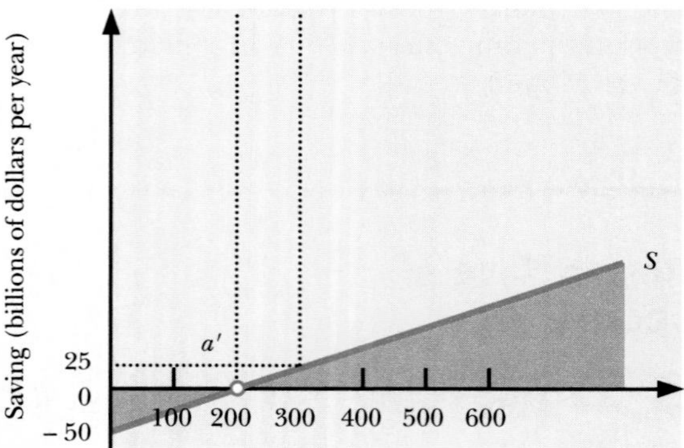

The consumption/income curve, *C*, is graphed in panel *a* from the data in Table 1 and shows the amount of desired consumption at different levels of income. The slope of the *C* curve is the marginal propensity to consume, MPC, which in our example equals 0.75.

At any income measured on the horizontal axis, the vertical distance to the 45-degree line equals that income. The vertical distance to the *C* curve equals consumption; the vertical distance between the 45-degree line and the *C* curve equals saving. At the intersection of the 45-degree line and the *C* curve (point *a*), where income equals $200 billion, saving is zero. To the right of *a*, saving is positive; to the left of *a*, saving is negative (the economy is dissaving). In panel *b*, the saving/income curve, *S*, shows the amount of real saving at each level of income. Saving is positive to the right of *a*′ and negative to the left of *a*′.

Nonincome Factors That Affect Consumption

Income is not the only determinant of consumption. A number of nonincome factors can also affect consumption. If any of these other factors change, the entire consumption/income curve will shift. It is important to distinguish between *movements along* the consumption/income curve and *shifts* in the consumption/income curve.

> A **movement along** the consumption/income curve occurs when income changes—with all other factors that affect consumption held constant. A **shift** in the consumption/income curve occurs when a factor other than income affects consumption changes.

In Figure 2, a change in income from y_1 to y_2 will cause a movement along the consumption/income

FIGURE 2
Shifts in the Consumption/Income Curve

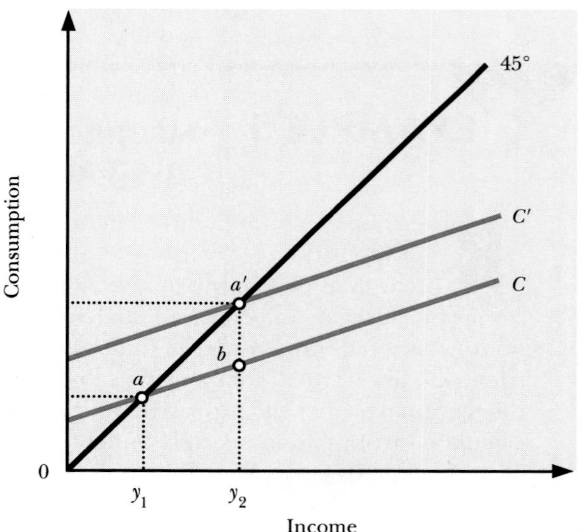

The original consumption/income curve, *C*, is drawn holding constant certain nonincome factors that affect consumption. Upward shifts in *C* are caused by increases in financial assets, reductions in the price level, reductions in taxes, a lowering of the average age of the population, a change in the distribution of income in favor of the poor, or the development of a more negative attitude toward thrift.

FIGURE 3
Saving and the Rate of Interest

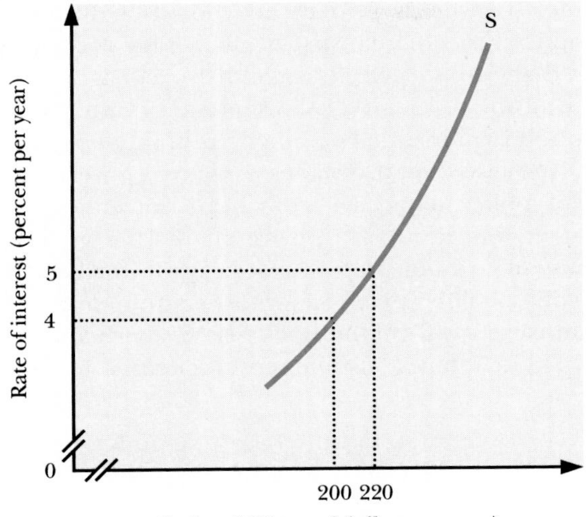

When the rate of interest increases, the amount people desire to save generally increases. An increase in the rate of interest from 4 to 5 percent might increase saving from $200 billion to $220 billion.

curve from *a* to *b*. A change in a factor other than income shifts the entire curve from *C* to *C′*. The most important factors that can cause a shift in the consumption/income curve are interest rates, expectations, stocks of assets, the price level, taxation, age, income distribution, and attitudes toward thrift.

Interest Rates. The rate of interest that people earn on their savings has a significant impact on how they allocate their income between saving and spending. The higher the rate of interest, the more expensive it is to buy a house or a car or to purchase goods with a credit card. In general, a higher interest rate encourages people to save more today in order to have more money for retirement, a vacation, or a car in the future. It has been estimated that an increase in the rate of interest from, say, 4 percent to 5 percent could increase private saving by as much as 10 percent. Figure 3 illustrates the positive relationship between the rate of interest and the amount of saving for a given level of income. A higher interest rate means, *ceteris paribus,* more saving and less consumption.

Expectations. People form expectations about how rapidly prices will rise, about the likelihood of becoming unemployed, or about whether a war will cause shortages of goods. People who feel their jobs are secure may spend more than those (earning the same income) who fear they will lose their jobs. If people become convinced that inflation will accelerate, they may increase their consumption spending—to buy before prices rise too high.

The consumption/income curve can shift upward or downward when expectations change. In the real world, inflationary expectations, for example, can change dramatically. Accordingly, the consumption/income curve shifts upward when inflationary expectations increase and downward when inflationary expectations fall.

Stocks of Assets. Changes in the wealth of consumers can also cause shifts in the consumption/income curve. The wealth of individuals is the net money value of the assets they own (stocks, cash balances, real estate). As the money value of these assets rises, people feel that they are better off, and they are likely to increase their consumption expenditures, *ceteris paribus.* When the stock market rises, stock owners may increase their consumption spending, even though their income has not changed. When wealth rises, people need not save as much out of current income to meet future needs. (See Example 2 regarding Black Monday.)

The Price Level. Financial assets, such as money, savings deposits, and money market mutual funds, are fixed in *nominal* value. Thus, when the price level rises, the purchasing power of nominal financial assets falls. As prices fall, their purchasing power rises. For example, if the price level doubles, the purchasing power of $100 in cash is reduced by exactly half.

> The higher is the price level, the lower is the purchasing power of financial assets fixed in nominal value.

When the purchasing power of financial assets increases, people who hold currency and money in checking accounts feel better off and may increase their consumption spending even if their real income remains the same. For example, if your nominal income falls by 10 percent and prices fall by 10 percent but the amount of money in your checking account remains the same, the purchasing power of your income will remain constant while the purchasing

EXAMPLE 2 Black Monday and Consumer Spending

October 19, 1987 is known as Black Monday because stock prices fell by almost one-quarter in one day's time. Personal wealth dropped by hundreds of billions of dollars. This chapter teaches that people cut back on consumption spending when their wealth declines; hence, many experts predicted that the U.S. economy would enter a severe downturn as consumption spending dropped in the wake of Black Monday. Subsequent events showed that such fears were unfounded. People continued to spend at previous rates, and an economic downturn did not materialize.

Three factors explain why Black Monday failed to have a stronger effect on the economy. First, the effect of declining stock prices on consumer spending was weak. Second, after Black Monday the stock market began a slow recovery that caused people's wealth to rise again. Third, unlike the 1929 stock market crash, as economist Christina D. Romer has pointed out, "... the last several decades of activist government policy may have convinced consumers that in the event of a severe crisis, [the government] would step in to prevent further declines." This, in effect, removed the cloud of uncertainty from the stock market crash and helped maintain consumer confidence.

Source: Christina D. Romer, "U.S. Business Cycles Between the Two World Wars," *NBER Reporter,* National Bureau of Economic Research, Inc., Fall 1988, 8–10.

power of your money holdings will increase by 10 percent. The rise in the real value of your money holdings makes you feel better off, and you might increase your consumption spending.

Taxation. As income taxes rise, disposable income falls, *ceteris paribus.* As taxes increase, one would expect less consumption spending for the same amount of income. As income taxes are cut, disposable income rises, *ceteris paribus;* thus, one would expect more consumption spending from the same income.

The consumption/income curve should shift upward when income taxes are cut. It should shift downward when income taxes are increased.

Other Factors. Other nonincome factors can cause the consumption/income curve to shift. Typically, the younger the population, the higher is the percentage of income consumed. Younger families buy washing machines, cars, and other consumer durables. They must raise and educate their children. Older families have already accumulated durable goods; their children are on their own. They spend a smaller portion of their income on consumption. To prepare for their retirement years, they build up a nest egg by saving.

High-income families have a lower average propensity to consume than poor families. If the distribution of income were changed (say, by means of a tax reform) to raise the disposable income of the rich proportionately more than that of the poor, the consumption/income curve would shift down. If the distribution of income changed in favor of the poor, the consumption/income curve should shift upward.

If public attitudes toward saving and thrift change, the consumption/income curve will shift. Although attitudes toward thrift may change suddenly, the age composition and income distribution of the United States change slowly and do not cause rapid shifts in the consumption/income curve.

THE THEORY OF INVESTMENT

Figure 4 shows that over the years, real investment spending has fluctuated more than real GDP. Why is investment so unstable? We can answer this question by looking at the determinants of business investment.

FIGURE 4
The Instability of Investment Compared to GDP

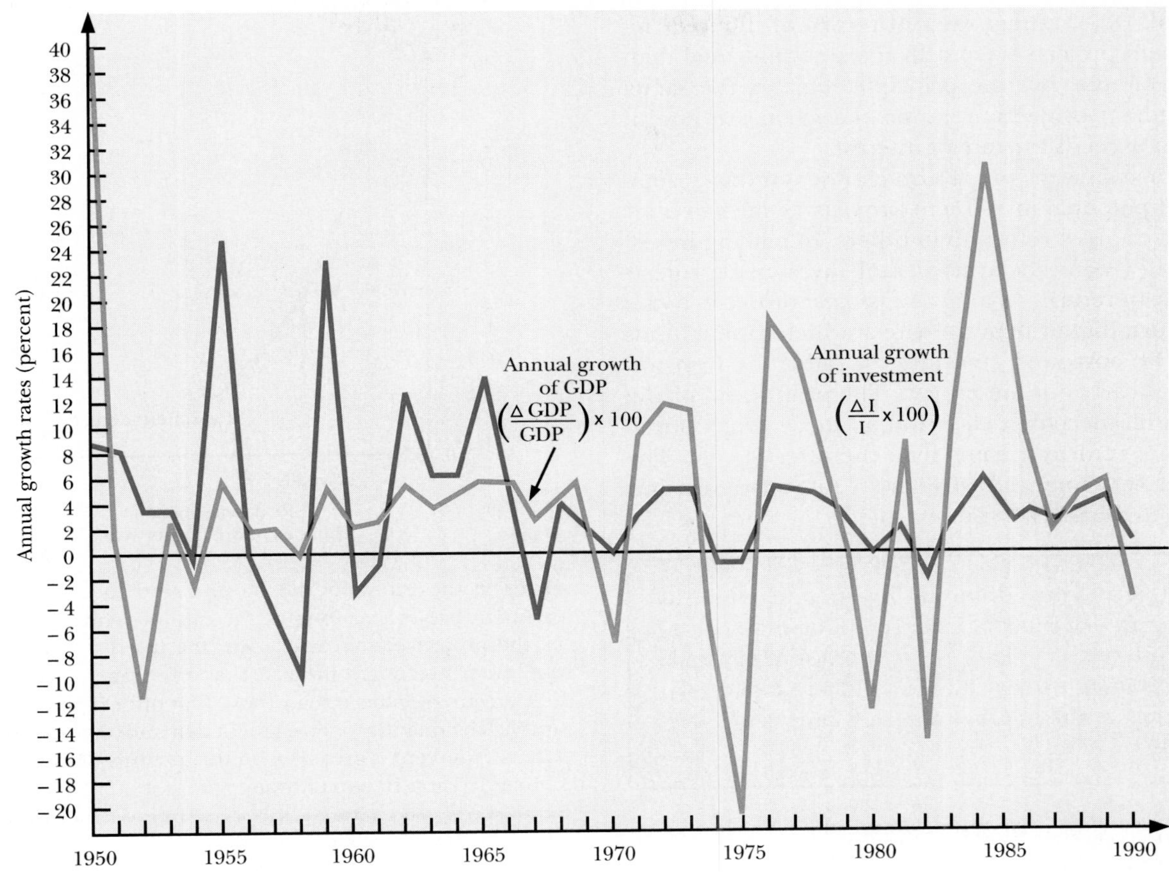

The data for the past 40 years show that the growth rate of investment fluctuates much more than the growth rate of GDP.

Source: *Economic Report of the President.*

The Investment Demand Curve

The profit-seeking firm will add to its capital stock (invest) following the same rules it follows when buying materials, renting land, or hiring labor. It compares the marginal costs and marginal benefits of acquiring more or less of the resource in question—in this case, capital.

Investment is undertaken to increase or maintain sales: The greater the increase in expected sales, the more profitable is new investment. But the firm also incurs costs when it invests. The firm's cost of acquiring additional capital is, basically, the prevailing cost of borrowing loanable funds, or *the interest rate.*

The amount of investment a typical firm will want to make at different interest rates depends upon the *rates of return* that the firm believes it can earn on the various investment projects suggested by its engineers and managers.

Suppose a $10 million investment project promises to add $1 million to profits each year for a very long (almost infinite) period. The rate of return on this $10 million investment, in this special case, is 10 percent—the annual addition to profit divided by the cost of the project. The project will be carried out if the interest rate is less than 10 percent because the rate of return will exceed the cost of acquiring capital. Determining rates of return of different investment projects is typically more complicated than this example, but the principle remains the same: Investment projects are approved when the rate of return exceeds the rate of interest.

In any given year, a firm chooses among a number of potential investment projects. Some will offer higher rates of return than others. In making investment decisions, the firm will rank investment projects by rate of return. As long as a project promises a rate of return higher than the rate at which capital funds must be borrowed (the interest rate), the firm will want to carry out the project. The profit-maximizing firm will, therefore, carry out all those projects that promise returns greater than the interest rate. The last project financed will have a rate of return just equal to the market interest rate.

Firms carry out additional investments as long as their rate of return (R) exceeds the market rate of interest (r). Therefore, the last (marginal) investment project should yield a rate of return equal to the market interest rate, such that $R = r$.

The firm's **investment demand curve** should be negatively sloped just like its other demand curves (see Figure 5). At high rates of interest, there are fewer projects that offer rates of return equal to or greater than the interest rate. The lower the interest rate, the greater is the number of investments that the business will wish to undertake. In this case, what holds for individual firms also holds for the economy as a whole: At low interest rates, there is a greater quantity demanded of investments than at higher interest rates.

The **investment demand curve** shows the amount of investment desired at different interest rates.

The negative slope of the investment demand curve illustrates that *the amount of investment increases as the interest rate falls.* In Figure 5, an interest rate of 10 percent yields an investment demand of $100 billion.

FIGURE 5
The Investment Demand Curve for an Entire Economy

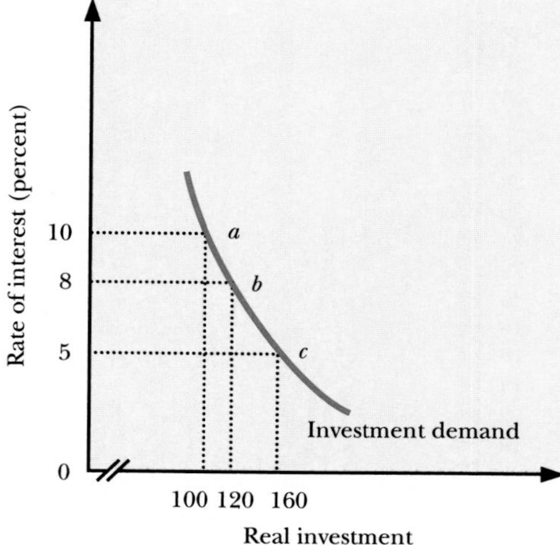

Firms in the economy will be prepared to carry out investment projects as long as the rate of return promised by the project equals or exceeds the interest rate. There are fewer investment projects that offer rates of return of 10 percent and above than those that offer 5 percent and above. The quantity of investment demanded at an interest rate of 5 percent is greater than the quantity of investment demanded at a 10 percent rate.

An interest rate of 8 percent yields an investment demand of $120 billion.

Expectations and Business Psychology

Just as expectations can influence individuals' savings and spending behavior, so can changing expectations about the future alter business investment decisions. Insofar as rate-of-return calculations depend upon perceptions of prices, costs, and profits in the often-distant future, a shift in expectations toward a more pessimistic outlook, for example, can reduce investment demand. Consequently, since the degree of pessimism or optimism can be unstable, the investment demand function might be expected to be more unstable than the consumption/income schedule.

Animal Spirits. John Maynard Keynes wrote that business psychology played a key role in determining desired investment. Keynes, however, attributed most fluctuations in business investment to disturbances in the "animal spirits" of business entrepreneurs. Shifts in investment can occur even if, on objective grounds, nothing changes in the business environment. As time passes, the captains of industry accumulate much elusive information about future products, future technology, and the future attitude of government toward business. Much of this information is qualitative and subjective. Investment demand increases or decreases when the collective intuition of business entrepreneurs turns optimistic or pessimistic. (See Example 3.)

According to Keynes, spontaneous changes in "animal spirits" mean:

> ... not only that slumps and depressions are exaggerated in degree, but that economic prosperity is excessively dependent on the political and social atmosphere which is congenial to the average business man.... In estimating the prospects of investment, we must have regard, therefore, to the nerves and hysteria and even the digestions and reactions to the weather of those upon whose spontaneous activity it largely depends.[2]

Stock Market Speculation. Keynes also believed that stock market speculation increased the instability of business investment. On the organized stock markets, company assets that have been accumulated through past investments are constantly being revalued. For example, IBM stock sold for about $160 a share in June 1987. In early 1992, IBM stock could have been purchased for about $90 a share. Although there had been no significant reduction in the capital assets of IBM, the market's valuation of these assets changed significantly. Such revaluations of capital assets can influence current investment decisions. As Keynes said, "there is no sense in building up a new enterprise at a cost greater than that at which a similar existing enterprise can be purchased" on the stock market.

If the prices of stocks are determined by irrational processes, business investment will be unstable because it responds to shifts in stock prices. According to Keynes, the stock market devoted far too much attention "to anticipating what average opinion expects the average opinion to be."

Modern experts claim that the prices of stocks roughly reflect what the company is worth at any given time. In a world of uncertainty, the financial community revalues old investments from day to day in light of the information provided by a constant stream of news about profits, technology, and opportunities. To the extent that unfolding news is misleading, it may still be the case that stock market speculation leads to excessive fluctuations in investment. According to Keynes:

> Speculators may do no harm as bubbles on a steady stream of enterprise. But the position is serious when enterprise becomes the bubble on a whirlpool of speculation. When the capital development of a country becomes a by-product of the activities of a casino, the job is likely to be ill-done.[3]

MONEY

What impact does money have on macroeconomic behavior? Money is defined as an acceptable means of payment for goods or debts. We shall see in the chapter on money, prices, and interest that the form of money can range from large stones to paper currency. In a modern economy, money consists of bank accounts and cash. Every person and firm has a certain amount of money. The key concept that economists measure is the **money supply** at any given time. We will be more precise later on, but for now we will define an economy's money supply to be the sum of the money balances of each household and firm.

> The **money supply** in an economy is the sum of all bank accounts and cash held by individuals and nonbank firms.

The money supply in each country is measured in terms of the legal currency unit. It might be the

[2]See John Maynard Keynes, *The General Theory of Employment, Interest, and Money* (New York: Harcourt, Brace and Company, 1936), chap. 12, from which all the quotes in this section are taken.

[3]Keynes, *The General Theory of Employment, Interest, and Money*, chap. 12.

EXAMPLE 3 Animal Spirits and Spending Volatility

Keynes felt that capital spending plans were characterized by "animal spirits"—wild swings from periods of optimism to periods of pessimism that affected businesses' desire to invest and consumers' willingness to purchase durable goods.

The attached figures illustrate the notion of animal spirits in two types of markets: the business market for capital goods and the consumer market for consumer durables such as automobiles and homes. Both figures are based on surveys of intentions to purchase. They show that business plans to buy capital goods vary erratically over time. One month businesses plan to expand at a rapid rate; the next month they plan to contract. Likewise, one month consumers are anxious to buy homes and cars; the next month they intend to withdraw from the market entirely.

Source: Panel *a*: U.S. Department of Commerce, Bureau of the Census. Panel *b*: The Federal Reserve Bank of Cleveland.

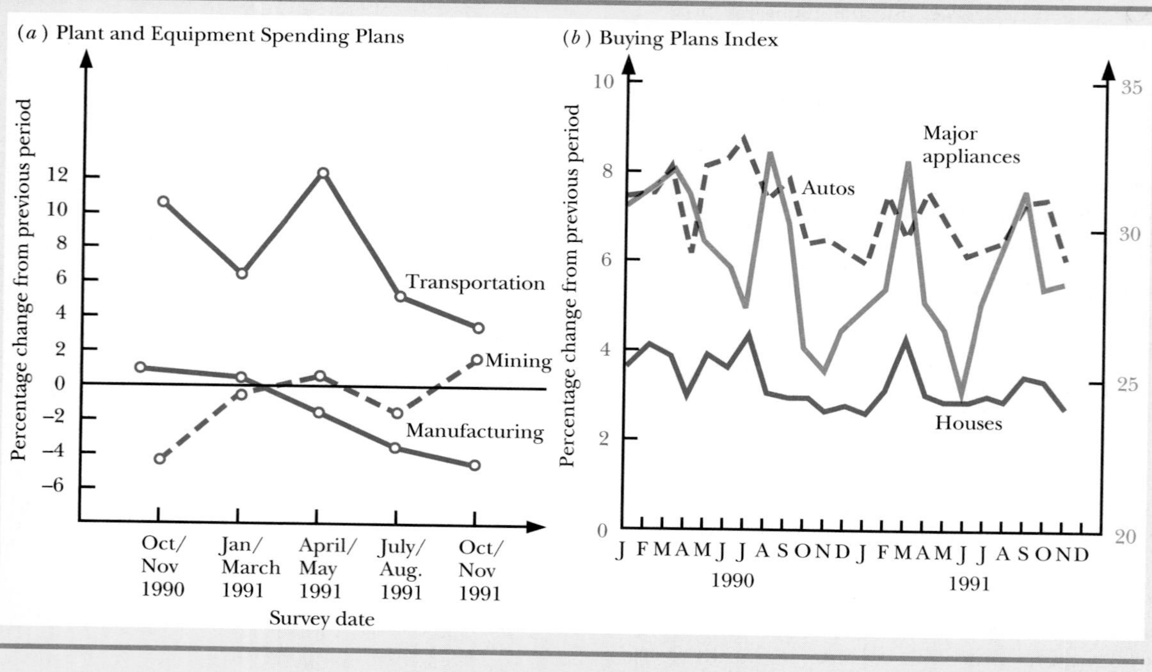

dollar, the pound, the mark, the yen, or the rial. The money supply in the United States in early 1992 was around $900 billion, or the equivalent of $3500 in bank deposits and cash for every adult and child. In the course of this book we will try to explain how the money supply is actually determined. In other words, how does money get into the economy?

For the moment we will give a very simple answer to this question. Money enters an economy through an institution that is given a monopoly over the printing of money. In the United States, this institution is the Federal Reserve System—your banker's bank (which we will examine in the chapter on commercial banking). The Federal Reserve System ultimately introduces money into the U.S. economy by *spending* the money it prints. This mechanism, which is used in some form by all countries, is as simple as the actions of an individual who, given the sole right to print money, would rush to spend it, thereby passing it on to other people.

Figure 6 shows the history of the money supply and GDP from 1981 to 1991. Notice that the money supply has more than doubled while GDP has almost doubled. Recently the ratio of the money supply to GDP has been about 15 percent. This means that for every dollar of income, people hold about $0.15 in money balances over the course of the year.

The law of scarcity means people always want more than they have. A naive question arises: Why don't we eliminate scarcity by printing more money and give it to all but the very rich? It costs only a few pennies to print a dollar. Why not print enough to enable people to buy whatever they want? This question gets to the heart of what money is and what money is not. The answer is that people sustain themselves with goods and services, not money. In turn, as we saw in the last chapter, income and output are different sides of the same coin. If you were marooned on a deserted island, with no hope of ever returning to civilization, you would happily start a fire with a $100 bill in order to cook your dinner. But you would still want to earn income by producing various goods and services such as fish, fish nets, and coconuts.

Goods are not made valuable by the money gained from their sale; rather, goods give money value. In other words, money is valuable only because we can use it to purchase goods and services. Think once again about being stranded on that island: All of your money would be worthless. Yet even though money has no intrinsic value, it is still an extremely crucial part of our economy. Modern money cannot be eaten or worn, but it can cause havoc through its relationship to spending.

The major link between the money supply and spending is the interest rate. A higher money supply (holding other factors constant) lowers interest rates; a lower money supply raises interest rates. A larger money supply lowers interest rates because, if there is more money available, people in the business of lending money must lower their interest rates to remain competitive. As discussed earlier in this chapter, lower interest rates stimulate spending on both consumer goods and investment goods.

FIGURE 6
Money and GDP

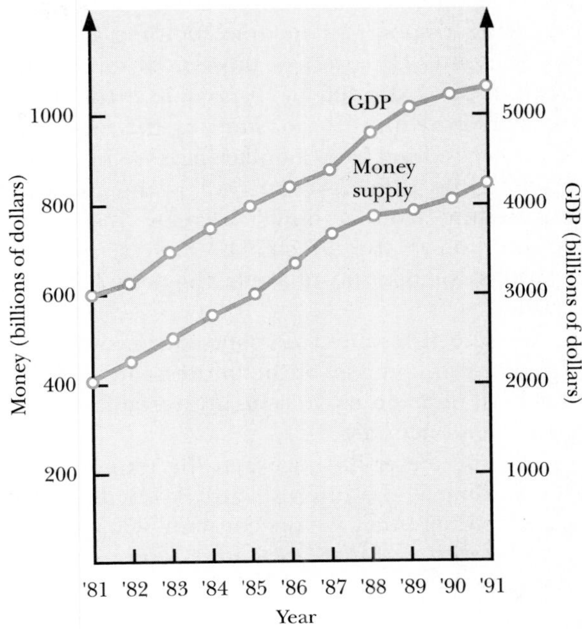

There is a strong relationship between the money supply and GDP. In the period from 1981 to 1991, the money supply tended to be about 15 percent of GDP.

Source: Department of Commerce.

There is also a direct link between the amount of money people hold and their consumption spending. The higher are money balances, everything else constant, the higher is wealth; thus, higher money balances directly increase consumption. But an extra dollar of money balances will not increase consumption by as much as an extra dollar of disposable income will. As we have seen, people spend about $0.93 out of every dollar of disposable income on consumption. But another dollar in money balances may only increase consumer spending by a few cents because a dollar in the bank earns only a few cents in income. Therefore, a dollar of income is more powerful than a dollar of wealth.

The next chapter explains the theory of aggregate demand and supply. It shows how the price level and the level of output are jointly determined in both the short run and the long run.

SUMMARY

1. The consumption/income and saving/income schedules show how desired consumption and saving respond to income, holding the price level constant. The average propensity to consume is consumption divided by disposable income. The marginal propensity to consume is the extra consumption resulting from a dollar increase in income. The marginal propensity to save is the extra saving resulting from a dollar increase in income. Consumption is also affected by interest rates, expectations, the quantity of assets, the price level, and taxation.

2. The investment demand curve shows that desired investment rises as the interest rate falls. The investment demand curve is highly unstable because the future is uncertain.

3. The major link between the money supply and spending is the interest rate. A higher money supply, holding other factors constant, will lower the rate of interest and increase both consumption and investment spending.

KEY TERMS

consumption/income schedule
saving/income schedule
average propensity to consume (APC)
marginal propensity to consume (MPC)
marginal propensity to save (MPS)
dissaving
investment demand curve
money supply

QUESTIONS AND PROBLEMS

1. If the consumption/income schedule shifts upward, what will happen to the saving/income schedule?
2. What is the marginal propensity to consume? How is it related to the marginal propensity to save?
3. Use the consumption/income schedule in Table A to answer each of the following.

TABLE A

Income (billions of dollars), *Y*	Consumption (billions of dollars), *C*
0	50
100	100
200	150
300	200
400	250

   a. Calculate the saving/income schedule.
   b. Determine the marginal propensity to consume (MPC) and the marginal propensity to save (MPS).
   c. Determine at what level of income the break-even point of zero saving is reached.
4. Explain why changes in expectations concerning the future can shift the investment demand curve.
5. How will the following factors affect the consumption/income curve or schedule?
   a. An increase in interest rates
   b. A reduction in the wealth or assets held by the public
   c. An increase in income
   d. An increase in the price level
6. In January 1991, the money supply in the United States was $827 billion; in December 1991, the money supply was $898 billion. The increase in the money supply was about 9 percent. What do you expect happened to interest rates? What happened to spending?

SUGGESTED READINGS

"Saving: Are the Japanese Beating Us?" *The Margin* (March/April 1990): 11.

Duesenberry, James S. *Income, Saving, and the Theory of Consumer Behavior.* Cambridge, MA: Harvard University Press, 1949, chaps. 3 and 4.

Hall, Robert E., and John B. Taylor. *Macroeconomics*, 3rd ed. New York: W. W. Norton, 1991, chap. 10.

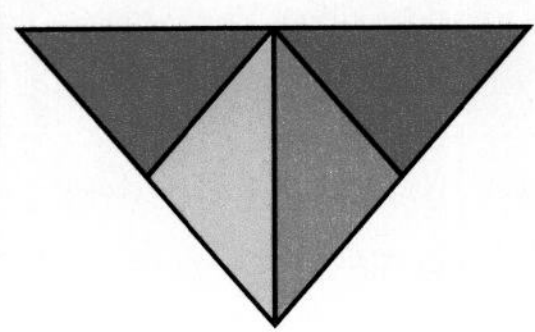

9 Aggregate Demand and Supply

CHAPTER INSIGHT

In microeconomics, the movements of prices and quantities of individual products are explained by supply and demand. Similarly, in macroeconomics changes in the overall price level and the aggregate amount of output—real GDP—are explained by the conditions of aggregate demand and aggregate supply. For example, between 1933 and 1942 real GDP more than doubled, whereas it took a quarter of a century for real GDP to double from 1966 to 1991. The source of the difference between these two historical episodes lies in the concept of the aggregate supply curve. Thus, the earlier episode was mostly due to increases in the aggregate quantity supplied out of relatively constant resources. During the 25 years from 1966 to 1991, the change in real GDP was due to growth in the size of the economy: productivity, the capital stock, and the labor force increased.

This chapter examines the mechanics of aggregate demand and supply in the short run and the long run. It shows how changes in aggregate demand can change output and prices. We address the question of whether the economy can emerge from a recession without the assistance of government.

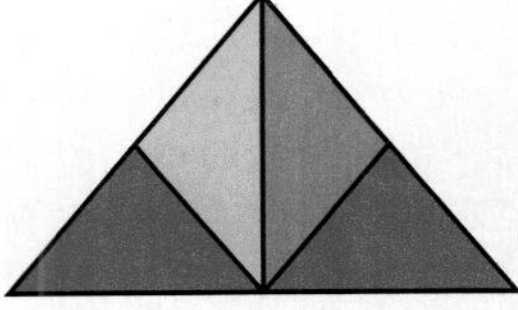

AGGREGATE DEMAND

The GDP of an economy measures its output or, equivalently, the income of its productive factors. On the income side, GDP is simply the sum of all incomes. On the output side, GDP $= C + I + G + (X - M)$. This section focuses on the basic determinants of the **aggregate demand curve (AD)**. Essentially, the aggregate demand curve shows the level of output (real GDP) that people are willing to buy at different price levels. Figure 1 shows how the demands for the various components of GDP are added to derive the aggregate demand curve. For example, the curves labeled C and $C + I$ are, respectively, demand for consumer goods at different price levels, and the sum of consumption plus investment at different price levels. The dark blue line in Figure 1 shows that the aggregate demand curve is downward sloping—the lower the price level, the higher the aggregate quantity demanded.

> The **aggregate demand curve (AD)** shows the levels of real GDP that agents (households, businesses, government, and foreigners) are prepared to buy at different price levels.

Broadly speaking, the aggregate demand curve is negatively sloped because as the price level falls, the purchasing power of the money supply increases. As a result, people feel richer, and people and firms can borrow money more easily, thus stimulating consumption and investment. A lower price level also facilitates exports to other countries.

These consequences point to three major factors that cause aggregate demand to decline as the price

FIGURE 1
The Aggregate Demand Curve

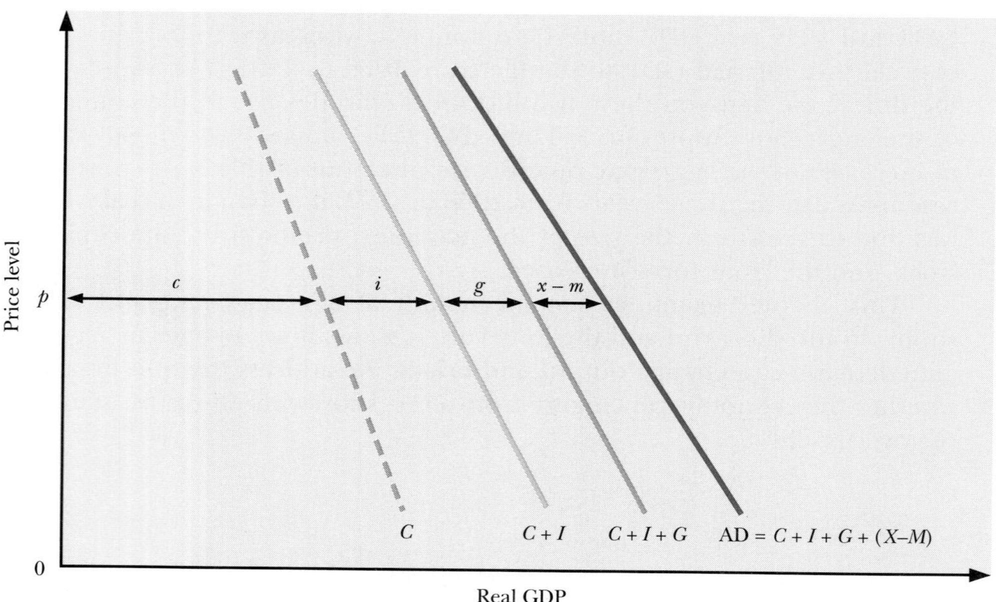

The aggregate demand curve AD $= C + I + G + (X - M)$ shows that people are willing to purchase larger aggregate quantities of goods at lower prices. At the particular price level p, people buy the quantities c, i, g, and $(x - m)$ of consumption, investment, government goods, and net exports (assumed positive for illustration purposes only), respectively. The AD curve shows a larger response to a price change than any of the components because it reflects the real-balance, interest-rate, and foreign-trade effects of a lower price level.

level rises: the real-balance effect, the interest-rate effect, and the foreign-trade effect.

The Real-Balance Effect

Individuals hold money balances as part of their individual wealth. The purchasing power of money balances rises and falls with the price level. If prices are generally falling, people realize that their money balances can buy more. Falling prices, therefore, motivate individuals with money holdings to conclude that they are better off, so they tend to increase their purchases of goods and services. Similarly, rising prices reduce the purchasing power of money balances; people conclude that they are worse off, so they reduce their purchases of goods and services. The effect of the change in the price level on real consumption spending is called the **real-balance effect.**

> The **real-balance effect** occurs when desired consumption falls as increases in the price level reduce the purchasing power of money balances, holding other factors constant.

The Interest-Rate Effect

Interest rates are determined by the demand for credit. The higher the demand for credit, the higher are interest rates. As the price level rises, the demand for credit to buy such goods as cars, plants, equipment, inventories increases; businesses and households must borrow more. This increased demand for credit raises interest rates, discouraging business investment. The **interest-rate effect** represents the change in the aggregate quantity demanded that results from changes in the level of spending on consumer durables and business investment. Thus, as prices rise, interest rates rise and real investment declines. People invest less in housing, plants, equipment, and inventories, and the aggregate quantity demanded decreases. As the price level falls, interest rates fall, investment increases, and the aggregate quantity demanded increases.

> The **interest-rate effect** occurs when desired spending decreases as increases in the price level push up interest rates in credit markets.

The Foreign-Trade Effect

As the domestic price level rises relative to foreign price levels, holding constant the exchange rate (the value of the dollar in terms of foreign currencies), exporters will face stiffer competition and imports will appear cheaper. As a consequence, exports (X) will fall and imports (M) will rise. Thus, net exports ($X - M$) will fall. For example, if the U.S. price level rises, *ceteris paribus*, American farmers can export less of their wheat and American consumers will be encouraged to buy more Japanese cars and Swiss watches. As a consequence of this **foreign-trade effect,** an increase in the domestic price level will cause net exports to fall. If the price level falls, the aggregate quantity demanded will increase because net exports will increase.

> The **foreign-trade effect** occurs when a rise in the domestic price level (holding foreign prices and the exchange rate constant) lowers the aggregate quantity demanded by pushing down net exports ($X - M$).

The real-balance, interest-rate, and foreign-trade effects cause the aggregate demand curve to have a negative slope.

The Slope of the Aggregate Demand Curve

The slope of the aggregate demand curve shows the aggregate responsiveness of the various components of demand to changes in the price level. In Figure 1, at the particular price level p, the economic agents purchase the specific quantities c, i, g, and $(x - m)$ of domestic goods. The real-balance, interest-rate, and foreign-trade effects explain why consumption, investment, and net exports rise as the price level falls. Consumption increases as the price level falls because of the real-balance effect on consumption and the interest-rate effect on the demand for consumer durables. Investment is the horizontal distance between the C curve and the $C + I$ curve; as the price level falls, the distance grows. Net exports, represented by the horizontal distance between the $C + I + G$ curve and the AD curve itself, also grow when P falls. The AD curve is flatter than the component curves because it reflects all of the reasons why the aggregate demand curve is downward sloping.

FIGURE 2
Shifts in the Aggregate Demand Curve

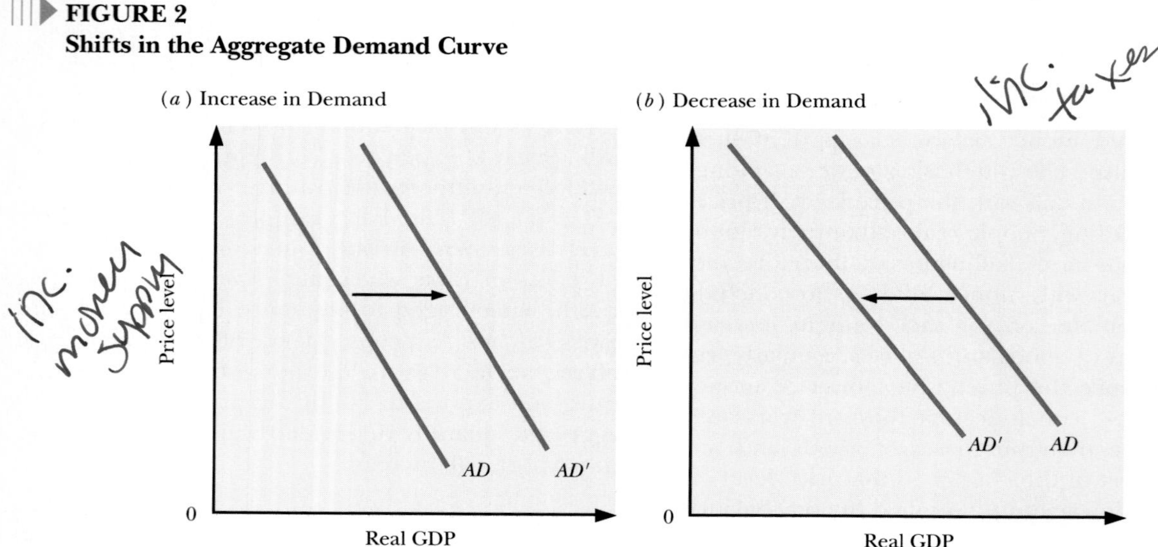

Panel *a* shows an increase in aggregate demand from AD to AD′; panel *b* shows a decrease in aggregate demand from AD to AD′.

It is clear that the aggregate demand curve will be flatter the larger the real-balance effect, the more sensitive investment is to interest, the easier it is to lower interest rates in response to credit availability, and the larger the price sensitivity of foreign trade (both exports and imports).

The Conditions of Aggregate Demand

Along the aggregate demand curve certain factors are held constant. Since government spending is a component of GDP, and private spending is influenced by the taxes that agents face, the spending and taxation policies of the government are taken as given. Private spending is also influenced by the amount of money in the economy. Since the money supply is determined in part by the government, we can say that government monetary policies are taken as given along a particular aggregate demand curve.

The aggregate demand curve also holds constant certain features of the private demand for domestic goods and services. The thriftiness and wealth of consumers must be held constant. People spend more if they become less thrifty or have greater wealth. The optimism of businesses toward the profitability of investment must also be held constant. If business firms expect greater profits from investment, they will spend more on plants and equipment. Finally, the ability of the economy to compete with the rest of the world, as represented by the costs of production and the availability of goods and services at home and abroad, must be held constant.

The aggregate demand curve will shift when any of these underlying conditions changes. For example, panel *a* of Figure 2 illustrates the effects of, say, an increase in the money supply or government spending on the aggregate demand curve: The entire curve shifts to the right. Panel *b* of Figure 2 illustrates the effects of, say, an increase in tax rates or a reduction in government spending on the aggregate demand curve: The entire curve shifts to the left.

AGGREGATE SUPPLY

The demand side of the macroeconomy rests on what output people will buy: Will people buy the output that is being produced at prevailing prices? By contrast, the supply side of the macroeconomy is based on the aggregate amounts of goods and services that are produced from the available resources with the available technology: Will businesses produce the quantity that people wish to buy at prevailing prices?

The aggregate supply of goods and services depends on the employment of labor and the productivity of labor. The greater the employment of labor, the greater is aggregate supply; the greater the productivity of labor, the greater is aggregate supply. In the study of economic growth (Chapter 22) we will focus on the determinants of labor productivity over decades (capital accumulation and technological progress). In this and the next few chapters, we focus on the employment of labor itself. To understand aggregate supply, it is necessary to investigate the natural rate of unemployment, introduced in Chapter 6.

The Natural Rate of Unemployment

The economy is in constant flux. Some industries are expanding, others are contracting. The labor force is being shuffled from industry to industry and from job to job. In a completely static economy, the full-employment level of output would correspond to that level of employment at which each and every worker would be allocated to his or her best job; unemployment would be essentially zero. Zero unemployment, however, is not possible in a complicated, dynamic economy. The aggregate levels of consumption, investment, government spending, and exports and imports constantly fluctuate. There is a constant search for new workers and new jobs.

Unemployment arises naturally from the frictions inevitably present in labor markets in which people are constantly looking for jobs and firms are constantly looking for workers. The natural rate of unemployment was defined in Chapter 6 as that unemployment rate at which there is an approximate balance between the number of unfilled jobs or vacancies and the number of unemployed workers qualified to fill those jobs. How do we know when this balance has been achieved? There is no way to estimate the match directly, but it can be determined indirectly by observing what happens to the price level (inflation) at different unemployment rates. When the unemployment rate falls below the natural rate, inflationary pressures intensify. If the unemployment rate is above the natural rate, inflationary pressures will weaken. The relationship between inflationary pressures and the unemployment rate offers an indirect definition of the **natural rate of unemployment.**

The **natural rate of unemployment** is that rate of unemployment that can be sustained without accelerating or decelerating inflation.

In the labor market, wages will behave differently at different rates of unemployment. When the unemployment rate exceeds the natural rate of unemployment (when the number of qualified people looking for work exceeds the number of unfilled jobs), the current rate of wage increase or inflation will tend to fall. When the unemployment rate falls short of the natural rate (when the number of unfilled jobs exceeds the number of qualified people looking for work), the current rate of wage increase or inflation will tend to rise.

The behavior of wages in absolute terms depends on the momentum of wages and prices. For example, suppose there is zero wage or price inflation and that the economy is at the natural unemployment rate. Wages and prices have been steady for some time, and everyone expects them to remain stable in the future. For purposes of illustration, assume that the natural rate of unemployment is 5 percent. If the unemployment rate rises above 5 percent, wages will begin to fall; if the rate of unemployment falls below 5 percent, wages will begin to rise. (See Example 1.) Only at 5 percent will wages remain stable. In another scenario, suppose wages have been rising steadily at 10 percent per year for a number of years. At the natural rate of 5 percent unemployment, this rate of wage inflation will continue. If unemployment rises above 5 percent, the rate of wage inflation will decelerate below 10 percent but still increase in absolute terms. If unemployment falls below 5 percent, inflation will accelerate above 10 percent. This illustration makes the important point that an economy can be at its natural rate of unemployment at different rates of inflation.

The natural rate of unemployment does not depend on the rate of inflation. The natural rate of unemployment is consistent with different rates of inflation.

The natural rate of unemployment depends not on the price level, but on long-run demographic and cost factors that will be discussed in Chapter 18.

EXAMPLE 1 What Is the Natural Rate of Unemployment?

The unemployment rate rose during the recession from 1990 to 1992, to around 7.4 percent by May 1992. How does this compare to the natural rate of unemployment? Recall that the natural rate is that rate of unemployment at which inflation shows no tendency to change. The natural rate can be estimated by examining the historical relationship between the inflation rate and the unemployment rate. Economists who have studied this issue tend to think that the natural rate is about 6 percent. Robert Gordon of Northwestern University has argued that the natural rate has been at the 6 percent level since the mid-1970s. By this criterion the 1990–92 recession was extremely mild. The recession provides evidence that unemployment above the natural rate drives down the rate of inflation: The rate of inflation fell from about 6 percent in 1990 to about 3 percent in 1991.

Source: "Natual Unemployment Holds Steady," *The Margin* 8 (Spring 1992): 13.

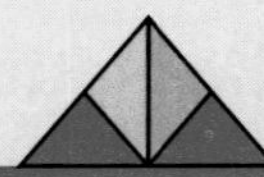

Natural Real GDP

Corresponding to the natural rate of unemployment is the **natural level of real GDP** (y_n).

> The **natural level of real GDP** (y_n) is the output produced when the economy is operating at the natural rate of unemployment.

At output levels above the natural output level, y_n, the unemployment rate will be below the natural rate of unemployment; wage inflation and price increases will accelerate. If output is below natural output, the unemployment rate will be above the natural rate; wage and price inflation will decelerate.

Consider an economy where prices have been holding steady for a number of years, where the economy is at the natural rate of unemployment, and where the real output corresponding to the natural rate is $6 trillion. If output rises above $6 trillion, prices will rise. If output falls below $6 trillion, prices will fall. Only at the natural output level will prices remain stable.

Aggregate Supply in the Short Run

In the long run (say several years), all prices and wages are perfectly flexible, both upward and downward. Example 2 shows the price levels of Germany, Great Britain, and France over the period from 1820 to 1913—before the onset of the sustained inflation experienced in modern times. Prices on the average rose about as often as they fell.

In the short run, however, some prices are not perfectly flexible. They are not free to respond to changing economic conditions because they are fixed by contract or institutional practice. For example, a firm may hire a worker with the understanding or explicit contract that the worker's wage may be changed at intervals of 3 months, 6 months, or 1 year. Some farmers might sign a contract with a miller to sell their forthcoming wheat crop at a fixed price. Over the next few months, the miller of wheat, might, in turn, face several fixed input prices from employees and from the wheat that will be turned into flour.

The wages that are fixed in the short run are powerfully conditioned by the expectations of future inflation. The future inflation rate is simply the percentage increase in the current price level to some future price level. The expected future price level (or future inflation rate) becomes an anticipated price level (or inflation rate) when it is reflected in various contracts for wages and credit. (See Example 3.)

In general, the **short-run aggregate supply curve (SRAS)** shows how changes in the price level affect the quantity of real output supplied, holding constant the anticipated price level. The SRAS curve relates the actual price level to the output that business firms are prepared to produce.

EXAMPLE 2 Long-Run Price Flexibility

The nineteenth century illustrates long-run price flexibility because it was not a period of sustained inflation. The accompanying table shows price indexes for major European countries throughout most of the nineteenth century. In France and Great Britain prices were from 10% to 20% *lower* in 1913 than in 1820. In Germany, prices were the same in 1908 as they were in 1820. As is evident, prices were flexible during that period of time, with extreme upward and downward movements in prices taking place regularly. Part of this price flexibility was due to the greater importance of agriculture in the nineteenth century. Agricultural prices tended to be more volatile than other prices in both an upward and downward direction.

Source: B. R. Mitchell, *European Historical Statistics, 1750–1970.*

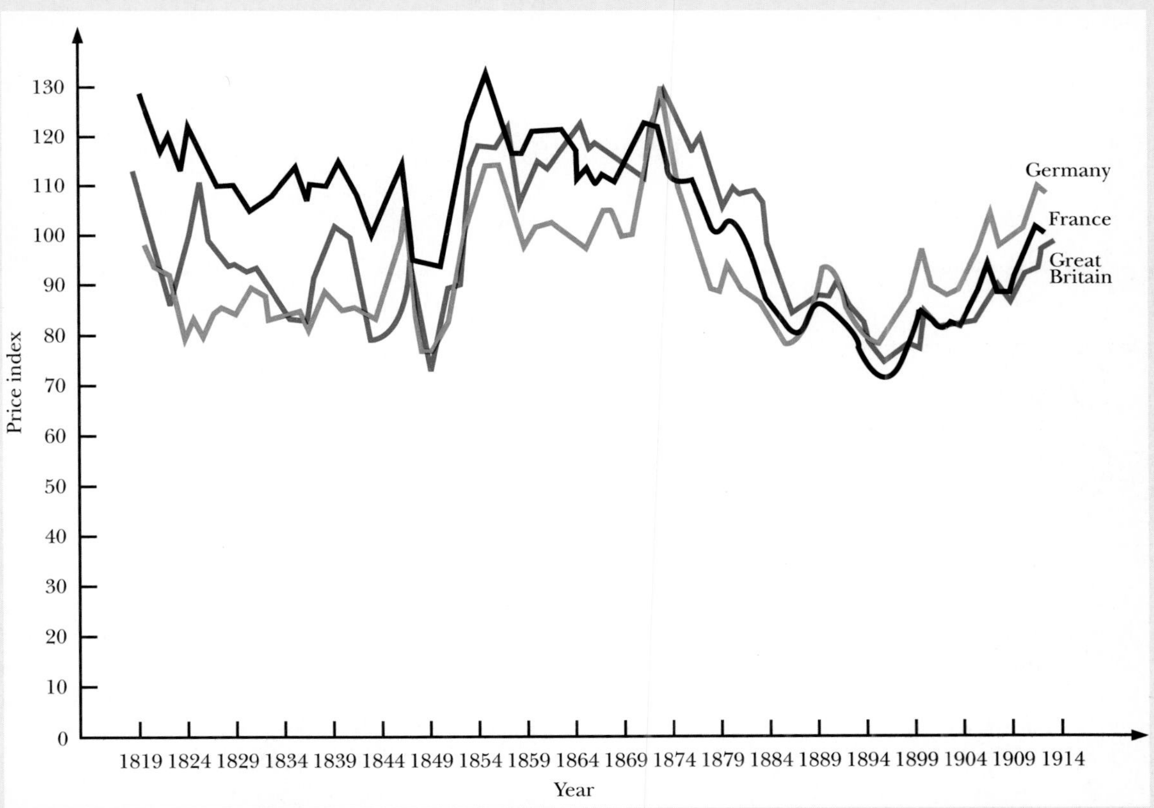

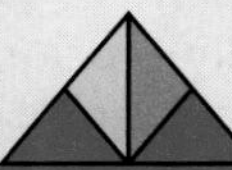

EXAMPLE 3 Is Wage Flexibility Increasing?

This chapter argues that the speed with which wages and other costs adjust to changes in economic conditions is important. Many economists believe that wages are becoming more flexible and that changes in labor market conditions affect worker compensation more quickly than they did in the past. Economists cite several institutional changes as causes of this increase in the flexibility of wages. First, a decreasing proportion of the labor force is employed in contract-type labor markets. In highly unionized branches such as manufacturing, transportation, utilities, and construction, compensation is typically set by contract 3 years in advance, in anticipation of future labor market conditions. However, an increasing proportion of the labor force now works in nonunionized sectors, such as services, that are not subject to long-term employment contracts. Second, more and more union contracts include "reopener clauses" that allow the wage contract to be renegotiated in the case of significant changes in labor market conditions. Third, the share of fringe benefits as a percentage of total compensation has declined since 1980. Fringe benefits tend to be relatively fixed costs that cannot respond to changes in economic conditions. Fourth, almost 70 percent of union contracts include significant compensation payments (such as bonuses) that depend on the economic performance of the employer. These extra payments are not part of the base pay upon which future wage increases are calculated.

Source: Erica L. Groshen, "What's Happening to Labor Compensation?" *Economic Commentary*, Federal Reserve Bank of Cleveland, May 15, 1988.

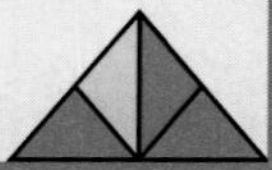

The **short-run aggregate supply curve (SRAS)** shows the levels of real GDP that firms are prepared to sell at different price levels, holding the anticipated price level and other factors constant.

Figure 3 shows the short-run aggregate supply curve. Why is it upward sloping? The SRAS curve, in the short run, takes the anticipated price level as given. In Figure 3, for example, the anticipated price level is taken to be 100, so the curve is labeled $SRAS_{100}$. The anticipated prices are reflected in level of wages agreed upon between employers and workers. Firms' incentive to produce depends on profit, which, in turn, depends on the margin by which selling prices exceed production costs. An increase in prices relative to costs can motivate profit-minded businesses to increase production and employment. Thus, in the short run, the aggregate supply curve is upward sloping, or positively sloped, because a general rise in the price level can raise prices more rapidly than contractual business costs.

When the actual price level equals the anticipated price level, the economy must be at the natural level of output and the natural rate of unemployment. In Figure 3, when the actual price level equals the anticipated price level ($P = 100$), the economy operates at the natural level of output, y_n. Recall that the natural rate of unemployment is sustained without accelerating or decelerating inflation. Thus, when output is at the natural level we can suppose that prices are rising at the rate people anticipate or, in terms of price levels, that the actual price level equals the anticipated price level.

We can now see how the output level can exceed or fall short of the natural level of output. If the price level rises above 100, holding the anticipated price level constant, it becomes more profitable for business firms to increase production. Thus, business firms will hire more workers or call back workers from layoffs. The more the actual price level exceeds the anticipated price level, the higher the desired output

FIGURE 3
Short-Run Aggregate Supply

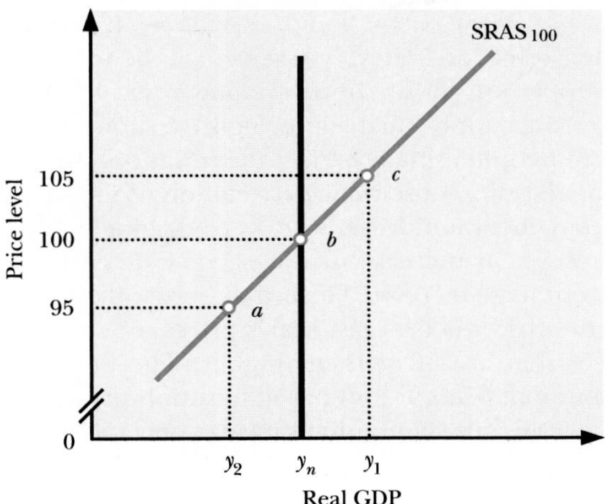

The short-run aggregate supply curve $SRAS_{100}$ is based on an anticipated price level of 100. At point *b*, the actual price level equals the anticipated price level, so the economy is at the natural level of output, y_n. If inflation rises to a level higher than anticipated—say, to a price level of 105—output rises to y_1. Unanticipated inflation stimulates output because prices of products rise faster than producing firms' costs. When prices fall more than anticipated—say, from 100 to 95—output falls to y_2. Unanticipated deflation discourages output because prices of products fall slower than producing firms' costs.

FIGURE 4
Short-Run Macroeconomic Equilibrium

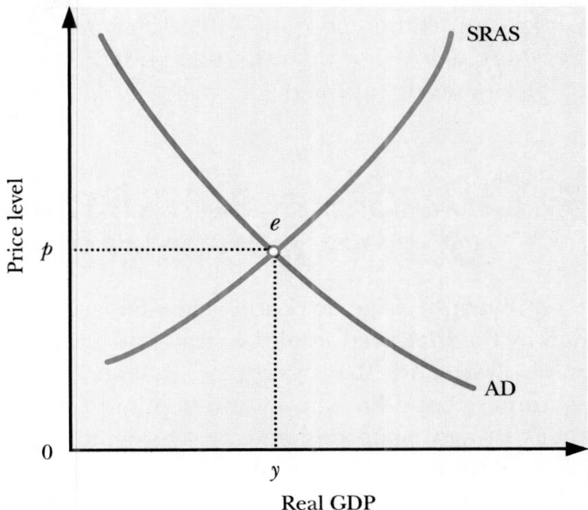

Short-run macroeconomic equilibrium occurs where the SRAS and AD curves intersect. If the price level is below *p*, the aggregate quantity demanded exceeds the aggregate quantity supplied; if the price level is above *p*, the aggregate quantity demanded falls short of the aggregate quantity supplied.

level and the lower the rate of unemployment. In Figure 3, an actual price level of 105 causes output to rise from y_n to y_1, holding the anticipated price level constant at 100.

If the price level falls below the anticipated level—say from 100 to 95 in Figure 3—business profitability will fall. Workers are paid according to contracts calling for fixed or rising wages on the basis of some anticipated price level; moreover, firms have negotiated the purchase of some materials at fixed prices. When the actual price level does not attain the anticipated level, selling prices fall relative to business costs. Firms will respond by producing less, firing some workers, and laying off other workers not currently needed. The rate of unemployment will exceed the natural rate and the level of output will fall short of the natural level. Thus, in Figure 3 when the price level falls from 100 to 95, the level of output falls from y_n to y_2.

> Output exceeds the natural level if the actual price level exceeds the anticipated price level; output falls short of the natural level if the actual price level is less than anticipated; and output equals the natural output level when the actual price level is anticipated.

Figure 4 graphs the short-run aggregate supply curve together with the aggregate demand curve. A **short-run macroeconomic equilibrium** occurs where the SRAS and AD curves intersect.

> **Short-run macroeconomic equilibrium** occurs at that output and price level at which short-run aggregate supply equals aggregate demand.

If the economy were to attempt to settle at a price level at which the aggregate quantity demanded exceeded the aggregate quantity supplied, the price level would rise and output would increase. If the economy tried to settle at a price level at which the aggregate quantity demanded fell short of the aggregate quantity supplied, the price level would drop and output would fall. Such adjustments would take place until the economy settled at an equilibrium where aggregate quantity demanded equaled aggregate quantity supplied.

CHANGES IN EQUILIBRIUM OUTPUT AND PRICES

The equilibrium price level and real GDP are determined by the intersection of the short-run aggregate supply curve and the aggregate demand curve. As in microeconomic supply-and-demand analysis, changes in aggregate demand or aggregate supply alter equilibrium prices and quantities. Inflation (a rising price level) results when aggregate demand increases or when aggregate supply decreases. Falling real GDP occurs when aggregate supply falls or when aggregate supply falls. In this section, we discuss those factors that cause shifts in the short-run aggregate supply curve and in the aggregate demand curve.

Shifts in Short-Run Aggregate Supply

The short-run aggregate supply curve shows what happens to output as the price level rises or falls in an unanticipated manner. It shows that the quantity of output supplied rises and falls with the price level in the short run. Like the aggregate demand curve, factors other than the price level can affect aggregate supply. When these factors change, the aggregate supply curve will shift. Any event that changes the price level at which the business sector is willing to supply a given volume of real output causes a leftward or rightward shift in the SRAS curve.

Some factors that change aggregate supply are slow moving, and their effects are seen only over a long period of time. Technological improvements lower production costs and cause firms to be willing to supply more output at the same price. Changes in labor market conditions (such as a decline in unionism or an influx of foreign workers) also affect firms' willingness to supply output at prevailing prices. Both of these factors, however, change slowly and would not be expected to cause rapid shifts in the short-run aggregate supply curve.

Two factors that can cause shifts in the SRAS curve are changes in inflationary expectations and supply shocks.

Changes in Inflationary Expectations. If the anticipated price level rises, businesses will be less willing to supply output at the prevailing price level, and aggregate supply will decline. Figure 5 shows the case where people initially expect the inflation rate to be zero, and then raise their expectation of inflation to 10 percent. Employees, who were originally willing to accept no increase in wages, now demand a 10 percent wage increase. Firms that were willing to supply their products at last year's prices, now demand prices that are 10 percent higher. The amount of output that firms are prepared to supply at any given price level falls when inflationary expectations rise.

> Rising inflationary expectations shift the short-run aggregate supply curve to the left.

FIGURE 5
The Effect of Inflationary Expectations on the Short-Run Aggregate Supply Curve

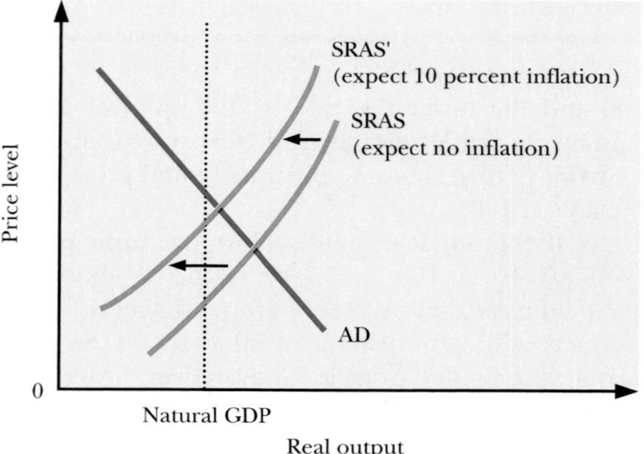

The initial short-run aggregate supply curve is SRAS, which prevails when people expect a zero rate of inflation. It intersects aggregate demand above the natural level of output. If people raise their inflationary expectations to 10 percent per annum, firms will supply less output at the same price levels as before. An increase in inflationary expectations, therefore, shifts the short-run aggregate supply curve to the left (to SRAS').

Because inflationary expectations affect aggregate supply, it is important to understand how inflationary expectations are formed. The formation of inflationary expectations is discussed in Chapter 17.

Supply Shocks. Supply shocks occur when an event occurs that alters the input costs of businesses. Examples of such events include the creation of a monopoly over an important natural resource, natural disasters, and poor worldwide harvests. These changing business input costs, in turn, alter the price level at which businesses are willing to supply output. Either **adverse** or **beneficial supply shocks** can result.

> An **adverse supply shock** occurs when the short-run aggregate supply curve shifts to the left, raising the price level and reducing output.

> A **beneficial supply shock** occurs when the short-run aggregate supply curve shifts to the right, reducing the price level and raising output.

Panel *a* of Figure 6 shows the effect of an adverse supply shock on prices and real output in the short run. The economy is initially operating at point *e* (the intersection of SRAS and AD curves), where the level of output is *y* and price level is *p*. People expect this situation to continue, but bad harvests occur on a worldwide basis or the prices of imports (such as oil) rise sharply. Because these price increases represent cost increases to producers, the short-run aggregate supply curve shifts to the left, from SRAS to SRAS′. The new equilibrium price level is p' and the new equilibrium GDP is y'. Thus, the end result of an adverse supply shock is a one-time inflationary episode (a shift from p to p') and smaller real output.

FIGURE 6
Supply Shocks

(*a*) Adverse Supply Shock

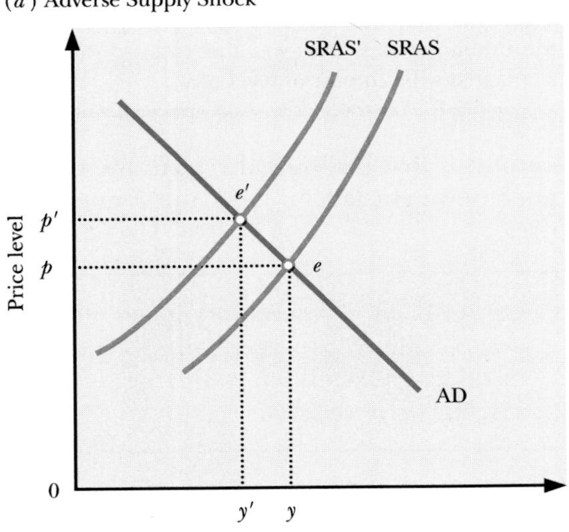

(*b*) Beneficial Supply Shock

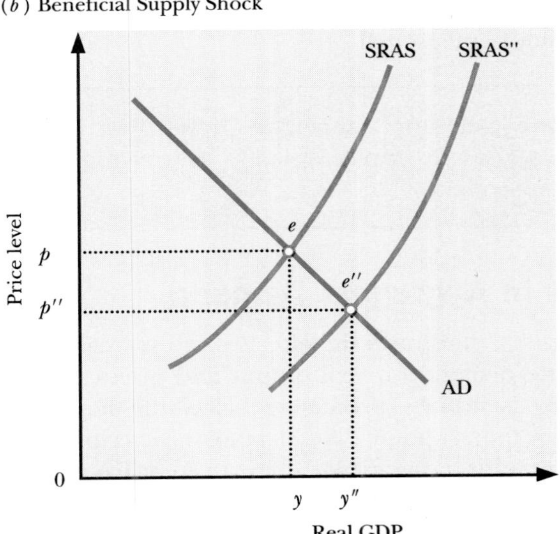

The economy is initially operating at point *e* in panel *a*. Aggregate supply is reduced (from SRAS to SRAS′) by disastrous harvests. At the original price level, *p*, aggregate demand exceeds aggregate supply and prices begin to rise. As prices rise, the economy moves along AD (from *e* to *e*′) until a new equilibrium is established at *e*′. Adverse supply shocks reduce real output and raise prices in the short run.

Panel *b* shows a beneficial supply shock. The economy is initially operating at point *e*, where the AD and SRAS curves intersect. Because of a good harvest or a reduction in the price of imported oil, the SRAS curve shifts right to SRAS″. The short-run equilibrium price level falls from p to p'' and real output rises from y to y''.

Such supply-side inflation occurred when OPEC raised the price of oil in 1973–74 and 1980–81. The substantial rise in oil prices raised costs of production, reducing aggregate supply. The fall in real output was accompanied by a reduction in employment (an increase in unemployment rates).

> An adverse supply shock yields the worst of both worlds. It raises both inflation and unemployment.

Panel *b* of Figure 6 illustrates the effects of a beneficial supply shock. The economy is initially operating at point *e*, where the output level is y and the price level is p. Good harvests occur on a worldwide basis, or the prices of imports fall. Because these price decreases represent cost decreases to producers, the short-run aggregate supply curve shifts to the right, from SRAS to SRAS″. The price level falls from p to p'' and real GDP increases from y to y''. A beneficial supply shock will cause supply-side deflation and raise employment (or lower the unemployment rate). A beneficial supply shock occurred in 1985–86 when the price of oil dropped from more than $30 a barrel to about $10 a barrel. In 1986, the inflation rate fell to it lowest level (2.7 percent) in two decades. Unemployment also fell.

> A beneficial supply shock yields the best of both worlds. It lowers inflation and reduces unemployment.

Shifts in Aggregate Demand

Figure 7 illustrates the effects of an increase in aggregate demand on real output and prices. The economy is initially producing below the natural level of output, at point *e*. An increase in government spending shifts the aggregate demand curve from AD to AD′. At the initial price level, p, aggregate quantity demanded exceeds short-run aggregate quantity supplied, so the price level begins to rise. As the price level rises, there is movement up the short-run supply curve, SRAS, from *e* to *e*′. The new equilibrium is established at *e*′, where the economy is producing output y_n at price level p'.

The effect of the increase in aggregate demand in the short run (starting below the natural level of output) is that real output rises to the natural level, unemployment falls to the natural rate, and prices rise.

FIGURE 7

The Effect of an Increase in Aggregate Demand on Short-Run Equilibrium

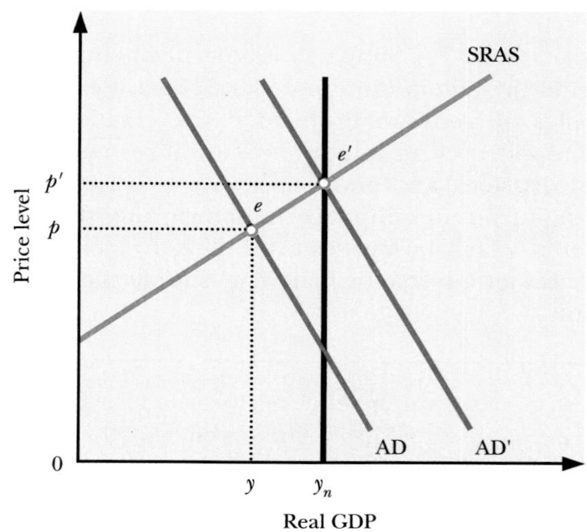

The economy is initially producing y at the price level p. Government expenditures increase and aggregate demand shifts from AD to AD′. As prices begin to rise, the economy moves along its short-run aggregate supply curve until a new equilibrium is established at *e*′. The increase in aggregate demand raises output and prices and lowers the unemployment rate—in this case, to the natural rate associated with an output level of y_n.

> For an economy operating below the natural level of output, an increase in aggregate demand can raise output to the natural level but at a higher price level.

SHORT-RUN INFLATIONARY AND DEFLATIONARY GAPS

Macroeconomic equilibrium occurs where the SRAS and AD curves intersect. In the short run, because these curves are independent of each other, the

FIGURE 8
Inflationary and Deflationary Gaps

(*a*) Deflationary Gap

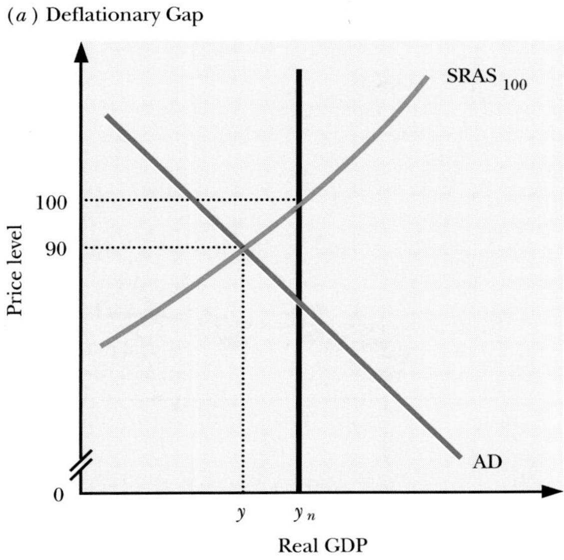

(*b*) Inflationary Gap

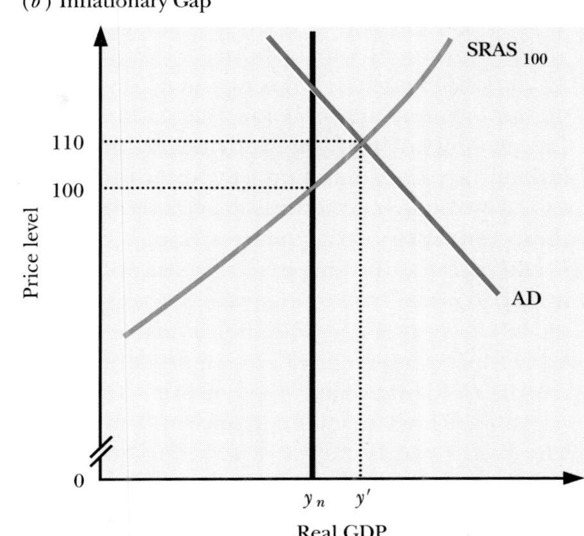

Panel *a* shows a deflationary gap. The anticipated price level is 100. The $SRAS_{100}$ curve intersects the AD curve to the *left* of the natural level of output, and y is less than y_n, the natural output level. The equilibrium level is 90.

Panel *b* shows an inflationary gap. The anticipated price level is 100. The $SRAS_{100}$ curve intersects the AD curve to the *right* of the natural level of output and y' exceeds y_n. The equilibrium price level is 110.

equilibrium level of output may be larger or smaller than the natural level of output. The equilibrium output, y, in panel *a* of Figure 8 falls short of the natural level of output, y_n. In panel *b*, the equilibrium level of output, y', exceeds y_n. Differences between actual output and y_n indicate a **deflationary gap** or an **inflationary gap.**

> A **deflationary gap** exists when the equilibrium level of output falls short of the natural level of output.
>
> An **inflationary gap** exists when the equilibrium level of output exceeds the natural level of output.

If a deflationary gap exists, as in panel *a* of Figure 8, the unemployment rate exceeds the natural rate of unemployment. If an inflationary gap exists, as in panel *b*, the unemployment rate falls short of the natural rate of unemployment. Deflationary and inflationary gaps set into motion movements in the price level. When a deflationary gap is present, the unemployment rate exceeds the natural rate; the rate of inflation of wages and prices will begin to drop. When an inflationary gap is present, the unemployment rate is less than the natural rate. Inflationary pressures build up in labor markets, and the rate of increase of wages and prices will accelerate. (See Example 4).

Chapter 12 will show how fiscal policy might be used to remove an inflationary or deflationary gap. Fiscal policy regulates aggregate demand by changing government spending and taxes. A rightward shift in the AD curve could remove a deflationary gap. Similarly, a leftward shift in the AD curve could remove an inflationary gap.

EXAMPLE 4 Inflationary and Deflationary Gaps: 1930 to 1991

This chapter explains that a *deflationary gap* is present when the actual unemployment rate is above the natural rate. An *inflationary gap* is present when the actual unemployment rate is below the natural rate. The accompanying figure provides estimates of inflationary and deflationary gaps from 1930 to the present. Economists may disagree with these estimates of the natural rate, but most would agree with the general trends shown in the figure. The orange areas are periods of deflationary gaps. The blue areas are periods of inflationary gaps. The figure shows the enormous deflationary gaps of the Great Depression, which persisted from 1930 to 1942. The World War II era was a period of inflationary gaps, as most able-bodied males were drawn into military service, creating exceptionally low unemployment. The 1950s and late 1960s were periods of inflationary gaps, whereas the early 1960s and the period from 1975 to 1984 were characterized by deflationary gaps.

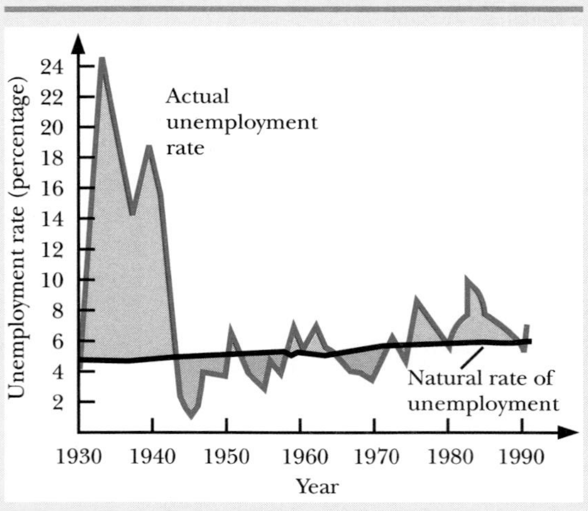

Source: Robert Gordon, "Inflation, Flexible Exchange Rates, and the Natural Rate of Unemployment," in *Workers, Jobs, and Inflation*, edited by Martin N. Bailey (Washington, D.C. Brookings, 1982); and Gordon, *Macroeconomics*, 5th ed. (New York: HarperCollins, 1990), Appendix A. The 1986–91 figures are estimated by the authors.

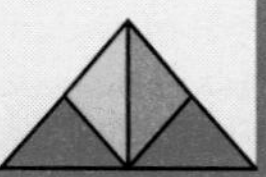

THE SELF-CORRECTING MECHANISM

We have discussed shifts in short-run aggregate supply and aggregate demand curves and their effects on prices, real output, and unemployment. Shifts in short-run aggregate supply and aggregate demand can cause inflationary or deflationary gaps. The *short run* is a period of time so short that wages and prices are not perfectly flexible and people cannot adjust their expectations to the change in the inflation rate. The short-run aggregate supply curve is upward sloping simply because people have not fully anticipated the change in prices. In the short run macroeconomic equilibrium, people initially expect the prevailing price level to continue into the future. Unanticipated inflation catches workers off guard with wage contracts that fail to protect them from the unanticipated inflation. Business firms have contracts for the purchase of inputs at prices that are rising less rapidly than selling prices.

The economy moves automatically to the natural level of output when people have time to adjust inflationary expectations; a *self-correcting mechanism* removes deflationary and inflationary gaps. Macroeconomists generally agree that the automatic process works, but they disagree over how long the process takes.

The Automatic Removal of a Deflationary Gap

The adjustment to a long-run equilibrium for a deflationary gap is illustrated in panel *a* of Figure 9. The economy is initially operating at point *e*, where the output level, y_1, is less than the natural level, y_n. In other words, the unemployment rate exceeds the natural rate of unemployment.

With a deflationary gap, prices will fall (or the rate of inflation will fall). In the long run, wage and

FIGURE 9
Self-Correcting Deflationary and Inflationary Gaps

(*a*) Deflationary Gap

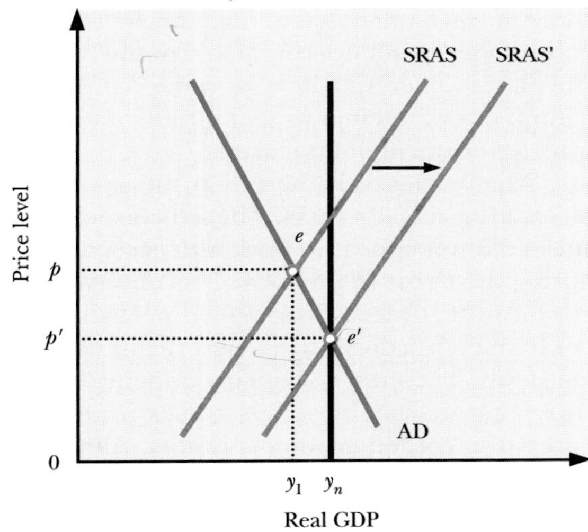

(*b*) Inflationary Gap

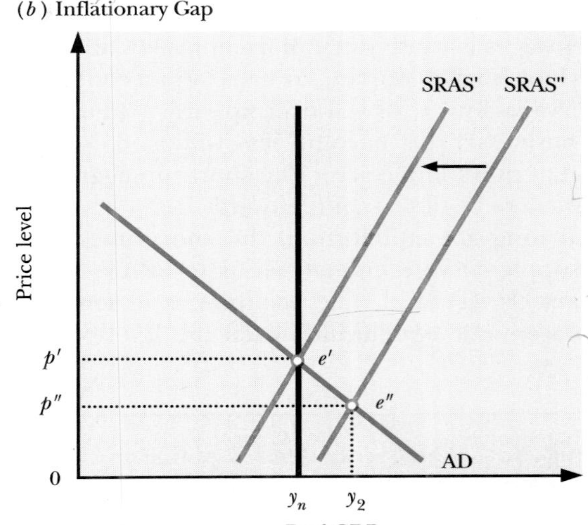

In panel *a*, the economy's short-run aggregate supply curve, SRAS, intersects the aggregate demand curve, AD, at point *e*. At this point, y_1 is less than y_n, and the unemployment rate exceeds the natural rate. Wages and prices fall. As the inflation rate drops, individuals and businesses adjust downward their inflationary expectations and become willing to supply more output at the same price level as before the drop in expected prices. Thus, the short-run aggregate supply curve shifts rightward, to SRAS′, causing the economy to move down AD toward e'. The long-run equilibrium occurs at the intersection of the AD and SRAS′ curves where the natural level of output, y_n, is produced. At this point, e', there is no longer any tendency for prices to fall. The fall in the price level from p to p' brings about this automatic adjustment.

In panel *b*, the economy's short-run aggregate supply curve, SRAS″, intersects the aggregate demand curve, AD, at point e''. At this point, there is an inflationary gap because y_2 exceeds y_n and unemployment is less than the natural rate. Wages and prices rise. In the long run, the short-run aggregate supply curve shifts leftward to reflect the higher level of expected prices. The long-run equilibrium occurs at the intersection of the AD and SRAS′ curves where the natural level of output, y_n, is produced.

supply contracts expire; firms can strike new bargains that reflect the general decline in prices throughout the economy. Firms will be able to pay workers lower wages because unemployment is high and real wages look high to workers covered by old contracts. As wages and costs adjust downward in the long run, business firms will increase their supply of output at prevailing prices. When this happens, the short-run aggregate supply curve shifts to the right. Falling prices will move the economy down the negatively sloped aggregate demand curve, AD, from point *e* toward point e'. As long as the economy's output is less than y_n, prices will continue to fall and move the economy closer and closer to y_n. This process stops when the economy reaches SRAS′ and produces y_n at price level p'.

> As long as the unemployment rate remains above the natural rate, falling wages and prices will in the long run move the economy to the natural rate of unemployment. This adjustment is self-correcting; it takes place automatically without any change in macroeconomic policy.

The Automatic Removal of an Inflationary Gap

Panel *b* of Figure 9 shows how the self-correcting mechanism can automatically eliminate an inflationary gap. The initial level of output is y_2 and the price level is p''. Although existing wage and supply contracts prevent wages and material prices from rising as rapidly as inflation, the inflationary gap eventually drives the price level upward. In the long run, wage and supply contracts must be renegotiated. As old wage contracts expire, workers bargain for higher wages because unemployment is low and real wages look small to workers covered by past contracts. Thus, wages and costs will drift upward. When costs rise, business firms become less willing to supply output at prevailing prices. The short-run aggregate supply curve begins to shift leftward.

In long-run equilibrium, the short-run aggregate supply curve eventually shifts to SRAS′ where it intersects AD at e'. The economy is in **long-run macroeconomic equilibrium** when the level of output is y_n.

> **Long-run macroeconomic equilibrium** is achieved when inflationary or deflationary gaps are no longer present. This occurs when SRAS intersects AD at the natural level of output.

There is an asymmetry between the automatic removal of an inflationary gap and the automatic removal of a deflationary gap. The elimination of deflationary gaps requires falling wages and prices, whereas removing inflationary gaps requires rising wages and prices. Generally speaking, in the short run, wages and prices are far more flexible in the upward direction than in the downward direction. Workers and business firms do not like to accept lower wages and prices even if those cuts do not represent real wage or price cuts. On the other hand, workers and firms will eagerly accept higher money wages and prices to prevent real wages or prices from falling or even to increase real wages or prices. A wage cut may cause a strike or extended negotiation. A wage increase will be praised. Thus, it may take longer to remove a deflationary gap by relying on the self-correcting mechanism.

Does the Self-Correcting Mechanism Really Work?

The self-correcting mechanism carries a soothing message: In the long run, economies will automatically return to the natural rate of unemployment (full employment). The theory of the self-correcting mechanism does not tell us how quickly this return will occur (whether it will take a few months or 5 years?), but it does appear to rule out long-run economic disasters such as an ever-worsening unemployment rate. It recognizes that economies will be buffeted from all sides—by supply shocks, by fluctuations in investment spending, and by accelerating government spending—but that movements in wages and prices will eventually restore the economy to the natural rate of unemployment without any assistance from government policymakers.

What evidence is there that the self-correcting mechanism actually works? The self-correcting mechanism did not appear to work with acceptable speed during the Great Depression. This observation does not mean that the self-correcting mechanism would not have eventually worked—just that it was working too slowly. The most convincing evidence that a self-correcting mechanism exists comes from the long sweep of recorded economic history. Although reliable statistics on unemployment rates from the late nineteenth through the early twentieth centuries are hard to produce, the available evidence suggests that there was no long-term trend in unemployment rates from the 1880s to the Great Depression. Unemployment rates fluctuated from year to year, but they seemed to return to a fairly "normal" unemployment rate. In France, for example, the unemployment rate ranged from a low of 4.7 percent to a high of 10.2 percent from 1895 to 1913, yet it appeared to return after such fluctuations to a 6.5 percent unemployment rate. The German unemployment rate ranged from 0.2 percent to 7.2 percent between 1887 and 1922, yet always seemed to return to a rate of around 2 percent. From 1887 to 1920, the English unemployment rate ranged from 0.4 percent to 7.8 percent but seemed to return to a rate of around 3 percent. From 1890 to 1929, there was no discernible trend in the U.S. unemployment rate, which ranged from a low of 1.4 percent to a high of 18.4 percent and tended to return to an unemployment rate in the range of 4 to 5 percent. (See Example 5).

The late nineteenth and early twentieth centuries witnessed many kinds of supply and demand shocks—wars, investment booms and busts, shifts of employment from agriculture to industry and services, stock market binges, major technological changes, new resource discoveries. It was also a period of laissez-faire macroeconomic policy. Governments did not consciously attempt to use monetary and fiscal policy to eliminate inflationary or deflationary

EXAMPLE 5 The Recovery from the Great Depression

The U.S. economy recovered from the Great Depression by about 1942. In that year, unemployment was 4.2 percent, and real GDP was up 50 percent from 1929. The money supply had increased from $20 billion to $55 billion. Was the recovery due to the self-correcting mechanism or to government-induced increases in aggregate demand?

Ben Bernanke and Martin Parkinson argue that the self-correcting menchanism was robust during the recovery. In a study using quarterly data from 1924 to 1941, they estimated that at any time about one-half of the difference between actual and natural unemployment would have been corrected within three quarters even without any stimulus from aggregate demand as measured by unexpected inflation. The growth of aggregate demand played a role, but the self-correcting mechanism was the "engine of recovery."

Source: Ben Bernanke and Martin Parkinson, "Unemployment, Inflation, and Wages in the American Depression: Are There Lessons for Europe?" *American Economic Review* (May 1989): 210–14.

gaps. The evidence from the nineteenth and early twentieth centuries is consistent with the theory of the long-run self-correcting mechanism.

This chapter has presented a view of macroeconomics that is broad enough to accommodate various macroeconomic schools of thought. The next chapter summarizes the classical and Keynesian schools of macroeconomics.

SUMMARY

1. The aggregate demand curve shows the real GDP that agents willingly demand at different price levels. It is downward sloping because of the real-balance effect, the interest-rate effect, and the foreign-trade effect.

2. The natural rate of unemployment is the unemployment rate that can be sustained indefinitely without accelerating inflation or deflation. The natural level of real GDP is the real GDP that is produced when the economy is operating at the natural rate of unemployment.

3. The short-run aggregate supply curve (SRAS) curve is upward sloping. The SRAS curve is upward sloping because unanticipated increases in the price level relative to business costs encourage firms to produce more.

4. Short-run macroeconomic equilibrium occurs where the aggregate demand curve intersects the SRAS curve. Adverse supply shocks shift the SRAS curve leftward, raising prices and lowering real output. Beneficial supply shocks shift the SRAS curve rightward, lowering prices and raising real output.

5. A deflationary gap prevails if the short-run equilibrium real GDP falls short of the natural level. An inflationary gap prevails if short-run equilibrium real GDP exceeds the natural level. Long-run equilibrium occurs when the short-run aggregate supply curve shifts sufficiently to remove inflationary or deflationary gaps.

6. In the long run, there is a self-correcting mechanism that automatically removes an inflationary or deflationary gap. Inflationary gaps may be removed more quickly than deflationary gaps. How quickly the self-correcting mechanism works depends on the flexibility of wages and prices.

KEY TERMS

aggregate demand curve (AD)
real-balance effect
interest-rate effect
foreign-trade effect
natural rate of unemployment
natural level of real GDP (y_n)
short-run aggregate supply curve (SRAS)
short-run macroeconomic equilibrium
adverse supply shock

beneficial supply shock
deflationary gap
inflationary gap
long-run macroeconomic equilibrium

QUESTIONS AND PROBLEMS

1. Give three reasons why the aggregate demand curve is downward sloping.
2. Explain the interest-rate effect on aggregate quantity demanded when the price level falls.
3. What is the difference between the interest-rate effect and the real-balance effect when the price level falls? How are they similar?
4. Assume a country is engaged in foreign trade. Both the nominal money supply and the domestic price level fall by 10 percent. If foreign prices and exchange rates remain the same, describe what would likely happen to the various components of aggregate quantity demanded.
5. Why are wages and prices more inflexible in the short run than in the long run?
6. Assume that during a period when nominal wages are fixed, the price level begins to fall. What effect will this drop in prices have on real wages and on the employment decisions of firms and of workers?
7. Can actual unemployment be less than the natural rate of unemployment? How?
8. How is an increase in the expected price level reflected in short-run aggregate supply?
9. Explain why the SRAS curve is upward sloping.
10. What would happen to the slope of the SRAS curve if the workers in the economy were covered by fewer long-term wage contracts?
11. How is the SRAS curve affected by each of the following events?

    a. An increase in the anticipated price level.
    b. An increase in the price level in the short run.
    c. A reduction in the price of imported steel.
    d. An increase in labor productivity.

12. Assume that the price level people anticipate is 110 and the actual price level is 100. Under these conditions, what will be the relationship between aggregate demand and aggregate supply? Will the economy be in long-run macroeconomic equilibrium?
13. What does an inflationary gap imply about:

    a. The unemployment rate?
    b. The actual versus the anticipated price level?

14. Explain how the self-correcting mechanism drives unemployment to the natural level. Will the self-correcting mechanism work faster when wages and prices are inflexible? Why?
15. In 1933, the GDP price deflator was 11.2 (1982 = 100) and real GDP was $499 billion. In 1942, the price level was 14.7 and real GDP was $1080. Draw the AD and SRAS curves.
16. Explain why inflationary gaps may be eliminated more quickly than deflationary gaps.
17. Explain how shifts in the aggregate demand curve might be used in place of the self-correcting mechanism to eliminate a deflationary gap.

SUGGESTED READINGS

Gordon, Robert J. *Macroeconomics,* 5th ed. New York: HarperCollins, 1990, chap. 6.

Mankiw, N. Gregory. *Macroeconomics.* New York: Worth Publishers, 1992, chaps. 8 and 9.

Tregarthen, Timothy. "Do Sticky Prices Gum Up the Economy?" *The Margin* 7 (Fall 1991): 32–33.

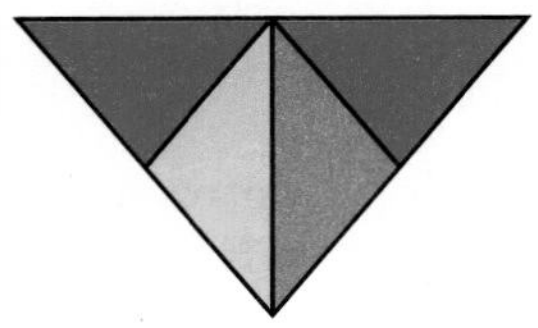

10

Classical and Keynesian Macroeconomics

CHAPTER INSIGHT

Classical economics owes its origin to David Hume (1711–1776), Adam Smith (1723–1790), David Ricardo (1772–1823), and J. B. Say (1767–1832). They concentrated on the conditions of aggregate supply and the explanation of inflation. The classical economists were aware of, but did not focus on, the business cycle and unemployment, issues that preoccupy modern economists.

The business cycles that occurred prior to the Great Depression of the 1930s were relatively mild. For example, from 1870 to 1929, the economy experienced a number of recessions, but in each case the decline in output was modest.[1] The Great Depression, however, shook the foundations of classical economics, leading John Maynard Keynes (1883–1946) to revolutionize the field by focusing on the conditions of aggregate demand. In particular, Keynes differed with the classical economists mainly over the issue of price flexibility.

This chapter discusses the three key elements of classical macroeconomics: the idea that supply creates its own demand, the assumption of price flexibility, and the quantity theory of money. It also explains how Keynes shifted the focus of economics from aggregate supply to aggregate demand.

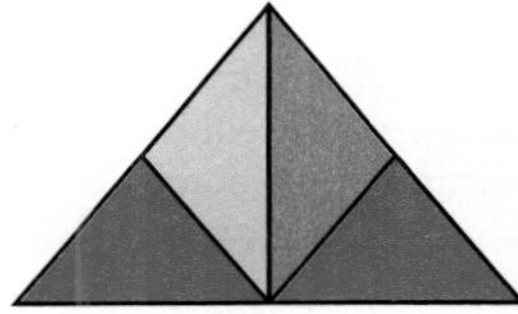

SAY'S LAW

According to the classical economists, whatever GDP can be produced will be demanded (**Say's law**), and unemployment can only be the short-term consequence of money wages being temporarily too high. The determination of GDP was no mystery to the classical theorists because they assumed that the economy operated near the full-employment level; they believed that full employment was the norm.

> According to **Say's law**, whatever aggregate output producers decide to supply will be demanded in the aggregate.

The classical theorists derived Say's law from the relationship between aggregate supply and aggregate demand. As Chapter 7 explained, national income and national product are two sides of the same coin. When an economy produces $6 trillion worth of final goods and services, it also produces the income with which these goods can be purchased. National income accounting demonstrates that it is always and everywhere true that *actual* aggregate income equals *actual* aggregate expenditures, but classical theorists went one step further. They argued that *supply creates its own demand.*

Say's law does not deny that an economy could produce too many quarts of milk or too many loaves of bread. If the price of milk or bread is too high, the demand will fall short of supply. The classical economists "recognized that there may be depressions, unemployment, or unsold goods."[2] Say's law asserted only that the demand for all goods and services could be counted on to purchase the supply of all goods and services.

To the classical economists, Say's law proved that economic growth had no natural limit: No matter how much the economy produced, the demand for the goods would be forthcoming. As Say himself pointed out, "Otherwise how could it be possible that there should now be bought and sold in France five or six times as many commodities as in the miserable reign of Charles VI?"[3]

How could the classical theorists believe that consumers and firms will want to buy however much aggregate output is produced? Consider a hypothetical economy with no government and no net exports that produces $600 billion worth of final goods and services, creating a total of $600 billion worth of income paid to land, labor, capital, and entrepreneurship. What happens if households want to spend $500 billion on consumer goods and save $100 billion? The $100 billion represents a withdrawal from the spending stream, so that saving creates a potential difference between aggregate spending and aggregate production.

According to Say, the desired saving of $100 billion will be exactly matched by desired investment of $100 billion. In this way, out of the $600 billion of income, households desire to spend $500 billion on consumption, and business firms desire to spend $100 billion on investment. Investment spending injects the saving of households back into the spending stream.

Figure 1 shows how the $100 billion worth of desired saving becomes $100 billion worth of desired investment. The rate of interest is measured on the vertical axis, and desired saving and investment are measured on the horizontal axis. The saving curve shows how saving responds to the interest rate. The higher is the interest rate, the higher is desired saving. The higher is the interest rate, the greater is the incentive to save more and spend less on personal consumption. The investment curve shows how desired investment responds to the interest rate. Generally speaking, the higher is the interest rate, the less business managers and others want to invest in buildings, trucks, inventories, and equipment.

As Figure 1 shows, the interest rate equates *desired* saving and *desired* investment. Thus, in the classical model, the interest rate coordinates saving and investment decisions. In Figure 1, the interest rate that

[1]GNP estimates for dates before 1930 are controversial. See Christina D. Romer, "The Prewar Business Cycle Reconsidered: New Estimates of Gross National Product, 1869–1908," *Journal of Political Economy* 97 (February 1989): 1–37; and Nathan S. Balke and Robert J. Gordon, "The Estimation of Prewar Gross National Product: Methodology and New Evidence," *Journal of Political Economy* 97 (February 1989): 38–92. From 1892 to 1894 Romer estimates a 2 percent reduction in real GNP, whereas Balke and Gordon estimate a 3.5 percent reduction.

[2]Thomas Sowell, *Classical Economics Reconsidered* (Princeton, NJ: Princeton University Press, 1974), 43.

[3]Thomas Sowell, *Classical Economics Reconsidered* (Princeton, NJ: Princeton University Press, 1974), 60.

FIGURE 1
The Interest Rate Equates Desired Saving and Desired Investment in the Classical Model

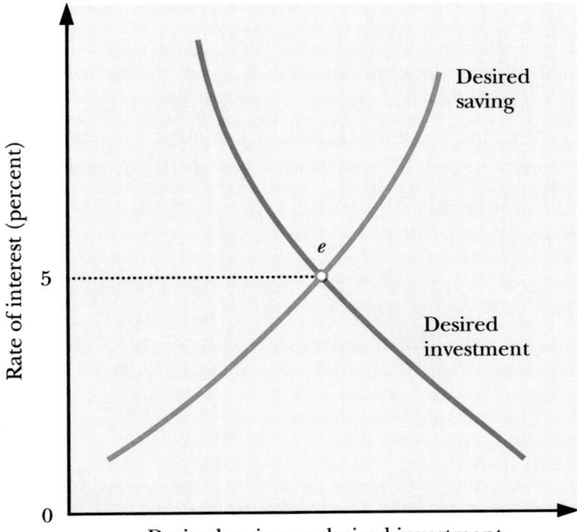

This figure measures the interest rate on the vertical axis and the amount of desired saving and desired investment on the horizontal axis. The saving curve shows the amount of desired saving at different interest rates. The higher is the interest rate, the greater is the amount of desired saving. The investment curve shows the amount of desired investment at different interest rates. The higher is the interest rate, the lower is the amount of desired investment. The interest rate equates the amount of desired investment and the amount of desired saving. In this example, the interest rate that equates desired saving and desired investment is 5 percent. At any interest rate above 5 percent, desired saving will exceed desired investment and the interest rate will fall. At any rate below 5 percent, desired investment will exceed desired saving and the interest rate will be driven up.

equates desired saving and desired investment is 5 percent. At any interest rate above 5 percent, desired saving will exceed desired investment, and the interest rate will fall. At any rate below 5 percent, desired investment will exceed desired saving, and the interest rate will be driven up.

According to the classical model, in equating desired saving and the desired investment, the interest rate automatically equates desired aggregate expenditures and aggregate income. If saving increases spontaneously, consumption falls by the amount of the saving decline. The increase in saving withdraws consumption expenditures from the spending stream. The increase in saving, however, lowers the interest rate, raising desired investment. The interest rate will fall until the increase in investment is enough to offset the decline in consumption. (See Example 1.)

PRICE/WAGE FLEXIBILITY

The classical economists assumed the existence of a highly competitive world in which prices and wages were determined in extremely flexible markets. Prices and wages were assumed to quickly adjust to changes in the conditions of demand and supply providing another line of defense for Say's law.

Price flexibility means that excess demand and excess supply are temporary conditions. When an excess demand for a particular good or service exists, competing buyers are unable to satisfy their demands from the prevailing offers of sellers. Thus, unsatisfied buyers bid up the price until the quantity demanded adjusts to equal the quantity supplied. When an excess supply of a particular good or service from unsatisfied sellers exists, more of the good or service is offered on the market than is demanded. Thus, competing sellers bid down the price until the quantity supplied matches the quantity demanded.

To the classical economists, unemployment was voluntary. Unemployment, in their opinion, could be looked upon as an excess supply of labor, which, like an excess supply of wheat or any other product, results when the price is too high. In the case of labor, the price is the wage rate. If unemployed workers would accept a lower wage they would quickly be put back to work by eager employers. Unemployment was a problem that the unemployed themselves could correct by accepting lower wages. In other words, unemployment would not be a problem if wages and prices were sufficiently flexible.

THE SIMPLE QUANTITY THEORY OF MONEY

The third component of classical macroeconomics is the simple quantity theory of money. The quantity theory was first put forth by David Hume in 1752,

EXAMPLE 1 The German Approach to Economic Policy

Germany is one of the world's most successful economies. It provides ample growth and relatively low levels of unemployment and inflation for its citizens. Its per capita gross domestic product is one of the highest in the world.

Say's law has been the underpinning of much of German economic thought. Since 1963, the German government has been advised by the German Council of Economic Experts. The council sees growth largely in terms of Say's law, emanating from supply-side developments in technology and capital accumulation. According to the Council, "the primary impetus for expansion often originates in supply, which automatically creates equivalent demand." A member of the council summarized its version of Say's law as follows: "the right kind of supply invariably creates its own demand." The "right kind of supply" refers to consumer and producer goods that incorporate modern technology and can be sold at competitive prices.

Source: Ernst Helmstädter, "The Irrelevance of Keynes to German Economic Policy and to International Economic Cooperation in the 1980s," in Walter Etis and Peter Sinclair, *Keynes and Economic Policy* (London: The Macmillan Press Ltd., 1988), 411–27.

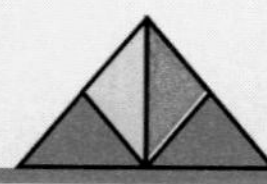

but it was developed in detail by the two most famous economists of the early twentieth century, America's Irving Fisher (1867–1947) and Britain's Alfred Marshall (1842–1924). The theory not only explains the relationship between money and prices but also gives a simple theory of aggregate demand.

In Chapter 8 we defined the *money supply* as the quantity of cash and checking accounts held by the nonbanking public. We will let M represent the supply of money (it will always be clear from the context when M stands for the supply of money and when it stands for imports). At any given time, there is always a certain amount of money in an economy. The money may be made of a high quality material (like gold) or simply of paper.

Basically, the simple quantity theory of money postulated that the general level of prices would be proportional to the quantity of money in exsistence. The quantity theory is the antecedent of important modern macroeconomic theories. It is especially useful because it provides a powerful though simplified view of how the macroeconomy works. The key lesson to be learned is that the value of money is determined more by its *quantity* than by its *quality*.

Velocity of Circulation

The concept of **velocity of circulation** is essential to an understanding of the quantity theory.

> The **velocity of circulation** is the number of times the average dollar is spent on final goods and services in 1 year's time.

In 1991, American GDP was approximately $5700 billion, which means that in 1991, households, government, and businesses spent this sum on final goods and services. The average 1991 supply of money (M) was about $850 billion. In order for the economy to make $5700 billion worth of purchases in the course of one year with a stock of money of $850 billion, each dollar was spent, on average, 6.7 times (6.7 = $5700 billion ÷ $850 billion). In other words, each dollar financed the purchase of $6.70 worth of final goods and services in the course of that year.

> The velocity of circulation (V) is the ratio of GDP to the money supply (M):
>
> $$V = \frac{\text{GDP}}{M}$$

The higher is the velocity of circulation, the faster people are turning over the available stock of money. Velocity can rise or fall with changing economic conditions. During hyperinflation, for example, velocity tends to rise as people try to spend their money as fast as possible before its value declines even further. When the rate of inflation is falling, people are more inclined to hold on to their money longer.

In recent years, velocity has been rising. For example, between 1988 and 1991, velocity rose from 6.15 to 6.7—an 8 percent increase in the rapidity with which money circulated. Because the money supply increased by about 15 percent from 1988 to 1991, the 8 percent rise in velocity increased the impact of the expansion in the money supply on inflation by about one half.

Because nominal GDP equals real GDP (denoted here by Q) multiplied by the price level (P), the velocity of circulation can also be expressed as:

$$V = \frac{PQ}{M}$$

where M represents the money supply.

The Equation of Exchange

By multiplying both sides of the velocity of circulation equation by M, the equation becomes

$$MV = PQ$$

This equation is known as the *equation of exchange.*

In effect, the equation of exchange says that the amount of final purchases in the economy (GDP) must equal the amount of money in circulation multiplied by the average number of times each dollar changes hands. Were this not true, then the observed amount of final spending would not have been possible.

The equation of exchange can be used to explain the quantity theory. Irving Fisher and Alfred Marshall both believed that the equation of exchange summarized the relevant factors determining the link between the money supply and the price level.

Changes in Money Supply and Prices

The equation of exchange does not guarantee that money supply and the price level will rise at the same rate. If V rises while M is constant, total spending (PQ) must rise. Unless Q rises to take up the slack, P must rise. Thus, P could rise without there being any increase in M. The simple quantity theory assumes that

1. The velocity of circulation, V, is fixed.
2. Real GDP, Q, is fixed in the short run.

With these assumptions, the equation of exchange becomes a theory—known as the *simple quantity theory of money.* The equation of exchange shows that if both Q and V are fixed, then P will be proportional to M. The equation of exchange, rewritten to solve for P, is

$$P = MV/Q$$

If Q and V are both fixed, V/Q will be a constant. Therefore, an x percent increase in M will cause an x percent increase in P. With V and Q constant (no matter what their values), a 5 percent increase in M will cause a 5 percent increase in P; a 10 percent increase in M will cause a 10 percent increase in P. With Q and V both fixed, the quantity theory concludes that P is strictly proportional to M, or, in other words, that inflation is strictly a monetary phenomenon.

> The basic message of the quantity theory of money is that the price level is proportional to the money supply and has nothing to do with the quality (that is, whether the money is paper money or gold) of the monetary unit.

The quantity theorists did not assume that velocity was unalterably fixed.[4] They simply supposed that velocity was relatively stable over long periods of time. They felt that velocity was determined by the monetary habits, experiences, and institutions of the community. A country with a large number of money substitutes would have a high velocity of circulation; a country with few money substitutes would have a low velocity. A country with frequent pay periods would have a high velocity; a country with few pay periods would have a low velocity. A country with a high rate of inflation would have a higher velocity than one with a low rate of inflation.

The quantity theorists believed that the size of real GDP is determined in the short run by the size

[4]Thomas Sowell, *Classical Economics Reconsidered* (Princeton, NJ: Princeton University Press, 1974), 60.

and productivity of the resources (land, labor, and capital) of the country. Land, labor, and capital grow slowly over the long run, but at any point in time they are essentially fixed in supply. The real output of the economy is fixed because resources will tend to be fully employed, particularly the most important resource—labor. In this view, changing resource prices ensure the full employment of resources. If workers are involuntarily unemployed, the wage rate will automatically adjust downward until all those willing to work at the going wage will be employed. Over time, as the labor force expands and technology improves, real output will rise. But in the short run, real output is fixed by the resource base and by technology.

The Real Sector and the Money Sector

The simple quantity theory divides the economy into two sectors: a *real sector* and a *monetary sector.* In the real sector, resources are combined to produce full-employment output. The same amount of output will be supplied no matter what the price level. What counts is not the height of the general price level but the adjustment of relative resource prices to bring the economy to full employment. In the monetary sector, the price level is established by the amount of money in the economy. According to the simple quantity theory, the two sectors do not overlap. Changes in money supply are not associated with changes in employment or real output, and vice versa.

Aggregate Supply and Aggregate Demand in the Quantity Theory

What types of aggregate demand and aggregate supply curves are suggested by the quantity theory? To obtain the quantity theory aggregate demand curve, the quantity equation $MV = PQ$ can be rearranged as $Q = MV/P$. With this arrangement, the aggregate quantity demanded (Q) is a negative function of the price level (P). A higher P causes a smaller Q to be demanded, *ceteris paribus.* Like microeconomic demand curves, the aggregate demand curve gives the relationship between output and price level when all other factors that affect demand are held constant. According to the simple quantity theory, velocity is already constant, so the aggregate demand curve will shift only if the money supply changes.

FIGURE 2
The Simple Quantity Theory

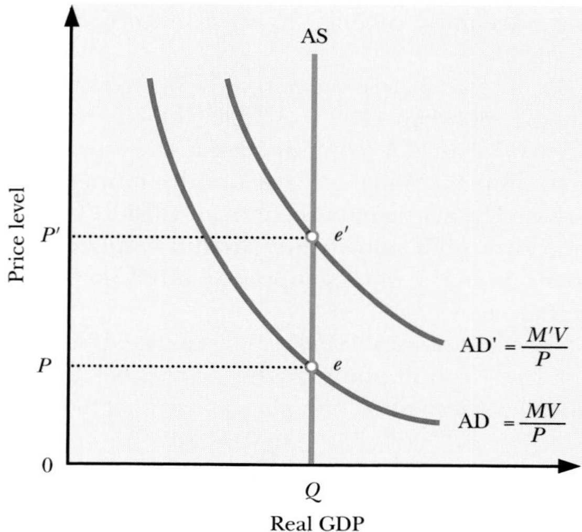

The aggregate quantity demanded of goods and services at each price level, according to the simple quantity theory, is simply MV/P, where V is a constant and M is held constant. Because real GDP is fixed, the aggregate supply curve (AS) is vertical. If the money supply increases from M to M', AD shifts to the right, and the equilibrium price level increases proportionately from P to P'.

Thus, when money supply increases, aggregate demand increases (AD shifts to the right). The demand equation, $Q = MV/P$, shows that when M increases, more will be demanded *at each price level.*

Figure 2 shows the aggregate demand and aggregate supply curves according to the simple quantity theory. The aggregate demand curve (AD) is negatively sloped, and the aggregate supply curve (AS) is a vertical line. AS is vertical because, according to the simple quantity theory, real GDP is fixed at full employment. Real GDP, therefore, cannot increase as the price level increases; all resources are already fully employed. With real GDP already determined, the intersection of AD and AS determines only the price level.

When the money supply increases, the aggregate demand curve shifts right proportionately, and the equilibrium price level, P, rises to P'. If M' is twice M, then P' will be twice P.

According to the quantity theory, *price level depends on the quantity of money, not on the stuff from*

EXAMPLE 2 Hyperinflations

Some countries have experienced dramatic episodes of runaway inflations, or hyperinflations. Hyperinflations essentially make the money of a country worthless. The economy must resort to barter or seek out other types of money, often foreign currencies.

How well do the historical episodes of hyperinflation support the quantity theory of money? The cause of each hyperinflation is well documented: The government printed too much money, often to finance wars or to pay the bills of past wars. Hyperinflations have been caused by excessive monetary growth. In each hyperinflation, the cure was achieved only when the government slowed down the growth of the money supply.

The last American hyperinflation was experienced by the confederate states during the American Civil War. In both the North and the South, paper money was printed to finance wartime expenditures. In the South, the supply of confederate money increased from an index of 100 in early 1861 to 2000 by April 1865. The supply of Northern currency, greenback dollars, roughly doubled during the same period. The growth of the money supply was rapid in the North, but it was slow relative to the burst of money growth in the South.

The equation of exchange predicts that inflation would have been more rapid in the South than in the North, as was indeed the case. In the North, the price level about doubled between 1861 and 1865 (it grew at about the same rate as the money supply), whereas in the South, the price level jumped from an index of 100 in early 1861 to an index of 9200 in April 1865. For the period as a whole, prices rose 10 percent per month, but by the end of the war, prices were increasing daily. In the South, prices grew much more rapidly than the money supply. Why? The equation of exchange shows that prices rise more rapidly than money when velocity is also rising. As people in the South started raising their expectations of inflation, they became increasingly unwilling to hold confederate money, which changed hands at faster and faster rates. As it became clear that the South would lose the war, velocity accelerated even more because people knew that confederate money would soon become worthless. On the day of armistice, the confederate dollar had fallen to about 1 percent of its original value.

Sources: E. M. Lerner, "Money, Prices, and Wages in the Confederacy, 1861–1865," *Journal of Political Economy* 63 (February 1955), cited in Gary M. Walton and Ross M. Robertson, *History of the American Economy*, 5th ed. (New York: Harcourt Brace Jovanovich, 1983), 304-5; *Historical Statistics of the United States from Colonial Times to the Present.*

which money is made. Money is valuable because of what it can buy. According to the quantity theory, it makes no difference whether the money is made out of gold, platinum, or just plain old paper on which some engravings of old men have been made. If the quantity of money is limited, the price level will be low, and money, as the generally accepted medium of exchange, will have value. (See Example 2.)

This conclusion has policy implications. Why waste resources using goods such as gold or silver as money? Why not just print limited quantities of money in a way that is difficult to counterfeit? Critics of this view doubt the ability of governments to resist the lure of printing too much money. For these critics, the cost of resources involved in using, say, gold is less than the inflationary costs of a too-rapidly growing money supply.

LAISSEZ-FAIRE POLICY

The classical economists' views of aggressive supply and demand and the source of unemployment caused them to advocate a **laissez-faire** economic policy for government.

> **Laissez-faire** means a hands-off government policy towards the economy. Government intervention in macroeconomic affaris should be strictly limited.

As long as aggregate supply creates its own aggregate demand, the government need not play a role in regulating the amount of aggregate demand. Aggregate demand will always equal the aggregate amount of production. As long as unemployment is caused by wages that are too high, the government need not intervene to create jobs. Sufficient jobs will be created simply by letting wages adjust to the equilibrium levels.

> Classical economists believed the economy was capable of healing itself by allowing flexible wages, prices, and interest rates to adjust to eliminate unemployment. No one needed to worry about an insufficiency of aggregate demand because Say's law ensured that supply creates its own demand. Government actions to regulate employment and real GDP were considered unnecessary.

KEYNESIAN ECONOMICS

Between 1929 and 1933, real GDP in the United States declined by 30 percent. The 1929 output level was not regained until 1939. Unemployment rose from 3.2 percent of the labor force in 1929 to 24.9 percent in 1933 and was still 17.2 percent in 1939. Such a substantial downturn appeared to contradict the teachings of classical economics. There had been economic recessions and depressions before, but none so severe or sustained.

The Great Depression of the 1930s caused a watershed in macroeconomic thought because it showed that economies could operate for extended periods of time with high unemployment. British economist John Maynard Keynes (1883–1946) offered an explanation of why economies could operate below their production potential for long periods of time. Keynes shifted the focus of macroeconomics from aggregate supply to aggregate demand. He agreed with the classical theorists that aggregate supply determines real GDP, output, and employment in the long run, but he pointed out that "in the long run, we are all dead." Keynes was more interested in what determined real GDP in the short run.

Keynes saw two major flaws in the classical theory. The first was that money wages did not, in fact, have the necessary downward flexibility to eliminate unemployment. The second flaw was Say's law, which Keynes rejected. Keynes believed that desired saving depended on interest rates in only a minor way. Instead, Keynes argued that desired saving depended primarily on disposable income. Thus, the interest rate alone could not be relied on to equate desired saving and desired investment. Keynes did not believe that supply creates its own demand, as Say's law predicted.

To understand Keynes's analysis of the Great Depression, however, one must first understand his view of the labor market.

The Keynesian Labor Market

Recall that the classical economists assumed that wages and prices were sufficiently flexible to maintain full employment of all resources. Keynes drew a picture of labor markets that is much different from the flexible labor market of the classical theorist. According to Keynes, the labor market is inflexible because economic and institutional factors prevent money wages from falling when unemployment exists. The main economic factor is the difficulty of instituting across-the-board wage cuts when wages are set in many different labor markets. Workers do not like to accept wage cuts unless others accept them, and firms do not want to be the first to cut wages. The institutional factors include union contracts that fix wages for several years, minimum-wage laws, and unemployment insurance that gives unemployed workers a financial backstop. These factors make money wages sticky in the downward direction. "Sticky" money wages do not fall when the demand for labor falls. Instead, they remain at a rate high enough to cause unemployment. (See Example 3.)

This picture was not unreasonable for Great Britain at the time of Keynes's writing. From 1890 to 1918, the unemployment rate in Great Britain averaged less than 5 percent, but from 1921 to 1936, it varied between 9.7 percent and 22.1 percent. From 1921 to 1929, the British unemployment rate averaged 12 percent; from 1930 to 1936, it averaged 17.8

percent. Throughout the 1920s and 1930s, prices declined very slowly and money wages remained more or less at the same level.

The Keynesian Aggregate Supply Curve

Remember from Chapter 9 that the aggregate supply curve shows the levels of real output (real GDP) that are supplied by businesses at different price levels. Keynes considered how this aggregate supply curve would look in a severe depression. In a depression economy, it is possible to coax more production out of existing resources without raising wages and prices. A large number of people are unemployed and are willing and anxious to work at the going wage rate. In addition, much plant and equipment capital is idle because factories are not running at capacity. The firm need not raise wages to get more workers; it simply puts the unemployed worker back on the job. Because unemployed workers are willing to work at the going money wage, it is possible to expand output without raising the price level. *At less than full employment, real GDP can increase without an increase in the price level.*

Figure 3 shows a simplified Keynesian aggregate supply curve. At levels of output less than full-employment output, wages and prices are sticky in the downward direction. There are unemployed workers willing to work at prevailing wages and prices. Therefore, the supply of real output can be increased

EXAMPLE 3 Unemployment, Wages, and Prices During the Great Depression

The classical model predicted that high unemployment would be self-liquidating. If a large number of people were involuntarily unemployed, they would be willing to work for less. Wages would fall; thus, unemployment would fall. However, during the Great Depression, which began in the late 1920s in Europe and spread to the United States in 1929, this prediction did not hold true. In Germany, France, the United States, and the Scandinavian countries, unemployment rates rose to 25 percent or even higher in the early 1930s. In Europe and the United States, unemployment rates stubbornly remained high for a decade. The accompanying diagrams show unemployment rates and wage and price indexes in Great Britain, the United States, and Germany during the Great Depression.

The figures for Great Britain clearly show why Keynes believed the classical model was not working: The British unemployment rate was higher than 10 percent from 1925 to 1937, rising to more than 20 percent in the early 1930s. During this same period, money wages in industry scarcely fell despite massive unemployment. Prices did decline somewhat, meaning that English real wages (money wages after adjustment for inflation) were actually rising during the Great Depression! It is no wonder that Keynes worried about the automatic self-correcting forces of falling wages and prices. The picture in the United States was slightly different. Money wages did fall substantially during the early 1930s, and prices fell more rapidly. The surprising feature of the U.S. experience was the fact that both wages and prices were rising in the mid-1930s, despite massive unemployment. The German case appears to conform most closely to the classical model. As the German unemployment rate rose to 30 percent of the labor force, the wage rate plummeted, falling more sharply than prices. Falling real wages accompanied high unemployment. Of the three cases, the German unemployment rate returned most quickly to pre-Depression levels. There are a number of reasons for this pattern (many cite Hitler's rearmament of the German military), but flexible wages and prices may have played a role.

Sources: Historical Statistics of the United States, Series D1–10; D802–810; B.R. Mitchell, *European Historical Statistics, 1750–1970,* Tables C–2, C–4.

(*continued*)

EXAMPLE 3 (*Continued*)

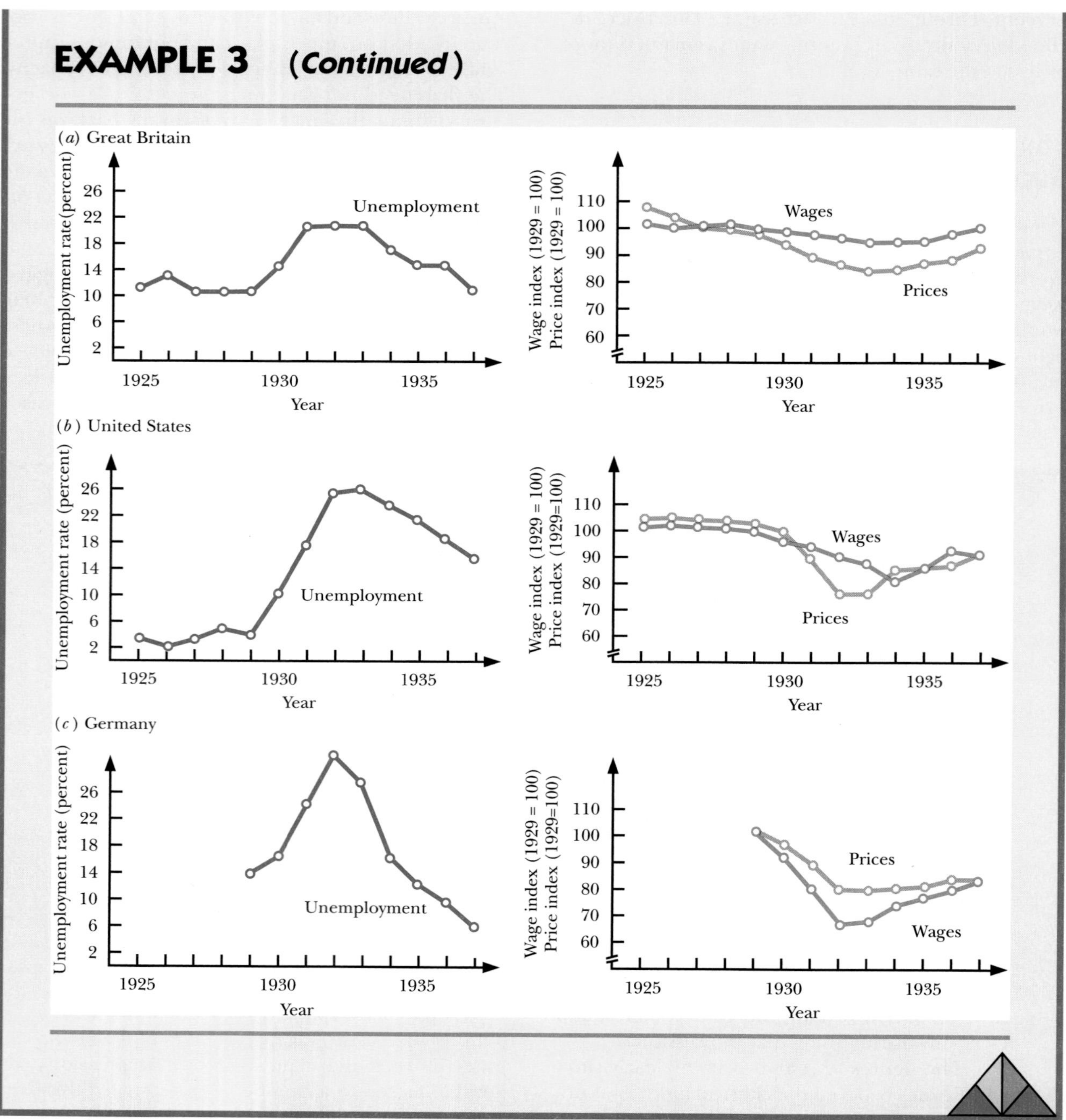

without an increase in prices. For this reason, the Keynesian aggregate supply curve is *horizontal* below the level of full-employment output, indicated by point *f* in Figure 3.

The picture changes when the economy reaches full employment. The simplified Keynesian aggregate supply curve is vertical at full-employment output. At full employment, any further attempt to increase real output will raise money wages. There is no involuntary unemployment, and it is not possible to increase real output any further because resources are already fully employed. Instead, employers bid among themselves for labor and drive up wages; prices rise at the same rate as wages. Because wages and prices rise at the same rate, *real wages* remain the same. Despite the rising price level, the economy

FIGURE 3
The Keynesian Aggregate Supply Curve

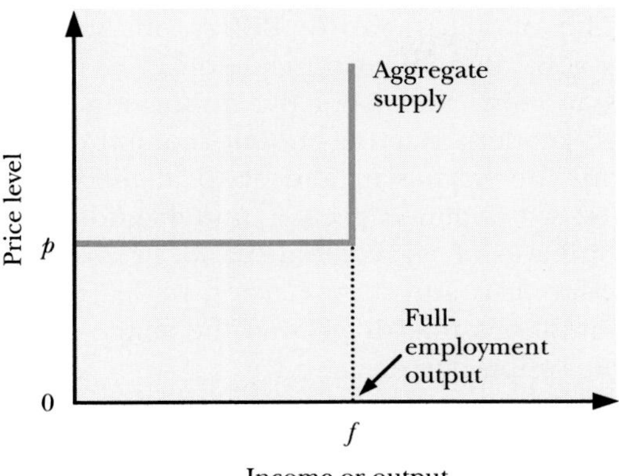

The Keynesian aggregate supply curve is horizontal at less than full-employment output (point f) because money wages are "sticky" in a downward direction. Money wages do not fall in response to rising unemployment; therefore, different rates of aggregate supply (at less than full employment) are consistent with the same price level. Once the economy is at full-employment output, money wages rise, but prices are driven up at the same rate, and employment does not increase. At full-employment output, the supply curve becomes vertical. Thus, the Keynesian aggregate supply curve is a right-angled curve.

FIGURE 4
A Keynesian Equilibrium during a Depression

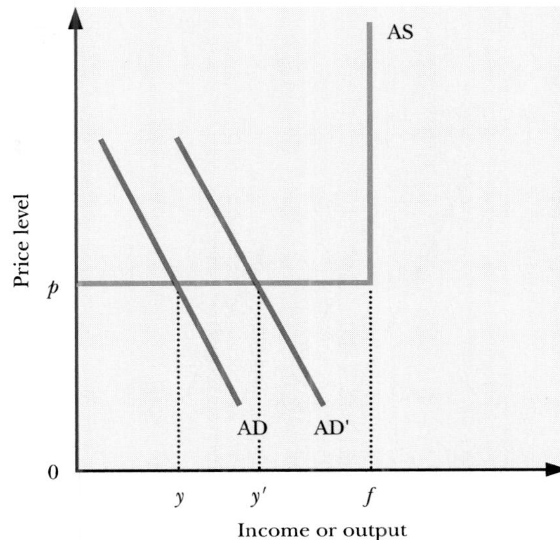

During a depression, the equilibrium level of output in the Keynesian model occurs when the aggregate demand curve intersects the horizontal portion of the aggregate supply curve, where significant unemployment exists. When aggregate demand shifts from AD to AD$'$, output rises from y to y'.

cannot produce more output because all labor is employed.

Keynesian Aggregate Supply and Aggregate Demand Together

Keynes combined an aggregate demand curve with his version of the aggregate supply curve to explain why an economy can fall into a depression (see Figure 4). Chapter 9 introduced the aggregate demand curve (the quantity of real GDP demanded at different price levels) and showed that the equilibrium output and price level are determined by the intersection of the aggregate demand and aggregate supply curves. When the aggregate demand curve, AD, intersects the backward-*L*-shaped aggregate supply curve on its horizontal portion, the economy will operate below full employment. The farther to the left of the full-employment output is the intersection of AD and AS, the greater is the amount of unemployment. As Keynes saw it, the basic problem of an economy caught in a depression is too little aggregate demand. As aggregate demand increases (as AD shifts to AD$'$), output rises and unemployment falls. Keynes, therefore, devoted himself to explaining the determinants of aggregate demand.

Figure 5 shows a Keynesian aggregate supply curve modified by the existence of bottlenecks. Bottlenecks occur when, as the economy expands, some sectors reach capacity before others. As long as output is below point b, increases in aggregate demand rasie output without inflation. The shift in aggregate demand from AD to AD$'$ simply raises output from y to y'. But the increase in aggregate demand from AD$'$ to AD$''$ raises both output and the price level because upward pressure is exerted on wages and prices in the sectors causing the bottlenecks.

The next chapter examines in greater detail a Keynesian equilibrium in which the aggregate demand curve intersects the aggregate supply curve in the horizontal portion. With a fixed price level it is better to focus on the relationship between spending and income rather than between spending and the price level.

FIGURE 5
Keynesian Aggregate Supply with Bottlenecks

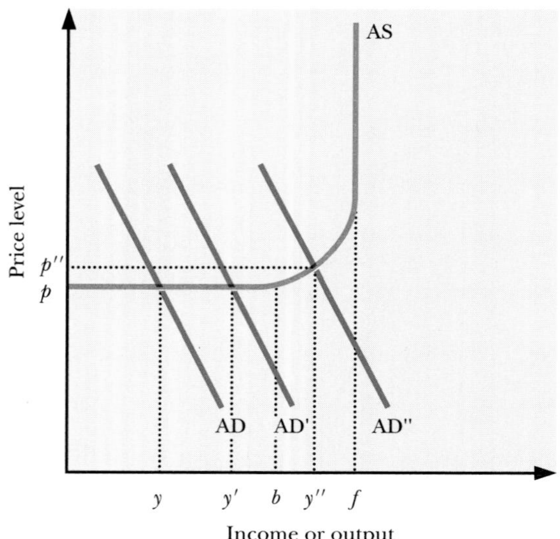

As the economy approaches full-employment output, the aggregate supply curve begins to slope upward (at the output associated with point b) as resource bottlenecks are experienced in some sectors of the economy. Thus, a shift in the aggregate demand curve from AD to AD′ does not affect the price level, but a shift from AD′ to AD″ raises prices because of bottlenecks.

KEYNES VERSUS THE CLASSICAL ECONOMISTS

John Maynard Keynes and the classical economists presented two distinct pictures of the macroeconomy. Each version was particularly suited to the conditions of its time. The classical model reflected the 19th-century world in which prices and wages responded quickly to changing supply and demand conditions. The classical model was not equipped to explain the occurrence of a deep and persistent drop in output and employment during which wages and prices remained stubbornly fixed. The Keynesian model was suited to the depression of the 1930s, when output and employment dropped precipitously due to declining aggregate demand. Because the restoration of employment and output under these conditions was simply a matter of pumping up aggregate demand, Keynesian economics (discussed in the next chapter) focused on how to increase demand during conditions of depression.

The modern world differs in many ways from both the 19th-century world of the classical economists and from the depressionary 1930s. Hence, modern macroeconomics combines features of both the Keynesian and classical models. From Keynes, we obtained greater understanding of the determinants of aggregate demand. From the classical economists and from Keynes, we learned about the conditions that determine the shape of the aggregate supply curve.

The next chapter discusses the aggregate expenditure model of Keynes. Subsequent chapters return to the discussion of aggregate supply and aggregate demand in modern economies.

SUMMARY

1. Say's law holds that supply creates its own demand. In the classical model, saving and investment are coordinated by changes in the rate of interest.

2. To the classical economists, unemployment could not occur because wages and prices were sufficiently flexible.

3. The simple quantity theory of money suggests that changes in money supply and price level will be strictly proportional. This conclusion follows from the equation of exchange ($MV = PQ$) and from the assumptions that velocity and output are fixed.

4. The Great Depression of the 1930s prompted Keynes to study economies operating with unemployed resources in which increases in aggregate expenditures could cause increases in real output and employment. He rejected Say's law that supply creates its own demand and believed that wages and prices were not sufficiently flexible to eliminate involuntary unemployment.

5. Keynes assumed money wages were sticky in the downward direction. When there is substantial unemployment, additional workers are available at the going set of wage rates. Thus, the Keynesian aggregate supply curve is horizontal below the full-employment output level. In this case, Say's law is reversed: Aggregate demand creates its own supply.

KEY TERMS

Say's law
velocity of circulation
laissez-faire

QUESTIONS AND PROBLEMS

1. Describe how classical economists would have responded to the following statement: "Savers and investors are different people. There is no way desired saving will equal desired investment."
2. Explain why the classical theorists believed that there would be no long-term involuntary unemployment.
3. What is Say's law?
4. How could the classical theorists believe that aggregate supply creates its own demand?
5. If prices are rising 5 percent per year, what is happening to the value of money?
6. Assume that real GDP is increasing at a rate of 20 percent per year and that the supply of money is increasing at a rate of 10 percent per year. What would you expect to happen to the value of money and to prices?
7. Answer the following questions, assuming $M = \$100, Q = 400$ units, and $P = \$2$ per unit.
    a. What is the value of V?
    b. Determine the aggregate demand schedule when velocity is 8 times for a price level of \$1, for a price level of \$2, and for a price level of \$3.
    c. If the money supply rose to \$150, what would the aggregate demand schedule be for each of the three price levels listed in part *b*?
    d. Use this example to illustrate the basic proposition of the simple quantity theory.
8. Suppose that the money supply doubles but that velocity falls by one-half. What will happen to the price level, assuming output remains the same?
9. How did the behavior of wages in Great Britain in the 1920s and 1930s affect the Keynesian view of labor markets?
10. Why is the Keynesian aggregate supply curve horizontal when there is substantial unemployment?
11. How does the Keynesian aggregate supply curve differ from the aggregate supply curve of the classical model?

SUGGESTED READINGS

Sowell, Thomas. *Classical Economics Reconsidered.* Princeton, NJ: Princeton University Press, 1974, chap. 2.

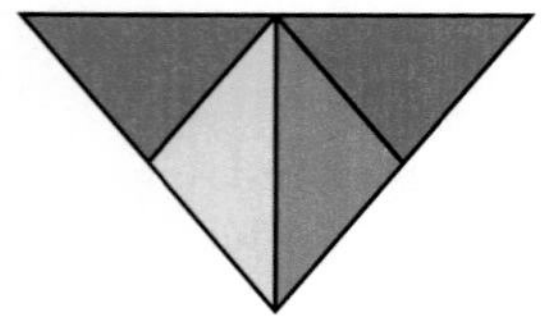

11

Keynesian Economics: The Multiplier

CHAPTER INSIGHT

It is often said that if you make a large purchase such as a car or a house, your expenditure will be "good for the economy." Classical economists would disagree because they believe that your expenditure is made at the expense of other individuals; your entrance into the housing market drives up the prices for everyone. The Keynesian vision, however, holds that, if you increase your demand by \$100, aggregate demand will increase by more than \$100 because the price level remains fixed. This magic is called the multiplier. Your \$100 puts someone else to work who, in turn, increases his or her spending by less than \$100, and so on. In the Keynesian world, an increase in aggregate demand is good for the economy because it allows aggregate output to increase.

This chapter focuses on Keynes's income/expenditure model of real-GDP determination. Unlike the classical model, the Keynesian model assumes inflexible prices. An appendix discusses the Keynesian model (called the *IS/LM* model), in which both interest rates and output are mutually determined.

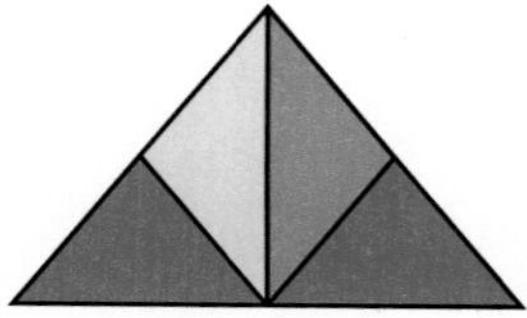

THE INCOME/EXPENDITURE MODEL

The aggregate demand and aggregate supply approach is useful when the price level must be determined simultaneously with the level of output. But if the price level is constant, as Keynes assumed, the income/expenditure model is more appropriate. Keynes based this approach to the determination of real GDP on the relationship between income and expenditures. His model explains the equilibrium level of GDP at a given price level (a point on the aggregate demand curve) by building on the components of aggregate expenditure. The model stands on its own as a description of an economy in a deep depression with fixed prices (and wages). (See Example 1.)

The Keynesian income/expenditure model explains the determination of real output, *Y*. Remember that the Keynesian model deals with an economy operating below full employment in which more

EXAMPLE 1 Why Are Wages Rigid?

Two views have developed to explain why wages are rigid, rather than responsive to each movement in labor market conditions. One view is that rigid wages are the natural outcome of the way that wages are set in a market economy; the other is that rigid wages are caused by the institutional circumstances that have been imposed on the economy by government policy. Each view lays a foundation for Keynesian economics, although the latter view provides more options for government policy.

The first view stems from the decentralization of the wage-setting process in a market economy. Workers will resist any attempt to lower wages, despite the possibility of greater employment, due to the impossibility of coordinating a wage cut on a large scale. A worker might be willing to accept a wage cut only if everyone else does. But since wages are set by millions of individually negotiated contracts, a large-scale wage cut is impossible to coordinate. This coordination problem is present everywhere and is an example of the fallacy of composition; what is true for all is not true for one. Accepting a cut in wages is like trying to see a spectacular play in football by remaining seated—if everyone stands, it is necessary to stand.

The existence of unemployment benefits is a second reason for the fixity of nominal wages. If a worker loses his or her job, the pressure to accept a lower wage is significantly reduced by the prospect of extended unemployment benefits. In Great Britain, unemployment benefits rose by almost 200 percent between 1920 and 1931, when commodity prices were collapsing. Between World War I and World War II, British money wages remained more or less constant, despite record levels of unemployment. Aggregate demand dropped after World War I, and money wages fell by a considerable amount from 1920 to 1923. But money wages subsequently stabilized in the face of a progressive liberalization of unemployment insurance: Nominal benefits were raised and eligibility requirements were eased over the decade of the 1920s. The plan was curtailed slightly in 1931 because the unemployment fund ran short, but by 1934 unemployment benefits had returned to the pre-1931 levels. By 1938, covered workers could receive unemployment benefits of nearly 60 percent of their average weekly wages for an indefinite period. Unemployment benefits became an important alternative to seeking work or accepting lower wages.

Sources: D. Benjamin and L. Kochin, "Searching for an Explanation of Unemployment in Interwar Britain," *Journal of Political Economy* 87 (June 1979): 441–70; Patrick Minford, "Wages and Unemployment Half a Century On," in W. Etis and P. Sinclair, *Keynes and Economic Policy: The Relevance of the General Theory after Fifty Years* (London: Macmillan Press, 1988), 45–64.

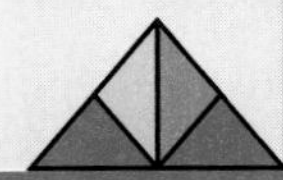

output can be produced without driving up the price level. The Keynesian model explains the determination of real output but not the level of prices.

To explain real output determination, one must explain total expenditures, not just consumption expenditures. Consumption (C) is only one component of total expenditures, although it is the most important. Total expenditures also include investment (I), government spending (G), and net exports ($X - M$). To keep the model simple, we first consider a hypothetical economy that makes only consumption and investment spending. Later we add the other two components of expenditures, government spending, and net exports.

Consumption and Saving

At the foundation of the income/expenditure approach are the consumption/income and saving/income curves introduced in Chapter 8. A brief review is given here. Panel *a* of Figure 1 shows how desired consumption rises with income. Where the consumption/income curve intersects the 45 degree line is the break-even point at which disposable income equals consumption. Panel *b* of Figure 1 shows how desired saving rises with income. Saving is zero where the saving/income curve crosses the horizontal axis. The two curves are complementary because $C + S$ equals disposable income: If you know consumption you can determine saving, and vice-versa. For each level of income, the consumption/income or saving/income curve shows the amount of consumption or saving that households are prepared to undertake.

In Chapter 8 we also defined the slope of the consumption/income curve as the marginal propensity to consume (MPC)—the amount of each additional dollar of disposable income devoted to consumption. Similarly, the slope of the saving/income curve is the marginal propensity to save (MPS)—the amount of each dollar of disposable income saved by households. Since $C + S = Y$, it follows that MPC + MPS = 1: Another dollar of disposable income can be devoted to either consumption or saving.

FIGURE 1
The Consumption/Income and Saving/Income Curves

(*a*) The Consumption/Income Curve

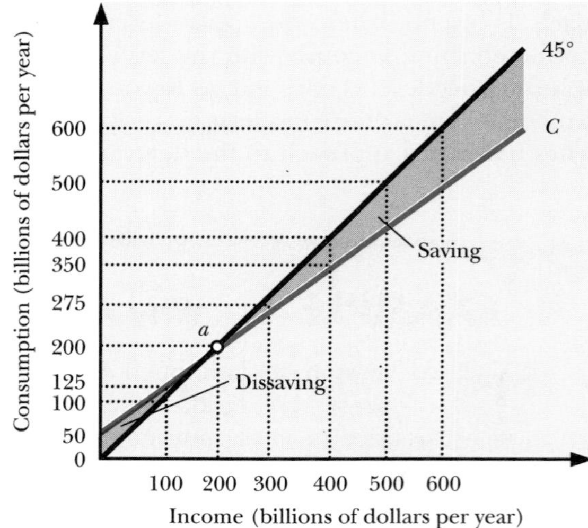

(*b*) The Saving/Income Curve

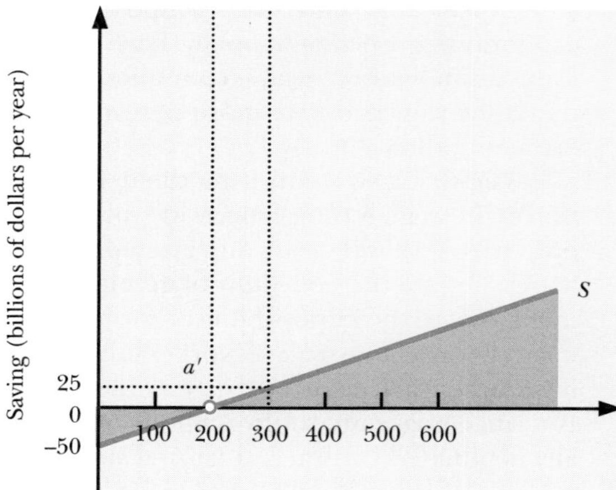

The consumption/income curve, *C*, shows the amount of desired consumption at different levels of income. The slope of the *C* curve is the marginal propensity to consume, MPC. In the lower panel, the saving/income curve (labeled *S*) shows the amount of real saving at each level of income. The slope of the *S* curve is the marginal propensity to save, MPS. Saving is positive to the right of a' and it is negative to the left of a'.

The Aggregate Expenditure Schedule

In the hypothetical economy described in Table 1, the business sector desires to spend a fixed amount

TABLE 1
The Aggregate Expenditure Schedule with No Government Spending and No Government Taxes (billions of dollars)

Output = Income, Y (1)	Consumption, C (2)	Saving, S (3)	Investment, I (4)	Desired Aggregate Expenditures, AE (5) = (2) + (4)	Unintended Investment, $S - I$ (6) = (3) − (4)
100	125	−25	50	175	−75
200	200	0	50	250	−50
300	275	25	50	325	−25
400	350	50	50	400	0
500	425	75	50	475	25
600	500	100	50	550	50

Columns 1 and 2 show the consumption/income schedule for our hypothetical economy. There are no taxes, so income and disposable income are the same. The marginal propensity to consume (MPC) in this example is 0.75 because for every $100 billion increase in income, consumption increases by $75 billion. The marginal propensity to save (MPS) is 0.25 because for every $100 billion increase in income, saving increases by $25 billion.

Aggregate expenditures equal the sum of desired consumption and desired investment at each income level. Desired investment is assumed to be constant at $50 billion. Unintended investment is the difference between desired saving and desired investment at each income level. Only at an income of $400 billion does desired saving equal desired investment or does the desired aggregate expenditure level equal aggregate output. The equilibrium income is, therefore, $400 billion.

on real investment—$50 billion—at each level of income (and output) produced by the economy. In this hypothetical economy, the government collects no taxes and purchases no goods or services, and the economy has zero net exports ($G = 0$, $T = 0$, $X - M = 0$). The consumption/income schedule is the same as Table 1 in Chapter 8.

Because investment is the same for each income level, desired **aggregate expenditures (AE)** at each income level are simply desired consumption plus desired investment, or the sum of columns 2 and 4 in Table 1.

A schedule of **aggregate expenditures (AE)** shows the relationship between the desired amount of total spending $[C+I+G+(X-M)]$ and income.

To understand Keynesian income/expenditure analysis, it is important to understand that *desired* decisions are not necessarily *realized.* Whether they are indeed realized depends upon the relationship between desired aggregate expenditures and actual aggregate output.[1]

Consider what would happen if this economy attempted to produce an output of $500 billion. This decision is made by the hundreds of thousands of producers acting independently of one another. As Chapter 7 on national income accounting demonstrated, the act of producing $500 billion worth of output will create an income of $500 billion. If the economy were to continue to produce output at this rate, at the end of 1 year it will have created $500 billion worth of income. At an income level of $500 billion, this economy would desire to spend $475 billion on consumption and investment, as shown in column 5 of Table 1. Desired aggregate expenditures would fall short of aggregate output by $25 billion, as shown in column 6 of Table 1.

The output rate of $500 billion per year is, therefore, not an equilibrium output because the economy is producing output at a rate faster than

[1]The terms *ex ante* (before) and *ex post* (after) are sometimes used to describe desired (*ex ante*) and actual (*ex post*) levels.

purchasers in the economy are buying. Producers will realize that too much output is being produced because excessive inventories of unsold cars, TV sets, sewing machines, and the like will build up. This accumulation will signal to business firms that their current production rates are higher than the market is prepared to purchase. Producers will have to slow down the rate of output production. (Remember, producers are operating in a Keynesian economy in which prices do not drop to rid the economy of unsold goods.)

If business firms reduce their rate of production from \$500 billion to \$300 billion worth of output, desired aggregate expenditures will now *exceed* the rate of output by \$25 billion. Producers will realize that there is too little output because purchasers want to buy more than is being produced. Inventories of goods—such as cars or TV sets—will fall below normal levels. Inventories can be replenished only be speeding up production.

Whenever aggregate production exceeds desired aggregate expenditures, the rate of production (and the rate of income creation) slows down. Whenever production falls short of desired aggregate expenditures, the rate of production (and income creation) speeds up. By adjusting the rate of output in response to total spending, the economy moves towards **Keynesian equilibrium.**

Keynesian equilibrium occurs when the economy produces an output that equals desired aggregate expenditures.

FIGURE 2
Equilibrium Output

(*a*) Equilibrium Showing Desired Aggregate Expenditure Equal to Aggregate Production

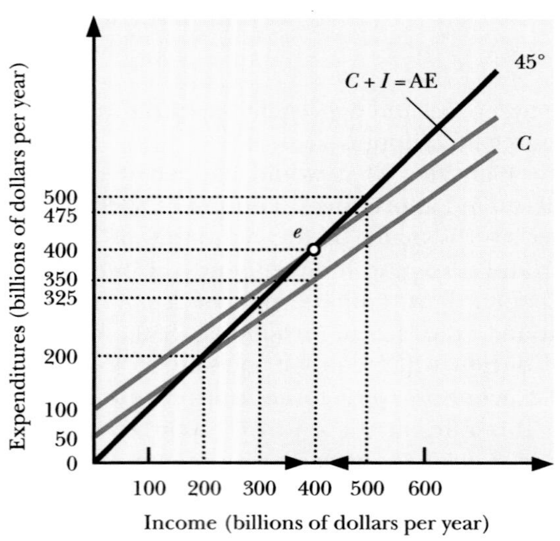

(*b*) Equilibrium Showing Desired Investment Equal to Desired Saving

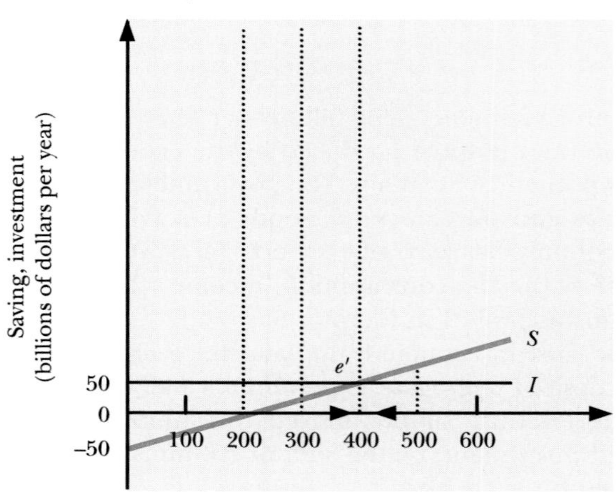

This figure is drawn from the data in Table 1. In panel *a*, the intersection of the AE curve with the 45-degree line occurs at an income of \$400 billion (point *e*). If the economy were to attempt to produce an income greater than \$400 billion (to the right of *e*), aggregate output would exceed desired aggregate expenditures and income would fall. If the economy were to attempt to produce an income less than \$400 billion (to the left of *e*), desired aggregate expenditures would exceed aggregate production and income would rise. Panel *b* contrasts desired investment and desired saving to show how the economy reaches equilibrium. At levels of income above \$400 billion (*e*′), desired saving exceeds desired investment. Unintended inventory investment (the difference between desired saving and desired investment) signals firms to slow down their rate of output. At levels of income below \$400 billion, desired investment exceeds desired saving. Unintended inventory disinvestment signals firms to increase their rate of production. Equilibrium income is reached at \$400 billion, when aggregate production equals aggregate expenditures, or when desired saving equals desired investment.

Panel *a* of Figure 2 gives a graphical picture of how equilibrium output is determined. The aggregate expenditure (AE) curve is simply the consumption/income curve (C) shifted upward by the amount of investment. The AE curve and the 45-degree reference line (which represents the set of all possible equilibrium points) show the relationship between *actual* aggregate output (or income) and *desired* aggregate expenditures at each output level. Aggregate income (or output) can be measured along the horizontal axis or by the corresponding vertical distance from the axis to the 45-degree reference line at that level of income (or output). Point *e*, which is the intersection of the aggregate expenditure curve with the 45-degree line, is the point where desired aggregate expenditures equal aggregate output. To the right of point *e*, more output is produced than the economy wishes to purchase; desired spending falls short of output at every income level. To the left of point *e*, less output is being produced than the economy wishes to purchase. The economy responds to such a disequilibrium by adjusting output until it equals $400 billion (at point *e*).

Saving and Investment

Investors and savers are typically different individuals. Although some businesses finance their investments out of their own saving, many must borrow outside funds. The primary source of such funds is the saving of individual households who consume less than their disposable income. However, without a coordinating mechanism, there is no reason why desired saving (S) should equal desired investment (I) in the economy at any time. The classical theorists supposed that desired saving would be equated with desired investment by the rate of interest. If desired investment exceeded desired saving, the interest rate would rise to reduce investment and increase saving. In the Keynesian model, by contrast, desired investment and desired saving are equalized by changes in output.

Returning to Table 1, the business community desires to invest $50 billion at all levels of income (or output). The amount of desired saving depends upon the amount of income. If firms in the economy are producing an output of $500 billion, desired saving equals $75 billion because consumption equals $425 billion. Desired saving exceeds desired investment by $25 billion at this output. At an output of $500 billion, there is too much saving; $25 billion of output is unsold and accumulates as unintended inventory investment. (*Inventory investment* is the addition to the inventories of goods and materials held by business firms.) When goods are unsold (because aggregate expenditures are insufficient), actual investment exceeds planned investment by the sum of unintended inventory investment. The unintended accumulation of inventories raises actual investment to $75 billion (the sum of desired and unintended investment) to equal desired saving. **Unintended investment** is shown in column 6 of Table 1.

Unintended investment is the difference between desired saving and desired investment at a given level of income.

Whenever unintended investment in unwanted inventories exists (caused by too little aggregate expenditures) or unintended reduction in inventories occur (caused by too much aggregate expenditure), producers change their rate of production. When output (and income) changes, desired saving changes as well. (See Example 2.)

When unintended investment is taking place, output begins to fall. With prices fixed (as Keynes assumed), businesses have only one way to cut back on the amount of unsold goods piling up in unwanted inventories: they cut back on production. Because desired saving depends upon income, as output falls so does saving. As this adjustment continues, the disparity between desired investment and desired saving diminishes until income (or output) is $400 billion.

When desired saving is less than desired investment, there is too little saving. The withdrawal of saving from the spending stream is smaller than the injection of investment back into the spending stream. Businesses will see their inventories being drawn down to low levels, and there will be unintended *disinvestment* in inventories. Again, with prices fixed, firms have only one way to build their inventories back up: they increase production. As income increases, desired saving increases along with income, and the gap between desired saving and desired investment disappears. This analysis suggests a second definition of **Keynesian equilibrium**.

Keynesian equilibrium is attained at that output at which desired investment equals desired saving.

EXAMPLE 2 Inventories and Output

In the Keynesian income/expenditure model, the buildup of inventories in the form of unintended investment signals to business firms to produce less output. The attached figure for the period 1950 to the present shows how this mechanism works in practice. As slowdowns in business activity start, businesses find themselves holding more inventories than usual. As business activity slowed in 1956, the ratio of manufacturing inventories to shipments rose from 1.74 to 1.90. As business activity slowed in 1982, the ratio rose from 1.74 to 1.91. The unusual feature of the early 1990s is that the decline in business activity has not been accompanied by an increase in inventories to levels above "normal."

Source: Department of Commerce

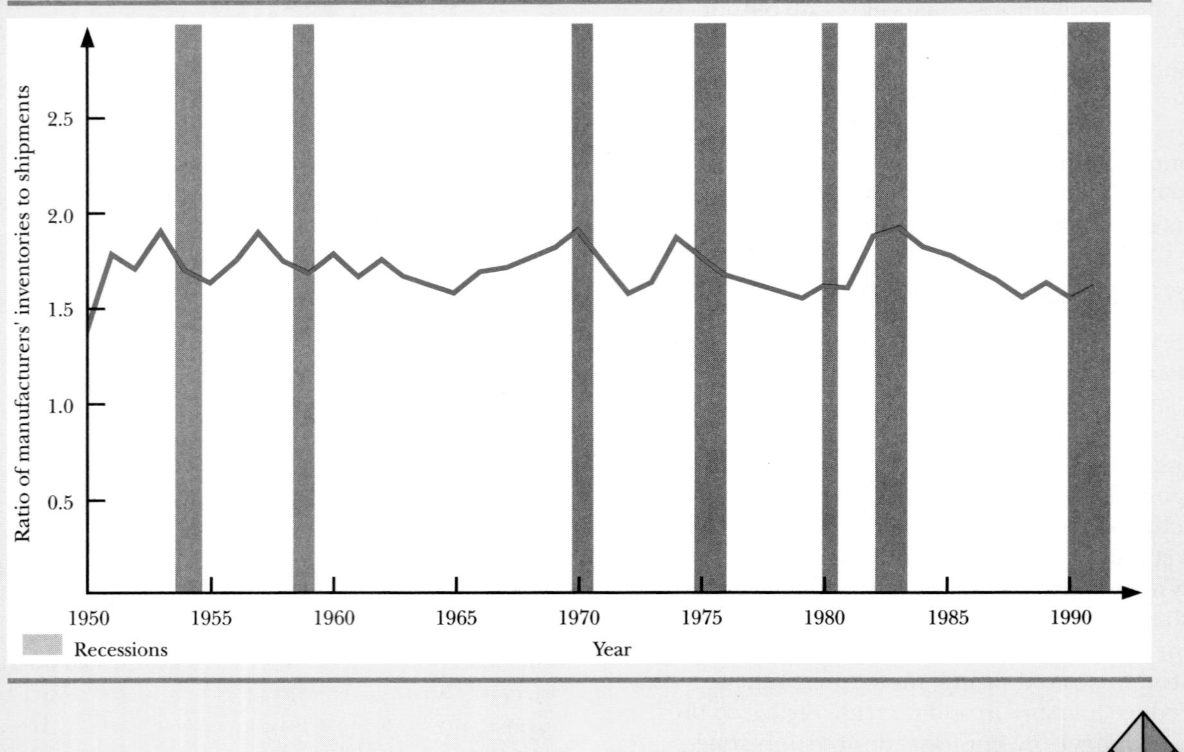

In Figure 2, panel *b*, the movement to equilibrium output is shown by the relationship between desired saving and desired investment. Point e' is the intersection of the horizontal investment curve with the saving/income curve (at an output of $400 billion). At levels of income to the right of e', the withdrawal of saving from the spending stream exceeds the injection of investment) back into the spending stream. Aggregate production exceeds desired aggregate expenditures; unsold goods accumulate in unintended inventories; and this accumulation signals producers that they are producing too much. At levels of income to the left of e', the injection of investment exceeds the withdrawal of saving. Desired aggregate expenditures exceed aggregate production; unwanted inventory disinvestment takes place;

and firms are signaled to increase output. The level of income (or output) adjusts until desired investment equals desired saving.

In the simple Keynesian model, equilibrium is achieved when either of these equivalent conditions is true:

1. Aggregate output equals desired aggregate expenditures (Y = AE).
2. Desired investment equals desired saving ($I = S$).

As this chapter has demonstrated, these two conditions are really different ways of looking at the same thing. When desired investment equals desired saving, output equals desired aggregate expenditures. Saving is the withdrawal households make from the spending stream, and investment is the injection firms replace into the spending stream. Whenever desired saving exceeds desired investment, more is withdrawn from spending than is replaced (desired aggregate expenditure is less than output). Because saving must equal investment, paradoxically, an increase in the desire to save will not increase actual saving if, for example, income drops.

EQUILIBRIUM WITH GOVERNMENT SPENDING AND TAXES

To keep matters simple, the preceding model disregarded government spending (G), taxes (T), and net exports ($X - M$) by setting them equal to zero.

Panel *a* of Figure 3 shows how taxes affect desired aggregate expenditures, AE. Raising taxes decreases aggregate expenditures at each level of income because the higher the taxes, the lower the disposable income. Disposable income (DY) is the difference between income and tax payments: DY = $Y - T$. Taxes have an *indirect effect* on aggregate expenditures. An income tax reduces disposable income by the amount of the tax; as disposable income is reduced, consumption declines at all levels of income. The decrease in consumption depends on the marginal propensity to consume (MPC). Consumption will fall by an

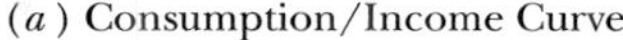

FIGURE 3
Keynesian Equilibrium with Government Spending and Taxes

(*a*) Consumption/Income Curve

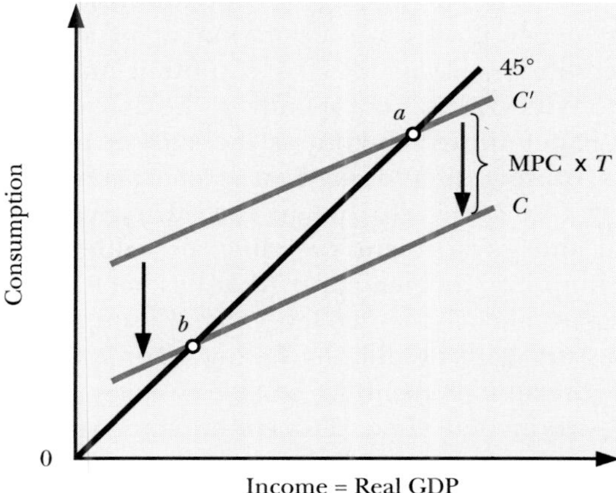

(*b*) Aggregate Expenditure Curve

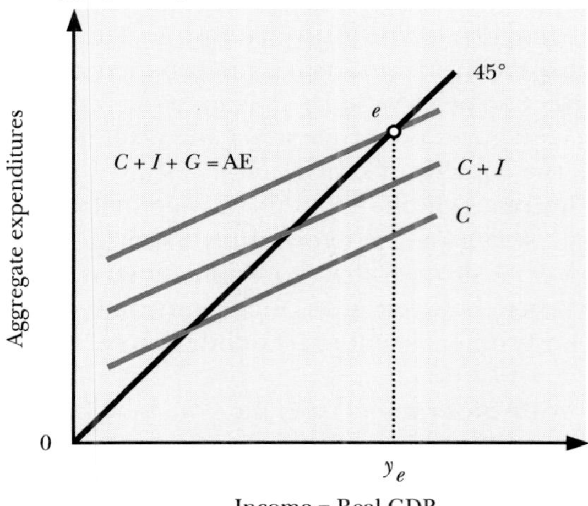

In panel *a*, the introduction of taxes lowers disposable income by the amount of the tax. At each income level, consumption is lowered by MPC times the level of taxes. The introduction of taxes shifts the consumption/income curve downward from C' to C. Panel *b* shows how desired aggregate expenditures (AE) are obtained at each income level. Government expenditures (G) and investment (I) are added to the C curve, shifting it upward by those amounts. Panel *b* shows that the equilibrium level of output (y_e) is determined where the AE curve (which includes taxes, government spending, and investment) intersects the 45-degree reference line at point *e*.

amount equal to MPC multiplied by the decline in disposable income. Thus, the consumption/income curve in panel *a* will shift downward by MPC $\times T$, or from C' to C. For example, if taxes increase by \$100, consumption falls by \$75 when MPC is 0.75.

Panel *b* of Figure 3 shows the effect of government spending on aggregate expenditures. Government expenditures are a component of aggregate expenditures, along with consumption and investment. With government spending, the desired aggregate expenditure schedule is the sum of the three types of spending desired at each income level: AE $= C + I + G$. To obtain the AE curve, investment and government spending are added to the consumption/income curve (that has been adjusted for taxes) at each income level. Panel *b* simplifies the discussion considerably by letting both investment and government spending be fixed sums that do not vary with income. The AE curve in panel *b* of Figure 3 represents the sum of C, I, and G at each level of income.

The Keynesian equilibrium in an economy with government spending and taxes occurs where desired aggregate expenditures (which now include government spending) equal aggregate production (at the intersection of AE with the 45-degree reference line).

With government spending and taxes in the picture, the equality of saving and investment is still an equilibrium condition, but now saving includes both private saving (S) and government saving ($T - G$). Chapter 7 showed that government saving is the difference between government income—taxes—and government spending. Equilibrium occurs when $I = S + (T - G)$.

With government spending included, desired aggregate expenditures ($C + I + G$) equal aggregate production (Y). With taxes included, aggregate income (Y) is used either for consumption, taxes, or saving and, therefore, equals $C + S + T$. Because aggregate production (Y) and aggregate income (Y) are the same,

$$C + I + G = C + S + T$$

or, to simplify,

$$I + G = S + T$$

Therefore,

$$I = S + (T - G)$$

With net exports excluded, investment equals the sum of private (S) and public saving ($T - G$) when an economy is at equilibrium.

EQUILIBRIUM IN AN OPEN ECONOMY

The hypothetical economy studied to this point has been a "closed" economy with no exports or imports. Let us now consider the equilibrium conditions that characterize an "open" economy with exports and imports. An open economy differs from a closed economy in two ways: (1) exports of domestic goods to foreign countries add to aggregate expenditures on domestic goods, and (2) the domestic demand for foreign goods—imports—subtracts from the aggregate expenditures on domestic goods. Thus, equilibrium occurs when

$$Y = C + I + G + (X - M)$$

The term $(X - M)$ represents net exports, or the net demand for domestic goods and services that arises from foreign trade. The net exports term may be positive or negative.

Figure 4 shows a Keynesian equilibrium for an open economy. The only difference between Figure 4 and Figure 2 (panel *a*) and Figure 3 (panel *b*) is that net exports $(X - M)$ have been added to Figure 4. Clearly, to analyze the open economy we must know what determines X and M.

Exports

The quantity of exports is determined by four factors: domestic prices, foreign prices, the exchange rate, and foreign income. Domestic income does *not* influence export demand. (U.S. exports of wheat to Taiwan depend on Taiwanese incomes rather than on U.S. incomes.)

1. Higher domestic prices, *ceteris paribus*, make it more difficult for domestic producers to compete with foreign producers. Thus, higher domestic prices discourage exports to the rest of the world.

FIGURE 4
Keynesian Equilibrium for an Open Economy

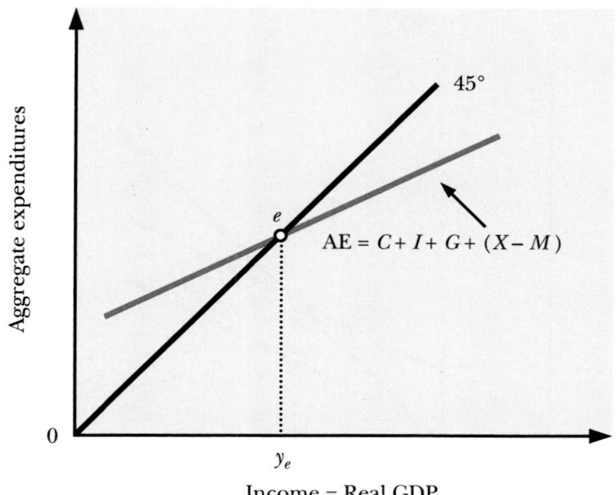

When the economy is open to foreign trade, the aggregate expenditure curve, AE, equals $C + I + G + (X - M)$ because exports (X) add to the demand for domestic output, and imports (M) subtract from the demand for domestic output. The Keynesian equilibrium is still determined by the intersection of AE and the 45-degree line, yielding the income level, y_e.

2. Higher foreign prices, *ceteris paribus*, make it more difficult for foreign producers to compete with domestic producers. Thus, higher foreign prices encourage exports to the rest of the world. Thus, exports from the United States are stimulated if U.S. prices are rising more slowly than German or Japanese prices, and U.S. exports are discouraged if U.S. inflation exceeds foreign inflation rates.

3. The exchange rate—the value of the dollar in terms of foreign currencies—determines how expensive U.S. goods appear to foreign buyers. For example, a bushel of wheat selling for \$3 in the United States will cost a German resident 6 deutsch marks (DMs) if the dollar is worth 2 DMs. If the dollar's value increases to 3 DMs, then the same bushel of wheat will cost a German resident 9 DMs. If the dollar has a high value, American goods will appear expensive and exports will be discouraged; if the dollar has a low value, American goods will be cheaper to foreigners and exports will be encouraged. Therefore, exports will increase or decrease as the exchange value of the domestic currency falls or rises.[2]

4. The higher are foreign incomes, the higher are domestic exports. Thus, the richer is Europe, the greater will be the demand for American wheat, airplanes, or computers.

Imports

The quantity of imports is also determined by four factors: domestic prices, foreign prices, domestic income, and the exchange rate. Notice that *foreign* income does not affect imports. (U.S. imports of Toyotas depend on U.S. income and not on Japanese income.)

Imports will be encouraged by higher domestic prices (as Americans substitute foreign goods for U.S. goods), lower foreign prices, a higher exchange value of the domestic currency (as foreign goods appear cheaper to U.S. residents), and a higher level of domestic income.

With net exports added as a fourth component of aggregate expenditures, the Keynesian equilibrium is now attained when output equals $C + I + G + (X - M)$. Using the same logic as in the preceding section, (remembering that income equals the sum of C, S, and T), we note that equilibrium is achieved when

$$C + S + T = C + I + G + (X - M)$$

This reduces to a new investment/saving equality

$$I = S + (T - G) + (M - X)$$

With both government and net exports included in the model, equilibrium requires that desired investment equal the sum of private saving (S); public saving, or dissaving if a negative number, $T - G$; and net imports or foreign saving ($M - X$). Net imports, $M - X$, are paid for by borrowing foreign savings. There are thus three sources of investment finance: private saving, public saving, and foreign saving.

[2]Domestic prices, foreign prices, and the exchange rate can be summarized in only one factor—the real exchange rate. Nominal exchange rates are observed in foreign-exchange markets. The real exchange rate is the nominal exchange rate adjusted for changes in domestic and foreign prices. For example, if domestic prices rise by 10 percent relative to foreign prices and if the nominal exchange rate falls by 10 percent, then the real exchange rate is constant. A higher real exchange rate for the U.S. dollar discourages U.S. exports.

In an open economy, equilibrium is achieved at that income level at which desired investment equals the sum of desired private saving, government saving (or dissaving), and foreign saving.

CHANGES IN EQUILIBRIUM OUTPUT

We have explained the determination of equilibrium output in the Keynesian model. We are now prepared to tackle an even bigger question: What causes that equilibrium output to increase? The answer is found in changes in the components of aggregate expenditures.

Consider an economy with considerable unemployed resources, where output can be increased without raising prices. As long as desired aggregate expenditures do not change, the equilibrium level of output will remain the same. Figure 5 shows that any change that shifts the aggregate expenditure (AE) curve will change equilibrium income. If the AE curve shifts upward, desired aggregate expenditures $[C + I + G + (X - M)]$ will exceed the initial equilibrium output, y. In Figure 5, an increase in government spending shifts the AE curve to AE′. The economy is now purchasing output at a rate faster than output is being produced; firms respond by increasing production. Upward shifts in AE, therefore, shift equilibrium from e to e' and increase output from y to y'.

Had AE shifted downward, desired aggregate expenditures would have fallen below the original equilibrium output, y, and the economy would have moved to a lower output.

A change in investment, government spending, or net exports will directly change desired aggregate expenditures. If one or all of these factors increase, there will be more desired aggregate expenditures at each level of income. Graphically, a change in investment, government spending, or net exports will cause a vertical shift in the AE curve by the amount of the change in I, G, or $(X - M)$. Expenditures that shift the level of desired aggregate expenditures are called **autonomous expenditures** if they are independent of the level of income.

FIGURE 5
The Effect of a Shift in Aggregate Expenditures on Equilibrium Output

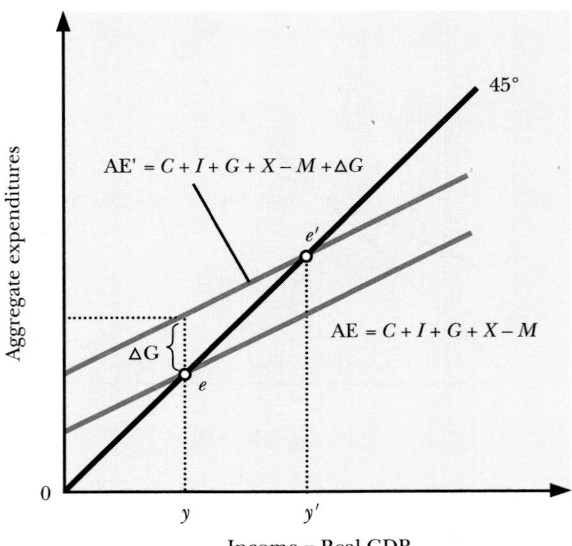

An increase in government spending (ΔG) shifts the aggregate expenditure curve from AE to AE′. This causes desired aggregate expenditure to exceed output at the old equilibrium income, y, and producers are signaled to increase production. The new equilibrium income is reached at an output of y', where output and desired aggregate expenditures are again equal.

Autonomous expenditures are expenditures that are independent of income changes.

Changes in government spending result when federal, state, and local governments change their level of expenditures for goods and services. Changes in investment occur when the business community decides to either increase or decrease its investment spending. Net exports change when foreign income changes relative to U.S. income.

Autonomous changes in consumption are caused by changes in interest rates, expectations, taxes, or the real value of financial assets. Changes in consumption that result from changes in income are *induced* rather than autonomous. Induced consumption changes cause a *movement along* the aggregate expenditure curve rather than a *shift* in the curve.

TABLE 2
Keynesian Equilibrium with an Autonomous Increase in Investment (billions of dollars)

Output = Income, Y	Consumption Spending, C	Investment Spending, I	Government Spending, G	Aggregate Expenditures $AE = C + I + G$
(*a*) With I at \$100 billion; equilibrium Y = \$400 billion				
100	25	100	50	175
200	100	100	50	250
300	175	100	50	325
400	**250**	**100**	**50**	**400**
500	325	100	50	475
600	400	100	50	550
700	475	100	50	675
800	550	100	50	700
(*b*) With I at \$200 billion; equilibrium Y = \$800 billion				
100	25	200	50	275
200	100	200	50	350
300	175	200	50	425
400	250	200	50	500
500	325	200	50	575
600	400	200	50	650
700	475	200	50	725
800	**550**	**200**	**50**	**800**

Panel *a* shows that when I = \$100 billion and G = \$50 billion, the equilibrium level of income (shown in bold numbers) is Y = \$400 billion. The last column shows $AE = C + I + G$. When $Y >$ \$400 billion, $AE < Y$; when $Y <$ \$400 billion, $AE > Y$. In panel (*b*), when investment spending increases to I = \$200 billion, the equilibrium output increases from Y = \$400 billion to Y = \$800 billion. The multiplier is $\Delta Y/\Delta I$ = \$400 billion/\$100 billion = 4.

SIMPLE MULTIPLIERS

The Autonomous Expenditure Multiplier

Table 2 shows the effects of a change in autonomous investment on equilibrium output. We first consider the simple Keynesian model where changes in autonomous spending affect neither the price level nor interest rates. In panel *a*, the first two columns show the consumption/income schedule. The marginal propensity to consume (MPC) is 0.75 (every \$1 increase in income results in a \$0.75 increase in consumption), desired investment is constant at \$100 billion, and government spending is constant at \$50 billion. There are no taxes and no net exports; they will be added later. Equilibrium output is \$400 billion, the level at which desired aggregate expenditures equal total output. The initial aggregate expenditure curve is labeled AE_1 in Figure 6.

Panel *b* of Table 2 shows what happens when there is a \$100 billion autonomous increase in investment spending (from \$100 billion to \$200 billion). The AE curve shifts upward, to AE_2 in Figure 6, by the vertical distance of the change in investment. Similarly, a \$100 billion increase either in government spending or in a combination of investment and government spending would have the same effect on desired aggregate expenditures as the \$100 billion increase in investment spending—shifting the AE_1 to AE_2.

FIGURE 6

The Effect of an Autonomous Increase in Investment on Equilibrium Output

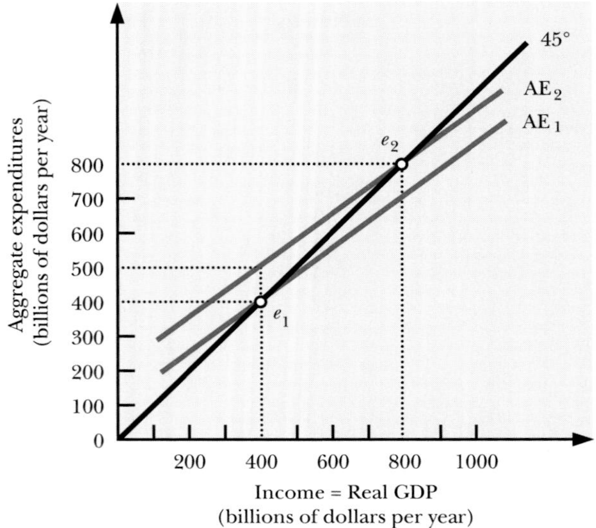

A $100 billion increase in investment shifts the aggregate expenditure curve up vertically by $100 billion, from AE$_1$ to AE$_2$. At the original equilibrium, output is $400 billion; desired aggregate expenditures now exceed aggregate production, and desired saving exceeds desired investment. Equilibrium is restored at an output of $800 billion. The $100 billion increase in investment has caused a $400 billion increase in output. In this case, interest rates and the price level are held constant.

The position of the AE$_2$ curve shows that desired aggregate expenditures are now greater at each income level than along AE$_1$. Point e_1 represents the initial equilibrium for curve AE$_1$. When increased investment shifts AE$_1$ to AE$_2$, the initial equilibrium output of $400 billion is less than the new desired expenditure level, $500 billion, for that level of income. The economy raises output until it arrives at its new equilibrium at point e_2, where it produces $800 billion worth of output. The output of $800 billion is the new equilibrium output because at that output, desired aggregate expenditures are also $800 billion.

Notice that the $100 billion increase in investment spending causes a $400 billion increase in output (from $400 billion to $800 billion). The increase in output is *4 times* the increase in investment. Keynes called the tendency for an increase in autonomous spending to cause magnified increases in output the **multiplier**. In general, any shift in the AE curve caused by an autonomous change in investment, government spending, consumption, or exports will have a multiplier effect on GDP.

> The **autonomous expenditure multiplier** **($\Delta Y/\Delta I$)** is the ratio of the change in output to the change in autonomous investment, government consumption, or net export spending.

Why should a relatively small autonomous change in investment cause such a large change in output? When investment expenditures are increased by $100 billion, incomes in the economy immediately increase by $100 billion. These expenditures, after all, end up in the pockets and purses of the suppliers of the factors of production that produced the $100 billion worth of investment goods. If this immediate effect were the only effect, then the increase in investment would cause only an equivalent increase in output. But the process does not stop here. *People whose incomes have gone up by a total of $100 billion will increase their consumption spending.* When income increases, consumption increases by the economy's marginal propensity to consume—by MPC times the increase in income. Aggregate incomes again increase by the amount of the increase in consumption, and the recipients of this extra income again increase their consumption by MPC times the amount of the income increase. This process continues until the successive increases in spending dwindle to zero. (See Example 3.)

Table 3 calculates how an increase in investment leads to a magnified increase in output. A $100 billion increase in investment immediately creates $100 billion worth of additional income. With a marginal propensity to consume of 0.75, this increase in income causes consumption to increase by $75 billion. In round 2, this $75 billion increase in consumption creates another $75 billion in income. Of this $75 billion, 75 percent ($56.25 billion) is spent on additional consumption, creating $56.25 billion of additional income. In round 3, this $56.25 billion worth of new income stimulates a consumption increase of another $42.19 billion, and so the process continues until the full effect of the multiplier is felt. In our example, the multiplier is 4 because the $100 billion increase in investment eventually causes a $400 billion increase in income.

EXAMPLE 3 The Multiplier and the Creation of Jobs

Businesses like to cite statistics such as the following: "The travel industry has created more than 400,000 new jobs in New Hampshire," or, "If the XYZ Steel Plant closes, OurTown USA will lose 10,000 jobs." These figures are cited even though it is clear that employment in the New Hampshire travel industry is less than 400,000 or the XYZ Steel Plant employs only 2000 employees. Such statistics are derived using the simple multiplier notion. For every $1000 spent directly on tourism, recipients of that money increase their purchases; their recipients increase their purchases; and so on. For every $1 million order of steel from the XYZ Plant, employees and suppliers will increase their purchases; the people who make these sales will increase their purchases, and so on.

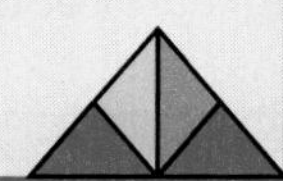

TABLE 3
The Multiple Principle Illustrated (billions of dollars)

Round	Amount of Increase in Income (ΔY)	Amount of Increase in Consumption (ΔC)	Leakages (increase in saving) (ΔS)
1	**100.00**	75.00	25.00
2	75.00	56.25	18.75
3	56.25	42.19	14.06
4	42.19	31.64	10.55
5	31.64	23.73	7.91
6	23.73	17.80	5.93
All other	71.19	53.39	17.80
Totals	400.00	300.00	**100.00**

A $100 billion increase in investment sets the multiplier process into motion. (Here, the marginal propensity to consume is 0.75.) The $100 billion increase in investment creates $100 billion in additional income, 75 percent of which is spent in round 1. In round 2, the $75 billion extra consumption enters as a $75 billion increase in income, and 75 percent of this increase (56.25 billion) is spent on additional consumption. This $56.25 billion enters as additional income in round 3, and 75 percent of this income is spent on additional consumption. This process continues through a large number of rounds until income has increased by $400 billion and consumption has increased by $300 billion. The process continues until the sum of leakages into saving equals the initial increase in investment. In this case, the investment multiplier equals 4 because a $100 billion increase in investment has caused a $400 billion increase in income.

At each stage, income is leaking out of the circular flow of expenditures in the form of saving. As Table 3 shows, of the initial $100 billion increase in income, $75 billion is consumed and $25 billion is saved. At the next stage, $56.25 billion is consumed and $18.75 billion of the newly generated $75 billion in income is saved. These saving leakages limit the ultimate increase in income that occurs in response to an increase in autonomous spending. Income stops increasing when the total leakages equal the initial $100 billion increase in investment. The same multiplier (4) would have been obtained for an increase in government spending rather than in investment. In this simple case, the investment and government expenditure multipliers have the same numerical value.

One can see in Table 3 that the MPC determines the value of the multiplier. If the MPC had been 0.9 rather than 0.75, the initial increase in consumption would have been larger in the first and in subsequent rounds. The smaller the leakages (or the larger the MPC), the greater the amount of additional income created at each stage, and the larger the multiplier. The larger the leakages (or the smaller the MPC), the smaller the amount of income generated at each stage, and the smaller the multiplier.

The multiplier formula ($\Delta Y/\Delta I$) is

$$\frac{\Delta Y}{\Delta I} = \frac{1}{1 - \text{MPC}} = \frac{1}{\text{MPS}}$$

where there are no taxes (MPC + MPS = 1 in the absence of taxes). If investment increases by $1, in the new equilibrium, saving must also increase by $1 because $S = I$. If MPC equals 0.75, then

MPS = 0.25, and \$4 of extra income is necessary to increase saving by the \$1 necessary to match the \$1 increase in investment.

The higher the MPC, the higher the multiplier. An MPC of 0.75 yields a multiplier of 4; an MPC of 0.9 yields a multiplier of 10. The economy's response to autonomous expenditures, therefore, depends on the MPC (or MPS). The higher the MPC, the higher the induced expenditures from any given rise in income. In other words, the higher the MPC and the lower the MPS, the more income must change in order to get the saving leakages to match the injection of new investment.

> The higher the MPC, the higher the multiplier. The lower the MPC, the lower the multiplier.

The Algebra of the Multiplier

The relationship between the marginal propensity to consume and the multiplier can be demonstrated with some simple algebra.

The multiplier is the ratio of the increase in income (Y) to the increase in investment (I). The increase in Y equals the increase in I plus the change in C, or

$$\Delta Y = \Delta C + \Delta I \tag{1}$$

But ΔC equals MPC times ΔY:

$$\Delta C = \text{MPC} \times \Delta Y \tag{2}$$

Substituting equation 2 into equation 1 yields:

$$\Delta Y = \text{MPC} \times \Delta Y + \Delta I \tag{3}$$

or

$$\Delta Y(1 - \text{MPC}) = \Delta I \tag{4}$$

Dividing both sides by (1 − MPC) yields:

$$\Delta Y = \frac{\Delta I}{1 - \text{MPC}} \tag{5}$$

Equation 5 gives the expenditure multiplier formula when both sides are divided by ΔI:

$$\frac{\Delta Y}{\Delta I} = \frac{1}{(1 - \text{MPC})} = \frac{1}{\text{MPS}} \tag{6}$$

A simpler derivation is to note that $\Delta S = \Delta I$. Because $\Delta S = \text{MPS} \times \Delta Y$, it follows that $\Delta I = \text{MPS} \times \Delta Y$, or $\Delta Y / \Delta I = 1/\text{MPS}$.

The above multiplier assumes no foreign trade; an increase in income, however, can stimulate imports and lower the multiplier.[3]

The Tax Multiplier

The effect of changes in taxes can differ from the effect of changes in autonomous spending. Because taxes affect aggregate expenditures only indirectly, through their effect on consumption expenditures, taxes do not lower consumption expenditures dollar for dollar. Therefore, the **tax multiplier** will be smaller than the expenditure multiplier.

> The **tax multiplier ($\Delta Y/\Delta T$)** is the change in output divided by the change in the tax.

Figure 6 showed the effect of a \$100 billion increase in investment in an economy with no taxes. Figure 7 now illustrates the effect of a permanent \$40 billion increase in taxes (from \$0 to \$40 billion) on output.

At each level of income, the tax increase reduces disposable income by \$40 billion. Consumption will, therefore, fall by the MPC (0.75) times the fall in disposable income (\$40 billion), or by \$30 billion. The reduction in consumption is less than the increase in taxes. In Figure 7, the increase in taxes lowers the consumption/income curve from C_1 to C_2 in panel *a* and lowers aggregate expenditures from AE_1 to AE_2 in panel *b*. The \$30 billion downward shift from C_1 to C_2 in panel *a* corresponds to the \$30 billion downward shift from AE_1 to AE_2 in panel *b*.

Point e_1 represents the initial equilibrium, where output equals desired expenditures at \$400 billion. When aggregate expenditures decline by \$30 billion to \$370 billion while output is still \$400 billion, the economy is buying at a rate slower than the economy is producing, so firms cut back on production. The

[3]The impact of a higher GDP on imports is summarized in the *marginal propensity to import* (MPM), which is the increase in imports per dollar increase in GDP. The higher is the MPM, the flatter is the AE curve. A higher MPM deflects expenditures away from domestic goods toward foreign goods, reducing the impact that an increase in GDP has on the aggregate expenditures for domestic goods.

FIGURE 7
The Effect of an Increase in Taxes on Equilibrium Output

(*a*) The Consumption/Income Curve

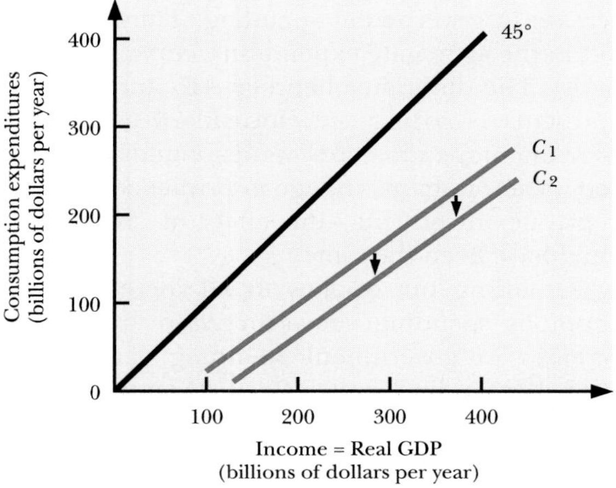

(*b*) The Aggregate Expenditure Curve

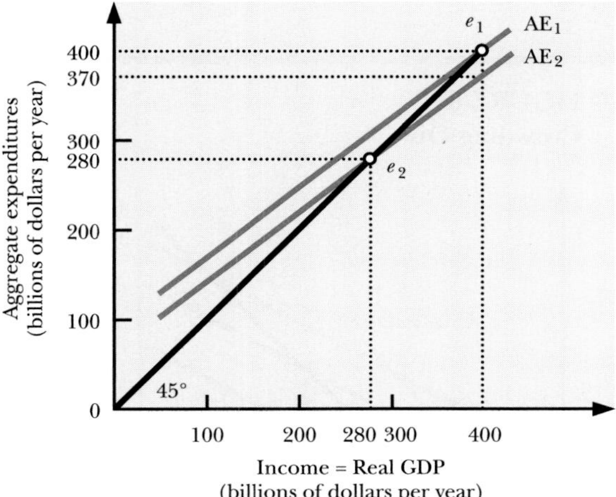

In this example, taxes rise from $0 to $40 billion. In panel *a*, the original consumption/income curve, C_1, shifts downward to C_2, but the vertical downward shift in the consumption/income curve is less than the $40 billion increase in taxes. The tax increase reduces disposable income by the amount of the tax increase, but with an MPC of 0.75, consumption spending falls by only $30 billion. In panel *b*, aggregate expenditures shift downward (from AE_1 to AE_2) by $30 billion, the amount of the decrease in consumption spending. Equilibrium output will be restored at $280 billion. Output has fallen by $120 billion as a consequence of the $40 billion increase in taxes; the equilibrium point has shifted from e_1 to e_2. Interest rates and the price level are held constant in this example.

new equilibrium is established at point e_2, where output equals desired expenditures at $280 billion.

The tax multiplier is smaller than the ordinary spending multiplier for the same size change. In the above example, the tax multiplier equals −3. The $40 billion increase in taxes reduces output by $120 billion. The tax multiplier is a negative number because *increases* in taxes cause *reductions* in output. The investment and government spending multipliers are positive because *increases* in investment or government spending cause *increases* in output.

A $1 tax shifts the AE curve by −MPC. In other words, expenditures *fall* by $1 × MPC. Thus, the tax multiplier is

$$\frac{\Delta Y}{\Delta T} = \frac{-\text{MPC}}{1 - \text{MPC}}$$

> Because MPC is less than unity, tax changes cause shifts in consumption that are less than the change in taxes. Accordingly, changes in taxes cause shifts in desired aggregate expenditures that are less than the change in taxes.

The Balanced-Budget Multiplier

The absolute value of the tax multiplier subtracted from the expenditure multiplier is 1.

$$\frac{1}{1 - \text{MPC}} - \frac{\text{MPC}}{1 - \text{MPC}} = \frac{1 - \text{MPC}}{1 - \text{MPC}} = 1$$

Since the expenditure multiplier is 1 greater than the tax multiplier in absolute value, then, surprisingly, *equal changes in government spending and taxes will change income by the amount of the change in government spending.*

The multiplier effect of equal changes in government spending and taxes is called the **balanced-budget multiplier.**

> The **balanced-budget multiplier** is the multiplier when there are equal changes in government spending and taxes. It always equals 1.

Because the balanced-budget multiplier is 1, tax-financed government spending can still increase output. For example, if private investment were to fall by $100 billion, a multiplier of 4 would cause GDP to fall by $400 billion. The balanced-budget multiplier implies that to maintain constant GDP, a $400 billion increase in tax-financed government spending would be necessary.

THE CROWDING OUT OF EXPENDITURES

To this point, we have discussed **simple multipliers**, which are based on the assumption that increases in autonomous spending (for example, increases in *I*, *G*, or *X*) affect neither the price level nor interest rates.

> A **simple multiplier** shows the impact on income of a change in autonomous spending or taxes when the price level and interest rates are not affected by such changes.

In the real world, increases in autonomous spending are indeed likely to raise interest rates and prices, and multiplier analysis needs to take these effects into consideration. Moreover, increases in government spending may affect private spending decisions. Thus, it is now time to drop the assumption that interest rates remain constant when autonomous expenditures change. We continue to assume that the price level is constant.

When autonomous spending increases, output rises. With output rising, the demand for credit increases on the part of business and consumers, and interest rates rise. As interest rates rise, the quantity of investment demanded will be reduced. Higher interest rates force some business investment out of the market. Thus, increases in autonomous spending (higher government or investment spending) will cause **crowding out** of private spending. The upward shift in the aggregate expenditure curve that would have resulted from a spending increase will be restrained by the impact of the rising interest rate.

> **Crowding out** occurs when an increase in autonomous spending pushes up interest rates and crowds out some of the private investment spending that would otherwise have taken place.

Figure 8 shows the effect of an autonomous increase in government spending, ΔG, when there is crowding out. Ignoring crowding out, the aggregate expenditure curve shifts upward, from AE_1 to $AE_1 + \Delta G$. But the fall of investment spending resulting from the higher interest rate partially offsets the increase in government spending. Thus, the actual shift in the aggregate expenditure curve is from AE_1 to AE_2. The difference between AE_2 and $AE_1 + \Delta G$ represents crowding out. Instead of a change in government spending, ΔG, we also could have considered an autonomous change in private consumption or private investment—the effect of crowding out would have been the same.

Crowding out applies to all increases in autonomous spending—government or private. But increases in government spending can have additional crowding out effects. Simple-multiplier analysis assumes that when government expenditure increases by one dollar, private spending remains the same at each level of income. However, this assumption may hold only for certain types of government ex-

FIGURE 8
Crowding Out

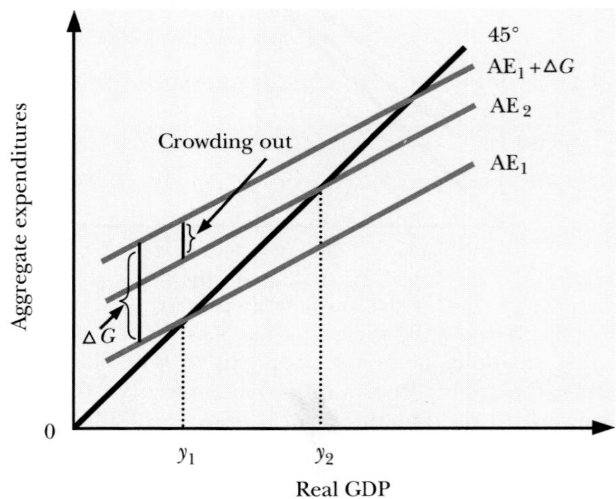

An increase in government spending or autonomous investment spending of ΔG will shift the aggregate expenditure curve from AE_1 to only AE_2 because of the crowding out of some private expenditures (through higher interest rates). Along curve AE_2, the interest rate is higher than along curve AE_1. The equilibrium level of GDP rises by the simple multiplier of the vertical shift from AE_1 to AE_2.

penditure (for example, national defense). It is quite possible that government expenditures on health care, education, police protection, roads, and parks will directly reduce some private expenditure. Thus, when government purchases and provides at a low cost goods that are substitutes for private goods, increasing government expenditures on those substitutes will likely reduce private spending on those goods.

Real-world multipliers show the effects of changes in autonomous spending or tax rates after crowding out has taken place. Some estimates of real-world multipliers are given in Example 4.

THE AGGREGATE DEMAND CURVE: ANOTHER LOOK

Chapter 9 explained that the aggregate demand curve is downward sloping because when the price level falls, the real-balance effect encourages more consumption spending, interest rates fall to stimulate investment, and exports increase relative to imports. The aggregate demand curve was defined as showing the level of output that economic agents are prepared to purchase at different price levels. In more precise terms, the aggregate demand curve shows the equilibrium level of GDP for each price level.

The link between the income/expenditure approach and the aggregate demand/aggregate supply approach is shown in Figure 9. As the price level rises, holding the money supply constant, real-money balances decrease. In panel *a* of Figure 9, when the price level rises from p to p', the aggregate expenditure curve shifts downward, from AE to AE′. The equilibrium level of output, thus, decreases from y to y' as the price level rises from p to p'. The combinations of points (p, y) and (p', y') lie on the aggregate demand curve (AD) in panel *b* of Figure 9. In other words, each price level is associated with a unique aggregate expenditure curve and a unique equilibrium output. The association between the given price level and the equilibrium value of aggregate expenditure constitutes the aggregate demand curve.

Although the aggregate demand curve follows from the Keynesian model of equilibrium output determination, there is a clear distinction between the aggregate demand curve and the aggregate expenditure curve.

FIGURE 9
The Derivation of Aggregate Demand

(*a*) A Change in Price Level Shifts the Aggregate Expenditure Curve

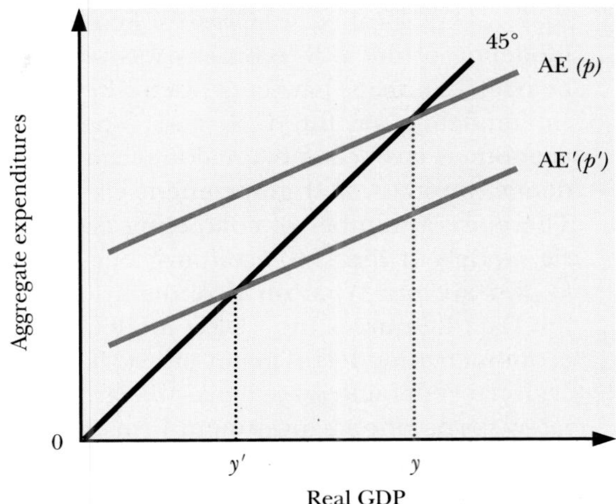

(*b*) Aggregate Demand as Equilibrium Output for Each Price Level

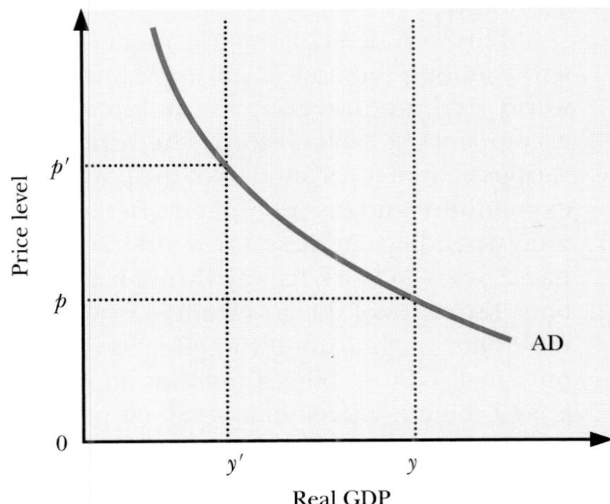

Panel *a* shows that an increase in the price level from p to p' will shift down the AE curve as a result of the interest-rate and real-balance effects. The aggregate demand curve (AD) in panel *b* associates each price level with the corresponding equilibrium GDP; thus, a price level of p corresponds to an output of y, and p' corresponds to y'.

EXAMPLE 4 Multipliers and Econometric Models

The branch of economics that estimates actual expenditure and tax multipliers is called *econometrics.* Econometric modeling of the U.S. economy was pioneered by Nobel laureate Lawrence Klein. Econometric modeling of the U.S. and other world economies has become a major activity of academic, business, and government economists. There are a number of competing econometric models of the U.S. economy, but the best known are the Wharton Econometric Model, the Data Resources Inc. (DRI) model, and the econometric models of major private banks and regional Federal Reserve banks that are used by many corporations, investment firms, and government agencies. Unlike the simple-multiplier models discussed in this chapter, econometric models often consist of hundreds of equations that describe the behavior of the U.S. economy.

The various econometric models do not agree among themselves on the values of real-world expenditure and tax multipliers. The accompanying table records the estimates of various econometric models of the government expenditure and tax multipliers after a government spending increase (or tax decrease) has had 2 years to work its way through the economy. Estimates of the government expenditure multiplier range from 0 (no effect on real output) to 2.7 (a $1 billion increase in *G* causes a $2.7 billion increase in real output). The various models illustrate the theory that the tax multiplier is less (in absolute value) than the expenditure multiplier. The tax multipliers range from a low of 1.1 to a high of 2.1.

Econometric Model	Government Expenditure Multiplier $\Delta Y/\Delta G$	Tax Multiplier $-\Delta Y/\Delta T$
Bureau of Economic Analysis	2.2	1.4
Brookings	2.7	1.6
University of Michigan	1.4	1.1
Data Resources, Inc.	0.9	1.1
Federal Reserve Bank of St. Louis	0	n.a.*
MPS Model, University of Pennsylvania	2.2	2.1
Wharton Model	2.4	1.7
H-C Stanford University	1.4	n.a.*

* Information is not available.

Despite their disagreement, econometric models perform a valuable function: They allow participants in the economy to look into the future, albeit imperfectly, and attach probabilities to different economic outcomes. The fact that American business spends large sums on econometric forecasting suggests that econometrics is performing a positive function. The main source of forecasting errors is the necessity of predicting the future on the basis of what has happened in the past. Although past behavior is often a good guide, it is far from foolproof.

Sources: Gary Fromm and Lawrence Klein, "A Comparison of Eleven Econometric Models of the United States," *American Economic Review* (May 1973); Robert Gordon, *Macroeconomics,* 5th ed. (New York: HarperCollins, 1990), 469–72.

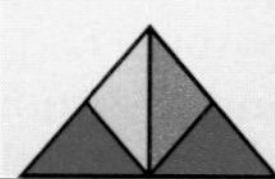

> The aggregate expenditure (AE) curve shows *desired* aggregate expenditures at *each level of income.* The aggregate demand (AD) curve shows *equilibrium* aggregate expenditures at *each price level.*

Shifts in Aggregate Demand

Revealing the determinants of the aggregate demand curve is Keynes's fundamental contribution to macroeconomics. Figure 10 illustrates a situation that results in an increase in aggregate demand. Panel *a* shows an upward shift in the aggregate expenditure curve from AE_1 to AE_2. The curve shifts upward because of an increase in autonomous expenditure (perhaps a combination of increased government, consumption, and private investment). In panel *b*, at the fixed price level *p*, the aggregate demand curve shifts from AD_1 to AD_2 because the Keynesian equilibrium has increased from y_1 to y_2. The horizontal shift in the aggregate demand curve at the price level *p* is exactly the full multiplier effect of the vertical shift in the aggregate expenditure curve.

> The horizontal shift in the aggregate demand curve is the multiplier times the change in autonomous spending (net of any crowding out effects), or the vertical shift in the aggregate expenditure curve.

FIGURE 10
Shifts in Aggregate Demand

(*a*) A Shift in the Aggregate Expenditure Curve

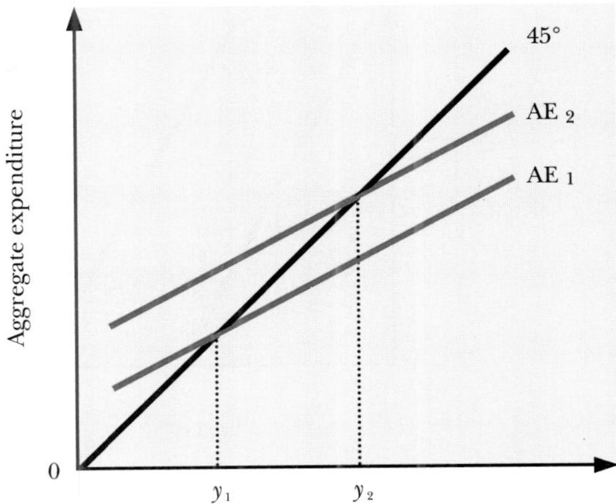

(*b*) The Resulting Shift in the Aggregate Demand Curve

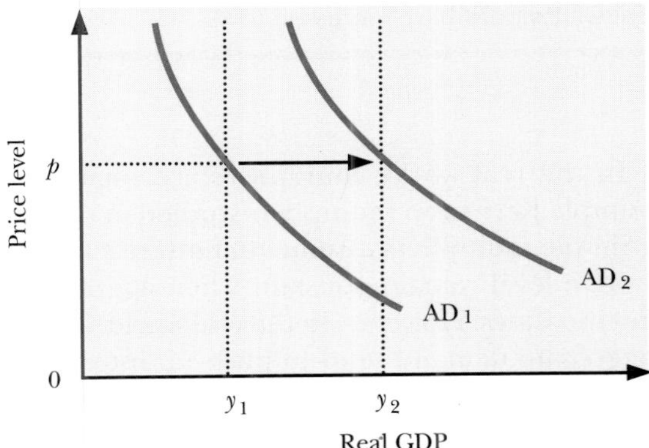

When autonomous expenditure (government, consumption, or investment spending) increases, the aggregate expenditure curve shifts upward from AE_1 to AE_2, inclusive of the crowding out of other expenditures by high interest rates. For the given price level (*p*), the equilibrium level of GDP increases from y_1 to y_2. The AD curve shifts to the right by a distance equal to the full multiplier times the vertical shift in the AE curve.

Figure 11 shows that the size of the effect that a shift in the aggregate demand curve has on output depends on the shape of the aggregate supply curve. Panel *a* shows the Keynesian case, in which the aggregate supply curve is horizontal. A rightward shift in the aggregate demand curve raises output by the full amount of the shift because the equilibrium price level remains the same.

Panel *b* of Figure 11 shows that if the aggregate supply curve is upward sloping, a rightward shift in the aggregate demand curve raises output by less than the full amount of the shift because the rise in the price level discourages some consumption and investment spending. When the aggregate demand curve shifts to the right from AD to AD′, output increases from y to y'' and the price level rises to p'. Had the price level remained constant at p, output would have increased to y', as in panel *a*. The difference between y' and y'' results from the increase in the price level from p to p'. When the aggregate supply curve is upward sloping, an increase in aggregate demand raises aggregate output less than in the Keynesian case because part of the increase is absorbed in higher prices.

FIGURE 11
The Effect of Aggregate Supply on Equilibrium Output

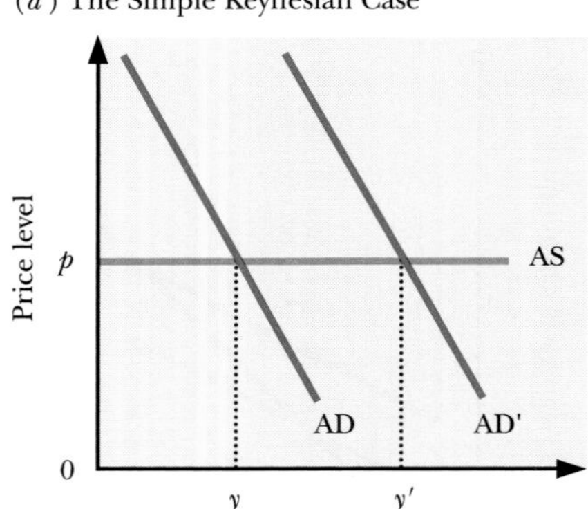

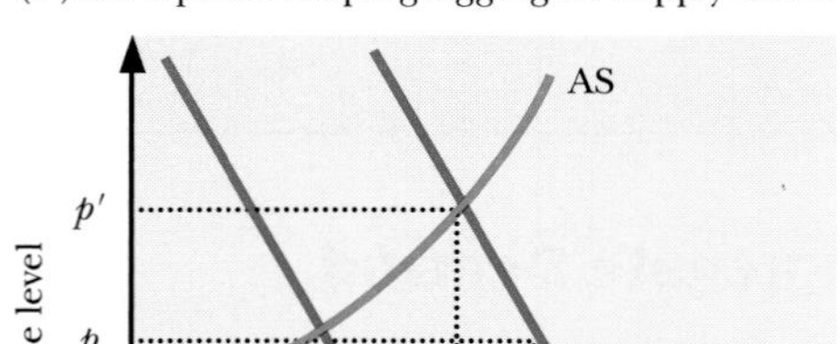
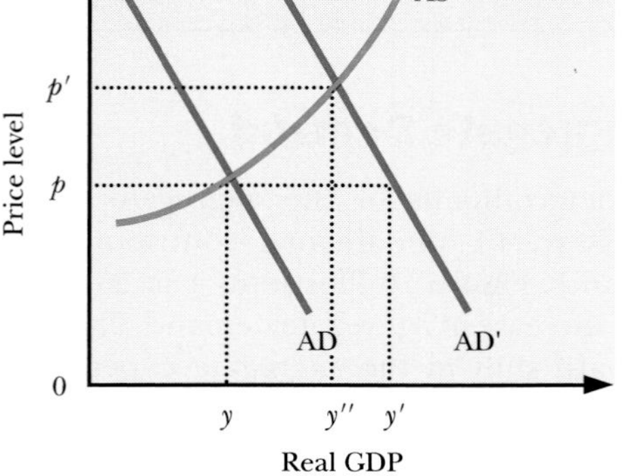

Panel *a* shows that when the price level is constant, an increase in aggregate demand from AD to AD′ has the maximum impact on equilibrium real GDP. Panel *b* shows that when the aggregate supply curve is upward sloping, an increase in aggregate demand raises real GDP from y to y'' and raises the price level from p to p'. Had the price level remained at level p, real GDP would have increased to y'.

In the real world, multipliers are smaller than the simple Keynesian multipliers studied in this chapter. Simple multipliers assume that interest rates and the price level remain constant when aggregate demand increases. However, in the real world, increases in aggregate demand tend to push up interest rates and prices. As interest rates rise, investment is discouraged and the multiplier effect is diminished (crowding out). As the price level rises, the real-balance effect discourages consumption, and the foreign-trade effect discourages net exports. If the aggregate supply curve is steep enough, the "multiplier" can be zero.

The next chapter examines the short-run and long-run effects of fiscal policy.

SUMMARY

1. The income/expenditure model assumes that prices are fixed. The aggregate expenditure (AE) curve shows the amount of desired aggregate expenditures, $C + I + G + (X - M)$, at each income level. The economy will produce that income at which: (1) aggregate production equals desired aggregate expenditures, and (2) desired investment equals desired saving. These two statements are equivalent versions of equilibrium conditions.

2. When government spending is introduced into the income/expenditure model, the same two equilibrium conditions still determine output: Aggregate production equals desired aggregate expenditures, and desired investment equals desired saving. Saving, however, now includes both public $(T - G)$ and private (S) saving.

3. In an economy open to foreign trade, the aggregate expenditure curve is simply $AE = C + I + G + (X - M)$, where the term $(X - M)$ represents net exports to the rest of the world. A higher domestic price level lowers $(X - M)$; a higher foreign price level raises $(X - M)$. In equilibrium, investment equals the sum of private saving, government dissaving, and foreign saving.

4. Changes in autonomous expenditures—those that are determined independently of income changes—change desired expenditures dollar for dollar. The simple expenditure multiplier indicates by how much output will change for each change in government spending or investment. The value of the multiplier depends upon the marginal propensity to consume; the higher is the MPC, the

higher is the multiplier. The expenditure multiplier formula is $1/(1 - \text{MPC})$, or $1/\text{MPS}$. The simple tax multiplier indicates by how much output will fall for each \$1 increase in taxes. The tax multiplier is $-\text{MPC}/(1-\text{MPC})$. The tax multiplier equals (in absolute value) the expenditure multiplier minus 1. For this reason, the balanced-budget multiplier equals unity.

5. Crowding out occurs when an increase in autonomous spending crowds out some private spending because of the increase in interest rates.

6. Keynesian economics provides the foundation for the theory of aggregate demand. Indeed, the aggregate demand curve graphs the Keynesian equilibrium for each price level. Rightward shifts in the aggregate demand curve raise output less than the simple multiplier because both interest rates (crowding out) and the price level will be pushed up.

KEY TERMS

aggregate expenditures (AE)
Keynesian equilibrium
unintended investment
autonomous expenditures
multiplier ($\Delta Y/\Delta I$)
tax multiplier ($\Delta Y/\Delta T$)
balanced-budget multiplier
simple multiplier
crowding out

QUESTIONS AND PROBLEMS

1. The country of Friedmania has no government spending and no taxes. Its consumption schedule is given in Table A.

TABLE A

Income (billions of dollars), *Y*	Consumption (billions of dollars), *C*
0	10
50	50
100	90
150	130
200	170
250	210
300	250

a. What is the MPC? What is the MPS?
b. What is the equilibrium income when investment spending is \$30 billion? What is the equilibrium income when I = \$50 billion?
c. What is the investment multiplier?

2. Assume that in Friedmania, investment spending is \$30 billion.
   a. What is the effect on income of introducing government spending in the amount of \$20 billion (but with no taxes!)?
   b. What is the effect on income of introducing government spending of \$20 billion and taxes of \$25 billion?

3. Define *unintended inventory investment.* How will businesses respond to unintended investment in the simple Keynesian model? If prices were flexible, would the response of businesses to unintended inventory investment be different?

4. In Keynesian theory, what mechanism coordinates business investment and consumer saving?

5. What would happen to the aggregate expenditure curve in each of the following cases?
   a. Investment demand increases.
   b. The money supply increases.
   c. The price level increases.
   d. Consumers anticipate a sharp increase in prices in the next year.

6. Suppose the consumption schedule is C = \$100 billion + $0.75Y$.
   a. Draw the consumption/income schedule for income levels of \$200 billion, \$400 billion, \$600 billion, and \$800 billion. What is the marginal propensity to consume?
   b. What is the equation for saving?
   c. If I = \$50 billion, what is the equilibrium level of output?

7. If there were no government spending, even though the government collected taxes, what would the saving/investment equality look like?

8. Assume that in economy Z, I = \$25 billion and the relationship between consumption and income *without taxes* is given in Table B.
   a. What is the MPC? What is the MPS?
   b. What is the equilibrium output?
   c. Now assume T = \$100 billion and G = \$125 billion. What is the new consumption/income schedule?
   d. When T = \$100 billion, G = \$125 billion, and I = \$25 billion, what is the equilibrium output?

TABLE B

Income (billions of dollars), Y	Consumption (billions of dollars), C
0	75
100	150
200	225
300	300
400	375
500	450
600	525

9. Consider an economy with the same consumption/income curve as in Table B. Assume that I = $60 billion and that there is no government. Let exports (X) equal $30 billion, and assume that imports (M) are determined by the schedule shown in Table C. What is the equilibrium output?

TABLE C

Income (billions of dollars), Y	Imports (billions of dollars), M
0	5
100	10
200	15
300	20
400	25
500	30
600	35

10. Will a cut in personal income taxes of $100 billion raise or lower equilibrium real output? Does the answer depend upon whether there are unemployed resources in the economy? Will the effect on equilibrium output be larger if the marginal propensity to save is 0.2 or 0.1? Explain.
11. Evaluate the validity of the following statement: "Changes in attitudes toward thrift and in personal income taxes both affect the consumption/income curve. Therefore, a $100 billion increase in taxes will have the same effect as a $100 billion decrease in desired consumption expenditures caused by an increase in thrift."
12. The economy of Hoover Island has substantial unemployed resources. The marginal propensity to save out of disposable income is 0.25. Government spending increases by $100 billion, and taxes are lowered by $100 billion. Using the Keynesian multiplier analysis, by how much would you expect equilibrium output to change?
13. What assumptions are made in simple-multiplier analysis?
14. Is the following statement true or false? "There will be no crowding out of government spending if interest rates are fixed."
15. Explain the difference between the aggregate expenditure curve and the aggregate demand curve. What is being held constant along each of these curves?

SUGGESTED READINGS

Gordon, Robert. *Macroeconomics,* 5th ed. New York: HarperCollins, 1990, chap. 3.

Hall, Robert E., and John B. Taylor. *Macroeconomics,* 3rd ed. New York: W. W. Norton & Co., 1991, 132–48.

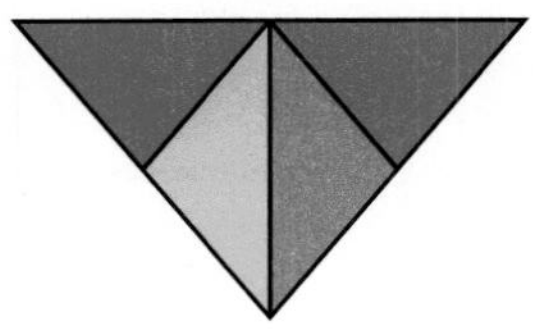

APPENDIX 11A

The *IS/LM* Model

APPENDIX INSIGHT

The aggregate demand curve shows how the Keynesian equilibrium varies with different price levels. The description of the Keynesian equilibrium in Chapter 11 is inexact because interest rates are determined simultaneously with income. This appendix describes the *IS/LM* model, which shows how both the interest rate and the level of real GDP are the outcome of two equilibrium conditions: the goods market equilibrium and the money market equilibrium. The *IS/LM* approach explicitly incorporates crowding-out effects and clearly separates monetary factors from fiscal factors in the determination of output. It also can be used to rigorously derive the aggregate demand curve.

The following analysis is conducted under the assumption that the price level is fixed. This assumption will be relaxed when the aggregate demand curve is discussed.

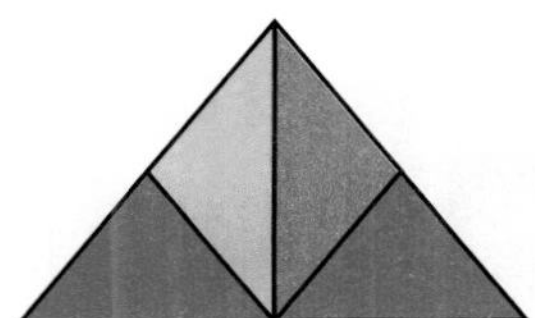

THE *IS* CURVE: GOODS MARKET EQUILIBRIUM

Consider a simple economy with no government spending, no taxes, and no foreign trade. When aggregate production equals desired aggregate expenditure, the market for goods is in equilibrium. The condition for equilibrium is that desired investment (I) must equal desired saving (S). The ***IS* curve** answers a simple question: How is the equilibrium level of income related to the interest rate, holding the price level constant? Thus, the *IS* curve shows, for each interest rate, the level of real GDP that is consistent with equilibrium in the market for goods and services.

> The ***IS* curve** shows all the combinations of interest rates and real income that are consistent with goods market equilibrium (in which desired investment equals desired saving).

Panel *a* of Figure 1 shows how higher interest rates lower the aggregate expenditure curve (because of the induced reduction in desired investment). Consider three interest rates, r_1, r_2, and r_3, and assume that $r_3 > r_2 > r_1$. Higher interest rates discourage investment. Clearly, the higher is the interest rate, holding the price level constant, the lower will be the aggregate expenditure curve. Thus, as the interest rate rises, the aggregate expenditure curve shifts downward from AE_1 to AE_2 to AE_3. Thus, the three interest rates are associated with three equilibrium levels of income—y_1, y_2, and y_3.

The *IS* curve in panel *b* of Figure 1 relates each interest rate to the corresponding equilibrium level of real output. The *IS* curve is negatively sloped because higher interest rates lower the equilibrium level of real GDP.

FIGURE 1
The *IS* Curve

(*a*) The Aggregate Expenditure Curve Shifts Downward as the Interest Rate Rises

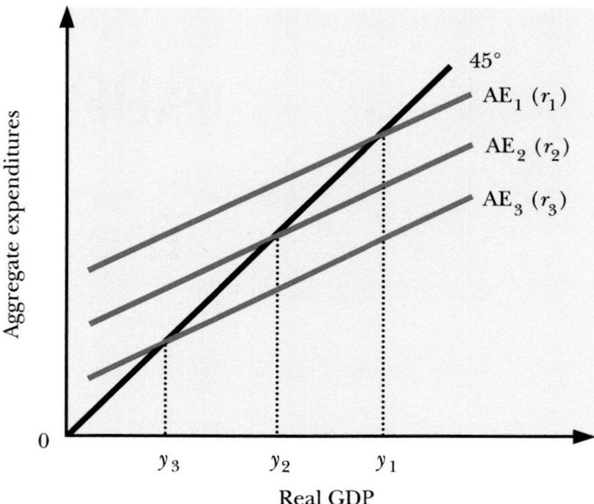

(*b*) Equilibrium Output Falls as the Interest Rate Rises

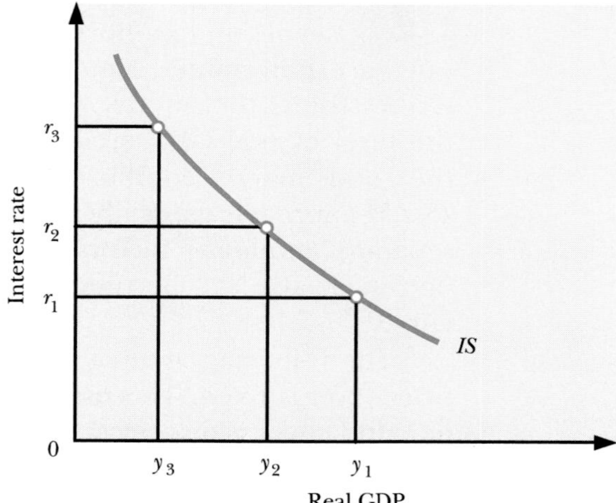

Panel *a* shows that as interest rates rise from r_1 to r_2 to r_3, the aggregate expenditure curve shifts downward, from AE_1 to AE_2 to AE_3. The *IS* curve in panel *b* associates the corresponding equilibrium levels of income to each interest rate.

THE *LM* CURVE: MONEY MARKET EQUILIBRIUM

The *LM* curve takes its name from the fact that when the money market is in equilibrium, the demand for money (often denoted by L in economics) equals the supply of money (often denoted by M in economics). The demand for real money balances depends on two factors: the nominal interest rate and real income, or GDP. Because the price level is assumed to be fixed, the expected inflation rate is 0, making the nominal

FIGURE 2
The *LM* Curve

(*a*) Higher Real Output Raises Money Demand

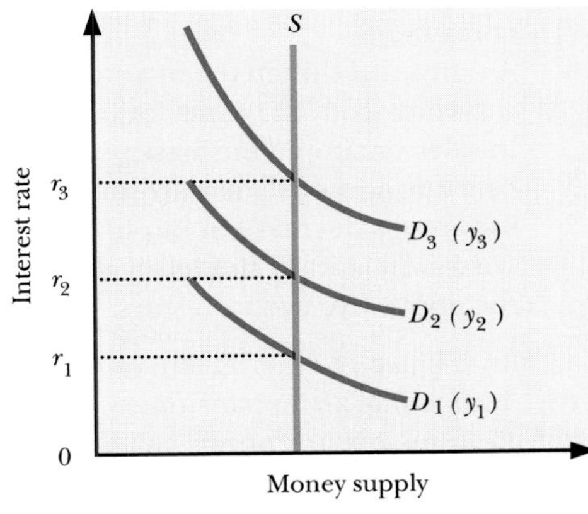

(*b*) Equilibrium Interest Rate Rises as Income Rises

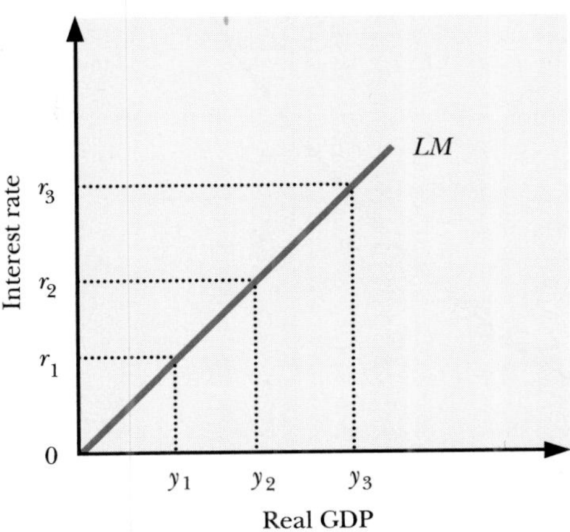

Panel *a* shows that as real income rises from y_1 to y_2 to y_3, the demand for money shifts upward from D_1 to D_2 to D_3. Thus, as income rises, the interest rate equating the fixed supply of money balances, *S*, to the quantity of money demanded increases from r_1 to r_2 to r_3. The *LM* curve in panel *b* associates each equilibrium interest rate to each level of real income.

rate of interest equal to the real rate of interest. The ***LM* curve** answers the question: For a given supply of real money balances, how does the equilibrium interest rate respond to changes in real income? Thus, the *LM* curve shows, for each interest rate, the level of real GDP that is consistent with equilibrium in the money market.

> The ***LM* curve** shows all the combinations of interest rates and real income that bring about equality between the demand for money and the supply of money.

Panel *a* of Figure 2 measures the interest rate on the vertical axis and real money balances on the horizontal axis. The demand for money depends on the level of income and the rate of interest. The demand curve for money shows that the quantity of money demanded rises as the interest rate falls, holding the level of income constant. The reason for this downward slope is that the interest rate measures the cost of holding non-interest-bearing money: the lower the cost (the interest rate) of holding money, the higher the quantity of money demanded. Higher income requires larger money balances to carry out the increased transactions. Thus, increasing income shifts the entire demand curve for money to the right.

Consider three levels of real income: y_1, y_2, and y_3. The demand curves D_1, D_2, and D_3 in panel *a* of Figure 2 illustrate how the demand for real balances increases as the level of real income rises. Because $y_1 < y_2 < y_3$, the demand curve D_3 is to the right of D_1. The supply of real money balances is shown by the vertical line, *S*. When the real income level is y_1, the interest rate that brings about money market equilibrium is r_1. When the real incomes are y_2 and y_3, the equilibrium interest rates are r_2 and r_3, respectively. Clearly, the interest rate that equates the quantity of money demanded to the quantity of money supplied rises as the level of real income rises.

The *LM* curve in panel *b* of Figure 2 shows the combinations of interest rates and real income that are consistent with money market equilibrium. The curve is upward sloping because increases in real income raise the demand for real money balances, so that higher interest rates must also rise to maintain equilibrium. In other words, higher interest rates are required to choke off the extra demand for money created by a higher level of real income.

FIGURE 3
The *IS/LM* Equilibrium

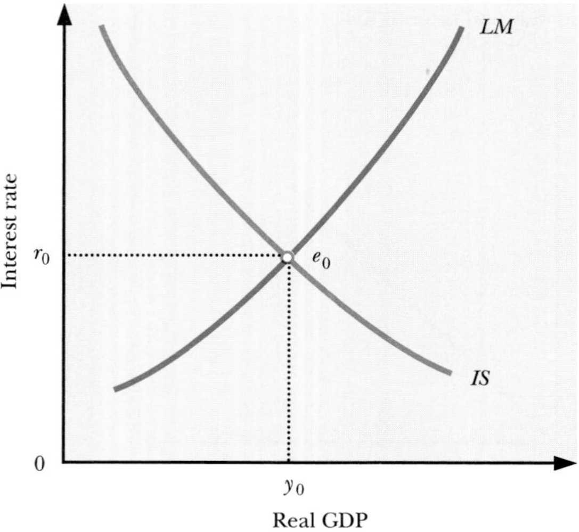

The combination of the interest rate r_0 and the income level y_0 brings about equilibrium in both the goods market and the money market, because e_0 falls on both the *IS* and *LM* curves.

THE *IS/LM* EQUILIBRIUM

Figure 3 combines the *IS* and *LM* curves on the same graph. Point e_0 represents the equilibrium level of interest rate and real income. The interest rate r_0 and the income level y_0 are the only levels compatible with equilibrium in both the goods market and the money market simultaneously.

Shifts in the *IS* Curve

Shifts in the *IS* curve can be explained by shifts in the aggregate expenditure curve that are not caused by changes in the rate of interest. As explained in Chapter 11, an increase in the aggregate expenditure curve by the amount ΔA will increase the equilibrium level of output by $\Delta Y = \Delta A/(1 - \text{MPC})$. Thus, the *IS* curve shifts by the simple multiplier of the change in autonomous spending.

Figure 4 shows a rightward shift in the *IS* curve, from IS_0 to IS_1. This rightward shift can result from any of the following events:

1. An increase in the real level of government spending
2. A decrease in tax rates that shifts the consumption/income curve upward
3. An upward shift in the consumption/income curve resulting from an increased propensity to consume
4. A rightward shift in the investment demand curve resulting from the expectation of an acceleration in sales or simple business psychology
5. An autonomous increase in exports or an autonomous decrease in imports. Obviously, the *IS* curve will shift to the left if the reverse of any of the above five events occurs.

In Figure 4, the *IS* curve shifts from IS_0 to IS_1, indicating an expansionary fiscal policy or an autonomous expansionary change in consumption, investment, or net exports. The equilibrium interest rate rises from r_0 to r_1 and the equilibrium level of real GDP rises from y_0 to y_1. Notice that the change in real GDP is *smaller* than the horizontal shift in the *IS* curve (the full multiplier effect of the change in autonomous spending). The explanation, of course,

FIGURE 4
The Effects of a Shift in the *IS* Curve

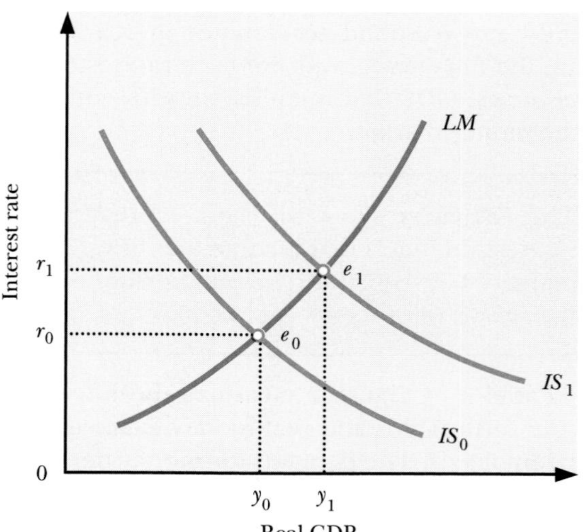

If the *IS* curve shifts to the right from IS_0 to IS_1—because of, say, an increase in government spending or a reduction in tax rates—the equilibrium level of real income will rise from y_0 to y_1 and the equilibrium interest rate will rise from r_0 to r_1 along a given *LM* curve.

is that interest rates rise and crowd out some private investment (or even consumption) spending.

Shifts in the *LM* Curve

To simplify the discussion, assume that an increase in the supply of real money balances has a negligible effect on private consumption. Thus, changes in the real money supply can exert only indirect effects on the goods market.

Shifts in the *LM* curve are caused by (1) fluctuations in the demand for money that are not a result of changes in interest rates or real income and (2) changes in the real supply of money. An increase in the money supply requires a larger real GDP to equate money supply and demand at a constant interest rate. Alternatively, an increase in the money supply lowers the interest rate needed to maintain money market equilibrium for a constant real GDP. Thus, an increase in the money supply will shift the *LM* curve to the right; a decrease in the money supply will shift the *LM* curve to the left.

Suppose the nominal supply of money increases. If the price level is assumed fixed, the real money supply will rise. Figure 5 shows a rightward shift in the *LM* curve, from LM_0 to LM_1, that results from an increase in the real supply of money. The equilibrium interest rate falls from r_0 to r_1 and the equilibrium level of real GDP rises from y_0 to y_1. The mechanism underlying the increase in real GDP, of course, is that the higher supply of real money balances lowers interest rates, increasing the quantity of investment demanded.

The *LM* curve can also shift if the demand for money changes. For example, if the demand for money falls because of the introduction of money substitutes, the *LM* curve will shift downward.

FIGURE 5
The Effects of a Shift in the *LM* Curve

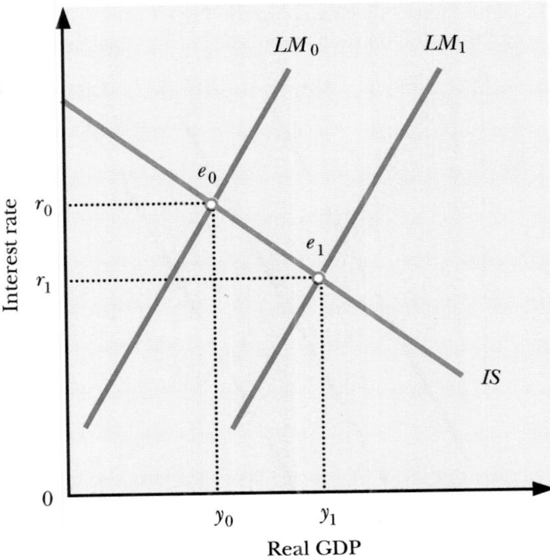

If the *LM* curve shifts to the right from LM_0 to LM_1—because of an increase in the nominal money supply (holding the price level constant)—the equilibrium level of real income will rise from y_0 to y_1 and the equilibrium interest rate will fall from r_0 to r_1 along a given *IS* curve.

DERIVING THE AGGREGATE DEMAND CURVE

The foregoing analysis assumes that the price level is fixed. What happens when the price level changes? The effect is similar to a change in the money supply. If the money supply is fixed and the price level is reduced from p_0 to p_1 to p_2, the real money supply will rise because the purchasing power of the given nominal money supply increases. Thus, just as in the preceding analysis of monetary policy, the *LM* curve shifts to the right each time the price level falls. In panel *a* of Figure 6, LM_0, LM_1, and LM_2 are the *LM* curves for the price levels p_0, p_1, and p_2, respectively. As the price level falls, real income rises and the interest rate falls.

Panel *b* of Figure 6 associates each price level with the resulting equilibrium level of real GDP. Thus, p_0, p_1, and p_2 are associated with the real GDP levels of y_0, y_1, and y_2, respectively. The underlying mechanism is that a lower price level increases the real money supply, which in turn lowers interest rates and encourages private investment spending. The output level associated with the *LM/IS* equilibrium point for each price level is plotted against that price level to generate the aggregate demand curve relating different price levels to the Keynesian level of equilibrium GDP.

> The aggregate demand curve is derived by plotting the association between each price level and the equilibrium level of real GDP corresponding to the *IS/LM* equilibrium for each price level.

FIGURE 6
The Derivation of Aggregate Demand

(*a*) The Effect of a Change in the Price Level on the *IS/LM* Equilibrium

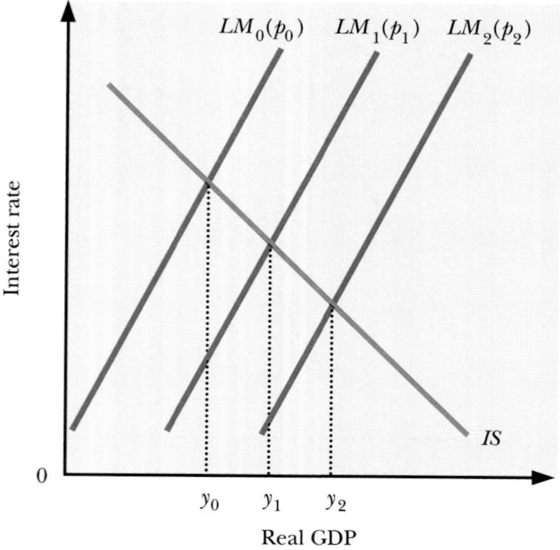

(*b*) The Aggregate Demand Curve

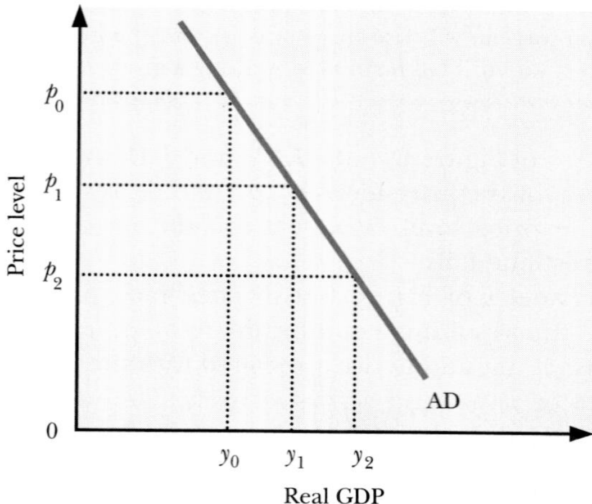

Panel *a* shows that the *LM* curve shifts to the right each time the price level falls, from p_0 to p_1 to p_2 (holding the nominal money supply constant). Thus, LM_0, LM_1, and LM_2 are associated with p_0, p_1, and p_2, respectively. Panel *b* plots the corresponding levels of real income against each price level, forming the aggregate demand (AD) curve.

Shifts in the aggregate demand curve are caused by changes in the nominal money supply (which change the *LM* curve) or any of the factors that cause shifts in the *IS* curve. Unlike a shift in the *IS* curve, the aggregate demand curve will shift by *less* than the full multiplier effect of a change in autonomous spending because for any price level, a rightward shift in the *IS* curve will drive up interest rates and choke off some investment demand, which partly offsets the initial change in autonomous expenditure.

SUMMARY

1. The *IS* curve shows all the combinations of interest rates and real income that are consistent with goods market equilibrium (in which desired investment equals desired saving).
2. The *LM* curve shows all the combinations of interest rates and real income that bring about equality between the demand for money and the supply of money.
3. The *IS/LM* intersection point shows the interest rate and income level compatible with equilibrium in both the goods market and the money market. An expansionary fiscal policy that raises real GDP will also raise interest rates. An expansionary monetary policy that raises real GDP will lower interest rates.
4. The aggregate demand curve is derived by plotting the association between each price level and the equilibrium level of real GDP corresponding to the *IS/LM* equilibrium for that price level.

KEY TERMS

IS curve
LM curve

QUESTIONS AND PROBLEMS

1. Why is the *IS* curve downward sloping?
2. What factors are held constant along the *IS* curve?
3. Why is the *LM* curve upward sloping?
4. What factors are held constant along the *LM* curve?
5. Describe the impact of increasing tax rates on the *IS/LM* equilibrium.
6. Describe the impact of reducing the money supply on the *IS/LM* equilibrium.
7. How is the simple multiplier modified by the *IS/LM* model?

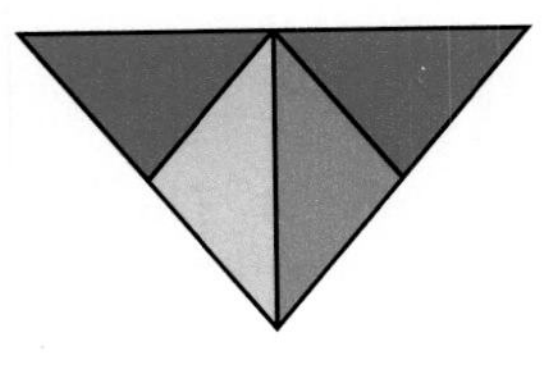

12 Fiscal Policy

CHAPTER INSIGHT

Each year, the federal government spends almost $1.5 trillion: nearly $8000 for every person in the United States. Government spending clearly affects our lives in many ways: It helps determine the education we receive, the size of our national defense, and the strength of our legal system. But how does government expenditure of such a vast amount of money affect the health of our economy? Does the government spend in a way that will avoid recessions and inflations and provide for economic growth?

In 1936, Keynes introduced the notion that government spending and taxation should consider not only the costs and benefits of public finance but also its impact on the business cycle. He proposed that government spending and taxation be coordinated to eliminate the ups and downs of recessions, depressions, and inflations.

This chapter discusses fiscal policy. It shows how the federal budget process works; examines the automatic stabilizers used to prevent unhealthy swings in business activity; and considers some of the reasons fiscal policy may not be an effective weapon against the business cycle.

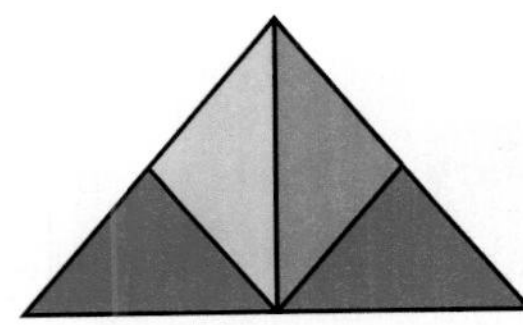

FISCAL POLICY: A DEFINITION

This chapter studies how **fiscal policy** can be used to affect macroeconomic conditions.

> **Fiscal policy** is the use of government spending and taxation to pursue macroeconomic goals.

Most government spending and taxation is unrelated to fiscal policy. Governments spend to provide for the national defense, to care for the poor and the hungry, and to provide for public education. Government tax policy may aim to equalize the distribution of income or to promote some activities and discourage others. Such spending and taxation decisions are made independently of their impact on output and employment. Fiscal policy, by contrast, is the *deliberate* control of government spending and tax policy for the purpose of affecting output, employment, or inflation.

THE BUDGET PROCESS

The decision makers of the U.S. government use the budget system as the basis for deciding what resources to allocate to the requirements of the nation and how to maintain effective financial control and accountability.[1]

Phases of Budgeting

The budget process has three interelated phases: (1) executive formulation and transmittal; (2) congressional action; and (3) budget execution and control.

Executive Formulation and Transmittal. The budget sets forth the president's financial plan and priorities for the federal government. The budget focuses primarily on the next fiscal year for which the Congress needs to make appropriations. However, it is developed in the context of a multiyear planning system that covers the four years following the budget year.

The president transmits the budget to Congress early in each calendar year, 8 to 9 months before the next fiscal year begins on October 1. The formulation process begins not later than the spring of each year, at least 9 months before the budget is transmitted and at least 18 months before the budget fiscal year begins. During formulation, the president, the Office of Management and Budget (OMB), other executive office units, and the various government agencies continually exchange information, proposals, evaluations, and policy decisions. Decisions are influenced by economic projections jointly prepared by the Council of Economic Advisors, OMB, and the Treasury.

Congressional Action. Congress can approve, modify, or disapprove the president's budget proposals. It can change funding levels, eliminate programs, or add programs as well as enact legislation affecting taxes and other sources of receipts.

Before making appropriations, Congress usually enacts legislation that authorizes an agency to carry out a particular program and, in some cases, includes limits on the amount that can be appropriated for the program. Some programs require annual authorizing legislation. Others are authorized for a specific number of years or indefinitely.

In making appropriations, Congress does not vote on the level of outlays directly, but rather on the *budget authority* granted to agencies of the executive branch to incur obligations. Spending programs can either be voted on annually or be placed under permanent budget authority, which makes funds available annually without further congressional action. In recent years, more programs have been funded by permanent appropriations than by current actions of the Congress. Therefore, most outlays in any year are not controlled through appropriations actions in that year. Currently, more than three-quarters of federal government appropriations are for *uncontrollable* items specified in permanent appropriations. The dominance of this form of federal spending makes it difficult to effect major changes in federal spending in a short period of time.

Congressional budget resolutions do not require presidential approval. Frequently, however, the congressional leadership and the administration consult informally because the specific legislation developed to attain congressional budget targets must be sent to the president for approval. The House of Representatives is the first congressional body to consider requests for appropriations and changes in revenue laws. The Appropriations Committee, through its subcommittees, studies the requests for

[1]This section is adapted from *The United States Budget in Brief.*

appropriations and examines in detail each agency's performance. The Ways and Means Committee reviews proposed revenue measures. Each committee then recommends a course of action for the House of Representatives. After the budget resolution passes, a point of order can be raised to block consideration of bills that would breach a committee's targets, as set by the resolution.

After the appropriations and tax bills are approved by the House, they are forwarded to the Senate, where a similar review follows. In case of disagreement between the two Houses of the Congress, a conference committee (consisting of members of both bodies) meets to resolve the differences. The report of the conference committee is returned to both Houses for approval. When the measure is agreed to, first in the House and then in the Senate, it is ready to be transmitted to the president.

The president must either accept or veto Congressional appropriation bills. Because U.S. presidents lack **line-item veto authority**, they cannot veto individual spending items within the budget.

> **Line-item veto authority** is presidential authority to veto specific spending appropriations.

U.S. presidents have requested line-item veto authority from Congress consistently for the past two decades, but Congress has refused on the ground that such authority conflicts with the Constitution's delegation of spending authority to Congress. (See Example 1.)

Budget Execution and Control. Once approved, the president's budget, as modified by Congress, becomes the basis for the financial plan for the operations of each agency during the fiscal year. Under the law, most budget authority and other budgetary resources are made available to the agencies of the executive branch through an apportionment system. To ensure the effective use of available resources, the director of OMB distributes appropriations and other budgetary resources to each agency by time periods and by activities.

EXAMPLE 1 The Limited Impact of the Line-Item Veto

Current budgetary practices do not allow U.S. presidents to exercise a line-item veto: They must either sign budget legislation passed by Congress in total or veto the entire appropriation bill. In the absence of a line-item veto, Congress can attach to spending bills riders that would be unacceptable if considered separately but that must be accepted as part of the overall bill. Would the amount of federal government spending be reduced if the president had line-item veto authority?

The line-item veto was an innovation of the Confederacy. The first line-item veto legislation was proposed to Congress in 1876 and has been proposed more than 150 times since. Line-item veto authority has been incorporated into most, but not all, state constitutions. Only one state allows the governor no veto authority, six limit the governor to an all-or-nothing veto, and 33 states have a simple line-item veto.

When researchers compare the spending behavior of states with line-item vetoes to those that lack such veto authority, they find no significant differences between spending in states with line-item vetoes and states without line-item vetoes. As one researcher quoted by Carter and Schap writes, "In general, the line-item veto does not appear to significantly alter, on average, the outcomes of the budgetary process."

The fact that the line-item veto does not affect state budgetary processes suggests that granting the president such authority would not increase the flexibility and effectiveness of federal fiscal policy.

Source: John R. Carter and David Schap, "Line-item Veto: Where Is Thy Sting?" *Journal of Economic Perspectives* (Spring 1990): 103–118.

Changes in laws or other factors may indicate the need for additional appropriations during the year, and supplemental requests may have to be sent to Congress. On the other hand, amounts appropriated may be withheld temporarily from obligation under certain limited circumstances. The executive branch must report to Congress any effort through administrative action to postpone or eliminate spending provided by law. Deferrals, which are temporary withholdings of budget authority, may be overturned by an act of the Congress at any time.

The Timing of the Budget Process

The planning, formulation, passage, and execution of the federal government's budget is a time-consuming process. The federal budget is for the fiscal year, which runs from October 1 to September 30. The president's formulation of budget priorities and proposals takes place in the months of March through January preceding the fiscal year. Congressional consideration of the budget begins in January, 9 months before the start of the fiscal year. The budget is enacted in the course of the fiscal year, and if Congress fails to enact a new budget by September 30, the federal government will operate on the basis of temporary appropriations. (See Figure 1.)

The federal budget process is like a slow-moving train. The budget is planned and deliberated over an 18-month period preceding the actual execution of the budget. Moreover, the vast bulk of appropriations considered in any particular budget year are based on permanent resolutions that do not require Congressional approval.

AUTOMATIC STABILIZERS AND DISCRETIONARY POLICY

Whether the result is intended or not, the continuous process of governmental spending and taxation affects aggregate demand. Two types of government spending and tax policies contribute to this effect: **automatic stabilizers** and **discretionary fiscal policies**.

> **Automatic stabilizers** are government spending or taxation actions that take place without any deliberate government control and that tend automatically to dampen the business cycle.

FIGURE 1
The Federal Budget Process

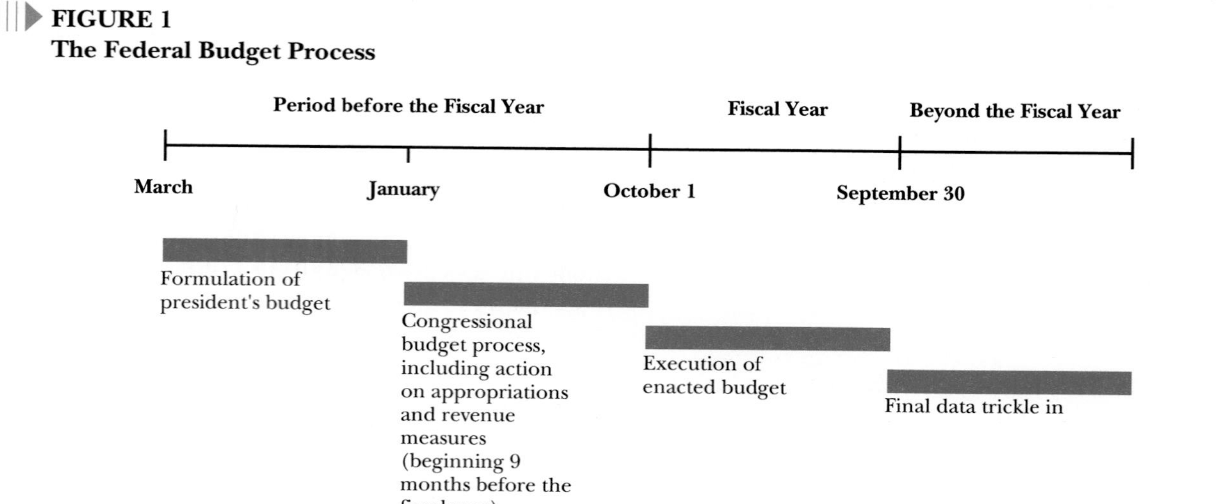

A minimum lead time of 20 months is required between the planning and execution of the federal budget. This lag makes it difficult to conduct discretionary fiscal policy. Final data trickle in throughout the following year; e.g., final GDP data are in 9 months after the year ends.

Discretionary fiscal policies are government spending and taxation actions that have been deliberately taken to achieve macroeconomic goals.

Many actions mandated by fiscal policy take place automatically and require no policy decisions on the part of government—as in the case of an **entitlement program,** such as Social Security or unemployment compensation payments.

An **entitlement program** requires the government to pay benefits to anyone who meets eligibility requirements.

To receive entitlement payments, recipients need only demonstrate that they qualify under legislated rules. Once the rules are set, the government cannot dictate the magnitude of such payments: they depend on general economic conditions. At the federal level, 75 percent of all federal outlays in the early 1990s were for relatively uncontrollable items like entitlements, permanent appropriations, and interest on the national debt.[2] Similarly, once income tax rates and rules concerning depreciation and personal exemptions are set, government tax revenues also depend on general economic conditions.

Despite relatively uncontrollable items, the government can raise or lower revenues and outlays through deliberate, discretionary decision making—for example, by changing the rules of eligibility for entitlement programs, raising or lowering income tax rates, or initiating major new defense expenditures or public-works programs.

Automatic Stabilizers

The income tax system and unemployment compensation and welfare programs automatically moderate cyclical disturbances by moving taxes and spending against the current of the business cycle. These automatic stabilizers depend entirely upon prevailing economic conditions and require no discretionary action by policymakers.

Income Taxes as Automatic Stabilizers. The amount of income tax revenues a government collects is determined by applying the average tax rate to the economy's taxable income. If an economy has an average tax rate of 20 percent of income and total taxable income is $100 billion, the government collects $20 billion in income taxes (20 percent times $100 billion). If total taxable income rises to $150 billion, the government collects $30 billion (20 percent times $150 billion). Income taxes rise and fall with income.

If the economy goes into a recession, personal incomes start to fall. Even if Congress maintains current tax rates, government tax receipts will fall. Take a family with a taxable income of $100,000, paying a tax rate of 34 percent. After paying $34,000 in taxes, it has $66,000 of income to spend. If its income falls by $20,000 as a result of the general decline in business activity, its tax bill falls to $27,200, and it has $52,800 to spend after taxes. Its after-tax income has fallen by $13,200, not by the full $20,000 reduction in income. If as a result of the drop in income, the family moves into a lower tax bracket (say 30 percent), the decline in after-tax income will be even less.

The tax system thus acts as an automatic stabilizer, moderating cyclical disturbances. A sudden drop in income leads to a corresponding drop in tax collections, which moderates the drop in after-tax income.

Unemployment Compensation and Welfare Payments. When an economy moves into recession, more people are unemployed and eligible for unemployment entitlement benefits. Moreover, families whose incomes have declined because of fewer hours of work or unemployment become eligible for welfare assistance. Unemployment compensation and increased welfare payments soften cyclical effects by limiting the decline in consumption expenditures. Unemployment compensation and welfare programs also soften the business cycle on the upswing by dampening the increase in consumption. Welfare recipients are taken off the welfare and unemployment compensation rolls as they find jobs, and increased deductions from payrolls (to state and local programs and union employment funds) reduce the amount of disposable income available to employed workers.

[2]Stanley E. Collender, *The Guide to the Federal Budget, 1986* (Washington, DC: The Urban Institute Press, 1986), 5–6.

EXAMPLE 2 Social Security Surpluses and Fiscal Drag

Fiscal policy is determined by the spending and taxation legislation of Congress. Tax increases can exert a "fiscal drag" on the economy by reducing disposable income. In 1983, Congress raised Social Security taxes to create surpluses to handle the substantial claims that will be made on Social Security when the baby boom generation retires early in the twenty-first century. By 1993, the annual Social Security surplus is projected to be $100 billion, and by 2020, the accrued surplus is projected to be well over $2 trillion measured in 1992 dollars.

Some economists have argued that the growing Social Security surpluses will so depress private consumption that economic growth will be depressed. Says economist Robert Kuttner, "You don't stimulate growth just by putting money in the piggy bank." Other economists do not fear the impending fiscal drag of Social Security. They argue that Social Security surpluses will add to national saving, raise investment, and actually stimulate economic growth.

Source: Robert Kuttner, "What Makes the Debate over Social Security So Curious," *Business Week*, August 8, 1988, 14.

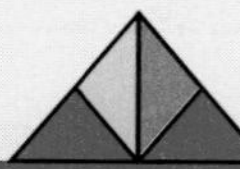

Government spending tends to rise automatically during recessions as more people become eligible for entitlement programs. Some forms of government spending therefore act as automatic stabilizers.

Automatic stabilizers cannot fully neutralize the business cycle. If spending falls, automatic stabilizers can neutralize only a part of the decline in output. The effect of taxes, unemployment compensation, and other welfare payments restore only a portion of lost disposable income. (See Example 2.)

Discretionary Fiscal Policy

Proponents of **policy activism** believe that discretionary actions should be taken to eliminate or further soften the forces of the business cycle.

Policy activism is the deliberate use of discretionary fiscal or monetary policy to achieve macroeconomic goals.

Activist fiscal policy operates through **autonomous changes** in tax rates and government expenditures.

Autonomous changes in taxes and government spending are independent of changes in income.

The proponents of activist (discretionary) fiscal policies believe that macroeconomic policy should go beyond setting up automatic stabilizers. Policy activists believe that better macroeconomic results can be achieved if policymakers use fiscal policy (or monetary policy, as will be discussed in Chapter 16) to eliminate inflationary and deflationary gaps.

Figure 2 illustrates how fiscal policy could be used to close gaps. Panel *a* shows an economy in a deflationary gap; the intersection of the aggregate demand (AD) and short-run aggregate supply (SRAS) curves occurs below the natural level of output at *e*. If government spending and taxes could be manipulated to raise the aggregate supply–aggregate demand equilibrium from *e* to *e′*, the deflationary gap would disappear. The increase in aggregate demand raises both output and prices. The self-correcting mechanism would have eventually yielded the same output (at point *a*) but with a lower price level. A fiscal policy that increases aggregate demand is called an **expansionary fiscal policy.**

FIGURE 2
Fiscal Policy with Deflationary and Inflationary Gaps

(*a*) Expansionary Fiscal Policy for a Deflationary Gap

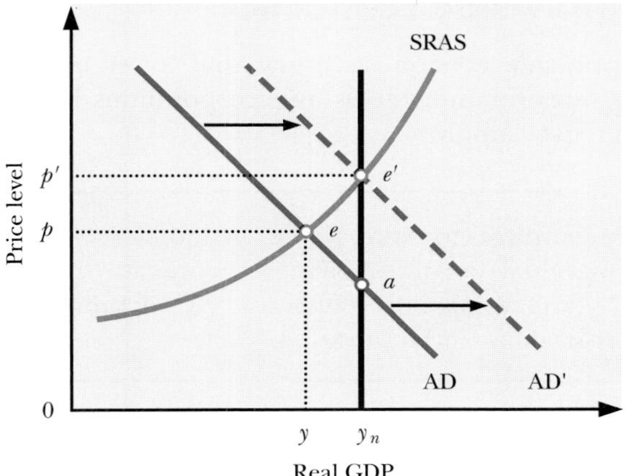

(*b*) Contractionary Fiscal Policy for an Inflationary Gap

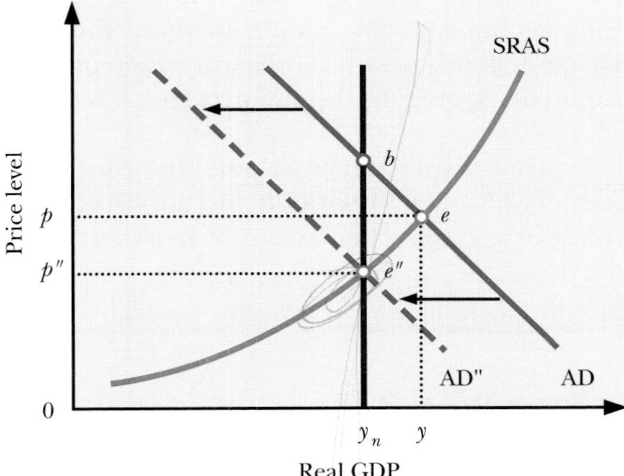

Panel *a* shows how expansionary fiscal policy could be used to eliminate a deflationary gap. By an increase in antonomous government spending or an autonomous reduction in taxes, the aggregate demand curve could be shifted to the right (from AD to AD′), restoring the economy to the natural rate of output, y_n. Panel *b* shows how contractionary fiscal policy could be used to eliminate an inflationary gap. By a reduction in autonomous government spending or an autonomous increase in taxes, the aggregate demand curve could be shifted to the left (from AD to AD″) to restore the economy to the natural rate of output.

An **expansionary fiscal policy** increases aggregate demand by raising government spending and/or by lowering tax rates.

Panel *b* illustrates the use of **contractionary fiscal policy** to eliminate an inflationary gap. In this case, fiscal policy aims to lower aggregate demand sufficiently to achieve an AD-SRAS equilibrium at the natural level of output.

A **contractionary fiscal policy** lowers aggregate demand by lowering government spending or by raising tax rates.

According to policy activists, if an inflationary gap is present, government should cut government spending or raise tax rates. If a deflationary gap is present, the government should raise spending or cut tax rates to raise output. If government spending and tax-rate actions are properly timed and of the correct magnitude, activist policies will cause inflationary or deflationary gaps to disappear.

Fiscal policymakers have a number of instruments: In the case of a deflationary gap (Figure 2, panel *a*), the government could raise its expenditures above the level of increase dictated by the automatic stabilizers (such as unemployment compensation and welfare programs). For example, additional money could be spent on dams, national defense, public parks, or increased police protection; unemployment compensation rules could be liberalized and eligibility requirements for welfare lowered to raise the incomes of the unemployed and the poor; or tax rates could be lowered. These actions would raise aggregate demand and close the deflationary gap. In the case of an inflationary gap (panel *b*), the government could lower discretionary spending, tighten entitlement rules, and raise tax rates. These actions should reduce aggregate demand and close the inflationary gap.

Expansionary and contractionary fiscal policies have different political costs and benefits. Expansionary fiscal policies win many friends and make few enemies. Tax rates are lower; entitlement benefits are easier to qualify for; members of Congress find it easier to get their favorite spending programs funded. Contractionary fiscal policies make many enemies and win few friends. The voters do not like tax increases or stricter eligibility requirements for entitlement benefits. Special-interest groups oppose the nonpassage of pork-barrel spending legislation. For these reasons, the government tends to prefer a fiscal policy that is expansionary rather than contractionary.

THE ROLE OF TAXES IN FISCAL POLICY

Tax policy can affect both aggregate demand and aggregate supply because changes in tax rates can affect economic behavior. These changes alter **average tax rates** and **marginal tax rates.**

> The **average tax rate** is the tax payment divided by taxable income.
>
> The **marginal tax rate** is the increase in the tax payment caused by a $1 increase in taxable income.

A taxpayer who pays $10,000 in taxes on a $50,000 income has a 20 percent average tax rate. If that person's tax payment rises to $15,000 when income rises to $60,000, the marginal tax rate is 50 percent. The $10,000 increase in income has caused a $5000 increase in taxes—for a marginal tax rate of 50 percent.

Supply-side Economics

Supply-side economists argue that lower marginal tax rates for individuals and corporations increase aggregate supply.

> According to **supply-side economics**, lower marginal tax rates increase aggregate supply by increasing work effort and by encouraging risk taking and innovation.

Supply-side economists believe that individuals respond to lower marginal tax rates by working more, taking more risks, and perhaps saving more. Businesses respond to investment incentives by investing in new technology. As people increase their work effort and as businesses modernize their plant and equipment, aggregate supply increases. (See Example 3.)

Figure 3 contrasts the two potential effects of discretionary tax cuts. In panel *a*, the tax cuts cause an increase in aggregate demand only. In panel *b*, the tax

EXAMPLE 3 Did the 1981 Tax Reform Work?

The 1981 tax reform, which lowered marginal tax rates by significant amounts, was a direct result of the supply-side economic philosophy that influenced the Reagan presidency. Supply-side theorists argued that if marginal tax rates were cut, people would have increased incentives to work and engage in risk taking, and economic growth would increase.

By 1992, enough evidence from the period after 1981 had been amassed to evaluate how well the 1981 tax reform performed in the vital area of labor supply. The overall conclusion is that the lower marginal tax rates did indeed raise labor supply. Increases were most substantial among women, whose behavior as second-income earners was most sensitive to a lower marginal tax rate. The decline in hours worked by men halted after 1986. The statistical evidence, as is usually the case, is not conclusive. Some of the largest increases in labor supply occurred among low-income workers whose marginal tax rates were not changed by the 1981 tax reform.

Source: Barry Bosworth and Gary Burtless, "Effects of Tax Reform on Labor Supply, Investment, and Saving," *Journal of Economic Literature* 6 (Winter 1992): 3–25.

FIGURE 3
Demand-side versus Supply-side Views of the Effects of a Tax Cut

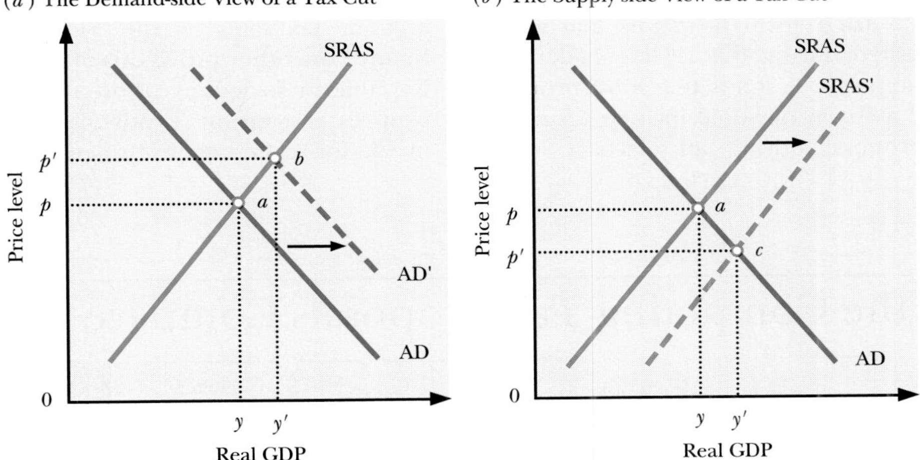

According to the demand-side view illustrated in panel *a*, a tax cut will affect output and prices through an increase in aggregate demand (from AD to AD′). The increase in aggregate demand raises both output and prices. The supply-side view, in panel *b*, is that the tax cut affects output and prices through an increase in short-run aggregate supply (from SRAS to SRAS′). The increase in short-run aggregate supply raises output and lowers prices.

cuts cause an increase in short-run aggregate supply only. In general, when tax rates fall, both aggregate demand and short-run aggregate supply increase. If the aggregate demand increase dominates, output increases and *prices increase.* If the aggregate supply increase dominates, output increases but *prices fall.* If authorities could cut taxes and count on substantial increases in short-run aggregate supply, the result would be the best of both worlds: more output and employment and lower prices.

Tax Policy and Economic Growth

Economists lack the historical perspective to evaluate the supply-side effects of tax cuts, although supply-side advocates of lower marginal tax rates and investment tax credits to stimulate economic growth cite the vigorous economic expansions of the 1960s and 1980s following tax reforms that lowered personal income tax rates and provided investment incentives.

There appears to be a consensus that tax policy affects long-term economic growth. If the tax system penalizes innovation and risk taking with exceptionally high marginal tax rates, long-term economic growth suffers. If the tax system encourages businesses to acquire modern capital equipment (through various tax incentives), economic growth is promoted.

The issue of economic growth and tax policy played a major role in the 1992 presidential campaign, with the Republicans and Democrats putting forward their own "growth-oriented" tax proposals. (See Example 4.) These tax reform packages focused on lower personal income taxes, investment tax credits, and incentives to save through tax-exempt retirement accounts.

THE EFFECTIVENESS OF FISCAL POLICY

The aim of discretionary fiscal policy is to eliminate inflationary or deflationary gaps more quickly than the self-correcting mechanism does. Critics of discretionary fiscal policy believe that (1) fiscal policy is too slow moving, cumbersome, and often counterproductive; (2) the effects of fiscal policies (especially tax policies) on aggregate demand are uncertain and

EXAMPLE 4 Competing Tax Proposals During an Election Year

The accompanying chart shows the various tax reform proposals that were floated during the 1992 presidential election campaign. It shows that most proposals favored a cut in personal income taxes—a popular proposal during an election year. Democratic proposals, however, called for increasing tax rates on the "rich" in order to finance the other provisions of the tax reform. Republican programs favored investment incentives and various proposals to provide tax breaks for real estate investments.

How the Competing Tax Proposals Compare

	President Bush	Representative Rostenkowski	Senator Bentsen	Liberal Democrats (Gore-Downey)	Conservative Republicans (House GOP)
Middle-class Tax Cut	Increase personal exemption by $500 per child	Tax credit of up to $400 for workers for two workers	$300 tax credit per child	$800 tax credit per child	None
Investment Incentive	15% first year write-off on equipment purchased this year	Favors some temporary investment incentive*	Favors some temporary investment incentive*	None	Increase expense limit for small companies to $18,200 from $10,000
Capital Gains	15.4% rate on assets held for three years	None	None	None	15% rate; index gains for inflation
Real Estate	Allows passive loss deduction for those materially participating in real estate	None	Might support a limited restoration of passive loss deduction*	None	Might support a limited restoration of passive loss deduction*
Retirement Accounts	$2,500 a year, nondeductible, in IRAs; tax-free earnings	None	Restore deductible IRAs to upper income taxpayers; new accounts with tax-free earnings	None	$2000 a year, nondeductible, in IRA's ; tax-free earnings
Cost Offsets	Cut government benefit programs	New 35% top rate; 10% surtax on millionaires	Cut defense spending	New 36% top rate; 15% surtax on highest incomes	None

* Specific proposals haven't been introduced.

Source: "Proposals Indicate Bush Is Willing to Bend on the Issue of the Deficit," *Wall Street Journal,* January 30, 1992, A6.

in some cases negligible; (3) increased government spending may crowd out private investment and reduce the long-run growth of the economy.

Lags in Fiscal Policy

Because changes in taxation and government spending must be approved by Congress and supported by the president, they often take several years or more from inception to enactment. Public-works programs must be approved by Congress and are often handled on a case-by-case basis. Lacking line-item veto authority, the president must either accept or veto budgets forwarded by Congress, and logrolling often overrides considerations of stabilization.

The lags that impede fiscal policy fall into three categories. First, Congress and the president may be slow to recognize the need for a change in fiscal policy. Reliable statistics on real output become available only 6 months after the fact. No one is certain whether a downturn is temporary or the start of a serious recession. It is therefore difficult to recognize when a change in fiscal policy is required. This *recognition lag* makes fiscal policy difficult to initiate on a timely basis.

Second, fiscal policy is subject to a substantial *implementation lag*—by the time the program goes through Congress and is implemented, the policy may no longer be correct. By the time a tax cut has been passed, a tax increase may have been more appropriate.

Third, the *effectiveness lag* is the amount of time it takes between implementation of a fiscal policy action and an actual change in economic conditions. Statistical evidence on the length of the effectiveness lag is mixed, but it appears to be long.[3] Critics of activist fiscal policy ask whether a country can carry out effective activist fiscal policy when substantial time lags and political delays are involved.

Permanent Income

The effects of discretionary tax policy can be reduced by *permanent-income effects.* Tax cuts affect aggregate demand only if lower tax payments shift the consumption/income curve up. (See Chapter 8.) As long as the marginal propensity to consume (MPC) remains stable, tax-induced changes in disposable income should elicit predictable changes in consumption: Lower tax rates mean more disposable income for consumption spending. But how stable is the consumption/income relationship? Keynes believed it was one of the most stable relationships in the whole economy, but economists after Keynes have come to question this proposition.

Many modern economists, such as Nobel laureates Franco Modigliani and Milton Friedman, argue that people tend to base their consumption decisions on life-cycle income, or **permanent income,** not on transitory changes in current income.

Permanent income is an average of the income that an individual anticipates earning over the long run.

A transitory change in this year's income—resulting from a *temporary* tax increase—will have a minimal effect on current consumption. This is because the impact of the tax on long-run income is so small that few people will change their current consumption.

When people base their spending decisions on permanent income, the relationship between this year's income and this year's consumption can thus be quite unstable. With its effects on private spending unknown, discretionary tax policy is therefore difficult to pursue.

Crowding Out

Chapter 8 pointed out that an increase in aggregate demand may crowd out private investment by pushing up interest rates. When this crowding out occurs, the growth of the nation's capital stock is retarded, and the long-run growth of the economy is reduced. Moreover, because the amount of crowding out is hard to anticipate, the exact effects of a fiscal stimulus are difficult to predict.

Increases in government spending can have other crowding-out effects, as well. For example, government expenditures on health care, education, police protection, roads, and parks could directly reduce some private expenditure. Thus, when government purchases and provides goods at a low cost as substitutes for private goods, an increase in

[3]Robert L. Gordon. *Macroeconomics,* 5th ed. (Boston: Little, Brown and Company, 1987), 524.

FIGURE 4
Fiscal Policy and Crowding Out

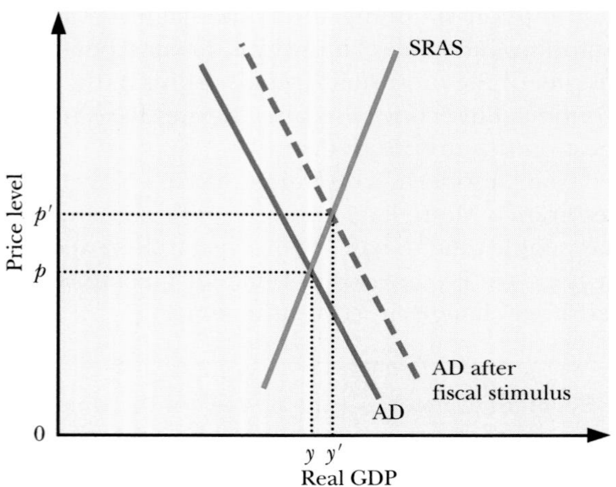

In response to fiscal stimulus (more government spending or lower taxes), aggregate demand increases, with a steep-sloped short-run aggregate supply curve, the price level is pushed up and interest rates may rise. These changes reduce consumer spending and business investment and thereby limit the increase in real GDP. If increased government spending *directly* causes less consumer spending, the initial shift in AD will be even less and real GDP will increase even less.

government expenditures on those substitutes will likely cause the **direct crowding out** of some private expenditures.

> **Direct crowding out** occurs when an increase in government spending substitutes for private spending by providing similar goods.

If direct crowding out is complete, there can be no increase in aggregate expenditures when government spending increases. Complete crowding out means that the *increase* in government spending causes an equal *decrease* in private spending.

Figure 4 illustrates the effects of crowding out. It shows an increase in aggregate demand caused by either an increase in government spending or a reduction in tax rates. With a steep-sloped short-run aggregate supply curve, the increase in *AD* pushes up prices (and probably interest rates), thereby crowding out consumption and investment spending. The resulting increase in real GDP is, in this case, relatively modest. If, in addition, the increase in government spending *directly* causes people to spend less on private consumption, the increase in AD will be even less (zero if complete crowding out occurs). This is why critics of activist fiscal policy say that its effects are both unpredictable (we do not know how much crowding out will occur) and weak.

EXAMPLE 5 1990: A Reversal of Keynesian Fiscal Policy?

The traditional Keynesian approach to fiscal policy is to increase discretionary government spending during recessions. In the fall of 1990, when the economy was clearly in a recession and unemployment was rising, Congress passed a substantial tax increase and pushed for lower federal spending. Both measures were touted as necessary for economic recovery.

Did Congress and the president's economic advisors reject Keynes's notion of activist fiscal policy? The 1991 *Economic Report of the President* stated that fiscal policy should ignore the short-run effects of the business cycle and focus on creating conditions for economic growth. The report warned that short-sighted discretionary reactions could potentially do more harm than good (due to the lags, crowding out, and other effects discussed in this chapter) and argued that the goal of fiscal policy should be to devise credible and systematic policies.

Source: "Fiscal Policy Focuses on the Long Run," *The Margin* (Fall 1991): 20–21.

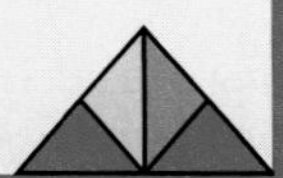

The debate over fiscal policy is not about its effects on economic growth but about the ability of discretionary fiscal policy to smooth out the wrinkles in the business cycle. Given its slow-moving nature, it becomes increasingly apparent that fiscal policy cannot be used to counter every turn in the business cycle. Rather, it is better used to create a climate that is conducive to economic growth. (See Example 5.)

The next chapter examines the economics of deficits and the public debt—a topic closely related to fiscal policy, which determines the nature of government deficits.

SUMMARY

1. The objective of discretionary fiscal policy is to eliminate inflationary and deflationary gaps. Fiscal policy is the deliberate control of government spending and taxation to achieve macroeconomic goals.

2. The federal budgeting phase takes almost two years and consists of three phases: executive formulation, congressional action, and budget execution and control.

3. A portion of government spending and tax colletion depends upon income. Tax collections fall as income falls; welfare payments and unemployment compensation rise as income falls. Such automatic stabilizers soften the business cycle, but they cannot eliminate it. Cyclical disturbances can be fully counteracted only by discretionary policies.

4. Supply-side economists argue that tax cuts that lower marginal tax rates increase aggregate supply.

5. Critics question the effectiveness of fiscal policy because of lags, permanent-income effects, and the crowding out of private investment.

KEY TERMS

fiscal policy
line-item veto authority
automatic stabilizers
discretionary fiscal policies
entitlement program
policy activism
autonomous changes
expansionary fiscal policy
contractionary fiscal policy
average tax rate
marginal tax rate
supply-side economics
permanent income
direct crowding out

QUESTIONS AND PROBLEMS

1. Economy Y is operating below the natural rate of output when autonomous government spending is increased by $50 billion. As a consequence of this action, private spending is reduced by $50 billion. How will the increase in government spending affect output and employment?
2. Evaluate the validity of the following statement: "If wages and prices are flexible in both inflationary and deflationary gaps, there is no need for activist macroeconomic policy."
3. What is the difference between automatic stabilizers and discretionary fiscal policy? Are they not the same because they both work through government spending and taxes?
4. Use the permanent-income hypothesis to predict which type of tax cut is more likely to affect aggregate output: a 1-year tax surcharge or a permanent lowering of tax rates.
5. Why is crowding out important to the debate over activist policy?

SUGGESTED READINGS

Barro, Robert J. *Macroeconomics*, 3rd ed. New York: John Wiley & Sons, 1990, chap. 15.

Collander, Stanley E., ed. *The Guide to the Federal Budget, 1986*. Washington, DC: The Urban Institute Press, 1986.

Mills, Gregory B., and John L. Palmer. *The Deficit Dilemma: Budget Policy in the Reagan Era*. Washington, DC: The Urban Institute Press, 1983.

Pechman, Joseph A. *Federal Tax Policy*, 5th ed. Washington, DC: The Brookings Institution, 1987, chaps. 1–3.

Schultz, George P., and Kenneth W. Dam. *Economic Policy beyond the Headlines*. New York: W.W. Norton, 1977, chaps. 2 and 3.

Thomas, Lloyd B., Jr. *Money, Banking, and Economic Activity*, 3rd ed. Englewood Cliffs, NJ: Prentice Hall, 1985, chap.18.

The United States Budget in Brief, fiscal year 1991.

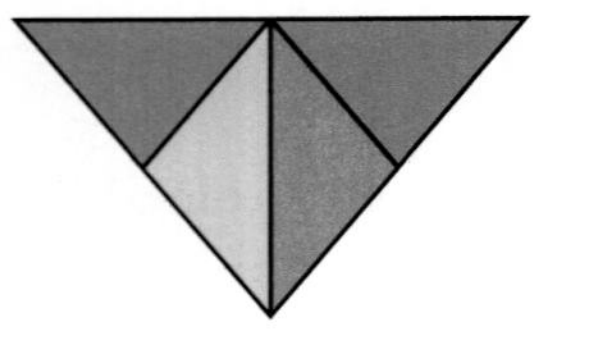

13 The National Debt

CHAPTER INSIGHT

Few economic issues generate as much emotion as the national debt. People complain, "We are going to bankrupt our children and grandchildren it we can't get the federal deficit under control." Others ask, "If we have to live within our means, why can't the government live within its means?"

Regardless of these widely expressed concerns and fears, the postwar period has seen only one year of federal government surpluses. Despite legislative efforts and numerous campaign promises, the federal deficit continues to rise.

This chapter examines government deficits and the government debt that results. It explores the various measures of deficits, shows how deficits relate to the level of economic activity, and examines how government deficits affect the overall economy.

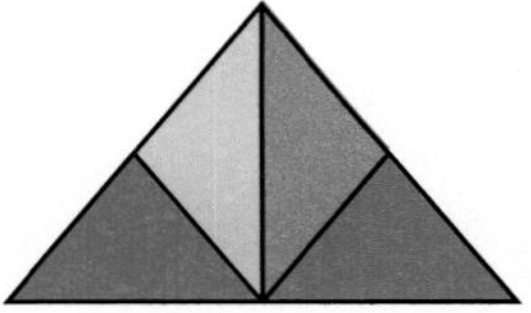

GOVERNMENT FINANCES

There are more than 82,000 federal, state, and local government units in the United States: one federal government, 50 state governments, and more than 82,000 township and county and municipal governments. Each government unit carries out a spending program and collects revenues through a variety of taxes and fees; some sell goods and services to residents—although sales revenues tend to be relatively minor compared to tax revenues.

The Federal Budget

The proposed 1993 budget of the U.S. government is shown in Table 1. Federal government receipts are made up primarily of personal tax receipts and contributions to social insurance programs. Corporate income taxes make up a relatively small portion of the federal government's receipts. On the expenditure side, only one-third of federal government expenditures are for purchases of goods and services. About 40 percent of spending goes for transfer payments to individuals, and the remainder goes for grants to state and local governments and for interest payments on the national debt.

About two-thirds of federal government spending transfers income from one person or organization to another. *Transfer payments to persons* shift income from taxpayers to recipients of welfare payments, unemployment insurance, and Social Security benefits. *Grants in aid to states and local governments* transfer income from the federal government to state and local governments. *Interest payments* on the national debt transfer income from taxpayers to the owners of government bonds both at home and abroad.

Surpluses and Deficits

The finances of a government unit are like those of a household. Both governments and households have revenues. Households receive income through factor payments and transfer payments; government units take in income by collecting taxes, receiving transfer payments from other government units, and selling services (such as municipal water or sewage connections, or tuition at state universities). Both governments and households spend their income. Households spend income on consumer goods and services; governments spend their income on purchases of goods and services and on transfer payments. When a household spends more than its income, it is *dissaving*. Dissaving occurs when the household must borrow money (or draw down accu-

TABLE 1
The 1993 Federal Budget

Category	**Amount (billions of dollars)**		**Percent**	
Total receipts		**1165**		**100**
Personal tax and nontax receipts	515		44.0	
Corporate income taxes	103		8.5	
Indirect business taxes, estate and gift taxes, miscellaneous receipts	100		8.5	
Social-insurance contributions	447		39.0	
Total expenditures		**1498**		**100**
Purchase of goods and services	508		34.0	
Transfer payments to persons	599		40.0	
Grants-in-aid to state and local governments	165		11.0	
Net interest payments and other expenditures	226		15.0	
Deficit (total revenues minus total expenditures)		**333**		

Source: Office of Management and Budget, *The United States Budget in Brief.*

EXAMPLE 1 Are We Really Running a Surplus?

Robert Eisner argues that we should calculate government debt as we calculate business debt. If a business borrows $1 million to build a new plant, it has not increased its overall indebtedness. It owes an additional $1 million, but has acquired an asset worth $1 million. and the two cancel each other.

Eisner argues that government investments in buildings, airports, dams, and tunnels should be treated in the same manner. He provides the following calculations for the year 1989:

Federal budget deficit	$152 billion
Federal government investments	−70
Federal deficit adjusted for investment	82
State and local budget surplus	−47
Total government deficit	$ 35 billion

After adjustment for federal government investments and the surpluses of state and local governments, the total government deficit of the United States, according to Eisner, is only one-fifth of the official federal deficit figure.

Eisner further notes that inflation reduces the real value of debt. With 1989 inflation at 4.1 percent. holders of the debt suffered an inflation tax of $87 billion. If this inflation tax is subtracted, the total government deficit becomes a surplus of $52 billion!

Source: Robert Eisner, "Deficits and Us and Our Grandchildren," in *Debt and the Twin Deficits Debate,* ed. James M. Rook (London: Bristelcone Books, 1991), 83.

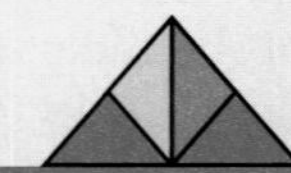

mulated savings). Similarly, when a government unit spends more than it takes in, it is dissaving. When such dissaving occurs, the government typically must borrow money (or draw down accumulated savings).

The difference between the total revenues and total outlays of a government unit is either a **government deficit** or a **government surplus.**

> A **government deficit** is an excess of total government spending over total revenues.
>
> A **government surplus** is an excess of total government revenues over total spending.

If total government revenues from taxes and fees equal total government expenditures, the government unit has a *balanced budget.*

Although the measurement of government deficits appears straightforward, in fact many ambiguities are involved. (See Example 1.)

Trends in Government Finance

Figure 1 shows government expenditures, revenues, surpluses, and deficits as a percentage of GDP since 1960, with blue areas for years of deficits and the rare orange areas for years of surpluses. This figure reveals some basic facts about government finance. First, the expenditures and revenues of total government (federal, state, and local) have generally risen as a percentage of GDP, with expenditures rising more rapidly than revenues. Second, government deficits are far more common than government surpluses. Since 1960, there have been only 3 years of small surpluses for total government and only 1 year of surplus for the federal government. Federal deficits have grown larger over time (in nominal dollars)—from $13 billion in the 1950s to $75 billion in the 1970s and to $350 billion in 1992. Third, government deficits widen during recessions. Fourth, the blue areas in the bottom part of the figure (representing federal deficits) are generally larger than the blue areas in the top part (representing deficits of total government). The deficits of the federal government dominate the picture, although state and local governments have run some small surpluses that partially offset federal deficits.

The rising government share of GDP is not unique to the United States. The government share has been growing in the major industrialized countries, and deficits are more common than surpluses. (See Figure 2.)

FIGURE 1
Government Expenditures, Revenues, and Deficits as a Percentage of GDP

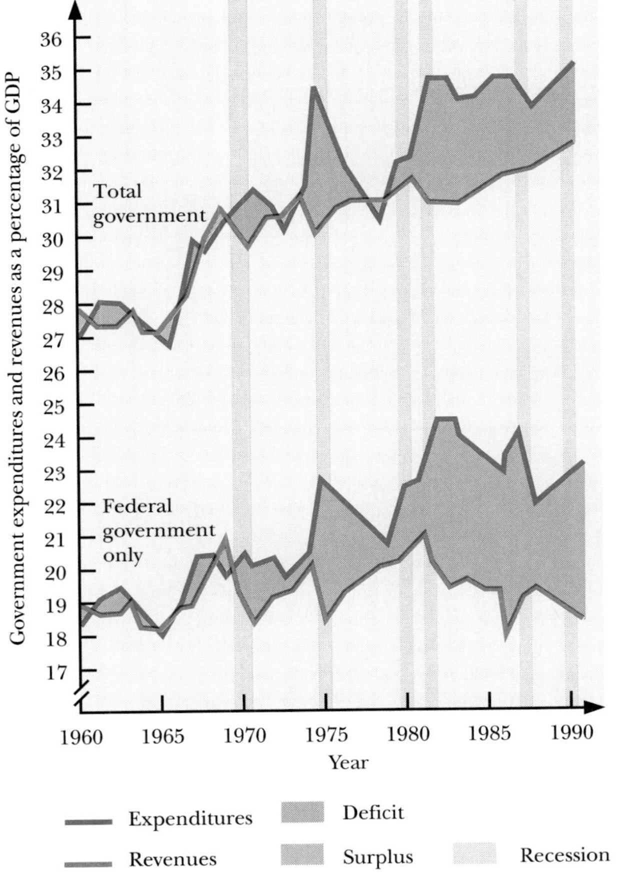

This figure shows that, since 1960, deficits tend to be associated with recessions. During recessions, government revenues fall while expenditures rise. The late 1960s (the Vietnam years) were an exception to this rule.

Source: *Economic Report of the President.*

THE FULL-EMPLOYMENT DEFICIT

The previous chapter demonstrated that taxes and government expenditures respond automatically to changes in output. Hence, the direction of fiscal policy cannot be gauged simply by looking at government spending, taxes, and the actual government surplus or deficit. During periods of declining real GDP, the government deficit tends to become larger. As income falls, tax revenues fall, but government obligations, in the form of unemployment compensation payments and welfare transfers, rise.

> Rising expenditures and falling taxes automatically push the government budget in the direction of deficits during recessions.

Federal deficits are shown by the orange line in Figure 3. During recessionary periods, the budget deficit typically follows a sharp *V* curve. The deficit widens during the recession and narrows during the recovery period to form a spike. The business cycle clearly affects the federal deficit. Prosperity brings rising tax revenues and declining transfer payments. Recessions bring falling tax payments and rising transfer payments. Because changes in the deficit that are induced by changes in the business cycle obscure discretionary changes in fiscal policy, it is useful to distinguish between the **cyclical deficit** and the **structural deficit.**

> The **cyclical deficit** is the part of the deficit caused by movements in the business cycle.
>
> The **structural deficit** is the deficit that would occur if there were no business cycle and the economy were operating at the natural level of real GDP.

It is possible to separate the effects of the business cycle from structural factors by comparing the actual deficit (or surplus) with the **full-employment deficit** (or **surplus**), illustrated by the blue line in Figure 3.

> The **full-employment deficit** (or **surplus**) is what the government budget surplus or deficit would have been had the economy been operating at the natural level of output (full employment).

To understand how the full-employment deficit is calculated, assume that the natural rate of unemployment is 6 percent and the economy has 8 percent

FIGURE 2
Selected Developed Countries: Government Receipts, Outlays, and Balances as a Share of GDP, 1960–1987

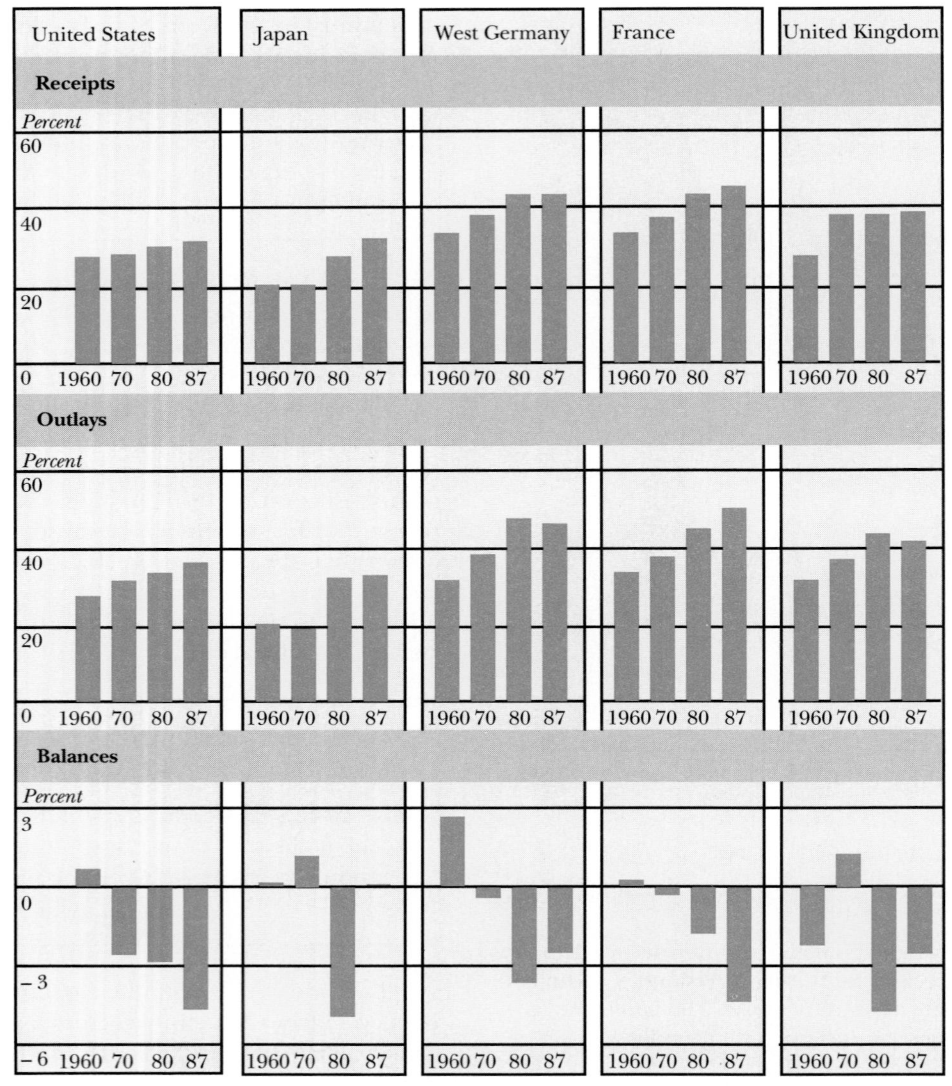

Source: *Handbook of Economic Statistics,* 1990, 17.

unemployment. Because the economy is 2 percentage points below full employment, the government must make extra payments for welfare and unemployment compensation, and it collects fewer tax dollars. The actual budget deficit (actual revenues minus actual expenditures) is $40 billion, but at full employment, revenues would have been $15 billion more and expenditures would have been $10 billion less. The full-employment deficit is therefore $15 billion (= $40 − $15 − $10)—much less than the actual deficit.

Because the effects of the cyclical deficit have been removed, the full-employment budget is able to reveal the direction of activist (discretionary) fiscal policy. When the deficit is calculated as if the economy were steadily operating at the natural rate, any changes in that deficit must be caused by discretionary changes in government spending, eligibility requirements for entitlements, and tax rates. The movement from a full-employment surplus in the early 1960s to a full-employment deficit by the late 1960s signals a movement toward expansionary fiscal policies (associated with a tax cut in 1964 and accelerated military spending during the Vietnam War). The mid-1970s was a period of contractionary fiscal policies (as the full-employment deficit narrowed), but the fiscal policies of the 1980s and early 1990s were expansionary (as taxes were cut and military spending expanded).

The actual budget deficit (or surplus), shown by the orange line, tends to move with the full-employment deficit (or surplus), shown by the blue line. During periods of low unemployment (as in most of the 1960s and the late 1980s), the two budget figures are close. During periods of high unemployment (as in recessions), the two lines diverge. For example, during the recession of 1958, the actual deficit was greater than 2 percent of GDP, while the full-employment budget was in balance. In the recession of 1982, the actual deficit was more than twice as large as the full-employment deficit. The differences between the two deficit measures show the cyclical deficit. The vertical distance between the two budget figures represents the cyclical component of the deficit.

Budget Policies

Using discretionary fiscal policy to eliminate deflationary or inflationary gaps has implications for government deficits. Expansionary fiscal policies tend to drive down government revenues (by lowering tax

FIGURE 3
The Actual Budget versus the Full-employment Budget of the United States

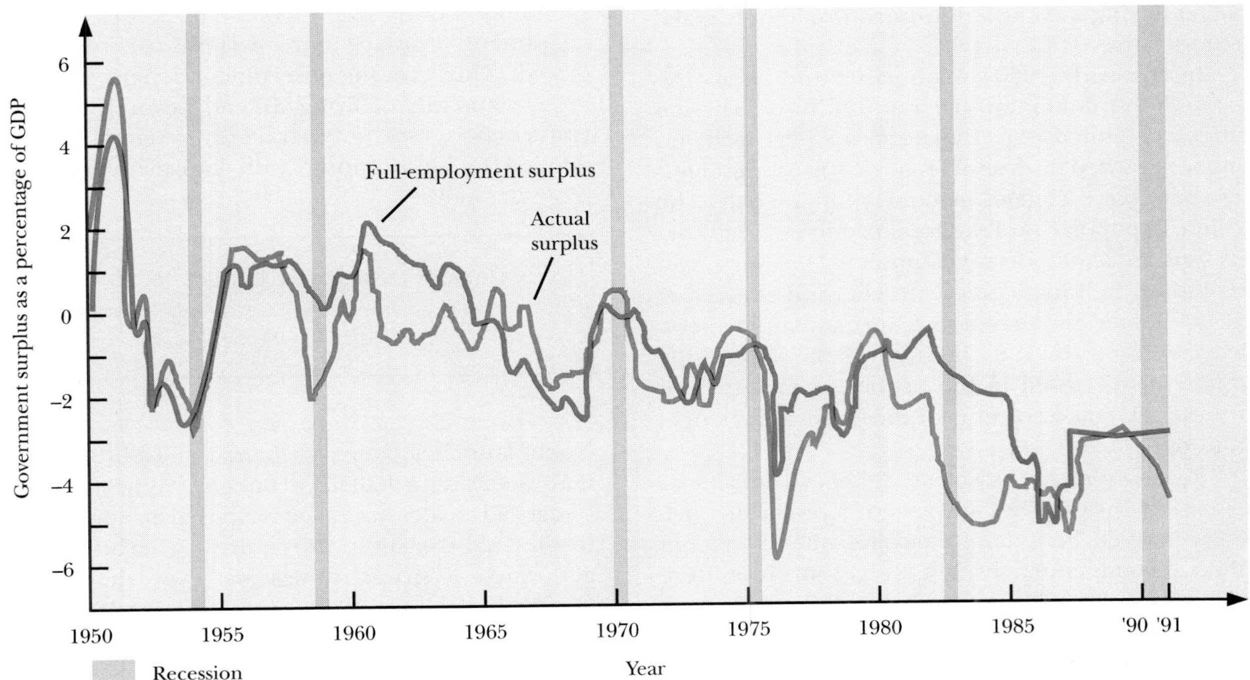

The orange line shows the actual federal government surplus or deficit for the period 1950 to 1991. The blue line gives the full-employment surplus or deficit for the same years. The full-employment budget should reveal changes in discretionary fiscal policy over this period. The shaded bars are periods of recession.

Source: Robert J. Gordon, *Macroeconomics,* 5th ed. (New York: HarperCollins, 1990), Appendix A. Updated by authors.

rates) while increasing government spending, hence adding to the budget deficit. Recessions tend to increase deficits by lowering tax revenues.

Keynesian Budget Policy. The proponents of activist fiscal policy maintain that government expenditures and taxes should be set to induce the economy to produce at full employment. If required to raise output to full employment, budget deficits (or surpluses) are a price that must be paid. The actual size of the government surplus or deficit is not critical in any one year. The budget surplus or deficit should not be allowed to stand in the way of important macroeconomic goals.

According to this budgetary philosophy, espoused by Keynes, it would be very unwise to adopt the goal of a balanced federal budget. If the economy is experiencing a cyclical downturn (say, a reduction in private investment) that reduces output below full employment, tax revenues decline along with output. Therefore, to balance the budget, government expenditures must be reduced by the amount of the reduction in tax collections. To pursue a balanced budget during a cyclical downturn would only make matters worse.

In the early 1960s, economists and public officials almost unanimously embraced the Keynesian budgetary philosophy. Balanced budgets were no longer regarded as desirable *per se*; instead, budgets were supposed to meet macroeconomic goals. The decline in popularity of the balanced-budget philosophy signaled an important triumph for the Keynesian revolution. In 1964, taxes were cut, and the deficit was deliberately increased to reduce unemployment. Taxes were cut in 1981 because of the supply-side arguments discussed in the previous chapter. Both of these tax cuts were tests of the Keynesian budget philosophy.

Keynes did not advocate *sustained* deficits or surpluses. Instead he advocated a cyclically balanced budget. Periods of excessive unemployment called for budget deficits, but budget surpluses were required during inflationary upswings. Therefore, although there was no rule that the budget should be balanced each year, it was expected that budget surpluses and deficits would even out in the long run—especially because cyclical upturns last longer than cyclical downturns.

In fact, some economists in the 1950s and 1960s worried about the *fiscal drag* of automatic stabilizers. With generally rising income, government tax revenues would automatically rise. They worried that government spending might lag behind government revenues.

As Figure 1 shows, a long-run balanced budget has not materialized. Since 1960, the federal budget has had only 1 year of surplus. In recent years, public alarm over the growing size of the federal deficit has grown, setting off bitter political struggles.

The Classical Case for Balanced Budgets. The Keynesian argument against a strict balanced-budget rule was a substantial departure from the philosophy of the classical economists. If, as they maintained, economies tend to operate at full employment, increases in government expenditures could not raise real GDP. Rather, increased government spending would push up interest rates and would be perfectly offset by an equivalent reduction in investment. Every extra dollar of government spending would crowd out a dollar in private investment.

In the classical view, increased government spending occurs at the expense of investment, and long-run economic growth suffers if government spending crowds out investment. Lower rates of investment translate into lower rates of economic growth. Thus growing government deficits can mean lower standards of living. In the Keynesian model, rising deficits raise output and living standards when applied to an economy with considerable unemployed resources.

> The classical case against budget deficits is that government spending crowds out investment spending and hence, lowers economic growth.

The Public-Choice Case for a Balanced Budget. Nobel laureates James Buchanan and Milton Friedman advocate a balanced budget. Some balanced-budget advocates have even proposed an amendment to the U.S. Constitution requiring a balanced budget. Such a proposal was narrowly defeated in Congress in June 1992. Although modern advocates of a balanced budget fear that government deficits will crowd out private investment, they are primarily concerned that elected politicians will not be able to limit government spending to socially necessary programs. Rational politicians know that spending programs that aid special-interest groups bring in votes. The average voter is generally poorly informed about government spending programs;

special-interest legislation hurts each of a large number of voters in only a minor and poorly understood way; logrolling and vote trading are therefore facts of life in the political arena. With the bias toward spending, balanced-budget advocates fear that borrowing to pay for government programs will offer the easy way out for politicians. If the budget had to be balanced over the business cycle, the public would be more likely to want less government spending because of the unwillingness to accept higher taxes.

> Public-choice economists argue that a balanced-budget requirement would limit government spending to socially necessary programs.

This is called a public-choice approach because it studies the way politicians and bureaucrats make decisions on how to raise and spend public funds.

PUBLIC DEBT, DEFICITS, AND SAVING

As Figure 3 shows, the federal government has run a deficit in 29 of the last 33 years. The federal government will doubtless continue to run deficits for the foreseeable future. Although many economists had hoped that the budget would be balanced over the business cycle, this has not occurred. The federal budget has been in deficit during periods of rising prosperity as well as recession.

When the federal budget is in deficit, the federal government is *dissaving.* Like individuals who dissave, the federal government must typically borrow to finance the difference between expenditures and revenues. The federal government borrows by selling IOUs (government bonds or bills) to private individuals (both at home and abroad), to banks, to corporations, and to the Federal Reserve banks. (The Federal Reserve is the U.S. central bank, discussed in Chapter 15.) The cumulative outstanding debt of the federal government is the **national debt.**

> The **national debt** is the sum of outstanding federal government IOUs upon which interest and principal payments must be made.

The *federal deficit* is the *annual addition* to the national debt. If the 1992 federal deficit is $350 billion, the national debt will grow by that amount each year. (See Example 2.)

Chapter 7 listed three forms of saving (or dissaving): private (household and business) saving, foreign saving, and government saving. If all government units combined are running a surplus, government as a whole is saving. If all government units combined are running a deficit, government is dissaving.

Table 2 shows the total of government, foreign, and private saving of the U.S. economy in the year 1991. Total saving (private saving plus foreign saving minus government dissaving) equaled $673 billion. Households and businesses as a whole saved a total of $771 billion, while government dissaved −$121 billion. The federal deficit was $156 billion, while state and local governments ran a combined surplus of $35 billion. Hence, government as a whole reduced the sum of saving by $121 billion. The $23 billion of foreign saving, on the other hand, provided an increase in the amount of saving available to the economy.

The fact that government deficits reduce the amount of saving available to the economy is viewed as one of the negative features of government deficits.

TABLE 2
Private, Foreign, and Public Saving 1991

Saving Category		Amount of Saving (+) or Dissaving (−) (billions of dollars)
Personal saving		170
Business saving		601
Government dissaving		−121
Federal deficit	−156	
State and local surplus	35	
Foreign saving		23
Total saving		**673**

Source: *Survey of Current Business,* U.S. Department of Commerce.

EXAMPLE 2 Who Buys the National Debt?

When the U.S. government runs a deficit, the U.S. Treasury must sell government debt in the form of bonds or bills. Who actually buys U.S. government debt? From the accompanying table, it appears that the debt's buyers are different from year to year. During some years (1986, for example), foreigners are the predominant buyers. During other years (1985), state and local governments have dominated. In 1983, the largest purchasers were banks and households.

The table shows that the Federal Reserve Bank (known as the Fed) can also be a major buyer of U.S. government debt. In 1986, for example, the Fed purchased about 15 percent of U.S. government debt. Such purchases expand the money supply and are felt to have an inflationary effect on the economy.

Although some people worry that the federal government has run up substantial debts abroad, foreigners remain a minority owner of the national debt.

Source: "All Micawber Needed Was Treasury's Luck," *Wall Street Journal*, June 20, 1988. (Based on data compiled by Paul Getman of WEFA Associates from Federal Reserve data.) Updated by authors from the *Federal Reserve Bulletin*.

		Buyers of National Debt				
Year	Net New Supply of National Debt	Federal Reserve	All Foreign	State & Local Govt.	Comm. Banks	Households
1980	$ 79.8	$ 3.9	$12.4	$ 0.7	$16.1	$18.7
1981	87.8	9.6	7.9	−1.8	1.8	36.6
1982	162.1	8.4	12.8	4.8	19.4	52.7
1983	186.7	12.6	15.7	16.7	47.8	69.9
1984	199.0	8.9	27.7	4.5	1.9	79.5
1985	223.7	20.5	19.6	66.3	12.1	31.1
1986	214.7	30.0	42.8	24.1	5.3	10.8
1987	142.3	11.2	36.7	2.9	8.6	28.3
1990	411.8	31.2	32.2	−9.1	13.4	8.5

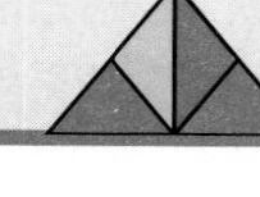

WHY PEOPLE FEAR DEFICITS

People fear deficits for a number of reasons, some justified, others not. In fact, the persisting strong public concern over government deficits is a matter of record. Public opinion polls show that people regard government deficits as a concern that sometimes rivals crime and world peace in importance.

People are concerned about the national debt because deficits create inflation, raise interest rates, place a high tax burden on future generations, and hurt the balance of trade.

Deficits and Inflation

When the federal government runs a deficit, it must sell IOUs to someone. If the IOUs are sold to the public, the government increases the demand for credit in credit markets, and there is a danger that interest rates will rise. If the government wishes to finance its deficits without pushing up interest rates, it can essentially create more money (and credit) by "printing money." In this respect, government differs from households and businesses. Only governments can print money to finance their deficits. As Chapter 8 showed, when the nation's supply of money expands, prices are bid up and inflation accelerates. In this way, deficits can lead to inflation.

If deficits cause inflation, there should be a significant correlation between changes in deficits and inflation. The facts (discussed in Chapter 17) show that the year-to-year relationship between deficits and inflation is weak over the course of the business cycle. During the recession phase, the deficit grows, but product and labor markets are weak and prices remain stable. During the recovery stage, the deficit falls, but product and labor markets are tight and inflation heats up. Cyclical effects tend to mask the effects of deficits on inflation. Chapter 17 shows that when cyclical effects are averaged over the long run, there is a positive relationship between deficits and inflation.

FIGURE 4
The Federal Deficit and Interest Rates

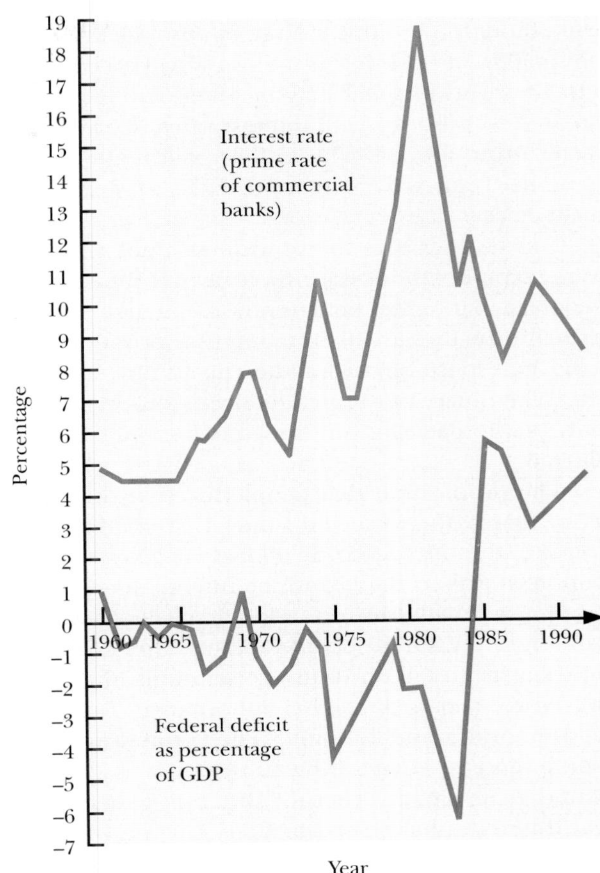

This figure fails to demonstrate a positive relationship between the federal deficit as a percent of GDP and interest rates.

Source: *Economic Report of the President.*

Deficits and Interest Rates

Do large deficits push up interest rates? The logical argument is that when the U.S. government runs a deficit, it must borrow funds in credit markets just like any other borrower. When the U.S. government runs a large deficit, it increases the demand for credit and raises interest rates. As interest rates rise, private businesses reduce their borrowing for investment purposes, and the federal deficit crowds out private investment.

Although this proposition has gained wide acceptance, the empirical relationship between federal deficits and interest rates is surprisingly weak. Figure 4 plots interest rates and the federal deficit (as a percent of GDP) from 1960 to the present, and it does not reveal the expected positive relationship. When interest rates rose in the late 1960s, the federal deficit was falling. Interest rates fell in the early 1970s as the deficit was rising. In the early 1980s, the deficit was rising while interest rates were falling. In the early 1990s, interest rates fell and the deficit rose. The high interest rates in the mid-1970s did, however, correspond to rising federal deficits.

A number of reasons have been advanced to explain the weak relationship between federal deficits and interest rates. First, deficits are highest during recessions, when credit demand is low. Therefore, government borrowing may not necessarily push up interest rates during periods of weak credit demand. Second, as Figure 1 reveals, the deficits of total government (including state and local government) have been smaller than federal deficits. Budget surpluses at the state and local level have offset a portion of the federal deficit. Third, there has been an internationalization of credit markets since 1960. People with funds to loan can now place them in London, New York, Tokyo, Hong Kong, or Latin America on a moment's notice. Cast in this global perspective, the large U.S. deficits of the 1980s and 1990s make up only a small percentage of the credit demand in world credit markets. It may be that U.S. deficits (even though they appear large in absolute size) are too small to affect interest rates in world credit markets. In a world capital market, when rising deficits threaten to push up U.S. interest rates, saving is attracted from abroad. The in-flow of foreign saving therefore returns U.S. interest rates to prevailing world-market rates.

Fourth, increases in government debt may motivate taxpayers to increase their saving. If taxpayers recognize that higher deficits now mean higher taxes in the future, they are likely to increase private saving to be in a position to handle the future tax burden. When increases in private saving offset increases in public dissaving, interest rates should be unaffected.

The proposition that people increase their saving to match the expected future increase in taxes is called the *Ricardo-Barro equivalence theorem* after economist Robert Barro and the nineteenth-century economist David Ricardo, who first ventured this proposition. Even if people expect the resulting higher taxes to fall on future generations, they may save more to pass on higher inheritances for their children and grandchildren.[1] The proposition that people increase their saving in response to government deficits is controversial.[2] Different generations bear different lifetime tax burdens. Currently, older generations are expected to pay taxes lower than the benefits they will receive, while younger generations will bear a substantial tax burden. (See Example 3.)

[1] See Robert J. Barro, *Macroeconomics,* rev. ed. (New York: John Wiley and Sons, 1987), chap.15; Robert J. Barro, "Are Government Bonds Net Wealth?" *Journal of Political Economy* 82 (November/December 1984): 1095–1117.

[2] The main evidence in favor of the equivalence theorem is the weak association between deficits and interest rates. On this, see Paul Evans, "Do Large Deficits Produce High Interest Rates?" *American Economic Review* 74, 1 (March 1985); 68–86. For a more direct test of the evidence, see Roger Kormendi, "Government Debt, Government Spending, and Private Sector Behavior," *American Economic Review* 73 (December 1983): 994–1010. The skeptics point out that people are unlikely to take such a long-run view of future tax obligations, and they point to the decline in private saving that accompanied the large deficits of the 1980s. For a critic's view, see Robert L. Gordon, *Macroeconomics,* 5th ed.(New York: HarperCollins, 1990), 415–16.

The Burden of Debt

Probably the most widespread public concern is that high deficits will eventually result in a national debt that is "too large" to handle. The burden of national debt can be measured in the same way that the burden of private debt is measured. The person who goes to a bank to borrow money will be asked about income and existing liabilities. The borrower with an income of $100,000 and no outstanding debts will be able to borrow much more than one with a $15,000 annual income and large debts. Debt must be judged relative to the ability of the debtor to pay the interest and principal on the debt.

What determines the U.S. government's ability to carry debt? Insofar as tax collections (the government's income) are closely tied to GDP, ultimately the federal government's income depends upon the amount of GDP produced. Government tax receipts since 1960 have averaged around 20 percent of GDP. The 1992 GDP of almost $6 trillion gave the federal government an income of more than $1 trillion. A GDP of $10 trillion in the year 2000 would yield the government about $2 trillion. The amount of GDP produced now and in the future is a critical factor in determining the burden of the national debt.

As Figure 5 indicates, public debt as a percentage of GDP has declined since the end of World War II. In 1945, public debt was 1.2 times GDP. By 1981, the ratio of debt to GDP had fallen to 34 percent. Between 1981 and 1991, the national debt rose from 34 percent to about 60 percent of GDP. By comparison, the average American family has personal debt equal to three-quarters of one year's income after taxes.

The burden of the public debt can also be measured by the proportion of current income required to pay interest and principal on the debt. In 1991, 17 percent of federal government expenditures was devoted to interest payments on the national debt. For the average American family, approximately 17.5 percent of personal disposable income was devoted to interest payments on mortgages and consumer debt in the same year. The burden of private debt appears to be about the same as national debt.

Will the United States ever go bankrupt by accumulating too much debt? As long as GDP grows as rapidly as debt, the burden of the debt will remain the same. If GDP outgrows debt, the burden of the debt falls.

EXAMPLE 3 The Burden of the Debt on Different Generations

In an effort to determine the remaining net-payment burden placed on each generation by the present national debt, under current fiscal policies, the Congressional Budget Office has developed "generational accounts." These accounts, which include federal, state, and local government debt, also compute the average net-payment burden that will have to be imposed on members of all future generations if the government debt is eventually to be paid off.

The accompanying chart depicts these amounts for selected generations as of 1989. Note that older generations are expected to be net recipients, since they pay low taxes but receive substantial Social Security and Medicare benefits. Younger generations will likely pay more than they receive because of their greater income, payroll, and sales taxes. Men aged 30 in 1989 can expect to pay out almost $200,000 more in taxes than they receive in benefits.

For both newborn and future generations, these numbers represent net-payment burdens to be paid over their entire lifetimes. A comparison of the results reveals a substantial generational imbalance.

Source: Federal Reserve Bank of Cleveland, *Economic Trends,* January 1992; Congressional Budget Office; *Budget of the United States Government,* fiscal year 1992.

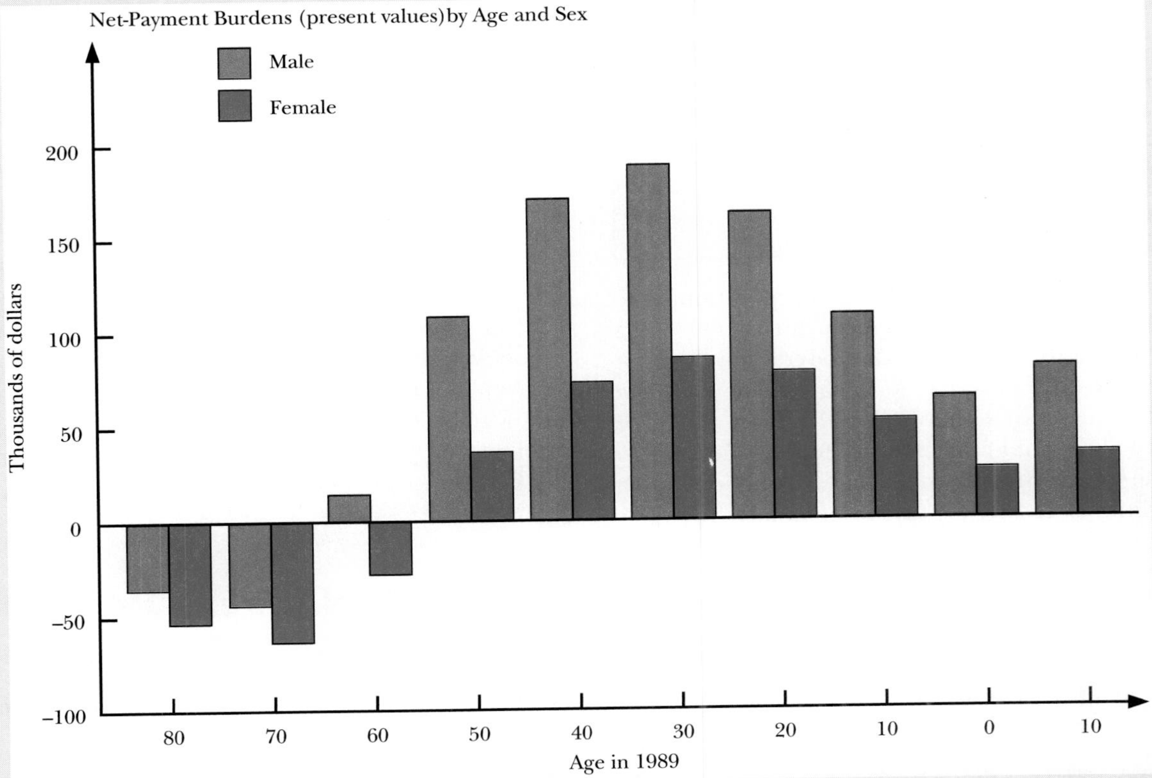

Net-Payment Burdens (present values) by Age and Sex

Male

Female

Thousands of dollars

200

150

100

50

0

–50

–100

80 70 60 50 40 30 20 10 0 10

Age in 1989

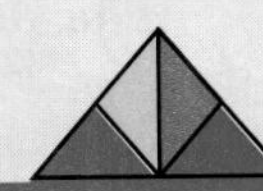

FIGURE 5
Public Debt as a Percentage of GDP

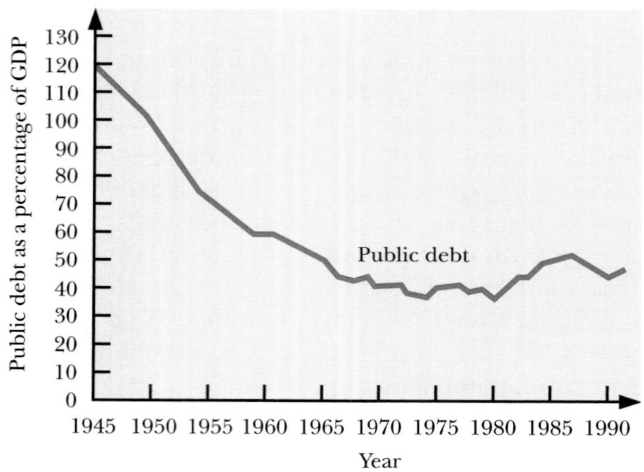

Despite growing concern about its absolute size, public debt as a percentage of GDP has been falling throughout the postwar period, although the percentage did rise between 1981 and the present.

Source: *Economic Report of the President.*

> A growing economy is the best protection against an increasing burden of national debt.

Unlike private individuals or corporations, the federal government has a special guarantee of its ability to handle its debt. If the federal government runs a $50-billion deficit in a particular year, the U.S. Treasury can either sell $50 billion worth of bonds to the public or ask the Federal Reserve to buy the bonds, thereby pumping $50 billion worth of additional reserves into the economy. In other words, the federal government can finance its deficit by printing money.

Budget Deficits and Trade Deficits

Government deficits are thought to affect the **trade deficit.**

> A **trade deficit** is an excess of imports over exports.

People worry about these "twin deficits"; they are afraid that a soaring federal deficit will contribute to a rising trade deficit.

The impact of the federal deficit on the trade deficit is by no means certain, however. The federal budget deficit is economically linked to the trade deficit through the exchange rate (how many German marks or Japanese yen it takes to buy one U.S. dollar). A higher exchange rate means U.S. wheat or commercial aircraft cost more to foreign buyers. A lower exchange rate lowers the price of U.S. goods to foreign buyers. A higher federal deficit represents a greater demand for the savings of the public. As U.S. interest rates are bid up above foreign rates, capital flows into the United States from foreign countries. Eventually this flow of capital eliminates the U.S. interest-rate differential. Meanwhile, as foreigners buy U.S. dollars to take advantage of higher U.S. interest rates, the exchange value of the dollar increases. The higher dollar exchange rate discourages exports and encourages imports, and the U.S. trade deficit increases.

Figure 6 shows the relationships between the trade deficit, the federal budget deficit (as a percentage of GDP), and the exchange value of the U.S. dollar. When the federal deficit decreased from 1970 to 1980 (in panel *a*), the exchange value of the U.S. dollar also increased (in panel *b*). When the federal deficit increased from 1980 to 1985, the dollar soared in value. The drop in the dollar from 1985 to 1987 was accompanied by a modest decline in the deficit. The substantial rise in the dollar in 1989 was accompanied by a relatively stable trade deficit and a modest reduction in the federal deficit. In 1991, the federal deficit rose, the trade deficit fell, and interest rates fell. Thus the relationship between the federal deficit and the trade deficit is complex. The trade deficit appears to depend on many additional factors.

INTERNAL VERSUS EXTERNAL DEBT

Any country can have either **internal debt** or **external debt.**

> **Internal debt** is national debt owned by the citizens of that country.

FIGURE 6
The Trade Deficit, the Federal Deficit, and the Dollar

(*a*) The Trade Deficit and the Federal Deficit

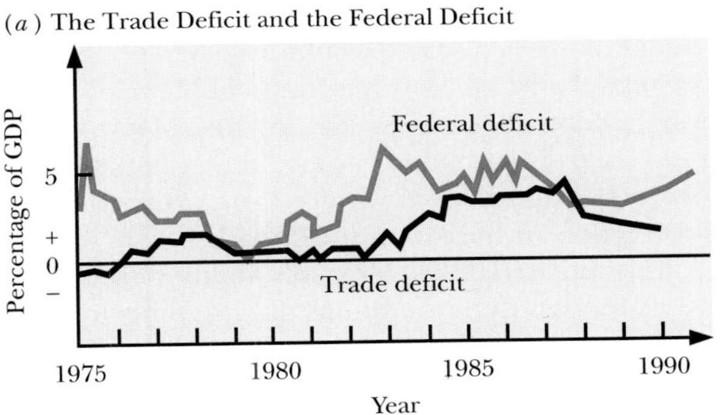

(*b*) The Dollar

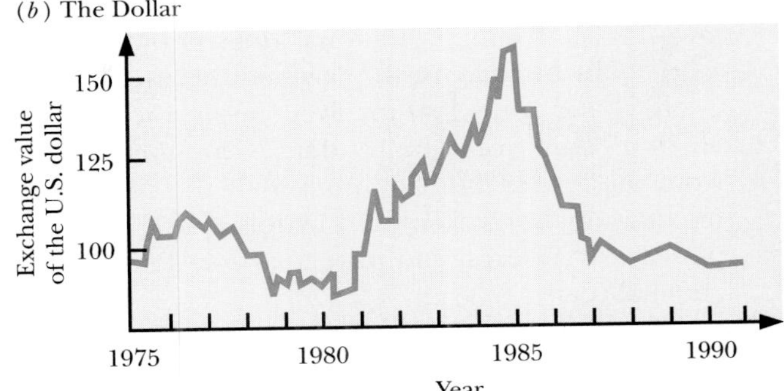

In panel *a*, the trade deficit (measured as the current account divided by GDP) and the federal deficit divided by GDP are shown from 1975 to the present. There is no apparent link between the two deficits. Panel *b* shows the exchange value of the U.S. dollar as measured by an index of the weighted average exchange value of the U.S. dollar against the major industrial countries plus Switzerland.

Source: *Federal Reserve Bulletin.*

External debt is national debt owned by citizens of other countries.

If the debt is *internal*, the United States basically owes itself. When interest payments are made on the national debt, income is transferred from one U.S. citizen to another. The taxpayers' dollars are used to pay interest to the owner of the government bond. Insofar as recipients of interest payments are also taxpayers, the *net transfer* of income is small. Internal debt payments do not alter the amount of income in the country; they affect only the distribution of income between debt owners and nonowners.

An *external* debt works differently: Interest payments represent transfers of income from U.S. taxpayers to residents of other countries. The amount of income left in the country is affected by this type of transaction. In the 1950s, only 5 percent of national debt was owned by foreigners. By the early 1990s, the proportion exceeded 20 percent. Foreign ownership of the national debt has increased over the years for many reasons. The main reason is that the United States has come to be regarded as a safe haven by foreign investors.

External debt is not necessarily bad. Had the United States not borrowed abroad, U.S. interest rates might have been higher and private investment much lower. For other countries, such as those in Central and Latin America, external ownership of the debt is so large that interest payments abroad account for a large share of GDP. (See Example 4.)

Problems of Deficit Reduction

Over the last decade, the impact of deficits on the economy has been hotly debated. Politicians, economists, and the general public favor deficit reductions. Although several U.S. presidents have made strong deficit-reduction pledges in their campaigns, over the past 15 years, no president has been able to produce a balanced federal budget. Why is it so difficult to achieve a balanced budget?

First, approximately 75 percent of all federal government spending is for relatively uncontrollable outlays—government expenditures whose level is determined by existing statutes, by contracts, or by other obligations. Federal government outlays for nondefense discretionary programs accounted for only 17 percent of the total in 1991. To cut the size of the

EXAMPLE 4 External versus Internal Debt: Mexico and the United States

If a country's national debt is owned by its citizens, the payment of interest and prinicipal involves simply a transfer of income from one resident to another or from one generation to another. If the country's national debt is owned by foreigners, the payment of interest and prinicipal transfers income abroad.

Consider the following comparison of the national debts of Mexico and the United States (for 1990):

	United States	Mexico
National debt owned by foreigners as a percentage of GDP	15%	78%
Interest and principal payments abroad as a percentage of GDP	1.4%	9.4%

With almost 80 percent ownership of national debt by foreigners, approximately 10 percent of Mexico's GDP would have had to be transferred abroad each year to meet Mexico's foreign debt obligations. To do this, Mexico would have either had to earn sufficient net exports to pay the necessary interest and principal to foreigners or borrow more abroad.

In the early 1980s, Mexico's ability to service its foreign debt ran out as did its ability to borrow new funds abroad. It simply could not afford to transfer 10 percent of its income abroad. Accordingly, an international bailout of Mexico and much of Latin America and Central America had to be arranged by the International Monetary Fund and other international financial institutions to prevent disorderly defaults on loans. In the course of these bailouts, a major portion of the debt was either canceled or rescheduled.

The financial difficulties of Mexico and much of Latin America vividly illustrate the difference between external and internal debt.

Source: Kenneth Jameson, "Latin America's Burden: The Debt," in *Debt and the Twin Deficits Debate*, ed. James K. Polk, (London: Bristlecone Books, 1991), 55–77.

federal deficit, federal revenues must be increased, federal outlays must be reduced, or a combination of the two must take place. In any particular year, budgetary authorities have little leeway for reduction. In addition to relatively uncontrollable outlays, tax revenues are also largely out of the control of budgetary authorities, insofar as they depend upon the state of the economy (with given tax rates).

There is no popular way to reduce the deficit. Spending cuts are vigorously opposed by those who benefit from the spending program; tax changes that raise government revenues are just as vigorously opposed by those who would pay higher taxes. Affected parties are able to lobby their elected officials, who then find it difficult to vote in favor of unpopular spending cuts or tax increases. Tax-increase proposals are further complicated by the need to raise only those tax items that will not reduce work effort or capital formation. If work effort and capital formation drop, income drops and there is less income to tax. Although everyone favors deficit reduction, few are willing to pay the personal price of a lower deficit, particularly when it comes to giving up spending and tax programs that are of benefit to that individual. This fact, more than any other, explains why it is difficult to substantially reduce the deficit. (See Example 5.)

The next chapter examines the role of money in the economy and effect of money on inflation.

EXAMPLE 5 Deficit Reduction: Gramm-Rudman versus the Budget Enforcement Act

The most notable legislative attempt to reduce the federal deficit was the Gramm-Rudman-Hollings Deficit Reduction Act of 1985, which was intended to balance the federal budget by 1993. The most recent attempt was the Budget Enforcement Act of 1990, designed to keep the federal deficit to manageable proportions. So far, none of the budget-balancing acts has worked.

Gramm-Rudman set yearly targets for federal deficit reductions so that by 1993 (eight years after the passage of the act), the federal budget would be balanced. In each year, Congress's Office of Management and Budget was to estimate the projected budget deficit; if it exceeded the Gramm-Rudman budget target for that year, automatic spending cuts were to go into effect.

Legislators found various ways to avoid the automatic budget reductions called for by Gramm-Rudman. Rosy projections of federal revenues were the main device used to avoid automatic cuts. Each year, an unrealistically low deficit projection permitted Congress to avoid spending cuts. Creative budgetary accounting techniques were also used to reduce the measured deficit.

The Budget Enforcement Act of 1990, which placed annual caps on defense, international, and domestic discretionary spending replaced Gramm-Rudman. The 1990 act placed no restrictions on entitlement spending for Social Security, Medicare, and unemployment compensation. The new act proved a weaker restraint on government spending than Gramm-Rudman for a number of reasons. First, spending caps were set very high (discretionary spending was allowed to increase more rapidly than inflation). Second, entitlement spending programs did not have caps, whereas under Gramm-Rudman they were supposed to increase at about the rate of inflation. Third, a number of emergency and special provisions allowed Congress to exceed the caps. Fourth, the continued weakness of the U.S. economy in 1992 caused electioneering politicians to push for popular spending programs and tax cuts.

The policeman of the 1990 act is the White House budget director, who has the authority to impose across-the-board cuts if spending caps are exceeded.

Although Gramm-Rudman failed to eliminate the federal deficit, it appears to have caused the federal deficit to decline as a percentage of GDP. (In 1989, the deficit declined to 3 percent of GDP). Under the Budget Enforcement Act, the federal deficit is projected to equal 7 percent of GDP in 1992 and 6 percent in 1993, after which it is supposed to decline.

The failure of both Gramm-Rudman and the Budget Enforcement Act shows how difficult it is to reduce federal budget deficits. There are many pressures for spending and few pressures to raise revenues and/or reduce spending.

Source: "Bring Back Gramm-Rudman—It Worked," *Wall Street Journal*, August 12, 1991.

SUMMARY

1. Government budgets show the relationship between government revenues and outlays. A budget deficit occurs when the government unit is dissaving; a surplus occurs when the government unit is saving. Currently, the federal government is running deficits while state and local governments combined run surpluses.

2. Economists use the full-employment budget as a yardstick to measure changes in discretionary fiscal policy. The full-employment budget is the surplus or deficit that would have prevailed had the economy

been producing full-employment output. Keynesian economists argue that deficits should be accepted if necessary to achieve full employment. Friedman and other public-choice economists argue for a balanced budget.

3. The national debt is the sum of outstanding federal government IOUs. People fear the national debt because they believe it may cause inflation, high interest rates, national bankruptcy, or a negative trade balance. Deficit reduction is difficult because most federal spending is relatively uncontrollable in the short run. In the long run, deficit reduction requires unpopular spending cuts and unpopular tax increases.

KEY TERMS

government deficit
government surplus
cyclical deficit
structural deficit
full-employment deficit (surplus)
national debt
trade deficit
internal debt
external debt

QUESTIONS AND PROBLEMS

1. In Economy Z, private saving is \$500 billion. Expenditures of the federal government are \$700 billion, and its revenues are \$650 billion. The combined expenditures of state and local government are \$300 billion, and their combined revenues are \$350 billion. There is no foreign saving. What is the total amount of saving in the economy?
2. When an economy goes into a recession, tax collections fall. What would you expect to happen to government spending?
3. If actual government expenditures are \$200 billion and actual government revenues are \$100 billion, and if the economy is at less than full employment, would the full-employment budget show a larger or smaller deficit than the actual budget? Explain.
4. Contrast the Keynesian position on balanced budgets with that of the classical economists.
5. Explain why the U.S. government can afford to carry a heavier debt burden than private individuals.
6. In 1997, the actual deficit in Economy X is \$100 billion, and the full-employment deficit is \$80 billion. In 1998, the actual deficit is \$200 billion, and the full-employment deficit is \$80 billion. From these figures, speculate about what has happened to Economy X during this time.
7. If deficits are highest during recessions, explain why the link between large deficits and inflation may be weak.
8. Explain why supporters of activist fiscal policies would oppose a balanced-budget amendment to the Constitution.
9. Consider the reasons people fear deficits. Which of these fears appears to be most justified?
10. Explain why one would expect a positive relationship between budget deficits and trade deficits.

SUGGESTED READINGS

Aronson, J. Richard, and John L. Hilley. *Financing State and Local Governments.* Washington, DC: The Brookings Institution, 1986.

Barro, Robert J. *Macroeconomics,* 3rd ed. New York: John Wiley & Sons, 1990.

Eisner, Robert. *How Real Is the Federal Deficit?* New York: Free Press, 1986.

Feldstein, Martin. *The Budget Deficit and the Dollar,* National Bureau of Economic Research Working Paper No. 1898, 1986.

Rook, James M., ed. *Debt and the Twin Deficits Debate.* London: Bristlecone, 1991.

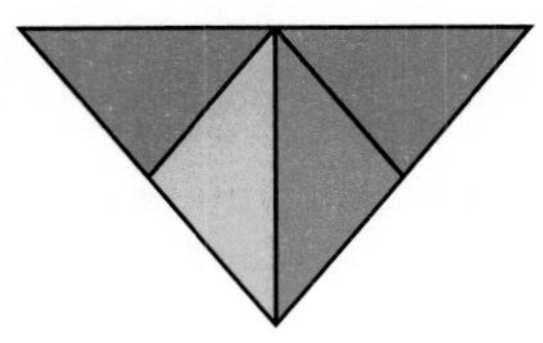

14 Money, Prices, and Interest

CHAPTER INSIGHT

Everyone uses money, but few understand its nature. The most important lesson about money is that what we use as money need not have intrinsic value. In days past, money consisted of gold and silver coin. The money that we use today is a piece of paper or an entry in a bank account. What accounts for this change? To understand the way in which we now use money, we must study the basic characteristics of a monetary economy.

This chapter examines the functions of money, the relationship between money and prices, and the relationship between interest rates, inflation, and the prices of bonds.

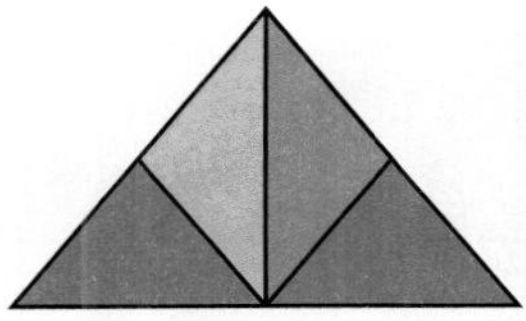

THE FUNCTIONS OF MONEY

Money facilitates trade and commerce in economies that are characterized by specialization and exchange. In such economies, money performs four functions. Money serves as

1. A medium of exchange
2. A unit of value
3. A standard of deferred payment
4. A store of value

By performing these functions, money allows people to specialize according to their comparative advantage and exchange goods and services with others. Thus, money allows people to earn higher incomes and, hence, to consume more goods and services than would otherwise be possible. In the language of Chapter 2, the use of money shifts the production possibilities curve outward. By performing its four functions, money increases the efficiency of the economy.

Money as a Medium of Exchange

The most important function of money is to serve as a medium of exchange. In a modern economic system, money enters almost all market transactions. The existence of a common object acceptable to all sellers eliminates the need for the *double coincidence of wants* that is necessary for barter transactions. In a barter economy, in which goods are traded directly for other goods, a seller of wheat who wants to buy sugar must find a seller of sugar who wants to buy wheat. Because such a double coincidence of wants is rare, in a pure barter economy a series of transactions would be required to obtain what one wants. The seller of wheat might first have to settle for potatoes, trade the potatoes for an ax, and then finally trade the ax for some sugar. The efficiency of the economy suffers as the efforts of the wheat grower (who wants sugar) are diverted from wheat cultivation into a long string of barter transactions. (See Example 1.)

> Money's most important function is to serve as a generally acceptable means of payment (for buying things and paying debts).

Money eliminates the need for costly intermediate exchanges. Because intermediate exchanges are so difficult, customs and laws designate something to serve as the medium of exchange, or money. Thus, the wheat farmer can sell wheat for money and use the money to buy sugar. Converting money into sugar is easy, and the wheat farmer is free to concentrate on growing wheat. Likewise, the sugar grower is left free to concentrate on sugar cultivation.

Money is a social contrivance. The object that society uses as money or the medium of exchange can be almost anything. The list of things that have been used as money staggers the imagination. American Indians used *wampum* (a string of shells); early American colonists used tobacco, rice, corn, cattle, and whiskey. Gopher tails were used as money in North Dakota in the 1880s. Cigarettes have served as money in prisoner-of-war camps. Farther from home, more exotic items have been used as money: whale teeth in Fiji, sandalwood in Hawaii, fish hooks on the Gilbert Islands, reindeer in parts of Russia, red parrot feathers on the Santa Cruz Islands (as late as 1961), silk in China, slaves in Africa, rum in Australia. Money can be grown, walk, talk, fly, be eaten, or be drunk. Our modern paper money is boring by comparison.

Money as a Unit of Value

The value of a good or service equals that for which it can be exchanged in the market. In a barter economy; a cow might sell for two pigs, for an acre of land, for 50 bushels of corn, for a motorcycle, or for dozens of other things. It is of course, inconvenient to keep track of the value of a cow, or anything else, in terms of every other thing for which it would trade. Barter is also impractical when the units cannot be divided, as in a case where a pig is worth half a cow. Choosing a common unit of value—money—saves much time and energy in keeping track of the relative price or values of different things and solves the problem of converting units. When the money prices of common objects are known, it is easy to appraise the *relative* price of any item just from its money price. If an apple costs $0.50, an orange costs $0.25, and a banana costs $0.10, we know immediately that an apple is twice as expensive as an orange and five times as expensive as a banana and that an orange is 2.5 times as expensive as a banana. Money prices can also be used to add together apples and oranges. By reducing different economic entities to their dollar

EXAMPLE 1 To Russia with Toothpaste

The official Russian currency unit is the ruble. Under the communist system, the government printed rubles to cover the losses of its state-owned enterprises. The system was convenient because new rubles entered the Russian economy through the wages paid to workers. At the same time, the Russian economy suffered from severe shortages of shoes, soap, toothpaste, cigarettes, vodka, and many other consumer items. Such shortages occurred because, at the state-controlled prices, the quantity demanded exceeded the quantity supplied. The scarce supply was rationed by favoritism and the ability to wait in long lines. Before the August 1991 revolution, at least, very important persons could often purchase goods without waiting in line. The resentment of the ordinary citizen played a role in the ultimate downfall of communism.

This system left the country with a huge overhang of rubles in the wake of the communist regime. Because people could not spend their rubles, they preferred to obtain goods that could be quickly traded or used. A tube of toothpaste or a package of American cigarettes could be used to purchase something without waiting in line. Young beggars in Russia asked for gum, not rubles; they were even likely to refuse rubles. The inability to use the official money resulted in the extensive use of barter in the Russian economy. Barter extended even to dealings between enterprises. For example, a clothing manufacturer in St. Petersburg, a wine producer in Georgia, and a brick producer in Moscow would rather barter their goods than accept rubles.

This situation complicates Russia's conversion to a free-market economy. The government must first raise ruble prices so that markets clear and the ruble can be used as a medium of exchange. Yet, the Russian public desires low prices that will enable them to buy goods. In the long run, these problems may disappear if the democratic revolution in Russia can put the economy back on the right track.

values, consumers can add apples and oranges, firms can subtract expenses from revenue to obtain profit, and accountants can subtract liabilities from assets.

> Money serves as the common denominator in which the values of all goods and services are expressed.

Money as a Standard of Deferred Payment

When something is used as the medium of exchange, it is almost inevitable that it will also be used as the standard of deferred payment on contracts extending over a period of time. Numerous contracts extend into the future: home mortgages, car loans, all sorts of bonds and promissory notes, charges on credit cards, salaries, home rents. That which serves as money will also be that in which payments deferred into the future will be made. If in the Santa Cruz Islands red parrot feathers are money, an agreement to pay for a cart 1 year in the future might call for payment 1 year hence in red parrot feathers. If dollars are money, contracts to pay for some good in the future will call for payment in dollars. When a home is purchased on credit, the mortgage loan calls for interest and principal payments over the loan period in dollars.

> Money is a standard of deferred payment on exchange agreements extending into the future.

Inflation complicates money's role as the standard of deferred payment. When inflation occurs, deferred payments will be made in "cheaper" dollars because a unit of money buys fewer goods and ser-

vices than it did before. The impact depends on the extent to which inflation is anticipated.

Chapter 6 showed that unanticipated inflation can redistribute wealth. Unanticipated inflation will benefit debtors and harm creditors who have not had the foresight to demand a higher interest rate to compensate them for the effects of inflation. Unforeseen inflation tends to redistribute wealth from those who receive deferred payments to those who make them.

If inflation is foreseen, parties entering into deferred-payment contracts can build in safeguards. The parties may agree that the deferred payment will be adjusted upward at the same rate as inflation (a cost-of-living adjustment). Interest rates, rental payments, or even salary payments may include a premium to compensate the recipient of deferred payments for the anticipated rate of inflation. When inflation is foreseen, there are ways to protect money's role as a standard of deferred payment.

Money as a Store of Value

People, on average, do not consume all their income. When a family consumes less than its income, it saves or (to say the same thing), it accumulates wealth. People can accumulate wealth in virtually any form that is not perishable—paintings, gold, silver, stocks, bonds, land, buildings, apartments, and money. A desirable characteristic of any *asset* (any possession that has value) is that it should maintain or increase its value over time. During periods of rising prices, the value of money is eroded because the amount of goods and services a unit of money will purchase falls. Paper currency or coins that have a face value greater than the value of the substance of which they are made are particularly vulnerable to this erosion. Nevertheless, money, like other assets, serves as a store of value. If people accumulate wealth in the form of money, they can use this money at some future date to purchase goods and services. The effectiveness of money as a store of value depends upon the rate of inflation. The higher is the rate of inflation, the less value money will retain.

> Because money is a medium of exchange, it can also be used as a means of storing wealth.

THE SUPPLY OF MONEY

Money is anything that performs the four functions of money. As we have seen, different objects and substances have served as money at different times and in different parts of the world. Historically, money ranges from things that have no intrinstic value (such as a dollar bill) or little intrinsic value (such as a dime) to things that have considerable intrinsic value (such as gold coins).

Types of Money

Money comes in three basic varieties: commodity money, fiat money, and bank money.

Commodity Money. Historically, the most important **commodity money** has been gold and silver. Although gold and silver have nonmonetary uses in jewelry and industry, they can be easily coined, weighed, and used for large and small transactions. In early history, governments started minting gold and silver coins to avoid costly weighings each time a transaction occurred. When gold or silver serve as commodity money, private citizens can produce money simply by taking mined gold to the government mint! In a commodity money system there can also be paper currency, but the paper can be exchanged for gold at a fixed rate.

> **Commodity money** is money whose value as a commodity is as great as its value as money.

A commodity money system is formally established when the commodity content of a unit of money is set at a fixed rate—say, $100 equals one ounce of gold. If the amount of gold mined increases (because of new discoveries), there is likely to be more money in circulation, prices of goods and services are bid up, and a unit of money buys less. (The relationship between money and prices will be discussed later in this chapter.) In this case, gold's value as money has fallen. If the nonmonetary demand for the commodity increases (if the demand for gold fillings increases), there is less money in circulation, prices fall, and a unit of money buys more. In this case, gold's value as money has risen. In this way, the value of gold as a commodity and as money are kept equal. People can never place a value on commodity money that is higher than its monetary value; dentists would never be willing to pay $110 for an ounce of gold when its monetary value is $100 per ounce because gold would be shifted to commodity use whenever its commodity price threatened to exceed its value as money.

As we noted, historically (and in some primitive societies today), agriculture products, such as rice, cattle, wheat, or sugar, have served as money. Whatever the commodity—gold, silver, rice, sugar, or cattle—the commodity value of money will be the same as its money value.

Commodity money suffers from an inherent problem, known as **Gresham's law.**

> **Gresham's law** states that *bad money drives out good.* When depreciated, mutilated, or debased currency is circulated along with money of high value, the good money will either disappear from circulation or circulate at a premium.[1]

When people start to shave or mutilate gold and silver coins, the bad currency will circulate along with the good currency. The lesser-valued coins will be the ones spent while the more valuable coins will be hoarded. The use of tobacco money in colonial Virginia illustrates Gresham's law. Initially, both good and poor quality tobacco circulated as money. As predicted by Gresham's law, people hoarded the good tobacco and used only the worst tobacco as money. Eventually, the tobacco used as money in colonial Virginia was the scruffiest and foulest tobacco in the entire state. This opportunism tends to raise the cost of using commodity money as a medium of exchange because sellers of goods become suspicious of the money in use.

The basic cost to society of using commodity money is that society must devote real resources to producing the commodity money. Gold and silver mines must be discovered and operated to produce gold or silver commodity money. This gold and silver must then be set aside to circulate as money so that it will not find its way into use as jewelry or dental fillings (See Example 2.)

Fiat Money. If society uses something as money that costs little or nothing of society's resources (such as pieces of engraved paper), resources can be devoted to other activities. For this reason, governments create **fiat money.**

> **Fiat Money** is a government-created money whose value or cost as a commodity is less than its value as money.

Governments must have a monopoly over the issue of fiat money for a simple reason: If everyone were allowed to produce fiat money, so much fiat money would be issued that its value as money would fall to its production cost. If anyone could go to private engravers and order paper currency that could be exchanged for goods and services, the consequent flood of paper money would saturate the economy and push up prices. The rush to print money would cease only when the purchasing power of a unit of money equaled the bill's commodity value, or the cost of producing the unit of paper money (which is very low). When the amount of fiat money in circulation is determined by government, however, fiat money exchanges for more than its cost of production. People require money for transactions, but the government monopoly limits the supply of money. Because money is useful, people are willing to exchange goods and services for money in excess of its commodity value.

The two basic forms of fiat money are coins and paper currency. U.S. coins are issued by the U.S. Treasury, and the value of the metal plus the cost of minting is less than the value of the coins used as money. Sometimes such coins are called *token money*. The most important example of fiat money in the United States is paper currency—called *Federal Reserve Notes* because they are issued by the Federal Reserve System rather than by the U.S. Treasury. (See Example 3.)

An advantage of fiat money is that it uses up little of society's resources. Critics of fiat money argue that it has one major flaw: because fiat money is so cheap and easy to produce, governments, which have a monopoly over printing fiat money, are constantly

[1]Gresham's law is named after Sir Thomas Gresham (1519–1579). He was a successful banker and merchant, accumulated a great fortune, and endowed Gresham's College in London. Gresham's methods of making money were described as more effective than ethical. It may be that Gresham formulated his law on the basis of firsthand observation.

EXAMPLE 2 The Stone Money of the Island of Yap

Anything accepted by the population as a medium of exchange can serve as money. The island of Yap is a tiny U.S. trust territory in the South Pacific, 500 miles from Guam. For money, the Yapese—10,000 strong—use stone wheels, from 1 foot to 12 feet in diameter, made from stones found only on distant islands. Most of the stones are 2 to 5 feet in diameter. Each stone has a hole in the middle so it can be carried on a tree trunk. A private citizen could produce money only by making what was often a treacherous sea journey. Thus, Yap money could be called a commodity money. Interestingly enough, the value of the stones is related to their size as well as to their scarcity and the difficulty of acquiring them.

Each stone has its own history. A stone brought over during the days of the Yap empire is the most valuable. Next in line are stones fashioned in the 1870s by David Dean O'Keffe, a shipwrecked American sailor. Last in value are those few mechanically chiseled by German traders around 1900.

Physical possession is not necessary for ownership. A particular large stone may be owned by many residents, each of whom has received some part of the stone in exchange for some product or service. Larger stones, thus, stay put, with legal ownership being transferred from person to person. How the Yapese keep their bookkeeping straight is not known. On at least one occasion, a family was considered wealthy because an ancestor was known to have discovered an extremely large and valuable stone that a storm sent to the bottom of the sea!

The Yapese have several media of exchange in addition to stone money: U.S. dollars, necklaces of stone beads, and large sea shells. The sea shells and stone beads are used as small change in traditional transactions, but U.S. dollars must be used to make deposits in banks or to buy goods in one of the few retail stores. Will the stone money last? Probably not. The informational requirements of stone money are too great (each stone has a history) for a complicated world. As retailing and banking displace traditional person-to-person exchange, stone money will doubtless become extinct.

As this example illustrates, money can be without intrinsic value, but it must be scarce. What works as money in one society need not work as money in another. However, as societies become more complex and impersonal, money must become more standardized.

Source: William Fumess III, *The Island of Stone Money* (New York: J.B. Lippincott Company, 1910), 92–100: "Fixed Assets, Or: Why a Loan in Yap is Hard to Roll Over.," *Wall Street Journal*, March 29, 1984.

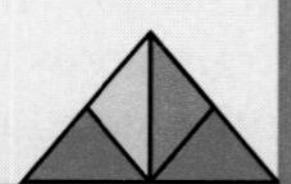

tempted to produce more fiat money to pay their bills. However, as more fiat money floods the market, prices will be bid up throughout the economy, and the value of a unit of fiat money will fall.

> One criticism of a fiat money system is that the absence of constraints on the government to issue more paper currency increases the chances of inflation.

Bank Money. In a modern economy, most transactions are conducted using **bank money.**

> **Bank money** consists of deposits in checking accounts.

About 90 percent of all transactions in the United States, by dollar value, are carried out by the writing of a **check.**

EXAMPLE 3 The Dollar and "In God We Trust"

The Federal Reserve System is a public agency charged with regulating the money supply and serving as the bankers' bank (the central bank). The Federal Reserve issues the paper currency of the United States, called *Federal Reserve Notes.* Nothing backs Federal Reserve Notes. If you examine one of these notes you will find that it states, "This note is legal tender for all debts public and private." You will also notice along the top of the note the phrase, "In God We Trust." Not too long ago, the legal declaration contained a promise. The old declaration read, "This note is legal tender for debts public and private and is redeemable in lawful money at any Federal Reserve Bank." This statement, of course, was an empty promise because the Federal Reserve Notes themselves were the lawful money of the United States! In the 1950s, a Cleveland man tested this promise by requesting that a $20 bill be converted into lawful money. The Federal Reserve Bank sent him two $10 bills! The man persisted, sending in one of the $10 bills, and ended up with two $5 bills and a letter explaining that "lawful money" was not defined. Soon after this incident, the promise for redemption was dropped and the phrase "In God We Trust" was added!

A **check** is a directive to the check writer's bank to pay lawful money to the bearer of the check.

Payments can be made more safely by check. Checks are a better record of transactions, and money is more secure from theft if it is in a checking account rather than in someone's wallet. A checkable deposit at a local bank is money, simply because it is a generally acceptable medium of exchange. The next chapter describes how bank money is created.

A customer's deposit at a bank can be either a **demand deposit** (a checking account) or a **time deposit** (a savings account).

A **demand deposit** is a deposit of funds that can be withdrawn ("demanded") from a depository institution (such as a bank) at any time without restrictions. The funds are usually withdrawn by writing a check.

A **time deposit** is a deposit of funds upon which a depository institution (such as a bank) can legally require 30 days notice of withdrawal and on which the financial institution pays the depositor interest.

In recent years, the distinction between demand deposits and other types of bank deposits has become less pronounced, complicating the definition of bank money.

Definitions of Money Supply

The United States has no commodity money, so the U.S. money supply is the sum of fiat money and bank money. Note that the fiat money *held by banks* should not be considered part of the money supply. When someone cashes a check, the bank money that the person holds in a checking account is converted to fiat money. Thus, the supply of fiat money in circulation has increased by the same amount as the supply of bank money has decreased. The fiat money that the bank holds as cash is not counted in the money supply until it is held by someone outside the bank.

People hold their assets in different forms: as currency, as a deposit in a checking account or a savings account, as stocks or bonds, as real estate, and so on. These assets vary according to their **liquidity.**

Liquidity is the ease and speed with which an asset can be converted into a medium of exchange without risk of loss.

The most basic characteristic of money is that it is perfectly liquid—it is already a medium of exchange. People are prepared to accept money as a means of payment. Thus, currency and demand deposits are perfectly liquid. They are a medium of exchange, a store of value, and a unit of account. There is no question that they should be included in the money supply. But other types of assets can be converted to cash with varying degrees of ease. Money-market funds and savings deposits on which checks may be written can be converted into cash quickly. Time deposits with a fixed maturity date can be converted to cash but with some penalty. Government and corporate bonds can also be converted into cash quickly, but only when the banks are open or when the bond market is open. Also, when these bonds fall in value, they have to be sold at a loss. Even assets such as land or old paintings can be converted into cash, though a substantial loss may be incurred if one cannot wait for the right buyer to come along. Where does one draw the line between money and nonmoney?

Because it is difficult to draw the fine line dividing money and nonmoney, U.S. financial authorities use different definitions of the U.S. money supply for different purposes.

Table 1 shows the two definitions of the U.S. money supply that are most frequently used by financial authorities: **M1** and **M2.**

> **M1** is the sum of currency (paper money and coins), demand deposits at commercial banks held by the nonbanking public, travelers' checks, and other checkable deposits, such as NOW (negotiable order of withdrawal) accounts and ATS (automatic transfer services) accounts.
>
> **M2** equals M1 plus savings and small time deposits, money-market mutual-fund shares, and other highly liquid assets.

TABLE 1
The U.S. Money Supply, M1 and M2, January 1992

Component	Amount (billions of dollars)
Currency and coin	269
Demand deposits[a]	294
Travelers' checks	8
Other checkable deposits[b]	339
M1	**910**
Savings deposits at all depository institutions	1045
Small time deposits at all depository institutions[c]	1061
Money-market mutual-funds shares	543
Other	800
M2	**4359**

[a] Demand deposits at all commercial banks other than those due to other banks, the U.S. government, and foreign official institutions.

[b] Other checkable deposits include NOW and ATS accounts, credit union share-draft balances, and demand deposits at mutual-savings banks. NOW (negotiated order of withdrawal) accounts pay interest and are otherwise like demand deposits. ATS (automatic transfer sevices) accounts transfer funds from savings accounts to checking accounts automatically when a check is written.

[c] A small time deposit is one issued in a denomination less than $100,000.

Source: *The Federal Reserve Bulletin*

M1 is the most frequently cited measure of the money supply. In 1992, M1 amounted to $910 billion. It consists of the most liquid assets available in the economy. In the U.S. economy, the medium-of-exchange function is carried out by currency and coin, checkable deposits, and travelers' checks. Checkable deposits consist of ordinary noninterest-bearing demand deposits and other checkable deposits that do pay interest. The latter include NOW accounts, which are simply checkable deposits that pay interest, and ATS accounts, which allow automatic transfers out of savings into special checking accounts. These accounts (especially NOW accounts) are included in the category of "other checkable deposits" in Table 1. They represent about 37 percent of the nation's money supply; in 1992, such accounts were even larger than currency in circulation (Table 1).

M2 amounted to $4359 billion in 1992. It includes, in addition to M1, assets such as savings and other time deposits that are less liquid than the items in M1. For example, many of these accounts have penalties for withdrawal before a specified maturity date. The largest component of M2 is small time deposits ($1061 billion).[2]

The $3449 billion difference between M1 and M2 is made up of savings deposits, money-market funds, and other highly liquid assets.

Savings accounts can be converted into currency or checking account money simply by going to the bank and withdrawing cash or by depositing the cash in a checking account. Banks typically allow depositors to withdraw small time deposits with little or no penalty. Money-market funds may, likewise, be converted quickly into cash. Because such funds are close substitutes for M1, people have a tendency to shift assets back and forth between M1 and M2. Therefore, M1 may change while M2 does not change at all.

The inclusion of NOW accounts in M1 is subject to some debate. Because money-market mutual-fund shares are accounts on which checks can also be written, it may be argued that M1 should also exclude NOW accounts or that M1 should include money-market accounts. The justification for putting money-market accounts in M2 and NOW accounts in M1 is that money-market accounts are subject to more restrictions (such as the size of the minimum balance, the number of checks that can be written per month without penalty, and the minimum size of the check); NOW accounts are used more for ordinary transactions than are money-market accounts. Thus, the difference between NOW and money-market accounts is simply in the degree to which the accounts are used as vehicles for transactions and savings. As we shall see in Chapter 15, much of the growth in M1 in recent years is explained by the simple shift of savings into NOW accounts.

BOND PRICES, INTEREST RATES, AND ANTICIPATED INFLATION

The money supply is intimately connected with interest rates. This section looks at how interest rates are related to bond prices and how inflationary expectations affect interest rates. The following section examines how changes in the money supply affect interest rates.

Bond Prices and Interest Rates

The financial pages of the daily newspaper describe the relationship between interest rates and bond prices in the following way: "Bond prices drifted lower yesterday as interest rates moved up for the second day in a row. Last week, bond prices were higher and interest rates lower." As such statements indicate, there is an inverse relationship between bond prices and interest rates.

A *bond* is a promise to pay future dollars. The issuer of the bond promises to pay a prescribed number of dollars at specified dates in the future. Bonds promise a stream of future returns. For example, the simplest bond is the 3-month Treasury bill (called a *T-bill*). In the case of a 3-month T-bill, the U.S. Treasury promises to pay the face amount of the bill —$1000—in 3 months. The price of the T-bill will be some discount from $1000; otherwise, the buyer would earn no interest. If the price of the bill were $985, the buyer would earn $15 ÷ $1000 = 1.5 percent interest over 3 months, or 6 percent per year (there are four 3-month periods in a year). If the annual interest rate increased to 12 percent, the buyer would pay only $970 for the T-bill ($30 ÷ $1000 = 3 percent; 4 × 3 percent = 12 percent). Clearly, the interest rate on a T-bill rises if the price of the T-bill falls (and vice versa).

The same relationship between the bond prices and interest rate holds for any bond, but the calculations are more complex if bonds pay interest periodically over several years. Whatever the case, the lower is the price of the bond today, the greater is the return the investor is making because the bond specifies fixed dollar payments in the future.

> Because bonds promise fixed dollar payments in the future, the lower is the current price of the bonds, the higher is the interest rate yielded. Similarly, the higher is the current price of bonds, the lower is the interest rate.

A bond-market *rally* (bond prices rising rapidly) means that interest rates are falling. When the news-

[2]The Fed defines even broader categories. For example, M3 includes M1, M2, and such items as time deposits in excess of $100,000 and dollar-dominated deposits of U.S. citizens in English and Canadian banks as well as foreign branches of U.S. banks worldwide.

paper talks about the bond market being *bearish* (bond prices falling), one knows that interest rates are rising.

Real versus Nominal Interest Rates

Because bonds are promises to pay future dollars, bondholders are interested in what these future dollars can buy. If the prices are expected to rise rapidly, future dollars will buy less. When people make borrowing or lending decisions, they must weigh the extra dollars they will receive in the future against the anticipated decline in what these dollars will buy if inflation occurs.

The interest rate earned on interest-bearing assets (such as bonds) is a **nominal interest rate.** Nominal interest rates do not take into account the changing value of the dollar.

> The **nominal interest rate** is the interest rate paid on interest-bearing assets expressed in current dollars (unadjusted for inflation).

Basically, borrowers and lenders are interested in the **real interest rate**—the nominal interest rate adjusted for inflation. For example, if a person anticipates a 4 percent inflation rate, a 9 percent nominal interest rate means that the real interest rate is 5 percent. Consider what happens to $100 invested at 9 percent. In one year, the $100 will grow to $109. But with 4 percent inflation it takes $104 to buy the same goods and services that $100 initially purchased. Thus, investing $100 at 9 percent yields the ability to buy only $5 more in goods and services. The real rate of interest is 5 percent in this case.

> The **real interest rate** is the nominal rate minus the anticipated rate of inflation and is expressed in constant dollars (adjusted for inflation).

Figure 1 compares the nominal interest rate with the anticipated rate of inflation, measured by the average of the inflation rates over the past 3 years. It uses the interest rate on triple-A (Aaa) corporate bonds (the long-term bonds of the most creditworthy corporations, such as General Motors, IBM, and Ford). Figure 1 confirms that the anticipated inflation rate and the nominal interest rate move together. Increases in the anticipated inflation rate push up nominal interest rates. When anticipated inflation falls, nominal interest rates fall.

FIGURE 1
Anticipated Inflation and Interest Rates

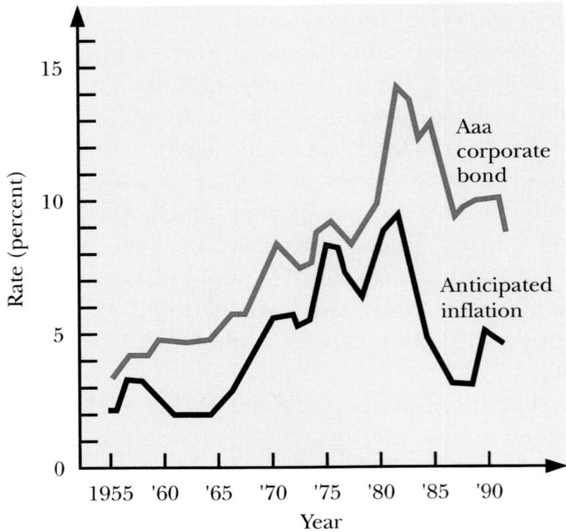

The anticipated inflation rate is here measured as the average of actual inflation over the preceding three years. Notice how the anticipated inflation rate and the nominal interest rate, measured by the Aaa corporate-bond yield, move together.

Source: Data on nominal interest rates and inflation from *Economic Report of the President.*

People must pay income taxes on the interest they earn. Thus, income tax rates also affect nominal interest rates. One way to untangle tax effects from anticipated inflation effects is to look at municipal bonds. Municipal bonds are the IOUs of state governments, water districts, school districts, and other government units. They differ from other bonds in that their interest is tax-free. Between 1955 and 1991, the real interest rate on high-grade bonds varied from a low of −1.2 percent in 1976 to a high of about 5 percent in 1984 (see Figure 2). The average real (tax-free) rate was only 1.6 percent over the entire period.

Figure 2 compares the real interest rates on corporate bonds and high-grade municipal bonds. The real interest rate on corporate bonds varied

FIGURE 2
Real Interest Rates

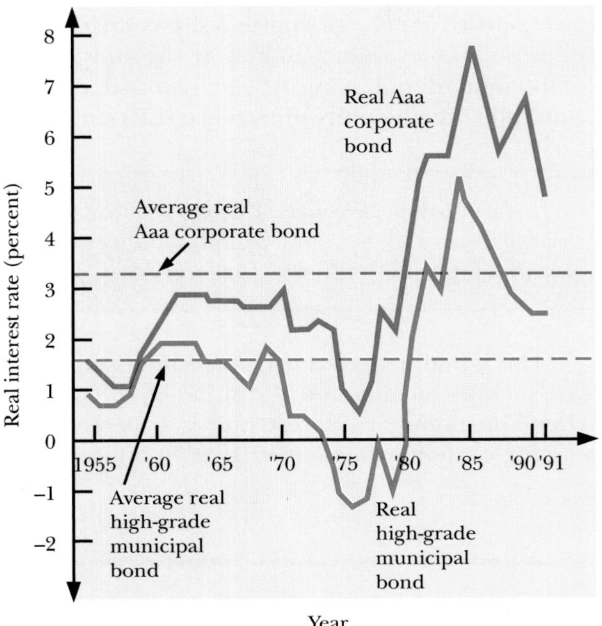

What is remarkable about real interest rates is how low they have been. Real yields on Aaa corporate bonds have averaged 3 percent and real yields on high-grade municipal bonds have averaged about 1 percent. Real interest rates were at historic highs in the early 1980s.

Source: Data on nominal interest rates and inflation from *Economic Report of the President.*

from a low of 0.6 percent in 1976 to a high of 8 percent in 1984. On the average, the real interest rate on corporate bonds from 1955 to 1991 was only 3.3 percent, with the nominal rate averaging 7.6 percent. The average anticipated inflation rate was 4.3 percent. Clearly, the largest component of the nominal interest rate is the anticipated rate of inflation.

In looking at the overall behavior of real interest rates over the past 36 years, two things stand out: First, real interest rates are very low—especially after adjustment for taxes. (The average real rate after taxes was only slightly above 1 percent.) Second, changes in nominal interest rates mostly reflect changes in the anticipated rate of inflation.

THE DEMAND FOR MONEY

To understand the link between money and interest we need to examine the demand for money.

The Motives for Holding Money

The main motive for holding money is that money is required for transaction purposes. Money is a perfectly liquid asset. As already mentioned, liquidity is the ease and speed with which an asset can be converted into a medium of exchange without the risk of loss. One can measure the liquidity of an asset by the speed of its conversion to money or the ease of its acceptance as money. The holder of money does not have to go through the time and expense of selling a less liquid asset (like a stock certificate or a bond) in order to get money. Assets such as land, apartment buildings, and paintings may serve as good stores of value, especially during inflationary periods, but they are not liquid because some time or expense is involved in converting them to cash. Because people have to carry out regular transactions, they must hold part of their wealth in the form of money.

Keynes discussed two other motives for holding money: the precautionary and the speculative. People hold money as a precaution against unforeseen emergencies, although credit cards have nearly eliminated this motive. People have a speculative motive when they hold money to take advantage of opportunities to profit from market fluctuations. Today, the speculative motive is not important in the demand for M1 because speculative funds could be kept in highly liquid Treasury bills or money-market funds.

Liquidity Preferences and Interest Rates

Although there are many benefits to holding money, there is also an opportunity cost. The basic opportunity cost of holding ("demanding") money is that one is passing up the opportunity to accumulate other forms of wealth that promise higher returns. For example, if an individual holds $10,000 in cash or in a noninterest-bearing checking account, that individual sacrifices the opportunity to buy goods now or to put that money into stocks, bonds, or real estate.

The opportunity cost of holding money is the nominal interest rate on perfectly safe securities. The real interest rate measures the opportunity cost of spending versus saving: it represents the difference between what we give up tomorrow and what we give up today by spending one dollar now. The nominal interest rate measures the opportunity cost of holding assets in the form of money as opposed to holding interest-bearing assets. Inflation affects the real value of money and nominal interest-bearing assets equally. For example, a 3 percent inflation rate erodes $300 from both a $10,000 bond and $10,000 in cash. Thus, the difference between the bond and cash is the nominal interest rate.

The nominal interest rate is really the *price* of holding assets in the form of money. (As Table 1 shows, almost two thirds of M1 do not earn interest.) According to the law of demand, quantity demanded falls when prices rise. This rule holds for the demand for money just as it holds for the demand for other commodities. People would be expected to hold (demand) more money at low interest rates (a low opportunity cost) than at high interest rates, *ceteris paribus*. Panel *a* of Figure 3 shows the demand curve for money. Since money is the most liquid component of one's assets, the demand curve is often called the **liquidity preference (LP) curve.**

> The **liquidity preference (LP) curve** shows the demand for money as the nominal interest rate changes, holding other factors constant.

The liquidity preference curve holds other factors, such as income and the price level, constant. When the nominal interest rate is 6 percent, the quantity of money demanded is $800 billion; when

FIGURE 3
The Demand for Money: Liquidity Preference

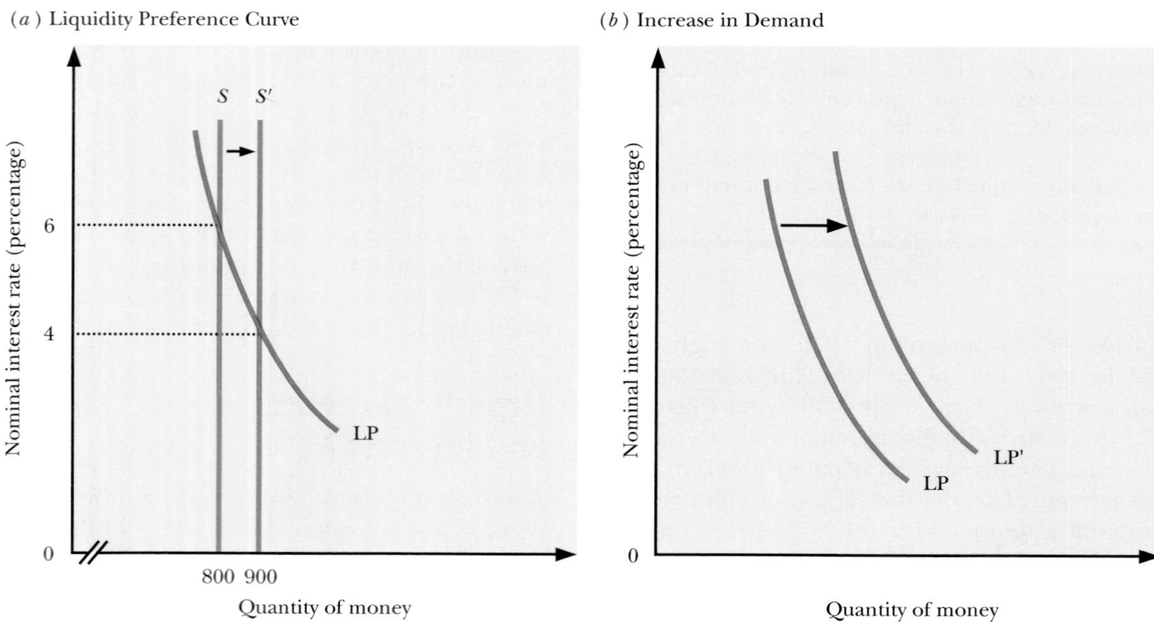

Panel *a* shows a typical liquidity preference (LP) curve, which graphs the demand for money. Panel *b* shows the impact of an increase in real GDP or the price level on the LP curve. The demand for money rises with GDP and *P*, and falls with the nominal interest rate.

the nominal interest rate is 4 percent, the quantity of money demanded is $900 billion.

> The nominal interest rate is the opportunity cost (price) of holding money. Therefore, the quantity of money demanded would be expected to vary inversely with the nominal interest rate.

Figure 3, panel *a*, also demonstrates how changes in the money supply affect the rate of interest for a given liquidity preference or demand curve for money. We show the money supply (S) as a vertical line because at any given time the rate of interest has a negligible effect on how much money is in the economy. The negative relationship between the nominal interest rate and the quantity of money demanded means that a higher money supply will lower the rate of interest. When the money supply increases from $800 billion to $900 billion, the nominal interest rate must fall from 6 percent to 4 percent in order to induce people to hold the higher supply of money. The next chapter will study how the money supply itself increases.

Other Factors Affecting the Demand for Money

The demand for money depends not only on nominal interest rates but also on real GDP and the price level. If either real GDP or the price level increases, the total value of all transactions will increase. If people spend more dollars to pay higher grocery or clothing bills, the demand for money will increase in order to carry out those transactions.

Panel *b* of Figure 3 shows an increase in the demand for money. The liquidity preference curve shifts from LP to LP′ as real GDP or the price level increases. At each interest rate, there is a greater quantity of money demanded.

The anticipated rate of inflation also affects the demand for money, but its role is already partly reflected in the nominal rate of interest. A rise in the anticipated inflation rate increases nominal interest rates and, thus, lowers the quantity of money demanded. If we try to determine the impact of the anticipated rate of inflation by itself on the demand for money, the impact may be only about one-fifth as important as the impact of the nominal rate of interest.[3]

> The major factors affecting the demand for money are real GDP, the price level, and the nominal rate of interest.

THE RELATIONSHIP BETWEEN MONEY AND PRICES

Chapter 10 introduced the quantity theory of money. This section applies the quantity theory to show how inflationary expectations are related to monetary growth.

The Quantity Theory Revisited

The quantity theory sheds light on the relationship between the stock of money and prices. Remember the equation of exchange from Chapter 10 that

$$MV = PQ$$

where M is the stock of money, V is the velocity of its circulation, P is the price level, and Q is the quantity of real output or GDP. The quantity theory supposes that V and Q are constant. By dividing both sides of the equation of exchange by V, we obtain

$$M = \frac{PQ}{V}$$

The term (PQ/V) can be thought of as the demand for money; all the above factors operating on the demand for money must work through P, Q, or V. Higher expected inflation or interest rates will raise the cost of holding money and, thus, raise velocity. As the cost of holding money rises, people attempt to reduce their money holdings by spending them and turning them over more rapidly. As everyone tries to spend money balances, velocity rises. The term on the left-hand side is the supply of money. The

[3]Milton Friedman and Anna J. Schwartz, *Monetary Trends in the United States and the United Kingdom,* National Bureau of Economic Research (Chicago: University of Chicago Press, 1982), 277, Table 6.N.3.

quantity theory says that price level adjusts until the demand for money equals the supply of money. If the money supply doubles, the price level doubles.

How does an increase in the money supply increase the price level? The new money is injected into the economy whenever the agency charged with controlling the money supply buys something. Once the money is in the economy, it is impossible for the rest of the community to get rid of the money balances (unless it gives the money back to the money-supply agency). When one person purchases a good with money, the seller's cash balance rises as the buyer's balance falls. Money is simply passed from one person to another without changing the economy's supply of money. Individuals can spend excess cash balances, but the whole community cannot. As each person tries to get rid of an excess supply of money, prices are driven up because there are more dollars chasing the same number of goods. As prices rise, the community as a whole requires more money for its transactions. Thus, rising prices increase the demand for money until the excess supply of money disappears. Equilibrium is restored when the supply of money equals the quantity of money people want to hold, and prices stop rising.

The *value* of money is determined by what one can buy with it. The value of money is declining when each unit of money (say, each dollar) buys fewer goods. If the price of a candy bar is $0.25, $1 is worth 4 candy bars. If the price of a candy bar rises to $0.50, $1 is worth only 2 candy bars. In terms of candy bars, the value of $1 is 1 divided by the price of a candy bar. Thus, the value of money falls when prices rise, and the value of money rises when prices fall.

One of best examples of inflation happened in Germany after World War I, when prices were doubling every few weeks. The quantity theory gives a perfectly simple explanation: the German government was printing paper money so fast that it caused a hyperinflation. As Example 4 indicates, the value of money fell so low in the German hyperinflation that a truckload of paper money was needed to meet the payroll of a typical company. Yet, the advantages of a monetary economy are so great that the German people still used their near-worthless currency as a medium of exchange.

The key idea of the quantity theory is that the value of money depends on its quantity, not the quality of the material (paper, gold, silver, lead) of which it is composed. What determines the value of money is simply the law of supply and demand. As the supply of the anything rises relative to the demand, its value falls to maintain equality of quantity supplied

EXAMPLE 4 The Inconvenience of Hyperinflation

One of the worst inflations ever to befall the world occurred in Germany after its World War I defeat. Prices doubled every few weeks. The following anecdote from a contemporary tells how it was:

> At eleven o'clock in the morning a siren sounded and everybody gathered in the factory forecourt where a five-ton lorry was drawn up loaded brimful with paper money. The chief cashier and his assistants climbed up on top. They read out names and just threw out bundles of notes. As soon as you caught one you made a dash for the nearent shop and bought just anything that was going.

This illustrates two points. First, the value of money is largely determined by its quantity. Second, even in a hyperinflation a medium of exchange is useful. Even viutually worthless money buys goods. However, one of the costs of hyperinflation is that people have to take a lot more shopping trips! Indeed, hyperinflation robs money of its role in lowering the costs of engaging in economic exchange.

Source: William Guttman and Patricia Meehan, *The Great Inflation, Germany 1919-1923* (Farnborough, England: Saxon House, 1975), 57–58.

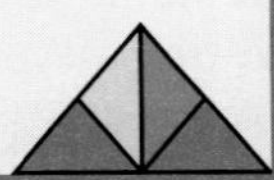

EXAMPLE 5 Velocity

Velocity is defined as GDP divided by the money supply. But which definition of the money supply should be used: the broad measure, M2, or the narrow measure, M1? The attached figure shows the behavior of velocity since 1959 based on both definitions. The velocity of M2 has barely fluctuated from the average value of 1.65. But the velocity of M1 has varied from about 3.5 to about 7. It appears, therefore, that to predict the price level it may be better to choose M2, the broad measure.

Source: John B. Carlson and Susan M. Byrne, "Recent Behavior of Velocity: Alternative Measures of Money," *Economic Review*, Federal Reserve Bank of Cleveland, 28 (1992 Quarter 1): 2–10.

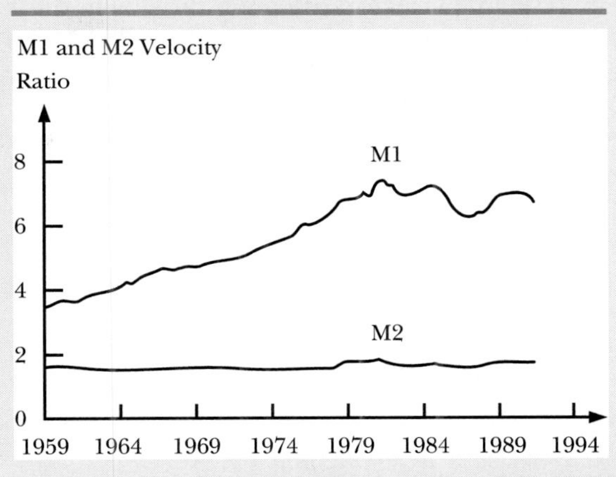

with quantity demanded. This concept applies to money just as much as it applies to goods or services.

Modern Quantity Theory

Economists do not accept the simple quantity theory that P and M are strictly proportional because Q and V are not considered constants. (See Example 5.)

Modern monetary theory argues that velocity changes if people generally anticipate a change in the rate of inflation. If people expect inflation to rise, velocity rises. If people expect inflation to fall, velocity falls. Similarly, velocity should rise or fall with interest rates. If there is no change in inflationary expectations or interest rates, velocity remains the same. In effect, modern monetary theory argues that M and V can move together. Excess monetary growth sets off inflation, which causes inflationary expectations to rise. As inflationary expectations rise, velocity rises.

Modern monetary theory also maintains that the money supply can indeed affect output and employment, but more so in the short run than in the long run. The major effects of money on employment and output occur when people have not correctly anticipated inflation. The effects of unanticipated inflation on output and employment are discussed in Chapters 17 and 18.

Although increases in anticipated inflation raise velocity, massive changes in the institutions of money and banking can also cause substantive changes in velocity. During periods when many new money substitutes are being created, the velocity of old money will increase as people switch from old money to new forms of money.

The next chapter will examine how the money supply is actually determined in a modern economy and will describe the role of the banking system.

SUMMARY

1. Money is the medium of exchange used in market transactions. In addition, money serves as a unit of value, a standard of deferred payment, and a store of value. People may be able to safeguard against inflation when they use money as a standard of deferred payment.

2. Commodity money's value as a commodity is as great as its value as money. Fiat money's value as a commodity is less than its value as money. Bank money consists of checking deposits. M1 is the narrow measure of the money supply, excluding such items as savings deposits and other highly liquid assets; M2 is a broader measure of the money supply.

3. Bond prices are inversely related to interest rates. The real rate of interest is the nominal rate of interest minus the anticipated rate of inflation.

4. The major factors affecting the demand for money are nominal interest rates, real GDP, and the price level. The liquidity preference curve shows how a higher nominal interest rate lowers the quantity of money demanded, holding real GDP and the price level constant. A higher level of prices or real GDP increases the demand for money by shifting the liquidity preference curve to the right.

5. Economists no longer accept the simple quantity theory that M and P are rigidly linked. Through the impact on inflationary expectations, M and V can move together. In the short run, an increase in the money supply can affect real GDP.

KEY TERMS

commodity money	liquidity
Gresham's law	M1
fiat money	M2
bank money	nominal interest rate
check	real interest rate
demand deposit	liquidity preference (LP) curve
time deposit	

QUESTIONS AND PROBLEMS

1. Evaluate the validity of the following statement: "Anything is money that is legally declared by the government to be money."
2. During hyperinflations, money loses its value as a medium of exchange, as a store of value, and as a standard of deferred payment. What would you expect to happen to the overall efficiency of the economy when this decline in value happens?
3. Evaluate the validity of the following statement: "It is foolish to talk about the demand for money. People want all the money they can get their hands on."
4. Explain why the value of fiat money is determined by its relative abundance. What is the lower limit to which the value of fiat money can fall?
5. Discuss the social costs of having a commodity money system. What are the benefits? How does Gresham's law enter into this issue?
6. How does M1 differ from M2?
7. Explain why houses are not money.
8. Assume that in a prisoner-of-war camp, cigarettes are used as money. What will happen to the price level if a health scare motivates people to reduce their commodity demand for cigarettes?
9. Economy A uses gold as money, and Economy B uses paper money without any commodity backing. Economy A's money supply is growing at a rate of 10 percent per year; Economy B's money supply is growing at a rate of 5 percent per year. Use quantity theory to predict which economy will have the largest rate of inflation. Explain your reasoning.
10. How might a fiat money system result in more inflation over the long run than, say, a commodity money system?
11. What are the major differences between a simple quantity theorist and a modern quantity theorist?
12. If a bond pays—in perpetuity—$100 a year in coupon payments and if the interest rate is 20 percent, what should be the price of the bond?
13. Historically, what has been the most important component of nominal interest rates?
14. If the equilibrium real rate of interest is 5 percent and the equilibrium nominal interest rate is 7 percent, what is the anticipated inflation rate?
15. Explain the relationship between bond prices and interest rates.
16. If the newspaper reports, "The bond market is in the doldrums; it has been depressed all week," what is happening to interest rates?

SUGGESTED READINGS

Feldstein, Martin. "Inflation, Income Taxes, and the Rate of Interest." *American Economic Review* 66 (December 1976): 809–20.

Fisher, Irving. *The Theory of Interest.* New York: Macmillan, 1930.

Friedman, Milton. *Money Mischief.* New York: Harcourt Brace Jovanovich, 1992.

Galbraith, John K. *Money.* Boston, MA: Houghton Mifflin, 1975.

Ritter, Lawrence S., and William L. Silber. *Money*, 5th ed. New York: Basic Books, 1984, chaps. 1, 2, 3, 22, and 23.

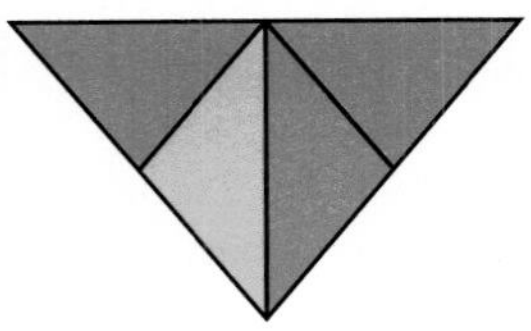

15 Commercial Banking and the Federal Reserve

CHAPTER INSIGHT

The last chapter defined both the functions and the supply of money, and it related money and inflation to interest. This chapter will explain how and by whom the money supply is determined. Why does the money supply increase or decrease? Or, in other words, where does money come from and where does it go? How stable is the banking system where we put our money?

The money supply can increase or decrease very rapidly. From 1929 to 1933, the money supply fell by a gigantic 25 percent, from $26.6 billion to $19.9 billion, yet the amount of currency held by the public actually increased. What happened to the missing $6.7 billion? Those who lived through the Great Depression might argue either that people had it under their mattresses or that Rockefeller had it all.

In order to see how the money supply expands or contracts, one must understand the business of banking and the relationship between banks and the Federal Reserve System (the Fed). It is also necessary to study the role of deposit insurance and bank regulation.

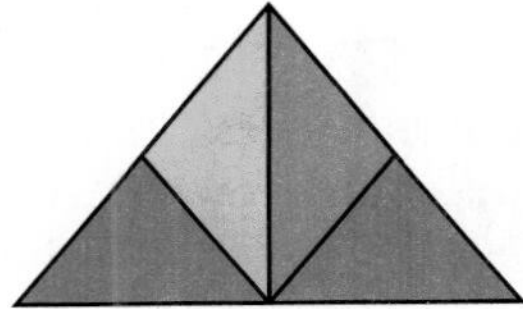

THE BUSINESS OF BANKING: THE BENEFITS OF FINANCIAL INTERMEDIATION

Most of us have had some experience with banks: a commercial bank cashes our checks; a savings and loan association handles our savings account; the credit union at our place of work will give us a loan for new furniture. What services do these banks perform for us? How do they earn profits?

A savings and loan association, an insurance company, a commercial bank, a mutual savings bank, a credit union, a retirement fund, and a mutual fund are all examples of **financial intermediaries,** or financial institutions that mediate between borrowers and lenders.

> **Financial intermediaries** borrow funds from one group of economic agents (people or firms with savings) and lend to other agents.

Financial intermediaries serve a useful purpose in our economy. With financial intermediation, borrowers and lenders do not have to seek each other out. The lender does not have to accept the borrower's IOU, investigate the borrower's creditworthiness, or pass judgment on the wisdom of the borrower's spending plans. The commercial bank, for example, accepts a deposit with the promise to pay the depositor a specified interest rate and then lends these funds to a borrower at a higher interest rate. Borrowers and lenders thus pay a price for using the services of a financial intermediary. If they had sought each other out, the lender would have received more and the borrower would have paid less.

Is the cost of financial intermediation worth its benefits? Financial intermediation offers at least three benefits: information processing, risk reduction, and high liquidity.

Information Processing

Banks process information about the creditworthiness of borrowers. In order to make profitable loans, banks must thoroughly investigate the health, management, and future prospects of a firm. Hence, if a firm announces that it has received a bank loan, as opposed to issuing new stocks or bonds, the stock market value of that firm will generally rise.

Banks are acting as intermediaries between thousands of small savers—the ultimate lenders—with those of borrowers. For example, if a large company wishes to borrow $5 million, it would be very costly to the firm to borrow $5000 from 1000 different lenders. Likewise, it would be very inefficient for 1000 separate lenders to make their own credit investigations. The bank facilitates the transaction by offering appropriate terms to ultimate lenders investigating the creditworthiness of the company wanting to borrow $5 million.

Risk Reduction

For lenders, it is better not to put all of their eggs in one basket. If Jack lends $1000 to Jill and Jill cannot pay, Jack loses all his money. But if Jack lends $1 each to 1000 different Jills, Jack can reduce his risks substantially by pooling risks. The financial intermediary pools the smaller savings of individuals and loans these savings to a diversified group of borrowers. When a financial intermediary makes loans to different borrowers, risks can be reduced because the chances that all borrowers will not repay are much smaller than the chances that any one of the borrowers will not repay. If one borrower out of 100 defaults, the loss is still relatively small. Financial intermediaries can spread the pooled funds of their depositors over a variety of borrowers, whereas individual depositors with small sums of money to lend cannot. (See Example 1.)

High Liquidity

A final benefit of deposit intermediaries, such as commercial banks, savings and loan associations, and mutual savings banks, is that they *borrow short* and *lend long*. Borrowers usually prefer to borrow for a long term (*to borrow long*), because the services of the house, car, or business plant for which the borrowed funds are paying last a long time. But lenders prefer to lend funds for a short period of time (*to lend short*) because unexpected needs could always arise. Thus, people in general prefer to lend short and borrow long. Financial intermediaries fill the gap between borrowers and lenders with their willingness to borrow short and lend long. Finan-

EXAMPLE 1 Creating a Commercial Banking System: Russian Banks

A bank is an institution that makes loans and accepts deposits. In market economies, banks intermediate between savers and investors. In Russia, under the old central planning system, the state budget automatically transferred funds collected through taxes to finance enterprise investment according to a central plan. As the old system of budget finance collapsed, new businesses were unable to obtain investment funds either from the state budget or from state banking institutions.

The need for financial intermediation between people with money to lend and people who needed to borrow sparked the spontaneous development of a new banking system. Cooperative, state, and private enterprises resolved this problem by forming their own banks. By pooling their deposits, they built up reserves to fund various investment projects. At first these enterprises lent money primarily to themselves but then later they began to lend to outsiders.

For example, one of the first private Russian commercial banks, Inkombank, is owned by 129 shareholders who contributed 500 million rubles in capital, which serves as a reserve against Inkombank's 10 billion rubles in outstanding loans. Most of Inkombank's loans are short-term—for no more than six months. Inkombank's biggest problem is determining who should get loans. In the new market environment, it is difficult to determine which projects will succeed and which will fail.

Source: "The Roulette of Russian Banking," *New York Times*, February 29, 1992.

cial intermediaries offer deposits that are highly liquid. They borrow money from depositors, who can withdraw their funds at any time. Financial intermediaries may then lend to home buyers, for example, on 30-year mortgages.[1]

The above functions highlight the contribution of financial intermediaries to economic efficiency. The individual household saves monitoring costs, lowers risks, and increases its liquidity.

The different types of financial intermediaries compete with each other for borrowers and lenders. Savings and loan associations, mutual savings banks, and credit unions offer checkable accounts that compete with commercial banks. Financial intermediaries compete among themselves to make loans to qualified borrowers. Profit rates in banking are comparable to the returns earned, for example, in retailing or the aerospace industry.

COMMERCIAL BANKS

Commercial banks are more important than the other financial intermediaries. In 1992, commercial banks held more assets than all the other financial intermediaries combined.

> **Commercial banks** are banks that have been chartered either by a state agency or by the U.S. Treasury's Comptroller of the Currency to make loans and receive deposits.

Thrift institutions, such as savings and loan associations, mutual savings banks, and credit unions, cater

[1]During periods of unanticipated inflation, financial intermediaries may become less willing to borrow short and lend long. In the late 1970s and early 1980s, savings and loan associations were stuck with large volumes of outstanding mortgage loans at 7 to 10 percent when they were borrowing short at 10 to 15 percent. For this reason, financial intermediaries became cautious about making long-term loan commitments at a fixed rate of interest during this period.

to noncommercial customers. In the past, thrift institutions could not offer checking account services; instead, they could offer only various types of savings accounts (hence, the name *thrift* institution). However, thrift institutions are now able to offer checking accounts to both families and commercial firms. Legislation passed in the early 1980s also enables the thrift institutions to make limited commercial loans and to make direct investments in real estate.

Commercial banks still held virtually all the checkable deposits included in M1 at the beginning of 1992, though most thrift institutions offered such accounts.

How Commercial Banks Make Profits

Commercial banks make profits by borrowing from customers in the form of demand deposits and time deposits and then relending these funds in the form of automobile loans, real estate loans, business loans, and student loans. Commercial banks earn profits by borrowing money at low interest rates and lending money at higher interest rates. The difference between the rate at which banks borrow and the rate at which they lend is called the *interest-rate spread.*

Balance Sheets

The concept of a **balance sheet** is essential to an understanding of how banks operate.

A **balance sheet** summarizes the current financial position of a firm by comparing the firm's *assets* and *liabilities.*

The **assets** of a firm can be buildings, equipment, inventories of goods, money, or even IOUs. A balance sheet lists the claims to these assets.

Assets are anything of any value that is owned.

The **liabilities** of a company include unpaid bills, tax obligations, and outstanding debt.

Liabilities are anything owed to other economic agents.

The value (or net worth) of a company is measured as the excess of assets over liabilities. If a company owns assets worth $1 million and has liabilities of $900,000, the net worth of the company is $100,000.

Net worth = Assets − Liabilities

A bank's assets consist primarily of IOUs of one kind or another—the loans it has made to persons and firms, the government bonds it has purchased, and the deposits it has with other banks. Its liabilities consist principally of the various deposits that its customers have made—demand deposits, savings deposits, and time deposits.

The combined balance sheet of America's commercial banks as of January 1992 is shown in Table 1. As of that date, transaction-account liabilities accounted for about 20 percent of liabilities, and savings and time deposits accounted for about 55 percent. Balance sheets are often called ***T*-accounts.**

***T*-accounts** show bank assets and liabilities.

The fact that commercial bank transaction-account liabilities are less than their savings and time-deposit liabilities is a recent development attributable to the increased use of credit cards and the rise of money-market mutual funds and NOW accounts. Historically, demand-deposit liabilities exceeded time deposits. In other words, commercial banks have become more like thrift institutions.

The asset side shows how commercial banks serve as financial intermediaries. Commercial bank deposits are loaned to individuals and businesses and are used to purchase securities. The asset statement shows that commercial banks are primarily in the business of making loans.[2]

A large fraction of a bank's liabilities are *demand liabilities,* or obligations that can be called in by depositors. Any customer who withdraws a deposit is paid out of the bank's **reserves.**

[2]Further discussion of the bank balance sheet and recent changes can be found in Bruce R. Dalgaard, *Money, Financial Institutions, and Economic Activity* (Glenview, IL: Scott, Foresman and Company, 1987), chap. 5.

TABLE 1
Consolidated Balance Sheet of All Commercial Banks, January 1992

Assets (billions of dollars)		Liabilities plus Net Worth (billions of dollars)	
Vault cash	31	Transaction deposits	644
Reserves at Fed	24	Savings deposits	668
		Time deposits	1138
Loans and investments	3011	Other borrowings	810
Other assets	430	Net worth	236
Total	**3496**	**Total**	**3496**

Source: *Federal Reserve Bulletin.*

Reserves are the funds that the bank uses to satisfy the cash demands of its customers.

Bank reserves consist of two components: vault cash, which is simply currency and coin in the vaults of the bank, and the bank's balances with the Federal Reserve System (explained below).

The combined balance sheet in Table 1 shows that bank reserves are much less than the liabilities of the banking system. In January 1992, bank reserves equaled $55 billion, or 8.5 percent of the transaction-deposit liabilities to the nonbanking public. When savings deposits are included (because, in practice, banks also pay out these funds on demand), the ratio of reserves to deposits falls by almost 4 percent.

Why are depositors and the banks not alarmed by the imbalance between bank reserves and transaction-deposit or savings-deposit liabilities? On an ordinary business day, some customers deposit money in their checking accounts. Others withdraw money from their accounts by writing checks through ATMs. If deposits come in at the same pace as withdrawals, bank reserves do not change. Reserves rise when deposits exceed withdrawals; they fall when withdrawals exceed deposits. The normal course of banking is for withdrawals and deposits to proceed at roughly the same rate.

Is it not precarious for bank reserves to be such a small fraction of deposits? What would happen if suddenly there were no deposits—only withdrawals? The reason why people have demand deposits is that checking account money is safer and more convenient than currency and coin for many transactions. As long as depositors know that they can get their money from the bank, they will want to leave it on deposit. The moment they feel that they cannot get their money, they will want to withdraw it. Thus, people want their money if they can't get it and don't want their money if they can!

This paradox of banking has made commercial banks subject to *bank panics* at times. The history of banking is filled with episodes where large numbers of depositors lose confidence in the banks and demand their cash; when the banks cannot pay, a rash of bank failures occurs. In the Great Depression, bank failures reached unprecedented levels. The federal government's Federal Deposit Insurance Corporation (FDIC) was established in 1933 to deal with this problem. Currently, in banks and thrift institutions that are members of the FDIC, each deposit account is insured up to $100,000. However, bank failures in the 1980s revealed weaknesses in the system. Later in this chapter, we study the issue of bank reform.

THE FEDERAL RESERVE SYSTEM

Bankers use the FDIC as their insurance agent and the Federal Reserve System as their banker. The *Federal Reserve System*—or *the Fed*—is the central bank of the United States. All modern countries have a central bank. The first was the Bank of Sweden. The Bank of England, the Banque de France, the

Deutsche Bundesbank, and the Bank of Japan are prominent in world financial circles.

The United States did not have a central bank throughout most of the nineteenth century and into the second decade of the twentieth century. During this period, the United States became the most important industrial nation in the world. A number of financial panics, culminating in the financial panic of 1907, convinced Congress that a central bank was needed to supervise and control private banks. The Federal Reserve System became a reality in 1913 when President Woodrow Wilson signed the Federal Reserve Act.

Functions of the Fed

The Fed—like other central banks throughout the world—performs two primary functions:

1. The Fed controls the nation's money supply.
2. The Fed is responsible for the orderly working of the nation's banking system. It supervises private banks; it serves as the bankers' bank; it clears checks; it fills the currency needs of private banks; it acts as a lender of last resort to banks needing to borrow reserves.

The Fed's most important function is to control the money supply. Because the supply of money is believed to have an important effect on prices, output, employment, and interest rates, the Fed wields great economic influence. Therefore, the control of the money supply places the Fed in a position to influence inflation, output, unemployment, and interest rates.

The Structure of the Federal Reserve System

The 1913 Federal Reserve Act divided the country into twelve districts, each with its own Federal Reserve bank. These banks are located in Boston, New York, Philadelphia, Cleveland, Richmond, Atlanta, Chicago, St. Louis, Minneapolis, Kansas City, Dallas, and San Francisco. Each Federal Reserve bank issues currency for its district, administers bank examinations, clears checks, and is the banker to depository institutions in the district.

The Federal Reserve System is controlled and coordinated by a seven-member Board of Governors (formerly known as the Federal Reserve Board) located in Washington, D.C. This powerful group is appointed by the President of the United States. Each member of the board serves a 14-year term. Terms are staggered so that the appointees of a single U.S. President cannot dominate the board. The President appoints the chair of the board, who is the most powerful member and serves for 4 years. The Federal Reserve System has much more independence than other government agencies. Independence is insured in part by the long terms of the board members and because the Fed is self-financing.

Reserve Requirements

A prudent banker knows that sufficient reserves must be on hand to meet the cash demands of customers. Private profit-maximizing banks would choose voluntarily to hold a portion of their assets in reserves. The Bank of England did not impose legal reserve requirements on private banks for several centuries, yet British banks held prudent levels of reserves, and England developed an excellent reputation for its banking services. In the United States, however, the Fed imposes uniform **reserve requirements** on all commercial banks, savings and loan associations, mutual savings banks, and credit unions. U.S. banks are required by law to hold reserve levels that meet a standard **required-reserve ratio.**

> **Reserve requirements** are rules that state the amount of reserves that a bank must keep on hand to back bank deposits.
>
> A **required-reserve ratio** is the amount of reserves required for each dollar of deposits.

A required-reserve ratio of 0.1 (10 percent) means that the bank must hold $0.10 in reserves for each dollar of deposits. Transaction accounts, such as checking accounts, have required-reserve ratios ranging from 3 percent to 12 percent, depending on the size of the bank. The reserve requirements on time and savings accounts range from 0 percent to 3 percent, depending on the size of the account and its maturity. The Fed has the power to raise or lower these required-reserve ratios and to impose supplemental requirements.

Borrowing from the Fed

Any depository institution holding reserves with the Fed is entitled to borrow funds from the Fed. A bank that is allowed to borrow from the Fed, in the jargon of banking, has access to the *discount window.*

Banks do not have unlimited access to the discount window. They must have exhausted all reasonable alternative sources of funds before coming to the Fed. The discount window is available for temporary and immediate cash needs of the banks.

The rate of interest the Fed charges banks at the discount window is called the *discount rate.* The Fed sets the discount rate and can encourage or discourage bank borrowing by raising or lowering the discount rate. If the spread between the rate at which the banks themselves borrow (the discount rate) and the rates at which they lend is small, the bank's incentive to use the discount window is reduced.

The Federal Open Market Committee

The control of the money supply is the responsibility of the Federal Open Market Committee (FOMC). The FOMC meets monthly and holds telephone conferences between meetings. It consists of the seven members of the Board of Governors and presidents of five of the regional Federal Reserve banks. The president of the New York Federal Reserve Bank is always one of these five; the presidents of the other regional Federal Reserve banks rotate in the four remaining slots.

The Monetary Base

The Fed can do something that other institutions cannot do: it can print money, a power delegated to it by Congress. Because the Fed can print money, whenever the Fed buys something, it puts money into the economy; whenever the Fed sells something, it takes money out of the economy. Imagine, for the moment, that you could print money; whenever you bought something with the money you printed, everyone else (taken together) would have more money; whenever you sold something, you would get some of your money back and everyone else (taken together) would have less money. Similarly, Fed purchases inject money into the economy; Fed sales withdraw money.

As the next chapter will show, the Fed normally buys and sells government securities. It is simpler, however, to consider a more elementary case. For example, suppose the Fed hires a computer programmer, Jane, and pays her with a check for $5000. Jane deposits the check in her commercial bank—the First National Bank of Clear Lake. The Fed's check is different from other checks. When the First National Bank of Clear Lake sends the check to the Fed for collection, its balance sheet changes in two ways. On the asset side, the Bank of Clear Lake's "reserves with the Fed" increase by $5000; on the liability side, the Bank of Clear Lake's "demand deposits due Jane" increase by $5000, as shown in Table 2 (part *a*). The *T*-accounts in this table show only the *change* in bank assets and liabilities that result from the transaction under discussion.

At this point, the money supply has increased by $5000. Jane's bank account has increased by $5000. Everyone else's bank acount has remained the same, and the currency in circulation (outside banks) is still the same. (Remember the *money supply* is the quantity

TABLE 2
Sample *T*-Accounts for the First National Bank of Clear Lake: Results of $5000 Purchase by the Fed

	Changes in Assets		Changes in Liabilities	
(*a*) Jane deposits the Fed's $5000 check	Reserves at the Fed	+$5000	Demand deposits due Jane	+$5000
(*b*) The bank converts $5000 of Fed reserves into $5000 in vault cash.	Vault cash Reserves at the Fed	+$5000 −$5000	No change	
(*c*) Jane withdraws $5000 cash.	Vault cash	−$5000	Demand deposits due Jane	−$5000

These *T*-accounts show that when the Fed buys something (in this case, something for which it pays $5000), three things can happen: First, the receiving bank's reserves at the Fed can increase (a); second, the bank's vault cash can increase (b); or third, cash in circulation can increase (c).

of checkable deposits plus the currency in circulation held by the nonbanking public.)

Had anyone but the Fed hired Jane for $5000, the money supply would have remained the same. Jane's bank account would have increased by $5000, and the purchaser's account would have fallen by $5000. The two transactions would have canceled each other.

Suppose the Bank of Clear Lake does not wish to hold its new reserves as deposits at the Fed. Instead, the bank decides that it needs $5000 more in vault cash. So the bank wires the Fed to send the $5000 in cash. The Fed prints $5000 in Federal Reserve Notes and issues this $5000 to the Bank of Clear Lake. At this point, the Fed lowers the Bank of Clear Lake's deposit balance by $5000. This conversion of reserve balances with the Fed into vault cash (another Fed liability) shown in part *b* of Table 2, has no impact on the money supply because neither total demand deposits nor the currency outside of banks has changed.

Finally, suppose that Jane goes to the bank and cashes a check for $5000 on her account. Again, nothing happens to the money supply. Her demand-deposit account with the Bank of Clear Lake has fallen by $5000, and the Bank of Clear Lake's vault cash has fallen by $5000. Because there is $5000 more in currency in circulation and $5000 less in checkable deposits, the money supply is unchanged, as shown in part *c* of Table 2.

Of these three transactions, the only one that changes the money supply is the one in which Jane deposited the Fed's check for $5000 in her bank. The same effect would have occurred if the Fed had simply printed $5000 and issued the $5000 to Jane in cash.

In hiring Jane, the Fed is purchasing something and is injecting money into the economy. When the Fed sells something, it withdraws money from the economy. If Joe bought a $5000 used car from the Fed's fleet of cars, the money supply would immediately fall by $5000. Joe's bank account would fall by $5000, and the bank's reserves at the Fed would be reduced by that amount. The $5000 that the Fed received for the used car would be in the form of reduced liabilities (reserves at the Fed). If Joe had paid in cash, then the Fed would receive some of the currency it already issued and currency in circulation would fall by $5000. Whatever the case, the Fed's sale of an asset reduces the money supply.

Purchases by the Fed: (1) raise reserves at the Fed, (2) increase vault cash, or (3) increase currency in circulation.

Sales by the Fed: (1) reduce reserves at the Fed, (2) reduce vault cash, or (3) reduce currency in circulation.

Our simple example shows that the Fed can inject money into the economy by purchasing something; it can withdraw money from the economy by selling something. Fed purchases and sales alter the **monetary base.**

The **monetary base** is the sum of reserves on deposit at the Fed, all vault cash, and the currency in circulation.

Only by calculating the monetary base can one gauge Fed injections or withdrawals of funds from the economy. The Fed can control the monetary base by varying the amounts of things it buys or sells (whether these things are goods and services or government bonds).

Figure 1 compares the monetary base with the money supply (M1). The money supply is greater than the monetary base. In January 1992, for example, the money supply M1 was $910 billion, and the monetary base was $328 billion. Where did the $582 billion difference between M1 and the monetary base come from? To answer this question, one must consider how banks create money.

HOW BANKS CREATE MONEY

Banks can create bank demand deposits (money) by lending out the money that people and firms have deposited. Each bank is simply trying to make a profit from financial intermediation. By examining how banks create money, one can understand why the money supply exceeds the monetary base and how the Fed controls the money supply.

The Goldsmith

The creation of money can be illustrated by considering an historical parable about how banking first got

FIGURE 1
The Monetary Base and the Money Supply, January 1992

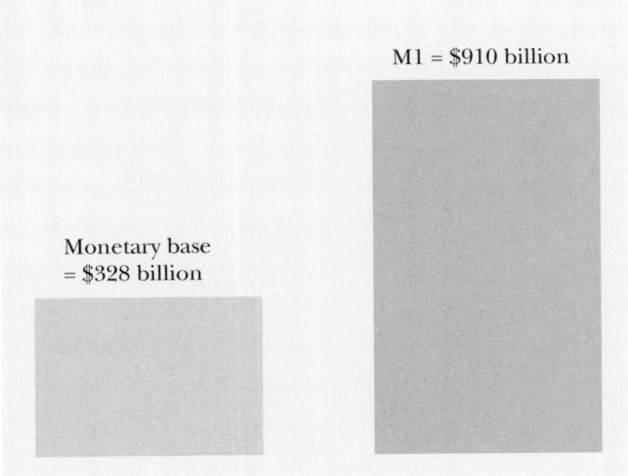

This diagram illustrates the relative size of the monetary base in relation to the money supply as of January 1992.

Source: *The Federal Reserve Bulletin.*

started. Imagine an ancient goldsmith in the business of shaping gold into fine products used by kings, lords, princes, and wealthy merchants. The goldsmith must keep inventories of gold on hand and, therefore, must have safe storage facilities to prevent theft. Because the goldsmith has such facilities, people find it useful to store gold with the goldsmith. In return, the goldsmith might charge a fee to defray storage costs. When people deposit their gold with the goldsmith, they want a receipt, and the goldsmith returns the gold only when a receipt is presented.

Assume that the gold is in the form of uniform bars. People do not care whether the goldsmith returns those same gold bars that they deposited. By not having to keep track of who owns which bar, the goldsmith can hold down storage costs.

The goldsmith soon discovers that only a small amount of gold is needed to accommodate the gold withdrawals on any given day. Each day customers bring in more gold to exchange for storage receipts; each day customers bring in storage receipts to exchange for their gold. The goldsmith can keep most of the gold in the back room under strict lock and key, collecting dust, and maintain only a small inventory to service his customers. As long as they receive the correct amount of gold upon presentation of a storage receipt, they are content.

As the custom of storing gold with the goldsmith becomes more and more widespread, people find it convenient to use the storage receipts themselves, rather than the bulky gold, for transactions. Although storage receipts are mere pieces of paper, because they are accepted as a medium of exchange, they serve as money just like circulating gold. As long as the goldsmith keeps the gold in the back room, the money supply in such a world is the gold in circulation (outside the goldsmith's back room) plus the storage receipts issued by the goldsmith. But the storage receipts only add up to the amount of gold stored in the back room.

Now imagine one fine day the goldsmith discovers a method of making additional profit. A friend of the goldsmith says, "Because all the gold is just sitting in the back room collecting dust, why not lend me some of it?" The goldsmith at first objects that this gold is somebody else's, but a sufficiently high interest rate convinces the goldsmith to lend out some of the gold left to him for safekeeping. The friend gives the goldsmith an IOU; the goldsmith gives the friend some gold. The moment this transaction occurs, the money supply increases by the amount of the loan. The money supply now consists of the storage receipts, the gold previously in circulation, and the gold loaned out by the goldsmith. The goldsmith has *monetized* the debt by giving out gold in exchange for an IOU.

To make a long story short, the friend is even willing to take a storage receipt instead of gold. Why? The storage receipt circulates as money. Indeed, what is to prevent the goldsmith from issuing many times his gold reserve in storage receipts as long as he knows that very few storage receipts are going to be presented for gold? The goldsmith bank can create money provided that: (1) the storage receipts circulate as money and (2) the goldsmith makes loans. If either condition is not satisfied, it is impossible for the goldsmith to create money.

Modern banks do not issue storage receipts for gold; they accept demand deposits and allow customers to write checks (or use an automatic teller machine) on those deposits. Checking account money does not circulate like the storage receipts of the goldsmith. Indeed, the only time checking account money has any real existence is when a check is being written. Most checking account money is simply an entry on the books of some bank.

TABLE 3
The Effects of a $100 Cash Deposit and a $90 Loan

	Change in Assets		Change in Liabilities	
Bank A				
(*a*) After $100 cash deposit:	Cash in vault	+$100	Demand deposits	+$100
(*b*) After $90 loan but before funds are spent:	Reserves Loans	+$100 +$ 90	Demand deposits	+$190
(*c*) After $90 loan proceeds are deposited in Bank B:	Reserves Loans	+$ 10 +$ 90	Demand deposits	+$100
Bank B				
(*d*) After the $90 deposit but before the new loans are made:	Reserves	+$ 90	Demand deposits	+$ 90

The cash deposit in part *a* does not create money because cash in the vault is not part of the money supply. The $90 loan and corresponding $90 demand deposit in part *b* creates $90 worth of new money because demand deposits have increased and currency in circulation has remained the same. When the $90 loan is deposited in Bank B in parts *c* and *d*, no new money is created until Bank B makes a loan.

Loaning Out Reserves

Modern banks are prohibited from printing their own money like the goldsmith's storage receipts. (See Example 2.) They can only make loans and accept deposits. How do modern commercial banks create money?

Consider what happens when someone deposits $100 in currency in Bank A. (Suppose the depositor has been keeping the cash in an old shoe.) Prior to the deposit, the bank was in equilibrium—it was neither making new loans nor calling in old loans. The moment the $100 cash deposit is made, Bank A's balance sheet changes as shown in part *a* of Table 3. Both vault cash and demand deposits have gone up by $100.

Nothing happens to the money supply as long as Bank A remains in this position. Currency in circulation has fallen by the amount that demand deposits have increased; the total money supply outside banks remains the same.

It is likely that Bank A will not be content to stay in this position. Banks have learned through experience that only a small fraction of deposits must be kept as reserves—the rest can be loaned out. The bank is not making any profit from the $100 cash in its vault. Because the bank is interested in making profits, the $100 deposit will allow Bank A to expand its loans. What fraction of the new deposit will Bank A keep? In the United States, banks must maintain the required-reserve ratio of reserves to demand deposits imposed by the Fed. If the Fed requires a reserve ratio of 10 percent, banks must keep $10 as reserves for each $100 of demand deposits.

The Fed's reserve requirements have typically been more conservative than the reserve ratio a profit-minded banker would consider safe and prudent. Hence, reserves above required reserves would likely be considered **excess reserves.** Excess reserves will usually be loaned out. Banks that have no excess reserves are said to be "loaned up."

Excess reserves are reserves in excess of required reserves. Excess reserves equal total reserves minus required reserves.

Suppose that prior to the $100 cash deposit, the required reserves of Bank A equaled actual re-

EXAMPLE 2 The Free Banking Era, 1837–1863

In America's Free Banking Era, from 1837 to 1863, banks operated something like the goldsmith—they issued paper currency. In the free banking period, it was as easy to enter the banking business as to open a hamburger stand. It is often said that so many banks tried to get into the profitable business of issuing notes that it became impossible to determine the legitimacy of their bank notes. Banks would set up business where only the "wildcats lived." If people tried to redeem their notes, the wildcat bank could simply close. This conventional view alleges that (1) bank failures were numerous; (2) banks were fly-by-night affairs in business for a short period; and (3) bank notes were not safe.

Arthur Rolnick and Warren Weber reexamined these allegations and found that the conventional view is highly exaggerated. In the states examined, only about 15 percent of the free banks failed. About two-thirds of the banks that failed redeemed their notes fully. Moreover, the average bank stayed in business over six years. This compares favorably with the average length of time ordinary businesses remain in operation today.

Rolnick and Weber concluded that it is "misleading to characterize the overall free banking experience as a failure of laissez-faire banking." Since free banking worked very well in New York but not in Wisconsin or Michigan, it appears that the peculiarities of different state laws may have played a role in the success or failure of free banking.

Source: Arthur J. Rolnick and Warren E. Weber, "New Evidence on the Free Banking Era," *American Economic Review* (December 1983).

serves (Bank A was loaned up). Assume the Fed's required-reserve ratio is 10 percent. Because the new $100 deposit would require a $10 increase in required reserves, the bank would have $90 in excess reserves after the deposit. The bank, therefore, makes $90 worth of new loans to eliminate the $90 of excess reserves. The moment the $90 loan is made, the borrower's demand-deposit account is credited with $90. Before the borrower spends this $90, Bank A's balance sheet changes as shown in part *b* of Table 3.

Notice that in part *b* the money supply has increased by exactly $90. Bank A has created money! The bank exchanged the borrower's IOU for a demand deposit. The borrower's IOU is *not* money, but the bank's IOU—the $90 demand deposit—*is* money. The bank has created money by monetizing debt. If demand deposits were not used as money, or if the banks made no loans, banks could not create money.

> Banks can create money when (1) demand deposits are used as money, and (2) banks make loans out of excess reserves.

Part *c* of Table 3 takes this process a step further. When the loan recipient spends the $90, Bank A loses $90 of its reserves. The department store, grocery store, or plumber who is paid the borrowed $90 will either cash the $90 check or deposit the $90 check in some other bank.

Whether the $90 ends up in cash that remains in circulation or in a checking account in another bank, the money supply has still increased by $90 as a result of the loan. If the check is cashed, the amount of cash in circulation goes up by $90 and Bank A's deposit liabilities go down by $90. If the check is deposited in another bank, the increase in the depositor's account equals the decrease in the check writer's account. Most transactions (in terms of dollar value) are in checks, and the $90 will likely end up as a checking account deposit in another bank.

Multiple-Deposit Creation

The expansion of the money supply does not end with the $90 increase in the money supply as long as transactions continue to be in the form of checks (as long as people do not cash their checks). In our example, we assume that when Bank A loses the $90 in reserves, some other bank—Bank B—gains the entire amount in new deposits. Our example assumes that there is no **cash leakage** from the banking system to the public.

> A **cash leakage** occurs when a check is cashed and not deposited in a checking account. This cash remains in circulation outside of the banking system.

In this example, people are paid in checks, and they deposit these checks in their checking accounts.

Because Bank B receives $90 in new deposits, its balance sheet changes as shown in part *d* of Table 3. The transfer of $90 from Bank A to Bank B has no immediate impact on the money supply. The amount of demand-deposit liabilities remains the same, and no additional money is created.

If Bank B were originally in equilibrium with no excess reserves, it would now have excess reserves of $81. Because deposits increased by $90, required reserves increased by $9 with a 10 percent reserve requirement. Like Bank A before it, Bank B will loan out its excess reserves of $81. When the recipient of Bank B's loan spends this $81 (with zero leakages of cash), Bank C will receive a new deposit of $81.

The moment Bank B made the loan of $81, the money supply increased by that amount. Bank C will keep 10 percent of the $81 deposit as reserves and lend out the rest—$72.90—which again increases the money supply. When the borrower of $72.90 spends the funds, Bank D receives a new deposit of that amount (again assuming zero leakages of cash).

The $100 increase in reserves has set into motion a pattern of multiple expansion of the money supply. If there are no leakages of cash out of the banking system, the original $100 cash deposit in Bank A leads to demand deposits of $90, $81, $72.90, and so on, with each succeeding figure being 90 percent of the previous deposit. If one sums $100 + $90 + $81 + $72.90 and so on down to the smallest amount, one obtains the total of $1000.

Table 4 shows what happens to each bank as a consequence of a $100 cash deposit in Bank A. The original $100 cash deposit has led to the creation of $900 in additional deposits, or a **multiple expansion of deposits.**

TABLE 4
The Multiple Expansion of Bank Deposits

Bank	New Deposits	New Loans or Investments	Required Reserves
Bank A	$ 100.00	$ 90.00	$ 10.00
Bank B	$ 90.00	$ 81.00	$ 9.00
Bank C	$ 81.00	$ 72.90	$ 8.10
Bank D	$ 72.90	$ 65.61	$ 7.29
Bank E	$ 65.61	$ 59.05	$ 6.56
Sum A–E	$ 409.51	$368.56	$ 40.95
Sum of remaining banks	$ 590.49	$531.44	$ 59.05
Total for whole banking system	$1000.00	$900.00	$100.00

The banking system as a whole can create a multiple expansion of bank deposits; a single bank can create only as much money as it has excess reserves. If the reserve requirement is 0.10 (10 percent), a fresh deposit of $100 will lead to $1000 in total deposits and $900 in new money, provided there are no cash leakages and no bank keeps excess reserves. The original deposit of $100 in Bank A leads to a $90 deposit in Bank B (because of Bank A's new loans), and so on. Thus, $10 is manufactured out of $1, or $9 is created by the multiple expansion of bank deposits.

> A **multiple expansion of deposits** of the money supply occurs when an increase in reserves causes an expansion of the money supply that is greater than the reserve increase.

Notice that one bank out of many cannot create a multiple expansion of bank deposits. (See Example 3.) Each single bank can lend out only a fraction of its new deposits. In the above example, each bank can create new money at a rate equal to only 90 percent of any fresh deposit; that is, each bank can loan out only its excess reserves. But when there is no leakage of cash out of the system, an original cash deposit of $100 will lead to a multiple expansion of deposits. As long as the extra cash reserves are in the banking system, they provide the required

EXAMPLE 3 Canada: Multiple Expansion and Banking Concentration

This chapter explains that a single bank can lend out only its excess reserves. If it loaned out more than its excess reserves, the loan proceeds would be deposited in another bank, and its reserves would fall short. Things would be different if there were only one bank in an economy. A monopoly bank could lend out a multiple of its excess reserves because it knows that loan proceeds will be redeposited in the bank. Whether a single bank can lend more than its excess reserves depends upon that bank's share of total deposits. In the United States, the business of banking is less concentrated than in many other countries. The top five U.S. banks account for less than 20 percent of all bank deposits. In England, Germany, Japan, Canada, and Switzerland, however, only a few banks account for most deposits. In Canada, for example, the top five banks (The Royal Bank of Canada, Canadian Imperial Bank, Bank of Montreal, Bank of Nova Scotia, and Toronto Dominion) account for 80 percent of deposits. In effect, the top five banks of Canada constitute the banking system and, collectively, they can create a multiple expansion of the money supply. Moreover, any single bank can lend more than its excess reserves because it knows a portion of its loans will be redeposited in the bank.

Source: Data supplied by the Royal Bank of Canada.

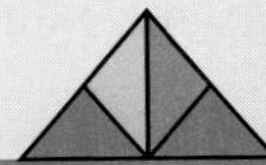

reserves against deposits. If the reserve requirement is 10 percent, a $100 reserve increase will support $1000 worth of additional deposits. When each bank lends out its excess reserves, it loses those reserves to other banks; these reserves then become the basis for further expansion of the money supply by other banks. The $100 initial cash deposit continues to be passed through the banking system until $900 in new money is created for a total of $1000 in deposits.

> One bank can lend out only its excess reserves. However, the banking system as a whole can lend out a multiple of any excess reserves.

Thus, what is true of all banks taken together is not true of any single bank.

The Deposit Multiplier

Table 4 showed how the banking system was able to turn a $100 increase in reserves into $900 of new money, for a total increase in demand deposits of $1000. The factor by which demand deposits expand is the **deposit multiplier.**

> The **deposit multiplier** is the ratio of the change in total deposits to the change in reserves.

A deposit multiplier of 10 indicates that for every $1 increase in reserves, demand deposits will increase by $10. We have already calculated the deposit multiplier when the required-reserve ratio is 10 percent (and when there are no cash leakages). With a 10 percent required-reserve ratio, banks will always lend out 90 percent of their excess reserves. Each dollar of new reserves adds $1 to deposits in Bank A, $0.90 to deposits in Bank B, $0.81 to deposits in Bank C, and so on. When all these deposits are added together, the result is a $10 increase in deposits for each $1 increase in reserves.

If the required-reserve ratio had been 20 percent in our example, the $1 increase in reserves would still add $1 to deposits in Bank A, but would now add $0.80 in Bank B, $0.64 in Bank C, and so on, for a total increase of $5 in deposits. With a required-reserve ratio of 20 percent, the deposit multiplier is 5. These two examples suggest a formula for the deposit multiplier.

The deposit multiplier is the reciprocal of the reserve ratio (r) maintained by the banking system:

$$\text{Deposit multiplier} = \frac{1}{r}$$

When the reserve ratio is 10 percent, $r = 0.10$, and the deposit multiplier is 10. If the reserve ratio is 5 percent, $r = 0.05$, and the deposit multiplier is 20. As the formula suggests, the deposit multiplier varies inversely with the reserve ratio.

Expansion of the Money Supply in the Real World

Our discussion of the multiple expansion of bank deposits assumed that no cash ever leaked out of the banking system and that banks kept excess reserves at zero. Neither assumption is strictly true.

Cash Leakages. The public does not hold all of its money balances in demand deposits. When banks begin to create new demand deposits, it is likely that the public will also want to hold more currency. Thus, there will be leakages of cash into hand-to-hand circulation as the multiple creation of bank deposits takes place.

Cash leakages reduce the deposit multiplier. Returning to our numerical example, when \$100 was initially deposited in Bank A and \$90 was lent out, the next generation of banks—Bank B—might receive only \$80 in new deposits rather than \$90. Thus, Bank B could create only \$72 in new deposits rather than \$81. This erosion would occur all along the line in Table 4 and would reduce the deposit multiplier accordingly.

If one knows the total cash leakage that will take place, one can apply the deposit multiplier ($1/r$) to the amount of the new reserves that are left with the banking system. Suppose that out of the \$100 originally deposited with Bank A, \$20 would eventually leak into hand-to-hand circulation. Because \$80 of new reserves would remain in the banking system, \$800 of deposits must result from the \$100 deposit. Thus, the 10-to-1 multiplier applies to the quantity of reserves permanently left with the banking system.

The effect of cash leakages on the total money supply explains the mysterious disappearance of \$6.7 billion during the Great Depression noted at the beginning of this chapter. As already stated, the Fed controls the monetary base through its purchases and sales. From 1929 to 1933, the Fed did not attempt to pump reserves into the banking system, but the public did draw cash out of the banking system—partially in response to a loss of confidence in banks. These cash withdrawals lowered bank reserves and led to a multiple *contraction* of bank deposits. The \$6.7 billion disappeared into thin air. Thus, the deposit multiplier works both in forward and in reverse. If reserves contract, demand deposits will fall by a multiple of the fall in reserves. Banks will call in some loans or simply allow existing loans to be paid in full without relending.

Excess Reserves. If r in the deposit multiplier formula is interpreted as the required-reserve ratio, the formula applies only when there are no excess reserves. However, since banks hold excess reserves, the r in the formula must be interpreted as the *desired-reserve ratio* of banks. The desired-reserve ratio will depend on the required-reserve ratio and on the profitability of making loans.

Excess reserves are only about 2 percent of total reserves. Excess reserves are small for two reasons. First, banks can usually borrow from the Federal Reserve System at the official discount rate to meet any reserve deficiency. Second, banks can always borrow reserves from other banks. The *federal-funds market* is a market in which any bank with excess reserves can lend its reserves to banks with deficient reserves at the federal-funds rate.

BANK REGULATION AND REFORM

We now understand how banks help determine the supply of money and deposits. The money supply depends on the public's desire for currency relative to deposits, the banking system's desire for reserves relative to deposits, and the monetary base (currency outstanding plus bank reserves). The stability of the money supply depends on the stability of these three fundamental factors. Therefore, the confidence of the public in the banking system, as well as the reliability of bank lending practices, plays a major role in the monetary system.

This brings us to our final topic: bank regulation and reform. The stability of the supply of money and credit depends in part on the way in which banks are regulated.

Bank Regulation

It is useful to examine the key developments in bank regulation in the United States in order to understand the current system.

Restriction of Interest Payments on Deposits. The Banking Acts of 1933 and 1935 imposed limits on the interest rates banks could pay on demand, savings, and time deposits. These acts prohibited interest payments on checking accounts and provided for the Fed to adjust the other rates periodically. The United States began to phase out these interest-rate ceilings in the early 1980s.

Deposit Insurance. In the Great Depression, government-guaranteed deposit insurance was instituted for both commercial banks and savings and loans associations. The FDIC (Federal Deposit Insurance Corporation) insured bank deposits; and the FSLIC (Federal Savings and Loan Insurance Corporation) insured savings and loan deposits. In 1989, the two were merged under the FDIC.

Restrictions on Permissible Activities. Until the early 1980s, savings and loan associations were restricted to making mortgage loans. Commercial banks were free to make consumer loans, commercial loans, and mortgage loans and to buy government securities. The Glass-Steagall Act of 1933 separated the activities of commercial banks from the securities industry. Commercial banks were prohibited from selling corporate securities. Investment banks (who could deal in corporate securities) were prohibited from engaging in commercial banking. Thus, the distinction between savings and loan associations, commercial banks, and investment banks is a legal one.

Capital Requirements. All depository institutions must meet certain minimum capital requirements. There are two ways to finance the acquisition of assets: drawing the owner's equity or capital, and borrowing. Historically, there have been diverse capital requirements, depending on the size and location of the bank. Since 1983, the Fed and the Comptroller of the Currency have established the minimum capital requirement of 6 percent of a bank's assets. In other words, 6 percent of a bank's assets should be financed by the owners of the bank. This presumably makes the bank safer in case the bank enters a period of negative profits. Federal bank regulators have some discretion in enforcing the requirement for individual banks.

Inspection and Control of Riskiness. The government has the power to examine depository institutions to determine the riskiness of their assets and liabilities.

Entry Restrictions. To create a new bank, a new branch of an old bank, or a new savings and loan association, it is necessary to obtain permission from federal and state regulators.

Bank Deregulation

The United States experienced high inflation rates in the late 1970s and early 1980s. During 1980, the rate of inflation was about 13 percent. This put a squeeze on savings and loan associations. Interest rates on home mortgages rose, but savings and loans had difficulty attracting deposits because of government regulation of interest paid on deposits. The savings and loans had loaned out substantial sums on residential real estate in the 1970s, but at relatively low, fixed interest rates. Industry losses mounted to about $6 billion in 1980. From 1970 to 1982, the number of savings and loan associations dropped by about one-third.

In the early 1980s Congress deregulated banking, in the hope of solving the savings and loan crisis and making the banking system more efficient. Both commercial banks and thrifts were deregulated. The Depository Institutions and Monetary Control Act of 1980 and the Garn–St. Germain Act of 1982 jointly reduced the legal distinction between banks and thrifts and removed many restrictions on their investment activities and the interest rates paid on deposit accounts. For example, competitive interest rates could be paid on checking accounts; and banks could lend real estate developers in excess of 100 percent of their construction costs.

Banking Crises

The combination of deregulation and deposit insurance proved lethal, and unintended consequences followed. Basically, the FDIC method of insuring deposits creates an incentive problem. Banks or thrifts pay a fixed fee as a percent of their deposits. Even though there is a $100,000 nominal limit on an insured deposit, any amount can be insured through the use of deposit brokers, who spread $100,000 accounts over many banks. With such deposit insurance there is no incentive for banks to provide, nor for consumers to demand, information on how well the bank is doing. Deposits are as safe in a poorly-run bank as in the most well-run bank. One can get an insured deposit from a failed or failing bank. This is similar to buying fire insurance while your house is burning or after it has burned down. Thus, banks and thrifts could and did invest in wild schemes without imposing any costs on depositors or even on themselves. Who monitors the banks and thrifts? Since depositors have no incentive to monitor banks or thrifts, that role falls on the shoulders of bank regulators. But deregulation effectively meant that nobody was watching the store.

Banks lent money to real estate developers without carefully examining the creditworthiness of their projects. In one example among many, banks lent the flamboyant Donald Trump about $2 billion without even auditing him! Why? The competition for loans became fierce as thousands of thrifts began to make loans to real estate developers with cheap, government-insured funds. When these investments failed, so did banks and thrifts. Bank failure rates in the late 1980s and early 1990s increased tenfold over the bank failure rates in the 30 years from 1950 to 1980.

> Government-insured deposits severed the link between a bank's performance and the ability of a bank to attract deposits. Bank performance deteriorated in the 1980s due to a combination of deposit insurance and deregulation.

Can Banks Be Too Big to Fail?

The rationale for federal deposit insurance and the discount window is that bank safety is more important than the safety of your local grocery or hardware store. To protect the individual depositor and banks from bank failures is to prevent such widespread failures from destroying the economic system. Bank panics spread when small banks draw deposits out of larger banks, banks cut back on loans and investments, and rumor feeds on rumor. The possibility exists that a bank failure, unlike the failure of a shoe store, represents a risk to the entire economic system—a **systemic risk.**

> A **systemic risk** is the additional risk imposed on the economy as a whole arising from the failure of one bank or business unit.

The policy of the FDIC has been to bail out failing banks by guaranteeing not only insured deposits but the vast majority of uninsured deposits. At banks with over $1 billion in assets, the FDIC has fully protected all depositors. For example, in the 1984 failure of the Continental Illinois Bank, no depositor lost a cent even though 90 percent of all deposits were uninsured. This was the beginning of the too-big-to-fail doctrine: even though a large bank made bad loans, that bank was not allowed to fail, because the ripple effects of such a failure would have hurt too many people.

The FDIC has not bailed out all uninsured depositors. In one of its most controversial decisions, the FDIC allowed uninsured depositors (mostly charities) at Harlem's Freedom Bank to lose $11 million. Evidently, this bank was not "too big to fail."

The FDIC's liberal policy for the big banks, along with a rash of bank failures in Texas and New England, caused the insurance fund to dwindle from $18 billion in 1987 to near insolvency in 1991. Eventually taxpayers will have to bail out the FDIC. In 1991, the cost of bailing out banks was estimated to be in the vicinity of $70 billion. It is hoped that, in the future, banks will repay this one-time advance through increased insurance premiums. Congress provided an additional $80 billion to the Resolution Trust Corporation (RTC), the Federal agency charged with handling closed savings and loan associations; and the RTC may need still another $80 billion.

What Type of Banking Reform?

Clearly, some type of banking reform is needed. Many plans have been proposed. We discuss three such plans: the free market plan, the Tobin plan, and the Treasury plan.

The Free Market Plan. The simplest plan calls for the elimination of deposit insurance. If banks are

EXAMPLE 4 Problems with the National Banking System

If the National Banking System worked so well, why was it changed? The system had two problems: First, the supply of currency was inelastic, because there was no central bank to change the quantity of the monetary base in response to seasonal needs. Second, illiquidity in country banks often led to illiquidity in city banks. Small banks held reserves in large banks and large banks held reserves in gigantic banks. When a panic occurred in the country, due to a crop failure, it could spread to the big cities as small banks pulled their reserves out of the larger banks. This put a liquidity squeeze on banks up and down the line.

The above two problems and frequent financial panics led Congress to pass the Federal Reserve Act in 1913. It was felt that a central bank could act as a lender of last resort and provide an elastic supply of currency.

Milton Friedman and Anna Schwartz have pointed out that the Federal Reserve Act failed miserably in its objectives when it allowed the money supply to fall by one-third from 1929 to 1933. About 10,000 banks closed their doors during the Great Depression.

Source: Milton Friedman and Anna Schwartz, *A Monetary History of the United States, 1867–1960* (Princeton, NJ: Princeton University Press, 1963), 327–28.

not unique and must compete with other financial institutions, why should the government subsidize the banking industry through deposit insurance? Deposits are to a bank what labor and capital are to a firm. Thus, it is argued, banks should not be subsidized more than other firms in the economy.

History provides several examples of banking without much regulation or deposit insurance. The experience that is most relevant for the United States today occurred from 1863 to 1913, during the National Banking Era. This was the period of time between the National Bank Act of 1863 and the Federal Reserve Act of 1913. Nationally chartered banks were subject to reserve requirements, and banks were restricted in their investments. But deposits were not insured and there was no central bank.

How well did the National Banking Era work?[3] Contrary to popular views, banks failed less than nonbanks in that period. In the worst banking panic of the period (in 1873), 1.3 percent of banks failed, and the depositors of those banks lost only 2.1 cents of every dollar of deposits. If a bank was in trouble, it might stop converting notes and deposits into gold. But the bank would not usually close; it would continue to make and service loans.

Because there was no deposit insurance, banks held larger reserves, invested a larger fraction of their assets in safe securities, and maintained more capital to meet contingencies. These factors reduced the impact of a financial panic. Financial panics seemed to affect the insolvent banks, but when the public realized that a particular bank was safe, that bank was not pulled down by the panic. Example 4 discusses the shortcomings of the National Banking Era.

The Tobin Plan. James Tobin, a Nobel laureate in economics, proposed a plan that has much in common with the free market plan. Tobin's plan is a minimal government plan, involving both insured and uninsured deposits.

First, Tobin's plan backs insured deposits by safe assets, such as Treasury securities, that are specifically dedicated to the redemption of those deposits. Second, the plan lets banks and savings and loan associations give depositors the option of keeping their money in uninsured deposits. Uninsured deposits would offer higher yields and be subject to the usual regulations of the banking authorities. Third, the plan would not bail out insolvent institutions, no matter how big, or pay off uninsured depositors. In

[3]The following discussion of the National Banking Era is based on "The Banking Industry: Withering Under the Umbrella of Protection," *Federal Reserve Bank of Cleveland Annual Report*, 1990.

this two-tiered scheme, there is no required limit on deposit insurance. If a charity wanted to keep $2 million in an insured account, the entire amount could be redeemed if the bank went bankrupt because the $2 million would be backed by Treasury securities.

If this plan were adopted, an industry could potentially develop to privately insure federally uninsured deposits. Although it is difficult for individuals to monitor single banks, insurance companies could grade the banks according to risk and sell consumers private insurance policies to cover federally uninsured deposits.

The Treasury Plan. The U.S. Treasury and Congress have considered plans that would reform the current system in three ways:

1. Deposit insurance premiums would depend partly on banks' estimated risk.
2. The scope of insurance would be reduced by limiting coverage to a certain amount and by protecting uninsured depositors less often when banks fail.
3. Banks would be closed before their reported capital (net assets) falls to zero.

The first aspect of the plan would work with regulators estimating the risk of a bank by taking a weighted average of the bank's assets in four risk categories. The FDIC would decide on the premium for each risk level.

The second aspect would entail limiting each depositor to two insured accounts of $100,000 or less per bank, making it illegal for wealthy investors to fully insure large amounts of money by using deposit "brokers" to spread that money among different banks in lots of $100,000. Regulators would still determine on a case-by-case basis when uninsured deposits would be covered.

The third aspect of the plan would involve a complicated scheme of regulation and supervision depending on a bank's ratio of capital to its risky assets.

The Treasury plan may be better than current law, but it still gives the FDIC the power to distinguish between big banks and small banks. Many economists feel that this distinction is inefficient because it favors the establishment of larger banks and does not promote competition. Usually, political, rather than economic, concerns drive regulators to favor large banks over small ones.

This chapter explained the relationship between the Federal Reserve System and the money supply. This chapter also studied the role of bank regulation and possible plans for reform of the banking system. The next chapter examines the role of monetary policy in the broader context of controlling aggregate demand.

SUMMARY

1. Banks are financial intermediaries. Financial intermediaries borrow money from ultimate lenders and lend this money to ultimate borrowers. Most lending in the United States is done by financial intermediaries. Financial intermediaries offer three advantages over direct lending from lenders to borrowers: they process information about the creditworthiness of borrowers, they pool risks, and they offer liquidity to lenders by borrowing short and lending long.

2. Commercial banks are chartered by state banking authorities or by the U.S. Treasury. Commercial banks offer their customers checking account services and savings accounts. They earn money by loaning out funds they have borrowed or by investing these funds in government securities. Banks make profits by borrowing at a lower rate of interest than that at which they lend or invest. Bank balance sheets summarize the claims on the assets of a bank. Banks must maintain reserves to meet the cash needs of their depositors. Reserves are held in two forms: cash in the vault and reserve balances at the Fed. Reserves are typically much less than the demand-deposit liabilities of the bank. The FDIC insures deposits and gives depositors the necessary sense of security.

3. The Federal Reserve System, established in 1913, is the central bank of the United States. The Fed imposes reserve requirements on banks and thrift institutions. Depository institutions can borrow from the Fed to meet their temporary cash needs, and the interest rate at which they borrow is called the discount rate. By buying and selling things, the Fed injects money into the banking system and takes money out of the banking system. The monetary base equals reserve balances with the Fed, vault cash, and currency in circulation. The monetary base is smaller than the money supply.

4. Banks create money by monetizing debt. Banks can use reserves to make loans, and in the process of making loans, they create money. Private banks have the ability to create money because demand deposits are money and because banks make loans out of new deposits. An increase in reserves leads to a multiple expansion of deposits. Although any one bank can lend out only its excess reserves, the banking system as a whole can lend out a multiple of an increase in reserves. The deposit multiplier is the ratio of the change in deposits to the change in reserves. The deposit multiplier is the inverse of the desired-reserve ratio.

5. The Depository Institutions and Monetary Control Act of 1980 and the Garn–St. Germain Act of 1982 reduced the legal distinction between banks and thrifts, removed restrictions on investment activities, and allowed competitive interest rates on deposit accounts. Bank deregulation combined with the system of deposit insurance precipitated bank and thrift failures in the 1980s and 1990s. Although systemic risk is a possible justification for federal deposit insurance, bank reform seems called for.

KEY TERMS

financial intermediaries
commercial banks
balance sheet
assets
liabilities
T-accounts
reserves
reserve requirements
required-reserve ratio
monetary base
excess reserves
cash leakage
multiple expansion of deposits
deposit multiplier
systemic risk

QUESTIONS AND PROBLEMS

1. Evaluate the validity of the following statement: "Banks get away with murder. They pay you no interest on your checking accounts, and then they turn around and lend your money to some poor borrower at 18 percent."
2. Commercial banks hold only about 10 percent of their transaction deposits in reserves. Explain how banks can get by with so few reserves.
3. Explain why bankers would maintain reserves even without required-reserve ratios.
4. Assume that the Fed sells all its old office furniture to XYZ Corporation for $10 million. What effect will this sale have on the money supply? What will happen if the Fed sells XYZ Corporation $10 million worth of its holdings of government securities?
5. Explain why banks can create money only if bank deposits are accepted as money and only if banks are willing to make loans. Explain what is meant by the monetization of debt.
6. Assume that the required-reserve ratio is 0.4 (40 percent) and that there are no cash leakages. The Fed buys a government security from Jones for $1000. Explain, using *T*-accounts, what will happen to the money supply. Answer the same question assuming only that Jones (and only Jones) takes payment from the Fed as follows: $500 cash (which he puts under his mattress) and a $500 check. There are no more cash leakages.
7. Rework Table 3 on the assumption that $r = 0.2$. In this case, the deposit multiplier is 5, so that the $100 fresh deposit in Bank A will ultimately lead to $500 in total deposits, or $400 in new money.
8. What will happen to the money supply if the Fed sells a large fleet of used cars to a car dealership?
9. What would you predict would happen to commercial bank borrowing from the Fed if the Fed were to raise the required-reserve ratio?
10. Assume that between year 1 and year 2, the amount of currency in circulation increased while the amount of vault cash and reserves at the Fed remained the same. Was the Fed purchasing or selling securities?
11. During the Christmas season, the public tends to withdraw large sums of cash from checking accounts. What effect do these withdrawals have upon the nation's money supply?
12. How were the savings and loan associations hurt by the inflation of the 1970s?
13. Evaluate the validity of the following statement: "Central banking is only as good as the people who run it."
14. What effect did the deregulation of the 1980s, combined with federal deposit insurance, have on banking in the United States?
15. Evaluate the various plans for reforming the banking system.

SUGGESTED READINGS

Campbell, Tim S. *Money and Capital Markets.* New York: HarperCollins, 1988.

Dalgaard, Bruce R. *Money, Financial Institutions, and Economic Activity.* Glenview, IL: Scott, Foresman and Company, 1987.

"The Banking Industry: Withering Under the Umbrella of Protection," *Federal Reserve Bank of Cleveland Annual Report,* 1990.

Mayer, Martin. *The Bankers.* New York: Ballantine Books, 1980.

Mayer, Thomas, et al. *Money, Banking, and the Economy,* 3rd ed. New York: W. W. Norton, 1987.

Ritter, Lawrence S., and William L. Silber. *Money,* 5th ed. New York: Basic Books, 1984.

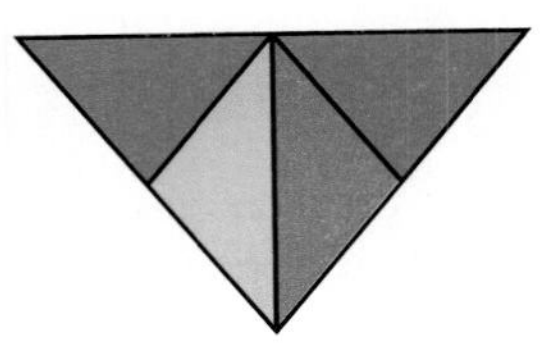

16

Monetary Policy

CHAPTER INSIGHT

When the U.S. economy was in recession from 1990 to 1992, the Fed was expected to take action to end it. Experts studied the tea leaves to try to figure out when the Fed would lower interest rates to stimulate spending. They expected the Fed to follow the typical pattern for the last few recessions: If unemployment figures looked dismal, the Fed would lower interest rates; if unemployment figures looked good, the Fed would let interest rates rise. Is the Fed really so all-powerful? This chapter examines the means by which the Fed attempts to control the money supply and the degree to which it is successful.

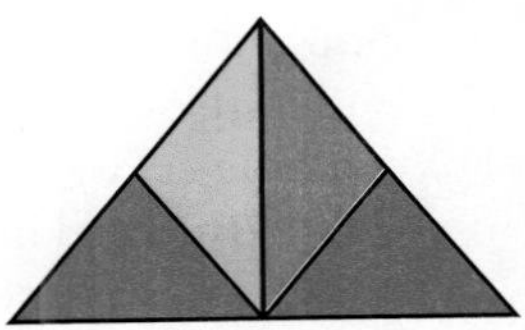

FEDERAL RESERVE POLICY

The most important function of the Fed is to control **monetary policy.**

> **Monetary policy** is the deliberate control of the money supply and, in some cases, credit conditions for the purpose of achieving macroeconomic goals such as a certain level of unemployment or inflation.

The quantity of money can affect prices, output, and employment; therefore, the Fed controls—to some degree—the pulse rate of the economy. By expanding the money supply, the Fed can speed up the pulse rate; by contracting the money supply (or by slowing down its rate of growth), the Fed can slow down the pulse rate.

The Fed controls money and credit by

1. Controlling the monetary base through open-market operations
2. Controlling reserve requirements
3. Setting the discount rate
4. Applying moral suasion
5. Imposing selective credit controls
6. Setting margin requirements

Open-Market Operations

As already mentioned, the Fed can inject or withdraw money from the economy by buying or selling. An injection of money leads to a multiple expansion of deposits; a withdrawal of money leads to a multiple contraction of deposits.

The Fed controls bank reserves by buying and selling federal government securities on the open market as directed by the Federal Open Market Committee. The Fed already owns a large sum of government securities. In 1992, the Fed owned more than $260 billion worth of government securities.

A substantial portion of the Fed's open-market operations are purely defensive. The Fed responds to changes in the currency-holding habits of the public. For example, a large seasonal influx of cash from the public into the banking system tends to automatically increase bank reserves. When people deposit cash in their checking accounts, bank reserves rise and excess reserves are created. If the Fed does not take countermeasures, banks begin to loan out excess reserves. Likewise, spontaneous cash drains from the banking system cause a contraction of the supply of money in the absence of offsetting action by the Fed. When depositors write checks to obtain cash, bank reserves fall, and banks can be left with insufficient reserves.

The mechanics of Fed open-market transactions are the same whether the Fed is simply offsetting actions in the private economy to hold money supply steady or whether it is embarking on a course of monetary expansion or contraction.

Open-Market Sales. Suppose the Fed sells $10,000 worth of government securities to an individual (by means of some intermediary). The individual sends a personal check written on a commercial bank to the Fed (although the exact same effect is achieved if the individual pays cash). Panel *a* of Table 1 shows what happens to the balance sheet of the individual, the commercial bank, and the Fed. The individual's total assets stay the same. The individual's bonds increase by $10,000, and demand deposits decrease by $10,000. The commercial bank finds that its demand-deposit liabilities fall by $10,000. Its reserves with the Fed also fall by $10,000 because when the Fed receives the check drawn on the commercial bank, it reduces the bank's account by that amount. The Fed's stock of government securities falls by $10,000, and its reserve-balance liability to the commercial bank falls by $10,000.

As a consequence of the Fed sale, the money supply falls by $10,000 because demand deposits fall by that amount. In addition, the monetary base falls by $10,000; by selling $10,000 in securities, the Fed extinguishes $10,000 in reserves. Writing a check to the Fed, unlike writing one to someone else, destroys money instead of transferring it.

The extinction of $10,000 in reserves (monetary base) will cause a multiple contraction of deposits. With a deposit multiplier of 10, deposits will fall by $100,000 (assuming no cash leakages).

Open-Market Purchases. Now suppose the Fed purchases $10,000 worth of securities from a person (by means of some intermediary). That person receives a check from the Fed and deposits it in his or her bank. Panel *b* of Table 1 shows what happens to the balance sheets of the person, the commercial bank, and the Fed. The individual's total

TABLE 1
Two Open-Market Transactions

***(a)* Effects of an Open-Market Sale of $10,000 in Government Securities**

	Changes in Assets		Changes in Liabilities	
(1) Individual or household	Securities Demand deposits	+$10,000 −$10,000	No change	
(2) Commercial bank	Reserves at Fed	−$10,000	Demand deposits	−$10,000
(3) The Fed	Govenment securities	−$10,000	Reserve balances of banks	−$10,000

***(b)* Effects of an Open-Market Purchase of $10,000 in Government Securities**

	Changes in Assets		Changes in Liabilities	
(1) Individual or household	Securities Demand deposits	−$10,000 +$10,000	No change	
(2) Commercial bank	Reserves at Fed	+$10,000	Demand deposits	+$10,000
(3) The Fed	Govenment securities	+$10,000	Reserve balances of banks	+$10,000

Panel *a* of this table shows the effect of an open-market sale by the Fed. Rows 2 and 3 of panel *a* show that commercial bank reserves fall by the amount of the sale. Thus, Fed sales of government securities lower commercial bank reserves. Panel *b* shows the effect of an open-market purchase by the Fed. Rows 2 and 3 show that commercial bank reserves rise by the amount of the purchase. Thus, Fed purchases of government securities raise commercial bank reserves.

assets remain the same: demand deposits increase by $10,000, and government bonds decrease by $10,000. The commercial bank finds that its demand deposits rise by $10,000, as do its reserves with the Fed. Finally, the Fed's government securities and reserve balances of commercial banks both rise by $10,000. The monetary base rises by the amount of the purchase. This expansion of bank reserves sets into motion a multiple expansion of deposits.

As a comparison of panels *a* and *b* of Table 1 shows, open-market purchases have the exact opposite effects as open-market sales.

Advantages of Open-Market Operations. The chief advantages of open-market operations as a tool of monetary policy are

1. Open-market operations give the Fed more precise control over the monetary base. By purchasing or selling a given dollar amount of government securities, the Fed adds or subtracts exactly that amount to or from the monetary base.
2. Flexible monetary control is possible through open-market operations because the Fed can buy or sell securities each day. The Fed can reverse itself if new information becomes available.

Thus, it is hardly surprising that the Fed relies more heavily on open-market operations than on any other tool of monetary control.

> Open-market purchases increase the monetary base; open-market sales lower the monetary base. Open-market operations are flexible because they can be transacted quickly and in almost any desired amount. Open-market operations are powerful because they have a magnified impact on the money supply as banks create new money from new reserves.

Changes in Reserve Requirements

The Fed's power to change reserve requirements within broad limits is another tool for controlling the money supply. For example, increasing reserve requirements from 10 percent to 12.5 percent would force banks to contract demand deposits by 20 percent. Recall that the deposit multiplier is $1/r$. When $r = 0.10$, \$40,000 in reserves would support \$400,000 in demand deposits. If reserve requirements were raised to $r = 0.125$, \$40,000 in reserves would support only \$320,000 in demand deposits; demand deposits would have to contract by \$80,000. Conversely, lowering reserve requirements can result in a massive increase in the money supply.

Traditionally, the Fed has been reluctant to use this tool of monetary policy. One argument against reserve-requirement changes is that they are too blunt an instrument. An open-market operation, for example, can be carried out to offset a seasonal currency drain without any fanfare or comment from the press. But a reduction in reserve requirements that is used to offset a seasonal currency drain might be interpreted by the financial press as a fundamental change in monetary policy. However, in April 1992 the Fed did lower reserve requirements against checking account deposits, from 12 percent to 10 percent. The Fed made it clear that the purpose was to increase bank profits, not to increase the supply of money and credit.

> Increases in reserve requirements reduce the money supply; reductions in reserve requirements increase the money supply. Changes in reserve requirements, however, are a seldom-used instrument of monetary policy.

The Setting of the Discount Rate

Recall from Chapter 15 that depository institutions, such as commercial banks and savings and loan associations, can borrow from the Fed at the *discount rate.* When banks borrow from the Fed, they are said to be using the *discount window.* The amount that banks borrow from the Fed directly affects the monetary base. As depository institutions borrow more or less from the Fed, the monetary base increases or decreases. A key feature of the discount rate is that it is lower than bank lending rates. For example, in early 1992, banks on the average charged their best customers 6.5 percent per year, while they could borrow from the Fed at a discount rate of about 4.5 percent. Thus, banks normally have an economic incentive to borrow from the Fed and then lend those funds at a higher rate.

The Fed, of course, does not want depository institutions to make opportunistic use of their borrowing privileges. By administrative action, the amount banks can borrow at the discount window is limited to their seasonal borrowing needs, except for banks in financial trouble. The Fed takes a close look at depository institutions that use the discount window too frequently, and it can refuse to make loans. Nevertheless, the higher are market interest rates relative to the discount rate, the greater is the incentive of depository institutions to borrow from the Fed.

To limit the incentive of depository institutions to use the discount window, the Fed attempts to keep the discount rate in line with market interest rates. Therefore, as market interest rates rise or fall, the discount rate is raised or lowered.

Some have suggested that the discount rate can be used to indicate the Fed's future monetary policy. Increases in the discount rate are said to be indicative of tight monetary policy, and decreases are said to suggest an easy monetary policy. Thus, changes in the discount rate can have an *announcement effect.* Economists are usually suspicious of this argument, however, because no one has yet shown that changes in the discount rate can be used to predict the future monetary base or money supply.

The Fed's use of the discount rate as a tool of monetary policy has been criticized by many economists. First, the ability to borrow from the Fed reduces the Fed's control over the monetary base. If banks borrow when the Fed is interested in lowering the monetary base, the Fed must sell government bonds to offset such borrowing. Second, allowing banks to borrow at an interest rate that is lower than the market interest rate amounts to a subsidy to those depository institutions. Generally speaking, the banks that avail themselves of the discount window are usually in financial trouble. Critics argue that imprudently run banks should not be subsidized.

Other Instruments of Control

In addition to the three major instruments just mentioned, the Fed has three minor tools for controlling money supply: moral suasion, selective credit controls, and margin credit.

Moral Suasion. The chairperson of the Fed has been known at times to urge banks to expand their loans or to adopt more restrictive credit policies. *Moral suasion* is the process by which the Fed tries to persuade banks to voluntarily follow a particular policy.

Selective Credit Controls. The Fed can use *selective credit controls* to affect the distribution of loans rather than the overall volume of loans. The Fed can dictate terms and conditions of installment credit and requirements for consumer credit cards. Until 1986, the Fed could set interest-rate ceilings on deposits at commercial banks, and these ceilings could affect bank deposits.

Margin Credit. When investors buy stocks, they are permitted to buy a portion on credit (this practice is called *buying on margin*). This credit, supplied by stockbrokers, is called *margin credit.* The Fed sets margin requirements. Current margin requirements allow purchasers of stock to finance 50 percent of the purchase with margin credit. In the speculative stock market boom of the 1920s, speculators could purchase stocks with as little as 10 percent down; the rest was financed with margin loans. Studies show margin requirements to be relatively ineffective as a tool of monetary policy because stocks can always be purchased with money borrowed from alternative sources.

PROBLEMS OF MONETARY CONTROL

When the monetary base increases, banks have a larger base on which to make loans. As loans increase, the money supply increases. Chapter 15 showed that if there is no drain of reserves into circulating currency and if the ratio of reserves to deposits is 10 percent, then a $1 increase in the monetary base will increase the money supply by $10. As explained in Chapter 15, the deposit multiplier equals $1/r$, where r is the reserve/deposit ratio.

In reality, increasing the monetary base by $1 will not raise the money supply by $10. People hold their money balances in both checking accounts and currency. As the quantity of checking accounts expands, currency in circulation will also increase. Thus, as banks make loans out of additional reserves, some of those reserves will leak out into currency in circulation. If Bank A receives $1 in extra reserves as a result of a Fed openmarket purchase, the money supply will rise by $1. When Bank A then increases its loans by $0.90, the money supply increases again, this time by $0.90 (as explained in Chapter 15). If the proceeds of this loan end up entirely as currency in circulation, the process of money expansion stops. In this case, the money supply increases by a total of $1.90 as the result of a $1 open-market purchase. Consequently, a $1 increase in the monetary base can increase the money supply by any amount between $1.90 and $10, depending on the cash leakage from the system. Historically, an increase in the monetary base of $1 increases the money supply (M1) by between $2.75 and $3.00.

A given increase in the monetary base will increase the money supply by more, the smaller the amount of currency people hold per dollar of deposit and the smaller the reserve/deposit ratio. If people hold less currency, the banking system will gain more new reserves from any given increase in the monetary base; and the smaller the reserve/deposit ratio, the larger the deposit multiplier for any given increase in reserves.[1]

The ratio of currency to deposits can vary unpredictably from month to month. Thus, even if the Fed

[1]The money supply formula, for interested students, is derived as follows: Assume banks wish to hold the ratio r of Fed and vault reserves (R) to deposits (D). Thus, $R = rD$. Assume the public wishes to hold the ratio k of currency (C) to deposits (D). Thus $k = C/D$ and $r = R/D$. The monetary base $(H) = R + C$. The money supply $(M) = C + D$. Thus,

$$\frac{M}{H} = \frac{D + C}{R + C} \tag{1}$$

Nothing is changed by dividing D into the numerator and denominator

$$\frac{M}{H} = \frac{(1 + k)}{r + k} \tag{2}$$

For example, if one assumes that the currency/deposit ratio (k) is 0.4 and the reserve/deposit ratio is 0.1, the result is a money multiplier (the money/reserve ratio) of $M/H = (1 + 0.4)/(0.1 + 0.4) = 2.8$. If the currency deposit ratio fell by exactly one half, the money multiplier would increase from 2.8 to 4 $[= (1 + 0.2)/(0.1 + 0.2)]$. But if k remained at 0.4 while the reserve deposit ratio (r) fell by one half, to $r = 0.05$, the money multiplier would increase from 2.8 to only 3.11 $[= (1 + 0.4)/(.05 + 0.4)]$.

has precise control over the monetary base, it does not have precise control over the money supply. One month a 3 percent increase in the monetary base may be accompanied by a 4.7 percent decrease in the money supply (June 1989); another month a 5.9 percent increase in the monetary base may coincide with a 9 percent increase in the money supply (March 1991). In the short run, the Fed can never be sure how the money supply will respond to a change in the monetary base. In the long run, the Fed has much more control over the money supply because the ratio of currency to deposits is not as unpredictable.

> The Fed does not have direct control over the money supply. It can control only the monetary base. The money supply itself will depend on: (1) the reserve/deposit ratio that banks hold, which depends in part on the reserve requirements imposed by the Fed as well as on the excess reserves desired by depository institutions, and (2) the public's desired currency/deposit ratio. The Fed's short-run control is less effective than its long-run control.

KEYNESIAN MONETARY POLICY

The income/expenditure model pioneered by Keynes viewed the role of money much differently from the classical simple quantity theorists, whose views were summarized in Chapter 10. The classical economists believed that the supply of money affected the level of money expenditures directly. With velocity (V) constant and the economy tending to operate automatically at full employment, the equation of exchange ($MV = PQ$) showed that aggregate expenditures rise at the same rate as the money supply (M). However, classical quantity theorists did not believe that the quantity of money had any effect on real GDP or employment because of the natural tendency for economies to operate at full employment. Rather, they argued that increases in money supply translated into proportionate increases in the price level.

Keynes viewed the link between the money supply and desired aggregate expenditures in a different light. He rejected the two classical notions of fixed velocity and full employment. Keynes believed that velocity could fluctuate unpredictably, as could real GDP; therefore, he believed the direct link between the money supply (M) and aggregate expenditures (PQ) was weak and unstable.

Instead, Keynes proposed an indirect link between the money supply (M) and real GDP (Y). This indirect relationship would operate through the effect of money supply on interest rates. By affecting real investment and perhaps even real consumption expenditures, changes in the interest rate would have an indirect effect on real output. (See Example 1.)

> In the Keynesian model, monetary policy affects output indirectly through interest rates.

The following sections will trace these indirect linkages between money and output, starting with the relationship between money and interest rates.

From Interest Rates to Aggregate Demand

Given the relationship between bond prices and interest rates (explained in Chapter 14), Fed open-market operations can have a direct impact on interest rates. When the Fed purchases government securities, the increased demand for those bonds will drive up their prices and, thus, lower interest rates. When the Fed sells government securities, the increased supply of those bonds will drive down their prices and, thus, raise interest rates. A similar phenomenon occurs if banks purchase or sell government securities. If banks expand the money supply by buying government securities, bond prices will rise and interest rates will fall. If banks contract the money supply by selling government securities that they own, bond prices will fall and interest rates will rise.

The exact impact that changes in the money supply have on interest rates depends on the responsiveness of the quantity of money demanded to the rate of interest. Chapter 14 explained the Keynesian liquidity preference theory of the demand for money. According to this theory, monetary authorities can control interest rates by controlling the supply of money. By increasing the money supply, monetary authorities can drive down the rate of interest. By reducing the supply of money, monetary authorities can raise the rate of interest.

EXAMPLE 1 The Money Supply and Bank Loans

Bank loans to businesses and consumers are a major channel through which monetary policy affects the economy. Loans made to businesses finance new investment, and loans made to consumers finance durable goods purchases. Loans constitute about three-fourths of the banking system's interest-earning assets (one-fourth of the total is commercial, almost one-third is for real estate, and about one-seventh is for individuals).

After the United States went into recession in 1990, the Fed moved to lower interest rates. In September 1990, 3-month Treasury bills yielded 7.36 percent annually; by September 1991, the rate had fallen to about 5.25 percent annually. This easing of monetary policy, as markets perceived it, apparently had little effect on bank loans. An economist for the Bank of America, Steven A. Wood, took such evidence as suggesting that the Fed has "less ability to stimulate the economy today than it had in the past."

Some experts think that one of the reasons the Fed may have had difficulty getting banks to increase the number of loans is that capital requirements were increased in response to the banking crises of the late 1980s and early 1990s. Yet, this requirement could be overcome by providing more reserves than would otherwise be necessary. A deeper analysis suggests that the breakdown in the short-run relationship between the money supply and bank loans was due to bank deregulation in the early 1980s. Economist George A. Kahn of the Kansas City Fed stated: "Since the removal of interest rate ceilings on deposit accounts in the early 1980s, a greater proportion of the monetary aggregates pay a market-related rate of interest." Thus, a given increase in the monetary base will cause a smaller increase in the money supply because lower interest rates lead to a smaller increase in M2. This does not mean that the Fed has lost its ability to affect the money supply in the long run, but its short-run impact may have been lessened. This may be another unintended consequence of the deregulation of the early 1980s.

Sources: George A. Kahn, "Does More Money Mean More Bank Loans," *Economic Review of the Federal Reserve Bank of Kansas City* (July/August 1991); Kenneth Gilpin, "Uneven Economic Recovery Shakes Faith in Fed's Power," *New York Times*, September 3, 1991.

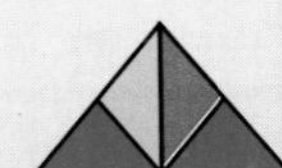

In Figure 1, the money demand curve is shown by the liquidity preference curve, LP. The intersection of the money demand curve with the money supply curve determines the current interest rate. Thus, the interest rate falls from r to r' when the money supply increases from M to M', *ceteris paribus.* A greater supply of money induces lending institutions (banks, savings and loan associations, insurance companies) to make more loans, which drives down the market rate of interest. The extent to which the interest rate falls depends on the responsiveness of the money demand to the rate of interest. If the LP curve is very flat, so that the quantity of money demanded is highly responsive to the interest rate, a very small change in the rate of interest is enough to induce people to hold a larger stock of money. If the LP curve is very steep, so the quantity of money demanded is relatively insensitive to the interest rate, a very large change in the rate of interest is needed to induce people to hold a larger stock of money.

> An increase in the supply of money drives down interest rates as long as the money demand—or liquidity preference—curve is constant.

Figure 2 shows that at higher interest rates, less investment is demanded and that at lower interest rates, more investment is demanded. Figure 3 shows how the interaction between money and investment markets depicted in Figures 1 and 2 can affect the economy's level of output.

FIGURE 1
The Demand and Supply of Money and the Interest Rate

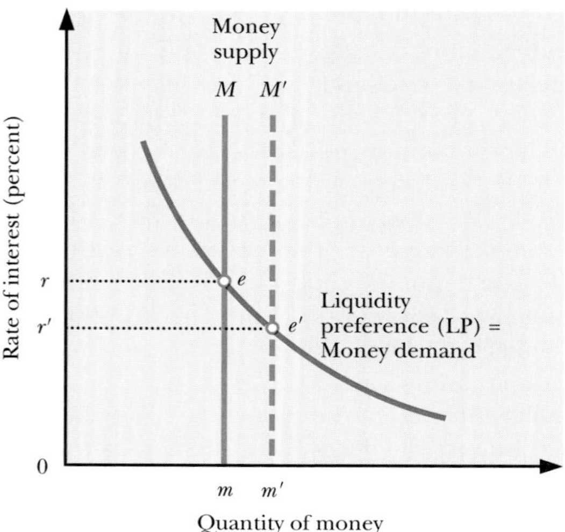

The money demand curve, or liquidity preference curve, has a negative slope. The amount of money demanded by the economy is greater at low rates of interest than at high rates of interest because the interest rate is the opportunity cost of holding money. The supply of money is determined by monetary authorities. The market interest rate (r) will be the equilibrium rate at which the quantity of money demanded (m) equals the quantity of money supplied. As monetary authorities increase the supply of money from m to m', the interest rate falls from r to r', *ceteris paribus.*

FIGURE 2
The Effect of Interest Rate Changes on Investment

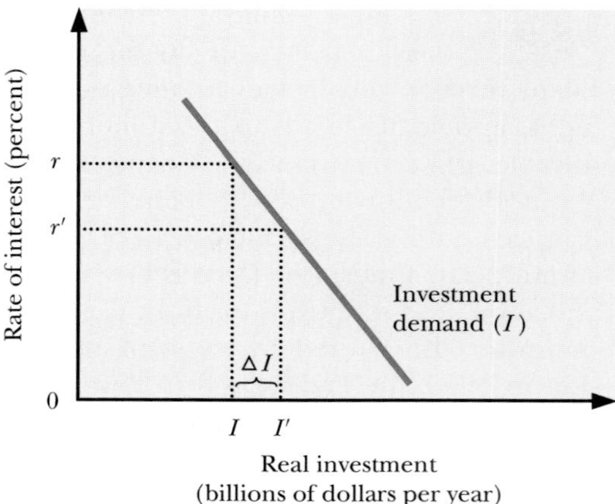

More real investment takes place at lower rates of interest than at higher rates of interest, *ceteris paribus.* Any monetary policy that lowers the interest rate will stimulate investment, *ceteris paribus.*

If the Fed increases the money supply, the rate of interest falls and the quantity of investment demanded increases. This increased investment shifts the aggregate demand (AD) curve to the right. Figure 3 shows what happens when the money supply doubles if the initial price level is p_0. As the AD curve shifts horizontally (from AD to AD′), the economy moves from point e_0 to e_1, thereby increasing its output level at the initial price level p_0 from y_0 to y_1. The AD curve will shift to the right for any increase in the money supply as long as a decline in interest rates occurs and is accompanied by increasing investment.

The case of doubling the money supply allows us to examine the vertical distance between the AD curve and AD′ curve. To determine the vertical shift in the aggregate demand curve, we can ask what would keep aggregate expenditures the same when the money supply changes? Figure 3 shows that a doubling of prices would allow the economy to stay at y_0 when the money supply doubles. Even though money balances have doubled, the doubling of prices leaves *real money balances* (the supply of money adjusted for inflation) the same as before. People who now hold twice as much money as before may recognize there has been no real change. Accordingly, the interest rate and the quantity of investment demanded will remain at their original levels. Thus, when M doubles and p_0 doubles to $2p_0$, equilibrium output stays the same at y_0. The new aggregate demand curve, AD′, must, therefore, pass through the price level $2p_0$ at the income level y_0.

> When the money supply increases, the *horizontal* shift in the AD curve depends on the sensitivity of interest rates and investment to the money supply and on the marginal propensity to consume. The *vertical* shift will be in proportion to the change in the money supply.

FIGURE 3
The Effect on Aggregate Demand of Doubling the Money Supply

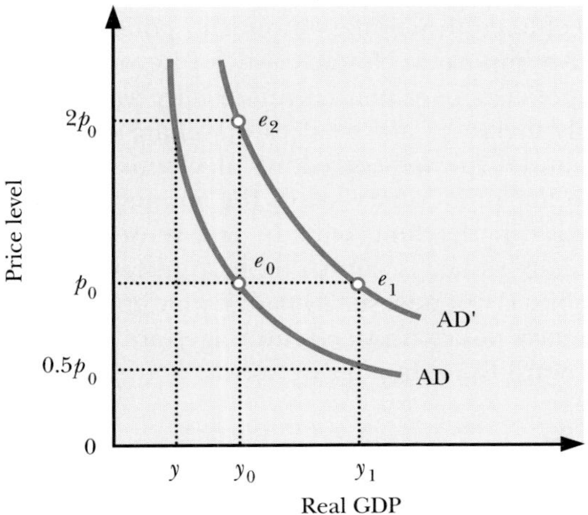

When the money supply increases, the interest rate falls, increasing investment and causing a rightward shift in the AD curve. The vertical shift in the AD curve is in the same proportion as the increase in the money supply. If the money supply doubles, AD′ will be exactly twice as high as AD.

FIGURE 4
Removing a Deflationary Gap

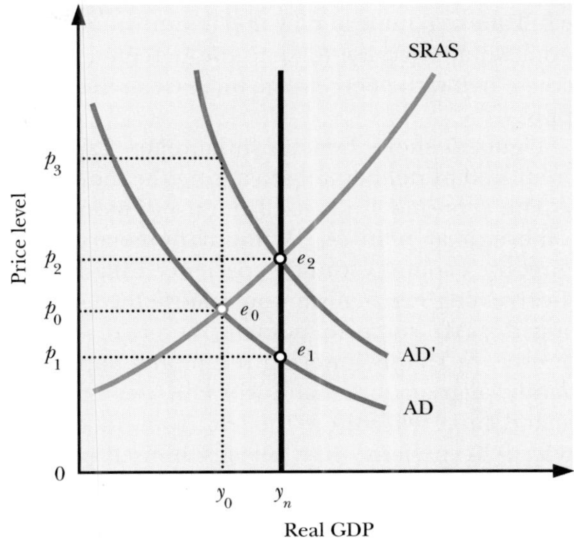

The economy is originally in short-run equilibrium at e_0, where the AD curve intersects the SRAS curve. A deflationary gap exists because y_0 is less than the natural level of output, y_n. The self-correcting mechanism would require deflation until the economy reaches e_1 on the AD curve. Increasing the money supply sufficiently, however, could shift the AD curve to AD′, thereby eliminating the deflationary gap.

Removing Deflationary and Inflationary Gaps

Chapter 9 explained that if there were a deflationary gap, monetary and fiscal authorities could follow a policy of nonaction, trusting that the self-correcting forces of deflation would return the economy to the natural level of output. In Figure 4, the economy finds itself in such a deflationary gap where the aggregate demand (AD) curve intersects the short-run aggregate supply (SRAS) curve to the left of the natural level of GDP. The self-correcting mechanism would eventually move the economy (through rightward shifts in the SRAS curve as prices fall) from point e_0 at price level p_0 to point e_1 at the lower price level p_1, restoring the economy to full-employment output, y_n.

Keynes believed that waiting for deflation to solve the problem wasted far too many economic resources. Instead of letting the self-correcting mechanism use deflation to return the economy to the natural level of output (which could be slow and painful), Keynes thought the money supply should be increased immediately. As shown in Figure 4, an appropriate increase in the money supply could shift AD to AD′, where the deflationary gap would be removed when the economy moved along the SRAS curve to e_2. Output would increase from y_0 to y_n and the price level would rise from p_0 to p_2. Notice that the increase in the price level from e_0 to e_2 does not correspond to the increase in the price level (from p_0 to p_3) that would be in proportion to the increase in the money supply, given the shift in the demand curve. Keynes differed with the simple quantity theory (described in Chapter 10) concerning the proportionality of the increases in the money supply and the price level. The simple quantity theory stated that increasing the money supply by, say, 10 percent would merely raise prices by 10 percent (because V and Q were assumed to be constant in the equation

$MV = PQ$). Keynes showed that with unemployed resources (a deflationary gap), an increase in the money supply would cause a less-than-proportionate change in the price level. Instead of prices rising by the full amount indicated by the quantity theory, real output would increase to keep the percentage price increase below the percentage increase in the money supply.

Figure 5 shows how an inflationary gap could be removed by deliberately changing the money supply. The economy finds itself in an inflationary-gap equilibrium at point e_0. Without monetary policy action, the economy would experience inflation; the self-correcting mechanism would move the economy along the AD curve to point e_2 at price level p_2. However, by simply lowering the money supply sufficiently, aggregate demand will fall (the aggregate demand curve will shift to the left, from AD to AD′). Modern Keynesians (like Keynes himself) believe that inflationary gaps will be removed more quickly than deflationary gaps by the self-correcting mechanism. Prices and wages rise more readily than they fall. Hence, Keynesians tend to be more activist with respect to expansionary monetary policy than with respect to contractionary monetary policy.

FIGURE 5
Removing an Inflationary Gap

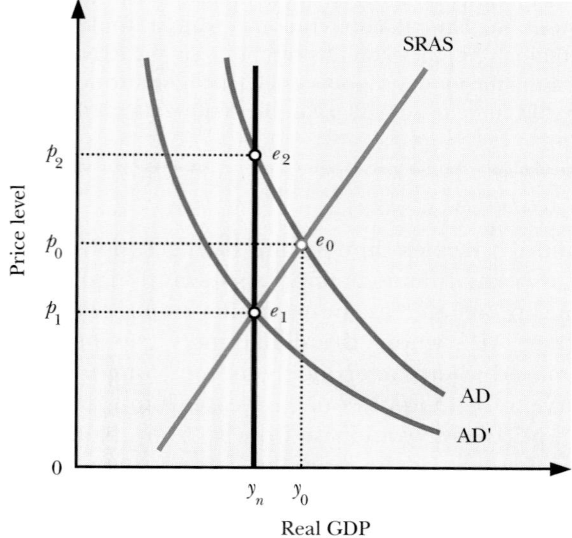

The economy is originally in short-run equilibrium at e_0, where the AD curve intersects the SRAS curve. An inflationary gap exists because y_0 exceeds the natural level of output, y_n. The self-correcting mechanism would require inflation until the economy reaches e_2 on the original AD curve. A sufficient decrease in the money supply, however, can shift the AD curve to AD′, thereby eliminating the inflationary gap.

An important characteristic of Keynesian monetary policy is its potential *inflationary bias.* If money supply increases are used to eliminate deflationary gaps and if the self-correcting mechanism is used to eliminate inflationary gaps, the money supply will increase in the long run. In this sense, Keynesian monetary policy is said to have an inflationary bias. This bias is not necessarily bad; it may be the optimal monetary policy if prices and wages are less flexible downward than they are upward.

Credit Rationing

In the Keynesian model, monetary policy works primarily through interest rates. When the Fed reduces the money supply, interest rates rise to choke off some investment. **Credit rationing** can, however, be used as a subsidiary instrument of monetary policy.

> **Credit rationing** occurs when interest rates are not allowed to rise to the rate at which the demand for loans equals the supply of loans. In this situation, the demand for investment funds at the prevailing interest rate exceeds the supply.

Credit rationing limits investment by making investment funds unavailable to some firms that are prepared to invest at prevailing interest rates. Although credit rationing and a decrease in the money supply work generally in the same direction, there is an important difference. A decrease in the money supply raises the interest rate, and as the interest rate rises, less investment is demanded. Credit rationing operates differently: controls on interest rates prevent them from rising to a new equilibrium when the supply of money is reduced. Firms are discouraged from investing not because of a reduced demand for investment, but because of a reduced availability of loans. Moreover, credit rationing typically tends to be less evenhanded than a decrease in the money supply. Often rules as to which customers will be granted credit are set by the Fed or by the lending institutions themselves.

THE FED'S MONETARY POLICY: TARGETS AND GOALS

Countercyclical versus Procyclical Monetary Policy

According to Keynesians, **countercyclical monetary policy** is preferable to **procyclical monetary policy.**

> A **countercyclical monetary policy** increases aggregate demand when output is falling too much (or when its rate of growth is declining) and reduces aggregate demand when output is rising too rapidly.
>
> A **procyclical monetary policy** decreases aggregate demand when output is falling and increases aggregate demand when output is rising.

The countercyclical prescription is clear: If there is a deflationary gap (a recession), increase the money supply; if there is an inflationary gap (a boom), reduce the money supply. In an economy where, over time, the resource base and the natural level of real GDP grow, these policy rules translate into changes in the *rates of monetary growth.* In recessions, the Fed should raise the rate of monetary growth; in booms, the Fed should lower the rate of monetary growth.

Has Fed monetary policy been countercyclical in actuality? We shall use the term *targets* to refer to monetary targets such as controlling M1, M2, or the monetary base. The term *goals* will refer to such objectives as reducing unemployment or reducing inflation. What have been the Fed's goals? The ultimate goals of monetary policy could include the achievement of certain levels of unemployment or output, a certain rate of inflation, a certain interest rate, or perhaps even a certain exchange rate for the U.S. dollar (how many French francs or British pounds it takes to buy a U.S. dollar). This chapter will concentrate on the output goals of monetary policy. Other chapters will examine how monetary policy can affect inflation, the interaction of inflation and unemployment, interest rates, and the value of the dollar.

FIGURE 6
Yearly Growth Rates in M1: 1960–1991

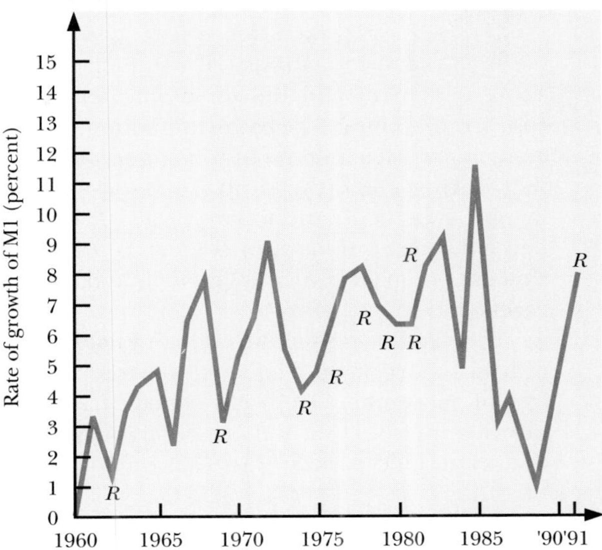

Yearly growth rates in the money supply (from December of the preceding year to December of the given year) from 1960 to 1984 fluctuated between highs (peaks) and lows (troughs). With the exceptions of 1982 and 1991, years of recession (marked with an *R*) were accompanied by troughs in the rate of monetary growth. In later years, policy apparently became countercyclical. In 1984, monetary growth was relatively low, yet the economy was booming.

Sources: *Economic Report of the President; Federal Reserve Bulletin.*

Figure 6 shows the yearly rates of growth in the money supply (measured from December of the previous year to December of the indicated year) from 1960 to 1991. The graph shows that until recently, the Fed did not pursue a countercyclical monetary policy.[2] Notice that the rate of monetary growth passed through various peaks and troughs. If monetary policy were countercyclical, the peaks of monetary growth should correspond to recessions and the troughs of monetary growth should

[2]See Robert J. Gordon, *Macroeconomics,* 5th ed. (New York: HarperCollins, 1990). For a more detailed study, see Alan S. Blinder, *Economic Policy and the Great Stagflation* (New York: Academic Press, 1979).

EXAMPLE 2 The 1990–1992 Recession

The period of recession from 1990 to 1992 followed an 8-year period of expansion. Industrial production fell about 5 percent and the unemployment rate rose from about 5.5 percent to about 7.3 percent, making it a mild recession. Figure 6 shows that during 1989, the supply of money grew by only 1 percent; and during 1990, by only 4 percent. Some might even conjecture that the slow rate of growth in 1989 contributed to the recession.

The Fed's response was very dramatic. The official report of the Fed's open-market meeting of November 13, 1990 stated that "the information reviewed at this meeting suggested that economic activity was weakening in the fourth quarter." Without revealing its hand, the report suggested a completely ambiguous policy: "slightly greater reserve restraint might or somewhat lesser reserve restraint would be acceptable . . . " The Fed then began to increase the monetary base at a very rapid pace. In January 1991 the monetary base grew at an annual rate of over 20 percent! A few months later the rate of monetary growth increased substantially. Over the year, from January 1991 to January 1992 the monetary base increased by about 7.4 percent, a larger than average increase. As a consequence, M1 increased by almost 9 percent.

Source: *Federal Reserve Bulletin,* February 1991, 102–103.

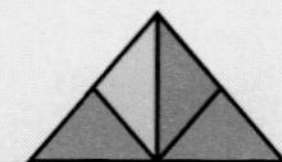

correspond to inflationary gaps. In general, the opposite holds: monetary policy has been procyclical (troughs of monetary growth correspond to recessions, and peaks of monetary growth correspond to booms).

Each recession (a period in which growth rates in real GDP were either negative or significantly less than average) is marked by an *R* on the curve. With only two exceptions (1982 and 1991), the recessions occur at the troughs of monetary expansion. Instead of rapid monetary growth that pulls the economy out of a recession, the historical record shows that monetary growth has been slow during the recession stage of the business cycle. The two exceptions indicate that the Fed now appears to be following a countercyclical policy. Example 2 shows that in the recession from 1990 to 1992, the Fed acted vigorously to increase the supply of money and credit.

The 1986 boom in the money supply represents a special case. In 1986, the economy was in the fourth year of a business-cycle expansion period. The main reason that the Fed kept the money supply pumped up is that the demand for M1 was increasing abnormally because of the inclusion of NOW accounts in the definition of M1.

> Historically, the Fed has followed policies that are procyclical (that is, growth rates of the money supply have decreased in recessions or increased in booms). Recent Fed behavior has been more countercyclical.

Control Interest Rates or Control the Money Supply?

Why did the Fed historically follow a procyclical monetary policy? One answer is that until recently, the Fed has preferred to set an **interest-rate target** rater than a **monetary-aggregate target.**

> An **interest-rate target** is a rate of interest that the Fed seeks to achieve through its monetary policy.
>
> A **monetary-aggregate target** is a particular money supply or growth rate of the money supply that the Fed seeks to achieve through its monetary policy.

According to the Keynesian model, monetary policy works through interest rates. Should monetary policy try to set interest rates and not worry about how much the money supply must rise or fall to achieve the desired interest rate? Or should monetary authorities set a target money supply and not worry about the effect of this money supply on interest rates? *Monetary economists generally favor controlling the money supply* without excessive worry about interest rates. They argue that the pursuit of interest-rate targets destabilizes the economy.

Assume, for example, that the economy is in a boom period and that monetary authorities, following an interest-rate target policy, decide to hold interest rates constant. But economic expansion increases the demand for credit, and this increased demand starts to drive up interest rates. To hold interest rates down, therefore, the Fed must create even more money. The increased money supply will further feed the boom. Likewise, when the economy is depressed, the demand for credit will contract and threaten to push down interest rates. For monetary authorities to hold the interest rate constant, they must reduce the supply of money, thereby depressing economic conditions even further.

> The pursuit of rigid interest-rate targets exaggerates the business cycle by leading to a procyclical monetary policy.

Setting flexible interest-rate targets could work if the Fed knew the interest rate that would lead to full employment. The Fed could then change the money supply until that interest-rate target was achieved. Unfortunately, it is very difficult to know the right interest rate. Recall from Chapter 14 the distinction between nominal and real interest rates: *Nominal interest rates* are the explicit rates charged by banks or earned (in nominal dollars) on various bonds; *real interest rates* are the nominal interest rates adjusted for inflation. The rate of interest the Fed should target to obtain full employment is the anticipated real interest rate (the nominal interest rate minus the anticipated inflation rate) that generates the level of investment demand corresponding to the natural level of real GDP. *But nobody knows the anticipated inflation rate that people have in mind at every point in time.* The Fed can affect only the nominal rate of interest. The Fed does not control inflationary expectations, and economists can only guess at the expected inflation rate. Thus, any interest-rate target is likely to be wrong at any given time.

Prior to October 1979, the Fed's monetary policy was directed toward setting interest-rate targets. This policy meant that the growth of the money supply was dictated by the interest-rate targets and the demand for money. If very rapid growth of the money supply was required to achieve a target rate of interest, so be it.

The procyclical behavior of the money supply observed in Figure 6 is clearly consistent with the hypothesis of interest-rate targeting by the Fed. As we pointed out, the pursuit of interest-rate targets is likely to speed monetary expansion during booms (since the demand for money is high) and to slow monetary expansion during recessions (since the demand for money is low).

The Experiment with Money Supply Targeting: 1979–1982

In October 1979, the Fed made the important decision to base monetary policy on monetary-aggregate targets and let interest rates settle at the level dictated by the targeted money supply. The Fed set a target range of growth rates for the money supply and used its control of the money supply to keep monetary growth within these target ranges. The Fed's move was inspired by then Fed Chairman Paul T. Volcker, who argued that control of the money supply was necessary to control the rate of inflation (in 1979, inflation was running at an annual rate of 9 percent). According to the operating procedure adopted in October 1979, the Fed would set specific target growth rates for the money supply. Although the Fed had set money growth targets prior to 1979 (see Table 2), the Fed decided to stop manipulating interest rates and to start focusing on the money supply targets. The Fed still planned to monitor interest rates, but only to prevent wild swings in interest rates arising from short-run changes in the demand for money.

The Fed's experiment with strict money-supply targeting did not last long. Initially, inflation increased from 9 percent in 1979 to 9.7 percent in 1981 (measured by the GDP price deflator). But the reduced rate of growth in the money supply from 1979 to 1981 helped push the inflation rate, as well as real GDP, down by 1982. The inflation rate dropped to 6.4 percent in 1982, and unemployment rose to

TABLE 2
M1 and M2 Growth versus Fed Targets

Time Period*	Targeted Range for M1 (annual percentage)	Targeted Range for M2 (annual percentage)	Actual M1 Growth (annual percentage)	Actual M2 Growth (annual percentage)
1977–1978	4–6.5	6.5–9	7.3	8.0
1978–1979	1.5–4.5	5–8	5.5	7.8
1979–1980	3.5–6	6–9	6.7	8.9
1980–1981	3–5.5	5.5–8.5	5.1	9.9
1981–1982	2.5–5.5	6–9	8.5	9.0
1982–1983	4–8	7–10	10.4	12.2
1983–1984	4–8	6–9	5.8	8.0
1984–1985	4–7	6–9	11.9	8.7
1985–1986	3–8	6–9	15.3	8.5
1986–1987	3–8	5.5–8.5	5.8	3.9
1987–1988	—	4–8	3.5	5.3
1988–1989	—	3–7	1.0	5.0
1989–1990	—	3–7	4.0	3.7
1990–1991	—	2.5–6.5	8.0	3.0

*Time periods are from the fourth quarter of the start year to the fourth quarter of the end year, except for 1982–1983.

Source: St. Louis Federal Reserve Bank, *Federal Reserve Bulletin,* various issues

9.5 percent. As the economy moved into a recession, the Fed suspended its 1982 target range of 2.5 percent to 5 percent and allowed the money supply to rise by 8.5 percent during 1982. In 1983, the inflation rate dropped to 3.8 percent and unemployment remained high. The Fed again suspended its 1982 target range of 4 percent to 8 percent and increased the money supply by more than 10 percent.

The experiment in money supply targeting seemed to represent a turning point in Fed policy. It marked the transition between a fairly definite procyclical policy to one that now appears to be countercyclical (see Example 2 again).

Current Fed Targeting

The Fed's actual behavior since 1977 is recorded in Table 2. The table shows that the Fed has departed significantly from its M1 growth targets, but not much from its M2 growth targets. Since 1979, the Fed has exceeded its M1 target range five times out of seven and has exceeded its M2 target range only two times.

One simple explanation for the Fed's behavior is that although it still abides by the October 1979 decision, recent financial innovations have increased the importance of M2 and reduced the importance of M1. As pointed out in Chapter 14, interest-bearing NOW accounts are now a major component of M1. The Fed has maintained that such accounts are in part savings accounts rather than transactions accounts. Thus, including them in M1 overstates the extent to which the money supply is really increasing. Because NOW accounts diluted the meaning of M1, the Fed decided in 1987 not to establish specific targets for M1. Fed policy now emphasizes M2. (See Example 3.)

THE EFFECTIVENESS OF MONETARY POLICY

The Limitations of Monetary Policy

The old saying, "You can take a horse to water but you can't make him drink" has been applied to monetary policy. Basically, all the Fed can do to expand the money supply is to make additional monetary reserves available to the banking system. It cannot

EXAMPLE 3 Understanding the Behavior of M2

The Fed's recent reliance on M2 is based on some impressive statistical evidence. In a study prepared by Fed economists, the changes in the demand for M2 could be readily explained by nominal GDP, personal consumption expenditures, and the opportunity cost of holding M2. Since most M2 balances pay interest, the opportunity cost of holding M2 is defined as the 3-month Treasury bill rate minus the average rate paid on M2 deposits. The Fed study found that M2 demand "unfolded smoothly over time" in response to changes in the above variables. It takes less than 1 year for M2 demand to respond to changes in GDP, and about a year and a half to respond fully to changes in opportunity costs. But they found that the response of M2 demand to changes in opportunity cost was relatively small: a 10 percent increase in opportunity costs would reduce the demand for M2 by only $\frac{1}{2}$ of 1 percent.

Source: "Understanding the Behavior of M2 and V2," *Federal Reserve Bulletin*, April 1989, 237–44.

force banks to lend out these reserves and expand the money supply. Nor can it force businesses to increase their investment borrowing when interest rates drop. The use of monetary policy to induce the economy to increase investment can be like pushing on a string. If banks do not loan out additional reserves or if business firms do not invest more when interest rates drop, the monetary authorities are pushing on a string. Monetary authorities may be more effective when they *pull* on the string. When they wish to contract the money supply, authorities can withdraw reserves and force a contraction of the money supply. If firms do not respond to higher interest rates by investing less, the monetary authorities can always use credit rationing to restrict investment.

The links on the chain connecting the money supply and desired aggregate expenditures in the Keynesian model can be very fragile. A link can break at any point in the chain. If increases in the money supply fail to lower interest rates or if changes in interest rates fail to elicit changes in investment, changes in the money supply will exert no pressure on desired aggregate expenditures. Moreover, even if the chain is not broken, the effects may be very weak or take some time to occur. Interest rates may respond only weakly to changes in the money supply; investment demand may be very insensitive to changes in interest rates.

For these reasons, Keynes believed that monetary policy would be less effective than fiscal policy in combating severe unemployment.

The Problem of Lags

If the monetary authorities can recognize an inflationary or a deflationary gap, and if the effects of the change in the money supply take place *before* the self-correcting mechanism solves the problem, discretionary monetary policy can stabilize the economy. One possible problem with discretionary monetary policy is that there is a **recognition lag** and an **effectiveness lag** between a monetary-policy action and its desired effect.

A **recognition lag** is the time it takes the Fed to decide to change the supply of money in response to a change in economic conditions.

An **effectiveness lag** is the time it takes the change in the money supply to affect the economy.

Modern economics, even with extensive data-gathering facilities, can never be sure of *current* economic conditions. We do not have an accurate estimate of GDP until several months after the fact. Unemployment and inflation data come in more quickly but they are still a couple of months old. Thus, nobody knows for sure what is happening at the current moment. The recognition lag may be about 4 months (as estimated by Robert Gordon). In other words, the Fed may need 4 months to identify an inflationary or deflationary gap and to initiate the appropriate technical procedures to expand or contract the money supply.

Estimates of the effectiveness lag vary widely. Robert Gordon estimates the effectiveness lag as short—from 5 to 10 months. Milton Friedman estimates the effectiveness lag as long and variable—from 6 months to 2 years.

The total lag (the sum of the recognition and effectiveness lags), according to Gordon, varies from 9 to 14 months; according to Friedman, the total lag varies from 10 months to more than 2 years. Who are we to believe? It could be that both are right. Gordon's estimates are based on recent business-cycle experience; Friedman's estimates are based on averages over nearly a century. It is possible that, as a result of improvements in communication and information, the lags have become shorter in recent years. Time will tell whether the lags are short but variable or long but variable.

If lags are short, the argument for activist monetary policy is strong. With short lags, the monetary authorities stand a better chance of adopting the correct countercyclical policy. If a deflationary gap develops (threatening a recession), a 5-month effectiveness lag means that an expansionary monetary policy will be felt 5 months after recognition of the problem. A 2-year lag means that the effects of the policy will be felt 2 years after recognition of the problem. By that time, the economy may be in a boom that requires a contraction in the money supply. Keynesian economists tend to believe that lags are short and that activist policy can be used to iron out many fluctuations in real GDP.

Even if lags are short but variable, monetary policy should not try to smooth out every small inflationary or deflationary gap. If a deflationary gap is relatively small, the self-correcting mechanism may do its work before the effects of monetary policy can take place. Thus, most Keynesians now believe that policymakers should not try to fine-tune the economy but rather, should aim at correcting only significant inflationary or deflationary gaps.

The Monetarist Response to Monetary-Policy Limitations

If lags are long but variable, what monetary policy should be followed? Milton Friedman has argued that the Fed should follow a **constant-money-growth rule:** the money supply should grow at a fixed percentage (Friedman usually says 3 percent) per year.

> The **constant-money-growth rule** states that the money supply should increase at a fixed percentage each year.

The justification for the constant-growth rule is that if the monetary lag varies between 10 months and 28 months, by the time the effects of any monetary policy are felt, the original reasons for the policy may have disappeared through the self-correcting mechanism. More likely than not, by the time the policy is felt, it may be that the exact opposite of the policy is required. The choice of a constant growth rate (whether it be 2, 3, or 4 percent) depends on the long-term growth of real GDP (which, historically, has averaged about 3 percent per year). Friedman argues that if we knew more about the economy (for example, if we knew the length of the effectiveness lag), we could possibly control the business cycle better, but given present knowledge and the lags involved, an activist monetary policy (and also fiscal policy) may be destabilizing. The nonactivist policy of Milton Friedman and economists such as Karl Brunner and Allan Meltzer is known as **monetarism.**

> **Monetarism** is the doctrine that monetary policy should follow a constant-money-growth rule.

Some economists, journalists, and politicians have identified the Fed's self-imposed constraints on monetary growth rates from 1979 to 1982 as an experiment in monetarism. Franco Modigliani has argued that this interpretation is not correct, because the growth rate of the money supply was far from constant. (See Example 4.)

The debate between the monetarists and the Keynesians over whether or not to pursue an activist monetary policy is an important one and will be discussed extensively in the next section and the next few chapters.

EXAMPLE 4 Modigliani on the Fed's "Monetarist Experiment"

In October of 1979, the Fed decided to change from interest-rate targeting to targeting growth rates of money. It also decided to target gradual reductions in the growth of money over the next few years. Although many experts felt that the Fed had embraced monetarism, experience has shown that this was far from a monetarist experiment. Monetarism is a belief that the macroeconomy is relatively stable and can correct itself without outside intervention. The foundation of monetarism is the belief in a constant growth of the money supply irrespective of current economic conditions.

Nobel laureate Franco Modigliani has reviewed the "monetarist experiment" of the Fed from 1979 to 1983 and concludes that the Fed never embraced monetarism during this period. First, Modigliani finds that the Fed adopted broad target ranges of monetary growth throughout the period. Typically, the Fed set money-growth targets that had ranges of from 2.5 to 3 percentage points. With a target growth of 3 percent, such broad ranges mean that growth rates of from zero to 6 percent would be within the acceptable range. This range is far from the constant money-growth target that the monetarists desire. Second, the Fed typically set growth targets for four monetary aggregates, and these targets generally could not be expected to be consistent. The setting of four targets meant that the Fed could use its discretion to decide which targets to meet. Third, Modigliani finds that the Fed's decision to target monetary aggregates (rather than interest rates) was based on convenience rather than on monetarism. With high and variable inflation, it was proving difficult to set the appropriate interest rate, particularly with interest rates changing in response to inflationary expectations. Moreover, for political reasons, the Fed felt that it could not directly vote for interest rates that would be high enough to dampen inflation. Hence, by voting to slow the growth of the money supply, the Fed could raise interest rates indirectly without having to approve interest rates that would be politically unacceptable.

Source: Franco Modigliani, "The Monetarist Controversy Revisited," *Contemporary Policy Issues* 6 (October 1988): 3–17.

PRICE LEVEL STABILITY

Keynesian monetary policy suggests that the ultimate target of monetary policy should be the real interest rate. With a deflationary gap, the authorities should increase the money supply, lower the real rate of interest, and stimulate the economy through more spending on plant, equipment, housing, and durable consumer goods.

Milton Friedman, however, questioned whether the Fed had the ability to control real interest rates and, by extension, the economy because of lags and uncertainty. Recent monetarists argue that even if such lags were not present, there is no basis for using monetary policy to control the economy. Indeed, economists from Adam Smith to Irving Fisher considered real interest rates to be determined by factors such as productivity and thrift, not the money supply. In a recent summary of the evidence, British economists Terence Mills and Geoffrey Wood reported that for interest rates on longer-term assets there was no association between monetary growth and real interest rates in the United Kingdom between 1972 and 1984.[3] They summarized studies based on complicated statistical techniques that enable economists to see what would have happened if such factors as industrial production, unemploy-

[3]Terence Mills and Geoffrey Wood, "Interest Rates and the Conduct of Monetary Policy," in W. Eltis and P. Sinclear, *Keynes and Economic Policy* (London: Macmillan Press, 1988), 246–67.

ment, and the exchange rate had remained constant. Support for Mills' and Wood's results can be found in recent U.S. experience. Figure 7 shows virtually no relationship between quarterly M2 growth and changes in the 10-year yield on government bonds over 12 quarters. This evidence can, of course, be criticized for committing the *ceteris paribus* fallacy, but the work cited by Wood and Mills is not subject to this criticism.

If money growth cannot be expected to lower interest rates, what should be the objective of monetary policy? In previous chapters we have documented a fairly close relationship between the supply of money and the price level. Therefore, an appropriate objective of monetary policy would be a stable price level.

How stable should the price level be? Some economists think that the appropriate standard should be zero inflation. The reasons for this objective would be (1) unemployment tends to the natural rate in even a zero inflation world and (2) inflation makes comparison shopping more difficult for buyers and sellers. The first point follows from the analysis of the self-adjusting mechanism. The second follows from the fact that inflation complicates the problem of calculating relative prices. For example, outdated information may cause a shopper to think that one store charges more for a given product than another store. According to Mills and Wood:

> The step from a barter economy to a monetary one is enormous. Anything which makes money a less efficient conveyor of information about relative prices imposes great efficiency losses. Hence we should seek to stabilize the value of money. That is the only desirable objective of monetary policy.

FIGURE 7
The Money Supply and the Interest Rate

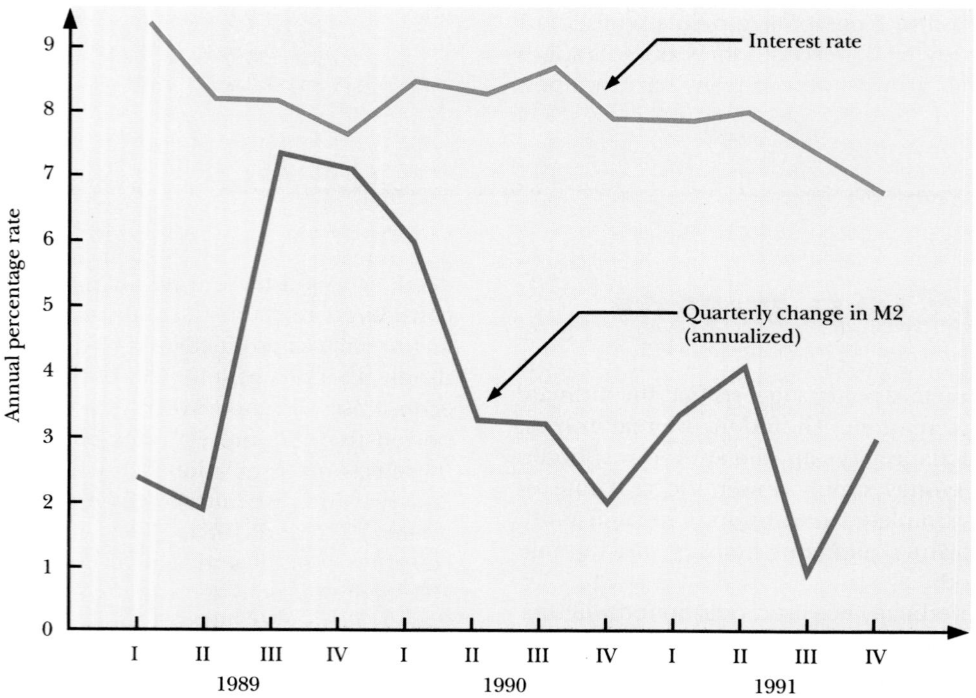

There is virtually no relationship between quarterly changes in M2 and interest rates on government bonds.

Keynesian economists sharply disagree with the objective of zero inflation. They believe that zero inflation may increase unemployment for the sake of an objective that does not seem that important. Keynesians do not think that a mild inflation of several percentage points is anything to worry about. After all, inflation just means higher prices on goods, services, and labor. Higher unemployment, by contrast, usually signifies that average living standards are falling.

THE INDEPENDENCE OF THE FED

Monetary policy is the responsibility of the Fed. The Fed's power to set money-supply and interest-rate targets is independent of Congress and the executive branch of the government. Recall from Chapter 15 that the Fed does not require financing from Congress; it is self-supporting. Moreover, members of the Board of Governors have 14-year, nonrenewable terms. The Fed can make decisions that the Secretary of the Treasury, the President of the United States, and congressional leaders all oppose. The authors of the 1913 Federal Reserve Act believed the Fed should be independent of political pressures. Opponents of an independent Fed disagree.

The Case for Fed Independence

The basic case for independence rests on three observations. First, if the Fed were under the direct control of politicians, the Fed would exhibit a stronger inflationary bias because, it is argued, politicians like to spend money but do not like to tax. With a cooperating Fed, government deficits could be easily financed by money expansion and inflation would be encouraged. Many countries with high rates of inflation have a central bank that is not independent. Nonelected, relatively anonymous central bankers can more easily adopt anti-inflationary policies than can elected officials.

Second, proponents of independence argue that the Fed can carry out long-term plans, whereas politicians can see no farther than the next election. There are fears of a so-called "political business cycle" (discussed in Chapter 19): politicians may try to engineer Fed policy to help them get reelected.

Third, proponents of Fed independence argue that the Fed will never go too strongly against the wishes of the electorate because the real independence of the Fed is somewhat constrained by political reality. If the Fed got out of hand, Congress could pass legislation reducing the Fed's independence.

The Case Against Fed Independence

Critics of Fed independence cite two important arguments. First, independence means that what may be the most important flexible policy tool available to the government is out of the hands of the electorate. Even if the public does not like Alan Greenspan (the Fed chairperson appointed by President Reagan in 1987 and reappointed by President Bush in 1991) or the other members of the Board of Governors, it can do nothing. The Fed cannot be thrown out of office like an unpopular and, perhaps, incompetent politician. Many believe that in a democracy, policy should be sensitive to the wishes of the public.

Second, critics of Fed independence point out that monetary policy and fiscal policy should be coordinated. Under the current system, it is possible for monetary and fiscal policy to work at cross-purposes. For example, imagine there is a large government deficit. The U.S. Treasury may want the Fed to expand the money supply rapidly to stimulate economic growth and, thus, reduce the deficit through increased tax revenues. If the Fed maintains a low rate of growth of the money supply, the government deficit is likely to increase.

The next chapter examines how fiscal policy and monetary policy can be used to control inflation.

SUMMARY

1. The Fed has an arsenal of weapons to control the money supply: open-market operations, control of the discount rate, control of the required-reserve ratio, and selective credit controls. By buying government securities, the Fed injects reserves into the system and expands the money supply. By selling government securities, the Fed withdraws reserves, and the money supply contracts. Changing reserve requirements can have a large impact on the money

supply because it creates excess reserves (when the rate is lowered) and because it creates reserve deficiencies when the rate is raised. This tool, however, is seldom used. Changes in the discount rate have a modest effect on bank reserves.

2. The money supply depends on the monetary base, the currency/deposit ratio, and the reserve/deposit ratio. The Fed's short-run control over the money supply is subject to unpredictable changes in the behavior of the public and banks. In the long run, the Fed can take changes in these factors into account.

3. Keynesian monetary policy is based on the indirect link between money supply and real GDP. Because bond prices and interest rates move inversely, increases in the money supply (in the short run) lower interest rates. The quantity of investment demanded rises when interest rates fall. In principle, inflationary and deflationary gaps can be removed by changes in the money supply.

4. In the past, the Fed's use of interest-rate targets rather than monetary growth targets tended to make changes in the money supply procyclical. Prior to October 1979, the Fed's interest-rate targets had priority over money growth targets, and Fed policy tended to destabilize the economy. After October 1979, the Fed's policy has been more flexible. Current policy appears to be countercyclical.

5. Keynesians believe that monetary policy should be used actively to remove major deflationary and inflationary gaps. Monetarists believe that lags in the effectiveness of monetary policy imply that a constant-money-growth rule should be used and that activist monetary policy can destabilize the economy.

6. Some monetarists maintain that the evidence shows that central banks cannot control real interest rates. To maintain the efficiency of a monetary economy in conveying relative price information, they believe that the central bank should simply try to stabilize the price level, an objective that seems to be within the power of the central bank. Keynesians believe that some inflation may be desirable to keep unemployment low.

7. Defenders of Fed independence stress that being independent reduces the inflationary bias of government policy and allows the Fed to have a longer time horizon than politicians have. An independent Fed can follow politically tough policies. Critics of Fed independence worry about the Fed being irresponsible to the electorate and working at cross-purposes with fiscal policy.

KEY TERMS

monetary policy
credit rationing
countercyclical monetary policy
procyclical monetary policy
interest-rate target
monetary-aggregate target
recognition lag
effectiveness lag
constant-money-growth rule
monetarism

QUESTIONS AND PROBLEMS

1. Describe briefly how the Fed uses its three major instruments of monetary control.
2. What is the most important instrument of monetary policy and why?
3. Evaluate the validity of the following statement: "The Fed controls the monetary base precisely, but not the money supply."
4. Explain what happens to interest rates if the Fed engages in open-market purchases of government securities.
5. If the newspaper reports, "The bond market is in the doldrums; it has been depressed all week," what is happening to interest rates?
6. Compare the impact on interest rates of a change in the money supply when
   a. The quantity of money demanded is highly responsive to interest rates.
   b. The quantity of money demanded is relatively insensitive to interest rates.
7. How does a change in the money supply increase real GDP?
8. What problems could arise to reduce the impact of a change in the money supply on real GDP?
9. Explain why the vertical shift in the aggregate demand curve attributable to monetary policy equals the percentage increased in the money supply.
10. What decision did the Fed make in October 1979? Did this decision result in a lasting change?
11. Why might rigid interest-rate targeting destabilize the economy?
12. Historically, has the Fed been Keynesian or monetarist in its approach to monetary policy?
13. Describe recent Fed policy.
14. How do lags in the effectiveness of monetary policy affect the design of a good monetary policy?

15. What are the arguments for targeting the price level as the only reasonable objective of monetary policy?
16. How can Fed independence reduce inflation?
17. How can Fed independence result in poor monetary policies?

SUGGESTED READINGS

Bryant, Ralph C. "Money and Monetary Policy." *The Brookings Review* (Spring 1983).

Friedman, Milton. *Money Mischief.* New York: Harcourt, Brace, Jovanovich, 1992.

Gordon, Robert J. *Macroeconomics,* 5th ed. New York: HarperCollins, 1990, chaps. 15 and 16.

Olsen, Leif H. "Is Monetarism Dead?" *The Cato Journal* (Fall 1986): 461–76.

"How Fed Reserve under Volcker Finally Slowed Down Inflation." *Wall Street Journal,* December 7, 1984.

"U.S. Monetary Policy in Recent Years: An Overview." *Federal Reserve Bulletin,* January 1985.

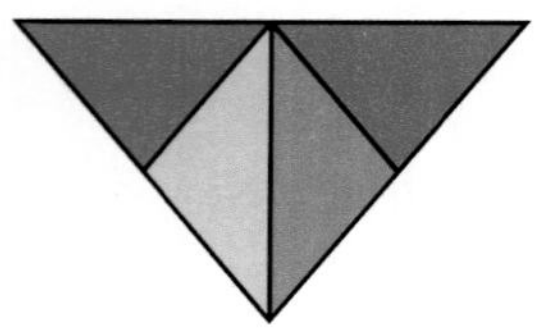

17

Inflation

CHAPTER INSIGHT

Rapid and accelerating inflation strikes great fear in people when it occurs, overshadowing other concerns, such as unemployment, the threat of nuclear war, or crime. During most periods, prices rise at a relatively slow pace. At other times, however, prices rise sharply. For example, between 1947 and 1972, it took a quarter of a century for the price level to double. Yet, between 1974 and 1984—a span of only a decade—the price level doubled again. Why did it take 25 years for prices to double in one period and only 10 years in another period? Why is inflation so variable?

This chapter focuses on the causes of inflation. It considers the relationships between the money supply and inflation, between government deficits and inflation, and between supply shocks and inflation. This chapter describes the causes of the wage/price spiral and spells out various approaches to curbing inflation, detailing the costs of each approach. Inflation's impact on income distribution was discussed in Chapter 6, and *stagflation*—the combination of high unemployment and rapid inflation—is the focus of Chapter 19.

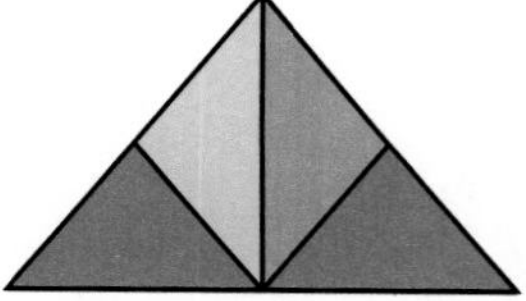

THE FACTS OF INFLATION

It is useful to begin a discussion of inflation with five basic facts:

1. Inflation is not inevitable.
2. Money and prices are positively associated.
3. Inflation rose in the 1970s and fell in the 1980s.
4. Inflation and interest rates are positively associated.
5. An inflationary trend has existed since the 1930s.

Inflation Is Not Inevitable

Figure 1, which shows the U.S. price level from 1800 to the present, demonstrates that, over the very long run, inflation is not inevitable. Prices in 1943 were about the same as prices in 1800! Until World War II, there was no definitive upward trend in prices. Rather, periods of inflation were followed by periods of deflation; the two tended to cancel each other out. Over the entire nineteenth century, the general price level went up and down again and again. In the mid-1930s, when the U.S. economy began its recovery from the Great Depression, prices began to rise. Since then, there have been few episodes of falling prices. Instead, the question has been whether prices are rising slowly or rapidly.

Some may argue that under present circumstances inflation is a fact of life. However, objective economic science cannot regard inflation in the same way as it regards the laws of scarcity or diminishing returns. Scarcity will always be present, as will

FIGURE 1
The U.S. Price Level, 1800–1992

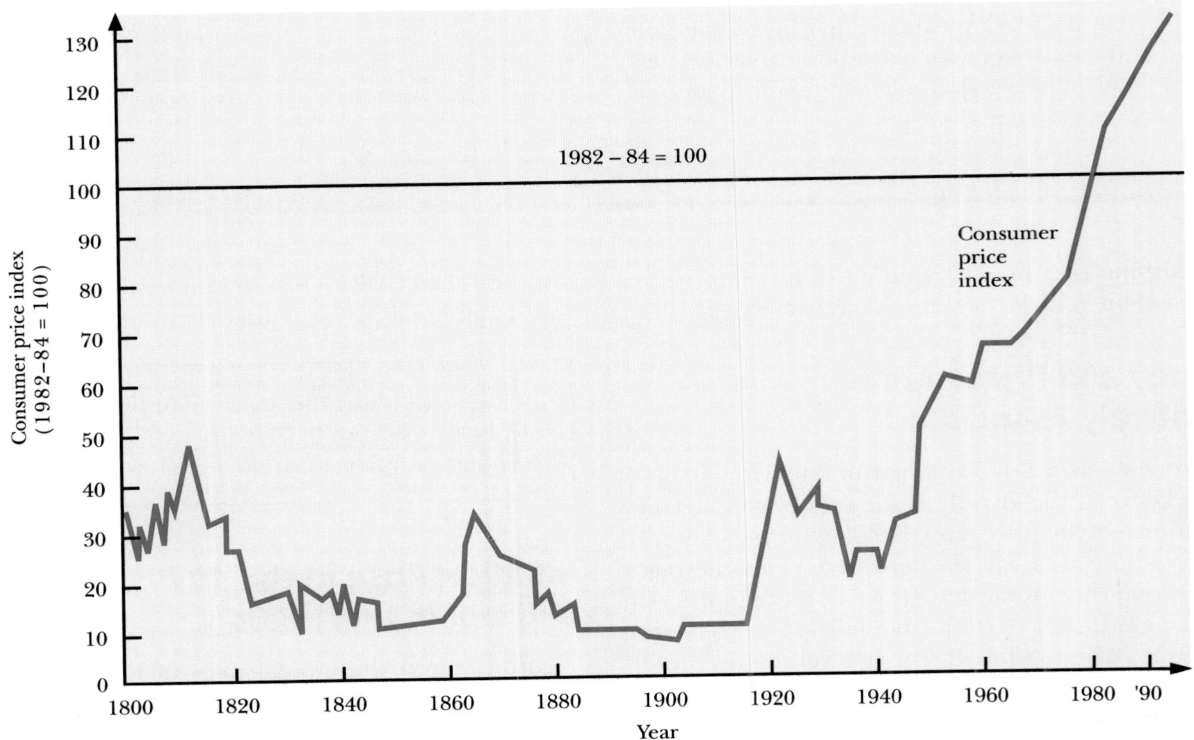

The price level has continuously risen since World War II, deviating from the pattern of the preceding 140 years.

Sources: *Historical Statistics of the United States; Economic Report of the President.*

EXAMPLE 1 The Case for Zero Inflation

Since the early 1980s, the United States has experienced inflation rates between 3 percent and 5 percent. It is clear that double-digit inflation, such as that experienced in the mid- and late 1970s, is destructive and should be avoided. Is moderate inflation, however, a sufficient worry to warrant adopting policies to achieve zero inflation?

Proponents of zero inflation make the following arguments:

1. Even moderate inflation causes people to engage in economically unproductive activities, such as investing in land or precious metals, instead of making more productive investments in plant and equipment. These unproductive activities reduce economic efficiency and growth.
2. Through the tax system, moderate inflation reduces long-term gains on invested capital. An investment that has earned 20 percent over a four-year period, earns virtually nothing after adjustment for moderate inflation, especially after investment earnings have been taxed.
3. Moderate inflation causes price system distortions. When prices are generally rising, information on relative prices becomes obscured. People do not know what the cheapest input combinations are or what the best buys are. When the price level is stable, however, people can be well informed about relative prices and make "good" economic decisions.

Advocates of zero inflation also point to the empirical finding that inflation tends to be negatively related to economic growth. The economies of countries with high inflation grow more slowly than those with low inflation. Proponents cite this finding as evidence that countries should aim for a zero rate of inflation.

Source: Lee Hoskins, "Defending Zero Inflation," *Quarterly Review*, Federal Reserve Bank of Cleveland, Spring 1991.

diminishing returns. The amount of inflation is, to some extent, a social decision. (See Example 1.)

Money and Prices Are Positively Associated

Figure 2 shows a positive long-run empirical association between the growth of the money supply and the growth of the price level. Despite this association, money and prices have not grown at the same rate in the long run; money has grown faster than prices. Between 1915 and 1991, the money supply (M1) rose by about 70 times while the price level rose by more than 13 times. The average annual rate of inflation since 1915 has been about 3.3 percent. The quantity theory (Chapter 10) predicted this relationship. The money supply grows more rapidly than the price level because more money is required to accommodate the larger quantity of real GDP. Between 1915 and 1991, real GDP increased 12 times.[1] More money was required just to keep prices constant.

> In the long run, the money supply tends to increase more rapidly than prices because rising real output holds down price increases.

Inflation Rose in the 1970s and Fell in the 1980s

Figure 3 shows the annual rates of inflation since 1951. The inflation rate, measured by either the

[1]The equation is $MV = PQ$. In the long run, Q rises with advancing technology and growth in the labor force. So M must rise to accommodate more Q, with V and P constant.

FIGURE 2
The Growth of the U.S. Money Supply and the Price Level, 1915–1991

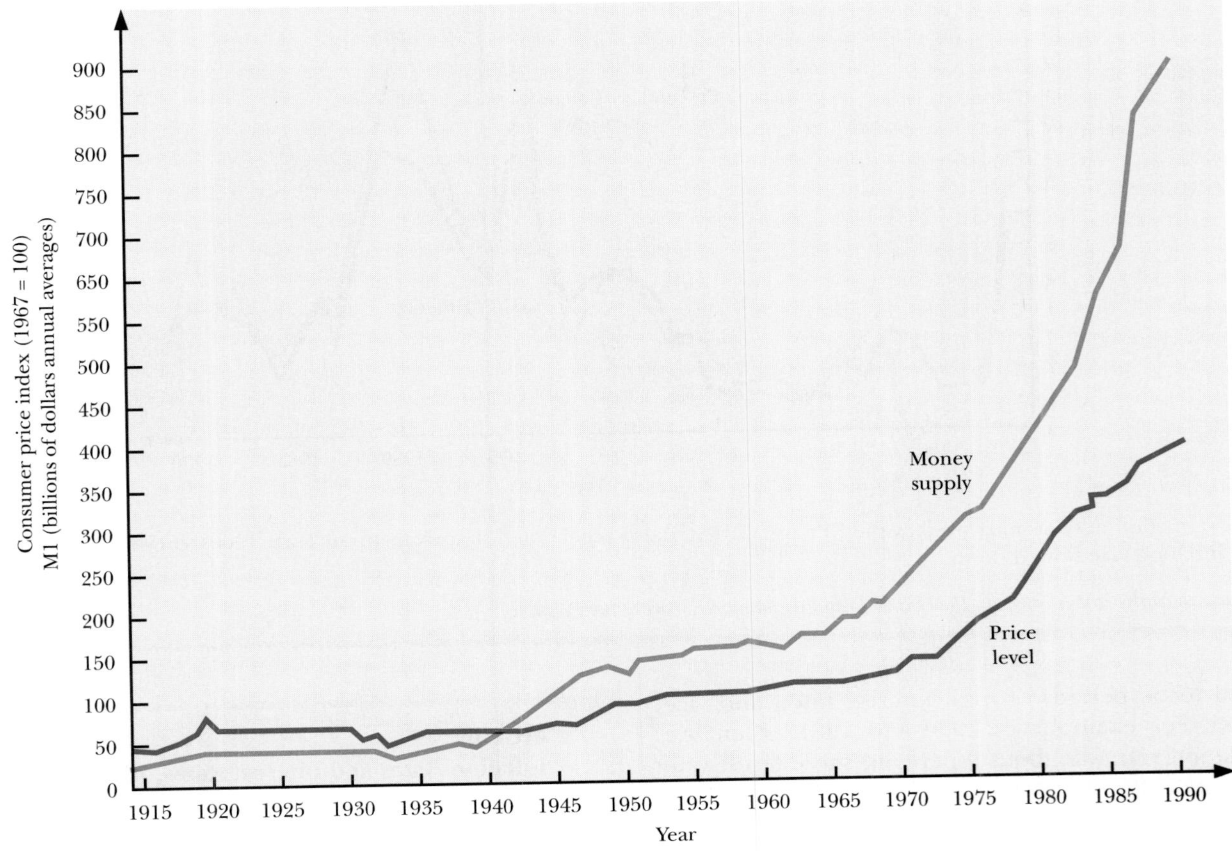

Changes in the money supply and changes in the price level have tended to move together, although without exact agreement. M1 has grown faster than the price level because the increase in real GDP over time absorbs some of the increase in M1.

Sources: *Historical Statistics of the United States,* 1970, 210–11, 992; *Economic Report of the President.*

consumer price index or the GDP deflator, rose throughout the 1970s, fell throughout the 1980s, and rose slightly in the early 1990s. Measured by the CPI, inflation reached a peak of 13 percent in 1980 (but only 9 percent when measured by the GNP deflator). From 1988 to 1991, the average inflation rate was about 4 percent, which was only slightly above the long-run average for this century. This chapter will explain why the inflationary experiences of the 1970s were so different from the 1980s and early 1990s.

Inflation and Interest Rates Are Positively Associated

Figure 4 shows the relationship between inflation rates and the interest rate for the period 1966 to 1991. If the relationship between inflation and interest rates is positive, the graph should show that interest rates tend to be high when inflation is high and low when inflation is low. The scatter diagram confirms a strong positive relationship: periods of rapid inflation

FIGURE 3
Inflation Trends, 1951–1991

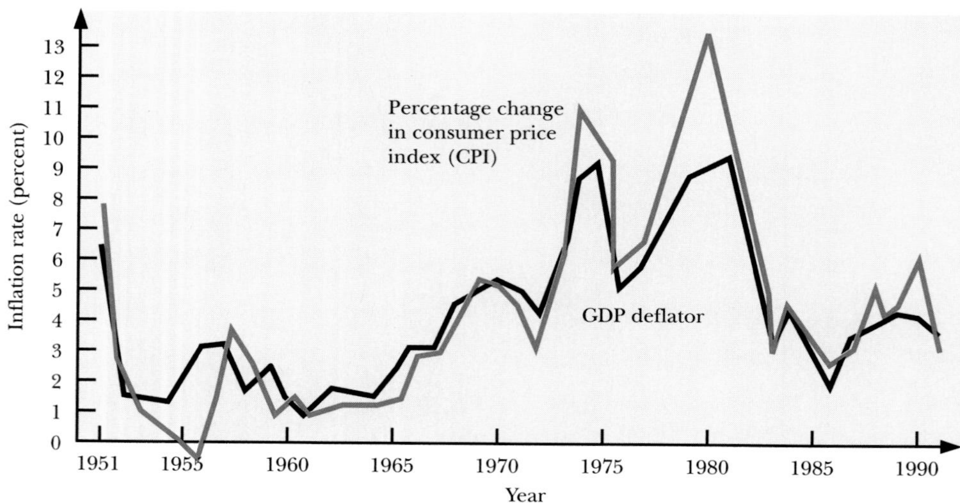

The rate of inflation as measured by the CPI and GDP deflator accelerated sharply from the early 1960s to 1981. After 1981, the inflation rate slowed down.

Sources: *Statistical Abstract of the United States; Economic Report of the President.*

tend to be periods of high interest rates, and vice versa. For example, in 1980 and 1981, when the inflation rate was about 9 percent, the interest rate was between 12 and 14 percent. In 1971 and 1972, when the inflation rate was between 4 and 5 percent, the interest rate was less than 5 percent. In 1991, the inflation rate was about 3 percent and the interest rate was about 5.5 percent. Figure 4 demonstrates that the relationship between inflation and interest rates is not simple. The fact that the dots do not lie on a straight line shows that factors other than the current rate of inflation also affect nominal interest rates.

FIGURE 4
Inflation Rates and Interest Rates, 1966–1991

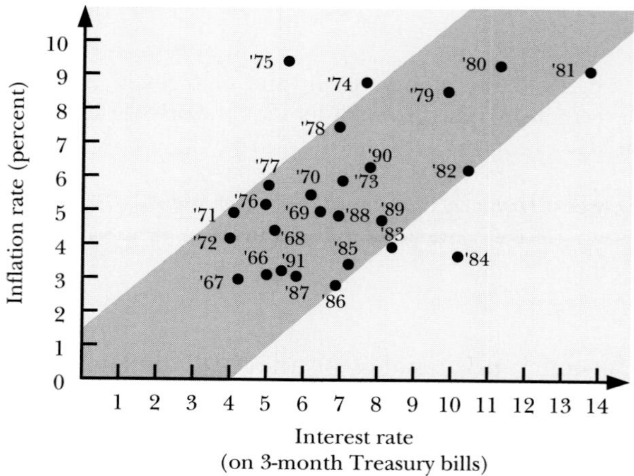

This scatter diagram reveals a strong positive relationship between rapid inflation and high interest rates.

Sources: *Economic Report of the President; Federal Reserve Bulletin.*

An Inflationary Trend Has Existed Since the 1930s

Figure 1 showed no clear-cut trend in the price level from 1800 to the 1930s. For more than a century, prices were as likely to decrease as to increase. Since the mid-1930s, there has been a clear inflationary bias in the United States. Periods of declining prices (deflation) have ceased to cancel out periods of rising prices. Since the early 1930s, the question has been

not whether prices would rise but by how much. This chapter will explain why the past 60 years have been characterized by the presence of inflation and the absence of deflation.

THE CAUSES OF INFLATION

Any good theory of inflation should account for the above five facts of inflation. The previous chapters used aggregate supply and aggregate demand to explain how real output, employment, and the price level are determined. They showed why the short-run aggregate supply curve is positively sloped, why the aggregate demand curve is negatively sloped, and why economies tend to produce the natural level of output in the long run.

Aggregate supply-and-demand analysis suggests the existence of two general types of inflation: **demand-side inflation** and **supply-side inflation.**

> **Demand-side inflation** occurs when aggregate demand increases and pulls prices up.
>
> **Supply-side inflation** occurs when aggregate supply declines and pushes prices up.

Figure 5 illustrates both types of inflation using the tools of aggregate supply-and-demand analysis. These diagrams show short-run effects only; they do not show what happens to prices, output, and employment as the self-correcting mechanism does its work.

Demand-side Inflation

In panel *a* of Figure 5, the economy is initially operating at point *e*, where output is y and the price level is p. Chapter 9 explained in detail why increases in the price level induce the economy's firms to pro-

FIGURE 5
Demand-side versus Supply-side Inflation

(*a*) Demand-side Inflation

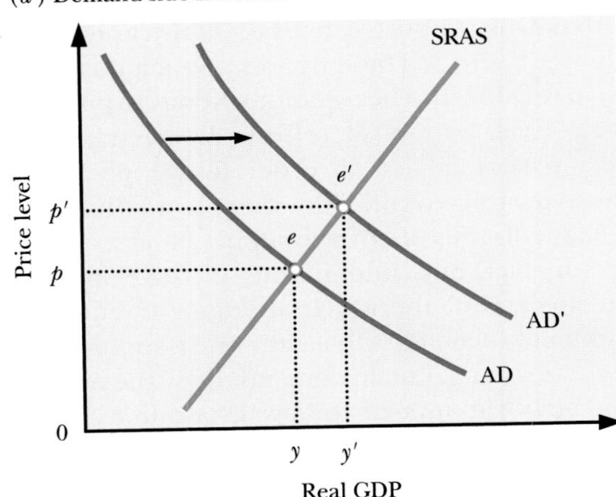

(*b*) Supply-side Inflation

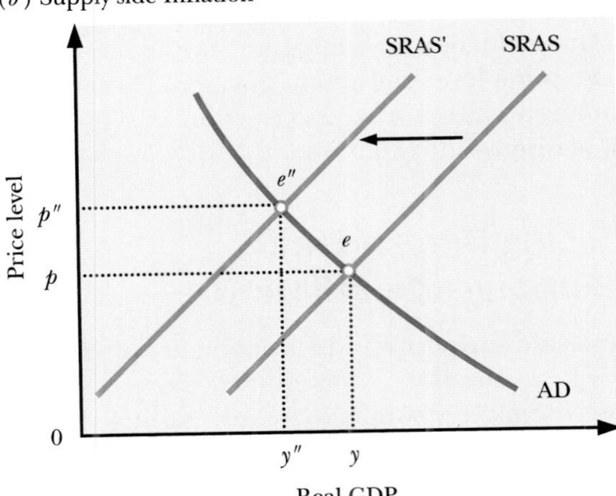

Panel *a* illustrates demand-side inflation. The economy is initially in equilibrium at point *e*. Aggregate demand increases from AD to AD′ and raises the price level from p to p' as the economy moves up along the short-run aggregate supply curve, SRAS, to point e'. In the short run, output increases from y to y'. The increase in aggregate demand has pulled prices up.

Panel *b* illustrates supply-side inflation. The economy is initially in equilibrium at point *e*. A reduction in short-run aggregate supply from SRAS to SRAS′ causes a movement back along the aggregate demand curve, from point *e* to point e''. Prices rise from p to p''; output declines from y to y''; unemployment increases. The reduction in short-run aggregate supply has pushed prices up.

duce more output in the short run. The short-run aggregate supply curve, SRAS, is positively sloped—which means that the economy will produce more output only at a higher price level. If aggregate demand increases—through an increase in the money supply, a lowering of taxes, an increase in government spending, or an autonomous upward shift in consumption—the aggregate demand curve, AD, will shift to the right. At the new equilibrium, e', more output (y') is produced (and unemployment falls). The increase in demand has caused the equilibrium price level to rise (to p'). In panel *a*, the inflation caused by the increase in aggregate demand is demand-side inflation.

Supply-side Inflation

In panel *b* of Figure 5, the economy is initially operating at point *e* again, producing output *y* at price level *p*. A reduction in aggregate supply—because of a decline in productivity, poor harvests, or autonomous increases in energy prices—shifts the aggregate supply curve to the left, from SRAS to SRAS′. The drop in aggregate supply disrupts the initial equilibrium of output and prices and shifts the equilibrium to e''. At price level *p*, aggregate demand exceeds aggregate supply, so prices rise (from *p* to p''). As prices rise, the economy moves back along the aggregate demand curve; output falls to y'', and the unemployment rate rises. The reduction in aggregate supply has raised both the price level and unemployment. In panel *b*, the inflation caused by the reduction in aggregate supply is supply-side inflation.

Confusing Demand-side and Supply-side Inflation

Demand-side and supply-side inflation are often confused when inflation is moderate. For example, suppose the money supply increases, raising the aggregate demand for goods and services throughout the economy. As each sector seeks to meet the increase in demand, its prices and wages rise. Individual businesses will not see the increase in the money supply; they will see only that their wage costs, material costs, and interest charges are rising, and they will raise prices as best they can in response to higher costs. Thus, on an individual level, pure demand-side inflation may look like supply-side inflation.

> To individuals and firms, moderate demand-side inflation looks like supply-side inflation. To determine whether inflation is demand-side or supply-side, one must know the source of rising wages and prices.

When inflation is excessive and there is widespread knowledge that the money supply is expanding at a rapid rate, there is less chance observers will think the demand-side inflation is really supply-side inflation. In hyperinflations, people understand that the runaway inflation is caused by runaway aggregate demand. In order to decide on the best inflation cure, it is important to know whether inflation is caused by demand-side or supply-side forces.

DEMAND-SIDE INFLATION: MONEY AND INTEREST

Protracted and sustained inflation (such as the United States has experienced since the early 1930s) is primarily a monetary phenomenon. Protracted and sustained inflation is most likely caused by persistent increases in aggregate demand resulting from excess monetary growth. The proposition that excess monetary growth is the prime cause of protracted inflation is supported by the empirical evidence in Figures 2 and 3. These figures reveal a positive long-term relationship between the money supply and the price level. Supply-side effects, by contrast, tend to be one-shot affairs. In order for supply shocks to cause protracted inflation, there would have to be a sustained series of adverse supply shocks.

In fact, any autonomous increase in expenditures can shift the aggregate demand curve to the right; monetary growth is only one potential cause of increases in aggregate demand. Only the money supply, however, appears to have grown in a sufficiently rapid and sustained manner to be responsible for protracted inflation. From 1933 to the present, the price level increased by 11 times; the supply of money increased by 33 times; real government and investment spending increased by 8 times—at about the same rate as real GDP. The relatively rapid growth of the money supply makes it the most likely source of the autonomous increases in expenditures required to continuously raise aggregate demand. To explain the inflationary bias of the past 60 years, economists look first at the monetary theory of inflation.

Inflationary Expectations, Interest, and Velocity

Chapter 10 introduced the simple quantity theory. It is now time to reconsider the quantity theory's equation of exchange, allowing for systematic changes in the velocity of the circulation of money. Recall the equation of exchange, $MV = PQ$, where M is money supply, V is velocity, P is the price level, and Q is real output.

The effects of monetary growth on prices, output, unemployment, and interest rates can be determined using the tools of aggregate supply-and-demand analysis. The effects of money supply on the price level would be simple to predict if velocity and real output were constant, but in reality, changes in velocity complicate the relationship between money supply and prices. Much of modern inflation theory is devoted to explaining the determinants of velocity through the effects of inflationary expectations.

Inflationary expectations affect the relationship between money and prices. Changes in the anticipated rate of inflation can change velocity. It is, therefore, important to consider how people form inflationary expectations and how the expected rate of inflation affects velocity through interest rates. The following sections explore the different effects of anticipated and unanticipated inflation on interest rates and the effect of changes in velocity on the inflationary aspects of monetary growth.

Unanticipated Inflation with a One-Shot Monetary Injection

Inflation is not likely to be anticipated if it is caused by a one-shot or once-and-for-all increase in aggregate demand. Consider a hypothetical economy that has had stable prices for a number of years—the people are not likely to anticipate inflation. Although we have experienced inflation (sometimes low, sometimes high) for a long period of time, examination of a permanent, one-shot increase in demand starting from a stable price level simplifies the understanding of demand-side inflation. After this section, we will turn to the more common case of continuing inflation.

In Figure 6, a once-and-for-all increase in the money supply causes a one-shot, permanent increase in aggregate demand. People do their best to anticipate inflation, but in a situation where prices have been stable for years, people will expect prices to remain stable. In this example, they do not know of the impending increase in the money supply that will cause prices to rise. The increase in aggregate demand will have both short-run and long-run effects.

The Short Run. In panel *a* of Figure 6, the economy is initially operating at point *a*, producing the natural level of output, y_n, at a price level of 100. In panel *b*, the increase in money supply (from M to M') adds reserves to the commercial banking system. Banks can use these excess reserves to make loans and other investments. The increase in the supply of credit brings down the interest rate along the money demand or liquidity preference (LP) curve (discussed in Chapter 14) from 10 percent to 7 percent.

In order to keep the interest rate this low, the price level and real output would have to remain unchanged after the increase in aggregate demand. Interest rates, however, are unlikely to remain so low, because the increase in aggregate demand should push up both the price level and real output. As the price level rises, the demand for money rises, pushing interest rates back up. An increase in real output will also push interest rates back up by increasing the demand for money. Thus, as aggregate demand increases, output rises to y' and the price level rises as the economy moves from *a* to *b*. As the price level rises, the demand for money increases, and the interest rate rises from a' to *b* in panel *b*.

> An increase in the money supply can initially lower interest rates, but the resulting increase in prices and output pushes interest rates back up in the short run.

The Long Run. As explained in Chapter 9, an increase in aggregate demand can raise output and employment in the short run above the natural rate, but in the long run, both output and employment will return to the natural rate through the self-correcting mechanism. Is there an equivalent rule for interest rates?

FIGURE 6
The Effects of Increases in Money Supply on Interest Rates, Output, and Prices

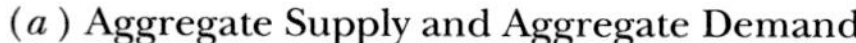

(*a*) Aggregate Supply and Aggregate Demand

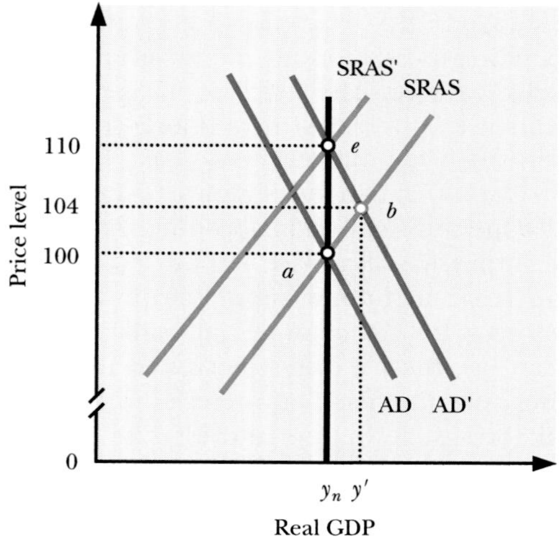

(*b*) The Money Market

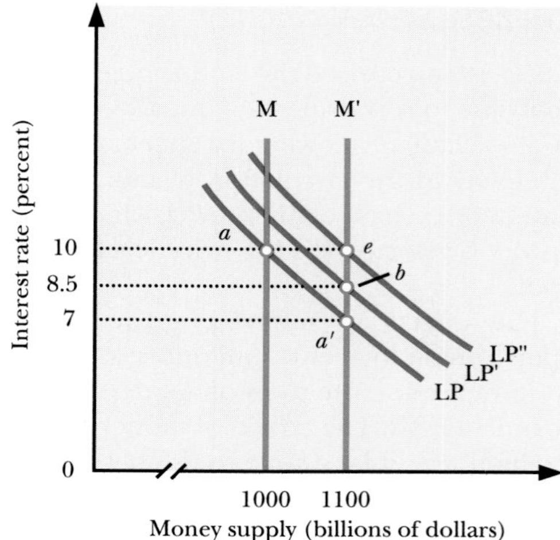

In both panels, the economy is initially operating at point *a,* producing an output of y_n with an interest rate of 10 percent. As a result of an unanticipated move by the Fed, money supply increases, and the interest rate drops to 7 percent. At the lower interest rate, aggregate demand increases (because of higher investment spending) from AD to AD′. As aggregate demand shifts up along SRAS, both prices and output rise. As prices start to rise, the demand for money increases (the liquidity preference curve starts to shift to the right). As the price level rises initially from 100 to 104, the money demand curve shifts from LP to LP′ to establish a higher interest rate (8.5 percent) in the money market. The interest rate has risen from 7 percent to 8.5 percent but is still below its original rate of 10 percent. However, the economy is now operating above the natural level of output at point *b;* therefore, the price level continues to rise. As the price level continues to rise, people expect a higher price level. The economy is restored to producing y_n when the short-run aggregate supply curve shifts all the way to SRAS′. The movement of the price level to 110 affects the credit market by continuing to increase the demand for money. Eventually, the liquidity preference curve shifts all the way to LP″. At the intersection of LP″ and M′ (at point *e*), the interest rate is restored to the original 10 percent rate. Long-run equilibrium occurs at point *e* in both diagrams. (The diagram ignores the effect on the LP curve of the temporary increase in output from y_n to y'.)

At point *b* in panel *a,* output is above the natural level, and the price level begins its long-run ascent toward point *e* where output equals the natural rate (y_n). As prices rise, people need more money to carry out their transactions; the demand for money increases as LP′ shifts towards LP″. The interest rate rises as the demand for money increases; it will continue to rise as long as prices are rising. Prices rise until point *e* is reached (at a stable price level of 110). The interest rate rises as long as prices are rising. In panel *b,* when the price level reaches 110 (at point *e*), prices no longer rise (the inflation rate goes back to zero), and output is restored to y_n. The interest rate is restored to its original rate (10 percent) at point *e* in panel *a.* The economy is operating with the same real income and the same rate of inflation (zero) as before the increase in money supply. The only change is that the price level has risen.[2] The economy has moved from one stable price level to another stable, but higher, price level.

When the inflation rate is zero, both the nominal and real interest rate are equal (at 10 percent in this example). In the long run, a once-and-for-all

[2]To simplify the above explanation, we have ignored the shifts in the liquidity preference curves that result from the temporary changes in real GDP. In the long run, real GDP is y_n—the natural level. Thus, LP, LP′, and LP″ are drawn on the assumption that real GDP equals y_n. LP assumes the price level is 100; LP′ assumes the price level is 104; LP″ assumes the price level is 110.

permanent change in the nominal money supply has no impact on real GDP, the real interest rate, or the real money supply. Thus, in the long run, the interest rate tends to be restored to its original rate after a one-shot change in the money supply. Increases in money supply drive down interest rates only in the short run.

> If the economy starts from a long-run equilibrium, an unanticipated *one-shot* increase in the money supply (that people expect to be permanent) lowers the rate of interest (and raises output above the natural rate) only in the short run. But in the long run, the self-correcting mechanism returns the economy to the natural level of output and to the original interest rate.

Anticipated Inflation with Steady Monetary Injections

Instances of one-shot unanticipated inflation like the one described in Figure 6 are rare. Because both the money supply and real GDP typically grow continually, people come to expect a certain rate of inflation and they do their best to anticipate the inflation rate. How do people form inflationary expectations? There is no way to know for sure the mental process by which inflationary expectations are formed, but economists have developed two competing hypotheses.

Adaptive Expectations. One hypothesis economists offer to explain how inflationary expectations are formed is that of **adaptive expectations.**

> **Adaptive expectations** are expectations of the future that people form from past experience and modify only gradually as experience unfolds.

For example, if the annual inflation rate has been 10 percent each year for the past 10 years, people will probably expect the inflation rate to remain at 10 percent. If the inflation rate jumps to a steady 15 percent, the adaptive expectations hypothesis says that people will not immediately adjust their expected rate of inflation up to 15 percent. In the first year, they might raise their expectation to 11 percent or 12 percent. As the rate of inflation continues at 15 percent, people will adjust upward until they finally reach a 15 percent expected inflation rate.

The main implication of the adaptive expectations hypothesis is that *it takes time to adjust to a new rate of inflation. In the meantime, there will be a difference between the actual and the anticipated rate of inflation.* If the rate of inflation rises, the anticipated rate of inflation will rise by less than the actual increase. If the rate of inflation falls, the anticipated rate of inflation will fall by less than the actual decrease. Only gradually will people bring their anticipated rate of inflation in line with the actual rate of inflation.

Rational Expectations. The adaptive expectations hypothesis maintains that people change their expectations of inflation slowly in response to changing circumstances. The **rational expectations** hypothesis assumes that people can change their expectations more quickly by using more information to form their expectations.

> **Rational expectations** are expectations that people form by using all available information, relying not only on past experience but also on their predictions about the effects of present and future policy actions.

A major difference between adaptive and rational expectations is the speed of adjustment of expectations. It is conceivable that people could change their rational expectation of inflation simply on the basis of a policy pronouncement from monetary or fiscal authorities. If they believe a change in policy will raise a current 10 percent inflation rate to a permanent 15 percent rate, they will immediately raise their inflation projection to 15 percent.

Many people and businesses do indeed study the latest economic projections, money supply growth statistics, and fiscal policy changes. Banks, investment firms, labor unions, and small investors gather information that they hope will allow them to anticipate the future. It is, therefore, entirely possible that expectations are, in actuality, formed according to the rational expectations hypothesis. Which hypothesis is correct is an empirical issue that has been the subject of much research and controversy. Chapter 21 considers rational expectations in more detail.

FIGURE 7
Velocity and Inflation

(*a*) The Relationship Between Anticipated Inflation and Interest Rate 1966–1991

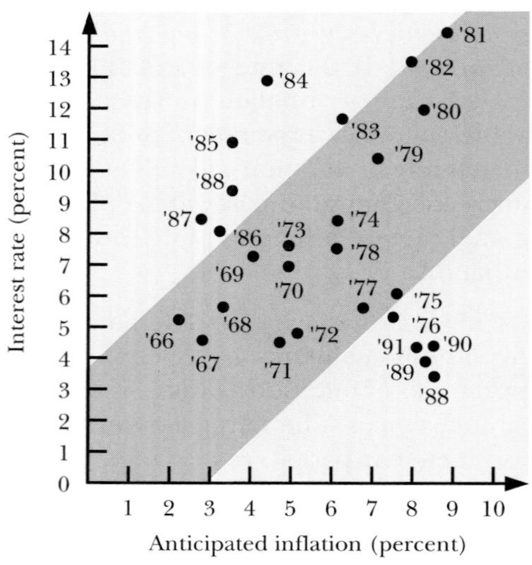

(*b*) The Relationship Between the Interest Rate and Velocity 1966–1991

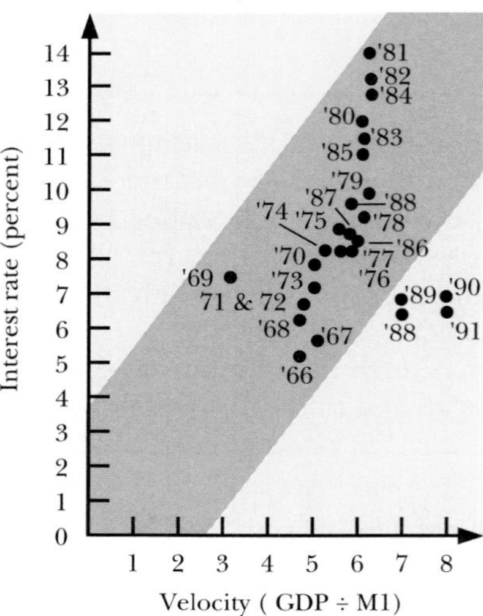

In panel *a*, the anticipated inflation rate is measured as the average inflation rate over the last 3 years. The interest rate in both panels is the interest rate on 10-year U.S. government bonds. The positive slope of the scatter diagram in panel *a* reveals a positive relationship between anticipated inflation and the interest rate. In panel *b*, velocity is the ratio of GDP to M1. This scatter diagram clearly shows a positive relationship between interest rates and velocity. The results of panels *a* and *b* together show that velocity tends to increase as anticipated inflation rises.

Anticipated Inflation, Velocity, and Interest Rates

Consider an economy in which inflation has been present for some time and in which people are attempting to anticipate the rate of inflation. We will assume that they form their expectations adaptively.

Chapter 14 explained that when people anticipate more inflation, the nominal interest rate rises. Lenders become less willing to lend at prevailing interest rates because they will be paid back with cheaper dollars. Borrowers become more anxious to borrow at prevailing interest rates because they can pay back their loans with cheaper dollars.

As noted earlier, the interest rate is the opportunity cost of holding money. The higher is the opportunity cost of money, the lower is the quantity of money balances people wish to hold. Higher interest rates cause people to reduce their money balances, which they attempt to do by increasing their spending. As people generally try to reduce their money balances, money turns over faster. Higher interest rates should, therefore, raise velocity.

How can we measure the anticipated rate of inflation? One simple way is to say that the anticipated inflation rate is the average of the inflation rates that have occurred over the past few years.[3] This measure of anticipated inflation can then be compared with interest rates, and interest rates can be compared with velocity.

Panel *a* of Figure 7 shows the relationship between this measure of the anticipated rate of inflation and the rate of interest for the period from 1966 to 1991. The scatter diagram of anticipated inflation and interest rates shows a strong positive relationship between the two.

[3]For example, if the inflation rate in the current year is 10 percent and if it was 9 percent last year and 8 percent the year before, people would expect 9 percent (the average of 10, 9, and 8) for the next year. If the inflation rate jumps to 14 percent, the new expected inflation rate is 11 percent (the average of 14, 10, and 9).

> The higher is the anticipated rate of inflation, the higher is the rate of interest.

Panel *b* of Figure 7 shows the effects of interest rates on velocity. Theory predicts a strong positive correlation between velocity and interest rates. At high interest rates, velocity should be high because the opportunity cost of holding cash balances is high. The scatter diagram confirms a positive relationship between interest rates and velocity.

In listing the facts of inflation, we noted the substantial difference between the 1970s (a period of high inflation) and the 1980s (a period of declining inflation). In the latter half of the 1970s, prices rose more rapidly than the money supply. In the 1980s, the money supply generally rose faster than prices. Why? As the inflation rate rose during the 1970s, inflationary expectations pushed up interest rates and velocity. With rising velocity, a given increase in the money supply yielded a larger increase in prices. The normal relationship between monetary growth and inflation (prices rising slower than money supply rises) was disrupted by rising inflationary expectations, which raised velocity.

The sharp reduction in inflation in the mid-1980s caused inflationary expectations to fall. As interest rates dropped, velocity fell. With declining velocity, a given increase in the money supply yielded a smaller increase in prices. The normal situation (money growing faster than prices) was restored.

Monetary Growth and Interest Rates

Figure 6 showed that a one-shot increase in the money supply lowers the interest rate in the short run, but the ensuing rise in the price level restores the economy to the original interest rate (at a stable but higher price level).

An economy that is experiencing continuous excess monetary growth (as opposed to a one-shot permanent increase in the money supply) experiences a similar result. If there is an unanticipated *permanent* acceleration in monetary growth that unexpectedly raises the inflation rate, interest rates should drop in the short run. Because the acceleration of inflation is unanticipated, lenders expect the prevailing rate of inflation to continue and do not cut back on their willingness to lend. Borrowers also expect the prevailing rate of inflation to continue and do not increase their willingness to borrow. Yet the increase in the growth rate of money has speeded up the injection of credit into credit markets, pushing interest rates down.

If the higher inflation that is brought about by the faster growth in money supply is anticipated, however, the interest rate will not fall at all. In this case, lenders and borrowers anticipate that prices will increase; lenders will be more reluctant to lend money at prevailing interest rates, and borrowers will be more eager to borrow at prevailing interest rates. These actions cause the nominal interest rate to rise.

By contrast, the real interest rate (the nominal interest rate minus anticipated inflation) need not change when the rate of monetary growth is increased. Consider an economy that has had an annual growth of money supply of 5 percent for the last 5 years. Real GDP has been rising at 2 percent per year, and the annual inflation rate has been 3 percent. The nominal interest rate has been steady at 7 percent, and the real interest rate is 4 percent. Monetary growth accelerates unexpectedly to a permanent 8 percent, which eventually raises the inflation rate to 6 percent. Initially, the anticipated inflation remains at 3 percent, and the increased growth of money temporarily drives down the interest rate below the original 7 percent. The drop in the interest rate will be only temporary, however. As people come to expect higher inflation, the interest rate rises. In the long run, people come to anticipate the higher 6 percent rate of inflation. The nominal interest rate rises to 10 percent (the 6 percent anticipated rate of inflation plus the 4 percent real interest rate). The economy has returned to the original real rate of interest, but at a higher inflation rate.

> In the long run, an increase in monetary growth raises the nominal interest rate but not the real interest rate.

The Dilemma Faced by Monetary Authorities

Monetary authorities face a dilemma during periods of rapid and anticipated inflation. When inflation is high, nominal interest rates will have to be high enough to incorporate a premium for anticipated inflation. There will be a public outcry against high interest rates, and pressure will build on the Fed to lower interest rates. In order to lower nominal interest rates when inflationary expectations are high, monetary authorities must lower inflationary expectations.

With adaptive expectations, people lower their inflationary expectations slowly as they see inflation actually dropping. In this situation, the Fed must lower actual inflation to reduce inflationary expectations. In an inflation, both the money supply and the price level are rising; to lower inflation, the Fed must, therefore, reduce the growth of money supply. The demand for money remains strong because people require more money to carry out their transactions with rising prices. The resulting imbalance between money growth and money demand growth pushes interest rates up.

> To lower nominal interest rates in an environment of steady anticipated inflation requires that nominal interest rates be *raised* in the short run. When monetary authorities reduce the growth of money supply, nominal interest rates rise further. When the rate of inflation slows, inflationary expectations begin to fall, and only then will nominal interest rates come down.

The U.S. experience with rising interest rates in 1979 and 1980 illustrates the dilemma faced by monetary authorities during a stagflation. Interest rates were driven up in the short run when monetary authorities cut the growth of the money supply during a period of high inflation and high inflationary expectations. The Fed decided in October 1979 to reduce money growth rates in order to combat inflation. Table 1 shows that from 1978 to 1980, the rate of monetary growth was gradually reduced from 8.2 percent per year to 6.4 percent per year. During this same time period, the rate of interest (on 3-month Treasury bills) rose from 9.1 percent in December 1978 to 15.7 percent in December 1980. As one would expect, interest rates rose when monetary growth was reduced in the presence of high inflationary expectations. But as the anti-inflation policy began to take hold in 1982 and 1983 (at the cost of driving unemployment up from 6.1 percent in 1978 to 9.7 percent in 1982), interest rates started to fall. The inflation rate fell to less than 4 percent per year in the mid-1980s from a peak inflation rate of 9.7 percent in 1981. As inflation fell, people lowered inflationary expectations and interest rates began to fall. Interest rates in late 1983 and late 1984 (9 percent and 8.2 percent, respectively) were about the same as when the Fed anti-inflation action began. By 1985, the drop in inflationary expectations lowered interest rates below 1978 levels. The conditions of the recession from 1990 to 1992 were quite different. Interest rates and inflation were both low in 1991. The Fed could expand the money supply without worrying excessively about inflation.

The experience of the period from 1978 to 1988 vividly displays the Fed's dilemma. To lower interest rates when inflation rates are high, the economy must first be put through a short-run upsurge in interest rates. In this case, the upsurge lasted 2 years, and the interest rate in the third year was still quite high.

Government Deficits and Inflation

Although it has become increasingly popular to blame inflation on the government deficit, the relationship between the deficit and inflation is not clear. As already noted, U.S. inflation was falling after 1982 despite record U.S. deficits. What is the relationship between inflation and deficits? The connection appears to depend on whether short-run or long-run periods are examined.

The Short Run. The short-run relationship between government deficits and inflation is ambiguous because deliberate fiscal policy, automatic stabilizers, and monetary policy often work in opposite directions. On the one hand, deficits produced by deliberate increases in government spending or reductions in tax rates raise the rate of inflation as aggregate demand increases. On the other hand, deficits produced by falling tax revenues induced by a weak economy (falling aggregate demand caused by reductions in private spending) are associated with a falling rate of inflation. A tight money policy will also reduce inflation and increase the deficit by driving up unemployment and decreasing government tax revenues. Thus, in the short run, the empirical association may be positive or negative, depending on the factors at work.

The scatter diagram in Figure 8 plots deficits (measured by the yearly percentage increases in the national debt) against inflation rates for the period from 1975 to 1991. The years of lowest inflation (1983 and 1986) were also years of larger-than-average increases in the national debt! The government's anti-inflation policy lowered the rate of inflation in

TABLE 1
Money Growth, Inflation, Unemployment, and Interest Rates 1978–1991

	Year-to-Year Growth Rate in M1 (percent)	Inflation Rate: GDP Deflator (percent)	Yearly Average Unemployment (percent)	Year-end Rate for 3-Month T-Bill (percent)
1978	8.2	7.3	6.1	9.1
1979	7.7	8.9	5.8	12.1
1980	6.4	9.0	7.1	15.7
1981	7.0	10.0	7.6	10.9
1982	6.6	6.2	9.7	8.0
1983	11.1	4.8	9.6	9.0
1984	6.6	4.4	7.4	8.2
1985	12.0	3.7	7.2	7.5
1986	17.0	2.6	7.0	5.2
1987	3.5	3.2	6.2	5.8
1988	4.8	3.9	5.4	8.2
1989	1.2	4.3	5.2	7.5
1990	3.9	4.2	5.4	6.8
1991	8.7	3.6	6.6	4.2

Sources: *Economic Report of the President; Federal Reserve Bulletin.*

1983 and 1984, but at the expense of driving up unemployment and increasing the deficit. The scatter diagram, therefore, reveals a negative relationship between inflation and the deficit. It appears that between 1975 and 1991, the impact of the Fed's anti-inflation policy and the workings of the automatic stabilizers dominated the relationship between inflation and the deficit.

The Long Run. Is there a long-run positive relationship between inflation and the deficit? Economists have advanced three theories that claim that there is.

1. The federal deficit can contribute to inflation indirectly *through its effect on the money supply.* If the newly issued government bonds are sold only to the public, the money supply is not affected, but interest rates may be driven up as government and private borrowers compete for available investment funds. If, however, there is an unwillingness to raise interest rates in the short run, the Fed—although it is not obligated to do so—can purchase the federal debt. When the Fed purchases government bonds, it injects new reserves into the banking system and the money supply expands. In effect, the government deficit is financed by "printing money."

> Deficits can cause inflation by forcing an expansion of the money supply.

2. The federal deficit can contribute to inflation indirectly *if increases in the national debt cause people to spend more.* If people treat the government IOUs that they own as net wealth, a larger national debt means that people will spend more. In other words, if people look only at their increased holdings of federal government IOUs and ignore the future taxes that must be collected to finance the debt, an increase in the national debt may motivate them to spend more and, thus, drive up prices.

3. *Inflation can cause the deficit, rather than vice versa!* This argument is simple: Higher inflation rates—in the long run—raise interest rates. Higher interest rates increase the federal deficit by increasing the interest cost of the national debt.

The scatter diagram in Figure 9 shows a positive long-run relationship between inflation and federal deficits. When changes in the national debt over 5 years (the accumulated deficit over 5 years) are compared to 5-year changes in the price level, the

FIGURE 8
The Yearly Change in the Price Level versus the Yearly Change in National Debt, 1975–1991

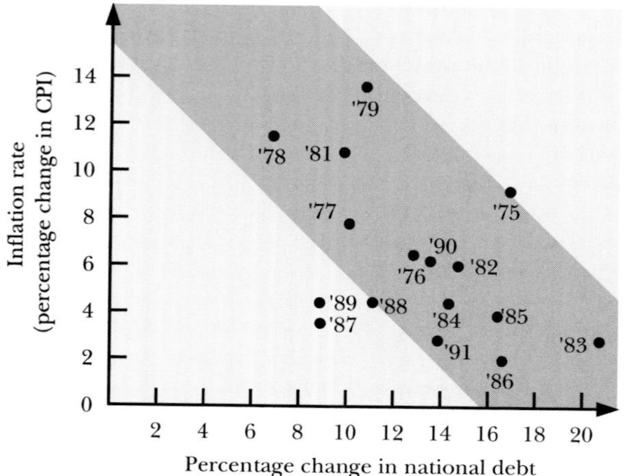

The evidence from the last 13 years suggests that in the short run there may be a negative relationship between inflation rates and the deficit (as indicated by changes in the national debt), but a positive relationship is also possible.

Source: *Economic Report of the President.*

FIGURE 9
The 5-Year Change in Prices versus the Change in National Debt, 1950–1990

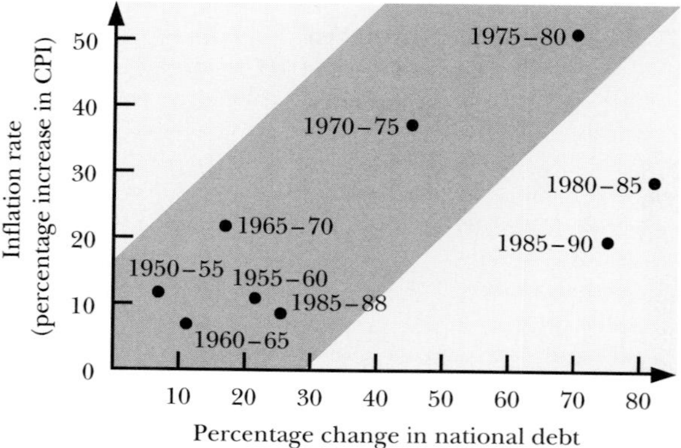

This scatter diagram reveals a positive relationship between percentage changes in the price level and percentage changes in the national debt over 5-year intervals. If a 5-year period can represent the long run, there is a long-run positive association between deficits and inflation.

Sources: *Economic Report of the President; Statistical Abstract of the United States.*

two rates of change are positively related between 1950 and 1990. A combination of the preceding three theories likely explains the long-run empirical relationship between inflation and deficits.

> In the short run, cyclical factors obscure the relationship between deficits and inflation. In the long run, there appears to be a positive relationship between deficits and inflation.

THE SUPPLY SIDE: SUPPLY SHOCKS

Supply-side inflation occurs when there is a reduction in aggregate supply—when the SRAS curve shifts to the left, as in panel *b* of Figure 5. The drop in aggregate supply moves the economy up the aggregate demand curve to a lower level of output and to a higher price level. Unlike demand-side inflation, which tends to raise output and employment in the short run, supply-side inflation brings the worst of both worlds: rising prices *and* lower output and employment.

Shifts in aggregate supply can be expected or unexpected. For example, the generally rising trend in technological advances would be expected to increase aggregate supply over time in a fairly predictable manner. Of greater interest is an unexpected shift in aggregate supply, called a **supply shock.**

> A **supply shock** is an unexpected shift in the short-run aggregate supply curve.

An *adverse supply shock* reduces aggregate supply (the short-run aggregate supply curve shifts to the left). A *favorable supply shock* increases aggregate supply.

Causes of Supply-side Inflation

There is no single cause of supply-side inflation. Any factor that decreases aggregate supply can initiate supply-side inflation. Changes in labor productivity, autonomous increases in raw-material prices, crop failures, and changes in the way labor and product markets work can all reduce aggregate supply.

If the costs of production rise spontaneously, the economy will experience an adverse supply shock. Firms, on average, will supply fewer goods and services than before at prevailing prices, and aggregate supply will fall. As the aggregate supply curve shifts to the left, the price level is pushed upward.

The most dramatic case of supply-side inflation in recent years was the 1475 percent rise in the price of imported oil between 1973 and 1980. When the Organization of Petroleum Exporting Countries (OPEC) discovered the magic of cartel pricing in 1973, the oil-importing countries of the world were hit with an enormous adverse supply shock. OPEC inflicted leftward shifts in the aggregate supply curves of every oil-importing country. The oil-induced reductions of supply pushed up the general price level. Table 2 supplies data on the price of OPEC oil and the average inflation rate of seven major countries.

The upsurge of world inflation rates coincided with the increase in energy prices in the mid- and late 1970s. World inflation rates abated in the 1980s as oil prices stabilized or dropped. Although OPEC was not the only cause of the upsurge of inflation in the 1970s, the oil shocks were a major contributor.

Price shocks can also emanate from agriculture. Poor weather and bad harvests can raise agricultural prices, and because agricultural goods are a major input for the world economy, such a price increase can shift the aggregate supply curve. The year 1973 brought with it not only the beginning of the oil shock, but also an increase in the price of wheat from $70 per ton to $140 per ton—largely as a result of a poor harvest in the United States in 1973 and a crop disaster in the Soviet Union the year before.

Supply shocks can also lower the rate of inflation when the SRAS curve shifts to the right. Table 2 shows that as the OPEC cartel weakened in the early 1980s, price inflation dropped.

TABLE 2
OPEC Crude Oil Prices and Average Inflation Rates in the Big Seven Countries (U.S., Germany, Japan, France, Canada, Italy, and the U.K.)

Year	Oil Price (dollars per barrel)	Average Inflation Rate (percent)
1971–73	2.13	6.4
1974	10.77	14.5
1975	10.72	13.0
1976	11.51	10.0
1977	13.12	10.1
1978	12.93	7.6
1979	18.67	9.7
1980	30.87	9.1
1981	34.50	10.1
1982	33.63	8.4
1983	29.31	6.0
1984	28.70	5.4
1985	28.14	3.2
1986	15.35	2.5
1987	17.70	3.8
1988	19.00	3.3
1989	19.63	4.7
1990	20.47	5.0
1991	21.42	4.5

Sources: *Handbook of Economic Statistics,* 1984, 53; James Griffin and Henry Steele, *Energy Economics and Policy* (New York: Academic, 1980), 18; *Economic Report of the President; Handbook of Economic Statistics,* 1988.

Ratification of Supply-side Inflation

As Figure 5 demonstrated, supply-side inflation reduces output and, hence, increases unemployment. Demand-side inflation, on the other hand, may increase both output and employment. The combination of rising prices and rising unemployment characteristic of supply-side inflation puts pressure on government to do something about rising unemployment.

In Figure 10, the economy is initially producing an output of y_1 at a price level of p_1 (at point e_1). The economy now suffers a supply shock; accordingly, the aggregate supply curve shifts to the left (from SRAS to SRAS′). If aggregate demand is unchanged, the economy moves to e_2, producing less output at higher prices (prices rise from p_1 to p_2). As output declines, the unemployment rate also rises.

FIGURE 10
The Ratification of Supply Shocks

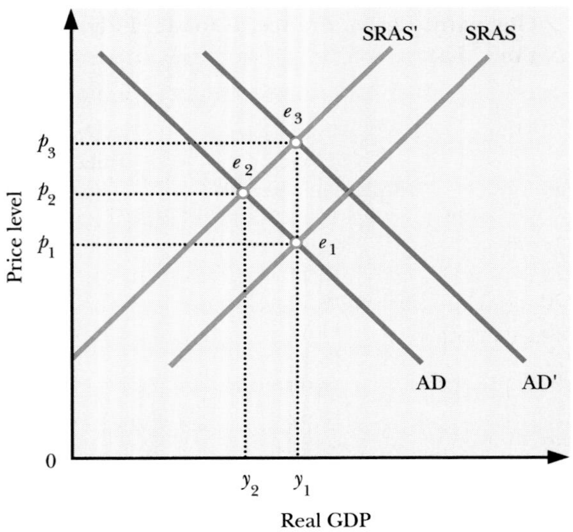

The economy is initially operating at point e_1, producing an output of y_1 at price level p_1. When short-run aggregate supply falls from SRAS to SRAS′, the price level rises to p_2 and output falls to y_2 (unemployment rises). The government ratifies the supply-side inflation by increasing aggregate demand from AD to AD′. The price level rises to p_3, and output (and unemployment) returns to its original level.

If the government succumbs to pressure to combat rising unemployment, it raises the money supply, thereby increasing aggregate demand (from AD to AD′). As a result, the price level rises even further (from p_2 to p_3), and the economy returns to its original level of output and unemployment. The process of responding to adverse supply shocks by increasing monetary growth is known as the **ratification of supply-side inflation.**

Ratification of supply-side inflation results if the government increases the money supply to prevent supply-side shocks from raising unemployment.

As a consequence of ratification, the supply-shock-induced unemployment is eliminated, but the price level is driven up even further.[4] If nothing else happens, the price increase stops at p_3. If ratification continues, a wage/price spiral can result.

THE WAGE/PRICE SPIRAL

When inflation continues for some time, it no longer catches workers and firms off guard; they attempt to anticipate inflation. Contracts between workers and their employers reflect the anticipated rate of inflation. Workers who anticipate a 10 percent annual inflation rate over the life of a wage contract will negotiate contracts that protect them from this amount of inflation. When inflation is anticipated, firms will be willing to pay the higher wages that are demanded. In an inflationary setting, firms can pass wage increases along in the form of higher prices. Sellers factor the anticipated rate of inflation into their sales contracts.

In such a situation, the economy gets caught in a **wage/price spiral.** Workers anticipate inflation and demand higher wages. Higher wages raise production costs and shift the aggregate supply curve in Figure 10 to the left. To prevent unemployment from increasing, monetary authorities ratify the supply-side inflation and drive prices even higher. Workers now anticipate a higher price level; they demand higher wages; aggregate supply falls again; and the whole process repeats itself.

The **wage/price spiral** is the phenomenon of higher prices pushing wages higher and then higher wages pushing prices higher, or vice versa. This spiral is sustained when the monetary authorities ratify the resulting supply-side inflation.

As long as monetary authorities ratify the increase in wages, the wage/price spiral can continue indefinitely. A necessary component of the wage/price spiral is the accompanying rise in the money supply.

[4]Our example illustrates a perfectly matched demand response of monetary policy to the supply shock. In practice, this match may be difficult to achieve.

Is the wage/price spiral supply-side or demand-side inflation? If workers did not demand higher wages, it would not be necessary to ratify this supply-side inflation by increasing the money supply. Or, if the money supply had never increased and the economy were not on an inflationary path, workers would not demand wage increases in excess of productivity advances. In a wage/price spiral, the growth of the money supply is always present but so is the supply-side element of anticipated inflation that forces up wage contracts. The debate over who caused the wage/price spiral is like the argument over which came first, the chicken or the egg.

An economy that aims to maintain full employment can be subject to wage/price spirals. If the economy suffers an adverse supply shock, monetary authorities must increase the money supply to prevent unemployment from rising, and prices will be bid up even more. Any action that threatens to raise unemployment will be counteracted by increasing aggregate demand. Government policy is more likely to prevent price declines than price increases, building an inflationary bias into the economy.

The wage/price spiral cannot be halted painlessly. If the government ceases to ratify supply-side inflation (by refusing to let the money supply grow), the wage/price spiral will be broken; but the economy will have to live with unemployment until the self-correcting mechanism works.

INFLATION CURES

The U.S. economy has experienced both rising and falling rates of inflation over the past 40 years. The 1950s through the mid-1960s were years of modest inflation by today's standards. The late 1960s witnessed an acceleration of the inflation rate. The 1970s were a decade of high inflation with bursts of even higher price increases in the mid- and late 1970s. The 1980s were a period of moderating inflation, with inflation rates reminiscent of the 1960s. The early 1990s saw a slight resurgence of inflation. U.S. policymakers have experimented with different approaches to moderating inflation. In the late 1960s, a tax increase was used to depress aggregate demand. Wage and price controls were used in the early 1970s. The Fed adopted new operating procedures in 1979 to restrict monetary growth. Fed credit controls have also been tried as instruments of inflationary control.

Economists differ in their approach to controlling inflation. Keynesians favor a mixed approach of restraining aggregate demand and incomes policies. Monetarists favor strict limitations on monetary growth. Supply-side economists favor tax and investment policies that increase aggregate supply.

The Keynesian Solution

There is no unique Keynesian solution to the problem of rapid inflation because Keynesians do not believe in a single cause of inflation. Most believe that the best way to control inflation is through activist restraint of aggregate demand combined with **incomes policy.**

> An **incomes policy** is a set of government rules, guidelines, or laws that influence wage and price increases.

Keynesians, as represented by Paul Samuelson, Franco Modigliani, James Tobin, and the late Arthur Okun, would fear that a pure anti-inflation strategy (such as monetarism) would result in excessive unemployment. They would cite the experience of the early 1980s: When the Fed tightened monetary policy after 1979, unemployment rose from 5.8 percent in 1979 to 9.7 percent in 1982 until the rate of inflation dropped. Critics of such a pure anti-inflation strategy would ask: Was the drop in inflation worth the resulting rise in unemployment?

Nobel Prize laureate James Tobin argues, along with many other Keynesians, that moderate inflation is not nearly as bad as unemployment. The basic cost of inflation is that people move away from money. Anticipated inflation motivates people to hold smaller money balances per dollar of expenditure. Hence, people shop more and make extra trips to the bank. In effect, the costs of moderate inflation are not great. Why risk unemployment to reduce inflation?

When inflation approaches the double-digit rates of the late 1970s to 1981, the crawl from money becomes more serious. In such circumstances, Keynesians suggest using a combination of restrictive monetary and fiscal policy. This restraint has to be tempered, though, with an eye to the unemployment rate. Countercyclical policy cannot be forgone in an inflationary world. If a recession threatens, expansionary policies must be used. Keynesians hope that in a recession an incomes policy will help keep the inflation rate down when expansionary policies are applied.

Wage and Price Controls. One approach to controlling the inflationary wage/price spiral is the use of wage and price controls, or government-imposed rules and laws that govern prices and wages. In their mild form, such controls could be an incomes policy of voluntary rules and guidelines concerning wage and price increases. For example, the government may decree that prices can be raised only at the same rate as costs; it may say that wages and prices cannot increase by more than a given percentage in a given year; it may set rules on profit margins. These rules can be mandatory or voluntary. The use of wage and price controls often requires a substantial bureaucracy to monitor compliance.

A more extreme form of control is the use of rigid wage and price freezes that prohibit raising wages and prices above the level at which they stand on a certain date prior to the freeze. Such freezes are usually not all-inclusive; agricultural commodities and imports, whose prices are set in world markets, are typically exempted.

The principal argument for wage and price controls is that they can break inflationary expectations. Adaptive expectations fall only slowly as inflation rates fall. As long as inflationary expectations remain high, interest rates remain high and workers continue to demand wage increases. Wage and price controls can put an immediate damper on inflationary expectations.

The principal argument against rigid wage and price controls is that they can cause the productive efficiency of the economy to decline. If relative wages and prices are not allowed to move freely, higher relative wages will no longer signal which sectors of the economy are growing. Branches experiencing rising demand will not raise their prices sufficiently to equate supply and demand, and shortages will develop. Economic activity will tend to spill over into industries that are not frozen—such as agriculture and imports and even the underground economy. Supply and demand pressures will encourage the evasion of rules.

Economists agree that rigid wage and price controls cannot be used over an extended period because of their effect on efficiency. They can be applied only in the short run. If people are aware that these controls are of limited duration, they will attempt to anticipate what will happen to inflation when the controls are lifted. If people generally expect a price explosion when the program ends, they will not reduce their inflationary expectations. If the controls program fails to wind down inflationary expectations, it will not have accomplished its goal, as illustrated by the results of the U.S. experiment with wage and price controls in the early 1970s. (See Example 2.)

Monetarism: Monetary Rules

The major proponent of monetarism, Milton Friedman, argues that "inflation is always and everywhere a monetary phenomenon"—that inflation cannot persist unless it is supported by monetary growth. According to Friedman, supply-side inflation is just a temporary phenomenon that is important only in the short run. Protracted inflation is caused by demand-side factors, primarily excess monetary growth. From 1915 to 1991, the average annual growth in the money supply (5.5 percent) exceeded real GDP growth (3.1 percent) by 2.4 percent.

If inflation is "always and everywhere" caused by excess monetary growth, it is easy to predict Friedman's solution: strict limitation of the growth of the money supply. Insofar as real GDP over the long run has grown at about 3 percent per year, Friedman would limit the rate of growth of the money supply to about 3 percent per year. (The details of monetarism will be discussed in Chapter 20.)

Friedman's "3 percent rule" is that the Fed should increase the money supply by 3 percent every year, give or take some small margin of error. The fixed rate of monetary growth could be any other small number—anywhere from 3 percent to 5 percent—depending on the output growth rate. Friedman's constant-money-growth rule is sometimes called the "*k* percent rule." Under these circumstances, the Fed's decision-making power would be reduced to mere technical matters. The Fed's sole job would be to expand the money supply at the designated rate.

Friedman's rationale for the constant-money-growth rule is as follows.

1. Studies of the business cycle reveal that recessions and depressions are usually associated with prior sharp reductions in monetary growth. Hence, monetarists argue that monetary instability is largely responsible for the business cycle. Under a constant-money-growth rule, cyclical ups and downs would still exist, but their magnitude would be smaller.

EXAMPLE 2 The U.S. Wage and Price Controls Program from 1971 to 1974

On August 15, 1971, President Richard Nixon announced a 90-day freeze on almost all wages and prices. Controls were introduced because the 5.1 percent inflation rate from 1969 to 1971 appeared alarming in those days and because the unemployment rate had roughly doubled between 1969 and 1971. It was hoped that controls would reduce inflationary expectations, leaving the government free to fight unemployment.

The controls program ran through four phases and was dismantled in late 1973 and early 1974. Phase I was a 90-day freeze from which only taxes, mortgage interest rates, and raw agricultural commodities were exempted. Phase II began in November 1971. A Pay Board was established to enforce Phase II, which set a standard for wage increases of 5.5 percent per year. A Price Board operated on the rule that firms would be allowed to pass a percentage of cost increases on in the form of higher prices. Phase III began in January 1973. The Pay and Price boards were abolished; the 5.5 percent wage-increase standard was retained, but standards for passing on cost increases were loosened. Inflation accelerated alarmingly during Phase III, and a second freeze was announced in June of 1973. Freeze II froze prices but not wages! Phase IV went into effect in August 1973, and the standards and regulations of this phase were very much like those of Phases II and III. On April 30, 1974, the President's authority to control wages and prices lapsed, and the experiment with wage/price controls ended.

The controls program must be judged on the basis of what happened to inflation and unemployment. During Phase I, prices were basically unchanged. During Phase II, the inflation rate averaged 3.6 percent. There was an alarming resurgence of inflation during Phase III—inflation rose to a 9.1 percent annual rate. At the end of the controls program (1974), the inflation rate averaged 9.4 percent. In the 2 years after controls were lifted (1975 and 1976), inflation averaged 5.9 percent. Unemployment remained between 5 percent and 6 percent during the controls program. After the controls were lifted, the unemployment rate rose to 8.5 percent.

The controls program failed to bring down inflation and unemployment at the same time. One of the most important explanations for this failure was that nothing was done to prevent a price catch-up as the controls were being lifted. The rate of growth of the money supply accelerated from 6.6 percent in 1970 to 7.1 percent in 1971 to 7.5 percent in 1972 and then down to 5.0 percent in 1973. If inflation is a monetary phenomenon, why should prices not "catch up" after the controls are lifted? Economists conclude that the controls likely held down the inflation rate somewhat when they were in effect, but they raised the inflation rate after the controls were removed.

Source: Alan Blinder, *Economic Policy and the Great Stagflation* (New York: Academic Press, 1979), chaps. 3 and 6.

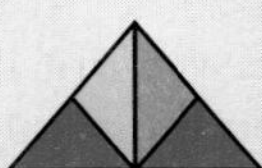

2. The empirical relationship between changes in the rate of monetary growth and nominal GDP growth is lagged. Friedman argues that the lag between money supply and GDP is long and variable (sometimes 6 months; sometimes 2 years). Because the business cycle cannot be forecasted accurately, attempts to use countercyclical policy can destabilize the economy. The growth of money supply at a fixed rate would bring more stability than would countercyclical policy.

3. The historical relationship between excess monetary growth and inflation is close and cannot be denied. (See Example 3.) If excess monetary growth causes inflation, then inflation can only be cured by eliminating excess monetary growth.

The Supply-side Program

The equation of exchange shows that inflation will be lower, *ceteris paribus,* the higher is the rate of growth of output. Supply-side economists claim that inflation can be moderated by increasing the growth of real output. The appeal of this proposition is enormous because it obviates the need for pain and suffering (in the form of high unemployment or high interest rates) while curing inflation. If inflation can be eliminated by expanding real output, unemployment will fall along with the inflation rate.

Tax Incentives. Supply-side economists (such as Arthur Laffer) believe it is possible to use tax reform to increase the growth of output. Progressive taxes discourage people from working and business firms from investing in plants and equipment. Lowering tax rates will therefore raise real output.

The "Laffer Curve" shows the relationship between tax rates and tax collections. If tax rates were to rise to 100 percent of income, there would be little or no output because all incentives to produce and work would disappear. At a 100 percent tax rate, tax revenues would be zero because there would be no income. At the other extreme, if the tax rate were 0 percent of income, incentives to work and produce output would be at their greatest. Although incomes would be high, zero taxes would be collected. Tax collections would be zero at both a 100 percent and a 0 percent tax rate. Accordingly, there must exist some tax rate between 0 and 100 percent at which tax revenues are maximized. For example, one might argue that if the tax rate rises from 40 percent to 50 percent, tax revenues might actually fall because people's work effort and earnings would fall off more rapidly than the tax rate would increase.

If an economy has a tax rate above the rate that yields maximum tax revenues, it can attack inflation by reducing the tax rate. Such a reduction will lead the economy to produce more real output because of improved economic incentives; the government might actually gain tax revenues from the lower tax rate. Both of these effects will reduce inflation. The increase in real output increases the supply of goods and services, and the increase in tax collections reduces the budget deficit.

Former President Ronald Reagan was much influenced by the ideas of the supply-side school. Indeed, the tax cut passed in 1981 was designed to stimulate work effort by lowering marginal tax rates and offering investment incentives to business firms. The tax reform legislation of 1986 also lowered marginal tax rates, but it eliminated certain investment incentives.

Return to the Gold Standard. Supply-side economists favor a return to the gold standard as an inflation cure. As noted in Chapter 14, the money supply is no longer backed by gold. The price of gold, like that of other raw materials, is set by market forces. It rises and falls relative to the value of the dollar as the market dictates.

The ideal gold standard as proposed by supply-siders would work as follows. The value of the dollar would be fixed in terms of gold—say, one ounce of gold would equal $400. The U.S. Treasury would guarantee the value of the dollar in terms of gold. Anyone with $400 could always buy one ounce of gold from the U.S. Treasury. Likewise, the U.S. Treasury would always stand ready to sell one ounce of gold for $400. By buying and selling gold at a fixed price, the relative price of dollars for gold would be fixed.

Under a gold standard, the money supply would be tied to the underlying stock of gold. Monetary authorities would no longer be free to expand or contract the money supply. The control of the money supply would effectively be taken out of their hands.

Under a gold standard, when inflation threatened, gold production would slack off because the value of gold would fall (a dollar would purchase fewer goods). The supply of gold and, hence, the money supply would no longer grow rapidly, and the rate of inflation would fall. As prices fell, the produc-

EXAMPLE 3 Milton Friedman's 100-Year Evidence for Monetarism

Monetarists, led by Nobel laureate Milton Friedman, maintain that the best way to control inflation is for the Fed to increase the money supply at a constant rate equal to the real growth of GDP. The accompanying diagram summarizes 100 years of empirical evidence for this position. The money supply figure measures *excess* monetary growth. When the figure is positive, money is growing more rapidly than real GDP; when it is negative, money is growing more slowly than real GDP.

Friedman's diagram shows that, over the past century, inflation and excess monetary growth have generally moved together. Periods of high excess monetary growth have been generally associated with rapid inflation. However, the relationship is by no means perfect over a short-run period. At times, the two series move closely together; at other times, excess monetary growth accelerates well before inflation. Friedman argues that because the exact timing of the relationship between excess monetary growth and inflation is variable and unpredictable, discretionary monetary policy is unpredictable and potentially dangerous. In his view, it is better to pursue a steady course of constant monetary growth. As Friedman writes, "The quantity of money is not a magic tool. On the contrary, the attempt to use it as such has added to the economy's instability rather than reduced it."

Source: Milton Friedman, "Monetary History, Not Dogma," *Wall Street Journal*, February 12, 1987,: 22.

GDP Deflator

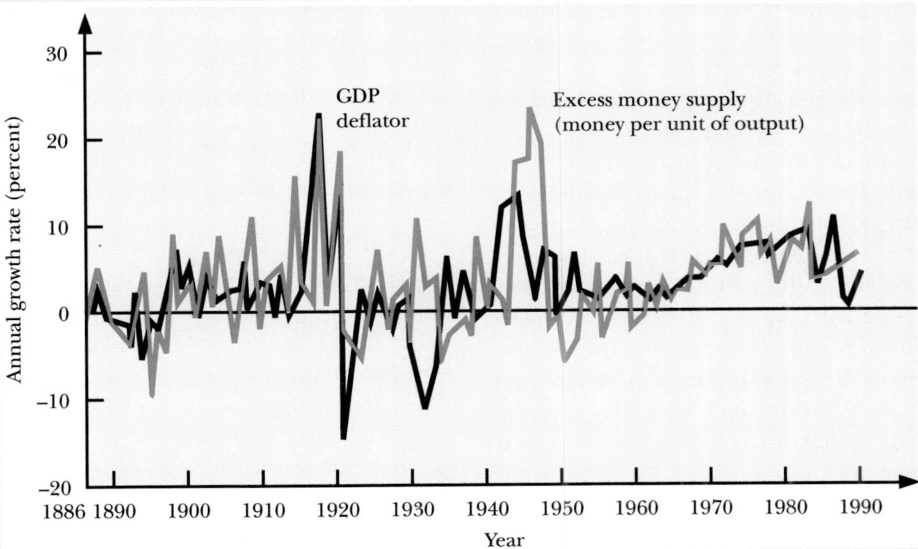

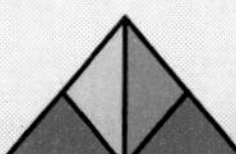

tion of gold would become more profitable because of the increasing value of the dollar. The gold supply would increase more rapidly, and prices would stabilize. Although it is assumed that inflation or deflation would still exist under the gold standard, it is also assumed that private producers of gold would engage in the appropriate anti-inflationary or anti-deflationary monetary policy. Inflation would discourage gold production; deflation would encourage gold production (as long as the price of gold remained fixed in terms of the dollar).

Criticisms. Critics of the supply-side approach point out two problems. First, most economists are skeptical about the possibility of obtaining sustained increases in real output from tax incentives. Tax reductions are likely to bring about relatively small, one-shot increases in real output, not sustained increases. Historically, it is very difficult to raise the growth rate of output; very substantial increases in resources or efficiency are required to raise the annual real growth rate by even 0.5 percent per year. Even under the most favorable circumstances, supply-side increases will not have much of an effect on inflation.

Second, critics of the gold-standard plank of the supply-side school argue that a return to the gold standard would make the money supply a hostage of the two leading gold-producing countries, South Africa and Russia. It also seems unwise to dig up gold and then turn around and bury it again in Fort Knox simply to restrain monetary growth. There must be cheaper ways of limiting monetary growth.

The basic problem with the gold standard is that the economy is still subject to the random shocks of wars, changes in gold production, or crop failures. The United States (along with other industrialized countries) was on the gold standard from 1879 to 1914. During this period, prices fell 47 percent from 1882 to 1896 and then rose 41 percent from 1896 to 1913. Economies on the gold standard went through painful periods of deflation and inflation and depression. As noted earlier, prices were anything but stable during these periods.

Both monetarists and Keynesians would tend to be suspicious of returning to the gold standard. Monetarists would be opposed because the gold standard could not guarantee a steady and moderate rate of money growth. Keynesians would be opposed because the gold standard disallows the use of monetary policy as a discretionary instrument of economic policy.

This chapter explored the facts, causes, and possible cures of inflation. The next chapter will analyze unemployment.

SUMMARY

1. The five facts of inflation are the non-inevitability of inflation, the positive historical relationship between the money supply and the price level, the correlation between high inflation and high interest rates, the inflationary trend in recent years, and the fact that inflation of the 1970s was higher than can be explained by the historical relationship between money supply and prices.

2. Demand-side inflation is caused by increases in aggregate demand. Supply-side inflation is caused by decreases in aggregate supply.

3. In the short run, an increase in the money supply will drive down interest rates, but in the long run, interest rates will return to their original level.

4. Excess monetary growth occurs when the growth of money supply exceeds the growth of output. The growth of the price level will equal the growth of money supply minus the growth of output with constant velocity. When inflation is anticipated, monetary authorities can lower interest rates in the long run only by raising interest rates in the short run. In the long run, deficits and inflation appear to be positively related.

5. Supply-side inflation is caused by supply shocks. Ratification of supply-side inflation occurs when aggregate demand is raised to prevent unemployment from rising as a consequence of a supply shock.

6. The wage/price spiral is caused by anticipated inflation and the ratification of supply-side inflation by monetary authorities.

7. The proposals to cure inflation include the monetarist constant-money-growth rule; the Keynesian package of demand management, incomes policy, and antirecession policies; and supply-side economics.

KEY TERMS

demand-side inflation
supply-side inflation
adaptive expectations
rational expectations
supply shock
ratification of supply-side inflation
wage/price spiral
incomes policy

QUESTIONS AND PROBLEMS

1. The owner of the apartment you are renting complains: "Wages, utilities, and other costs are rising too rapidly. I have no choice but to raise your rent." Is this increase in price a case of supply-side inflation?
2. Economists classify inflation as either supply-side inflation or demand-side inflation. Using aggregate supply-and-demand analysis, explain the differences between these two types of inflation. Is it possible to distinguish between the two types of inflation from observed information on output, employment, and prices?
3. In Friedmania, the money supply has been growing at 8 percent per annum and output has been growing at 3 percent per annum. If velocity is constant, what is the rate of inflation? If velocity is declining at a rate of 2 percent per year, what is the rate of inflation?
4. Explain why increases in money supply that are unanticipated are likely to lower the interest rate. Why may the drop in the interest rate be short-lived? If the increase in money supply is fully anticipated, what will happen to interest rates?
5. Using the adaptive expectations hypothesis, what do you think the expected rate of inflation would be in 1992 if past inflation rates were 6 percent in 1991, 4 percent in 1990, and 1 percent in 1989?
6. If the Fed reduces monetary growth during a period of rapid inflation, would adaptive expectations or rational expectations be expected to cause a more rapid drop in inflation?
7. What should happen to velocity as inflationary expectations increase? What is the actual relationship between velocity and anticipated inflation?
8. Why is the short-run relationship between inflation and government deficits ambiguous?
9. What are some reasons for a long-run relationship between inflation and the government deficit?
10. Using aggregate supply-and-demand analysis, explain why adverse supply shocks combine the worst of two worlds: more inflation and higher unemployment. Also explain why governments tend to ratify supply-side inflation.
11. The wage/price spiral is blamed both on friction between unions and management and on expansionary economic policy. Explain why it is difficult to assign the blame for the wage/price spiral.
12. Evaluate the validity of the following statement: "Both the Keynesians and monetarists believe that inflation is caused primarily by demand-side factors. Therefore, there really is no difference between the two schools' approaches to the inflation problem."
13. What are some arguments for and against wage and price controls?
14. Describe the costs and benefits of a monetary policy based on the gold standard.
15. If you believe in the monetarist approach, do you see in Table 1 any evidence that inflation will increase in the mid-1990s?
16. Critically evaluate: "Inflation is caused by too much money chasing too few goods. We can't reduce our 10 percent inflation rate by monetary policy, because that would increase unemployment. But we can reduce the inflation rate to perhaps 3 or 4 percent by increasing the supply of goods through supply-side tax and work incentives."

SUGGESTED READINGS

Blinder, Alan. *Economic Policy and the Great Stagflation.* New York: Academic Press, 1979.

Colander, David, ed. *Incentive-Based Incomes Policies, Advances in TIP and MAP.* Cambridge, MA: Ballinger Publishing Company, 1986.

Friedman, Milton. "Monetary Policy in a Fiat World." *Contemporary Policy Issues* 4, 1 (January 1986): 1–9.

Kahn, George A., and Stuart E. Weiner. "Has the Cost of Disinflation Declined?" *Federal Reserve Bank of Kansas City Economic Review* (May/June 1990).

Lerner, Abba P. "Stagflation—Its Cause and Cure." *Challenge* 20 (September/October 1977): 14–19.

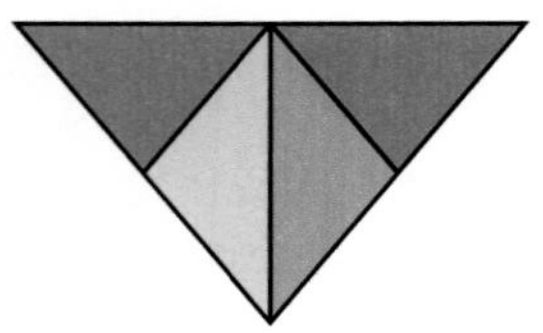

18

Unemployment

CHAPTER INSIGHT

The Employment Act of 1946 committed the federal government to "maintain useful employment opportunities . . . for those able, willing, and seeking work." The full-employment goal was reaffirmed by the Full Employment and Balanced Growth Act of 1978 (also called the Humphrey-Hawkins Bill), in which Congress declared the achievement of full employment a national economic objective. The goal of full employment, unlike other macroeconomic goals, such as price stability or economic growth, has thus been clearly established by federal legislation.

Chapter 6 discussed the facts of unemployment: its rising trend, its cyclical nature, and its complex interaction with employment. In this chapter we turn to the determinants of unemployment, the different types of unemployment (frictional, structural, and cyclical), and the problems of defining unemployment. This chapter examines how people search for jobs and how job searches are affected by inflation. It shows how layoff unemployment differs from other types of unemployment, and it analyzes the natural rate of unemployment as well as its private and social costs.

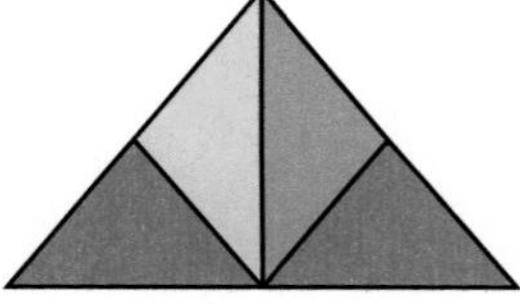

DEFINING UNEMPLOYMENT

The definition of unemployment was introduced in Chapter 6. To be counted as unemployed, a person must meet three conditions.

> A person 16 years or older is unemployed if he or she (1) did not work at all during the preceding week, (2) has actively looked for work during the previous 4 weeks, and (3) is currently available for work.

Persons aged 16 or older who are not unemployed fall into two other categories. They can be either *employed* or *not in the labor force.* Employed persons are either currently working at jobs or have jobs but are currently not working because of bad weather, labor disputes, illness, or other temporary factors. Persons not in the **labor force** remain *voluntarily* outside the labor force because they wish to raise children or attend school, or because they have retired or are suffering from a long-term illness. Some workers remain outside the labor force involuntarily, as will be explained later in a discussion of *discouraged workers.*

> The **labor force** consists of employed and unemployed persons 16 years of age or older who either have jobs or are looking for and available for jobs.

The flow of persons into and out of the labor force and into and out of employment are shown in Figure 1.

Layoffs

There is one exception to the rule that a person without a job and currently available for work must be "actively searching" for a job in order to be classified as unemployed. Workers who are unemployed as a result of a **layoff** and are waiting to be recalled are counted as unemployed even though they are not actively looking for another job.

> A **layoff** is a suspension of employment, without pay and without prejudice, that lasts 7 days or more. The laid-off worker may be recalled to his or her job if economic conditions improve.

Laid-off workers may choose not to search for new jobs because they expect to be recalled within a reasonable period of time and feel that another job would not provide the same pay or benefits.

Problems of Definition

The definition of unemployment raises a number of questions that underscore the difficulty of measuring this phenomenon. It is often a close judgment call whether a particular person is unemployed, employed, or not in the labor force. The unemployment rate is supposed to be a measure of persons who are *involuntarily* without jobs. Yet unemployment has both voluntary and involuntary elements. For example, in the case of an unemployed head of household, willing to accept virtually any paying job but unable to find work, the involuntary element clearly dominates. Conversely, in the case of the spouse of a well-paid executive casually looking for a job compatible with his or her social position, there is a stronger voluntary element. Indeed, in most cases there is a mixture of voluntary and involuntary elements that cannot be separated without knowing an individual's thoughts. (See Example 1.)

There are no accepted ground rules for differentiating unemployment that is less voluntary from unemployment that is more voluntary. The issue of voluntariness in unemployment is thus highly controversial in macroeconomics.

Intensity of Job Search. One criterion we cannot use to distinguish among the unemployed is intensity of job search. Some people may be looking perfunctorily for employment (as in the case of a high-school student casually looking for an after-school job). Other persons may be conducting a very intensive job search, spending 15 hours a day on the telephone, reading want ads, visiting employment agencies, and attending interviews. The Bureau of Labor Statistics gathers data on job-search methods (see Table 1), but these data shed little light on the intensity of job search.

FIGURE 1
Flows Into and Out of the Labor Force

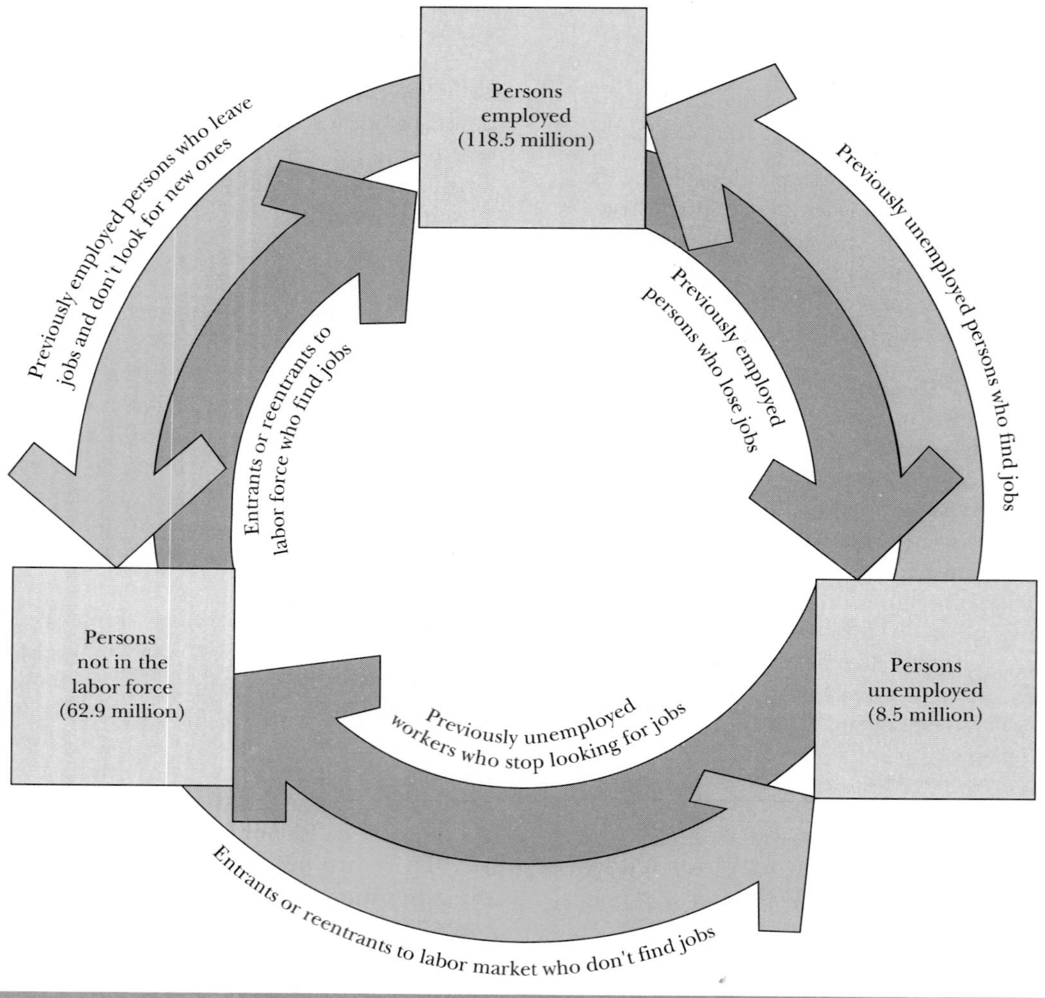

Persons can enter the ranks of the unemployed either by moving from the ranks of the employed or by not finding a job upon entering the labor force. People can drop out of the labor force either by departing from jobs or by giving up the job search once unemployed.

Source: *Employment and Earnings,* April 1987. The data are for 1991.

Matching Jobs and Qualifications. People seek jobs that are consistent with their education, skills, qualifications, and work experience. The unemployed ditchdigger does not seek work as a certified public accountant. The unemployed aeronautical engineer would like to find employment in aeronautical engineering—and may choose to remain unemployed until a suitable position becomes available. Whether a person accepts or rejects a job opportunity that is not consistent with his or her background and abilities depends upon the magnitude of the mismatch (the job of janitor is a greater mismatch for the automotive design engineer than the job of automotive assembly engineer) and upon

EXAMPLE 1 Salient Unemployment

One way to gauge the seriousness of a period of unemployment is to see whether people remember it later. The Work Experience Survey conducted by the U.S. Department of Labor at periodic intervals asks about the number of weeks of unemployment people remember for the preceding calendar year, using the same unemployment definitions as the Labor Department uses in its monthly survey of unemployment. In the Work Experience Surveys, respondents must rely on memory to report labor-market experiences 2–14 months after the event.

Analysts who have compared unemployment rates from the Work Experience Survey with the monthly survey rates find that there are serious recall problems even over this short time period. Most notably, they find that respondents tend to filter out periods of unemployment that were *not salient* (not memorable). The amount of unemployment that people do not remember after the period has passed ranges from 10 to 19 percent.

Some economists argue that salient unemployment is a better measure of unemployment than unemployment data gathered at the time of the unemployment. If people cannot even remember the period of unemployment, it was not very significant.

Source: George A. Akerlof and Janet L. Yellen, "Unemployment Through the Filter of Memory," *Quarterly Journal of Economics* 100, 3 (August 1986): 247–73.

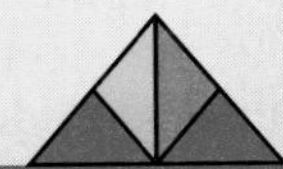

TABLE 1
Job-Search Methods of Unemployed Workers (percent using method)

	By Sex		By Age				
Method	**Men**	**Women**	**16–19**	**20–24**	**25–34**	**35–44**	**45–54**
Public employment agency	27.7	20.7	12.6	27.8	25.6	28.6	31.3
Private employment agency	7.4	6.1	3.1	5.9	8.4	9.1	6.3
Direct contact with employer	76.3	74.1	89.3	76.6	74.5	70.9	73.8
Friends or relatives	18.8	15.4	13.7	17.0	18.2	19.3	18.1
Want ads	33.1	38.1	27.5	35.2	37.0	40.4	37.8
Other	5.4	3.5	2.3	4.5	4.3	6.0	4.7
Average number of methods used	1.69	1.58	1.43	1.67	1.68	1.74	1.72

Source: *Employment and Earnings,* March, 1987.

personal preferences. The problem of matching available jobs with worker qualifications again underscores the difficult distinction between voluntary and involuntary unemployment. The matching problem also explains why unemployment exists even in an economy with a large number of unfilled positions.

> High unemployment combined with a large number of unfilled positions means a mismatch of available jobs with available skills.

Underground Workers. Official unemployment figures fail to capture the hundreds of thousands, or perhaps millions, of people who work in the underground economy. As Chapter 7 demonstrated, the underground economy is a multibillion-dollar business that employs a large number of people. Most people working in the underground economy also have regular jobs and are counted as employed, like the electrician or plumber who also does cash business under the table or the drug smuggler who may have a regular job to cover illegal activities. The **underground workers** missed by official employment statistics, however, are those who are officially counted as "not in the labor force." The retired carpenter who continues a thriving under-the-table home-repair business, the homemaker who runs an unreported word-processing service in the home, full-time college students who moonlight as waiters (and whose earnings go unreported) are all officially counted as not in the labor force even though they have underground employment. Some of the people who are counted as unemployed may also have underground employment. The "unemployed" construction worker may work off the books on a construction project. An "unemployed" domestic worker may work full time on a cash-only basis.

> An **underground worker** is one whose income is unreported or not fully reported to the government.

Because workers in the underground economy have a strong incentive to conceal their activities, government statisticians cannot estimate the size of underground employment. We do not know by how much the inclusion of underground workers would lower the amount of unemployment or affect its changes over time.

Discouraged Workers. People who stop looking for work because they conclude they cannot find suitable jobs represent another problem in measuring unemployment. **Discouraged workers** are considered not in the labor force because they are not actively looking for jobs.

> A **discouraged worker** has stopped looking for a job after becoming convinced (after an unsuccessful job search) that it is not possible to find a suitable job.

Some economists maintain that discouraged workers should be included in the ranks of the unemployed. They argue that there is a big difference between the voluntarily retired person or the full-time homemaker and the discouraged worker, all of whom are classified as not being in the labor force. Although discouraged workers are not counted among the nation's jobless, separate statistics on their numbers are gathered (see Table 2). If discouraged workers were counted as unemployed, the unemployment rate would rise substantially. In 1991, 8.5 million persons were unemployed. Adding the 1.1 million discouraged workers would have raised the number of unemployed to 9.6 million, and the unemployment rate would have increased from 6.8 percent to 7.4 percent.

Involuntary Part-Time Work. According to the official definition, a person is counted as employed even if that person wishes to work full time but can get only a part-time job. Employment is an either/or

TABLE 2
Why Job Wanters Are Not Job Hunters

Reason	Total (thousands)	Percent
School attendance	1412	23.8
Ill health, disability	1010	17.0
Home responsibilities	1300	21.9
Belief that job can't be found	1094	18.4
Other reasons	1117	18.9
Total	**5933**	**100.0**

Source: *Employment and Earnings,* January 1992. Data are for 1991.

proposition: You are either employed or not. There is no such thing as being half employed. Statistics are available, however, for people on voluntary and involuntary part-time work schedules. In November of 1991, for example, 14.9 million people worked on a voluntary part-time basis (70 percent of them were women); 6.5 million were on part-time schedules for "economic reasons" (such as slack work, inability to find full-time work, job changing during the reference week, and material shortages).[1]

For the decade of the 1980s, the average unemployment rate was 7.2 percent according to the official definition. Adjustment for discouraged workers and for involuntary part-time employment raised the average unemployment rate to 10.6 percent.[2]

Types of Unemployment

Economists identify three types of unemployment—*frictional unemployment, cyclical unemployment,* and *structural unemployment*—that differ in their degree of voluntariness. These distinctions are useful in thinking about unemployment.

Frictional Unemployment. Business conditions change constantly. Employment opportunities are created in one business, region, or industry at the same time that they are lost elsewhere. Employed workers are usually on the lookout for better jobs; employers are usually on the lookout for better workers. Yet each worker possesses incomplete information about job opportunities, and each employer possesses incomplete information about prospective employees. It therefore takes time for people to match themselves to jobs.

People are constantly entering and leaving the labor force. In this sense, the labor market is like a revolving door. At any given time, some workers will be changing jobs. Some will be entering the labor force for the first time or reentering after an absence; others will be leaving the labor force. The result of this flux is **frictional unemployment.**

> **Frictional unemployment** is associated with the changing of jobs in a dynamic economy.

In the case of frictional unemployment, there is no great imbalance between the number of qualified job seekers and the number of unfilled jobs. Frictional unemployment will always be with us. Its magnitude depends upon the age, sex, occupational, and racial composition of the labor force and upon how rapidly the economy itself is changing. Typically, frictional unemployment concerns economists and policymakers less than other types of unemployment. Frictional unemployment can even improve economic well-being in some ways: if the frictionally unemployed use this time to locate better jobs, they (and society) benefit.

Frictional unemployment would disappear only if people were frozen into their current jobs by the lack of opportunity for job advancement or if no one left jobs until they had already found new ones. Although frictional unemployment is always present in a dynamic economy, there are ways to limit it. Measures that increase information about job opportunities or that speed up the search for jobs reduce frictional unemployment.

Cyclical Unemployment. During cyclical downturns, fewer goods and services are purchased, employers cut back on jobs, and people find themselves without jobs. Many workers in basic industrial employment (steel, auto, and farm equipment manufacturing) will be unemployed until the economy improves. Unlike frictional unemployment, **cyclical unemployment** involves largely involuntary job changes. People become unemployed because their jobs evaporate in a generally declining economy.

> **Cyclical unemployment** is unemployment associated with general downturns in the economy.

In the case of cyclical unemployment, general declines in business activity reduce the number of unfilled positions, making it more difficult for job seekers to locate jobs. With cyclical unemployment, there is a mismatch between the number of unfilled jobs and qualified job seekers. People are unemployed for longer periods as business worsens. Family incomes fall; marriages break apart; even the suicide rate rises during periods of cyclical unemployment. People become worried about their jobs and express their dissatisfaction at the ballot box by voting against incumbents.

A smoothly functioning labor market matches people to jobs for which they are suited, and does

[1] *Statistical Abstract of the United States, 1991,* Table 664.

[2] *Monthly Labor Review,* U.S. Department of Labor (January 1992): 86.

so within a reasonable amount of time. In individual cases, this process breaks down. Even after searching for jobs for 6 months, a year, or longer, the chronically unemployed still cannot find jobs.

Although jobs affected by cyclical conditions pay higher wages than comparable jobs, cyclical unemployment offers few or no benefits to the unemployed or to society. Having otherwise productive workers sitting on the sidelines without jobs reduces the efficiency of resource utilization and causes the economy to produce less output than it is capable of producing.

Structural Unemployment. In a dynamic economy, some industries, companies, and regions experience rising economic fortunes at the same time that others experience a long-term decline. In declining industries—particularly those concentrated in specific regions of the country—employees suffer **structural unemployment.**

> **Structural unemployment** results from the long-run decline of certain industries in response to rising costs, changes in consumer preferences, or technological change.

In the case of structural unemployment, the task of matching people and jobs is more difficult than in frictional unemployment as people must move from a declining industry to an expanding industry to find jobs.

Long-term structural unemployment is especially prominent when it is concentrated in a specific region of the country. An example would be the high unemployment in the oil industry in the mid-1980s. People hit hardest by structural unemployment are those who find it most difficult to relocate. Workers over 50 years old with a lifetime of work in the

EXAMPLE 2 Elections and the Jobless Issue

In late 1991, the U.S. unemployment rate was 6.2 percent, the Canadian rate was 9.7 percent, and the German rate (not counting eastern Germany) was 7.2 percent. In each country, the unemployment rate was the highest in nearly a decade. The puzzling feature of the high unemployment in 1991 was its small political effect. In the U.S., Congressional attempts to extend unemployment coverage went without sponsors, and in Canada and Germany, the parliamentary majorities of the ruling conservative parties were not threatened. In 1958, with a 6.8 percent unemployment rate, then Senator John Kennedy argued passionately for extending unemployment benefits, and his defense of the unemployed is credited with helping him win the 1960 presidential election. In 1991, sponsors of similar bills feared being labeled "big spenders" by their constituents.

The pending 1992 election caused a reversal of lax attitudes toward unemployment. As the unemployment rate continued to rise to 7.1 percent and the election drew closer, President Bush declared his deep concern and sympathy for the unemployed. He dropped his opposition to extending unemployment benefits, and the Emergency Unemployment Compensation Act of 1991 was passed in December. This emergency program provided 13 or 20 weeks of federally funded unemployment benefits to claimants who had exhausted their regular benefits. States were also permitted to pay unemployment benefits between school years and terms to school employees. Waiting periods for unemployment benefits were dropped for veterans.

State officials, also concerned about reelection, began to extend state unemployment benefits to ensure that the long-term unemployed remained eligible for unemployment benefits.

Sources: "Jobless Issue Becomes a Puzzle for Democrats," *New York Times,* April 28, 1991; "Changes in Unemployment Insurance Legislation in 1991," *Monthly Labor Review,* U.S. Department of Labor (January 1992): 64–69.

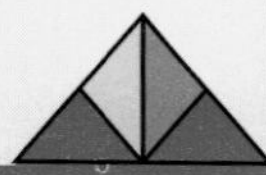

oil industry would find it difficult (and perhaps not economically worthwhile) to move to another industry in another region. Declining defense spending is expected to cause structural unemployment in California, Texas, and New York in the 1990s.

People fear both cyclical and structural unemployment. The 1946 Employment Act reflects public concern about high unemployment. (See Example 2.)

THE THEORY OF CYCLICAL UNEMPLOYMENT

Cyclical unemployment occurs when there is a general decline in the number of vacant jobs relative to the number of qualified job seekers. Chapter 6 showed a distinct pattern of employment and unemployment during recessions and recoveries. During the downturn, the unemployment rate rises, employment falls, and people drop out of the labor force. During recoveries and booms, unemployment falls, the growth of employment accelerates, and people return to the labor force as either job holders or job seekers. Table 3 shows that during cyclical downturns, the duration of periods of unemployment and the proportion of long-term unemployment rise. During periods of prosperity, the duration of periods of unemployment shortens.

Cyclical unemployment occurs when the short-run aggregate supply curve intersects the aggregate demand curve below the natural rate of unemployment (see Figure 2). It can be caused either by a reduction in aggregate demand or in short-run aggregate supply. This section uses a reduction in aggregate demand to explain cyclical unemployment.

If the economy is initially operating at the natural rate of unemployment (and, accordingly, producing the natural level of output), a reduction in aggregate demand (from AD to AD′) moves the economy to an output level below the natural level (from *a* to *b*). The price level is lower at the new short-run equilibrium, and the economy is in a *deflationary gap*. The upper horizontal axis (in color) measures *the unemployment rate associated with each level of output.* The level of output is measured along the lower horizontal axis. The natural rate of unemployment (u_n) coincides with the natural level of output (y_n) by definition. Note that because output and the corresponding rate of unemployment move in opposite directions, the unemployment rate starts out at u_n and gets progressively lower as it moves to the left of u_n Figure 2 shows that the unemployment rate rises above the natural rate as the aggregate demand falls, starting from an initial equilibrium at the natural rate of unemployment.

TABLE 3
Proportion of Unemployment by Duration during Contractions and Expansions

		Percentage of Unemployed Out of Work for:		
Year	**Cycle**	**Less than 5 Weeks**	**27 Weeks or More**	**Average Duration of Unemployment (weeks)**
1959	Expansion	44.4	15.3	14.4
1961	Contraction	38.3	17.1	15.6
1965	Expansion	48.4	10.4	11.8
1975	Contraction	37.0	15.2	14.2
1978	Expansion	46.2	10.4	11.9
1981	Contraction	41.7	14.0	13.7
1984	Expansion	39.2	19.1	18.2
1986	Expansion	41.9	14.4	15.0
1991	Contraction	39.3	13.1	13.8

Source: *Economic Report of the President.*

FIGURE 2
How a Reduction in Aggregate Demand Raises Unemployment and Lowers Real GDP

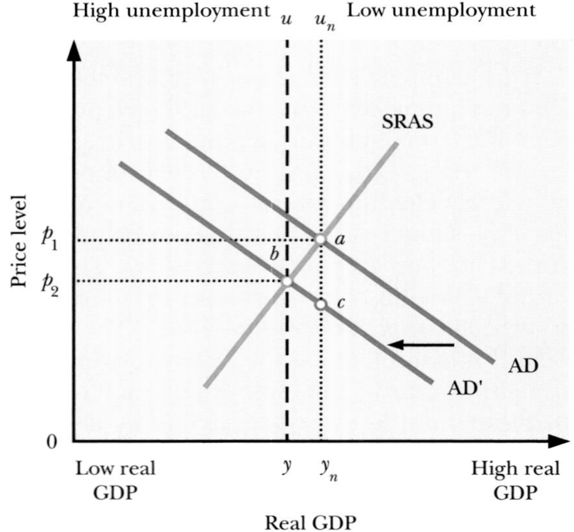

A reduction in aggregate demand (the movement of AD to AD′) reduces real output from the natural level of output (y_n) to a level (y) below the natural rate. The horizontal axis that appears at the top of the diagram shows the movements in unemployment that accompany movements in output level. As output falls below y_n, the unemployment rate rises above the natural rate of unemployment (from u_n to u).

> Cyclical unemployment occurs when aggregate demand falls to the extent that the economy produces less than the natural level of output and hence operates above the natural rate of unemployment.

JOB SEARCH AND UNEMPLOYMENT

When the economy is in a deflationary gap (actual output is less than the natural level of output), the number of qualified job seekers exceeds the number of unfilled jobs. Job seekers find it more difficult to find appropriate jobs; the job search takes longer, and periods of unemployment are longer. People search for jobs when the economy is at the natural level of output, but at this level there is a general match between the number of unfilled jobs and the number of qualified job seekers.

LABOR MARKET SEARCH

When people become unemployed, they do not automatically step into their next job. If they did, there would be little unemployment. Instead, they begin a job search—which can be short or long. They must search because they cannot possibly know about all possible jobs for which they are qualified. They find out about these jobs by telephoning, hiring professional placement counselors, networking, going to factory gates, and so on. They must decide whether to take a job that is below their expectations or to search further for a better job.

People use common sense in making these decisions. If they pass up a job, they don't earn the income from that job. There are opportunity costs to continuing the search. People continue to search as long as they expect to gain more from searching than it costs.

How people search for jobs has a considerable effect on unemployment. If something happens to make people shorten their job search, unemployment drops. If something happens to make people prolong their job search, unemployment rises.

How People Become Unemployed

The labor market is a vast information-processing network that must match an incredible variety of jobs—from brain surgeon to store clerk—to an equally impressive variety of workers. In a world where everyone possessed complete information, matching jobs to people would be a relatively simple task. Everyone would be aware of all jobs in the economy, and employers would know the skills and qualifications of all potential employees. There would be little or no unemployment except in periods of cyclical unemployment.

Unemployment evokes the image of job losses (firings and layoffs). These are indeed important sources of unemployment, but there are other ways of becoming unemployed. Table 4 shows the sources of unemployment during a year of cyclical expansion (1989) and a year of cyclical contraction (1991). (See also Figure 1 for a graphic illustration.) Of those unemployed, 34 to 38 percent were unemployed not because they had been fired or laid off but because they had not found jobs upon entry (or reentry) into the labor force. The entry and reentry of people into the labor market goes on all the time and accounts for a significant percentage of total unemployment. With the exception of laid-off workers who are waiting to be recalled, the unemployed are all searching for a job.

How people become unemployed is affected by the business cycle. As shown in Table 4, during business expansions, the proportion of those fired or laid off falls, and the proportion of those who quit jobs rises. During the prosperous late 1960s, job losses accounted for only 40 percent of unemployment while 14.5 percent were quits. During the recession of 1981, 59 percent were job losses and 8 percent were quits. Figure 3 shows how quits move with the business cycle (rising in importance during prosperity and falling during recessions), whereas layoffs move *counter* to the business cycle.

TABLE 4
How People Become Unemployed

Reasons for Unemployment	1989 Expansion (percent)	1991 Contraction (percent)
Lost job—layoff or firing	46	54
Left job	16	12
Did not find job upon entering the labor force	10	9
Did not find job upon reentering the labor force	28	25
Total	**100**	**100**

Source: *Monthly Labor Review.*

The Theory of Job Search

By definition, those who are unemployed are actively searching for employment. Firms are also searching for workers. The economic theory of job search maintains that both individuals and firms search the labor market in a rational manner.[3]

The Rational Search for Jobs. People cannot know about all the jobs that are available now or may become available in the future. Taking a job now may mean passing up the opportunity to find a better job. If a person knew all the unfilled jobs that were available, there would be no need to search. People could immediately move to new and better jobs without a job search. Entrants to the job market could instantly accept the best of all jobs open to them. In a world of perfect job information, there would be little frictional unemployment.

In the real world, people do not have perfect information about jobs. Job seekers must make decisions based upon uncertain information. To gain job information, job seekers must read newspaper ads, telephone, set up interviews, travel to distant cities, hire private placement firms. Gathering such information is costly, both in time and money. The most significant cost of continued job search is the opportunity cost of not accepting a job offer. The longer the search, the greater the cost. Presumably, a longer search also yields greater benefits in the form of a higher-paying and more satisfactory job. The theory of job search maintains that rational people will weigh these costs and benefits in deciding on the amount of search time. They will search for jobs only as long as the benefits outweigh the costs.

> The rational worker searches in the labor market as long as the expected benefits from more searching (the marginal benefits) exceed the expected costs of more searching (the marginal costs).

The Search for Employees. Firms searching for employees use the same general logic as workers looking for jobs. Firms have a variety of jobs through

[3]The theory of the economics of search was developed by Edmund Phelps, Martin Feldstein, Dale Mortensen, Ronald Ehrenberg, and George Neumann. For a survey of this literature, see Ronald Ehrenberg and Robert Smith, *Modern Labor Economics,* 4th ed. (New York: HarperCollins, 1991), chap. 15.

FIGURE 3
Quit Rates and Layoff Rates

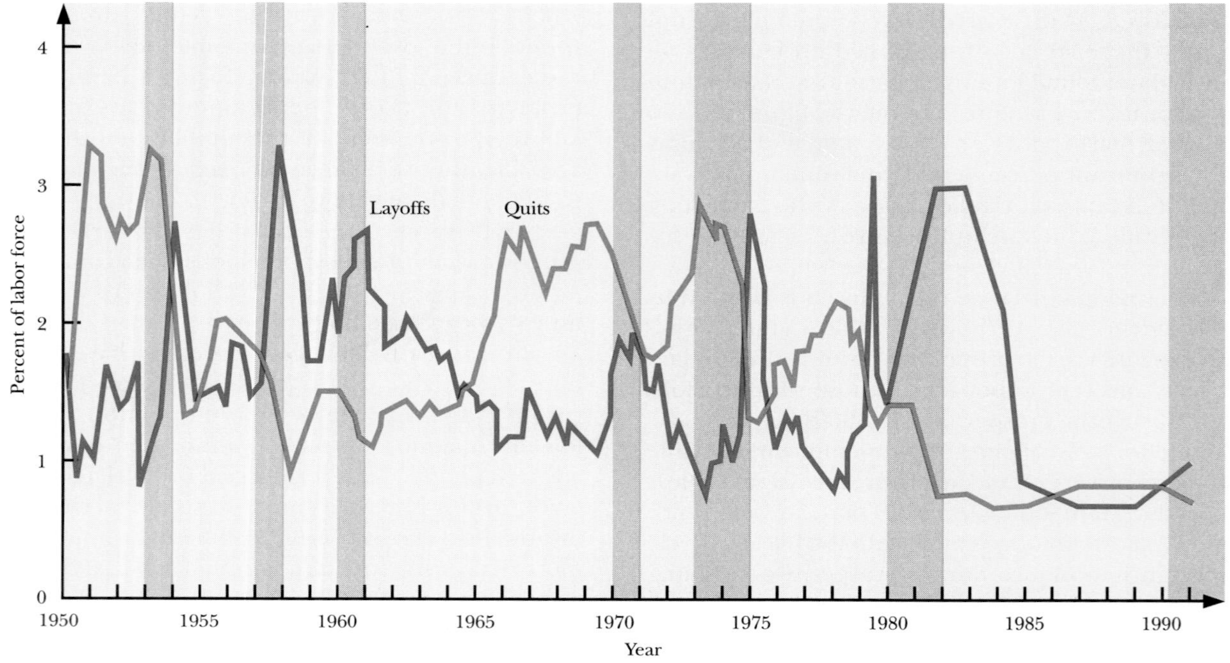

Quit rates tend to drop and layoff rates tend to rise during periods of recession.

Sources: *Economic Report of the President; Survey of Current Business; Employment and Earnings.*

quits, layoffs, firings, and general business expansion. They wish to staff available jobs with the best possible people, but they do not know everything about potential employees. To gather such information, they search for new employees, but searching incurs search costs: Ads must be placed in newspapers, management personnel must be assigned to recruiting committees, the training costs of new employees must be paid. Moreover, the firm incurs an opportunity cost by leaving positions vacant and continuing to search.

The firm benefits from search because careful selection procedures identify new employees whose benefits to the firm exceed their wage plus their hiring costs. The longer the search takes, the more likely the firm will be to acquire the most qualified employees. The rational firm will search for employees until the marginal costs of further search equal marginal benefits. (See Example 3.)

> Firms search for new employees as long as the cost of more searching (marginal cost) is less than the expected benefits of more searching (marginal benefits).

The Duration of Unemployment

The extent of the search that job seekers and firms undertake depends upon its marginal costs and benefits. When a search is less extensive, job seekers accept jobs more quickly and firms hire more quickly.

> The duration of periods of unemployment falls when job seekers and firms reduce their search time. For the economy as a whole, shorter search time means lower unemployment.

EXAMPLE 3 Search Methods: Interviewing and Hiring New Employees

Search theory postulates that employers search for employees in a rational manner by balancing the marginal costs and marginal benefits of search. The existence of systematic employer search procedures has been documented by a 1980 survey of 3100 employers who had recently hired new employees. Employers were asked: How many hours were spent recruiting, screening, and interviewing? How many job applicants were interviewed? How many people turned down offers? What was the current starting wage of the job?

Analysis of these results reveals that larger employers are more efficient at interviewing (their marginal costs are lower) and they interview more applicants per job but spend less time per interview. The greater the level of training that must be given the new employee (the higher the marginal benefits of search), the more the employer searches. The marginal benefits of selecting the right professional or technical employee are greater than those of selecting the right blue-collar worker, and employers do indeed devote more search time to hiring professional and technical workers.

Source: John M. Barron, John Bishop, and William Dunkelberg, "Employer Search: The Interviewing and Hiring of New Employees," *Review of Economics and Statistics* 67, 1 (February 1985): 43–52.

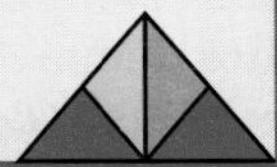

Shorter searches result in lower unemployment rates. Longer searches translate into higher unemployment rates. Decisions to quit searching altogether and withdraw from the labor force translate into lower unemployment rates. To explain unemployment, economists must therefore concentrate on the factors that affect search costs and benefits for the economy as a whole rather than for single individuals or firms. Two such factors are unanticipated inflation and unemployment benefits.

Unanticipated Inflation. Unanticipated inflation affects the duration of unemployment in three ways. First, it causes workers to accept jobs more quickly because they get more offers that exceed their **reservation wage.**

> A **reservation wage** is the minimum wage offer that a job searcher will accept.

Workers who are searching for jobs enter the job market with a preconceived reservation wage. The reservation wage is a *real wage,* for workers base their employment decisions on real, not nominal, wages. (The real wage is the nominal wage adjusted for inflation.) They will accept the first job that offers a wage greater than or equal to their reservation wage. The higher the worker's reservation wage, the longer the search (the period of unemployment) will last.

How do workers go about determining their reservation wages? Job-searching workers have some idea of the distribution of wages in their occupation (the highest possible wage, the lowest possible wage, the average wage), but the job searcher does not know which firms are offering which wages. To obtain this information, the job searcher must search the job market to obtain job offers.

Unanticipated inflation can therefore shorten job searches. With wages rising generally throughout the economy, firms start to raise their money-wage offers. Because a greater number of wage offers equal or exceed the reservation wages of job searchers, job seekers are more willing to accept jobs, and the unemployment rate falls. The increase in money-wage offers makes workers (who anticipate no inflation) think that real-wage offers have increased. The perceived increase in real wages raises the opportunity cost of not accepting job offers.

Second, firms affect the duration of unemployment by shortening their search time during unanticipated inflation. In labor markets governed by fixed union-wage contracts, unanticipated inflation raises selling prices faster than costs. Rather than leave positions unfilled, firms step up their hiring of new workers. Fearing that fewer and fewer qualified workers will be available, firms are also motivated to hold on to current employees. As firms shorten their search time, the unemployment rate falls.

> Unanticipated inflation causes unemployment to fall by reducing the search time of job seekers and firms.

Third, as we shall see in the next section, unanticipated inflation also shortens search time by eroding unemployment benefits.

Unemployment Benefits. Unemployment benefits help to determine the duration of unemployment by affecting the marginal costs of job search. Workers must compare the opportunity cost of earnings from jobs that they have not accepted with unemployment benefits to determine their net marginal search costs. If unemployment benefits fall, the opportunity cost of turning down jobs rises. A decline in unemployment benefits raises the cost of remaining unemployed. Workers therefore accept jobs more readily. (See Example 4.)

> A reduction in unemployment benefits reduces both the duration and amount of unemployment by raising the costs of job search.

Unlike unanticipated inflation, unemployment benefits do not fluctuate substantially over short periods of time. In the short run, however, inflation can alter the costs of unemployment by eroding unemployment benefits, which tend to lag behind inflation. When rising inflation lowers real unemployment benefits, it raises the costs of remaining unemployed, and people cut short their job searches.

> The relationship between unanticipated inflation and unemployment should be negative.

EXAMPLE 4 Unemployment and Jobless Benefits in Europe

From the 1950s through the 1970s, Europe was a region of very low unemployment rates; in the 1980s and 1990s, it has had relatively high unemployment rates. Between 1973 and 1990, the average unemployment rate in Western Europe rose from 3 to around 10 percent. Economists have puzzled over the causes of the rise in European unemployment and have isolated a number of factors. Researchers who have investigated this issue, such as British economists Richard Layard and Stephen Nickell, have concluded that the unconditional payment of unemployment benefits for an indefinite period is a major cause of high European unemployment. Researchers report the case of an unemployed chauffeur who collected Belgian unemployment benefits for 15 years while turning down jobs as a taxi and truck driver. In England, libraries make available pamphlets with the title, "Leaving School: What You Should Know about Social Security Benefits." In the Netherlands, where unemployment benefits can be drawn virtually indefinitely, a new law will require young people through the age of 20 to work if they are not in school.

The magnitude and duration of unemployment benefits determine the "cost" of unemployment. This chapter teaches that the duration of job searches depends upon both the costs and benefits of unemployment.

Sources: Olivier Blanchard and Lawrence Summers, "Beyond the Natural Rate Hypothesis: Why Is Unemployment So High In Europe?" *American Economic Review* 78 (May 1988): 182–93; Richard Layard and Stephen Nickell, in *The Rise in Unemployment,* ed. Charles Bean et al. (London: Basil Blackwell, 1987).

The next chapter explores the relationship between inflation and unemployment.

LAYOFF UNEMPLOYMENT AND IMPLICIT CONTRACTING

Search theory does not apply to laid-off workers waiting to be recalled to their former jobs.[4] Why are some workers willing to wait to be recalled while others search the labor market?

In specific industries, typically unionized industries such as automobiles and steel, workers have an **implicit contract** with their employers that motivates them not to search for jobs when they have been laid off.

> An **implicit contract** is an agreement between an employer and employees concerning conditions of pay, employment, and unemployment that is unwritten but understood by both parties.

Industries that use implicit contracting are subject to the ups and downs of the business cycle. During business expansions, more jobs are available. During downturns, fewer jobs are available. The employers require a long-term labor force composed of workers who have gained skills specific to that industry. When business is bad, they do not want to lose their skilled workers permanently. Workers, on the other hand, have acquired skills that are more valuable to that particular firm than to outside firms. They know that they will earn their highest wages in that industry.

To cope with this situation, workers and employers strike an implicit bargain. Employers agree to pay workers a higher wage than they could earn elsewhere as long as they are employed. In return, workers agree to wait to be recalled when laid off during bad times, and the employer agrees that laid-off workers will be the first to be recalled when business conditions improve. The employer will not necessarily reduce the wages of those who remain employed during business downturns. Rather, wages are held steady throughout the cycle. Improvements in business conditions—not lower wages—cause jobs to reappear.

Implicit labor contracts explain the tendency of wages to remain stable during periods of high unemployment. If a large proportion of the labor force operates according to such implicit contracts, laid-off workers do not enter the job market. The presence of laid-off workers therefore need not drive down wages in the industry from which they have been laid off.

> Implicit contracting explains how wages can remain steady during periods of high unemployment.

Implicit labor bargains are most prevalent in unionized industries, which account for about one-fifth of employment. It is difficult to determine how closely both sides stick to the implicit bargain. Do employers start to shave wages when business conditions are bad? Do unemployed workers not search for other employment during layoffs?

[4]The theory of implicit contracting was developed by Arthur Okun in *Prices and Quantities* (Washington, D.C.: Brookings Institution, 1981).

CAUSES OF RISING UNEMPLOYMENT

Chapter 6 noted that the U.S. unemployment rate has been generally rising over the last 40 years. In Europe, unemployment has risen steeply since 1970. (See Figure 4.) This section explores possible explanations.

The Changing Composition of the Labor Force

The composition of the American labor force has changed dramatically since the end of World War II. In 1950, women accounted for 30 percent of the labor force; in 1991, they accounted for 45 percent (see Table 5). In 1950, only 1.4 million women with young children were in the labor force; by 1991, their number had increased to almost 5 million. Table 5 also shows that the labor force share of persons aged 16–24 has increased as well.

FIGURE 4
The Rise in Unemployment in the Industrialized Countries

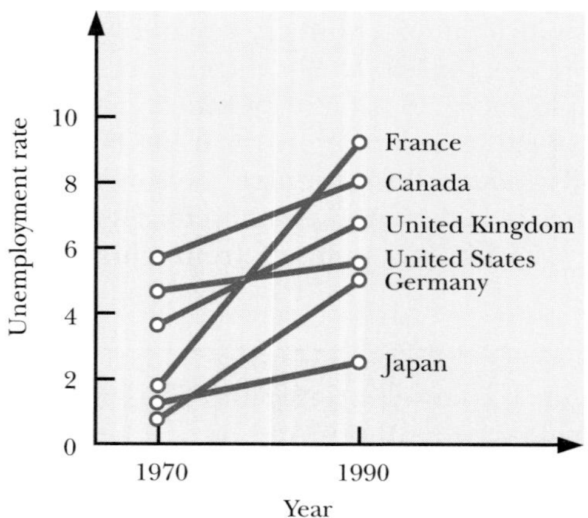

Sources: OECD, *Historical Statistics,* 1960–1981, Table 2.15; *Monthly Labor Review* (January 1992): 48.

Figure 5 shows that different groups of workers have different rates of unemployment. The unemployment rate of married men, while varying from year to year, has not increased over the long run. The unemployment rates of males and females 20 years and older have risen only slightly. The unemployment rates of young people 16–19 years of age reveal a distinct upward trend, as do the unemployment rates of women who maintain families. The unemployment rates of experienced wage and salary workers have risen less than those of blue-collar workers.

TABLE 5
Shares in the Labor Force by Sex and Age

	Percent	
Category	**1950**	**1991**
Men	70	55
Women	30	45
Persons aged 16–24	18	23
Persons aged 35–44	22	20

The labor-force shares of women and young workers have increased over the past 35 years; women and young people also tend to have higher unemployment rates.

Source: *Monthly Labor Review.*

To what extent can the rise in the unemployment rate be explained by the rising labor-force shares of women and young workers, who have higher-than-average unemployment rates? One study shows that approximately one-third of the increase in the unemployment rate between the late 1950s and the mid-1970s was explained by changes in the composition of the labor force.[5] One must look to other factors to explain the remaining two-thirds of the rise in the unemployment rate.

Changing Private Costs and Private Benefits

Modern economists maintain that much unemployment can be explained in cost/benefit terms: If the costs of being unemployed are reduced, the unemployment rate should rise. The costs of unemployment are affected by a number of factors, including multiple-earner households, unemployment insurance, taxes, minimum-wage laws, and progressive taxation.

Multiple Earners. In 1960, about 23 percent of the U.S. female population over the age of 16 was employed. By 1991, this figure was close to 50 percent. The trend toward two or more working members in a household has changed the costs of unemployment. Before 1960, the unemployment of a household head usually meant an almost total loss of family income. In the 1990s, the earnings losses to a household of one unemployed member are cushioned by the earnings of other employed members. In the recession year of 1982, for example, only 28 percent of families with an unemployed member had no employed person in the family. Only in single-parent families with children was there a high percentage of families with unemployment and no employed member (47 percent for single-parent families headed by females and 37.5 percent for single-parent families headed by males).

[5]N. J. Simler has calculated what the 1976 unemployment rate would have been had the labor-force composition not changed over the preceding 20 years. Simler finds that the 1976 unemployment rate would have been only one-third lower. See Simler, "Employment and Unemployment," Federal Reserve Bank of Minneapolis *Review,* April 1978, 13.

FIGURE 5
Selected Unemployment Rates

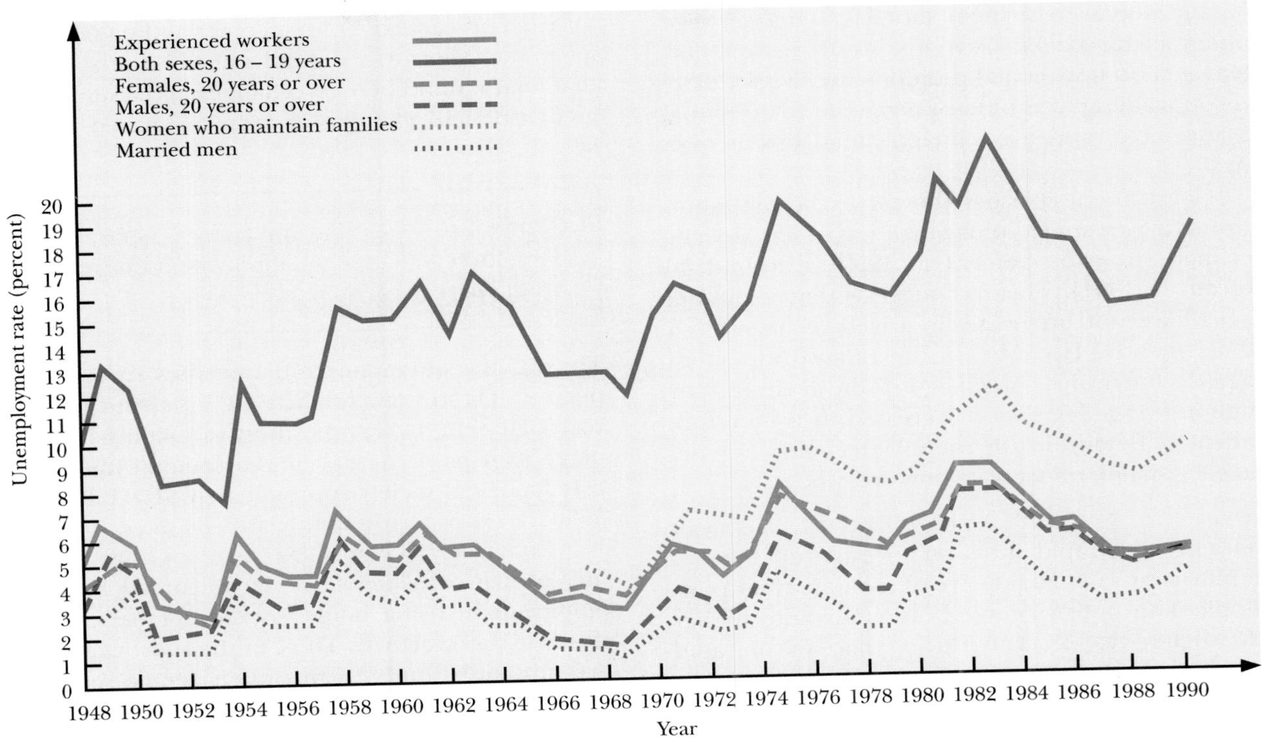

Unemployment rates vary for different segments of the labor force. Teenagers and women who maintain families have experienced rising unemployment rates in recent decades.

Source: *Economic Report of the President.*

Unemployment Insurance. Rising coverage and rising benefits offered by unemployment insurance have altered the costs of unemployment over the past 25 years. Some economists have argued that the substantial decline in the personal costs of unemployment explains much of the rise in the unemployment rate.[6]

Over the past quarter century, the proportion of *covered employment* (workers and employees covered by state and federal unemployment insurance) has risen. In 1950, 58 percent of the labor force was covered. By 1991, 88 percent of the labor force was covered. In 1950, the average weekly unemployment benefit represented 39 percent of average weekly earnings when working. In 1991, it accounted for about 46 percent.

Unemployed workers who are eligible for unemployment compensation can count on state and federal programs to cover roughly one-half of after-tax wage income. Employer-provided benefits and union unemployment funds raise benefits above 50 percent of former earnings in certain instances.

The long-term trend toward rising protection of unemployed workers reversed in the mid-1970s with the tightening of eligibility requirements and the rise of individual ineligibility due to employment in service industries and part-time positions. (Refer back to Example 4 on unemployment benefits and unemployment in Europe.)

[6]Martin Feldstein, "The Economics of the New Unemployment," *Public Interest* 33 (Fall 1973).

Minimum-Wage Laws. Figure 5 shows, teenage unemployment is significantly higher than adult unemployment. Many economists argue that this is the result of a minimum wage that is too high to encourage employers to spend money training teenage employees for skilled positions. As a consequence, teenagers occupy menial positions, receive little on-the-job training, see little opportunity for eventual advancement, and leave unappealing jobs at high rates.

Government statistics show that the minimum wage as a percentage of average wages has actually declined (from 54 percent in 1950 to around 40 percent in 1991). This fact suggests that minimum wages have not progressively priced teenagers out of the market. However, as the relative minimum wage declined, the percentage of those covered by minimum-wage legislation increased. It is therefore difficult to determine the overall effect of minimum-wage legislation on teenage unemployment.

Progressive Taxation. A progressive tax system can combine with rapid inflation to push up the unemployment rate. Highly progressive tax rates push middle- and upper-income households into higher and higher tax brackets during periods of rapid inflation. As inflation moves people into higher tax brackets, the after-tax rewards to employment are reduced. Moreover, the costs of unemployment increase when unemployment benefits are taxed. In addition, the combination of inflation and progressive taxes pushes people into the underground economy where, although they are actually working, they may not be counted as employed.

The Tax Reform Act of 1986 reduced the progressivity of the U.S. federal income tax. Lessening progressivity plus indexing tax rates for inflation would be expected to reduce unemployment.

THE SOCIAL COSTS OF UNEMPLOYMENT

During the contraction phase of the business cycle, the unemployment rate rises above the natural rate. If cyclically unemployed resources had been productively employed, more output could have been produced, and society could have had a higher standard of living, *ceteris paribus*. The aggregate loss of income and output attributable to cyclical unemployment is the social cost of cyclically unemployed resources.

Economist Arthur Okun measured the social cost of unemployment in terms of the loss of output for each percentage point increase in the unemployment rate above the natural rate. The relationship that Okun found between changes in the unemployment rate and changes in output is called **Okun's law.**

> **Okun's law** states that for every 1 percentage point increase in the unemployment rate, there is a 2.5 percent drop in real GDP.

Thus, if the unemployment rate rises from 6 to 7 percent, Okun's law predicts a 2.5 percent drop in real GDP.[7] In 1991, according to Okun's law, a 1 percentage point increase in the unemployment rate cost American society approximately $150 billion, or $630 for every person in the United States.

Conversely, Okun's law assumes that cyclical increases in *employment* are accompanied by rising employment, rising hours worked per person, and increased productivity. Thus, in the short run, there are substantial output gains when people return to productive employment. Idle capital is utilized more efficiently, and people doing part-time work return to full-time jobs.[8]

The private costs of unemployment are not evenly distributed across society. The long-term unemployed with minimal unemployment-insurance protection bear a substantial burden of the private unemployment costs, especially if they place a low value on their leisure time. The unemployed with generous unemployment benefits suffer less. Employees in declining industries who must pull up stakes to find employment must also pay a personal cost.

[7] Arthur Okun, in "Upward Mobility in a High-Pressure Economy," Brookings Papers in Economic Activity (1973:2), estimates the ratio to be 3. More recent estimates place the ratio at 2.5.

[8] Okun's law applies only to cyclical fluctuations in the unemployment rate. It overstates the effects of a permanent increase in the natural rate of unemployment. In the long run, the sole effect of the increase in the unemployment rate is the decrease in the number of workers employed; long-run effects on productivity and hours worked are not expected. In the long run, a 1 percentage point increase in the natural rate of unemployment should yield about a 1 percent reduction in real GDP.

EXAMPLE 5 The Human Costs of Unemployment

Economists typically concentrate on the easily measurable dollar costs of unemployment. Unemployed workers lose income and, when the unemployment rate exceeds the natural rate, society loses output that could have been produced without heating up inflation. Researchers find that unemployment also has human costs that rise during periods of high cyclical unemployment. Scientific statistical studies and newspaper accounts report that family conflict and child-abuse rates, alcoholism, and divorce rates rise as the unemployment rate rises. Unemployed workers often lose their health insurance. Statistical studies find that a 1 percent increase in the unemployment rate is associated with 920 more suicides, 650 more homicides, 20,000 more heart attacks, and 4000 additional admissions to mental hospitals.

Source: Barry Bluestone and Bennett Harrison, *The Deindustrialization of America* (New York: Basic Books, 1982), chap. 3.

The worker in a cyclically depressed industry must bear the anxiety of waiting to be recalled and the belt tightening associated with layoffs. It is obviously not pleasant to be unemployed, except when it is a short interruption to move up the job ladder. (See Example 5.)

REDUCING UNEMPLOYMENT

Can the government do anything to control long-term unemployment? If programs can be enacted to improve the efficiency of labor markets and provide job skills to those with limited training and experience, the long-term unemployment rate should decline.

The Employment Act of 1946 gave the federal government responsibility for fighting excessive unemployment, but monetary and fiscal policy cannot affect the structural unemployment that results from a declining industry or a severe lack of employable skills. For this reason, the federal government—in conjunction with state governments—has instituted a series of job programs designed to combat structural unemployment.

The most ambitious programs of the federal government in the area of labor-force training were enacted during the Johnson administration's drive for the "Great Society." Programs such as the Job Corps, Manpower Training and Development, and Neighborhood Youth Programs were enacted in the 1960s. The first full-scale government training program was the 1962 Manpower Development and Training Act, designed to provide vocational and remedial training for persons with low skills and high unemployment rates (particularly disadvantaged youths). The intent of the various job-training programs has been to train workers to do jobs in high demand. In 1971, the Public Employment Program was passed, and in 1973, the Comprehensive Employment and Training Act (CETA) was enacted.

In 1978, almost 1 million workers—mainly under age 20—were enrolled in federally funded classroom or on-the-job training programs at a cost of around $2000 per person. In 1982, the CETA program was abolished. How successful were these programs? As noted above, the unemployment rates of those whom the training programs were designed to help—particularly teenagers—*increased* over a period of time when large government outlays were being devoted to training. These statistics do not demonstrate the failure of such programs—the rise in unemployment could have been much worse without them—but they do not indicate outstanding successes either. The training programs of the 1980s and early 1990s (Jobs Corps, Summer Youth Employment Program) under the Job Training and Partnership Act were less ambitious. In the early 1990s, only $3 billion per year was spent on such programs.

The next chapter analyzes the stagflation (the combination of rising inflation and rising unemployment) of the 1970s and early 1980s.

SUMMARY

1. A person is unemployed if not currently working, if actively looking for work, and if available for work. Persons on layoff waiting to be recalled are counted as unemployed. The amount of unemployment is difficult to measure because of differing intensities of job search, problems in matching qualifications to jobs, underground employment, discouraged workers, and involuntary part-time work. The unemployment rate is the number of unemployed divided by the total labor force.

2. The three types of unemployment are frictional unemployment, structural unemployment, and cyclical unemployment. Unemployment is the problem of matching people with jobs. When the economy is at the natural rate of unemployment, there is a rough balance between the number of unfilled jobs and the number of job seekers. When the economy is operating above the natural rate of unemployment, the result is cyclical unemployment.

3. Cyclical unemployment occurs when the economy operates above the natural rate of unemployment. In the long run, the economy should return to the natural rate. Unemployed people usually search for jobs. People become unemployed not only because of quits, firings, and layoffs but also because they do not find jobs upon entering or reentering the labor force. Both job seekers and employee-seeking firms will search in the labor market until the marginal costs of search equal the marginal benefits. When people and firms choose to search less, the unemployment rate falls. Unanticipated inflation tends to reduce search time. Reductions in unemployment benefits raise search costs to individuals and lower search time.

4. When employers and employees in a certain industry strike implicit bargains that laid-off workers will be recalled to high-wage jobs in return for not seeking jobs elsewhere, wages in that industry tend to remain steady during periods of high unemployment.

5. Only about one-third of the rise in the unemployment rate is explained by the changing composition of the labor force. The rise in the long-term unemployment rate has likely been affected by changing unemployment benefits, the increase in the percentage of families with more than one income earner, minimum-wage laws, and progressive taxation.

6. The principal social cost of unemployment is the loss of output that unemployed labor would have produced. Okun's law states that in the short run, every 1 percentage point increase in the unemployment rate reduces output by 2.5 percent. Unemployment yields benefits to society when workers move to better jobs and when the overall allocation of labor improves.

7. Government programs that improve the efficiency of labor markets and provide job skills to those with limited training and experience might reduce unemployment.

KEY TERMS

labor force
layoff
underground worker
discouraged worker
frictional unemployment
cyclical unemployment
structural unemployment
reservation wage
implicit contract
Okun's law

QUESTIONS AND PROBLEMS

1. To what extent can the different types of unemployment—cyclical, structural, and frictional—be considered voluntary or involuntary?
2. Brown is prepared to take a job that pays $50,000 per year with a 2-week paid vacation in the first year, but Brown cannot find such a job. Would Brown be classified as unemployed?
3. Explain why it is unlikely for cyclical unemployment to account for the long-run rise in unemployment in the United States.
4. "Economists are on the wrong track when they say that unemployment decisions are based upon cost/benefit analysis. Cost/benefit analysis applies to most economic decision making, but not to unemployment. Able-bodied people want to work." Evaluate this statement.
5. Using cost/benefit analysis, explain why rising coverage for unemployment benefits may affect the unemployment rate.
6. Assume that tax rates are substantially reduced. In which direction would you expect the natural unemployment rate to change?
7. Okun's law underlines the high costs of unemployment. Yet this chapter stated that unem-

ployment has a positive side as well. Are these two views of unemployment inconsistent?

8. Explain, using job-search theory, why the duration of unemployment is lower for teenagers than for adult workers.
9. What happens to the number of people not in the labor force during recessions? Give some reasons for this pattern.
10. Draw a diagram showing the relationship between the marginal costs and marginal benefits of job search for a laid-off worker who decides not to search for a new job in order to be available for recall.
11. Assuming that the Bureau of Labor Statistics could detect all underground employment and thus exclude underground workers from the officially unemployed, which of the following cases would be considered an example of unemployment?
    a. A full-time student is detected working on an unreported basis as a waiter.
    b. An electrician is caught installing wiring after hours on an unreported basis.
    c. A woman who gives her occupation as a homemaker is found to be conducting an unreported cosmetics business from her house.
12. Explain how the unemployment rate can fall when unemployment is rising.
13. How should each of the following affect search time?
    a. The amount of time an unemployed worker can draw unemployment benefits is lowered from 6 months to 3 months.
    b. The spouse of an unemployed worker loses his or her job.
    c. State employment offices increase the amount of information they make available on job vacancies.
    d. Wages fall generally in the economy, and many perceive them to be decreasing more rapidly than prices.
14. What shifts in the composition of the American labor force have contributed to rising unemployment?
15. If laid-off union workers in an industry decide not to wait to be recalled to their former jobs, what effect would this decision have on wage rates in other industries?
16. Explain what would happen to search and unemployment if the reservation wages of unemployed workers began falling.
17. What effect would an unanticipated deflation have on the search behavior of unemployed workers and hiring firms?
18. Explain why unemployed workers need to search for jobs and why this search can take a long time. How does the search vary according to the amount of job information?

SUGGESTED READINGS

Benjamin, Daniel K., and Lewis A. Kochin. "Searching for an Explanation of Unemployment in Interwar Britain." *Journal of Political Economy* 87 (June 1979): 441–74.

Ehrenberg, Ronald G., and Robert S. Smith. *Modern Labor Economics,* 4th ed. New York: HarperCollins, 1991, chaps. 15 and 16.

Employment and Earnings, U.S. Department of Labor, Bureau of Labor Statistics.

Feldstein, Martin. "The Economics of the New Unemployment." *Public Interest* 33 (Fall 1973).

Feldstein, Martin. "The Private and Social Costs of Unemployment." *American Economic Review* 68 (May 1978): 155–58.

Handbook of Labor Statistics, U.S. Department of Labor.

Monthly Labor Review, U.S. Department of Labor, Bureau of Labor Statistics.

Okun, Arthur. *Prices and Quantities.* Washington, DC: Brookings Institution, 1981.

Phelps, Edmund S. *Inflation Policy and Unemployment Theory.* New York: W. W. Norton, 1972.

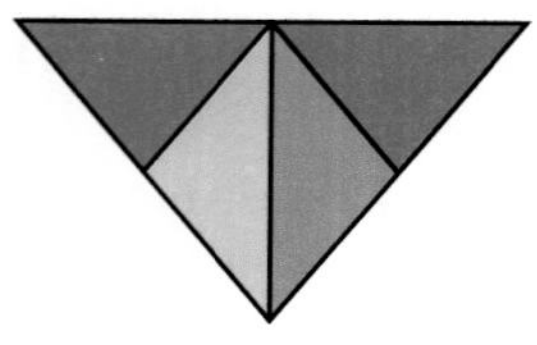

19

The Phillips Curve: Inflation and Unemployment

CHAPTER INSIGHT

The combination of high unemployment and high inflation (stagflation) in the 1970s and early 1980s shattered belief in an inevitable trade-off between inflation and unemployment and prompted a search for new understanding of the relationship between inflation and unemployment. Frustrated commentators of the 1970s proclaimed that the "laws of economics" were no longer working. How could inflation and unemployment rise together?

The stagflation of the 1970s was not limited to the United States. Virtually all industrialized countries experienced both rising inflation and rising unemployment during this period. Figure 1 shows how inflation and unemployment rose together in the 1970s.

Stagflation presents a serious policy dilemma. As preceding chapters showed, contractionary monetary and fiscal policies are the traditional remedy for inflation, whereas high unemployment calls for expansionary policies. If an economy has both unemployment and inflation, what should policymakers do? If they fight high unemployment, they will worsen inflation. If they fight inflation, they will worsen unemployment.

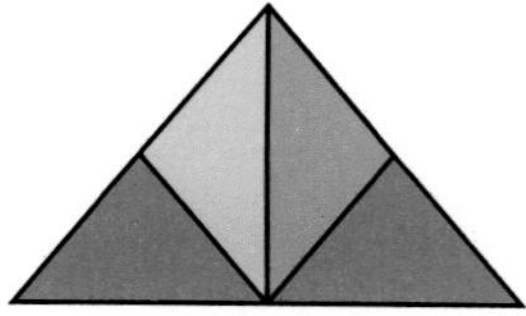

STAGFLATION

Just as the Great Depression of the 1930s motivated Keynes to question the theories of the classical economists, the stagflation of the 1970s and early 1980s motivated economists to revise their views of the relationship between inflation and unemployment.

The 1970s and the early 1980s showed that high unemployment and high inflation could occur simultaneously. A new term entered the economist's vocabulary: **stagflation.**

> **Stagflation** is the combination of high unemployment and high inflation.

FIGURE 1
World Stagflation: Unemployment and Inflation in the 1960s and 1970s.

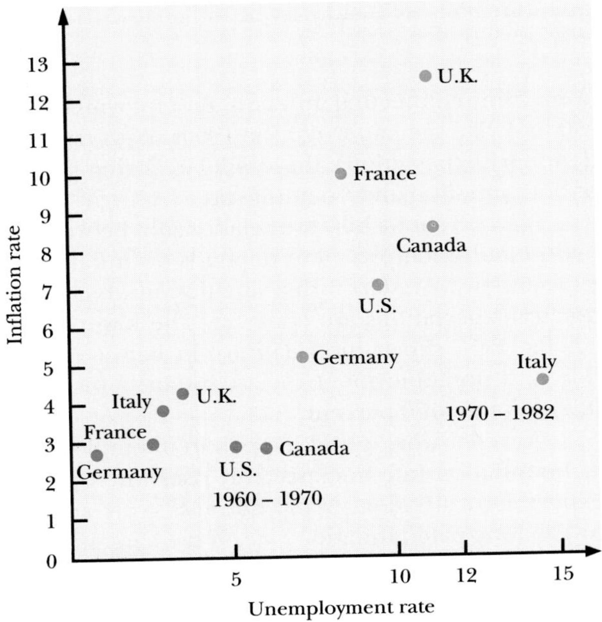

Source: *Economic Report of the President*, selected years.

Stagflation was particularly troubling because it represented the worst of all possible worlds: high inflation and high unemployment. Journalists and politicians began to speak of a "misery index"—the sum of inflation and unemployment.

The Phillips Curve

Data on U.S. inflation and unemployment from 1961 to 1991 (Figure 2) show why stagflation surprised economists and politicians in the early 1970s. Previously, high unemployment had usually been accompanied by low inflation and vice versa. The pioneering research of A. W. Phillips for England had shown a negative relationship between inflation and unemployment that appeared to change little over time. Similar studies conducted for the United States found a stable trade-off between inflation and unemployment.

The economic conditions of the 1960s seemed to bear out this assumption. The combinations of inflation and unemployment rates for the 1960s are connected with a blue line in Figure 2. The 1960s dots show that unemployment fell from a 5–7 percent level in the early 1960s to a 3–4 percent level in the late 1960s, while inflation rose from 1–2 percent in the early 1960s to 4–5 percent in the late 1960s.

The combination of high unemployment with low inflation (or high inflation with low unemployment) found in the 1960s appears logical. At low rates of unemployment, labor markets become "overheated" and push up wage inflation. Conversely, at high rates of unemployment, labor markets are "loose," and wages tend to fall.

The line connecting the 1960s dots traces out a negatively-sloped curve called the **Phillips curve** after the pioneering researcher in this field, A. W. Phillips. (See Example 1.)

> The **Phillips curve** shows a negative relationship between the unemployment rate and the inflation rate.

The policy implication of the Phillips curve was that inflation could be eliminated only if society was prepared to tolerate an unemployment rate well above full employment. Inflation was the price of low unemployment!

FIGURE 2
Inflation and Unemployment in the United States, 1960–1991

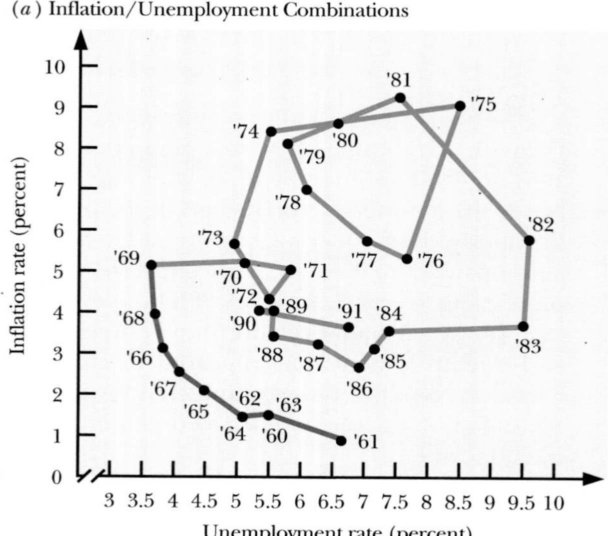

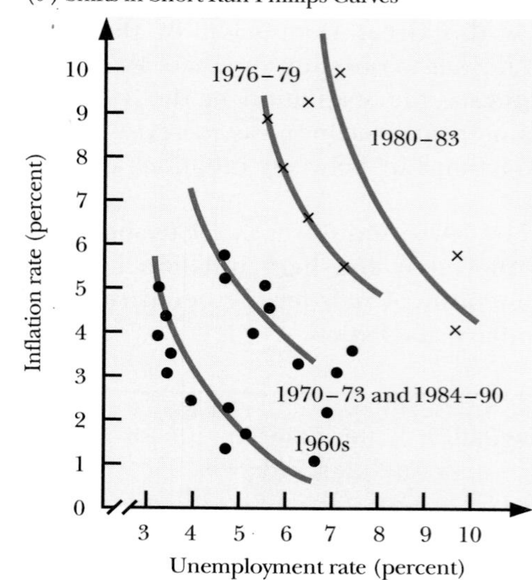

Panel *a* plots the inflation/unemployment combinations for the period 1960–1991. The 1960s are connected with a blue line that shows a negatively sloped Phillips curve. The orange line connecting the 1970s and 1980s reveals a swirling pattern, rather than the expected trade-off between inflation and unemployment. In panel *b*, freehand curves are drawn through the dots for the 1960s, early 1970s, late 1970s, and early 1980s, and late 1980s. These curves show shifts in the short-run Phillips curves as inflationary expectations change.

The Breakdown of the Phillips Curve

As Figure 2 shows, the combinations of inflation and unemployment for the 1970s and 1980s fail to reflect a neat trade-off between higher inflation and lower unemployment. The orange line connects the years 1969 to 1991. Instead of the neat negative relationship of the blue 1960s line, the orange line of the 1970s, 1980s, and early 1990s dissolves into a *swirling pattern*. For the 1970s as a whole, both unemployment and inflation rose together.

The New Phillips Curve

Why is there a trade-off between inflation and unemployment in one period and stagflation in another period? The explanation provided by Milton Friedman and Edmund S. Phelps is that a *trade-off* will exist when inflationary expectations are *constant* and *stagflation* will be present when inflationary expectations are *rising*. With stable inflationary expectations, a line connecting inflation-unemployment dots will look like the pattern of the 1960s. With rising inflationary expectations, there will be a rising pattern of both inflation and unemployment.

Figure 3 shows how the relationship between inflation and unemployment depends on inflationary expectations. We start with a situation in which inflationary expectations are constant. The lower curve, labeled PC_0, shows the relationship between inflation and unemployment for a constant anticipated inflation rate of 0 percent.

Consider what would happen to unemployment if the inflation rate unexpectedly rises when people expect zero inflation. Many business costs are tied to the anticipated inflation rate. Wage bargains were based on the expectation of zero inflation. As inflation pushes up the prices of the things a firm sells, business profits rise. Firms raise their production, and unemployment falls. *Higher-than-expected inflation reduces unemployment.*

EXAMPLE 1 The Original Phillips Curve

In 1958, A. W. Phillips of the London School of Economics published a paper that Nobel laureate James Tobin called "the most influential macroeconomic paper of the last century." In this paper, Phillips collected data on the relationship between wage inflation and unemployment in the United Kingdom for the years 1861 to 1913. When Phillips fit a curve to the 1861–1913 data, he found that it sketched out a relationship much like the experience of the United Kingdom through 1957. The *Phillips curve* suggested a stable and long-lasting trade-off between inflation and unemployment.

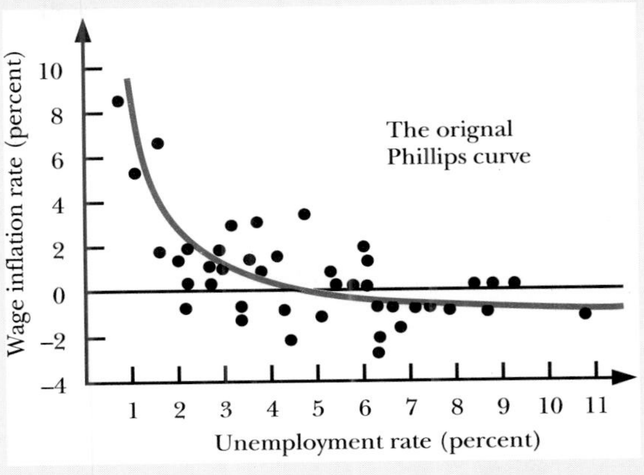

The accompanying figure reproduces the original Phillips curve. It shows a scatter diagram of the rate of change of wage rates and the unemployment rate in the United Kingdom for the years 1861 to 1913. Each dot represents a single year. The vertical height of each dot shows the average rate of change of money wages during the year; the horizontal distance between the vertical axis and the dot shows the average unemployment rate for the year. The Phillips curve has a negative slope: Low unemployment rates are accompanied by high inflation, and high unemployment is accompanied by low inflation rates.

Phillips's work in England motivated economists to examine the relationship between inflation and unemployment in other countries. American economists Paul Samuelson and Robert Solow fit a Phillips curve to the American experience from 1935 to 1959. Instead of looking at wage inflation, as Phillips did, they drew a Phillips curve relating the rate of price inflation and unemployment. Samuelson and Solow discovered that the U.S. data told the same story: To lower inflation, the unemployment rate must rise. They estimated that an unemployment rate of between 5 and 6 percent was required for an inflation-free economy. The socially acceptable unemployment norm in 1960 was perhaps 3.5 percent (which sounds low today but did not then). The American Phillips curve therefore implied a difficult social choice: Inflation could be eliminated only if a society was prepared to tolerate an unemployment rate well above full employment. Inflation was the price of low unemployment!

Sources: A. W. Phillips, "The Relation between Unemployment and the Rate of Change of Money Wages in the United Kingdom, 1861–1957): *Economica* 25 (November 1958): 283–99; Paul A. Samuelson and Robert M. Solow, "Analytical Aspects of Anti-Inflation Policy," *American Economic Review* 50 (May 1960): 177–94.

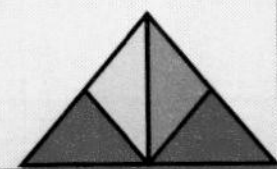

FIGURE 3
The New Phillips Curve

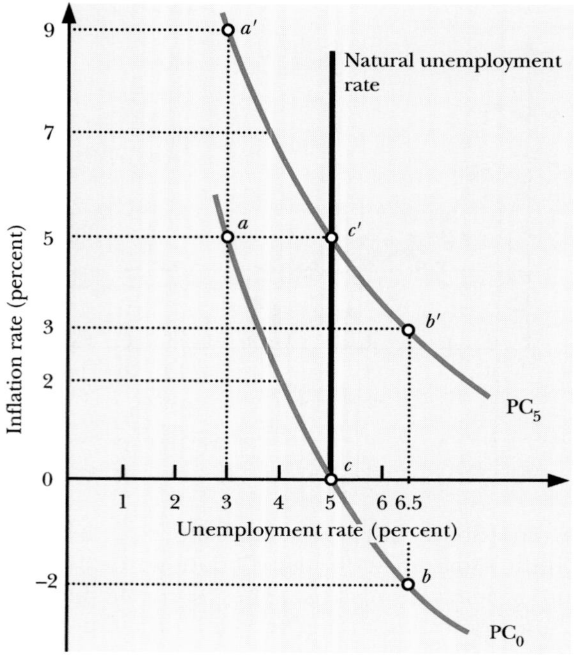

The economy is initially operating at the natural rate (assumed to be 5 percent) at point *c* on the Phillips curve PC_0. The actual and anticipated inflation rates are 0 percent. An increase in aggregate demand raises the inflation rate to 5 percent, and the unanticipated inflation moves the economy to point *a,* where the unemployment rate is 3 percent. If the economy had instead been at point *c′* with an anticipated inflation rate of 5 percent, the Phillips curve would be PC_5. On PC_5, a 9 percent inflation rate is required to move the economy to point *a′* where the unemployment rate is again 3 percent.

The relationship between inflation and unemployment when inflationary expectations are constant is called the **short-run Phillips curve.**

> The **short-run Phillips curve,** which shows the relationship between inflation and unemployment when inflationary expectations are constant, yields a negative relationship between inflation and unemployment.

In Figure 3, PC_5 is the short-run Phillips curve when people expect an inflation rate of 5 percent. It is drawn *above* the short-run Phillips curve for an anticipated inflation of 0 percent, PC_0. If people expect an inflation rate of 5 percent and the actual inflation rate is greater than 5 percent, output expands and unemployment falls for the same reasons this occurs in the PC_0 curve. (See Example 2.)

> There is a different short-run Phillips curve for different expected inflation rates.

Upward Shifts of Short-Run Phillips Curves

Why did we draw PC_5 above PC_0? An increase in the anticipated inflation rate causes short-run Phillips curves to shift up. As this occurs, both unemployment and inflation rise—the phenomenon of stagflation. Let us consider why this happens.

Recall from Chapter 6 that the natural rate of unemployment is the point at which the number of qualified job seekers and the number of vacant jobs balance. Inflationary pressures are constant, with no increase or decrease in the prevailing inflation rate. People can therefore properly anticipate inflation; workers and firms are aware that real wages or the relationship between costs and selling prices are not changing. Businesses know that the same increase in both wages and selling prices will not change the real profitability of employment.

Whether the actual inflation rate is minus 10 percent, 0 percent, or plus 10 percent, as long as actual and anticipated inflation are the same, there will be no change in output, employment, and unemployment.

> Workers and firms do not change employment or output decisions if there are no changes in real wages or in the ratio of business costs to selling prices. If inflation is correctly anticipated, there will be no change in output or employment.

Figure 3 shows that short-run Phillips curves shift up when anticipated inflation increases. There is an entire family of short-run Phillips curves—one for

EXAMPLE 2 Oil Shocks and Stagflation

Some economists argue that the stagflation of the 1970s and early 1980s can be explained by supply shocks. This opinion is based on aggregate supply-and-demand analysis. Adverse supply shocks, like energy shocks, make the short-run aggregate supply curve shift to the left, causing inflation and unemployment to rise simultaneously. If price and wage rigidities are factored in, the aftereffects of supply shocks could be felt for several years.

The accompanying figure shows the relationship between domestic crude oil prices and recessions for the postwar period. If we examine the stagflation period (1970 to the early 1980s), we see that crude oil prices accelerated before and during the 1969–1970 recession, skyrocketed before the deep 1974–1975 recession, and rose just prior to the brief 1980 recession. Crude oil prices skyrocketed again in 1981, one year before the 1981–1982 recession. In each case, energy shocks appear related to recession.

Source: Gerald Anderson, Michael Bryan, and Christopher Pike, "Oil, the Economy, and Monetary Policy," *Economic Commentary*, Federal Reserve Bank of Cleveland, November 1, 1991.

Domestic Crude Oil Prices and Recessions, 1947–1985

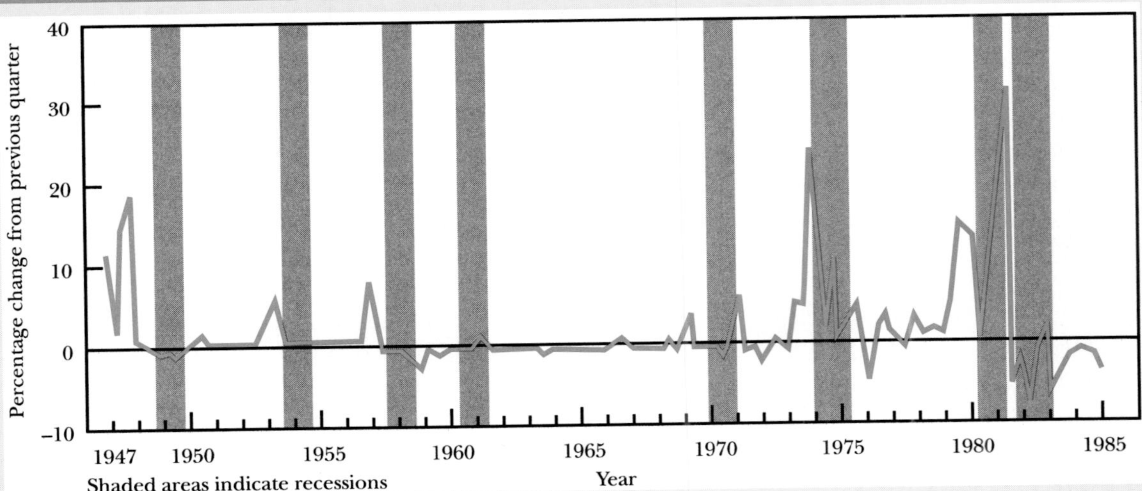

Shaded areas indicate recessions.

Sources: U.S. Department of Labor, Bureau of Labor Statistics; and National Bureau of Economic Research.

each anticipated rate of inflation. We have already shown that an inflation rate greater than anticipated moves the economy up the short-run Phillips curve. An inflation rate less than anticipated moves the economy down the short-run Phillips curve. When actual inflation is different from anticipated inflation, a trade-off exists between inflation and unemployment. In the long run, however, the economy comes to anticipate a higher rate of inflation, and the short-run Phillips curve shifts up as anticipated inflation increases.

At point *c* on PC_0, the economy is at the natural rate of unemployment and people expect zero inflation. An actual inflation rate of 5 percent is thus 5 percentage points above the anticipated inflation rate. In response to the unexpected rise in inflation, the unemployment rate falls from 5 percent to 3 percent (the movement from *c* to *a*).

> Unexpected inflation pushes the actual unemployment rate below the natural rate.

As inflation continues at 5 percent, people eventually come to anticipate this rate. Eventually, new wage and supply contracts are based on the higher (correctly anticipated) inflation rate of 5 percent. Firms that had been encouraged by the unexpected inflation to provide more employment now find that their wages and production costs are rising at the same rate as their selling prices. They accordingly reduce their output, and unemployment rises. As inflationary expectations rise from 0 to 5 percent, the short-run Phillips curve shifts up from PC_0 to PC_5.

> An increase in inflationary expectations causes the short-run Phillips curve to shift up.

Labor Markets and the Phillips Curve

If inflation changes nominal wages but not real wages, why should inflation change employment decisions throughout the economy? The previous chapter, which examined the effects of inflation on labor-market behavior, explained that unanticipated inflation can indeed affect unemployment.

Unanticipated Inflation and Unemployment. If inflation rises above the anticipated rate, labor-market search activities are affected in a number of ways.

1. When prices and wages are rising faster than expected, wage offers start to become more attractive to people looking for jobs. If wages and prices both rise by 7 percent while people anticipate a 5 percent inflation rate, workers will think they are being offered higher real wages, and job seekers will take jobs sooner. Unanticipated inflation causes people to think that their job offers equal or exceed their reservation wage (see previous chapter). Recipients of unemployment insurance find that wages are rising relative to insurance benefits (which respond slowly to rising living costs), and they accept jobs more quickly.
2. As wages rise more rapidly than expected, firms are more likely to keep marginal workers (who are a known quantity). Tight labor markets reduce the probability of finding willing prospective employees. As firings slow down, the actual tightness of the labor market increases.
3. Firms and employees set wage contracts on the basis of anticipated inflation rates. When the actual inflation rate exceeds the anticipated rate, employees are stuck with contracts that do not fully protect them from inflation. Firms find that selling prices (which are being pulled up by inflation) are rising faster than production costs because wages are rising slower than prices. Firms thus have an incentive to hire more and to fire less.
4. Unanticipated inflation reduces the amount of layoff unemployment by motivating firms to worry about the loss of their career labor force. If workers are laid off when positions are hard to fill, their alternative employment opportunities are good, and they are more likely to take jobs with other firms. The anticipation of difficulty filling positions tends to be a self-fulfilling prophecy as employers become increasingly wary of laying off workers and start recalling laid-off workers.

> There is an inverse relationship between unanticipated inflation and unemployment.

Anticipated Inflation and Unemployment. As long as inflation is properly anticipated, it does not change real variables. Rather, it is fully factored into multiyear contracts so that nominal wages and selling prices rise at the same rate. People and firms do not take rising nominal wages as a sign that jobs are easier for workers to find or harder for employers to fill. Workers on layoff understand that inflation has not altered the prospects of recall, and their employers understand that inflation does not affect the prospects of losing their career labor force. Anticipated inflation therefore does not affect the natural rate of unemployment.

> Anticipated inflation does not affect the natural rate of unemployment.

Understanding the Swirls

We are now in a position to make more sense of the confusing swirls of Figure 2(a). We superimpose five freehand curves over the dots in Figure 2(b): one each through the dots of the 1960s, the early 1970s, the late 1970s, the early 1980s, the late 1980s, and the early 1990s. The result is four short-run Phillips curves (the late 1980s curve coincides with the early 1970s curve), each with a negative slope. These freehand representations show how the short-run Phillips curve shifted upward as inflationary expectations rose from the 1960s to the early 1980s and then shifted back down in the mid-1980s and early 1990s as inflationary expectations fell.

Note the tendency for the short-run Phillips curves to shift both up *and* to the right. The rightward shift reflects the long-run rise in the unemployment rate discussed in the previous chapter. The tendency of the short-run Phillips curve to shift with inflationary expectations appears to explain the confusing inflation/unemployment relation after the 1960s. Example 2 provides an alternate explanation. The tendency of the short-run Phillips curve to shift with inflationary expectations appears to explain the confusing inflation/unemployment relation after the 1960s.

Accelerating Inflation

The new Phillips curve implies that any attempt to maintain unemployment below the natural rate will increase inflation faster and faster. A permanent reduction in unemployment below the natural rate thus *accelerates* inflation.

FIGURE 4
Accelerating Inflation

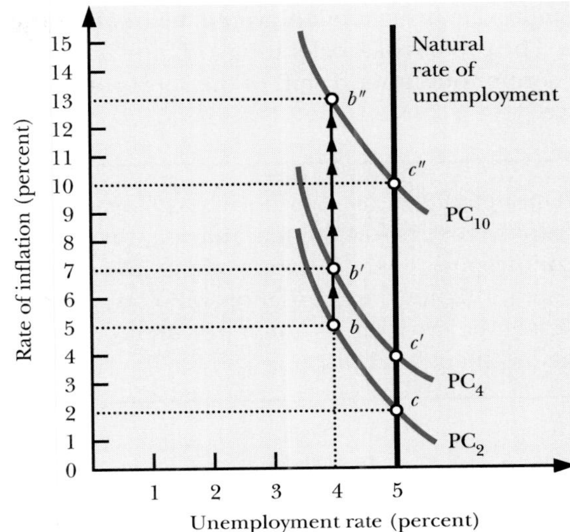

Maintaining a 4 percent unemployment rate causes accelerating inflation. For unemployment to fall below the natural rate, actual inflation must exceed anticipated inflation, but this requirement increases the anticipated rate of inflation. Hence, the Phillips curve shifts ever upward.

Suppose the economy is operating at point *c* in Figure 4. The inflation rate, 2 percent, is the anticipated inflation rate, and unemployment is at the natural rate of 5 percent. The government now decides to lower the unemployment rate to 4 percent and hold it at that level. By increasing aggregate demand, the inflation rate rises unexpectedly to 5 percent (there is a 3 percent unanticipated inflation), and the unanticipated inflation lowers the unemployment rate to 4 percent. The economy has moved along the established short-run Phillips curve, PC_2, from *c* to *b*.

At a 5 percent inflation rate, however, people raise their inflation expectations, initially perhaps from 2 to 4 percent. When the anticipated rate of inflation rises, the entire short-run Phillips curve shifts up (from PC_2 to PC_4). With the new and higher short-run Phillips curve, PC_4, a 7 percent inflation rate is required to keep the economy at a 4 percent unemployment rate (point *b*′ on PC_4).

A 7 percent inflation rate shifts the Phillips curve up again, and an even higher inflation rate is required to keep the economy at a 4 percent unemployment rate. Figure 4 warns of the inflationary implications of attempting to bring unemployment below the natural rate. The process of accelerating inflation is shown by the continuous upward shift of the short-run Phillips curve.

> If monetary and fiscal authorities try to hold unemployment below the natural rate, they must continuously keep inflation above the anticipated inflation rate. Inflation will continue to accelerate as long as unemployment is held below the natural rate.

Stop-and-Go Policies

The world does not proceed as smoothly as in Figure 4. As the government sees the inflation rate accelerating, political pressures build to stop inflation. Hence, it is likely that the government will respond to accelerating inflationary pressures by cutting the growth of the money supply. For example, the U.S. economy experienced accelerating inflation from 1964 to 1968. The growth of the money supply trended upward, and by 1968, money was growing at an 8 percent annual rate. In the next year, 1969, money-supply growth was cut to 3 percent per year. When money-supply growth is cut, inflation does not tend to fall immediately; instead, it will first peak and then eventually slow down.

As the inflation rate falls, the actual rate will fall below the anticipated rate. As already demonstrated, unemployment rises under these circumstances. Then the problem becomes rising unemployment, not inflation. As political pressure builds to combat high unemployment, monetary authorities may be persuaded to step up the growth of the money supply once again. For example, in 1982, when the unemployment rate was 9.5 percent, the monetary authorities began speeding up the rate of monetary growth. By 1986, the money supply was growing at an annual rate of more than 15 percent—the highest monetary growth rate since World War II. (See Example 3.)

Figure 5 illustrates such stop-and-go policies. First, the unemployment rate is pushed below the natural rate (at point *a*) by expansionary policies that create unanticipated inflation. As the inflation rate accelerates (at point *b*), the monetary authorities become concerned about inflation and cut back on monetary growth, pushing the economy to point *c*, where unemployment is high but the inflation rate is falling. Monetary authorities respond to high unemployment by stepping up the growth of the money supply and moving the economy to *d*. Accelerating inflation again becomes a problem at *e*, and authorities reduce monetary growth, moving the economy to *f*. The cycle may repeat itself.

The spiral movements in Figure 5 look uncannily like those of Figure 4, with one important difference. The U.S. data in Figure 4 reveal stop-and-go movements with the unemployment rate trending up—unlike our hypothetical stop-and-go diagram with fluctuations around a stable natural rate of unemployment.

FIGURE 5
Stop-and-Go Economic Policies

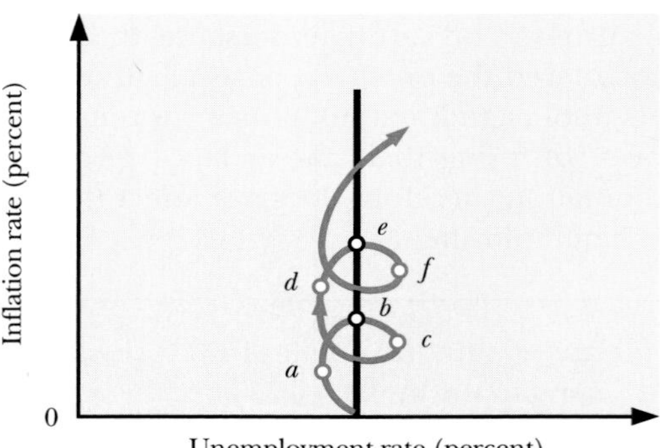

The economy is initially experiencing unanticipated inflation that drives the unemployment rate below the natural rate (point *a*). Accelerating inflation moves the economy to point *b*. Political pressure builds to stop inflation, and the growth of the money supply is reduced. Unanticipated deflation causes unemployment, and the economy moves to point *c*. Monetary authorities are now pressured to fight unemployment. The growth of the money supply is speeded up, and the economy moves to point *d*, where inflation becomes the major political problem once again. This process may repeat itself.

EXAMPLE 3 Public Opinion and Stop-and-Go Policies

Changes in public opinion are responsible for the stop-and-go policies discussed in this chapter. People worry more about inflation when inflation is high. They worry more about unemployment when unemployment is high. The accompanying figure illustrates how public opinion shifts. In 1975, people were even split about whether inflation or unemployment was the more serious problem. As inflation accelerated in the late 1970s, fear of inflation grew relative to fear of unemployment. In 1980 and 1982, people were again evenly split, but after 1982, people began to forget inflation, and a considerable majority (as high as three quarters) viewed unemployment as the cause of more serious hardship.

Sources: John L. Goodman, Jr., *Public Opinion during the Reagan Administration* (Washington, DC: Urban Institute Press, 1983), 9. Data for diagram from University of Michigan Survey of Consumer Attitudes.

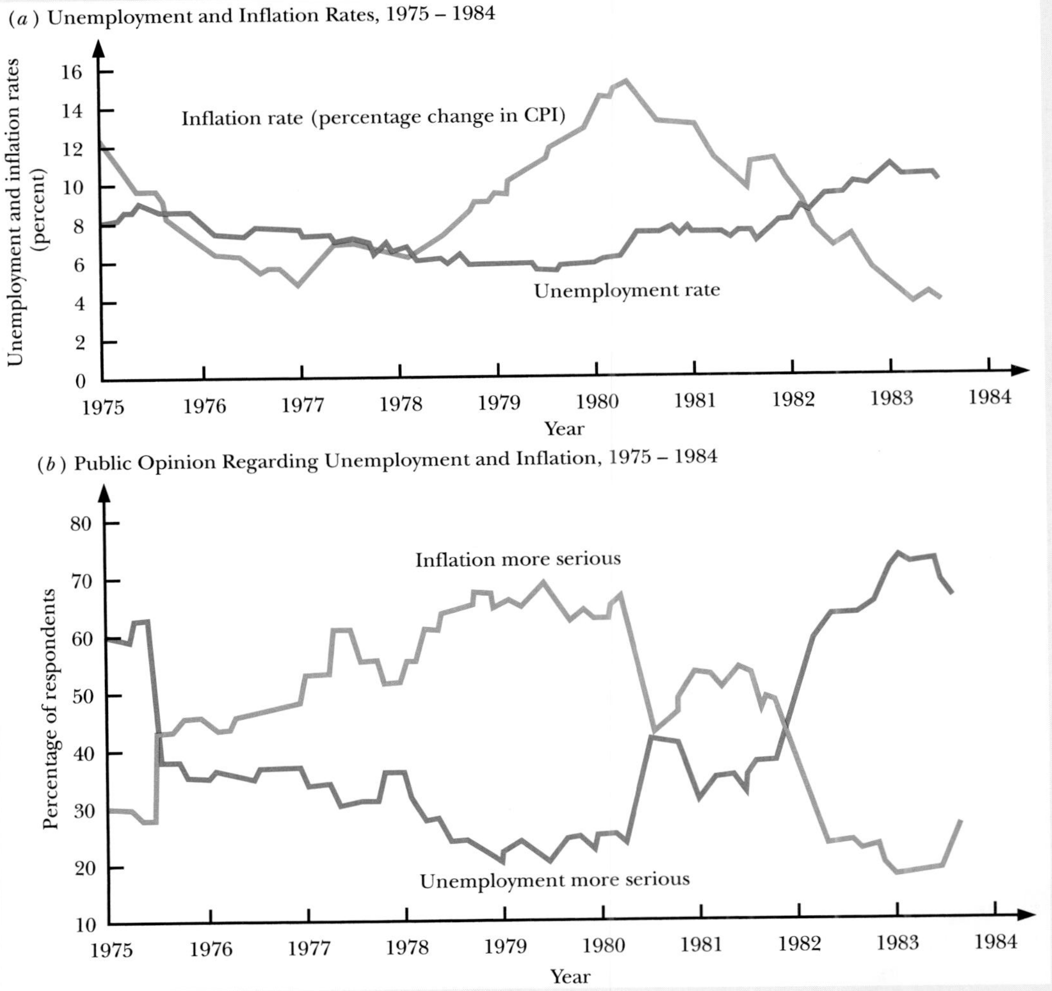

(*a*) Unemployment and Inflation Rates, 1975 – 1984

Unemployment and inflation rates (percent)
16
14
12
10
8
6
4
2
0
Inflation rate (percentage change in CPI)
Unemployment rate
1975 1976 1977 1978 1979 1980 1981 1982 1983 1984
Year

(*b*) Public Opinion Regarding Unemployment and Inflation, 1975 – 1984

Percentage of respondents
80
70
60
50
40
30
20
10
Inflation more serious
Unemployment more serious
1975 1976 1977 1978 1979 1980 1981 1982 1983 1984
Year

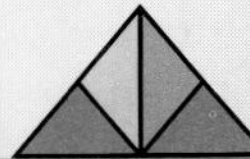

Political Business Cycles

Stop-and-go policies can generate **political business cycles.**

> **Political business cycles** occur when the executive branch and Congress select expansionary policies that they believe will increase their chances of reelection.

When inflation is singled out as public enemy number one, politicians who are up for reelection put pressure on monetary authorities to reduce the inflation rate. When unemployment is seen as the main villain, they pressure the Fed to lower the unemployment rate. The tendency of the executive branch and the Congress to alternate the focus of their economic policies between fighting inflation and fighting unemployment leads to the spiral motions of Figure 5.

Is it in the interests of democratic governments to induce business cycles? Underlying the political business cycle model is the assumption that voters are irrational—that they do not understand what is going on. Politics is usually considered a short-run business. In good times, the politicians in power are usually rewarded by reelection; in bad times, they are penalized by losing their offices. Voters do not have long memories and are impatient for good times to reappear. A politician who enacts a policy of slowly reducing inflation and unemployment over a 10-year period would stand little chance of reelection—even though the problem of anticipated inflation may have been decades in the making. The politician who wants to get reelected must act now. The price of immediate action to achieve a low unemployment rate at election time may be a high rate of inflation in the future. But the vote-maximizing politician cannot afford to worry about such long-range concerns. The politician's attitude often is to worry about tomorrow when tomorrow comes.

The evidence on the political business cycle is still inconclusive. (See Example 4.) If there is a political business cycle, what can be done about it? One proposal is to increase the terms of the president from 4 to 6 years and to limit the president to one term in office. The advocates of this proposal maintain that this system would allow the president to pursue more long-term economic goals without worrying about reelection.

POLICY CHOICES

Experience has shown that countries can face a high inflation rate, a high unemployment rate, or both (stagflation). How does a country fight inflation without raising unemployment or lower unemployment without causing more inflation?

Lowering Inflationary Expectations

The new Phillips-curve analysis suggests that reducing inflation may result in substantial unemployment costs if expectations are slow to adjust. Anti-inflationary monetary policy raises the unemployment rate if inflationary expectations do not drop at the same rate as inflation. If actual inflation is below anticipated inflation, unemployment rises.

How do policymakers lower the anticipated inflation rate without first lowering the actual inflation rate and causing more unemployment?

Two solutions have been proposed. One method is for the government to use wage and price controls to attempt to encourage the public to lower its expectations of inflation. The United States attempted wage and price controls in the early 1970s, but that policy failed because it did not bring down inflationary expectations. (Money growth remained rapid, with continued upward pressure on prices).

A second method for reducing inflationary expectations is for the government to persuade the public that it will follow a policy of slow monetary growth. In response, the public lowers its anticipated inflation rate. The most famous example of this case occurred during the serious hyperinflation that Germany experienced after World War I. To lower inflation without substantially raising unemployment, Germany announced a monetary reform (changing the monetary unit and balancing the government budget) that convinced the public that it was serious—the monetary reform ended the hyperinflation without sending the economy into a deep recession.

The Unemployment Costs of Lowering Inflation

Unless the public can somehow be convinced to lower their inflationary expectations immediately, an

EXAMPLE 4 Macroeconomic Performance, the Political Business Cycle, and Presidential Elections

Edward Tufte, a political scientist, has found that the presidential incumbent has typically been reelected when real personal income after taxes was growing at an annual rate of 3.4 percent or greater. Economist Ray Fair found that the rate of growth of real GDP 6 to 9 months before election day and the inflation rate 2 years before election day are significant determinants of the election outcome. Michael Lewis-Beck, a political scientist, has found that the presidential incumbent has won in all elections when the unemployment rate was falling in the second quarter of the election year.

Most experts agreed in mid-1992 that the state of the economy had made the presidential election contestable and that President Bush's reelection depended in a significant way on whether the economy was visibly recovering from the recession on election day.

These findings have caused political scientists, including the originator of the political business cycle theory, to conclude that any administration facing reelection would attempt to boost the economy by expansionary monetary and fiscal policies. Tufte found that, excluding the Eisenhower years of 1953 to 1960, about 80 percent of the election years showed an increase in the growth of real disposable income and about 80 percent of the nonelection years showed a decrease in the rate of growth of real disposable income. According to Tufte's findings, this phenomenon is not unique to the United States: A similar pattern appeared in 27 different democratic countries. Although this study has been challenged by others, it turned attention to the idea that the business cycle can have political as well as economic causes. The political business cycle theory contradicts Keynesian thinking. Keynes felt that it was the responsibility of government to eliminate the business cycle. Tufte's work shows that the government may deliberately cause business cycles.

Sources: Edward Tufte, *Political Control of the Economy* (Princeton, NJ: Princeton University Press, 1978); "Experts Ponder Politics of Declining Incomes," *New York Times,* March 9, 1992, C6.

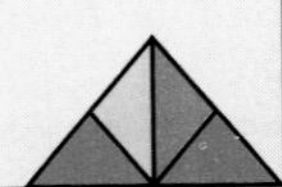

anti-inflationary program will raise unemployment. It will also raise interest rates. Any program that raises both unemployment and interest rates will likely face political opposition.

Figure 6 illustrates this problem. The economy is initially operating at the natural rate of unemployment (5 percent) with an inflation rate of 10 percent. Actual and anticipated inflation are equal. How can the economy move from a high rate of inflation to a 0 rate of inflation without raising unemployment (how can it move from c' to c)?

According to the new Phillips-curve analysis, getting from c' to c is very difficult because inflationary *expectations* must be brought down to 0 percent! If expectations are adaptive, the actual rate of inflation will remain below the anticipated rate for a number of years. But during this period unemployment will rise.

While actual inflation is less than anticipated inflation, a simplified picture of the path of the economy might look something like the curve $c'bc$. The economy starts at c' with inflation at 10 percent, unemployment at 5 percent, and the anticipated inflation rate at 10 percent. When contractionary policies are applied, the economy moves to point b. At this intermediate point, the unemployment rate has risen to 8 percent and the inflation rate has dropped to 4 percent, but the anticipated inflation rate is 8 percent. Unemployment above the natural rate has been caused by an anticipated rate of inflation higher than actual inflation. The hardships of unemployment at point b may be considerable. As

FIGURE 6
The Unemployment Costs of Reducing Inflation

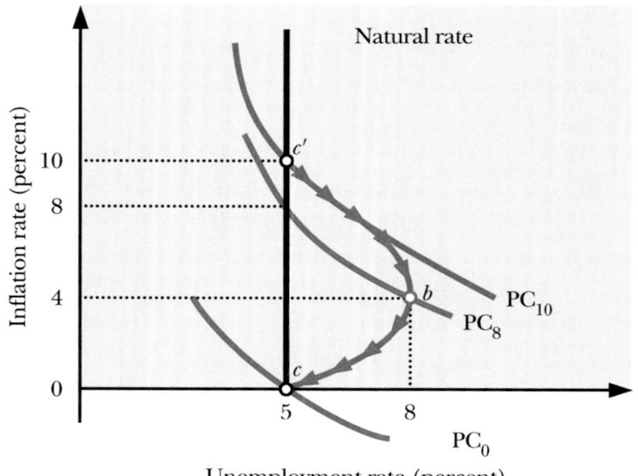

The economy is initially operating at point c'—at the natural rate of 5 percent unemployment with an anticipated inflation rate of 10 percent (which equals the actual inflation rate). Monetary authorities reduce the growth of the money supply, and the rate of inflation begins to slow. The economy begins to move along the curve $c'bc$. Point b is a representative intermediate point where the inflation rate is 4 percent, but the anticipated inflation rate is 8 percent; unemployment is 8 percent. Until the expected rate of inflation falls to 0 percent, the economy will continue to experience unemployment above the natural rate.

the inflation rate continues to drop toward 0 percent, inflationary expectations will continue to drop. Once the economy reaches point *c*, the natural rate of unemployment is restored, and the actual and anticipated rates of inflation are both 0 percent.

Gradualism

To move from c' to c in Figure 6 requires a drastic reduction in the rate of growth of the money supply. Even if this is accomplished all at once—say the rate of growth of money supply is cut from 13 percent to a permanent 3 percent—the economy may require 3 to 5 years to move along $c'bc$ to c. During these years, the economy would have to endure considerable unemployment. A **gradualist policy** might reduce the impact on unemployment.

> A **gradualist policy** calls for steady reductions in monetary growth spread over a period of years to combat accelerating inflation.

Instead of reducing the growth of the money supply from 13 percent to 3 percent all at once, monetary authorities might do it gradually over a period of, say, 5 years. Moreover, in order to persuade the public to lower its expectations about inflation, the monetary authorities would announce in advance the scheduled reductions in the rate of monetary growth. If people's expectations are rational—when people believe the government policy announcements—they will immediately lower the anticipated rate of inflation. If the people do not believe the government's monetary-growth plans will be carried out (they may have long ago lost faith in such pronouncements), the anticipated inflation rate will drop only when people see the actual inflation rate dropping.

Human-Resource Policies

The stagflation policy problem has been made more difficult by the long-run rise in the natural unemployment rate. The changing composition of the labor force, multiple-earner families, unemployment benefits, and a variety of other factors explain this increase. To limit the rise, governments can use **human-resource policy.**

> **Human-resource policy** is the use of government training programs and unemployment services to lower the natural rate of unemployment.

Human-resource policies aim at reversing long-run trends that have raised the natural rate of unemployment. These policies, which include government-sponsored vocational training programs, jobs corps, and government employment commissions, attempt to improve the efficiency of labor markets and provide job skills to those with limited training and experience. If human-resource programs are successful, the rightward shift of the short-run Phillips curve should be halted, and policymakers should be less likely to try to hold the actual unemployment rate below the natural rate because the natural rate would be falling.

This chapter and the preceding one examined issues of inflation and unemployment and suggested possible policies to reduce the rate of inflation with minimal effects on unemployment. If the problem of inflation were solved, the economy would still be subject to ups and downs in unemployment—the business cycle. The next chapter explores how the business cycle can be stabilized.

SUMMARY

1. Stagflation is the combination of high unemployment and high inflation. The original Phillips curve showed a stable negative relationship between unemployment and inflation. It predicted that to reduce inflation, a higher unemployment rate had to be accepted and that to reduce unemployment, a higher inflation rate had to be endured. The Phillips-curve relationship held for the 1960s but not for the 1970s, when increasing inflation was accompanied by increasing unemployment.

2. Milton Friedman and Edmund Phelps argued that the short-run Phillips curve would shift up with the anticipated rate of inflation. Only if inflationary expectations are constant would there be a trade-off between inflation and unemployment.

3. An actual inflation rate that is greater than the anticipated rate will cause the unemployment rate to fall because less searching is required. An actual inflation rate that is less than the anticipated rate will cause unemployment to rise because more searching is required. Layoff unemployment also rises when actual inflation is less than anticipated.

4. If the government attempts to hold the unemployment rate below the natural rate, inflation will accelerate. Unanticipated reductions in the rate of inflation increase unemployment. Therefore, political pressures will encourage the government to use stop-and-go economic policies that may lead to a political business cycle.

5. Reducing unemployment without increasing inflation is difficult. It may be possible to lower the anticipated rate of inflation by using price and wage controls or a preannounced policy of monetary restraint, but such policies are difficult to implement. Inflation can be reduced by permanently lowering the rate of growth of the money supply, but until inflationary expectations fall, the unemployment rate will rise. The unemployment costs of fighting inflation can extend over a period of years. Gradualism is one solution to the problem of fighting inflation without creating too much unemployment.

KEY TERMS

stagflation	political business cycles
Phillips curve	gradualist policy
short-run Phillips curve	human-resource policy

QUESTIONS AND PROBLEMS

1. What should happen to the short-run Phillips curve when there is a long period of deflation?
2. Explain why anticipated inflation is unlikely to affect real behavior (the job choices of individuals, the production decisions of firms). Why does unanticipated inflation affect real behavior?
3. How are actual and anticipated inflation related when unemployment is above the natural rate? When unemployment is below the natural rate?
4. Explain why the short-run Phillips curve shows a negative relationship between inflation and unemployment. Explain under what conditions the short-run Phillips curve shifts up.
5. If the rate of inflation anticipated by workers is 5 percent but the actual rate of inflation turns out to be 10 percent, how would this surprise affect employment decisions?
6. What will be the consequences when monetary authorities attempt to hold the unemployment rate permanently below the natural rate?
7. In the inflation/unemployment scatter diagram (Figure 2), the dots for 1974 and 1975 are unusual. Explain why.
8. Explain why a firm would be more reluctant to lay off workers when it becomes harder to fill positions with qualified applicants.
9. What happens to the unemployment rate in the following situations?

   a. Initially, the anticipated rate of inflation is 5 percent, and the actual rate of inflation is also 5 percent.
   b. In the next period, there is an unexpected decline in the inflation rate to 2 percent. Show what then happens to the unemployment rate.
   c. In the following period, inflationary expectations drop to 2 percent, and the actual inflation rate is also 2 percent.

10. Explain what happens to the costs of job search from the perspective of the unemployed job seeker when there is unanticipated inflation. What happens when inflation is anticipated?
11. Why would a laid-off worker behave differently from a worker who has been fired? What factors determine whether the laid-off worker actively searches for a different job?
12. This chapter considered the consequences of monetary and fiscal authorities aiming for an unemployment rate below the natural rate. What would happen if they aimed for an unemployment rate above the natural rate?
13. Explain why some reformers believe that lengthening the term of the presidency would help eliminate the political business cycle.
14. Why might lowering the inflation rate be more difficult politically than raising the inflation rate?

SUGGESTED READINGS

Friedman, Milton. *Dollars and Deficits.* Englewood Cliffs, NJ: Prentice Hall, 1968.

Okun, Arthur. *Prices and Quantities.* Washington, DC: Brookings Institution, 1981.

Phelps, Edmund S. *Inflation Policy and Unemployment Theory.* New York: W. W. Norton, 1972.

Tobin, James. "Inflation and Unemployment." *American Economic Review* 62 (March 1972): 1–18.

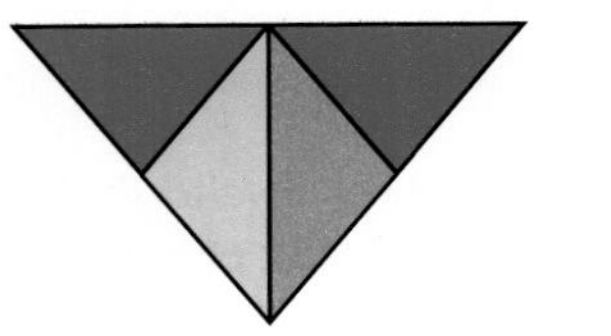

20 Stabilizing the Business Cycle

CHAPTER INSIGHT

The most controversial question in macroeconmics today is how to stabilize business cycles. Economists agree generally about many things, but they have many disagreements on how best to control inflation, unemployment, and the business cycle. These issues worry the average person who looks to policymakers and economists for answers.

Activists argue that monetary and fiscal policies should be used deliberately to moderate the business cycle. *Nonactivists,* on the other hand, argue that deliberate countercyclical policies should be replaced by a stable monetary and fiscal framework based on fixed rules. Activist economists follow the tradition of Keynes; nonactivists are monetarists or proponents of *rational expectations theory* (described in detail in Chapter 21).

This chapter focuses on the main features of business cycles, the main theories of the business cycle, and the activist/nonactivist debate. It presents the cases for and against activism and nonactivism. It also describes actual macroeconomic policy over the past quarter century in terms of the activist/nonactivist debate.

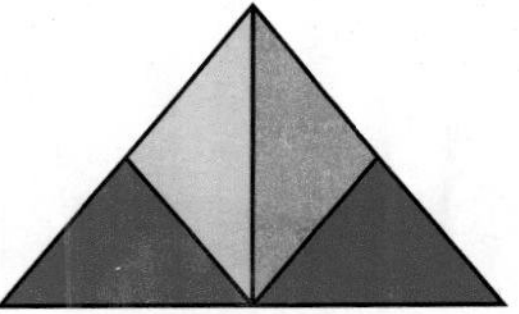

BUSINESS CYCLES

The business cycle refers to recurring fluctuations in output and employment. Perhaps the two most important facts about business cycles are (1) they are national and sometimes international in scope; and (2) they last several years, long enough to allow cumulative movements upward or downward. These two facts can be observed in the historical experiences of the United States, Great Britain, France, and Germany. Business cycles are different from other fluctuations in economic outputs (e.g., a reduction in wheat output) because they are "larger, longer, and more widely diffused."[1] (See Example 1.)

Main Features of Business Cycles

When there is a business expansion or contraction, most industries or sectors move in the same direction. In other words, there is a high degree of conformity in the activities of different industries. Two exceptions to this trend are agriculture, which depends on the weather, and the production of mineral resources. But durable producer goods and consumer goods experience large, simultaneous fluctuations in production, employment, and inventories. Within this conformity, durable goods production fluctuates more than nondurable production; manufacturing fluctuates more than wholesaling; and wholesaling fluctuates more than retailing. By the same token, industrial prices fluctuate more than retail prices and wages.

Financial factors also exhibit certain regularities. The rate of growth of the money supply usually falls before or at the same time as a recession or depression. Short-term interest rates rise with business expansions and fall with business contractions. Short-term interest rates experience larger fluctuations than do long-term interest rates. During a recession, the short-term rate is usually below the long-term rate; and when the economy is at a business cycle peak, short-term rates can exceed long-term rates.

Productivity and wages behave procyclically. A key feature of business cycles is that during economic upswings, real wages and labor productivity tend to rise, whereas the opposite occurs during recessions.

What Causes Business Cycles?

In the last century at least two dozen explanations of the business cycle have emerged. These explanations include monetary theories, overinvestment theories, underconsumption theories, and psychological theories. In an influential article, Robert Lucas pointed out (after surveying facts similar to those we just discussed) that

> [B]usiness cycles are all alike. To theoretically inclined economists, this... suggests the possibility of a unified explanation of business cycles, grounded in the general laws governing market economies.[2]

In this chapter, we will discuss only two basic theories of the business cycle: the Keynesian theory and real business cycle theory.

The Keynesian Theory. The Keynesian theory states that the business cycle is demand-driven. With wages being sticky, increases or decreases in aggregate demand can cause multiplier effects on real GDP and employment. Investment demand is highly unstable because animal spirits sometimes propel investors in unpredictable directions. This is basically the theory we explained in Chapters 9 and 11.

A historical problem of the demand-driven theory about business cycles is that real wages have behaved procyclically in actual business cycles. This contradicts the demand-driven theory, which holds that the incentive for firms to hire more workers must be lower than real wages. Recall that in the upward-sloping aggregate supply schedule, the price level changes relative to fixed money wages. If aggregate demand increases, the price level increases relative to wage rates, meaning that real wages must be falling. Thus, the Keynesian theory of business cycles would predict that real wages should behave countercyclically: the higher the real GDP, the lower

[1]The next three paragraphs in this section are based on Victor Zarnowitz, "Recent Work on Business Cycles in Historical Perspective," *Journal of Economic Literature* (June 1985).

[2]Robert Lucas, "Understanding Business Cycles," in *Stabilization of the Domestic and International Economy*, ed. Karl Brunner and Allen Meltzer, Carnegie-Rochester Conference, vol. 5 (Amsterdam: North-Holland, 1977).

EXAMPLE 1 Booms and Busts

The severity of recessions and depressions is measured by two dimensions: their duration and the magnitude of the drop in real output. Although there is considerable debate about whether the drops in real output are becoming less severe, there is convincing evidence that business cycle downturns are becoming shorter and shorter. The accompanying figure of 200 years of business cycle history, prepared by the eminent business cycle analyst, Geoffrey Moore, shows that, over time, the recession phase of the business cycle has become shorter and shorter.

Moore attributes this trend to several developments. The increasingly service-oriented U.S. economy of the twentieth century is less dominated by agriculture and manufacturing, which are subject to more frequent ups and downs. In addition, automatic stabilizers—such as unemployment insurance and progressive taxes—have lessened the severity of cycles. Moore also believes that the countercyclical policies of the government have reduced the duration of recessions.

Source: Geoffrey Moore, "200 Years of Booms and Busts," *Wall Street Journal*, August 8, 1991. Data for the figure was supplied by the National Bureau of Economic Research.

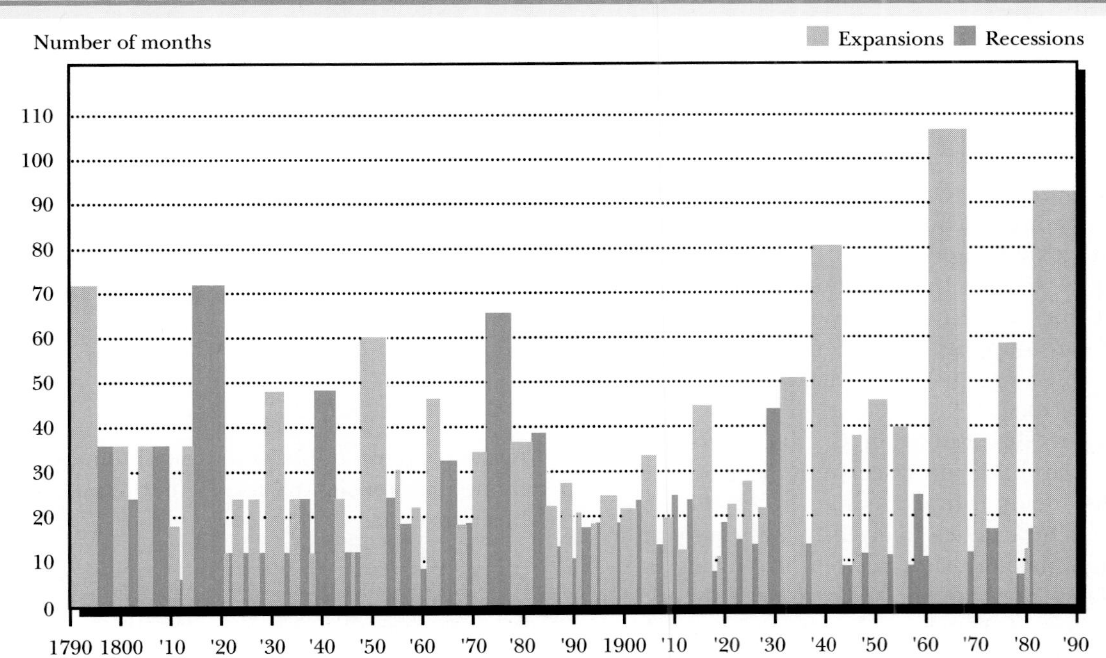

are real wages; the lower the real GDP, the higher are real wages.

The main theoretical advantage of the Keynesian theory of business cycles is that it can account for such factors as optimism, cumulative expansions and contractions, monetary factors, and psychology. Finally, from a policy perspective, the Keynesian theory offers the hope that the business cycle can be controlled by demand management.

Real Business Cycle Theory. The theory of the real business cycle comes down through the work of many people, but it was inspired by the work of Robert Lucas. Finn Kydland, Edwin Prescott, John Long, and Charles Plosser actually developed a model in which the business cycle emerges out of the interaction of supply shocks and capital-using production methods. Random shocks to the rate of technological progress cause the cycle. The model is called **real business cycle theory** because it abstracts from all monetary facts, such as the banking system, money, fixed nominal prices and wages, and so forth.

> **Real business cycle theory** supposes that cyclical fluctuations arise from large random shocks to the rate of technological progress.

Real business cycle theory can account for the essential features of business cycles just by focusing on profit-maximizing consumers and producers in a pure market setting. In this framework, the business cycle becomes a natural response of the equilibrium levels of consumption, investment, production, productivity, and wages to the inevitable shocks that any economy faces.

Imagine that Robinson Crusoe is isolated on a desert island. He produces only fish. Sometimes he catches many fish; sometimes he catches only a few. When he catches many fish, he spends much more time making fishnets; when the fishing is not so good, he does not make as many fishnets. His consumption of fish varies, but he tries to stabilize his consumption by storing fish caught when times are good so that he will have food when times are bad. Thus, his fish consumption will be more stable than his fish production. Likewise, his investment in fishnets will fluctuate more than his consumption of fish. When the fish are biting, Robinson will work more than when the fish are not biting. As in the real world, Robinson's investment and hours of work will fluctuate more than his consumption.

Real business cycle theorists have surprised economists with their ability to replicate many of the features of actual business cycles by experimenting with different "shocks" to their simple models of the economy. One interesting implication of such models is that labor productivity and real wages rise in booms and fall in recessions. This implication is more consistent with actual data than is the Keynesian theory of business cycles.

In spite of this achievement, the real business cycle theory has serious weaknesses. Bennett McCallum of Carnegie-Mellon University argues that the most serious weakness is the theory's view of the economy as a single, homogenous industry driven by supply shocks. In the actual economy, however, the ebb and flow of technological improvements has a negative impact on the productivity of only a few products at any given time. Moreover, new production techniques will increase the output of other goods at any given time. Thus, supply shocks to a few sectors average out over the entire economy to be relatively insignificant.[3]

The implications of real business cycle theory for economic policy are very different from the implications of the Keynesian theory. We now look at the policy options, policy instruments, and case for and against using demand management to try to stabilize the business cycle.

THE POLICY OPTIONS

Activism

Activist policy deliberately manipulates fiscal and monetary policies to iron out fluctuations in the business cycle.

> An **activist policy** selects monetary and fiscal policy actions on the basis of the economic conditions and changes that are perceived as economic conditions change.

[3]See Bennett McCallum, "The Role of Demand Management in the Maintenance of Full Employment," in *Keynes and Economic Policy*, ed. W. Etis and P. Sinclair (London: The Macmillan Press, 1988), 30.

The objective of activist policy is to soften the business cycle. Activists argue that it is too costly to sit on the sidelines and wait for the economy to cure itself. They argue that tools are available to moderate the ups and downs of economic activity. Activist policies can be carried out either through *feedback rules* or *discretionary policy*.

Feedback Rules. Activist policy can be rigid if policy dials are set to respond in a predetermined manner to changes in the state of the economy through the use of a **feedback rule.**

A **feedback rule** establishes a feedback relationship between activist policy and the state of the economy.

For example, a simple monetary policy feedback rule might be to raise monetary growth by 1 percent for every 1 percent increase in the unemployment rate above a specified unemployment-rate target. A fiscal policy feedback rule might be to increase government expenditures by a certain percentage for every 1 percent increase in the unemployment rate above a target rate. Feedback rules prescribe which monetary and fiscal policies to undertake once the state of the economy changes in a specified manner.

Discretionary Policy. Feedback rules are fixed. Opponents of fixed rules argue that different economic situations may call for subtle policy variations. The optimal feedback rule may be difficult to determine. If policy-making is an art rather than a science, it is better to let the country's best economic experts decide what monetary and fiscal policies are appropriate. Economic policymakers can look at a number of indicators of the state of the economy—inflation, unemployment, interest rates, the trade balance, and political factors—to determine monetary and fiscal policy.

How active should activist policies be? Should stabilization policies respond only to major disturbances or also to small changes in the business cycle? In the heady days of the 1960s, economists spoke of **fine-tuning.**

Fine-tuning is the frequent use of discretionary monetary and fiscal policy to counteract even small movements in business activity.

Today, few economists argue for fine-tuning; most believe that the policy dials should be adjusted only in response to major movements in real GDP and inflation. Feedback rules could be written to allow for a range of fluctuations in real GDP and unemployment to occur before any policies are activated.

Nonactivism

The major spokesperson for nonactivism, Milton Friedman, argues for a stable monetary and fiscal framework without activism. In the view of nonactivists, attempts to deliberately manage monetary and fiscal policy are ineffective and even harmful; rather, **nonactivist policy** will yield macroeconomic results that are superior to activism.

A **nonactivist policy** is independent of prevailing economic conditions and is held steady when economic conditions change.

Friedman's proposal for nonactivism consists of two parts.

1. There should be a fixed monetary rule that requires constant (or nearly constant) growth of the nominal money supply year after year at a rate equal to the long-run average growth rate of real GDP.
2. The federal budget should be balanced over the business cycle. Surpluses during the recovery phase should cancel out deficits during the recession stage. Government spending should be dictated by the need for public spending and not by the needs of discretionary fiscal policy.

Nonactivists argue that such a stable monetary and fiscal framework would provide the proper setting for long-run economic stability. The self-correcting mechanism would work at its maximum efficiency under a fixed monetary rule and a cyclically balanced budget.

The Self-Correcting Mechanism versus Activist Policy

The differences between activism and nonactivism can be illustrated using the now-familiar tools of aggregate demand and short-run aggregate supply. Figure 1 shows an economy (at point *a*) that is

FIGURE 1
The Policy Options

How Activist Policy Can Restore the Economy to the Natural Rate of Output

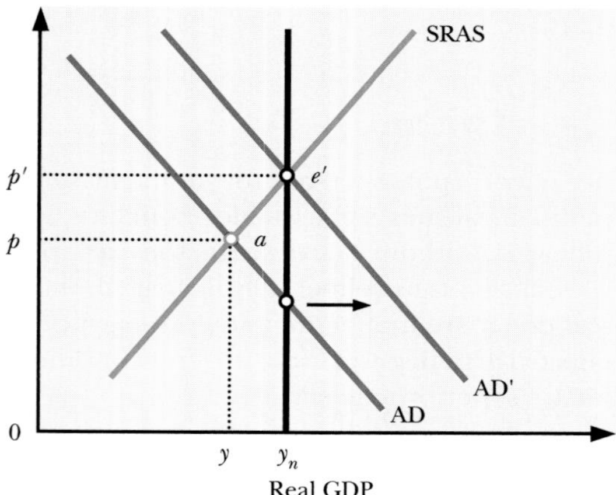

(b) How Nonactivist Policy Can Restore the Economy to the Natural Rate of Output

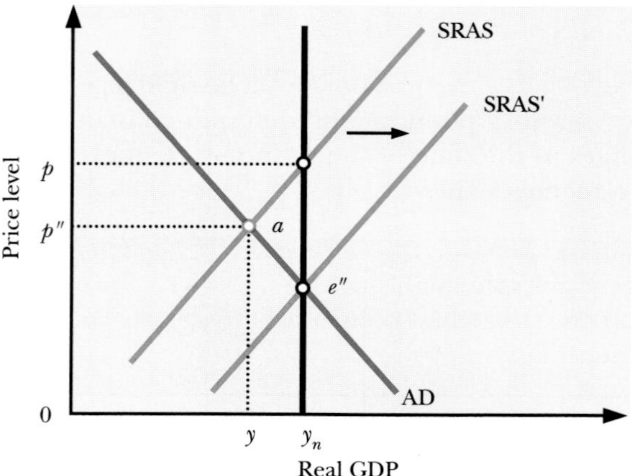

Panel *a* shows how activist policy can be used to return an economy that is in a deflationary gap (producing output below the natural level) to the natural level of output. Activist policy can be used to increase aggregate demand (shifting AD to AD′). At the higher aggregate demand, the economy produces y_n, and the price level has risen from p to p'. Panel *b* shows how nonactivism (working through the self-correcting mechanism) restores the economy to the natural level of output. Because the economy is producing less that y_n, the price level falls. As prices and wages fall, short-run aggregate supply increases from SRAS to SRAS′. The economy is restored to producing y_n, and the price level has fall from p to p''.

in a deflationary gap—producing output below the natural level of output. The goal is to return the economy to the natural level of output. Panel *a* depicts the activist approach. In response to the prevailing deflationary gap ($y < y_n$), expansionary monetary and fiscal policies are applied. Aggregate demand increases from AD to AD′. The economy moves up the short-run aggregate supply curve from *a* to *e′*, and the economy returns to producing the natural level of output y_n. The increase in aggregate demand has raised the price level (from p to p').

Panel *b* shows the nonactivist approach. It begins with the economy operating below the natural level of output. As the price level drops, short-run aggregate supply increases until the natural level of output is reached.

> Activism uses shifts in aggregate demand to restore the economy to the natural level of output, whereas nonactivism uses the self-correcting mechanism.

As these diagrams show, both approaches (if followed properly) yield the same output result: the economy ends up producing the natural level of output. In the activist case, there has been an increase in the price level (from p to p'). In the nonactivist (self-correcting) case, the price level has fallen (from p to p'').

Real business cycle theory does not require a self-correcting mechanism or activism. It simply assumes that output is always at the natural level. Although the natural level of output fluctuates over time in response to different shocks, the economy is always at full employment.

POLICY INSTRUMENTS

Previous chapters have described the **policy instruments** that can affect output, employment, and prices.

Policy instruments are variables—such as the money supply, government spending, or tax rates—that affect output, employment, and prices.

The two major types of macroeconomic policy instruments are monetary policy instruments and fiscal policy instruments. Monetary policy is the deliberate control of the money supply (and sometimes credit conditions) for the purpose of achieving macroeconomic goals. Fiscal policy is the deliberate control of government spending and taxation for the purpose of achieving macroeconomic goals.

The fact that a variety of policy instruments exist means that policymakers may be able to select what they consider to be the appropriate blend of monetary growth, credit restrictions, government spending level, and tax rates to achieve their macroeconomic goals.

Differences in Flexibility

Monetary policy in the United States is conducted by the Federal Reserve. As noted in Chapter 16, the Fed was designed to be insulated from current political pressures. Although in practice, the Fed must take major political factors into consideration, it is generally agreed that the Fed is more independent of political pressures than the president, the Treasury, or Congress. The Fed is also in a position to act quickly (quietly buying or selling government securities) to change the money supply. The Fed can buy or sell government securities daily or only once a year, largely hidden from public view. On a more visible level, the Fed can raise or lower the discount rate, change reserve requirements, and even impose credit controls. As earlier chapters have shown, the Fed's control of the money supply is not perfect (especially in the short run), but the Fed does possess the flexibility to change monetary policy on short notice.

The two instruments of fiscal policy are discretionary government spending and tax policy. The president of the United States submits spending budgets to Congress, but only Congress can grant actual spending authorization. The president must either sign or veto the spending bills approved by Congress. The president does not have the authority to cut out parts of approved spending packages; instead, the president must accept or reject the entire bill. On occasion, the president can simply not spend the money authorized by Congress (called *impounding*), but the constitutional legality of this practice has been questioned, and Congress can force appropriated funds to be spent. Although Congress has sought to develop procedures for gearing the total amount of federal spending to specific macroeconomic goals, this approach has never worked well in practice. Given the current appropriation system, it is very difficult to conduct macroeconomic policy by manipulating the amount of federal government spending.

Tax policy is also determined by Congress. Proposals for tax changes can be made by the Treasury, or they can originate within the Congress. The current tax system is very complex and has developed in response to special-interest pressures. Nevertheless, in the past Congress has passed a number of tax bills specifically designed to achieve macroeconomic goals. Taxes were lowered in 1964, 1975, and 1981 for the express purpose of stimulating economic activity. The tax reform passed in 1986 was designed to change tax rates and deductions rather than to manipulate aggregate demand.

Because of Fed independence and the flexibility of open-market operations, the money supply is the most flexible policy instrument. Monetary policy is the preferred instrument of modern activists because of its greater flexibility and the ability of the Fed to act quickly. Because of the inflexibility and uncontrollability of federal spending, the major instrument of fiscal policy is tax policy.

THE CASE FOR ACTIVISM

The key conflict between the activists and nonactivists is whether or not deliberate monetary and fiscal policy should be used to stabilize the economy. Modern Keynesians support an activist policy. Monetarists believe that activist policy is ineffective at best and destabilizes the economy at worst. Rational expectations economists believe that activist policy cannot stabilize the economy in the long run and will, at best, have only a short-run effect when the activist policy is not anticipated.

The GDP Gap

Modern Keynesian economists believe that the self-correcting mechanism does indeed operate in a stable monetary and fiscal framework. The private economy can generate enough steam on its own power to reach the natural rate of unemployment in the long run. No change in monetary or fiscal policy is required for this correction to occur; the adjustment to the natural rate is automatic. Even Keynes believed that the economy would tend toward full employment in the long run. However, modern Keynesian economists also assert that sharp fluctuations in real GDP and employment will naturally occur if monetary and fiscal policy are held constant, in spite of the operation of the self-correcting mechanism. The economy is subject to all kinds of shocks. Investment is naturally unstable because of changing expectations; supply shocks can disrupt the economy; unpredictable shifts in consumer demand take place. Changes in autonomous spending induce magnified changes in real GDP and unemployment through the multiplier. If the economy is beset by adverse supply shocks, both unemployment and prices can be pushed up.

The modern Keynesian rationale for activist stabilization policy is that *waiting for the economy to cure itself by wage and price adjustments (the self-correcting mechanism) is too costly.* As Keynes remarked, "In the long run, we are all dead." When the economy is subjected to an adverse demand or supply shock, the economy does not operate at full employment. In addition to the private anguish of unemployment, society must bear a social cost—the cost of lost output. Okun's law (explained in Chapter 18) measures the loss in output resulting from an increase in unemployment. If the economy had been operating at full employment, a larger real GDP would have been produced. The **GDP gap** measures this loss of output.

> The **GDP gap** is the difference between current GDP and potential GDP (the output the economy would conceivably have produced at full employment) and is a measure of the social cost of unemployed resources.

No one knows the exact size of the GDP gap. First, full employment is difficult to define exactly. Second, it is difficult to estimate what unemployed resources would have produced had they been employed. A rough estimate for 1991 is that the GDP gap was around $370 billion.

> The GDP gap is the price society must pay while waiting for the self-correcting mechanism to operate. Activists prefer to use activist policies to limit the private and social costs of unemployed resources by speeding up the economy's adjustment toward full employment.

Wage and Price Rigidities

Activists question how rapidly the self-correcting mechanism works. As evidence, they point to the Great Depression, when wages and prices failed to respond to unemployment, thereby keeping economies in deep depression. Activists also cite the downward inflexibility of wages introduced by overlapping multiyear contracts. Wages set in multiyear contracts are not free to respond to changing economic conditions. Moreover, laid-off workers operating with implicit labor contracts wait to be recalled to their former jobs. By not searching for new jobs, they do not depress wages generally throughout the economy.

Activists point out that important wages and prices are not set in **auction markets.** Instead, key wages and many prices are set in long-term contracts.

> An **auction market** is a market in which the market price is renegotiated on a regular basis.

For example, the prices of stocks are determined in auction markets (the various stock exchanges) in which prices are renegotiated every minute. Likewise, the wage rate of day laborers who gather at hiring halls every morning is determined daily. Most basic commodities (wheat, cotton, coffee, sugar, corn, soybeans, cattle, oats, gold, silver) are bought and sold in auction markets.

If most wages and many input prices are set in long-term contracts, wages and prices become inflexible. When wages and prices are rigid (or slow to adjust) in the downward direction, the self-correcting mechanism of deflation (or disinflation) will be very slow in restoring the economy to full employment.

Activists emphasize wage and price rigidities that slow down the operation of the self-correcting mechanism as justifications for their policies.

Activism versus Doing Nothing

Proponents of activism acknowledge that discretionary activist policy is difficult to conduct. They readily admit that mistakes have been made in the past and will continue to be made. Proponents, however, argue that the best criterion for judging activism is whether it has produced results that are better than those that nonactivism would have produced.

Five arguments have been advanced in favor of activism.

1. The historical data show that, although the business cycle has not been eliminated, it has become less severe since activist policies came into use. Figure 2 plots the annual rates of growth of real GDP and unemployment rates from 1890 to 1991. Episodes of negative real growth still occur, but severe depressions have been avoided. The 1930s was the period of greatest cyclical instability, but the period before 1930 showed much greater instability in growth rates and unemployment rates than the period after World War II. According to Keynesians, the experience of the last 40 years provides important evidence that activist policy has reduced the amplitude of economic fluctuations.

2. The experience of the mid-1970s shows what happens when there is no activist response to a severe adverse supply shock. In the mid-1970s, the energy shock pushed up inflation and unemployment; yet monetary authorities pursued roughly constant monetary growth. The absence of activism led to excess unemployment.[4] If activist monetary expansion had been used instead, the costs of high unemployment and lost output could have been avoided, and the economy would have eventually returned to lower inflation as the energy shock subsided.

3. Discretionary tax cuts have been applied successfully to stimulate employment and economic growth. Keynesian tax policy was given its first test in the 1960s. The first major use of discretionary fiscal policy occurred when the Revenue Act of 1964 cut personal taxes by 20 percent and corporate taxes by 8 percent. The 1950s had seen two recessions, and the unemployment rate was in the 5 to 7 percent range in the early 1960s. Although such unemployment rates do not appear alarming by today's standards, they were high to an economy accustomed to 3 percent unemployment. The tax cut enacted in 1964 was designed to lower unemployment and raise the growth of real GDP. According to the calculations of Arthur Okun—one of the architects of economic policy during the 1960s—the 1964 tax cut succeeded in increasing real GDP by about 6 percent and pushing down unemployment. The 1968 tax increase and the 1975 tax reduction were less successful, but critics point out that they were both billed as one-time tax changes and were unlikely to change permanent disposable income. The 1981 and 1986 tax cuts may have fueled the 8-year expansion from 1982 to 1990.

4. Activists argue that the known is better than the unknown. The United States has had 40 years of activism without major economic catastrophes such as a deep depression or a hyperinflation. Without activist policies, the United States might not be able to respond to some major economic emergency in the future with a suitable policy. Activists argue that there is no way to know how the economy will behave if policymakers commit themselves to fixed rules. With a cyclically balanced budget rule, what would happen if a severe recession drove down government revenues? How would policymakers know when to suspend a fixed budgetary rule? With fixed monetary growth rules, how should the Fed respond to unforeseen types of new monies that the banking system is so good at creating?

Activists argue that nonactivism poses unknown risks in a modern economy.

5. Activists argue that our ability to carry out effective activist policy is improving over time, as we learn more about how the economy functions. The data-gathering and data-processing ability of private and government agencies is also improving. Policymakers have learned from past mistakes. In the past quarter century, a number of important social experiments have been tried. There have been four discretionary tax changes. The operating rules of the Fed have been changed, and the Fed's countercycli-

[4] Franco Modigliani, "The Monetarist Controversy, or, Should We Foresake Stabilization Policy?" *American Economic Review* (March 1977): 1–19.

FIGURE 2
GDP Growth and Unemployment in the United States

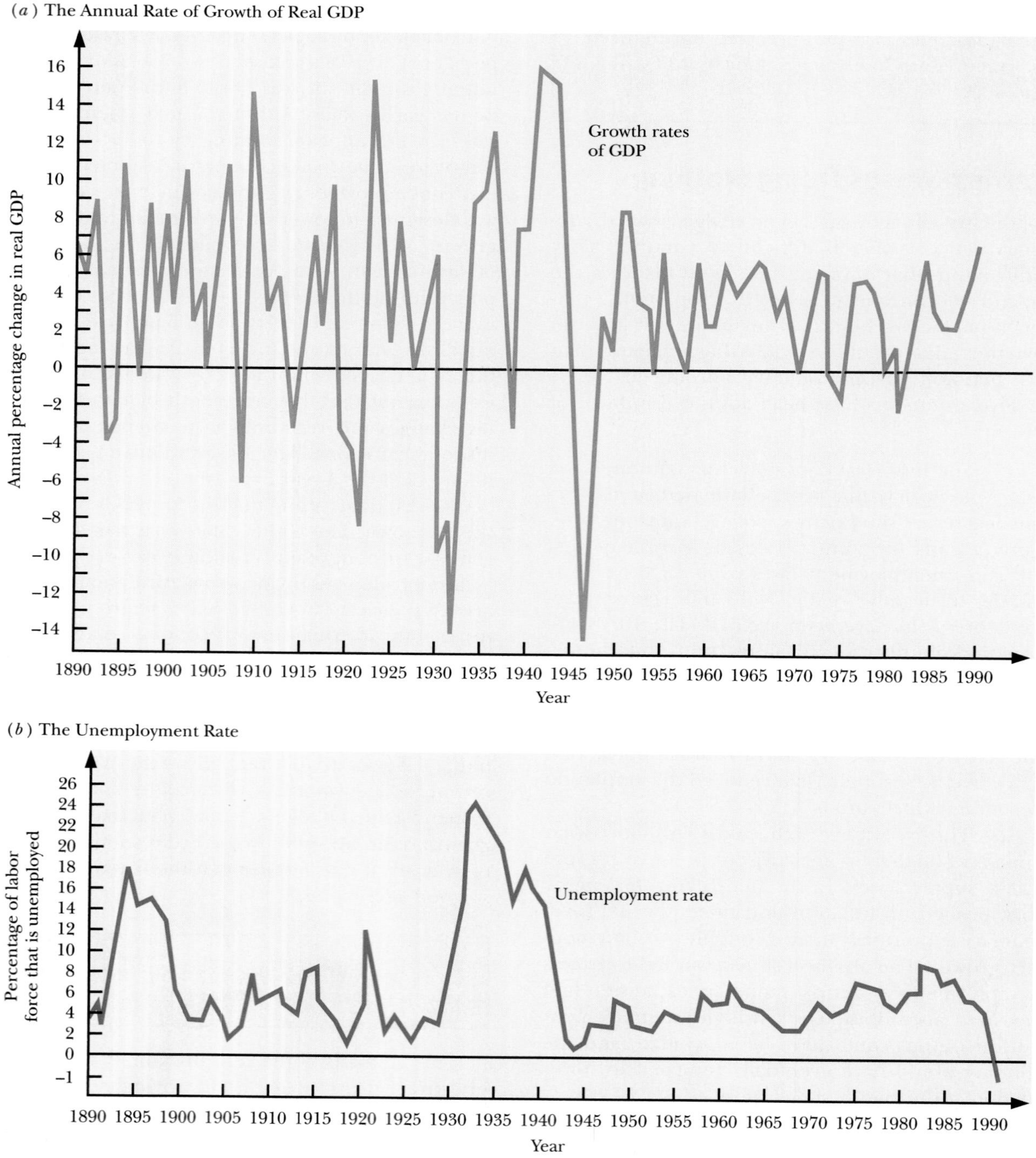

(a) The Annual Rate of Growth of Real GDP
Annual percentage change in real GDP
16
14
12
10
8
6
4
2
0
−2
−4
−6
−8
−10
−12
−14
Growth rates of GDP
1890 1895 1900 1905 1910 1915 1920 1925 1930 1935 1940 1945 1950 1955 1960 1965 1970 1975 1980 1985 1990
Year
(b) The Unemployment Rate
Percentage of labor force that is unemployed
26
24
22
20
18
16
14
12
10
8
6
4
2
0
−1
Unemployment rate
1890 1895 1900 1905 1910 1915 1920 1925 1930 1935 1940 1945 1950 1955 1960 1965 1970 1975 1980 1985 1990
Year

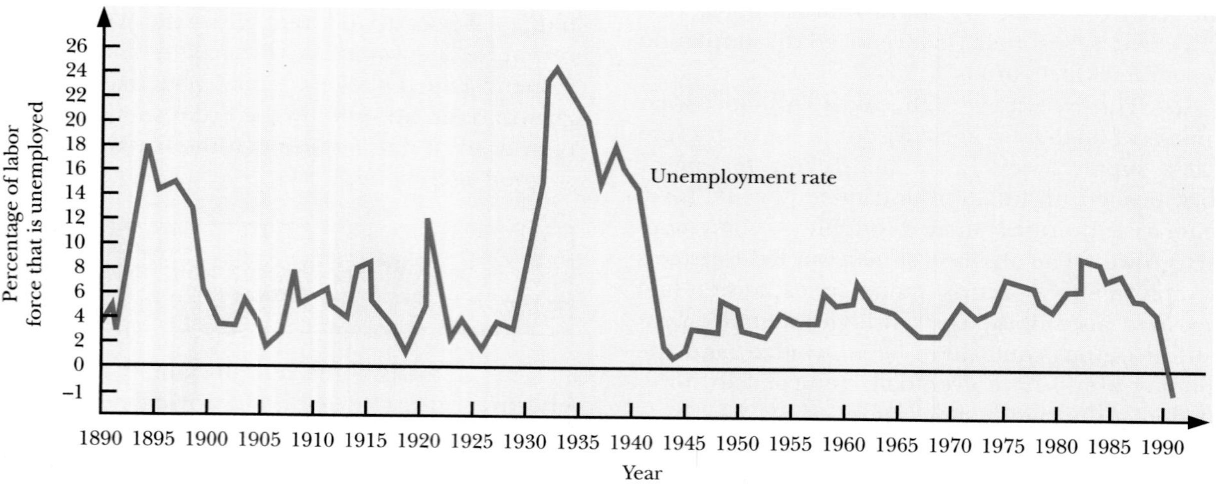

Both the GDP growth rate data in panel *a* and the unemployment data in panel *b* show less cyclical volatility after 1948.

Sources: *Historical Statistics of the United States; Economic Report of the President.*

cal performance may have improved after 1979. We have lived with both high and low federal deficits. The experiences gained from each of these social experiments form the basis for better activist policy today and in the future.

THE CASE FOR NONACTIVIST RULES

Monetarists, rational expectations economists, and real business cycle theorists offer policy prescriptions that differ radically from Keynesian activism.

> The monetarist, rational expectations, and real business cycle theories hold that it is better to do nothing in the face of demand and supply shocks.

The monetarists, led by Milton Friedman, Karl Brunner, and Allan Meltzer, maintain that activist policies either fail to improve the business cycle or actually make the cycle worse. The real business cycle and rational expectations school, led by Robert Lucas, Thomas Sargent, Ed Prescott, and Robert Barro, maintains that activist policies affect only inflation, not cyclical unemployment. Activist policies can make inflation better or worse but have no lasting effect on reducing real GDP fluctuations.

The case for nonactivism rests upon four claims: (1) it is too difficult to select appropriate activist policies; (2) activist policies are likely to make matters worse rather than better; (3) rational expectations may defeat activist policies; and (4) the business cycle is itself an equilibrium response to all sorts of economic shocks.

The Difficulty of Devising Activist Policy

Although the proponents of activism could defend activist policy by saying the biggest policy blunders were made when economists did not understand how the economy works, nonactivists give four reasons why countercyclical policy is destabilizing even in this modern age.

1. *There are long and variable lags in the effect of money on the economy.* If monetary authorities decide to increase the growth of the money supply in order to combat a rising unemployment rate, the monetary expansion will not have an immediate effect on real output and unemployment. Milton Friedman's own research suggests that there is a 6-month to 2-year lag before changes in money supply affect GDP. Thus, monetary authorities can never be sure when the change in money supply will begin to affect real output and employment. If the lag is short, the chances are less that the monetary policy will be inappropriate, but if the lag is long (say, 2 years), the policy may take effect when contraction rather than expansion is required.

2. *The effects of fiscal policy are uncertain.* Because of permanent-income and crowding-out effects, it is virtually impossible to predict the impact of fiscal policy. An accurate estimate would require advance knowledge of the amount of crowding out and the effects of tax changes on consumption expenditures. Moreover, like monetary policy, fiscal policy affects the economy only after a lag. Not only is fiscal policy difficult to implement because of recognition lags and implementation lags, fiscal planners must also be able to determine when the change in fiscal policy will affect economic activity.

3. *It is difficult for activist policymakers to know if the economy is approaching a recession.* It is very important to be able to anticipate changes in the business cycle. If policymakers knew 6 months in advance, for example, that a recession was coming, it would be much easier to devise countercyclical policy. But recessions vary in length and in predictability. Policymakers attempt to anticipate recessions through econometric models and indexes of leading indicators, but these models and indexes are far from accurate guides to the future. Monetary and fiscal authorities who attempt to carry out activist countercyclical policies at the wrong time run the risk of actually destabilizing the economy. Monetarists believe policymakers do not possess sufficient information to diagnose and cure the disease before it spontaneously corrects itself. By acting without adequate information, they may actually use the wrong medicine and make the patient even worse. (See Example 2.)

4. *Activist policies can aim for the wrong target.* Most modern economists agree that the appropriate target of activist policy is the natural rate of unemployment. If the economy is operating with an unemployment rate above the natural rate, expansionary policies can lower unemployment without accelerating inflation. But policymakers may not

EXAMPLE 2 Forecasting the Business Cycle: Leading Indicators

Literally hundreds of indicators may be used to measure the rhythm of the business cycle. They include the length of the average work week, the layoff rate, unemployment, total output, personal income, industrial production, stock prices, the number of new private housing units started, and the volume of commercial and industrial loans. Such indicators tend to move together, but they do not move in exactly the same rhythm as the business cycle. Some indicators lead the basic cycle; some are coincident with the cycle; others lag behind the basic cycle. The *leading indicators* of business activity are the most important indicators because they may give information about the future. They tend to rise or fall prior to the general rise or fall in business activity.

The accompanying figure shows the composite (combined) index of 12 leading indicators. The combined index is a weighted average of the 12 component indexes. The darkly shaded bands show recession phases of the business cycle; the lightly shaded bands show expansion phases of the business cycle. Also shown are 4 of the 12 components of the composite index of leading indicators: new building permits, net change in inventories, stock prices, and the money supply.

How well do the leading indicators warn of forthcoming recessions? Prior to each of the eight recessions shown in the accompanying figure, the index of leading indicators indeed dropped—but the amount of time between the drop and the recession varied. Sometimes the composite index began to drop a year or more before the recession (2 years before the 1957–1958 recession); other times it began to drop just before the recession (4 months before the 1953–54 recession). Often, drops in the index of leading indicators are not followed by recessions. For example, the 1960s was a decade of

The Index of Leading Indicators and Four of Its Major Components (1967 = 100)

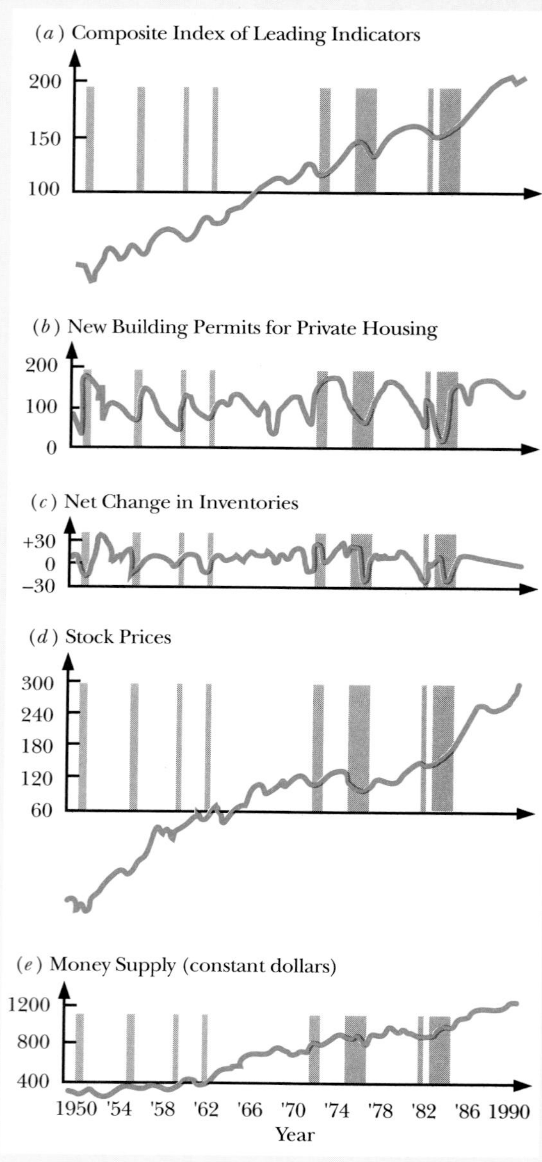

Source: Department of Commerce, *Business Conditions Digest*.

uninterrupted expansion, yet the index of leading indicators predicted three recessions during the 1960s. Another problem is that the components of the composite index of leading indicators do not move together in exactly the same rhythm.

Sound macroeconomic policy requires reliable and timely information about the timing, depth, and severity of recessions. The failure of the index of leading indicators to be a guide to the future provides ammunition to opponents of activism.

always know what the natural rate is at any point in time. Because the natural rate itself changes from year to year, it is difficult to chase it with deliberate policy actions. As Chapter 19 showed, aiming for a natural-rate target that is too low (a rate that is below the natural rate) causes inflation to accelerate.

The Counterproductive Effects of Activism

Figure 2 shows that the swings of the business cycle have narrowed in the postwar period—after activist policies were used to moderate the business cycle. The trauma of the Great Depression has not been repeated. According to the monetarists, the cycle was *not* moderated by countercyclical policy. Friedman and Schwartz, in their study of the U.S. business cycle over one century, conclude that discretionary policy actually had a *destabilizing* effect on the economy. In their view, the Great Depression began as a business downturn that turned into a severe depression because of a series of incredible government blunders. (See Example 3.)

Keynesians maintain that activist countercyclical policy is responsible for the reduced fluctuations in real GDP after World War II. Monetarists counter that the reduced amplitude of the business cycle is a consequence *not* of countercyclical policies but of a reduction in the amplitude of money supply growth. The major episode of cyclical instability prior to World War II—the Great Depression—was itself caused by improper monetary policy, not by natural cyclical forces.

The monetarist evidence is presented in Figure 3, which shows the annual growth rate of the money supply since 1890. Comparison of money growth (in Figure 3) and output growth (in Figure 2) reveals that the reduction in the amplitude of GDP fluctuations coincides with the sharp reduction in the amplitude of money supply growth. From this evidence, the monetarists conclude that the greater relative stability over the past 40 years is the result not of activist policy but of the increased stability of the growth rate of the money supply.

The monetarists cite a large number of cases in which activism has resulted in the choice of the wrong policy. Correct activist policy would call for monetary growth to expand during cyclical downturns. The correct activist policy was definitely not used in the late 1920s and early 1930s. Figure 3 shows that, beginning in 1926, the growth *rate* of money supply was reduced almost every year until 1933. This pattern holds up in the postwar period as well; postwar recessions were usually preceded by reductions in the rate of growth of money supply. This includes the 1990–1992 recession: In 1989 the money supply grew by a little more than 1 percent. From this evidence, monetarists conclude that activist monetary policy causes rather than cures recessions.

If the business cycle is caused by fluctuations in the growth rate of money supply, monetarists believe that cyclical instability can be reduced or eliminated by stabilizing the growth pattern of the money supply. This belief is the rationale for Milton Friedman's 3 percent rule, which states that monetary authorities should be forced to expand the money supply at a constant rate year in and year out and that monetary authorities should be denied the use of activist monetary policy.

Monetarists argue that monetary authorities should be ordered to expand the money supply at a constant annual rate year in and year out. If the growth of money supply is held constant at a rate equal to the long-run growth of real GDP, cyclical instability and inflation could be reduced at the same time.

FIGURE 3
The Annual Growth Rate of the Money Supply in the United States

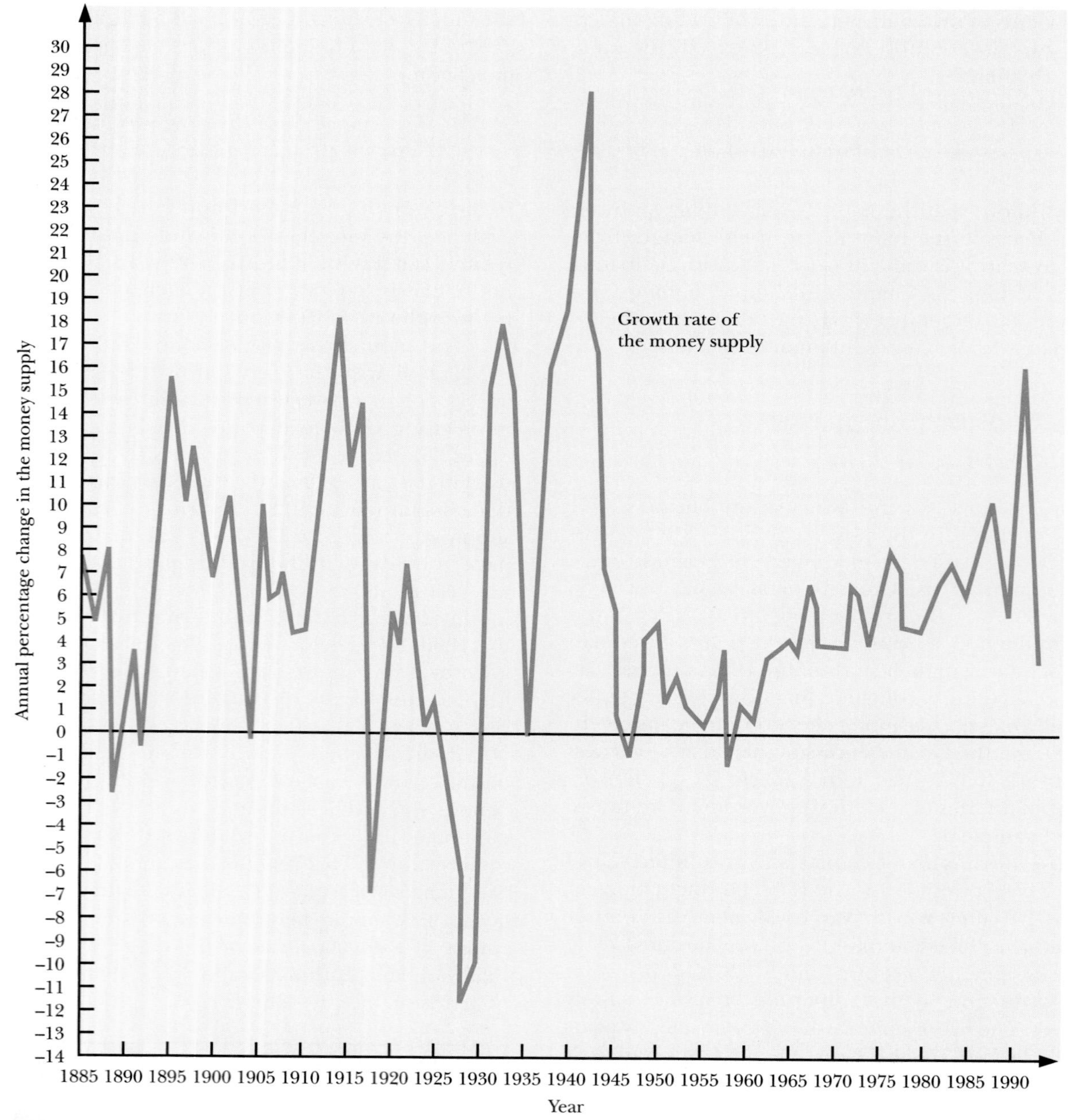

A comparison of this figure with panel *a* of Figure 2 shows that the reduction in the amplitude of GDP fluctuations coincides with the reduction in fluctuations in the growth rate of money supply in the past 40 years.

Sources: *Historical Statistics of the United States; Economic Report of the President; Survey of Current Business; Federal Reserve Bulletin.* The percentage growth rate in money supply is based on M1 for the years from 1915 to 1981 and includes time deposits (formerly M2) for the years from 1890 to 1915.

EXAMPLE 3 The Policy Blunders of the 1930s

Nonactivists point to the policy blunders of the 1930s as a reason for relying on fixed rules rather than discretion. The policy blunders of the 1930s were as follows.

1. From 1929 to 1933, the nominal supply of money (M1) fell 25 percent. The price level also fell nearly 25 percent. Therefore, there was no change in the real money supply, even though an increase in the real money supply was needed to get the economy moving again. If monetary policy had been stable in the early 1930s, falling prices would have increased the real money supply; the economy would not have fallen into the Great Depression.

2. As Nobel Prize winners James Tobin and Milton Friedman have pointed out, various government actions taken by Roosevelt's New Deal program raised wages and prices after 1933 amid massive unemployment, even though the self-correcting mechanism required falling wages and prices. The New Deal increased the power of labor unions, gave more monopoly power to business firms, and encouraged them to raise prices. In short, from 1933 to 1936, a supply-side inflation in the middle of a deep depression retarded the move toward full employment.

3. In 1937, in an incredible act of self-destruction, the Federal Reserve System doubled reserve requirements. The banking system did have large excess reserves at the time, but excess reserves were being held by banks because of the prevailing economic situation. Accordingly, the increase in the reserve requirement brought the needed money growth to a halt and sent the economy into another recession within the Great Depression.

4. Large tax increases were passed in 1932 and 1937 during periods of massive unemployment.

The nonactivists blame these four policy blunders for the Great Depression. They believe that if policymakers had pursued a policy of steady monetary growth and nonintervention in wage and price determination, the Great Depression would have been avoided.

Sources: James Tobin, "Inflation and Unemployment," *American Economic Review* 62 (March 1972): 14; Milton Friedman, *Dollars and Deficits* (Englewood Cliffs, NJ: Prentice Hall, 1968).

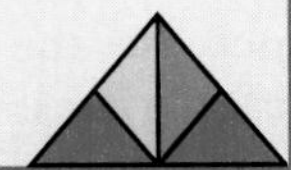

Rational Expectations and Activist Policy

The rational expectations theory argues that activist policies—*if predictable*—will have no impact on the business cycle.

For example, suppose monetary and fiscal authorities adopt activist expansionary policies and increase aggregate demand in order to reduce unemployment. As aggregate demand increases, the price level rises. As earlier chapters have demonstrated, if the inflation set off by rising aggregate demand is unexpected, it can indeed raise output and reduce unemployment. If wages are rigid because of multiyear contracts or layoff unemployment, then selling prices are pushed up more rapidly than costs, and firms expand their hiring and reduce layoffs. The unanticipated inflation reduces unemployment and expands real output.

Rational expectations theory goes one step further and maintains that unanticipated inflation can raise output and reduce unemployment *even if wages and prices are fully flexible.* People and firms can process only a limited amount of information on prices and wages, so they specialize in the wages and prices most important to them. People typically know by how much their wages are changing but, because they buy hundreds or thousands of different goods and services, they have trouble keeping up with changes in the prices of the things they buy. Businesses sell a few things but must buy many things to produce their products. Hence, businesses can keep up with the prices of the things they sell better than the prices of the things they buy. Because price information is unevenly distributed, unanticipated inflation can fool people and firms into taking actions they would not otherwise have taken.

Unanticipated inflation can fool the wage earner into thinking that his or her real wage has risen (the wage earner knows that the nominal wage has gone up but is uncertain about what has happened to prices). The perceived rise in real wages motivates people to accept job offers more readily and remain out of work for shorter periods of time. Unanticipated inflation can fool the firm into thinking that its selling prices are rising faster than its costs. Accordingly, the firm expands its employment and output.

> Rational expectations theory argues that unanticipated inflation causes people and firms to mistake nominal wage and price changes for real wage and price changes. Accordingly, activist policies can affect employment and real output if they cause *unanticipated* changes in inflation.

According to rational expectations theory, if people anticipate the inflationary effects of activist policies, activist policies will not affect output or unemployment. Suppose that people and firms have come to recognize that when monetary authorities increase the growth of money, the inflation rate usually rises. They know that excess growth of money leads to higher inflation and, accordingly, they expect a higher rate of inflation. When the higher inflation actually materializes, it is fully anticipated. People expect higher inflation, and they recognize that rising wages and rising selling prices are a part of the general rise in prices. Unless people can be fooled into thinking their real wages have changed, or unless firms can be fooled into thinking their prices are rising faster than costs, there will be no change in output, employment, or unemployment. If people correctly anticipate the effects of expansionary policies on wages and prices, they realize that real wages are not rising and that prices are not rising more rapidly than costs. Workers and firms will raise prices right along with the expansion of aggregate demand. At the economy-wide level, real GDP will not change, and unemployment will not change. The expansionary policies will cause nominal GDP to rise as a consequence of rising prices, but real GDP will remain unchanged.

Rational expectations theorists object to activist policy on the grounds that the activist policies work only if people do not understand their effects. Initially, monetary expansions or tax cuts might cause real changes in the economy because people do not immediately understand how they work. After several uses, however, people should start to catch on and anticipate the effects of these policies. Once the effects are anticipated, activist policies have no impact on output or employment. Rational expectations theory adds another degree of complexity to activist policy. Policymakers must not only be able to select the correct policy with the proper timing, they must also know whether people and firms will be able to anticipate the effects of these policies. Because people are likely to catch on quickly, policymakers must develop new policy instruments with which people are unfamiliar. Becuse there are, however, only a limited number of policy instruments (tax policy, government spending, monetary policy), it will prove impossible for policymakers to fool the public over the long run.

The Business Cycle Is Due to Supply Shocks

The final argument on behalf of nonactivism comes from the real business cycle theorists. This theory makes three assumptions: (1) the business cycle is caused by random shocks to the rate of technological innovation; (2) observed changes in employment are simply the result of people choosing to work more or less in response to temporary opportunities (for example, Robinson Crusoe spends more time fishing when the fish are biting than when they are not biting); and (3) financial factors are not crucial.

To support this view of the economy, nonactivists cite evidence collected by Christina Romer. Romer's evidence shows that cyclical instability has remained fairly constant over the very long run. Romer challenged the historical data in Figure 2 that shows that, whether measured by unemployment rates or rates of growth in real GDP, economic volatility was greater before 1929 than after 1947. According to Romer, this conclusion is based on a simple fallacy: As we go back in time, the quality of economic data deteriorates. The consequence is that unless we are very

EXAMPLE 4 The Great Debate: The Evidence for Real Business Cycle Theory

Before 1929, the rate of change in real GDP was much more volatile than after 1947 (see Figure 2, panel *a*). This comparison excludes the Great Depression and World War II as special cases. This has been the conventional wisdom for many years, giving support to the role of demand management in stabilizing the economy. Using conventional data, it has been estimated that the period from 1869 to 1928 is about 85 percent more volatile than the period from 1947 to 1986.

This conclusion, however, is somewhat shaky because no primary annual real GDP data exist before 1909. According to Christine Romer, conventional pre-1909 data made the unrealistic assumption that GDP moved one for one with the output of commodities—agriculture, mining, and manufacturing. Thus, Romer developed new estimates that allowed for changes in the importance of commodity production. Using these estimates, she found that the 1869–1928 period is only about 25 percent more volatile than the 1947–1986 period. Since statistical errors are involved, this difference is not significant.

Romer's evidence supports the contention of the real business cycle theory that monetary factors are unimportant determinants of the business cycle. Figure 3 shows that before 1929 the rate of growth in the money supply was more volatile than after 1947. If Romer is correct in stating that real GDP is just as stable in the postwar period as in the pre–Great Depression years, the conclusion that monetary factors played a small role in this stability seems inescapable.

The text cited Romer's earlier work on unemployment, which showed a similar result. However, Romer's conclusion must still be regarded as tentative. Nathan Balke and Robert Gordon of SMU and Northwestern, respectively, disputed her conclusions about GDP (but not unemployment) by arguing that one cannot rely on estimates of commodity output alone. Balke and Gordon take into account the role of construction as well as transportation. They reaffirm traditional conclusions.

It is difficult to say which set of estimates will stand the test of time. But it will be interesting to follow this Great Debate over the next few years.

Sources: Christina D. Romer, "The Prewar Business Cycle Reconsidered: New Estimates of Gross National Product, 1869–1908," *Journal of Political Economy* 97 (February 1989): 1–37; Nathan S. Balke and Robert J. Gordon, "The Estimation of Prewar Gross National Product: Methodology and New Evidence," *Journal of Political Economy* 89 (February 1989): 38–92.

careful, the increase in the quality of the data may show less volatility.[5]

In one study, Romer studied unemployment data prior to the Great Depression. Romer showed that if unemployment rates of the last quarter century are calculated with the same crude types of data and methods used to estimate unemployment before 1930, they are just as volatile as the long-run historical rates. Example 4 discusses her more controversial study of real GDP.

Romer's evidence strongly supports real business cycle theory because it suggests that the business cycle is not the dance of the dollar that many economists have believed it to be. Recall that most economists believe that monetary instability was greater before 1930 than after 1947 (see Figure 3), causing greater pre–Great Depression fluctuations in the business cycle. If, however, the business cycle has remained

[5]Christina Romer, "Spurious Volatility in Historical Unemployment Data," *Journal of Political Economy* 94 (February 1986): 1–37.

unstable throughout the twentieth century, then, evidently, money does not affect real GDP.

Real business cycle theorists explain the apparent unimportance of money with the same argument used by early Keynesians. They argue that it is not money that causes the business cycle, but rather the reverse. As economic activity expands, so does the demand for loans. Since the creation of loans increases the money supply, an increase in the pace of economic activity can increase the rate of growth of the money supply.

A REDUCTION IN DIFFERENCES?

The disagreement between activist Keynesians on the one hand, and nonactivist monetarists, rational expectationists, and real business cycle theorists on the other, appears profound. One side believes in activist policy; the other side says that countercyclical policies either have no effect on economic activity or make matters worse.

Signs of agreement between activists and nonactivists are beginning to emerge. First, the two positions have come much closer in the last 40 years. At one time Keynesians argued that fiscal policy affected the business cycle but money did not. Monetarists argued the opposite until Keynesians reversed their position, agreeing not only that money did indeed matter, but also that fiscal policy was not as important as monetary policy. But now we have come full circle. The real business cycle theorists are repeating the old Keynesian refrain that money doesn't matter! All groups agree that money and the cycle move together. The question is: does money cause the cycle or the reverse? The answer is not obvious.

The fundamental monetarist critique of activist policy is that it is more likely to do harm than good. Activists also realize that policymakers have committed costly errors in the past. It is unlikely that policy blunders as large as those committed in the 1930s will ever be repeated. Presumably, the ability to forecast the business cycle improves over time; economists learn from experience about the effects of past policies. Yet economists are far from reaching the point where monetarists would be satisfied that policymakers know enough to devise error-free activist policy.

Monetarists and rational expectations economists have shown that Keynes's original multiplier analysis paints too simple a picture. To devise correct activist policy, policymakers must know what the multipliers are and how soon multiplier effects will be felt. With crowding out, lags, and unpredictable inflationary expectations, the effects of any monetary or fiscal policy will be difficult to predict.

As a consequence, modern Keynesians have largely abandoned the notion of fine-tuning—the constant fiddling with the dials of discretionary policy. Instead, it is agreed that activist policy should respond only to major cyclical disturbances.

The activists have pointed out the potential weaknesses of fixed rules. If a balanced-budget rule is followed, what kind of provisions must be made to trigger its suspension? Would a war or severe recession be sufficient cause to suspend the balanced-budget rule? If money substitutes can be created, which money concept is to be used in applying fixed monetary growth rules? Activists have outlined the difficulties faced by the Fed in setting monetary growth targets during a period of rapid changes in financial institutions. The growth of money substitutes makes it difficult for monetary authorities to know whether interest-bearing deposits are used for savings or transactions. The choice among alternative money supply definitions complicates the fixed monetary growth rule.

The concern over which money supply concept to use as a policy instrument has encouraged proponents of activism to consider new and unusual instruments. Monetarists have long argued in favor of money supply targeting using a fixed monetary growth rule. As long as the money supply grows steadily at a reasonable rate, the economy can operate at the natural rate without high inflation. The Keynesian activists have long favored aiming for a level of real GDP close to the natural level of GDP. Such an outcome would keep unemployment at the natural rate without accelerating inflation.

The discussion of appropriate targets has prompted innovative suggestions that seem to bridge the gap between monetarists and Keynesians. One is to target nominal GDP. The Fed should raise interest rates when forecasted nominal GDP exceeds the target, and lower interest rates when nominal GDP is expected to fall below the target. The Fed would then determine the long-run inflation rate and its policies would not destabilize the economy.

The activists and the nonactivists do share an important common ground. They wish to achieve the same targets: full employment, moderate inflation, and real economic growth. Both schools dislike unnecessary unemployment; both recognize the private and social costs of recessions. They agree that, in the long run, nonactivism would yield the desired end result; both believe that the self-correcting mechanism works in the long run. The disagreement is basically over the amount of time it takes for the self-correcting mechanism to work. Activists argue that it is important to use discretionary policy to speed up the return to full employment. According to them, the self-correcting mechanism works slowly, and activist policy (however imperfect) can return the economy to equilibrium more quickly than reliance on automatic forces. Nonactivists maintain that the self-correcting mechanism works with sufficient speed. Even if the self-correcting mechanism were slow-moving, the nonactivists argue that the likelihood of activist policy blunders is too great to warrant interfering with automatic forces.

Real business cycle theory has been criticized for assuming that money does not affect real economic activity and that unemployment is a voluntary response to temporary random shocks to technology. Yet, the theory has created a new standard for a theory of business cycles. Such theory should have a microeconomic underpinning in which profit-maximizing producers and consumers are linked by the impersonal forces of supply and demand. Instead of looking at real business cycle theory in terms of what it does not accomplish, we should evaluate the theory in terms of its basic achievement: It gives a minimal equilibrium explanation of a business cycle without the special features emphasized in the model of aggregate supply and aggregate demand. Under its terms, the business cycle can occur even if money wages are perfectly flexible and the monetary system never impinges on the real economy—production, employment, investment, and consumption. Actual business cycles may reflect the importance of money, periods of psychological optimism, fixed money contracts, and simple mistakes in business investments. The burden of empirical work is to determine the relative importance of these different factors.

ACTIVISM AS THE CHOICE OF U.S. POLICYMAKERS

This chapter and previous chapters have shown that U.S. policymakers have historically chosen the activist policy approach. Monetary growth rates have fluctuated considerably over the years, although the fluctuations have decreased in recent years. Activist monetary policy (either directed toward interest-rate targets or monetary growth targets) has aimed at moderating the business cycle. The Fed has never followed a fixed monetary growth rule—even after October 1979 when the Fed placed a higher priority on monetary growth targets. There is an important distinction between monetary growth targets (which can be changed as economic conditions change) and a fixed monetary growth rule. Activist monetary policy is perfectly consistent with monetary growth targets.

U.S. policymakers have made relatively frequent use of activist tax policy since the 1964 tax cut. In the postwar era, there have been four tax revisions that have been passed largely for activist policy reasons. These tax revisions have had different degrees of success, but it is clear that U.S. policymakers regard tax revision as a major instrument of activist fiscal policy. The data presented earlier in this book on federal deficits clearly demonstrate that U.S. policymakers have not followed the balanced-budget rule advocated by the nonactivists. In fact, the inability of policymakers to balance the budget over the cycle, despite the best intentions of several Presidents, makes one skeptical about our ability to implement any balanced-budget rule.

This chapter discussed how to stabilize the business cycle over the short-run. The next chapter turns to the subject of the long-term growth of real GDP.

SUMMARY

1. Business cycles are broad in scope and last several years. Most industries move up or down together. Durable goods production fluctuates more than nondurable production. Short-term interest rates are highly procyclical. The rate of growth in the money supply often falls sharply before a recession. Productivity and real wages behave procyclically.

2. There are many theories of the business cycle. The two main theories are the Keynesian theory, in which the cycle is driven by demand shocks, and real business cycle theory, in which the cycle is driven by supply shocks.

3. The two main macroeconomic policy options are activism and nonactivism. Activist policies

aim to stabilize the business cycle; they can be either discretionary or can use feedback rules. Nonactivist policy uses fixed rules. The two rules suggested by Friedman for nonactivism are (a) let the money supply grow at a constant rate and (b) have a cyclically balanced budget.

4. The policy instruments of macroeconomic policy are monetary policy and fiscal policy. Monetary policy is the most flexible policy instrument. In order to devise perfect activist policy, policymakers must know about impending changes in the business cycle, know the natural level of output, be able to use policy instruments in a timely fashion, and know when policy changes will affect the economy.

5. The chief argument for activism is that the self-correcting mechanism is too slow. The main evidence in favor of activism is the long-term reduction in GDP fluctuations since World War II.

6. The case for nonactivism rests on the following points: (1) instability has been caused by policy blunders; (2) the reduced GDP fluctuations since World War II are the result of smaller fluctuations in monetary growth or measurement errors in earlier periods; (3) activist policy tends to be destabilizing; and (4) the business cycle is due to supply shocks rather than demand shocks.

7. Modern Keynesians now take into account many of the monetarists' points, such as crowding out, permanent income, accelerating inflation, and the role of expectations. Monetarists increasingly recognize the difficulty of using the money supply as a policy target when financial innovations create new types of money. More economists now favor nominal GDP targeting.

8. U.S. policymakers have used activist policy to try to moderate the business cycle and have been unable to follow a cyclically balanced-budget rule.

KEY TERMS

real business cycle theory
activist policy
feedback rule
fine-tuning
nonactivist policy
policy instruments
GDP gap
auction market

QUESTIONS AND PROBLEMS

1. The 1990–1992 recession was preceded by a dip in the growth rate of the money supply to a scant 1 percent from 1988 to 1989 (down from nearly 5 percent from 1987 to 1988). Was this a typical pattern?
2. List some of the features of business cycles.
3. What are the main points of real business cycle theory?
4. A typical feature of business cycles is that real wages rise in booms and fall in recessions. How does this fact fit into real business cycle theory? Keynesian theory?
5. Evaluate the validity of the following statement: "Real business cycle theory assumes that fluctuations in employment reflect changes in the amount people want to work."
6. If, as most economists believe, there is a self-correcting mechanism that automatically moves the economy toward full employment, how can anyone advocate discretionary policy? Will the economy not take care of itself?
7. This chapter pointed out that the advocates of nonactivism must demonstrate that activist policies tend to worsen the business cycle. What evidence is there that activism actually makes matters worse?
8. How could we have had the Great Depression of the 1930s if there is a self-correcting mechanism at work in the economy?
9. The rational expectations argument states that expectations can defeat activist policy. Assume that Congress decides to pass a tax cut to stimulate the economy. How could rational expectations defeat the purpose of the tax cut?
10. Explain the difference between monetary targets and monetarism. Is it correct to call the Fed's October 1979 decision to follow monetary growth targets a victory for monetarism?
11. This chapter showed that the conditions required for conducting ideal activist policy cannot be met in the real world. What is the activist policy's defense, given the fact that conditions are imperfect?
12. Both activists and nonactivists cite the greater stability of the economy after World War II to support their positions. Explain how both sides can use the same data to support entirely different positions.
13. This chapter explained how the economic policies of the mid-1930s forced up wages and prices, even though the unemployment rate was high. Use aggregate supply and aggregate de-

mand curves to show the effect of these policies on real output.

14. Suppose that, to combat inflation, Congress passes a tax increase. Will the expected effect be greater if the bill calls for a permanent increase in tax rates or for a 1-year increase in tax rates?
15. Explain why both activists and nonactivists appear to agree that monetary policy is the most important policy instrument.
16. Earlier chapters explained that unanticipated inflation raises output and employment. Explain how the rational expectations school uses this argument to support its view that activist policy may have no real effect on output and employment.

SUGGESTED READINGS

Carlson, Keith, and Roger Spencer. "Crowding Out and Its Critics." Federal Reserve Bank of St. Louis, *Review,* December 1975, 2–17.

Friedman, Milton. *A Program for Monetary Stability.* New York: Fordham University Press, 1983.

Gordon, Robert J., ed. *Milton Friedman's Monetary Framework: A Debate with His Critics.* Chicago: University of Chicago Press, 1982.

Lucas, Robert. "Understanding Business Cycles." In *Stabilization of the Domestic and International Economy,* ed. Karl Brunner and Allen Meltzer. Carnegie–Rochester Conference, vol. 5. Amsterdam: North-Holland, 1977.

Mankiw, N. Gregory. "A Quick Refresher Course in Macroeconomics." *Journal of Economic Literature* (December 1990).

Meltzer, Allan H. "Monetarism and the Crisis in Economics." *The Public Interest* (Special Issue, 1980), 35–45.

Modigliani, Franco. "The Monetarist Controversy, or Should We Forsake Stabilization Policies?" *American Economic Review* 67 (March 1977): 1–19.

Zarnowitz, Victor. "Recent Work on Business Cycles in Historical Perspective." *Journal of Economic Literature* (June 1985).

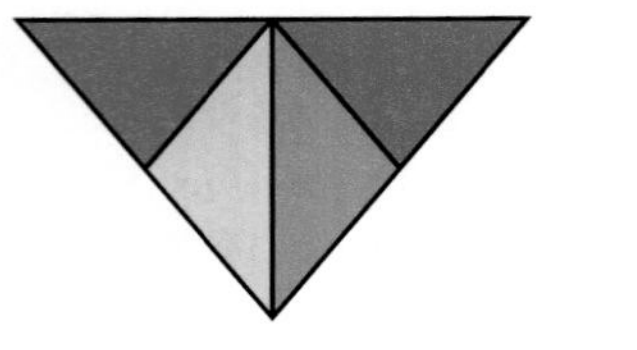

21 Rational Expectations

CHAPTER INSIGHT

Twenty-five years ago, macroeconomists had reached a consensus on how economic policy should respond to fluctuations in output and employment. If unemployment was rising and output was falling, the money supply should be expanded, government spending should be accelerated, or taxes should be cut. Policymakers were confident that they could spend their way out of recessions at the price of higher inflation. As a policy choice, they had to decide whether it was better to have more unemployment and less inflation or vice versa.

Just as the Great Depression of the 1930s gave rise to the Keynesian revolution, the stagflation of the 1970s spawned the new classical economics, or rational expectations theory, to explain why traditional remedies could not combat the combination of high unemployment and accelerating inflation. Economists and government officials complained that "things don't work the way they used to!" Officials responsible for monetary and fiscal policy were puzzled by the apparent ineffectiveness of their macroeconomic tools.

The new classical economics has sought to close the gap between microeconomic principles and macroeconomic practice. Rational expectationists argue that macroeconomic theories must be firmly based upon an understanding of the way individual participants in the economy—households and businesses—behave.

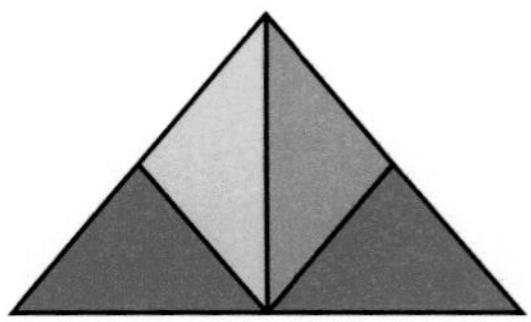

THE NEW CLASSICAL MACROECONOMICS

The classical economists believed that the economy would naturally remain at or near the natural rate of unemployment. Flexible wages and prices would adjust to prevent significant deviations from full employment. Keynes rejected the old classical quantity theory as unrealistic. The Great Depression supported Keynes's criticism of classical economics and clearly established the need to explain large fluctuations in real GDP.

The new classical economics was developed in response to two flaws—one theoretical, one empirical—in the Keynesian view of the world. The theoretical flaw was that Keynesian economics left a "chasm between microeconomic principles and macroeconomic practice that was too great. . . ."[1] The Keynesian model viewed households and businesses as nonthinking automatons—responding in an automatic fashion to changes in government policy and remarkably unconcerned with anticipating the future. The empirical flaw was that Keynesian economics could not adequately explain the rising rates of inflation and unemployment that occurred during the 1970s.

The central idea of rational expectations theory, as pioneered by Robert Lucas, John Muth, Thomas Sargent, and Robert Barro, is that consumers and business managers are more than just passive observers of the economic scenery. People are active observers; they *think*. A person will, in making economic decisions, not only take objective economic data into account but also form **rational expectations** about the future course of economic activity and government policy.

Rational expectations are expectations that people form about the inflation rate and the unemployment rate using their knowledge about current and future monetary and fiscal policy, business and consumer spending plans, and the behavior of the macroeconomy.

[1] N. Gregory Mankiw, "A Quick Refresher Course in Macroeconomics," *Journal of Economic Literature*, 33, 4 (December 1990): 1647.

Rational expectations theory assumes that people use their best available information about what the government (or other people) is going to do in the future. People then combine the information they have about how the economy works to form expectations about the future. If government policy changes, people will change their view of the future. If people expect the government to increase the growth of the money supply by a substantial amount, they will raise their inflationary expectations. If people expect a monetary reform to halt a hyperinflation, they will lower their expectations of inflation. In fact, evidence suggests that the general public is able to anticipate and recognize macroeconomic events. (See Example 1.)

Households and business firms use the best available information to try to anticipate what is going to happen. Employers and employees negotiate wage contracts not only on the basis of current prices and costs but also on the basis of wages and prices they expect to prevail in the future. Business firms base their output decisions on current as well as expected prices and costs. Workers and firms benefit from correctly anticipating inflation. They lose when they guess wrong. The stakes are high. It is not surprising that people devote effort and resources to anticipating the future.

The difference between adaptive expectations and rational expectations was explained in Chapter 17 on inflation. Adaptive expectations are formed on the basis of what is happening now and what has happened in the past. Rational expectations are based not only on what has happened in the past but also on people's analysis of current economic theories, conditions, and policies.

Do People Anticipate Policy?

Do consumers and producers form expectations concerning government monetary and fiscal policy from which they rationally forecast expected wages and prices? Many individuals and businesses subscribe to newsletters and commercial reports or use the services of macroeconomic forecasting firms, such as Data Resources, Inc., or Wharton Econometrics. A large number of public and private forecasters provide predictions for real GDP, the inflation rate, and the unemployment rate. Business firms and labor unions hire economists to make macroeconomic predictions. Generating information and projections

EXAMPLE 1 How Well Can the Public Predict the Future?

According to the new classical economics, people and businesses use all available information to predict the economic future. There is surprising evidence that the general public may do a better job of predicting the economic future than professional economic forecasters. When the U.S. economy began its latest recession in July 1990, the Blue Chip Consensus Forecast of professional economic forecasters was predicting that the recession would not begin until 1992. The Department of Commerce's Index of Leading Indicators was also predicting continued economic expansion as late as August 1990. Meanwhile, two polls of American public opinion, the ABC News/Money Magazine Consumer Comfort Index and the University of Michigan Survey of Consumer Confidence, both slid sharply in July 1990. The general public recognized the onset of recession better than economic forecasters.

Surveys of consumer confidence have also outperformed professional economic forecasters by not responding to false signs of recession. For example, Blue Chip Forecasters cut their forecast of economic growth by almost one-half 3 weeks after the 1987 stock market crash. The ABC/Money Magazine index, on the other hand, correctly shrugged off the stock market crash as not affecting the economy.

Why can average Americans predict the course of the economy? Pollsters say Americans have a strong personal interest in the economy and are good at picking up signals of change in the economy. They observe what is going on at their workplaces and in their neighborhoods. They see pay raises, hiring freezes, tighter credit, rising prices, and cutbacks on overtime. Although individuals may miss these signs, a random national sample does not overlook signs of recession and recovery.

Source: "The Public Can Predict What Economists Can't," *Wall Street Journal*, May 1, 1991.

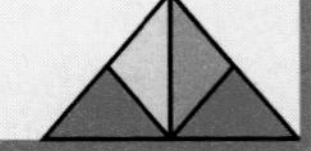

about the government monetary and fiscal policy has become a big business.

Most people are reasonably knowledgeable about taxes and are informed about tax policy. People worry about the national debt and form expectations about deficit reductions. Even though most people do not make elaborate economic predictions, they use data available to them to form rational expectations about future prices and wages. Even average citizens, whether they are aware of it or not, form expectations or guesses concerning government economic policies. To say that people do not attempt to anticipate economic policy is almost like saying that they are not interested in their own well-being.

People Specialize in Price Information

The next key hypothesis of the new classical macroeconomics is that no single person has perfect information. This mundane observation has profound implications when combined with another observation: *People are more specialized in their selling activities than in their buying activities.* The number of products a business manager sells is much smaller than the myriad of products that manager purchases in order to produce and market the product line. The wheat farmer sells wheat but buys fertilizers, rents land, hires workers, and purchases tractors and equipment. Workers sell only the services of their labor, but they buy hundreds of consumer goods. Thus, virtually every economic agent—whether a firm or a worker—sells fewer things than it buys.

> The typical producer (worker, business firm, farm) knows the prices of the things it sells better than the prices of the things it buys.

Because people have less information about buying prices than about selling prices, they can be confused by price and wage movements. They mistake changes in nominal wages and prices for changes in real wages and relative prices. Even if prices and wages adjust very quickly during inflations, people may still change their employment and output decisions if they confuse nominal and real price changes.

ANTICIPATED VERSUS UNANTICIPATED POLICY

Chapter 20, on stabilization policy, questioned whether activist policies should be used to stabilize the economy. The new classical macroeconomics makes a novel argument against policy activism: Activist policies will achieve desired results only if people are surprised or fooled. For the effect to be long lasting, people must be continuously fooled. If the policy is anticipated, it will have no effect on output and employment.

Price-Level Surprises

A *price surprise* occurs when the actual price is different from the expected price. Just as individuals experience price surprises, so the economy as a whole can experience a **price-level surprise.** The price level (P) is a weighted average of the prices of all the individual goods and services the consumer or firm purchases and is measured by a price index, such as the CPI or a wholesale price index. When prices are higher than people expect (on the average), the actual price level is higher than the price level that people expect. The price level that people expect is called the *expected price level* (P_e).

> A **price-level surprise** occurs when the actual price level, P, is not equal to the expected price level, P_e.

People form expectations about future prices. If they guess wrong, they will suffer price-level surprises. (See Example 2.)

Demand and Supply Shocks

A price-level surprise is caused either by a **demand shock** or by a *supply shock.*

> A **demand shock** is an *unanticipated* shift in the aggregate demand schedule.

If people are indeed interested in anticipating inflation, they must attempt to anticipate changes in aggregate demand. Demand shocks can arise from monetary policy, fiscal policy, investment, consumer spending, and exports. People will try to anticipate monetary policy—how rapidly the Fed will increase the money supply. People will try to anticipate tax policy and government spending. If monetary policy and fiscal policy are correctly anticipated, price surprises can be largely avoided. *The fact that people attempt to anticipate changes in aggregate demand does not necessarily mean that they will succeed.* Given so many sources of demand shocks, anticipating future inflation will always be a difficult task.

A price surprise can also be caused by a **supply shock.**

> A **supply shock** is an unanticipated shift in the aggregate supply curve.

For example, the unanticipated fourfold increase in OPEC oil prices in 1974 was a supply shock that caused an extensive price-level surprise. The decline in OPEC oil prices after 1982 (which accelerated in the late 1980s) set into motion a price-level surprise in the opposite direction: Prices rose less rapidly than anticipated. The 1988 drought was a supply shock that cut agricultural supplies. Both supply shocks came out of the blue and could not be anticipated.

Adjustment with Price Surprises

Figure 1 shows an economy that is initially in long-run equilibrium at point a. It is producing the natural level of output (it is at the natural rate of unemployment), and there are no price-level surprises ($P = P_e$). People are correctly anticipating the price level (or, equivalently, they are correctly anticipating the inflation rate).

As preceding chapters have shown, an *unanticipated* increase in aggregate demand (from AD to AD_1, in Figure 1) would set off an increase in prices that would catch people off guard. Prices are greater than expected. Workers on multiyear contracts find that their wages rise less than prices. Employers increase

EXAMPLE 2 Can Consumers Predict Inflation?

The University of Michigan conducts its Survey of Consumers on a monthly basis. Each month a sample of households is asked what it expects the consumer inflation rate to be over the next 12 months. The mean response of consumers to the Michigan survey is the most widely used measure of inflationary expectations.

The accompanying figure, which compares expected inflation with actual inflation, shows that consumers can generally anticipate rises and falls in the inflation rate, but sometimes overestimate or underestimate future inflation by significant margins. These periods of inaccurate prediction occur when there is a sharp change in the inflation rate. Consumers underestimated the runup of inflation in the mid- and late 1970s and failed to anticipate the sharp drop in inflation in the early 1980s.

Expected versus Actual Inflation

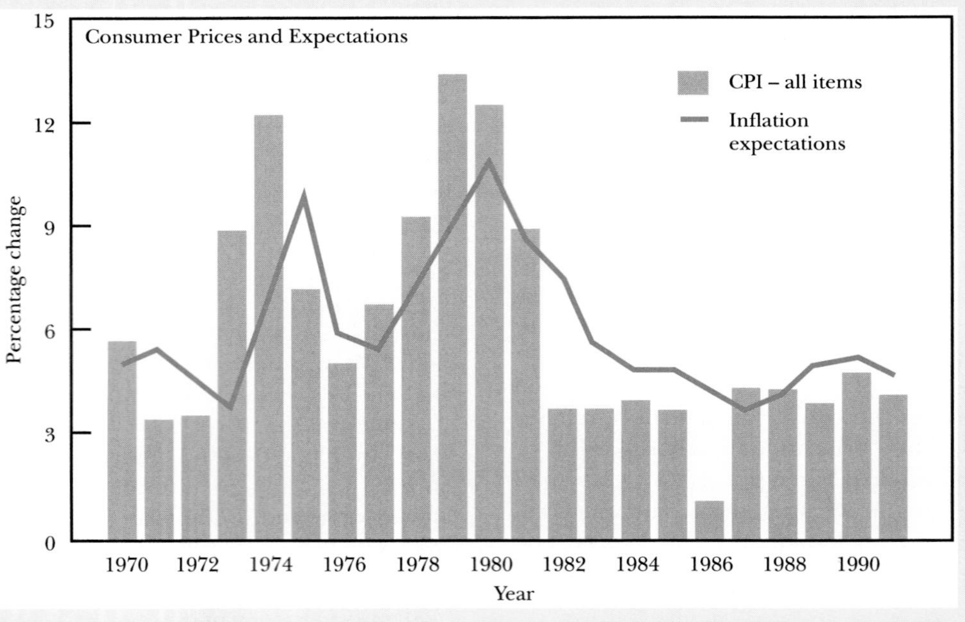

their hiring because of the decline in real wages. Firms find that their selling prices rise faster than costs and increase their output. The novel feature of the new classical macroeconomics model is that there need not be any long-term contracts or other sources of price or wage inflexibility for unanticipated inflation to increase output—all wages and prices could be perfectly flexible upward or downward.

Rational expectations theorists argue that people know the prices of the things they sell better than the things they buy. If prices are higher than people have anticipated, the sellers of products (firms) or of labor (workers) will think that the prices of the goods they sell have risen *relative* to the things they buy. This mistaken belief will induce producers to supply more real GDP. Sellers will think they are be-

FIGURE 1
Rational Expectations Theory in Terms of Aggregate Supply and Demand

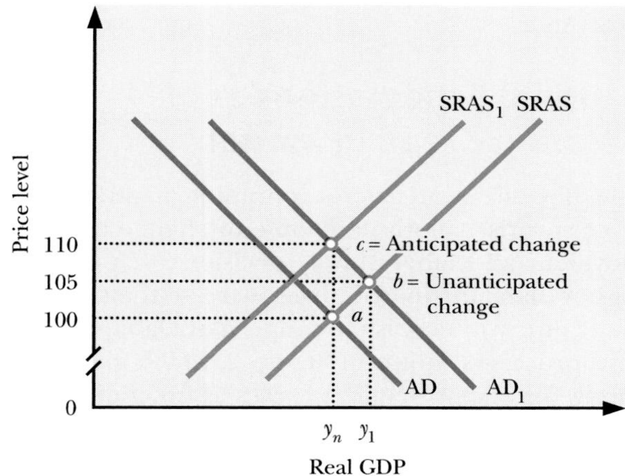

The initial equilibrium of aggregate supply and aggregate demand occurs at point *a*, where the AD curve intersects the SRAS curve. The AD curve shifts upward to AD_1 as a result of monetary or demand-side fiscal policy. If the increase in aggregate demand is not anticipated, people and firms are caught off guard by inflation, and the economy moves along the SRAS curve from *a* to *b*. If the policy is anticipated, the rational expectations hypothesis implies that the short-run aggregate supply curve shifts up at the same time to $SRAS_1$. The new equilibrium is then at point *c*, with the same GDP but a higher price level. When policy is anticipated, the economy adjusts directly from *a* to *c*.

ing offered a good deal in the marketplace and will try to take advantage of it by increasing their output (for example, labor will work harder). In response to positive price surprises, people will try to "make hay while the sun shines."

Consider day-labor construction workers, who assemble every morning at a hiring hall. Their employers build small shopping centers on a speculative basis. There has been a long period of low inflation, and both the day laborers and their employers expect low inflation to continue. An unexpected increase in aggregate demand pushes up wages and prices generally throughout the economy, raising the wages of the construction workers, who know more about the wage increase than about the increase in the prices of the things they buy. They *mistake* the nominal wage increase for a real wage increase. More of them are now willing to work at prevailing wages. The construction firm is now able to sell its small shopping centers at higher-than-expected prices. It knows that its selling prices are increasing, but is less aware of what is happening to all its costs—such as construction materials or wages of skilled craftspersons. The firm *mistakes* the increase in its selling prices for an increase in its real prices and therefore increases its hiring and raises the number of shopping centers under construction. In this example, *unexpected inflation has increased real output and employment even though wages and prices are perfectly flexible.*

The unexpected increase in aggregate demand from AD to AD_1 (Figure 1) sets off a price surprise. People think that real wages and relative prices have changed when they have not. The economy moves up the short-run aggregate supply curve (from *a* to *b*). The economy produces more output (output increases from y_n to y_1), and the price level rises (from 100 to 105).

Figure 1 shows how business cycles can occur even when wages and prices are flexible. The unexpected increase in aggregate demand set off a price surprise, which increased output and employment as people and firms were "fooled" into actions they would not have taken had they had perfect information. If, in the next period, prices rise slower than expected, output and employment are reduced below the levels that would have prevailed with perfect information on prices and wages.

> The new classical macroeconomics explains the business cycle in terms of price surprises. Price increases greater than anticipated raise real output and employment. Price increases less than anticipated lower real output and employment.

The new and old classical macroeconomics do not disagree on the long run. Eventually, both agree, firms are no longer fooled into thinking their selling prices are rising faster than costs, and people are no longer fooled into thinking real wages have changed. If there has been surprise inflation, workers insist on higher nominal wages in the new round of contracts. When these long-run adjustments are made, short-run aggregate supply falls (there is a leftward move of the SRAS curve to $SRAS_1$.) As short-run aggregate supply falls, prices are pushed up further. The increase in prices stops only when the economy returns to the natural level of output (at point *c*). At the natural level of output, the prevailing price level (or the prevailing rate of inflation) remains constant.

> The long-run self-correcting mechanism restores the economy to the natural rate by gradually eliminating the effects of price surprises from the economy.

The economy moves from point *a* to point *b* in Figure 1 because of price surprises. It then moves from point *b* to point *c* because, in the long run, price surprises are eliminated automatically as people adjust price expectations.

Adjustment with No Price Surprises

Let us now consider what happens if the increase in aggregate demand is *fully anticipated.* The demand increase raises prices, but if the increase in aggregate demand is fully anticipated, there are no price surprises. Firms recognize that their selling prices are not rising more rapidly than costs. Consumers recognize that income and prices are rising at the same rate. Workers do not mistake nominal wage increases for real wage increases. Union contracts having anticipated the rise in prices, nominal wages are set to rise at the same rate as prices. Because people realize that real wages and prices are not changing, there is no change in output or employment. *The economy continues to produce the natural level of output even though prices are rising.* In Figure 1, there is no movement up the short-run aggregate supply curve (from *a* to *b*) to moderate price increases. Instead, the short-run aggregate supply curve shifts immediately to the left (from SRAS to $SRAS_1$) to offset the increase in aggregate demand, and prices rise (from 100 to 110) immediately to the new long-run equilibrium at point *c*. There is no short-run effect on output and unemployment (there is no short-run movement from *a* to *b*). The economy moves directly from the initial position at point *a* to the final position at point *c*. *An anticipated expansionary policy raises the price level without raising real GDP.*

> Anticipated fiscal and monetary policies simply raise (or lower) the price level without any change in real GDP. Without price surprises, real GDP stays at the natural level of output.

When people correctly anticipate price-level changes, *the automatic adjustment mechanism works instantaneously.* Firms and workers anticipate the full magnitude of the price increase, and the short-run aggregate supply curve shifts immediately from SRAS to $SRAS_1$.

Rational Expectations as a Market-Clearing Model

The new classical macroeconomics maintains that price surprises motivate people to change their employment and labor supply decisions. If prices are higher than anticipated, firms increase their employment, and workers wish to supply more labor to firms. This process is shown in Figure 2, which gives labor supply and labor demand curves as functions of the real wage. If the real wage rises, workers wish to supply more labor to firms, and if the real wage falls, firms wish to hire more workers. Initially, the labor market is in equilibrium at point *a*. Unanticipated inflation drives up nominal wages, and workers *believe* their real wage has increased. Accordingly, workers move up their supply curve to point *b*. On the demand side, unanticipated inflation raises selling prices, and firms *believe* the real wage has fallen. Accordingly, firms move down their demand curve to point *c*. *Workers think real wages have risen, and firms think real wages have fallen.* Unanticipated inflation has caused simultaneous increases in the quantity of labor demanded and the quantity of labor supplied. The labor market continues to clear because the quantity of labor demanded equals the quantity of labor supplied.

As people and firms continue to be surprised by the unanticipated inflation, they are content to remain where they are on their respective labor supply and labor demand curves. Unanticipated inflation has driven the labor market to a higher equilibrium level of employment.

> Unanticipated inflation raises the *equilibrium* level of employment. As long as workers are fooled into thinking the real wage has risen and firms are fooled into thinking that the real wage has fallen, the labor market remains at the higher equilibrium level of employment. This is a market-clearing model because the quantity of labor demanded equals the quantity supplied at the higher level of employment.

FIGURE 2
The New Macroeconomics as a Market-Clearing Model

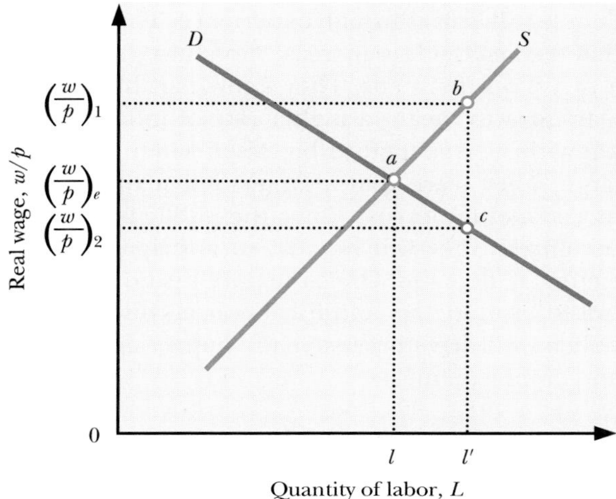

Labor supply (S) and labor demand (D) curves are functions of the real wage, w/p. Initially, the labor market is in equilibrium at point a, where the equilibrium quantity of labor is l and the equilibrium real wage is $(w/p)_e$. If the real wage rises, workers wish to supply more labor to firms; if the real wage falls, firms wish to hire more workers. Unanticipated inflation drives up nominal wages, leading workers to believe their real wage has increased to $(w/p)_1$. Accordingly, workers move up their supply curve to point b. On the demand side, unanticipated inflation raises selling prices, and firms believe the real wage has fallen to $(w/p)_2$. Accordingly, firms move down their demand curve to point c. A new equilibrium is established at l', which is the quantity of labor corresponding to both b and c. Unanticipated inflation thus causes more workers to be hired and more output to be produced.

Once workers and firms realize that they have been fooled by the unanticipated inflation, they return to the initial equilibrium employment level (point a) because they realize that the real wage has not really changed.

Note the distinction between the views of rational expectationists and modern Keynesians. The latter argue that demand shocks affect real output and employment through price and wage rigidities and other institutional factors. When aggregate demand increases, wages and prices cannot immediately adjust to their new equilibria. Wages are set in multiyear wage contracts; price increases are restricted by existing delivery contracts. In the modern Keynesian model, real output increases becauses labor markets and product markets are prevented from clearing by various rigidities. These temporary disequilibria cause real output to increase when aggregate demand rises and to fall when aggregate demand falls.

RATIONAL EXPECTATIONS AND POLICY INEFFECTIVENESS

The most controversial conclusion of the new classical macroeconomics is that activist monetary and fiscal policies, if anticipated, will have no effect on real output and employment. The only lasting effect will be on inflation. Anticipated expansionary policy increases inflation but does not change real output and employment. Anticipated contractionary policy lowers inflation but does not change real output and employment.

Anticipated Policy

A monetary policy is anticipated when the public correctly anticipates the rate of growth of the money supply. Output and employment decisions do not change, because there are no price surprises. Even though the supply of money is increasing, the public realizes it is no better off in real terms, and there is no reason for aggregate quantity demanded to increase in real terms.

With fully anticipated inflation, there is no change in real interest rates. The nominal interest rate simply increases by the increase in the inflation rate. The real rate of interest is unaffected, and the amount of desired business investment is unchanged.

> According to the new classical macroeconomic theory, an anticipated increase in the money supply will leave real GDP unchanged but will *raise* the rate of inflation and the nominal rate of interest.

Expectations can defeat fiscal policy as well. Consider, once again, the aggregate demand and short-run aggregate supply curves in Figure 1. The initial equilibrium is point a, where the equilibrium price level is 100. An increase in real government expenditures shifts the aggregate demand curve from AD to AD_1.

When aggregate demand increases to AD_1, short-run aggregate supply decreases to $SRAS_1$: firms and workers anticipate that prices and wages will rise in response to expansionary fiscal policy and they know there is no change in real wages or in relative prices. At the new price level of 110, real GDP doesn't change, but the mix of public and private spending does change. In other words, the higher price level *crowds out* a quantity of private expenditures equal to the increase in government expenditures.

Unanticipated Policies and Learning from the Past

If the public is fooled by monetary and fiscal policy, real output and employment can be affected. Obviously, the public cannot always anticipate government policy. The future is uncertain, and the government may, without warning, change the monetary and fiscal rules under which it operates. For example, in October 1979, the Federal Reserve System changed from interest-rate objectives to monetary-growth targeting. As a consequence, monetary growth was much slower than expected in 1980 and 1981.

If the Fed surprises the public with an *unanticipated increase* in the money supply, the public sees its money balances increasing but fails to recognize that price increases will soon wipe out any real gains. Real spending therefore increases. The increase in the money supply starts to drive down interest rates, and savers (who fail to anticipate the impending increase in inflation) do not require an added inflation premium on interest rates. The interest rate falls, and real business investment increases.

A similar effect results from unanticipated fiscal policy. If the public has had no prior experience with deficit financing and the government adds $20 billion worth of spending to its budget without raising taxes, the unanticipated fiscal policy would raise aggregate demand.

The public, however, learns from these experiences. As Abraham Lincoln said, "you can't fool all the people all the time." Policy surprises occur because the public doesn't anticipate policy changes. After the public recognizes that they were fooled (that monetary growth was higher than expected or that deficit financing raises future taxes), they make adjustments, and the economy returns to the natural level of output.

Rational expectations theorists predict that it will become increasingly difficult to surprise the public with unanticipated monetary and fiscal policies. People will learn through experience. They will learn that the Fed tends to increase monetary growth when a recession threatens. They know that higher monetary growth means a higher rate of inflation. They know that taxes tend to be raised when deficits are large. They learn that a larger deficit today means more taxes tomorrow. Once the public becomes experienced, they will be able to anticipate shifts in aggregate demand. Once the public is no longer surprised by monetary and fiscal policy, countercyclical policies will have no systematic impact on real GDP and employment.

> The new classical macroeconomics argues that countercyclical policy cannot be used to stabilize flucuations in real GDP unless the public can be fooled or fails to learn from experience.

The Good News about Stopping Inflation

Chapter 17 discussed two different views about the means by which inflationary expectations are formed: adaptive expectations and rational expectations. The adaptive expectations approach says that people form inflationary expectations on the basis of their experiences of the recent past. Their predicted value of inflation, for example, might be an average of inflation over the past 3 or 4 years. If expectations are formed adaptively, the motion of inflation will be like that of a freight train. The faster the train moves, the longer and harder the braking action will be. An accelerating inflation builds up its own momentum that can be broken only by extreme measures. If the Fed slams on the monetary brakes during an accelerating inflation, the cost of the cure will be a substantial rise in unemployment until inflationary expectations are pulled down.

The rational expectations approach claims that it is easier to stop the momentum of inflation. Because people form expectations on the basis of current policy (as well as experience), if they are convinced that policy actions are being taken that will stop inflation, inflationary expectations can be pulled down quickly. There are ample historical examples of hyperinflations that have been stopped virtually overnight when governments adopt policies that people were convinced would stop inflation.

> Rational expectations theory argues that it is possible to reduce inflationary expectations quickly by adopting policies that convince people that inflation will stop.

To halt accelerating inflation, the government might announce, for example, that there will be a stable monetary-growth policy of 4 percent per year for the next decade. Or it might announce that all government spending increases will have to be covered by tax increases, so that the deficit will remain constant. Because people will understand that these preannounced policies can lower future rates of inflation, inflationary expectations will drop instantly, and the economy will settle down to the natural level of real GDP with a low rate of inflation.

The prescription of preannouncing anti-inflationary monetary and fiscal policies is attractive if it works. The problem lies in convincing the public that the preannounced policy will actually be implemented. As long as monetary and fiscal policy are discretionary, policymakers are free to change their minds. What is to prevent them from ignoring monetary and fiscal targets once people have changed their inflationary expectations? An example of public disbelief was the sharp increase in unemployment in late 1981 and 1982 after the Fed announced in 1979 that it intended to pursue a rigorous policy of slower monetary growth. The public did not believe the Fed, and unemployment shot up when inflation slowed down. (See Example 3.)

As long as policy is discretionary, the public's disbelief of government promises is entirely rational. Therefore, many rational expectations theorists believe in fixed constitutional rules that constrain the government's actions.

EXAMPLE 3 The End of the German Hyperinflation

Rational expectations theorists cite the rapid termination of historical hyperinflations to demonstrate that inflationary expectations can be broken by decisive changes in government policies. The end of the German hyperinflation in late November 1923 is a classic case. In the preceding month, prices had increased 100 times, but they increased only 72 percent in December, and they actually fell after December 1923. On October 15, 1923, a monetary reform was announced in which a new unit of currency called the *Rentenmark* replaced the old *Reichsmark*. One unit of the new currency was set equal to an amazing 1 trillion units of the old currency. More significantly, a new bank was established to take over the function of note issue. The decree establishing the new bank put binding limits on the number of units of new currency that could be printed and a maximum amount that could be issued to the government. In December 1923, these decrees were tested by the government, and it became clear that the new bank would stick to its limits. As the public became convinced that the new measures would be effective, they cut back on their inflationary expectations, and the hyperinflation stopped. Notably, the end of the German hyperinflation was accompanied by increases in ouput and reductions in unemployment.

Source: Thomas J. Sargent, *Rational Expectations and Inflation* (New York: Harper and Row, 1986), 79–94.

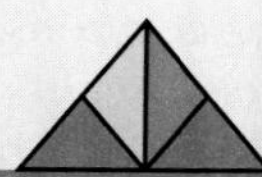

EVALUATING THE NEW MACROECONOMICS

The new theory of classical macroeconomics portrays the world quite differently from the activist Keynesian model. Evidence can be cited for and against rational expectations.

Supporting Evidence

It is very difficult to test the rational expectations model against real-world data. The basic hypothesis of the new classical macroeconomics is that only unanticipated policy affects output and employment. In order to test this proposition, one must know (1) to what extent a policy has been anticipated and (2) if it has been anticipated, whether people properly understand how the policy will affect the economy.

First, the most direct evidence of rational expectations can be seen in the rather dramatic endings to the hyperinflations that have plagued the world. Following World War I, Austria, Germany, Hungary, and Poland experienced hyperinflations. For example, in Germany prices were doubling or tripling *each month*. Each hyperinflation stopped suddenly without causing deep recessions. In each case, the governments took concrete and widely announced steps to end government deficits and runaway monetary growth. By changing the name of the monetary unit and by radically reconstructing the monetary and fiscal rules of the game, they brought inflation to an abrupt halt. (Refer again to Example 3.) In 1985, Argentina changed the name of its currency from the *peso* to the *austral*, letting 1000 old pesos equal 1 austral, to end a hyperinflation of 1000 percent per year.

Second, evidence that only unanticipated monetary policy affects real GDP and employment has been compiled by Robert Barro, who compared unanticipated increases in the rate of growth of the money supply with the rate of unemployment. Figure 3 shows that when money growth was higher than anticipated, the unemployment rate fell—which supports the view that only unanticipated monetary policy will affect real GDP and employment.

Third, experience with postwar fiscal policy appears to be generally consistent with the rational expectations hypothesis. The 1964 tax cut was the first use of discretionary tax policy. Since people would have had great difficulty anticipating its effect, it is commonly credited with raising output and employment. Subsequent tax changes, however, did not appear to affect output and employment, and this result is consistent with the rational expectations scenario. Once people understand how tax cuts work, tax cuts would affect only inflation. The impact of subsequent tax changes would be easier to predict and, hence, offset.

Fourth, the evidence concerning the new Phillips curve is consistent with the new classical macroeconomics which says that inflation and unemployment trade off only when inflation is unanticipated.

Criticism

There is little disagreement among modern economists that people attempt to anticipate inflation. To do otherwise would be to behave irrationally, and economists believe that people behave rationally in the conduct of their economic business. The heart of the dispute between activist Keynesians and the new classical macroeconomists, however, concerns whether people can anticipate the inflationary implications of policy changes and how people react to policy changes.[2]

The Keynesians argue that people understand quite well the prevailing institutional arrangements that govern wage and price contracts. In the real world, most wages and prices are not set in auction markets in which wages or prices are renegotiated frequently. Instead, most wages and many prices are set in long-term contracts or are subject to other rigidities. Unions negotiate multiyear contracts. Utility rates change slowly because of regulatory delays. Crude-oil prices are set in long-term delivery contracts.

If key wages and input prices are set in long-term contracts, people recognize that policy changes cannot bring about quick changes in wage and price inflation. If union wage contracts are predetermined over a 3-year period, when the Fed puts on the monetary brakes, union wages do not respond until

[2]The literature on testing the rational-expectations theory is surveyed in Steven M. Shefrin, *Rational Expectations* (New York: Cambridge University Press, 1983); and in Frederick S. Mishkin, *Rational Expectations Approach to Macroeconomics* (Chicago: University of Chicago Press, 1984).

FIGURE 3
The Relationship Between Unanticipated Growth in the Money Supply and Unemployment

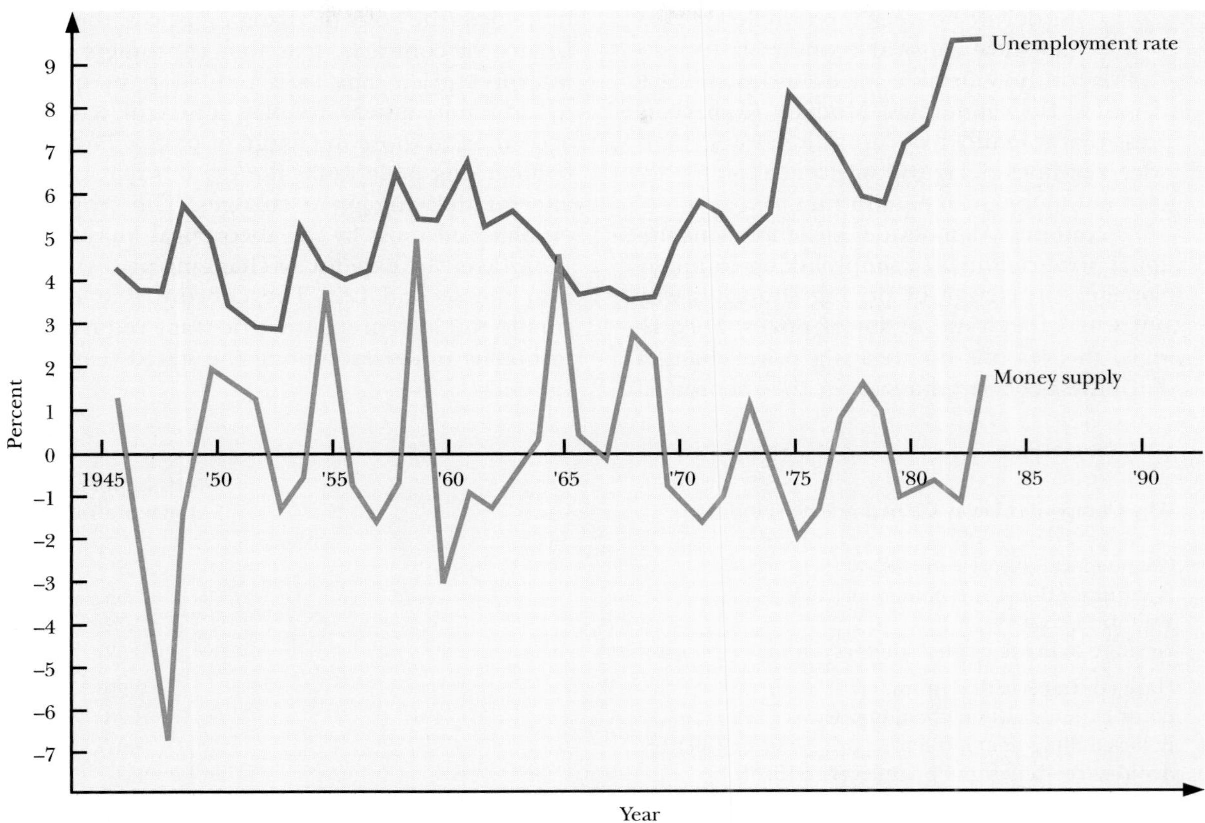

Robert Barro's estimates of the money surprise are based on the unanticipated rate of growth of the money supply (measured as the actual money growth rate minus the anticipated money growth rate). These estimates assume that people believe the rate of growth of the money supply depends on past rates of growth, the unemployment rate, and the federal fiscal deficit. The unemployment rate tends to fall when there is unanticipated growth of the money supply.

Sources: Based on Robert Barro, "Unanticipated Money, Output, and the Price Level in its Natural State," *Journal of Political Economy* 86 (August 1978). Updated by Mark Rush, "On the Policy Ineffectiveness Proposition and a Keynesian Alternative," unpublished paper, University of Florida.

the contract is renegotiated. People may simply be unable to realize their actual inflation expectations because prior contracts have frozen historical, rather than current, price expectations. (See Example 4.)

As long as wages and prices are set in long-term contracts, inertia is built into the system. Even if there are substantial changes in policy that people correctly anticipate, many wages and prices cannot respond quickly because they are not set in auction markets.

Because of these rigidities, Keynesians argue that discretionary monetary and fiscal policy should be used to stabilize the economy. The main problem, as the Keynesians see it, is that the government often follows the wrong monetary and fiscal policies. Keynesians cite the 1981–1982 tax cut and the Fed's 1982 easing of monetary policy as examples of successful discretionary policy. They argue that we are in a better position today to avoid the policy errors of the past.

EXAMPLE 4 Why Prices Are Inflexible

The debate between modern Keynesians and new classical economists focuses on how flexible wages and prices are in real-world economies. Modern Keynesians stress that a number of institutional wage and price rigidities delay the macroeconomy's adjustment to long-run equilibrium.

Economist Alan Blinder has studied institutional price rigidities by simply asking company managers in charge of pricing strategies why and when they raise or lower prices. Surprisingly, the reasons for delaying price changes that have been emphasized in the theoretical literature (the costs of changing prices, the existence of contracts, fear that consumers will interpret price cuts as a reduction in quality) do not appear to play much of a role according to those in charge of prices. The accompanying table ranks the reasons managers cite for delaying price changes. The reasons emphasized most by the theoretical literature (contracts, the expense of changing prices) fall into the second tier. The concern that consumers will interpret lower prices as a reduction in quality ranks last among the stated reasons for delay.

Why Companies Delay Changing Prices	**Mean Importance (on scale 1–4)**
Change level of service instead	2.86
Wait until other firms change prices	2.85
Wait until costs rise	2.72
Hesitate to break implicit understanding with customers	2.52
Have contracts with customers	2.29
Incur expenses when changing prices	2.28
Believe falling demand makes price cuts ineffective	1.97
Avoid exceeding some price levels: $19.95	1.97
Change inventory levels instead	1.72
Have constant marginal costs	1.56
Feel delayed by corporate bureaucracy	1.54
Worry that consumers will think quality is lower	1.45

Source: Elizabeth Corcoran and Paul Wallich, "The Analytical Economist," *Scientific American* (March 1991): 114.

While emphasizing the importance of price rigidities, activist Keynesians question whether it is indeed possible for price surprises to have a significant effect on output and employment. In the new classical macroeconomic model, price surprises affect real output because people confuse nominal wage and price changes with real wage and relative price changes. Keynesians concede that people can confuse nominal and real changes, but they believe such effects are fleeting and insignificant. Workers have information on general movements in prices, such as the CPI, and firms should be able to keep track of changes in costs just as well as changes in selling prices. If workers and firms experience price surprises, they will not last long. It is unlikely that an entire business cycle could be explained by price-surprise effects.[3]

[3]Frederic S. Mishkin, *A Rational Expectations Approach to Macroeconometrics* (Chicago: University of Chicago Press, 1983).

This chapter completes our analysis of the basic workings of the macreconomy. The next four chapters turn to broader aspects of the world economy: economic growth and development, international finance, international trade, and protection.

SUMMARY

1. Rational expectations theory offers an explanation for why countercyclical policy appears not to have worked well in recent years. The central idea of rational expectations theory is that people use all the information available to them to attempt to anticipate the future. People combine their knowledge of the macroeconomy with forecasts of government policy to form their expectations about future prices. The typical producer knows about the prices of the things it sells better than the prices of the things it buys. General inflation or deflation can therefore cause errors in judgment.

2. A price surprise occurs when the actual price level is different from the expected price level. Price-level surprises are caused by supply and demand shocks. A supply shock is an unexpected shift in aggregate supply. A demand shock is an unexpected shift in aggregate demand. Unanticipated changes in policy (policy shocks) are an important source of demand shocks. When a shift in aggregate demand is anticipated, it will have no affect on output or employment. It will affect only the price level; the self-correcting mechanism works instantaneously. Because the resulting change in the price level is anticipated, the economy will move immediately to the higher price level but will remain at the same level of real GDP. Only when the demand change is not anticipated will there be a change in output. Demand shocks change real output only temporarily.

3. Only if people fail to learn from past experience will they be continuously surprised by policy. Anticipated monetary and demand-side fiscal policy should have no effect on real output and employment. Rational expectations theorists argue that there may be no short-run trade-off between unemployment and inflation.

4. The evidence on the rational expectations hypothesis is still being gathered. Evidence in favor of rational expectations theory is found in the quick ends to historical episodes of hyperinflation and the apparent effect of unanticipated monetary growth on real output and employment. Keynesians argue that institutional arrangements prevent inflationary expectations from adjusting quickly, and they doubt that price surprises can be significant or long lasting.

KEY TERMS

rational expectations	demand shock
price-level surprise	supply shock

QUESTIONS AND PROBLEMS

1. Evalute the validity of the following statement: "I do not know much about economics. In fact, before this course, I did not even know that the Fed controls the money supply, and I am not much different from other people. How can the rational expectations theory claim that people in general attempt to anticipate the effects of monetary and fiscal policy?"
2. Consider a very simple economy that consists of four people. One anticipates that prices will rise 10 percent; another thinks prices will not rise at all; the other two expect prices to rise 5 percent. The actual price increase turns out to be 7 percent. What is the expected price increase? What is the price-level surprise?
3. Evaluate the validity of the following statement: "How can there be price-level surprises in the economy? All we have to do is turn on the radio or television to learn how rapidly prices are rising."
4. Suppose that in a secret session of Congress, the president and Congress agree on a 20 percent tax cut. Would this tax cut affect real output and employment?
5. Explain why the long-run response to the tax cut described in question 4 may be different from the short-run response.
6. Under which of the following conditions would people be more likely to rapidly adjust their inflationary expectations?

   a. All prices are set in auction markets.
   b. Wage rates are set in 3-year contracts.

7. A weakness of the old classical theory was that it could not explain the business cycle. How does the new classical macroeconomics explain the business cycle?

8. If there were only three products in the economy, what would happen to the basic argument of rational expectations theory? Would there still be price surprises?
9. Contrast the positions of the quantity theory, Keynesian economics, and rational expectations theory concerning the self-correcting mechanism.
10. How can rational expectations negate the effects of activist policy?
11. Assume there is an expansion of aggregate demand as a consequence of increased government spending that is financed by raising the federal deficit. Why would the effect of this action on output depend upon the extent to which people change their view of their future tax liabilities?
12. Would policy surprises be more likely in the case of monetary or fiscal policy? Explain your answer.
13. Using a diagram of aggregate supply and aggregate demand curves, illustrate the adjustment to long-run equilibrium after a negative price surprise (in which the actual price level is below the anticipated price level).
14. Explain the conditions under which preannounced policies would be effective in stopping inflation quickly. Explain the conditions under which preannounced policies would be no more effective than policies that were not announced in advance.
15. What are some of the major criticisms of the rational expectations approach to macroeconomics?

SUGGESTED READINGS

Begg, David. *The Rational Expectations Revolution in Macroeconomics.* Baltimore: The Johns Hopkins University Press, 1982.

Fisher, Stanley, ed. *Rational Expectations and Economic Policy.* Chicago: University of Chicago Press, 1980.

Forman, Leonard. "Rational Expectations and the Real World." *Challenge* (November/December 1980).

Gordon, Robert J., "What is New Keynesian Economics?" *Journal of Economic Literature,* 33, 3 (September 1990): 1115–1171.

Holden, K., D. A. Peel, and J. L. Thompson. *Expectations: Theory and Evidence.* Basingstoke: Macmillan, 1985.

Maddock, Rodney, and Michael Carter. "A Child's Guide to Rational Expectations." *Journal of Economic Literature* 20 (March 1982): 39–51.

Mankiw, N. Gregory. "A Quick Refresher Course in Macroeconomics." *Journal of Economic Literature,* 33, 4 (December 1990): 1645–1660.

McCallum, Bennett. "The Significance of Rational Expectations Theory." *Challenge* (January/February 1980): 37–43.

Mishkin, Frederic S. *A Rational Expectations Approach to Macroeconometrics.* Chicago: University of Chicago Press, 1983.

Sargent, Thomas J. *Rational Expectations and Inflation.* New York: Harper and Row, 1986.

Willes, Mark H. "'Rational Expectations' as a Counterrevolution." *The Public Interest,* Special Issue 1980, 81–96.

International Economics

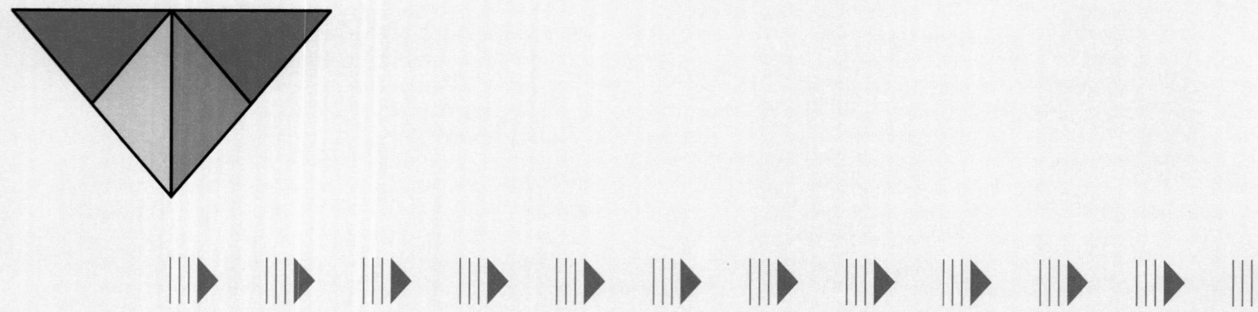

III

The World Economy

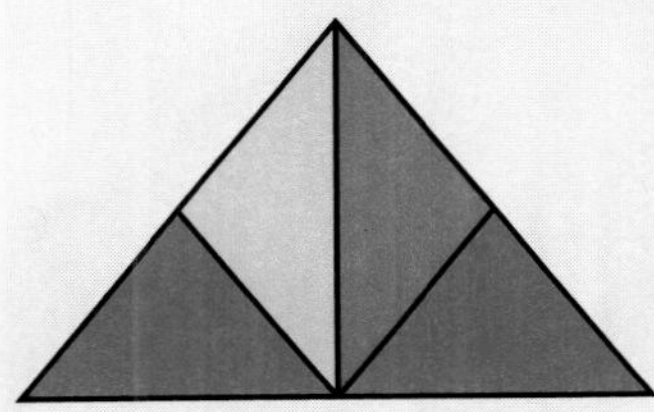

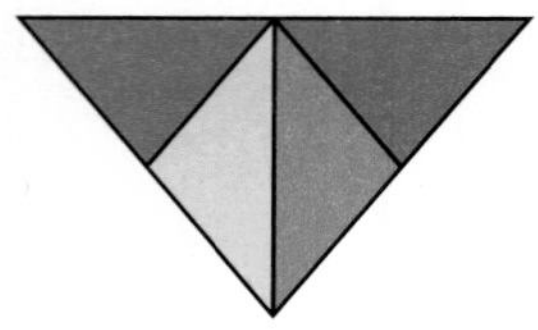

22

Productivity, Growth, and Development

CHAPTER INSIGHT

Sometime in the early eighteenth century, the United Kingdom began to experience the world's first case of sustained economic growth and industrialization. The world had previously seen transitory periods of economic growth in the rises and falls of the great civilizations of Egypt, Greece, and the Roman Empire. Yet, each of these experiments failed to produce the sustained economic growth necessary to improve living standards. By contrast, the United Kingdom's industrial revolution raised living standards to unprecedented levels.

From the United Kingdom, the industrial revolution spread to the European continent and to North America and Australia, but then it stopped. It failed to move to Latin America, Asia, and Africa. Since the initial industrial revolutions in the eighteenth and nineteenth centuries, only a few countries have successfully made the transition from poverty to affluence. The most prominent example is Japan, and the most recent contenders are Taiwan, Singapore, South Korea, and Hong Kong. This chapter examines the mystery of economic development. What are the sources of economic growth? Why is sustained economic growth and prosperity confined to such a small percentage of the world's population?

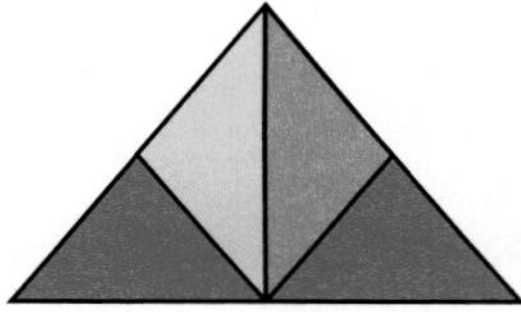

ECONOMIC GROWTH

Economic growth is defined in terms of changes in real GDP in two ways.

> **Economic growth** is an increase in real GDP from one period to the next.
>
> Economic growth is an increase from one period to the next in *real GDP per capita,* which is real GDP divided by the country's population.

When economists study economic growth, they are interested in the growth of real output (or output per capita) over an extended period of time. Long-term economic growth is the long-term trend in real output, ignoring the short-run deviations around this trend caused by the business cycle. In effect, economic growth is the expansion of the natural level of real GDP.

The two measures of economic growth provide different information about economic performance. The growth of real GDP measures the rate at which total output is expanding. As such, it measures the degree to which an economy is growing in both scale and importance. For instance, Japan's phenomenal growth after World War II allowed it to join the select group of advanced industrialized nations. (See Example 1.) If the current rapid growth of countries such as Taiwan and South Korea continues, they too will soon be advanced industrialized countries. The growth of real GDP per capita measures the growth of average living standards. People who live in countries with high per capita GDP are better off materially (on average).

The two rates of economic growth can be quite different. Some countries with rapid GDP growth also have rapid population growth; such countries can have a smaller increase in living standards than a country in which GDP growth is more modest but in which there is little or no population growth. The difference between the two measures of economic growth is evident from comparisons of small, rich countries with large, poor countries. The total output of the People's Republic of China in 1985 was $354 billion; Switzerland's output was $92 billion. On a per capita basis, the output of China was $346 and that of Switzerland was $14,154. Although the total output of Switzerland was less than that of China, Swiss living standards were 40 times those of China.

THE HAVES AND THE HAVE NOTS

The modern world is divided into "have" and "have not" nations, according to the **level of economic development.**

> The **level of economic development** is measured by per capita GDP, industrial structure, population dynamics, and the health and education of the population.

Although there is no single indicator of the level of economic development, per capita GDP comes as close as possible to being the most comprehensive. However, a country can have a high GDP per capita and yet lack the other characteristics of economic development, such as a highly educated population or an industrial structure geared to industry and services.

The industrialized countries of North America, Europe, Australia, and Japan have attained a high level of economic development. The **less developed countries (LDCs)** have not.

> **A less developed country (LDC)** is a country with a per capita income far below that of a typical advanced country.

Figure 1 shows that approximately 3 out of every 4 persons lives in an LDC. Only 15 percent of the world's population lives in the highly developed capitalist countries of the United States, Canada, Australia, Japan, and Western Europe, and 10 percent of the world's population lives in the former communist countries of the U.S.S.R and eastern Europe. The LDCs' share of world population has been rising since 1900 and is projected to rise throughout the twenty-first century.

A comparison of the distribution of world population with the distribution of world income dramatizes how unequally income is distributed among

EXAMPLE 1 Are Economic Growth Rates Increasing?

A lesson of this chapter is that an economy can experience growth in per capita output because of capital accumulation and technological progress. Measured by the growth rate of real per capita GDP, the advanced capitalist countries appear to have experienced increasing growth rates over the past several centuries. Angus Maddison has collected the best available data on GDP and populations for 14 advanced capitalist countries going back to 1820. The accompanying table shows that from 1820 to 1870 the annual growth rate of the 14 countries averaged only 0.9 percent, but from 1870 to 1989 the average annual growth rate was 1.6 percent.

Paul Romer has explained the increase in growth rate by the basic nature of technological change. Inventions are carried out to make a profit, but every new product or invention lowers the cost of additional inventions or products. For example, the invention of the cathode ray tube lowered the cost of inventing television; the invention of the gasoline engine lowered the cost of developing the automobile. Each new invention may contribute to a new idea consisting of all previous ideas. Technical progress can thus accelerate, causing the rate of growth of the economy to increase.

The Romer vision may, however, be overly optimistic. Critics might point out that since 1973 growth rates have headed downward. Romer would reply that his theory deals with long-run growth rather than short-run cyclical developments.

Growth Rates of Real Per Capita GDP (annual average)

	1820–1870	1870–1989
Australia	1.9	1.2
Austria	0.6	1.8
Belgium	1.4	1.5
Denmark	0.9	1.8
Finland	0.8	2.3
France	0.8	1.8
Germany	0.7	2.0
Italy	0.4	2.0
Japan	0.1	2.7
Netherlands	0.9	1.5
Norway	0.7	2.2
Sweden	0.7	2.1
United Kingdom	1.2	1.4
United States	1.5	1.9
Average	**0.9**	**1.6**

Sources: Paul Romer, "Increasing Returns and Long-Run Growth," *Journal of Political Economy*, 95 (October 1986): 1002–1037; Angus Maddison, *Dynamic Forces in Capitalist Development* (New York: Oxford University Press, 1991).

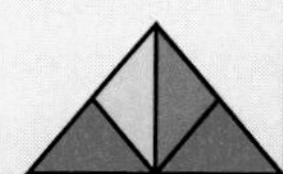

the different countries of the globe. As Figure 1 shows, the developed countries, which account for only 25 percent of the world's population, account for 83 percent of the world's GDP. The LDCs account for 75 percent of world population but only 17 percent of world GDP. World output is concentrated in the United States, western Europe, and Japan. The unequal distribution of income among countries also leads to an unequal consumption of natural resources between the rich and poor countries. The industrialized capitalist countries, for example, consume 71 percent of the world's oil production. Only 9 percent of the world's oil production is available for the LDCs.

The LDCs' share of world production has been falling as its share of world population has been rising. In 1800, the LDCs accounted for 44 percent of world production. By 1900, the LDCs' share of world production had fallen to 19 percent. The declining LDCs' share of world production has been the result

FIGURE 1
The Share of Less Developed Countries in Population and Production, 1800–1990

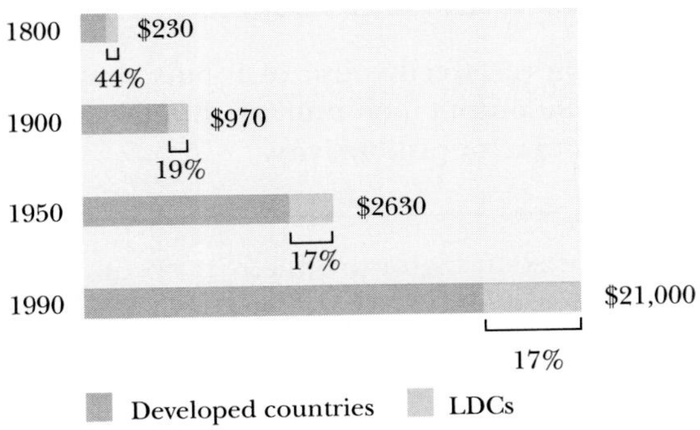

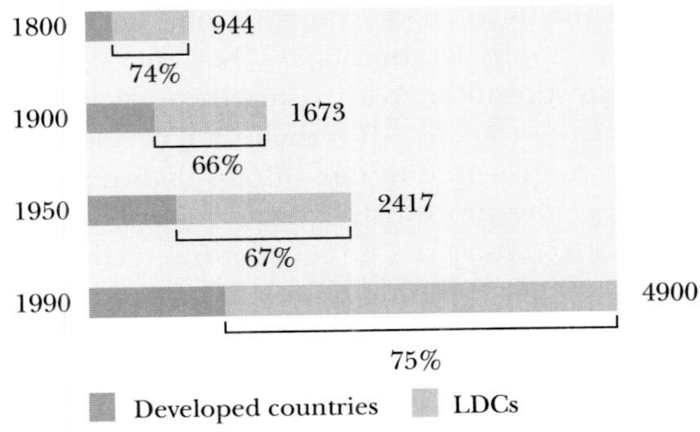

This exhibit shows that the less developed countries' share of the world's population far exceeds their share of income. It also shows the decline in their share of world output since 1800.

Sources: Adapted from World Bank, *World Development Report 1984,* 6, and from *Handbook of Economic Statistics,* 1990.

of rapid growth in the developed countries combined with slow or stagnant growth in the LDCs after 1800.

Life in a low-income LDC is very different from life in the United States. Only 1 of 5 people in a low-income LDC lives in an urban area (as opposed to 78 percent in the industrial market economies). One out of every 7 children dies before the age of 4 (as compared with 1 out of every 200 in the industrial market economies). In a community of 6000 people, there is 1 physician (as opposed to 11 in the industrial market economies). Life expectancy is 58 years in a typical low-income LDC and 75 years in a typical industrial market economy. In an LDC, only 1 out of every 2 adults can read or write, and only 1 out of 4 school-age children attends secondary school. There is a better than 50/50 chance that a girl will never attend school. Only 2 out of every 100 persons own their own radio, and a private automobile is a virtually unheard-of luxury. LDC residents come from large families and plan on having a large number of children, many of whom will not survive their infancy.[1]

[1]These figures are from World Bank, *World Tables,* Vol. II, 3rd ed., 1983, 142–45.

ECONOMIC GROWTH OF THE HAVES

The industrial revolution discussed in the chapter opener resulted in the acceleration of the growth of real GDP and of population. The growth of output exceeded the growth of population, and per capita GDP began to grow at a sustained or increasing rate.

The principal feature of modern economic growth has been its sustained nature. There is no simple explanation for why the industrialized world began to sustain economic growth in the eighteenth century, for the first time in human history. The industrial revolution was accompanied by a technological revolution. Productivity-increasing inventions produced by eighteenth- and nineteenth-century science, including the steam engine, the mechanized cotton spindle, and the blast furnace, help explain modern economic growth. Modern economic growth was also accompanied by the expansion of trade and the growth of free-market institutions.

Modern economic growth brought about substantial changes in lifestyles. The share of economic activity devoted to industry and services rose;

the share of agriculture declined. These changes in the structure of the economy were accompanied by rising urbanization; the typical worker was no longer a farmer but an industrial laborer. Rising per capita income made it possible for real wages to rise, and items that had previously been available only to the rich—quality textiles, long-distance transportation, phonographs, automobiles—became available for mass consumption. With rising living standards, birth rates began to fall. After the initial acceleration of population growth, the rate of population growth began to decline in industrialized countries. In the late twentieth century, a number of affluent countries even worry about declining population.

Extensive and Intensive Growth

Since the beginning of modern economic growth, industrialized economies have experienced sustained growth of GDP and of GDP per capita. Although there have been cyclical episodes of zero or negative growth—such as the Great Depression of the 1930s—the industrialized economies have grown consistently over the long run. (See Table 1.)

Economies expand their real GDP because of both **extensive growth** and **intensive growth.**

> **Extensive growth** occurs when the total amount of land, labor, and capital inputs expands.
>
> **Intensive growth** occurs when available inputs are used more effectively.

The more effective use of inputs shows up as increases in output per unit of input—that is, as increases in **factor productivity.**

> An increase in **factor productivity** occurs when more output is produced per unit of factor input.

To expand labor inputs, people must sacrifice leisure or household production to produce more market output. To expand capital inputs, people must sacrifice current consumption for future consumption. Compared to these costs of extensive growth, the costs of intensive growth are smaller. Such sacrifices are not necessary when output is increased through intensive growth.

TABLE 1

Long-Term Average Annual Growth of Real GDP and Real GDP Per Capita for Selected Industrialized Countries, 1929–1990

	1929–1950 Growth Rate (percent)		1950–1960 Growth Rate (percent)		1960–1990 Growth Rate (percent)	
Country	GDP	GDP per Capita	GDP	GDP per Capita	GDP	GDP per Capita
United States	2.9	1.8	3.2	1.4	3.3	2.1
Canada	3.2	1.8	4.6	1.9	4.4	3.0
France	0.0	−0.1	4.6	3.6	3.7	3.2
West Germany	1.9	0.7	8.0	6.4	3.1	2.9
Italy	1.0	0.3	5.5	4.8	4.0	3.4
Japan	0.6	NA	8.0	6.9	6.4	5.4
United Kingdom	1.6	1.2	2.8	2.4	2.5	2.3
U.S.S.R.	5.4*	3.5*	6.0	4.2	3.4	2.0

*1928–1940

Sources: *Statisitical Abstract of the United States; Handbook of Economic Statistics.*

The Role of Productivity

Does economic growth result from the growth of inputs or from the growth of productivity? Table 2 supplies long-term data for American economic growth. The first column gives the growth rates of real GDP for different periods from 1800 to 1988. The next two columns give the corresponding growth rates of labor inputs (measured in hours) and of capital inputs. The fourth column gives the growth rates of labor and capital combined. From data on real GDP growth and factor input growth, one can calculate productivity.

Three measures of productivity are shown in Table 2: **labor productivity, capital productivity** and **total factor productivity.**

> **Labor productivity** measures output per unit (usually per hour) of labor input.
>
> **Capital productivity** measures output per unit of capital input.
>
> **Total factor productivity** measures output per unit of combined labor and capital input.

The three measure of productivity are usually expressed as rates of growth. The growth rate of labor productivity measures the growth rate of output per unit of labor input. The growth rate of total factor productivity measures the growth rate of output per unit of combined inputs. *The growth rate of productivity is approximately the growth rate of real output minus the growth rate of the factor input.*

By comparing the growth of real GDP, factor inputs, and factor productivity, one can determine how much economic growth is attributable to the expansion of inputs (extensive growth) and how much is due to the expansion of productivity (intensive growth). Because inputs grew at an annual rate of 1.5 percent between 1948 and 1988 in the United States, 47 percent (1.5/3.2) of the annual output growth is explained by the growth of inputs. The remaining 53 percent is accounted for by productivity growth. The data for the periods 1855 to 1948 (the period of U.S. industrialization) show that productivity growth explains the major portion of U.S. economic growth. (See Example 2 for an international perspective.)

Labor Productivity

Figure 2 shows the annual rate of growth of labor productivity from 1958 to 1990. Labor productivity growth—as measured by the rate of growth of real GDP per hour of labor—flucuates significantly from year to year. These flucuations make it difficult to see long-run trends in labor productivity. The period from the late 1950s through the mid-1960s was one of high labor productivity growth. From the late 1960s to 1991, labor productivity growth was erratic, generally falling with recessions and rising with recoveries.

Figure 2 illustrates why fears of a long-term productivity decline were widespread in the 1970s and early 1980s. From high and steady productivity growth in the 1960s, the economy experienced negative productivity growth in the mid- and late 1970s. The economic recovery after 1982 generated positive and reasonably rapid labor productivity growth, underscoring the fact that labor productivity is heavily dependent upon the state of the business cycle. We do not know whether the 1990s will be a time of steady and high or slow and erratic labor productivity growth.

Table 3 shows that fears of a long-term decline in labor productivity may not be justified. Productivity growth since 1973 has been close to the long-run average for earlier periods. In fact, the early postwar period was one of exceptionally high labor productivity growth.

Productivity and Policy: Supply-side Economics

Productivity growth determines whether the economy is expanding rapidly or slowly. Can economic policy affect productivity growth? Proponents of supply-side economics argue that economic policy can be used to stimulate productivity growth. Higher productivity growth will yield higher growth of real GDP, will lower inflation, and will raise general prosperity. Supply-side economics asserts that productivity can be raised by changing the tax system to provide greater incentives to work harder and take more risks.

Specifically, supply-side economists maintain that distortions in the tax system and high marginal tax rates discourage the efficient allocation of resources. If workers have to pay $0.50 out of every extra $1.00 earned in taxes, they have little incentive

TABLE 2
Growth Rates of U.S. GDP, Factor Inputs, and Productivity, 1800–1988

	Annual Growth Rate (percent)								
Period	Real GDP (1)	Labor Inputs (hours) (2)	Capital Inputs (3)	Combined Inputs (4)	Labor Productivity (5) = (1) − (2)	Capital Productivity (6) = (1) − (3)	Total Factor Productivity (7) = (1) − (4)	Proportion of Growth Explained by Inputs (percent) (8) = (4) ÷ (1)	Unexplained Residual (percent) (9) = (5) ÷ (1)
1800–1855	4.2	3.7	4.3	3.9	0.5	−0.1	0.3	93	7
1855–1898	4.0	2.8	4.6	3.6	1.1	−0.6	0.3	90	10
1899–1919	3.9	1.8	3.1	2.2	2.0	0.7	1.7	46	54
1919–1948	3.0	0.6	1.2	0.8	2.4	1.6	2.2	20	80
1948–1988	3.2	0.9	3.7	1.5	2.3	−0.2	1.7	47	53

Sources: John W. Kendrick, "Survey of the Factors Contributing to the Decline in U.S. Productivity Growth," Federal Reserve Bank of Boston, *The Decline in Productivity Growth,* Conference Series No. 22, June 1980, 2; U.S. Department of Labor, Bureau of Labor Statistics, *Trends in Multifactor Productivity, 1948–81,* September 1983, 24; Edward Denison, *Trends in American Economic Growth, 1929–1982* (Washington, DC: Brookings, 1985); *World Development Report 1991,* 43–44.

EXAMPLE 2 Productivity as a Source of Growth: World Experience

This chapter explains that economic growth can be either extensive (resulting from the growth of capital and labor inputs) or intensive (resulting from technology advances, better business methods, and so on). The example of the industrialized West shows that productivity growth, rather than the growth of inputs, has been the most important source of economic growth.

The accompanying table, prepared by the World Bank, shows that the poor regions of the world, Africa, Latin America, and East Asia, have a different long-term growth experience from the industrialized countries. Africa and Latin America had no growth of factor productivity between 1960 and 1987. In South Asia, there was only slight growth of factor productivity. Hence, virtually all growth in these regions was extensive in nature. In the industrialized countries, on the other hand, more than half of the growth was accounted for by factor productivity growth.

Source: *World Development Report 1991: The Challenge of Development* (New York: Oxford University Press, 1991), 43–45.

The Growth of GDP, Inputs, and Total Factor Productivity, 1960–1987

Region, Group, or Economy	GDP	Capital	Labor	Total Factor Productivity	Percentage of Growth Explained by Factor Productivity
Developing economies					
Africa	3.3	6.3	2.2	0.0	0
East Asia	6.8	10.2	2.6	1.9	28
Latin America	3.6	6.3	2.6	0.0	0
South Asia	4.4	7.7	2.1	0.6	14
Sixty-eight economies	4.2	7.2	2.3	0.6	14
Industrial economies					
France	3.9	4.8	−0.2	1.7	78
Germany[a]	3.1	4.2	−0.6	1.4	87
United Kingdom	2.4	3.1	−0.2	1.2	78
United States	3.0	3.4	1.8	0.5	50

Note: Estimates for developing countries are based on a sample of sixty-eight economies. Estimates for industrial economies are based on data from 1960 to 1985.

[a]The Federal Republic of Germany before reunification with the former German Democratic Republic.

Source: *World Development Report 1991*, 43–44.

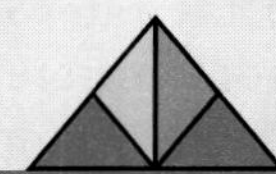

FIGURE 2
Annual Growth Rates of U.S. Labor Productivity, 1958–1990

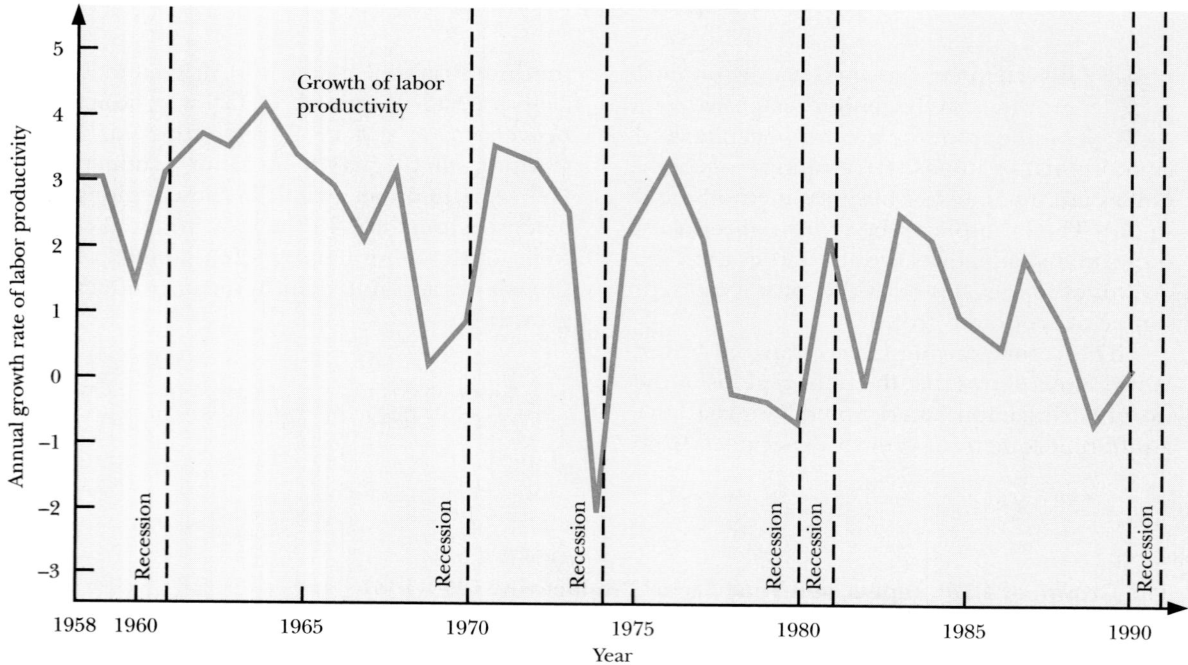

The growth rate of labor productivity tends to fluctuate from year to year. Productivity growth was high from the late 1950s through the late 1960s, fell during the recessions of the 1970s and early 1980s, and rose sharply during the recovery phase of the cycle.

Source: *Economic Report of the President.*

to work more intensively. If entrepreneurs have to pay high marginal tax rates on their earnings, they will have less of an incentive to take risks and to innovate. If the tax system favors one industry over another, the economy will not invest in an optimal manner, opting for a lower-return investment in the tax-favored industry.

The Reagan administration (1980–1988) was heavily influenced by these supply-side arguments. In 1981, tax rates were lowered and were indexed to the rate of inflation. It was hoped that the lowering of tax rates would stimulate extra work effort and more entrepreneurship, thereby raising real output, earnings, employment, and tax revenues. In 1986, tax rates were lowered again, and the favorable tax treatment of specific industries (such as construction) was eliminated. However, corporate income tax rates were raised and some incentives to take risks (the preferential treatment of capital gains) were eliminated. It is too early to tell whether these important changes in the U.S. tax system will yield increases in productivity over the next decade.

WHY THE LDCs ARE POOR

Sustained productivity growth explains why the developed countries are affluent. What explains why the LDCs are poor? The "stationary state" of the classical economists provides a first explanation of LDC poverty.

TABLE 3
Long-Term Trends in U.S. Labor Productivity Growth

Period	Average Annual Growth Rate in Output per Hour (percent)
1900–1916	1.5
1916–1929	2.3
1929–1948	1.6
1948–1965	3.3
1965–1973	2.3
1973–1990	1.4

Source: Michael Darby, "The U.S Productivity Slowdown: A Case of Statistical Myopia," *American Economic Review* (June 1984): 302. Darby's figures are updated from *Economic Report of the President.*

The Classical Growth Model

Economists first became interested in economic growth in the late eighteenth and early nineteenth centuries. The classical economists—particularly David Ricardo and Thomas Malthus—sought to explain why predominantly agricultural economies reach an upper limit to economic growth, which they called a *stationary state.* From the perspective of the classical economists writing at the very beginning of the industrial revolution, the stationary state of zero growth seemed to be the normal state of affairs; there was very little growth of output or of population prior to 1750, the approximate starting point of modern economic growth in Great Britain.

Diminishing Returns. The classical economists were interested in explaining the growth of a traditional agrarian economy. In such an economy, modern science and technology had yet to be applied to agriculture, and capital equipment (such as hoes or plows) was a relatively minor input. Output was produced primarily by combining land and labor, and agricultural land was essentially fixed in supply.

The *law of diminishing returns* applies to situations in which more and more units of a variable factor (labor) are being added to a fixed factor of production (land). According to the law of diminishing returns, at low levels of population and labor force, increases in labor initially yield fairly substantial increases in output, but as more and more labor is combined with a fixed amount of land, additional inputs of labor bring in smaller and smaller additions to output. The average product of labor, after first rising, falls as diminishing returns set in.

Panel *a* of Figure 3 shows the aggregate output of an economy in which more and more units of a variable input (labor) are combined with a fixed input. Initially, output rises at an increasing rate, but the increase in output tapers off as more units of labor are added. Panel *b* shows how the average product of labor first rises but then declines.

The law of diminishing returns suggests that an agricultural economy with a fixed amount of land, primitive technology, and rudimentary capital resources should avoid excessively large inputs of labor insofar as these labor injections drive down the average product of labor. Labor productivity determines real wages; therefore, an economy whose population and labor force are too large should expect to experience falling real wages and falling living standards.

Malthusian Population Laws. Because of the writings of Thomas R. Malthus, whose *Essay on the Principle of Population* was published in 1798, classical economics came to be called the "dismal science." Malthus believed that there would be a long-term disproportion between the rate of growth of population and the rate of growth of food production. Population, Malthus argued, tends to increase at *geometric* rates (in which the *ratio* between each number and its predecessor is constant) because the "passion between the sexes" and factors such as disease and war remain constant throughout human history. On the other hand, food production tends to increase at *arithmetic* rates (in which the *difference* between each number and its predecessor is constant), following the law of diminishing returns. Because a geometric series, such as 1, 2, 4, 8, 16,... grows at a faster rate and will inevitably overtake an arithmetic series, such as 10, 11, 12, 13,..., Malthus believed that humanity would usually find itself on the verge of starvation, living at subsistence wages.

The crux of the Malthusian population problem is that wages can never rise above the subsistence level for long periods of time because when they do, reproduction tends to increase. Thus, once wages rise above the subsistence level, the population and labor force will expand geometrically, and the increase in the supply of labor will drive wages back

FIGURE 3
The Classical Growth Model

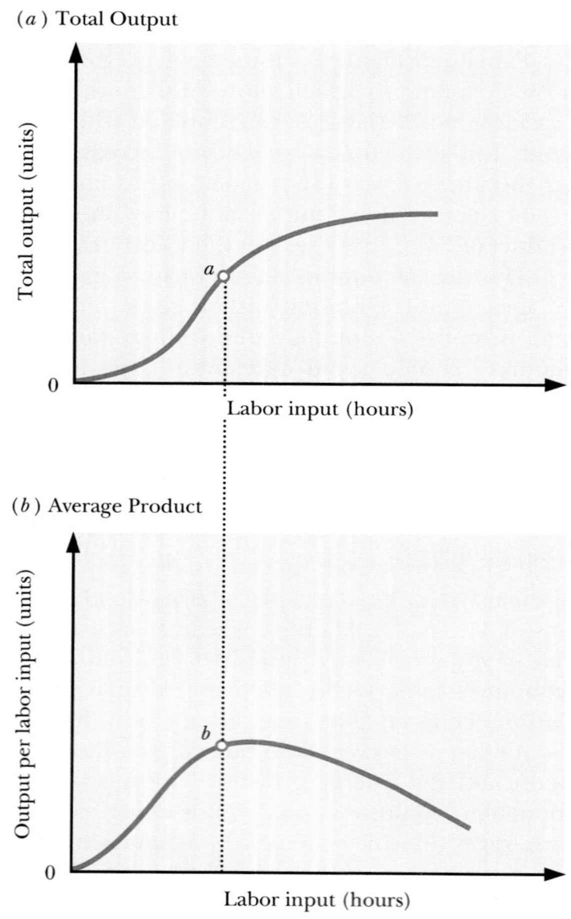

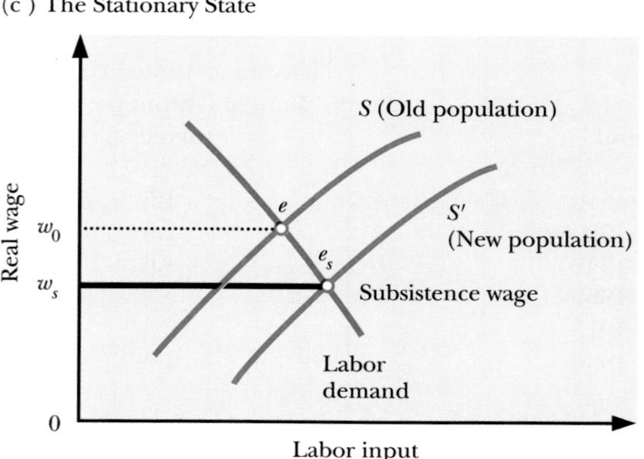

In this economy, the amount of agricultural land is fixed. As the variable factor—labor—is combined with the fixed factor, output initially rises at an increasing rate. Panel *a* shows that as more and more units of the variable factor are added beyond point *a*, the rate of increase in output slows. Panel *b* shows that the average product of labor first increases and then decreases. Panel *c* shows that in the short run, the market wage rate will be w_o—the equilibrium wage rate. The horizontal line shows the subsistence wage rate, w_s. If the market wage is above the subsistence level, as it is in this case, population will expand, and the labor supply curve will shift to the right (supply will increase). As long as the market wage remains above the subsistence level, population will continue to expand, thereby driving wages down even further. Population growth will cease when the market wage is driven down to the subsistence level. At this point, the economy is in a stationary state. The growth of output ceases, and wages are stuck at the subsistence level.

down to the subsistence level. If wages fall below the subsistence level, famine and higher mortality rates will reduce the population and allow wages to rise back to the subsistence level.

The Stationary State. The classical economists came to the pessimistic conclusion that there are distinct limits to growth. In the long run, economies would end up in a stationary state characterized by (1) a zero growth rate of output, population, and per capita output and (2) subsistence wages.

In panel *c* of Figure 3, the downward-sloping labor demand curve shows the economy's demand for labor at different wage rates, and the upward-sloping labor supply curve shows the amounts of labor supplied at different wage rates. The subsistence wage (w_s) is drawn as a horizontal line.

In the short run, the supply of labor is determined by the size of the population and by the proportion of the adult population that works—both of which change slowly over time. In the short run, wages can rise above the subsistence level; they are determined by the forces of supply and demand. If the wage rate rises above the subsistence level, the birth rate will rise and death rates will fall as a result of better nutrition and health. The increase in population will increase the labor supply (the curve will shift to the right), thereby driving down the equilibrium wage rate. Population growth will not cease until population growth shifts the labor supply curve to S'. At this point, wages stabilize at the subsistence level.

If a severe famine or war reduces the number of workers, wages will temporarily rise above the subsistence level, the population will begin to reproduce, and wages will be driven back to the subsistence level. During the Black Death plague of the Middle Ages, which destroyed one-third of Europe's population, real wages rose substantially but declined thereafter as population growth accelerated.

The Sources of LDC Poverty

The classical growth model has relevance to today's LDCs. The economies of LDCs are typically characterized by a reliance on agricultural output for income, a limited supply of arable land, a rapidly growing population, and limited technological improvements. Thus, LDCs have the basic ingredients of a stationary state. Population pressure forces LDCs to operate with diminishing returns as technological progress fails to offset declining labor productivity. Wages are kept near the subsistence level, and population growth is regulated by rising and falling mortality rates. Good harvests cause lower mortality rates but increase population pressure. Poor harvests cause higher mortality rates but relieve population pressure.

The classical model suggests some measures that could be taken to release the LDCs from the stationary state.

1. If the rate of population growth were to decline, the pressures of diminishing returns would be abated.
2. If capital formation could be accelerated, labor productivity could be raised.
3. If technological progress could be achieved, diminishing returns could be avoided.

Population Pressures. The rate of growth of per capita GDP equals the rate of growth of GDP minus the rate of growth of population. Per capita growth can, therefore, be accelerated either by increasing the growth of GDP or by decreasing the growth of population. This simple arithmetic explains why many analysts of LDCs tend to regard rapid population growth as an enemy of economic development.

Why is population growth more rapid in the LDCs than in the developed countries? Demographers have long studied a "law" of population growth called the **demographic transition.**

> The **demographic transition** is the process by which countries change from rapid population growth to slow population growth as they modernize.

In a country's premodern era, there is little or no population growth because the birth rate and death rate are roughly equal. However, as modernization begins, population growth accelerates. Modernization brings with it better health care and nutrition, and the death rate, especially the infant mortality rate, declines. In addition, rising incomes may cause birth rates to rise. The first phases of modernization are, therefore, characterized by an acceleration in the rate of population growth.

As modernization proceeds, further reductions in the death rate become harder to achieve. Mortality due to infectious diseases has already declined, and medical science is left with harder-to-combat chronic diseases, such as heart disease and cancer. Modernization eventually causes the birth rate to decline. As married couples become more educated, they use contraception to regulate the number of births. The desired number of children decreases. In modern societies, a larger number of children is no longer the ticket to old-age security. The reduction of infant mortality eliminates the need to have many children to ensure that some will survive to adulthood. Employment opportunities for women improve, and the opportunity costs of having children increase. All of these factors combine to reduce the birth rate.

These forces cause a demographic transition from high rates of population growth to low rates. The Malthusian specter of overpopulation is removed, and advanced societies must even worry about underpopulation, or negative population growth.

The LDC's have failed to participate in the demographic transition for a number of reasons.

1. Unlike the industrialized countries, declines in death rates in the LDCs were not coordinated with rising modernization and prosperity. Instead, public-health improvements (such as typhoid and cholera immunizations) were introduced by the colonial powers prior to significant economic development. Improved health care and sanitization in the LDCs caused significant declines in mortality *prior* to modernization.
2. In many LDCs—which remain rural societies without government old-age security programs—children are still the only guarantee that one will be looked after in one's old age. Parents that have many children stand a better chance of health and income security in their old age.
3. In many LDCs, century-old traditions favor large families. The proof of manhood may be the number of children fathered. Having many children, grandchildren, and great-grandchildren is regarded as an assurance of immortality.
4. As long as a country remains underdeveloped and employment opportunities continue to be found primarily in agriculture, the opportunity costs to women of having additional children are low. In many LDCs, having a baby means the loss of only a few days or weeks in the fields. At an early age, the child becomes productive in the fields and helps his or her parents.

For these reasons, the LDCs are caught in a vicious circle: rapid population growth inhibits increases in per capita income; without substantial increases in per capita income (and the modernization that accompanies rising incomes), it is difficult to bring about substantial reductions in birth rates. There is no simple relationship, however, between per capita income growth and population growth. Example 3 shows that some countries can have both rapid population growth and rising affluence, whereas others have low population growth and economic stagnation.

Capital Formation Problems. The LDCs encounter another vicious circle in the area of capital formation. The major portion of a nation's saving is carried out by the affluent; the poor save little or nothing. Therefore, if a whole country is poor—with most of its population living near a subsistence level of income—its saving rate will be low. Moreover, the wealthy in the LDCs tend to invest their savings in nonproductive areas such as land speculation, precious metals, and foreign bank accounts. The wealthy are simply reacting to the realities of LDC life: the uncertain political climate and the apparently poor development prospects of their own countries.

Modern economic growth began in the developed countries after centuries of preparation. Canals, schools, roads, and cathedrals had been built in the centuries that preceded the industrial revolution. By the time of the industrial revolution, the developed countries had accumulated an impressive stock of *social overhead capital.* The LDCs have not had the luxury of centuries of steady accumulation of social overhead capital which, in effect, may be required before real economic development can take place.

Technological Backwardness. On the surface, it would appear that the LDCs should simply borrow the modern technology already developed by the industrialized countries. However, the technology of the industrialized countries represents a response to the factors that are present in these countries. Relative to the LDCs, capital is abundant in the developed countries; the quantity of labor is scarce, but the quality of each worker (in training, health, and education) is quite high. Because of these factor endowments, the industrialized countries have developed technologies that emphasize labor saving and require inputs of highly skilled labor and capital.

The modern production techniques of the developed countries are, therefore, not well suited to the LDCs. The LDCs require technologies that take advantage of unskilled labor and do not place heavy burdens on their more limited resources—skilled labor and capital. Although a wealth of sophisticated technology is on hand in the industrialized countries, the LDCs remain in the ironic position of having to develop their own technologies. There is evidence that Japan was successful in adapting modern technology to its particular needs, but most LDCs have been less successful.

Signs of Progress?

Is material life in LDCs getting better? Have there been significant improvements. Table 4 gives data on

EXAMPLE 3 Population Growth and Per Capita Income

Many policymakers and economists assume that there is an inverse relationship between population growth and the growth of per capita income for the LDCs. It would appear that rapid population growth should depress the growth of per capita income. However, the accompanying figure shows that there is no discernible relationship between per capita income growth and population growth for LDCs. Some countries combine high population growth with high per capita income growth. Others have high population growth and low per capita income growth.

The accompanying figure shows that the relationship between population growth and per capita income is complex and depends upon a variety of factors. Experts suggest that large, resource-rich countries can combine high population growth with high growth of per capita income. Small, resource-poor countries, on the other hand, trade off population growth and per capita income growth.

The choice of an "optimal" rate of population growth is not as simple as it seems. Countries that automatically pursue a policy of lower population growth may even cause per capita income growth rates to fall.

Source: Allen C. Kelley, "Economic Consequences of Population Change in the Third World," *Journal of Economic Literature* 31, 4 (December 1988): 1685–1728.

Income Per Capita Growth and Population Growth in LDCs, 1970–1981

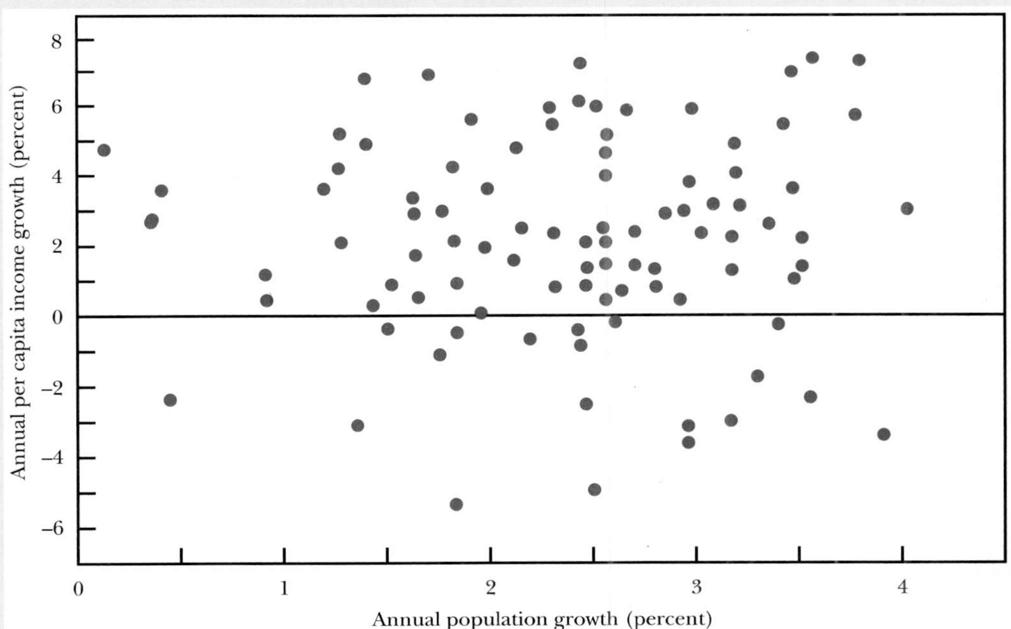

This figure shows no correlation between growth of per capita income and population growth.

Source: World Bank (1983).

TABLE 4
A Comparison of Developed Countries and Less Developed Countries (LDCs)

	1950–1960	1960–1970	1970–1980	1980–1989
Rate of population growth				
Developed countries	1.2	1.0	0.7	0.7
Middle-income LDCs	2.4	2.5	2.4	2.1
Low-income LDCs	2.0	2.4	1.9	2.1
Rate of per capita GDP growth				
Developed countries	2.5	4.0	2.3	2.3
Middle-income LDCs	2.8	3.7	3.0	0.5
Low-income LDCs	1.8	2.1	1.0	4.1
	1960	**1970**	**1980**	**1986**
Life expectancy (years)				
Developed countries	68.9	71.8	74.9	75.0
Middle-income LDCs	50.6	54.9	59.9	60.0
Low-income LDCs	40.8	45.3	58.4	59.0
Adult literacy (per 100)				
Developed countries	96.9	98.3	98.9	99.0
Middle-income LDCs	44.0	56.2	65.2	67.0
Low-income LDCs	22.6	31.0	51.0	53.0

Sources: World Bank, *World Tables;* World Bank, *World Development Report 1991,* published for the World Bank by Oxford University Press.

average rates of growth of population and per capita GDP and on changes in two social indicators from 1960 to 1986. On the whole, there is little evidence that the LDCs are catching up with per capita incomes in the developed countries. The low-income LDCs have fallen further behind since 1950 (although they grew rapidly in the 1980s), while the middle-income LDCs have just about held their own. LDCs have clearly experienced more rapid population growth than the developed countries. Both the low- and middle-income LDCs have experienced GDP growth as rapid or more rapid than that of the developed countries, but more rapid population growth has meant equivalent or slower per capita GDP growth.

In terms of life expectancy and literacy, the LDCs have indeed been catching up with the developed countries. The developed countries are approaching natural upper limits (one cannot raise the literacy rate above 100 percent, and human beings are mortal), and the LDCs have succeeded in improving the health and education of their populations. Moreover, a number of countries have made significant progress in achieving agricultural self-sufficiency.

SOLUTIONS TO WORLD POVERTY

The LDCs are poor because they have fewer economic resources—skilled labor, entrepreneurs, capital, and technology—than the developed countries. Moreover, cultural traditions, religious taboos, and bureaucratic restrictions have prevented them from utilizing their limited resources as effectively as the industrialized countries. The LDCs are caught in a vicious circle: Low income prevents them from accumulating new resources, and the failure to accumulate new resources leaves them poor.

Trade Policies

The examples of Great Britain in the nineteenth century and Hong Kong, Taiwan, and Singapore today show how extensive international trade can bring many benefits to a country. Trade harnesses the power of specialization to raise national income beyond what is possible in isolation. Some LCDs have tried to grow by denying the benefits of specialization and have attempted to copy the industrialized countries. They want their own automobile and steel industries even though it is cheaper to purchase cars and steel indirectly by producing goods for which the economy's resource base is suited (textiles, natural resources). Countries such as Argentina and India have attempted to follow the inward-looking policy of **import substitution.**

> **Import substitution** occurs when a country substitutes domestic production for imports by subsidizing domestic production through tariffs, quotas, and other devices.

Cases of successful import substitution are rare, primarily because the products manufactured with the assistance of tariffs and other forms of protection are not competitive.

An alternative course followed by countries such as Hong Kong, South Korea, Taiwan, Brazil, and Singapore has been the outward-looking policy of **export promotion**—encouraging exports through various types of incentive schemes.

> **Export promotion** occurs when a country encourages exports by subsidizing the production of goods for export.

In general, those LDCs that have followed export-promotion policies have done better as a group than those that followed import-substitution policies. The major success stories in the third world are those countries that have become fully integrated into the world economy, competing successfully with more affluent countries in the area of manufacturing.

External Assistance

Can the LDCs realistically expect to develop on their own, or must they have outside assistance? The issue of assistance from the industrialized countries is an explosive one in the third world. Direct foreign assistance is one means by which the industrialized countries assist the LDCs. The LDC bloc in the United Nations expresses the view that the current level of foreign assistance is grossly inadequate. The LDCs call for a doubling of foreign assistance, requiring the industrialized countries to donate approximately 1 percent of their GDP to the LDCs. Few industrialized nations, including the United States, contribute anything close to the 1 percent figure.

Most LDCs trade raw materials, and they feel that their dependence upon raw-material export places them at a disadvantage in the world economy. Their earnings from raw materials—coffee, rubber, flax, sugar, ores—fluctuate more than the prices of manufactured goods. The LDCs believe that there is a long-run tendency for the prices of raw materials to fall relative to manufactured goods. To deal with these problems, the LDCs have called for a new international economic order. The cornerstone of the new order would be a commodity stabilization program that guarantees the LDCs stable earnings from raw-material production.

In addition to more foreign aid and commodity stabilization, the LDCs have called for improved access to the markets and technology of the industrialized countries and for reforms of the international monetary system.

Capitalism, Socialism, and Economic Growth

The planned socialist economies of the former Soviet Union, Eastern Europe, and China represented an important experiment concerning the economic system and economic growth. The Soviet administrative-command model developed by Stalin in the early 1930s sought to direct resources into high-growth activities through a system of centralized planning. It was thought that such a model would generate higher growth rates than could be achieved under market capitalism. Planners could insure high investment rates, massive human capital programs, and high rates of labor force participation, especially of women. The Stalinist model was imposed on Eastern Europe after World War II and was adopted in part in China.

FIGURE 4
Annual Growth Rates of Real GDP in the Former Soviet Union and Eastern Europe, 1950–1990

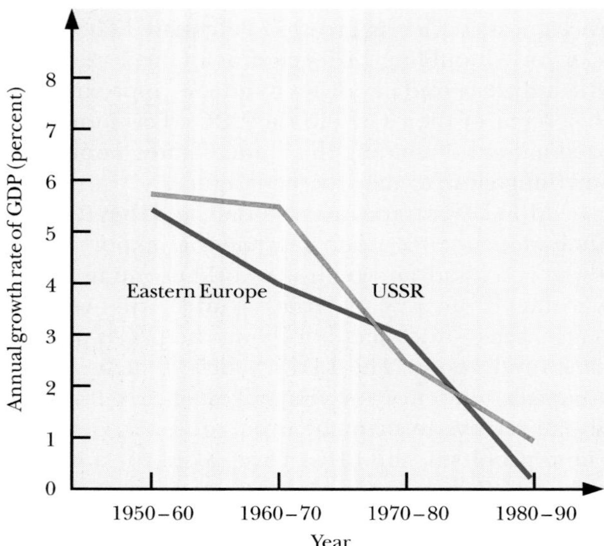

Sources: *Handbook of Economic Statistics;* Central Intelligence Agency, "Eastern Europe: Coming Around the First Turn," Joint Economic Committee, May 1991.

The communist experiment was a bold attempt to generate rapid growth for the purpose of overcoming economic backwardness relative to the industrialized West. At the height of the communist experiment in the mid 1950s, one Soviet leader, sensing success, promised that communism would bury capitalism by proving it to be an inferior economic system.

Figure 4 shows the annual growth rates achieved by Eastern Europe and the Soviet Union after 1960. It shows why the former Soviet Union and Eastern Europe opted to abandon the Stalinist command model in favor of a stronger element of market resource allocation. From rapid growth in the 1950s, economic growth in this region declined steadily, coming to a virtual halt in the 1980s. The decade of the 1980s witnessed negative growth of factor productivity as labor and capital inputs grew more rapidly than output.

The failure of the Stalinist model of economic development is best seen in the decisions to abandon this model throughout the communist world in the 1980s and early 1990s. The Stalinist administrative-command model has few remaining supporters (primarily Cuba and North Korea). Elsewhere, the former administrative-command economies are seeking an appropriate path of transition from planned socialism to market capitalism. Whereas earlier the Stalinist model exercised considerable appeal in the LDCs as a means of accelerating economic development, it has few remaining adherents in Africa, Asia, and Latin America.

DOOMSDAY FORECASTS

The sustained growth of GDP per capita over a long period of time has provided Americans with a high standard of living. The average citizen of the United States enjoys a comfortable standard of living. In recent years, some social critics have come to question the wisdom of further economic growth. They argue that economic growth increases environmental problems (more factories create more pollution) and that economic growth threatens to exhaust the globe's scarce natural resources. Since there are only finite supplies of natural resources, clean air, and pure water, economic growth may some day threaten our very existence.

Modern doomsday forecasts are reminiscent of the predictions of the classical stationary state; but rather than seeing agricultural land as the limiting factor of production, doomsday forecasters see natural resources (arable land, minerals, air, and water) in this role. A famous doomsday model was published by the Club of Rome in 1972.[2]

The Club of Rome computer model—like the stationary state models of the nineteenth century—predicts that continued economic growth will put such a severe strain on our natural resources and on our environment that, shortly after the turn of the twenty-first century, GDP per capita will begin to decline. The basic conclusion of this doomsday model is that our planet cannot sustain further economic growth and that humanity should adopt social policies to stop the growth of GDP and population in order to avoid catastrophe.

[2]Dennis Meadows et al., *The Limits to Growth* (Washington, DC: Potomac Associates, 1972).

EXAMPLE 4 An Economist's Critique of Doomsday Forecasts

Economist Julian Simon has conducted a careful investigation of charges that our globe is running out of resources and that there is a growing disproportion between the world's resources and its population.

Simon finds that these charges are based upon very flimsy evidence:

1. Contrary to doomsday claims that economic growth is robbing the world of arable land, the quantity of arable land has actually increased markedly in recent years. In fact, the amount of land taken out of cultivation by the much publicized urban sprawl has been more than offset by the amount of arable land added by swamp drainage and land improvement.
2. Contrary to doomsday forecasts, Simon finds that the incidence of famine is actually decreasing rather than increasing. In reality, per capita food production has been increasing at nearly 1 percent per year—25 percent over the last 25 years—and even countries like India are becoming increasingly self-sufficient in grains.
3. Contrary to doomsday warnings against overpopulation, Simon finds no negative statistical correlation between population growth and per capita income growth.
4. Contrary to doomsday warnings that we are running out of natural resources and raw materials. Simon finds that the most direct measure of rising scarcity—rising relative prices—does not support the thesis of growing shortages of natural resources and raw materials. Relative to other prices paid by consumers, raw materials and natural resources are growing cheaper, not more expensive.

Source: Julian Simon, *The Ultimate Resource* (Princeton, NJ: Princeton University Press, 1981).

How much credence should one attach to the dire predictions of the doomsday philosophers? Economists can raise certain legitimate questions about the assumptions of their models. First, such doomsday models are based upon the assumption that the world economy will continue to use resources at the same rates as they have been used in the past. If past petroleum usage grew at the same rate as real GDP, the doomsday prophets assume that this relationship will continue in the future. Economists, using the elementary laws of supply and demand, argue that when a natural resource becomes short in supply, its relative price will rise, thereby reducing its quantity demanded. For example, the rising relative price of oil resulted in a major shift in the amount of oil used per dollar of GDP. The oil/GDP ratio dropped substantially during the energy-price explosion. Most economists, therefore, maintain that a freely functioning price system will retard the depletion of scarce natural resources. (See Example 4.)

Second, the doomsday models—like the models of Malthus and Ricardo—assume static technology. However, in the twenty-first century, the world economy may very well develop new energy-saving technologies or discover good substitutes for natural resources that are rising in relative price. If the world supply of petroleum and natural gas threatens to run out, for example, scientists may develop new energy sources that will be economically feasible.

Only the future will show whether the predictions of the doomsday philosophers will prove true or whether technological progress will continue to save the day, as it did in the case of the classical stationary state. Economists tend to be skeptical of doomsday models because they believe that a correctly functioning price system will motivate people and firms to economize on the use of scarce resources and will create incentives to develop new technologies to replace depleted resources. Our experience with rising energy prices suggests how market economies will deal with future shortages of natural resources.

Rising relative prices forced our economies to combine economic growth with declining usage of petroleum inputs. In this case, economic growth was proven to be compatible with declining usage of a scarce natural resource.

The next three chapters will examine international economics, beginning with an exploration of the advantages of international trade.

SUMMARY

1. Economic growth is an increase in real GDP or an increase in real GDP per capita.

2. The industrialized countries have grown at a sustained rate since the mid-eighteenth century. Modern economic growth is characterized by sustained growth of per capita GDP and by structural changes in the economy.

3. Economies grow because the total amount of factor inputs increases and because output per unit of input (productivity) increases. The major factor causing economic growth is the growth of productivity.

4. Classical economists David Ricardo and Thomas Malthus predicted that economies would reach a stationary state of zero growth and subsistence living standards. The stationary state would be caused by the law of diminishing returns and by the tendency of the population to expand whenever wages rose above the subsistence level.

5. The classical stationary state model provides a first explanation of LDC poverty. The combination of rapid population growth and limited technological progress has caused diminishing returns to be a serious problem in LDCs. Possible solutions to the diminishing returns problem are reduced population growth, increased capital formation, and more rapid technological progress. The demographic transition is the process by which countries change from rapid to slow population growth during the course of modernization. The LDCs as a group have yet to experience the demographic transition. The LDCs suffer from inadequate capital formation. The advanced technology of the developed countries is generally not well suited to the factor endowments of the LDCs.

6. The LDCs must choose between import substitution and export promotion policies of economic development. The LDCs have asked the industrialized countries for more foreign aid, commodity stabilization programs, and improved access to markets. The LDCs must decide whether planned or market allocation systems offer them a better chance for economic development.

7. Events of the 1980s have shown that the Stalinist administrative-command model did not generate satisfactory growth of output or productivity.

8. Doomsday forecasts predict that economic growth cannot be sustained because the exhaustion of scarce natural resources and the increase of pollution will cause a new stationary state to be reached. Doomsday predictions, however, are based upon the unsupported assumption that scarce resources will continue to be used at the same rate as in the past.

KEY TERMS

economic growth
level of economic development
less developed countries (LDCs)
extensive growth
intensive growth
factor productivity
labor productivity
capital productivity
total factor productivity
demographic transition
import substitution
export promotion

QUESTIONS AND PROBLEMS

1. Explain why the two measures of economic growth can yield different results.
2. The amount of land in the world is fixed. The law of diminishing returns indicates that, with a fixed input, the marginal productivity of variable inputs will ultimately decline. Will we not ultimately reach Ricardo's stationary state?
3. Malthus maintained that whenever wages rise above the subsistence level, the population will grow. Has this prediction proven to be true in the industrialized countries? Why not?
4. Explain why intensive growth is less costly than extensive growth.
5. In the economy of Malthusia, over a 10-year period, real output grew at 5 percent per year, combined inputs at 2 percent per year, and population at 1 percent per year. What is the annual growth rate of per capita GDP? What is the annual growth rate of factor productiv-

ity? What proportion of the 5 percent growth rate is explained by productivity growth (the residual)?

6. Economists criticize the doomsday models on the grounds that they don't take into account the effects of relative prices. Why should prices matter if the supply of natural resources is fixed?
7. From 1973 to 1981, capital grew twice as fast as labor hours (approximately). If capital had grown at three times the rate of labor hours, what would you expect to happen to labor productivity?
8. Describe the characteristics of the classical stationary state.
9. In the economy of Gregoria, the number of hours worked grew by 2 percent per year, and the capital stock grew by 5 percent per year. What effect would these trends have on labor productivity?
10. Explain why GDP or GDP per capita can be an imperfect measure of the level of economic development in a country.
11. Evaluate that validity of the following statement: "The stationary state of Ricardo and Malthus is not an accurate description of the situation in industrialized countries. On the other hand, it does appear to describe accurately conditions in the LDCs."
12. Describe the demographic transition. Why has the demographic transition not occurred in many of the LDCs?
13. Contrast the different trade policies that an LDC might pursue in trying to promote its economic development.
14. Evaluate the validity of the following statement: "The LDCs should not have any problem with technology. All they have to do is adopt the technologies that have been developed in the industrialized world."
15. Using the data presented in this chapter, indicate which area—economic growth or social indicators—the LDCs have made the most progress relative to the industrialized world.

SUGGESTED READINGS

Baily, Martin N., and Gordon, Robert J. "Measurement Issues, the Productivity Slowdown, and the Explosion of Computer Power." *Brookings Papers on Economic Activity* 19, 2 (1988): 347–420.

Denison, Edward F. *Trends in American Economic Growth, 1929–1982.* Washington, DC: The Brookings Institution, 1985.

Gordon, Robert J. *Macroeconomics,* 5th ed. New York: HarperCollins, 1990, chap. 12.

Solow, Robert M. "Growth Theory and After." *American Economic Review* 78 (June 1988): 307.

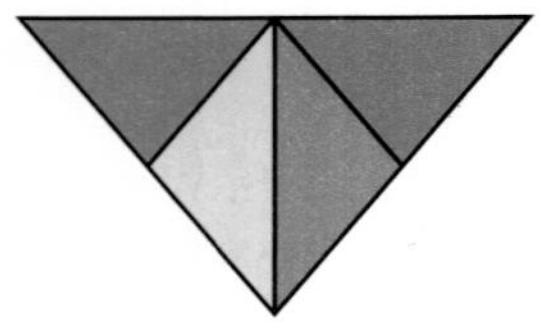

23 International Trade and Comparative Advantage

CHAPTER INSIGHT

International trade has changed the way we live. Traders throughout history have helped transmit knowledge and inventions. Today, foreign products from Sony, BMW, Mitsubishi, and Chanel are as familiar to us as U.S. products from General Electric, Chevrolet, and IBM. Yet, people continue to debate whether or not trade is beneficial. In the early 1990s, television news showed an angry American worker destroying a Japanese car with a sledgehammer because of the fear that imports were taking away American jobs. Some politicians were seeking office by appealing to sentiments favoring protectionism—the artificial restriction of imports.

It is easy to fall prey to the fallacy that imports eliminate domestic jobs. People often fail to realize that ultimately exports pay for imports. Indeed, it was conventional wisdom in the sixteenth and seventeenth centuries that a country should encourage exports and discourage imports. But in 1817 David Ricardo developed the law of comparative advantage, which demonstrates the benefits of international trade. This chapter will explain the workings of the law of comparative advantage and how it applies to the United States.

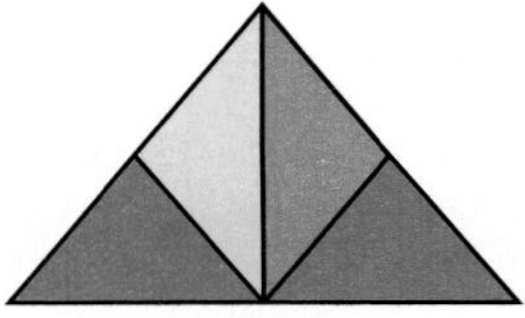

THE GLOBAL ECONOMY

The production of goods and services throughout the world has become truly global. Many Japanese cars are built in America. The Smith Corona typewriter—an American product—is produced in Singapore. International production has obscured the dividing line between "American" goods and "foreign" goods. Electronic components are shipped to Asian countries and return as completed computers or calculators. American companies form alliances with foreign companies: Chrysler has an alliance with Mitsubishi, General Motors with Toyota, and International Business Machines (IBM) with Toshiba. Almost all large companies have foreign branches. For example, the Ford Escort is produced in Europe and Ford owns Jaguar.

Since the end of World War II, world trade has increased faster than world output, due to low trade barriers, smaller transportation costs, and dramatic reductions in the costs of international communication, achieved through the use of space satellites.

How extensive is world trade? In 1988 world GDP was almost $20 trillion. World trade was over $3 trillion. By way of comparison, the United States was by far the largest economic unit, with a 1988 GDP of $4.5 trillion. Japan ran a distant second with a 1988 GDP of $1.5 trillion in comparable U.S. dollars. West Germany was third with a 1988 GDP of $770 billion in comparable U.S. dollars.[1] Thus, world trade was more massive than the second and third largest economies combined!

THE REASONS FOR INTERNATIONAL TRADE

This book has emphasized that people benefit from specialization. People increase their incomes by specializing in those tasks for which they are particularly suited. Different jobs have different intellectual, physical, and personality requirements. Because people are different and because each person has the capacity to learn, it pays to specialize. As Adam Smith stated:

> It is the maxim of every prudent master of a family never to attempt to make at home what it will cost him more to make than to buy.

Trade among persons succeeds primarily because each individual is endowed with a mix of traits that are different from most other people. Some of these traits are an inherent part of the individual that cannot be shared with other individuals. Trade between individuals has much in common with international trade between countries.

Each country is endowed with certain characteristics: a particular climate, a certain amount of fertile farmland, a certain amount of desert, a given number of lakes and rivers, and the kinds of people that comprise its population. Over the years, some countries have accumulated large quantities of physical and human capital, whereas other countries are poor in capital. In short, each country is defined in part by the endowments of productive factors (land, labor, and capital) inside its borders. Just as one person cannot transfer intelligence, strength, personality, or health to another person, one country cannot transfer its land and other natural resource deposits to another country. Similarly, the labor force that resides within a country is not easily moved; people have friends and family in their native land and share a common language and culture with their fellows. Even if they wish to leave, immigration laws may render the labor force internationally immobile.

It is easier to transfer to another country the goods and services produced by land, labor, and capital than to transfer the land, labor, and capital themselves. Thus, to some degree each country will possess land, labor, and capital in different proportions. A country like Australia has very little labor compared to land and, hence, devotes itself to land-intensive products, such as sheep farming or wheat production. A country like Great Britain tends to produce goods that use comparatively little land but more labor and capital. Sweden's Nobel Prize-winning economist Bertil Ohlin pointed out that when each country specializes in those goods for which its factor proportions are most suited, international trade in goods and services substitutes for movements of the various productive factors.

[1]These GDP comparisons are based on a common set of prices so that real output can be compared. See Robert Summers and Alan Heston, "The Penn World Table (Mark 5): An Expanded Set of International Comparisons, 1950–1988," *Quarterly Journal of Economics* 106 (May 1991): 327–68.

> The fundamental fact upon which international trade rests is that goods and services are much more mobile internationally than are the resources used in their production. Each country will tend to export those goods and services for which its resource base is most suited.

International trade allows a country to specialize in the goods and services that it can produce at a relatively low cost and to export those goods in return for imports whose domestic production is relatively costly. Through international trade, as John Stuart Mill (1806–1873) said:

> ... a country obtains things which it either could not have produced at all, or which it must have produced at a greater expense of capital and labor than the cost of the things which it exports to pay for them.

As a consequence, international trade enables a country—and the world—to consume and produce more than would be possible without trade. We shall later show that a country can benefit from trade even when it is more efficient (uses fewer resources) in the production of *all* goods than any other country.

Trade has intangible benefits in addition to the tangible benefit of providing the potential for greater totals of all the goods and services the world consumes. The major intangible benefit is the diversity trade offers to the way people live and work. The advantages of particular climates and lands are shared by the rest of the world. The United States imports oil from the hot desert of Saudi Arabia so its people can drive cars in cool comfort. Americans can enjoy coffee, bananas, and spices without living in the tropics. The economy and durability of Japanese cars can be enjoyed without driving in hectic Tokyo. Thus, international (and interregional) trade enables us to enjoy a more diverse menu of goods and services than we could enjoy without trade. World trade also encourages the diffusion of knowledge and culture because trade serves as a point of contact between people of different lands.

THE LAW OF COMPARATIVE ADVANTAGE

Chapter 3 used the **law of comparative advantage** to explain the benefits people enjoy from specialization. Individuals are made better off by specializing and engaging in trade with other people. The law of comparative advantage can also help explain the gains from international specialization. In 1817, David Ricardo proved that international specialization pays if each country devotes its resources to those activities in which it has a comparative advantage.

> The **law of comparative advantage** states that people or countries specialize in those activities in which they have the greatest advantage or the least disadvantage compared to other people or countries.

Profound truths are sometimes difficult to discover; the real world is so complex it can hide the working of these truths. Ricardo's genius was that he was able to provide a simplified model of trade without the thousands of irrelevant details that would cloud our vision. He considered a hypothetical world with only two countries and only two goods. The two "countries" could be America and Europe; the two goods could be food and clothing. For the sake of simplicity, let us also assume the following.

1. Labor is the only productive factor, and there is only one type of labor.
2. Labor cannot move between the two countries (this assumption reflects the relative international immobility of productive factors compared to goods).
3. The output from a unit of labor is constant (in other words, productivity is constant no matter how many units of output are produced).
4. Laborers are indifferent about whether they work in the food or clothing industries, provided that wages are the same.

Table 1 shows the hypothetical output of food or clothing from 1 unit of labor in each of the two countries. America can produce 6 units of food with 1 unit of labor and can produce 2 units of clothing with 1 unit of labor. Europe can produce either 1 unit of food or 1 unit of clothing with 1 unit of labor. America is 6 times more efficient than Europe in food production (it produces 6 times as much with the same labor); America is only twice as efficient in clothing production (it produces twice as much with the same labor).

We have deliberately constructed a case in which America has an **absolute advantage** over Europe in all lines of production.

TABLE 1
Hypothetical Food and Clothing Output from 1 Unit of Labor

Country	Units of Food Output from 1 Unit of Labor	Units of Clothing Output from 1 Unit of Labor
America	6	2
Europe	1	1

Trade patterns depend on comparative advantages, not on absolute advantages. In our hypothetical example, America is 6 times more efficient than Europe in food production and twice as efficient in clothing production. America has an absolute advantage in both food and clothing but has a comparative advantage only in food production. Europe has an absolute disadvantage in the production of both goods but has a comparative advantage in cloth-production. Europe will export clothing to America in return for food, and both will gain by this pattern of trade. Each country exports the good in which it has the greatest efficiency advantage (in the case of America) or the smallest inefficiency disadvantage (in the case of Europe).

A country has an **absolute advantage** in the production of a good if it uses fewer resources to produce a unit of the good than any other country.

Even under these circumstances, however, both countries stand to benefit from specialization and trade according to comparative advantage, as we will proceed to demonstrate.

The Case of Self-Sufficiency

Assume that each country in our hypothetical world is initially self-sufficient and must consume only what it produces at home.

America. A self-sufficient America must produce both food and clothing. American workers can produce 6 units of food or 2 units of clothing from 1 unit of labor (see Table 1). Thus, in the marketplace, 6 units of food will have the same value as 2 units of clothing, or, to simplify, 3 units of food (F) will have the same value as 1 unit of clothing (C). Hence, in order to acquire 1 unit of clothing, a worker must sacrifice 3 units of food. In other words, America's opportunity cost of 1 unit of clothing is 3 units of food:

$$3F = 1C$$

Under conditions of self-sufficiency, the American price of a unit of clothing will be 3 times the price of a unit of food.

These same facts are shown in panel *a* of Figure 1, which graphs America's production possibilities frontier. Labor is the only factor of production, and a total of 15 units of labor are assumed to be available to the American economy. America's production possibilities frontier is a straight line because opportunity costs are constant in our example. If everyone worked in clothing production, $30(= 15 \times 2)$ units of clothing could be produced. If everyone worked in food production, $90(= 15 \times 6)$ units of food could be produced. The economy would likely produce a mix of food and clothing to meet domestic consumption. Such a combination could be point *a*, where 45 units of food and 15 units of clothing are produced and consumed. Thus we can say that without trade, America consumes $45F$ and $15C$, the combination that reflects America's preferences in this case.

Europe. In a self-sufficient Europe, workers can produce 1 unit of food or 1 unit of clothing with 1 unit of labor. A unit of clothing and a unit of food have the same costs, and hence, the same price. In other words, Europeans must give up 1 unit of food to get 1 unit of clothing. Thus, Europe's opportunity cost of 1 unit clothing is 1 unit of food.

$$1F = 1C$$

Panel *b* of Figure 1 shows Europe's production possibilities frontier. In our example, Europe is more populous than the United States; it has 50 units of labor available. Europe also has a straight-line production possibilities frontier, and it can produce either 50 units of food, 50 units of clothing, or some combination of the two. A likely situation would be for Europe to produce and consume at a point such as *e*, where 30 units of food and 20 units of clothing are produced. Thus we can say that without trade, Europe consumes $30F$ and $20C$, the combination that reflects Europe's preferences in this case.

Without trade, each country must consume on its production possibilities frontier. To produce (and

FIGURE 1
Hypothetical American and European Production Possibilities Frontiers

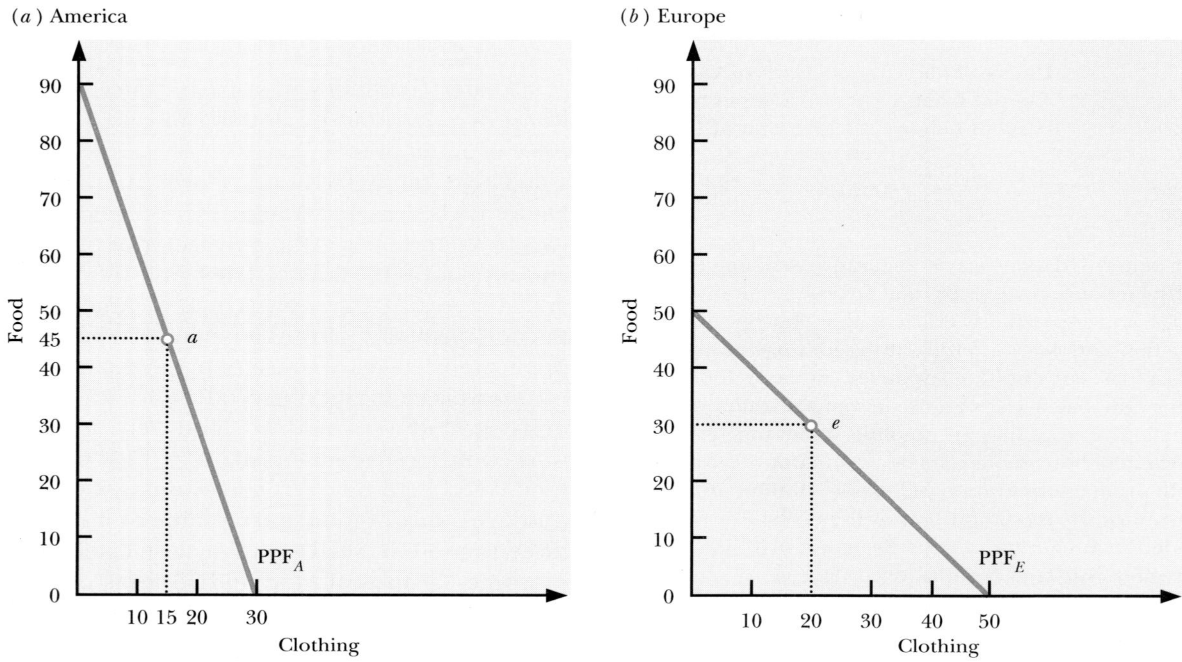

Panel *a* shows a hypothetical production possibilities frontier for America. Based on the labor productivity rates in Table 1, if 15 units of labor are available and labor is the only factor of production, America could produce either 30 units of clothing, 90 units of food, or some mixture of the two—such as the combination represented by point *a*, where 45 units of food and 15 units of clothing are produced. Panel *b* shows a hypothetical PPF for Europe, where 50 units of labor are available. Again, based on the labor productivity rates in Table 1, Europe could produce 50 units of clothing, 50 units of food, or a combination—such as that represented by point *e*, where 30 units of food and 20 units of clothing are produced.

consume) more requires either a larger labor force or an increase in the efficiency of labor.

The World. If both Europe and America were self-sufficient, the total amount of food and clothing produced would be the amount produced by America ($45F$ and $15C$) plus the amount produced by Europe ($30F$ and $20C$). Thus, the total amount of food produced would be 75 units ($45F + 30F$), and the total amount of clothing produced would be 35 units ($15C + 20C$).

The Case of International Trade

Before trade opens between Europe and America (as described in Table 1), a potential trader would find that 1 unit of clothing sells for 1 unit of food in Europe but sells for 3 units of food in America. If the trader then applies 1 unit of labor in American food production and ships the resulting 6 units of food to Europe, he or she can obtain 6 units of clothing instead of the 2 obtained by producing it at home! It makes no difference that clothing production is half as efficient in Europe. What matters is that in Europe, food and clothing production use the same amount of labor, so food and clothing sell for the same price in Europe.

Americans would soon discover that clothing could be bought more cheaply in Europe than at home. The law of supply and demand would then do its work. Americans would stop producing clothing in order to concentrate on food production, and they would begin to demand European clothing. This increased demand would drive up the price of

European clothing. Europe would presumably shift from food production to clothing production; eventually the pressure of American demand would lead Europe to produce only clothing. The end result would be that Americans would get clothing more cheaply (at less than $3F$ for $1C$) than before trade, and Europeans would receive a higher price for their clothing (at more than $1F$ for $1C$).

In making decisions about trading, people in each country need to know the **terms of trade,** or how much clothing is worth in terms of food.

> The **terms of trade** are the rate at which two products can be exchanged for each other between countries.

The terms of trade between Europe and America will settle at some point between America's and Europe's opportunity costs, although the final equilibrium terms of trade cannot be determined without knowing each country's preferences. If America's opportunity cost of 1 unit of clothing is 3 units of food and Europe's opportunity cost of 1 unit of clothing is 1 unit of food, the final terms of trade will settle between $1C = 3F$ and $1C = 1F$. Europe is willing to sell 1 unit of clothing for at least 1 unit of food; America is willing to pay no more than 3 units of food for 1 unit of clothing.

The cheap imports of clothing from Europe will drive down the price of clothing in America. When Europe exports clothing to America, the price of clothing in Europe will rise. If the world terms of trade at which both Europe and America can trade are set by the market at $2F = 1C$, Americans will no longer get only 2 units of clothing for 1 unit of labor; instead, they can produce 6 units of food and trade that food for 3 units of clothing (because $2F = 1C$) in Europe. Europeans will no longer have to work so hard to get 1 unit of food. They can produce 1 unit of clothing and trade that clothing for 2 units of food instead of getting only 1 unit of food per unit of clothing.

When the terms of trade in the world are $2F = 1C$, Americans will devote all their labor to food production and Europeans will devote all their labor to clothing production. (If increasing, rather than constant, opportunity costs had been assumed, the two countries need not have been driven to such complete specialization).

THE GAINS FROM TRADE

When American workers specialize in food production and European workers specialize in clothing production, the gains to each may be measured by comparing their sacrifices before and after trade. Americans, before trade, sacrificed 3 units of food for 1 unit of clothing. After trade, Americans need sacrifice only 2 units of food for 1 unit of clothing (with terms of trade at $2F = 1C$). Europeans, before trade, sacrificed 1 unit of clothing for 1 unit of food. After trade, Europeans need sacrifice only half a unit of clothing per unit of food (because clothing sells for twice as much as food after trade).

The gains from trade are shown more dramatically in Figure 2. Before trade, America is at point *a* in panel *a,* and Europe is at point *e* in panel *b.* When trade opens at the terms of trade $2F = 1C$, America moves its production to point x_A (specialization in food production), as the arrows show. Thus, America increases its food production from 45 units to 90 units. America can now trade each unit of food for half a unit of clothing. America trades 40 units of food for 20 units of clothing. Now America consumes at point c_A, with consumption at 50 units of food and 20 units of clothing. Trade enables America to consume above its production possibilities frontier. In this example, trade shifts consumption from *a* to c_A. The dotted line shows the consumption possibilities available to Americans when $2F = 1C$ in the work market.

As column 1 of Table 2 shows, America produces $45F$ and $15C$ before trade. The opening of trade shifts American labor entirely out of clothing production. As column 2 shows, America produces only food ($90F$) after trade opens. Columns 3 and 4 describe America's trade: America keeps $50F$ for domestic consumption and sells $40F$ for $20C$. Column 5 shows consumption after trade, and column 6 shows America's benefits from trade. As a result of trade, America increases its consumption of each product by 5 units.

Europe's story is told in panel *b* of Figure 2. Europe shifts production from *e,* where $30F$ and $20C$ are produced, to point x_E, where 50 units of clothing are produced. The terms of trade are $2F = 1C$; when Europe trades 20 units of clothing for 40 units of food, Europe's consumption shifts from *e* to c_E, which is above the original production possibilities

FIGURE 2
The Effects of Trade

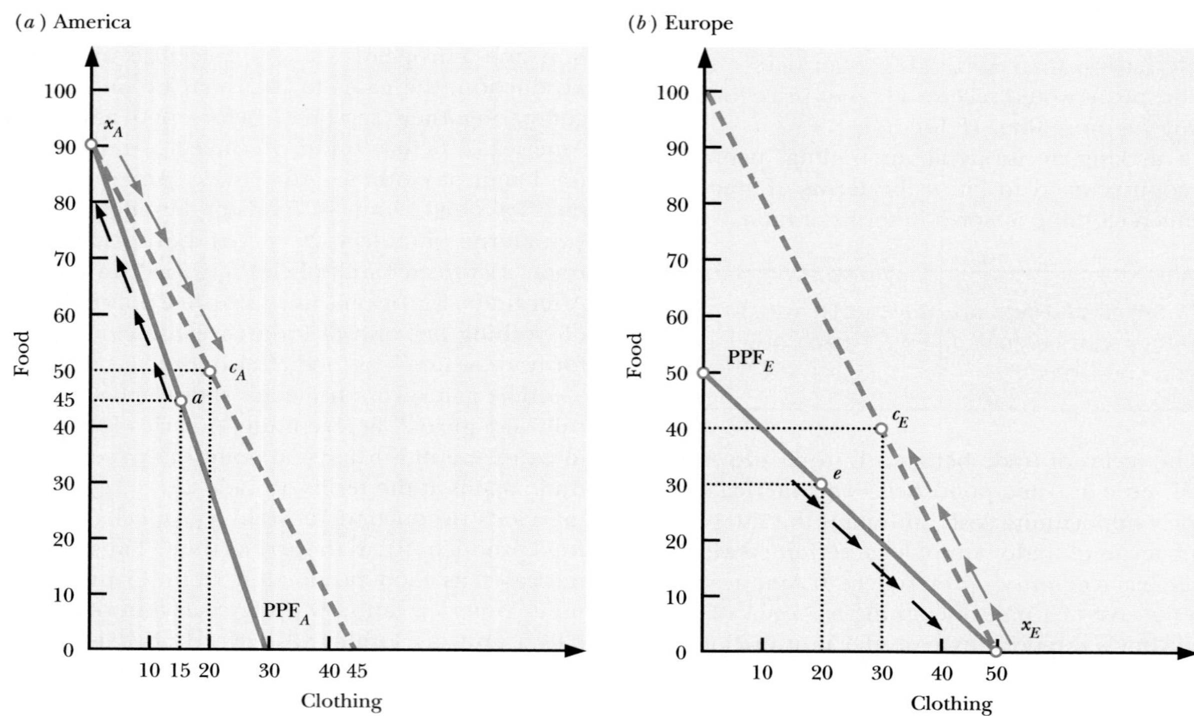

As shown in panel *a*, before trade, America produces and consumes at point *a*. When trade opens at the terms of $2F = 1C$ (where F = units of food and C = units of clothing), America produces at x_A, specializing in food production, and trades 40 units of food for 20 units of clothing. America, therefore, consumes at point c_A, where it consumes 50 units of food and 20 units of clothing. Trade shifts American consumption from *a* to c_A. As shown in panel *b*, before trade, Europe produces and consumes at point *e*. When trade opens, Europe shifts production to x_E, specializing in clothing production, and trades 20 units of clothing for 40 units of food. Europe, therefore, shifts consumption from *e* to point c_E, where 30 units of clothing and 40 units of food are consumed. In both panels, the black arrows show the effects of trade on domestic production, and the orange arrows show the effects of trade on domestic consumption. Both countries consume somewhere on the dashed line above their original production possibilities frontiers.

frontier. Like America, Europe is better off with trade. Row *b* of Table 2 tells the same story in simple arithmetic. Columns 3 and 4 show that Europe's trade is consistent with America's. For example, America exports 40F and Europe imports 40F. The dotted line in Figure 2 shows the consumption possibilities available to Europeans when $2F = 1C$ in the world market.

In this simple world, the benefits of trade are dramatic. America consumes 5 units more of both food and clothing; Europe consumes 10 units more of both food and clothing. Row *c* of Table 2 shows that the world increases its production of food by 15 units, or by 20 percent (from 75 to 90 units), and increases its production of clothing by 15 units, or by 43 percent (from 35 to 50 units). Everybody is made better off; nobody is hurt by trade in this case. Trade has the same effect on consumption as an increase in national resources or an improvement in efficiency of resource use. As a consequence of trade, countries are able to consume beyond their original production possibilities frontiers. (See Example 1).

TABLE 2
The Effects of International Trade

	Consumption and Production before Trade (1)	Production after Trade (2)	Exports (3)	Imports (4)	Consumption after Trade (5)	Gains (6)
(a) America	45*F*	90*F*	40*F*	0*F*	50*F*	5*F*
	15*C*	0*C*	0*C*	20*C*	20*C*	5*C*
(b) Europe	30*F*	0*F*	0*F*	40*F*	40*F*	10*F*
	20*C*	50*C*	20*C*	0*C*	30*C*	10*C*
(c) World	75*F*	90*F*	—	—	90*F*	15*F*
	35*C*	50*C*	—	—	50*C*	15*C*

F = units of food
C = units of clothing

EXAMPLE 1 Freer Trade for Less Developed Countries

There is perhaps no clearer example of the benefits of international trade than a comparison of the less developed countries that have encouraged trade with those that do not.

In 1960, India, South Korea, and Thailand were at about the same stage of development—extreme poverty. South Korea and Thailand instituted policies that encouraged expanded international trade, both exports and imports, whereas India looked inward and emphasized the protection of domestic industries from cheaper foreign imports. The consequences have been dramatic. By 1988, South Korea's per capita income was seven times that of India; and Thailand's per capita income was four times that of India.

Because of experiences like these, many developing countries are jumping on the free-trade bandwagon. In July, 1990, Brazil dropped import bans on more than 1000 products and promised to lower tariffs from an average of 80 percent in 1990 to 20 percent by 1994. Mexico once banned many imports, required hard-to-obtain import licenses, and levied tariffs above 100 percent on some goods. With the free-trade movement in Latin countries, tariffs have been slashed so much that the average tariff in Mexico was only about 10 percent in 1991—extremely low by third-world standards. In 1991, Mexico sought a free-trade pact with the United States and Canada.

Sources: "Adding up the World Trade Talks: Fail Now, Pay Later," *New York Times,* December 16, 1990: "Texas Farmers Say They Don't Fit in to Plans with Mexico," *Houston Post,* April 8, 1991; "Free Trade Imperils a Free-Trade Zone in Brazil," *New York Times,* December 17, 1990; "In Mexico, Fears of Free-Trade Melt," *New York Times,* September 22, 1991.

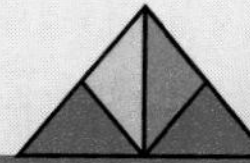

The advantages of international trade are sometimes obvious and sometimes subtle. They are obvious when trade enables a country to acquire some good that it cannot produce (such as tin or nickel or manganese in the United States) or that would have an exorbitant production cost (such as bananas, coffee, or tea in the United States). As Adam Smith pointed out:

> By means of glasses, hotbeds, and hotwalls, very good grapes can be raised in Scotland, and very good wine can be made of them at about thirty times the expense for which at least equally good can be bought from foreign countries.

The advantages of trade are subtle when a country imports goods that can be produced at home with, perhaps, the use of fewer resources than the resources used abroad for the same goods. This would be the case of producing textiles, television sets, and videocassette recorders in the United States. We can produce these things, but (to paraphrase John Stuart Mill) at a greater expense of capital and labor than the cost of the goods and services we export to pay for them.

In the real world, imports of goods from abroad displace the domestic production of competing goods, and in the process, some people may find that their income falls. Because the Ricardian model assumes only one factor of production, the model simply cannot account for changes in the distribution of income. The model does demonstrate that in a world with many factors and shifts in distribution of income, trade increases average real income. Since trade makes the average person better off, the people who are made better off could compensate those who are made worse off.

LOW-WAGE AND HIGH-WAGE COUNTRIES

U.S. hourly wages are about seven times higher than Mexican hourly wages. Japanese hourly wages are more than three times higher than Korean hourly wages. Yet the United States and Japan are two of the world's largest exporting countries; Korea and Mexico are comparatively small exporting countries. The law of comparative advantage explains how high-wage countries can compete with low-wage countries.

Table 1 assumed that America is six times as productive in food and two times as productive in clothing production as Europe. Since wages reflect productivity, American wages should be between six and two times as high as European wages. When the world terms of trade are $2F = 1C$, the price of clothing is twice that of food. In our example, the price of food could be $3 per unit and the price of clothing could be $6 per unit. If Americans specialize in food production, food is $3 per unit, and 1 unit of labor produces 6 units of food, then wages must be $18 (= $3 × 6 units) per unit of labor in America.

Europeans specialize in clothing production. Because the price of clothing is $6 per unit and 1 unit of European labor produces 1 unit of clothing, wages must be $6 (= $6 × 1 unit) per unit of labor in Europe. (Prices are measured in dollars to avoid currency differences.) Thus, with the given terms of trade, American wages are three times European wages.

Assertions that high-wage countries like the United States cannot possibly compete with low-wage countries like Taiwan or Korea are nonsense. Wages are higher in the United States because productivity is higher. Reports that people who live in low-wage countries cannot compete with high-productivity countries like the United States are also nonsense. When comparative advantage directs the allocation of resources, both high-wage and low-wage countries share in the benefits of trade. The high-productivity country's wage rate will not be high enough to completely wipe out the productivity advantage or low enough to undercut the low-productivity country's comparative advantage. Likewise, the low-productivity country's wage will neither be high enough to make it impossible to sell goods to the rich country nor low enough to undercut the rich country's comparative advantage.

Given the hypothetical case in Table 1, American wages will be somewhere between 6 and 2 times as high as European wages (depending on the terms of trade). If American money wages were 7 times higher than European money wages, American money prices would be higher than European money prices for both food and clothing because America's labor-productivity advantage could not offset such a high wage disadvantage. This situation could not persist. The demand for American labor would dry up while the demand for European labor would rise. With American wages 7 times European wages, forces would be set into operation to reduce

American wages and raise European wages until the ratio of American to European wages returned to a level between 6 and 2. With market-determined wages, all countries can compete successfully.

OTHER REASONS FOR INTERNATIONAL TRADE

Differences in comparative advantage are one reason for international trade. Two other reasons for trade are (1) decreasing costs, or economies of scale, and (2) differences in consumer preferences.

Economies of Scale

The discussion thus far assumed that food and clothing were produced under constant returns to scale. If America and Europe could produce food and clothing with the same labor costs but with **decreasing costs** as production increases (economies of scale), advantages of large-scale specialization would be gained if each product were produced by only one country.

> **Decreasing costs** are present when the cost of production per unit decreases as the number of units produced increases.

Decreasing costs play a vital role in what is called *intraindustry trade.* Many products come in different varieties, such as cars, television sets, clothing, watches, and furniture. Germany exports ultraluxury sports cars, whereas Japan has traditionally exported economy cars (but Japan is successfully invading Germany's territory). The same generic products, cars or furniture, can be both exported and imported. There is two-way trade. This intraindustry trade often involves decreasing costs: When many varieties of a good are produced, an increase in the production of any one variety spreads fixed overhead costs (such as rent, machinery, and administration) over more units. As a result, each country can specialize in a particular variety of some generic product.

Preference Differences

If our two countries had identical productivities but were subject to **increasing** (opportunity) **costs** of production, there would be no trade *unless consumer preferences in the two countries were different.*

> **Increasing costs** are present when opportunity cost per unit increases as the number of units produced increases.

If America's preference for clothing increased relative to Europe's preference for clothing in the absence of international trade, the relative price of clothing would increase in America compared to Europe. If trade were opened, America would import clothing and export food.

For example, some Asian countries can produce rice easily because they have the necessary rainfall, but some of these countries actually import rice because of the enormous importance of rice in their diets. Indonesia is a traditional rice importer and yet devotes about one third of its resources to agricultural output. The United States, which devotes less than 3 percent of its resources to agriculture, is a rice exporter. This rice trade is explained in part by preference differences.

TRADING BLOCS AND FREE TRADE

The European Community

The best example of free trade within a group of nations, called a trading bloc or a common market, is the European Community (EC). The EC formally began with the 1957 Treaty of Rome between six nations—Belgium, West Germany, France, Italy, Luxembourg, and the Netherlands. The purpose of the EC was to create a region of free trade. By 1968 all tariffs among the member states were eliminated. From 1958 to 1972 the EC's total real GDP grew at about 5 percent per year while intraEuropean trade expanded at about 13 percent per year. The success of the EC attracted more nations. Between 1972 and 1985 six more countries joined—Denmark, Ireland, Britain, Greece, Spain, and Portugal.

But from 1972 to 1985, the member states did not do nearly as well as the original six. The oil price shocks in the 1970s, a slowdown in European economic growth, and rising European unemployment reversed the trend towards integration. Member states began to impose new barriers to trade with the outside world as well as with other EC countries. The growth rate in real GDP fell by about one-half.

Europe 1992

Europeans became convinced that rising trade barriers were partially responsible for their economic ills. Thus, in 1986 the 12 nations of the European Community signed the Single European Act. In 1992, the EC member countries became a single market for goods, financial services, capital, and labor movements. This new, unified market is called Europe 1992.

Europe 1992 eliminates many types of barriers to trade. First, countries must share the same set of standards for safety and consumer protection. Second, the large differences in tax rates must be reduced. For example, in 1987 Spain had a 12 percent value-added tax, whereas Denmark has a 22 percent value-added tax. Spain must increase its rate to at least 14 percent, and Denmark must lower its rate to 20 percent at most. Third, border controls must be minimized. For example, in the past truck drivers had to show border officials up to 100 documents—invoices, forms for import statistics, and tax reports. Now truck drivers can go through customs showing only a single document.

In addition to eliminating the above barriers, Europe 1992 creates a single market for financial services. For example, a bank established in one EC country can operate a branch in another EC country, and EC firms in one country can borrow in another. EC citizens can keep bank accounts in any member nation. Thus, capital will flow freely throughout the bloc.

Fortress Europe

Many have expressed the fear that Europe 1992 will become Fortress Europe against the rest of the world by erecting more trade barriers between EC countries and non-EC countries. Will other countries find access to the huge European market—which is one-third larger than the U.S. market—cut off? About 28 percent of U.S. exports go to the EC. If Europe imposed restrictions, the U.S. terms of trade would deteriorate because the demand for its exports would be reduced. At this stage no one knows what Europe will do.

North American Free-Trade Bloc

The United States has responded to the EC by forming its own trading bloc. (See Example 2.) The United States signed a free-trade agreement with Canada in 1989 and is seeking a free-trade agreement with Mexico. The Canada–United States agreement generated little debate in the United States, but much in Canada. The proposed free-trade agreement between Mexico, the United States, and Canada has been opposed by some labor and farm groups.

Table 3 shows the dramatic difference between the EC and a North American trade bloc. By and large, the EC is a trading bloc among equals—France, West Germany, the United Kingdom, and Italy are about the same size. The United States is 10 times larger than either Canada or Mexico. This does not mean that the North American trading bloc is doomed to fail. But it does mean that gains from intra-bloc specialization should be much larger in the EC countries than in a North American trading bloc. Moreover, since Mexico and Canada are much smaller than the United States, these two countries stand to gain more than the United States because of economies of scale.

Labor groups have expressed the fear that a pact with Mexico would lower U.S. wages because Mexican wages are only about one-seventh as high. Yet, even though more international trade can lower some wages, the principle of comparative advantage tells us that average U.S. wages will rise. As a country specializes in the goods in which it has a comparative advantage, its average real income—and wages—rise, not fall. In fact, the United States is more productive than Mexico. Only lower wages enable Mexico to compete in spite of the absolute advantages of the United States. Moreover, much of the impact of freer trade with Mexico has already taken place. Beginning in 1986 Mexico unilaterally opened its markets to foreign goods. Since that time American exports to Mexico have doubled. (See Example 3.)

THE U.S. COMPARATIVE ADVANTAGE

According to Bertil Ohlin, a country tends to export those goods that intensively use the abundant productive factors with which that country is blessed. The Ohlin theory is based on the relative abundance of

EXAMPLE 2 Paths to Free Trade

The law of comparative advantage implies that free trade promises the most efficient allocation of the world's scarce economic resources. Free trade is the goal of the 108-nation General Agreement on Tariffs on Trade (GATT). Since 1948, GATT has been the world's forum of trade talks among nations. The hallmark of GATT has been the most-favored-nation principle that promises equal access for all countries to any market.

GATT negotiations have run into so many serious difficulties that it has become known as the General Agreement to Talk and Talk. First, it has been impossible to convince countries to lower impediments on the imports of agricultural goods. For example, potent farm lobbies insist that Europe and Japan protect highly inefficient agricultural industries. Second, it has been very difficult to remove barriers to trade in services such as banking, securities brokerages, and insurance. Third, the United States continues to subsidize its own farmers and protect sugar growers from more efficient foreign competition.

Regional trading blocs such as the European Community, the emerging United States–Mexico–Canada free-trade zone, and trading blocs in Asia have become substitutes for GATT. These trading blocs reduce or eliminate trade taxes or quotas on trade between bloc members. The difficulty with trading blocs is the possibility of world economic inefficiency: such blocs might shift production from lower-cost sources outside the bloc to higher-cost sources inside the bloc. This trade diversion is not only economically inefficient for the world, but it also hurts those countries most in need of export markets—third world countries with comparative advantages in textiles. For example, East Asia, not Mexico, has the lowest-cost textiles. Yet, a free-trade bloc encompassing North America could exclude textiles produced in East Asia. In the intermediate run, the bloc should still benefit the United States, Canada, and Mexico though the world may be worse off as a whole. In the long run, however, the trading bloc might backfire because the engine of the world's economic growth is Europe and Asia, not Mexico or Canada: it might be far better for the United States to continue pushing for free trade with these dynamic countries than to retreat into its own bloc.

Sources: "Blocs Replacing Free Trade," *New York Times*, August 26, 1991; "Adding Up the World Trade Talks: Fail Now, Pay Later," *New York Times*, December 16, 1990.

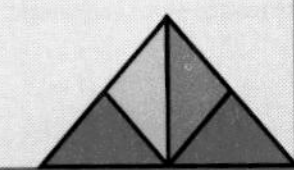

different productive factors. For instance, if a country has a large quantity of labor relative to land or capital, its wages will tend to be lower than wages in countries with abundant land or capital. Even if technical know-how were the same across countries, countries with cheap labor would have a comparative advantage in the production of labor-intensive goods. Whereas the Ricardian theory assumes only one factor and takes cost differences as given, the Ohlin theory explains comparative advantage as the consequence of differences in the relative abundance of different factors.

Compared to other countries, the United States is rich in agricultural land. This lowers the cost of agricultural goods compared to other countries. Despite protection abroad, the United States exports large quantities of goods such as wheat, soybeans, corn, cotton, and tobacco.

The United States also has an abundance of highly skilled, technical labor. The United States tends to export goods that use highly skilled labor. The United States, thus, has a comparative advantage in manufactured goods that require intensive investment in research and development (R&D); industries with relatively high R&D expenditures contribute most to American export sales. Chemicals, nonelectrical or electrical machinery, aircraft, and professional and scientific instruments are the major

TABLE 3
The European Community versus North America, 1988

Country	Real GDP (billions of U.S. dollars)	Population (millions)	Real GDP Per Capita (U.S. dollars)	Annual Growth Rates (percent)		
				1960–1973	1973–1980	1980–1988
European Community						
Belgium	115	9.9	11,500	4.8	2.4	1.2
Denmark	60	5.1	12,100	4.4	1.6	2.0
France	680	55.9	12,200	5.7	2.6	1.6
West Germany	770	61.0	12,600	4.4	2.1	1.6
Greece	60	10.0	5900	7.9	3.2	1.3
Ireland	20	3.6	6200	4.9	3.2	0.7
Italy	670	57.5	11,700	5.1	4.2	2.3
Luxembourg	5	.4	13,900	4.0	1.7	2.9
Netherlands	170	14.8	11,500	5.2	2.9	1.5
Portugal	55	10.1	5300	6.9	3.8	2.4
Spain	290	39.0	7400	7.7	1.8	2.2
United Kingdom	680	57.0	12,000	3.2	1.1	2.9
North America						
United States	4500	245.9	18,300	4.0	2.1	3.3
Canada	420	26.1	16,300	4.8	3.8	3.2
Mexico	417	83.6	5000	6.8	6.6	0.4

Figures have been rounded.

Source: Robert Summers and Alan Heston, "The Penn World Table (Mark 5): An Expanded Set of International Comparisons, 1950–1988," *Quarterly Journal of Economics* 106 (May 1991): 327–68.

R&D-intensive industries. These industries generate a trade surplus, with exports exceeding imports. The manufacturing industries that are not in this category—such as textiles, paper products or food manufactures—generate a trade deficit (a surplus of imports over exports).

The products of R&D industries tend to be new products, which are nonstandardized and not well-suited to simple, repetitive, mass-production techniques. As time passes, the production processes for these products—such as personal computers—become more standardized. The longer a given product has been on the market, the easier it is for the good to become standardized and the lesser the need for highly trained workers. When new goods become old goods, other countries can gain a comparative advantage over the United States in these goods. The United States then moves on to the next new product generated with its giant research establishment and abundant supply of engineers, scientists, and skilled labor in order to fulfill its comparative advantage. The U.S. comparative advantage in manufacturing is in new products and processes.

This chapter studied the global economy, the law of comparative advantage, the gains from trade, how high-wage countries compete with low-wage countries, regional trading blocs, and the pattern of U.S. trade. The next chapter will examine the arguments for and against free trade.

EXAMPLE 3 U.S. Trade with Mexico

After Canada and Japan, Mexico is the third largest trading partner of the United States. Mexico supplies 5 percent of U.S. imports and buys 6 percent of U.S. exports. U.S. trade with Mexico consists primarily of two-way trade in manufactured goods. In 1989, the four largest U.S. exports to Mexico were auto parts, processed food, electronic components, and electrical switchgear. Excluding oil, the four largest U.S. imports from Mexico were autos and auto parts, electrical distributing equipment, telecommunications equipment, and electrical switchgear.

About 60 percent of Mexico's manufacturing exports to the United States come from its *maquiladora* program. *Maquiladoras* are plants that are exempt from paying import duties on raw materials and parts that are used in their products.

This description of U.S. trade with Mexico suggests that a free-trade pact with Mexico will dislocate very little production within the two countries. When trade consists of two-way trade in different varieties of certain manufactured products (for example, electrical switchgear or auto parts), greater international trade is likely to result in each country producing more of fewer varieties of the same generic product. Because it is easy to switch from one type of electrical switchgear to another, little production will be dislocated.

Sources: *Economic Report of the President, 1991* (Washington, DC: Government Printing Office, 1991), chap. 7; *U.S. Foreign Trade Highlights, 1990,* U. S. Department of Commerce, 1990.

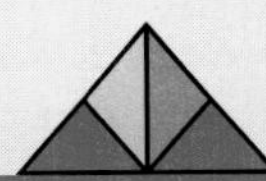

SUMMARY

1. Just as trade and specialization can increase the economic well-being of individuals, so specialization and trade between countries can increase the economic well-being of the residents of the trading countries. The basic reason for trade is that countries cannot readily transfer their endowments of productive factors to other countries. Trade in goods and services acts as a substitute for the transfer of productive resources among countries. The Swedish economist Bertil Ohlin has demonstrated that a country specializes in those goods for which its factor proportions are most suited. In 1817, David Ricardo formulated the law of comparative advantage, which demonstrates that countries export according to comparative—not absolute—advantage. Countries export those goods that they are the most efficient (or the least inefficient) at producing, compared to the rest of the world.

2. In a simple two-country, two-good world, even if one country has an absolute advantage in both goods, both countries can still gain from specialization and trade. If the two countries were denied the opportunity to trade, they would have to use domestic production to meet domestic consumption. With trade, specialization allows each to consume beyond its domestic production possibilities frontier by producing at home and then trading the product in which it has a comparative advantage. Countries will specialize in those products whose domestic opportunity costs are low relative to their opportunity costs in the other countries. Through trade, countries are able to exchange goods at more favorable terms than those dictated by domestic opportunity costs.

3. Money wages are set to reflect the average productivity of labor in each country. Higher average labor productivity is reflected in higher wages. Money wages ware not set in such a manner as to undercut each country's comparative advantage. Economies of scale and preference differences are also reasons for trade among countries.

4. Regional trading blocs abolish trade barriers among member nations. The most important blocs are the European Community and the proposed

North American free-trade pact between Canada, Mexico, and the United States.

5. The United States has an abundance of agricultural land and highly skilled, technical labor. This gives the United States a comparative advantage in agricultural goods and high-technology research and development products.

KEY TERMS

law of comparative advantage
absolute advantage
terms of trade
decreasing costs
increasing costs

QUESTIONS AND PROBLEMS

1. Adam Smith noted: "What is prudence in the conduct of every private family can scarce be folly in that of a great kingdom. If a foreign country can supply us with a commodity cheaper than we ourselves can make it, better buy it from them with some part of the produce of our own industry." Strictly speaking, a fallacy of composition is involved in Smith's famous remark. But when applied to international trade, what is true of the family is also true of the kingdom. Why is it true that the fallacy of composition does not apply?
2. Suppose that 1 unit of labor in Asia can be used to produce 10 units of food or 5 units of clothing. Also suppose that 1 unit of labor in South America can be used to produce 4 units of food or 1 unit of clothing.
   a. Which country has an absolute advantage in food? In clothing?
   b. What is the relative cost of producing food in Asia? In South America?
   c. Which country will export food? Clothing?
   d. Draw the production possibilities frontier for each country if Asia has 10 units of labor and South America has 20 units of labor.
   e. What is the range for the final terms of trade between the two countries?
   f. If the final terms of trade are 3 units of food for 1 unit of clothing, compute the wage in Asia and the wage in South America, assuming that a unit of food costs $40 and a unit of clothing costs $120.
3. What happens to the answers to parts *a*, *b*, and *c* of question 2 when the South American productivity figures are changed so that 1 unit of labor is used to produce either 40 units of food or 10 units of clothing?
4. In Congressional hearings, American producers of such goods as gloves and motorcycles claim that they are the most efficient in the world but have been injured by domestic wages that are too high compared to foreign wages. Without disputing the facts of their case, how would you evaluate their plight?

SUGGESTED READINGS

Ellsworth, P. *International Economics.* New York: Macmillan, 1938, chaps. 1–4.

Grunwald, Joseph, and Kenneth Flamm. *The Global Factory.* Washington, DC: Brookings Institution, 1985.

Kreinin, Mordecai E. *International Economics,* 5th ed. New York: Harcourt Brace Jovanovich, 1987, chaps. 11–12.

Lindert, Peter H., and Charles P. Kindleberger. *International Economics,* 7th ed. Homewood, IL: Richard D. Irwin, 1982, chaps. 1–4.

Porter, Michael. *The Competitive Advantages of Nations.* New York: The Free Press, 1989.

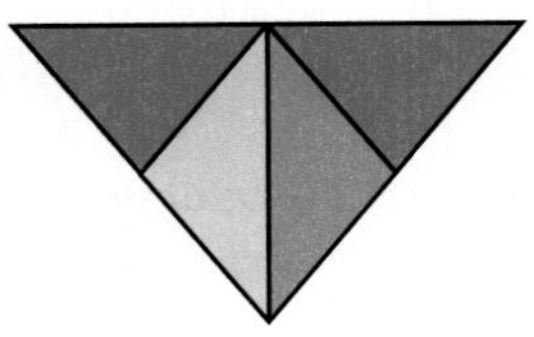

24 Protection and Free Trade

CHAPTER INSIGHT

This chapter examines the economics of trade barriers. The American dairy industry contends that imported cheese and ice cream are bad for its business. Americans love cheese and ice cream, but the government loves the dairy industry even more. It therefore limits the imports per American to a pound of dairy cheese and a spoonful of ice cream each year. The same happens in other industries. Limits on imports double the price of sugar. American peanut farmers have prevailed upon the government to limit imports to no more than seven peanuts per year per American. These are examples of trade barriers.

When a country specializes and trades according to comparative advantage, it can consume more than would be possible if it had to produce everything itself. As the last chapter showed, in the absence of trade barriers or with free trade, a country can consume above its production possibilities frontier.

Is it to the country's advantage to adopt complete free trade, or should a country impose some trade barriers between itself and the rest of the world? This chapter discusses the nature of trade barriers, the case against protection, the arguments for trade barriers, and American trade policies.

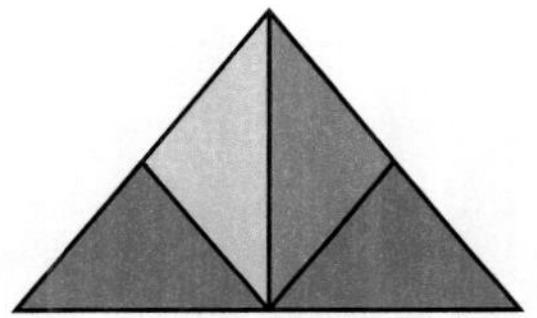

TRADE BARRIERS

Trade barriers consist of tariffs, quotas, and various technical standards and practices.

Tariffs

An import **tariff** raises the price paid by domestic consumers as well as the price received by domestic producers of similar or identical products.

> A **tariff** is a tax levied on imports.

A tariff on clothing from Taiwan will raise the prices paid by American consumers of clothing imports and the prices received by American clothing producers.

Suppose a country levies a $1 tariff on imported shoes that cost $10 in the foreign market. If domestic and foreign shoes are the same, both imported and domestically produced shoes will sell for $11 in the home market. Because consumers will pay more for shoes, the tariff discourages shoe consumption. Because the domestic producer of shoes will be able to charge more for shoes, the $1 tariff encourages domestic production and discourages shoe imports and foreign shoe production.

The same result (discouraging shoe consumption and encouraging domestic production) could be accomplished by taxing domestic consumption of shoes by $1 and giving every domestic firm a $1 subsidy per pair of shoes produced.

Import Quotas

An **import quota** sets the number of units of a particular product that can be imported into the country during a specified period of time. For example, U.S. import quotas on steel might specify the number of tons of a specified grade that can be imported into the United States in a particular year.

> An **import quota** is a quantitative limitation on the amount of imports of a specific product during a given period.

Generally speaking, importers of products that fall under quota restrictions must obtain a license to import the good. When the number of licenses issued is limited to the number specified by the quota, the quantity of imports cannot exceed the maximum quota limit.

Import licenses can be distributed in a variety of ways. One option is for import licenses to be auctioned off by the government in a free and fair market. If import licenses are scarce (more importers want licenses than are available), they will sell for a price that reflects their scarcity. In such a case, an import license is similar to a tariff: It restricts imports and raises revenue for the government.

Import licenses may also be handed out on a first-come-first-served basis, on the basis of favoritism, or according to the amount of past imports by the importer. When import quotas are not auctioned off, the potential revenue that the government could collect goes to the lucky few importers who get the scarce import licenses. For this reason, some importers, especially those who are likely to obtain import licenses, prefer import quotas to tariffs. Instead of the government collecting the revenue, the importers can cash in on the scarcity value of the import licenses. The license permits them to buy a product cheaply in the world market and then to sell it at a handsome profit in the home market. For example, as indicated earlier, the U.S. sugar quota keeps domestic sugar prices at almost twice the level of world sugar prices. The importers collect the difference! American consumers pay higher prices, and the government gains no revenues.

Voluntary Export Restraints

A **voluntary export restraint** is a popular trade barrier in use by the United States.

> A **voluntary export restraint** is an agreement between two governments in which the exporting country voluntarily limits the export of a certain product to the importing country.

The U.S. government has negotiated a number of voluntary export restraints with foreign governments that limit the foreign country's volume of commodity exports to the U.S. market. Unlike tariffs or import quotas, voluntary export restraints generate no revenue for the importing country or its

EXAMPLE 1 The Impact of Tariffs and Quotas on Prices

Tariffs are inefficient because they subsidize domestic production and raise prices to consumers. The Institute of International Economics has made a study of the impact of tariffs and quotas on particular industries. The following table compares the free-market price of selected products to the price with trade restraints. Blue jeans cost $18 with trade restraints instead of $14.50; rubber boots cost $12 instead of $10; cars cost $10,000 instead of $7500; a box of candy costs $5 instead of $2; and a leather purse costs $44 instead of $40.

Item	1985 Free-market Price	1985 Price with Trade Restraints
Blue jeans	$14.50	$18
Rubber boots	10	12
Vinyl purse	10	12
Leather purse	40	44
Box of candy	2	5
Automobile	7500	10,000

Sources: Gary Clyde Hufbauer, Diane T. Berliner, and Kimberly Ann Elliot, *Trade Protection in the United States: 31 Case Studies* (Washington, DC: Institute for International Economics, 1986); Clyde Farnsworth, "Trying to Shield Injured American Industries," *New York Times*, January 18, 1987.

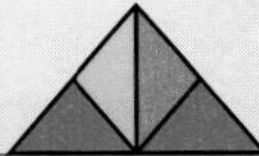

government. Instead, the foreign exporter or the foreign government collects the scarcity value of the right to export to the huge American market.

Voluntary export restrictions are particularly widespread in textiles. An agreement among 50 countries restricts trade in textiles. The importing country induces the exporting country to impose export quotas under the threat of tariffs or import quotas. Under these quota agreements, not all those who wish to export textiles to the United States can do so. First, they must acquire scarce export licenses. The privilege to export textiles to the United States is a property right that can be bought and sold in several Asian countries. The voluntary export quotas imposed by Japan on automobile exports to the United States is another example. Under the U.S. threat of an import quota, the Japanese government ordered its auto companies to voluntarily limit exports to the United States to about 1.8 million units a year from 1981 to 1985.[1] A Brookings Institution study concluded that the Japanese-American curb boosted the average car prices by about $2500. (See Example 1.)

Over the last decade, animal feeds, brooms, color TV sets, cattle, cotton, crude petroleum, dairy products, fish, meat, peanuts, potatoes, sugar, candy, textiles, stainless-steel flatware, steel, wheat and wheat flour, and automobiles have been subjected to import quotas or voluntary export quotas. According to C. Fred Bergsten, a Washington-based trade expert, "The U.S. now has an array of quotas and 'voluntary' export restraints that have an even greater price effect than tariffs.[2]

Like import tariffs, import quotas and voluntary export restraints limit the quantity of foreign goods available in the domestic market. Such nontariff barriers raise the price paid by domestic consumers and the price that can be charged by domestic producers on their import-competing products. Domestic producers benefit from quotas by being able to charge higher prices. The gains go to the importer who receives a license to buy cheap imports: or, if licenses are auctioned, the gains go to the government in the form of revenue. The loser is the consumer, who pays higher prices because such quotas exist.

[1]Keith Maskus, "Rising Protectionism and U.S. International Trade Policy," Federal Reserve Bank of Kansas City, *Economic Review* (July/August 1984): 9.

[2]C. Fred Bergsten, *The Cost of Import Restrictions to American Consumer* (New York: American Importers Association, 1972).

Other Nontariff Barriers

The importance of nontariff barriers in world trade has grown in the last decade. It has been estimated that nearly 50 percent of world trade is conducted under some sort of nontariff barrier. Import and voluntary export quotas are not the only nontariff barriers. Three other major impediments to trade are government procurement practices, technical standards, and domestic content rules. Governments tend to give preferential treatment to domestic producers when they purchase goods and services. Further, the free flow of products can be impeded by technical standards that imported products must meet. For example, imported cars must pass American pollution control and safety standards; imported foods and drugs must meet U.S. food and drug standards. European countries ban American beef treated with growth-inducing hormones. (See Example 2). Recent talks among the major trading nations indicate a desire to limit such nontariff barriers, but no agreements have been forthcoming on limiting import quotas or voluntary export restraints.

Tariffs and nontariff barriers raise costs to consumers and protect the domestic producers of import-competing products. The following discussion of the economics of protection focuses on tariffs, but also applies to quotas and nontariff barriers.

THE CASE AGAINST PROTECTION

According to one study, 94 percent of economists agree that tariffs and quotas lower real income. Probably no other issue in economics commands so much

EXAMPLE 2 Measuring the Costs of Protection

The accompanying table shows the annual cost to consumers for each job protected in a few selected industries and draws on studies by M. Morkre, D. Tarr, M. Weidenbaum, M. Munger, R. Crandall, and Wharton Econometrics. Trade barriers protect jobs in particular industries at the cost of higher prices for consumers. What is the ratio of annual costs to benefits? The table shows that the ratio of cost to benefits ranges from 10 for citizen's band transceivers to 3.5 for carbonized steel. In other words, the trade barrier for citizen's band transceivers costs consumers $85,539 for each $8500 in earnings saved! The trade barrier for carbonized steel costs consumers $85,272 for each $24,329 in earnings saved. Thus, the hidden costs of protection far exceed the visible benefits.

Source: Keith E. Maskus, "Rising Protectionism and U.S. International Trade Policy," Federal Reserve Bank of Kansas City, *Economic Review* (July/August 1984): 3–17.

Product and Restriction	Number of Jobs Protected	Average Earnings	Cost per Job	Ratio of Cost to Earnings
Citizen's band transceivers (tariffs, 1978–81)	587	$ 8,500	$85,539	10.1
Apparel (tariffs, 1977–81)	116,188	6,669	45,549	6.8
Footwear* (tariffs and quotas, 1977)	21,000	8,340	77,714	9.3
Carbon steel* (tariffs and quotas, 1977)	20,000	24,329	85,272	3.5
Autos* (proposed local content law, 1986–91)	58,000	23,566	85,400	3.6

*In 1980 dollars.

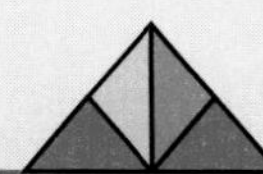

support among economists,[3] whose enthusiasm for free trade has remained steadfast for more than 210 years.

The Costs of Protection

According to the law of comparative advantage, specialization benefits the country as a whole, while tariffs or quotas eliminate or reduce those gains from specialization. The argument for free trade presented thus far has rested on the rather simple Ricardian model of the last chapter, which, for simplicity, ruled out the existence of different types of land, labor, and capital. In the real world, when trade opens, some people are hurt. The import of Japanese cars keeps domestic car prices lower and car buyers happy but certainly hurts domestic auto producers, their suppliers, and auto workers. The export of American wheat keeps domestic prices of bread higher but makes wheat farmers happy. The law of comparative advantage, however, guarantees that the *net* advantages are on the side of trade rather than protection.

Figure 1 shows why consumers benefit from lower prices. If the price of a video game is $36, the demand curve in Figure 1 shows that 6000 games are demanded. If the price of the game were to fall to $24, about 9000 games would be demanded. The gain to consumers of the lower price is the area $G+H$. The people who would have bought 6000 units at $36 have to pay only $24 and therefore save $12 per unit. Their gain is $12 × 6000, or $72,000 (area G). When the price is $24, new customers come into the market who buy 3000 additional video games. The average new customer would have been willing to pay $30 (the average of $36 and $24). Since new customers are paying only $24 per game, their gain is $6 × 3000 or $18,000 (area H). Thus, if the price falls from $36 to $24 per game, consumers gain $G + H$. Conversely, if the price rises above $24 to $36, consumers lose $G + H$.

Whereas the demand curve in Figure 1 showed how consumers benefit from lower prices, the supply curve in Figure 2 shows how producers benefit from higher prices. If the price of a ton of coal is $140, 9 million tons of coal will be supplied. If the price of coal is $200, 12 million tons will be supplied.

[3]Richard Alston, Michael B. Vaughn, and J. R. Kearl, "Is There a Consensus Among Economists in the 1990s?" *American Economic Review* 82 (May 1992).

FIGURE 1
Consumer Benefits from Lower Prices

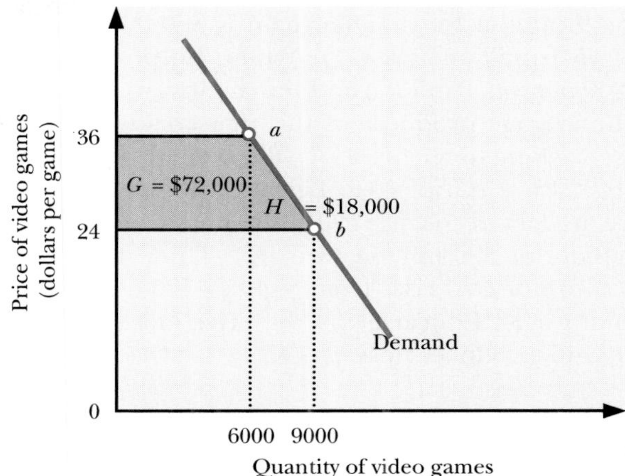

When the price falls from $36 to $24 per video game, consumers benefit by the area $G + H$. Those who would buy 6000 units at $36 (point a) benefit by area G because they save $12 per unit. Those new customers who buy the 3000 additional units when the price is $24 (point b) benefit by area H.

FIGURE 2
Producer Benefits from Higher Prices

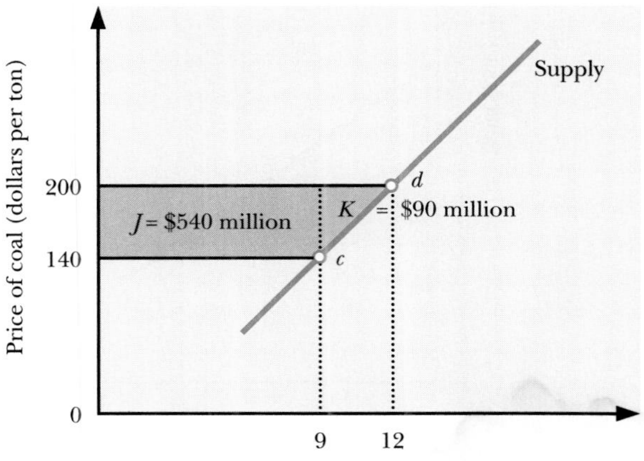

When the price rises from $140 to $200, producers benefit by the area $J + K$. Those who would sell 9 million tons at $140 per ton (point c) benefit by area J. Those new suppliers who sell 3 million additional tons when the price is $200 per ton (point d) benefit by area K.

The gain to producers from raising the price from \$140 to \$200 is the area $J + K$. Coal producers who would have supplied 9 million tons at a price of \$140, receive \$200 per ton (a \$60 gain on each of the 9 million tons). Their gain is \$60 × 9 million, or \$540 million (area J). When the price rises to \$200 per ton, 3 million additional tons are produced. The average producer of this new coal would have been willing to receive \$170 (the average of \$200 and \$140) for a ton of coal. Because the new suppliers are in fact receiving \$200, their gain is \$30 × 3 million, or \$90 million (area K). Thus, if the price of a ton of coal rises from \$140 to \$200, producers gain $J + K$. Conversely, if the price falls from \$200 to \$140, producers lose $J + K$.

A Prohibitive Tariff. The costs of protection are easiest to understand by examining the effects of a **prohibitive tariff** (as opposed to a **nonprohibitive tariff**).

> A **prohibitive tariff** is a tariff that is high enough to cut off all imports of the product.
>
> A **nonprohibitive tariff** is a tariff that does not wipe out all imports of the product.

Panel *a* of Figure 3 shows the hypothetical demand-and-supply situation in America for shirts; panel *b* shows the hypothetical demand-and-supply situation in Europe for shirts. For each "country," the supply curve shows the quantity of shirts supplied by domestic producers at each price, and the demand curve shows the quantity demanded by domestic consumers at each price. For simplicity, we will assume that American and European shirts are the same and that the European currency is the pound, where \$2 equals £1. For simplicity, we will also assume that Europe and America are the only countries in the world economy.

FIGURE 3
The Costs of a Prohibitive Tariff

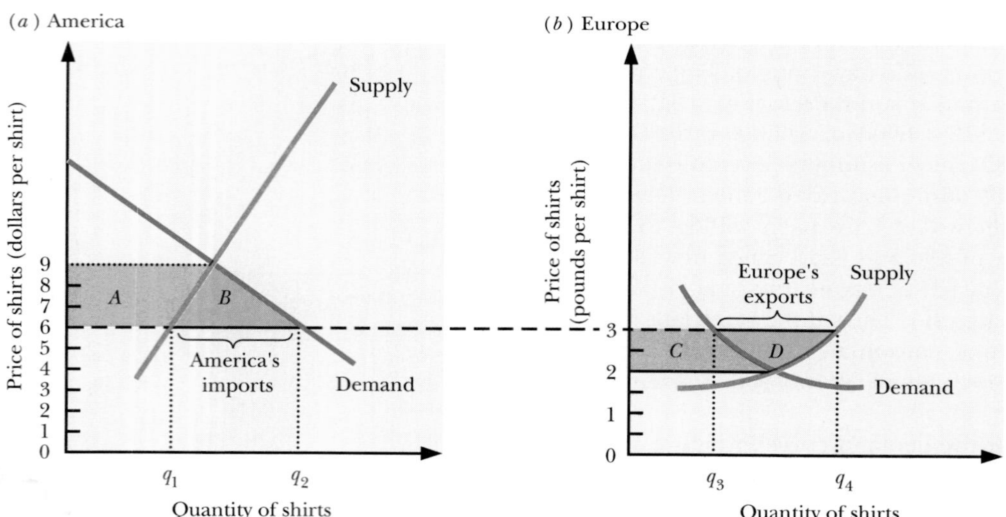

With a prohibitive tariff, the prices paid in each country are determined by the supply and demand curves in each country. To compare prices, we assume that \$2 = £1. If there were no tariff, prices would be the same in the two countries. The prohibitive tariff in America raises the price in America from \$6 to \$9. Consumers lose area $A + B$, but production gain area A. The net loss to America is area B. In Europe, prices fall from £3 to £2; and producers lose area $C + D$ while consumers gain area C. The gain to consumers is less than the loss to producers. The net loss to Europe is area D.

Using these simple assumptions, we can determine the gains from trade in shirts. With free trade, the price of shirts would be the same in America and Europe. If prices were different, importers would buy in the cheap market and sell in the expensive market until prices equalized. In our example, the price in America under free-trade conditions would be \$6 (in Europe £3.) America would be importing shirts from Europe. America's excess of consumption over production (imports) would just match Europe's excess of production over consumption (exports).

Suppose America imposed a prohibitive tariff high enough to cut off all shirt imports. With no trade, the prices in the two countries would diverge; they would be determined exclusively by domestic supply-and-demand conditions. Europe's price of shirts would be £2 (or the equivalent of \$4), and America's price would be \$9 (or the equivalent of £4.5).

Without trade, the difference between American and European shirt prices is \$5. Thus, if America imposed a tariff exceeding \$5, the incentive to trade would be wiped out because imported shirts would cost more than the domestic price (\$4 plus the tariff of more than \$5).

As demonstrated earlier, the increase in price from \$6 (with trade) to \$9 (with a prohibitive tariff) would result in consumers losing the shaded areas $A + B$. America's shirt consumers lose but American producers gain as a consequence of higher prices. The producers of shirts in America would gain area A. In panel *a* of Figure 3, the cost of tariff protection to consumers $(A + B)$ exceeds the gains to producers (A). The net cost of tariff protection to the whole American economy is area B.

Europe also loses from a prohibitive tariff, as shown in panel *b*. With free trade, Europe's price of shirts is £3 (or \$6). A prohibitive tariff eliminates exports, and the European price must equate domestic supply with domestic demand. If Europe cannot export shirts, the price of its shirts must be £2. The prohibitive American tariff hurts European shirt producers by the area $C + D$ but benefits European shirt consumers by area C. The gain to consumers (C) is less than the loss to producers $(C + D)$. Thus, Europe suffers a net loss of area D.

A Nonprohibitive Tariff. Unlike prohibitive tariffs, nonprohibitive tariffs do not eliminate imports entirely. Figure 4 shows the supply-and-demand conditions in a country whose imports of a particular

FIGURE 4
The Effects of a Nonprohibitive Tariff

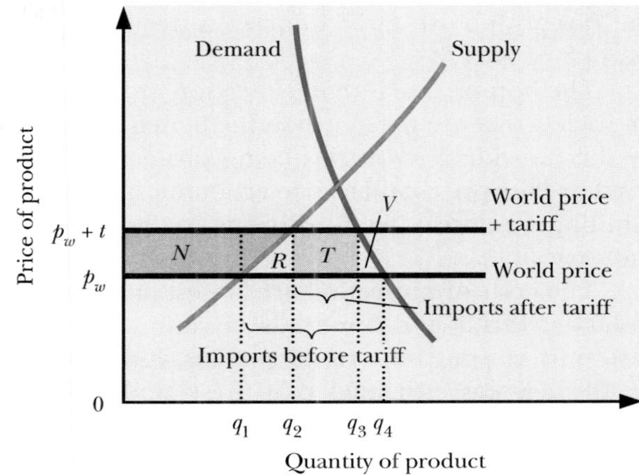

Before the nonprohibitive tariff, the price of the product is p_w. The tariff raises the price to $p_w + t$—that is, the world price plus the amount of the duty. Consumers lose area $N + R + T + V$. Producers gain area N. The government gains the tariff revenue of area T, which equals the tariff per unit times the quantity of imports. The net loss is area $R + V$. The tariff lowers imports from $(q_4 - q_1)$ to $(q_3 - q_2)$.

good are so small relative to the world supply that the world price (p_w) is taken as given. The amount imported by this country will not affect the world price.[4]

With a zero tariff, consumers can purchase all they want at the prevailing world price, p_w. According to Figure 4, the quantity represented by the distance between q_1 and q_4 would be imported because it constitutes the difference between the quantity demanded at p_w, and the quantity supplied by domestic producers.

When a tariff (t) is imposed, the price rises to $p_w + t$; the new domestic price equals the world price plus the tariff rate. The country now imports only that quantity represented by the distance between q_2 and q_3.

The tariff benefits domestic producers by the area N. The government (or public) benefits by area T—which equals the revenue from the tariff (the

[4]Note that this assumption is not satisfied in Figure 3: There are only two countries, and the number of shirts imported by America affects the world price of shirts.

tariff rate times the quantity of imports). The loss to consumers from the increase in price is the sum of areas $N + R + T + V$. If the gains (area $N + T$) are subtracted from the losses (area $N + R + T + V$), the nonprohibitive tariff imposes a net loss to the country of area $R + V$.

The bottom line is that protection imposes costs on society that are greater than the benefits received by the individual industries being protected. Trade barriers raise prices and lead to economic inefficiency (shifting resources from efficient to less efficient industries).

The costs of protection are largest in the textile industry. Tariffs and hundreds of voluntary export restraints restrict imports of textiles and clothing. In 1987, it was estimated that these trade barriers cost American consumers about $11 billion while benefiting textile producers by only about $4 billion. Thus, the net cost to the American economy was $8 billion just for the textile industry.

Import restrictions on other products also impose more costs on consumers than they bestow on the producers they protect. Example 2 shows estimates of the annual costs to consumers per job protected by different trade barriers. In general, the cost per job is more than twice as much as the average earnings in that job. In other words, if trade barriers save a $20,000-a-year job, that job costs the rest of the community more than $40,000.

Such losses may be an underestimate, according to economists Gordon Tullock and Anne Krueger. Tullock and Krueger argue that because producers have an incentive to expend resources to get the tariff passed, the import-competing industry may form a committee, lobby Congress, or advertise the plight of its industry. When the color TV industry was hurt by imports, the industry formed COMPACT (the Committee to Preserve American Color Television). Such expenditures reduce gains to protected producers and thus further increase the costs of protection.

Exports Pay for Imports

A country imports goods, services, and securities. It does not pay for these imports by sending money abroad but by exporting goods, services, and securities. A security is basically a piece of paper promising future payments. The difference between exporting a good and exporting a security is that a security represents giving up future income or command over future goods. The difference between importing a good and importing a security is that the security represents future imports of goods. Exports of all things subtract from domestic consumption (present or future); imports of all things add to domestic consumption (present or future). The gains from trade consist of imported goods that can be gained more cheaply by importing them than by producing them at home.

The preceding chapter described a simple, hypothetical world where America trades only with Europe and simply ships food in return for clothing. In this case, American exports of food are paying for clothing imports from Europe. The more food America exports, the more clothing imports are brought in, and vice versa. The reason exports of goods and services must pay for imports of good and services is that, in the long run, countries want each other's goods, not each other's money. The next chapter describes how a surplus of imports over exports must be financed by foreign investment in domestic industries.

If the United States, or any country, restricts imports, it necessarily restricts exports. In other words, subsidizing import-competing industries by means of tariff or nontariff barriers penalizes a host of unseen export industries. Imports can be more visible than exports.[5]

If tariffs impose a cost on the community, why do they exist? Why would a representative democracy, which is supposed to represent consumer interests, establish trade barriers?

The main explanation for tariffs is that the costs imposed by a tariff are highly diffused among millions of people, while the (smaller) benefits are concentrated among specific sectors of the economy associated with the protected industry. The costs imposed on the community are large in total but so small per person that it is not worth the trouble to any one person to join a committee to fight tariffs on each imported good, while the benefits to protected sectors are well worth the costs of lobbying. For example, assume people devote about 0.5 percent of all consumption to sugar (in all its forms). A trade

[5]One of the authors was once on a flight to Europe to sell his services to a foreign university for a short time (exporting). Sitting next to him was an engineer off to Europe to sell his engineering talents. Even the Boeing 747 was an export to the foreign airline. The engineer fretted that the United States "can't export anything and imports too much." The author decided it was better to have a pleasant trip than win a debating point!

barrier that raises the price of sugar by 50 percent helps domestic sugar producers enormously, but it raises the cost of living by only 0.25 percent (50 percent of 0.5 percent). To the consumer, this cost is too small to worry about. The costs of assembling a fighting coalition against each request for protection are prohibitive.

The people with an incentive to lobby Congress heavily would be the foreign competitors of the domestic import-competing industry seeking protection. But these foreign competitors have comparatively little political clout in the United States.

PROTECTIONIST ARGUMENTS

Preventing Unfair Foreign Competition

The economy gains from foreign trade because it can obtain goods more cheaply from abroad than from domestic sources. The domestic producers of goods that are close or perfect substitutes for these imports try to convince their governments, and others, that such competition is unfair. This argument takes many forms and is probably the most widely used protectionist argument.

Low Foreign Wages. According to the theory of comparative advantage, high-wage countries can export to or compete effectively against low-wage countries in those industries in which their productivity advantage more than offsets their wage disadvantage. Likewise, low-wage countries can export to or compete effectively against high-productivity countries in those industries in which their wage advantage more than offsets their productivity disadvantage (see the preceding chapter). In the high-wage country, the industries that can export are those in which the country has a comparative advantage; the industries that cannot compete, because of their low-productivity advantage, are those in which the country has a comparative disadvantage. Every country has some industries in which it has a comparative advantage and others in which it has a comparative disadvantage. If one country could undercut every other country in every good, its wages (relative to the rest of the world) would be bid up until it would begin to import.

In the more developed countries, the industries that cannot compete complain that they are subjected to unfair competition because of the low wages abroad. Some years ago, during a House committee hearing, Representative Noah Mason observed:

> We have just listened to the American Knit Handwear Association and the America Seafood Association and the Harley-Davidson Motorcycle Co. representative, and all three state that they represent an industry that is most efficient in the world, as compared to the industries abroad. But they all three stated that they are being injured because of imports from abroad . . . because . . . of low wages there, high wages here.
>
> If our people are to compete against the people of the other countries then we have got to cut our wages in half.

To some business managers and politicians, it seems unfair to be more efficient in productivity yet unable to compete because wages are too high. If this view were sound, it would be necessary to erect trade barriers so that all the industries in which the United States had a comparative disadvantage could supply the home market. The erection of such barriers, however, would destroy U.S. export trade and severely lower the real income of the American people. One could argue that it is unfair to erect trade barriers that would raise the incomes of those hurt by import competition but would lower the incomes of the rest of the community even more. This trade-off is a key element of the theory of comparative advantage. As observed by American economist Frank W. Taussig (1859–1940), the reason that we continue to import goods (such as textiles) for which we have an absolute advantage compared with the rest of the world is that such industries "cannot meet the pace set by those in which the labor of the country, is *more* productively applied."

Dumping. Another version of the complaint that foreign competition is unfair alleges that foreign goods are "dumped" on the home market at less than the foreign cost.

The **dumping** complaint is even enshrined in law. The U.S. Tariff Act of 1930, as amended by the Trade Agreements Act of 1979, provides for special antidumping duties to be imposed when foreign goods are sold in the home market for less than the price they would fetch in the foreign market. The original Anti-Dumping Law was passed in 1921. (See Example 3.)

EXAMPLE 3 The U.S. Antidumping Law

In a global economy, antidumping laws are often inconsistent and give rise to a great deal of costly legal manueuvering as one company files suit against another. The examples are striking.

Smith-Corona typewriters (52 percent American-owned; 48 percent British-owned) had traditionally been produced in the United States. Recently, Smith-Corona located half of its assembly operations in Singapore and Indonesia. Its products compete with Brother typewriters, a Japanese company.

Historically, Smith-Corona has asked for and received antidumping duties against Brother. To escape these duties, Brother moved the final assembly of its typewriters to its Tennessee factory. However, the parts and design still come from Japan or Japanese-owned plants in Asia. After Smith-Corona moved some of its typewriter assembly to Singapore, Brother turned the tables and filed an antidumping complaint against Smith-Corona! The suit was dismissed by the International Trade Commission.

Global production causes other anomalies. Chrysler filed a formal complaint that Japan was dumping its minivans into the United States. But Chrysler has a kind of station wagon—the Colt Vista or Eagle Summit—that is produced by Japan's Mitsubishi. Is this a station wagon or a minivan? Chrysler attempted to have the federal definition of a minivan changed so that its imported product could be designated a station wagon. If it does not succeed, Chrysler is filing suit against itself!

Source: "Fair-Trade Case Has Twist: Japanese Charge U.S. Rival," *New York Times*, August 12, 1991.

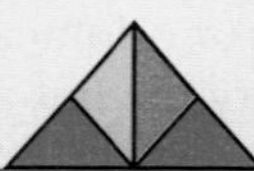

Dumping occurs when a country sells a good in another country for less than the price charged in the home country.

Public attitudes toward dumping are peculiar. As Charles P. Kindleberger has pointed out, most people appear to have a subconscious producer's bias, which leads them to applaud antidumping actions. When dumping occurs, however, domestic consumers are buying goods more cheaply than foreign consumers. The beneficiaries are the domestic consumers, and the losers are the domestic firms competing with the dumped products. The theory of comparative advantage points out that the advantage of foreign trade is that a country (as a whole) is made better off if it can obtain goods more cheaply abroad than at home: The cheaper the foreign goods, the greater the consumer benefit.

International-trade economists are suspicious of antidumping laws. The case against these laws has been made by Charles Kindleberger:

> Countervailing measures against alleged dumping are obnoxious because they reduce the flexibility and elasticity of international markets and reduce the potential gain from trade. From 1846 to 1913, when Britain followed a free-trade policy, distress goods in any part of the world could be disposed of in London . . . to the benefit of the British consumer and the overseas producer. With antidumping tariffs everywhere, adjustment after miscalculations which result in overproduction is much less readily effected.[6]

The only time antidumping duties might be appropriate is in the case of predatory dumping, where the foreign firm monopolizes the domestic market by temporarily lowering prices and then raising them to an even higher level after the domestic competitors have been driven out of business. However, predatory dumping may be difficult to prove. The costs of screening the valid claims from the frivolous ones may exceed any potential gains.

[6]Charles P. Kindleberger, *International Economics*, 5th ed. (Homewood, IL: Richard D. Irwin, 1973), 156.

Foreign-Export Subsidies. One of the most important arguments for protection in today's world is similar to the dumping complaint, but the "dumping" is caused by the actions of a foreign government rather than the actions of a foreign firm. Business managers who must compete against foreign imports argue that if a foreign government provides export subsidies to their exporters, domestic firms face unfair competition. This argument, like the dumping argument, is supported by the U.S. **countervailing duty.**

> **A countervailing duty** is a duty imposed on imports subsidized by the governments of the exporting country.

When a foreign government subsidizes exports to, say, the United States, the ultimate beneficiaries are the American people. The losers are the residents of the foreign country and the special interests in the United States that produce domestic import substitutes. Textiles from Argentina, radial tires from Canada, sugar from the European Community, molasses from France, tomato products from Greece, refrigerators from Italy, and chains from Spain are examples of goods exported to the United States that have received government subsidies. Even the United States, which has a solid comparative advantage in commercial aircraft, subsidizes the export of aircraft through below-market loans to the Boeing Company and McDonnell Douglas Corporation.

Those who desire protection from subsidized foreign exports have a powerful political argument, but there is no economic argument for countervailing duties. The benefit of foreign trade is imports; the opportunity cost of foreign trade is exports. Protectionists reason that exports are good and imports are bad. This reasoning is true for the businesses that must compete with foreign imports but not for the economy as a whole. Foreign-export subsidies are a gift to the American people. To offset this gift by imposing countervailing duties is a perverse policy—like the dog biting the hand that feeds it.

Protecting Infant Industries

Alexander Hamilton, the first U.S. Secretary of the Treasury, argued that the "infant" or new industries of newly developing economies need protection in their initial stages. This Hamiltonian argument is repeated today by many economists and politicians interested in accelerating the economic development of nonindustrialized countries. There are two versions of the infant-industry argument. One version is difficult to defend in terms of economic theory; the other makes more sense.

The most common infant-industry argument amounts to a disguised brand of simple protectionism. It is argued that in many industries, economies of scale are present and that an initial stage of learning by doing is necessary to make the plant competitive on an international basis. A small, new plant must face higher costs than its foreign rivals, who are larger and have been in the business a long time. Hence, some argue that it is necessary to protect new industries until they can stand on their own feet.

This argument ignores the fact that in virtually every business enterprise, the first few years of activity are characterized by losses. Until businesses become known externally, until a competent staff is acquired, and until early production difficulties are overcome, it is difficult to make a profit. Most successful businesses are characterized by losses in the first few years and profits thereafter. It is not unusual to wait 5 or 10 years or even more for a business venture to pay off. Capital markets allow business firms to borrow the funds from lenders or venture capitalists to finance their investments. If these investments paid profits from the beginning, it would not be necessary to borrow.

To argue that the government must protect an industry from foreign competition implies that the private market has failed to see the profit opportunities in the infant industry. Given the way information is distributed in this world, the argument is highly improbable. Information is costly to acquire. Those who are most likely to have information are those who would benefit the most from it. Thus, it is very unlikely that a government bureaucracy or a House committee would have more valuable information about the future course of profits in an industry than would potential investors.

Economists Leland Yeager and David Tuerck have found that, historically, new industries do not need protection:

> Manufacture of iron, hats, and other goods got a foothold in Colonial America despite British attempts at suppression. Manufacture of textiles, shoes, steel, machine tools, airplanes,

and countless other goods has arisen and flourished in the American West and South despite competition under internal free trade with the established industries of the Northeast.[7]

Another version of the infant-industry argument is that a particular industry may yield external benefits to the rest of the community for a certain period of time. These benefits cannot be captured by the initial investors and thus will not be included in private profitability calculations. A new firm might have to adapt from foreign to local conditions. The knowledge it acquires about new technology would not be patentable, and later users could take full advantage of their experience. The knowledge acquired by the one firm could be used by all; hence, public action in the form of protection may be called for to promote this activity.

Robert Baldwin of the University of Wisconsin has pointed out that even this reason for supporting an infant industry does not justify import duties. Baldwin argues that even if external benefits are present, a tariff does not guarantee that the most desirable type of knowledge-acquisition expenditures will be made. It may be better to subsidize firms who make the initial contacts or first acquire the knowledge to use new technology.

Tariffs are also a poor device for subsidizing an industry because they raise costs to consumers. Hence, if it is desirable to stimulate some industries, a direct subsidy that can be easily measured and does not lead to higher costs to consumers would be preferable.

Economists, however, do not adamantly oppose temporary protection of infant industries in selected circumstances where it is apparent that a country has a long-run comparative advantage.

Keeping Money in the Country

Some protectionist arguments are grossly false. The first is attributed (perhaps incorrectly) to Abraham Lincoln: "I don't know much about the tariff. But I do know that when I buy a coat from England, I have the coat and England has the money. But when I buy a coat from America, I have the coat and America has the money."

While this argument may be appealing at first glance, it contains an error in logic. It supposes that money is somehow more valuable than goods. This *mercantilist fallacy* was committed by the mercantilist writers of the seventeenth and eighteenth centuries who feared that unrestricted trade would lead to the loss of gold. Writers such as David Hume and Adam Smith pointed out that this argument confuses ends with means. The end of economic activity is consumption: Money is only a means to that end. When England sells an American a coat, the money is eventually used to buy, say, American wheat. The cost is the wheat, not the money.[8]

Saving Domestic Jobs

Another false protectionist argument is that imports deprive Americans of jobs: "The American market is the greatest in the world, and necessarily it should be reserved for American producers . . . ," we hear from a 1952 Senate speech. An American senator once explained the mysterious mechanism by which foreign imports cause unemployment:

> The importation of . . . foreign beef is not a stimulant to our economy. For foreign producers do not employ American labor; they do not buy our feed grain and fertilizers; they do not use our slaughterhouses; they do not use our truckers; they do not invest in or borrow from our banks; they do not buy our insurance; they do very little to stimulate the national economy.[9]

As already demonstrated, if each country specializes according to its comparative advantage, every country has more real GDP. The presumption the senator makes is that when a job is lost through import competition, a job is lost forever to the economy—which is simply untrue.

In the long run, a country must export in order to import. Even in the short run, the exports of

[7]Leland B. Yeager and David G. Tuerck, *Trade Policy and the Price System* (Scranton, PA: International Textbook Company, 1966). This excellent book contains almost all the arguments pro and con for free trade but is strongly opposed to protection.

[8]Under the existing international monetary system, trade imbalances do not even lead to the loss of money (currency) to other countries. The "prices" of foreign currencies are set in foreign-exchange markets, where the supply and demand for each currency are equated. A foreign currency is demanded to pay for goods purchased from the foreign country. No actual money crosses foreign borders. Transactions in each country must be carried out in that country's currency, not in the currency of another country.

[9]The quotations in this section from Yeager and Tuerck, *Trade Policy and the Price System.*

goods, services, and securities must equal the imports of goods, services, and securities. Jobs destroyed by competition from imports are eventually restored by increased exports or increased investment. Foreign trade increases economic efficiency. In the long run, import barriers simply make it costlier to purchase the goods and services. The enormous efficiency changes over the last century did not result in permanent unemployment but rather in a higher standard of living for all. Trade, according to comparative advantage, raises economic efficiency. A country would not benefit by forgoing long-term efficiency gains for short-term reductions in unemployment. Even if there is a trade deficit (imports greater than exports), greater unemployment is not the result.

NONPROTECTIONIST ARGUMENTS FOR TARIFFS

Protectionists argue that tariffs should be used to benefit certain special interests (at the public expense). Four arguments for tariffs are not protectionist in nature.

The National-Defense Argument

One nonprotectionist argument for tariffs states that an industry essential to the national defense should be subsidized to encourage it to produce at a prudent level for the public safety. Although this argument does make some sense, it is not entirely applicable to the United States. A look at the comparative advantage of the United States reveals that the manufacturing industries in which this country excels—chemicals, machinery, transportation equipment, aircraft—are the same ones that would be important in times of war. Significant exceptions to this, perhaps, are shipbuilding (which the United States does subsidize), semiconductors, and steel.

In some cases, protection even appears contrary to defense interests. Consider oil imports. The United States protected domestic oil by a tariff from the 1950s to the early 1970s. One could argue that it would be better to import foreign oil, save domestic oil reserves, and follow a policy of stockpiling imported oil in the case of war. The U.S. policy, instead, used up American oil.

Many industries that have little to do with national defense have used the national-defense argument as a rationale for protection. These industries are, to name but a few, gloves, pens, pottery, peanuts, paper, candles, thumbtacks, pencils, lacemaking, tuna fishing, and even clothespins.

If an industry is deemed essential for the national defense, the domestic-production subsidy would be a better way to obtain more peacetime production by that industry. Such subsidies could be handed out by the Department of Defense, where the experts on defense presumably reside. As noted, a tariff has the same effect as the combination of a production subsidy and a consumption tax. A direct subsidy is almost always better than a tariff because the tariff also raises the cost of living of consumers.

The Foreigner-Will-Pay Argument

International economists have long recognized that it is logically possible for a country to raise tariffs and so shift the terms of trade to raise the country's real income. If a country imports widgets under free trade at a price of $10 a widget and this country is a major importer of widgets, the less the country imports, the lower is the world price. In an extreme case, a $1 tariff might drive down the world price of widgets from $10 to $9. The country's consumers would still pay a $10 price for widgets, but the country could then import them for $9 and fill the national treasury with the tariff revenues, benefiting the entire country.

A famous turn-of-the-century British economist, Francis Edgeworth, warned that the foreigner-will-pay argument is like a bottle of poison that is useful in small doses: One should always label it *Danger.* The argument presupposes that the rest of the world cannot retaliate. Very special circumstances would have to be present for one country to be able to beat down everybody else's terms of trade by tariffs while the rest of the world could not respond. Once the possibility of retaliation is present, countries that try to use this policy could start a tariff war that would leave everybody worse off.

The Diversification Argument

An argument closely related to the infant-industry argument is that free trade may lead an economy to specialize too much and expose it to the risks of putting all its eggs in one basket. When an economy is highly dependent on only one export good—as is Ghana on cocoa, Bolivia on tin, or Colombia on coffee—the fortunes of the country wax and wane with the price of the main export good. Such cyclical fluctuations in raw-material prices allegedly impose hardships on the specialized economy.

Raul Prebisch, a well-known Latin American economist, has argued that if such countries impose tariffs to protect their domestic industry, this protection would permit them to diversify their industrial base. A greater range of goods produced would reduce the risk imposed on the economy by price changes.

One seldom hears this argument in fair weather, only in foul. No one questioned the wisdom of the oil-exporting countries' specialization in oil. Kuwait is heavily dependent on oil exports and is one of the richest countries in the world (on a per capita basis) because of this specialization. When prices are going up, the diversification theorists remain strangely quiet. Private investors find it profitable to invest in the goods that promise the highest return. In nondiversified economies, investors have concluded that only a few goods are worthy of their attention. To conclude that diversification should be forced by government policy is sound only if the policy-maker has more information about the future of an economy than private investors. It is difficult to determine which industries will be profitable in the future. If one industry is much riskier than another, private investors will demand a risk premium in the risky industry—such as copper in Chile or cocoa in Ghana. A case can be made for deliberate diversification only if governments can make better decisions than investors about future comparative advantage.

The Tariffs-for-Revenue Argument

Tariffs provide protection and raise government revenue. The two goals are partly in conflict. A perfect protectionist tariff would eliminate trade entirely and so eliminate tariff revenue!

A nonprohibitive tariff does raise government revenue. Tariffs are not an important source of revenue in the United States (slightly more than 1 percent of the federal government's revenue), but in some countries, tariff revenue is significant. Indeed, nineteenth-century America relied heavily on tariff revenues.

A revenue tariff has special justification if it is difficult for a country to raise revenues in other ways. In a poor country where tax avoidance and nonmarket transactions restrict the amount of revenue yielded by income taxes, the government may be forced to collect its revenues by imposing taxes on traded goods. Customs officers located in airports and ports may be able to collect tax revenue to pay for roads, education, and other public goods. A tariff probably has greater justification under these circumstances than in any other case.

U.S. TRADE POLICIES

The tariff history of the United States is depicted in Figure 5, which shows that tariffs have fluctuated with the ebb and flow of protectionism in the U.S. Congress. In modern times, tariffs hit their peak with the infamous Smoot-Hawley tariff of 1930. Economists were so appalled by the prospect of this tariff bill that in a rare show of agreement 1028 of them signed a petition asking President Hoover to veto the bill. Because politics tends to override economics in tariff legislation, the bill was signed.

The Trade-Agreements Program and GATT

The Smoot-Hawley tariff, like most of the preceding 18 tariff acts stretching back to 1779, was the result of political *logrolling* in the U.S. Congress. Logrolling occurs when some politicians trade their own votes on issues of minor concern to their constituents in return for other politicians' votes on issues of greater concern to their constituents. Tariffs, historically, are the best example of the sacrifice of general interests for special interests.

Having established the highest tariff rates in U.S. history, the Smoot-Hawley Act triggered angry reactions overseas, as predicted by economists. As one nation after another erected trade barriers, the volume of world trade declined more than it would have in response to the Great Depression alone. The export markets of the United States shrunk at the time of a very deep domestic depression. Example 4 considers some modern examples of trade wars.

In order to secure a large market for U.S. exports, Congress amended the Tariff Act of 1930 with the Reciprocal Trade Agreements Act of 1934. The president was authorized to negotiate reciprocal agreements that promised to lower U.S. trade

FIGURE 5
Average U.S. Import Duties, 1920–1992

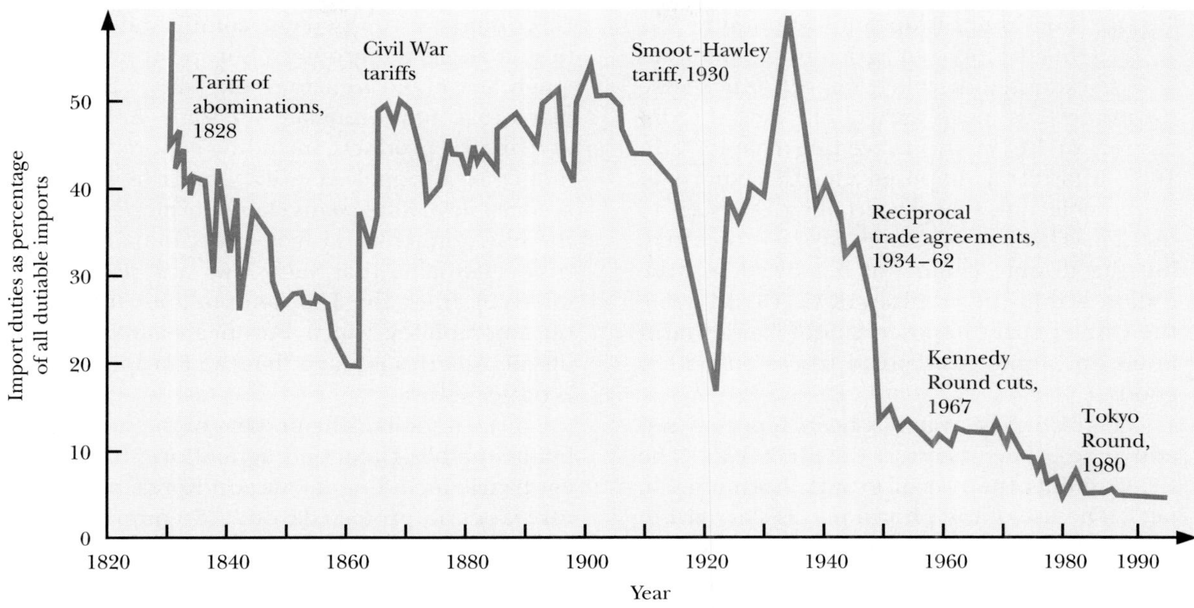

As attitudes toward free trade and protectionism have fluctuated in the United States, average tariff rates have also fluctuated but have shown a distinct downward trend.

Sources: *Historical Statistics of the United States; Statistical Abstract of the United States.*

barriers or tariffs in return for similar concessions abroad. The fact that Congress did not have to approve the tariff cuts marked a significant change in the power of special interests to influence U.S. tariff policy.

The trade agreements program has been broadened under successive extensions and modifications. The Trade Expansion Act of 1962 gave the president the power to reduce tariffs by up to 50 percent and to remove duties of less than 5 percent. Under the authority of this act, the United States engaged in multilateral negotiations, known as the Kennedy Round, which resulted in an average reduction of 35 percent on industrial tariff rates. The Trade Reform Act of 1974 allowed the president to reduce tariffs by up to 60 percent and to eliminate duties of less than 5 percent. This act resulted in the Tokyo Round (1980) of multilateral reductions, in which the United States agreed to cut tariffs on industrial goods by 31 percent, the European Community agreed to cut tariffs by 27 percent, and Japan agreed to cut tariffs by 28 percent. The Trade and Tariff Act of 1984 authorized the president to enter into a new round of multilateral reductions in trade barriers (called the Uruguay Round).

Clearly, the trade agreements program has been an enormous success. In 1932, the average tariff rate was about 59 percent; today, the average tariff rate is about 5 percent. The trade agreement obligations of the United States and other countries are carried out under the General Agreement on Tariffs and Trade (GATT), established in 1948. GATT spells out rules on the conduct of trade and procedures to settle trade disputes. It is also the forum in which international tariff negotiations now take place. (Also see Example 2 in the preceding chapter.)

Escape Clauses

The president's authority to reduce tariffs in reciprocal trade agreements can be used only if the anticipated increases in imports are considered

EXAMPLE 4 Trade Wars: Chicken or Beef?

Then the European Community was first formed, an agricultural policy was adopted in which import duties were to protect European agriculture (see the discussion of EC in the preceding chapter). In 1962, a tariff was imposed on U.S. exports of frozen chickens, sharply curtailing U.S. sales to the EC. The United States strongly objected, but the dispute could not be solved by arbitration within the confines of GATT. In 1965, the United States imposed Smoot-Hawley tariff levels on brandy, assembled trucks and other goods.

The Chicken War has been repeated several times. The lastest is the Beef War. The EC prohibits the use of growth hormones in beef. The use of such hormones is standard in the United States, because a $1 expenditure on hormones will lower cattle-fattening costs by as much as $20. There is also a widespread black market in Europe. Beginning January 1, 1989, the EC prohibited U.S. imports of beef treated by such hormones. While this will affect only $105 million in U.S. exports of beef to the EC, if other countries follow suit, about $1 billion of U.S. beef exports would be at risk. The stakes are high, and the U.S. retaliated, just as in the Chicken War. On January 1, 1989, the U.S. imposed 100 percent countervailing duties on a selected group of European products (such as canned tomatoes and tuna). Europe plans to counter-retaliate on some American agricultural products, including exports of hormones to Europe! America claims hormones are harmless; Europeans claim hormones harm the environment and may affect humans. Europe maintains that such laws are really no different from the U.S. antipollution devices on automobiles, which European automakers install. Americans claim that the European law is protectionist.

Free trade is difficult. One of the most difficult stumbling blocks is agriculture. In many countries, including Japan and Korea, agriculture is heavily protected from U.S. competition. For some reason, farmers are able to argue that agriculture is somehow different and is required for the national security and identity. Food has a symbolic meaning, and the farmer is often regarded as the backbone of society.

Sources: "Beef Dispute: Stakes High in Trade War," *New York Times*, January 1, 1989; "U.S. and Europe Near Trade War over Hormone Use in Beef Cattle," *New York Times*, November 20, 1988; John A. C. Conybeare, *Trade Wars*, (New York: Columbia University Press, 1987), chap. 7.

unlikely to threaten or cause serious injury to a domestic industry. Protectionists can now use this "escape clause" to avoid competition from cheaper foreign imports. But an escape clause (Section 201 of the Trade Act of 1974) can be invoked only if three conditions are met: (1) imports must be increasing, (2) the domestic import-competing industry must be (or must potentially be) seriously injured, and (3) the increased imports must be a substantial cause of the serious injury or threat to the domestic import-competing industry. Escape-clause cases are initiated by petition from the industry to the U.S. International Trade Commission.

The escape clause cannot be invoked simply because the increased imports adversely affect a domestic industry or because the domestic industry is seriously depressed. For example, the Trade Commission did not grant the U.S. automobile industry escape-clause protection because the major difficulties in the auto industry have been caused by the reduced demand for automobiles. Even if imports had not increased their penetration, the U.S. auto industry would have been depressed in the early 1980s.

Economists tend to be critical of escape clauses because the expectation of greater net social gains from tariff cuts results in a larger reallocation of resources away from the import-competing industries into export industries and other industries. Thus, escape clauses are presumably invoked in those industries where trade gains may be the greatest.

In recent years, escape-clause protection has been granted sparingly.

Trade-Adjustment Assistance

When tariffs are lowered and, say, textile or auto workers are thrown out of jobs, hardships are imposed on them. If escape-clause action is inefficient, an alternative is to assist workers and firms to adjust to the changed conditions by supplementing unemployment insurance, giving job counseling and training, or providing grants for moving expenses.

A case can be made that government trade-adjustment assistance is necessary because a government policy (tariff reductions) brought about the short-term unemployment of workers. The question is how to provide this assistance without discouraging the transfer of resources from declining, protected sectors into the exporting sectors of the economy. (See Example 5).

From 1975 to 1981, the United States had a liberal trade-adjustment program. The program basically extended unemployment insurance benefits and did little to encourage workers to move from declining to expanding industries. Another problem with the program was that the benefits were for the most part given to only one industry—the automobile industry. The Trade Bill of 1988 authorized a $1-billion worker-assistance program for retraining workers displaced by imports.

Dumping and Protectionism

Recall that dumping occurs when a foreign company charges a lower price in an export market than in the home market. We argued early that antidumping laws make little sense because they ignore the consumer and simply protect certain producers from foreign competition.

While the United States has pursued free-trade agreements with Mexico and Canada and encouraged lower tariffs around the world, the laws against dumping have been strictly enforced and expanded by Congress and the Commerce Department. Other

EXAMPLE 5 How to Move to Free Trade

Although most economists recommend free trade, they recognize that moving to free trade will dislocate industries and workers. Robert Z. Lawrence and Robert E. Litan of the Brookings Institution have designed a scheme for easing the transition between a world of tariffs and quotas and one with completely free trade.

Lawrence and Litan propose a three-step process. First, all quotas should be converted into tariffs. Every quota has a tariff equivalent—namely, the tariff rate that would bring about the same level of imports as the quota. Second, all tariffs should be phased out over a 10- or 15-year period, giving industries and workers nearly a decade to adjust to the new competition from foreign imports. Third, trade-adjustment assistance (TAA) should be granted to workers who have lost their jobs because of foreign competition. To avoid the problems with previous TAA programs (which gave workers an incentive to remain unemployed), Lawrence and Litan suggest that TAA benefits take the form of earning insurance. Workers would then be compensated for a proportion of their loss in earnings when they accept a new job. For example, a worker who loses a $20,000-a-year job may be able to find a job paying only $12,000 a year. Giving the worker, say, 50 percent of his or her wage loss—or $4000—for a period of 2 years would give the worker an incentive to find a new job as quickly as possible.

Source: Robert Z. Lawrence and Robert E. Litan, "Ending the 'Lunacy' of Trade Protection," *New York Times*, April 27, 1986.

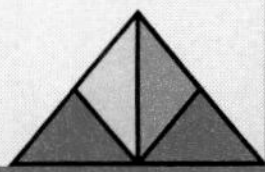

nations and GATT have been calling for eliminating or trimming antidumping laws.[10]

The Commerce Department has been convicting foreign companies for small or trivial price differences even when the prices are really the same. Small price differences can arise just because exchange rates change. Thus, a company can be subject to antidumping duties even though it had no intention to dump.

As a result of exchange rate changes, quality differences, taxes, distribution costs, and so forth, it is very difficult to accurately compare the prices paid in the foreign company's home market with the prices paid in the export market. But the Commerce Department has no trouble! An Italian company was convicted of dumping exports of pads for woodwind instruments. The Commerce Department compared the price of the smaller pads sold in the United States with the larger pads sold in Italy. If the Commerce Department has difficulty comparing the prices, it uses a cost-of-production proof. The department assumes that foreign profits should be 8 percent. If a foreign company selling in the United States makes a 7 percent profit, it is assumed that dumping has occurred.

The Commerce Department can require a company to pay duties on any goods exported in the past. In a sporting event, if an umpire misses a foul, there is no foul. Not so with the antidumping laws. In 1989, the Commerce Department required a Japanese ball-bearing company to pay a 67 percent duty on its U.S. exports from 1975 to 1979.

Antidumping laws are difficult to apply in a world of global production of goods and services. The same company that initiates an antidumping investigation at one time may itself be subject to an antidumping duty a few years later. (See Example 3.)

From 1980 to 1989, there were 451 antidumping cases in the United States—and more than half resulted in antidumping duties. More than half of all cases are in the iron and steel industry and the chemical industry. The target countries were Japan, West Germany, Taiwan, Korea, Italy, Canada, and Brazil (in order of importance). The antidumping laws and countervailing duty laws are now the favorite vehicle for protectionist demands.

This chapter examined the nature and consequences of trade barriers. Imports are bought with money; exports are sold for money. The next chapter will examine how monetary relationships fit into the international exchange of goods and services.

SUMMARY

1. The major trade barriers are tariffs, import quotas, voluntary export restraints, and other nontariff barriers. A *tariff* is a tax levied on imports. It raises both the price paid by the domestic consumer and the price received by the domestic producer of the import-competing product. *Import quotas* limit the amount of imports of specified products. They raise the prices paid by domestic consumers and the prices received by domestic producers of import-competing products. Quotas are normally regulated by import licenses. If import licenses are sold to importers, the government receives their scarcity value. If they are not sold, private importers benefit from their scarcity value. *Voluntary export restraints* direct governments to restrict their exports to another country.

2. The basic argument against protection is that its costs outweigh its benefits. The loss to consumers from a tariff is greater than the gain to the protected producers. Additional losses include the costs of lobbying for tariff or quota protection.

3. Politics explains why tariffs are passed. Although the costs of tariffs are large in total, these costs are small per person. Special-interest groups therefore lobby and spend funds to obtain tariff protection. The major economic arguments for protection are that it is necessary to avoid unfair foreign competition (low foreign wages, dumping, foreign-export subsidies), to protect infant industries, to keep money in the country, and to save domestic jobs.

4. The nonprotectionist arguments for tariffs are the national-defense argument, the foreigner-will-pay argument, the diversification argument, and the tariffs-for-revenue argument. The national-defense argument is potentially valid but tends to be misused and applied to industries of little importance to national defense. The foreigner-will-pay argument normally works only if the nation's trading partners fail to retaliate against protective tariffs.

[10]The following is based on James Bovard, "No Justice in Anti-Dumping," *New York Times,* January 20, 1990; Peter Passell, "Cement Shoes for Venezuela," *New York Times,* September 25, 1991.

The diversification argument fails to take into account the fact that private investors prefer to specialize their investments in specific domestic industries. The tariff-revenue argument may have a special justification in poor countries that have difficulty raising revenues through other means.

5. U.S. trade policies have changed over the years. The Smoot-Hawley tariff of 1930 caused a further restriction of trade during the Great Depression by setting very high tariff rates. Since then, legislation has been passed that allows the U.S. president to negotiate tariff reductions. Existing legislation does contain escape clauses that can reverse the trend toward free trade. The U.S. antidumping laws appear to have become more protectionist in recent years.

KEY TERMS

tariff
import quota
voluntary export restraint
prohibitive tariff
nonprohibitive tariff
dumping
countervailing duty

QUESTIONS AND PROBLEMS

1. What are the differences between an import duty and an import quota? What are the similarities?
2. What is the difference between an import quota and a voluntary export restraint?
3. Economists agree that tariffs hurt the countries that impose them. Yet nearly all countries impose tariffs. Is something wrong with the economists' argument?
4. Assume a country can export all the wheat it wants at the world price of $5 per bushel. Using an analysis parallel to the discussion of Figure 4 in the text, show the impact of imposing a $1-per-bushel export tariff on every bushel exported. Does the benefit to consumers and government exceed the cost to producers of wheat? (*Hint:* An export tariff means that if a foreigner purchases wheat, he or she must pay the domestic price plus the $1 export duty.)
5. What are the best arguments that can be made for tariffs? What are the worst arguments that can be made for tariffs?
6. Frederic Bastiat, a nineteenth-century French economist/journalist, called tariffs "negative railroads." In what respects are tariffs negative railroads? In what respects is the analogy faulty?
7. Evaluate the validity of the following statement: "Ignoring political considerations, importing from China may not benefit the United States because under communism, prices need not correspond to the true Chinese comparative advantage."

SUGGESTED READINGS

Bergsten, C. Fred. *The Cost of Import Restrictions to American Consumers.* New York: American Importers Association, 1972.

Bhagwati, Jagdish. *Protectionism.* Cambridge, MA: The MIT Press, 1990.

Bovard, James. *The Fair Trade Fraud.* New York: St. Martin's Press, 1991.

George, Henry. *Protection or Free Trade?* New York: Schalkenbach, 1980.

Kreinin, Mordechai. *International Economics,* 5th ed. New York: Harcourt Brace Jovanovich, 1987, chaps. 13 and 14.

Weidenbaum M., and M. Munger. "Protection at Any Price?" *Regulation* (July/August 1983): 14–18.

Yeager, Leland B., and David G. Tuerck. *Trade Policy and the Price System.* Scranton, PA: International Textbook, 1966.

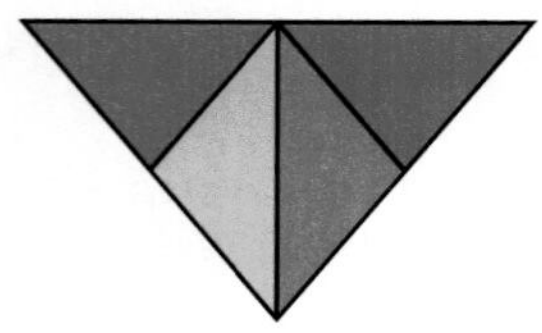

25 The International Monetary System

CHAPTER INSIGHT

From 1988 to 1991 the United States bought an average of $108 billion more foreign goods than it sold abroad. With such trade deficits many people claimed that America had lost its ability to compete internationally. America had to borrow from foreign countries to pay for its profligate spending on foreign cars, television sets, oil, and so forth. In addition to these perceived failures, the value of the U.S. dollar dropped by almost 50 percent from its peak value in 1985 to its Gulf War low in January 1991.

This chapter will examine the monetary mechanism behind the international exchange of goods and services. What causes trade deficits? How does the foreign-exchange market work? What happens when a currency depreciates? Why are exchange rates between the currencies of different countries allowed to fluctuate? What are the advantages and disadvantages of the present international monetary system?

These questions and others will be answered as this chapter discusses the U.S. balance of payments, international capital movements, exchange rates, the gold standard, the International Monetary Fund (IMF), and the coordination of monetary and fiscal policies among countries.

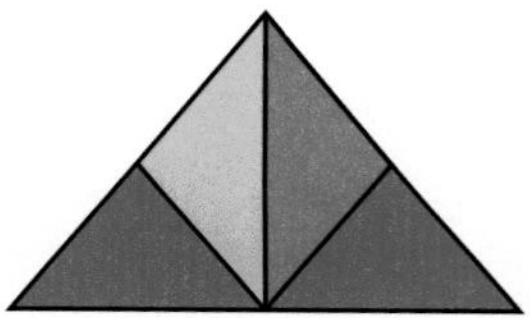

INTERNATIONAL MONETARY MECHANISMS

Money is the medium of exchange for domestic transactions because it is accepted by all sellers in exchange for their goods and services. Each seller generally wants the national currency of his or her own country. Thus, Americans want U.S. dollars, the English want pounds sterling, the Japanese want yen, Germans want marks, and the French want francs.

The Foreign-Exchange Market

When an international transaction takes place, buyers and sellers reside in different countries. An American farmer sells wheat to a British miller, or a British firm sells a bicycle to an American cyclist. To make the purchase, the buyer needs the currency of the seller's place of residence. The currency needed for international transactions is called **foreign exchange.** Normally, foreign exchange consists of bank deposits denominated in the foreign currency, but it may sometimes consist of foreign paper money when foreign travel is involved.

> **Foreign exchange** is the national currency of another country that is needed to carry out international transactions.

The buyer of international goods and services obtains his or her currency requirements from the foreign-exchange market. This market is highly dispersed around the world. Exchange between different currencies takes place between large banks and brokers. For example, an American importer of a British bicycle priced in pounds sterling pays in sterling that is deposited in a British bank. The money is transferred by a check or draft or cable that is purchased with dollars from the importer's American bank that holds a sterling deposit in a British bank. Where does the America bank get these sterling deposits? They come from British importers of American goods who want dollars and supply pounds.[1]

[1]For a further discussion of the foreign-exchange market, see Peter H. Lindert and Charles P. Kindleberger, *International Economics,* 7th ed. (Homewood, IL: Richard D. Irwin, 1982), 243–62.

> America's demand for foreign exchange comes from its demand for the things that residents of the United States want to buy abroad: America's supply of foreign exchange comes from the demand by foreign residents for the things that they want to buy in the United States.

The price of one currency in terms of another is the *foreign-exchange rate.* These rates change from day to day and from hour to hour. In the second week of April 1992, the British pound cost about $1.75, the German mark about $.62, the French franc about $.19; $1 was worth about 133 Japanese yen and 3060 pesos.

Foreign-exchange rates are needed to convert foreign prices into American prices. When the exchange rate is expressed in terms of dollars per unit of foreign currency, the rate can be multiplied by the foreign price to obtain the American price. For example, if a British bicycle costs 90 pounds (£), the American importer pays $144 when the pound is worth $1.60 (because $144 = $1.60 × 90). When the exchange rate is expressed in terms of foreign currency per dollar, the foreign price can be divided by the rate to obtain the American price. For example, a Japanese car costing 900,000 yen costs $6000 when 150 yen equal $1.

Floating Exchange Rates

How the exchange rate is determined depends upon whether it is a **fixed exchange rate** or a **floating exchange rate.**

> A **fixed exchange rate** is set by government decree or intervention within a small range of variation.
>
> A **floating exchange rate** is freely determined by the interaction of supply and demand.

The real world is a blend of these two polar cases. The floating system is easier to understand and roughly corresponds to the present regime adopted by the United States, Great Britain, Canada, Japan, and other nations (about 27 countries in total). Many small countries maintain fixed exchange rates against the dollar, the English pound, the French franc, or some basket of currencies. Eight European countries (including France, Germany, and Italy) have formed a European Monetary System and maintain fixed exchange rates relative to each other, but not relative to the United States. About 20 countries have adopted a dual exchange-rate system involving multiple exchange-rate quotations (depending on what is exchanged).

Americans demand foreign exchange to buy imported commodities; to use foreign transportation services and insurance; to travel abroad; to make payments to U.S. troops stationed abroad; to remit dividends, interest, and profits to the foreign owners of American stocks, bonds, and business firms; to grant foreign aid; and to make short-term and long-term investments in foreign assets.

America's supply of foreign exchange is generated by foreigners' demand for American dollars to buy American exports: to travel in America; to pay American owners of stock, bonds, and businesses: and to invest in American assets.

To simplify the explanation of the foreign-exchange market, imagine again that the world consists of two countries: America and England. The American demand for foreign exchange is thus a demand for British pounds sterling. Also assume that exports and imports of goods and services are the only things traded internationally.

FIGURE 1
The Foreign-Exchange Market

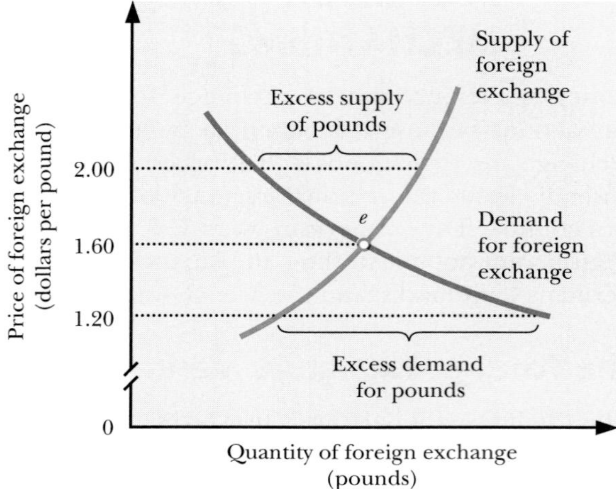

The dollar price of a British pound is measured on the vertical axis; the flow of pounds on the foreign-exchange market per unit of time is measured on the horizontal axis. The equilibrium exchange rate is $1.60 = £1. If the exchange rate were $2.00 = £1, the excess supply of pounds on the market would drive down the price. At a price of $1.20 per pound, there would be an excess demand for pounds on the market, bidding the price up.

Figure 1 shows the demand curve for foreign exchange by Americans. The dollar price of pounds is measured on the vertical axis; the flow of pounds into the foreign-exchange market during the relevant period of time is measured on the horizontal axis. The demand curve is downward sloping because as the price of pounds in dollars rises, *ceteris paribus,* the cost of British goods to American importers rises as well. For example, if a British bicycle costs 90 pounds and the pound price rises from $1.60 to $2.00, the bike's price rises from $144 to $180 for the American importer. This price increase will induce Americans to buy fewer bikes or switch to an American-made brand. Thus, as the price of pounds rises, the quantity of foreign exchange demanded by Americans decreases.

The American supply curve of foreign exchange depends on British importers of American goods. When the English buy American wheat, they supply pounds to the foreign-exchange market (because pounds must be exchanged to buy U.S. goods). The supply curve is upward sloping because when the dollar price of pounds rises—or when the dollar falls in value—American goods appear cheaper to foreigners. As a result, they will buy more American goods, thereby increasing the quantity of pounds supplied to Americans in the foreign-exchange market. For example, if a bushel of U.S. wheat costs $3.60, a fall in the value of the dollar from £1 = $1.20 to £1 = $1.60 will lower the cost of a bushel of wheat to foreigners from £3 to £2.25. The English will then shift their demand for wheat from British to American wheat and increase wheat consumption, stimulating American exports.

When the price of pounds is $2, Figure 1 shows that there is an excess supply of pounds on the foreign-exchange market. At the $2 exchange rate, desired U.S. exports exceed U.S. imports. With a floating exchange rate, the dollar price of a pound could not be high enough to cause an excess supply. An excess supply of pounds bids the price of pounds down, as in any competitive market. Similarly, at a price per pound of $1.20, there would be an excess demand for pounds, and the price of pounds would be bid up. The market-clearing price of $1.60 per pound in Figure 1 not only equates the supply and demand for foreign exchange but also maintains an equilibrium between U.S. exports and imports. Equilibrium between imports and exports is achieved because they are the mirror image of the demand and supply for foreign exchange.

Exports and imports will be equal only if there are no factors other than exports or imports (tourism, paying dividends, foreign investments) entering the foreign-exchange market. Suppose, in addition to exporting and importing, some foreigners wish to invest in American securities. The demand curve (D) in Figure 2 reflects America's foreign-exchange requirements for imports of goods. The desire to make new investments in America shifts the supply curve of foreign exchange outward to S'. The dollar price of pounds falls, or the dollar rises in value. This appreciation in the dollar, or depreciation in the pound, makes American goods more expensive, and brings about the required excess of imports over exports needed to accomodate the inflow of foreign capital to America.[2]

A currency is said to *depreciate* if it falls in value on the foreign-exchange market (if it buys less foreign exchange) and to *appreciate* if it rises in value on the foreign-exchange market (if it buys more foreign exchange). In our example, the appreciation of the dollar is the same as the depreciation of the pound because the dollar/pound exchange rate reflects the relative values of the two currencies: when one goes up, the other must go down.

In the actual world, of course, the dollar can rise in terms of the pound while falling in terms of the franc or the mark. For this reason, the value of the dollar on the foreign-exchange market as a whole is best expressed as an average of the major currencies against which the dollar trades. For example, the most well-known average is the Fed's index of the value of the U.S. dollar. The index uses a trade-weighted average of the value of the dollar in 10 industrial countries. The index is constructed so that when it *rises*, the value of the dollar is rising, or the average value of the currencies in the index is falling. Figure 3 shows the history of the Fed's index of the value of the U.S. dollar since 1973.

[2]An alternative approach to explaining the foreign-exchange market is the *monetary approach to the balance of payments*. This approach focuses on the total demand and supply for each national money. The exchange rates must induce people to hold the various national stocks of money. An excellent introduction can be found in Lindert and Kindleberger, *International Economics*, 319–35.

FIGURE 2
The Effect of an Increase in Foreign Investment in America

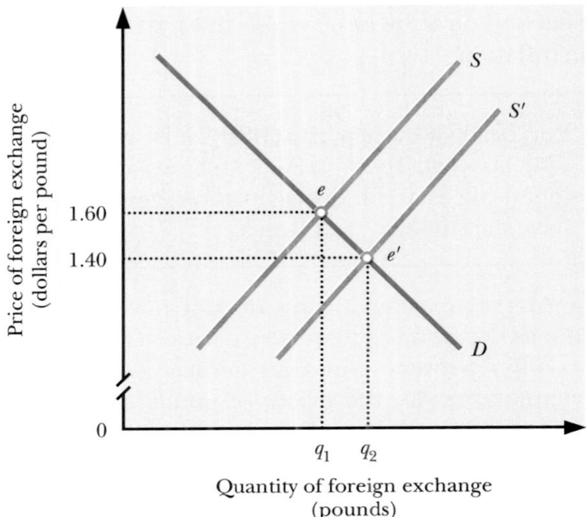

If foreigners decided to invest more in America, the supply curve for foreign exchange would shift from S to S'. The equilibrium price of pounds would fall to \$1.40 and would allow a surplus of imports over exports.

Purchasing-Power Parity

Inflation rates in different countries play an important role in determining floating exchange rates. Countries that have enormous rates of inflation can still trade with the rest of the world because the exchange rate reflects the relative purchasing power of the two currencies in their respective countries.

This theory, popularized by Sweden's Gustav Cassel around 1917, works well when the inflation rates between two countries are quite different. When differentials are small, exchange-rate movements are dominated by other developments, such as fluctuations in the business cycle, capital movements, and changes in comparative advantage.

Suppose England and America were in equilibrium with an exchange rate of \$1.20 = £1. If England doubles its supply of money while America maintains a constant money supply, there will be a tendency for the price of all English goods to double. If the price of the pound falls to a mere \$0.60 (if the pound price falls to one-half its previous exchange value),

English prices appear exactly the same to Americans. The British bike that used to cost £60 rises to £120, but since the pound falls from $1.20 to $0.60, the bike still costs Americans $72. The exchange rate has maintained its **purchasing-power parity** (PPP). A dollar still buys the same goods in England as before the inflation.

Purchasing-power parity (PPP) is the exchange rate between the currencies of two countries that is necessary in order for those countries to have the same costs of living.

Market exchange rates do not have to be the same as the purchasing-power parities (PPP). Prices can differ between countries because even with international trade, the prices of goods and services differ between countries when compared with market exchange rates. For example, a luxury room at the Plaza hotel in New York City was $245 in 1991, but a similar room at the George V hotel in Paris cost $460. One reason prices differ is that some goods (like hotel rooms) are not traded. Another reason is that countries levy different domestic taxes, tariffs, and quotas. When compared to most advanced countries, the United States has a lower cost of living. Example 1 shows that when PPP rates are used, the United States in 1988 had a higher per capita GDP than Japan, Norway, Switzerland, or Sweden—countries that have higher apparent or nominal per capita GDP.

The Behavior of the Dollar

The theory of flexible exchange rates helps explain the behavior of the dollar since the first use of a floating system. Two general factors determine exchange rates: inflation differentials and real interest-rate differentials. When inflation in the United States is higher than in the rest of the world, the U.S. dollar should fall to maintain purchasing-power parity. When real interest rates in the United States are rising relative to real interest rates abroad, the U.S. dollar should rise as investors seek to place their funds in the United States. As the dollar rises in value, as in Figure 2, net exports fall to accommodate the net capital inflow. The net capital inflow brings about an excess of imports over exports.

Figure 3 traces the value of the U.S. dollar from 1973 to 1991. Beginning in 1976, the dollar began to depreciate. The reason for this depreciation was that U.S. inflation increased relative to an average of foreign inflation rates from early 1977 to 1979. Accordingly, to maintain purchasing-power parity, the dollar depreciated.

In the 1980s, inflation differentials stabilized as U.S. inflation was broadly similar to the average of other industrial countries. For example, from 1982 to 1986, the U.S. inflation rate fell from 6.2 percent to 1.9 percent per year; over the same period, the average inflation rate of the industrial countries fell from 7.4 percent to 2.3 percent per year. The principal determinant of the value of the U.S. dollar after 1980 became the differential between U.S. and foreign real interest rates.

Figure 4 shows the real interest-rate differential between the United States and the other industrial countries. From 1980 to 1984, the real interest rate increased in the United States relative to the other countries. As Figure 3 showed, the value of the dollar steadily increased until early 1985. Subsequently, the dollar fell sharply as the real interest-rate differential fell against the U.S. rate. From the beginning of 1985 to April 1992, the dollar depreciated by almost 50 percent.

The dollar's real appreciation up to 1985 (beyond purchasing-power parity) had both costs and benefits. On the benefit side, a higher dollar meant that imports were cheaper to Americans. This price decrease raised American living standards by lowering the U.S. inflation rate relative to the increase in U.S. incomes. Moreover, the fact that the United States was attracting so much capital from abroad meant that Americans could consume and invest more than they otherwise could. Despite a massive government deficit and an unusually low rate of private saving, foreign investment in the United States enabled Americans to continue to build plant and equipment for the future.

While economic theory suggests that an improvement in a country's terms of trade that results from incoming foreign investment has more benefits than costs, there are important costs of a dollar appreciation. First, a higher dollar makes America's exports of wheat and other goods much more expensive in foreign markets. Cutting exports causes hardships in those export industries. Second, when America repays its foreign debts, it will have to consume and invest less sometime in the future. Any country that borrows today is trading future goods against more present goods: more today, less tomorrow. The

EXAMPLE 1 How Rich Are Americans?

A common newspaper headline states that several countries have higher per capita incomes than Americans. Such comparisons simply divide a country's per capita GDP by the market price of the U.S. dollar in terms of the country's currency. Using this as the criterion for the countries shown in the accompanying table, the United States is much "poorer" than Switzerland or Norway or Japan. On this basis, Swiss residents are 40 percent richer than Americans. But market exchange rates do not reflect purchasing-power parities—what foreigners' currencies will buy in their own countries compared to the United States. Column 2 shows the PPP rate for the selected countries. For example, the Swiss paid 1.463 Swiss francs for a dollar in 1988—that was the average market exchange rate. But at this exchange rate, Swiss domestic prices are 60 percent higher than American prices. Accordingly, the PPP rate is 2.33 Swiss francs to the dollar. On this basis, which gives a more accurate comparison, American per capita GDP is 14 percent higher than Switzerland's! The same is true for Norway, Japan, and Sweden.

In 1988, the only country with a higher per capita GDP than the United States was the United Arab Emirates—a country literally soaked with oil!

Source: Robert Summers and Alan Heston, "The Penn World Table: An Expanded Set of International Comparisons," *Quarterly Journal of Economics* 106 (May 1991): 327–68.

Purchasing-Power Parities, 1988

	Market Exchange Rate (1)	PPP (2)	Per Capita GDP/PPP (3)	Per Capita GDP/Market (4)
Switzerland	1.463	2.33	$16,155	$25,686
Norway	6.517	10.21	14,976	23,467
Japan	128.15	219.39	12,209	20,902
Sweden	6.127	8.90	12,991	18,837
United States	1.0	1.0	18,339	18,339
West Germany	1.756	2.37	12,604	17,053
France	5.957	7.45	12,190	15,250
United Kingdom	0.562	0.62	11,982	13,219

Column 1 shows the average 1988 market exchange rate—how many currency units buy 1 U.S. dollar; column 2 shows the purchasing-power-parity (PPP) exchange rate; column 3 shows per capita GDP in dollars, using PPP or internationally comparable prices; column 4 shows per capita GDP in dollars, using market exchange rates.

FIGURE 3
The Value of the U.S. Dollar, 1973–1992

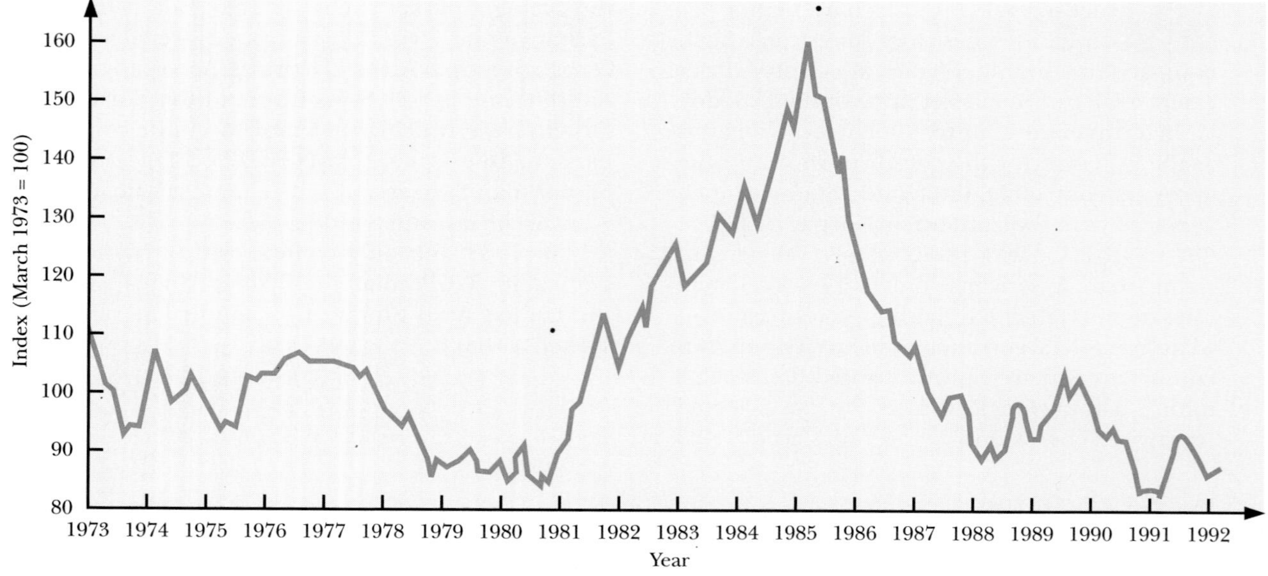

Source: Federal Reserve Bank of Cleveland.

advantage is that the investment allows the country to build its productivity capacity. If the investment's yield exceeds the borrowing costs, the economy benefits.

Fixed Exchange Rates and the Gold Standard

The gold standard is the prototype of the fixed exchange-rate system. The classical gold standard was in its heyday before World War I, from about the 1870s to 1914. The United Kingdom was on the gold standard as far back as the 1820s and used both gold and silver during the eighteenth century—the century in which David Hume and Adam Smith lived.

A fixed exchange-rate system does not have to use gold, silver, or any commodity, but *each country must adopt monetary rules that correspond to those of the classical gold standard.*

When Spain conquered the New World, it brought back enormous amounts of gold. As the quantity theory predicts, a major consequence of the inflow of gold into Spain was inflation of wages and production costs. This inflation made it more difficult for Spain to compete with other European countries in world markets. Thus, Spain developed an excess of imports over exports and shipped gold to pay for the difference. Eventually, this gold caused inflation elsewhere, and Spain's exports and imports were brought into approximate balance.

The blueprint for an international gold standard, brilliantly outlined by David Hume in 1752, showed how a fixed exchange-rate system can work to maintain equilibrium in the balance of payments with the rest of the world.

The gold-flow mechanism can be explained with our hypothetical two-country world. If America defined the dollar as equal to 1/20 of an ounce of gold, and England defined the pound as equal to 1/4 of an ounce of gold, an English pound would contain 5 times as much gold as a U.S. dollar. England would convert gold into pounds (and vice versa) at the established rate of £1 = 1/4 of an ounce of gold; America would convert gold into dollars at the rate of $1 = 1/20 of an ounce of gold. Under these circumstances, the exchange rate would be $5 = £1.

FIGURE 4
Real Interest-Rate Differentials

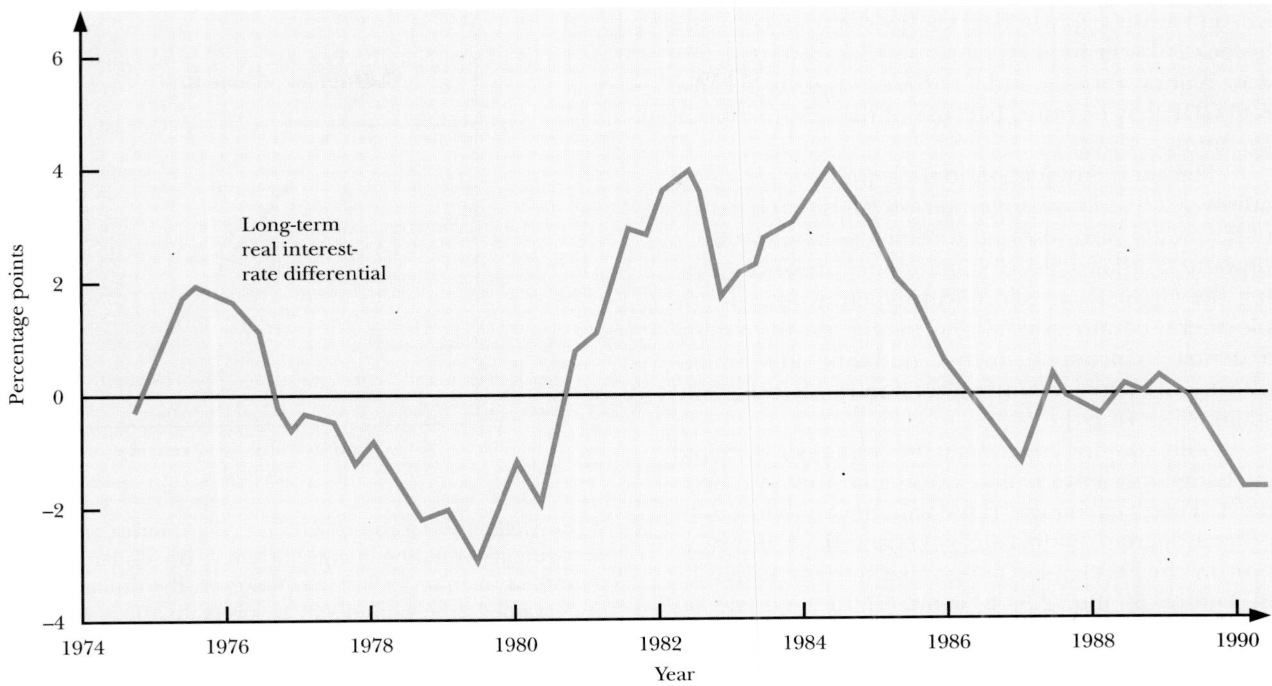

Source: Federal Reserve.

No rational person would pay more than \$5 for an English pound, because \$5 would buy 1/4 of an ounce of gold from the U.S. Treasury and that amount of gold would buy one pound note from the British Treasury.[3] The next key ingredient of the gold standard is that England and America let their money supplies depend on how much gold is in their national treasuries.

If America had a surplus of exports over imports in our hypothetical world, gold would be shipped from England to America to pay for the surplus of exports over imports. This gold shipment would raise the money supply in America and reduce the money supply in England. As a result, inflation of costs and prices would occur in America, and a deflation of costs and prices would occur in England. Thus, America's exports would become less competitive, and England's exports would become more competitive. As America's exports decreased and England's exports increased, America's surplus of exports over imports would disappear—as long as the rules of the gold-standard game were followed.

The equilibrating mechanism of the international gold standard is the *relationship between the domestic money supplies and the state of the balance of payments.* It is not actually necessary for gold or silver to be involved. If the country with a payments deficit allows its money supply to fall while the country with a payments surplus allows its money supply to rise, automatic adjustment mechanisms will tend to restore equilibrium.

In the country with a payments surplus, the expansion of the money supply will (1) lower exports because of higher prices and costs, (2) raise imports

[3]Because shipping gold back and forth between America and England is costly (transportation and insurance), the dollar price of pounds might range between \$5.02 and \$4.98, if it costs 2 cents to ship 1/4 ounce of gold between the countries. These upper and lower limits of exchange rate are called the *gold points.*

because prices and costs are now cheaper abroad, and (3) raise imports because real GDP may be increased because of the expansion in the money supply. In the deficit country, the contraction of the money supply will (1) raise exports because prices and costs are lower (2) lower imports because prices and costs are now higher abroad, and (3) lower imports because real GDP may be lower because of the contraction of the money supply.

The central objection to the equilibrating mechanism of a fixed exchange-rate system is that balance-of-payments surpluses and deficits may produce unwanted inflationary or deflationary pressures. During the Great Depression, with its enormous unemployment, countries could no longer afford to allow a deficit to produce further deflation and unemployment. Hence, country after country left the gold standard during the 1930s.

Gold is not necessary to establish a fixed exchange-rate system that works like the gold standard. Fixed exchange rates can be established by official decree reinforced by central-bank intervention in the foreign-exchange market. For example, in Figure 5, the U.S. is assumed to maintain its currency at a $2 exchange rate against the English pound, but the equilibrium exchange rate is $1.75. Thus, at the official rate, there is an excess supply of foreign exchange, because the pound is overvalued (or the dollar is undervalued). To maintain the $2 price of pounds, America's central bank must purchase the excess supply of pounds coming onto the foreign-exchange market. While the United States is experiencing this balance-of-payments surplus, the U.S. central bank is adding to its inventory of pounds. This inventory can later be used as international reserves to defend the value of the dollar when a deficit appears—when the supply and demand curves intersect above the $2 official price.

The surplus of exports over imports in this example will not persist if the United States and England follow the rules of the gold-standard game. If the United States lets its money supply rise and England allows its money supply to fall, mechanisms will be set in motion that will shift the demand curve to the right and the supply curve to the left. When the United States suffers inflation relative to England, the United States exports less (decreasing supply) and imports more (increasing demand). These changes will cause the demand and supply curves for foreign exchange in Figure 5 to shift until they intersect at the official $2 price.

FIGURE 5
American Balance of Payments

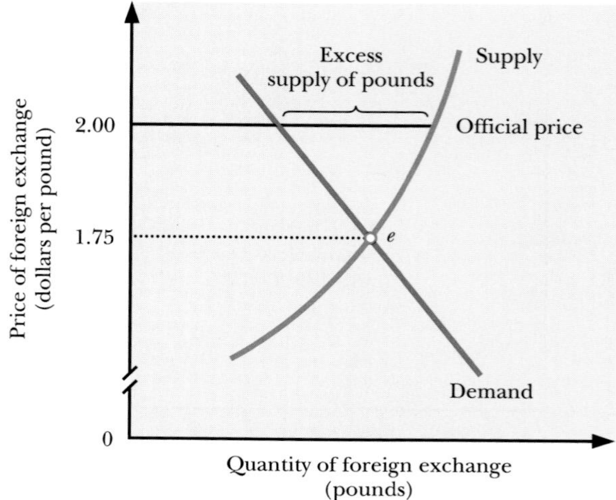

If the exchange rate were $1.75 = £1, America's balance of payments would be in equilibrium. If the dollar price of pounds is fixed at $2.00 = £1, however, the dollar will be undervalued (the pound will be overvalued), and America's balance of payments will be in surplus by the excess of supply of pounds on the foreign-exchange market. These pounds will have to be purchased by the central banks of either America or England.

The term *devaluation* refers to official changes in the exchange rate in a fixed exchange-rate system. Under the old gold standard, a devaluation of the dollar occurred when the price of gold rose. Today, a country with a fixed exchange rate devalues its currency simply by lowering the official price of its currency. The country announces that it will no longer defend the old price and sets a new price to maintain by official intervention.

In Figure 5, America has a surplus and England has a deficit at the official price of $2 per pound. This price can be maintained if the American central bank buys pounds or if the English central bank sells dollars (or if both actions take place). To avoid this inflation in America and deflation in England, England might, with America's agreement, decide simply to devalue its currency! In Figure 5, lowering the price of pounds to $1.75 will (temporarily, at least) solve England's deficit and America's surplus. When the official value of a currency is raised, a *revaluation* is said to occur. Thus, in this case, England *devalues* its currency, and America *revalues* its currency.

THE BALANCE OF PAYMENTS AND INTERNATIONAL CAPITAL MOVEMENTS

The Balance of Payments

A country's **balance of payments** is a summary of information about the country's exports, imports, earnings by domestic residents on assets located abroad, earnings on domestic assets owned by foreign residents, international capital movements between countries, and official transactions by central banks and governments.

> A country's **balance of payments** is a summary record of its economic transactions with foreign residents over a year or any other period.

The balance of payments is a two-sided summary of international transactions. Each transaction is recorded by standard double-entry bookkeeping. In other words, every transaction has two sides, each of which is entered on one of the two sides of the balance-of-payments account. For example, when America exports wheat, the foreign importer might simply give an IOU in exchange for the wheat. The wheat sale is recorded on the minus (debit) side, and the IOU is recorded on the plus (credit) side. Because each amount recorded on the minus side is also recorded on the plus side, the balance-of-payments record will always be *in balance.*

Although the balance of payments always balances if all transactions are considered, its specific *accounts* need not balance. U.S. merchandise exports need not equal U.S. merchandise imports, for example. Thus, a specific account of the balance of payments may have a surplus or deficit, but all the surpluses in the balance of payments as a whole cancel out the deficits. Because the balance of payments as a whole must balance, a deficit on one account implies a surplus on some other account.

These observations should serve as a warning that a deficit in a particular account should not be treated as unfavorable, nor should a surplus be treated as favorable to a country. Mercantilists—those seventeenth- and eighteenth-century writers whom Adam Smith and David Hume criticized—treated a surplus of exports over imports as a good thing and even called it a "favorable trade balance." That such a surplus benefits a country more than an "unfavorable" trade balance is a fallacy. A trade deficit may be a good thing. If a country is importing more than it is exporting, more goods are being brought in than are being sent out. Mercantilists committed the fallacy of treating exports as business sales and imports as business expenses. This fallacy still lingers in many press reports and in the minds of many people.

International-trade economists view exports as the cost of imports. The exports of everything—goods, services, and IOUs—must equal the imports of everything.

As noted, the balance of payments records each transaction on two sides: the credit side and the debit side. In the plus, or credit, column is placed the part of the transaction that increases the *supply* of foreign exchange: the payments for exports of merchandise or the income earned by providing services like transportation, insurance, and even capital to foreigners. In the minus, or debit, column is placed the part of a transaction that increases the demand for foreign exchange: payments for imports of merchandise and the income earned by foreigners when they provide domestic residents with transportation, insurance, or capital.

Exports and Imports. Table 1 shows the U.S. balance of payments for 1991. The most important categories are found under items 1 and 2. U.S. merchandise imports (item 2a) exceeded U.S. merchandise exports (item 1a) by $73 billion. The **merchandise trade balance** is sometimes called the *visible trade balance,* because it is easy to see physical movements of goods, such as wheat, cars, airplanes, computers, and steel.

> The **merchandise trade balance** equals exports of merchandise minus imports of merchandise. If positive, it is the *merchandise trade surplus.* If negative, it is the *merchandise trade deficit.*

TABLE 1
The U.S. Balance of Payments, 1991

Item	Amount (billions of dollars)	
1. Exports of goods and services		**+677**
a. Exports of merchandise	417	
b. Military sales	10.0	
c. Services	135	
d. Income from U.S. investments abroad	115	
2. Imports of goods and services		**−705**
a. Imports of merchandise	−490	
b. Military purchases	−16	
c. Services	−93	
d. Income on foreign investments in U.S.	−106	
3. Net unilateral transfers abroad		**+20**
4. Balance on current account		**−9**
5. Net capital movements		**+12**
a. U.S. capital outflow	−68	
b. Foreign-capital inflow	+80	
6. Allocations on new SDRs to U.S. by IMF		**0**
7. Statistical discrepancy		**−3**
8. Decrease (+) in U.S. official reserve assets		**+6**
9. Increase (+) in foreign official assets in the U.S.		**+19**
10. Total		**0**

Source: *Federal Reserve Bulletin,* May 1992.

The Current Account Balance. The visible trade balance may not give an accurate picture of what the United States exports and imports from abroad. There are also many invisible items in the balance of payments. The United States furnishes transportation, insurance, and capital to foreigners. Payments are received in exchange for these services. When the less visible items are taken into account, the United States imports more goods and services than it exports by only $28 billion (items 1 and 2).

If an American sends money to a relative in a foreign country, if the government gives money to a foreign country as a gift or grant, or if an American decides to retire in a foreign country and receives a pension check there, such transactions enter the balance of payments as *unilateral transfers.* Nothing concrete is exchanged for these payments, but these transactions do give rise to a demand for foreign exchange. In 1991, the United States received $20 billion worth of such transfers, reflecting the cash contributions made by foreign countries to finance the Persian Gulf War. The net difference between exports of goods and services and imports of goods and services minus net unilateral transfers is the **current account balance.**

> The **current account balance** equals exports of goods (merchandise) and services minus imports of goods (merchandise) and services minus net unilateral transfers abroad.

The current account deficit fell from $92 billion in 1990 to only $9 billion in 1991. From 1946 to 1991, the United States had 18 current account deficits and 27 current account surpluses. A current account deficit means that exports of goods and services fall short of imports of goods and services plus net unilateral transfers. To finance this deficit, the United States must be a net importer of capital.

Net Capital Movements. When Americans buy foreign bonds and stocks and invest in foreign factories, capital that would otherwise be available for investment at home is invested abroad. This capital outflow was $68 billion in 1991 (item 5a). When foreigners invest in U.S. stocks, bonds, and factories, there is a capital inflow. In 1991, the capital inflow into the United States was $80 billion. Capital outflows—sometimes called *capital exports*—are a debit item, because they give rise to a demand for foreign exchange and, like imports, represent an increase in a domestically held asset (the foreigner's IOU). Capital inflows—sometimes called *capital imports*—are a credit item, because they give rise to an increase in the supply of foreign exchange and represent an increase in U.S. liabilities to foreigners.

The excess of capital imports over capital exports—$12 billion (item 5)—is a new phenomenon for the United States. From 1917 to 1982—a period of about 65 years—the United States was a net capital exporter. Americans invested more in the rest of the world than foreigners invested in the United States. Beginning in 1983, the huge inflow of capital from the rest of the world swamped America's net-creditor position (accumulated over 60 years) and is turning America into a net debtor. Soon, the United States may no longer earn more from foreign investments than it pays out. In 1991, the United States still earned more from investments it made abroad than the investments foreigners made in the United States. U.S. net income from foreign investment—about $19 billion in 1991—-is a reflection of exporting more capital than was imported over many decades.

Item 7 in Table 1 is a *statistical discrepancy.* In 1991, the statistical discrepancy was a $3 billion debit item. This statistical discrepancy arose from the fact that when all the observable credits and debits were recorded, the credits outweighed the debit items by this amount. Thus, observed credits, such as spending by foreign tourists in America, hidden exports, or unnoticed capital inflows, must have occurred. As a dramatic example, business firms in Latin American countries, such as Argentina, falsify their reported exports and imports to the U.S. in order to acquire U.S. dollars (through over-invoicing exports and under invoicing imports). This represents hidden capital inflows into the United States.

Official Reserve Assets. A country's *official reserve assets* are its gold or special drawing rights (SDRs), its reserve position in the International Monetary Fund (discussed later), foreign exchange, or any financial assets held in official agencies, such as the central bank or treasury.

Item 9, *the increase in foreign official assets in the U.S.,* records the investments of official agencies of foreign countries in the United States. In 1991, official foreign agencies invested a net $19 billion in the United States.

Government agencies engage in buying and selling assets and foreign exchange. When official agencies like the central bank or the treasury take such an action, there is a presumption that the agency is demanding or supplying foreign exchange for the purpose of stabilizing the exchange rate. The $19 billion increase in foreign official assets in the United States (item 9) does supply foreign exchange and helps increase the value of the dollar.

The allocations of new special drawing rights by the International Monetary Fund (IMF) are included in item 6 and item 8. These new allocations can be used as an official reserve asset of the United States—namely, to buy foreign exchange. SDRs are allocated to every member of the IMF on a regular basis, but not in 1991.

When the deficits and surpluses on all the individual accounts are summed, the total deficit or surplus must be zero, as indicated earlier. For example, in 1991, the $9 billion deficit on the current account was offset by a $12 billion net capital inflow and the statistical discrepancy of more than $3 billion.

International Capital Movements

International capital movements considerably complicate what is happening to a country's balance of payments. Without such capital movements, exports would more closely approximate imports, and there would be fewer measures of deficit or surplus in the balance of payments.

Capital movements enable capital-importing nations to raise their physical capital stocks—dams, buildings, roads—above what such stocks would be in the absence of international capital flows. When a country exports capital, it is furnishing residents of another country with funds for financing investments in plant and equipment. Thus, capital exports divert one country's saving into investments in another country. Saving still equals investments in the world as a whole, but when international trade is involved, this equality need not hold for any individual country.

Recall from Chapter 7 that GDP = consumption (C) + government spending (G) + investment (I) + [exports (X) − imports (M)]. Because GDP equal income, GDP = consumption (C) + saving (S) + taxes (T). If government spending and taxes are assumed to be zero (for simplicity),

$$C + S = C + I + (X - M)$$

or

$$S = I + (X - M)$$

or

$$S - I = X - M$$

This equation shows that the excess of saving over investment in a country is reflected in the excess of exports over imports. The excess of saving over investment is the net export of capital to other countries. Thus, the export of capital is transferred into physical goods through the current account surplus. Similarly, an excess of investment over saving will

EXAMPLE 2 Trade Deficits and Unemployment

In 1991, the United States had a merchandise trade deficit of about $73 billion. Does this mean that the United States was losing jobs to workers in other countries? To the individual factory worker whose plant was closed down because of competition from imports, it must seem that the trade deficit does cause unemployment. However, what is true of the individual is not necessarily true for the economy!

Beginning in 1971, America's traditional trade surplus became a trade deficit. From 1971 to 1991, the trade deficit grew from a mere $2 billion to about $73 billion—a 3600 percent increase! During this 20-year period, U.S. employment grew by more than 1.9 percent per year. In the preceding 15 years (1956–71), the United States experienced trade surpluses, and employment grew by less than 1.5 percent per year. While the statistics do not prove that trade deficits are beneficial, they are consistent with the hypothesis that the trade deficit has not dragged down the U.S. economy. Historically speaking, it is difficult to achieve 1.9 percent annual employment growth (since 1947, employment has grown by about 1.6 percent per year on the average).

The trade deficit should have nothing to do with long-run employment opportunities. In the long run, as explained in Chapter 19, the economy tends toward the natural rate of unemployment. Long-run employment growth is the result of a great many factors—the growth in labor force, trends in the labor-force participation rate, and structural determinants of the natural rate of unemployment. But the foreign-trade deficit is not one of these factors.

The trade deficit of any country must be matched by borrowing from other countries. In fact, one reason for the U.S. trade deficit is that foreigners have invested heavily in the United States. The influx of foreign capital has financed the trade deficit. Indeed, the belief that foreign capital provides domestic jobs has muted protectionist sentiment in Congress. It is difficult for a member of Congress to take a strong position on imposing trade barriers when there are foreign-owned manufacturing and assembly plants in his or her state.

Source: "Influx of Foreign Capital Mutes Debate on Trade," *New York Times*, February 8, 1987.

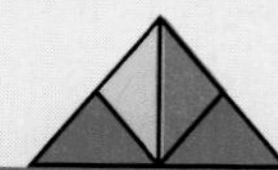

match the excess of imports over exports. This excess investment corresponds to the import of capital, which describes the U.S. position in the 1980s and early 1990s. (See Example 2.)

Capital movements take place for two reasons: Investors wish to take advantage of earning a higher interest rate on their capital, or investors wish to gain some measure of security. Capital seeks higher returns and lower risks.

The capital account of any country's balance of payments contains both capital inflows and outflows because investors are seeking to diversify their portfolios of investments and securities. A fundamental principle of sound investment strategy is not to put all of one's eggs in one basket. By holding a portfolio of international securities—for example, investments in German companies, Japanese companies, and American companies—an investor can reduce the risk of achieving a given expected rate of return.

Net capital movement is governed by the desire for higher interest rates. For example, in a simple world with no risks, investors would place their capital in the country that paid the highest interest rate (the highest rate of return on investments). This process of capital exportation would raise interest rates in low-interest-rate regions and lower interest rates in high-interest-rate regions. This allocation of capital gives rise to greater production everywhere in the world and thus a more efficient utilization of the world's scarce stock of capital.

Stages of the Balance of Payments. When a country first begins to export capital, its earnings on previous foreign investments are small or zero. To finance this export of capital, it is essential to generate a surplus of merchandise exports over merchandise imports. The merchandise trade surplus of such an immature creditor country enables the world to use the scarce capital stock efficiently. As time goes on, the country begins to collect on its investments. As it becomes a mature creditor country, it is able to import more than it exports. The United States was an immature creditor country in the 1920s; partly because it was a mature creditor country until 1984, it had a merchandise trade deficit year in and year out.

When a country first begins to import capital, its payments on past indebtedness are small or zero. Thus, an immature debtor country will be able to finance an excess of imports over exports (a trade deficit). As the debtor country matures, its interest obligations will grow relative to its net borrowing until it must generate an export surplus to pay for its borrowings. As indicated earlier, the United States recently become an immature debtor country. It has a trade deficit for two powerful reasons. First, it borrows more from foreigners than it lends to them; second, its income from foreign investments still exceeds its interest obligations to foreigners.

Why has the United States becomes a net capital importer? Will its net-debtor position become a permanent feature of the U.S. balance of payments? Several factors have played a role. First, as indicated earlier, high real interest rates in the United States relative to the rest of the world led to inflows of capital. Second, many foreign investors believe that the United States is a safe haven for their investments. Third, it has become easier for foreign residents to invest in the United States because of changes in the laws abroad. For example, the guidelines for foreign investment by Japanese and British institutions were loosened in the 1980s. Whether or not America remains a capital importer depends on the fundamental factors determining U.S. real interest rates—productivity and thrift. Higher productivity and lower thriftiness increase real interest rates. As Figure 4 demonstrates, U.S. real interest rates have fallen relative to foreign real interest rates in recent years. Thus, capital inflows into the U.S. have fallen dramatically.

Foreign Investment and Nationalism. When capital is exported from the United States, labor complains that the United States is giving employment to foreigners and depressing home wages. When capital is imported, capitalists complain that their rate of return is depressed. When a foreign country takes over a particular business firm, many people will regard this takeover as a bad thing. In recent years, for example, the Japanese have bought up some American banks, trading companies, hotels, and office buildings. Is it somehow to the disadvantage of the United States to allow foreigners to take over American businesses?

When foreign investment takes the form of actual control of a domestic firm, another issue is at stake: trade in entrepreneurial services.[4] Like trade in all goods and services, if the Japanese can operate American business more efficiently than the former management, the American people will benefit—just as they benefit from buying cheaper foreign imports of personal computers or cars.

THE EVOLUTION OF THE INTERNATIONAL MONETARY SYSTEM

In 1870, the world was not on an international gold standard; by 1900, the world had moved to an international gold standard. The gold standard was dead in 1945 and was replaced by a system of fixed but adjustable exchange rates. The postwar system was dead by 1973, and today the world is on a system of floating exchange rates with active exchange-rate stabilization policies by the major central banks. To understand the current system, it is useful to take a backward look at this evolution.

The Bretton Woods System

The International Monetary Fund (IMF) was established in 1947 after a 1944 conference in Bretton Woods, New Hampshire. The international monetary arrangements set up at this conference are now

[4] Indeed, there is no reason why the taking over of a domestic firm by a foreign firm should be associated with foreign investment, because a Japanese firm can take over an American firm by borrowing in the American capital market.

called either the "old IMF" system or the "Bretton Woods" system. It was set up to avoid the unstable exchange rates of the 1930s.[5]

Each member of the IMF was assigned a quota that was determined by its trade and national income. A country contributed 25 percent of its quota in gold or U.S dollars and 75 percent in its own currency. Thus, the IMF consisted of a pool of gold, dollars, and all other major currencies that could be used to lend assistance to any member country having balance-of-payments difficulties.

The Bretton Woods system was set up on the theory that balance-of-payments *deficits* and *surpluses*—reductions or increases in international reserves—were usually temporary in a fixed exchange-rate system. Thus, the discipline of the Hume reserve-flow mechanism—deflation for deficit countries and inflation for surplus countries—could in many cases be avoided. Each country pledged to maintain a par value of its currency in gold or in dollars that were worth $1/35$ of an ounce of gold and to maintain the exchange rate of its currency within 1 percent of this par value. Should a deficit develop, the country could rely on its international reserves to help it weather the storm until a surplus on the balance of payments developed. In the meantime, the country would not have to go through the adjustment of a domestic deflation.

If the deficit did not reverse itself, the country was considered to be facing a "fundamental disequilibrium" and was then allowed to adjust its exchange rate. A country in fundamental deficit could devalue its currency; a country in fundamental surplus could revalue its currency.

The Fall of Bretton Woods

The United States was the center of the Bretton Woods system. Under the old IMF system, countries tied their currencies to the U.S. dollar. The United States, in turn, tied the dollar to gold. Until 1971, the United States allowed foreign monetary authorities to convert dollars into gold at the rate of $35 an ounce. The dollar became a critical source of international reserves. Countries obtained dollars by accepting dollar payments in exchange for their goods and services. With other countries needing international reserves, the United States could run an import surplus, or a surplus of capital exports over capital imports, without too much difficulty. In other words, because the United States could buy the goods and factories of the rest of the world with its own dollars, it was in a very enviable position during this period.

The expectation was that when the U.S. import surplus came to an end, the Bretton Woods system would begin to work smoothly. In the 1950s and 1960s, the United States had a deficit in its official accounts virtually every year. The expectation of the deficit's turning into a surplus, or at least equilibrium, never materialized.

The fact that the U.S. dollar was the international money of the world also made it very difficult for the United States to adjust the value of its own currency. If the United States devalued the dollar, every country holding dollars as reserves would find itself losing a substantial fraction of its wealth. Thus, the most important member of the IMF could not use its safety value when its deficit was permanent.

Special Drawing Rights (SDRs). In the late 1960s, it was believed that part of the U.S. deficit problem was caused by inadequate international reserves. Thus, at the IMF's annual meeting in 1967, a new kind of international money was created—the *special drawing right* (SDR).

Basically, the IMF simply creates SDRs out of thin air and allocates them to the various member countries in accordance with their quotas. If a deficit country needs international reserves, it can transfer its SDR balance to other countries. The rate of exchange that a country gets for SDRs depends upon the prevailing value. At first, 1 SDR = $1. Later, the SDR's value was determined by making 1 SDR equal to a bundle of currencies. Now, the SDR rises or falls in terms of the dollar.

SDRs were essentially a stopgap measure. While SDRs may eventually become the basis for an international currency, this solution did nothing to solve the fundamental problem of the Bretton Woods system: speculation.

Speculation. In addition to the U.S. official deficit, another problem was that the currency adjustment system itself suffered from incompatibility with relatively free international capital movements. If a country had a fundamental deficit and needed to devalue its currency, speculators would know this better than anyone else. The chances that the coun-

[5]See Leland B. Yeager, *International Monetary Relations: Theory, History, and Policy*, 2nd ed. (New York: Harper & Row, 1976), chap. 18.

try would revalue or raise the value of its currency would be virtually zero. The speculators would be in a no-loss situation if they sold weak currencies with a vengeance and bought strong currencies. For example, the British pound was often weak and the German deutschmark (DM) was often strong. Accordingly, speculators would sell pounds and buys DMs. This exacerbated the deficit in the United Kingdom and the surplus in Germany.

In 1971, speculation against the U.S. dollar began. That August, President Nixon changed the fundamental character of the IMF system by severing the dollar's link with gold. No longer could countries convert dollars into gold at $35 an ounce; the dollar was essentially free to flucuate. After a few attempts to fix up the system, by March 1973, all major currencies of the world were on a managed floating system, and the Bretton Woods system was shattered.

The Current International Monetary System

The Jamaica Agreements. At a conference in Kingston, Jamaica, in early 1976, the original IMF charter was amended to legalize the widespread managed floating that replaced the Bretton Woods par-value system.

According to the new agreements, each country could adopt whatever exchange-rate system it preferred (fixed or floating). Countries were asked to "avoid manipulating exchange rates... in order to prevent effective balance-of-payments adjustment or to gain an unfair competitive advantage over other members." The IMF was directed to "oversee the compliance of each member with its obligations" in order to "exercise firm surveillance of the exchange-rate policies of its members." Monetary authorities of a country could buy and sell foreign exchange in order to "prevent or moderate sharp and disruptive fluctuations from day to day and from week to week," but it was considered unacceptable to suppress or reverse a long-run exchange-rate movement.

In principle, the current exchange-rate system is a managed float because the various central banks can intervene, and have done so, to effect day-to-day exchange rages. But official U.S. intervention in the foreign exchange markets has been sporadic and infrequent. Most of the intervention that has taken place has been by foreign central banks or governments. The most extensive U.S. intervention took place in 1989, when U.S. authorities sold $22 billion net in U.S. dollars and foreign central banks cooperated by selling $43 billion in U.S. dollars. The purpose of such sales was to lower the exchange value of the dollar to help correct the U.S. current account deficit. As Figure 3 showed, the U.S. dollar had been falling since 1985, but it reversed itself in early 1988. The dollar staged a minor rally until mid-1990. The rise in the dollar was believed to be counterproductive. While the 1989 interventions seem massive, they had comparatively little impact because private foreign-exchange trading is on the order of $50–$100 billion a *day* in New York alone.

Advantages. All the major countries float their exchange rates against the dollar. A number of small countries are tied to the dollar, and some others are tied to the French franc and the pound sterling. The 12 countries of the European Community have a European Monetary System with fixed exchange rates among themselves. Jointly, these rates float against the dollar. Thus, the entire system is one of individual floating, joint floating, and intervention in the foreign-exchange markets to keep the exchange rate from appreciating or depreciating too sharply. The advantages of this system are (1) monetary autonomy, (2) ease of balance-of-payments adjustment, (3) recycling of oil revenues, and (4) market efficiency.

When exchange rates are flexible, one country's monetary policy does not have to be dictated by the monetary policies of other countries. If everybody else wants to inflate, a country can maintain stable prices simply by following a long-run monetary policy of tight money (low monetary growth) and allowing its exchange rate to appreciate relative to the countries that choose to follow inflationary policies. Likewise, flexible exchange rates enable a country to follow highly inflationary policies by simply allowing its rate of exchange to depreciate.

Under a fixed exchange-rate regime, a deficit can be solved by internal deflation or unemployment. If this solution is not in the best interests of the country, a flexible exchange rate allows a country to depreciate its currency rather than undergo the discipline of Hume's reserve-flow mechanism. It is much easier to lower the value of a country's currency than to lower every internal commodity price and wage rate!

The most dramatic achievement of the current system occurred when the OPEC countries quadrupled the price of oil in 1973–74. The resulting shock to the world economy was absorbed by floating

EXAMPLE 3 Floating Exchange Rates: Bumblebees Cannot Fly

Economists are currently divided over whether governments should try to manage exchange rates. The argument for managing exchange rates rests on three points. First, the government can determine the fundamental equilibrium exchange rate. Second, floating exchange rates have been too volatile. Third, under floating exchange-rates, currencies can become significantly overvalued or undervalued.

The first and third points are related. If the information exists for determining whether an exchange rate is in "fundamental equilibrium," it is possible also to determine whether a currency is overvalued or undervalued (misaligned). A currency is overvalued if the exchange rate is higher than can be explained by changes in purchasing-power parity or improvements in the country's productivity relative to other countries.

Critics of floating rates also argue that excessive exchange-rate volatility reduces the volume of international trade by making international transactions more uncertain.

Supporters of the current system argue that the very concept of currency misalignment supposes that economists have the correct model of exchange-rate determination. Economists' exchange-rate models have not worked very well (such models focus on fundamentals), but is the exchange rate misaligned or are the models simply wrong? According to the law of aerodynamics, a bumblebee cannot fly. According to some economic models of exchange rates, the U.S. dollar is too high because of the trade deficit. Until better models of exchange rates are developed, economists should be slow in pronouncing whether an exchange rate is "overvalued" or "undervalued" (loaded terms).

Supporters of floating exchange rates point out that volatile exchange rates may or may not have reduced the volume of international trade. The evidence is mixed. Moreover, it is clear that exchange rates have shown excessive volatility. For example, in the United States, Canada, Germany, Great Britain, and Japan, both interest rates and their domestic stock markets have been more volatile than their exchange rates.

Sources: John Williamson, *The Exchange Rate System* (Cambridge: MIT Press, 1983); Jeffrey H. Bergstrand, "Is Exchange-Rate Volatility 'Excessive'?" Federal Reserve Bank of Boston, *Economic Review* (September/October 1983); Douglas K. Pearce, "Alternative Views of Exchange-Rate Determination," Federal Reserve Bank of St. Louis. *Economic Review* (February 1983).

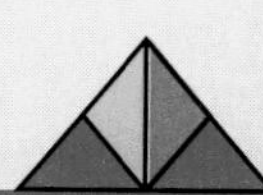

exchange rates. The enormous deficits that developed in the oil-importing countries and the necessity of the oil-exporting countries to invest their oil revenues meant that the foreign-exchange markets had a lot of recycling oil revenues to process. The previous Bretton Woods system could not have accomplished this recycling. Indeed, the Bretton Woods system could not take much smaller pressures. While exchange rates fluctuated dramatically after the oil shock, the system worked. It did not break down or cause crises like those that the world witnessed in the late 1960s and early 1970s. (See Example 3.)

Proponents of floating exchange rates argue that the foreign-exchange market, while volatile, is efficient. If a market is efficient, the price of the commodity being traded should reflect all currently available information. For example, on June 24, 1992, the British pound was worth \$1.880. The same day, a person could arrange a futures contract to buy a British pound in 90 days for \$1.851. Thus, on June 24, people expected the pound to fall slightly in 3 months. If the market works efficiently, such predictions (made daily) should not be biased one way or the other. Sometimes the futures price will overestimate the exchange rate and sometimes it will underestimate the exchange rate, but on the average, it will turn out to be right. This view appears to be supported by some studies of the foreign-exchange market, but other economists make exactly the opposite argument.[6]

Disadvantages. Critics of the present system of floating exchange rates claim that the system (1) is a nonsystem, (2) is characterized by exchange-rate volatility, (3) has increased world inflation, and (4) requires monetary unification for efficiency.

According to critics of floating rates, the world would be better off going back to the Bretton Woods system or to some system of managed exchange rates.[7] Establishing such a system, however, would require the monetary authorities of each country to set up and defend an exchange rate.

Others argue that it is impossible for the monetary authorities to know what the equilibrium exchange rate should be (see Example 4). Hence, any attempt by the monetary authorities to intervene in the foreign-exchange markets will inevitably reflect other goals. When an exchange rate appreciates, for example, exporters may complain that it is harder to sell in foreign markets. By moderating the appreciation of an exchange rate by purchasing foreign currencies, exporters are not hit quite as hard. Because each country has many domestic objectives, manipulation of exchange rates is inevitable and does not foster the achievement of long-run equilibrium. Because the economics of managing exchange rates is not well understood, it is difficult to evaluate this criticism.

It is not possible to determine whether floating exchange rates are too volatile. Some think they are too volatile simply because they are far from stable. For example, some economists would maintain that the 50 percent decline in the dollar from 1985 to early 1991 was just too much. But what is the criterion for such a judgment? We can compare the volume of trade under fixed exchange-rate periods with the volume of trade under floating exchange rates. Under this criterion, the evidence is mixed.[8] We can also compare exchange rates to other prices. It has been pointed out that exchange rates are no more volatile than the prices of stocks and bonds. Those prices are also determined on highly fluid, organized markets.

Some economists argue that floating exchange rates are inflationary. Under a fixed exchange rate, a country is constrained from following an inflationary policy because balance-of-payments deficits are produced. A floating exchange rate removes this constraint on domestic monetary policy. Hence, as a practical political matter, one should expect greater inflation with floating rates than with fixed rates. Economists Arthur Laffer and Robert Mundell are now suggesting that the United States should return to the gold standard in order to prevent inflation.

A final criticism of the present system is that the only way to enjoy the full benefits of a monetary economy is for every country to adopt the same currency. In other words, the current system is just a long detour away from the most efficient monetary arrangement. Presumably, in a world without nationalism and with free trade, the adoption of a truly international currency unit would come almost automatically. An international currency, however, requires the sacrifice of national monetary autonomy and other nationalistic goals. One unified world is a long way off.

POLICY COORDINATION: THE PLAZA AND PARIS AGREEMENTS

In September 1985, the *Group of Five* countries (the United States, Japan, West Germany, Britain, and France) met at the Plaza Hotel in New York City and agreed to reduce the value of the dollar. In October 1986, Japan and the United States agreed to coordinate their policies. Japan would stimulate its economy by cutting interest rates; the United States agreed to abandon its policy of driving down the dollar against the yen. Finally, on February 22, 1987, the Group of Five plus Canada met in Paris and agreed that the dollar was to be stabilized around current levels (keeping the dollar at the level of about 1.82 German marks and 153 Japanese yen), that Japan and West Germany would stimulate their economies, and that the United States would cut its budget deficit. Since that agreement both the mark and the yen have varied widely from those levels.

[6]It was confirmed in Jacob A. Frenkel, "Flexible Exchange Rates, Prices, and the Role of 'News': Lessons from the 1970s," *Journal of Political Economy* 89 (August 1981): 665–705.

[7]See John Williamson, *The Exchange Rate System* (Washington: Institute for International Economics, 1983).

[8]Leland Yeager, in *International Monetary Relations*, chap. 13, argues that exchange-rate fluctuations do not reduce trade. For the opposing view, see "International Trade Flows under Flexible Exchange Rates," Federal Reserve Bank of Kansas City, *Economic Review* 65 (March 1980): 3–10.

EXAMPLE 4 The European Monetary System

The countries of the European Community (except for Portugal and Greece) have agreed to keep their exchange rates fixed in terms of a single monetary unit, currently called the ECU. The exchange rates of each country are allowed to fluctuate only 2.25 percent above or below the fixed rates in terms of the ECU. For example, the official exchange rate between the French franc and the British pound is 15.16 francs to the pound. When the pound rises by 2.25 percent in terms of francs, the central banks of the two countries must intervene in the market to push the price of the pound down by selling pounds and buying francs. A fundamental rule of the European Monetary System is that countries cannot unilaterally devalue or revalue their currencies.

The basic mechanism of the European Monetary System is very similar to the Bretton Woods system established for the world economy after World War II. A necessary condition for the success of the European Monetary System is that countries give up a great deal of their monetary autonomy. Wildly different inflation rates are not possible. Since 1980, the countries of Europe have experienced convergence in their inflation rates. For example, in 1980 Italy's inflation rate was about 20 percent while Germany's was about 5 percent. By 1990 only 4 percentage points separated the inflation rates of the two countries.

The goal of the European Monetary System is to have a single European currency.

Source: *The Federal Reserve Bulletin,* October 1991, 769–83.

Attempts to intervene in exchange markets to stabilize the dollar/yen rate or the dollar/mark rate are probably destined for failure. As indicated earlier, the amounts that governments have available for exchange-rate stabilization are small relative to the enormous amounts of funds that private speculators can tap whenever they wish to bet on or against any particular currency.

The most important component of any agreement is the extent to which monetary and fiscal policies are coordinated. Policy coordination can stabilize exchange rates. There is always a mix of monetary and fiscal policies that will keep exchange rates stable. This is the lesson to be learned from David Hume's gold-or-reserve flow mechanism. For example, a sufficiently contractionary monetary policy can always bring exchange rates down; a sufficiently contractionary monetary policy can always improve a country's exchange rate. Thus, in a world of floating exchange rates, explicit policy coordination would be necessary to prevent exchange rates from becoming too volatile. If one country follows an expansionary monetary and fiscal policy while another country follows a contractionary monetary and fiscal policy, there should be considerable changes in the exchange rate.[9] (See Example 4.)

> As long as monetary and fiscal policies between countries are not coordinated, it is unlikely that exchange rates will stabilize.

SUMMARY

1. Foreign exchange is the national currency of another country that is needed to carry out international transactions. America's demand for foreign

[9]The discussion of policy coordination is based on *The Economic Report of the President, 1987,* chap. 3; Jacob A. Frenkel and Assaf Razin, "Real Exchange Rates, Interest Rates, and Fiscal Policies," *Economic Studies Quarterly* 37 (June 1986): 99–102; Jacob A. Frenkel, "Commentary on 'Causes of Appreciation and Volatility of the Dollar,'" in *The U.S. Dollar—Recent Developments, Outlook, and Policy Options,* Federal Reserve Bank of Kansas City, 1985; "Exchange Rates and Intervention after G-5," *The NBER Digest,* National Bureau of Economic Research, February 1987.

exchange increases when U.S. residents demand more foreign goods and services. America's supply of foreign exchange increases when residents of foreign countries demand more U.S. goods and services. The demand curve for foreign exchange is downward sloping because as the dollar price of foreign currency rises, there is a corresponding rise in the cost of foreign goods to American importers. The supply curve of foreign exchange tends to be upward sloping because as the dollar price of foreign currency rises, American goods appear cheaper to foreigners. Under a floating exchange-rate system, the exchange rate is allowed to float to the point where the demand for foreign exchange equals the supply. When the exchange rate reflects the relative purchasing power of the currencies of two different countries, purchasing-power parity prevails between the two currencies. Under a fixed exchange-rate system, equilibrium in the demand for and supply of foreign exchange is brought about by Hume's gold-flow mechanism.

2. A country's balance of payments provides a summary record of its economic transactions with foreign residents over a period of 1 year. It is a two-sided (credit/debit) summary that must always be in accounting balance. International capital movements raise the physical capital stocks in the capital-importing countries and lower them in the capital-exporting countries.

3. Today, the world operates on a system of floating exchange rates with active exchange-rate stabilization by the major central banks. The Bretton Woods system set up after World War II broke down because a currency-adjustment system is fundamentally in conflict with free international capital movements. Speculation destroyed the old Bretton Woods system. The new international monetary system involves a mixture of floating and fixed exchange rates. Since 1973, the U.S. dollar has floated with respect to all the major currencies of the world.

4. The international coordination of fiscal and monetary policies may be necessary to reduce exchange-rate volatility.

KEY TERMS

foreign exchange
fixed exchange rate
floating exchange rate
purchasing-power parity (PPP)
balance of payments
merchandise trade balance
current account balance

QUESTIONS AND PROBLEMS

1. Suppose the German mark is worth $0.55 (in U.S. dollars) and $1 is worth 150 Japanese yen. How much would a Mercedes-Benz cost in U.S. dollars if the German price were 30,000 deutschmarks (DM)? How much would a Toyota cost in U.S. dollars if the Japanese price were 1,200,000 yen?
2. Table A shows part of an actual newspaper report on the foreign-exchange market. Did the British pound rise or fall from Tuesday to Wednesday? Did the Japanese yen rise or fall from Tuesday to Wednesday? What happened to the U.S. dollar in terms of the pound? What happened to the U.S. dollar in terms of the yen?

TABLE A

	Foreign Currency in Dollars		Dollar in Foreign Currency	
	Wed.	**Tues.**	**Wed.**	**Tues.**
British pound	1.7475	1.7495	0.5722	0.5716
Japanese yen	0.00753	0.00749	132.77	133.00

3. If there were a floating exchange rate between Japan and the United States, which of the following events would cause the Japanese yen to appreciate? Which would cause the yen to depreciate? Explain your answers.
   a. The government of Japan orders its automobile companies to limit exports to the United States.
   b. The United States places a quota on Japanese automobiles.
   c. The United States increases its money supply relative to Japan's money supply.
   d. Interest rates in the United States rise relative to Japanese interest rates.
   e. More Japanese people decide to visit America.
   f. Japanese productivity growth rises relative to U.S. productivity growth.
4. Indicate whether each of the following transactions represents a debit (a supply of U.S. dollars)

or a credit (a demand for U.S. dollars) in the U.S. balance of payments.

a. An American commercial airline buys the European-made Airbus (an airplane competing with the Boeing 747).
b. A European airline buys an American Boeing 747.
c. An American makes a trip around the world.
d. A French company pays dividends to an American owning its stock.
e. An American buys stock in a French company.
f. An American company borrows from a European investor.
g. A Canadian oil company exports oil to Japan on an American tanker.
h. An American banker makes a loan to a European manufacturer.

5. Explain the mechanism under which U.S. restrictions on its imports will lead to fewer U.S. exports under a floating exchange-rate system.
6. What would happen if Mexico and the United States had a fixed exchange rate but for 20 years Mexico had more inflation than the United States?
7. What are some arguments for floating exchange rates?
8. What are some arguments against floating exchange rates?
9. Why can exchange-rate volatility probably be reduced more by international policy coordination than by market intervention?

SUGGESTED READINGS

Frenkel, Jacob A. "Commentary on 'Causes of Appreciation and Volatility of the Dollar' " in *The U.S. Dollar—Recent Developments, Outlook, and Policy Options,* Federal Reserve Bank of Kansas City, 1985.

Hakkio, Craig S. "Interest Rates and Exchange Rates—What Is the Relationship?" Federal Reserve Bank of Kansas City, *Economic Review,* November 1986.

Kreinin, Mordechai. *International Economics,* 5th ed. New York: Harcourt Brace Jovanovich, 1987, chaps. 2, 3, 4, and 7.

Lindert, Peter H., and Charles P. Kindleberger. *International Economics,* 7th ed. Homewood, IL: Richard D. Irwin, 1982, 243–62.

Microeconomics

IV

Product Markets

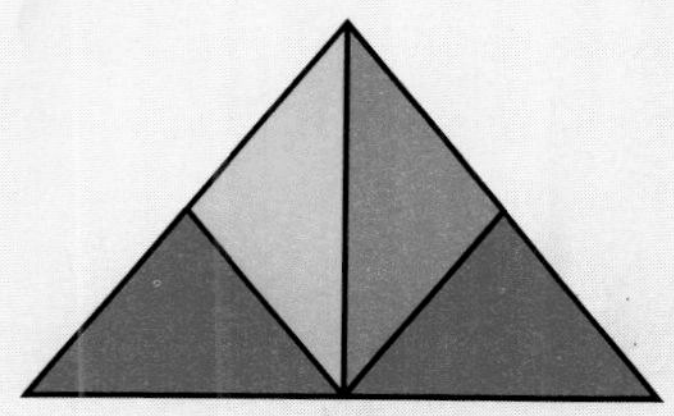

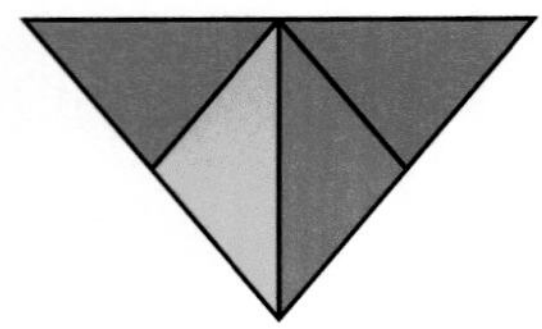

26

Elasticity of Demand and Supply

CHAPTER INSIGHT

A state once attempted to raise revenues with a 20 percent increase in tuition and fees at state universities and a 25 percent increase in the charge for vanity license plates. One year later, the state treasurer reported that revenues from tuition and fees from state universities were up 15 percent, while revenues from vanity license plates were down 10 percent.

This chapter uses the concept of price elasticity, which shows that the sensitivity of buyers to price increases varies from product to product, to explain why raising prices increased revenues from tuition and fees but decreased revenues from vanity license plates. The tuition raise at state universities caused only a few students (at least in the short run) to go out of state or switch to private universities, so revenues increased. However, when the price of vanity license plates was raised, many people switched to regular license plates (a perfectly good substitute), so revenues fell.

The elasticity concept applies not only to the responsiveness of quantity sold to changes in the good's own price but also to the responsiveness of demand to changes in income and in the prices of other goods. In addition, there are elasticity measures of the responsiveness of quantity supplied to changes in price.

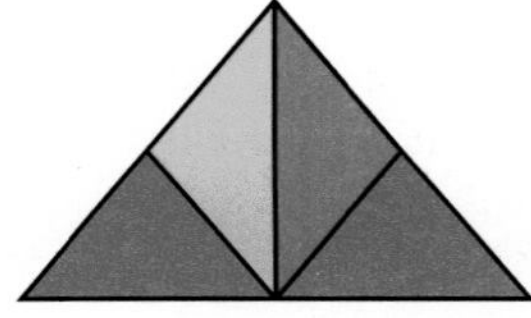

THE PRICE ELASTICITY OF DEMAND

Remember that the demand curve shows how quantity demanded responds to different prices, *ceteris paribus*, and the supply curve shows how quantity supplied responds to different prices, *ceteris paribus*. In panels *a* and *b* of Figure 1, the equilibrium intersection of *S* (the supply curve) and the demand curve (whether *D* or *D′*) is at point *e*, where price is $10 and quantity is 100 units. The only difference between the two diagrams is in the demand curve. *D* in panel *a* is much flatter than *D′* in panel *b*. The supply curves (*S*) are identical.

Suppose that there is a reduction in supply for one of the reasons discussed in Chapter 5. The supply curve shifts to the left, as illustrated in panels *a* and *b*. The supply shift from *S* to *S′* is the same in panels *a* and *b*. When supply decreases, equilibrium price rises and equilibrium quantity falls. The equilibrium point *e* moves in panel *a* to *e′* on *D* and in panel *b* to *e″* on *D′*. In panel *a*, the price increased (from $10 to $14) is relatively small compared to the substantial reduction in quantity demanded (from 100 units to only 20 units). In panel *b*, on the other hand, the price increase (from $10 to $20) is relatively large compared to the small reduction in quantity demanded from 100 to 80 units. The difference between the two demand curves in panels *a* and *b* is in the *responsiveness of quantity demanded to a price increase*. In panel *a*, quantity demanded is very responsive to the price change; in panel *b*, it is less responsive. The **price elasticity of demand (E_d)** is a measure of this responsiveness. (See Example 1.)

> The **price elasticity of demand (E_d)** is the percentage change in the quantity demanded divided by the percentage change in price.

Absolute changes in price or quantity demanded are poor measures of responsiveness. If a $1 increase in the price of coal lowers quantity demanded by 1 ton, we cannot determine whether these changes are large or small unless we know the initial price and quantity. If the initial price is $2 per ton, a $1 change in price represents a 50 percent increase in price. If the initial price is $1000, a $1 change in price is minuscule. The same principle applies to quantity

FIGURE 1
Response to a Reduction in Supply

(*a*) Quality Demanded Is More Responsive to Price Change

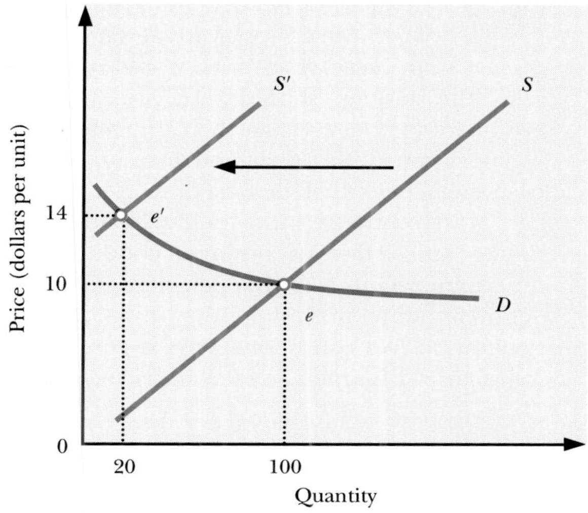

(*b*) Quality Demanded Is Less Responsive to Price Change

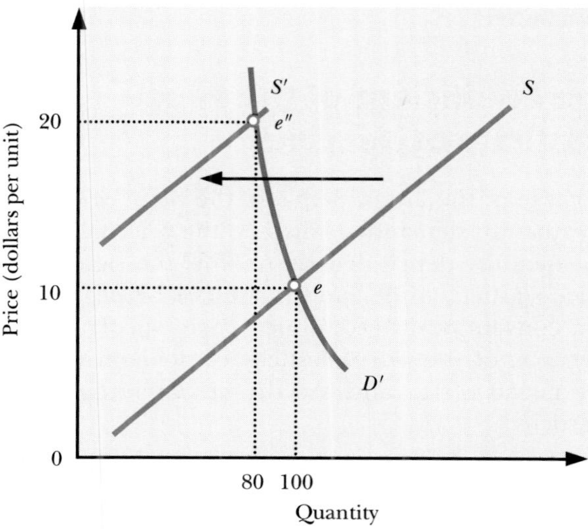

In both panels *a* and *b*, *S* intersects the demand curve at the equilibrium price/quantity combination of $10/100 units. The supply conditions are exactly the same in each diagram, but the quantity demanded is less responsive to price changes in panel *b* than in panel *a*. A decrease in supply from *S* to *S′* causes a sharper increase in the equilibrium price when quantity demanded is less responsive to price. Although the price increase in *b* from $10 to $20 is greater than the price increase in *a* from $10 to $14, quantity demanded falls more in *a* than it does in *b*.

EXAMPLE 1 How Businesses Know Price Elasticity

One of the most valuable pieces of information needed by businesses is, What would happen to sales if we raise prices? If an increase in price would devastate sales, the business should keep prices as they are or lower them. If, on the other hand, the business can raise prices and lose only a few customers, prices will be raised.

Most businesses use their executives' intimate knowledge of business conditions to determine whether to change prices. These executives, aware of competitive situations and general market conditions, have a good "feel" for what will happen to sales if prices change. The executives can consult the firm's sales representatives to confirm their own sense of what will happen. If the company's management lacks confidence about the price elasticity of demand, the firm can hire management consultants who use sophisticated interview techniques and experiments to predict how customers will react to a price change. These specialized services sell for $50,000 or more—a price that shows the importance of knowing the price elasticity of demand.

Source: Timothy Tregarthen, "Elasticities for Sale," *The Margin* (December 1987): 11.

changes. The measure of the response of quantity demanded to change in price must therefore be the relative (or percentage) change in price or quantity demanded.

The Coefficient of the Price Elasticity of Demand

Because of the law of demand, the price rises when the quantity demanded falls, and the price falls when the quantity demanded rises. Thus the sign of the price elasticity of demand will always be negative. It is a convention in economics when calculating the *coefficient* of the price elasticity of demand to drop the negative sign and use the *absolute value* of the elasticity.

The coefficient of the price elasticity of demand (E_d) is the absolute value of the percentage change in quantity demanded (ΔQ) divided by the percentage change in price (ΔP). The coefficient measures the percentage change in quantity demanded per 1 percent change in price:

$$E_d = \left| \frac{\%\Delta Q}{\%\Delta P} \right|$$

where $\%\Delta$ stands for percentage change.

For example, if P rises by 10 percent and Q falls by 20 percent, E_d equals 20 percent divided by 10 percent, or 2. An elasticity coefficient of 2 means that if prices were raised from the prevailing rate, the percentage change in quantity demanded would be 2 times the percentage change in price. The elasticity coefficient measures the percentage change in quantity demanded for each 1 percent change in price. With an elasticity coefficient of 2, a 5 percent increase in price means a 10 percent reduction in quantity demanded.

Calculating the Price Elasticity of Demand

Table 1 shows how to calculate the price elasticity of demand. The price of wheat changes from $4.50 per bushel to $5.50 per bushel, and the quantity demanded responds by falling from 105 to 95 bushels per month. We determine the price elasticity of demand by calculating the percentage changes in quantity demanded and price. This may seem simple, but there is a trick: We must calculate the percentage change on the basis of *average* quantity and *average* price. Why? We wish to calculate the same price elasticity whether the price rises or falls. For example, when the price rises from $4.50 to $5.50, the percentage increase is ($1/$4.50) × 100 = 22 percent. But when the price falls from $5.50 to $4.50, the percent-

TABLE 1
How to Calculate the Price Elasticity of Demand

	Prices (dollars per bushel)	Symbols
Initial price	\$4.50	P_0
Change in price	1.00	ΔP
New price	5.50	$P_1 = P_0 + \Delta P$
Average price	5.00	$P = (P_0 + P_1)/2$
Percentage change in price	20%	$(\Delta P/P) \times 100$
	Quantities (bushels per month)	
Initial quantity demanded	105	Q_0
Change in quantity demanded	−10	ΔQ
New quantity demanded	95	$Q_1 = Q_0 + \Delta Q$
Average quantity demanded	100	$Q = (Q_0 + Q_1)/2$
Percentage change in Q	10%	$(\Delta Q/Q) \times 100$
Price elasticity of demand	10%/20% = 0.5	$(\Delta Q/Q)/(\Delta P/P)$

age decrease is (\$1/\$5.50) × 100 = 18 percent. However, we don't want one price elasticity for raising the price and another for lowering the price; therefore, we calculate the percentage change on the basis of the average price, \$5 = (\$4.50 + \$5.50)/2. The percentage change in the price is then (\$1/\$5) × 100 = 20 percent. Similar reasoning applies to the percentage change in quantity demanded. The change in quantity demanded is 10 bushels; the average quantity demanded is 100 = (95 + 105)/2. The percentage change in quantity demanded is (10/100) × 100 = 10 percent. Accordingly, the price elasticity is E_d = 10 percent/20 percent = 0.5.

When we use the average price and average quantity to calculate the price elasticity of demand we are using the **midpoints elasticity formula**. This formula yields the same elasticity coefficient for an increase from a lower price to a higher price as for the decrease back from the higher price to the lower price.[1]

The **midpoints elasticity formula** for determining the elasticity of demand (E_d) for a given segment of the demand curve is

$$E_d = \frac{\text{Percent change in quantity demanded}}{\text{Percent change in price}}$$

$$= \frac{\text{Change in quantity demanded}}{\text{Average of two quantities}} \div \frac{\text{Change in price}}{\text{Average of two prices}}$$

Figure 2 shows an independent summary of the midpoints elasticity formula for any demand curve, D. The two prices are P_1 and P_2; the associated quantities demanded are Q_1 and Q_2.

Elasticity and Total Revenue

Economists typically divide elasticity coefficients into three broad categories:

1. When $E_d > 1$, demand is *elastic* (Q is strongly responsive to changes in P).
2. When $E_d < 1$, demand is *inelastic* (Q responds weakly to changes in P).
3. When $E_d = 1$, demand is *unitary elastic* (a borderline case).

[1]In symbols, if P_1 and P_2 are the two prices and Q_1 and Q_2 are the two quantities, the midpoints elasticity formula can be simplified as follows:

$$E_d = -\frac{Q_2 - Q_1}{(Q_1 + Q_2)/2} \div \frac{P_2 - P_1}{(P_1 + P_2)/2}$$

$$= \frac{Q_2 - Q_1}{P_1 - P_2} \times \frac{P_1 + P_2}{Q_1 + Q_2}$$

FIGURE 2
The Midpoints Elasticity Formula

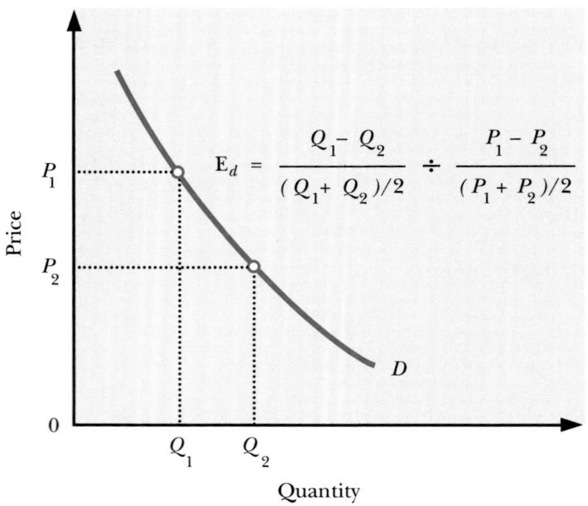

To calculate the elasticity of demand between any two prices, P_1 and P_2, along a given demand curve, *D*, requires three steps: (1) calculating the percentage change in quantity demanded by dividing the change in quantity by the average of the quantities, (2) calculating the percentage change in price by dividing the change in price by the average of the two prices, and (3) calculating the ratio of the percentage change in quantity demanded to the percentage change in price.

Coefficients for price elasticity of demand are divided in this way because total revenue responds differently to price changes in each category.

The coefficient of the elasticity of demand can be used to show what will happen to the **total revenue *(TR)*** of sellers or, in other words, what will happen to the total expenditures of consumers when price changes.

> The **total revenue *(TR)*** of sellers in a market is equal to the price of the commodity times the quantity sold:
>
> $$TR = P \cdot Q$$

Along a demand curve, price and quantity demanded will always move in opposite directions. While a fall in price lowers total revenue, the resulting rise in quantity demanded raises total revenue. Total revenue is caught in a tug-of-war between these conflicting forces. The outcome depends on the extent to which quantity demanded responds to changes in price. For example, a relatively small rise in quantity demanded will not offset the decline in revenue caused by a fall in price, but a substantial rise in quantity demanded could offset the revenue loss caused by a lower price. The response of total revenue to price changes depends on the price elasticity of demand.

Elastic Demand. If $E_d > 1$, the percentage rise in quantity demanded is greater than the percentage fall in price. Revenue *increases* because the increase in quantity demanded more than offsets the *decrease* in price. Price and revenue move in opposite directions.

> When $E_d > 1$, $|\%\Delta Q| > |\%\Delta P|$.
>
> If $|\%\Delta Q| > |\%\Delta P|$, *TR* will move in the opposite direction of price.

Inelastic Demand. If $E_d < 1$, the percentage rise in quantity demanded is less than the percentage fall in price. Revenue *falls* because the *decline* in price is not offset by the relatively small rise in quantity. Price and revenue move in the same direction.

> When $E_d < 1$, $|\%\Delta Q| < |\%\Delta P|$.
>
> If $|\%\Delta Q| < |\%\Delta P|$, *TR* will move in the same direction as price.

Unitary Elastic Demand. If $E_d = 1$, the percentage rise in quantity demanded equals the percentage fall in price. Revenue is unchanged because the decline in price is just offset by the rise in quantity.

> When $E_d = 1$, $|\%\Delta Q| = |\%\Delta P|$.
>
> If $|\%\Delta Q| = |\%\Delta P|$, *TR* will not change.

The Total Revenue Test. We can determine whether demand for a particular product is elastic, inelastic, or unitary elastic by applying the **total revenue test** to movements along a demand curve that combines the principles of elasticity already discussed.

TABLE 2
Total Revenue and Elasticity

	Price (dollars per unit) P (1)	Quantity (units) Q (2)	Total Revenue TR = $P \times Q$ (3) = (1) × (2)	Direction of Change in Revenue (4)	Percentage Change in Quantity Demanded $\frac{\Delta Q}{(Q_1 + Q_2)/2}$ (5)	Percentage Change in Price $\frac{\Delta P}{(P_1 + P_2)/2}$ (6)	Coefficient of Price Elasticity, E_d (7) = (5) ÷ (6)	Conclusion (8)
	9	15	135					
(a)	7	25	175	Increase	$\frac{10}{20} = 50\%$	$\frac{2}{8} = 25\%$	$\frac{50}{25} = 2$	Elastic
(b)	5	35	175	No change	$\frac{10}{30} = 33.3\%$	$\frac{2}{6} = 33.3\%$	$\frac{33.3}{33.3} = 1$	Unitary elastic
(c)	3	45	135	Decrease	$\frac{10}{40} = 25\%$	$\frac{2}{4} = 50\%$	$\frac{25}{50} = 0.5$	Inelastic

Columns 1 and 2 show a demand schedule. Column 3 is the total revenue of sellers—or the total expenditure of buyers. Column 4 shows what happens to revenue as *price falls.* Column 5 shows the percentage change in quantity using the midpoint between Q_1 and Q_2 as the base. Column 6 shows the percentage change in price using the midpoint between P_1 and P_2 as the base. Finally, column 7 shows the ratio of column 5 to column 6—the elasticity of demand, E_d. Notice that when demand is elastic ($E_d > 1$), revenue rises when price falls; when demand is inelastic ($E_d < 1$), revenue falls when price falls.

The **total revenue test** uses the following criteria to determine elasticity:

1. If price and total revenue move in different directions, $E_d > 1$ (demand is elastic).
2. If price and total revenue move in the same direction, $E_d < 1$ (demand is inelastic).
3. If total revenue does not change when price changes, $E_d = 1$ (demand is unitary elastic).

There are thus two ways to determine whether demand is elastic, inelastic, or unitary elastic. The first method is to calculate the coefficient of the price elasticity of demand from price and quantity information. The second method is to observe what happens to total revenue when price changes and apply the total revenue test. Although this second method also indicates whether demand is elastic, inelastic, or unitary elastic, it does *not* give a value for the coefficient.

In Table 2, column 3 shows total revenue (price times quantity) along the demand curve. Column 4 indicates whether total revenue rises or falls as prices decline from \$9 to \$7 to \$5 to \$3. This column summarizes the visual information contained in the colored areas of the graphs in Figure 3. In panel *a*, the price is reduced from \$9 to \$7; 15 units were sold at \$9, and now 25 units are sold at \$7. The blue area indicates the loss in revenue that occurred because the first 15 units had to be sold at the lower price of \$7. But more units are sold at \$7 than at \$9. The orange area indicates the revenue gained from the sale of more units. Total revenue rises because the orange area is larger than the blue area when demand is *elastic.* The revenue lost through the lower price is more than offset by the revenue gained by the sale of substantially more units.

The midpoints formula also shows that demand is elastic. In the segment of the demand curve where price falls from \$9 to \$7, quantity demanded rises from 15 to 25 units. The appropriate percent increase in quantity demanded is the change in quantity demanded, 10, divided by the average of the

FIGURE 3
Elasticity Rises as Price Increases

(*a*) Elastic Demand

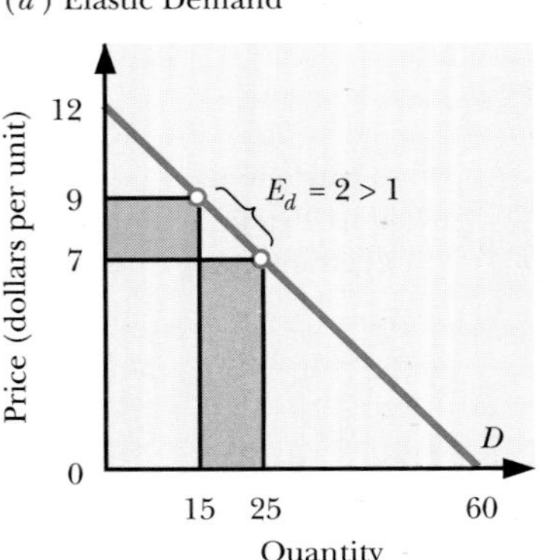

(*b*) Unitary Elastic Demand

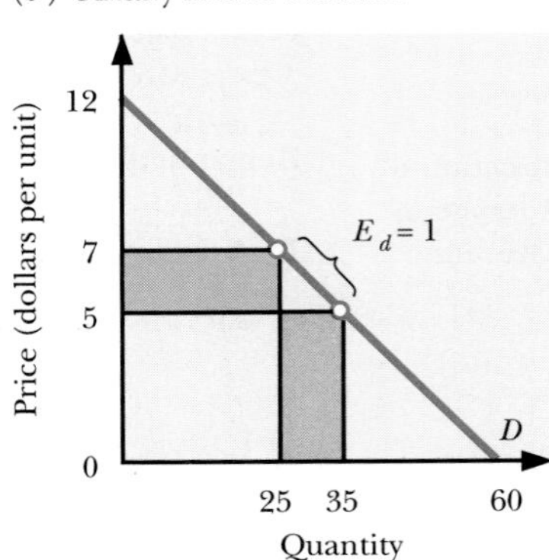

(*c*) Inelastic Demand

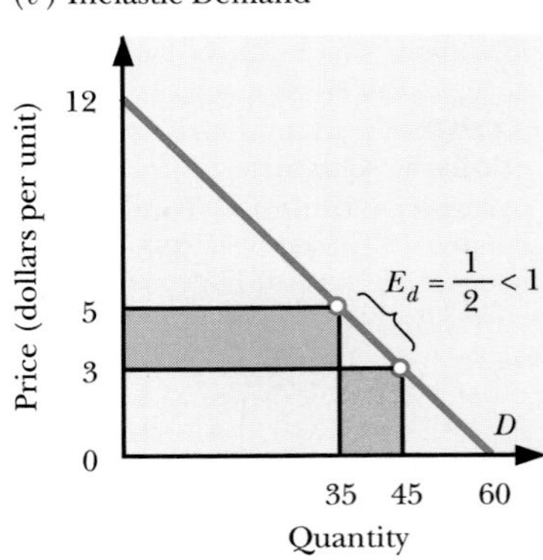

The linear demand curve, *D*, is the same in panels *a, b,* and *c.* Between the prices of \$9 and \$7, the elasticity of demand (E_d) is 2; demand is elastic. Panel *a* shows that a reduction in price raises revenue. The blue rectangle shows the revenue lost due to the lower price, and the orange rectangle shows the revenue gained due to the greater number of units sold. Because the orange rectangle has a greater area than the blue rectangle, more revenue is gained than lost.

Between prices of \$7 and \$5. E_d equals 1; panel *b* shows that the reduction in price has no impact on revenue. Finally, between the prices of \$5 and \$3, E_d is $\frac{1}{2}$; demand is inelastic. Panel *c* shows that the reduction in price lowers revenue because more revenue is lost (blue area) than gained (orange area). Thus, the elasticity of demand varies along a linear demand curve with constant slope. *Elasticity and slope are different.*

two quantities, $(15 + 25)/2 = 20$. Hence the percent change in quantity demanded is $10/20 = 50$ percent. The percent change in quantity demanded is given in column 5, and the percent change in price appears in column 6; so $E_d = 50/25 = 2$.

If price now falls from \$7 to \$5, as in panel *b* of Figure 3, demand is unitary elastic; in this case, revenue remains constant because the revenue lost (the blue area) equals the revenue gained (the orange area). As price falls further from \$5 to \$3, demand is inelastic. In panel *c,* the revenue lost (the blue area) exceeds the revenue gained (the orange area) from selling a few more units, so total revenue falls.[2] Column 7 shows that the coefficient of price elasticity is now 0.5.

[2]The total revenue test can be applied to the data listed in Table 2 and graphed in Figure 3. In line *a*, where price decreases and total revenue increases, $E_d (= 2) > 1$. In line *b*, where total revenue does not change when price changes, $E_d = 1$. In line *c*, where price and total revenue both decrease, $E_d (= 0.5) < 1$.

Perfectly Elastic or Perfectly Inelastic Demand Curves

The highest degree of elasticity possible—the greatest responsiveness of quantity demanded to price—is a perfectly horizontal demand curve. In Figure 4, any amount on demand curve *D* can be sold at the indicated price (\$5). Such a horizontal demand curve describes **perfectly elastic demand.**

A horizontal demand curve illustrates **perfectly elastic demand** ($E_d = \infty$), a condition in which quantity demanded is most responsive to price.

The elasticity formula shows that E_d is infinitely large ($E_d = \infty$) when the demand curve is horizontal: The quantity demanded can be increased indefinitely without a decrease in price. As a result, the elasticity formula yields an infinitely large coefficient of price elasticity of demand.

Although perfectly elastic demand curves represent an extreme, they are common in the real world. In perfectly competitive markets—defined in Chapter 5 as markets in which no single producer is large enough to influence the market price—each seller can sell all he or she wants to sell at the market price. Single sellers do not have to lower their prices to sell more. American corn or wheat farmers can sell all they want at the prevailing market price and can't sell anything at a higher price. Thus each seller can face a horizontal demand curve even though the market demand curve is downward sloping.

The lowest degree of inelasticity possible—the least sensitivity of quantity demanded to price—occurs when the demand curve is perfectly vertical. In Figure 4, the vertical demand curve D' demonstrates **perfectly inelastic demand.** With this demand curve, 75 units of the good will be sold regardless of the price. The coefficient of the elasticity of demand is zero because if the price were to rise above $5, the percentage change in the quantity demanded would be zero. When zero is divided by the percentage change in price, E_d is zero.

FIGURE 4
Perfectly Elastic and Perfectly Inelastic Demand Curves

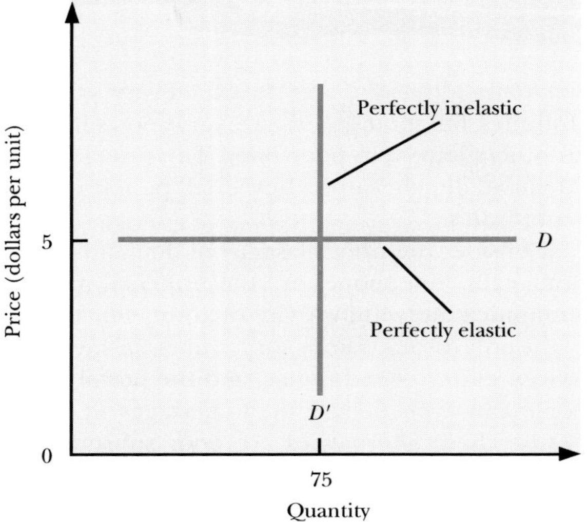

The demand curve D is perfectly elastic; it is perfectly horizontal, or parallel to the quantity axis. The demand curve D' is perfectly inelastic; it is perfectly vertical, or parallel to the price axis. The elasticity-of-demand coefficient of D is infinitely large along the entire demand schedule. The elasticity-of-demand coefficient of D' is zero along the entire demand curve.

> A vertical demand curve illustrates **perfectly inelastic demand** ($E_d = 0$). a condition in which quantity demanded is least responsive to price.

With a perfectly inelastic demand curve, no matter how high the price rises, consumers will not cut back on the quantity demanded. The demand curve of insulin for the diabetic is probably as close to perfectly inelastic as possible, but even in this case if the price rose higher and higher, diabetics might eventually reduce their dosages and accept some health loss or change their behavior by eating less or exercising more.

Demand curves can be perfectly inelastic *within a range of prices*. If insulin prices rose by 10 percent, the quantity demanded would probably not change. If the price of salt rose from $0.20 to $0.21 per pound, the quantity demanded would probably stay the same.

Elasticity versus Slope along a Demand Curve

Perfectly elastic and inelastic demand curves describe very special circumstances: the extremes of infinite response and no response. A vertical demand curve shows perfect inelasticity; a horizontal demand curve shows perfect elasticity. It might be tempting to conclude, by analogy, that demand is more elastic when the demand curve is "flat" than when the demand curve is "steep." This conclusion would be wrong.

In general, the law of demand holds: As price falls, quantity demanded rises. However, the price elasticity of demand is very different from the slope of the demand curve. Although both elasticity and slope measure the response of quantity demanded to change in price, the slope of the demand curve does not indicate the size of the response. For example, recall the demand schedule in columns 1 and 2 of Table 2 (depicted by curve D in Figure 3). Each time the price falls by $2, quantity demanded rises by 10 units. The slope of the demand curve is constant because the curve is a straight line. We showed earlier that when the price falls from $9 to $3, the

EXAMPLE 2 Why the Telephone Company Worries about Charging Too High a Price

The local telephone company does not have any close competitors. If we want to communicate with others in our city, our best choice is to use the telephone. Local telephone rates are generally regulated by government bodies (such as the state utilities commission or the local city council), but even if the telephone company could set its own rates, it would have to worry about charging too high a price.

We have seen that elasticity of demand increases as price increases. This is true for goods and services in general and for local telephone service in particular. For example, if the telephone company raised its rates by $10 per month starting at a very low monthly rate (such as $15 per month), it would lose few customers. An increase in rates would raise revenues. However, at some point after a series of successive price increases, an additional monthly increase would cause the telephone company to lose so many customers that its revenues would actually decline.

This example shows that even businesses that have the power to set just about any price are constrained by an increasing price elasticity of demand. Such businesses cannot set arbitrarily high prices because they could actually reduce their profitability by losing too many customers.

price elasticity of demand falls. Why? For the same price reductions, the percentage change in price is rising since P is falling; and for the same increases in quantity demanded, the percentage change in quantity demanded is falling since Q is rising. (See Example 2.)

Price elasticity of demand falls as one moves down a linear (straight-line) demand curve. For example, consumers are more responsive to price changes at high prices than at low prices. When ballpoint pens were introduced after World War II, they sold for about $90 (in 1992 dollars). The demand for them was very price elastic: When the price dropped, consumers eagerly increased the quantity demanded as they substituted ballpoint pens for messy and inconvenient fountain pens. Today, the price of ballpoint pens is very low: A reduction in price would bring about a comparatively small increase in quantity demanded.

Determinants of Price Elasticity of Demand

What determines the sensitivity of consumers to price? The four determinants of the price elasticity of demand for a good are (1) the availability of substitutes, (2) the relative importance of the good in the budget, (3) the amount of time available to adjust to the price change, and (4) the status of the good as a necessity or luxury.

The Availability of Substitutes. Every good has substitutes, but some goods have very good substitutes and others have very poor ones. The price elasticity of demand depends upon how easily people can turn to substitutes.

Consider the price elasticity of demand for telephone calls. Telephones are the principal means of communicating within a city or town, but they are not the only means. There are commercial messenger services, citizens-band radios, and the postal service. People can even deliver their messages in person. Because these alternatives are poor substitutes for the telephone, we would not expect a substantial percentage change in quantity demanded in response to a 1 percent change in price.

On the other hand, there are quite a few good substitutes for going to the movies, including subscribing to a cable TV service, watching commercial television, or renting a video. As a result, the elasticity of demand for movie tickets would probably be high. (See Example 3.)

EXAMPLE 3 Why Movie Producers Are No Longer Considered a Monopoly

In the 1950s, the U.S. Justice Department ruled that movie studios such as Paramount and Warner Brothers had a monopoly over the entertainment industry. The studios were ordered to sell off their chains of movie theaters. The Justice Department held that allowing studio executives to control the movie industry all the way from production to screening was against the public interest.

In 1986, the Justice Department reversed its 30-year ban against studio ownership of movie theaters. The department concluded that such ownership no longer constituted a danger to the entertainment-buying public. Why? In the early 1950s, movies dominated the entertainment industry. Television was in its infancy, and few communities had live theater. By the mid-1980s, the industry had become crowded. Consumers could now choose among movies, regular television, cable television, live theater, and videocassettes.

The broadening of the entertainment industry resulted in more viable substitutes for movies and raised the price elasticity of demand for movies. Movie makers and distributors must now think twice about raising their prices because customers can easily choose other forms of entertainment.

The availability of substitutes depends in part upon how broadly a good is defined. The elasticity of demand for automobiles is lower than that for Chevrolets. The demand for energy will be less elastic than the demand for coal. The demand for entertainment will be less elastic than the demand for movie tickets. The more narrowly defined the product (Chevrolets versus automobiles, coal versus energy, movie tickets versus entertainment), the greater the number of close substitutes (Plymouths for Chevrolets, natural gas for coal, cable TV for movies) and the higher the elasticity of demand. This principle can be applied as follows: The price elasticity of demand for lettuce has been estimated to be in the vicinity of 0.3; the demand is highly inelastic.[3] The demand for *Farmer Smith's lettuce,* however, would be very elastic (nearly perfectly elastic) because there are many perfect substitutes for the lettuce produced on Smith's farm: lettuce of equal quality and freshness produced on any other farm.

> The greater is the number of close substitutes for a good, the *more elastic* is its demand. The smaller is the number of close substitutes for a good, the *more inelastic* is its demand.

The Relative Importance of the Good in the Budget. Both gasoline and salt have few close substitutes. Which one should be more elastic?

Would an increase in the price of salt from \$0.40 to \$0.50 a package (a 22 percent increase by the midpoints method) have a substantial percentage effect on purchases of salt? The average consumer might buy two boxes of salt per year, so a 22 percent price increase would raise the family's cost of living by only \$0.20 per year. A 22 percent increase in the price of gasoline, however, translates into a price increase from \$1.20 per gallon to \$1.50 per gallon. The average family consumes about 1000 gallons of gas per year, so the cost of living of the average family would be increased by \$300 per year. Because consumers would scarcely notice the salt price increase, their purchases would hardly be affected. The gasoline price increase, however, would lower real income by a noticeable margin and would therefore depress gasoline purchases.

[3] George E. Brandow, "Interrelation among Demands for Farm Products and Implications for Control of Market Supply," Pennsylvania Agricultural Experimental Station Bulletin 680, 1961, Table 1.

As this comparison shows, the price elasticity of demand depends upon the relative importance of the good in the budget.

> Goods that represent a small fraction of the consumer's budget (salt, pepper, drinking water, matches) are more inelastic in demand than products that constitute a large fraction of the consumer's budget (automobiles, fuel oil, mortgage payments, television sets), other things being equal.

Time to Adjust to Price Changes. Demand becomes more elastic as consumers have more time to adjust to price changes. This pattern is explained by a number of factors. Consider the response of consumers to higher electricity prices. Immediately after electric utility rates are increased, consumers can do little more than lower their heating thermostats in the winter and raise their air-conditioning thermostats in the summer. As time passes, additional substitutes for electricity become available. Extra insulation and more energy-efficient heating and air-conditioning equipment can be installed. If natural-gas prices have not risen as much, the family can convert to natural-gas appliances when their old system needs to be replaced.

Many expenditures are determined by habits, which are often hard to break. The family may be used to setting the thermostat at 72 degrees: They may need time to adjust to cooler temperatures when prices rise. Families who are accustomed to having fresh vegetables may need time to switch to canned or frozen if the price of fresh vegetables rises substantially.

> Generally speaking, demand becomes more elastic as consumers have more time in which to adjust to changes in prices.

Necessities versus Luxuries. As we will discuss in more detail later in this chapter, economists make a basic distinction between necessities and luxuries. *Necessities* are products whose demand increases less rapidly than income. For example, according to *Engel's law,* families tend to spend a smaller portion of their income on food as their income rises.[4] *Luxuries,* on the other hand, are goods whose demand increases by a larger percentage than income. Foreign travel is an example of a luxury good.

Luxuries tend to have a higher price elasticity of demand than necessities. Chapter 5 noted that a reduction in price increases real income. Higher real incomes in turn stimulate the demand for luxuries more than the demand for necessities, if everything else (the availability of substitutes, the importance of the good in the budget, the time allowed for adjustment) is equal. Therefore, the income effect is larger for luxury goods than for necessities.

> The demand for luxury goods tends to be more elastic than the demand for necessities (*ceteris paribus*).

Actual Price Elasticities of Demand

The principles discussed in this section are illustrated by actual price elasticities, such as those described in Table 3. Most of the examples in this table were compiled by Hendrick Houthakker and Lester Taylor in their noted study of consumer demand in the United States. Two variants are calculated: the *short-run* E_d (where the consumer has not had much time to adjust to price changes) and the *long-run* E_d (where the consumer has had more time to adjust to price changes).

This evidence generally supports the claim that long-run elasticities are larger than short-run elasticities. In the case of electricity, E_d equals 0.13 in the short run (highly inelastic) but equals 1.89 in the long run (elastic). In the case of foreign travel, E_d rises from 0.14 in the short run to 1.77 in the long run. The elasticities in the table illustrate the important role of substitutes. Medical care has fewer good substitutes than most of the other products listed, and it therefore has lower short-run and long-run elasticities than products such as motion pictures, recreation equipment, gasoline, and foreign travel. In the short run, electricity has no good substitutes, and the short-run electricity E_d is low. Finally, necessities (such as water and gasoline) have lower

[4]Ernst Engel, a German statistician, conducted pioneering studies of European spending patterns in the mid-nineteenth century.

TABLE 3
Short-Run and Long-Run Price Elasticities

	E_d in Short Run	E_d in Long Run
Tobacco products	0.46	1.89
Jewelry	0.41	0.67
Toilet articles	0.20	3.04
Owner-occupied housing	0.04	1.22
China and glassware	1.55	2.55
Electricity	0.13	1.89
Water	0.20	0.14
Medical care and hospitalization	0.31	0.92
Tires	0.86	1.19
Auto repairs	0.40	0.38
Durable recreation equipment	0.88	2.39
Motion pictures	0.88	3.69
Foreign travel	0.14	1.77
Gasoline	0.15	0.78

Sources: Hendrick S. Houthakker and Lester D. Taylor, *Consumer Demand in the United States: Analyses and Projections* (Cambridge, MA: Harvard University Press, 1970), 166–67; James L. Sweeney, "The Demand for Gasoline: A Vintage Capital Model," Working Paper, Department of Engineering Economics, Stanford University.

price elasticities than luxuries (such as china and recreation equipment).

OTHER ELASTICITIES OF DEMAND

Chapter 5 showed that consumer demand depends not only on the product's own price, but also on consumer preferences, the prices of substitutes and complements, and consumer income. Although economists devote most of their attention to price elasticity of demand, the elasticity concept is also applied to the other factors affecting demand. Economists measure the responsiveness of demand to the prices of related goods (cross-price elasticity) and the responsiveness of demand to consumer income (income elasticity). The concepts of cross-price elasticity and income elasticity provide insights into the interrelationships of prices and the effects of income changes on consumer demands.

Cross-Price Elasticity

A change in the price of one product shifts the demand schedules of related products. This responsiveness of demand to other prices is measured by the **cross-price elasticity of demand (E_{xy}).**

> The **cross-price elasticity of demand (E_{xy})** is the percentage change in demand of the first product (x) divided by the percentage change in the price of the related product (y).[5]

Unlike the price elasticity of demand, which will always be negative (because of the law of demand), the cross-price elasticity can be either positive or negative.

A positive cross-price elasticity of demand means that an increase in the price of one product will cause an increase in the demand for the other product and vice versa. As the price of beef rises, the quantity of beef demanded falls, in part because substitutes have been purchased in place of beef. Chicken is a *substitute* for beef; therefore, the increase in the price of beef causes an increase in the demand for chicken. Generally speaking, the *better* the substitutes, the *higher* the cross-price elasticity.

A negative cross-price elasticity means that an increase in the price of one product will cause a decrease in the demand for the other product. Airline travel and auto rentals are *complements* because a large proportion of auto rentals are made by airline travelers. If the price of airline tickets rises, the number of airline passengers declines. As the number of air passengers declines, so does the demand for automobile rentals. Table 4 contains a few estimates of some actual cross-price elasticities.

> If the cross-price elasticity of demand is positive, the two products are *substitutes.* If the cross-price elasticity is negative, the two products are *complements.* If the cross-price elasticity is zero, the products are unrelated.

[5]The cross-price elasticity of demand is calculated by the same midpoints elasticity formula as the elasticity of demand. The only difference is that instead of the "own price" (P_x), the price of the related product (P_y) is in the denominator.

$$E_{xy} = \frac{Q_{x2} - Q_{x1}}{(Q_{x1} + Q_{x2})} \div \frac{P_{y2} - P_{y1}}{(P_{y1} + P_{y2})}$$

TABLE 4
Selected Cross-Price Elasticities

Good No. 1	Good No. 2	Elasticity Coefficient
Butter[a]	Margarine	.67
Natural gas[b]	Fuel oil	.44
Beef[a]	Pork	.28
Cheese[c]	Butter	−.61

Sources: [a]H. Wold and L. Jureen, *Demand Analysis* (New York: Wiley, 1953). [b]L. Taylor and R. Halvorsen, "Energy Substitution in U.S. Manufacturing," *The Review of Economics and Statistics* (November 1977). [c]L. Philips, *Applied Consumption Analysis* (Amsterdam: North-Holland, 1974).

Income Elasticity

A rise or fall in consumer income will affect the demands for different products. As consumer income rises, the demand for most products increases—but not always. The exception is inferior goods, which were defined in Chapter 5 as goods whose demand falls as income increases. This section examines goods whose demand increases with income. The responsiveness of demand to consumer income is measured by the **income elasticity of demand (E_i)**.

> The **income elasticity of demand (E_i)** is the percentage change in the demand for a product divided by the percentage change in income, holding all prices fixed.[6]

The income elasticity of demand is positive for most goods because higher consumer income usually means increased spending. If the income elasticity equals unity, each 1 percent increase in income will lead to a 1 percent increase in the demand for the good. Hence consumers would continue to spend the same fraction of their income on the good as before their income increased. For example, a consumer spends $10 on soft drinks out of $100 weekly income. If the income elasticity is 1, an increase in income to $110 will increase spending on soft drinks to $11; therefore, the fraction spent is still 10 percent. If the income elasticity exceeds 1, people will spend a larger fraction of their income on the good as income rises. If the income elasticity is less than 1, people will spend a smaller fraction of their income on that good as income rises. The definitions of **necessities** and **luxuries** given earlier in this chapter can be refined using the income elasticity of demand concept. (See Example 4.)

> **Necessities** are those products that have an income elasticity of demand less than 1.
>
> **Luxuries** are those products that have an income elasticity of demand greater than 1.

TABLE 5
Selected Income Elasticities

Good	Elasticity Coefficient
Motion-picture tickets[a]	3.4
Foreign travel[a]	3.1
Toys[a]	2.0
Automobiles and parts[b]	1.7
Clothing and shoes[b]	1.1
Furniture[b]	.9
Beef[c]	.5
Pork[c]	.3
Lard[c]	−.1

Sources: [a]H. S. Houthakker and L. D. Taylor, *Consumer Demand in the United States* (Cambridge, MA: Harvard University Press, 1970). [b]L. Philips, *Applied Consumption Analysis* (Amsterdam: North-Holland, 1974). [c]G. E. Brandow, "Interrelations among Demands for Farm Products and Implications for Control of Market Supply," Pennsylvania State University Agricultural Experiment Station Bulletin 680, 1961.

[6]The midpoints elasticity formula for the income elasticity of demand is

$$E_i = \frac{Q_2 - Q_1}{(Q_1 + Q_2)} \div \frac{I_2 - I_1}{(I_1 + I_2)}$$

where I denotes consumer income.

EXAMPLE 4 Engel's Law and Income Elasticities: Where Have All the Farmers Gone?

The income elasticity of demand is the percentage change in demand divided by the percentage change in income. If a product's income elasticity is greater than 1, its purchases tend to rise more rapidly than income, and its share of the total consumer spending increases. If a product's income elasticity of demand is less than 1, its purchases tend to rise more slowly than income, and its share of total consumer spending falls.

The nineteenth-century German statistician, Ernst Engel, noted a statistical regularity in his studies of family budgets in different countries. Engel found that as family income increases, the percentage of the budget spent on food declines. Subsequent statistical studies have confirmed this finding. This statistical regularity has come to be called *Engel's law.* In terms of income elasticity, Engel's law simply means that the income elasticity of demand for food is less than 1.

The inelastic income elasticity of demand explains a trend that characterizes virtually all economies. As income grows, the share of income devoted to purchases of agricultural goods falls. A smaller share of income is spent on goods produced by agriculture, and larger shares are spent on manufacturing and services. The factors of production therefore shift in relative terms from agriculture to manufacturing and services in response to the relative change in consumer demand.

Engel's law explains (at least partially) the declining shares of the farm population in industrialized societies. At the turn of the century, U.S. families spent \$0.30 of every dollar on food. In 1929, they spent \$0.25 of every dollar on food, and in 1988, they spent \$0.17 of every dollar on food. At the turn of the century, one in three workers was employed in agriculture. On the eve of World War II, only one in ten workers was employed in agriculture. By 1992, only two in every hundred workers were employed in agriculture.

Source: *Historical Statistics of the United States.*

Based on this criterion, goods such as food items would be necessities, and recreational vehicles would be luxury items. Notice, though, that the economist allows the terms *luxury* and *necessity* to be defined by the market choices people make rather than by individual perceptions about what is more "necessary" than something else. See Table 5 for some selected income elasticities ranging from movies (3.4) to lard (−0.1).

THE PRICE ELASTICITY OF SUPPLY

The price elasticity of demand measures the responsiveness of *consumers* to price change. The **price elasticity of supply (E_s)** measures the responsiveness of *producers* to price changes. The elasticity of supply is calculated in the same way as the elasticity of demand, only now Q refers to quantities *supplied,* not quantities demanded.

> The **price elasticity of supply (E_s)** is the percentage change in the quantity supplied divided by the percentage change in price.

According to the midpoints formula, E_s is calculated as

$$E_s = \frac{Q_2 - Q_1}{(Q_1 + Q_2)/2} \div \frac{P_2 - P_1}{(P_1 + P_2)/2}$$

Like the elasticity of demand, the E_s coefficients are divided into three categories: elastic ($E_s > 1$), unitary elastic ($E_s = 1$), and inelastic ($E_s < 1$). The direction of movement of total revenue along a supply curve, however, will not depend upon the value of E_s. The E_s coefficient is positive except in rare cases. Firms take maximum advantage of a higher price by producing more. Because both price and quantity supplied are rising, total revenues rise as well.

Perfectly Elastic and Perfectly Inelastic Supply Curves

The highest degree of elasticity possible for a supply curve is a perfectly horizontal supply curve. In Figure 5, supply curve S illustrates a case of **perfectly elastic supply.** At the price of $10, producers of the good (in the aggregate) are willing to supply any amount of the good to the market at that price.

> A horizontal supply curve illustrates **perfectly elastic supply ($E_s = \infty$)**; quantity supplied is most responsive to price.

FIGURE 5
Perfectly Elastic and Perfectly Inelastic Supply Curves

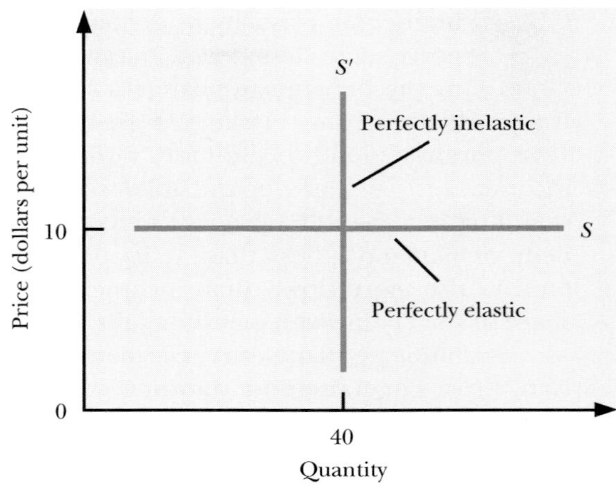

The supply curve S is perfectly elastic because at a price of $10 any quantity of output can be offered on the market by sellers. The supply curve S' is perfectly inelastic because no matter how much the price rises, the quantity supplied remains the same.

Most of the supply curves that the average consumer encounters are perfectly elastic. The grocery store is willing to sell any person all the milk, canned goods, and dairy products that person wants to buy at the prices set. Under normal circumstances, however, all buyers together (the market) must offer higher prices to induce producers to increase the quantity supplied.

The lowest degree of elasticity occurs when the supply curve is perfectly vertical, as shown in Figure 5 by supply curve S'. Such a supply curve demonstrates **perfectly inelastic supply.** The coefficient of E_s in this case equals zero. An increase in price has no effect on quantity supplied; therefore, the percentage change in quantity supplied is zero. A good example would be the fisher's catch of fresh fish. Here the supplier cannot go back out on the boat to increase that day's supply of fresh fish.

> A vertical supply curve illustrates **perfectly inelastic supply ($E_s = 0$)**; quantity supplied is least responsive to price.

Most market supply curves fall between the two extremes of perfect elasticity ($E_s = \infty$) and perfect inelasticity ($E_s = 0$).

Elasticity of Supply in Three Time Periods

Like elasticity of demand, elasticity of supply depends upon the amount of time the consumer has to respond to price changes.

> In general, the elasticity of supply increases as the producer has more time to adjust to changes in prices.

When prices change, economists distinguish between three time periods during which producers adjust their supply to the new prices: the **immediate run,** the **short run,** and the **long run.**

The **immediate run** is a period of time so short that the quantity supplied cannot be changed at all. In the immediate run—sometimes called the *momentary period* or *market period*—supply curves are perfectly inelastic.

The **short run** is a period of time long enough for existing firms to produce more goods but not long enough for existing firms to expand their capacity or for new firms to enter the market. Thus output can be varied, but only within the limits of existing plant capacity.

The **long run** is a period of time long enough for new firms to enter the market, for old firms to disappear, and for existing plants to be expanded. In the long run, firms have more flexibility in adjusting to price changes.

The amount of calendar time required to move from the short run to the long run varies with the type of industry. The electric power industry may require a decade to expand existing power generating facilities and bring new plants on line. On the other hand, the fast-food industry can construct and open a new outlet in a few months.

TABLE 6
Selected Estimates of Long-Run Supply Elasticities

Good	Elasticity Coefficient
Wheat[a]	.93
Corn[a]	.18
U.S. oil[b]	.76
Natural gas[c]	.20
Urban housing[d]	5.30

Sources: [a]M. Nerlove, "Estimates of the Elasticities of Supply of Selected Agricultural Commodities," *Journal of Farm Economics* (May 1956); [b]E. W. Ericson, S. W. Millsaps, and R. M. Spann, "Oil Supply and Tax Incentives," *Brookings Papers on Economic Activity* (1974); [c]J. D. Khazzoom, "The FPC Staff's Econometric Model of Natural Gas Supply in the United States," *The Bell Journal of Economics* (Spring 1971); [d]B. A. Smith, "The Supply of Urban Housing," *Journal of Political Economy* (1976).

Table 6 shows some selected long-run supply elasticities for some important goods. Compared to agricultural goods and energy, the supply of housing is extremely elastic.

ELASTICITY AND THE TAX BURDEN

Local, state, and federal governments tax a variety of goods and services, including tobacco, alcohol, gasoline, and various foreign imports. Elasticity of supply and demand explains how the burden of such taxes falls on consumers or producers. We shall see that the group with the lowest sensitivity to price will pay the largest share of the tax.

How the Tax Burden Is Shared

Suppose that a tax is imposed on a luxury good like perfume. Figure 6 shows the supply curve and the demand curve for perfume before the tax is imposed. The equilibrium price is $2 per gram, and the equilibrium quantity is 8 million grams per month at point *e* before the tax is imposed.

Suppose a tax of $1 per gram is imposed by the government. In order for sellers to earn $2, they must now charge $3; to earn $1.25 they must charge $2.25. The tax will shift the supply curve *up* by exactly $1—the amount of the tax. Before the tax, suppliers were prepared to supply 8 million grams per month at a price of $2 per gram, but after the tax, suppliers will be prepared to supply the same 8 million grams per month only if the price is $3 (because they will still receive $2 per gram after the tax). The tax does not change the demand curve. At each price (where the price now includes the $1 tax), consumers will continue to demand the same quantities. The new equilibrium price must be less than $3 (the original price of $2 plus the $1 tax) because at $3, the quantity supplied is the same as without the tax but the quantity demanded is lower.

The new equilibrium point is e' at a price of $2.25 and a quantity of 6 million grams. Buyers pay $2.25 for perfume, and sellers receive $1.25 after paying the $1.00 tax, with the government picking up the $1.00 difference. The government gets $6 million

FIGURE 6
The Burden of a Tax

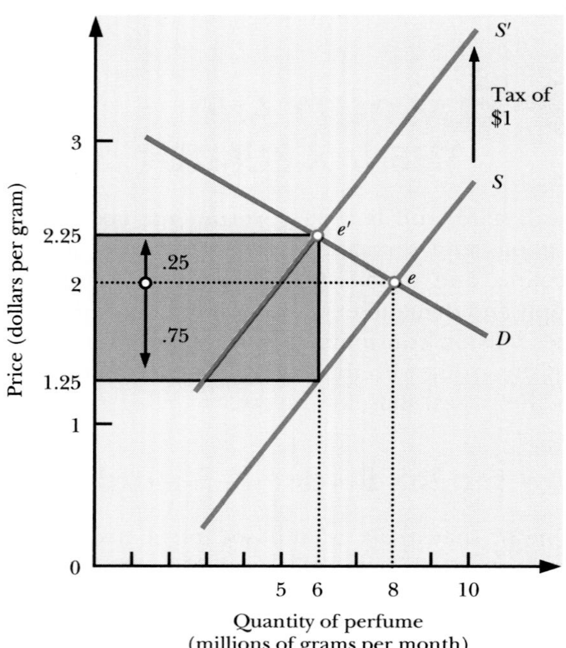

Curves D and S are the demand and supply curves for perfume before the tax; the equilibrium price is $2. A tax of $1 per unit on sellers shifts the supply curve upward by exactly $1 as sellers recoup their tax payments to the state. The new equilibrium price to buyers is found where the new supply curve, S', intersects the old demand curve, D, at point e'; thus, the new price is $2.25 to buyers. Sellers must send $1 (per gram sold) to the tax collector; hence, sellers keep only $1.25 after paying tax. Notice that one fourth of the burden of the $1 tax ($0.25) falls on buyers and three fourths of the burden ($0.75) falls on sellers. This incidence reflects the fact that the elasticity of demand is approximately 4 times greater ($E_d = 2.4$) than the elasticity of supply ($E_s = 0.6$).

($1.00 × 6 million grams) in taxes. The equilibrium price *paid* by consumers goes up only $0.25 (from $2.00 to $2.25), but the net price (price minus tax) received by producers goes down by $0.75 (from $2.00 to $1.25). In this particular case, the greater burden of the tax is on the sellers who pay three-quarters of the tax. Buyers pay only one-quarter of the tax.

Elasticities Determine Who Bears the Burden

Why does the producer bear a greater part of the burden than the consumer in our perfume example? The answer is found in the elasticities of demand and supply.

The demand curve in Figure 6 is more elastic than the supply curve in the vicinity of the equilibrium point *e*, as evidenced by the fact that curve S is steeper than curve D. Consumers therefore respond more to the price than do producers. Hence consumers have a greater opportunity to avoid the tax. In fact, the elasticity of demand along D between $2.00 and $2.25 is 2.4; the elasticity of supply along S between $1.25 and $2.00 is approximately 0.6.

Had the supply curve been more elastic than the demand curve, the consumer would have borne a greater burden of the tax. If consumers have a more inelastic demand, it is easier to shift the price forward to them and harder to reduce the price paid to producers. For the consumer to bear the greater burden of the tax requires that demand elasticities be *smaller* than supply elasticities—which in the long run, in many industries, is likely to be true (see the chapter on perfect competition). In fact, tax officials typically levy taxes on items like liquor, cigarettes, and gasoline because their price elasticity is relatively low. In such cases, the consumer bears more of the burden of the tax than the producer. (See Example 5.)

The concept of elasticity allows us to understand the extent to which changing prices and income affect supply and demand. The next chapter will look behind the demand curve to explain the law of demand and consumer surplus.

SUMMARY

1. The price elasticity of demand (E_d) is a measure of the responsiveness of consumers and producers to changes in price. It is the absolute value of the percentage change in quantity demanded divided by the percentage change in price. The price elasticity of demand can be either elastic ($E_d > 1$), unitary elastic ($E_d = 1$), or inelastic ($E_d < 1$). If demand is elastic, price and total

EXAMPLE 5 Sin Taxes versus Luxury Taxes

This chapter teaches that the burden of a tax can be passed on to consumers when the price elasticity of demand is low. When a good has an inelastic demand, consumers will not reduce quantity demanded very much even after the price has increased.

Over the years, "sin" taxes have proved very popular for two reasons. First, officials justify taxes on the sale of cigarettes, liquor, and beer on the grounds that such taxes improve public morality. Second, sin taxes are an excellent source of revenue. If the state raises the cigarette tax by 50 percent, cigarette consumers (with inelastic demand) reduce their purchases by a relatively small amount. The tax increase therefore brings in a considerable amount of new tax revenue.

Luxury taxes (such as the current federal tax on fur coats, luxury automobiles, and yachts) have been less successful in generating tax revenue. The demand for luxury cars, furs, and yachts is highly price elastic. When the luxury tax threatens to raise prices, the rich switch to substitutes. Purchases of furs, yachts, and luxury cars drop, and the state collects less revenue from the tax than expected.

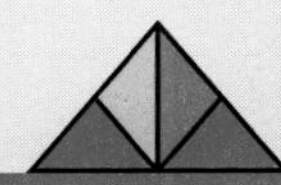

revenue move in opposite directions. If demand is inelastic, price and total revenue move in the same direction. If demand is unitary elastic, total revenue is not affected by price changes. E_d can be calculated by the midpoints elasticity formula; the change in quantity is divided by the average quantity, and the change in price is divided by the average price. The price elasticity of demand is determined by the availability of substitutes (more substitutes mean higher elasticity), the amount of adjustment time (more time means higher elasticity), the importance in the budget (the more important the good, the higher the elasticity), and the status of the good as a necessity or a luxury (necessities tend to have lower elasticities).

2. Elasticities can also be used to measure the responsiveness of consumer demand to changes in income and the prices of other goods. Cross-price elasticity is the percentage change in the demand of one good divided by the percentage change in the price of the other good. If this number is positive, the two goods are substitutes; if it is negative, the two goods are complements. Income elasticity of demand is the percentage change in the demand divided by the percentage change in income. If this number is greater than 1, the good is a luxury; if it is less than 1, the good is a necessity.

3. The price elasticity of supply is the percentage change in quantity supplied divided by the percentage change in price. Supply is perfectly elastic when the supply curve is horizontal; supply is perfectly inelastic when the supply curve is vertical. The price elasticity of supply depends upon the time period of adjustment. In the immediate run, supply is fixed and the supply schedule is perfectly inelastic. In the short run, firms can produce more or fewer goods, but they do not have sufficient time to alter their capital stock or enter or leave the industry. In the long run, supply can be altered through changes in capital stock and through the entry and exit of firms. Elasticity of supply is greater in the long run than in the short run.

4. Elasticity analysis explains whether producers or consumers will bear the greater burden of a tax on a particular good. The group with the smallest price elasticity pays the largest share of the tax.

KEY TERMS

price elasticity of demand (E_d)
midpoints elasticity formula
total revenue (TR)
total revenue test
perfectly elastic demand
perfectly inelastic demand
cross-price elasticity of demand (E_{xy})
income elasticity of demand (E_i)
necessities
luxuries

price elasticity of supply (E_s)
perfectly elastic supply
perfectly inelastic supply
immediate run
short run
long run

QUESTIONS AND PROBLEMS

1. Using the demand schedule in Table A, calculate the price elasticities of demand for each successive pair of rows.

TABLE A

Price (dollars)	Quantity (units)
5	1
4	2
3	3
2	4
1	5

2. Suppose the price elasticity of demand for rental housing of 0.6 and the average rent increases from $275 per month to $325 per month. At $275 per month, 100,000 rental units are rented. What percentage decrease in quantity demanded would you predict from this information? Approximately how many units would be rented at $325 per month?
3. Suppose the price of gasoline falls from $1.20 per gallon to $0.60 per gallon. Why would a consumer's short-run adjustment to this price change be different from the long-run adjustment?
4. Assume that the basic monthly charge for a private telephone is $10.50 per month. If the rate were to rise to $11.00, would you expect a substantial reduction in the quantity demanded? Explain your answer. If, on the other hand, the basic monthly charge were $250 per month and the rate were to rise by the same percentage as the lower rate, what is your prediction for the change in quantity demanded?
5. In the mid-1980s, the state of Texas raised the price of personalized automobile license plates from $35 to $70. The state's revenue from personalized license plates then fell. From this information, what can you say about the price elasticity of demand for personalized plates?
6. If the price of tennis balls went up, what impact would this price increase have on the quantity demanded of tennis rackets? What sign (+ or −) would the cross-price elasticity have? What sign would the cross-price elasticity of tennis balls and golf balls have?
7. The income elasticity of demand for all services taken together is greater than 1. As the economy grows, what would you expect to happen to the share of service industries in total output?
8. During economic recessions, used car sales typically rise and new car sales decline. Explain why.
9. Assume that oranges have the following characteristics. The elasticity of demand is 0.2, and the elasticity of supply is 2. If government imposes a tax of $1 per crate of oranges, who would end up paying more of the tax (bearing the larger burden of the tax): the consumer or the producer? Why? Draw a diagram illustrating your argument.
10. Evaluate the validity of the following statement: "The elasticity of demand for oranges is 0.2; therefore, California orange growers could raise their income by restricting their output."
11. Suppose the supply curve for product X shifts to the right (supply increases). What happens to the total expenditure of consumers under each of the following conditions?
    a. The demand for X is price elastic.
    b. The demand for X is price inelastic.
    c. The demand for X is perfectly elastic.
    d. The demand for X is perfectly inelastic.
12. Suppose the supply curve for product X shifts to the left (supply decreases). What happens to the total expenditure of consumers under each of the following conditions?
    a. The demand for X is price elastic.
    b. The demand for X is price inelastic.
    c. The demand for X is perfectly elastic.
    d. The demand for X is perfectly inelastic.
13. Suppose the demand for product X increases. What happens to the total revenue of sellers under each of the following conditions?
    a. The supply of X is elastic.
    b. The supply is X is inelastic.

14. Using the determinants of the price elasticity of demand, indicate which item in each of the following pairs of goods has the highest elasticity.

    a. Wheat and grains
    b. Soft drinks and beverages
    c. Cars and clothing
    d. Toothpicks and beef

15. Double the quantities demanded at each price in Table A above (for example, when the price is \$5, assume 2 units are demanded; when the price is \$4, assume 4 units are demanded; and so on). What happens to the slope of the demand curve? What happens to the elasticity of demand between each successive pair of prices?

16. Who bears the burden of a tax on a good in each of the following circumstances?

    a. The supply curve is upward sloping; demand is perfectly inelastic.
    b. The supply curve is upward sloping; demand is perfectly elastic.
    c. The demand curve is downward sloping; supply is perfectly inelastic.
    d. The demand curve is downward sloping; supply is perfectly elastic.

17. Calculate the price elasticity of demand for the market demand curve $Q = 100 - 2P$ when the price changes from $P = \$42$ to $P = \$38$.

SUGGESTED READINGS

Kohler, Heinz. *Intermediate Microeconomics: Theory and Applications,* 3rd ed. New York: HarperCollins, 1990.

Ruffin, Roy. *Intermediate Microeconomics,* 2d ed. New York: HarperCollins, 1992.

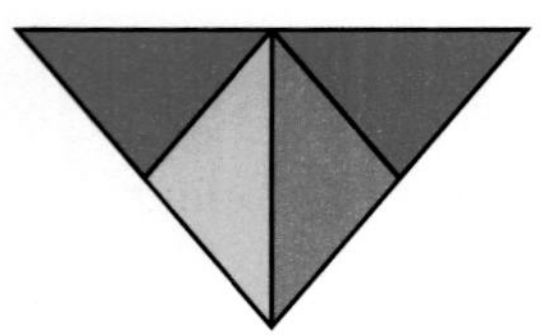

27 Demand and Utility

CHAPTER INSIGHT

Adam Smith, in *The Wealth of Nations* (1776), noted that "nothing is more useful than water; but it will purchase scarce anything; scarce anything can be had in exchange for it. A diamond, on the contrary, has scarce any value in use; but a very great quantity of other goods may frequently be had in exchange for it."

This chapter will explain Adam Smith's diamond/water paradox by building a theory of consumer behavior that illustrates how consumers spend income to maximize satisfaction. This rational consumer theory is used to derive the law of demand. This chapter will also show how to combine individual demand curves to determine market demand curves and how to measure the consumer gains and losses that result from price changes.

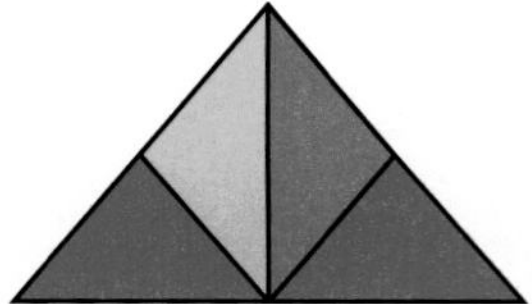

THE NATURE OF CONSUMER PREFERENCES

Economists make a clear distinction between *wants* and *demand. Wants* are those goods and services that consumers would purchase if they had unlimited budgets. *Demand* denotes those goods and services that consumers are prepared to buy given relative prices and income levels. Another factor that affects demand is consumers' tastes, or **preferences.** Some people might not want brussel sprouts even if they were given away free. The individual with a fear of flying will not want free airline tickets. The opera lover will welcome a free concert ticket but might throw away a free ticket to the World Series that a baseball fan would treasure. To understand why consumers are willing to buy a given quantity of a given good, it is necessary to first understand the nature of consumer preferences.

> **Preferences** are a person's evaluations of goods and services independent of budget and price considerations.

Consumer preferences—when broadly defined—are relatively stable. In a sense, the consumer wants the *services* that goods provide, not the goods themselves. Rather than an automobile, the consumer wants transportation. Rather than theater tickets, admission to bowling alleys, or tickets to sports events, the consumer desires the entertainment. Rather than a house or condominium, the consumer seeks shelter.

Consumer preferences for the services provided by different goods are more stable than preferences for the specific products that provide those services. The taste for transportation services may remain relatively constant, but because these services can be provided by a variety of goods (cars, taxis, buses, trains, airplanes, one's feet), the form in which these services are purchased will vary. The taste for entertainment may be quite stable, but the exact manner in which a consumer satisfies that the taste can change dramatically over time. One year a person listens to radio; a decade later the same person watches television.

Technology and innovations alter preferences for specific goods. For example, transportation innovations over the years have been spectacular: The consumer who was content to move about by horse 200 years ago may now prefer jet-powered transportation. To the casual observer, this transformation might seem like a radical change in preferences, but economists would argue that the preference for the transportation service itself has remained relatively stable.

THE CONCEPT OF UTILITY

Preferences indicate how a consumer would rank different commodity bundles (combinations of goods and services) in all conceivable situations. A simple criterion for evaluating a consumer's preferences or satisfaction is to use the **utility** of various commodity bundles.

> **Utility** is a numerical ranking of a consumer's preferences among different commodity bundles.

As defined by economists, utility measures the rank-order of different satisfactions rather than the magnitudes of those satisfactions. Utility is expressed in ordinal numbers (such as first, second, and third) because it is not possible to attach a "util-o-meter" to a person's arm to measure the satisfaction that is gained from consuming particular goods and services. In the nineteenth century, though, economists expressed utility in cardinal numbers, which indicate both rankings and magnitudes. For example, the concept of weight is a cardinal number. It makes a difference whether you tell someone that last week you gained 100 pounds or 10 pounds.

The appendix to this chapter demonstrates that an absolute measure of cardinal utility is not necessary for analyzing demand. However, it is useful to quantify preferences in order to measure differences in the utility of goods. For example, if we say that the utility of consuming 51 gallons of water per week is 3010 utils (hypothetical units of utility) and the utility of 50 gallons is 3000 utils, then we can quantify the **marginal utility** of increasing water consumption by one gallon as 10 utils.

The **marginal utility (MU)** of any good or service is the increase in utility that a consumer experiences when consumption of that good or service (and that good or service alone) is increased by 1 unit. In general,

$$MU = \frac{\Delta TU}{\Delta Q}$$

where TU is total utility and Q is the quantity of the good.

As we shall see, however, this absolute measure of marginal utility is only a tool for comparing the relative marginal utilities for two or more goods.

The Law of Diminishing Marginal Utility

The more of something people consume, the less valuable it becomes at the margin. The **law of diminishing marginal utility** states that generally, as more of a good or service is consumed, its marginal utility declines. Thus, the first gallon of water consumed in a given week, for example, has an enormous marginal utility because a person who has no water will consider 1 gallon to be very valuable. The 20th gallon of water has a relatively small marginal utility because a person who already has 19 gallons will not value a 20th as highly. The *total utility* from all 20 gallons of water is the sum of the marginal utilities of all units. Why does the marginal utility of water decline so rapidly as more water is consumed? The first gallon of water is essential to sustaining life; its marginal utility is therefore astronomical. As more water becomes available, water can be applied to less urgent uses: bathing, washing clothes, feeding pets, and eventually even to watering the lawn. By the time sufficient water is available for watering the lawn, the marginal utility of the last gallon is much smaller than the marginal utility of the first gallon.

The **law of diminishing marginal utility** states that as more of a good or service is consumed during any given time period, its marginal utility declines, if the consumption of everything else is held constant.

There are some rare exceptions (the marginal utility of the stamps of the stamp collector may rise for quite some time as additional stamps are acquired), but these do not concern us here because they do not change the general pattern of consumer behavior. The law does not say how rapidly marginal utility will decline as consumption increases; this rate will vary. For some goods (food products, for example), marginal utility declines rapidly. The marginal utility of the second hamburger is much less than that

EXAMPLE 1 Marginal Utility, "All You Can Eat for $10," and the Daily Newspaper

Many restaurants offer buffets where customers can eat all they want for a specified price. Such offers are possible because the marginal utility of food diminishes rapidly. Depending upon the individual's appetite, extra helpings yield smaller and smaller marginal utilities. In fact, they rather quickly yield negative marginal utility, in which the consumer's utility decreases with an extra helping. Although more food costs the consumer nothing, people will limit the amount of food they consume.

Rapidly diminishing marginal utility explains why the daily newspaper is dispensed from coin-operated boxes that permit people to take as many copies as they want. Newspaper companies know that the marginal utility of a second newspaper is zero for most people, so they don't worry about people taking more than one. Owners of coin-operated dispensers of other products (soft drinks, candies, etc.) know that they cannot give the customer the opportunity to take more than one.

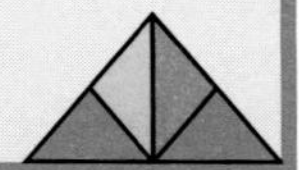

of the first. The marginal utility of the third hamburger will be very small or even negative. For other goods, such as collectors' items, marginal utility may decline slowly as consumption increases. (See Example 1.)

The Diamond/Water Paradox

In the quotation that opens this chapter, Adam Smith poses the famous *diamond/water paradox.* The question at the root of this paradox is why prices often fail to reflect the usefulness of goods. Goods such as water and salt, without which human beings would perish, have low relative prices, whereas goods that have little practical value, such as diamonds, gold, and high fashion, have high relative prices.

Why is it that diamonds, whose total utility is much less than that of water, have a higher relative price than water? The law of diminishing marginal utility provides the answer to this paradox. On the one hand, the consumption of water takes place at a low marginal utility because the supply of water is large; on the other hand, the supply of diamonds is usually so limited that consumption takes place at a relatively high marginal utility. Although water's total utility is high, its marginal utility is low. Therefore, no one will sacrifice very much for an additional gallon.

The terms of the diamond/water paradox hold under normal supply conditions, but what happens when these conditions are disrupted? In the confusion at the end of World War II, food supplies were interrupted, and people gladly exchanged diamonds and precious metals for bread and potatoes in parts of Europe. The availability of food products was so limited that food products yielded a higher marginal utility (by preventing malnutrition) than did diamonds and precious metals. Similarly, when the American West was being settled in the nineteenth century, range wars were fought (and people were killed) over the control of water holes, and in arid parts of the world (Africa, the Middle East), armed conflicts still break out over water.

MARGINAL UTILITY AND THE LAW OF DEMAND

The law of diminishing marginal utility explains the diamond/water paradox; relative prices reflect marginal utility rather than total utility. The exact relationship between the law of diminishing utility and the law of demand will be examined in this section.

Consider an individual consumer, Mr. Ruffgreg, who purchases only two goods, ale and bread. Ruffgreg's preferences for both goods are summarized in Table 1. Columns 2 and 6 show the total utility of ale (TU_A) and bread (TU_B), respectively; columns

TABLE 1
The Utility of Ale and Bread

Quantity of Ale (pints), Q_A (1)	Total Utility of Ale (utils), TU_A (2)	Marginal Utility of Ale (utils), MU_A (3)	Marginal Utility of Ale per Dollar (utils), MU_A/P_A (4)	Quantity of Bread (loaves), Q_B (5)	Total Utility of Bread (utils), TU_B (6)	Marginal Utility of Bread (utils), MU_B (7)	Marginal Utility of Bread per Dollar (utils), MU_B/P_B (8)
1	40	40	20	1	15	15	30
2	70	30	15	2	23	8	16
3	90	20	10	3	30	7	14
4	100	10	5	4	35	5	10
5	105	5	2.5	5	38	3	6
6	107	2	1	6	40.5	2.5	5

This table lists the quantities of ale and bread consumed per week by Ruffgreg, along with the utility Ruffgreg attaches to each quantity. The price of ale equals $2 per pint and the price of bread equals $0.50 per loaf. The marginal utility columns illustrate the *law of diminishing marginal utility:* the marginal utility of each product falls as the amount consumed increases.

FIGURE 1
Marginal Utility Schedule

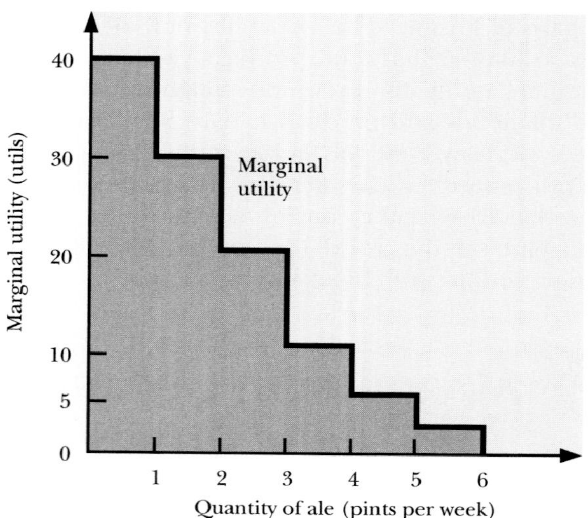

This figure graphs the data in columns 1 and 3 of Table 1. The width of each bar represents 1 pint of ale. The vertical height or area of each bar represents marginal utility for that extra unit of ale. Total utility up to some quantity of ale is the sum of the areas of the bars to the left of that quantity of ale. For example, the total utility of 2 pints equals 70 (= 40 + 30); the total utility of 5 pints equals 105 (= 40 + 30 + 20 + 10 + 5).

3 and 7 show the marginal utility of ale (MU_A) and bread (MU_B), respectively. These utility schedules apply to Ruffgreg's consumption over a particular time period—say, a week. For simplicity, we assume that the utility of ale does not depend on the consumption of bread, or vice versa. Both ale and bread obey the law of diminishing marginal utility.

Ruffgreg's marginal utility schedule for ale is depicted in Figure 1 and is based on the data in column 3 of Table 1. The first pint of ale (per week) yields Ruffgreg a marginal utility of 40 utils; the second, 30 utils; the third, 20 utils; and the fourth, 10 utils. The total utility from consuming different quantities of ale is the sum of the marginal utilities up to the quantity of ale consumed. The total utility from consuming 3 pints of ale during a week, for example, is 90 (= 40 + 30 + 20).

We cannot determine Ruffgreg's demands for ale and bread from his preferences alone. As noted in Chapter 5, demand depends not only on consumer preferences but also on consumer income and prices. To keep our example simple, let us assume Ruffgreg has $8 to spend on ale and bread per week. The price of ale (P_A) is $2 per pint, and the price of bread (P_B) is $0.50 per loaf. Ruffgreg could spend the entire $8 allowance on ale, buying 4 pints of ale, or he could spend all $8 on bread, obtaining 16 loaves of bread. The most likely case, however, is that Ruffgreg will spend part of the money on ale and part on bread. For instance, he could purchase 3 pints of ale per week, costing $6, and 4 loaves of bread per week, costing $2, for a total weekly expenditure of $8.

Maximizing Satisfaction

How will Ruffgreg allocate his $8 between ale and bread? All consumers (if they behave rationally) seek to obtain as much satisfaction as possible from the amount of income they have to spend. (See Example 2 on consumer rationality.)

> To achieve maximum utility the consumer allocates the budget on goods in such a way that it is impossible to obtain more utility by spending a bit more on one good and a bit less on another.

We will now demonstrate that Ruffgreg maximizes his satisfaction when his budget is spent so that *the last dollar spent on each product yields the same marginal utility*. The intuitive sense of this rule holds that if the marginal utility per dollar is not the same for two products, a consumer can increase total utility by switching an extra dollar to the good with the greater marginal utility per dollar.

> Satisfaction (utility) is maximized when the marginal utility per extra dollar of expenditure is equal for all goods purchased.

Marginal utility per dollar is calculated by dividing marginal utility by the price. For each quantity of ale, priced at $2 per pint, the marginal utility per dollar in column 4 of Table 1 is half of the marginal utility in column 3. For each quantity of bread, priced at $0.50 per loaf, the marginal utility per dollar in column 8 is twice the marginal utility in column 7.

EXAMPLE 2 Do People Actually Maximize Utility?

Economists have designed experiments in which subjects are given an income to allocate over different choices, as described by the theory of consumer behavior. The choices give the subjects (students) different monetary payoffs. Even if they are not told the payoffs until after each choice is made, subjects quickly reach the maximum total monetary payoff in less than 10 out of a possible 30 trials or attempts. This shows that even if consumers must learn about the marginal utilities of different goods and services, it does not take them long to arrange their consumption to achieve maximum utility.

Source: Don L. Coursey and Charles F. Mason, "Investigations Concerning the Dynamics of Consumer Behavior in Uncertain Environments," *Economic Inquiry* 25 (October 1987): 549–64.

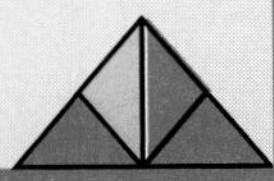

The **marginal utility per dollar** is the ratio MU/P and indicates the increase in utility from another dollar spent on the good.

Note that the concept of marginal utility per dollar is a rate measure similar to miles per hour. Just as one can drive 50 miles per hour without driving for a full hour, a given figure for marginal utility per dollar does not necessarily involve the expenditure of a full dollar.

Table 2 illustrates a step-by-step process through which Ruffgreg maximizes utility by making incremental expenditures for bread and ale until all of his income is allocated. At the point of the initial purchase, a loaf of bread, which costs $0.50, yields a marginal utility of 15 and a marginal utility *per dollar* of 30 (= 15/$0.50), and a pint of ale, which costs $2, yields a marginal utility of 40 but a marginal utility *per dollar* of only 20 (= 40/$2). Because bread has a higher marginal utility per dollar, Ruffgreg's first purchase is one loaf at a cost of $0.50, leaving $7.50 to spend. Ruffgreg now finds that the marginal utility per dollar is higher for a pint of ale (20) than for a second loaf of bread (16), so he purchases one pint for $2, leaving $5.50 to spend. Marginal utility per dollar is higher for a second loaf of bread (16) than for a second pint of ale (15), so Ruffgreg's third purchase is a second loaf of bread. Ruffgreg continues to select the product with the higher marginal utility per dollar until his budget is exhausted. Ruffgreg achieves **consumer equilibrium** when he buys 3 pints of ale and 4 loaves of bread; he has spent his entire income of $8 (3 pints at $2 each and 4 loaves at $0.50 each), and the marginal utility per dollar is 10 utils for both ale and bread.

Consumer equilibrium occurs when the consumer has spent all income and marginal utilities per dollar for each good purchased are equal ($MU_A/P_A = MU_B/P_B$). At this point, the consumer is not inclined to change purchases unless some other factor (such as prices, income, or preferences) changes.

The law of demand can be derived from this theory of consumer behavior. When the price of ale is $2, Ruffgreg purchases (demands) 3 pints of ale, given that his income is $8 and the price of bread is $0.50. The price/quantity combination of $2 and 3 pints of ale is point *r* on Ruffgreg's demand curve (Figure 2).

Other points on the demand curve can be calculated by repeating the whole process at different prices of ale, keeping income at $8 per week and the bread price at $0.50 per loaf.

If the price of ale falls from $2 to $1 per pint, the marginal utility per dollar for ale becomes greater than the marginal utility per dollar for bread at the

TABLE 2
The Steps to Consumer Equilibrium

	Available Choices	Decision	Income Remaining	
1st Purchase ↓	1st pint of ale: $MU_A/P_A = 20$ 1st loaf of bread: $MU_B/P_B = 30$	Buy 1st loaf of bread for \$0.50	\$8.00 − \$0.50 = \$7.50	
2nd Purchase ↓	1st pint of ale: $MU_A/P_A = 20$ 2nd loaf of bread: $MU_B/P_B = 16$	Buy 1st pint of ale for \$2.00	\$7.50 − \$2.00 = \$5.50	
3rd Purchase ↓	2nd pint of ale: $MU_A/P_A = 15$ 2nd loaf of bread: $MU_B/P_B = 16$	Buy 2nd loaf of bread for \$0.50	\$5.50 − \$0.50 = \$5.00	
4th Purchase ↓	2nd pint of ale: $MU_A/P_A = 15$ 3rd loaf of bread: $MU_B/P_B = 14$	Buy 2nd pint of ale for \$2.00	\$5.00 − \$2.00 = \$3.00	
5th Purchase ↓	3rd pint of ale: $MU_A/P_A = 10$ 3rd loaf of bread: $MU_B/P_B = 14$	Buy 3rd loaf of bread for \$0.50	\$3.00 − \$0.50 = \$2.50	
6th Purchase and 7th Purchase	3rd pint of ale: $MU_A/P_A = 10$ 4th loaf of bread: $MU_B/P_B = 10$	Buy 3rd pint of ale for \$2.00 and 4th loaf of bread for \$0.50	\$2.50 − \$2.00 = \$0.50 \$0.50 − \$0.50 = \$0	} Equilibrium

This table shows the step-by-step process by which a consumer makes purchasing decisions to maximize satisfaction. In this example, with data taken from Table 1, the consumer has \$8 to spend. At each step, the consumer chooses the commodity that has the highest marginal utility per dollar. The consumer ends up buying 3 pints of ale and 4 loaves of bread, which is the equilibrium combination because marginal utility per dollar is equal for the two goods at the last purchase, and all income is spent.

old equilibrium of 3 pints of ale and 4 loaves of bread. Expenditures will consequently be reallocated between the two goods until the \$8 is spent and marginal utilities per dollar are again equal—this time at 5 pints of ale and 6 loaves of bread. Thus, when the price of ale is \$1, the quantity demanded is 5 pints. This price/quantity combination of \$1 and 5 pints is point *t* on the demand curve. As the law of demand predicts, holding all other factors constant, a decrease in the price causes an increase in the quantity demanded.[1]

[1]The mathematics is as follows: Start with the consumer in equilibrium, with $MU_A/P_A = MU_B/P_B$. If P_A falls, $MU_A/P_A > MU_B/P_B$. To restore equilibrium, MU_A must also fall. The law of diminishing marginal utility states that MU_A will fall if consumption of *A* *increases*. From this, the negative relationship between P_A and Q_A is established.

FIGURE 2
The Individual Demand Curve Derived from Ruffgreg's Marginal Utility Schedule

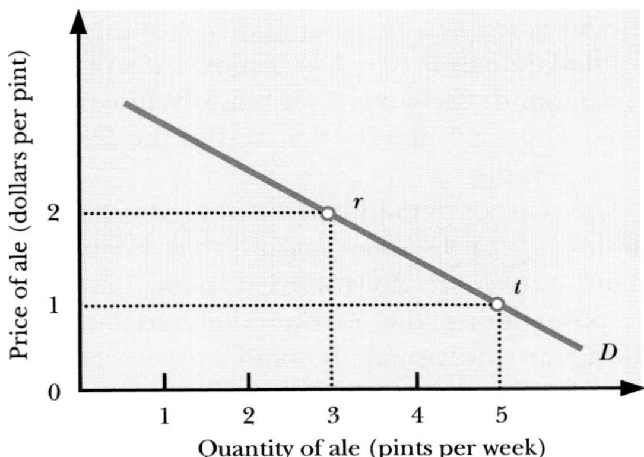

This curve shows Ruffgreg's demand curve for ale calculated from Table 1. Say the price of bread is $0.50 per loaf and weekly income is $8. The quantity required for consumer equilibrium when the price of ale equals $2 per pint is 3 pints (point *r*). The equilibrium quantity when the price of ale equals $1 per pint is 5 pints (point *t*).

Every point on a given consumer's demand curve satisfies the conditions that MU/*P* be the same for all goods the consumer purchases and that all income be spent. In other words, the consumer is maximizing utility at each price/quantity combination on the curve.

Income and Substitution Effects

A reduction in the price of a good has two effects. First, the savings that consumers gain can be used as income to purchase more goods. The part of the total increase in the quantity demanded of the reduced-price good that can be attributed to this extra income is called the **income effect.** Second, the cheaper good yields a higher marginal utility per dollar so consumers bent on maximizing satisfaction will substitute this now cheaper good for other products. This part of the increase in the quantity demanded of the cheaper good is called the **substitution effect.**

When the price of a good falls, people buy more of it because (1) the price reduction is like an increase in income that in itself normally results in larger demands for all goods and services (the **income effect**); and (2) consumers tend to substitute that good for other, relatively more expensive goods (the **substitution effect**).

Referring again to Table 2, before the price of ale dropped from $2 to $1, the consumer purchased 3 pints of ale and 4 loaves of bread for a total of $8 worth of ale and bread. At the lower price of ale, the consumer can purchase the same 3 pints of ale and 4 loaves of bread for $5, leaving $3 extra. This $3 represents an increase in real income that can be spent on either ale or bread. The effect of this increase on purchases of ale constitutes the income effect.

The price reduction is also accompanied by a drop in the relative price of ale (the ratio of ale price to bread price falls from 4 to 2). As a result, the consumer receives more marginal utility per dollar from ale than bread and, therefore, switches to buying more ale. This switch from bread to ale constitutes the substitution effect.

The size of the income effect from a price change depends on the amount of the good being consumed. A change in the price of a Rolls-Royce has no income effect for the vast majority of people because that ultra-luxury car lies far outside the limits of their budgets. However, a rise in the price of gasoline affects all drivers according to the amount they use. Thus, the income effects of price changes for food, clothing, and housing can be quite substantial. The income effects of price changes for goods that are relatively unimportant in the consumer's budget are small or trivial.

The size of the substitution effect also depends on the ease with which other goods can be substituted for a good. A Ford has more substitutes than a Rolls-Royce, so the substitution effect of a price change for Fords is correspondingly larger.

Is the Theory Realistic?

The theory of rational consumer behavior predicts that the law of demand holds and explains how people determine which goods and services they consume.

Do people really behave in the mechanical fashion depicted by this theory? After all, few people keep marginal utility schedules in their heads or calculate marginal utility per dollar to identify the best buys at every given moment.

Yet, people—on the average—do behave as predicted by the theory. Thus, it meets an important criterion for an acceptable scientific theory. (See Chapter 1.) The sharp-eyed customer sifting through the packages of meat at the supermarket is, in effect, calculating *best buys.* A best buy is the good that yields the highest marginal utility per extra dollar spent. A consumer may get the most marginal utility from a delicious T-bone steak, but that consumer gets the most marginal utility *per dollar* from simple hamburger meat. Thus, instead of buying the steak, the consumer may decide to buy the hamburger *and* take in a movie.

The actual decision-making process of the individual is far more complicated than described in this example. Yet when we cut through all the apparent inconsistencies and irrationalities of individuals (such as keeping up with neighbors), observed consumer behavior as a whole is consistent with the predictions of the theory.

MARKET DEMAND

The law of diminishing marginal utility implies that rational consumers will purchase less of a product, *ceteris paribus,* if its price rises. According to the law of demand, the demand schedules of individual consumers will have negative slopes.

The individual consumer, however, is only a small part of the total market in which prices are established. Recall from Chapter 5 that if the market is competitive, the actions of single participants have no impact on the price because each represents only a small share of the total pool of consumers. Individual demand curves must be combined to determine the **market demand curve** for a particular good.

> The **market demand curve** shows the total quantities demanded by all consumers in the market at each price. It is the horizontal summation of all individual demand curves in that market.

Figure 3 shows the demand curves for ale for two consumers, Smith and White, who, for simplicity, constitute all the buyers in the market for ale. At a price of $3 per pint, Smith demands 0 pints and White demands 1 pint. The total market demand at the $3 price can be obtained by adding the two individual demands ($0 + 1 = 1$ pint). At a price of $2 per pint, Smith demands 2 pints and White demands 3 pints. The total market demand at the $2 price is $2 + 3 = 5$ pints.

The market demand curve in Figure 3 is downward sloping for the same reasons that the individual demand curves are downward sloping. Likewise, at each point along the market demand curve, just as along an individual demand curve, consumers are maximizing their satisfaction. Thus, as price decreases, more consumers might be enticed to buy a product. In Figure 3, for example, when the price of ale is above $3, Smith is not in the market; at a price of $0.50, even more buyers may enter.

CONSUMERS' SURPLUS

We have demonstrated that a high-priced good (diamonds) has a proportionately higher marginal utility than a low-priced good (water). When consumers maximize their satisfaction, the consumption of each good is pushed to the point where the marginal utility per dollar (MU/P) is the same for all the goods consumers are buying. *The theory of consumer demand shows that price reflects marginal utility.*

> When consumers are in equilibrium, the price of a good is a *dollar measure* of the value of the *last unit* of the good (its marginal benefit).

Figure 4 pictures a market demand curve that is drawn in a series of steps because the product is available only in whole units (such as a radio or a piano). According to the demand curve, if only 1 unit of the product is available, some consumer is willing to pay $10 for it (point *h*). If only 2 units of the product are available, someone is willing to pay $9 for the second unit (point *i*). If 6 units are available, someone is willing to pay a price of $5 for the sixth

FIGURE 3
From Individual to Market Demand

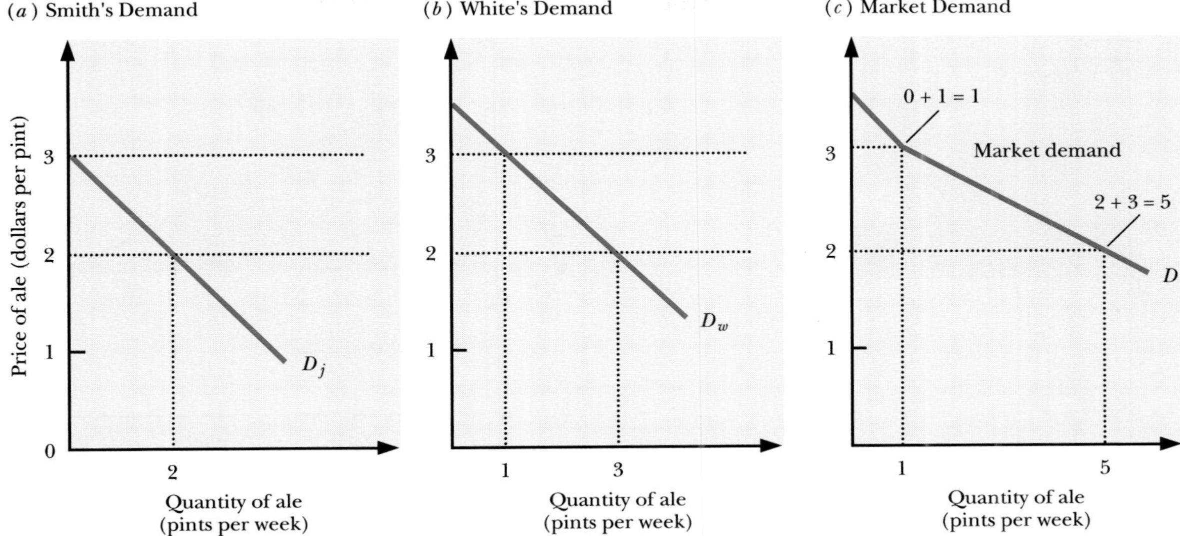

The market demand curve is the *horizontal* summation of all individual demand curves; it is calculated by summing the individual quantities demanded by all individuals at each price. Here, the market has only two consumers, but the principle applies to markets with any number of consumers.

unit. The current market price therefore reveals what consumers are willing to pay for the *last unit* of the product sold.

When the market price is $5 and the quantity demanded is 6 units (point *m*), the price paid by each consumer reflects the value of the sixth unit to the last purchaser, even though the first of those 6 units is still worth $10 to someone, the second is still worth $9 to someone else, and so on. The total value of the 6 units to consumers ($10 + $9 + $8 + $7 + $6 + $5 = $45) is greater than the total amount that consumers pay for them (6 × $5 = $30). Consumers enjoy a surplus on all the earlier units because they have a higher marginal value than later units. The surplus on each unit is the difference between the consumer's maximum willingness to pay and what the consumer must actually pay.

For example, at a price of $5 the first unit is worth $10 to someone but costs $5, so that person enjoys a surplus of $5 on the first unit. Someone enjoys a surplus of $4 on the second unit because the second unit is worth $9 to that person but costs $5. Only the last unit sold (the sixth) will yield no surplus, for its price will reflect exactly what that unit is worth to the consumer. Adding these surpluses together, one obtains a total **consumers' surplus** of $15.

> **Consumers' surplus** is the excess of the total consumer benefit that a good provides beyond consumer cost.

The great British economist Alfred Marshall (1842–1924) introduced the concept of consumers' surplus. It is a powerful tool that supplies a measure of the benefits that consumers obtain from markets and public works projects, as well as the price society pays for government policies.

As consumers move along a demand curve, the amount of consumers' surplus changes: If the price increases, consumers' surplus decreases; if the price falls, it increases. A lower price increases consumers' surplus because the same benefits can be purchased

FIGURE 4
Consumers' Surplus

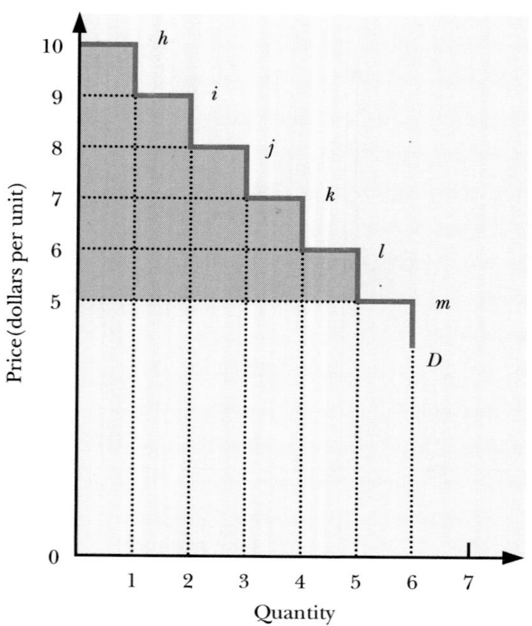

Say that the current market price is \$5 and the quantity demanded is 6 units. According to the demand curve, consumers were prepared to spend \$10 for the first unit, \$9 for the second unit, \$8 for the third unit, \$7 for the fourth unit, and \$6 for the fifth unit. When a total of 6 units are bought, however, consumers need pay only \$5 each for all 6 units. Thus, they pay for each of the 6 units only what the sixth unit is worth to them. The difference between what each unit is worth to consumers and what the consumers actually pay is shown by the height of the orange area for each unit. Adding these surpluses for all units yields a total consumers' surplus of \$5 + \$4 + \$3 + \$2 + \$1 = \$15.

FIGURE 5
The Gain in Consumers' Surplus Resulting from a Reduction in Price

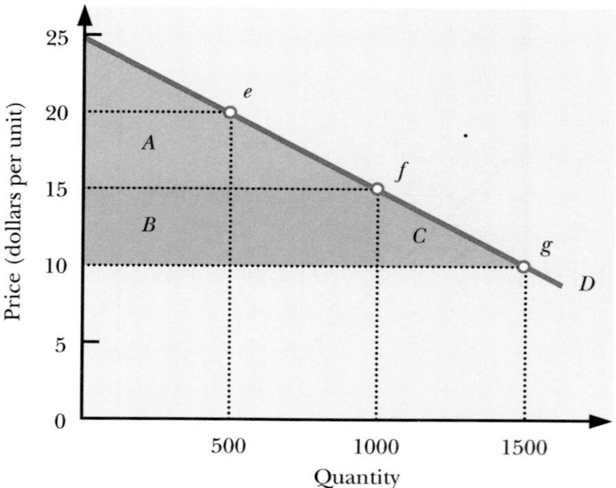

When price is \$15 and quantity demanded is 1000 units, the consumers' surplus is the orange triangle *A*, the excess of what people would be willing to pay beyond the actual cost. If the price falls to \$10, quantity demanded increases to 1500 units and consumers' surplus is the area $A + B + C$. Consumers' surplus, therefore, increases by $B + C$, or by \$6250.

at a lower cost. It follows that consumers' surplus measures consumer gains and losses from price changes along a given demand curve.

Figure 5 illustrates the calculation of consumers' surplus when the demand curve is a straight line. At point *f*, the price is \$15 and the quantity demanded is 1000 units. Consumers, therefore, pay a total of \$15,000 (\$15 × 1000 units) for the product. At quantities less than 1000 units, consumers would have been willing to pay more than \$15. This difference, measured by the vertical distance between the demand curve and the horizontal line at \$15, constitutes the surplus for each unit. For instance, the purchaser of the 500th unit would have been willing to pay \$20 instead of the \$15 actually paid (point *e*). Adding all the surpluses together for quantities less than 1000 yields the consumers' surplus, or the area of the orange triangle labeled *A*.[2]

What will happen to consumers' surplus if the market price drops to \$10? It will increase

[2] By changing quantity demanded in very small increments, the demand schedule approximates a smooth line. Thus, instead of adding a series of rectangles together as in Figure 4, consumer surplus is measured by the smooth area of triangle *A*.

As explained in Appendix 1A, areas of *rectangles* are computed by multiplying the horizontal width of the rectangle times the vertical height of the rectangle. The width of rectangle *B* is 1000; the height is \$5. Areas of triangles are calculated by multiplying the width of the triangle by its height and dividing by 2 (or multiplying by 1/2). The area of the triangle will be 1/2 that of the rectangle formed by the height and width of the triangle.

EXAMPLE 3 Consumers' Surplus: Why Directory Assistance Calls Are Not Free

In some states, telephone customers pay for calls to directory assistance. In states that do not charge for directory assistance calls, a fixed charge is incorporated into the basic monthly rate to cover the cost of providing the service.

Customers have resisted attempts by telephone companies to introduce a specific charge for directory assistance calls. This resistance stems from the customers' belief that they will be worse off if they are charged for something that was previously free. The concept of consumer surplus can help us see why this reasoning is not correct.

To keep the example simple, take the case of a phone company with 5 customers, each making no more than 1 call to directory assistance per week. The hypothetical demand schedule for directory assistance is given in the accompanying table.

Let us now compare the case where people are charged $0.20 per call to the case where they can make "free" calls but the per call cost of the service ($0.20) is ultimately included in their phone bills. According to the demand schedule, when the price per call is $0.20 (as it is when people are charged for each call), 3 calls would be made per week. The first customer has a surplus of $0.20, the second a surplus of $0.10, and the third pays exactly what the service is worth to that person. The total consumers' surplus is $0.30 per week. When the service is "free," 5 calls will be made per week. The total consumers' surplus equals $1.00 (the first customer has the full $0.40 because the price is zero, the second has $0.30, the third has $0.20, the fourth has $0.10, and the fifth has no surplus), but each customer must pay a fixed monthly charge of $0.20 to cover the cost of the service. Together, the 5 customers pay 5 × $0.20, or $1.00. Their consumers' surplus is eaten up entirely by the fixed charge.

We draw the conclusion that people are better off being charged directly for each directory assistance call. If the service is free, people who place a low (or even zero) marginal value on the service use it and then end up paying the average cost of providing the service. This makes them worse off than they would be under a direct-charge system.

Price of Directory Assistance (dollars per call)	Quantity Demanded (calls per week)
$0.40	1
$0.30	2
$0.20	3
$0.10	4
$0.00	5

Source: George Daly and Thomas H. Mayor, "Estimating the Value of a Missing Market," *Journal of Law and Economics* (April 1980).

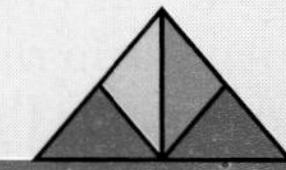

because a surplus will exist at all quantities less than 1500, whereas the surplus previously stopped at a quantity of 1000. Consumers' surplus at point *g*, where price is $10, is the area of the triangle formed by the demand curve and the horizontal line at $10, or the sum of the three areas $A + B + C$. Consumers' surplus at a price of $15 was area *A;* therefore, the *increase* in consumers' surplus as a consequence of the drop in price is $B + C$ = $5000 (area of *B*) +$1250 (area of *C*) = $6250.[3] (See Example 3.)

[3]The segment of the demand curve between *f* and *g* in this example was deliberately constructed to have an elasticity of demand of unity, so that the amounts of consumer spending at both points are equal. At both prices, consumers spend $15,000, but consumer surplus is $6250 greater at the lower price than at the higher price.

This chapter has examined the relationship between consumer behavior and the demand curve for goods and services. The next chapter will shift its focus to the supply side of the market for products. It will explore the different ways in which businesses are organized as well as the different types of markets in which firms operate.

SUMMARY

1. *Preferences* are people's evaluations of goods and services independent of budget and price considerations. Consumer preferences are fairly stable if they are defined as the services that goods provide. For example, the preference for transportation services fluctuates less than the demand for a particular type of transportation service.

2. *Utility* is a numerical ranking of a consumer's preferences among different commodity bundles. *Marginal utility* is the increase in total utility obtained when consumption of a good is increased by 1 unit. The *law of diminishing marginal utility* states that the marginal utility eventually declines as more of a good or service is consumed, holding the consumption of other goods constant. The fact that market prices reflect marginal utility rather than total utility explains the diamond/water paradox.

3. The law of diminishing marginal utility is consistent with the law of demand. When the rational consumer equates marginal utility per dollar on the last purchases of each commodity, the consumer is in equilibrium. If the price of one good falls, its marginal utility per dollar initially rises, and more of the commodity will be consumed. Rational consumers spend their money in a way that maximizes their satisfaction (utility). A drop in the price of a good has two effects: First, the use of the resulting increase in real income to purchase more of the good constitutes the *income effect.* Second, the increase in the amount of the good purchased that is due to the decrease in its relative price constitutes the *substitution effect.*

4. The *market demand schedule* is the horizontal summation of the demand schedules of all individuals participating in the market. The market demand schedule will have a negative slope because its individual components have negative slopes.

5. *Consumers' surplus* measures the extent to which consumer benefits exceed consumer costs for a particular product. Consumers' surplus follows from the law of diminishing marginal utility. Consumers pay the same market price for each unit they buy, but the market price reflects only the value of the last unit sold. The marginal benefit of earlier units, therefore, exceeds the market price. Adding these surpluses together yields total consumers' surplus. The concept of consumer surplus permits the measurement of consumer losses and gains from price changes.

KEY TERMS

preferences
utility
marginal utility (MU)
law of diminishing marginal utility
marginal utility per dollar
consumer equilibrium
income effect
substitution effect
market demand curve
consumers' surplus

QUESTIONS AND PROBLEMS

1. In some parts of Africa today, sick people go to witch doctors. In the United States, most people seek out medical doctors when they are ill; a few seek out faith healers. Does this variation mean that consumer preferences for medical care are basically unstable?
2. In the late 1970s and early 1980s, Americans began to buy smaller, fuel-efficient cars instead of large "gas guzzlers." In the 1990s, they switched back to buying larger cars; even Japan started exporting larger cars to the United States. Do these changes indicate that consumer preferences are unstable?
3. If the marginal utility of a good *A* were to increase as consumption of the good increased (in opposition to the law of diminishing marginal utility), would $MU_A/P_A = MU_B/P_B$ still be the equilibrium condition?
4. Use the marginal utility information in Table 1 to calculate the demand for ale at the price of $4 per pint. What do you do when marginal utility per dollar cannot be exactly equated for two goods on the last unit sold?
5. Again using Table 1, calculate the demand for ale at the price of $2 but at a weekly income of $11. Compare this result with the answer at $8. Which is larger? Why?
6. Assume that there are 1000 identical consumers in the market, each with the same income and the same preferences. When the price of *X* is

$50 per unit, the typical consumer is prepared to purchase 20 units. When the price is $40 per unit, the typical consumer is prepared to purchase 25 units. Construct from this information the market demand curve for *X* (assume the demand curve is a straight line). Then calculate the loss of consumers' surplus when the price rises from $40 to $50 per unit.

7. A consumer is spending an entire weekly income on goods *A* and *B*. The last penny spent on *A* yields a marginal utility of 10; the last penny spent on *B* yields a marginal utility of 20. Is it possible for the consumer to be in equilibrium? If so, what are the exact conditions?
8. Ms. White consumes only goods *X* and *Y*. Column 1 of Table A shows the marginal utility she derives from various units of *X*; column 2 shows the marginal utility she derives from various units of *Y*. Her income is $20, the price of *X* is $2 per unit, and the price of *Y* is $4 per unit. Use Table A to answer the following questions:

   a. How much of *X* and *Y* will Ms. White demand?

   b. Check your answer by using the consumer equilibrium conditions. (Is all income spent? Does $MU_x/P_x = MU_y/P_y$?)

TABLE A

(1)		(2)	
Units of *X*	MU_x	Units of *Y*	MU_y
1	20	1	2000
2	16	2	200
3	12	3	20
4	10	4	10
5	6	5	4

9. Can the equilibrium conditions be applied to more than two goods? How?
10. The price of ale is $10, the price of bread is $5, and the marginal utility of bread is 50 utils when the consumer is in equilibrium. Can you determine how much is spent on ale? Can you determine the marginal utility of ale?
11. The price of oranges is $0.25 each, and the price of grapefruit is $0.50 each. Assuming that all income is spent in each case, determine whether or not the consumer is in equilibrium in each of the following circumstances. If consumer equilibrium does not occur, determine which good the consumer will purchase in greater quantity and explain why.

    a. The marginal utility of oranges, MU_O, equals 10, and the marginal utility of grapefruit, MU_G, equals 15.

    b. $MU_O = 50$ and $MU_G = 100$.

    c. MU_O is twice that of MU_G.

    d. MU_G is twice that of MU_O.

12. *Optional Question.* Income and substitution effects can be measured. Suppose that the income elasticity of demand for housing is 1 and that the price elasticity of demand is 0.3 (these numbers are close to actual estimates). Furthermore, suppose that housing accounts for 20 percent of the average household's budget. A decrease in income of 2 percent would decrease the demand for housing by 2 percent because the income elasticity is 1. Now suppose that income is held constant and that the price of housing rises by 10 percent. Since the price elasticity is 0.3, a 10 percent increase in price will lower quantity demanded by 3 percent. What portion of this 3 percent decrease in quantity demanded is due to the income effect? What portion is due to the substitution effect? (*Hint:* A 10 percent increase in the price of housing raises the cost of living by 2 percent since there is a 10 percent increase in 20 percent of the budget. Observe also that a 2 percent increase in the cost of living has the same effects as a 2 percent reduction in income. Therefore, a 10 percent increase in the price of housing, holding income and other prices constant, is like a 2 percent reduction in real income.)

SUGGESTED READINGS

Jevons, William Stanley. *The Theory of Political Economy.* Baltimore: Penguin Books, 1970, chap. 3. Originally published in 1871.

Mansfield, Edwin. *Microeconomics: Theory and Applications,* 6th ed. New York: W. W. Norton, 1988, chap. 3.

Stigler, George. *The Theory of Prices,* 4th ed. New York: Macmillan, 1987, chap. 4.

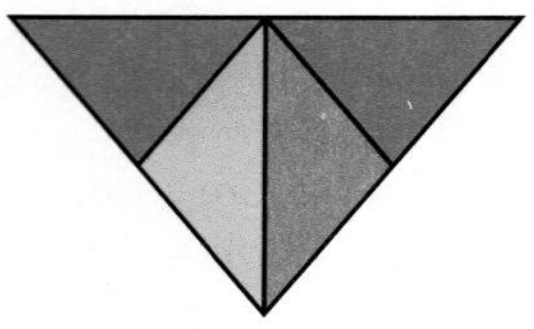

APPENDIX 27A

Indifference Curves

APPENDIX INSIGHT

The preceding chapter based the law of demand on the nineteenth-century conception of cardinal utility—a measure that reflects the magnitude as well as the rank of a consumer's satisfaction from different commodity bundles. Skepticism about the quantification of utility prompted economists to seek an alternative approach to understanding consumer behavior. The culmination of this search is the *indifference curve theory*. This theory assumes that consumers are able to *rank* their preferences for combinations of goods, but does not require that utility be measured in absolute terms. A consumer who does not prefer one combination to another is said to be *indifferent*. Indifference curve theory provides a convenient graphical approach for illustrating consumer response to income and price changes and for analyzing the breakdown of consumer behavior into substitution and income effects.

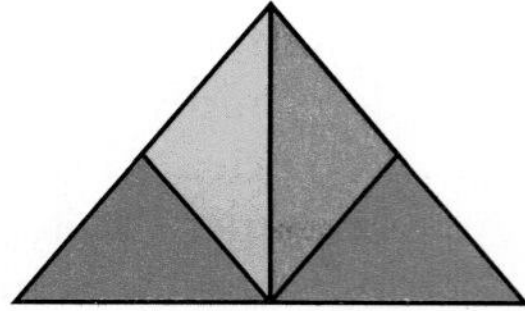

CONSUMER PREFERENCES

The indifference curve approach is based on an analysis of the amount of one good a consumer is willing to give up in exchange for 1 unit of another good without experiencing a loss in total satisfaction. When one combination of goods yields the same satisfaction as another, the consumer is indifferent between the two combinations.

Figure 1 diagrams the preferences of a particular consumer. The horizontal axis measures the quantity of ale consumed by the individual per week. The vertical axis measures the quantity of bread consumed by the individual per week. At point *a*, 6 loaves of bread and 1 pint of ale are consumed. At point *a*, the consumer is willing to give up 3 loaves of bread for 1 more pint of ale. Making this trade would move the consumer to point *b*, where 3 loaves of bread and 2 pints of ale are consumed. At point *b*, the consumer is willing to give up only 1 loaf of bread to acquire 1 more pint of ale. Making this trade would move the consumer to point *c*, where 2 loaves of bread and 3 pints of ale are consumed per week. Finally, to acquire 1 more pint of ale, the consumer at point *c* is willing to give up only half of a loaf of bread, which would result in the combination at point *d*. The consumer is indifferent between points *a, b, c,* and *d*.

A curve can be drawn through points *a, b, c,* and *d* to represent all possible consumption patterns that keep the consumer at the same level of satisfaction. This curve is called an **indifference curve.**

An **indifference curve** shows all the alternative combinations of two goods that yield the same total satisfaction to a particular consumer and among which the consumer is indifferent.

An indifference curve is downward sloping because both goods yield satisfaction. The consumer's satisfaction will remain constant when the consumption of one good increases only if consumption of the other good decreases.

FIGURE 1
An Indifference Curve

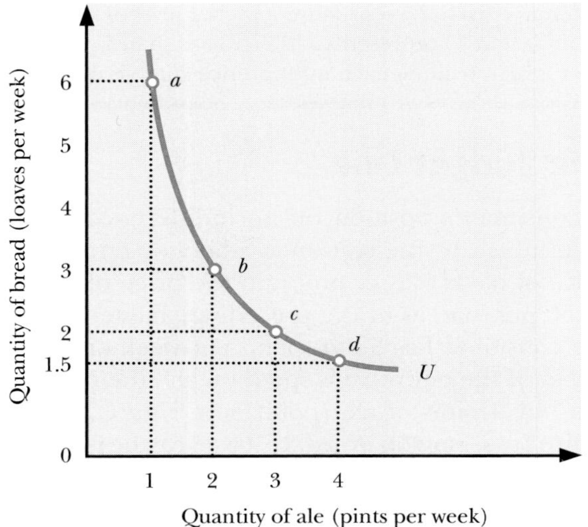

When given the choice among the commodity bundles along an indifference curve, the consumer is indifferent. Consumption pattern *a* yields the same satisfaction to the consumer as *b, c,* or *d*. The absolute value of the slope of an indifference curve is the marginal rate of substitution and shows—in this case—how much bread the consumer is just willing to sacrifice for one more pint of ale.

The Law of Diminishing Marginal Rate of Substitution

When indifference curves are used to analyze consumer preferences, the concept of marginal utility is replaced by that of the **marginal rate of substitution (MRS).**

The **marginal rate of substitution (MRS)** is how much of one good a person is just willing to give up to acquire one unit of another good.

Thus, the marginal rate of substitution is just a fancy name for an acceptable trade-off between two goods, for a person's *valuation* of an additional unit of one good in terms of another. For example, the amount of pizza a person would be willing to sacrifice for an additional hot dog indicates that person's valuation of hot dogs in terms of pizza.

An indifference curve is always convex when viewed from below. (This means that the curve bulges toward the origin). This convex curvature follows from the **law of diminishing marginal rate of substitution:** As more ale is consumed relative to bread, the consumer is willing to give up less and less bread to acquire additional units of ale because bread is getting more valuable and ale is getting less valuable. In Figure 1, when one moves from point *a* down to point *d* and beyond, the indifference curve gets flatter and flatter because the relative valuation placed on ale is decreasing compared to that of bread.

> The **law of diminishing marginal rate of substitution** states that as more of one good (*A*) is consumed, the amount of another good (*B*) that the consumer is willing to sacrifice for one more unit of good *A* declines.

The flatter is the slope of the indifference curve, the lower is the relative valuation the consumer places on *A* (compared to *B*) when *A* is on the horizontal axis. The slope of the tangent at any point on the indifference curve measures the marginal rate of substitution of good *B* for good *A*.

Indifference curves can be drawn to represent any level of satisfaction. Each consumer has an entire map of indifference curves, one for every level. Figure 2 shows three indifference curves for the same consumer. Higher indifference curves for any one consumer represent higher levels of satisfaction because more is usually better.

Indifference curves are subjective and unique to each person. Nevertheless, all indifference curves have the following five properties in common:

1. Indifference curves between two goods for which consumers derive positive benefits are downward sloping.
2. They are bowed toward the *origin* (the point where the axes meet), reflecting the law of diminishing marginal rate of substitution.
3. The consumer is better off when he or she moves to a higher indifference curve.
4. Indifference curves cannot intersect each other because an intersection would indicate that the consumer is simultaneously worse off and better off. (Even though indifference curves cannot intersect, they need not be parallel.)
5. Indifference curves do not shift in response to changes in market circumstances (income or prices).

FIGURE 2
Map of Indifference Curves

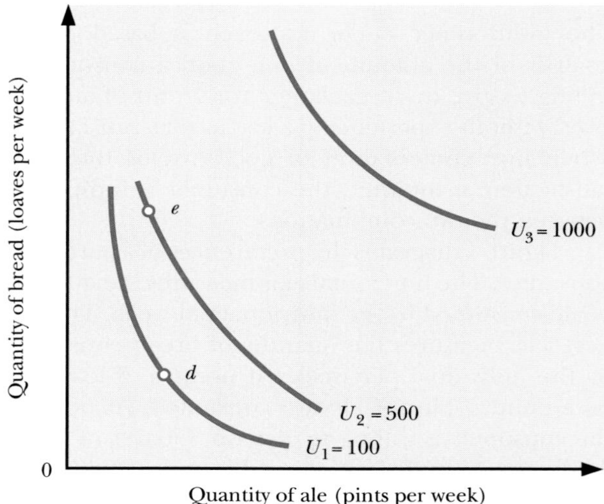

Each consumer has an infinite number of indifference curves. Three indifference curves for a particular consumer are shown here. The higher is the indifference curve, the greater is the well-being of the consumer. The indifference map shows that commodity bundle *e* is preferred to bundle *d* because the former is on a higher indifference curve. Indifference curve U_3 represents a higher level of satisfaction than U_2, and U_2 represents a higher level than U_1. The level of satisfaction along each indifference curve is constant.

The Budget Line

A consumer's position on an indifference curve is determined by the consumer's budget. Suppose the price of ale is $2 per pint and the price of bread is $0.50 per loaf, as in the preceding chapter. Assume the consumer has $8 to spend per week on ale and bread. If the entire $8 is spent on ale, the consumer can buy 4 pints of ale (point *m* in Figure 3). If the entire $8 is spent on bread, 16 loaves can be purchased (point *n*). The **budget line** connecting points *m* and *n* indicates all possible combinations of ale and bread that the consumer is able to purchase by allocating the entire $8 income between the two goods.

> The **budget line** represents all the combinations of goods the consumer is able to buy, given a certain income and set prices. The budget line shows the consumption possibilities available to the consumer.

FIGURE 3
The Budget Line

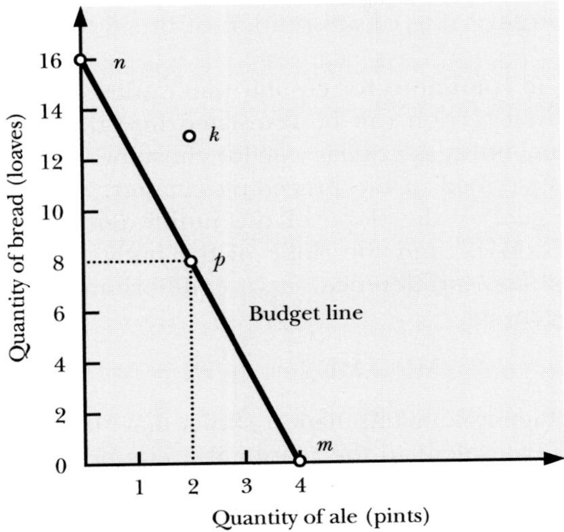

With a budget of \$8, the consumer can buy 16 loaves of bread at a price of \$0.50 per loaf or 4 pints of ale at a price of \$2 per pint. Spending \$4 on each good would buy 8 loaves of bread and 2 pints of ale (point *p*). The budget line shows the choices open to the consumer. The consumer can afford to buy any combination of goods on the budget line. Points above the budget line, such as *k*, cannot be purchased with the consumer's income. The slope of the budget line is the ratio of the price of ale to the price of bread—here, 4.

The budget line in Figure 3 has a slope with an absolute value of 16/4 = 4. This slope is the price of ale (the good on the horizontal axis) in terms of bread (the good on the vertical axis): $P_A/P_B = \$2/\$0.50 = 4$; it indicates that a consumer who wants to buy 1 more pint of ale must give up 4 loaves of bread.

Algebraically, point *m* in Figure 3 is income divided by the price of ale (Income/P_A) because it represents the maximum possible consumption of ale. Point *n* is income divided by the price of bread (Income/P_B). The absolute value of the slope of the line *nm* is then determined as follows:

$$\text{Slope} = \frac{\text{Income}}{P_B} \div \frac{\text{Income}}{P_A} = \frac{P_A}{P_B}$$

An indifference curve shows how the consumer ranks various commodity bundles; the budget line shows which bundles the consumer is able to buy. Combining the information represented by an indifference curve and the budget line reveals which combination the consumer *will* buy.

CONSUMER EQUILIBRIUM

The consumer achieves equilibrium by choosing a consumption pattern that maximizes satisfaction and lies on the budget line. The consumer is *able* to locate anywhere on the budget line, but *the rational consumer will select that consumption combination that falls on the highest attainable indifference curve.* Figure 4 illustrates the choice of an optimal consumption pattern. By consuming 4 loaves of bread and 3 pints

FIGURE 4
Consumer Equilibrium

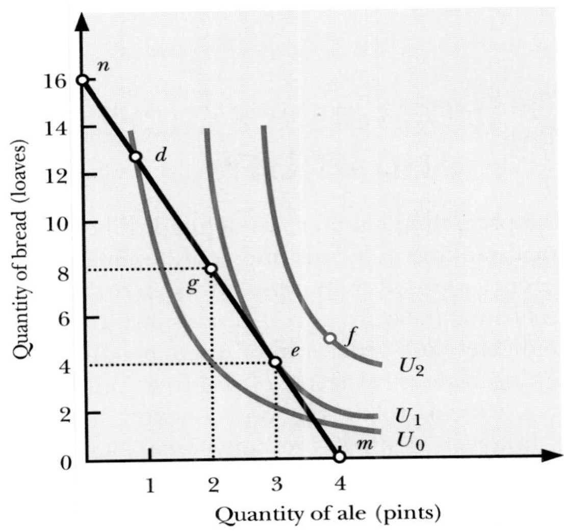

The consumer's optimal consumption pattern is at point *e*. A point like *d* is attainable (on the budget line) but is inferior to *e* because it places the consumer on a lower indifference curve (U_0). Point *f* is preferable to *e* (the consumer is on a high indifference curve, U_2) but is not attainable with the given set of income and prices. At *e*, the indifference curve U_1 is tangent to the budget line. Thus, the slope of the indifference curve equals the slope of the budget line. This tangency is equivalent to the marginal utility rule for maximizing utility ($MU_A/P_A = MU_B/P_B$) discussed in the preceding chapter.

of ale (point e), the consumer can reach indifference curve U_1. Any other point on the budget line will fall on a *lower* indifference curve. At this optimal consumption point, the budget line is tangent to (touches the curve only at one point and has the same slope as) the indifference curve.

In equivalent terms, consumer equilibrium occurs at that point on the highest attainable indifference curve where the marginal rate of substitution equals the price ratio. At point e, the consumer's marginal rate of substitution is 4 because the consumer is willing to trade off 4 units of bread for 1 unit of ale. The price ratio, as we have shown, is also 4.

> The consumer is in equilibrium when the budget line is just tangent to the highest attainable indifference curve. Two conditions are then satisfied: (1) The consumer is on the budget line. (2) The consumer's marginal rate of substitution of bread for ale equals the price ratio of ale to bread (P_A/P_B).

INDIFFERENCE CURVES AND UTILITY

In the preceding chapter, we defined utility as a numerical ranking of a consumer's preferences among different commodity bundles. We stated that utility is an ordinal measure of consumer satisfaction, used to indicate rank-order rather than magnitude. By assigning numerical levels of utility to indifference curves, we can relate the two concepts. (We must not, however, confuse the convenient language of utility theory with the assumption that utility is measurable.) Any numbers can be assigned as long as they are increasing for higher indifference curves. Thus, in Figure 2, indifference curve U_3 is assigned a higher number (1000) than U_2 (500) or U_1 (100).

Also in the preceding chapter, the quantification of utility allowed us to define the marginal utility (MU) of a good as the increase in utility per unit change in the consumption of the good, holding the consumption of other goods constant. Marginal utility theory and indifference curve analysis are linked by the ability to use the marginal utilities of two goods to calculate the marginal rate of substitution. For example, if the marginal utility of ale (MU_A) is 20 and the marginal utility of bread (MU_B) is 5, it takes 4 extra loaves of bread to compensate the consumer for the loss of only 1 pint of ale. But if $MU_A = 10$ and $MU_B = 5$, the marginal rate of substitution of bread for ale is only 2.

The conditions for equilibrium outlined in the preceding section can be translated into the equal marginal utility per dollar rule for consumer equilibrium described in the preceding chapter. At point e in Figure 4, the slope of the indifference curve is MU_A/MU_B, and the slope of the budget line is P_A/P_B. The indifference curve equilibrium rule is equivalent to

$$MU_A/MU_B = P_A/P_B$$

Some algebraic manipulation shows that this equation is equivalent to the marginal utility per dollar rule for equilibrium:

$$MU_A/P_A = MU_B/P_B$$

> The marginal rate of substitution of bread for ale ($MRS_{B/A}$) equals the ratio of the ale's marginal utility (MU_A) to the bread's marginal utility (MU_B):
>
> $$MRS_{B/A} = \frac{MU_A}{MU_B}$$

THE EFFECT OF AN INCOME CHANGE

The consumer's equilibrium position is affected by changes in income, the price of ale, and the price of bread. Figure 5 shows that a reduction in the consumer's income from \$8 to \$4 leads to a reduction in the demand for both ale and bread. We assume the price of ale stays at \$2 per pint and the price of bread remains at \$0.50 per loaf. The budget line shifts downward from nm to hj because the consumer can purchase a maximum of only 2 pints of ale or 8 loaves of bread with an income of \$4. Consumption decreases from 4 loaves of bread and 3 pints of ale to only 2 loaves of bread and 1.5 pints of ale at the new equilibrium (point e_0).

Notice that because prices are held constant, the slope of the budget line, P_A/P_B, remains the same. Thus, all budget lines for a given set of prices are

FIGURE 5
The Effect of an Income Change

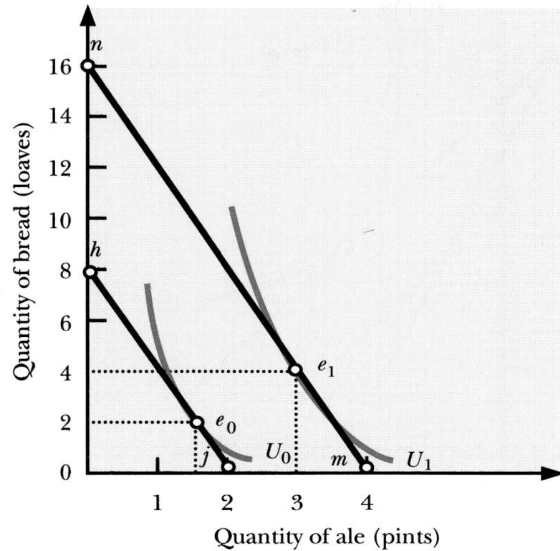

When the price of ale is \$2 per pint and the price of bread is \$0.50 per loaf, a fall in income from \$8 to \$4 causes a parallel shift in the budget line from *nm* to *hj*. The equilibrium point moves from e_1 to e_0, which is on a lower indifference curve (U_0).

FIGURE 6
The Effect of a Price Change on Consumer Equilibrium: The Law of Demand

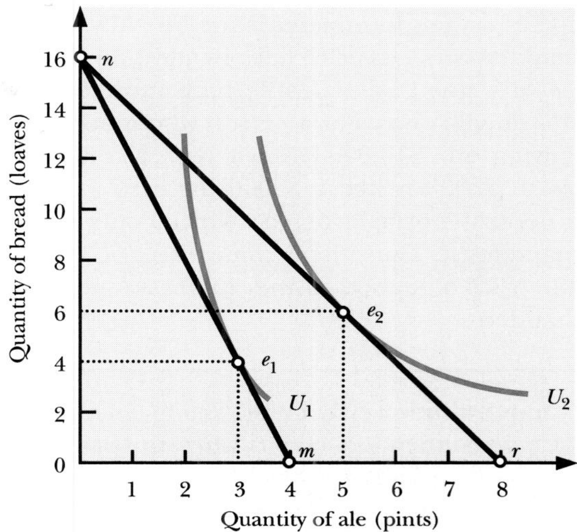

Assuming that income is \$8 and the price of bread is \$0.50, when the price of ale falls from \$2 to \$1 per pint, the budget line swings outward from *nm* to *nr* because the consumer is able to buy as many as 8 pints of ale. The consumer finds a new equilibrium combination, e_2, where indifference curve U_2 is tangent to the new budget line *nr*. A fall in the price of ale from \$2 to \$1, thus, increases the quantity of ale demanded from 3 pints at point e_1 to 5 pints at point e_2.

parallel, shifting downward when income falls and upward when income rises. Clearly, utility also rises and falls in concert with income.

THE EFFECT OF A PRICE CHANGE

Now consider the effects of a change in the price of one of two goods, holding income and the other price constant. Figure 6 shows that a fall in the price of ale from \$2 to \$1 per pint leads to an increase in the quantity of ale demanded. The initial equilibrium situation is represented by point e_1, where the price of ale is \$2 and the price of bread is \$0.50. Reducing the price of ale to \$1 allows the consumer to purchase as many as 8 pints of ale with the same income of \$8. The budget line swings outward from *nm* to *nr*.

At the new equilibrium position, point e_2, the consumer buys 5 pints of ale and 6 loaves of bread. Before the price change, the consumer bought 3 pints of ale and 4 loaves of bread. The law of demand is reconfirmed: lowering the price of ale increases the quantity of ale demanded.

Moreover, the consumer is made better off (moves to a higher indifference curve) by the fall in the price of ale. The lower is the price of a good bought by a consumer, holding income and other prices constant, the greater is the consumer's welfare.

> When the price of one good falls, an increase in real income occurs, represented by an outward swing of the budget line.

An analysis of the effect of a price change illustrates why demand curves are downward sloping. A downward slope on a demand curve implies that as the price of a good falls, the quantity demanded rises. The preceding chapter outlined two reasons for the law of demand: the **substitution effect** and the **income effect.** When the price of a good falls, people tend to substitute that good for other goods because its relative price decreases. Thus, the substitution effect tends to increase the quantity of a good demanded when its price falls. In addition, when the price of a good falls, people have more money to spend on all goods. For a person who is accustomed to buying one $10,000 car per year, a reduction in price to $8000 is like a $2000 increase in income. If a good is normal, increases in income raise the demand for it. Thus, the income effect of a decrease in the price of a good further increases the quantity demanded.

> The **substitution effect** is the change in quantity of *X* demanded that occurs when the price of *X* changes and the consumer's utility or welfare is held constant.
>
> The **income effect** is the change in the quantity of *X* demanded that is attributable to the welfare change that accompanies the price change.

FIGURE 7
Substitution and Income Effects

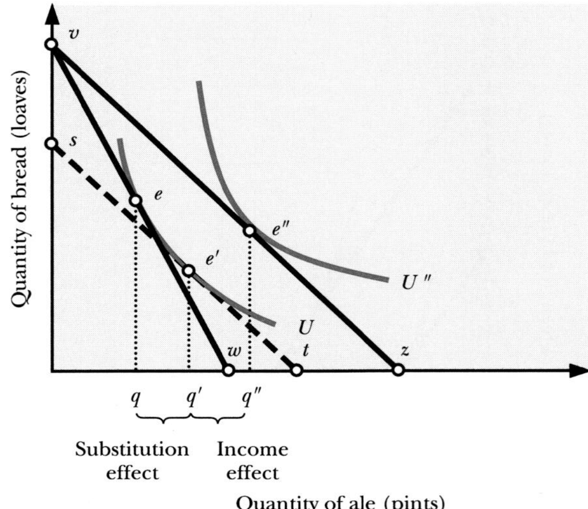

When income is $8 per week, bread costs $0.50 per loaf, and ale costs $2 per pint, the initial equilibrium is point *e*. When the price of ale falls from $2 to $1 per pint, the budget line swings outward from *vw* to *vz*. The new equilibrium is point *e''*. The substitution effect is obtained by drawing the budget line *st* parallel to *vz* but tangent to the original indifference curve, *U*. Thus, the substitution effect is the distance *qq'* and the income effect is the distance *q'q''*. In the case of a normal good, the income effect augments the substitution effect.

Figure 7 shows a consumer with an initial budget line *vw* and an initial equilibrium at point *e*, where the consumer is purchasing *q* units of ale. When the price of ale falls, the budget line shifts to *vz*. The quantity of ale demanded is now *q''* at the new equilibrium point, *e''*. The consumer is better off after the drop in the ale price because curve *U''* is higher than curve *U*. Indifference curve analysis can be used to isolate the roles of the substitution effect and the income effect on the change in the equilibrium position.

When the price of ale falls, the ratio of the price of ale to the price of bread changes. This new ratio is reflected by the budget lines *vz* and *st*. A consumer interested only in maintaining the same level of utility achieved on curve *U* would increase the quantity of ale demanded until he or she reached point *e'*, where line *st* is tangent to *U*. At *e'*, the consumer buys more ale and less bread without changing the level of satisfaction. This change in the quantity of ale demanded, from *q* to *q'*, constitutes the substitution effect of the change in the price of ale.

At point *e'*, however, the consumer is not spending all available income. The drop in the price of ale shifts the budget line outward to *vz*, which has the same ale price/bread price ratio as *st* but enables the consumer to choose a position on a higher indifference curve. Instead of remaining at *e'*, a consumer who wishes to maximize satisfaction will choose *e''*, a point on the highest indifference curve attainable given budget line *vz*. A consumer making this choice will further increase the quantity demanded of ale from *q'* at *e'* to *q''* at *e''*. This new equilibrium, unlike *e'*, does satisfy all the conditions of consumer equilibrium. The increase in quantity demanded from *q'* to *q''* constitutes the income effect of the change in the ale price.

The importance of the distinction between the substitution and income effects is that if a good is normal, the income effect reinforces the substitution effect. In Figure 7, the price of ale falls and the substitution effect increases quantity demanded from *q* to *q'* along the convex indifference curve *U*. The move from e' to e'' is like any income increase. If ale is a normal good, more ale will be consumed. In effect, a reduced price of ale gives the consumer more income to spend on both ale and bread. Thus, for a normal good, the income effect also indicates more ale will be consumed. It follows from the above analysis that if a good is normal, the demand curve for the good must be downward sloping.

SUMMARY

1. Indifference curve analysis requires only that consumers be able to state whether they prefer one combination of goods to another or whether they are indifferent. An indifference curve plots those combinations of goods that yield the same level of satisfaction to the consumer. In indifference curve analysis, the law of diminishing marginal rate of substitution replaces the law of diminishing marginal utility. It states that the greater is the quantity of good *X* that the individual consumes relative to good *Y*, the smaller will be the quantity of good *Y* that the consumer is willing to sacrifice to obtain 1 more unit of good *X*. The budget line shows the choices of goods open to the consumer.

2. Maximizing satisfaction requires that the consumer seek out the highest indifference curve that can be attained while remaining on the budget line. This point occurs at the tangency of the indifference curve and the budget line.

3. Indifference curves can be related to marginal utilities. The marginal rate of substitution of bread for ale is the marginal utility of ale divided by the marginal utility of bread.

4. A change in income causes a parallel shift in the budget line. The budget line shifts downward if income decreases and upward if income increases. The new equilibrium is simply the point of tangency between the new budget line and an indifference curve.

5. A reduction in the price of one commodity swings the budget line outward. The new equilibrium occurs at the point of tangency between a higher indifference curve and the new budget line. The consumer is made better off by the price reduction because the consumer is able to locate on a higher indifference curve. The effects of a price change on quantity demanded can be broken down into a substitution effect, which maintains the existing utility level, and an income effect, which results from the change in the consumer's level of utility.

KEY TERMS

indifference curve
marginal rate of substitution (MRS)
law of diminishing marginal rate of substitution
budget line
substitution effect
income effect

QUESTIONS AND PROBLEMS

1. Assume that a consumer's income is \$100, the price of ale is \$5 per pint, and the price of bread is \$4 per loaf.
   a. Draw the consumer's budget line.
   b. How does the budget line shift if the price of bread rises to \$10, holding the price of ale at \$5?
   c. How does the budget line shift if the price of ale rises to \$10, holding the price of bread at \$10?
   d. How does the budget line shift if income doubles to \$200, holding the prices of ale and bread at \$5 and \$10, respectively?
2. Why are indifference curves downward sloping? Why are they bowed toward the origin?
3. Why must the equilibrium position be a point of tangency between the budget line and an indifference curve?
4. Illustrate a situation in which income increases and the demand for one of two goods falls.
5. Derive the law of demand for a normal good using the distinction between substitution and income effects when the price of the good rises.
6. Assume that the marginal rate of substitution of good *X* for good *Y* is $MRS_{X/Y} = 6$, that the price of good *X* is \$1 per unit, and that the price of good *Y* is \$3 per unit.
   a. Illustrate the consumer's current position on the budget line relative to an indifference curve.
   b. Explain why the consumer would buy more of good *Y*.

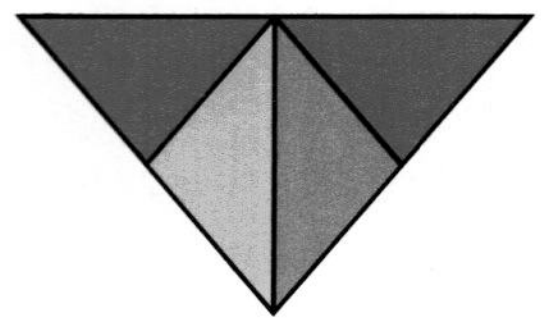

28

Business Organization, Corporate Finance, and Financial Markets

CHAPTER INSIGHT

Why are some businesses organized as corporations, while others are organized as partnerships? Why are some transactions handled through markets, while others are handled inside the business enterprise?

Business firms combine resources to maximize profit on the goods and services they produce. Much of this chapter focuses on one type of business firm—the corporation. Although some form of the corporation existed in ancient Rome and in medieval times, the modern corporation was not created until the sixteenth century, as a way to finance the expansion of Europe's lucrative but risky overseas trade. The corporation offered new ways of raising large amounts of capital by allowing individuals to purchase shares in the sea venture, while protecting the fortunes of those individuals if the venture failed. The advantages of the corporation have made it the dominant form of business organization in modern economies; however, other forms exist, such as sole proprietorships or partnerships. There are advantages and disadvantages to each form of business organization.

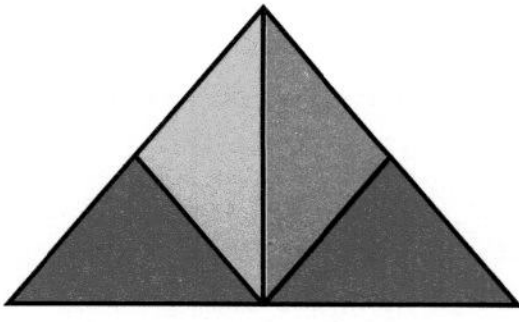

MANAGERIAL COORDINATION

All business firms, regardless of how they are organized, have some similar characteristics. In Chapter 3 a circular-flow diagram was used to show that firms can be involved in transactions with final consumers and in transactions with other firms. For example, IBM sells personal computers to households, while RCA sells parts and supplies to IBM. The first transaction enters the circular flow between businesses and households; the second transaction remains entirely within the business sector. Transactions with final consumers and transactions with other firms are conducted through markets that coordinate prices and quantities. Equilibrium prices coordinate the allocation of scarce resources.

Resources are allocated within the firm by **managerial coordination.** All business firms need a person or group of persons to make managerial decisions. The firm's managers allocate the capital and land that is owned or leased by the firm and issue directives to employees who work according to written or unwritten contracts.

> **Managerial coordination** is the disposition of the firm's resources according to the directives of the firm's manager(s).

Principals and Agents

Business firms enter into contractual relationships in which they can act either as a **principal** or as an **agent.**[1]

> A **principal** is a party that has controlling authority and that engages an agent to act subject to the principal's control and instruction.

> An **agent** is a party that acts for, on behalf of, or as a representative of a principal.

Firm A is a principal when it enters into a contract with Firm B. The contract requires that Firm B (the agent) supply Firm A with specified amounts of a product at specified prices over a specified period of time. Firm A is also a principal when it signs a contract with an employee (the agent) that calls for the employee to perform specific services at a specified wage for a specified period of time. Boeing Corporation acts as a principal when it contracts with Rolls-Royce (the agent) to supply jet engines for its aircraft. Chrysler Corporation acts as a principal when it hires Lee Iacocca (the agent) to serve as its chief executive officer. Jones acts as a principal when she signs a contract with a national moving firm (the agent) to move her household belongings from one city to another. Once an agency relationship is established, the principal is responsible for monitoring performance to ensure that the agent is providing the services specified in the agreement. When both the principal and the agent are motivated toward the same goal, or when the performance of the agent can be easily monitored, conflicts between the principal and the agent are unlikely to arise. However, when the parties have different goals and when monitoring is difficult, conflicts between principal and agent are expected.

Why Business Firms Exist

Earlier chapters discussed the role of *entrepreneurs*—individuals who combine the factors of production to produce output. Although it is possible for entrepreneurs to work entirely through markets and without business firms, such instances are rare. A single entrepreneur may build a home by contracting through markets with the numerous carpenters, plumbers, electricians, and lumber and glass suppliers; however, most homes are built by construction firms. The firm's agent, the manager, directs employees—carpenters, electricians, and unskilled laborers—to perform particular tasks.

There are four main reasons for the existence of business firms: Business firms can limit the costs of market transactions; they can take advantage of economies of scale; they can bear risk individuals are

[1]This distinction is made in Stephen A. Ross, "The Economic Theory of Agency: The Principal's Problem," *American Economic Review Papers and Proceedings* (May 1973): 134. The agency literature was developed by Robert Wilson, A. Michael Spence, Richard Zeckhauser, and Stephen Ross.

unwilling to bear; and they can provide monitoring of team production.

The Costs of Using Markets. Ronald Coase developed the first reason for the existence of business firms:[2] Market coordination has its costs. The participants in market-coordinated activities must negotiate contracts, complete paperwork, search out the best prices, and bear the legal expenses if contracts are not fulfilled. Imagine, for example, the enormous transactions costs of using market coordination instead of managerial coordination to produce a modern commercial jet aircraft. If market coordination were used, thousands of subcontracts would have to be negotiated to produce the instruments, the hydraulic control systems, the airframe, and the interior furnishings. Managerial coordination can reduce these transactions costs. Instead of negotiating thousands of market contracts, the manager simply directs employees to perform designated tasks, allocates the plant and equipment of the business enterprise, and works with fewer sub-contractors.

As long as the cost of organizing an activity inside the firm remains below the cost of organizing that activity using markets, the task is carried out within the firm.

Economies of Scale. As Adam Smith pointed out, business firms can take advantage of **economies of scale.**

> **Economies of scale** are present when large output volumes can be produced at a lower cost per unit than small output volumes.

Economies of scale are present in many production processes (Smith's example was a pin factory). The business firm brings together workers, land, and capital: the manager directs them to specialize in different tasks; output is produced in larger production runs and at a lower cost per unit.

Risk Bearing. Economist Frank Knight emphasized a third reason for the existence of business firms:[3] Some individuals are more willing to bear risk than others. Business ventures typically involve risk (demand can change, factor prices can fluctuate, and so on). The owner of the enterprise (the principal) is willing to bear the risk. The employees (the agents) are not. The employer hires workers and rents land and equipment at negotiated prices. The employer provides the suppliers of the factors of production with security. In return, they agree to follow the owner's business directives. If the business is successful, the owner will reap the rewards; if it fails, the owner will suffer the consequences.

The firm (as the principal) contracts with agents to perform services for and to represent the firm. The agents receive a fee (a wage, salary, or bonus) for their service. This contractual fee insulates them from risk and uncertainty. As long as the firm is solvent and the agency agreement is in effect, the agents will receive their fees even when the firm encounters financial difficulties. The principal bears the risks by absorbing business losses when they occur.

Figure 1 shows the trends in business failures from 1970 to 1991. During this period an average of 1 out of 100 businesses failed each year.

Monitoring Team Production. Armen Alchian and Harold Demsetz emphasize that business enterprises are formed when there are substantial gains from team production.[4] In many cases, employees working as a team can produce more output than employees working alone.

If team production is used, the performance of individual employees must be monitored by the owner/manager to ensure that no employees are shirking their responsibility. Because the owner of a firm is paid out of the gains of team production, the owner will be motivated to do a good job of monitoring. Moreover, the owner has the authority to change the production team by changing contractual arrangements between the business enterprise and its inputs.

Team monitoring is essential when agents have goals that differ from those of the principal. For example, the principal wants the firm to earn a maximum profit from its resources. Employees (agents) may want a lighter work load, or they may be un-

[2]Ronald H. Coase, "The Nature of the Firm," *Economica* 4 (1937): 386–405. Reprinted in George Stigler and Kenneth Boulding, eds., *Readings in Price Theory* (Homewood, Ill: Richard D. Irwin, 1952).

[3]Frank H. Knight, *Risk, Uncertainty, and Profit* (New York: Harper Torchbooks, 1957).

[4]Armen Alchian and Harold Demsetz, "Production, Information Costs, and Economic Organization," *American Economic Review* 57, no. 5 (December 1972): 777–95.

FIGURE 1
Business Failures in the United States, 1970–1991

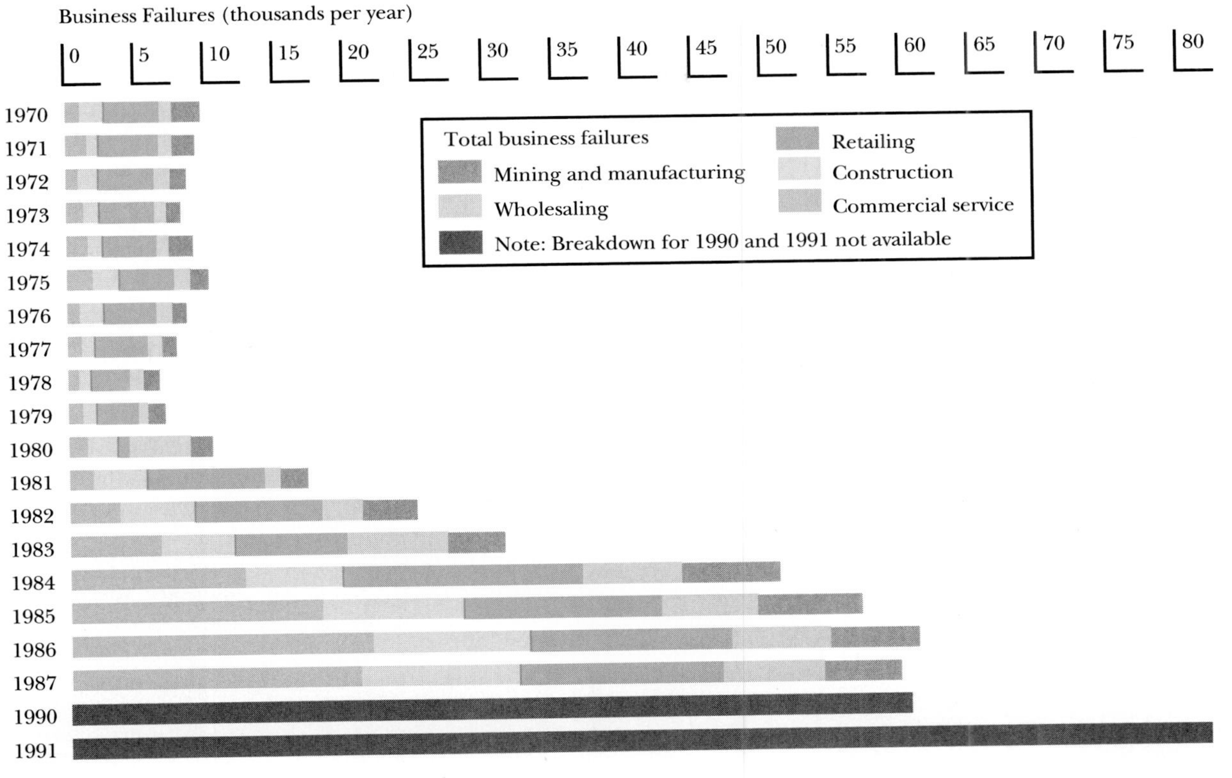

This figure shows the number of industrial and commercial failures resulting in some loss to creditors for the years 1970 to 1991. Retail failures are the largest. The substantial increase in business failures in the early 1980s resulted from the recessions of 1980 and 1982 and the easing of bankruptcy laws. During the 1980s, about 1 percent of all businesses failed each year. In the early 1990s, the increase in failures was a result of recession and a high number of bank failures.

Source: *Survey of Current Business;* Dun and Bradstreet Corp., Monthly Failure Report.

willing to acquire skills that only the principal would need. Hired managers (agents) may value job security more than profits. As long as the goals of agents are different from those of the principal, the principal must monitor the actions of agents.

Limits to Managerial Coordination

What reasons are there *not* to have managerial coordination of all resource allocation decisions? First, there are limits to economies of scale. If enterprises become too large, their costs of production per unit may be higher than those of a smaller firm. Second, as the number and scope of managerial decisions increase, so does the cost of managerial coordination. The manager is called upon to do too many things and to know too much about prices, equipment, and sales. As the business enterprise grows, an optimal size will be reached. Beyond this size the rising costs of managerial coordination will outpace the possible gains.

Realistically, managerial coordination must coexist with market coordination. Some activities are carried out within firms; other activities are the result of market coordination among firms. One automobile manufacturer will produce and market automobiles. Another automobile manufacturer will purchase engines and other parts from foreign and domestic manufacturers, assemble the automobile, and leave the marketing to independent distributors.

PROFIT MAXIMIZATION

What is the goal of a business firm? Most economists believe that the objective of all business firms (other than nonprofit organizations) is **profit maximization.** (See Example 1.)

> **Profit maximization** is the search by firms for the product quality, output, and price that give the firm the highest possible profits.

Opposing Theories

There are some prominent economists who have questioned the assumption that firms seek to maximize profits. William J. Baumol argues that firms seek to maximize their sales. Robin Marris maintains that firms seek to maximize the growth of the firm after they have insured the security of the management in its position. A. A. Berle and Gardner Means argue that the separation of ownership and management has allowed managers to neglect profit maximization and to concentrate on other objectives (such as the size of the firm). John K. Galbraith argues that modern companies are directed by a managerial elite—called the *technostructure*—whose goals are to limit risks and reduce uncertainty and surprises. Oliver Williamson maintains that managers will not pursue their own self-interests until they have kept profits and dividends at a level acceptable to shareholders. Finally, Richard Cyert, James March, and Herbert Simon argue that managers set a goal for satisfactory profits and then pursue other goals, including perhaps what they regard as their social responsibilities.

Natural Selection

The major defense of profit maximization is the **natural selection theory.**

> According to the **natural selection theory,** if business firms do not maximize profits, they will be unable to compete with other firms and will be driven out of the market or taken over by outsiders.

EXAMPLE 1 How to Measure Success: Revenues or Profits

The three major television networks are suffering from declining audience shares and rising costs. If the networks have a hit series, they enjoy the ratings success; however, network executives know that when the series contract is renewed, they will have to pay considerably more for each episode. Although hit series bring in high advertising revenue, their cost is $1 million per show. At the other end of the spectrum are low-cost news shows such as "Prime Time Live" and reality shows such as "Rescue 911." Although these shows do not have high ratings, they cost relatively little to produce. In purely economic terms, the most successful show of 1991 was probably "Rescue 911."

Businesses seek to maximize profits. If the higher advertising revenue generated by a hit series is neutralized by the higher cost of producing that series, no profits will be earned, even though millions of viewers are watching. On the other hand, if a series brings in modest advertising revenue but costs very little to produce, it may appear to be a "better deal" to network executives.

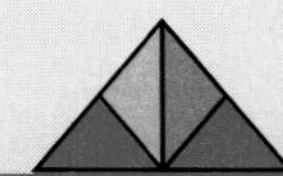

Any firm or management that does not seek to maximize profits may be forced to close its doors when competitors offer higher-quality products at lower cost. The natural selection argument is compelling in the case of firms that face competition. It is less compelling for monopolists who are partially insulated from competition. Business firms that do not earn maximum profits run another risk: They can be taken over by outsiders who believe they can earn higher profits.

FORMS OF BUSINESS ORGANIZATION

Business enterprises are classified into three categories: *sole proprietorships, partnerships,* and *corporations.* The form a business enterprise takes determines who makes business decisions, how capital is raised, who bears the risk of business failures, how principal/agent problems are resolved, and how profits are taxed. (See Table 1.)

Sole Proprietorships

The **sole proprietorship** is the least complex form of business enterprise.

> The **sole proprietorship** is owned by one individual who makes all the business decisions, receives the profits that the business earns, and bears the financial responsibility for losses.

Any individual can decide to go into business. The individual proprietor need not seek permission to enter into business except if business licenses are required, if health permits must be obtained, or if permission must be granted by zoning boards. No legal work is required to set up a sole proprietorship, although the individual proprietor will often seek legal and accounting advice.

The proprietor is responsible for all business decisions: how many employees to hire, how to reward those employees, what products to produce, and how to market those products. The only legal require-

TABLE 1
Types of Business Organization

Type of Firm	Advantages	Disadvantages
Individual Proprietorships	1. The business is simple to set up. 2. Decision making is clear-cut; the owner makes the decisions. 3. Earnings are taxed only once as personal income.	1. The owner has unlimited liability; the owner's personal wealth is at risk. 2. The company has a limited ability to raise financial capital. 3. The business dies with the owner.
Partnership	1. The business is relatively easy to set up. 2. More management skills are available; two heads are better than one. 3. Earnings are taxed only once as the personal income of the partners.	1. There is unlimited liability for the partners. 2. Decision making can be complicated. 3. The company has a limited ability to raise capital. 4. Partnerships can be unstable.
Corporation	1. There is limited liability for owners. 2. The company is able to raise large sums of capital through issuing bonds and stock. 3. The company has an eternal life. 4. The company is able to recruit professional management and to change bad management.	1. Corporate income is taxed twice: first as corporate profits and second as personal income (dividends). 2. There are greater possibilities for management disagreements. 3. There is the possibility of conflicting goals between the owners of the corporation (the *principals*) and management (the *agents*).

ments the owner must meet are observing the law and honoring contracts.

Advantages. The first advantage of the sole proprietorship is that decision-making authority is clear-cut: it resides with the owner. In making business decisions, the owner need not consult anyone.

The second advantage of the sole proprietorship is that it is easy to establish—there are no agreements with other owners.

The third advantage is that the profits of the company accrue to the owner; the earnings are taxed only once as personal income.

Disadvantages. The first disadvantage of the sole proprietorship is that the owner must assume *unlimited liability* (responsibility) for the debts of the company. The owner enjoys the profit of the business if it is successful; the owner is personally liable if the business suffers a loss. If the company borrows money, purchases materials, and incurs other bills that it cannot cover, the owner must personally cover the losses. The owner stands to lose personal wealth in paying off the debts of the company.

The second disadvantage of the sole proprietorship is its *limited ability to raise financial capital,* which explains why most proprietorships are small businesses. Most owners raise financial capital for the expansion of their companies in these ways: by reinvesting profits in the business; by dipping into personal wealth to invest in the company; or by borrowing money from relatives, friends, and lending institutions. The ability of the owner to borrow is determined by the owner's earning capacity (which will depend upon the success of the business) and personal wealth. Lending money to an individual proprietorship can be risky. If the proprietor dies, becomes incapacitated, or declares bankruptcy, the lender will have to stand in line with other creditors.

The third disadvantage is that the business will typically die with the owner. Since the firm does not have a permanent existence, it may be difficult to find reliable employees; many employees prefer to work in firms that will be around long enough to offer career advancement or provide for their retirement.

Partnerships

A **partnership** is much like an individual proprietorship, but it has more than one owner.

> A **partnership** is a business that is owned by two or more people (called partners) who make all the business decisions, who share the profits, and who bear the financial responsibility for any losses.

Like the individual proprietorship, partnerships are easy to establish. Most partnerships are based upon an agreement that spells out the ownership shares and duties of each partner. The partners may contribute different amounts of financial capital to the partnership; there may be an agreement on the division of responsibility for running the business; partners may own different shares of the business. One partner may make all the business decisions, while the other partner (a "silent partner") may simply provide financial capital. A partnership can be a corner gas station owned by three siblings or a nationally known law firm or brokerage house.

Advantages. The advantages of partnerships are much like those of the sole proprietorship. Partnerships are easy to set up. The profits of the company accrue to the partners and are taxed only once as part of their personal income.

Unlike the sole proprietorship, however, there is a greater opportunity to specialize and divide managerial responsibility. The partner who is the better salesperson will be in charge of sales. The partner who is a talented mechanical engineer will be in charge of production. Each partner offers different talents to the business enterprise. A partnership also can raise more financial capital than a sole proprietorship because the wealth and borrowing power of more than one person can be mobilized. If a large number of wealthy partners can be assembled, large sums of capital can be raised.

Disadvantages. First, the ability of the partnership to raise financial capital is limited by the amount of money the partners can raise out of their personal wealth or from borrowing.

Second, the partners have unlimited liability for the debts of the partnership. A business debt incurred by any of the partners is the responsibility of the partnership. Each partner stands to lose personal wealth if the company is a failure. A conflict in goals

EXAMPLE 2 The Crumbling of Finley, Kumble: The Instability of Partnerships

Law firms are usually organized as partnerships in which the firm's profits are distributed to the various partners. Historically, law firms have been organized on a local or regional basis. National law firms are a rare phenomenon. They are difficult to organize as partnerships; they can get too large to manage; and when partners disagree the partnership can be immobilized. Finley, Kumble, Wagner, Underberg, Manley, Myerson & Casey was the nation's fourth largest national law firm before its splintering in 1987. At its peak, Finley, Kumble employed more than 650 lawyers, 250 of whom were partners. Finley, Kumble had offices in Washington, Florida, New York, California, and London.

Internal dissension caused the breakup of Finley, Kumble. The firm expanded by recruiting new partners (in New York) whose $800,000 earnings were over four times those of more than half the firm's existing partners. This disparity so angered the existing partners that they sought to remove the managing partner and executive committee. Disgruntled partners left the firm, taking with them some of the firm's best lawyers. As a consequence of internal dissension, Finley, Kumble was forced into bankruptcy in 1991.

This example illustrates some reasons why partnerships are limited in size. The more partners there are, the more difficult it is to reach a consensus. The more geography the partnership covers, the more difficult it is to coordinate and manage.

Source: "The Splintering of Finley, Kumble," *New York Times*, November 15, 1987.

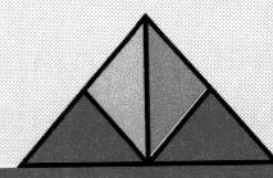

can arise when one partner is more risk-averse than another.

Third, decision making can become quite complicated if partners disagree. (See Example 2.) Partnerships where all partners are responsible for management decisions can be immobilized when partners disagree on fundamental policy. Decision making becomes even more complicated as the number of partners grows.

A fourth disadvantage is that partnerships can be unstable. If disagreements over policy cause one partner to withdraw from the partnership, the partnership must be reorganized. When one partner dies, the partnership agreement may have to be renegotiated.

Partnerships can involve a considerable risk for the individual partners. Although the sole proprietor bears unlimited liability for the debts of the company, at least he or she makes the business decisions—whether good or bad. However, in the case of the partnership, each partner is responsible for business debts incurred by another partner, even if that partner acted without consent of the other partners.[5] For this reason, partnerships are often made up of family members, relatives, and close personal friends who have come to trust one another over the years. Partnerships with more partners do have a greater ability to raise capital. However, because additional partners complicate decision making and increase the likelihood of an irresponsible act being committed by one partner, many partnerships have a limited number of partners.

Corporations

The **corporation** came into existence to overcome some of the disadvantages of the proprietorship and partnership.

[5]There are partnerships in which some partners have limited liability—as in real estate and sports, for example. In these partnerships, however, there must be one or more general partners with unlimited liability.

A **corporation** is a business enterprise that has the status of a legal person and is authorized by law to act as a single person. The stockholders elect a board of directors that appoints the management of the corporation.

Unlike sole proprietorships and partnerships that can be established with minimal paperwork, a *corporate charter* is required to set up a corporation. The laws of each state are different, but typically, for a fee, corporations can be established (incorporated) and can become legal "persons" subject to the laws of that state. According to state and federal laws, the corporation has the status of a legal person. Officers of the corporation can act in the name of the corporation without being personally liable for its debts. If corporate officers commit criminal acts, however, they can be prosecuted.

The corporation is owned by individuals (stockholders) who own shares of *stock* in the corporation. A stockholder's share of ownership of the corporation equals the number of shares owned by that individual divided by the total number of shares *outstanding* (owned by stockholders). If a person owns 100,000 shares of AT&T stock and there are 630 million AT&T shares outstanding, then the person owns 0.016 percent of AT&T. Stockholders have the right to vote for the board of directors and to vote on referenda items at meetings of the corporation. The corporation is required by law to issue periodic reports to its shareholders describing its financial and business activities during the reporting period. The stockholders may vote in person at meetings (the greater the number of shares owned, the greater the weight of the individual's vote), or they can vote *by proxy* (that is, authorize someone else to vote their shares).

In sole proprietorships and partnerships, the owners decide what to do with the profits. In corporations, the management determines whether to reinvest profits or disburse them as dividends. The stockholder who owns 1 percent of the stock of AT&T will receive 1 percent of the dividends the AT&T management chooses to pay to its shareholders out of profits. The shareholder who does not approve of the way management handles these profits can vote to change the current board of directors or can sell the stock.

Common stock, preferred stock, and **convertible stock** are three types of corporate stock.

Common stock confers voting privileges but no prior claim on dividends. Common stock dividends are paid only if they are declared by the board of directors in any given year.

Preferred stock confers a prior claim on dividends but no voting privileges. Dividends on preferred stock must be paid before paying common stock dividends.

Convertible stock is a hybrid between a stock and a bond. The owner of convertible stock receives fixed interest payments but has the privilege of converting the convertible stock into common stock at a fixed rate of exchange.

Corporations typically have thousands or millions of shares outstanding, and these shares are owned by a large number of stockholders. For example, billionaire H. Ross Perot's 11 million shares of General Motors stock made him GM's largest shareholder (with 2 percent of GM stock) before he sold his shares in 1987. In closely held corporations, the number of stockholders is limited, and each stockholder owns a substantial share of the corporation's stock. Unlike the sole proprietor or the partner, stockholders typically do not participate directly in the running of the corporation. Moreover, even if an effort were made to involve shareholders in corporate decision making, there would be too many of them, they would be geographically dispersed, and they would be too involved in their own business affairs to devote sufficient attention to corporate affairs.

For these reasons, there is usually a *separation of ownership and management* in the modern corporation. The board of directors appoints a management team (agents) that makes decisions for the corporation. If the corporation is successful, most likely the management team is allowed to continue. However, if the corporation is unsuccessful, the stockholders may vote out the current board of directors or the board of directors itself may decide to bring in a new management team.

Statistical studies of modern corporations have demonstrated the magnitude of the separation of ownership and management.[6] In most instances, the people who run the corporation own only a small portion of the shares. A 1986 survey of 512 large companies revealed that 9 percent of the chief executives owned no stock in their companies and 6 percent owned less than $100,000 worth.

Stockholders, however, can exercise substantial indirect control over management by simply selling their stock. The sale of stock by enough dissatisfied stockholders will depress the price of each share and invite possible takeovers by other corporate teams.

Advantages. The first advantage of the corporation is that the stockholders are not personally liable for the debts of the corporation. If a corporation incurs debts that it cannot meet, its creditors can lay claim to the assets of the corporation (bank accounts, equipment, supplies, buildings, and real estate holdings), but they cannot file claims against the stockholders. The worst thing that can happen to stockholders is that the value of their stock will decline (in extreme circumstances, it can become worthless).

Limited liability contributes to a second advantage of the corporation: corporations can raise large sums of financial capital by selling corporate bonds, by issuing stock, and by borrowing from lending institutions. (How corporations raise capital will be described in more detail later in the chapter.)

The third advantage of the corporation follows from its status as a legal person distinct from the officers of the corporation. A change in the board of directors, the death or resignation of the current president, or a transfer of ownership could destroy a partnership or sole proprietorship, but these events do not alter the legal status of the corporation. Continuity is an advantage in raising financial capital. Lending institutions are willing to make long-term loans to corporations because they expect the corporation to outlive its current owners and officers. In fact, U.S. corporations have loans that are not due until 2020. New stockholders (another source of financial capital) are willing to invest in the corporation because they know that its existence is not dependent upon the individuals that currently run it. Continuity also makes it easier for the firm to hire a career-minded labor force.

The fourth advantage of the corporation is a result of the separation of ownership and management. The owners of businesses (those individuals with money to invest) do not always make the best managers. In the modern corporation, talented officers who own little (or no) company stock can be brought into the business as managers. For example, Lee Iacocca, who was an "outsider" when he was appointed president of the Chrysler Corporation, helped save the car manufacturer from bankruptcy through his considerable skills in manufacturing and marketing cars (and in securing necessary government loan guarantees).

Disadvantages. The major disadvantage of the corporation is the double taxation of corporate income. The profits (earnings) of the corporation can either be distributed to shareholders as *dividends* or kept as *retained earnings* to be reinvested into the corporation. The profits of the corporation are subject to corporate income taxes. If the corporation chooses to reinvest all profits, corporate profits will be taxed only once, but if it distributes some of its profits to shareholders in the form of dividends, shareholders must pay personal income tax on these dividends. Therefore, corporate profits can be taxed twice—first by the corporate income tax and second by the personal income tax on dividends. Although the double taxation of corporate earnings is indeed a disadvantage, the advantages of corporate organization (most specifically, limited liability) can compensate for double taxation.

A second disadvantage of the corporation is its complexity. A modern corporation can have thousands or even millions of different owners (stockholders). Often ownership is so dispersed that it is difficult to mobilize the owners or get them to agree, even when important issues are at stake. Power struggles among shareholder factions can paralyze decision making. The costs of gathering information about the complex dealings of the corporation are high to individual shareholders, who are often poorly informed about the corporation.

A third disadvantage of the corporation is the possibility of conflicting objectives between the principals (the shareholders) and the agents (the corporation's management team). Shareholders are interested in maximizing the long-run profits of the corporation (thereby getting the best return from

[6]The pioneering study of the separation of ownership and management was A. A. Berle and Gardner Means, *The Modern Corporation and Private Property* (New York: Commerce Clearing House, 1932).

FIGURE 2
Proprietorships, Partnerships, and Corporations, 1991

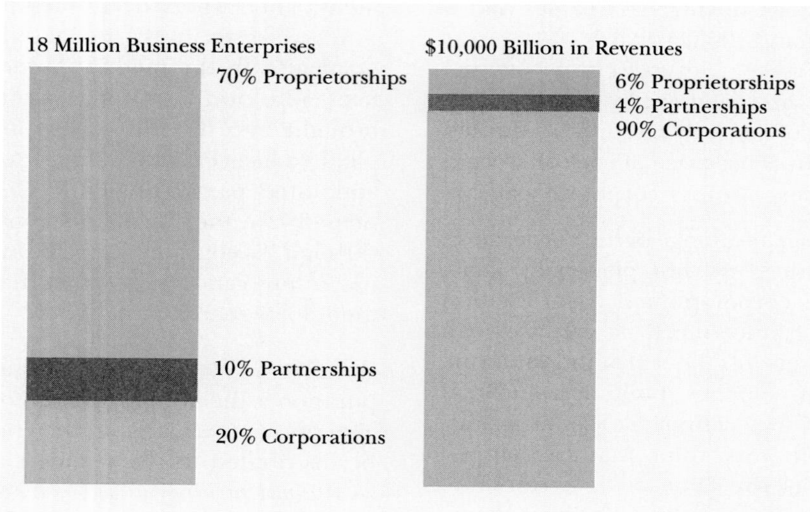

Source: *Statistical Abstract of the United States.* Updated by authors.

TABLE 2
Proprietorships, Partnerships, and Corporations, by Industry, 1991

	Number of Firms (thousands)			Business Revenues (billions of dollars)		
Industry	**Nonfarm Proprietorships**	**Partnerships**	**Corporations**	**Nonfarm Proprietorships**	**Partnerships**	**Corporations**
Total	12,320	1,760	3,520	712	473	10,111
Agriculture, forestry, and fishing	358	155	109	14	9	98
Mining	168	65	45	19	29	315
Construction	1,467	77	339	80	30	446
Manufacturing	304	27	312	17	24	3,873
Transportation, public utilities	551	21	138	37	11	995
Wholesale and retail trade	3,032	238	1,010	322	114	3,239
Wholesale	338	31	344	55	50	1,720
Retail	2,588	205	661	263	64	1,514
Finance, insurance, real estate	1,172	843	556	40	88	1,559
Services	5,211	324	986	177	108	582

Source: *Statistical Abstract of the United States.* Updated by authors.

their shares of stock). The management team may be more interested in preserving their jobs or in maximizing their personal income or perquisites than in profit maximization. The threat of takeovers by a rival management team may force management to act in the interests of its shareholders.

Business Enterprises in the U.S. Economy

In the United States, there are about 20 million business enterprises. (See Figure 2.) The overwhelming majority of these are proprietorships (70 percent); the rest are corporations (20 percent) and partnerships (10 percent). Although proprietorships dominate in number, their share of total business revenues is relatively small, accounting for only 6 percent. Corporations, on the other hand, account for 90 percent of business revenues.

Proprietorships are concentrated in the trade and services industries, where small family businesses are common. (See Table 2.) Corporations dominate the manufacturing and trade industries. Partnerships are active in trade, finance, and services industries.

The large corporation accounts for the most business sales and profits. The *absolute* size of giant U.S. corporations is awesome. The annual sales of large U.S. industrial corporations—such as General Motors, IBM, and Exxon—exceed the annual output of many industrial economies. The annual sales of General Motors, for example, equal the annual production of Belgium. The combined annual sales of the six largest U.S. industrial corporations exceed the annual production of the United Kingdom. The sales rankings of giant U.S. corporations change with the fortunes of the company and the industry.

The Multinational Corporation

As early as the late 1800s, many large U.S. companies expanded internationally. Singer licensed a French company to manufacture its sewing machines; Westinghouse started a shop in Paris; Western Electric set up an affiliate in Belgium; and Eastman incorporated a company in London to manufacture film. These international ventures were early examples of **multinational corporations.**

> A **multinational corporation** engages in foreign economic activities through its own affiliates located abroad, exercises direct control over the policies of these affiliates, and pursues business strategies that transcend national boundaries.[7]

Since World War II, the barriers to international trade and capital movements have been dismantled. International markets for goods, services, and capital have replaced national markets. Business enterprises that previously had to compete only with other domestic companies now must compete with companies from Japan, Germany, Taiwan, and Mexico.

The multinational corporation moves capital, technology, and entrepreneurial skills from areas where they are abundant to areas where they are scarce; it spreads new ideas, new products, and new ways of organizing production throughout the world. German and Swiss chemical companies introduce their products, ideas, and management skills to their affiliates in Taiwan and Brazil. Japanese automobile manufacturers introduce their manufacturing and quality control techniques to their U.S. affiliates. The multinational corporation has become an important instrument of change in the world economy.

The multinational corporation is the product of the internationalization of world business. Large corporations are no longer confined to the borders of their home country. They have foreign affiliates and foreign employees, and nationals from other countries are on their boards of directors.

CORPORATE FINANCE AND FINANCIAL MARKETS

Limited liability and continuity give corporations an edge in raising financial capital. Like proprietorships and partnerships, corporations can borrow money, and they can reinvest profits in the business. In addition to these traditional forms of raising capital, corporations can raise *equity capital* by selling

[7]This definition is adapted from Franklyn Root, *International Trade and Investment*, 5th ed. (Cincinnati: Southwestern, 1990), p. 583.

additional shares of stock, or they can sell **bonds** (also called issuing debt).

Corporate **bonds** are obligations that bind the corporation to pay a fixed sum of money (the principal) at maturity and also to pay a fixed sum of money annually until the maturity date. This fixed annual payment is called *interest,* or the *coupon payment.*

Present Value

Bonds are obligations to make specified payments at specific dates over a specified period of time. Bonds cannot be understood without knowledge of the present value of money.

A dollar today is worth more than a dollar tomorrow because it can earn interest.

For the sake of simplicity, assume that the annual interest rate is 10 percent. If $100 is deposited in a savings account, $10 interest will be earned at the end of 1 year. At 10 percent interest, $100 today will be equal to $110 a year from now. If the interest rate had been 20 percent, $100 today would be equal to $120 a year from now.

What would a person be willing to pay today in order to receive $110 in 1 year? At 10 percent interest, the most anyone would be willing to pay now to receive $110 in 1 year is $100. Why? Investing *more than* $100 at 10 percent interest yields *more than* $110 at the end of 1 year. Thus, the **present value (PV)** of a future payment of $110 is $100 at 10 percent interest.

The **present value (PV)** of money is the most anyone would pay today to receive the money in the future. The present value is sometimes called the *discounted value* because it is smaller than the amount to be received in the future.

The price (market value) of an IOU (such as a bond) that promises to make specified payments at specified future dates will be the present value of those payments. The present-value calculation can be summarized in a formula. The present value (PV) of each dollar to be paid in 1 year at the interest rate i (i stands for the rate of interest in decimals) is:

$$PV = \frac{\$1}{1+i}$$

If the interest rate is 10 percent, then $i = 0.10$ and $1 + i = 1.10$. The PV of each dollar equals $0.9091. If $10,000 is the sum to be paid in 1 year, the PV equals $9,091 ($10,000 times 0.9091).

The present-value formula becomes more complicated when the repayment period is greater than 1 year. At an interest rate of 10 percent, how much money would a person have to deposit today to have $121 at the end of 2 years? If the sum PV were deposited at interest rate i, it would be worth $PV \times (1+i)$ 1 year from now. At the end of the second year, it would be worth $PV \times (1 + i) \times (1 + i)$, or $PV(1 + i)^2$. Setting the sum, $PV(1+i)^2$ equal to $121 and dividing by $(1 + i)^2$ yields:

$$PV = \frac{\$121}{(1+i)^2}$$

At 10 percent interest, the present value of $121 to be received 2 years from now is $100 ($= \$121/1.1^2$).

This result can be generalized to show that the present value of a sum to be received in 3 years is that sum divided by $(1 + i)^3$; the present value of a dollar to be received in n years is:

$$PV = \frac{\$1}{(1+i)^n}$$

At a 10 percent interest rate, $100 received 1 year from now has a present value of $90.91; $100 to be received 5 years from now has a present value of only $62.27. The longer the repayment period, the lower the present value.

The further out in the future the money is to be paid, the lower is its present value.

The present value of money to be received in the future falls as the interest rate rises. In the preceding example, the present value of $121 to be received in 2 years is $100 at an interest rate of 10 percent—that is, $\$121 \div 1.1^2 = \$100$. At an interest rate of 20 percent, the PV of $121 to be received 2 years from now falls to $84; that is, $\$121 \div 1.2^2 = \$84$.

> The present value of a dollar to be received in the future falls as the interest rate rises and rises as the interest rate falls.

What is a bond worth that pays $100 per year in interest *in perpetuity* (forever)? If the interest rate were 10 percent, $1000 would earn $100 per year in interest income. This $1000 is the present value of the $100 perpetual income stream. If the interest rate doubled to 20 percent, $500 would earn $100 a year in perpetuity. Hence, $500 would be the present value at 20 percent interest.

The general formula for calculating the present value (PV) of a bond that yields a perpetual income stream is:

$$PV = \frac{R}{i}$$

where R = the annual income stream. At an interest rate of 10 percent, the present value of $100 a year in perpetuity is $100 ÷ 0.10, or $1000. (This formula is important in explaining stock prices, a topic discussed later in this chapter.)

Selling Bonds

By selling bonds, corporations acquire funds to finance business expansion. Once the bond is sold, the buyer can resell it, but sales of secondhand bonds do not add directly to the corporation's financial capital.

The interest or principal payments on corporate bonds represent a legal obligation for the corporation, just like any other debt. The purchaser of the bond has loaned the corporation money, and in return the corporation has promised to pay specified interest payments until maturity. Interest payments on corporate bonds have a claim on company earnings prior to dividends. The company must make interest payments unless it is declared to be in a state of **bankruptcy.**

> A corporation can be declared in a state of **bankruptcy** if it cannot pay its bills or its interest obligations.

Because corporate bondholders have prior claim on company earnings, bonds offer a relatively secure return. The bondholder will receive the promised annual coupon payment (as well as the principal payment at the date of maturity) as long as the corporation does not become bankrupt. (See Example 3.)

Nevertheless, corporate bonds are not a riskless investment because bond prices fluctuate in the secondhand market. If the bond owner sells the bond before the date of maturity, the price received for the bond may well be less than the price paid for the bond.

Bond prices are the present discounted value (PV) of the coupon payments and the maturity value. However, remember there is an inverse relationship between interest rates and present values. As interest rates rise, investors will pay *less* for the stream of coupon payments offered by a bond. As interest rates fall, investors will pay *more* for the stream of coupon payments offered by the bond.

One advantage corporate bonds have over stock is that bondholders have a prior claim on corporate profits. One disadvantage is that, unlike the shareholder, the bondholder cannot vote for the board of directors or receive larger dividends when profits rise.

Issuing Stock

A second means of raising financial capital is for the corporation to sell additional shares of stock. Suppose ZYX Corporation has 100,000 shares of stock that are already owned by stockholders. Each share of stock currently sells for $10 on the secondhand market (that is, the stock exchange or market) for stocks.

The corporation decides that it needs to raise $500,000 to build a new plant and arranges with an *investment bank* or an *underwriter* to sell 50,000 new shares of stock to investors. The company will prepare a *prospectus* (as required by the Securities and Exchange Commission) that describes to potential buyers the financial condition of the company and the proposed uses for the funds raised.

The amount of money investors will be willing to pay for the 50,000 new shares depends upon their assessment of the impact of the proposed investment on the earnings of ZYX Corporation. If investors expect the new plant to raise company earnings substantially, they will offer a higher price than if they expect the investment to have a small effect.

Experts believe that corporations will issue new stock only if they can avoid a decline in the price of the stock in the secondhand market. Suppose this is the case with ZYX Corporation. When the investment

EXAMPLE 3 Michael Milken: The Inventor of Junk Bonds—Genius or Crook?

Many view Michael Milken as the symbol of greed in the 1980s. Milken, a high-powered Wall Street investment banker, pioneered the "junk bond"—a concept that called for an outside group to take over a corporation that was underutilizing its profit potential by buying shares of that corporation through the sale of bonds to the public. Assume, for example, that Milken wished to take over XYZ Corporation by buying 51 percent of its outstanding shares for $50 million. Instead of paying $50 million cash, Milken would arrange to sell, say, $49 million in high-interest bonds to the public. The interest and principal payments on those bonds would be guaranteed by the future profits of XYZ Corporation. With new management, the rise in profits should be more than adequate to service the debt on the bonds. Because Milken would only have to put up $1 million of his own money (plus $49 million raised through junk bonds), the takeover of XYZ Corporation was called a "leveraged buy-out" (LBO).

Milken's supporters hailed him as the new prophet of Wall Street. He had apparently discovered an "efficient" way of installing new management in poorly managed corporations (through LBOs). However, Michael Milken was convicted of using "insider information" for personal gain and for the benefit of colleagues (such as Ivan Boesky). Typically, when an outside group seeks to gain control of a corporation by buying its stock, the stock price will shoot up (due to the increase in demand). Anyone who knows in advance that the stock price will rise, can buy stock early at a low price and resell it later. The use of insider information for this purpose is against the law.

The corporations that had been taken over through the sale of junk bonds did not fare well in the recession of the early 1990s. As corporate earnings dropped, there were not enough funds to service the high-interest junk bonds, and a number of corporations entered bankruptcy.

bank is able to sell the 50,000 new shares at the $10-per-share price, ZYX Corporation raises $500,000 through the stock issue. Unlike corporate bonds that legally obligate the corporation to pay fixed interest payments, there is no obligation to pay dividends.

Stock Markets

Stock prices are determined by supply and demand in **stock exchanges.**

> A **stock exchange** is a market in which shares of stock of corporations are bought and sold and in which the prices of shares of stock are determined.

There are many organized stock exchanges around the world; however, the most important stock exchanges are located in New York City, London, Denver, Frankfurt, Tokyo, Zurich, and Paris. In each stock exchange the shares of particular corporations are traded. The shares of French companies are traded in Paris, the shares of Japanese companies are traded in Tokyo, and so on. The world's largest stock exchanges are located on New York City's Wall Street: the New York Stock Exchange (NYSE) and the American Stock Exchange (ASE). The NYSE lists about 50 billion shares of stock, and most days millions of shares worth billions of dollars change hands. The shares of the largest American and multinational corporations are traded on the NYSE.

Stock Prices. Like any organized market, the NYSE brings together all buyers and sellers of a particular commodity—for example, the buyers and sellers of shares of IBM. The number of shares of IBM stock outstanding is fixed (unless IBM decides to issue new shares of stock), and the owners of these shares will be prepared to sell their shares at different prices. The supply curve of IBM shares on a given date is shown as curve *S* in Figure 3. The higher the price, the greater the number of IBM shares current owners will be prepared to sell; thus, the supply curve is positively sloped. On the demand side of the market are potential buyers of IBM stock. The demand curve for IBM shares, curve *D* in Figure 3, is negatively sloped. The lower the share price, the greater the number of IBM shares people will be prepared to buy. The equilibrium price of IBM shares is that price at which the number of shares demanded equals the number of shares supplied. The equilibrium number of shares traded (1 million) is referred to as the *volume* of IBM transactions.

Stock prices, like other market prices, are determined by supply and demand. When the supply or demand curves shift, stock prices change. For example, a rise in the price of IBM shares might be caused either by an increase in demand, a reduction in supply, or a combination of the two.

Figure 3 shows how stock prices are determined, but it does not explain what lies behind the supply and demand curves: the different assessments of the future profits of the corporation. The owner of a share of stock benefits from the profits that the corporation earns now and in the future. The share owner receives dividends that the corporation pays out of profits (if any) and benefits from reinvested profits, which may mean increased future profits. Share prices, therefore, depend upon the present and future earnings of the corporation. Present earnings are known, but future earnings are uncertain. They depend upon the general state of the economy, the quality of corporate management, and shifts in consumer demand. People have different views of what the future holds for a particular corporation. Some will see a bright future of rising profits and dividends. Others will see a bleak future of declining economic fortunes.

The price of a share of stock will depend upon the anticipated future profits per share of outstanding stock, called *earnings per share.* Suppose Jones, an optimist, expects earnings per share of ZYX Corporation to be $10 from now until eternity (in perpetuity). Smith, a pessimist, expects earnings per share of ZYX Corporation to be $5 from now until eternity. The anticipated future profits of ZYX Corporation need to be converted by both Jones and Smith into a present value. Applying the perpetuity formula (at a 10 percent interest rate), the present value of the anticipated profit stream of one share of stock is $100 ($10/0.10) for Jones and $50 ($5/0.10) for Smith. Jones would be a willing seller of ZYX stock at a price greater than $100 and a willing buyer at a price less than $100. Smith would be a willing seller at a price above $50 and a willing buyer at a price below $50. At a $75 price, Smith would sell and Jones would buy.

The demand and supply curves of stock show that potential buyers and sellers assess differently

FIGURE 3
Determination of IBM Stock Prices

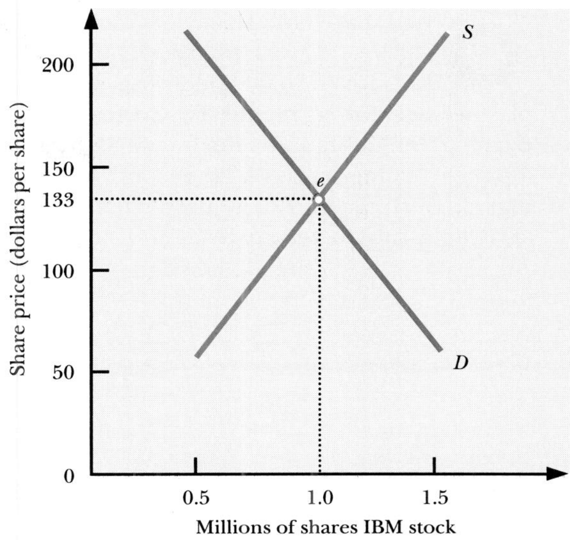

This figure diagrams the supply (*S*) and demand (*D*) curves for shares of IBM stock. The supply curve is positively sloped because owners of IBM stock will offer more shares for sale at high prices than at low prices. The demand curve is negatively sloped because buyers of IBM shares will be prepared to buy more at low prices than at high prices. The equilibrium price is that price at which the quantity demanded equals the quantity supplied. Share prices fluctuate daily because of shifts in supply and demand. The equilibrium price reflects the consensus present value of the future earnings per share of IBM.

EXAMPLE 4 One Share of Stock for $126,139?

One share of stock of Hoffman-La Roche, a Swiss pharmaceutical firm, sells for $126,000. How can one share of stock sell for so much? First, the earnings per share of Hoffman-La Roche are $4809—for a price/earnings ratio of 26. Second, the earnings of Hoffman-La Roche have been growing at a rapid rate in recent years and because of Hoffman-La Roche's record of successful innovation and product development, earnings are expected to continue to grow more rapidly than the earnings of other companies. Third, Hoffman-La Roche pays an annual dividend of $3600, for a percentage return of almost 3 percent—a return that is not low by Swiss interest-rate standards.

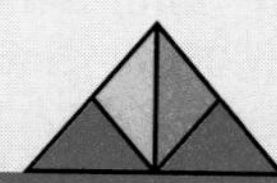

the future earnings of corporations. The share price settles at that price at which the quantity of shares demanded equals the quantity supplied. This equilibrium price is the consensus of participants in the market concerning the present value of the future earnings of the corporation. (See Example 4.)

> The price of a share of stock is the perceived present value of the future earnings per share of the stock.

The **price/earnings (PE) ratio** signals whether investors believe the profits of the company, or **earnings per share,** will rise or fall from current profit levels.

> The **price/earnings (PE) ratio** is the price of a share of stock divided by the earnings per share.
>
> **Earnings per share (EPS)** is the annual profit of the corporation divided by the number of shares outstanding.

If the average company has a PE ratio of 6, companies with a PE ratio greater than 6 are expected to have profits rising at above-average rates. Companies with a PE ratio less than 6 are expected to have profits rising at below-average rates.

> A high PE ratio indicates that investors believe that current profits understate the future profits of the corporation. A low PE ratio indicates that investors believe that current profits overstate the future profits of the corporation.

Stock Indexes. Stock market analysts compile **stock price indexes.**

> A **stock price index** (such as the Dow Jones Industrial Average, the Standard & Poor's Index, and the New York Stock Exchange Index) measures the general movements of stock prices.

The Dow Jones Industrial Average measures the movement of 30 industrial stocks (such as Exxon, AT&T, and Du Pont). The New York Stock Exchange Index measures the average price of all stocks traded on the New York Stock Exchange. Different stock price indexes usually agree on whether stock prices are rising or falling; however, they may disagree on the magnitude of the rise or fall. (See Example 5.)

What causes stock prices to fluctuate? If buyers and sellers of stocks expect corporate profits to rise more rapidly, average stock prices should rise. The present values of future corporate earnings would rise, and buyers would be willing to pay more for stocks. Rising optimism about future corporate

EXAMPLE 5 Stock Market Indexes and the World Capital Market

The world financial press provides up-to-date information on stock prices, interest rates, and currency exchange rates throughout the world. When we wake up in the morning, stock markets in Tokyo, Singapore, London, Frankfurt, and Zurich are open for trading of stocks, bonds, and currencies. When we go to bed at night, trading of financial securities is taking place elsewhere in the world.

The Dow Jones and New York Stock Exchange indexes are the most frequently used gauges of stock prices in the United States. Other major stock market indexes around the world include:

Nikkei Average (Tokyo)
Topix Index (Tokyo)
FT 30-share (London)
London 100-share (London)
Gold Mines (London)
DAX (Frankfurt)
Credit Suisse (Zurich)
CAC 40 (Paris)
Milan Stock Index (Milan)
ANP-CBS General (Amsterdam)
Affarsvarlden (Stockholm)
Bel-20 Index (Brussels)
All Ordinaries (Australia)
Hang Seng (Hong Kong)
Straits Times (Singapore)
Johannesburg Gold (Johannesburg)
General Index (Madrid)
Toronto 300 Composite (Toronto)
MSCI (Europe, Australia, and the Far East)

We live in a world of interrelated financial exchanges. Through modern telecommunications, buyers of securities can select among stocks and bonds offered on the world's major exchanges. A share of AT&T stock can be bought in New York, London, or Tokyo. A Siemens Corporation bond can be bought in London, Singapore, or Toronto. There is a world capital market that is not limited by national boundaries.

profits should cause the various stock price indexes to register increases. When interest rates rise, the present values of future corporate earnings fall (because of the inverse relationship between present value and interest rates). The falling present values of corporate earnings should generally depress stock prices. The tremendous rise in stock prices in the 1980s was accompanied by falling interest rates and by rising corporate profits.

Anticipated corporate profits and interest rates are not the only factors that explain movements in stock prices. Rumors of war, deaths of political leaders, drought, pronouncements of Wall Street gurus, and even trivial events can cause fluctuations in stock prices.

Stock Prices and Resource Allocation. The buying and selling of stock does not have a *direct* effect on the corporation's financial capital. However, the price of stocks does affect the allocation of capital resources. For example, if ZYX Corporation develops a promising anticancer drug and obtains Food and Drug Administration approval to market it, investors will realize that ZYX Corporation earnings will rise substantially; therefore, the price of ZYX stock will rise rapidly. Assume that prior to the development of this new drug the price of ZYX stock was $10. The company could raise $500,000 by selling 50,000 new shares of stock. However, if the prospect of the new drug raises the stock price to $50 (because the new plant would be built to manufacture the drug), the issue of 50,000 new shares would raise $2.5 million instead of $500,000.

As stock prices rise, corporations find it easier to raise financial capital. Likewise, corporations with falling stock prices find it difficult to raise money for expansion. In this sense, the secondhand markets for corporate stocks serve as barometers that signal the direction of the allocation of financial capital. Stockholders can express their dissatisfaction by selling their shares, which drives down the price of the stock. If dissatisfaction is widespread, the falling stock price prevents the firm from raising capital by selling new shares.

Taxation and Corporate Behavior

One important lesson gained from studying business enterprises is that taxes influence business behavior. The double taxation of corporate income influences whether a business will be set up as a partnership or as a corporation. If the advantages of the corporate form (limited liability, greater ability to raise capital) are not important, the business will likely be set up as a proprietorship or a partnership to avoid double taxation.

Double taxation forces corporations to invest in projects that offer higher rates of return than partnerships or proprietorships, and it also affects corporate dividend policies. Individuals invest in corporations because stocks offer two types of returns: a dividend and a **capital gain.**

> A **capital gain** is the increase in the market value of any asset (stocks, bonds, houses, automobiles, art) above the price originally paid. The capital gain is *realized* when the asset is sold.

Prior to 1987, realized capital gains were taxed at a lower rate than other forms of income (wages and salaries, dividends, interest) if the asset was held for more than 6 months. Preferential tax treatment of capital gains discourages dividends. If corporate earnings are not distributed as dividends but are reinvested in the company, the earnings of the company will grow (if the money is invested wisely), and eventually the market price of the stock will rise. Shareholders could then sell the stock for a capital gain, on which they pay a relatively small income tax. If the company instead paid out corporate profits as dividends, there would be less reinvestment, the value of the stock would rise more slowly, and the recipients of the dividend payments would have to pay a heavy tax on the dividends.

This chapter considered business organization as the first step in the study of the supply side of product markets. The next chapter will examine the role of production costs in determining product supply.

SUMMARY

1. Business firms allocate the land, labor, and capital resources they own or rent through the use of managerial coordination. Business firms work both through market allocation in their dealings with other firms and consumers and through managerial allocation. An agency relationship exists when one party—the *agent*—acts on behalf of another party—the *principal.* Principal/agent relationships are useful in describing the behavior of business firms. Firms exist to take advantage of economies of scale, to bear risk, to limit transaction costs, and to provide for team production.

2. Most economists assume that the goal of business firms is the maximization of profits.

3. The three forms of business organization are the *sole proprietorship* (a business owned by one individual), the *partnership* (a business owned by two or more partners who share in making business decisions), and the *corporation* (a business enterprise owned by stockholders). Although there are more sole proprietorships in the United States than there are partnerships or corporations, corporations (due to their larger average size) account for the bulk of business sales and profits.

4. A multinational corporation uses foreign affiliates to engage in foreign economic activities. It exercises direct control over foreign affiliates to pursue business strategies for the world market.

5. Corporations can raise capital by selling bonds or issuing more stock. Corporate bonds are IOUs that obligate the corporation to make fixed interest payments and to repay the principal at the date

of maturity. The amount of money a corporation can raise will depend upon its stock market price. These prices affect the allocation of capital to various industries and firms.

6. Taxation policies affect business behavior. Double taxation must be considered when establishing a business and formulating a corporate dividend policy.

KEY TERMS

managerial coordination
principal
agent
economies of scale
profit maximization
natural selection theory
sole proprietorship
partnership
corporation
common stock
preferred stock
convertible stock
multinational corporation
bonds
present value (PV)
bankruptcy
stock exchange
price/earnings (PE) ratio
earnings per share (EPS)
stock price index
capital gain

QUESTIONS AND PROBLEMS

1. You are deciding whether to build a home yourself or whether to hire an established building firm. What are the transaction costs of arranging to have the home built without the use of the building company? Under what circumstances would these costs be low enough for you to decide to build the home yourself?
2. Risk bearing is one function served by business firms. What risk does the owner of a new restaurant bear?
3. Generally, sole proprietorships are smaller than partnerships and partnerships are smaller than corporations. From what you know about the legal features of business organizations, explain why.
4. In limited partnerships, the liability of each partner for the debts of the company is limited. Explain why such partnerships may be more attractive than the traditional form of partnership.
5. Explain why corporations can issue bonds that mature in the next century while partnerships and proprietorships can borrow for only short periods of time.
6. Explain why a corporation would be reluctant to issue new shares of stock to raise capital when the price of the stock is at an all-time low.
7. One stock has a price/earnings ratio of 2; a second stock has a price/earnings ratio of 20. The average PE ratio is 10. What would be the investment community's best guess as to the course of future profits for each company?
8. You own 100 shares of ZYX Corporation, and the management of ZYX Corporation allows you to vote on whether stockholders will receive dividends or whether the management will reinvest earnings in the company. How would your tax bracket affect the way you vote?
9. ZYX Corporation offers to sell bonds maturing in 20 years at an interest rate of 15 percent. If you buy a $10,000 bond from ZYX, what would be the annual coupon payment? Would you be more likely to buy the bond if you expected interest rates to fall?
10. The 100 shares of ZYX Corporation that you purchased 2 years ago for $10 per share are now selling for $20 per share. If you sell the stock, what is the profit called? How will this profit be taxed?
11. For the following transactions, explain which party is the principal and which is the agent and why.
    a. Smith hires a remodeling company to add a room to her house.
    b. A university buys a computer from IBM.
    c. An engineer signs a contract with Aramco to work for a year in Saudi Arabia.
12. The price of one share of an airline stock is $4. The airline has not made a profit for 4 years. If share prices reflect corporate profitability, why is the price not $0?
13. Professional football teams take detailed films of each football game so that they can observe the performance of each player on each play. Using the Alchian/Demsetz theory, explain why they are monitoring player performance.
14. Assume an aerospace corporation does not manufacture its own jet engines. Instead, it buys them on subcontracts from other manufacturers. Using Coase's arguments about why firms exist, explain why Boeing would make this decision.

SUGGESTED READINGS

Alchian, Armen, and Harold Demsetz. "Production, Information Costs, and Economic Organization." *American Economic Review* 57, no. 5 (December 1972): 777–95.

Coase, Ronald H. "The Nature of the Firm." *Economica* 4 (1937): 386–405.

Demsetz, Harold, Mark Hirschey, and Michael Jensen. "The Market for Corporate Control." *American Economic Review: Papers and Proceedings,* May 1986.

Geneen, Harold. "Why Directors Can't Protect the Shareholders." *Fortune* (September 17, 1984).

Knight, Frank H. *Risk, Uncertainty, and Profit.* Chicago: University of Chicago Press, 1985.

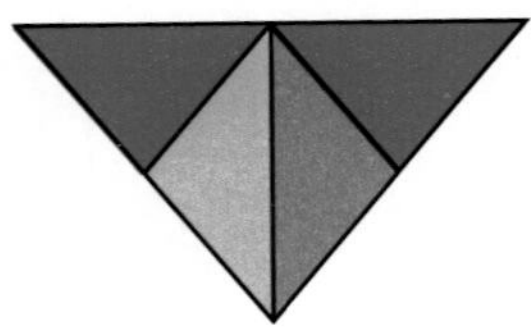

29

Productivity and Costs

CHAPTER INSIGHT

Once a business firm has chosen its basic organizational form (proprietorship, partnership, or corporation) it must get down to the main task—making a profit. Business activities may be complicated (like the production of a commercial jet airliner) or simple (like a teenager mowing lawns for summer earnings). To make a *profit* the business firm must earn revenues in excess of costs. The firm must understand revenues and costs to make sound business decisions.

This chapter examines costs: What are costs? What costs are important to business decisions? How is productivity related to costs? The next several chapters examine revenues.

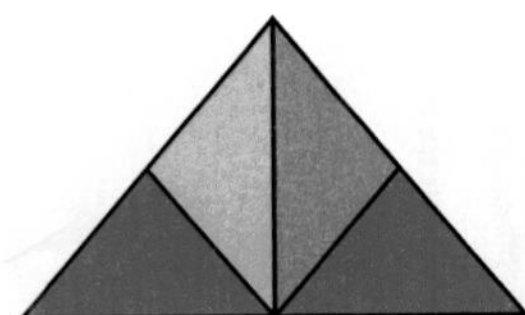

PRODUCTION

Production costs depend upon input prices and productivity. Production costs rise as input prices rise, and they fall as productivity improves. What happens to the costs of production as firms expand the level of output?

The Short Run versus the Long Run

A business firm expands the volume of its output by hiring or using additional resources. Every good or service is produced by a combination of resources (land, labor, capital, raw materials, entrepreneurial or managerial talent). The package of resources used depends upon three factors: (1) the productivity of the resources, (2) the prices of the resources, and (3) the time available to the firm for altering output. The first two are important because the business firm will try to keep costs as low as possible. The last is important because time is required to change the level of resource use. Some resources can be adjusted immediately. Other resources require considerable time to change.

A firm can obtain more labor resources quickly by asking each employee to work overtime. The firm may also be able to acquire additional raw materials immediately. But the installation of a new piece of capital equipment or the construction of a new plant may require a significant amount of time. Economists distinguish between the **short run** and the **long run** when considering the time necessary to change input levels.

> The **short run** is a period of time so short that the existing plant and equipment cannot be varied; such inputs are fixed in supply. Additional output can be produced only by expanding the variable inputs of labor and raw materials. The **long run** is a period of time long enough to vary all inputs.

The long run is not a specified amount of calendar time; it may be as short as a few months for a fast-food restaurant, a couple of years for a new automobile plant, or a decade or more for an electrical power plant. Engineering complexity determines whether the long run is a matter of weeks or years in actual calendar time.

The Law of Diminishing Returns

To understand the meaning of productivity, it is necessary to understand the concept of a **production function.**

> A **production function** summarizes the relationship between labor, capital, and land inputs and the maximum output these inputs can produce.

A production function is a technological recipe. It tells how much output can be produced from a given combination of inputs and tells by how much output will increase if one (or all) input(s) increase(s).

The prices of the land, labor, and capital used in the enterprise are determined by conditions outside the firm (in the markets for those resources). Except in unusual circumstances, input prices would not be affected by the decision of a firm to expand its output. The firm's production function is determined by the ability of the management team to absorb the engineering and technical knowledge relevant to the firm's business. The firm's production function dictates the relationship between increases in inputs and increases in outputs in the short run—a relationship that follows a distinctive pattern, called the **law of diminishing returns.**

> The **law of diminishing returns** states that as ever larger amounts of a variable input are combined with fixed inputs, eventually the extra product attributable to each additional amount of the variable input must decline.

The extra product that is attributed to an additional unit of an input, holding other inputs fixed, is called the **marginal physical product (MPP)** of the input.

> The **marginal physical product (MPP)** of a factor of production is the change in output divided by the change in the quantity of the input, holding all other inputs constant.

The law of diminishing returns asserts that as more of a variable input is used, diminishing or declining MPP must eventually be encountered by any firm. Alternatively, the law means that additional units of output become harder to produce when the point of diminishing returns is reached.

A shrimp boat along the Texas Gulf Coast illustrates the law of diminishing returns. The fixed inputs would be the boat, along with its engine and nets (and other fishing equipment), as well as the ocean. The variable inputs would be the number of workers (shrimpers) used. Table 1 shows the daily output (in bushels) as a function of the number of shrimpers. Figure 1, panel *a* shows the total output curve; Figure 1, panel *b* shows the marginal product curve.

If the boat is operated by only one shrimper, his or her time must be divided between piloting the boat, setting the nets, pulling in the nets full of shrimp, and unloading the nets. A lone shrimper catches 2 bushels per day. A second shrimper brings the total output to 12 bushels per day. The additional shrimper allows each person to specialize and save time switching from job to job. A third shrimper proves even more valuable, raising daily output to 32 bushels. The fourth shrimper raises output to 62 bushels, the fifth to 82, the sixth to 92, and so on.

TABLE 1
The Law of Diminishing Returns, Shrimp Fishing

Number of Shrimpers	Daily Output (in bushels)	Marginal Physical Product
0	0	
		2
1	2	**6**
		10
2	12	**15**
		20
3	32	**25**
		30
4	62	**25**
		20
5	82	**15**
		10
6	92	**7.5**
		5
7	97	**4**
		3
8	100	**2.5**
		2
9	102	**1.5**
		1
10	103	

FIGURE 1
The Law of Diminishing Returns

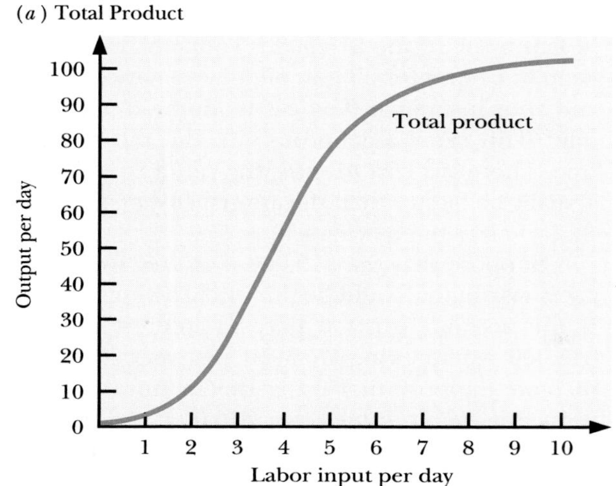

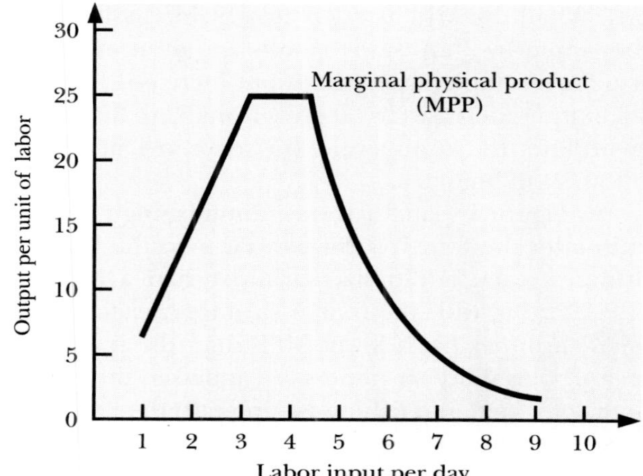

Panel *a* shows the total daily output; panel *b* shows the marginal physical product. Both graphs are based on the data in Table 1. When the total daily output is increasing rapidly, the marginal physical product curve (MPP) is increasing. When the total daily output is increasing, but at a slower and slower rate, the MPP curve is declining.

EXAMPLE 1 Diminishing Returns in Restaurants

The law of diminishing returns is observed on a regular basis in many restaurants. During slack periods, one or two waiters or waitresses can handle all the business more efficiently if part of the dining area is closed off. The fixed inputs are the one or two waitresses; the variable input is the dining room space. During slack times the marginal physical productivity of dining room space is not only declining but is negative—therefore, it pays the restaurant to reduce the amount of space available!

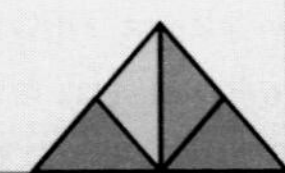

The MPP is the change in output per unit change in the input. Raising the input of shrimpers from 0 to 1 raises output by 2 bushels. Adding the sixth shrimper raises output from 82 to 92 bushels for an MPP of 10 bushels. Adding the tenth shrimper raises output from 102 to 103 bushels for an MPP of 1 bushel.

MPP can also be calculated for increases of more than one unit. Raising the input of shrimpers from 0 to 2 increases output from 0 to 12 bushels. MPP is the change in output (up 12 bushels) divided by the change in inputs (up 2 units)—or 6 bushels. The MPP of moving from 8 to 10 shrimpers is 1.5 units (3 bushels/2 shrimpers).

In Table 1 the MPP of increasing the number of shrimpers by one unit is given *in between* the relevant rows. When the MPP is calculated by increasing the labor input by 2 units, the results are given in boldface. For example, when the input increases from 4 to 6, output increases by 30 units from 62 to 92; thus, the MPP for the input level 5 (in between 4 and 6) is 15 (30/2) in boldface.

As Figure 1, panel *b* shows, diminishing returns set in after the fourth shrimper. Prior to the fourth shrimper, each additional shrimper had a higher MPP. Starting with the fourth shrimper, each additional shrimper has a lower MPP than the previous shrimper. As more shrimpers are added to the fixed inputs of a boat and fishing equipment, the benefits from specialization by each shrimper are soon exhausted. By the time the fifth shrimper is added, the variable inputs may start to get in each other's way. The tenth shrimper adds only 1 bushel of shrimp to the daily output.

The law of diminishing returns applies to the production of any good or service. When some inputs are fixed, adding more variable inputs means that each variable input has less of the fixed input with which to work. When the fixed input becomes "crowded" with variable inputs, the law of diminishing returns sets in. (See Example 1).

OPPORTUNITY COSTS

Suppose your rich aunt gives you a brand new Miata sports car, which has a market value of $15,000. She tells you, "This car is yours. You may keep it or sell it. If you sell it, the $15,000 is yours. As long as you keep it, I'll pay for all gas, oil, maintenance, repairs, and your insurance. The car is yours—free in every way." This car is a generous gift. But the car is not free. There is a cost to *using* the car, a cost that may actually be higher than the annual cost of a small car that you had to buy yourself.

Suppose that the $15,000 that the "free" sports car is worth now could be put into a savings account. If the account earns 6 percent interest per year, $15,000 would bring in $900 per year in interest income. Suppose that using the car for 1 year will reduce its resale value from $15,000 to $11,000—a cost to you of $4000. The total yearly *cost* of using the car is $4900. The lesson is that *costs are not necessarily what has been paid but what must be given up by taking one action rather than another.* **Opportunity cost** is the measure of what has been given up.

The **opportunity cost** of an action is the value of the next best forgone alternative.

The concept of opportunity costs was embodied in the production possibilities frontier studied in Chapter 2. When more of one good (such as tanks) is produced, a certain amount of some other good (such as wheat) must be given up.

Consider a business firm engaged in the production of some good. To produce the good requires resources. To acquire these resources, prices or payments must be paid to the owners of the resources because the resources have alternative uses. The minimum payments that are necessary to attract resources into the production of the good are the opportunity costs of production. Some of these payments are *explicit* (as money changes hands) and some may be *implicit.* The manager of the firm must also consider the implicit costs (the value of those resources if used elsewhere) of the resources owned by the firm.

SHORT-RUN COSTS

Fixed and Variable Costs

In the short run, some factors (such as plant and equipment) are fixed in supply to the firm; even if the firm wanted to increase or reduce them, it would not be possible in the short run. The firm pays these **fixed costs (FC)** even if it produces no output. In the short run, greater output is obtained by using more of the *variable inputs* (such as labor and raw materials); the costs of these variable factors are **variable costs (VC)**. The sum of variable and fixed costs is **total costs (TC)**.

Fixed costs (FC) are those costs that do not vary with output.

Variable costs (VC) are those costs that do vary with output.

Total costs (TC) are variable costs plus fixed costs:

$$TC = VC + FC$$

The short run may be defined as a period of time so short that some costs must be fixed. As the time horizon expands, more and more inputs can be varied. Thus, in the long run, all costs are variable–that is, fixed costs are zero.

Fixed costs and variable costs play different short-run roles in the behavior of the firm. The next chapter shows that rational firms should ignore fixed costs in the short run when making decisions because fixed costs are not affected by any actions the firm can take in the short run. Only variable costs affect short-run decisions: If the firm's revenues exceed variable costs in the short run, the firm has something left with which to pay part or all of its fixed costs.

In the long run, all costs are variable—that is, fixed costs are zero. In the short run, some costs are fixed. Total costs are variable plus fixed costs.

Marginal and Average Costs

The behavior of costs in the short run depends on the law of diminishing returns. Indeed, productivity and costs are inversely related. The higher productivity, the lower costs; the lower productivity, the higher costs.

Marginal Costs. As output increases, both total cost and variable cost increase by the same amount. Suppose, for example, that when the output of shrimp increases by 2 bushels, total (and variable) costs rise by \$10. The change in costs divided by the change in output is called the **marginal cost (MC)** of production. In this example, MC is \$5 (\$10 ÷ 2). In other words, MC is the increase in cost per unit of increase in output. If the increase in output is only one unit, the MC is simply the increase in costs associated with increasing output by one unit. MC can be determined for any increase in output.

Marginal cost (MC) is the change in total cost (or equivalently in variable cost) divided by the increase in output or, alternatively, the increase in costs per unit of increase in output.

$$MC = \frac{\Delta TC}{\Delta Q} = \frac{\Delta VC}{\Delta Q}$$

Average Costs. While marginal costs reflect the change in costs per unit of change in output, average costs spread total, variable, or fixed costs over the entire quantity of output.

To determine whether the firm should operate in the short run or temporarily close down, the firm must consult its **average variable cost (AVC)**. The AVC is obtained by dividing variable costs by output. Fixed cost per unit produced is called **average fixed cost (AFC)** and is calculated by dividing fixed costs by output. To determine whether the firm is making economic profit on each unit produced, the firm must calculate its **average total cost (ATC)** by dividing total cost by output. Alternatively, ATC is the sum of AFC and AVC.

Average variable cost (AVC) is variable cost divided by output:

$$AVC = VC \div Q$$

Average fixed cost (AFC) is fixed cost divided by output:

$$AFC = FC \div Q$$

Average total cost (ATC) is total cost divided by output, or the sum of average variable cost and average fixed cost:

$$ATC = TC \div Q = AVC + AFC$$

The Average/Marginal Relationship

The relationship between *average* values or quantities and *marginal* values or quantities is an important one. (This chapter examines the relationship between average costs and marginal costs; later chapters will discuss the relationship between average revenues and marginal revenues.) There is a common arithmetical background to all average/marginal relationships. It will be useful to examine this arithmetical relationship before discussing costs.

FIGURE 2
Average and Marginal Relationships

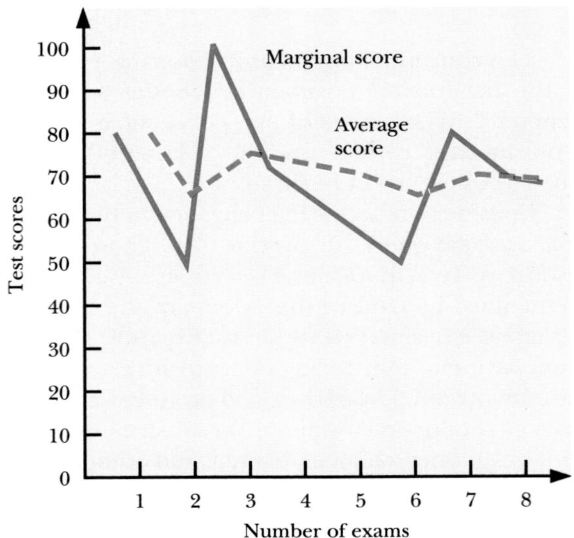

This figure graphs the data on hypothetical test scores given in Table 2. Whenever the marginal score is less than the previous average score, the average score declines. Whenever the marginal score is greater than the previous average score, the average score rises. If the marginal score equals the previous average score, the average score will not change.

Suppose you are taking a course in chemistry and there are eight equally weighted examinations. Your performance for the course is determined by your average score on all exams. Table 2 shows how the average score is computed, and Figure 2 graphs both marginal and average scores. On test number 1, you score 80 points; your average is 80. On test number 2, you score only 50; your *total* score is now 130 (80 + 50), and your average falls to 65 (130/2). Your average is the total accumulated points scored divided by the number of exams taken.

The marginal score is simply your score on the last examination taken. On the first exam your average and marginal scores are the same: 80. The second exam score is 50, which is below the previous average of 80. What will happen to the new average? *Whenever the marginal value is below the previous average value, the new average will fall.* In this case, the average falls from 80 to 65 because it is *pulled down* by the low marginal (last) test score. The third exam score is 100, well

TABLE 2
Average and Marginal Relationships: Test Scores

Test	Test Score = Marginal Score	Average Test Score	Explanation
0		0	
	80		
1		80	Average and marginal values are the same.
	50		
2		65	When the marginal score is below the previous average, the new average falls.
	100		
3		76.67	When the marginal score is above the previous average, the new average rises.
	70		
4		75	When the marginal score is below the previous average, the new average falls.
	60		
5		72	When the marginal score is below the previous average, the new average falls.
	50		
6		68.22	When the marginal score is below the previous average, the new average falls.
	80		
7		70	When the marginal score is above the previous average, the new average rises.
	70		
8		70	When the marginal score equals the previous average, the new average is unchanged.

above the 65 average to that point. What will happen to the new average? *When the marginal score is above the previous average test score, the new average will rise.* The average will be *pulled up* by the high marginal score.

Whenever the marginal value exceeds the previous average value, the new average value will rise. Whenever the marginal value is below the previous average value, the new average value will fall.

A second rule is illustrated by the final marginal test score. The average test score of the first seven exams is 70. The eighth exam score is 70. Because the marginal score, thus, *equals* the previous average score, the new average will remain the same because the marginal value will pull the average neither up nor down.

If the marginal value equals the previous average value, the new average will be unchanged.

Another example: Suppose the average height of the students in a classroom is 5′8″. If a new student arrives, what happens to the average? If the new (marginal) student has a height that exceeds 5′8″, the average height of the class will increase; if the student has a height that is less than 5′8″, the average height of the class will fall; and if the student is exactly 5′8″, the average height of the class will remain the same as before.

The Cost Curves

The average/marginal relationship can help us to understand costs. Table 3 and Figure 3 show cost and output information for a hypothetical firm that produces a single product. The costs shown include all opportunity costs (explicit and implicit). The firm is operating in the short run because it has fixed costs of $48 per day. The fixed costs consist primarily of the interest on the firm's capital, lease payments, and depreciation. As more output is produced, variable costs must rise because more inputs, such as labor and raw materials, must be acquired. Figure 3, panel

TABLE 3
The Short-Run Costs of a Hypothetical Enterprise

Quantity of Output (units), *Q* (1)	Variable Cost (dollars), VC (2)	Fixed Cost (dollars), FC (3)	Total Cost (dollars), TC (4) = (2) + (3)	Marginal Cost (dollars), MC (5)	Average Variable Cost (dollars), AVC (6) = (2) ÷ (1)	Average Fixed Cost (dollars), AFC (7) = (3) ÷ (1)	Average Total Cost (dollars), ATC (8) = (4) ÷ (1) = (6) + (7)
0	0	48	48			∞	∞
				20			
1	20	48	68	**15**	20	48	68
				10			
2	30	48	78	**8**	15	24	39
				6			
3	36	48	84	**5**	12	16	28
				4			
4	40	48	88	**6**	10	12	22
				8			
5	48	48	96	**10**	9.6	9.6	19.2
				12			
6	60	48	108	**16**	10	8	18
				20			
7	80	48	128	**26**	11.4	6.9	18.3
				32			
8	112	48	160	**38**	14	6	20
				44			
9	156	48	204				

This table shows the family of cost schedules for a hypothetical business enterprise operating in the short run with total fixed cost of $48. The table shows the basic data. *Variable cost* (column 2) rises with the level of output. *Total cost* (column 4) is the sum of total fixed cost and total variable cost. *Marginal cost* is shown in column 5, and *average variable, average fixed, average total cost* are shown in the remaining columns.

a graphs total costs, variable costs, and fixed costs; Figure 3, panel *b* graphs average variable costs, average total costs, and marginal costs.

In Table 3, variable and total costs are shown in columns 2 and 4. The marginal cost figures in column 5 are shown *in between* the various output levels, because they are in this case the extra cost of going from one output level to another. The boldface figures are the marginal costs of increasing output by 2 units and are shown in between the respective output levels. For example, the MC of going from 0 units to 2 units of output is $15. This $15 MC figure between the output levels of 0 units and 2 units is displayed at the output level of 1. Similarly, the MC of going from output level 5 to output level 7 is $16, because the increase in variable cost is $32 (from $48 to $80) and the increase in output is, again, 2. Thus, the MC figure for $Q = 6$ is $16 ($32/2).

In the example, MC at first falls and then rises. When MPP is rising, each additional worker produces a larger addition to output than the previous worker. When each worker is paid the same wage, the addition to cost (MC) will decline. When MPP is falling, each additional worker produces a smaller addition to output; therefore, the addition to cost (MC) will rise. Thus, according to the law of diminishing

FIGURE 3
The Short-Run Costs of a Hypothetical Enterprise

(*a*) Fixed, Variable, and Total Costs

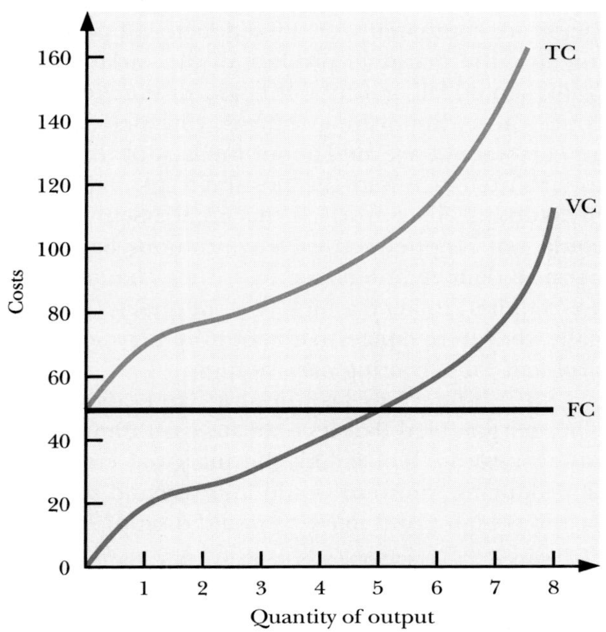

(*b*) Marginal and Average Costs

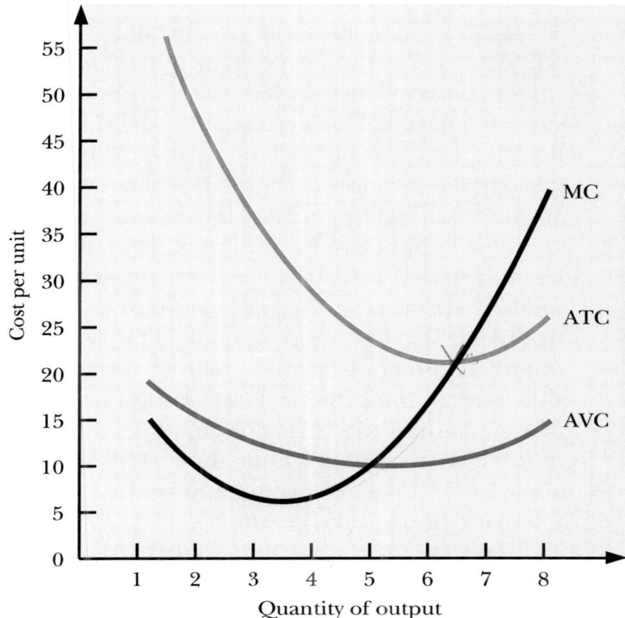

In Figure 3, the marginal and average figures (except for average fixed cost) are graphed from data in Table 3. Average total cost is the sum of average variable cost and average fixed cost. Note that ATC approaches AVC as output grows and that MC intersects both curves at their minimum points.

returns, MC will eventually rise in the short run as output is expanded.[1] (See Example 2.)

> According to the law of diminishing returns, marginal physical product will fall as output expands in the short run. But marginal cost rises when marginal physical product falls. Therefore, marginal cost will rise as output expands in the short run.

In column 6 of Table 3, variable costs are divided by output to arrive at AVC. In column 7, fixed costs are divided by output to arrive at AFC. Notice that AFC declines throughout because the same fixed cost is being spread out over more units of output. In column 8, total cost—column 4—is divided by output to obtain ATC.

Figure 3, panel *b* shows the graphical relationship between MC and AVC or between MC and ATC. Recall that when MC is below AVC (or ATC), the margin is pulling down the average. Thus, in increasing output from 3 units to 4 units, AVC falls from \$12 to \$10, and ATC falls from \$28 to \$22. The MC of \$4 is below AVC and ATC and pulls them both down. When output is 5 units, MC is slightly above AVC, and so just begins to pull AVC upward. When output is larger than 5 units, MC exceeds AVC and is pulling AVC up. When output is smaller than 5 units, MC falls short of AVC and is pushing AVC down.

Cost curves show what happens to costs of production as the level of output changes. Figure 3,

[1]The formula for calculating marginal cost from MPP is MC = W/MPP where W denotes the wage rate.

EXAMPLE 2 Chrysler's Gamble Against Diminishing Returns

Chrysler's minivan has been its most consistent source of profit in recent years. The restyled 1991 minivan was expected to yield $2000 gross profit per vehicle. Because of the minivan's popularity, Chrysler decided to increase its annual production by 10 percent (50,000 units). How would this increase in production be achieved? One option was to retool an existing plant for minivan assembly. However, this would cost financially troubled Chrysler $500 million. The second option, chosen by Chrysler, was to go to a three-shift operation at the St. Louis minivan plant. Chrysler would run three 7-hour shifts instead of the customary two 8-hour shifts. This would allow for 18 hours of production per day, with the plant closed only on Sunday.

The law of diminishing returns suggests that when more and more units of a variable factor are combined with a fixed factor of production, the marginal product of the variable factor should fall. In Chrysler's case, production could cause diminishing returns. Chrysler engineers were concerned about the lack of time for maintenance and the possibility of major breakdowns. They worried that final assembly could not be operated on a continuous basis because daily maintenance and filter changes are required to keep a high level of quality. Finally, they were concerned about the logistical problems of delivering parts at night.

In shifting to continuous operation, Chrysler gambled that it could stave off diminishing returns. If it failed, the marginal costs of producing minivans would increase and the previous high profit margins would disappear.

Source: "Chrysler Wants to Go Nonstop," *New York Times* (November 20, 1990).

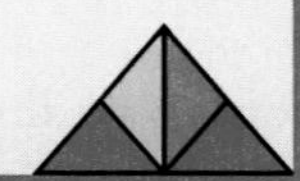

panel *b* illustrates an important principle: the MC curve intersects the AVC and ATC curves at their minimum points because of the average/marginal rule. At the minimum point, the average value is neither rising nor falling; therefore, the marginal and average values must be equal.

Minimum ATC occurs after the minimum AVC because when AVC reaches its minimum point, MC is equal to AVC and is still below ATC. Thus, when AVC is minimized, the ATC curve must still be falling by the average/marginal rule. When the ATC curve reaches its minimum point, the plant is being operated at its most efficient level.

Because ATC = AVC + AFC, the distance between the AVC and ATC curves represents AFC. As a given fixed cost is spread over a larger output, AFC gets smaller. Thus, the AVC and ATC curves get closer together as output rises.

The MC curve intersects the AVC curve and the ATC curve at their respective minimum values. AVC is at its lowest value when marginal cost equals average variable cost. ATC is at its lowest value when marginal cost equals average total cost.

LONG-RUN COSTS

Enterprises have no fixed factors of production in the long run; therefore, they do not have any fixed costs. In the long run, the business enterprise is free to choose any combination of inputs to produce

EXAMPLE 3 Flight Management Systems and Cost Minimization

Advanced commercial aircraft produced by Boeing and Airbus, the two major producers, have on-board computers that help airlines minimize their operating costs. The flight management system (FMS) contains several dozen microprocessors that analyze the entire flight plan.

First, the pilot types in the route, wind information, altitude, and the plane's weight. The FMS regulates the speed to meet the most efficient fuel budget. There is even a cost index that balances the cost of paying a flight crew against the cost of fuel. When fuel is relatively cheap, the computer increases the airspeed to reduce pilot and crew hours; when fuel is relatively expensive, the computer lowers airspeed. In other words, there is an optimal speed that minimizes the total cost of fuel and flight crew hours.

Businesses combine resources to minimize the cost of providing a particular good or service. Finding minimum-cost combinations is one of management's most important functions. In this example, airlines program computers to minimize operating costs. In most other businesses, management must figure out how to minimize operating expenses.

Source: *Scientific American* (July 1991): 99.

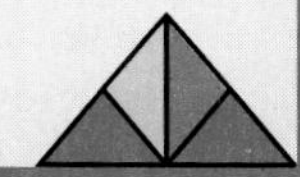

output. All costs are variable. However, once long-run decisions are executed (the company completes a new plant, the commercial-farming enterprise signs a 10-year lease for additional acreage), the enterprise again has fixed factors of production and fixed costs. Long-run cost-minimizing decisions are based on the prices the firm must pay for land, labor, and capital. (See Example 3.)

Shifts in Cost Curves

Acme Steel Company, which produces steel tubes, can determine the ATC curves it would face with different size plants. With a small plant and highly unspecialized machinery, Acme Steel would face the cost curve ATC_1 (see Figure 4). In this cost curve, ATC reaches its lowest point at output level q_1. With a slightly larger plant and somewhat more specialized equipment, Acme Steel's ATC would be lower for sufficiently larger levels of output, such as at q_2. The cost curve associated with the larger plant and more specialized equipment is ATC_2. The remaining ATC curves show the average costs for even larger plants. The curve ATC_3 yields the most efficient plant size.

At output level q_3, ATC is at its lowest point. (See Example 4.)

The Long-Run Cost Curve

For each level of fixed input, there is a different ATC curve. For every plant size, there is a different ATC curve. If there are an infinite number of fixed input levels from which to choose, there are an infinite number of associated ATC curves. Because all costs are variable in the long run, there is no distinction between long-run variable costs and long-run total costs—there is only **long-run average cost (LRAC).**

> **Long-run average cost (LRAC)** consists of the minimum average cost for each level of output when all factor inputs are variable (and when factor prices and the state of technology are fixed).

In the long run, the enterprise is free to select the most effective combination of factor inputs because none of the inputs is fixed. The LRAC curve

EXAMPLE 4 Shifts in Cost Curves: The Case of Nuclear Power

Nuclear power has been one of the most controversial issues of the last two decades. Environmental groups oppose nuclear power on safety and environmental grounds. Government regulatory agencies have been slow to license nuclear power plants. Public utilities with nuclear power plants have suffered severe declines in profits.

Although most people credit public relations and politics for the problems of nuclear power, some experts argue that it is more a matter of economics. We have learned that when capital capacity expands, short-run cost curves shift out. Once the investment has been undertaken, the industry operates on a new cost curve and cannot return to its original cost curve even if demand does not expand. In the case of electrical power, there is a substantial lag between the decision to build generating plants and their completion. Electrical utilities must make decisions based upon the projected demand for electrical power 10 years hence. Most nuclear power plants were planned during the late 1960s and early 1970s when the demand for electricity was expanding rapidly. Electrical utilities started constructing nuclear power plants while anticipating steady increases in demand. With growing demand, the shifting out of the cost curve would mean that the industry could operate at lower average costs. In fact, the first nuclear power plants became operational during a period of expanding demand, and they proved quite profitable.

The energy crisis of the mid- and late 1970s had a profound impact on electricity demand. With rising energy prices, consumers cut back on energy usage, and the demand for electricity stopped growing. New power plants could not be operated efficiently at the lower-than-anticipated demand levels of the late 1970s and early 1980s.

The accompanying figure shows an electrical utility that expected to be generating 600 megawatts of electricity in 1988. Therefore, it built a nuclear power plant to expand its capacity. The completion of the nuclear power plant shifted its cost curve from ATC to ATC′. ATC′ yields a much lower cost for generating 600 megawatts than ATC. However, the 1988 demand for electricity was much less than expected. Only 400 megawatts were generated. The electrical utility (now located on ATC′) generated this lower-than-expected output at high cost.

Source: "Public Utilities Desperate to Recoup Money Invested in Nuclear Power," *The Christian Science Monitor* (November 3, 1987).

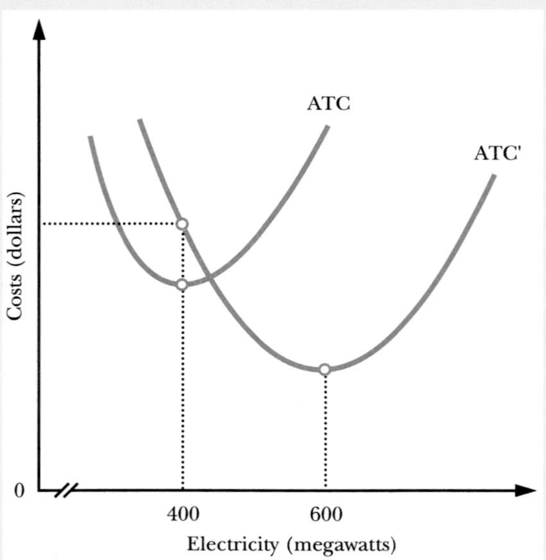

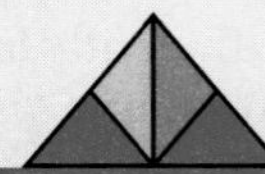

FIGURE 4
Shifts in Cost Curves with Changing Plant Size

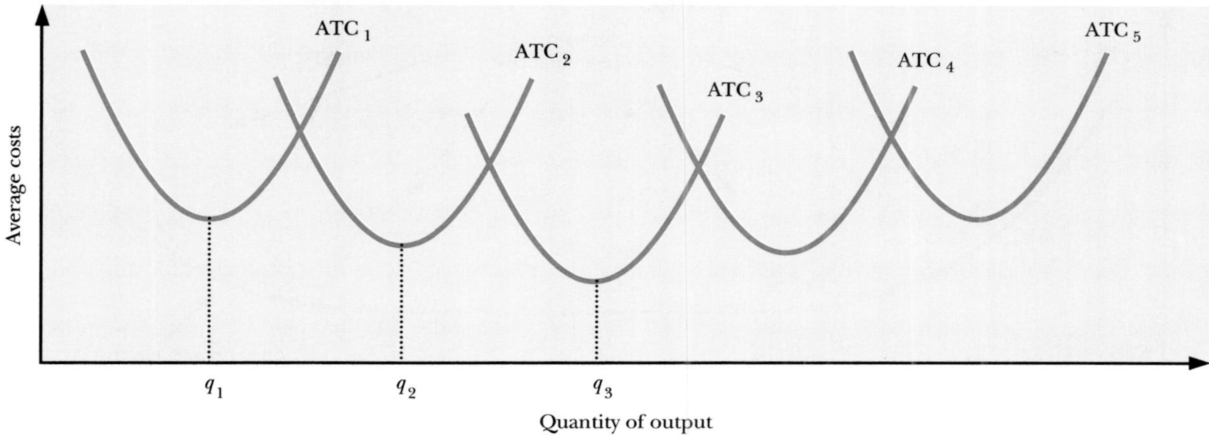

Economies of scale are achieved with larger plant sizes up to the plant size ATC_3. When diseconomies of scale are encountered, larger plant sizes entail larger unit costs, as with ATC_4 and ATC_5.

"envelopes" the short-run average total cost (SRATC) curves, forming an LRAC curve that touches each SRATC curve at only one point, as shown in Figure 5. In the short run, the fact that some factors of production are fixed causes the SRATC curve to be U-shaped. The law of diminishing returns does not apply in the long run because all inputs are variable.

Economies and Diseconomies of Scale

The LRAC curve will also be U-shaped, as show in Figure 5. Long-run average costs first decline as output expands and then later increase as output expands even further. Firms experience first economies of scale, then constant returns to scale, and finally diseconomies of scale as output expands.

Economies of Scale. The declining portion of the LRAC curve is due to economies of scale that arise out of the indivisibility of the inputs of labor and physical capital goods or equipment. In a large firm, the division of labor will be much more specialized than in a small firm. People are indivisible; it is difficult for one employee of a small firm to be one part mechanic, two parts supervisor, and three parts electrician and still remain as efficient as one who specializes in just one of these tasks. In a large firm, workers increase their productivity or dexterity through experience and save time in moving from one task to another.

The principles of specialization also apply to machines. A small firm might have to use general-purpose machine tools whereas a large firm might be able to build special equipment or machines that will substantially lower costs when large quantities are produced. Small-scale versions of certain specialized machines simply cannot be made available.

Economies of scale can occur because specialization allows for greater productivity in any of a variety of areas, including technological equipment, marketing, research and development, and management. The optimal rate of utilization for some types of machinery may occur at high rates of output. Some workers may not be able to perfect specialized skills until a high rate of output allows them to concentrate on specific tasks. As the output of an enterprise increases with all inputs variable, average costs will decline because of the **economies of scale** associated with increased specialization of labor, management, plant, and equipment. (See Examples 5 and 6.)

FIGURE 5
The Long-Run Average Cost Curve as the Envelope of the Short-Run Average Total Cost Curves

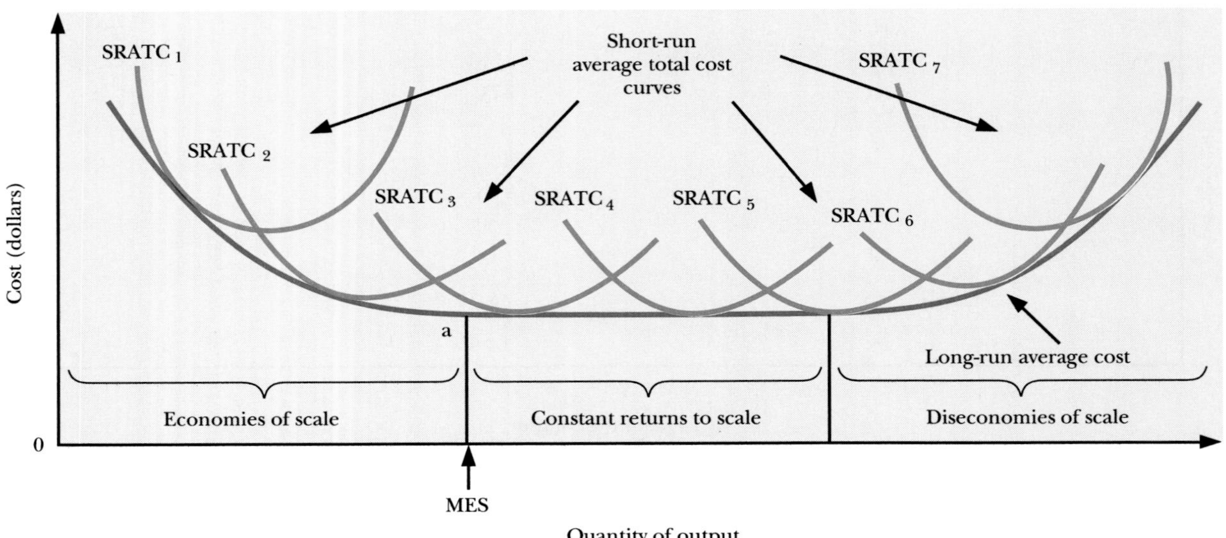

For each level of fixed input, there is a corresponding short-run average total cost curve. The long-run average cost curve is the envelope of the short-run average total cost curves. The long-run average cost curve is U-shaped. The declining portion shows economies of scale. The rising portion shows diseconomies of scale. The horizontal portion shows constant returns to scale.

EXAMPLE 5 The Do-It-Yourself Car: Economies of Mass Production

Classic Motor Carriages, located in Florida, sells a kit of automobile parts that can be assembled in one's own garage. Designed for do-it-yourself hobbyists, the kit does not include the automobile drive train. The drive train, which contains the engine and transmission, can be obtained already assembled. Even with the advantage of an assembled drive train, Classic Motor Carriages estimates that it would take a person 200 hours to assemble the car. The advantages of specialization and large-scale production in this case are obvious. For example, in 1978 the General Motors' assembly plant in Tarrytown, New York employed 2000 workers per 8-hour shift and turns out approximately 1 car per minute (about 500 cars per day). Dividing 500 cars by the 2000 workers yields 1 car for every 4 workers—or, one-fourth of a car per worker per day. Under conditions of specialization, large capital use, and mass production, the average worker produces 1 complete car every 4 days. The difference between 4 days (or 32 hours) per worker and 200 hours per worker dramatically illustrates the concept of economies of large-scale production.

Sources: Roger W. Shmenner. *Production/Operations Management: Concepts and Situations* (Chicago: SRA, Inc., 1981). chap. 5; and the authors.

EXAMPLE 6 Economies of Scale: Why the Small Airlines Have Disappeared

If there are significant economies of scale, you would expect industries to be populated by large firms. Small firms would have average costs that are too high for them to survive in competition with larger firms. The deregulation of the nation's airlines in the late 1970s and early 1980s gave both large and small airlines the opportunity to compete for air-passenger dollars. This competitive struggle provides a setting for studying economies of scale.

From 1978 to 1991, 130 small airlines were certified to compete for passenger dollars. Of these, less than 20 remained in operation by the end of 1990. The others either went out of business or were taken over by large carriers. Of the small low-cost airlines, only America West and Southwest Airlines can be regarded as successful. The disappearance of small airline companies demonstrated that large airlines could fly passengers at a much lower cost per passenger than small airlines. First, small airlines could not afford sophisticated computerized reservation systems, whose costs had to be spread over millions of passengers. Without computerized reservation systems, small airlines could not differentiate between high-paying business customers and vacation travelers, and they could not adjust fares to fill up empty flights. Second, small airlines could not offer enough flights to develop "hub-and-spoke" systems, whereby passengers from different originating points would be flown through "hub" cities, such as Chicago or Atlanta, for connecting flights. By using this system, large airlines could fly to many different locations at relatively low costs. Experts estimate that a carrier needs at least 20 planes to establish one hub. Third, small airlines could not offer the same frequency of service between two cities as large airlines. Whereas a large airline might offer ten flights per day between Boston and Chicago, a small airline may offer only two. Business travelers, in particular, preferred the convenience of many return flights.

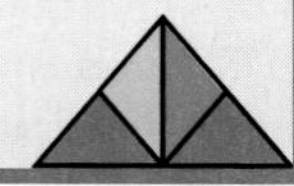

Economies of scale are present when an increase in output causes long-run average costs to fall.

Constant Returns to Scale. Economies of scale will become exhausted at some point when expanding output no longer increases productivity. For a large range of outputs, there will be **constant returns to scale.**

Constant returns to scale are present when an increase in output does not change long-run average costs of production.

Diseconomies of Scale. As the enterprise continues to expand its output, eventually all the economies of large-scale production will be exploited, and long-run average costs will begin to rise. The rise in long-run average costs as the capital stock of the enterprise expands is the result of **diseconomies of scale.**

Diseconomies of scale are present when an increase in output causes long-run average costs to increase.

Diseconomies of scale can be caused by a series of factors. As the firm continues to expand, management skills must be spread over a larger and larger firm. Managers must assume additional responsibility, and managerial talents may eventually be spread so thin that the efficiency of management declines. The problem of maintaining communications within a large firm grows, and red tape and cumbersome bureaucracy become commonplace. Large firms may find it difficult to correct their mistakes. Employees of large firms may lose their identity and feel that their contributions to the firm are not recognized. As the output of an enterprise continues to increase, average cost will eventually rise because of the diseconomies of scale associated with the growing problems of managerial coordination.

Minimum Efficient Scale

Why are some companies more profitable than others? Why are some industries more concentrated than others? Why is a particular company doing well or poorly? Economies of scale can help provide answers for these questions.

The LRAC curve in Figure 5 is flat over a large range. Empirical studies for a number of industries suggest that such constant returns to scale occur over a significant range of output. The output level at which average costs are minimized (at point *a*) is called the **minimum efficient scale (MES)** of the firm.

> The **minimum efficient scale (MES)** is the lowest level of output at which average costs are minimized.

Economies of scale differ substantially among industries. Some industries experience economies of scale up to output levels that are a high proportion of total industry sales. These industries tend to have a small number of firms because larger firms can drive smaller firms out of business.

Studies show that some industries (electricity, automobiles) have significant economies of scale,[2] while others, such as women's garments and concrete, do not. Table 4 reports the results of studies of selected industries that show that the minimum efficient firm size is as high as a 21 to 30 percent market share in the case of diesel engines and as low as a market share of only 0.2 percent in the case of shoe sales.

TABLE 4
Estimates of the Minimum Efficient Scale (MES) in Selected U.S. Industries

Industry	MES as a Percentage of U.S. Demand
Diesel engines	21–30
Electronic computers	15.0
Refrigerators	14.1
Cigarettes	6.6
Beer brewing	3.4
Bicycles	2.1
Petroleum refining	1.9
Paints	1.4
Flour mills	0.7
Bread baking	0.3
Shoes (nonrubber)	0.2

Sources: F. M. Schere, Alan Beckenstein, Erich Kaufer, and R. D. Murphy. *The Economics of Multiplant Operation* (Cambridge, MA: Harvard University Press, 1975). 80–94. Leonard W. Weiss, "Optimal Plant Size and the Extent of Suboptimal Capacity," in Robert T. Masson and P. D. Qualls, eds., *Essays on Industrial Organization in Honor of Joe S. Bain* (Cambridge, MA: Ballinger, 1975) 128–31; adapted in part from C. F. Pratten, *Economies of Scale in Manufacturing Industry* (Cambridge, England: Cambridge University Press, 1971).

Productivity Advances and the Cost Curves

The cost curves reflect the productivity and prices of the factors of production. A factor's *productivity* is the amount of output that can be obtained from a given level of its input. The production function shows how much output can be produced from any given set of inputs. A *productivity advance* results when *more* output can be produced with the *same* inputs. For example, when American farm productivity increased by over 50 percent from 1960 to 1990, the production functions for grains, dairy products, poultry and eggs, and meat animals changed in such a way that fewer inputs were needed to obtain the same output. As a

[2]Some techniques for measuring economies of scale are discussed in William G. Shepherd, *The Economics of Industrial Organization* (Englewood Cliffs, NJ: Prentice Hall, 1979), chap. 12; and James V. Koch, *Industrial Organization and Prices*, 2nd ed. (Englewood Cliffs, NJ: Prentice Hall, 1980), chap. 6.

FIGURE 6
The Effect of a Productivity Advance on the Long-Run Average Cost Curve

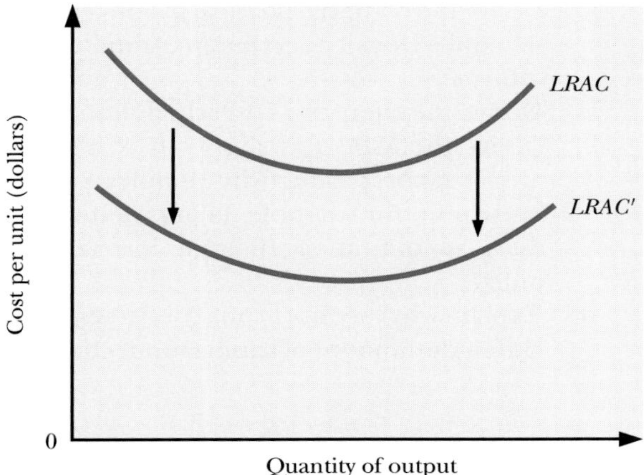

An improvement in technological knowledge can cause an advance in productivity, where more output can be produced with the same inputs or where the same output can be produced with fewer inputs. The basic consequence is that the long-run average cost (LRAC) curve shifts down. Thus, productivity advances imply that unit production costs fall for each level of output, assuming that factor prices are constant.

consequence, for any level of output and for given prices of the inputs, productivity advances will result in lower unit costs of production.

Figure 6 shows what happens to the LRAC curve as productivity improves, holding input prices constant. For each level of output, unit production costs fall. Thus, the entire LRAC curve shifts downward. The minimum efficient scale of the firm may rise or fall, depending on the type of technological breakthrough that has taken place. To illustrate, Henry Ford's assembly-line production of the famous Model T required a larger scale of plant, but a move away from assembly-line production with the use of modern industrial robots may involve a smaller minimum efficient scale.

Because unit production costs fall for each level of output, productivity advances are different from cost reductions arising from economies of scale. The fall in costs arising from economies of scale is a movement along a given LRAC curve, while a fall in costs resulting from a productivity advance is a downward shift in the entire curve.

This chapter examined how production costs behave in the short and long runs. The next chapter will study how competitive firms use these costs to determine their output level.

SUMMARY

1. In the short run, existing marginal physical product is the increase in output divided by the change in the quantity of an input, holding all other inputs constant. The law of diminishing returns states that as one input is increased (holding other inputs constant), the marginal physical product of the variable input will eventually decline. Plant and equipment cannot be varied; in the long run, all inputs are variable.

2. The opportunity cost of an action is the value of the next best forgone alternative. The average of a series of values falls when the marginal value is below the previous average value; the average stays constant when the marginal value equals the previous average; the average rises when the marginal value exceeds the previous average.

3. Variable costs are those costs that vary with output; fixed costs do not vary with output. In the long run, all costs are variable. Marginal cost (MC) is the increase in cost divided by the increase in output. Average variable cost (AVC) is variable cost divided by output; average total cost (ATC) is total (fixed plus variable) cost divided by output. The AVC and ATC curves tend to be U-shaped with the MC intersecting AVC and ATC at their minimum values.

4. In the long run, a firm can alter the size of its plant. For each plant size, there is a particular short-run average total cost (SRATC) curve. The envelope of all such SRATC curves is the long-run average cost (LRAC) curve, which gives the minimum unit cost of producing any given volume of output. Along the LRAC curve, the firm is choosing the least-cost combination of inputs. Economies of scale prevail when increasing output lowers average costs of production. Constant returns to scale prevail when increasing output does not change average costs of production—in which case, the LRAC curve is constant or horizontal. Diseconomies of scale prevail when increasing output lowers the average unit costs of production. A firm's minimum efficient scale is the lowest level of output at which average costs are minimized.

5. Advances in productivity shift the LRAC curve down (assuming input prices are constant).

KEY TERMS

short run
long run
production function
law of diminishing returns
marginal physical product (MPP)
opportunity cost
fixed costs (FC)
variable costs (VC)
total costs (TC)
marginal cost (MC)
average variable cost (AVC)
average fixed cost (AFC)
average total cost (ATC)
long-run average cost (LRAC)
economies of scale
constant returns to scale
diseconomies of scale
minimum efficient scale (MES)

QUESTIONS AND PROBLEMS

1. Your uncle gives you a "free" car and pays for the insurance, gas, oil, and repairs. You are told you may sell the car at any time. Assume the car is now worth $20,000 and will have an estimated value of $12,000 after 1 year. If the interest rate is 10 percent, how much does it cost you to use the car for 1 year?
2. Explain the distinction between explicit costs and opportunity costs. Why are opportunity costs a better guide to resource-allocation decisions?
3. A firm's accounting costs are $15,000 per month. In addition, the firm's implicit opportunity costs are $5000. What are the firm's total opportunity costs? How much revenue must the firm generate in sales in order to stay in business over the long run?
4. If a baseball player enters a game with a batting average of 0.250 (25 hits per 100 times at bat) and goes 2 for 4 on that day, what happens to his batting average? Why?
5. Contrast the average total cost (ATC) curve of a firm that has very large fixed costs relative to variable costs with the ATC curve of a firm that has very small fixed costs relative to variable costs.
6. For a given production plan, a firm's fixed costs are zero and its variable costs are $1 million. Is the plan short run or long run? Explain.
7. Answer the following questions using the production-function information in Table A. Assume that 1 unit of labor costs $5 and 1 unit of capital costs $10.
   a. Derive the marginal physical product (MPP) schedule. Does it obey the law of diminishing returns?
   b. Derive the short-run cost schedules.
   c. Derive the MPP and short-run cost schedules if labor productivity doubles (with 1 labor unit, for example, being used to produce an output of 10 units instead of 5 units).
   d. Explain why the short-run cost curves would shift if the amount of capital input changed.

TABLE A

Labor (units)	Capital (units)	Output (units)
0	2	0
1	2	5
2	2	15
3	2	20
4	2	23
5	2	24

8. At the current output level, ATC is $25, AVC is $10, and marginal cost (MC) is $15. If output were increased by 1 unit, what would happen to the new ATC? To the new average variable cost (AVC)? If ATC were to stay at $25 and MC were to increase to $25, what would happen to the next ATC?
9. Suppose FC = $25, VC = Q, and MC = $2Q$. Draw the AFC, AVC, MC, and ATC curves. At what output level does the minimum ATC occur?
10. What is the role of the law of diminishing returns in explaining the shape of the cost curves? Construct a numerical example.
11. If MC rises, what conclusion can be drawn about whether ATC or AVC is rising or falling?
12. What is the opportunity cost of a worker to a firm that mistakenly pays the worker $40 an

hour instead of the worker's wage of $25 an hour?

13. Industry A, with $10 million in sales, is comprised of three equal-sized large firms. Industry B, also having $10 million in sales, is made up of 50 equal-sized firms. From this information, make rough sketches of the long-run average-cost curve of a typical firm in each industry. Also make predictions about the minimum efficient scale as a given percentage of industry output in both cases.
14. Suppose that the MPP of the third worker is 100 units of output per week and that the MPP of the fifth worker is 50 units of output per week. If each worker is paid $25 per week and labor is the only variable input, what is the MC associated with the output of the third worker? Of the fifth worker?
15. Using Table B, plot all the short-run total-cost and average-cost curves discussed in this chapter. Do the cost curves have the expected shapes? Explain your answer.

TABLE B

Output (units)	Fixed Costs (dollars)	Variable Costs (dollars)
1	10	5
2	10	8
3	10	12
4	10	20
5	10	40

SUGGESTED READINGS

Heyne, Paul. *The Economic Way of Thinking,* 5th ed. Chicago: SRA, 1988, chaps. 5 and 6.

Kohler, Heinz. *Intermediate Microeconomics: Theory and Applications,* 3rd ed. New York: HarperCollins, 1990.

Scherer, Frederic. *Industrial Market Structure and Economic Performance,* 3rd ed. Boston: Houghton Mifflin, 1980, chap. 4.

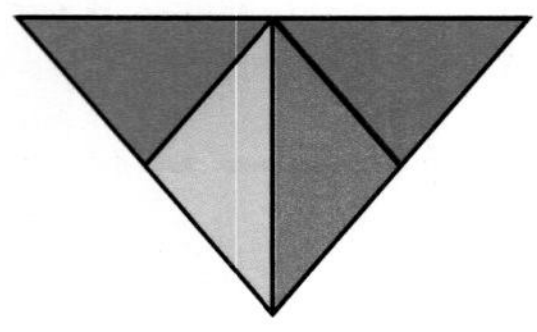

APPENDIX 29A

The Least-Cost Method of Production

APPENDIX INSIGHT

To choose the right combination of resources, a firm should use the *least-cost method* of production. This appendix will show how firms determine the level of output that uses the least costly combination of resources.

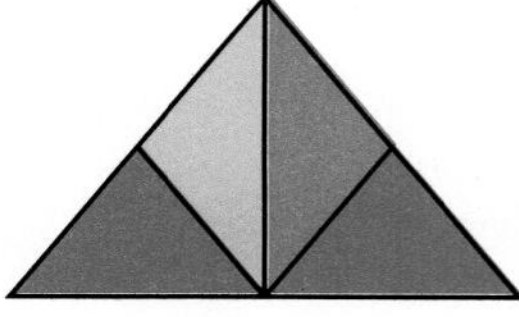

THE PRODUCTION FUNCTION

A production function shows the maximum output that can be achieved by a given combination of inputs. Figure 1 shows a hypothetical firm that employs only two factors—capital and labor—to produce its output. The horizontal edge measures the labor input from 1 to 8 workers; the vertical edge measures the capital input from 1 to 8 machines. The amount of output that can be produced from any combination of labor and capital is shown in the cells corresponding to the intersection of a row of capital input and a column of labor input. For example, 8 machines and 1 worker produce 50 units of output; 8 machines and 2 workers produce 71 units of output. Thus, the production function shown in Figure 1 gives the possible methods of producing the outputs shown at each intersection.

Marginal Physical Product

The marginal physical product (MPP) of a factor is the extra output associated with increasing input of the factor by 1 unit, holding all other factors constant. Suppose that the amount of capital is held constant at 4 machines. With 1 worker, output is 35 units; with 2 workers, output is 50 units; and so on. Clearly the

FIGURE 1
The Production Function

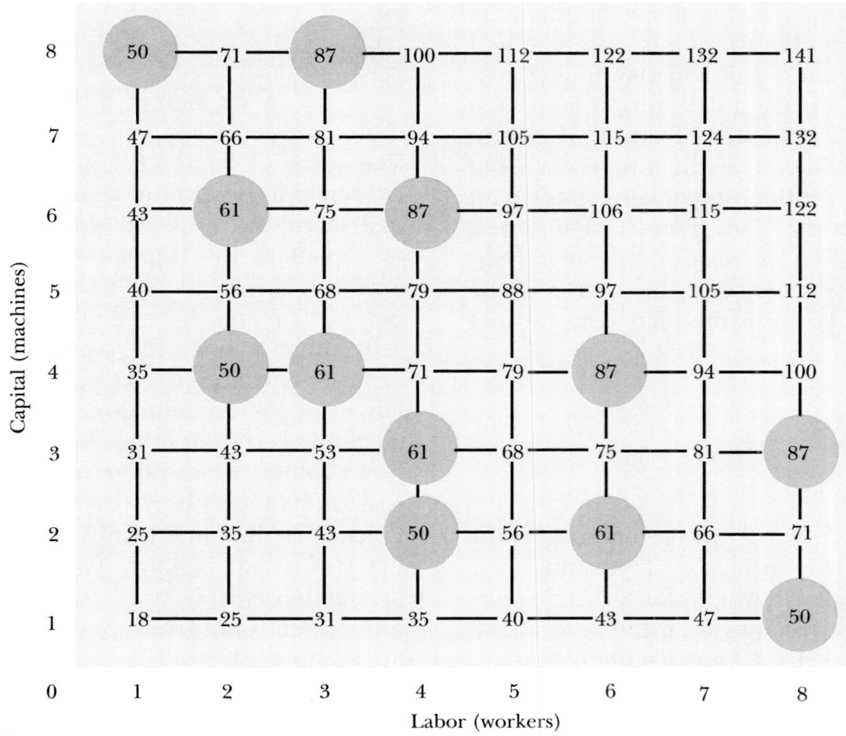

Capital inputs are measured vertically; labor inputs are measured horizontally. The number at the intersection of a row and column shows the output for that level of capital and labor input. For example, 4 machines and 2 workers produce 50 units of output. The law of diminishing returns can also be seen because, when the input of machines is held constant at 4 units, additional units of labor bring about smaller additions to output; thus, along a given row, output *increases* but at a *decreasing* rate.

marginal product of labor is 35 for the first worker and 15 for the second worker (because output rises from 35 to 50 units). The MPP of labor can be read in the figure by simply noting the difference between consecutive outputs along a given row. Using similar reasoning, the marginal product of capital could be determined by varying the machine input, holding labor constant.

The Law of Diminishing Returns

According to the law of diminishing returns, the MPP of a factor eventually declines as more of the factor is used, holding all other productive inputs constant. In Figure 1, when capital equals 4 machines, the MPP of the second worker is 15 and the MPP for the third worker is only 11.

The production function summarized in Figure 1 assumes constant returns to scale. When there are 3 units of capital and 3 units of labor, output is 53 units; when inputs double to 6 units of capital and 6 units of labor, output doubles to 106 units. When there are 3 units of capital and 3 units of labor, the fourth unit of labor has an MPP of 8 units, as output rises from 53 to 61. When there are 4 units of capital and 4 units of labor, the fifth unit of labor also has an MPP of 8 units, as output rises from 71 to 79. Thus, *the MPP of labor remains the same as long as the ratio of capital to labor remains the same.* The source of the law of diminishing returns is the increasing ratio of workers to machines.

The Principle of Substitution

Chapter 3 explained that there are substitutes for nearly everything. This principle of substitution is also illustrated in Figure 1, which shows that 50 units of output can be produced by four different combinations of capital and labor. These combinations are listed in columns 2 and 3 of Table 1.

From the information provided so far, there is no reason to choose the combination of 8 units of capital/1 unit of labor over the combination of 1 unit of capital/8 units of labor to produce 50 units of output. *The production function alone cannot tell us how to produce the 50 units of output.* Cost information must also be considered.

TABLE 1
Factor Combinations for Producing 50 Units of Output

	Output (units), Q (1)	Capital (machines), C (2)	Labor (workers), L (3)	Total Cost (dollars), TC (4)
a	50	8	1	250
b	50	4	2	200
c	50	2	4	250
d	50	1	8	425

Note: The price of capital is \$25 per machine; the price of labor is \$50 per worker.

LEAST-COST PRODUCTION

The price of labor (P_L) and the price of capital (P_C) help us determine what combination of capital and labor the firm will use. (Think of the price of capital as the implicit or explicit rental on a machine, truck, or building.) Suppose P_L = \$50 per worker and P_C = \$25 per machine. Column 4 of Table 1 shows the costs of each combination of labor and capital that yields 50 units of output. For example, combination *a* costs \$250 because 8 machines cost \$200 (8 × \$25) and 1 worker costs \$50. From Table 1 we can determine that the minimum-cost combination is *b*. This combination calls for 4 units of capital and 2 units of labor, the total cost (TC) of which is \$200. The average total cost of production is ATC = TC/Q = \$200/50 = \$4 per unit, which is the lowest possible cost per unit when total output is 50 units.

In moving from combination *a* to combination *b*, an extra unit of labor can be substituted for 4 machines without a loss of output. Labor costs \$50, but 4 machines cost \$100. Thus, the firm saves \$100 in machine costs by substituting 1 worker for 4 machines and spends \$50 on the added worker for a net gain of \$50 (without a loss in output). Clearly, it pays the firm to select *b* over *a*.

The Isoquant

These principles of least-cost production can be illustrated using graphs. Figure 2 plots combinations *a*, *b*, *c*, and *d* from Table 1 and connects these points by a smooth curve. The curve *abcd* shows all the combinations of capital and labor input that produce 50 units of output; hence, it can be called the **isoquant** for 50 units of output. (*Iso* means same, so *isoquant* means same quantity).

> An **isoquant** shows the various combinations of 2 inputs (such as labor and capital) that produce the same output.

Isoquant curves are very similar to the indifference curves studied in the appendix to the chapter on demand and utility. Just as the indifference curves were convex to the origin, so isoquants are convex to the origin. The ratio of the line segment af to fb is the amount of capital that is substituted for the extra unit of labor. The slope of the curve between *a* and *b* reflects the fact that the MPP of labor is four times the MPP of capital. The vertical distance af is four times the horizontal distance fb, which reflects the rate at which labor must be substituted for capital to keep output constant. The ratio of the marginal physical products measures the marginal rate of substitution (or the rate at which labor can be substituted for capital). This ratio equals the slope (in absolute value) of an isoquant between two points or the absolute slope of the tangent to any point of the equal-output curve.

FIGURE 2
The Isoquant

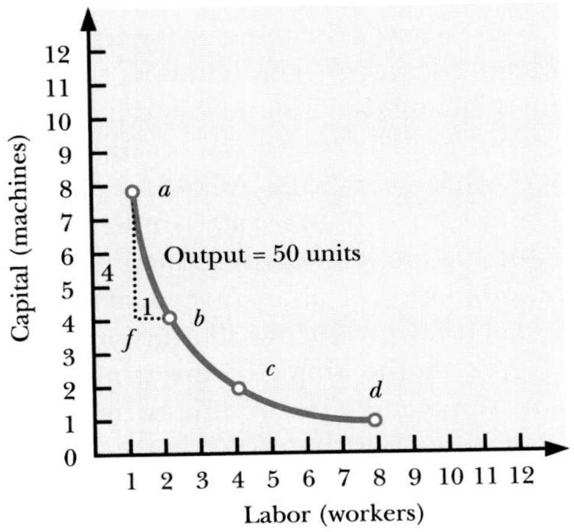

The isoquant shows all the combinations of labor (number of workers) and capital (number of machines) that produce the same amount of output. It is bowed toward the origin because the law of diminishing returns dictates that substituting capital for labor becomes easier as the ratio of workers to machines increases.

> The marginal rate of substitution of capital for labor
>
> $$= \frac{\text{MPP of labor}}{\text{MPP of capital}}$$
>
> $=$ The (absolute) slope of the isoquant

The isoquant is bowed toward the origin because when workers are substituted for machines, the MPP of labor falls relative to the MPP of capital; to keep output constant as labor is substituted for machines, fewer and fewer machines can be given up for each worker acquired.

Isocost Lines

Assuming that the price of labor (P_L) is \$50 per worker and the price of capital (P_C) is \$25 per machine, the total cost (TC) of production is

$$\text{TC} = (P_L \times L) + (P_C \times C) = \$50L + \$25C$$

where L = the number of workers and C = the number of machines. In Figure 3, the line TC = \$300 consists of all the combinations of labor and capital that cost \$300. For example, if $C = 12$ and $L = 0$, TC = \$300; if $C = 0$ and $L = 6$, TC = \$300; the combination of 6 machines and 3 workers also costs \$300. Thus, line TC is the **isocost line** for costs of \$300.

> The **isocost line** shows all the combinations of labor and capital that have the same total costs.

Figure 3 gives three illustrative isocost lines, but there is one for every level of total costs. These isocost

FIGURE 3
Isocost Lines

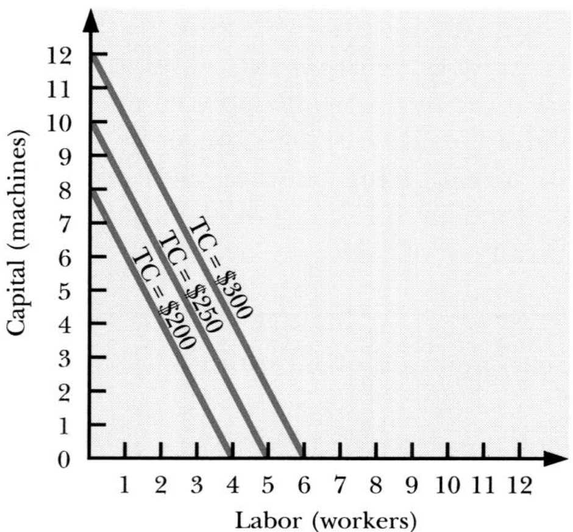

Isocost lines show all the combinations of labor and capital that cost the same amount. The line for TC = $300 shows all the combinations costing $300. The slope of each equal-cost line is measured by the ratio of the price of labor to the price of capital; in this case, labor is $50 per worker and capital is $25 per machine, so each equal-cost line has an absolute slope of 2.

FIGURE 4
The Least-Cost Rule

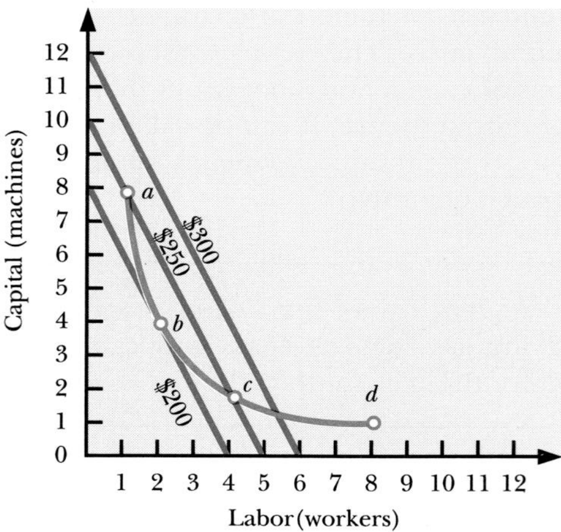

The least-cost method of producing 50 units of output can be found at the point where the isoquant, *abcd,* touches the lowest equal-cost line, TC = $200. At point *b,* the slope of the isoquant equals the slope of the isocost line because the two curves are tangent; here the ratio of the marginal physical product of labor to that of capital equals the ratio of the price of labor to the price of capital.

lines are parallel because each has the same slope. The absolute slope of any isocost line is simply P_L/P_C. In this example, the (absolute) slope is 2 since the price of 1 unit of labor is twice that of 1 unit of capital; therefore, 2 units of capital can be substituted for 1 unit of labor without increasing or decreasing total costs.

> The (absolute) slope of the isocost line is the price of labor divided by the price of capital, which represents the rate at which firms can substitute labor for capital without affecting total costs.

THE LEAST-COST RULE

Figure 4 shows how the firm minimizes the cost of producing a given volume of output (in this case, output is 50 units). When the isoquant for 50 units of output and the isocost lines for three representative cost levels are drawn on the same graph, one can determine the least-cost combination by observing where the isoquant *abcd* just touches the *lowest* isocost line (at point *b*). The lowest isocost line that curve *abcd* can reach is TC = $200. All other combinations of labor and capital on *abcd* cost more than $200. Thus, point *b* is the least-cost production point; it is the best combination of labor and capital (4 machines and 2 workers) for producing 50 units of output.

In Figure 4, the slope of the isoquant is the same as the slope of the isocost line because both are tangent (they touch without crossing) at that point. Thus

$$\frac{MPP_L}{MPP_C} = \frac{P_L}{P_C} \quad \textbf{(1)}$$

The least-cost rule can be rewritten in a second way:

$$\frac{MPP_L}{P_L} = \frac{MPP_C}{P_C} \quad \textbf{(2)}$$

In other words, the **least-cost rule** requires that the extra output from the last dollar spent on labor must equal the extra output from the last dollar spent on capital. A third way of writing the least-cost rule (by taking the reciprocals of equation (2)) is

$$\frac{P_L}{\text{MPP}_L} = \frac{P_C}{\text{MPP}_C} \qquad \textbf{(3)}$$

> The **least-cost rule** is that the least-cost combination of two factors can be found at the point where a given isoquant is tangent to the lowest isocost line. In other words, the least-cost combination of two factors can be found where
>
> $$\frac{P_L}{\text{MPP}_L} = \frac{P_C}{\text{MPP}_C}$$

The price of labor divided by the MPP of labor is labor cost per additional unit of output, which is simply the marginal cost of output using labor. (Recall that marginal cost is the extra cost of producing 1 more unit of output.) Similarly, the price of capital divided by the MPP of capital is the marginal cost of production using capital. According to the third equation, least-cost production (in the long run) requires using capital and labor in such a way that the marginal cost of production is the same whether output is increased using capital or using labor. If these two were not equal, one would be substituted for the other.

When $P_L/\text{MPP}_L = P_C/\text{MPP}_C$, since all cost-lowering substitution possibilities are exhausted, the long-run marginal cost of production is equal to the common value of the two ratios.

The Link Between the Short Run and the Long Run

The least-cost rule gives us the link between the short run and the long run. The long run is a period of time so long that both workers and machines can be varied. In the short run, the number of machines is fixed. It takes time to find the right machine, install it, and train workers to use it properly. So fixed costs would be the machine costs, and variable costs would be the labor costs. In the short run, marginal cost would be the ratio P_L/MPP_L. As shown in Table 2,

TABLE 2
Productivity and Costs

Capital (machines), C (1)	Labor (workers), L (2)	Marginal Physical Product of Labor (units), MPP_L (3)	Output (units), Q (4)	Marginal Cost (dollars), MC (5)	Fixed Cost (dollars), FC (6)	Variable Cost (dollars), VC (7)	Total Cost (dollars), TC (8)	Average Total Cost (dollars), ATC (9)
4	0		0		0	0	0	0
		35		1.43				
4	1		35		100	50	150	4.29
		15		3.33				
4	2		50		100	100	200	4.00
		11		4.54				
4	3		61		100	150	250	4.10
		10		5.00				
4	4		71		100	200	300	4.23
		8		6.25				
4	5		79		100	250	350	4.43

Note: The price of labor is $50 per worker; the price of capital is $25 per machine.

FIGURE 5
A Change in Factor Price

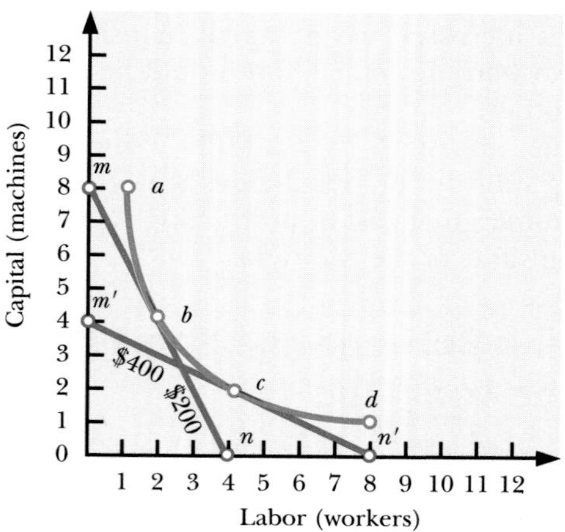

The isocost line *mn* shows the minimum cost of producing 50 units of output when capital is $25 per machine and labor is $50 per worker. (Line *mn* is the same as TC = $200.) If the price of capital rises to $100 per machine, the equal-cost line *m'n'* shows that the lowest cost of producing 50 units of output rises to $400 and the least-cost combination of capital and labor shifts from point *b* to point *c* as cheaper labor is substituted for machines.

the number of machines is fixed at 4 in the short run, and the number of workers can be varied from 0 to 5. The first four columns of Table 2 can be derived from Figure 1. Column 5 of Table 2 is the short-run marginal cost. Columns 6 through 9 show the short-run costs of production. Column 9 illustrates the average total cost (ATC) of production. Note that ATC hits its minimum at an output of 50 units where ATC = $4.00.

Applying the Least-Cost Rule

What would the firm do if the price of capital rises from $25 per machine to $100 per machine, while the price of labor remains at $50 per worker? If the firm continues to use 4 machines and 2 workers to produce 50 units of output, the new factor prices would cause total costs to be ($100 × 4) + ($50 × 2) = $500; average costs rise from $4 to $10 ($500/50). The firm, of course, would begin to substitute the now cheaper labor for the now more expensive machinery. The price of capital is now twice as great as the price of labor, so the slope of the new isocost lines is 1/2 instead of 2. Figure 5 shows what happens. The old TC line was *mn*—with the minimum-cost point *b*. The new minimum TC line is *m'n'*, which is tangent to point *c* on the isoquant. The least total cost of production is now $400 (4 units of capital now costs $400 and 8 units of labor costs $400). Because 50 units are still produced, the average cost of production is now $8 ($400/50). The firm saves $2 per unit of output by substituting labor for capital. Quadrupling the price of capital causes the average cost of production to double (from $4 to $8). The optimal ratio of machines to workers is now 2 machines per 4 workers, or 1/2 machine per worker. The production process has now become less capital intensive and more labor intensive.

SUMMARY

1. An isoquant shows all the combinations of two factors that will produce a given level of output.
2. An isocost line shows all the combinations of two factors that have the same total costs.
3. The least-cost combination of two factors can be found at the point where an isoquant is tangent to the lowest isocost line.

KEY TERMS

isoquant
isocost line
least-cost rule

QUESTIONS AND PROBLEMS

1. Why is an isoquant convex to the origin? Why is it downward sloping?
2. What should be the cost objective of the firm?
3. Show that raising the price of capital relative to labor will lead a firm to choose more labor-intensive techniques of production.
4. Assume a firm is hiring labor and capital until MPP_L = 3 and MPP_C = 15 units. Suppose P_C = $4 per unit and P_L = $10 per unit.
   a. Is the firm minimizing costs?
   b. Should the firm hire more capital and less labor or more labor and less capital? Explain your reasoning.

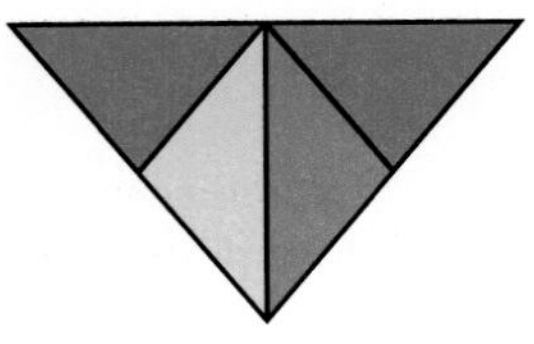

30 Perfect Competition

CHAPTER INSIGHT

Bernard Mandeville in the early eighteenth century posed the paradox of private vices being social virtues. Adam Smith later concluded that competitive forces function like an "invisible hand" to ensure that people pursuing individual interests simultaneously serve the interests of society. Competition among economic agents channels the narrow and sometimes selfish interests of each person in a socially desirable direction.

The theory of perfect competition suggests that the existence of positive economic profits in any given industry attracts new firms, thereby increasing supply and lowering the price to the point where a normal return is earned by the representative firm. Consider the videocassette recorder (VCR) industry. Sony introduced the VCR in 1975, with a price tag of $1400—about $3000 in 1992 dollars. The average VCR in 1992 cost $300. In 1975, there was one producer; in 1992, there were dozens.

This chapter will describe the manner in which a firm facing perfect competition will make its profit-maximizing decisions in both the short run and the long run, the process by which market prices are determined in both the short run and the long run, and the benefits that producers and consumers gain from trading in a competitive market.

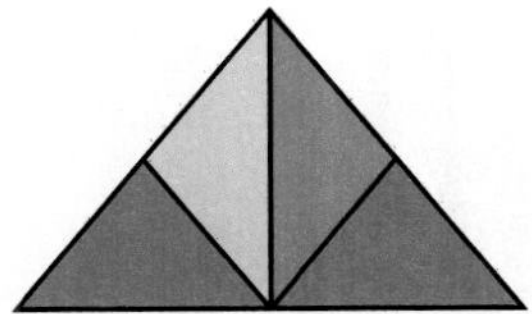

SCARCITY AND COMPETITION

In a world of scarcity, available resources are not adequate to satisfy everyone's wants. Competition for scarce resources is a necessary and unavoidable characteristic of any economy. We may dislike competition, but there is no way to avoid it. Competition, though, can take a variety of forms.

A free-for-all system of catch-as-catch-can or steal-as-much-as-one-can constitutes one possible scheme. In such a system, property rights do not exist; each person takes whatever he or she can find. It is easy to see that such a system would not work well. If property rights were not protected by law, people would have little incentive to buy or produce property. Likewise, such conditions would create a demand for security guards or mafia-style protection against the bullies and thugs who might prevail.

A system that allowed people to buy and sell property rights *freely*, with those rights protected by the state, would be more orderly. Firms would find it profitable to enter into market transactions with buyers, and all participants would attempt to strike the best deal for themselves. Such a system could exist under varying degrees of competition. This chapter studies firms operating in the most competitive markets possible.

COMPETITION AS A MARKET MODEL

An industry is a collection of firms producing a similar product (such as steel, aluminum, milk, wheat, or automobiles). A crucial characteristic of each industry is the extent to which competition is present. Economists distinguish among four basic market models: *perfect competition, monopolistic competition, oligopoly,* and *monopoly.* (See Table 1.) To briefly compare these models, perfect competition exists when individual firms in an industry have no control over the market price and new firms are free to enter the industry. Perfect competition is most likely found in an industry where there are many small producers of a homogeneous product. Farming is the classic example of perfect competition. Monopolistic competition prevails when there are many small producers of a differentiated product and new firms can enter freely. Local supermarkets and service stations are good examples of monopolistic competitors. When firms such as General Motors or Ford are large relative to the market and some impediments (such as sunk costs) to the entry of new firms exist, the industry is oligopolistic. For example, there are only a handful of large automobile companies, steel companies, soap manufacturers, and cereal producers in the United States. Finally, a monopoly exists when an industry's product is supplied by only one firm. Some examples of monopolies include local telephone or cable TV service; only one company in each industry is allowed to serve a community. Perfect competition is the subject of this chapter. The other three market models will be discussed in greater detail in later chapters.

In the real world, almost every seller exercises some influence over price; but the more competition the seller faces, the less control each individual seller can exercise over the prices charged. In the extreme case, the seller has absolutely no control over price. When the price is dictated to the individual seller by the market, the seller is said to be a **price taker.** In an

TABLE 1
Market Models

Type	Number of Firms	Product	Entry
Perfect competition	Many	Homogeneous	Easy
Monopolistic competition	Many	Heterogeneous	Easy
Oligopoly	Few	Not specified	Not easy
Monopoly	One	Irrelevant	Impossible

industry characterized by **perfect competition,** each individual seller faces so much competition from other sellers that the market price is taken as a given.

> A **price taker** is a seller that does not have the ability to control the price of the good it sells.
>
> In an industry characterized by **perfect competition:**
>
> 1. The market contains a large number of buyers and sellers.
> 2. Each buyer and seller has perfect information about prices and product.
> 3. The product being sold is homogeneous; that is, it is not possible (or even worthwhile) to distinguish the product of one firm from that of other firms.
> 4. No barriers obstruct entry into or exit from the market; that is, there is freedom of entry and exit.
> 5. All firms are price takers; no single seller is large enough to exert any control over the product price, so each seller accepts the market price as given.

In perfect competition, all firms in the industry sell a homogeneous or identical product. No firm exercises an advantage over other firms in terms of quality, location, or other product features. If Firm A charges a higher price than Firm B for the identical product, no rational buyer will buy from A. In a perfectly competitive market, buyers have perfect information about the prices charged by different sellers. Thus, every buyer will know that Firm B's price is lower than Firm A's price.

The difference between the perfectly competitive firm and the market (the industry as a whole) is illustrated in Figure 1. Panel *b* shows the market demand curve, *D*, for the product. When the market price is $7, the quantity demanded in the market is 10,000 units. The individual firm, shown in panel *a*, can sell all it wants (from a practical standpoint) at the going market price of $7. Whether the firm sells 3 units or 10 units, the price is still the $7 market price. (See Example 1.)

> The demand curve facing the perfectly competitive firm is *horizontal* or *perfectly elastic* at the going market price.

FIGURE 1
Market or Industry Demand versus Firm Demand

(*a*) The Representative Firm

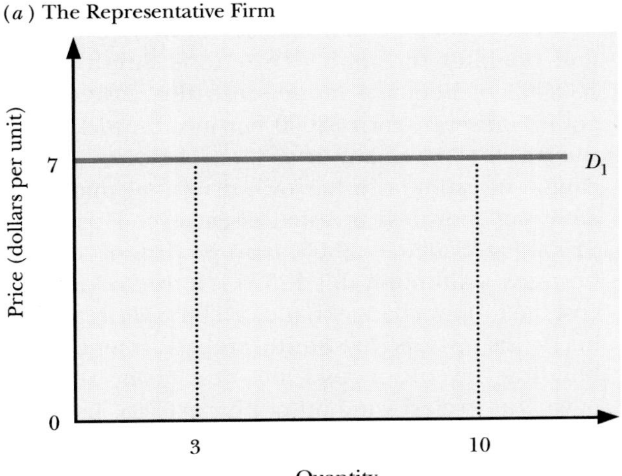

(*b*) The Market (or Industry) Demand

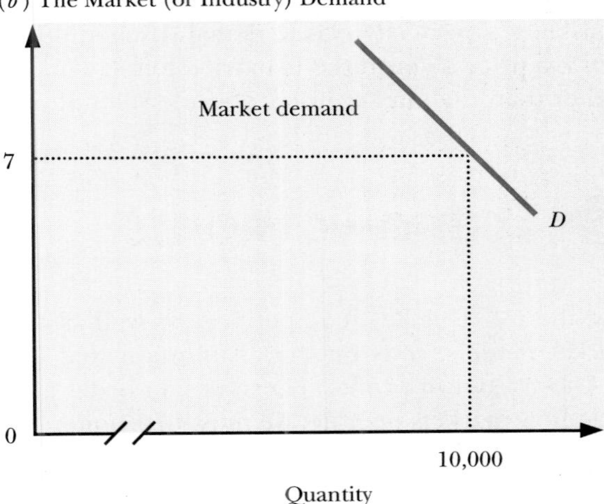

The market demand curve *D* in panel *b* shows the total market demand for a homogeneous product being produced by many relatively small firms. The demand curve D_1 in panel *a* shows how this demand is perceived by the individual firm. Because the individual firm is so small relative to the market, it cannot significantly influence the market price. The firm is, thus, a price taker and can sell all it wants at the going price.

EXAMPLE 1 Price Taking and Who Is to Blame?

The prices of basic farm products such as wheat, corn, and poultry are set on commodity exchanges. The world's most important commodity exchanges are located in Chicago, and they bring together under one roof all the potential buyers and sellers of particular commodities. For example, the price of wheat is set on the Chicago wheat commodity exchange, which brings together all the world's buyers and sellers of wheat. Brokers who arrange wheat transactions do so for a middleman's fee—typically less than 1 percent of the transaction.

When farm prices fell by 15 percent in 1986, farmers traveled to Chicago to protest. To their frustration, the farmers found no responsible party to whom they could complain. They could not blame the brokers who worked on the floor of the exchange; all the brokers did was to execute orders to buy and sell. They could not find buyers to blame; even the largest buyers of farm products (such as Nabisco and General Foods) accounted for such a small fraction of market purchases that they could not be blamed for falling prices. The farmers could not find sellers to blame because even the largest seller was too small to influence farm prices. For example, the largest egg farm in the United States, located in California, produces only 1 percent of U.S. egg output.

The farmers' experience illustrates the operating mechanism of competitive markets. Prices are set impersonally by the forces of supply and demand. No single buyer or seller is large enough to influence the price of any product.

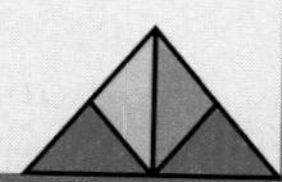

The individual firm in a perfectly competitive market produces very small amounts relative to the market as a whole. An individual firm cannot change the market price by altering the quantity of the good it offers in the marketplace. Because the individual firm faces a perfectly elastic demand schedule, the firm is a price taker. If the firm tried to sell at a price higher than the market price, it would sell nothing.

ECONOMIC PROFITS

The theory of perfect competition, as well as other market models, rests on the assumption that firms seek to maximize profits. Therefore, in order to analyze how markets operate, we must first understand the concept of profits.

Economists do not use the general term *profits* in the way most people do, nor do they always measure profits in the same manner as accountants. **Economic profits** indicate whether or not resources are being directed to their best use.

> **Economic profits** represent the amount by which revenues exceed total opportunity costs.

For example, pharmacist Smith is the owner and operator of Smith's Drugstore. Smith has put $60,000 of her own money into the business. She could, however, earn $2000 per month working as a pharmacist in a chain drugstore. Moreover, Smith's capital investment in her own drugstore might earn $500 per month if invested elsewhere. This sum of $2500 (= $2000 + $500) is an *implicit* cost of doing business. (Although this $2500 is a true opportunity cost, no money changes hands.) The *explicit* (accounting) costs involved are Smith's rent payments on the building, inventory costs, business taxes, and wage payments to clerks and other pharmacists. These add up to $37,000 per month. Smith's total monthly opportunity cost for operating her own drugstore is the sum of explicit costs ($37,000) and implicit costs ($2500), or $39,500.

Now suppose Smith's Drugstore has monthly sales of $40,000. Smith's accounting profits are $3000 per month (that is, sales = $40,000; accounting costs = $37,000). Smith's economic profit, however, is only $500 because total opportunity costs are $39,500. Accounting costs ignore the implicit costs that must be assigned to the use of Smith's entrepreneurial talents and funds. These implicit costs must be paid for the entrepreneur/owner to commit entrepreneurial resources and financial capital to the business. In this case, if accounting profits had been below $2500, Smith would not have entered the business because she would not earn a **normal profit,** which equals the cost of doing business.

A **normal profit** is the return that the time and capital of an entrepreneur would earn in the best alternative employment. It also equals the return that is earned when total revenues equal total opportunity costs.

THE SHORT-RUN SUPPLY CURVE

Perfectly competitive firms have no control over price; they are price takers. Therefore, the major decision they face is how much output to produce. In the short run, a perfectly competitive firm makes its output decisions by varying the quantities of variable inputs (such as labor, raw material, energy) that are combined with its fixed plant and equipment. The fixed level of plant and equipment is both a burden and a blessing. It is a blessing to established firms because in the short run fixed costs prevent new firms from entering the industry. Time is needed to build more plants, install more equipment, and find new locations. Yet, the fixed level of plant and equipment is also a burden. In the short run, the firm is obliged—even if the firm shuts down temporarily—to make certain contractual payments (taxes, rent payments, contractual obligations to some employees) and to forego interest receipts that could be earned if the plant and equipment could be sold.

In the short run, the firm must make two decisions: first, whether to temporarily shut down, and second, how much to produce if it decides not to shut down. In the long run, the firm has the additional options of building more plants and acquiring more equipment or leaving the business permanently.

How much does the firm produce at each price? The firm's supply curve indicates how much it is prepared to sell. For each price, the quantity supplied maximizes the firm's profit. The profit-maximizing rate of output depends on two factors: (1) the price in relation to average variable cost and (2) the marginal cost.

The Two Rules of Profit Maximization

When calculating the appropriate level of output, the firm is guided by the goal of profit maximization (or loss minimization). To maximize profit, the firm will follow some simple rules.

The Shutdown Rule. The first decision faced by the perfectly competitive firm is whether to shut down temporarily or produce some output. Surprisingly, it is not important whether or not the revenues that the firm earns cover fixed costs. Fixed costs should not affect decision making in the short run because they must be paid even if the firm shuts down. Only in the long run can fixed costs be avoided. Instead, according to the **shutdown rule,** the decision to shut down for the short run will depend on the relationship between revenues and variable costs.

The **shutdown rule** states that if a firm's revenues at all output levels are less than variable costs, it minimizes its losses by shutting down. If there is at least one output level at which revenues exceed variable costs, the firm should not shut down.

For example, brick manufacturer Smith has fixed costs of $1000 per week. She can sell $3000 worth of bricks per week while incurring a variable cost (VC) of $2900. Should the bricks be produced or should the plant be shut down? If no bricks are produced (the shutdown case), the fixed costs of $1000 must be paid anyway, so the manufacturer will incur a loss of $1000. By producing $3000 worth of bricks, the manufacturer can *reduce* her losses to $900 because producing bricks results in an excess of $100 of revenues ($3000) over variable costs ($2900). The reasoning behind the shutdown rule is that any excess of revenues over variable costs can be applied to cover a portion of fixed costs.

The Profit-Maximization Rule. Once the firm has decided not to shut down, what rule should it follow to maximize profits or minimize losses? The decision about *how much* to produce is guided by marginal analysis. If at any point producing another unit of output *raises the profit of the firm (or reduces its losses),* more output should be produced. Adjustments in the level of output will be made as long as each change increases profit or reduces losses.

What is the best output? As we learned in the preceding chapter, marginal cost (MC) is the increase in costs that results from increasing output by 1 unit. The marginal benefit of producing 1 more unit of output is measured by the firm's **marginal revenue (MR)**, which is the extra revenue brought about by a 1-unit increase in output. As long as an extra unit of output adds more to revenue than to costs, the profits of the firm increase (or its losses diminish) with greater production. If the marginal cost of an additional unit of output exceeds its marginal revenue, the firm's profits would be reduced (or its losses increased) by producing that extra unit. It follows that the **profit-maximization rule** holds that marginal revenue should equal marginal cost. This rule applies to all firms, be they perfectly competitive or monopolistic.

> **Marginal revenue (MR)** is the increase in total revenue (TR) that results from each 1-unit increase in the amount of output:
>
> $$MR = \frac{\Delta TR}{\Delta Q}$$
>
> The **profit-maximization rule** states that a firm will maximize profits by producing that level of output at which marginal revenue (MR) equals marginal cost (MC).

Because the competitive firm can sell all it wants without depressing the going market price, that price (P) is equivalent to the marginal revenue. Thus, for a competetive firm, the rule is to produce where $P = MC$.

Consider the hypothetical competitive firm described in Table 2. The costs are the same as the firm studied in Table 3 of the previous chapter. The firm's average variable costs (AVC) for different levels of output are listed in column 2; average total costs (ATC) in column 3; total costs in column 4; and marginal costs (MC) in column 5. Figure 2 presents the same information in graphical form. Notice that the difference between the ATC and AVC curves measures average fixed cost (AFC) and the MC curve intersects both the AVC and ATC curves at their minimum points.

The minimum points on the AVC and ATC curves are important to keep in mind. In Table 2, the minimum average variable cost listed in column 2 is \$9.60—which occurs when the output equals five units. The minimum average total cost listed in column 3 is \$18—which occurs when the output equals six units.

Whether or not the firm can make a profit depends upon the price. The competitive firm can sell all it wants at the going price. When the price

FIGURE 2
The Profit-Maximizing Firm

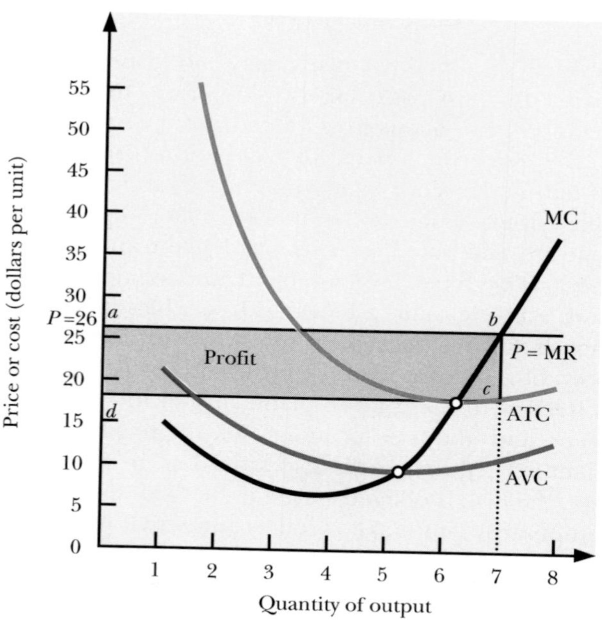

The market price is \$26. The firm maximizes profit at an output level of seven units (where $P = MC$). At $P = \$26$, price exceeds ATC by the distance *bc*. Total profit is the rectangle *abcd*.

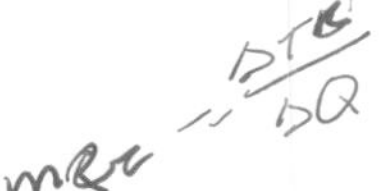

TABLE 2
The Profit-Maximizing Firm

Output (1)	Average Variable Cost (2)	Average Total Cost (3)	TC (4)	Marginal Cost (5)	P = Marginal Revenue (6)	Revenue (7)	Profit (8)
0	—	∞	$48		$26	$0	−$48
				$20			
1	$20	$68	68	**15**	26	$26	−42
				10			
2	15	39	78	**8**	26	52	−26
				6			
3	12	28	84	**5**	26	78	−6
				4			
4	10	22	88	**6**	26	104	16
				8			
5	9.6	19.2	96	**10**	26	130	34
				12			
6	10	18	108	**16**	26	156	48
				20			
7	11.4	18.3	128	**26**	26	182	54
				32			
8	14	20	160	**38**	26	208	48
				44			
9	17.3	22.7	204				

Profit is maximized where MR = MC. If P = MR = $26, the firm should produce 7 units.

exceeds the minimum ATC of $18, the firm can make a profit by producing six units of the good.

Three Cases

In the short run, the competitive firm's objective is either to maximize profits or, if necessary, to minimize losses. Once the market price is set, the firm will find itself in one of three positions:

1. The price may be high enough that the firm can make economic profits.
2. The price may be low enough that the firm stays in business but produces at a loss.
3. The price may be so low that the firm's best option is to temporarily shut down and hope for the price to rise.

The Profitable Firm. Let us start with a price of $26. Because the firm is perfectly competitive, P = MR = $26. Columns 4, 7, and 8 in Table 2 show the total cost, total revenue, and profit (positive or negative) of the firm. If the firm produces six units, minimizing average total costs at $18, it can make a profit of $48. However, at this output, MC equals $16. Since MR = $26, the firm can increase its profit by producing more units; the increase in revenue will exceed the increase in costs. If output is raised to seven units, profit increases to $54. This $6 increase represents the difference between the increase in revenue ($26) and the increase in costs ($20). Profit is maximized at $54 because when the output equals seven units, MR = MC.

The graph in Figure 2 tells the same story. At any point along the line P = MR, the firm's total revenue equals the price times the quantity produced. Profit is maximized where the P = MR line intersects the MC curve; when P = $26, this occurs at an output level of seven units. The vertical difference between the P = MR line and the ATC curve at that point—the distance *bc*— indicates profit per unit of output. Total profit is determined by multiplying this difference by the output of seven units and is measured by the

TABLE 3
The Loss-Minimizing Firm

Output (1)	Average Variable Cost (2)	Average Total Cost (3)	TC (4)	Marginal Cost (5)	P = Marginal Revenue (6)	Revenue (7)	Profit (8)
0	—	∞	$48		$16	$0	−$48
				$20			
1	$20	$68	68	**15**	16	16	−52
				10			
2	15	39	78	**8**	16	32	−46
				6			
3	12	28	84	**5**	16	48	−36
				4			
4	10	22	88	**6**	16	64	−24
				8			
5	9.6	19.2	96	**10**	16	80	−16
				12			
6	10	18	108	**16**	16	96	−12
				20			
7	11.4	18.3	128	**26**	16	112	−16
				32			
8	14	20	160	**38**	16	128	−32
				44			
9	17.3	22.7	204				

When P = $16, losses are minimized when output is 6 units.

rectangle *abcd*. Profit will not be maximized at any output other than seven units because MC will not equal *P* or MR.

The Loss-Minimizing Firm. Let us turn to the second case, in which the market price is not high enough for the firm to make a profit. A market price lower than the minimum ATC of $18 will result in losses. Consider a price of $16. Table 3 and Figure 3 use the same cost figures as the previous example, but columns 6, 7, and 8 of the table now reflect the lower price. The firm cannot make a profit; instead, it must worry about minimizing its losses. If the firm produces an output of zero, column 4 shows that total costs will still be $48—the firm's fixed costs do not disappear if it shuts down. The firm's revenue will be zero, as shown in column 7, and its loss (its negative profit) will be $48.

If the firm shuts down, it loses its entire fixed costs of $48. Can it do better? If the firm's revenue exceeds its variable costs, it will be able to cover some portion of its fixed cost. If the firm can pay even a small portion of its fixed costs it is better off staying in business than shutting down. The minimum AVC ($9.60) occurs when output is five units. By producing five units, the firm's price exceeds AVC by $6.40, revenue that can be used to cover some of the fixed costs. If the firm produces five units of output, its loss is $16, as shown in column 8, less than the $48 loss of shutting down. Yet, at an output of five units, the firm is still not minimizing its losses. The price of $16 exceeds the marginal cost of $10; an additional unit of output would add $16 to revenue and only $10 to costs. According to the profit-maximizing rule, the firm should increase production until P = MC. In Figure 3, this occurs at point *c*, where the P = MR line intersects the MC curve yielding an output of six units. At this point, the firm's losses per unit of output are measured by the distance *bc*, or $P-$ATC = $16 − $18 = −$2. The firm's total losses of $12 (the six units times the $2 loss per unit) are shown by the rectangle *abcd*.

FIGURE 3
The Loss-Minimizing Firm

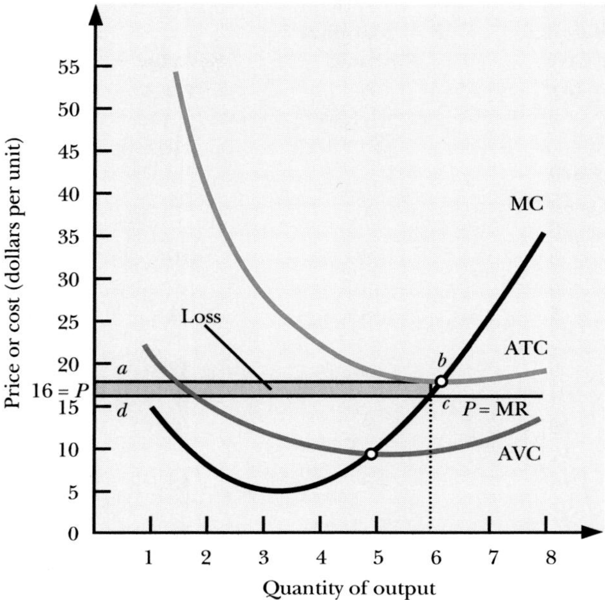

In this case, minimum ATC is \$18 and P = \$16, so the firm loses money. But the firm minimizes its losses by adjusting output to 6 units, where P = MC. At this level, it is able to cover not only its variable costs but also some portion of fixed costs. By shutting down, the firm would lose its fixed costs of \$48.

FIGURE 4
The Shutdown Case

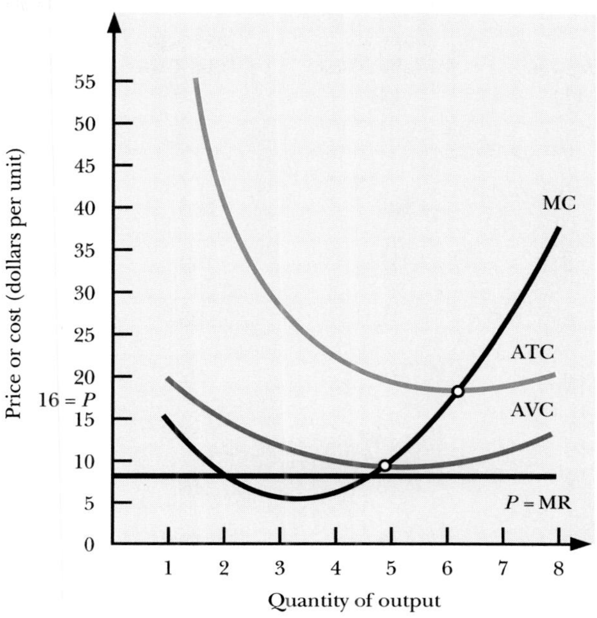

In this case, P = \$8 and the minimum AVC is \$9.60. The firm minimizes its losses by shutting down because the price is less than AVC.

> Perfectly competitive firms choose that level of output where P = MC—or, in graphical terms, where the P(= MR) line intersects the MC curve—provided price is greater than the minimum level of AVC. This holds whether the firm is maximizing its profit or minimizing its losses.

The Shutdown Case. In the previous two cases, the price of the product exceeded the minimum AVC of \$9.60. If, however, the price falls short of the minimum AVC, what should the firm do? A price below the average variable cost causes the firm's revenues to fall short of variable costs, so the firm should temporarily shut down. In this case, it loses not only its fixed cost, but also the portion of its variable cost that is not covered by dollar sales.

Table 4 and Figure 4 illustrate the situation of the competitive firm when the price is only \$8. Column 8 in Table 4 shows that its losses are minimized when output is zero. When the firm produces nothing, its losses are limited to its fixed cost of \$48. Any additional output, since the price does not cover AVC, will increase the firm's losses. By producing the first unit, for example, the firm's AVC is \$20. Since the price is only \$8, the firm loses \$12 on the first unit. Thus, its losses increase from \$48 to \$60 as output rises from zero to one unit. Figure 4 demonstrates graphically the rationale for a shutdown. The P = MR line is less than AVC for all outputs. Thus, for any positive level of output, the firm loses more money than by shutting down; the firm minimizes its losses by producing nothing.

The supply curve for a competitive firm shows the level of output that it is prepared to supply at each price. The three cases presented in this section illustrate that the profit-maximizing level of output increases as the price increases.

TABLE 4
The Shutdown Case

Output (1)	Average Variable Cost (2)	Average Total Cost (3)	TC (4)	Marginal Cost (5)	P = Marginal Revenue (6)	Revenue (7)	Profit (8)
0	—	∞	$48		$8	$0	−48
				$20			
1	$20	$68	68	**15**	8	$8	−60
				10			
2	15	39	78	**8**	8	16	−62
				6			
3	12	28	84	**5**	8	24	−60
				4			
4	10	22	88	**6**	8	32	−56
				8			
5	9.6	19.2	96	**10**	8	40	−56
				12			
6	10	18	108	**16**	8	48	−60
				20			
7	11.4	18.3	128	**26**	8	56	−72
				32			
8	14	20	160	**38**	8	64	−96
				44			
9	17.3	22.7	204				

When P = $8 (< AVC), losses are minimized by shutting down.

The competitive firm's supply curve is that portion of the firm's MC curve that lies above the AVC curve. It indicates the profit-maximizing level of output for the firm at different price levels. Because the marginal cost curve is positively sloped, the competitive firm's supply curve is also positively sloped.

Graphical Summary

A graphical summary of the competitive firm's supply curve is shown in Figure 5. The P = MR line intersects the MC curve above the minimum point on the AVC curve. If output is short of the intersection (point *e*), the firm can make the additional profit shown by the blue area, which represents MR in excess of MC. If the firm pushes output above point *e*, it loses the amount shown by the orange area, which represents MC in excess of MR. We know the firm is better off producing at point *e* than shutting down because *P* exceeds AVC. Since the firm is more than covering its variable costs, it is paying off at least some of its fixed costs.

The Industry Supply Curve

The behavior of the profit-maximizing firm explains the short-run behavior of the perfectly competitive industry of which it is a part. Recall that the short run is a period so short that old firms cannot build new plants and equipment; new firms cannot enter; old firms cannot leave. Thus, there are a fixed number of competitive firms of given sizes. Each individual firm's supply curve is its MC curve above its AVC curve. In the short run, the **industry** or **market supply**

FIGURE 5
Profit Maximization

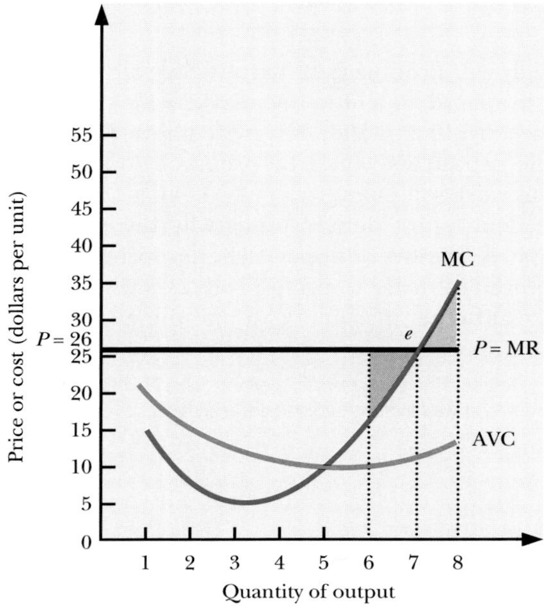

Profit is maximized where MR = MC. The blue area is lost if output is too low, and the orange area is lost if output is too high.

FIGURE 6
The Industry Supply Curve

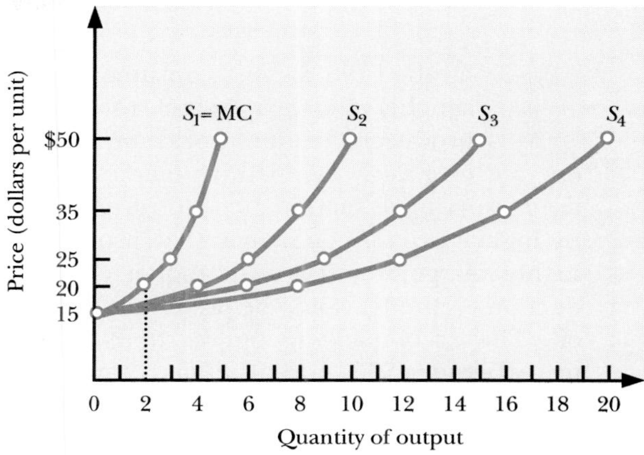

The industry supply curve is the horizontal summation of all individual firms' supply curves. In the present case, there are 4 identical firms. Each firm has the MC curve S_1. As additional firms are added, the supply curve shifts rightward to S_2 (for two firms), S_3 (for three firms), and finally to the market supply curve S_4 for all four firms.

curve is the sum of the profit-maximizing or loss-minimizing outputs of every firm at each price.

> In the short run, the **industry** or **market supply curve** is the horizontal summation of the supply curves of each firm, which in turn are those portions of the firms' MC curve located above minimum AVC.

Figure 6 illustrates how the market supply curve is derived in the case of four identical firms, but the principles are the same for any number of firms. We have considered an even simpler marginal cost curve than in the previous example. The marginal cost curve (above AVC) for a single firm is shown as S_1 = MC. The firm wishes to sell zero units at a price of \$15, two units at a price of \$20, three units at a price of \$25, four units at \$35, and five units at \$50. The curve S_4 is the market supply curve for all four firms.

Graphically, the market supply curve is the *horizontal* summation of each firm's supply curve. With four identical firms, no industry output is supplied at a price of \$15. At a price of \$20, eight units are supplied (the four firms at two units each). At a price of \$50, the industry is prepared to supply 20 units (four firms at five units each). The supply curves S_2 and S_3 show what the market supply curves would be with only two and three firms in the industry. The addition of firms simply shifts the market supply curve to the right. (See Example 2).

Short-Run Equilibrium

The market or industry equilibrium occurs at the market price that balances the market supply with the market demand for the good. Figure 7 demonstrates how the short-run equilibrium price is determined, using the hypothetical firm of Figures 2 through 4. Panel *a* of Figure 7 shows the individual firm, and panel *b* an industry consisting of 1000 such firms. The supply curve *S* in panel *b* is the horizontal summation of each individual firm's MC curve above AVC. For example, at a price of \$26 each firm sells seven

EXAMPLE 2 Marginal Costs, Oil Prices to 2100, and the Supply Curve

In the 1980s, oil consumers paid roughly $20 per barrel for oil. If producers in the world oil market operate in a fairly competitive market, $20 is the approximate marginal cost of production. At higher prices, companies that produce at higher marginal costs (using higher cost production methods) would be prepared to supply oil. The accompanying figure shows that at prices between $30 and $40 per barrel, marginal producers using the expensive enhanced oil recovery (EOR) method would be prepared to supply oil. Producers of extra heavy oil would be prepared to enter the markets at a price between $40 and $60. At a price above $50, oil shale producers would be prepared to supply oil to world oil markets.

The figure demonstrates why the supply curve is positively sloped. Higher prices are required in order to bring producers who produce at higher marginal cost into the market.

Source: "The Upper Limits," *Forbes* (June 27, 1988): 107. Chevron and Washington Analysis Corp. estimates.

Oil Price Outlook (constant 1987 dollars per barrel)

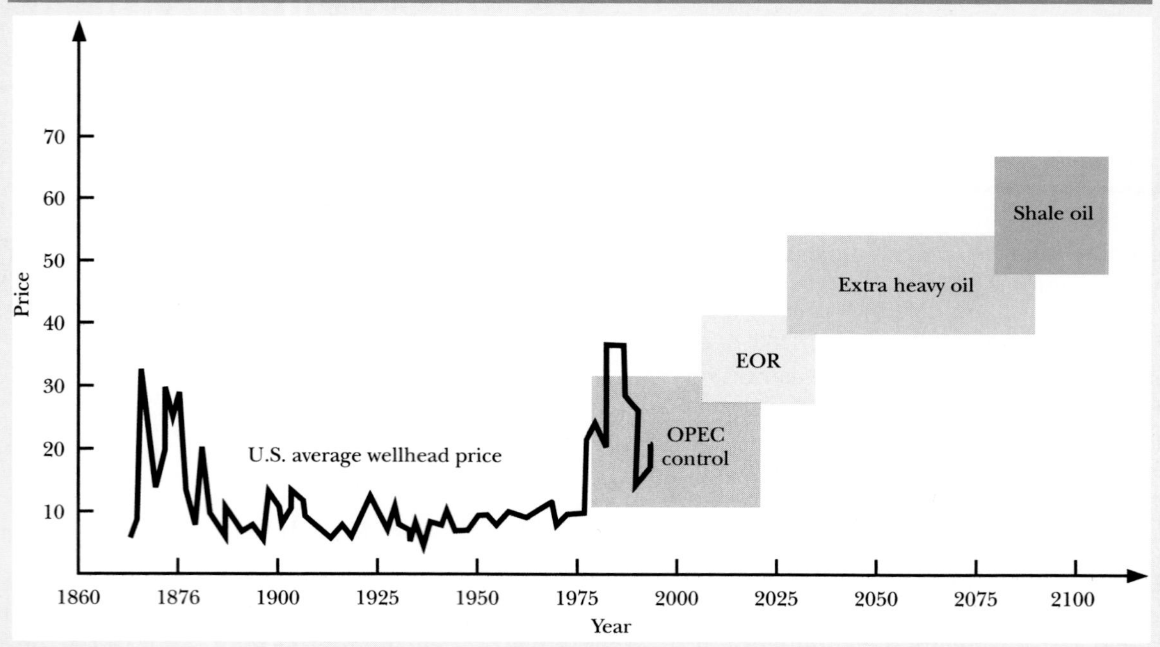

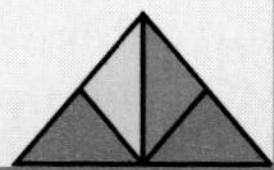

FIGURE 7
Short-Run Equilibrium: The Firm and the Market

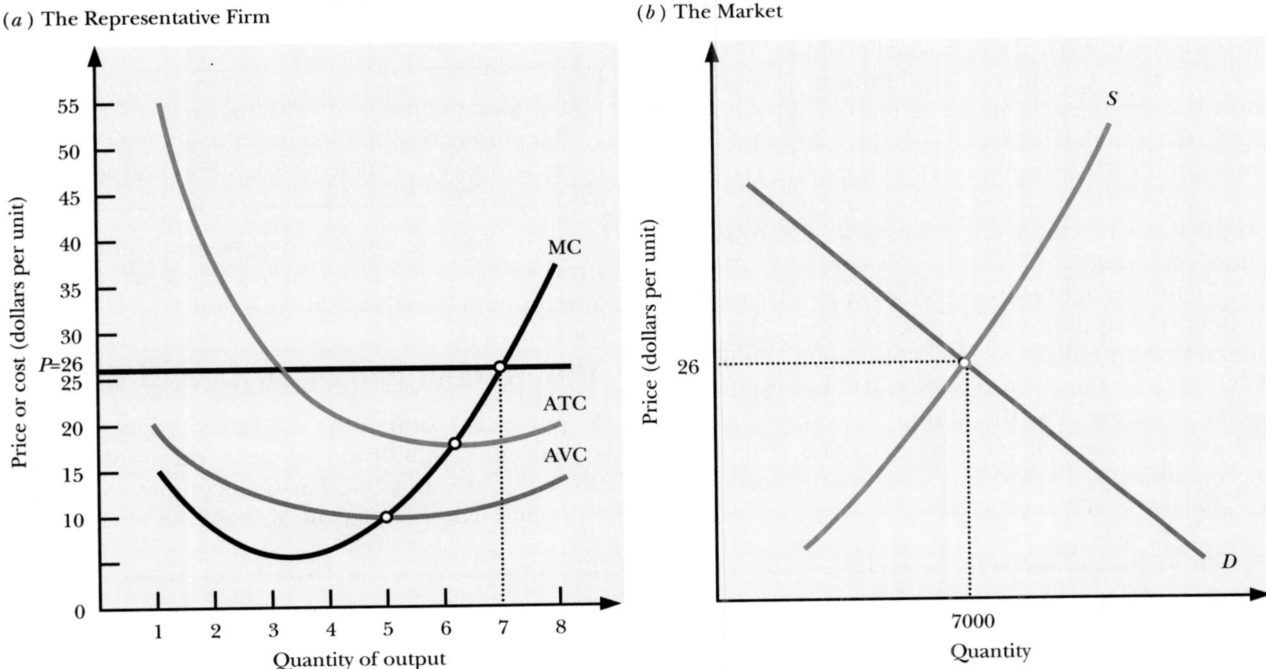

Panel *a* shows the representative firm; panel *b* shows the market, in which there are 1000 firms. Firm demand occurs at the point where market demand and supply are in equilibrium, in this case at a price of $26 and an output of 7000 units. The individual firm in panel *a* is making a short-run profit.

units and the industry sells 7000 units. If the market demand curve *D* intersects the market supply curve at the price of $26, then the quantity demanded also equals the quantity supplied (7000), and the $26 price becomes the individual firm's horizontal demand curve. In response to this price, the firm produces seven units, at the point where the MC curve intersects its demand curve. The profit-maximizing behavior of the individual firm is consistent with the profit-maximizing behavior of all the firms in the market.

Panel *a* shows a representative firm that is making an economic profit. ATC at the profit-maximizing output level of seven units is $18.30; therefore, the firm is making a per-unit profit of $7.70 (= $26 − $18.30) on each of the seven units for a total of $54 economic profit. The representative firm would experience economic losses if ATC were greater than the price. Even in such a case, however, the firm would not shut down in the short run as long as it could pay part of its fixed costs.

PERFECT COMPETITION IN THE LONG RUN

The effect of economic profits on perfectly competitive industries is felt primarily in the long run, when new firms can enter the industry and established firms can exit. As competitive firms respond to economic profits or losses, the industry short-run supply schedule shifts, and prices change.

Long-Run Equilibrium

The persistence of economic profits ($P >$ ATC) or economic losses ($P <$ ATC) is not a stable or equilibrium situation in the long run for a competitive industry. If losses continue to be sustained, the long run gives firms enough time to decide whether to escape fixed-cost obligations by leaving the industry. If economic profits continue to be made, there will be an incentive in the long run for new firms to enter the industry to earn above-normal profits.

A market in long-run equilibrium provides no incentive for new firms to enter or old firms to leave; the number of firms remains static. In long-run equilibrium, existing firms will operate at a level of output at which average costs are minimized; firms producing with inefficient plants will have dropped out of the market.

Figure 8 diagrams a perfectly competitive market in long-run equilibrium. In the long run, the firm operates at an efficient scale of operation. Thus, the ATC curve for the optimal plant will have a minimum average cost equal to the minimum average cost on the long-run average cost curve (LRAC). The long-run equilibrium for the representative firm occurs at q_0, where P = ATC = LRAC.

When P = MC and P = ATC = LRAC at the long-run equilibrium output, and when MC intersects ATC at its *minimum point,* the perfectly competitive firm is producing at the lowest average cost in the long run.

> Long-run equilibrium occurs for the competitive industry when economic profits are zero and long-run average costs are minimized.

This finding suggests that perfectly competitive firms will operate at maximum efficiency (produce at minimum LRAC) in the long run.

The Mechanism of Entry and Exit

A perfectly competitive industry adjusts toward a long-run equilibrium of zero economic profits through entry and exit. For the economy as a whole, entry and exit are opposite sides of the same coin. If

FIGURE 8
Long-Run Equilibrium: The Firm and the Market

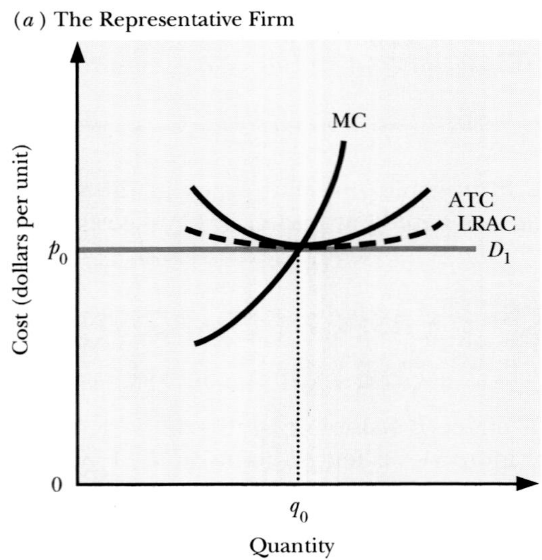

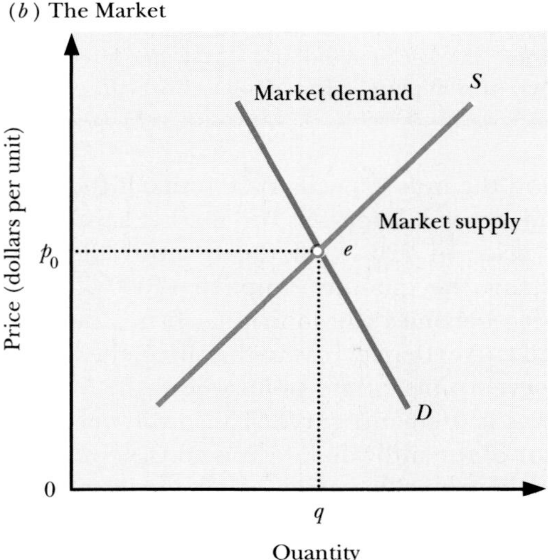

These graphs illustrate the relationship between the firm and the market in long-run equilibrium. Notice that three conditions are satisfied: (1) quantity supplied equals quantity demanded; (2) price equals marginal cost; and (3) price equals average total cost, which equals long-run average cost. (The representative firm makes zero economic profit.) The representative firm in panel *a* produces at the point where the D_1 curve intersects the MC curve (P = MC). Its profits are zero because price just covers the minimum average total cost of production. The market supply curve in panel *b* is based on the number of firms in existence in long-run equilibrium.

FIGURE 9

Free Entry Drives Economic Profits to Zero and Unit Costs to a Minimum

(*a*) The Representative Firm

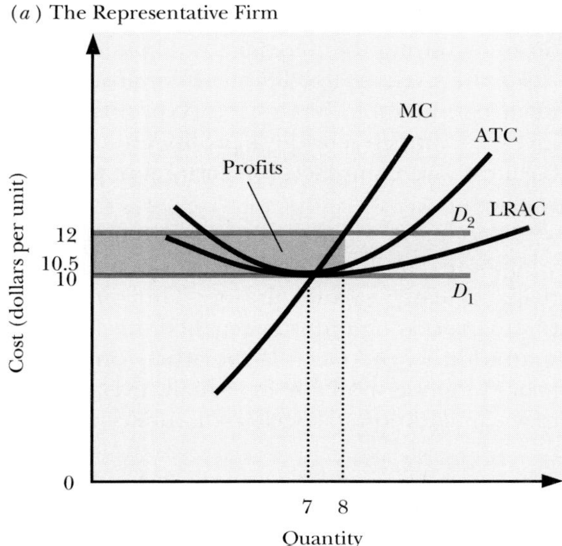

(*b*) The Industry

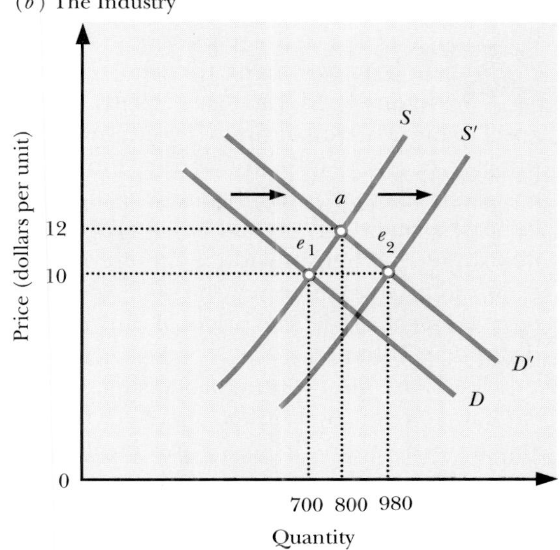

The initial long-run equilibrium is e_1, at the intersection of D and S in panel b. When demand shifts to D', the short-run equilibrium price rises to \$12 (point a), creating economic profits for the individual firm facing the new demand curve D_2 in panel a. In the long run, new firms enter the market until the supply curve shifts to S'. The long-run equilibrium is established at point e_2, where price again equals \$10. Each firm returns to producing seven units of output, but the number of firms rises from 100 (700 ÷ 7) to 140 (980 ÷ 7).

it is profitable to enter one industry, resources must be exiting another industry. In other words, if revenue exceeds opportunity costs in some industries, it falls short of opportunity costs in others.

This is difficult to see in a large economy, such as the United States. But in a small economy it would be obvious. For example, in Hawaii the success of the tourist industry crippled the pineapple industry through the effect of higher wages in the former. (See Example 5, Chapter 3.)

Entry. In the long run, the mechanism of free entry eliminates economic profits and ensures that goods are produced at minimum average cost with an efficient plant size.

Consider the perfectly competitive industry in Figure 9. Panel *a* graphs the ATC and MC curves of a typical firm in this industry; we assume ATC is the short-run average total cost curve for an efficient scale of plant. Panel *b* graphs the market supply curve derived by summing the supply curves of the 100 firms in the industry. When the market demand curve is *D*, the equilibrium price is \$10. At this price, the representative firm makes zero profits (a normal return). The demand curve facing the representative firm is D_1; each of the 100 firms produces seven units of the product, yielding a market output of 700 units. Point e_1 represents both a short-run and a long-run equilibrium.

Suppose that consumers increase their demand for the product, causing the market demand curve to shift from D to D'. The short-run equilibrium price rises to \$12, and the short-run equilibrium output of the industry rises to 800 units (point a).[1] At this higher price, the firm's short-run equilibrium occurs at eight units of output, where price and marginal

[1] Remember that in the short run, the number of firms is fixed. As market demand increases, movement occurs along the short-run supply schedule S. In the long run, new firms can enter, resulting in a rightward shift of the supply curve to S'.

EXAMPLE 3 Competition, Freedom of Entry, and One-Hour Photo Processing

As recently as 10 years ago, people had to wait overnight for film to be developed. In the early 1980s, French and Japanese manufacturers revolutionized the photo-processing industry by developing low-cost minilabs that could fit into a corner space in a pharmacy or any other small retail establishment. When introduced, these minilabs required an investment of $33,000. As technology was perfected, the price of the minilabs dropped substantially.

The one-hour photo-processing business is characterized by minimal barriers to entry. Anyone who wants to enter the business can do so by buying the necessary equipment. The first entrepreneurs to offer one-hour processing made considerable, but transitory, profits. Later investors, attracted by these profits, entered the business and competed for customers without restriction.

Economic theory states that entry into competitive businesses will cease when all participants earn normal profits. The one-hour photo-processing industry reached this level of saturation in the early 1990s, when one-hour processing was available in virtually every pharmacy, in addition to specialized outlets.

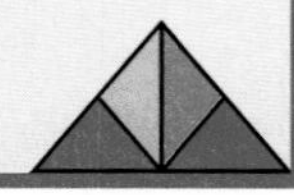

cost are equal. The typical firm now makes economic profits [= 8 × ($12 − $10.50) = $12]. In the short run, which may be a few months or many years, the individual firm will enjoy above-normal returns.

In the long run, above-normal profits will attract more firms. *As these new firms enter the market, the supply curve shifts to the right* because the market supply is the sum of individual supply curves. The entry of new firms will continue as long as economic profits remain positive. But as the supply curve shifts to the right (to S'), the market price falls, shrinking profits. Eventually, economic profits disappear. The new long-run (and short-run) equilibrium is point e_2, at the old equilibrium price of $10. The individual firm again produces seven units; but the total output is now 980 units, produced by 140 firms. (See Example 3.)

> In the long run, the number of firms in a perfectly competitive industry is not fixed. If the typical firm is making economic profits, the number of firms will expand. If the typical firm is sustaining economic losses, the number of firms will contract. In other words, if $P > \text{ATC}$, the number of firms will increase. If $P < \text{ATC}$, the number of firms will decrease.

Efficient Scale. Competition induces the perfectly competitive firm to produce at $P = \text{MC}$; free entry causes $P = \text{ATC} = \text{LRAC}$, thereby eliminating economic profits. Both forces combined result in *efficient* production, in which the good is being produced at the minimum cost to society. The firm in a competitive industry cannot be inefficient in the long run. For example, any firm in Figure 9 that is not the best possible size for producing seven units, will cease to exist in the long run.

Exit. The entry of some firms into profitable industries implies a simultaneous exit of other firms from unprofitable industries. Like entry, the mechanism of exit leads to a long-run equilibrium, with the average firm producing at the minimum average cost and with price equal to marginal cost. Just as entry into profitable industries is healthy for an economy, so is exit from unprofitable ones. *One of the most important lessons in all of economics is that entry and exit are different sides of the same economic mechanism.* Indeed, to say that economic profit attracts new entrants implies that those entrants were making economic losses elsewhere. Greater profits in one industry become the opportunity costs of other industries.

In Figure 10, the initial demand and supply curves are D and S in panel *b*. Point e_1 is both a short-run and a long-run equilibrium for an industry with

FIGURE 10
The Exit of Firms Eliminates Losses and Drives Unit Costs to a Minimum

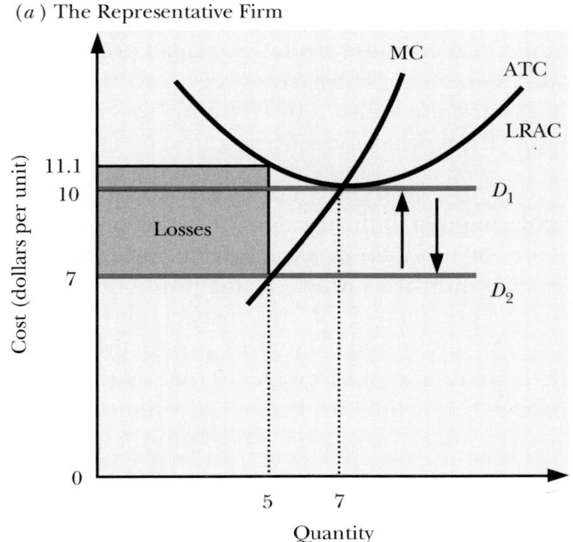

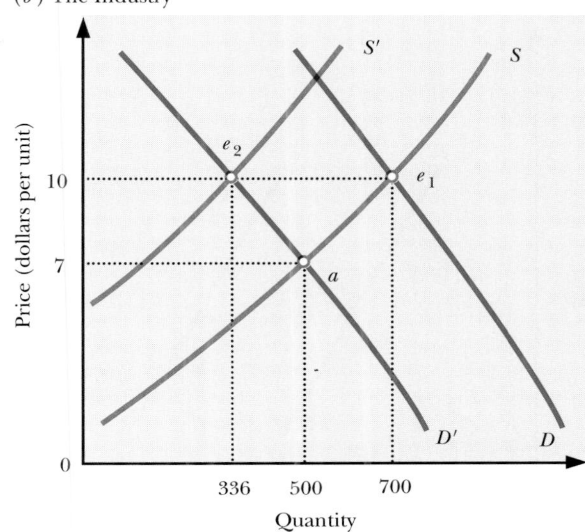

The initial long-run equilibrium is e_1, the intersection of D and S in panel b. Demand drops to D', causing the short-run equilibrium price to fall to \$7 (point a). The representative firm incurs losses as D_1 shifts downward to D_2. The exit of firms in the long run shifts the supply curve to S', which lifts the price back to \$10 and eliminates losses. Each firm returns to producing seven units of output, but the number of firms falls from 100 (700 ÷ 7) to 48 (336 ÷ 7).

100 firms. Point e_1 is a short-run equilibrium because, in panel *b*, the market quantity supplied equals the market quantity demanded and because, in panel *a*, P = MC for the representative firm. The market is in long-run equilibrium because when price is \$10 (the firm demand curve is D_1), the representative firm makes zero profits.

Suppose now that consumers reduce their demand for the product, causing the market demand curve to shift from D to D' in panel *b*. As a result, the short-run equilibrium shifts from point e_1 to point *a*, where the price is \$7 and the quantity is 500 units. The representative firm produces five units. Because \$7 is less than ATC, the representative firm has economic losses. In the long run, firms will begin to exit (the weaker ones first), shifting the industry supply curve to the left until economic losses are eliminated (at S') and price is driven back up to the original \$10. The new equilibrium is at point e_2, where total output is 336 units, and there are now only 48 firms who again produce an average of seven units each.

The Long-Run Industry Supply Curve

In Figures 9 and 10 increases or decreases in demand serve to raise or lower price in the short run. But in the long run, prices remain the same! In the case of Figure 9, the increase in demand triggers an increase in supply that drives the price back down to the original level. Similarly, in Figure 10, the decrease in demand results in a decrease in supply that drives the price back up to the original level. The **long-run industry supply curve** determines what happens to price when demand changes.

The **long-run industry supply curve** shows the quantities that the industry is prepared to supply at different prices *after* the entry and exit of firms is completed.

Constant-Cost Industries. The long-run industry supply curve corresponding to Figures 9 and 10 is perfectly elastic (horizontal) at the price of \$10,

FIGURE 11
The Long-Run Supply Curve for a Constant-Cost Industry

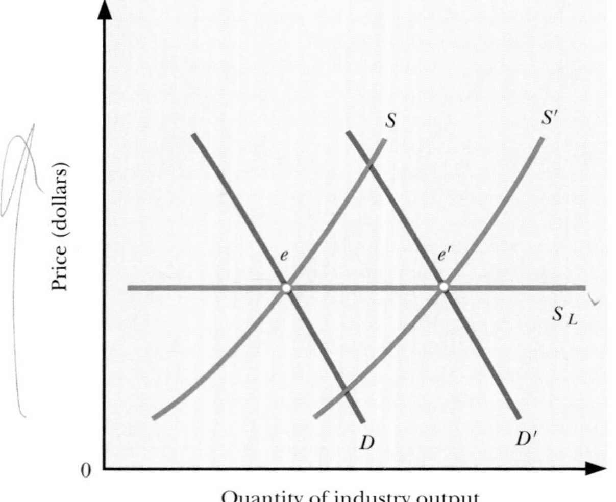

A constant-cost industry can buy all the inputs or productive factors it wants at constant prices; hence, the minimum average total cost of production is independent of industry size. When demand increases, as from D to D', the price stays the same in the long run; only quantity increases, due to the corresponding increase in supply, from S to S'. Price must stay the same to keep economic profits at zero. Thus, the long-run supply curve, S_L, is perfectly elastic.

which equals the minimum unit cost of production (minimum LRAC). The case of a perfectly elastic industry supply curve is illustrated in Figure 11, where S_L is the long-run industry supply curve. Shifts in demand, such as that from D to D', simply change the equilibrium quantity in the long run; they do not affect price or cost. When shifts in demand do not change price or cost in the long run, the industry is a **constant-cost industry.**

A **constant-cost industry** is relatively small and, hence, can expand or contract without significantly affecting the terms at which factors of production used in the industry are purchased. Hence, the long-run industry supply curve for a constant-cost industry is horizontal.

Why might an industry face constant-cost conditions? Firms in constant-cost industries can purchase labor, raw materials, land, and the like at the same prices whether the industry is expanding or contracting. This will occur if the industry's demand for resources constitutes a relatively small portion of the total demand for those resources, and if the industry's factor inputs are not so highly specialized that factors from other industries cannot be used.

Increasing-Cost Industries. As total output in an **increasing-cost industry** expands, the prices of the factors of production used by that industry are bid upward. Industries whose factor purchases make up a large percentage of the market and industries that use specialized factors of production are usually increasing-cost industries. Thus, as the industry expands, individual firms must pay higher prices for their resources—so their costs of production rise.

As industry output in an **increasing-cost industry** expands, the factor prices of resources used in the industry are bid upward. As industry output contracts, the prices of these factors fall. Hence, the long-run industry supply curve for an increasing-cost industry is upward sloping.

The long-run adjustment in an increasing-cost industry is illustrated in Figure 12. The initial demand curve is at D, with the equilibrium at point e_1. When the demand curve shifts to D', the price in the short run rises to the level indicated at point a. The typical firm now earns economic profits. New firms enter, the industry expands, and the price of the good itself falls, squeezing profits toward zero, as in a constant-cost industry. But factor prices are also bid up as the number of firms increases, causing the LRAC curve to shift upward from $LRAC_1$ to $LRAC_2$. In the final equilibrium, indicated at point e_2, profits have been shrunk to zero by the entry of new firms *and* rising costs combined. The long-run supply curve is shown as S_L.[2]

[2]There is yet a third category, the *decreasing-cost industry*. In decreasing-cost industries, prices paid for resources decline as the industry expands. Because decreasing-cost industries are rare and the causes of decreasing costs are complicated, we do not deal with them here.

FIGURE 12
The Long-Run Supply Curve for an Increasing-Cost Industry

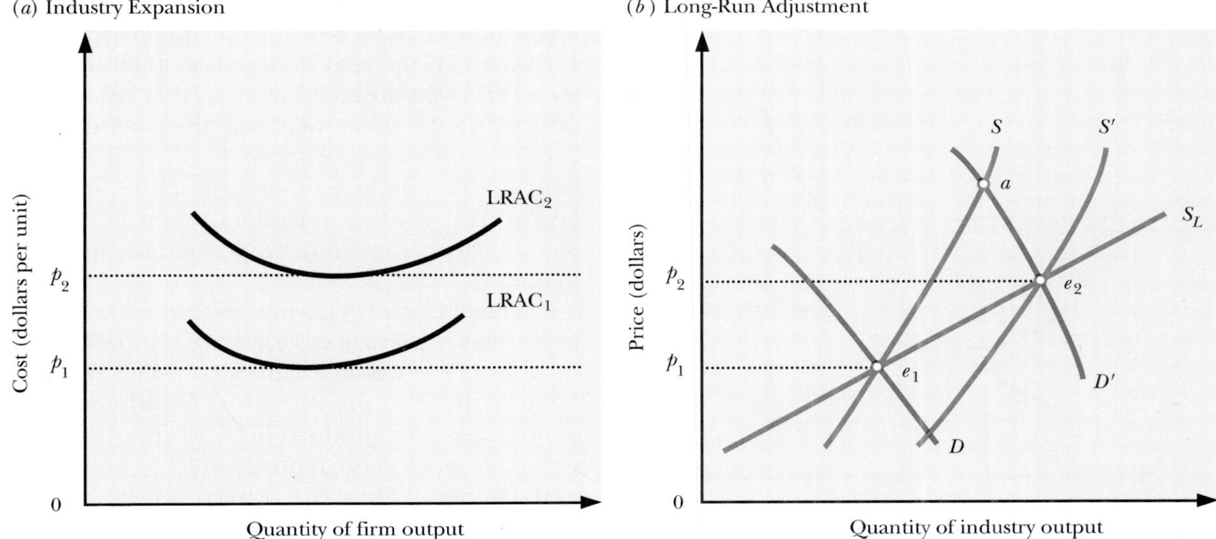

The expansion of an increasing-cost industry drives up important factor prices facing individual firms; hence, the cost curves shift upward as the size of the industry increases, as illustrated in panel *a*. When demand shifts from *D* to *D′*, the long-run equilibrium price increases from p_1 to p_2. The cost curve $LRAC_1$ in panel *a* corresponds to the equilibrium point e_1 in panel *b;* the cost curve $LRAC_2$ corresponds to point e_2. The long-run supply curve, S_L, is upward sloping but is still more elastic than the short-run supply curves, such as *S* or *S′*.

Differential Rents and the Representative Firm

Thus far we have assumed that perfectly competitive industries are composed of a large number of firms, all producing with *similar costs of production.* But is it not true that the production costs of competitive firms are quite different? One entrepreneur may have greater abilities and lower costs than another. One coal mine may offer rich veins just below the surface; another offers poor veins thousands of feet below the surface. One farm may have rich fertile land; another farm has poor soil. Do these natural differences result in large differences in average costs among different competitive firms in the same industry? The answer is, surprisingly, no.

Consider the two different coal mines in Figure 13. The superior mine in panel *a* has lower average variable costs at each level of output than the inferior mine in panel *b when the cost of renting the mine from its owner is excluded.*[3] Because coal mining is a competitive industry, the coal produced from Mine A will sell for the same price as the coal from Mine B (the demand is shown as *D* in both cases).

The operator of Mine A will choose to produce q_A units of output and the operator of Mine B will produce q_B units. *If there were no rental payment,* the operator of Mine A would make an economic profit represented by the orange area in panel *a;* the operator of Mine B would make a much smaller economic profit—the orange area in panel *b.*

Because Mine A is a superior mine with lower production costs, however, coal operators would

[3]Note that it does not matter whether the operator owns the mine or not. The operator who owns the mine incurs an opportunity cost in the form of sacrificing the opportunity to earn rental income from renting the mine to other operators.

FIGURE 13
Differential Rents on Coal Mines of Varying Richness

(*a*) Coal Mine A

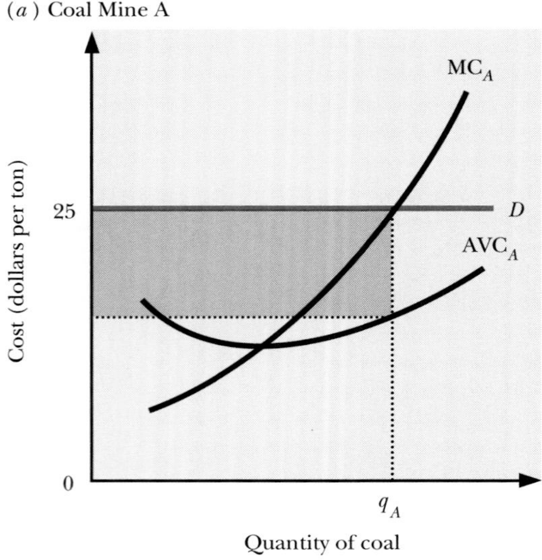

(*b*) Coal Mine B

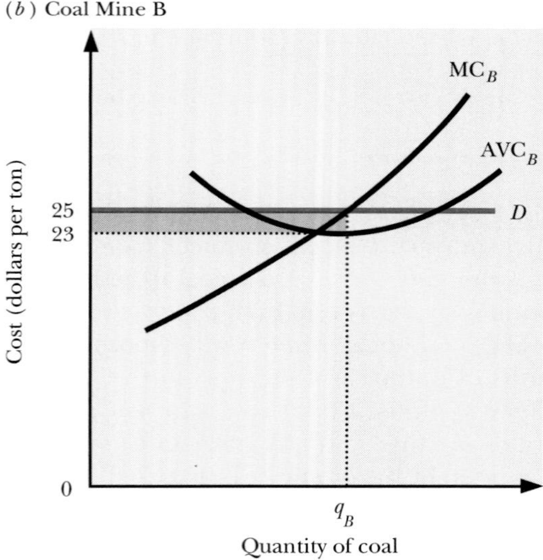

Coal Mine A, depicted in panel *a,* is easier to mine than Coal Mine B, depicted in panel *b.* Thus AVC$_A$ is lower than AVC$_B$. The average variable cost curves exclude the costs of paying the rent on the mine itself. The orange areas correspond to the rent that will be paid on each mine if the price of coal is $25 per ton. It will cost more to rent Mine A than to rent Mine B, equalizing the total costs of production.

be willing to pay a higher *rent* for the privilege of operating it. In both cases, an economic profit (an above-normal return) is earned even without a rental payment; operators would, therefore, be willing to pay the owners of the mine property a *rent equal to the orange area* for the privilege of using each mine. If the rent were greater than the orange area, ATC would exceed price so that below-normal returns would be earned and the operator would choose another occupation. If the rent were less than the orange area, above-normal returns would be earned, so other operators would be willing to pay a higher rent and would outbid the current operator.

The net result of paying rent for scarce resources is to equalize average costs among competitive firms. A higher rent would be paid for Mine A than for Mine B, and this *differential rent* would equalize the average costs of production. The return from this rental payment to the more productive mine accrues to the owner of Mine A, a scarce resource, not to the mine operator in the form of an economic profit. (See Example 4.)

This general principle can be applied to other competitive industries in which firms are different. A farmer who is located on particularly fertile land will earn more than neighboring farmers. A particular entrepreneur who is more ingenious than other entrepreneurs in the industry will earn a higher return. *These returns are included in accounting profits, but they are not considered economic profits.* Economists consider them *rents* paid to scarce factors of production.[4]

The theory of differential rent reconciles the zero-economic-profit property of perfect competition with the fact that some people earn large incomes in perfectly competitive industries in the long run. This situation is consistent with the conditions of perfect competition because the income of certain competitive coal mine owners, for example, constitutes rent rather than economic profit.

[4]This "differential rent theory" owes its origin to David Ricardo, who, in his 1817 classic, *The Principles of Political Economy and Taxation,* called attention to the fact that fertile farmland paid higher rents than marginal farmland. The theory of differential rent applies to other factors of production besides farmland. When applied to labor, the theory is called the law of comparative advantage, described in Chapter 3.

EXAMPLE 4 Kidd Creek: How Rents Equalize Costs

The giant Kidd Creek ore body, located in Ontario, Canada, is one of the great mines of the world. The owners of Kidd Creek can mine zinc, copper, and silver at average costs that are below those of other producers. The Kidd Creek reserve was discovered in 1964 and raised its first owner—Texasgulf—to prominence before it was sold to the Canada Development Corporation in 1981. Its current owner is Falconbridge, Ltd., a giant mineral producer, with worldwide mining operations, headquartered in Toronto.

Despite the vast riches of Kidd Creek, Falconbridge's profits have not been above normal for the mining industry. In fact, the corporation's profits have been depressed since it acquired Kidd Creek in 1986. The decrease in profits occurred because Falconbridge had to pay an economic rent of $615 million to acquire Kidd Creek. Unique resources that will bring the costs of production below those of rival firms are subject to competitive bidding for their acquisition. The resulting high economic rents for such resources equalize the costs of production among rival firms.

Source: "Wait and See," *Forbes* (June 30, 1986): 50–54.

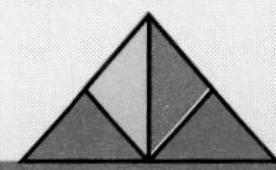

THE GAINS FROM VOLUNTARY EXCHANGE OR TRADE

The theory of perfect competition demonstrates that both producers and consumers can gain from voluntary exchange between many independent buyers and sellers.

Figure 14 shows a market that is in equilibrium when price is $9 and output is 400 units. Because the market supply curve begins at $5, the first unit can be coaxed out of some supplier by paying just $5; any price less than $5 would result in a zero output. To coax the 100th unit out of another supplier, a price of $6 must be paid; to elicit the 400th unit requires a price of $9. Although the market price is $9, some production of this good would have occurred even at a price less than $9. Those firms that would have been willing to supply the good at lower prices obtain a surplus return when the market price is $9. The supplier of the first unit receives a surplus of $4 (= $9 − $5); the supplier of the 100th unit, a surplus of $3 (= $9 − $6). The total surplus obtained by the suppliers of this good equals the area of the triangle *ceb.* Alfred Marshall, the great nineteenth-century British economist, called this area above the supply curve and below the price the **producers' surplus.** In the case of a constant-cost industry in the short run, producers' surplus is simply the revenue in excess of variable cost, summed over all firms.[5]

> **Producers' surplus** represents the amount that producers receive in excess of the minimum value the producers would have been willing to accept.

In Figure 14, when the market price is $9, producers' surplus is the area *ceb,* which equals $800.

The concept of producers' surplus is similar to the concept of **consumers' surplus** discussed in an earlier chapter.

> **Consumers' surplus** represents the consumer benefits (the dollar value of total utility) from consuming a good in excess of the dollar expenditure on the good.

[5]In the long run, producers' surplus is zero for a constant-cost industry. For an increasing-cost industry, in the long run, producers' surplus should be thought of as the sum of all the economic rents earned by all the factors employed in the industry.

FIGURE 14
The Gains from Trade

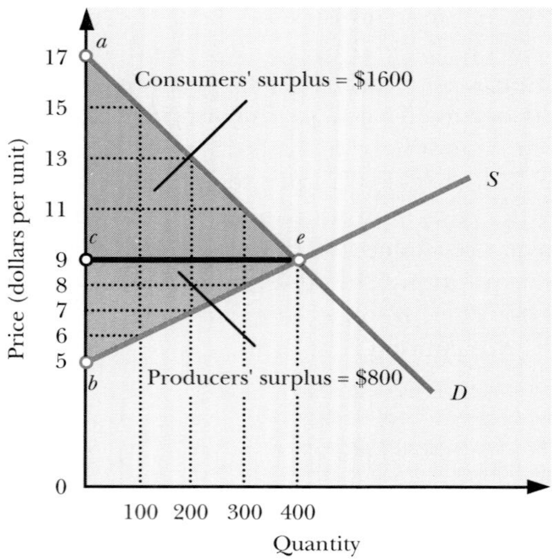

When the price is \$9, producers' surplus is the area *ceb*, and consumers' surplus is the area *cea*. The first unit is worth \$17 to buyers and costs \$5; it yields a gain of \$12 to society from trade. All 400 units of output at the \$9 price are worth the sum of the consumers' surplus and the producers' surplus, or area *aeb*. The total of consumers' and producers' surplus is \$2400 (area of triangle $aeb = \frac{1}{2} \times$ base $\times$ height $= \frac{1}{2} \times \$12 \times 400 = \$2400$).

In Figure 14, when the market price is \$9, the consumer surplus is the area *aec*, which equals \$1600.

What is the value of a market? In Figure 14, the first unit is worth \$17 to some consumer because the demand curve intersects the vertical axis at \$17. The first unit can be coaxed out of some producer for \$5. Thus, the first unit is worth approximately \$12 to society [(\$17 − \$9) + (\$9 − \$5)]. This \$12 that is gained from trade is shared by the supplier who values the first unit at only \$5 and the buyer who values the first unit at \$17. Similarly, the 100th unit is worth \$15 to some buyer and \$6 to some supplier, yielding a net gain of \$9 [(\$15 − \$9) + (\$9 − \$6)] at a market price of \$9. The 400th unit squeezes out all the gains from trade.

The value of the market, or the benefit of trade or voluntary exchange, to the economy is measured by the sum of producers' and consumers' surplus. Because the consumers' surplus aec = \$1600 and the producers' surplus ceb = \$800, society's net gain in the market illustrated in Figure 14 is \$2400. The triangle area *aeb* can be interpreted as the potential loss to society if this market were eliminated.

In the real world, the gains from trade are enormous. Through the mechanism of the market, people can specialize in the production of certain goods and trade them for resources that can, in turn, be traded for a wider variety of goods. The benefits of such specialization are represented by the triangle formed by the combination of the producers' and consumers' surpluses in each market. (This triangle is bounded by the demand curve to the left of the equilibrium quantity, by the supply curve to the left of the equilibrium quantity, and by the vertical axis).

Competitive markets coordinate the specialization of different economic units and ensure that goods will be produced at minimum average cost, provided that the mechanism of entry and exit is allowed to operate.

PERFECT COMPETITION IN THE REAL WORLD

Approximating the Conditions for Perfect Competition

Most industries are not perfectly competitive, but the conditions of perfect competition are met in a number of markets. Most agricultural markets—fibers, grains, livestock, vegetables, fruits—are perfectly competitive. Stock markets and commodity markets are also perfectly competitive. More important than these purely competitive markets are industries that closely *approximate* the conditions of perfect competition. In such industries, the number of producers may not be large enough to make each firm a perfect price taker, but the degree of control over price may be negligible. Information on prices and product quality may not be perfect, but consumers may have a significant amount of that information at their disposal. The product may not be perfectly homogeneous, but the distinctions between products may be inconsequential. The number of firms in the industry may not be exceptionally large, but many firms may be waiting in the wings to enter on short notice if economic profits are earned. An industry need not meet all the conditions of perfect competition for the theory of perfect competition to apply to its business behavior.

World Trade and Competition

The growth of world trade has ushered in a new era of competition. From 1970 to 1992, for example, world trade increased by more than 6 percent per year, about twice the growth rate of economic activity in general. For the most part, this high growth rate has resulted from the dismantling of barriers to international competition. Three important forces have been at work. First, explicit trade barriers such as tariffs and quotas have been relaxed by many countries. Second, international communications are now much cheaper due to the development of satellite technology, which allows telephone, television, and radio transmissions to be beamed almost anywhere in the world. Third, computer technology now makes it possible for companies to monitor developments all over the world. Consequently, firms in many countries are facing increasing competition in auto, TV, videocassette recorder (VCR), clothing, shoe, and hundreds of other industries.

> Increasing international competition in the last several decades has probably expanded the number of industries to which the perfectly competitive model is applicable.

For example, although there are only three major automobile manufacturers in the United States, they must compete against rivals located in Brazil, Japan, Germany, France, Italy, and Korea for customers throughout the world. Likewise, restaurants in Paris and Tokyo must compete for customers with McDonalds and Burger King.

A FINAL OVERVIEW

The theory of perfect competition tells us that economic profits will be eliminated in the long run by the entry of new firms and that when the markets are in equilibrium, price and marginal cost will be equal. It also states that short-run behavior will differ from long-run behavior. In the short run, firms will stay in business as long as the price covers average variable cost; in the long run, if the price fails to cover average costs (remember that in the long run there are no fixed costs), firms will leave the industry. In the short run, demand increases will lead to price increases; in the long run, the price will ultimately depend upon the costs of the representative firm. Finally, the theory tells us that extraordinary earnings can persist in the long run in competitive markets but that these earnings will be rental returns to the owners of scarce factors, not economic profit.

Two of the most important characteristics of perfectly competitive industries are (1) that perfectly competitive firms will operate at minimum average cost in the long run and (2) that perfectly competitive firms will produce that quantity of output at which price equals marginal cost in both the short run and the long run. These characteristics are important to remember when you evaluate the other types of markets—monopoly, oligopoly, and monopolistic competition—that will be studied in subsequent chapters. The next chapter will examine the behavior of firms that are able to exercise some control over price. Monopolists exercise considerable control over their prices; monopolistically competitive firms have only limited control over their prices.

SUMMARY

1. A market is perfectly competitive when it contains a large number of sellers and buyers, when buyers and sellers have perfect information, when the product is homogeneous, and when there is freedom of entry and exit. These conditions ensure that each seller will be a price taker. The price will be dictated to sellers by the market.

2. In the short run, the number of firms in an industry is constant, and the firm has fixed costs. In the long run, the number of firms can change through entry and exit, and fixed costs become variable costs. Profit-maximizing competitive enterprises face two decisions in the short run: first, whether or not to shut down; second, how much to produce, provided the enterprise does not shut down. If the market price covers average variable cost, the competitive firm will produce a positive level of output, the quantity at which price and marginal cost are

equal. The firm's supply curve is its marginal cost curve above average variable cost. The industry supply schedule is the horizontal summation of all the supply schedules of individual firms in the industry. The price at which the quantity supplied equals the quantity demanded is the market price. Each firm takes this market price as given.

3. In the long run, firms enter competitive industries where economic profits are being made and exit from industries where a below-normal profit is being earned. Economic profits must be zero for the competitive industry to be in equilibrium. In the long run, goods are produced at minimum average cost, with price equal to marginal cost for the average competitive firm. Returns to scarce factors of production like land or managerial skills are categorized as economic rents and are not included in economic profits.

4. The sum of consumers' surplus and producers' surplus represents the gain from voluntary exchange or trade.

5. The theory of perfect competition can explain the behavior of firms in an industry even when that industry does not meet all the conditions of perfect competition. The growth of world trade has ushered in a new era of international competition.

KEY TERMS

price taker
perfect competition
economic profits
normal profit
shutdown rule
marginal revenue (MR)
profit-maximization rule
industry or market supply curve
long-run industry supply curve
constant-cost industry
increasing-cost industry
producers' surplus
consumers' surplus

QUESTIONS AND PROBLEMS

1. Explain why each firm may not be a price taker in an industry in which there is product differentiation among firms.
2. A firm that is contemplating whether to produce its tenth unit of output finds its marginal costs for the tenth unit are $50 and its marginal revenue for the tenth unit equals $30. What advice would you give this firm?
3. A firm has fixed costs of $100,000. It receives a price of $25 for each unit of output. Average variable costs are lowest (equal to $20) at 1000 units of output. What advice would you give this firm in the short run? In the long run?
4. Explain the relationships between accounting profits, normal profits, and economic profits. Will they always be different amounts?
5. The representative firm in the widget industry, which is perfectly competitive, is making a large economic profit. What predictions can you make about what will happen in this industry in the long run?
6. Evaluate the following statement: "The theory of perfect competition claims that economic profits will disappear in the long run. This assumption is incorrect because I know a family that has a farm that earns more than $1 million per year."
7. What is the difference between a constant-cost industry and constant returns to scale (where the long-run average cost curve is horizontal)?
8. Jones is a genius at farming, knowing exactly what to plant and when. As a result, Jones's farm consistently earns higher profits than other farms. From the economist's perspective, do these represent higher profits or something else?
9. In Table 2, fixed costs are $48. If fixed costs were raised to $100, how would the supply schedule be affected in the short run? In the long run?
10. Imagine that a firm faces the cost schedule given in Table A.

TABLE A

Quantity, Q	Variable Cost, VC	Fixed Cost, FC	Total Cost, TC
0	$ 0	$5	$ 5
1	6	5	11
2	14	5	19
3	24	5	29
4	36	5	41

a. Calculate the firm's profit or loss for each level of output when the price is $5.99, when the price is $6.01, and when the price is $10.01.

b. Calculate how many units of output the profit-maximizing or loss-minimizing firm will produce at each of those three prices.

c. Graph the firm's supply schedule.

11. You observe that the (competitive) airline industry is incurring economic losses. What do you expect to happen to ticket prices, to the quantity of airline passengers, and to the number of airline companies as time passes?

12. You observe that a highly profitable new industry is manufacturing a product of advanced technology (such as computers). What do you expect to happen to the price of the product, to profits, to the industry's output, and to the number of firms as time passes?

13. Explain why, in the long run, the industry supply curve is perfectly horizontal in the case of a constant-cost industry.

14. What is the key difference between a constant-cost industry and an increasing-cost industry?

15. The long-run elasticity of supply for cucumbers has been estimated to be 2.20. Is the cucumber industry a constant-cost industry? Explain.

16. If dry cleaning is a constant-cost industry, what would you expect to happen to the price of dry cleaning in a particular town in both the short run and the long run as the size of the town increases?

SUGGESTED READINGS

Denzau, Arthur, *Microeconomic Analysis: Markets and Dynamics*. Homewood, IL: Irwin, 1992, chap. 17.

Kirzner, Israel. *Competition and Entrepreneurship*. Chicago: University of Chicago Press, 1978.

Weiss, Leonard. *Case Studies in American Industry*. New York: John Wiley, 1971, chap. 2.

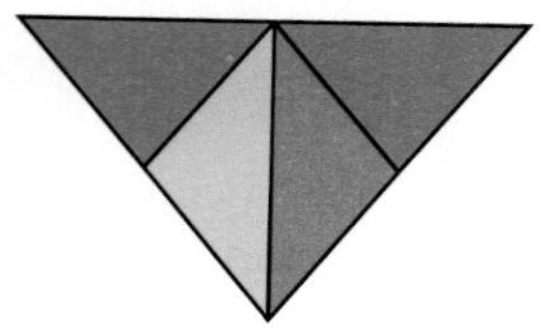

31 Monopoly and Monopolistic Competition

CHAPTER INSIGHT

For 60 years, the production and sale of beluga caviar were controlled by a secret monopoly arrangement between the Soviet Ministry of Fisheries and the Paris-based Petrossian S.A. company. The Petrossian family split profits from foreign sales of beluga with Soviet authorities, who placed strict limits on the quantity available for export. Although the annual catch was 2000 tons of caviar, Soviet authorities allowed only 150 tons to be sold abroad. In 1990, the Petrossian restaurant in Manhattan sold its best beluga caviar for $1000 per pound. The breakup of the Soviet Union in 1991 ended the caviar monopoly by multiplying the number of suppliers. Thus, in 1991 the official export price of beluga caviar fell 20 percent.[1]

This chapter examines monopoly and monopolistic competition. It explains how monopoly enterprises influence the price of goods by controlling the quantity offered to the market. Monopolies are price searchers, seeking out the price/quantity combination that maximizes profit. This chapter also analyzes the operation of firms under monopolistic competition, in markets with a large number of competitors and a limited control over price.

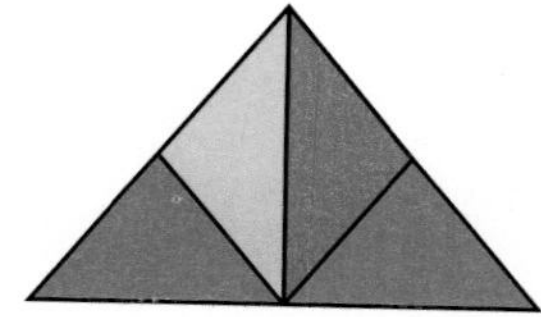

CONDITIONS FOR MONOPOLY

Monopoly literally means "single seller." A **pure monopoly** has the following characteristics.

> A **pure monopoly** exists when
> 1. There is one seller in the market for some good or service that has no close substitutes.
> 2. Barriers to entry protect the seller from competition.

Like perfect competition, examples of pure monopoly are rare, but the theory of pure monopoly does shed light on the behavior of firms that approximate the conditions of pure monopoly. (See Example 1.) Monopoly power allows the seller to have some control over the price of the product and is possessed to some degree by many firms. For example, a certain corner at a busy intersection may be the best spot in a town for a service station, giving one firm a locational monopoly at that spot.

Why Monopoly Is Rarely Pure

The rarity of pure monopoly stems from several sources. First, some kind of substitute exists for almost every product. Trucking can replace railroad freight; national magazines and TV news substitute for local newspapers, and stainless steel and copper substitute for aluminum. A pure monopoly requires that there be no good substitutes, but where does one draw the line between good and poor substitutes?

Second, a sole supplier in a particular market may not act like a pure monopolist if it fears the entry of rival firms. If the monopolist's economic profits become too high, rivals may find ways to overcome existing barriers to entry.

[1] "Horrors! Fine Caviar Now Could Become Cheap as Fish Eggs," *Wall Street Journal* (November 18, 1991).

Barriers to Entry

The basic source of pure monopoly is the presence of *barriers to entry*. The main barriers are:

1. Economies of scale
2. Economies of scope
3. Patents
4. Exclusive ownership of raw materials
5. Public franchises
6. Licensing

Economies of Scale. New firms have less production capacity than do established firms. If the industry is characterized by economies of scale, new firms will have higher average costs than established firms, thus inhibiting their entry. A *natural monopoly* occurs when economies of scale are so large that there is room for only one firm in the industry. Competition is either impossible or highly inefficient. Examples of apparent natural monopolies are the local public utilities that deliver telephone, gas, water, and electric service.

Economies of Scope. Sometimes it is cheaper to produce two related products in a single firm rather than in two separate firms. Cars and trucks, for example, use common inputs such as technical knowledge, engines, transmissions, and so forth. Thus, Ford, General Motors, and other major motor vehicle manufacturers produce both cars and trucks. Such **economies of scope**—like economies of scale—require firms to have a large size and capital investment, creating a barrier to entry.

> **Economies of scope** exist when it is cheaper to produce products A and B in the same firm than in two separate firms.

The automobile industry is not a natural monopoly. But it has been argued that cable television may be a natural monopoly due to economies of scope. Once one channel is made available, the cost of providing the subscriber others is trivial. The major cost is laying the cable and installing satellite dishes. (Example 4 in the following chapter examines the possibility of competition in the cable TV industry.)

Patents. American *patent* laws allow an inventor the exclusive right to use the invention for a period of 17

EXAMPLE 1 The Original Bell Telephone Monopoly

The key characteristic of a monopoly is its ability to charge a price much higher than its average costs. The original Bell patents on the telephone provided the American Telephone and Telegraph Company (AT&T) with a monopoly from 1877 to 1894. Consequently, telephone service was extremely expensive. The cost of basic telephone service for a residential customer was about 5 percent of a typical worker's wage. Today, basic local service costs less than 1 percent of a typical worker's wage.

The effect of competition on prices is illustrated by the events that occurred when the Bell patents expired in 1894. From 1894 to 1900, almost 2,000 new non-Bell telephone systems sprang up around the country. The number of telephones in the United States skyrocketed, from 240,000 in 1894 to over 6 million in 1907. In those areas where a Bell company competed with a non-Bell company, the price of basic telephone service dropped by about one-half. Bell's profits on stockholder equity plunged from a monopoly level of around 46 percent to about 8 percent.

Source: Gerald Brock, *The Telecommunications Industry* (Cambridge, MA: Harvard University Press, 1981).

years. The patent holder is thereby protected from competition during that period. The IBM Corporation's patents on tabulating equipment, Xerox's patents on copying equipment, and Smith Kline's patent on the drug Tagamet are examples of this type of entry barrier. The Bell System achieved a monopoly in the nineteenth century when Alexander Graham Bell obtained a patent for the telephone just hours before a rival inventor.

Exclusive Ownership of Raw Materials. Established companies may be protected from the entry of new firms by their control of raw materials. The International Nickel Company of Canada once owned almost all of the world's nickel reserves. Virtually all of the world's diamond mines are under the control of the DeBeers Company of South Africa. American Metal Climax Corporation controls most of the world's supply of molybdenum (a metallic element used in strengthening and hardening steel).

Public Franchises. State, local, and federal governments grant to individuals or organizations exclusive *franchises* to be the sole operator in a particular business. Competitors are legally prohibited from entering the market. The U.S. Postal Service is a classic example of a public franchise. States grant exclusive franchises to operate restaurants and service stations along tollways. Duty-free shops in airports and at international borders are also franchise operations. Many public utilities operate under state or local franchises.

Licensing. Entry into an industry or profession may be regulated by government agencies and autonomous professional organizations. The American Medical Association licenses medical schools and allocates hospital/staff privileges to physicians. The Federal Communications Commission licenses radio and television stations and controls entry into the lucrative broadcasting industry. Most countries license airlines and, thus, limit entry into the industry. In the United States, nuclear power plants must be licensed by the federal government.

PRICE-SEARCHING BEHAVIOR

The most fundamental difference between monopoly and perfect competition lies in the determination of price. The perfectly competitive firm is a *price taker;* it must accept whatever price the market dictates. The monopolist, however, is a **price searcher;** it has its own market demand curve along which it seeks the profit-maximizing price. Such price-searching behavior is not restricted to pure monopolies. Even the local grocery store has some ability to set a price that maximizes profit.

FIGURE 1
Price Searching versus Price Taking

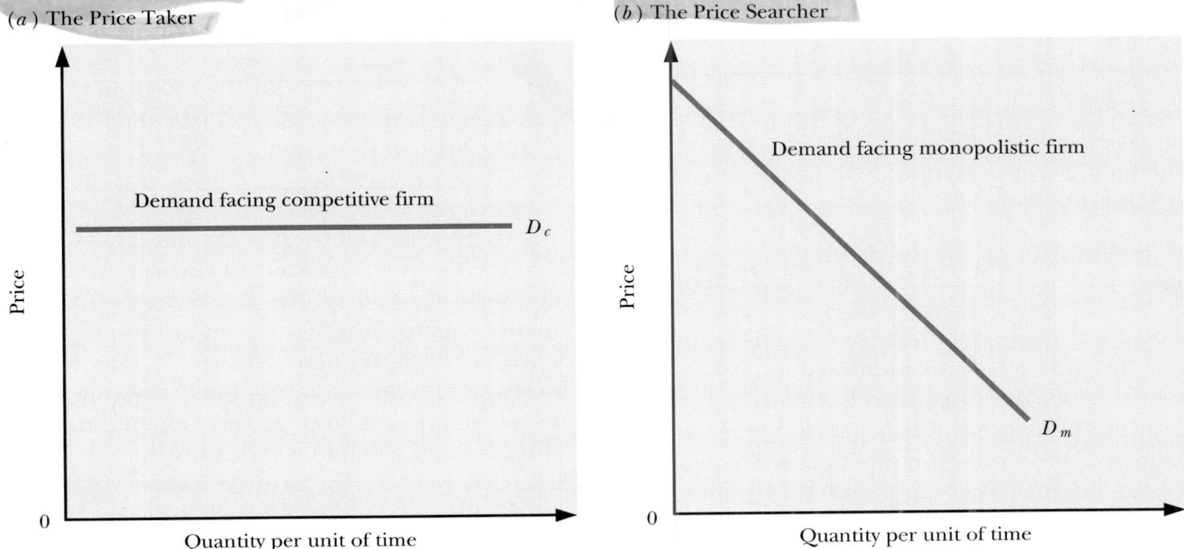

In panel *a*, the demand curve D_c facing the competitive firm is perfectly horizontal, meaning that the firm can sell as many additional units as it wants without lowering its price. In panel *b*, the demand curve D_m facing the monopolistic firm is downward sloping, meaning that the firm must lower its price in order to sell additional units.

A **price searcher** is a firm with some degree of control over the price of the good or service it sells.

The behavior of each price-searching firm is governed by certain general principles. First, *a price searcher faces a downward-sloping demand curve.* Unlike the perfect competitor, the price searcher cannot sell all it wants at the going market price. For the firm to sell more, it must lower the price of the product; if it raises its price, it will sell less.

Price searchers are sometimes called *price makers* because they have the power to set their own price. Indeed, if a firm is a monopoly, the term price maker is probably more accurate. If, however, the firm has only a small amount of monopoly power, the term *price searcher* seems more appropriate. The term price searcher is preferred by many economists because it has a neutral connotation regarding the extent of market power and it describes the actual process by which monopolists find the optimal price.

Figure 1 illustrates the difference between price takers and price searchers. The price taker's demand curve is perfectly elastic because the price is dictated by the market and more units can be sold without lowering the price. In contrast, the price-searching firm must lower its price on all units sold in order to sell more. If the revenue gains from selling one more unit of output outweigh the revenue losses of lower prices, the firm's **marginal revenue (MR)** will be positive.

Marginal revenue (MR) is the additional revenue raised per unit increase in quantity sold.

Like price takers, price searchers want to maximize profits by producing that level of output at which marginal revenue (MR) and marginal cost (MC) are equal. For the price taker, however, price equals marginal revenue; for the price searcher, price does not.

Price in Relation to Marginal Revenue

The perfect competitor can always sell additional output at the going market price.

> For a perfect competitor, because price is constant at every level of output, the extra revenue from selling one more unit (MR) is equal to the market price:
>
> $P = \text{MR}$

For the price searcher, price exceeds marginal revenue. In order to sell an additional unit of output per sales period, the price searcher must lower the price on the units previously sold at a higher price. Thus, the extra revenue generated per period equals the (new) price of the extra unit sold minus the revenue lost due to the lower price for the previous quantity of output.

> For a price searcher, because the price for all units must decrease to sell one more unit, price is greater than marginal revenue:
>
> $P > \text{MR}$

For example, suppose a price searcher faces a demand schedule in which 1 unit per week can be sold if the price is \$19; 2 units can be sold if the price is \$17. The total revenue generated is the number of units multiplied by the price per unit for that quantity. When 1 unit is sold, revenue is \$19 (= \$19 × 1); when 2 units are sold, revenue is \$34 (= \$17 × 2). The marginal revenue of a change in output from 1 to 2 units is \$34 − \$19 = \$15. Why is the marginal revenue of the second unit (\$15) less than the price for the second unit (\$17)? To sell two units per week, the firm must lower the price of the first unit from \$19 to \$17. The firm gains \$17 in revenue on the sale of the second unit but loses \$2 on the sale of the first unit. Hence, the marginal revenue of the second unit is \$17 − \$2 = \$15. In effect, selling 1 more unit "spoils the market" on the first unit because the price falls.

There is another way to explain why price exceeds marginal revenue. The chapter on productivity and costs described the relationship between average and marginal values. Recall that an average value falls if the marginal value is smaller than the previous average. This relationship can be extended to **average revenue (AR)** and marginal revenue (MR).

> **Average revenue (AR)** equals total revenue (TR) divided by output.

In general, TR = $P \times Q$, and TR = AR × Q. Hence, AR and P amount to the same thing when all units are sold at the same price. To say that the price searcher faces a downward-sloping demand schedule is to say that AR, or P, falls as output increases. In this case, marginal revenue must be below the previous average revenue, pulling it down. Thus, if AR is declining, MR must be less than AR. Since AR = P, P must be greater than MR.

Marginal revenue per additional unit sold is measured by taking the ratio of the change in revenue to the change in total units sold brought about by the change in price: that is, $\text{MR} = \Delta R/\Delta Q$. It is not necessary to change the number of units by increments of only one unit, as in the foregoing examples. To illustrate, imagine that a producer of chocolates can sell 500 boxes at \$10 per box and 600 boxes at \$9 per box. At a price of \$10, the firm's revenue is \$5000; at a price of \$9, the firm's revenue is \$5400. The change in revenue is \$400 and the change in quantity sold is 100. Thus, the marginal revenue is MR = \$400 ÷ 100 = \$4. Again, notice that the marginal revenue of \$4 is less than the new \$9 price.

Just as the demand schedule shows prices (or average revenue) for different quantities, the **marginal-revenue schedule** shows the marginal revenues for different quantities.

> The **marginal revenue schedule** shows how marginal revenue changes as the quantity of output changes.

Columns 1 and 2 of Table 1 give the demand schedule facing a price-searching firm. Column 3 lists the total revenue produced at each level of output ($P \times Q$), and column 4 gives the marginal revenue schedule.

TABLE 1
Monopoly Equilibrium

Output (units), Q (1)	Price or Average Revenue, $P = AR$ (2)	Total Revenue, $TR = P \times Q$ (3) = (1) × (2)	Marginal Revenue, MR (4)	Total Cost, TC (5)	Marginal Cost, MC (6)	Profit = TR − TC (7) = (3) − (5)
0	$21	$ 0		$10		−$10
			$19		$10	
1	19	19	**17**	20	**$8**	−1
			15		6	
2	17	34	**13**	26	**7**	8
			11		8	
3	15	45	**9**	34	**9**	11
			7		10	
4	13	52	**5**	44	**11.5**	8
			3		13	
5	11	55	**1**	56	**14**	−1
			−1		15	
6	9	54	**−3**	70	**16**	−16
			−5		17	
7	7	49	**−7**	87	**18.5**	−38
			−9		20	
8	5	40	**−11**	107	**21**	−67
			−13		22	
9	3	27	**−14**	129	**23.5**	−102
			−15		25	
10	1	10		144		−134

This table shows the demand and marginal revenue schedules of a price searcher. The demand schedule is given in the first two columns. Because all customers are charged the same price, price and average revenue are the same. Total revenue, in column 3, equals $P \times Q$. Marginal revenue is the increase in total revenue brought about by increasing output by 1 unit. The monopolist's profit is maximized by producing 3 units of output, where profit equals $11. If the monopolist had attempted to produce 1 more unit of output, total revenue would have increased by $7 and costs would have increased by $10, so profit would have fallen by $3. If the monopolist had produced 1 less unit, total revenue would have fallen by $11 and costs would have fallen by $8, reducing profit by $3. The firm expands outputs as long as MC does not exceed MR. Each MC and MR figure in boldface is the average of the preceding and following values.

The values in column 4 that are positioned vertically between the rows correspond to the marginal revenue for each change in output level in Table 1. Each number that appears in boldface in column 4 represents the marginal revenue when output is increased from the preceding to the following value. For example, the marginal revenue at an output level of 2 units is calculated over output from the increase in units 1 to 3, which increases revenue by $26. Since MR is the increase in revenue divided by the increase in output, MR is $13 (= $26 ÷ 2).

The demand and marginal revenue schedules for the firm in Table 1 are graphed as demand and marginal revenue curves in Figure 2.[2] The negative slope of the firm's demand curve, labeled *D*, shows that the firm is a price searcher (it must lower price to sell more quantity).

[2]The advantage of using an MR curve rather than a numerical schedule is that from a graph MR can be read at or between different levels of output.

FIGURE 2
Demand, Marginal Revenue, and Elasticity

(*a*) Demand and Marginal Revenue

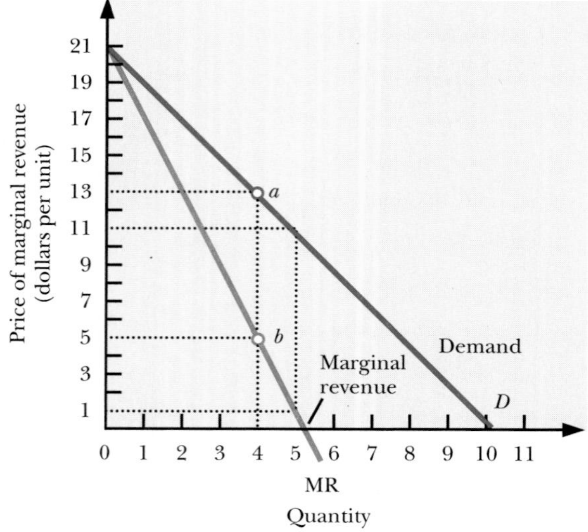

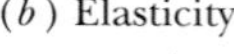

(*b*) Elasticity

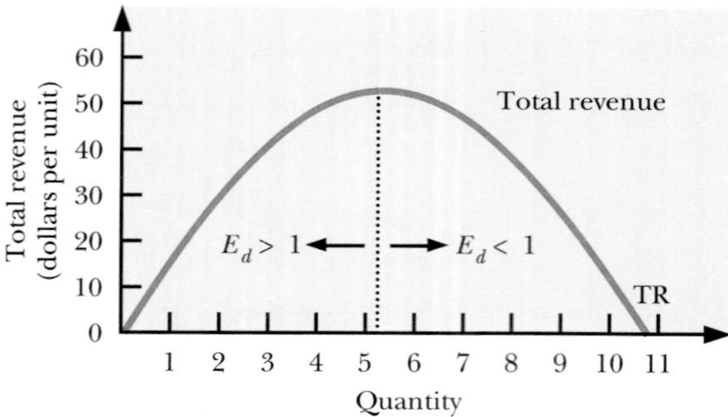

In panel *a*, the demand and marginal revenue schedules of Table 1 are plotted as *D* and MR. At an output level of 4 units, the price is $13 and the marginal revenue is $5. In other words, the value of MR for any given price is at that point on the MR curve directly below the point on the demand curve corresponding to that price. If the demand curve is a straight line, the marginal revenue curve will be located horizontally halfway between the demand curve and the vertical axis. In panel *b*, the total revenue schedule of Table 1 is plotted, showing the relationship between MR and total revenue. When MR is positive, total revenue is rising; when MR is negative, total revenue is falling; when MR is zero, total revenue reaches its highest value. When the price elasticity of demand (E_d) is greater than 1, total revenue is rising; when it is less than 1, total revenue is falling. Thus, when demand is elastic, reductions in price raise total revenue; when demand is inelastic, reductions in price lower total revenue.

The location of the MR curve below the demand curve shows graphically that price is greater than marginal revenue for any quantity of output (except for the first unit sold). Whenever the demand curve is a straight line, the MR curve will be horizontally halfway between the demand curve and the vertical axis because the slope of the MR curve is twice as steep as the slope of the demand curve. In Table 1, when price falls by $2, marginal revenue falls by $4. Accordingly, the marginal revenue curve intersects the horizontal axis halfway between the origin and the intersection of the straight-line demand curve with the horizontal axis, as shown in panel *a* of Figure 2. This relationship between the demand and marginal revenue curves is sometimes called the **halfway rule.**

> The **halfway rule** states that when the demand curve can be represented by a straight line, the marginal revenue curve bisects the horizontal distance between the demand curve and the vertical axis.

Marginal Revenue and Elasticity

Panel *b* of Figure 2 shows the behavior of total revenue ($P \times Q$) as output increases, graphing column's 1 and 3 of Table 1. Revenue increases as output rises, until the quantity of 5.25 units is attained; thereafter revenue decreases as output rises. The relationship between marginal revenue and total revenue is straightforward: When marginal revenue is positive, the total revenue curve is upward sloping; when marginal revenue is negative, the total revenue curve is downward sloping. Hence, the total revenue curve reaches its highest point when marginal revenue equals zero.

Whether marginal revenue is positive or negative for a given quantity depends on whether demand is elastic or inelastic at that point. Remember the total revenue test of elasticity from the chapter on the elasticity of demand and supply: *If demand is inelastic ($E_d < 1$), total revenue falls as price falls. If demand is elastic ($E_d > 1$), total revenue rises as price falls.* When demand is elastic, a reduction in price raises total revenue and marginal revenue is positive. When demand is inelastic, a reduction in price lowers total revenue and marginal revenue is negative.

Marginal revenue is positive when demand is elastic; marginal revenue is negative when demand is inelastic.

This rule indicates that a price searcher will always operate at a level of output where demand is elastic ($E_d > 1$). If the firm expands to the point where demand is inelastic, it will experience negative marginal revenue. Thus, profit-maximizing price searchers will not expand output into the inelastic range of their demand curve because an increase in output raises their costs as well as lowers their revenues.

The relationship between marginal revenue and elasticity is direct: For any given price, the higher is the elasticity of demand, the higher is the marginal revenue. In other words, if demand is highly price elastic, a given percentage increase in output can be sold with a proportionately smaller percentage reduction in price. Thus, the reduction in price on the previous units sold is relatively small, and marginal revenue is high (marginal revenue is close to price). The less elastic is the demand for a given price, the smaller is the marginal revenue. This means that if demand is highly price inelastic, a given percentage increase in output can be sold only with a proportionately larger percentage reduction in price. Thus, the reduction in price on previous units sold is relatively high, and marginal revenue is negative (marginal revenue is well below price).

All price-searching firms—be they monopolies, oligopolies, or monopolistic competitors—share three common characteristics:

1. For every price searcher facing a downward-sloping demand curve, $P >$ MR (except on the first unit sold) because the price must be lowered on previous units to sell additional units.
2. Marginal revenue is positive when demand is elastic; marginal revenue equals zero when the elasticity of demand is unity; marginal revenue is negative when demand is inelastic.
3. The higher is the elasticity of demand for a given price, the higher is the marginal revenue. The more elastic is the demand, the closer is marginal revenue to price.

MONOPOLY PROFITS

How Monopolies Determine Output

The monopolist is a special type of price searcher, distinguished from others by two characteristics. First, the monopolist is the sole producer of a product for which there are no close substitutes. Second, the monopolist is protected by barriers to entry.

The monopolist has a profit incentive to lower price and expand output when marginal revenue exceeds marginal cost. For example, if the marginal revenue of an additional unit of output is $10 and the marginal cost of the additional unit is only $6, the firm can add $4 to profit by producing the additional unit. Thus, the monopolist will cut prices when marginal revenue exceeds marginal costs.

If the monopolist finds that marginal revenue is less than marginal cost, it pays to lower output and raise price. If MC = $15 and MR = $9, a cut in output by 1 full unit would lower costs by $15 and revenue by only $9, so profits would rise by $6 (or losses would fall by $6). Thus, the monopolist maximizes profit by choosing an output level where marginal cost (MC) equals marginal revenue (MR).

The monopolistic firm can raise profit by expanding output (or by lowering price) when MR > MC. The firm can raise profit by cutting output (or by raising price) when MR < MC. The monopolist—or the price searcher in general—maximizes profit by producing that quantity for which MR = MC.

Table 1 gives cost schedules for the monopolistic firm that faced the demand and revenue schedules discussed in the previous section. Like the marginal revenue values in column 4, the values in column 6 that are positioned vertically *between* the rows correspond to the marginal cost for each change in output level. Again, each number in boldface is the marginal cost when output is increased from the preceding to the following value. What level of output will the monopolist choose to produce? Remember that the monopolist will expand output as long as marginal revenue exceeds marginal cost. The first unit of output raises total revenue by $19 (MR = $19) and raises costs by only $10 (MC = $10), thus contributing $9 toward paying the monopolist's $10 fixed cost

EXAMPLE 2 Choosing the Optimal Price: What Price a Cure for Baldness?

The Upjohn Company holds the patent to the drug Minoxydol, which in lotion form has been demonstrated to grow hair on balding patients. In those patients for which Minoxydol grows hair, treatment must be continued on a permanent basis, or else the hair will fall out. Following several years of safety tests, Upjohn intends to release Minoxydol for use as a cure for baldness.

In setting the price of Minoxydol lotion, Upjohn has had to consider the trade-off between a higher price and a smaller number of units sold. Although those who are losing their hair will be anxious to use this new drug, it is not a perfect cure. It is effective in only a minority of cases, and it tends to grow "peach fuzz" rather than thick hair. Persons in search of a cure for baldness can choose between a hair-growing solution, hair transplants, and a toupee. Because there are substitutes, the higher the price, the lower the sales. The price Upjohn has selected for Minoxydol is \$110 per bottle. A typical customer requires six bottles per year; so the annual cost of Minoxydol will be \$660. Upjohn has calculated that this price will maximize profits. If the price were set higher, profits would fall because revenue would fall faster than costs.

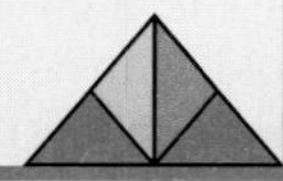

and reducing a \$10 loss at zero output to a \$1 loss at 1 unit of output. The second unit of output raises revenue by \$15 and adds \$6 to costs. The second unit, therefore, turns a \$1 loss into an \$8 profit. The third unit adds \$11 to revenue and \$8 to cost, adding \$3 to profit (now \$11). If the fourth unit were produced, only \$7 would be added to revenue but \$10 would be added to cost, decreasing profit by \$3. The monopolist should, therefore, produce 3 units of output. Profit is maximized at \$11, and MR = MC = \$9. (See Example 2.)

Once the monopolist selects an output level of 3 units, it will charge the price of \$15 dictated by the demand schedule. The monopolist can set either price or quantity. Once one is chosen, the other will be determined by the market demand schedule. Monopolists maximize profits *either* by selecting the profit-maximizing output level and letting the market set its price *or* by selecting the profit-maximizing price and letting the demand curve determine the quantity of output.

Figure 3 shows a graphical example of monopoly profit maximization. The demand schedule is graphed as the demand curve *D*; the marginal revenue schedule is graphed as curve MR. When output is 7000 units, marginal revenue exceeds marginal cost (point *m* is higher than point *n*), so profits rise if more than 7000 units are produced. When output is 10,000 units, marginal revenue is less than marginal cost (point *r* is lower than point *q*), so profits rise if fewer than 10,000 units are produced.

To maximize profit, the monopolist selects that output at which marginal revenue and marginal cost are equal. The MR and MC curves intersect at point *a*. The output level, price, and profit per unit of output can be determined by drawing a vertical line through *a*. Where the vertical line crosses the horizontal axis (at point *g*) is the monopolist's output level (8000 units). The price corresponding to the point where the vertical line intersects the demand curve (at point *c*) is the monopolist's price (\$10). Where the vertical line intersects the ATC curve (at point *b*) shows the average total cost of producing 8000 units (\$8). The distance between *c* and *b* (\$10 − \$8) represents the economic profit per unit of output (\$2). Total economic profit is, therefore, profit per unit times the number of units, or the blue area of the rectangle *cbed*. Algebraically, total economic profit = $(P - \text{ATC}) \times Q$ = (\$10 − \$8) × 8000 = \$16,000.

Monopoly Profits in the Long Run

When there is competition in an industry, the distinction between the short run and the long run

FIGURE 3
Monopoly Profit Maximization

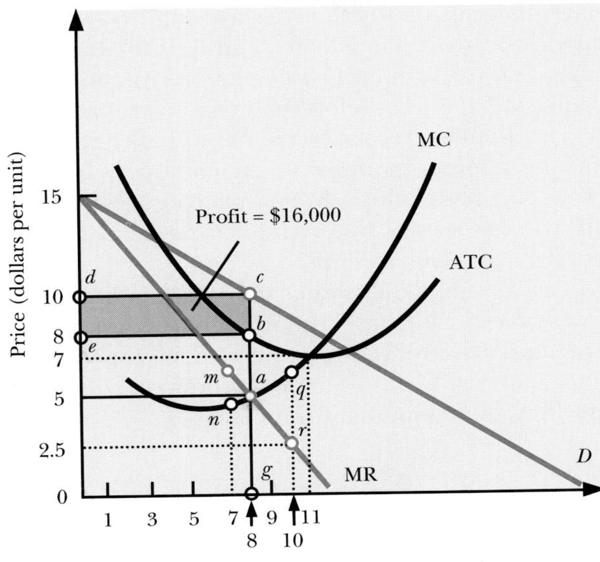

This monopolist has cost curves ATC and MC and faces demand curve *D*. Note that MC intersects ATC at its minimum point, where marginal cost and average total cost equal $7 and output is 11,000 units. However, the maximum profit occurs where MR = MC. The equilibrium price/quantity combination is found by drawing a vertical line from the demand curve through point *a*, where MR = MC, down to the horizontal axis. The output level represented by point *g*, where the vertical line hits the horizontal axis, gives the optimal output level (8000 units). The price corresponding to point *c*, where the vertical line hits the demand curve, is the optimal price ($8). Profits represented by the rectangle *cbed*, or the difference between price and ATC multiplied by the number of units ($\$2 \times 8000 = \$16,000$).

is critical. In the short run, the number of firms in the industry is fixed; in the long run, new firms can enter or old firms can exit in response to economic profits or losses. This long-run entry and exit of firms ensures that economic profits will be squeezed out of perfectly competitive industries. In the case of the monopolist, the distinction between the short run and the long run is not as important because barriers prevent new firms from entering the industry and systematically eliminating monopoly profits.

> Unlike competitive profits, monopoly profits can persist for long periods of time.

In the real world, it is difficult to find pure monopolies because actual or potential substitutes abound and because absolute barriers to entry are rarely present. Rather, most real-world monopolies are *near monopolies,* subject to the profit squeeze in the very long run, particularly if monopoly profits are exceptionally high.

Exceptional monopoly profits have historically inspired the development of closer substitutes for the monopolist's product. The railroads' monopoly over freight transportation was eventually broken by the emergence of trucking and air freight capabilities; the Bell System's monopoly over long-distance telephone service was broken by the advent of microwave transmission.

Although monopoly profits are systematically driven down to the normal return, there is a tendency for high monopoly profits to inspire the development of substitutes in the very long run. (See Example 3.)

So far we have considered monopolists that make a profit, but this need not be the case. Consider the monopolist pictured in Figure 4. The demand curve *D* passes between the average total cost (ATC) and the average variable cost (AVC) curves before it intersects the MC curve. In this example, the monopolist suffers a loss when producing at the 2000-unit output level where MR = MC because the price at 2000 units of output ($10) is less than the average total cost ($13). If this condition persisted in the long run, the monopolist would exit the industry.

FACTS ABOUT MONOPOLY

Our analysis sheds light on some basic facts concerning monopoly.

1. *Monopolists need not produce where average costs are minimized.* In the long run, perfectly competitive firms will be forced to produce that quantity of output at which average costs are minimized. Monopolists, however, both in the long run and in the short run, may produce a level of output that is smaller than or larger than the level necessary to minimize average costs. In Figure 3, average total cost is minimized at an

EXAMPLE 3 Intel's Microprocessor Monopoly

Intel Corporation's 80386 microprocessor is the chip of choice for IBM and IBM-compatible computers. Microprocessors are fingernail-sized wafers of silicon containing circuitry that functions as a personal computer's brain. Intel's virtual monopoly of the microprocessing industry stems from its Microcode patent, the strength of its brand-name identification (the 80386 name), and its reputation for technological innovation. Advances in processing speed and reductions in the cost of Intel's microprocessors have resulted in a steep drop in personal computer prices over the past decade.

Intel's monopoly is facing challenges on several fronts. First, Advanced Micro Devices has used reverse engineering to develop an 80386 clone with different circuitry that mimics the 80386. Second, Advanced Micro has received permission to call its reverse-engineered microprocessor the 80386. Third, Intel has been charged with antitrust violations by companies seeking to develop their own microprocessors. Intel has responded to these challenges with an attempt to maintain its monopoly by producing better chips. Its new microprocessor will run 51 percent faster and cost 34 percent less than previous versions.

This example illustrates the constant challenges faced by firms in monopoly positions. The most effective way to preserve a monopoly is to continually innovate and produce better products than potential competitors.

Source: "Intel is Facing New Challenges to its Microprocessor Monopoly," *Houston Chronicle* (November 13, 1990); "Intel Will Unveil Fast New Version of its 486 Chip," *Wall Street Journal* (June 24, 1991).

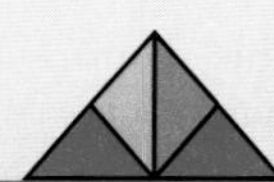

output of 11,000 units, but the monopolist produces only 8000 units. In this sense, monopolists are less efficient than perfectly competitive firms.

2. *Monopolists charge a price higher than marginal cost.* The monopolist equates marginal revenue and marginal cost, and price is greater than marginal revenue. Thus, in the case of monopoly, $P >$ MC.

3. *Monopolists produce where demand is elastic.* The profit-maximizing monopolist produces that quantity of output at which MR = MC. We have demonstrated that marginal revenue is positive only when demand is elastic. If the monopolist expanded into the inelastic portion of the demand schedule, total revenue would decline and the firm's profits would fall. This characteristic of monopoly pricing can be used as a partial test for the existence of monopoly behavior. If the demand for a product is inelastic at the current price, the seller is not behaving like a profit-maximizing monopoly.

4. *There is no supply curve for monopolists.* The monopolist supplies a certain quantity of output, given demand and cost conditions. The monopolist does not have a supply curve showing how much output will be supplied at different prices because marginal revenue, not price, determines the monopolist's optimal output. The same marginal revenue can be compatible with quite different prices, depending on the elasticity of demand.

MONOPOLISTIC COMPETITION

In reality, few price searchers are monopolies. Price searchers can be anything from a pure monopoly to a firm that bears a close resemblance to a perfect competitor. Their common characteristic is that they face a downward-sloping demand schedule for their product. In order to sell more, they must lower their price.

In the real world, there is usually some basis for distinguishing between the goods and services produced by different sellers. These distinctions may be based on the physical attributes of the product (hamburgers vary from restaurant to restaurant), on location (one gas station is more conveniently located than another), on the type of service offered (one dry cleaner offers 2-hour service; another offers

FIGURE 4
Monopoly Losses

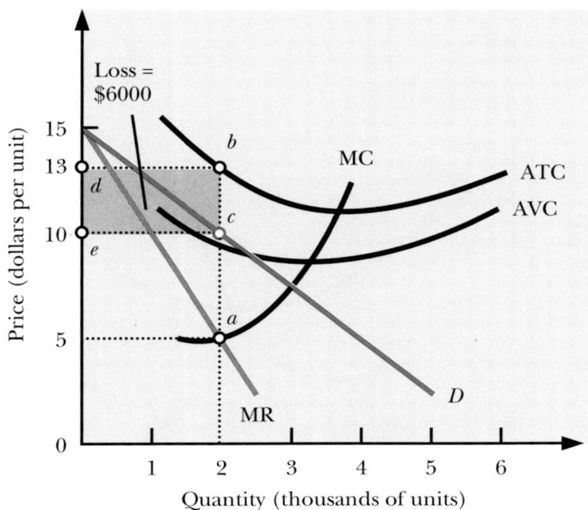

This monopolist minimizes losses (as long as price exceeds average variable cost) by producing 2000 units of output (where MC = MR). The monopolist must charge a price of $10 at an average total cost of $13. The monopolist loses $3 per unit of output for a total loss of $6000 (the rectangle *bced*).

1-day service), and even on imagined differences (one type of aspirin is "better" than another). The point is that there are differences among products. Sellers of each product have some monopoly power over the customers who have a preference for their product. The extent of their monopoly power depends upon the strength of this preference.

The theory of **monopolistic competition** was developed by the American economist Edward Chamberlin and the English economist Joan Robinson in order to describe markets that produce heterogeneous products. A monopolistically competitive industry is one that blends features of monopoly and competition.

The four essential characteristics of **monopolistic competition** are:

1. The number of sellers is large enough to enable each seller to act independently of the others
2. The product is differentiated from seller to seller
3. There is free entry into and exit from the industry
4. Sellers are price searchers

When sellers are acting independently, each presumes that its output or price decisions have no discernible effect on the rest of the market. Therefore, the monopolistic competitor need not worry about the reactions of rivals.

The price-searching characteristic follows from product differentiation; because products differ, the seller has some control over price. The degree of control may be quite limited, but it exists. The seller who raises the price will not lose all customers (as would the perfect competitor) because some will have such a strong preference that they will accept the higher price.

Profit Maximization by the Monopolistically Competitive Firm

To maximize profits, firms produce that quantity of output at which marginal revenue equals marginal cost. The monopolistic competitor is no exception to this rule. Like the monopolist, the monopolistic competitor faces a downward-sloping demand curve; marginal revenue is less than average revenue (price). It, therefore, selects the *quantity* at which marginal revenue equals marginal cost and charges the *price* that clears the market. Analytically, in the short run the theory of monopolistic competition is the same as the theory of the monopoly. The analysis of Table 1 and Figure 3 apply equally to monopolistic competition and monopoly in the short run.

Indeed, in the short run, the main difference between monopolistic competition and monopoly is the price elasticity facing the firm. Because a monopolistic competitor faces more competition from the substitute products of other firms in the industry, its price elasticity of demand will greatly exceed that of a typical monopolist.

In the long run, however, the two types of market organization are strikingly different. *Barriers to entry* protect the monopolist from competitors. The entry of new firms will not systematically squeeze out monopoly profits. Monopolistic competition, however, shares with perfect competition the characteristic of *freedom of entry*. Thus, if a monopolistic competitor earns economic profits in the short run, new firms can (and will) enter the market, gain access to those profits, and eventually drive them down to zero.

One example of a monopolistic competitor is a service station located on a busy intersection. It earns substantial economic profits in the short run. Like the monopolist, its price is greater than average total cost after equating marginal revenue and marginal cost. If the station were a monopolist (say, a gas station with an exclusive franchise along a tollway), new firms could not gain access to these profits, and the monopoly could continue to earn them for a long period of time. Not so with the monopolistic competitor.

In the long run, new firms can enter the monopolistically competitive market. Attracted by high profits, another service station can be built on the opposite corner of the intersection—a close but not perfect substitute. The two stations will differ in terms of access, number of gas pumps, friendliness of service, and operating hours. The entry of the second firm will have two effects on the demand schedule of the first: (1) When customers are attracted away from the first station, the demand schedule for its product will shift to the left. (2) Because buyers now have more substitutes for the product of the first station, its demand schedule will become more elastic. If both stations continue to make economic profits, even more gas stations will be built—perhaps one or two more at the same intersection. Each new entrant will reduce the demand facing other stations and increase its elasticity. As in the case of perfect competition, this adjustment process ends when economic profits have been eliminated.

The long-run equilibrium of a typical monopolistically competitive firm is shown in Figure 5. In the long run, new firms will enter until economic profits are driven down to zero. The relevant cost curve is the long-run average cost (LRAC) curve because revenue must cover costs in the long run. Graphically, profits equal zero at a point to the left of the lowest point on the LRAC curve, where the downward-sloping demand curve is tangent to the LRAC curve. In Figure 5, point *b*—where output is 600 units and price is $10—is the point of zero profits and, therefore, the point of long-run equilibrium. In Figure 5, 600 units is the quantity that equates marginal cost and marginal revenue, and $10 is the price that corresponds to 600

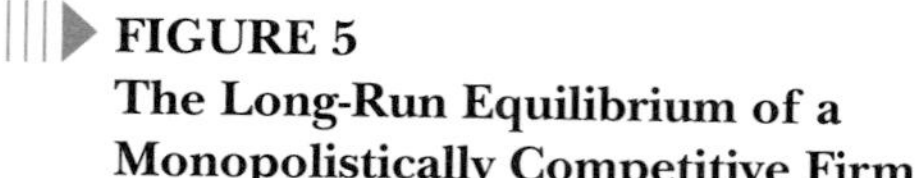

FIGURE 5
The Long-Run Equilibrium of a Monopolistically Competitive Firm

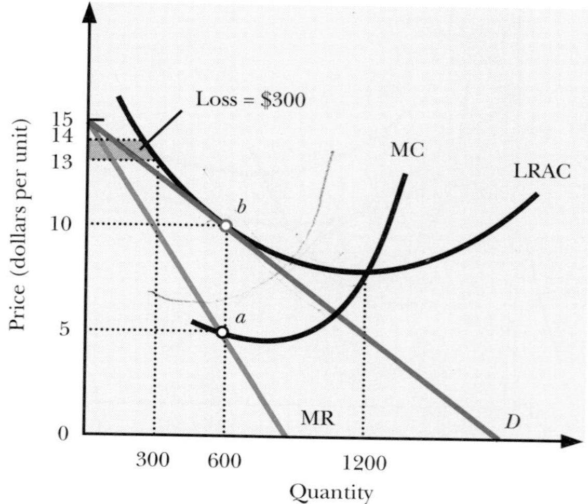

A firm engaged in monopolistic competition faces a downward-sloping demand curve such as *D*. In the long run, because of free entry, economic profits will be driven down to zero. Thus, the long-run equilibrium must be a point such as *b*, where *D* is just tangent to the LRAC curve. For any price other than $10, profits are negative. Profits, though equal to zero, are at a maximum when price is $10 and output is 600 units, indicating that marginal revenue must equal marginal cost at 600 units. Thus, the MC and MR curves must intersect directly below point *b*.

units on the demand curve. Therefore, point *b* is the point of maximum profit. Notice that because the demand curve is tangent to the LRAC curve at point *b*, price is less than long-run average cost to the left or to the right of point *b*. Thus, although profit is zero at point *b*, it is negative elsewhere. For example, at an output of 300 units, price is $13 and long-run average cost is $14, resulting in a loss of $1 per unit. We have already shown that profits are maximized where marginal cost equals marginal revenue. Accordingly, the MC and MR curves intersect directly below the tangency of the demand curve and LRAC curve at point *b*.

The minimum unit cost output, or optimum capacity, is clearly 1200 units in Figure 5 because at that output level, MC = LRAC. In long-run equilibrium, each firm in a monopolistically competitive industry will produce an output that is smaller than the optimal capacity. This smaller-than-optimal output results because the demand curve is downward sloping and tangent to the long-run average cost curve. Thus, there is *excess capacity,* making monopolistic competition less efficient than perfect competition. This need not mean that monopolistic competition is less socially desirable than perfect competition, since many regard such excess capacity as the price we must pay for variety.

Product Differentiation and Advertising

The threat of the entry of new firms and the loss of economic profits are facts of life for monopolistic competitors. If they can erect artificial barriers to entry (by exclusive government franchises, licensing, or zoning ordinances), they can delay the day when their economic profits are driven down to zero. Another tactic for protecting economic profits is to engage in **nonprice competition.** Since monopolistic competitors, by definition, produce goods and services that are somewhat different, if they can succeed in further differentiating their products from those of their competitors, they can gain loyalty. The stronger is this customer loyalty, the smaller will be the loss of customers as new firms enter and the less elastic will be the demand for a product.

Nonprice competition is the attempt to attract customers through improvements in product quality or service, thereby shifting the firm's demand curve to the right.

Advertising is frequently used to differentiate products in monopolistically competitive markets. In fact, nonprice competition can yield considerable short-run profits for a firm and offer potential long-run profits if new entrants cannot copy the nonprice attribute. Profits on some brand-name products, such as Bayer aspirin or Borden's condensed milk, have persisted for very long periods of time. In other cases, profits are transitory. If the gas station owner differentiates the product by staying open all night or by offering a free car wash with fill-ups, then competitors can do the same.

Market Size and Efficiency

Monopolistic competition has two important characteristics in common with perfect competition: freedom of entry and a large number of firms. In both types of markets, economic profits are driven down to zero in the long run. The major difference is that the product is homogeneous in the case of perfect competition and heterogeneous in the case of monopolistic competition. Monopolistic competition most closely approximates perfect competition *in large markets* that present consumers with a choice among many close substitutes.

Consider, for example, the large monopolistically competitive market constituted by service stations in a large metropolitan area. This market differs from service stations in a small market (such as a small town) by the variation in the kinds of service available at any given station: convenient location, self-service pumps, car repairs, automatic car wash, long hours of operation.

In a small town, the service station may be the only place that offers some of these services. In a large city, each service station faces far more competition. There are stations that specialize in car repair, car washing, or automobile service. In the large market, close substitutes are more widely available; the large number of service stations and specialist firms makes the demand curve for the product of any one service station quite elastic. In the small market, because each service station faces less competition from close substitutes, the demand curve for the product of any one service station is less elastic.

In large markets, the distinction between monopolistic competition and perfect competition becomes less pronounced.

In Figure 6, the small-town demand curve D is steeper (and less elastic) than the big-city demand curve D'. The small-market, long-run equilibrium occurs at point b, where price is $1.10 per gallon and output is 500 gallons. The large-market, long-run equilibrium occurs at b', where price is $0.90 and output is 800 gallons. If the large market continues to grow and the distinctions between the products of the different firms become negligible, eventually the demand curve will become perfectly elastic (D''). The market will become perfectly competitive, producing

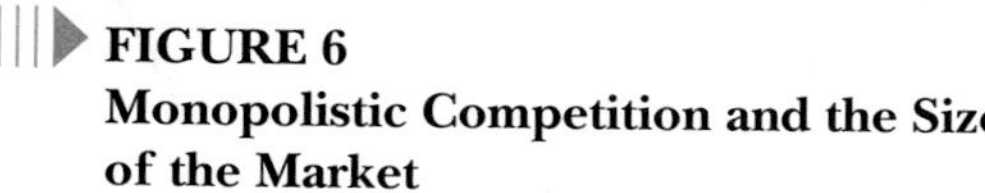

FIGURE 6
Monopolistic Competition and the Size of the Market

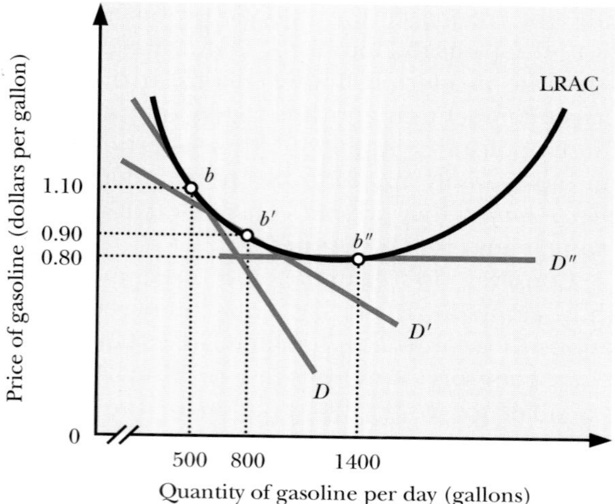

With a larger market for gasoline (more buyers), the demand curve is flatter because a smaller price cut is necessary to sell 1 more unit of the product. Thus, D' corresponds to the demand curve for a larger market than the market with demand curve D. Because in the long run profits are zero in monopolistic competition, a larger market brings with it a smaller price (b' as opposed to b) and a greater exploitation of economies of scale within the individual firm. The bigger is the market, the closer is the monopolistically competitive equilibrium to the perfectly competitive (long-run) equilibrium, illustrated by the horizontal demand curve D''.

in the long run an output of 1400 gallons at a price of $0.80 per gallon.

APPLICATIONS

The theories of monopoly and monopolistic competition explain a variety of behavior patterns exhibited by price-searching firms, including price discrimination, markup pricing, and discrepancies in product durability. These three examples, in particular, are accounted for by the theory of price searching, which holds that both monopolists and monopolistic competitors produce that quantity of output at which marginal revenue equals marginal cost.

Price Discrimination

Thus far, this chapter has assumed that the price searcher charges a single price to all buyers, but this is not always the case. Customers often pay different prices for the same product. Senior citizens typically pay less for movie tickets, airline fares, and sporting events; doctors and lawyers often charge wealthy clients more than poor clients. All of these situations are examples of **price discrimination.**[3]

> **Price discrimination** exists when the same product or service is sold at different prices to different buyers.

In order for firms to engage in price discrimination,

1. The seller must exercise some control over the price (price discrimination is possible only for price searchers).
2. The seller must be able to distinguish easily among different types of customers.
3. It must be impossible for one buyer to resell the product to other buyers.

If the firm is not a price searcher, it cannot control its price. The seller who cannot distinguish between customers will not know which buyers should be charged the lower price. The electric company meters electricity usage and can readily distinguish high-volume from low-volume users: doctors and lawyers can often identify wealthy clients on the basis of appearance, home address, and stated profession. If one buyer can sell to another, then low-price buyers can sell to high-price buyers and no one will be willing to pay the high price. Thus, poor clients cannot resell legal and medical services to the wealthy, and industrial users of electricity cannot sell their electricity to households.

If the foregoing conditions are met, the seller can divide the market into various noncompeting groups. A profit-maximizing seller will then charge prices according to the price elasticity of demand of each group. The higher is the price elasticity of

[3]For detailed discussions of price discrimination in the real world, see F. M. Scherer, *Industrial Market Structure and Economic Performance,* 2nd ed. (Boston: Houghton Mifflin, 1980), chap. 11; James V. Koch, *Industrial Organization and Price,* 2nd ed. (Englewood Cliffs, N.J.: Prentice-Hall, 1980), chap. 12.

demand, the lower will be the price charged. For example, if residential users of electricity have a more elastic demand for electricity than do industrial users, it pays the electric company to charge a higher price to industrial users.

To see how price discrimination raises profits, assume that the electric company initially charges the same price in both markets. Suppose that the demand of residential users is more price elastic than is the demand of industrial users. It is to the firm's advantage to lower the price to the more sensitive residential market segment and raise the price to the less sensitive industrial market segment. In terms of marginal revenue, such an adjustment will cause the electric company's marginal revenue from selling another unit to residential customers to exceed the marginal revenue lost from selling 1 less unit to industrial customers. Accordingly, it pays the firm to shift output from industrial users to residential users by raising the industrial price and lowering the residential price. The process of raising the price to the users with a low price elasticity of demand and lowering the price to users with a high price elasticity of demand continues until the firm earns the same marginal revenue in each market. Clearly, as long as marginal revenue differs between markets, it pays to reduce the quantity sold with a low marginal revenue and raise the quantity sold with a high marginal revenue. (See Example 4.)

Figure 7 graphs a specific case of price discrimination. Panel *a* shows the demand curve of residential users, D_R; panel *b* shows the demand curve of industrial users, D_I. The marginal revenue curve in panel *a* is MR_R and in panel *b* is MR_I. The marginal cost (MC) of a unit of electrical service is assumed to be $1 per 100 kilowatt hours.

The electric company equates marginal revenue and marginal cost in each market by charging $2 to residential users (whose price elasticity is 2) and by charging $3 to industrial users (whose price elasticity is 1.5). The $2 residential price corresponds to the output quantity that equates marginal cost and residential marginal revenue; the $3 industrial price corresponds to the output quantity that equates marginal cost and industrial marginal revenue. Thus, the monopolist exploits the differences in demand elasticities by charging different prices in order to earn more profit.

EXAMPLE 4 Price Discrimination: Manufacturers' Coupons

Grocery shoppers are familiar with manufacturers' coupons that arrive through the mail or can be clipped out of the daily newspaper. Economic theory explains why some manufacturers offer coupons and others do not. In effect, the holder of the coupon is entitled to buy the product at a lower price than others. If Nabisco places a coupon offering a 50-cent discount on one of their cereals in the daily newspaper, this means that a customer can buy the cereal at a lower price than other shoppers. Manufacturers' coupons are a form of price discrimination. The coupon issuer reasons as follows: Anyone taking the trouble to cut out the coupon has a higher elasticity of demand than other shoppers. Without the 50 cents off, many shoppers would not buy the cereal. The 50-cent reduction, therefore, brings about a substantial increase in quantity purchased from careful shoppers. Shoppers not taking the trouble to clip out the coupon have a lower price elasticity of demand. Their purchases are not strongly affected by the 50-cent price reduction. We have seen that price discrimination is possible only when the manufacturer has price-making power, when high-price elasticity customers can be identified, and when low-price buyers cannot resell the product. Manufacturers' coupons follow this pattern. Typically, manufacturers in highly concentrated markets (with only a few sellers), such as cereal or soap manufacturers, offer coupons. Such manufacturers exercise significant market power. Requiring coupons to obtain the lower price allows manufacturers to differentiate high-elasticity from low-elasticity customers. Although low-price buyers could theoretically sell to high-price buyers, the price difference usually is not great enough to yield this result.

FIGURE 7
Price Discrimination: Electricity

(*a*) The Residential Market

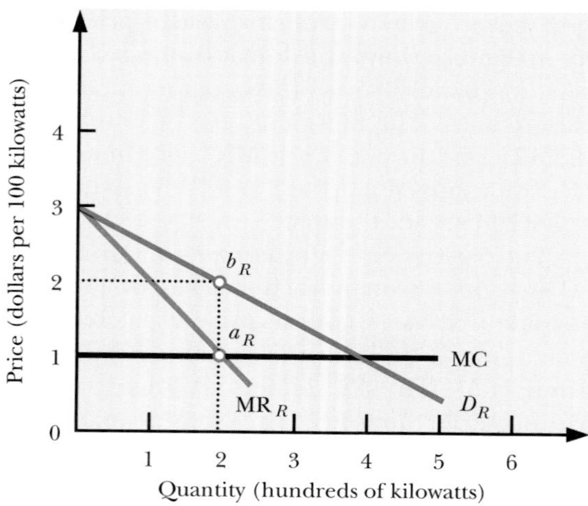

(*b*) The Industrial Market

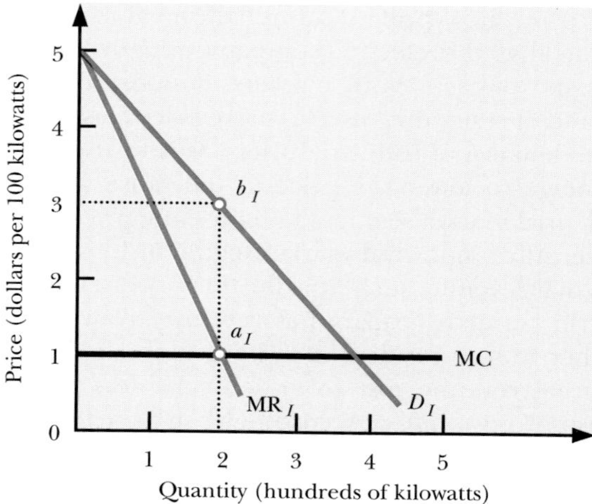

The demand and marginal revenue curves of residential customers are drawn as D_R and MR_R in panel *a*. They are more elastic than the demand and marginal revenue curves (D_I and MR_I) of industrial customers in panel *b*. The marginal cost of providing electricity is the same for industrial and residential customers and is constant at $1 per kilowatt. The electric company will maximize profits in each market by equating marginal revenue and marginal cost in each market. In the industrial market, MR = MC at a price of $3; in the residential market, MR = MC at a price of $2.

Markup Pricing

Retailers—supermarkets, drugstores, department stores, and specialty shops—are price searchers because they offer a service that is differentiated by location, hours of service, product lines, and friendliness of service. Retailers buy their goods at wholesale (from the producers) and sell them at higher retail prices; the percentage *markup* is the difference between the retail and wholesale prices divided by the wholesale price. Some products have high markups and other products, low markups. For example, in your local supermarket, school supplies have about a 50 percent markup, whereas coffee has a 10 percent markup. Economic theory explains why some products have higher markups than others.

As we know, a profit-maximizing firm sets prices to equate marginal revenue and marginal cost. Retailers can buy 1 more unit of the product at the wholesale price; therefore, neglecting handling costs, the wholesale price is the marginal cost to the retailer.

Figure 8 shows the demand curves for flour and envelopes facing individual supermarkets in a city. The price elasticity of demand for food staples (flour, sugar, vegetable oils) will be quite high to each supermarket. (Remember, the elasticity of demand facing a particular supermarket that must compete with other supermarkets is not the same as the elasticity of demand for an entire market.) Supermarkets compete among themselves for sales of such frequently purchased and well advertised items; slight changes in prices bring about large changes in sales.

The price elasticity of demand for discretionary items (envelopes, school supplies, beauty aids) will be less elastic to each supermarket. These items are purchased with less frequency; they are likely to be picked up because the shopper is already in the store; the shopper tends to be less aware of the prices of these items at competitive stores. Therefore, the demand curve for flour (D_F in Figure 8) is more elastic than the demand curve for envelopes (D_E) facing each store.

Assume that the marginal cost of flour (the wholesale price) is $0.20 and that the marginal cost of envelopes (also the wholesale price) is $0.20. The profit-maximizing supermarket manager will set prices to equate marginal revenue and marginal cost.

FIGURE 8
The Theory of Markup Pricing: Flour and Envelopes

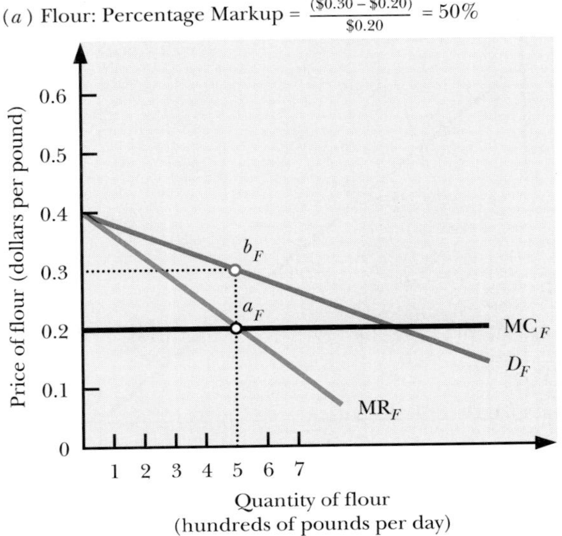

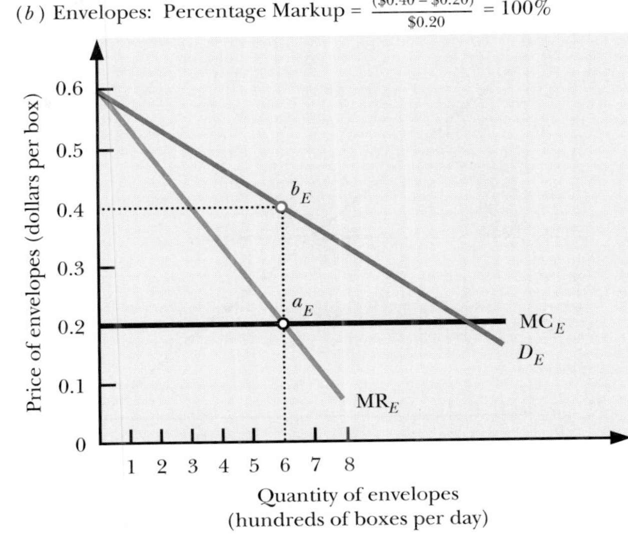

The demand for flour, D_F, facing the supermarket is elastic. The demand for envelopes, D_E, is less elastic. Because the supermarket maximizes profits by equating marginal revenue and marginal cost for each product, there will be a higher percentage markup for envelopes than for flour. Percentage markups tend to be higher the less elastic is the demand for the product.

In Figure 8, MR = MC at a price of $0.30 per pound for flour and a price of $0.40 per box for envelopes. The percentage markup is 50 percent for flour ([$0.30 – $0.20]/$0.20) and 100 percent for envelopes ([$0.40 – $0.20]/$0.20). Actual supermarket prices reveal that—as the theory predicts—the percentage markups of discretionary items tend to be higher than the percentage markups of staple items.[4]

> The percentage markup is negatively related to the elasticity of demand. If the price elasticity of demand is relatively high, the percentage markup will be small. If the price elasticity of demand is relatively low, the percentage markup will be high.

[4]For some examples, see "Emergence of Savvy Consumers Forces Painful Rethinking by Supermarkets," *Wall Street Journal* (September 29, 1980).

Product Durability

Do business firms suppress ways of increasing product durability in order to maintain long-run demand? How many of us have heard that there are tires that last twice as long, a lightbulb that lasts 10 years, more durable cars, motor oils that never have to be changed—but that these products have been suppressed to force consumers to buy less durable goods more often?

In fact, any monopolist would be happy to have lower costs of production. Imagine that a monopolist discovers a costless method of doubling the life of a lightbulb; that is, the monopoly learns that it can continue to produce a lightbulb for the same marginal cost, but the lightbulb will now last twice as many hours. Will the monopolist introduce the new lightbulbs? Clearly, this discovery would cut the cost of producing a *lightbulb hour* in half. This monopolist could increase its profits just by doubling the price of the (improved) product and cutting the output in half because the price of a lightbulb hour would remain the same. If the price of a 2-hour bulb were

FIGURE 9
Lightbulb Durability and Monopoly Profits

(*a*) 1 Lightbulb = 1 Lightbulb Hour

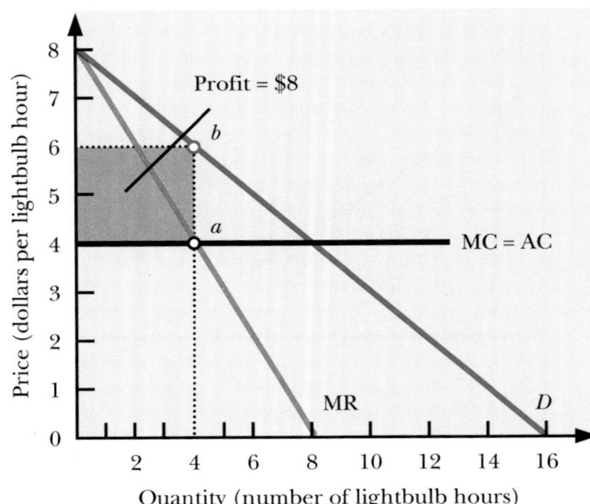

The demand curve *D* shows the demand for lightbulb hours (not lightbulbs). Panel *a* shows a situation where 1 lightbulb equals 1 lightbulb hour (each lightbulb burns only 1 hour). If the marginal cost of a lightbulb is $4, monopoly profits are maximized where output is 4 bulbs, where marginal revenue equals $4, and where price equals $6. Monopoly profits are $8. A costless doubling of lightbulb durability (to make 1 lightbulb burn 2 lightbulb hours) is shown in panel *b*. Marginal cost per lightbulb hour is now reduced to $2, but demand remains the same. The monopolist now maximizes profit at an output level of 6 lightbulb hours (= 3 bulbs). The monopoly price is now $5 per lightbulb hour, and monopoly profit equals $18.

twice the price of a 1-hour bulb, people could satisfy their demand by buying half as many lightbulbs each period as before. If the firm maintained the price of a lightbulb hour (by doubling the price of a lightbulb), the firm's profits would rise because revenue would stay the same while costs fell. As Figure 9 shows, however, the firm could do even better. Note that in Figure 9 everything is measured in terms of *lightbulb hours* rather than in terms of *lightbulbs.* Because the firm's marginal cost of producing lightbulb hours has fallen, it would pay the firm to reduce the price per lightbulb hour in order to equate marginal revenue and marginal cost. In Figure 9, the firm increases its profits by charging $5 per lightbulb hour ($10 per bulb) for its improved bulb.

Business firms do not extend the durability of more goods because of the cost involved. To produce a space vehicle with virtually no chance of breaking down costs millions of dollars; the cost could be reduced dramatically if all the backup systems and safety checks were eliminated. Similarly, to produce more durable cars requires certain trade-offs: either the car must have a higher price (like the Mercedes-Benz or Rolls-Royce), or other characteristics—such as style and handling performance—must be sacrificed (as in the Chevrolet).

This chapter has examined the price-seeking behavior of monopolists and monopolistic competitors. The chapter that follows will evaluate monopoly and monopolistic competition in relation to perfect competition. Characteristics that will be important in such a comparison include: (1) the fact that monopolists are not pressured to produce at minimum average cost in the long run and (2) the fact that price searchers do not equate marginal cost and price.

SUMMARY

1. A pure monopoly exists when a market contains only one seller producing a product that has no close substitutes. Barriers to entry keep out competitors. The monopolist is a price searcher with considerable control over price. Pure monopoly is rare in the real world due to the existence of substitutes and the absence of absolute barriers to entry, especially in the long run. Sources of monopoly

include economies of scale, economies of scope, patents, ownership of critical raw materials, public franchises, and licensing.

2. Price searchers face downward-sloping demand curves; they must lower their price in order to sell more. For price searchers, price exceeds marginal revenue. Marginal revenue is positive when demand is elastic; marginal revenue is negative when demand is inelastic.

3. Monopolists maximize profits by producing that output quantity at which marginal revenue and marginal cost are equal or by changing that price at which MR = MC.

4. Monopolists do not produce where price equals marginal cost. Monopolists need not produce in the long run where average costs are minimized. Monopolists produce where demand is elastic.

5. A monopolistically competitive industry has a large number of individual firms that are price searchers selling differentiated products, with freedom of entry and exit. Monopolistic competitors, like monopolists, produce where marginal revenue equals marginal cost. In the long run, the entry of new firms will drive profits down to zero. When profits are zero and MR = MC, the firm's output will be less than the minimum efficient scale; that is, unit costs are not minimized as in perfect competition. By engaging in nonprice competition—through product differentiation and advertising—monopolistically competitive firms can delay the disappearance of economic profits. In large markets, monopolistic competition approximates perfect competition.

6. Price searchers can raise their profits through price discrimination. Buyers with inelastic demand will pay higher prices than those with elastic demand. The practice of markup pricing is consistent with the MR = MC rule. The percentage markup will be negatively related to the elasticity of demand. Product durability will depend upon the cost of supplying durability.

KEY TERMS

pure monopoly
economies of scope
price searcher
marginal revenue (MR)
average revenue (AR)
marginal revenue schedule
halfway rule
monopolistic competition
nonprice competition
price discrimination

QUESTIONS AND PROBLEMS

1. Firm A can sell all it wants at a price of $5. Firm B must lower its price from $6 to $5 to sell more output. Explain why the marginal revenue of Firm A is not the same as the marginal revenue of Firm B even though they are both charging a $5 price.
2. Evaluate the validity of the following statement: "The shutdown rule applies only to firms operating in competitive markets and does not concern monopolies."
3. Explain why a price searcher can choose either its profit-maximizing output level or its profit-maximizing price. Why can it choose only one, not both?
4. A monopolist produces 100 units of output, and the price elasticity of demand at this point on the demand curve is 0.5. What advice would you give the monopolist? From this information, what can you say about marginal revenue?
5. A price searcher produces output at a constant marginal cost of $5 and has no fixed costs. The demand schedule facing the price searcher is indicated in Table A.

   a. Determine the price searcher's profit-maximizing output, price, and profit.
   b. What will happen to profit if the firm produces more output? Less output? Why?
   c. Explain what happens to marginal revenue when output is raised from 15 to 20 units.

TABLE A

Price (dollars)	Quantity Demanded (units)
12	0
10	5
8	10
6	15
4	20

6. A food concession in a sports stadium makes an economic profit of $100,000 in the first year of operation. Explain what will happen to profits in subsequent years under the following conditions.

a. The concessionaire is granted an exclusive franchise to stadium concessions.
b. Potential competitors have the freedom to set up concession stands in the stadium.

In the latter case, can the concessionaire do anything to protect long-run profits?

7. Prices of tickets to movies, sports events, and concerts are typically lower for children than for adults. Explain why, using the theory of price discrimination.
8. Explain why the entry of new firms into a monopolistically competitive market makes the demand curves of established firms more elastic.
9. Assume a monopoly is making an economic profit. The monopoly is sold to the highest bidder. Will the new owner make an economic profit? Why or why not?
10. Suppose the price at which a monopolist can sell its product is $P = 10 - Q$, where Q is the number of units sold per period. The monopolist's MC = ATC = $4.

    a. Graph the demand curve.
    b. Graph total revenue for output levels from 0 units to 10 units.
    c. Graph the marginal revenue at each output level.
    d. Which output level maximizes profit?
    e. How much is maximum profit?

11. A monopolist is making an economic profit of $100,000 per year. Explain what will happen to the monopolist's price and output if:

    a. The government imposes a fixed tax of $90,000 per year on the monopolist.
    b. The government imposes a fixed tax of $110,000 per year on the monopolist.

12. What advice would you give to a monopolist setting output to maximize revenue?
13. Evaluate the validity of the following statement: "The medical care industry is not a monopoly because the price elasticity of demand for medical care is less than unity. Monopolists would charge prices higher than current ones."
14. Explain why marginal revenue is less than price for a price searcher.
15. How does monopolistic competition differ from monopoly?
16. A natural water fountain is discovered in the middle of a city. The demand schedule for the drinking water is shown in Table B. There is no cost of production.

    a. Draw the demand curve.
    b. Use the halfway rule to derive the marginal revenue curve.
    c. How would the city maximize its revenues from the water fountain?

TABLE B

Price (cents per drink)	Quantity Demanded (drinks per day)
6	0
5	10
4	20
3	30
2	40
1	50
0	60

17. Why does a Mercedez-Benz dealer have a higher profit margin than a Toyota dealer? Explain in terms of the theory of markup pricing.
18. Which of the following are examples of price discrimination?

    a. Discount coupons
    b. First-class airline tickets
    c. Stand-by tickets
    d. More expensive seaside rooms in a hotel

SUGGESTED READINGS

Chamberlin, Edward H. *The Theory of Monopolistic Competition,* 6th ed. Cambridge, MA: Harvard University Press, 1980.

Coase, Ronald. "Durability and Monopoly." *Journal of Law and Economics* (April 1972): 143–149.

Kitch, Edmund W. et al. "The Regulation of Taxicabs in Chicago." *Journal of Law and Economics* (October 1971): 285–350.

North, Douglas C. et. al. *The Economics of Public Issues,* 8th ed. New York: HarperCollins, 1990, chap. 2.

Ruffin, Roy. *Intermediate Microeconomics,* 2nd ed. New York: HarperCollins, 1992, chap. 10.

Smith, Adam. *The Wealth of Nations.* Edited by Edwin Cannan. New York: The Modern Library, 1939, chap. 7.

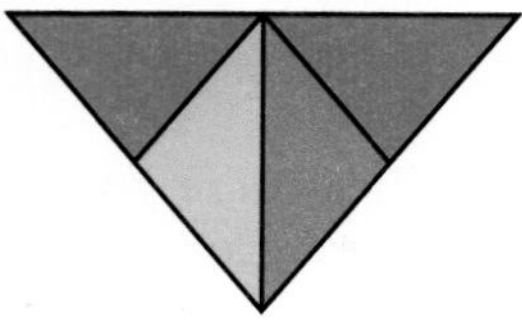

32 Monopoly and Competition Compared

CHAPTER INSIGHT

The development of prescription drugs is undertaken by research-oriented drug companies located primarily in the United States, Germany, and Switzerland. To protect its investment, the original manufacturer can obtain a patent granting it a 17-year monopoly over new prescription drugs. When the patent expires, other companies are permitted to manufacture the drug in its generic (chemical equivalent) form.

The case of drug patents illustrates the effects of monopoly and competition on prices. Faced with competition from the generic valium (diazepam) after Hoffman La Roche's patent expired in the early 1980s, the price of the notorious tranquilizer valium dropped by 50 percent. Likewise, when the patent on Lasix (the most widely prescribed drug for hypertension at the time) expired in 1985, its price dropped from $30 to $15 per prescription. The previous chapter showed that the price of beluga caviar fell when the Petrossian monopoly was broken in 1991.

There is ample evidence that when competition is introduced to a monopolistic market, prices fall, products are offered in greater quantities, and monopoly profits disappear. Does this mean that competition is preferable to monopoly?

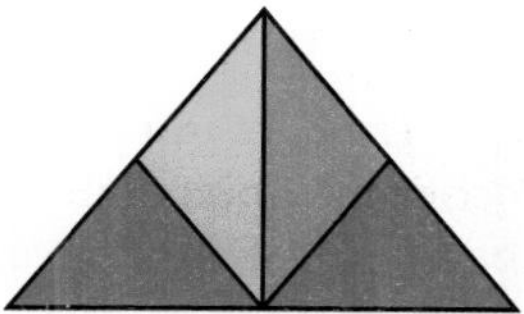

THE CASE FOR COMPETITION: EFFICIENCY

Ever since Adam Smith argued that the invisible hand of competition would guide profit-maximizing producers and utility-maximizing consumers to an efficient allocation of society's resources, economists have been captivated by its charm. The antitrust laws of the United States, for example, have attempted to make a competitive order the law of the land.

Economic Efficiency

The concepts of **economic efficiency** and **economic inefficiency** revolve around the notion of waste.

> **Economic efficiency** exists when it is impossible to make everyone better off by reallocating resources—in other words, making one person better off must necessarily be at the expense of someone else.
>
> **Economic inefficiency** exists when it is possible to make everyone better off by reallocating resources—in other words, when at least one person could be made better off without hurting anyone else.

To illustrate these definitions, consider the following examples.

1. Ann and Betty live on a deserted island with only 50 apples and 100 bananas per week upon which to subsist. Ann will not eat bananas, and Betty will not eat apples. Each has 25 apples and 50 bananas, and they do not trade.
2. Wheat, which requires little moisture, is being grown on Iowa land that receives plentiful rainfall. Corn, which requires more moisture, is being grown on dry Kansas land.
3. The price of wheat is $10 per bushel in Chicago and $2 per bushel in Kansas City. The wheat is used in the finest Illinois bakeries and as animal fodder in Kansas.

Each of these three cases is characterized by economic inefficiency. Both Betty and Ann would be better off if Ann gave Betty her bananas and Betty gave Ann her apples. Consumers and producers of wheat and corn would benefit if wheat were grown in Kansas and corn were grown in Iowa. Consumers in Illinois and producers in Kansas would benefit if wheat were shipped to Illinois. Such rearrangements would increase economic efficiency.[1]

The inefficiency in the preceding examples can be diminished if profitable trading opportunities are exploited. Ann can trade her bananas to Betty in return for Betty's apples. Similarly, farmers will make greater profits by devoting Kansas farmland to wheat and Iowa farmland to corn. Traders can buy wheat in Kansas City and sell it for a handsome profit in Chicago. Adam Smith theorized that individuals, guided by their own self-interest, will eliminate economic inefficiencies. The invisible hand operates to achieve economic efficiency for all through each person's individual quest for profit. (See Example 1.)

Efficiency and Competition

In perfectly competitive markets, economic efficiency results from the right balance between consumer utility and costs of production. The competitive price will reflect this balance.

Consumers buy a variety of goods—milk, shirts, cars, housing, bread, and so on. As discussed in the chapter on demand and utility, well-informed, rational consumers carry out their purchases of any particular good until the ratio of its marginal utility (MU) to price is the same as that for all other goods. Thus, individual consumers follow consumption patterns in which the prices of the goods they buy reflect the marginal utilities of those goods: low-priced goods have low MUs, and high-priced goods have high MUs. Thus, the price of a good is a dollar measure of the good's marginal utility to the individual; indeed, we can say that the marginal benefit of the good to the consumer equals its price. In a perfectly competitive market, the price is the same for all buyers and sellers, so each consumer pays the same price.

> The price of a good measures its marginal benefit to society because each utility-maximizing consumer equates the good's MU/P ratio to that of all other goods.

[1]This notion of efficiency was first developed by the Italian economist, Vilfredo Pareto. This concept of economic efficiency is named in his honor as *Pareto optimanty*.

EXAMPLE 1 Wasting Water

In California, farmers in the federally managed Central Valley Project pay as little as \$8 per acre-foot of water, whereas urban consumers sometimes pay as much as \$200 per acre-foot of water. Some urban districts have even considered building desalinization plants to produce clean water at a cost of about \$2000 per acre-foot. State law, however, prohibits farmers from selling their water to urban users.

This example presents a clear case of economic inefficiency. Farmers waste water; the alfalfa crop alone uses half as much water as all the urban districts combined. City dwellers hesitate to wash their cars or water their lawns.

Source: Ronald H. Schmidt, *Federal Reserve Bank of San Francisco Weekly Letter* (March 15, 1991); National Center for Policy Analysis, *Executive Alert* (July/August, 1991).

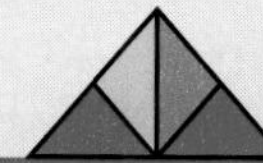

Now consider the other side of the market, the competitive firms that produce the various goods. Each producer will expand production until price and marginal cost are equal. As long as price exceeds marginal cost, the competitive producer finds profit opportunities. These are exhausted when diminishing returns drive marginal cost up to the level of price.

> In a perfectly competitive industry, every producer faces the same price and expands production to the point where marginal cost equals price. Therefore, each producer has the same marginal cost of production. The marginal cost of bread for one producer, which equals the marginal cost for other producers, is the same as the marginal cost of bread to society.

The use of society's resources to produce a good is minimized when each producer has the same marginal cost. If a good is produced by firms at different marginal costs, the same quantity of the total cost to society can be lowered by shifting production from high-marginal-cost producers to low-marginal-cost producers. Market equilibrium is the state in which a good is produced at minimum cost in a quantity that yields a marginal benefit (price) equal to marginal cost. An economy at market equilibrium is efficient; P = MC, markets have cleared, and opportunities to increase profits have been exhausted.

Removing Inefficiencies

Imagine that for some reason a good is being produced at a level where $P >$ MC. The difference between price and marginal cost not only represents a profit opportunity for individual producers but also signals a social opportunity. If $P >$ MC, society will benefit from producing more of the good. Remember that marginal cost is the opportunity cost at the margin—the value of what is being given up elsewhere. To say that price exceeds marginal cost is to say that the resources used in the production of this particular good have a higher marginal benefit to society in this use than in any other.

In Figure 1, the equilibrium quantity is 8000 units of output. Suppose for some reason that output is only 5000 units. The marginal cost to society is \$70 (at point *a*), and the marginal benefit to society is \$120 (at point *b*). Moving from an output of 5000 units to an output of 8000 units benefits society by the blue area *abc*. Point *c* is an efficient output level.

> If price does not equal marginal cost for all goods, there is inefficiency in the system. All people can be made better off (or at least some better off and none worse off) by reallocating resources until price equals marginal cost.

FIGURE 1
Perfect Competition and Social Efficiency

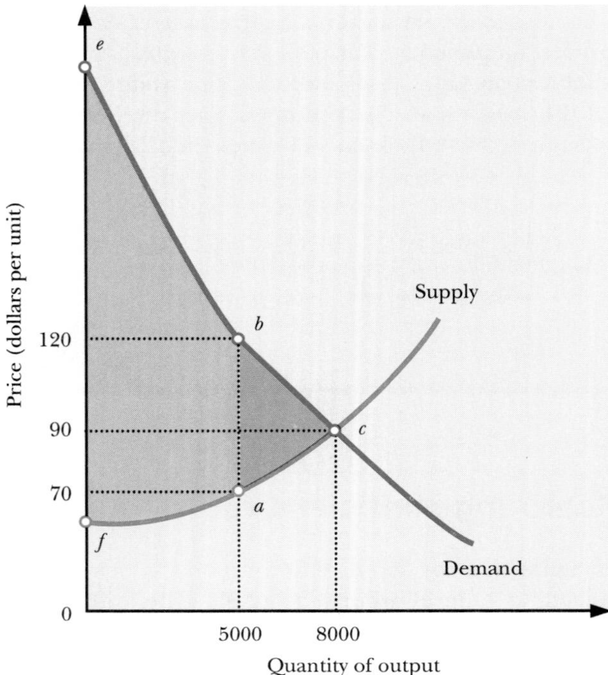

When output is restricted to 5000 units, the marginal cost of the 5001st unit of output is the price at point *a,* or \$70; the marginal benefit is the price at point *b,* or \$120. Moving to the equilibrium quantity of 8000 units results in a net gain to society of area *abc* because marginal benefits exceed marginal costs on the intervening 3000 units. Social welfare is maximized when the price is \$90 and the total of consumer and producer surplus equals area *ecf.*

THE LIMITATIONS OF COMPETITION

Even in the perfectly competitive world, the guidance of the invisible hand may not lead to the best of all possible worlds, for at least three reasons.

1. Perfect competition may lead to inequalities in the distribution of income that are not regarded by a democratic majority as equitable.
2. Perfectly competitive markets may not be efficient if economic actions have spillover or external effects on other people in the same neighborhood.
3. Perfect competition may not be conducive to a high rate of technological progress.

Equity versus Efficiency

As demonstrated in the previous section, perfect competition leads to economic efficiency, a state in which nothing is being wasted. In order to help one person, someone else must be hurt.

Efficiency can prevail even when the resulting distribution of income is widely believed to be unethical, unjust, or unfair. (There is no *equity* if some people are envious of others. Clearly, some inequities cannot be prevented.) Some people may live in a state of grinding poverty, while those owning large quantities of scarce resources may live in luxury. One person may inherit nothing; another may inherit a few acres of land in downtown Manhattan. One person may be a great typist; another may have the ability to write best-selling novels. Thus, there is no guarantee that resources will be divided equitably among the members of society. However, because there are no wasted resources in an efficient economy, the rich must be made worse off in order to help the poor.

In our real world of poverty and scarcity, a society that purposely enacts policies leading to inefficiencies (or wastefulness) might be just as negligent as an efficient society that ignores those people in real need. If society wishes to alter the distribution of resources among the members of society to achieve economic equity, it should seek to do so without sharply reducing economic efficiency. Later chapters will show that this is easier said than done.

Externalities

A perfectly competitive allocation of resources will be economically inefficient if **externalities** are present.

Externalities exist when an economic activity results in direct economic costs or benefits for third parties not immediately involved in the activity.

Externalities arise when a factory belches black smoke that raises the cost of laundry or medical care for those people living in the vicinity, when a chemical plant dumps wastes that affect fishing and agricultural production, when a pulp mill pollutes the air others must breathe, or when an airport pollutes an area with deafening noise.

In order to understand the effects of an externality, it is necessary to distinguish between **private costs** and **external costs** and between **private benefits** and **external benefits.**

> **Private costs** (or **benefits**) are the costs (or benefits) borne (or enjoyed) by the agent producing (or consuming) a good.
>
> **External costs** (or **benefits**) are the costs (or benefits) borne (or enjoyed) by someone other than the agent producing (or consuming) a good.

When externalities are present, the total cost to society of producing a good equals the sum of its private and external costs; the total benefit to society is the sum of its private and external benefits. The total costs or benefits to society of producing a good are the **social costs** or **social benefits.**

> **Social costs** are private costs plus external costs.
>
> **Social benefits** are private benefits plus external benefits.

The main effect of an externality is that the *marginal private cost* (MPC) of production does not necessarily reflect the *marginal social cost* (MSC). The marginal social cost of producing steel includes not only the marginal private costs of the steel mill but also the marginal external costs imposed on others (the extra laundry costs, medical care costs, and so on). A steel mill might not take these external costs into account when making its economic decisions.

Externalities result in economic inefficiency because the marginal social benefit of a good *as measured by its market price* is less than its marginal social cost.

Figure 2 shows the effects of externalities in steel production. The MSC curve measures marginal social costs and the supply curve measures only marginal private costs (MPC). At competitive equilibrium, 1 million tons are produced at a price of $100 per ton (point *a*). With a marginal social cost of $160 per ton, the equilibrium output level constitutes too much steel production from the standpoint of society. Marginal social costs ($160) do not equal marginal social benefits ($100) because externalities are present. Efficiency requires that 0.8 million tons of steel be produced (point *e*), yielding both a marginal social cost and a price of $120.

Economic activities can have external benefits as well as external costs. When one neighbor plants flowers, surrounding neighbors also benefit. The person who considers personal pleasure to be the sole benefit from growing flowers will plant flowers only to the point where marginal costs and marginal benefits are equal. The marginal costs to the person growing the flowers does not equal the marginal benefits enjoyed by society (the neighborhood) because other neighbors gain some marginal benefits as well. The

FIGURE 2
Externalities and Competition

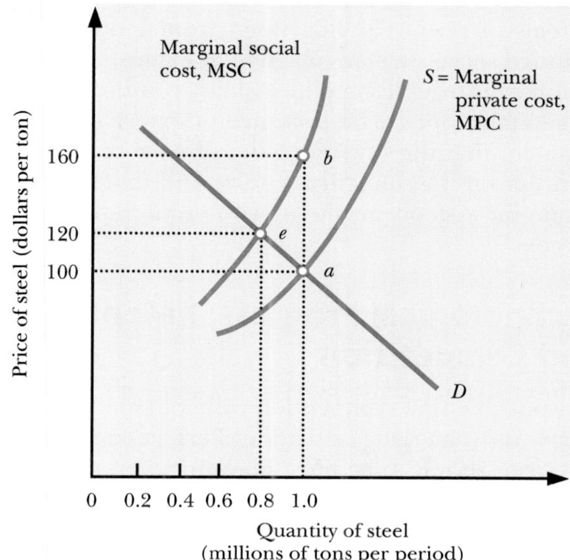

The supply and demand curves of this hypothetical steel industry intersect at the price/quantity combination of $100 per ton and 1 million tons of steel (point *a*). The supply curve, *S*, reflects only marginal *private* costs. The MSC curve shows marginal *social* costs. At the equilibrium point *a*, the marginal social cost of an extra ton of steel is $160, but the marginal social benefit is only $100, as measured by the height of the demand curve. Too much steel is produced from the society's point of view.

situation results in economic inefficiency because too few flowers get planted.

The problems created by externalities are not limited to conditions of perfect competition. All systems of resource allocation—from monopoly to planned socialism—are plagued by externalities. Pollution is as troublesome in socialist countries as it is in capitalist ones. The presence of externalities is a problem that the invisible hand of perfect competition does not automatically solve and that different economic systems may treat with varying degrees of success.

Technological Progress, Patents, and Competition

It is possible that competition will not be efficient in a *dynamic* (changing) situation. Perfect competition has been shown to be most efficient when resources and technology are *static* (unchanging). Some have argued that competition does not encourage the creation and promotion of technological change.

The major rationale for **patents**—which, in the United States, give a holder a legal monopoly on a product for 17 years—is that they are necessary to spur innovation. Why should a company or individual expend time and money on an invention that can be copied by a rival firm? Thus, patents are deemed to be a price society must pay for innovation. Basically, they protect the inventors by hindering the legal development of products related to ones which have been patented. For example, consider an electronics firm that has patented a production technology that gives it a cost advantage. Its rivals will find it difficult to develop a substitute technology that does the same thing but is different enough to avoid infringement on the patent.

> A **patent** is an exclusive right granted to an inventor to make, use, or sell an invention for a term of 17 years in the United States.

Economists Edwin Mansfield, Mark Schwartz, and Samuel Wagner studied the protection a patent actually provides from competition in the real world. They concluded that patents provide surprisingly little protection from competition. In a survey of 48 product innovations, 31 of them patented, Mansfield and his associates found that patents increased the cost of legally imitating the original invention by only 11 percent. They also found that 60 percent of the patented inventions were successfully imitated within 4 years—far less than the 17-year life of the patent. They further discovered that patent protection was not essential for the development and introduction of at least 75 percent of the inventions they studied. In fact, patents have played a relatively small role in the most innovative fields of the past 25 years, electronics and bioengineering. Companies in these two fields have relied more on secrecy than on patents to protect their inventions. The major exception to this trend is the prescription-drug industry, in which patents have effectively protected inventions for long periods of time.

The research of Mansfield and his associates raises a very important question: If patents do not effectively discourage imitation, are patents really necessary to encourage innovation? Secrecy may be more effective. For example, companies like Coca-Cola or McDonalds have made large profits for years by keeping their recipes secret.

Technological progress requires research and development. Is it necessary for firms to be large in order to be able to finance the development of new products and new methods of production? There is considerable controversy surrounding this question, which will be addressed later in this chapter.

THE CASE AGAINST MONOPOLY

Opponents of monopoly argue that monopoly is: (1) inefficient and (2) unfair.

Sources of Inefficiency in Monopoly

Monopoly has three sources of inefficiency. First, monopoly leads to contrived scarcities. Second, the resources used to acquire monopoly power can be better employed elsewhere in the economy. Third, monopoly does not encourage efficiency in production.

Contrived Scarcity. The main argument against monopoly is that monopolies maximize profit by restricting output to the scale where price exceeds marginal cost. Remember that monopolies maximize profit where MR = MC, but $P >$ MR. Therefore, price will exceed marginal cost at the output that maximizes monopoly profit.

> Price measures marginal social benefit, and marginal cost measures marginal social cost (if externalities are not present); therefore, when $P >$ MC, there is contrived scarcity in the economy.

Contrived scarcity occurs when the economy would be more efficient—in the sense of giving more to everyone—if more of the monopolized good were produced. When $P >$ MC, 1 more unit of output adds more to social welfare than to social costs, so it is possible to rearrange the allocation of resources (to produce more of the monopolized good and less of other goods) to make everyone better off.

> **Contrived scarcity** is the production of less than the economically efficient quantity of a good by a monopoly.

To compare monopoly with perfect competition, consider an industry in which both are possible. Figure 3 depicts an industry in which there are no economies of scale; average costs are the same for each level of output. Therefore, average cost and marginal cost are the same: AC = MC. Either one large firm (a monopoly) or a large number of small firms (a perfectly competitive market) could satisfy consumer demand at the same average cost. Marginal cost (= AC) is a constant $4 per unit. The monopoly output (300 units) is at the level where MR is also $4 (point *a*); the monopoly price is $7. Monopoly profits are represented by the blue-shaded area, which equals $900. Under conditions of perfect competition, meanwhile, free entry would squeeze out economic profits. The long-run competitive price would, therefore, be $4, and the competitive output would be 600 units (point *c*).

The cost of monopoly can be calculated from Figure 3. If this industry is transformed from a monopoly to perfect competition, the equilibrium price/quantity combination would shift from point *b* to point *c*, and the price would fall from $7 to $4. The increase in consumer surplus resulting from the shift is the sum of the blue-shaded area (the monopolist's profit of $900) and orange-shaded area ($450), equaling $1350. But the monopolist, who is also a member of society, loses monopoly profits of $900 in the process. Therefore, the net gain to society (the consumers' gain minus the monopolist's loss) is simply the orange-shaded triangle, which equals $450.[2] Notice that everyone involved is better

FIGURE 3
Monopoly and Competition Compared

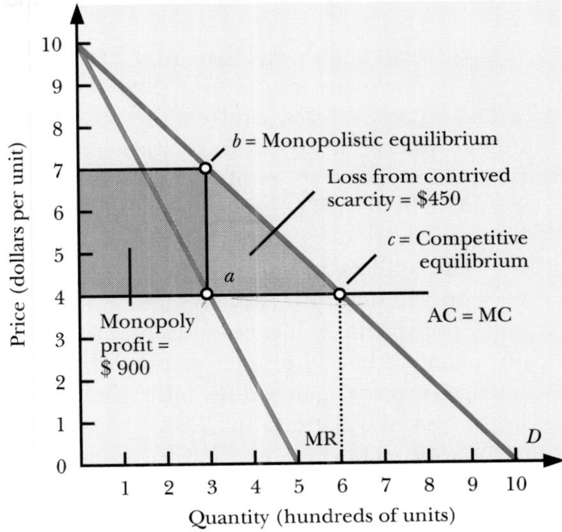

This industry has constant returns to scale where AC = MC = $4 for all levels of output. If the industry were perfectly competitive, price would be $4 and output would be 600 units. If this industry were a single-firm monopoly, price would be $7 and output would be 300 units, with a monopoly profit of $900 (= $3 × 300). Monopoly profit is the blue-shaded area. The monopolist creates profits via the contrived scarcity of 300 units (the monopolist produces 300 units less than the competitive industry). The loss from contrived scarcity is the orange area, which equals $450, or the deadweight loss to society. Moving from monopoly to competition creates consumer surplus of $1350 (which is the sum of $900 + $450) while destroying only $900 worth of profits for the monopolist. More is gained by all parties taken together than is lost.

[2]The deadweight loss can also be calculated another way. When Q = 300 and P = $7, the difference between marginal social benefits and marginal social costs is $3 ($7 − $4). Hence, it pays

EXAMPLE 2 Monopoly and Competition in the Skies over Europe

This chapter explains why a monopoly produces less output than a competitive industry and charges consumers higher prices. If an industry were converted from monopoly to competition, consumers would be better off because more output would be available at lower prices.

The effects of monopoly on prices can be seen when an industry changes from being monopolistic to being competitive. An example of an industry in such a transition is the European passenger airline industry. Prior to 1988, only the national airlines had the right to provide service between two cities in different countries. For example, only Swissair and Lufthansa were entitled to fly passengers between Frankfurt and Zurich. Moreover, prevailing rules required that each national airline provide the same number of flights and that revenues be divided equally between them. By blocking entry of competitors into these markets, this system allowed the national airlines to charge monopoly prices. Airfares within Europe have been more than double those in the United States, a market in which different airlines are allowed to compete for customers.

Following the American deregulation example, the European airlines have agreed to phase in competition over the next decade. More landing rights are to be given to private airline companies, and third-country national airlines will be allowed to serve markets from which they had previously been excluded (for example, Swissair would be allowed to fly between London and Copenhagen). If European airline deregulation proceeds as planned, European airfares should drop substantially. The national airlines will lose their monopoly profits, but the public will gain millions of dollars of consumer surplus from the lower fares. As Figure 3 in the text showed, the consumers' gain outweighs the loss of monopoly profits.

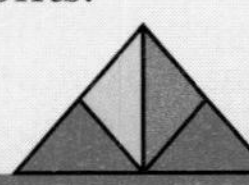

off under the move to perfect competition. Because consumers gain $1350 in consumer surplus, they can buy off the monopolist with a payment, say $901, greater than the original monopoly profit—which would make the monopolist better off by $1 and the consumers better off by $449. The $450 loss from monopoly is a **deadweight loss** because nothing is received in exchange for the loss. The deadweight loss of monopoly is equivalent to throwing away valuable scarce resources. (See Example 2.)

A **deadweight loss** is a loss to society of consumer or producer surplus that is not offset by anyone else's gain.

How large are losses from contrived scarcities in the American economy? Economist Arnold Harberger has estimated the deadweight loss from all monopolies to be a very small fraction of total U.S. output.[3] A number of other researchers roughly estimate these losses at about 1 percent of GDP.

society to expand output beyond the 300th unit. In effect, the 301st unit adds $3 to social welfare. The 601st unit adds nothing to social welfare because from $Q = 300$ to $Q = 600$, the extra benefit per unit declines from $3 to $0. Thus, on the average, the 300 additional units between 300 (the monopolist's output) to 600 (the output under perfect competition) add $1.50 each (the average of $3 and $0), or $450.

[3] Arnold Harberger, "Monopoly and Resource Allocation," *American Economic Review* 44 (May 1954): 77–87. We can mention only a few of the economists who have contributed to this estimate: David Schwartzman, Dean Worcester, Jr., David Kamerschen, and Michael Klass.

Monopoly Rent-Seeking Behavior. Anne Krueger and Gordon Tullock have argued that the previously cited estimates of the deadweight losses from monopoly represent lower bounds to the true loss of society from monopoly.[4] In terms of Figure 3, if the industry were perfectly competitive, the price/quantity combination would be $4/600 units, or point *c*, and there would be no deadweight loss. If someone could turn this industry into a monopoly through political activities, that person could gain the potential monopoly profit of $900 (blue-shaded area). People would be willing to spend real resources—or engage in **monopoly rent-seeking behavior**—to turn the industry into a monopoly and acquire the monopoly profit. The monopoly profit can be thought of as the rent received in return for expending the resources needed to turn a competitive industry into a monopoly or to maintain an existing monopoly.

> **Monopoly rent-seeking behavior** is the use of political power and its accompanying resources to achieve or maintain a monopoly in order to gain the monopoly profits, or "rent."

A prime example of monopoly rent-seeking behavior is the lobbying in Congress by American automobile manufacturers for protection from foreign imports. There are about 10,000 registered lobbyists in Washington, D.C. The offices they occupy, the secretarial services they employ, and their own labor could be used elsewhere in a world of scarcity. Instead, lobbyists use their resources to achieve and maintain monopolies through government charters, franchises, and regulation.

In the extreme case, *all* monopoly profits are spent by the persons engaging in monopoly rent-seeking behavior, thereby multiplying the deadweight loss of monopoly. Not only do consumers lose the orange-shaded area in Figure 3 (the loss of consumer surplus) but the monopolist does *not* gain the blue-shaded area (monopoly profit).

Monopoly rent-seeking behavior can lead to substantial social losses. To limit monopoly rent-seeking behavior, the government must act to substantially lessen the possibility of "buying" monopoly. This, however, is not an easy task. (See Example 3.)

X-Inefficiency. A controversial third loss from monopoly power is called ***X*-inefficiency,** a term coined by economist Harvey Leibenstein.[5] To understand *X*-inefficiency, recall that perfect competition forces enterprises to produce as cheaply as possible to avoid bankruptcy in the long run. What if the firm has a monopoly? Although it is beneficial to the monopolist to minimize costs of production, failure to do so will not drive it out of business. Hence, it is likely that "organizational slack" will develop in monopolistic industries.

> ***X*-inefficiency** refers to the organizational slack that results from the lack of competition in monopolies. It is characterized by costs that are higher than necessary.

Estimates of *X*-inefficiency as high as 2 percent of national output have been suggested by some industrial-organization experts, but accurate estimates are impossible to achieve.[6]

Some economists have argued that *X*-inefficiency is not a true deadweight loss. As British economist John R. Hicks once noted, "the best of all monopoly profits is the quiet life." Thus, the *X*-inefficiency costs of a monopoly are not a social cost; rather, they represent a gain to the owner or manager in the form of greater leisure. (See Example 4.)

Monopoly and Income Distribution

Does monopoly create an unfair excess profit for monopolists? What is the effect of monopoly on the distribution of income?

[4]Anne Krueger, "The Political Economy of the Rent-Seeking Society." *American Economic Review* 64 (June 1974): 291–303; Gordon Tullock, "The Welfare Cost of Tariffs, Monopolies, and Theft." *Western Economic Journal* 5 (June 1967): 224–32.

[5]Harvey Leibenstein, "Allocative Efficiency vs *X*-Inefficiency," *American Economic Review* 56 (June 1966): 392–415.

[6]Walter Primeaux conducted an interesting test of *X*-Inefficiency. He found that competition between at least two electric companies existed in 49 cities, and that the costs of those companies facing competition was 11 percent below those of monopoly suppliers. See Primeaux, "An Assessment of *X*-Efficiency Gained through Competition," *Review of Economics and Statistics* 59 (February 1977): 105–8.

EXAMPLE 3 Monopoly Rent-Seeking Behavior: Lobbying and Lawyers

Economists are just beginning to study the effect of monopoly rent-seeking behavior on the economy. Its impact is difficult to evaluate due to the complexity of calculating the value of the resources exhausted by lobbyists attempting to create monopolies. For example, in 1991 Texas began licensing "interior designers" but not "interior decorators." This distinction in the law resulted from a seven-year effort by lobbyists aiming to protect those who meet certain requirements. This story has been repeated many times in the realm of government regulations. The efforts of a vast number of researchers would be required to evaluate this wealth of information.

Stephen Magee, William Brock, and Leslie Young have attempted to estimate the effects indirectly. They argue that lawyers are the main resource employed by monopoly rent seekers. Although lawyers are generally useful, rent-seeking increases the demand for lawyers relative to other professions. Examining a group of 34 countries, the researchers discovered a strong negative correlation between national growth rates and the national ratios of lawyers to physicians. For example, income in the United States grew at a rate of 2.3 percent between 1960 and 1980, whereas the lawyer/physician ratio during the same period was over 1.25. By contrast, Japan and Hong Kong grew at nearly 7 percent per year and had lawyer/physician ratios of only about .1 and .3, respectively.

Source: S. Magee, W. Brock, and L. Young, *Black Hole Tariffs and Endogenous Political Economy in General Equilibrium* (Cambridge: Cambridge University Press, 1989), chap. 8.

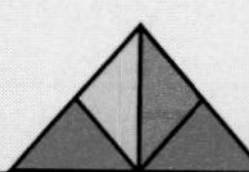

Certainly, the existence of monopoly profits affects the distribution of income among individuals. If the composition of an industry is transformed from that of several competitors to that of a monopoly, income is redistributed from the consumer to the monopolist. Yet, are monopoly profits fair? Economists are ill-equipped to answer this ethical question, but many people regard the transfer of income from the consumer to the monopolist as unfair.

What is the extent of the impact monopoly has on the distribution of income in the United States? Again, it is difficult to find reliable estimates, but one study of the wealthiest 0.25 percent of U.S. households revealed that their share of wealth would fall from 18.5 percent to between 12 and 14 percent if all monopoly power were eliminated.[7]

A normative objection to monopolies is that they can make above-normal, or economic, profits. Because the monopolist is protected from competition, its profits are secure from the inroads of competing firms.

Above-normal profits, however, can be redistributed to the poor through taxation. Thus, inefficiency, rather than monopoly profits, is the main economic objection to monopoly. As long as price is greater than marginal cost, society is not putting enough resources into the monopolized activity. Even if all monopoly profits are redistributed to society, monopoly remains inefficient.

THE CASE FOR MONOPOLY: INNOVATION?

Some economists believe that monopoly is more conducive to technological innovation than is a competitive order. If this were the case, the disadvantages of monopoly noted in the previous section—

[7]William Comanor and Robert Smiley, "Monopoly and the Distribution of Wealth," *Quarterly Journal of Economics* 89 (May 1975): 177–94.

EXAMPLE 4 Cable TV: Monopoly Pricing, Rent Seeking, and *X*-Inefficiency

Economist Thomas Hazlett uses cable-TV monopolies to demonstrate that a monopoly charges higher prices and has higher costs (*X*-inefficiency) than an industry that is competitive. The cable-TV industry also promotes monopoly rent-seeking behavior among firms wishing to earn monopoly profits.

Most cable companies ae protected from competition by exclusive franchises from local governments. Supporters usually justify cable-TV monopolies on efficiency grounds: economies of scale in laying cable allow one firm to operate more efficiently than two or more. The greater efficiency of the monopoly cable-TV company should guarantee customers better service at a lower price. Critics of monopoly cable TV, such as Hazlett, argue that any efficiencies of large-scale production are offset by monopoly pricing, *X*-inefficiency, and monopoly rent-seeking behavior.

Although most cable-TV companies are monopolies, instances of competition can be found, such as when cable companies enter into unincorporated areas (where no local licensing authority exists) or when a local government decides in favor of competition. In the future, there will be even more cases of cable-TV competition if the courts rule that exclusive franchises violate the First Amendment's guarantee of free speech. Cable TV provides a case study of the struggle between monopoly and competition.

According to Hazlett, competitive cable TV can offer subscribers lower prices. From 1971 to 1984, Bryan and College Station, Texas, had multiple cable-TV franchises, and subscribers had the lowest cable rates in the state. In unincorporated areas of California, Virginia, and Arizona, unfranchised cable firms offer lower prices and quality service. The political franchising process raises costs by requiring extra technological "whistles and bells." When local governments award cable-TV monopolies, they tend to require 100 channels, public-access facilities, two-way talk-back systems, and so on. These extras raise the cost of cable TV to customers, many of whom would not voluntarily pay for such extra services. The requirement to install little-used capacities and facilities, combined with the lack of competitive pressure, create *X*-inefficiencies in which cable services are provided at higher cost than in a more competitive situation.

Source: Thomas Hazlett, "Those Catchwords of Cable," *Wall Street Journal*, April 25, 1986.

inefficiency and unfair income distribution—might be offset by its dynamic advantages. Monopoly's contribution toward greater outward shifts in the production possibilities frontier over time could compensate for its failure to operate on the frontier at any single point in time.

Economists have asked what type of market structure—perfect competition or monopoly—fosters a more favorable atmosphere for innovation. Some prominent economists are convinced that big businesses, which resemble monopolies in their enormous market power and access to vast resources, are more likely to develop significant scientific inventions than are competitive businesses. Giant corporations such as AT&T, Du Pont, General Motors, Ford, and IBM maintain large, privately financed laboratories and employ thousands of scientists. Indeed, Nobel Prizes for the discovery of the laser and the transistor were awarded to scientists employed by giant corporations. The noted Austrian-born economist Joseph Schumpeter argued:

> As soon as we go into the details and inquire into the individual items in which progress was most conspicuous (since 1899), the trail leads not to the doors that work under conditions of comparatively free competition but precisely to

> the doors of the large concerns—which, as in the case of agricultural machinery, also account for much of the progress in the competitive sector—and a shocking suspicion dawns upon us that big business may have had more to do with creating (our high) standard of life than keeping it down.[8]

Why did Schumpeter refer to this conclusion as a "shocking suspicion"? Before Schumpeter's writings, economists maintained that monopolies are not especially innovative because they are not pressured by the forces of competition to innovate. Yet Schumpeter argued that monopolies are responsible for our important technological advances.

Schumpeter did not support the theory that innovation by monopoly yields a permanent competitive advantage or that it shields monopolists from long-run competition. Rather, Schumpeter believed in "creative destruction." This theory holds that innovations by monopolists, in spite of their large economic profits, spur economic progress because the monopoly position is only transitory. Eventually, another large concern will come up with a superior innovation, the original monopoly will lose out, a new monopoly will take its place until in turn, it is replaced by a more innovative monopoly.

Schumpeter's theory of the innovational efficiency of monopoly has been taken up by other economists. John K. Galbraith argued in a slightly different way:

> A benign Providence has made modern industry of a few large firms an almost perfect instrument for inducing technological change.... There is no more pleasant fiction than that technological change is the product of the matchless ingenuity of the small man forced by competition to employ his wits better than his neighbor. Unhappily, it is a fiction. Technical development has long since become the preserve of the scientist and engineer. Most of the cheap and simple inventions have, to put it bluntly, been made.[9]

What are we to make of the arguments for and against the dynamic efficiency of monopoly? On the one hand, it is argued that competition forces business firms to be innovative. On the other hand, we hear that monopoly and big business are essential to significant technological breakthroughs. Which view is correct?

In order to assess the validity of each position, we must consider the actual relationship between market structure and technological innovation over time.[10] Although the evidence is not overwhelming, we can safely say that it does not support the extreme Galbraith-Schumpeter position, despite the plausibility of their arguments.

In a major study, John Jewkes, David Sawers, and Richard Stillerman compiled case histories of 61 important twentieth-century inventions.[11] They found that less than one-third were discovered in large industrial laboratories. A little more than one-half were the product of academic investigators or of individuals working independently. In another study, Willard F. Mueller found that of the 25 most significant inventions pioneered by Du Pont, only 10 were developed in Du Pont laboratories. The rest came from small, independent researchers.[12]

F. M. Scherer summarized the evidence and its bearing on public policy: "No single firm size is uniquely conducive to technological progress. There is room for firms of all sizes. What we want, therefore, may be a diversity in sizes, each with its own special advantages and disadvantages."[13]

Diversity can be important to technological innovation. Basic ideas may come from small firms or even individuals, but a large laboratory may be required to develop the idea to the point where it can be put to practical use. A small firm may discover a new product or process, but the involvement of a large firm may be necessary to put the invention on the shelf for the consumer to enjoy.

[8]Joseph Schumpeter, *Capitalism, Socialism, and Democracy,* 2d ed. (New York: Harper and Brothers, 1942), 81–82.

[9]John K. Galbraith, *American Capitalism,* rev. ed. (Boston: Houghton Mifflin, 1956), 86.

[10]For a survey of this literature, see Morton Kamien and Nancy Schwartz, "Market Structure and Innovation: A Survey," *Journal of Economic Literature* 8, no. 1 (March 1975): 1–38.

[11]John Jewkes, David Sawers, and Richard Stillerman, *The Sources of Invention* (New York: St. Martins Press, 1959), 71–85.

[12]Williard F. Mueller, "The Origins of the Basic Inventions Underlying Du Pont's Major Product and Process Inventions," in *The Rate and Direction of Innovative Activity* (Princeton, NJ: Princeton University Press, 1962), 323–46.

[13]F. M. Scherer, *Industrial Market Structure and Economic Performance,* 2d ed. (Boston: Houghton Mifflin, 1980), 418.

THE EXTENT OF MONOPOLY: EVIDENCE FROM PRICE CEILINGS

This chapter noted earlier that the losses from monopoly in the U.S. economy have been estimated to be relatively small. One method for appraising the extent of monopoly is to compare how well the models for both monopoly and competition fit reality.

Chapter 5 demonstrated how price controls *in a competitive industry* cause shortages. Without controls, the competitive industry is in equilibrium when price equals marginal cost for each firm. Only at the equilibrium price will the quantity demanded by buyers equal the quantity supplied by firms. When a price ceiling is set below the equilibrium price, the quantity demanded exceeds the quantity supplied, and a shortage arises.

> In a competitive industry, price ceilings below the equilibrium price cause shortages.

However, the argument that price controls cause shortages depends on the existence of competition. *In the case of monopoly,* price ceilings below equilibrium do not necessarily result in shortages, as illustrated by Figure 4. The demand curve facing the monopoly is labeled *D*. For simplicity, assume MC = AC = \$4. The monopoly price/quantity combination is \$7/300 units (point *b*). If the ceiling price is set at \$6, the market demand will be 400 units. Clearly, the monopolist will want to sell all 400 units because profits (= \$800) will be larger than if any smaller quantity were sold at the price of \$6. For example, if the monopolist continued to produce 300 units at the \$6 ceiling price, profits would fall by \$200 (the area of the rectangle *acdg*). There is no reason for the monopolist not to sell the quantity demanded by the market at the ceiling price. Thus, in a monopoly, an effective price ceiling established below the uncontrolled monopoly price but above marginal cost will not cause a shortage.

> A price ceiling imposed on a monopoly below the monopoly price but above marginal cost will not cause a shortage.

FIGURE 4
The Effect of Price Ceilings on Monopoly

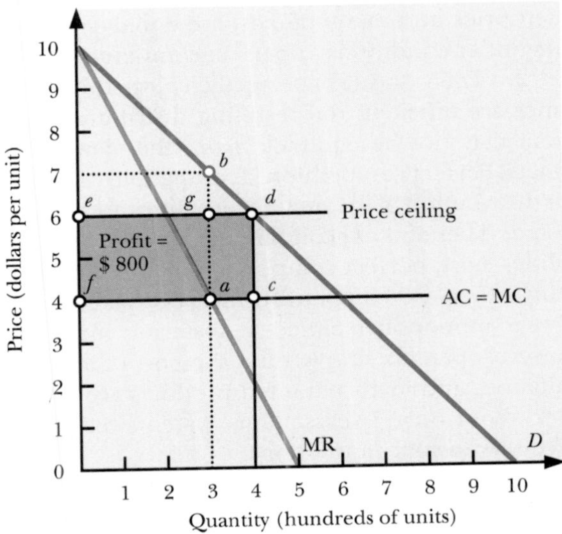

If there were no price ceilings, this monopolist would produce that output at which marginal revenue and marginal cost are equal—300 units—and would charge a price of \$7 per unit. If a price ceiling is imposed below the monopoly price but above marginal cost, the monopolist will sell more. At a price of \$6, the monopolist will sell 400 units because profits will be maximized (the area of the rectangle *edcf*) at that output. Price ceilings can increase output in the case of monopoly.

Historical evidence does not support the assumption that business behavior is, overall, monopolistic; virtually every price control that has been instituted in history has been associated with shortages. Although the real world is often a blend of both monopoly and competition, the example of price controls indicates the blend leans more toward the competitive side.

This chapter has compared the extremes of monopoly and competition under the assumption that both are feasible. The next chapter examines the many varieties of oligopoly behavior that combine elements of monopoly and perfect competition.

SUMMARY

1. In an ideal world, perfect competition would exist in every industry. Consumers would be well informed, and externalities would be absent.

Efficiency is present when society's resources are so organized that it is impossible to make even one person better off by any reallocation of resources without harming someone else. Efficiency prevails when price and marginal cost are equal—which occurs under conditions of perfect competition.

2. Even though perfectly competitive economies are efficient, the resulting distribution of income may not be equitable from the viewpoint of society. Perfect competition is compatible with an unfair distribution of income. Externalities are unpriced costs and benefits of economic activities. When externalities exist, perfect competition is not efficient. In many otherwise competitive markets, patents grant 17-year monopolies aimed at fostering innovation. However, patents simply raise the cost of successful imitation, and many patented products are imitated after about only 4 years. Thus, patents may not be necessary to spur innovations.

3. Sources of inefficiency in monopoly are contrived scarcity, monopoly rent-seeking behavior, and X-inefficiency. Monopoly may also result in an unfair distribution of income due to monopoly profits.

4. Schumpeter and Galbraith argue that large business firms or large concentrations of monopoly power are conducive to technological progress. Modern research, however, fails to support this view.

5. A price ceiling imposed on a monopoly below the monopoly price but above marginal cost will not cause a shortage. The historical association between price controls and shortages suggests that world markets behave more like competition than monopoly.

KEY TERMS

economic efficiency
economic inefficiency
externalities
private costs
external costs
private benefits
external benefits
social costs
social benefits
patent
contrived scarcity
deadweight loss
monopoly rent-seeking behavior
X-inefficiency

QUESTIONS AND PROBLEMS

1. Restate the reason why $P = \text{MC}$ is the condition for economic efficiency.
2. Give examples of positive external benefits and negative external costs.
3. Why do economists say that monopolists contrive scarcity?
4. The marginal cost of production in industry A is \$8 and is equal to the average cost. The demand schedule is linear and is given in Table A. What is the deadweight loss of monopoly that results from contrived scarcity in this case? What is the maximum monopoly rent-seeking loss?

TABLE A

Price (dollars per unit)	Quantity (units)
20	0
15	500
10	1000
5	1500
0	2000

5. Explain why monopolists produce too little output from the standpoint of economic efficiency.
6. Explain the resource allocation problem that would exist in a competitive market economy if the following undertakings had externalities: (a) the production of electricity by burning coal and (b) the immunization of children against communicable diseases. Draw a supply-and-demand diagram for each undertaking, indicating both the market allocation and the correct resource allocation result.
7. What does the historical evidence indicate about the relationship between the size of business firms and technological progress? Do large business enterprises hold a "monopoly" on technological innovation?
8. What is the difference between monopoly rent-seeking losses and losses that result when the monopolist produces where marginal revenue equals marginal cost?
9. Why is production at an output level where marginal cost equals marginal revenue socially inefficient for monopolies but socially efficient under perfect competition?
10. The marginal cost of production for a hypothetical drug is \$2 per dozen. The demand schedule for the drug is shown in Table B.

a. What is the monopoly price for the drug?
b. Compare the gains that consumers would receive to the losses that the monopolist would incur if the drug were sold competitively.
c. If a price ceiling of $4 were imposed, how would the monopolist's price and output change? Are consumers worse off or better off as a result of the ceiling price?

TABLE B

Price (dollars per dozen)	Quantity (dozens)
10	0
9	1
8	2
7	3
6	4
5	5
4	6
3	7

11. The Mafia obtains protection "rents" through the threat of violence, exacting payments in return for securing the physical or economic safety of one person against potential criminals or predators. Is this a form of economic rent seeking?

SUGGESTED READINGS

Galbraith, John Kenneth. *Economics and the Public Purpose.* Boston: Houghton Mifflin, 1973, parts I–III.

Harberger, Arnold. "Monopoly and Resource Allocation." *American Economic Review* 44 (May 1954): 77–87.

Kamien, Morton, and Nancy Schwartz. "Market Structure and Innovation: A Survey." *Journal of Economic Literature* 8, 1 (March 1975): 1–38.

Mansfield, Edwin. *Microeconomics: Theory and Applications,* 6th ed. New York: W. W. Norton, 1988, chap. 10.

Mansfield, Edwin, Mark Schwartz, and Samuel Wagner. "Imitation Costs and Patents: An Empirical Study." *Economic Journal* (December 1981): 907–18.

Schumpeter, Joseph. *Capitalism, Socialism, and Democracy,* 3rd ed. New York: Harper and Row, 1950.

Tollison, Richard D. "Rent Seeking: A Survey." *Kyklos* 35 (fasc. 4, 1982): 575–602.

Tullock, Gordon. "The Welfare Cost of Tariffs, Monopolies, and Theft." *Western Economic Journal* 5 (June 1967): 224–32.

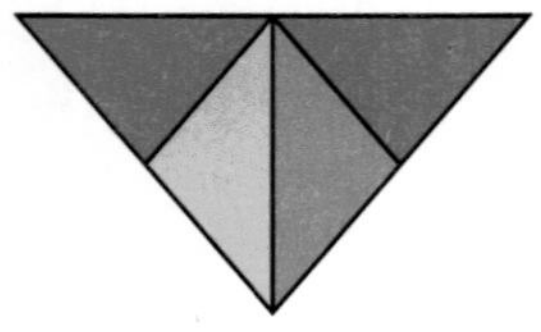

33

Oligopoly

CHAPTER INSIGHT

Strategy may be defined as behavior designed to influence one or more people in a manner that is favorable to the strategist. Jack may buy a new suit to increase the probability that Jill will go out with him. But Jack's rival, Jim, may, in turn, buy a new sports car. Clearly, Jack must consider Jim's likely response before he takes any competitive action. In other words, he must develop a strategy and act on it. Up to now we have not studied strategic behavior in this sense: The competitive firm sells at the market price; the price searcher selects from a given demand schedule the price that maximizes profit. No strategy is involved. But when IBM or General Motors (GM) prices a new product, they must worry about how their action might affect the pricing decisions of their competitors.

Strategic behavior is characteristic of the interaction between oligopolies. *Oligopoly* is an umbrella term that describes the market forms that fall between the extremes of monopoly and monopolistic competition. Oligopolistic behavior is rich and varied, and it presents many puzzles that require solutions. This chapter explains why some oligopolies behave like monopolies and others like competitive industries. It will describe the characteristics and behavior of oligopolies and the pitfalls of collusive behavior. Finally, this chapter also explains how game theory is used in the analysis of oligopoly.

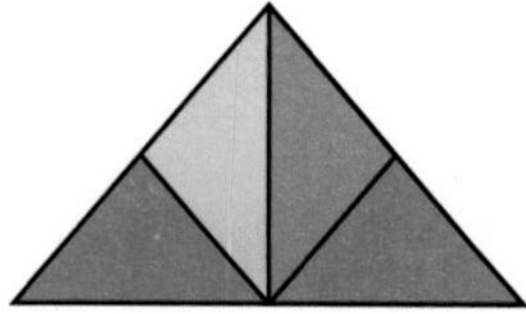

MUTUAL INTERDEPENDENCE

Many different industries are consistent with the definition of **oligopoly.**

> An **oligopoly** is an industry characterized by
>
> 1. Recognized mutual interdependence
> 2. Moderate to high entry barriers
> 3. Relatively few firms
> 4. Price searching (firms are able to exercise varying degrees of control over price)

As the definition points out, there is diversity among oligopolies. Some have high barriers to entry; others are characterized by more moderate barriers. The degree of price control varies. Some oligopolies produce a homogeneous product (aluminum); others produce a heterogeneous product (automobiles). The common denominator is mutual interdependence.

When there are relatively few firms in an industry, each firm is aware of the others on an individual basis (Ford is aware of General Motors, for example), and the industry is characterized by **mutual interdependence.**

> **Mutual interdependence** is the characteristic whereby the actions of one firm invite reactions by other firms in a given industry.

Mutual interdependence is the most important feature of oligopoly. In making decisions concerning prices, quantities, and qualities of output, mutually interdependent firms must consider the reactions of rival firms. Rival firms must, in turn, consider the possible reactions to *their* actions. In some cases, the pattern of reaction may be easy to anticipate by all participants; it may be dictated by custom or agreement. In other cases, reactions may be unpredictable, and participants must engage in strategic behavior to outguess and outmaneuver their rivals.

BARRIERS TO ENTRY

The mutual interdependence of oligopolistic firms results from the relatively small number of firms in the industry. If the numbers of firms were large, as in monopolistic competition or perfect competition, the actions of a single firm would not significantly affect other firms. The limited number of firms is due to **barriers to entry,** defined by pioneering researcher Joe S. Bain in the following way.[1]

> A **barrier to entry** is any advantage that existing firms hold over firms that might seek to enter the market.

Experts on industrial organization have attempted to classify industries according to the strength of barriers to entry. They have concluded that industries like distilled liquors, newspapers, drugs, automobiles, and heavy electrical equipment have had high barriers to entry. The clothing, printing, cement, and footwear industries have had low barriers to entry. Industries with high barriers are likely to have relatively few oligopolistic producers. Industries with low entry barriers are likely to have relatively numerous producers.

The chapter on monopoly studied barriers to entry, including economies of scale and scope, control over input supplies, government barriers to entry, large capital requirements, and technological advantages. In oligopoly, we also must pay attention to product differentiation and sunk costs.

Product Differentiation

The more highly differentiated a product is in the eyes of the consumer, the more difficult it is for new firms to enter an industry. Thus, although product differentiation will not create a monopoly, it makes oligopoly more likely. If the buyer is convinced that a particular brand of medication is superior to competing brands or that a particular brand of yogurt tastes better than others, the manufacturer has succeeded in erecting a barrier to entry.

[1]Joe S. Bain, *Barriers to New Competition* (Cambridge, MA: Harvard University Press, 1965).

One major means of differentiating products is advertising. If advertising successfully differentiates the product, the introduction of higher prices will not invite the entry of competitors who drive the price back down. For this reason, some economists view advertising as anticompetitive. Others consider advertising procompetitive because it increases the amount of product information available to the consumer.

Sunk Costs

Another important entry barrier is actually an exit barrier. Suppose a firm knows that some of the fixed costs it incurs when it enters the industry are **sunk costs** that it can never recover.

> **Sunk costs** are fixed costs that cannot be recovered even in the long run.

One example would be setup costs. When a firm enters a particular industry, it may have to pay to train its employees, hire attorneys to check for trademark or copyright violations, and purchase licenses to sell the product. These costs are often unrecoverable (although sometimes licenses can be resold competitively). The firm may also have to purchase specialized capital goods that have no use except in that particular industry. The salvage value of such machinery may be very small if it is difficult to sell to anyone outside the industry (for example, railroad tracks and certain kinds of telephone exchanges). The firm may have to advertise to let buyers know that it has entered the business. Clearly, if a firm goes out of business its losses may be enormous.

MEASURING CONCENTRATION

There is no magic formula for measuring the extent of oligopoly. Some economists believe that it is the predominant form of industrial organization; others argue that it is not so important. A tool economists use to gauge the extent of oligopoly is the **concentration ratio**. (See Table 1.)

> An *x*-firm **concentration ratio** is the percentage of industry sales accounted for by the *x* largest firms.

The four-firm sales concentration ratio, for example, is the percentage of industry sales accounted for by the four largest firms in the industry. Concentration ratios are an imperfect guide to the extent of oligopoly for four reasons. First, concentration ratios do not reflect competition from foreign producers or from substitute products at home. The four-firm concentration ratio of the U.S. automobile industry is 92 percent—a figure that fails to measure the competition of foreign imports. The four-firm concentration ratio in metal cans (50 percent) does not reflect the competition from stainless steel and plastic.

Second, concentration ratios may not measure concentration in the relevant market. The four-firm concentration ratio in the aircraft industry is 64 percent, but it is 97 percent in the commercial transport aircraft industry, where Boeing and McDonnell Douglas dominate sales.

Third, many markets, such as newspapers, cement, and real estate, are local or regional. Concentration ratios for percentages of national sales are misleading in such markets. A local or regional firm may dominate its relevant market, and this dominance would not necessarily be reflected by the national concentration ratio.

Fourth, concentration ratios do not measure *potential* competition. They do not indicate in which industries new firms can find ways and means to overcome existing barriers to entry if existing firms earn extraordinary profits. One airline may account for 90 percent of the flights between two cities, but the number of potential entrants into this market may be large.

Concentration ratios are a useful statistical tool for measuring the degree of market concentration. (See Example 1.) They can, however, be misleading because there is disagreement over how to define the relevant market and measure the effect of foreign competition.

> Economists do not agree how to measure oligopoly or whether a particular level of market concentration is harmful or not.

TABLE 1
Selected Concentration Ratios in Manufacturing, 1982

Industry	Four-Firm Concentration Ratio (percent)	Number of Firms
Motor vehicles and car bodies	92	284
Cereal breakfast foods	86	32
Photographic equipment	74	723
Tires and inner tubes	66	108
Aircraft	64	139
Metal cans	50	168
Soaps and other detergents	60	642
Cookies and crackers	59	296
Radio and TV sets	49	432
Farm machinery	53	1787
Blast furnaces and steel mills	42	211
Toilet preparations	34	596
Hardware	35	1085
Gray iron foundries	29	801
Men's footwear	28	129
Petroleum refining	28	282
Women's footwear	38	209
Periodicals	20	3143
Mobile homes	24	261
Paper mills	22	135
Pharmaceutical preparations	26	584
Canned fruits and vegetables	21	514
Tufted carpets	25	323
Men's and boys' suits	25	443
Radio and TV equipment	22	2083
Corrugated and solid fiber boxes	19	906
Sawmills	17	5810
Wood household furniture	16	2430
Nuts and bolts	13	780
Valves and pipe fittings	13	944
Women's dresses	6	5489
Ready-mixed concrete	6	8163

Source: U.S. Department of Commerce. "Concentration Ratios in Manufacturing," 1982 *Census of Manufacturers,* MC82-S-7.

Historical Trends in Concentration

There is a widespread false impression that the degree of concentration of the American economy has been increasing over time. In manufacturing, as column 1 of Table 2 shows, the share of manufacturing output accounted for by highly concentrated industries did not change markedly for more than 80 years. In fact, the share of highly concentrated industries in 1982 was virtually the same as in 1947. One reason for the impression of growing concentration is that the share of manufacturing output of the largest 100 companies grew from 23 percent in 1947 to 33 percent in 1982, as shown in column 2 of

EXAMPLE 1 The Herfindahl Index: Another Measure of Concentration

In 1982, the Justice Department began using the *Herfindahl index* to determine whether a merger would illegally restrain competition. The Herfindahl index (named for the late Orris Herfindahl) is the sum of the *squared values* of the market shares of all the firms in an industry. If an industry consists of firm one with a 60 percent market share and firm two with a 40 percent share, the Herfindahl index H is $(60)^2 + (40)^2 = 3600 + 1600 = 5200$. The general formula is:

$$H = (S_1)^2 + (S_2)^2 + (S_3)^2 + \cdots + (S_n)^2$$

where S_1 through S_n are the market shares (totaling 100 percent) of firms 1 through n.

Because the Herfindahl index squares market shares, large firms have a much larger impact on the index than small firms. For example, both the telephone equipment and lightbulb industries have four-firm concentration ratios of about 90 percent. Concentration ratios show them to be equally concentrated. AT&T's dominance of the telephone equipment industry, however, yields a Herfindahl measure of 5026, while the lightbulb industry has a Herfindahl measure less than half as large (2036) because the four largest firms are more equal in size in the lightbulb industry.

Industrial organization experts generally agree that an industry with 10 equally sized firms would be reasonably competitive. The Herfindahl index for an industry with 10 firms each of which has a 10 percent market share is 1000 ($= 10^2 \times 10$). In the 1982 Justice Department guidelines, a merger would not be challenged if the resulting Herfindahl index for the industry was less than 1000.

Source: Thomas M. Jorde, "Restoring Predictability to Merger Guideline Analysis," *Contemporary Policy Issues* 4, 3 (July 1988): 1–21.

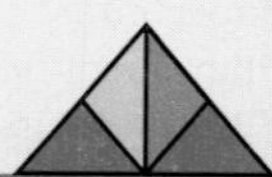

Table 2. This increase is largely the result of company mergers *across* industries, however, not of increasing concentration *within* a particular industry.[2]

Economist William G. Shepherd made a bold attempt to measure trends in the level of concentration for the U.S. economy as a whole from 1939 to 1980.[3] Using published data on concentration ratios in manufacturing and information provided by antitrust cases, government reports, research monographs, and specific articles, Shepherd classified each basic U.S. industry as a monopoly, an oligopoly, or a competitive industry. (See Table 3.)

Shepherd found that after virtually no decrease in concentration between 1939 and 1958, the U.S. economy became markedly more competitive (less concentrated) between 1958 and 1980. The average share of each sector of the economy that was "effectively competitive" rose from 56.4 percent in 1958 to 76.7 percent in 1980, with large increases in the competitiveness of the construction, manufacturing, trade, finance, insurance, real estate, and services industries. Between 1958 and 1980, the share of total output produced by monopoly fell only slightly, while the share produced by oligopoly fell dramatically from 40.6 percent to 20.8 percent of output. Shepherd concludes that three dominant factors—increasing import competition, antitrust actions, and deregulation—explain the rise in competition. (The last two factors will be discussed in a later chapter.)

[2]F.M. Scherer, *Industrial Market Structure and Economic Performance,* 2nd ed. (Boston: Houghton Mifflin, 1980), 67; James V. Koch, *Industrial Organization and Prices,* 2nd ed. (Englewood Cliffs, NJ: Prentice Hall, 1980), 181.

[3]William G. Shepherd, "Causes of Increased Competition in the U.S. Economy, 1939–1980," *Review of Economics and Statistics* (November 1982): 613–26.

TABLE 2
Trends in Concentration in American Manufacturing: Two Measures

Year	Percentage of Output by Firms with Four-Firm Concentration Ratio of 50 Percent or Above (1)	Percentage of Output of 100 Largest Firms (2)
1895–1904	33	*n.a.*
1947	24	23
1954	30	30
1958	30	32
1972	29	33
1977	28	33
1982	25	33

Sources: G. Warren Nutter. *The Extent of Enterprise Monopoly in the United States, 1899–1939* (Chicago: University of Chicago Press, 1951): 35–48, 112–50; F. M. Scherer, *Industrial Market Structure and Economic Performance* (Boston: Houghton Mifflin, 1980), 68–69; *Concentration Ratios in Manufacturing, 1977 Census of Manufacturing,* MC77-SR-9; *1982 Census of Manufacturing,* MC82-S-7.

Oligopoly versus Monopoly

Some economists think the distinctions between oligopoly and monopoly are small. In the words of John Kenneth Galbraith, "So long as there are only a few massive firms in an industry, each must act with a view of the welfare of all."[4] Although some oligopolies act like *shared monopolies,* many do not.

A shared monopoly in which all firms coordinate price or output decisions by agreed-upon rules is a *cartel.* Cartels are discussed in a later section of this chapter.

If an oligopoly were simply a complex monopoly, this chapter would be very short: It could just refer the reader to the chapter on monopoly theory. The truth is that oligopoly encompasses a broad range of market behavior and performance.[5] There is no single model of oligopolistic behavior. The task of oligopoly theory is to study the circumstances under which oligopoly might approximate either monopoly or competition.

VARYING DEGREES OF CONTROL OVER PRICE

Oligopoly theory is more complicated than the theories of perfect competition, pure monopoly, or monopolistic competition because no single theory of oligopoly exists. For example, in either perfect competition or monopoly, the firm need only equate marginal cost and a well-defined marginal revenue.

There are so few firms in oligopoly that each firm's action will influence the market as a whole and may also influence the behavior of rival firms. Because oligopolistic firms are interdependent, Firm A's behavior depends on Firm B's behavior, and Firm B's behavior depends on Firm A's behavior. The degree of control over price exhibited by an oligopolist industry varies according to which pattern of behavior the firms follow.

The Oligopolist's Demand Curve

Because firms in an oligopoly are mutually interdependent, the demand curve for an oligopolist's product cannot be defined until the behavior of rival firms is specified. This behavior can range from complete independence of other oligopolists to complete coordination with them.

Ford Motor Company, for example, produces cars and competes with a handful of other automobile manufacturers around the world. Suppose that at the current price of $8000 Ford is selling 1 million units of its compact car, with the comparable compact cars of Toyota, Volkswagen, Nissan, Chrysler, and General Motors selling for comparable prices.

Point *a* in Figure 1 describes the situation currently confronting Ford: It lies on Ford's demand curve because 1 million units are being sold at a price of $8000. What happens if Ford reduces its prices to $7000? Figure 1 shows two extreme scenarios. Point *b* represents Ford's quantity demanded if the rest of the industry (General Motors and foreign producers) behaves *in an exactly parallel fashion,* lowering prices by the same percentage as Ford. In this case, Ford

[4]John K. Galbraith, *American Capitalism,* rev. ed (Cambridge: The Riverside Press, 1956).

[5]Oliver Williamson, *Markets and Hierarchies: Analysis and Antitrust Implications* (New York: The Free Press, 1975), 234.

TABLE 3
Trends in Competition in the U.S. Economy, 1939–1980

Market Model		Share of Each Sector Characterized by Market Model (percent) 1939		1958		1980	
1. Pure monopoly		6.2		3.1		2.5	
2. Dominant-firm industries	Oligopoly	5.0	41.4	5.0	40.6	2.8	20.8
3. Tight-oligopoly industries	Oligopoly	36.4		35.6		18.0	
4. Effectively competitive industries		52.4		56.3		76.7	
Total		**100.0**		**100.0**		**100.0**	

Shepherd considered an industry to be (1) a pure monopoly if the market share was near 100 percent, entry barriers were high, and there was evidence of monopoly pricing; (2) a dominant-firm industry if the market share was between 50 percent and 90 percent, there was no close rival, entry barriers were high, and rates of return were above the competitive rate; (3) a tight-oligopoly industry if the four-firm concentration ratio was above 60 percent, market shares were stable, and there was a tendency toward cooperation; (4) an effectively competitive industry if the four-firm concentration ratio was below 40 percent, entry barriers were low, market shares were unstable, and prices were flexible. The extent of oligopoly in the economy is the measure of the combined shares of dominant-firm and tight-oligopoly industries.

Sources: William G. Shepherd, "Causes of Increased Competition in the U.S. Economy, 1939–1980," *Review of Economics and Statistics,* (November 1982): 613–26.

increases its sales to 1.25 million cars because auto prices in general have fallen relative to the prices of substitutes for autos. This point thus represents the *shared monopoly* effect on Ford's quantity demanded.

Point b' represents Ford's quantity demanded when the rest of the industry behaves *completely independently* of Ford: When Ford lowers its price, the rest of the industry continues to charge the same prices as before. In this case, there will be a large increase in Ford's sales to 1.75 million cars. The price of Ford cars has fallen relative to those of its closest substitutes. In Figure 1, points b and b' represent the extremes of the possible positions of the demand curve. The actual position could be anywhere between b and b', depending upon how competitors react.

If Ford raises its price to $9000, the same range of outcomes is possible. At point c on Ford's demand curve, pricing actions are completely coordinated by all oligopolists. In this case, Ford sales fall to 0.75 million cars. At point c', there is complete independence of actions, with the other oligopolists holding the line on prices. Ford sales might then fall considerably to point c, where only 0.25 million units are sold. The range of possible outcomes is represented by the line $c'c$.

In Figure 1, the demand curve for Ford's compact cars can be anywhere in the orange region of the two triangles. The slope of the demand curve can vary from the slope of the line cab to the slope of $c'ab'$. The demand curve and, hence, marginal revenue cannot be determined in oligopoly until the actions of rival firms are known.

The Kinked Demand Model

The behavior of an oligopoly can take many forms. One way to explain it is by the kinked demand curve, developed by Paul Sweezy. The kinked demand curve applies only to situations in which rivals match price cuts but do not follow price increases. For instance, suppose Ford discovers its rivals match its price *cuts* but hold their prices when Ford raises its price. In this

FIGURE 1
Why the Oligopolist's Demand Curve Is Indeterminant

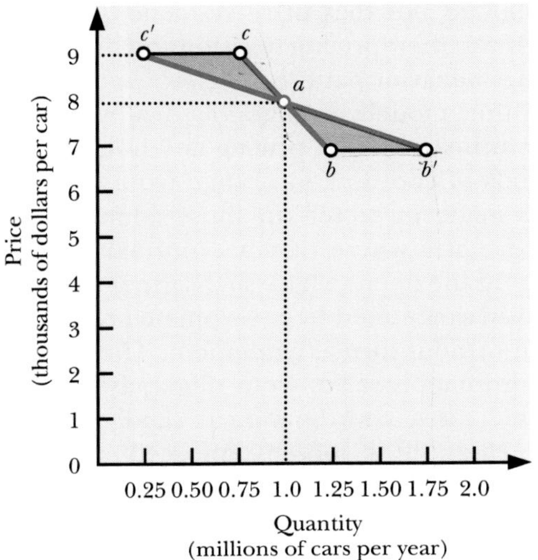

At point a, Ford sells 1 million cars at a price of $8000. If Ford lowers its price to $7000, what happens to sales depends upon how Ford's competitors react. Point b results when Ford's rivals match Ford's price reduction. Point b' results if they do not follow Ford's price reduction. If Ford raises its price to $9000, the effect on sales again depends upon the reactions of competitors. Point c' results if competitors keep their prices constant; point c results when they match Ford's increase.

FIGURE 2
An Oligopoly Firm Facing a Kinked Demand Curve

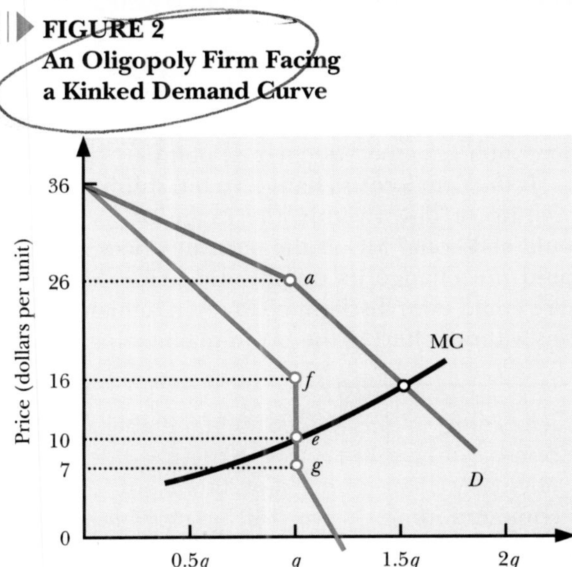

This firm's rivals will follow price reductions but not price increases. Therefore, for prices below the current $26 price, the demand curve, D, is less elastic than it is for prices above $26. The marginal revenue curve, MR, drops sharply from f to g. The MC curve can shift up or down (as long as it remains within this vertical portion of the MR curve) without changing the firm's price or output decisions. The kinked demand schedule is one explanation for the inflexibility of oligopoly prices.

case, Ford's demand curve would be $c'ab$ in Figure 1. The demand curve would have a "kink" in it at point a, the current price.

> A **kinked demand curve** results when other firms match a firm's price decreases but do not match its price increases.

The kinked demand model appears to hold for some industries (and firms) but not for others. In the airline industry, rival firms have tended to match fare cuts but not to follow fare increases. In the early 1980s, United Airlines (then the largest airline) had to abandon attempted fare increases when rival airlines failed to follow. In the early 1990s, most airlines had a policy of matching all fare reductions on rival airlines flying the same routes. Only relatively small carriers (such as Southwest) that offer a limited number of flights appear to be able to offer lower fares that are not matched by rival firms.[6]

Figure 2 shows an oligopoly firm facing a kinked demand curve. The firm's current price is $26. Because its price increases are not followed by rivals but its price cuts are matched, the firm's demand curve, D, is more elastic above the $26 price than below it. Thus the firm's demand curve has a kink at the current price. Because of the kink, the MR curve drops sharply at the price of $26. In Figure 2, marginal revenue is $16 at a price just above $26 and only $7 at a price just below $26. Because the marginal revenue curve has a vertical segment (feg) just below the

[6]Scherer, *Industrial Market Structure,* 184.

demand kink, a *range* of MR values is associated with the $26 price; the oligopolist is maximizing profits at the price of $26 if the MC curve intersects the MR curve anywhere in that range of values represented by the vertical segment *feg*. In this situation, the MC curve intersects the MR curve at point *e*.

If the firm's costs changed a bit, shifting the MC curve up or down within the range of *f* to *g*, MR would still equal MC at the current price. The firm would not change its output and price. Moreover, there could even be slight changes in demand conditions without altering the profit-maximizing price.

> According to the kinked demand theory: (1) prices will be more stable in a kinked demand oligopoly than under conditions of perfect competition: (2) prices will be more stable in a kinked demand oligopoly than in a pure monopoly because (as the monopoly chapter showed) monopoly prices change when costs change.

The kinked demand model raises as many questions as it answers. It applies only to situations in which price increases are not followed but price decreases are. It does not answer the most important question of all—namely, why the kink is located where it is.

The kinked demand model predicts that oligopoly prices will be more stable than in perfect competition *or* monopoly. Indeed, some studies have found that oligopoly prices on the average tend to change less than prices in other markets.[7]

[7]J. Fred Weston and Steven Lustgarten investigated price changes between 1954 and 1973 and found that, typically, the higher the concentration ratio, the lower the annual percentage price change. This study is one of a long series that followed the 1935 studies of Gardner Means, who coined the term *administered prices* to characterize inflexible oligopoly prices. The major challenge to the administered-price notion was mounted by George Stigler and James Kindahl, who maintain that the list prices of oligopoly products like steel, automobiles, and aluminum conceal many hidden discounts that understate oligopoly price flexibility. See J. Fred Weston and Steven H. Lustgarten, "Concentration and Wage-Price Changes," in eds. Harvey J. Goldschmid et al. *Industrial Concentration: The New Learning* (Boston: Little, Brown, 1974), 312; George Stigler and James K. Kindahl, *The Behavior of Industrial Prices* (New York: National Bureau of Economic Research, 1970.) For more recent work, see D.V. Carlton, "The Rigidity of Prices," *American Economic Review* (September 1986): 637–58.

Collusion

The kinked demand model of oligopoly assumes that there is no agreed-upon coordination among firms. Each firm knows that price increases will not be followed but that price reductions will be, and firms make their pricing decisions on the basis of this industry behavior pattern.

Other models of oligopoly deal with situations where firms *collude* on pricing and output decisions. Methods of coordination range from formal agreements made in secret (in those countries like the United States where they are normally against the law) or in the open (where such agreements are legal and even sanctioned by government) to tacit coordination without formal agreement. The effectiveness of coordination varies from oligopoly to oligopoly. In some cases, coordination is rigidly enforced; in other cases, it is loosely enforced and tends to break down.

The three major methods of oligopoly coordination are: (1) cartel agreements, (2) price leadership, and (3) conscious parallelism.

Cartel Agreements. The most direct way for an oligopoly to coordinate pricing and output policy is to enter a **cartel** agreement, binding on all parties, to set the prices or market shares of each producer. If successful, cartel agreements allow oligopolistic firms to operate as a shared monopoly—to earn monopoly profits for the industry as a whole.

> A **cartel** is an arrangement that allows the participating firms to operate the industry as a shared monopoly.

In effect, firms participating in the cartel coordinate their output and pricing decisions to yield the industry price and output combination that would have prevailed had this industry been a pure monopoly with each firm as a branch of one gigantic firm.

Consider an oligopolistic industry that consists of three identical firms (which the same costs and producing the same product). Barriers to entry are so high that the three established firms need not worry about attracting new entrants should profits be high. In this case, the three identical firms each agree to take one-third of the market and to charge the same monopoly price.

FIGURE 3
Collusive Oligopoly

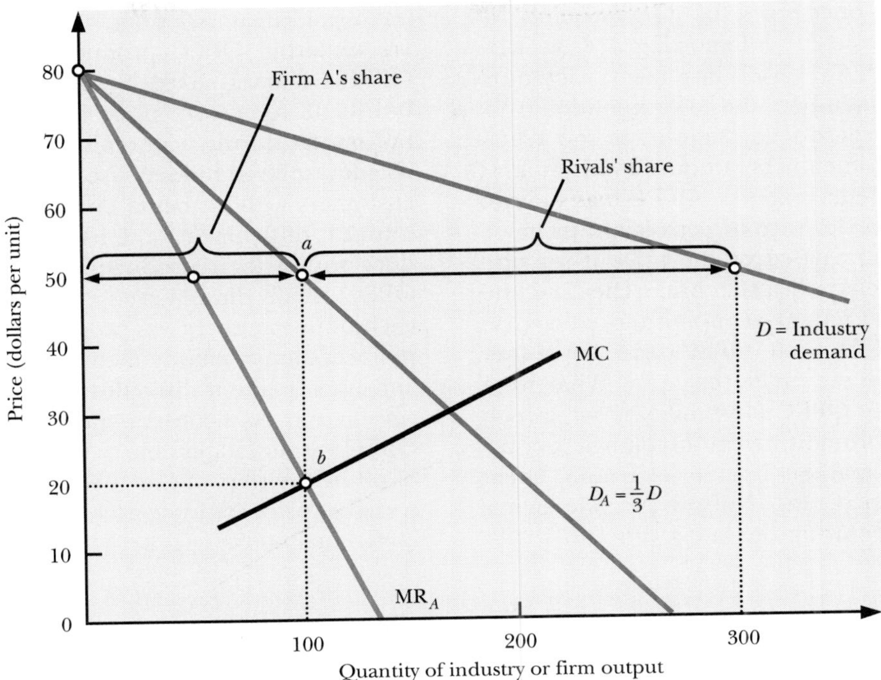

Curve D represents the industry demand curve. The industry consists of three oligopolistic firms that agree to share the market equally and charge the same price. D_A is the demand schedule of Firm A; it is one-third of the industry demand schedule. MR_A is the marginal revenue curve of Firm A. Firm A will maximize profits by producing that output at which MC equals MR, or 100 units at \$50 per unit (point a).

Why would Firm A be tempted to cheat on the agreement? If Firm A lowers price a little, it gains sales from its two rivals. As long as A's lower price exceeds A's marginal cost, Firm A's profits will increase. If all three firms cheat, however, a competitive bidding war should break out, and they could end up earning virtually no economic profits.

How each firm selects its profit-maximizing price is shown in Figure 3. The industry demand curve is D. Firm A's demand and marginal revenue curves (which are the same as those of firms B and C) are shown as D_A and MR_A. Because all three firms are part of a cartel agreement to share the market equally, Firm A's demand curve is D_A ($\frac{1}{3} \times D$). The monopoly price is determined by drawing the MR_A curve corresponding to D_A and locating its intersection with the MC curve. Firm A maximizes its profit by producing 100 units at a price of \$50 per unit (point a). The other two firms also charge \$50 and produce 100 units each. Industry output is 300 ($= 3 \times 100$).

Consider the position of Firm A. Its two rival firms are selling 200 units at the price of \$50. What would prevent Firm A from stealing some customers from the other firms by offering a slightly lower price? For instance, firm A could charge \$49.50 and possibly obtain a great deal more business. In effect, the cartel price approximately equals the marginal revenue to the cheating firm if it can make secret sales at slightly less than the cartel price. As long as its secret sales remain small and don't drive down the cartel price, \$49.50 is now essentially the cheating firm's marginal revenue. The marginal revenue of \$49.50 clearly exceeds marginal cost (\$20) to each firm. Hence, substantial gains accrue to the firm that breaks the cartel agreement. Firm A's cheating on the agreement has its long-run costs, however, because it may encourage the other two firms to break the

EXAMPLE 2 Cartel Instability: The Problems of OPEC

The once-powerful Organization of Petroleum Exporting Countries (OPEC) cartel has fallen victim to cheating by members and to competition from nonmember producing nations. In the 1970s, when OPEC members produced the bulk of world petroleum exports, OPEC was able to dictate the world price of petroleum. Its members generally abided by the price it set, and there was relatively little price cheating. Industrial organization economists predicted in the early 1970s that OPEC, like any other cartel, would eventually collapse. What were the sources of OPEC's instability? First, a high price of oil brought new nonmember producers into the market. The Soviet Union, Great Britain, Mexico, and Norway became major oil exporters during the late 1970s and 1980s. As "legal cheaters," such non-OPEC producers underbid OPEC producers and reduced OPEC's market share. Second, OPEC found it difficult to enforce price discipline and output quotas during economic downturns. Price cheaters offered hidden discounts or rebates to customers without being detected, and OPEC found it difficult to force its members to produce within their production quotas. In fact, OPEC usually did not even know how much oil each of its members was producing. Third, the political enmity among members (such as Iran and Iraq) made it difficult for OPEC to reach agreements. As a consequence of these factors, OPEC was no longer able to set the world price of oil by the start of the 1980s. What was once a mighty price-setting cartel was reduced to an ineffectual body.

agreement. Price warfare could erupt, and economic profit would be driven down. (See Example 2.)

Cartel theory has two great and contradictory themes: (1) Every cartel member can gain through the attainment of monopoly profits if every member adheres to the cartel agreement. (2) Each cartel member can gain by cheating on the agreement if the others do not cheat.

Most cartels are unstable because of the extreme difficulty of enforcing the cartel agreement. Greed leads firms into cartels; greed also leads firms to break up cartels. Very few cartels are successful over the long run. Most, like the ill-fated sugar, cocoa, tin, and coffee cartels, either disappear quickly or have no noticeable effect on prices. They become, instead, a forum for airing complaints about low prices. (See Example 3 for an exception.)

With some minor exceptions, formal price-setting agreements violate U.S. law. Nonetheless, a number of price conspiracy cases have come to light where oligopolistic producers have met in secret to set prices and distribute sales. The most widely publicized case was the electrical products conspiracy case of 1961 involving top executives from General Electric, Westinghouse, Allis-Chalmers, and other well-known companies. These executives met secretly to set prices and allocate contracts among companies participating in the agreement. In addition to paying stiff fines, the conspirators were sentenced to short prison terms. (Other, less risky means of coordinating prices, such as price leadership and conscious parallelism, are discussed in the next sections.)

Informal agreements can also be used to coordinate pricing and output decisions. The most notable historical case of informal agreement was the so-called Gary dinners of the early twentieth century. Mr. Gary, president of the U.S. Steel Corporation, would invite steel company executives representing more than 90 percent of industry output to dinner regularly to urge his guests to cooperate in holding prices where they were. Walter Adams describes the Gary dinners:

> He exhorted them like a Methodist preacher at a camp meeting to follow the price leadership of U.S. Steel. There was no need for any formal agreements. U.S. Steel simply

EXAMPLE 3 The Diamond Cartel: A Cartel That Works

The DeBeers Company, founded by Cecil Rhodes in 1871 in the diamond fields of South Africa, has proven to be the world's most lasting and effective cartel. DeBeers has controlled world diamond prices since the 1930s through its Central Selling Organization (CSO). The CSO is DeBeers' marketing arm, through which virtually all the world's diamonds are sold. Although only 15 percent of today's world diamond production originates in South Africa, the CSO has purchasing pacts with the world's major diamond producers (such as the former Soviet Union, Zaire and other African nations, and Australia). The diamond-producing countries give DeBeers a monopoly over the sale of diamonds in return for stable contracts and high diamond prices.

DeBeers controls diamond prices by regulating the supplies of diamonds it offers to world diamond buyers. When demand is weak, DeBeers holds diamonds off the market, building up a stockpile of unsold diamonds. In 1984, for example, DeBeers had a reserve of $2 billion worth of diamonds after a period of weak demand in the early 1980s. When demand is brisk (such as during the late 1980s), DeBeers offers diamonds to the world market only at a pace consistent with stable or rising prices.

How does DeBeers prevent the cheating that plagues other cartels? DeBeers prevents its *buyers* from cheating by inviting only a select group to its London sales every 5 weeks. Buyers must accept the cartel price or risk not being invited to subsequent sales. Jewelry manufacturers could not survive if cut off from DeBeers sales. DeBeers also prevents cheating by diamond *producers* by offering faithful members stable contracts, stable prices, and financial security. DeBeers agreements are accepted by world bankers as collateral for bank loans. Third, DeBeers has ways to punish disloyal members. When Zaire attempted to leave the cartel in 1981, DeBeers flooded diamond markets with low-quality diamonds similar to those from Zaire to drive their price down.

DeBeers is a rare example of a cartel that has remained successful in the long run by skillfully preventing cheating by both buyers and cartel members.

Source: "Why a Diamond Cartel is Forever," *New York Times*, September 7, 1986.

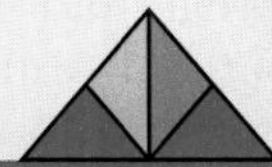

assumed the lead incumbent on a firm its size: its rivals followed, fully realizing the security and profitability of cooperation.[8]

Gary dinners and their like confirm Adam Smith's perception that "people of the same trade seldom meet together, even for merriment and diversion, but the conversation ends in a conspiracy against the public, or in some contrivance to raise prices."[9]

Price Leadership. A subtler method of collusion occurs when an oligopolistic industry has a recognized **price leader**, which keeps a sharp eye on market demand and costs common to all firms and whose price increases and decreases are followed by rival firms.

> A **price leader** is an oligopolist whose price changes are consistently imitated by other firms in the industry.

Examples of price leadership are plentiful. During the 1920s and 1930s, the "big three" cigarette manufacturers (R. J. Reynolds, American Tobacco,

[8]Walter Adams, *The Structure of American Industry,* 71.

[9]Adam Smith, *The Wealth of Nations,* ed. Edwin Cannan (New York: Modern Library, 1937).

EXAMPLE 4 Focal Points: Books for $4.95 or $4.99?

For the past 20 years, book publishers have set their price point at 95 cents. Books sold for $2.95 or $6.95 as opposed to $2.99 or $6.99. A book publisher explained that publishers adopted this pricing system years ago "precisely to differentiate books from the other things you buy in toy stores and at the gas pump."

The advent of book discounters has changed the rules of the book-pricing game. Books listed by the publisher at $22.95 might sell for $13.77 in a discount bookstore. In October 1990, Penguin USA announced that it would abandon the 95 cent price point: Books that previously cost $3.95 and $5.95 would now cost $3.99 and $5.99. Rival book publishers are also expected to adopt the 99 cent price point.

Why had no one announced a move to the 99 cent price-point standard sooner? Declared one publisher, "I've wondered about that since I've been in the business, and I guess the explanation is that book publishing is very traditional."

The 95 cent price-point tradition in book publishing is an example of the use of focal points. Traditional business practices dictated that books be priced at a dollar amount plus 95 cents. All participants in the market understood and followed this practice until the rules of the game changed. From now on, perhaps, the industry will follow the 99 cents price-point practice.

Source: "Penguin to Raise Prices Next Year by 4 Cents a Book," *New York Times*, October 19, 1990.

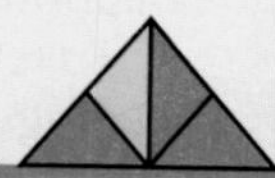

and Liggett & Meyers) set the classic pattern with R. J. Reynolds (Camels) serving as the price leader. In today's cigarette industry, Philip Morris has become the price leader by virtue of the market dominance of Marlboro cigarettes. In the ready-to-eat breakfast cereal industry, which includes Kellogg's, Post, and General Mills (the big three), Kellogg's leads for most product lines, and General Mills and Post each lead for their own best product lines.

Conscious Parallelism. The subtlest form of collusion is **conscious parallelism,** which uses *focal points* for price setting. A focal point is an obvious benchmark by which prices or output could be coordinated without an explicit agreement.

> **Conscious parallelism** occurs when rival firms follow the same pricing and output rules without formal agreement but in accordance with customary industry business practices.

Thomas Schelling uses the following general analogy to explain how focal points are discovered:

> You are to meet someone in New York City. You have not been instructed where to meet: you have no prior understanding with the person on where to meet: and you cannot communicate with each other.... You are told the date but not the hour of this meeting: The two of you must guess the place and exact minute of the day for the meeting.[10]

According to Schelling, given these instructions, most people familiar with New York City would choose the information booth at Grand Central Station at noon.

How do oligopolists use focal points? Oligopolistic firms are intimately acquainted with the way things work in their own industries. The focal points may be standardized business practices—such as common percentage markups, the use of round numbers, the charging of prices like $4.95, and policies like "splitting the difference" or changing high rates at the same time each year. As long as each oligopolist understands these standard practices, it can anticipate how rival firms will behave in given situations. (See Example 4.)

[10]Thomas Schelling, *The Strategy of Conflict* (Cambridge, MA: Harvard University Press, 1960), 56.

> Through conscious parallelism, the actions of producers can be coordinated within certain ranges without formal or even informal agreements. All oligopolists use their understanding of the industry to make their own decisions and anticipate the behavior of other oligopolists.

A possible example of conscious parallelism is the following experience of the U.S. Veterans Administration:

> On June 5, 1955, five different companies submitted sealed bids to fill an order for 5.640 100-capsule bottles of the antibiotic tetracyclin, each quoting an effective net price of $19.1884 per bottle.... But although one can never be certain, it is probable that there was no direct collusion connected with this transaction.... The curious price of $19.1884 per bottle was arrived at through the application of a series of round-number discounts to round-number base prices: $19.1884 is the standard trade discount of 2 percent of $19.58, which after rounding, is 20 percent off the wholesale price of $24.48, which in turn is 20 percent off the $30.60 charged to retail druggists, which is 40 percent off the prevailing retail list price of $51.00, which in turn reflected an earlier 15 percent cut from the original list price of $60.00 per 100 capsules.[11]

What appears to be an incredible coincidence explainable only by a secret price agreement may in fact be simply the application of focal points by the firms involved. Focal points may also help explain why oligopoly prices are sometimes inflexible. Firms accustomed to making decisions based on focal points may be reluctant to make large price changes that put them outside the customary range of focal points.

Obstacles to Collusion

Despite the considerable gains to oligopolists from cooperation, effective collusion may be difficult to achieve. The chances for effective and lasting collusion decrease when there are (1) many sellers, (2) low entry barriers, (3) product heterogeneity, (4) high rates of innovation, (5) high fixed costs, (6) opportunities for cheating, and (7) legal restrictions.

Many Sellers. The more sellers there are in the industry, the more difficult it is for the sellers to join a conspiracy to raise prices. The communication network becomes much more complicated as the number of conspirators grows. When there are two sellers, there is only one communication link. When there are three sellers, there are three different information links: A must agree with B; B must agree with C; C and A must agree. When there are 10 sellers, there are 45 ways information must flow! The number of information channels increases at a far greater rate than the rate at which the number of sellers increases. (See Example 5.) It becomes far more difficult to coordinate collusive actions as the number of colluders grows. [The formula for the number of information flows is $n(n-1)/2$, where n is the number of sellers.]

Low Entry Barriers. If it is easy for new firms to enter an industry, existing firms may not find it worthwhile to work out agreements to raise prices. Effective collusion would cause new firms to enter the industry.

High prices create profitable opportunities for new firms. For example, if an industry has constant returns to scale (no economies or diseconomies of scale), the average cost of production is the same whether there is one firm or many firms. Suppose that such an industry currently has two firms and the average cost of production—including a normal return—is $10. With complete free entry, the existing firms could not charge more than $10 in the long run. Any price above $10 would bring in new firms to capture above-normal returns. The entry of firms would eventually drive the price down to $10, where only a normal return is earned. The two existing firms would gain no lasting benefit by conspiring to raise the price above $10.

Product Heterogeneity. The more heterogeneous (differentiated) the product is from firm to firm, the more difficult it is for the industry to achieve coordination or collusion. Reaching an agreement creates both costs and benefits. It is costlier to reach an agreement if the product is not homogeneous. Because steel is homogeneous, an agreement on prices and market shares between two major steel producers may be fairly easy to conclude. (Again, see Example 5.) But an agreement between McDonnell Douglas and Boeing over the relative prices of the *MD–11*

[11]Scherer, *Industrial Market Structure,* 191.

EXAMPLE 5 Pricing Baby Formula

Almost everyone uses or has used baby formula. It is such an important product that the federal government finances the state-run Special Food Program for Women, Infants, and Children (WIC) to provide low-income families with formula. The program accounts for one out of every three cans of baby formula sold in the United States.

Three companies make up for the bulk of sales: Abbott (Similac), Bristol-Myers Squibb (Enfamil), and American Home Products (SMA brand). The wholesale prices charged by the three companies are virtually identical.

Until the mid-1980s almost all state WIC programs paid the full retail price for baby formula. The program would simply issue a voucher that could be used to purchase any brand of formula. The three companies have been happy with the program; they cooperate by giving away free formula to state hospitals and doctors. In turn, hospitals and doctors might recommend certain brands, even though federal law requires that baby formulas use standard ingredients. (Some hospitals treat the three brands as interchangeable.)

But prices of baby formula doubled from 1980 to 1991. State WIC programs had to be cut back. At this point, the Center of Budget and Policy Priorities in Washington urged state officials to try competitive bidding. In this case, the state program would issue a voucher only for the brand that gave the largest rebate to the state. In 1987, Texas, Oregon, and Tennessee announced competitive bidding; other states followed. Since Texas received a $1 per can rebate with competitive bidding, the state saved $35 million a year on formula and could serve an additional 110,000 residents.

Federal and state governments are investigating whether the three producers of formula have rigged bids on contracts. Both Abbott and Bristol-Myers heavily lobbied the various legislatures and doctors to keep the old system intact; one company even threatened that it might end its policy of giving away free formula to state hospitals. Another company (perhaps hoping to be a price leader) sent a letter to the WIC directors of several states announcing that its rebate (presented in sealed competitive bidding) would be 75 cents a can.

If collusion is established, it may have been fed by the small number of companies producing baby formula and the homogeneity of the product. The WIC program appears to have played a role in such collusion by allowing the companies to sell much of their product to a buyer that—at least until the late 1980s—paid too little attention to costs. Competition thrives on many sellers and many buyers shopping for the lowest price.

Source: "What Prompted Investigations into Pricing of Baby Formula," *New York Times*, January 19, 1991, 20.

and the Boeing 767 may be quite difficult because of the differences between the two planes. An agreement between the producers of high-quality goods and low-quality goods may break down because of differences of opinion over one good's quality relative to the other good's quality. It would be difficult for a fast-food chain like McDonald's to enter into a pricing agreement with a full-service restaurant chain like Red Lobster because of the difficulty of agreeing on the proper relative price.

High Rates of Innovation. If an industry has a high rate of innovation, collusive agreements are more difficult to reach. In unstable, quickly changing markets, oligopolies have more difficulty finding the joint profit-maximizing solution. The costs of reaching an agreement are higher in relation to benefits when the industry is constantly turning out new products and developing new techniques. For example, it would be difficult for Eastman-Kodak and Polaroid to reach an agreement because of the fast pace of technological change in the camera and instant-development industry. The same would be true of the personal computer market, which has been characterized by frequent advances in technology.

High Fixed Costs. As fixed costs become higher relative to total costs, collusive agreements become more likely to break down. Firms ask themselves what they can gain by cheating on the pricing agreement. If fixed costs are high, variable costs are a low percentage of total costs. As long as the price covers average variable costs, something is left over with which to pay fixed costs. By granting secret price concessions, firms may gain much in the short run if marginal costs are very low.

Opportunities for Cheating. If it is easy to cheat without being detected, firms will tend to break a collusive agreement. It is easier to cheat on price agreements when actual prices charged by one party cannot be known with certainty by the other parties to the agreement. For example, barbers can often agree upon and charge uniform prices within the same city because the prices of haircuts must be posted. It is easy for rival barbers to detect barbers who are undercutting the agreed-upon price. Thus, in many cities with a strong barbers' union, the price of haircuts is uniform, and there are few price wars. On the other hand, when the terms of price negotiations are not revealed (as in the cases of long-term oil delivery contracts or purchases of commercial aircraft by the airlines), it is easier to cheat on pricing agreements. When the cartel lacks an effective punishment for cheaters, enforcement of discipline is difficult.

Legal Restrictions. In the United States, the Sherman Antitrust Act (1890) holds that combinations in restraint of trade are illegal. The Sherman act and additional acts designed to prohibit and punish collusive behavior make up the antitrust laws of the United States (to be discussed in a later chapter). Antitrust laws reduce collusion by increasing the costs of forming agreements.

GAME THEORY

If the obstacles to collusion are sufficiently strong, oligopolists will engage in **noncooperative oligopoly behavior.** In such circumstances, each oligopolist must guess what its rivals will do under alternative circumstances. If McDonald's advertises heavily on television, can Wendy's or Burger King be expected to follow suit? If Kellogg's introduces a new breakfast cereal, will General Mills and Post also introduce new brands of cereal?

> **Noncooperative oligopoly behavior** occurs when mutually interdependent firms do not coordinate their actions but instead engage in strategic decision making.

When oligopolists do not collude, they must act strategically. Oligopoly is like a game. As in sports, poker, chess, or war, players must act in response to the strategies adopted by their opponents. In 1944, mathematician John von Neumann and economist Oskar Morgenstern together developed an approach for studying the strategic behavior of economic agents. Appropriately enough, their approach is called game theory.[12]

Nash Equilibrium

If oligopolists must guess what their rivals will do, at what point will they reach a state of equilibrium in which each rival is satisfied with its current strategy? The concept of equilibrium is as important to oligopoly as it is to perfect competition or monopoly. Firms will not be in equilibrium if they have guessed wrong about their rival's strategy. If one oligopolist cuts prices expecting the rival firm not to follow, the oligopolist will not have adopted the best strategy if the rival also cuts its prices.

Under what circumstances will noncooperating oligopolists eventually arrive at a state of equilibrium in which all parties are satisfied with their current strategy? While they are likely to guess wrong initially, noncooperating oligopolists can adjust their guesses about the rival's strategy. After a number of adjustments, they might be able to predict their rival's strategy. In a competitive market, price adjusts until suppliers and demanders are brought into balance. Would a firm's strategies also adjust in a noncooperative situation? An early nineteenth-century French

[12]Oskar Morgenstern and John von Neumann, *Theory of Games and Economic Behavior* (Princeton: Princeton University Press, 1944).

economist, Augustin Cournot, and later a modern game theorist, John Nash, suggested a way to analyze this situation. An oligopolistic industry will reach a **Nash equilibrium** when each firm's guess about the strategy of other firms is correct and each firm is able to employ the strategy best suited to the rival's correctly anticipated behavior.

> A **Nash equilibrium** exists in an oligopolistic industry if each firm's profit-maximizing behavior is based on a correct guess about the behavior of rivals.

An industry reaches a Nash equilibrium if no firm finds it advantageous to change its strategy as long as the others continue to behave the way the firm believes they are behaving.

Some types of oligopoly arrangements are basically unstable and cannot reach a Nash equilibrium. Rival firms are unable to settle on a stable behavior pattern. Cartels, for example, cannot achieve a Nash equilibrium. If everybody else is playing by the rules of the cartel game, it pays for each participant to break the rules. Similarly, focal-point pricing will not achieve a Nash equilibrium. If all sellers of a particular drug are submitting bids on the basis of costs plus 30 percent, it pays for one seller to submit a bid of costs plus 29 percent! When one seller breaks the focal-point pattern, other firms respond by altering their own strategy.

There are many examples of oligopoly behavior that achieves a Nash equilibrium. The kinked demand model achieves a Nash equilibrium when each oligopolist holds price steady in the expectation that its rivals will match price cuts but not price increases. As long as rivals persist in this behavior, the oligopolist cannot gain by raising or lowering price singlehandedly.

Four examples of behavior through which firms in an oligopolistic industry reach a Nash equilibrium are *the Cournot oligopoly game,* the *prisoners' dilemma game,* the *advertising game,* and the making of a *credible threat.*

The Cournot Oligopoly Game

One of the most important models of oligopoly was developed by a French economist, Augustin A. Cournot (1801–1877), in 1838. A **Cournot oligopoly** occurs when each firm in a group producing a homogenous product acts as though all other firms will continue to produce their current outputs. Thus a Cournot oligopolist supposes that if it increases its own output, the price of the product must fall by just enough to sell its planned increase in output since all rivals are expected to maintain their production levels. Similarly, if the firm cuts output, the price will rise by just enough to reduce market demand by the firm's planned reduction in output.

> In a **Cournot oligopoly,** (1) the product is homogenous; (2) each firm supposes that its rivals will continue to produce their current outputs independently of that firm's choice of outputs; and (3) there is a fixed number of firms.

Cournot himself used an example of two mineral springs supplied by an underground lake. The mineral water is accessible through two springs owned by Bob and Ted. Customers are indifferent about whether they buy mineral water from Bob or Ted, so Bob and Ted must sell at the same price. Figure 4 shows Ted's output on the vertical axis and Bob's on the horizontal axis. The line TM describes Bob's profit-maximizing response to Ted's output, and the line $T'M'$ describes Ted's profit-maximizing response to Bob's output. These *reaction curves* show the best response (or profit-maximizing response) of one firm to the other firm's output. In other words, they show the output level each firm would pick if it knew what the rival firm's output would be. The reaction curves are easy to understand. First, they are both downward-sloping because the more Ted produces, the less of the market remains for Bob (and vice versa). Second, when the output of one is zero, the other assumes he has a monopoly and produces accordingly. In Figure 4, the monopoly output is 3 units. Third, if one firm fully saturates the market, the other will produce nothing. We call this the *predatory output* because it drives the other firm out of business. In Figure 4, the predatory output of each firm is 6 units. This exceeds monopoly output because in monopoly the price exceeds marginal cost, leaving room for the other firm to make some sales. Therefore, the reaction curves must appear as in Figure 4. The two reaction curves intersect at the point where each firm's expectations about the other firm are fulfilled; it is an equilibrium because each firm

FIGURE 4
Cournot Strategies

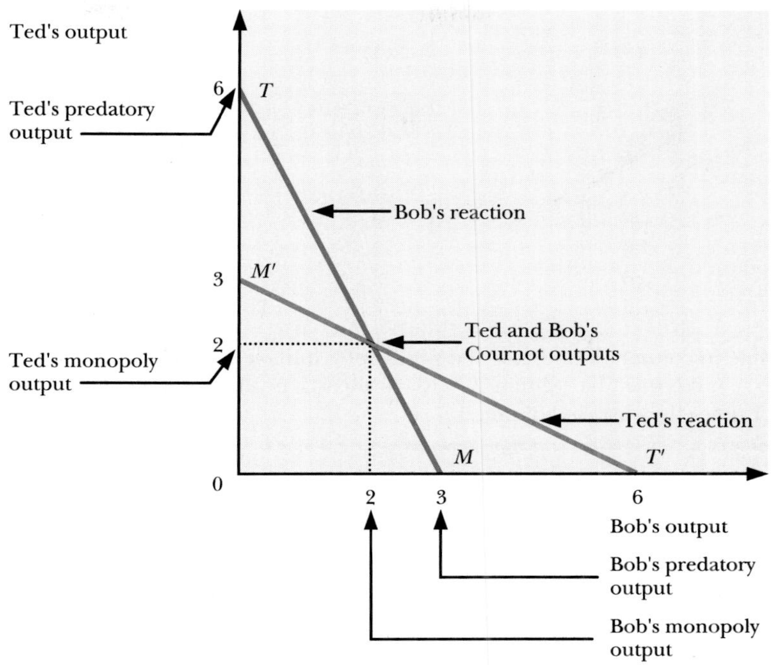

is doing the best it can given the other firm's choice of output. In the figure, the Cournot equilibrium occurs where each firm produces 2 units; the market therefore consists of 4 units.

The predatory and monopoly outputs of 6 and 3 used in Figure 4 can easily be rationalized by imposing simple demand and cost assumptions. Suppose it costs nothing to draw water from the springs. Marginal costs of production are zero. To keep matters simple, suppose packaging costs are also zero. With zero costs, revenue and profit are the same. The demand curve $P = 6 - Q$ gives the price that people will pay for mineral water. This means that predatory output is 6 for any firm because that output drives the price to zero (the level of costs).

Columns 1 and 2 of Table 4 show the demand curve. If either Ted or Bob has a monopoly, he will produce 3 units at a price of $3. Why? We showed in the chapter on monopoly that with a straight-line demand curve, revenue is maximized at the midpoint. This is shown again in column 3 of Table 4, when $Q = 3$ and profit (or revenue) is $9 (= $3 × 3). If 1 less unit is produced, so that $Q = 2$ and $P = 4$, profit would drop to $8; if 1 more unit is produced, so that $Q = 4$ and $P = \$2$, profit would again drop to $8.

Since the predatory and monopoly outputs in this example are 6 and 3 respectively, we have fully justified the reaction curves in Figure 4. The example contains an important lesson: You can always solve a Cournot problem by remembering that when the demand curve is a straight line and both firms face constant marginal costs, the predatory output is always twice the monopoly output. Thus, by computing each firm's predatory output, you can draw the reaction curves.

Table 4 gives an independent summary of the Cournot equilibrium. It shows what happens to Bob's profit if Ted produces 2 units and demonstrates that if Bob produces 2 units, he maximizes his profit at $4 by producing 2 units of output as well. Since Ted's situation is identical, Ted would maximize his profit by producing 2 units if Bob is producing 2 units. Thus the Cournot equilibrium occurs when each firm produces 2 units.

TABLE 4
A Cournot Model with Two Firms, Zero Costs, and Linear Demand

(1)	(2)	(3)	(4)	(5)	(6)
P	*Q*	*P* × *Q*	Ted's Output	Bob's Output	Bob's Profit
6	0	0	—	—	
5	1	5	—	—	
4	2	8	2	0	0
3	3	9	2	1	3
2	4	8	2	2	4
1	5	5	2	3	3

Given the demand schedule in columns 1 and 2, if Ted produces 2 units of output, Bob's profit is maximized when output is 2. The sum of columns 4 and 5 must be column 2. With zero costs, profits and revenue are the same. Thus column 6 is just the entry in column 1 times the entry in column 5.

The Cournot model shows that the price will be lower and the quantity higher in a duopoly (two firms) than in a monopoly. But the Cournot price will be higher than the competitive price. In our example, the competitive price is zero. With more firms, the price falls even more. Advanced analysis shows that most of the benefits of competition come from a handful of Cournot firms. For example, if our example included five Cournot firms, the equilibrium price would be $1, and each firm would produce 1 unit. Analysis of profits and consumer surplus demonstrates that this represents over 97 percent of all the possible benefits of the market. (At a zero price, consumer surplus is $18, but at a price of $1, consumer surplus is $12.50 and total business profit is $5 for a total benefit of $17.50.)

The Cournot game has been criticized for the assumption that firms suppose their rivals are passive, but experimental studies support this model. In one study, 16 pairs of undergraduates were given a Cournot game that would have resulted in a Cournot output of 40 (per subject). Surprisingly, the average output of each student firm, following their own rules, was approximately 40![13]

The Prisoners' Dilemma Game

The famous **prisoners' dilemma game** was developed by game theorists as a way to analyze a situation much like that often faced by oligopolistic producers. The game assumes that two bank robbers have been apprehended by the police; they are being interrogated in separate rooms. If both talk, both go to jail but with 5-year sentences. If one talks and the other remains quiet, the one who talks gets off with a 1-year sentence and the silent bank robber gets a 20-year jail sentence. If neither talks, both get 2 years for carrying a deadly weapon. Each prisoner has a dilemma. Each knows that if he or she keeps quiet, both can get a light sentence, provided the other remains quiet; but keeping quiet is risky, because the other prisoner might talk. Moreover, if the other prisoner remains quiet, confessing lowers the sentence from 2 years to 1 year. If the other prisoner confesses, the first must confess to avoid a 20-year sentence. A Nash equilibrium occurs if both bank robbers confess. If one believes the other will confess, his or her best strategy is also to confess. If both actually confess, each has guessed correctly about the other's behavior and is able to employ the best strategy for the situation in which the other confesses. If the prisoners could communicate and make a binding agreement, they would both be better off remaining quiet.

A **prisoners' dilemma game** is a game with two players in which both players benefit from cooperating, but in which each player has an incentive to cheat on the agreement.

[13]Lawrence Fouraker and Signey Siegal, *Bargaining Behavior* (New York: McGraw-Hill, 1963).

The prisoners' dilemma is much like an oligopolist's dilemma of deciding whether to collude or to act independently. In both cases, the consequences of one player's decision depends upon the decision of another player. Suppose Firm A and Firm B each sell a differentiated product. Suppose also that when the two products have equal prices, both firms enjoy exactly the same profit. If one charges a slightly lower price than the other, however, that firm will make large profits while the high-priced firm makes only a small profit.

Figure 5 illustrates the oligopolist's dilemma with a simple example. Each firm can choose a price of either $20 or $19. The prices Firm A might charge are shown down the left side of the figure; the prices Firm B might charge are shown along the top. The *profits* earned by each firm are the payoffs from any set of prices the *two firms together* might charge. Firm A's profit payoffs are shown in the lower left-hand corner of each box (in blue). Firm B's profit payoffs are shown in the upper right-hand corner of each box (in orange). When both charge $20, both earn $2500; when both charge $19, both earn $1500. When one charges $20 and the other charges $19, the lower-priced firm earns $3000, and the higher-priced firm earns only $1000.

FIGURE 5
Profit Payoffs to a Two-Firm Oligopoly

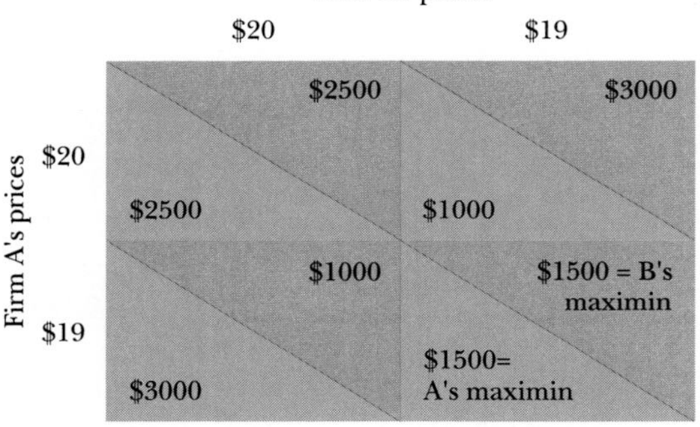

Each square (cell) shows the profits that each firm would earn when various combinations of prices are charged by the two firms. Firm A's profits are shown in blue in the lower left-hand corner of each cell, and Firm B's profits are shown in orange in the upper right-hand corner of each cell. For example, if A charges $19 and B charges $20, A would earn a profit of $3000 and B would earn $1000. What strategy will each pursue? There are two likely options: (1) If the two firms collude and each charges $20, they will both receive the maximum benefit of $2500. (2) Each firm might decide to use a *maximin* (maximize the minimum) strategy to find the best of the worst possible outcomes. If A charges $19, the worst that can happen to A is a profit of $1500. If A were to charge $20, the worst possible outcome for A is a profit of $1000. By charging a $19 price, A can insure that the worst outcome will not happen. B's best of the worst possible outcomes is the $1500 gained by charging $19. The maximin solution is for both firms to choose a price of $19. The maximin strategy also yields a Nash equilibrium: Each firm is worse off if it raises prices while the other firm sticks to its $19 price.

The two firms reach a Nash equilibrium when both firms charge $19. If each believes the other is charging $19, the best strategy for each is to charge $19. When both actually charge $19, each has guessed correctly, and each is able to employ the best strategy for the situation in which the other charges $19.

The Nash solution in which both firms charge $19, is also called the *maximin* (maximize the minimum gain) strategy. Firms following such a strategy choose the *best of the worst possible outcomes.* If Firm A charges $20, the worst that could happen to A is if B charged $19 because A's profits would then be $1000. If A charged $19, the worst that could happen to A would be a $1500 profit, which would result if B also charged $19. B's worst outcome for charging $19 is a profit of $1500. B's worst outcome for charging $20 is a profit of $1000. In this case, both firms will charge $19 and earn a $1500 profit, which for each is the best of the worst possible outcomes. If the conservative maximin strategy is followed, prices are rather stable, as in the kinked demand theory.

If A and B played this game repeatedly over a fairly long period of time, it is likely that A and B would eventually learn that they are both better off charging higher prices. They might learn to cooperate and choose the strategy that maximizes joint profits. In this case, both would charge $20 and earn profits of $2500 each. (See Example 6.)

The Advertising Game

If a firm's rival advertises "my product is better than all others," it is difficult for the firm to fail to respond with its own advertising message. Consider a rivalry between two hypothetical hamburger giants: Big Burger and Best Burger. Table 5 shows what the strategy of each hamburger company would be in

EXAMPLE 6 Tit-for-Tat and the Prisoners' Dilemma Game

Robert Axelrod has studied how best to play the prisoners' dilemma game, particularly when it is repeated over and over so that players can learn from experience. Axelrod invited 14 authorities on the game to compete in a prisoners' dilemma tournament. Each contestant was required to submit a strategy for the following game: For each of the 200 rounds of the game, each player's strategy should give either a C (cooperate) or D (don't cooperate—defect) response. If both players produced a C, then each received 3 points. If both produced a D, then each received 1 point. If one offered a D while the other offered a C, the defecting player got 5 points and the cooperating player 0 points. The winning program was the shortest program of all—called Tit-for-Tat by its author, Anatol Rapoport. The Tit-for-Tat strategy is very simple: Offer a C on the first move, and then do whatever your opponent did on the previous move. As long as your opponent cooperates, you cooperate too. If your opponent defects, you punish by defecting on the next move. The Tit-for-Tat program amassed the highest number of points in the first tournament and beat out 62 entrants from six countries in Axelrod's second tournament. The simplest winning strategy achieved its victory by being cooperative. Game theorists are studying whether or not people naturally employ cooperative behavior in real-life business "games" that are played frequently.

Source: William F. Allman, "Nice Guys Finish First," *Science* 84 (October 1984): 25–32.

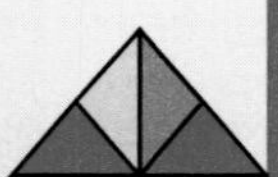

TABLE 5
Advertising Strategies

Big Burger's Strategies (ads per day)		Best Burger's Strategies (ads per day)	
Big Burger Optimum	**Best Burger Number**	**Best Burger Optimum**	**Big Burger Number**
3	0	4	0
6	8	8	6
9	16	12	12

This table shows the profit-maximizing number of TV advertisements for each hypothetical hamburger chain in response to its rival. The Nash equilibrium occurs when Best Burger runs 8 ads per day and Big Burger runs 6 ads per day because at this point each firm's profit-maximizing behavior is based on a correct guess about the other firm's behavior.

response to the various amounts of daily national television commercials run by its rival.

Big Burger strategists calculate that the company could maximize its profits by running 3 ads per day if Best Burger placed no ads per day, by running 6 ads if Best Burger placed 8 ads, and by running 9 ads if Best Burger placed 16 ads. The blue curve in Figure 6 graphs Big Burger's optimal strategies. On the other hand, Best Burger strategists calculate that the company could maximize its profits by running 4 ads per day if Big Burger placed no ads per day, by running 8 ads if Big Burger placed 6 ads, and by running 12 ads if Big Burger placed 12 ads per day. The orange curve graphs Best Burger's optimal strategies. The Nash equilibrium occurs where Best Burger's strategy curve intersects Big Burger's strategy curve. When Big Burger is running 6 ads a day and Best Burger is running 8 ads per day, there is a Nash equilibrium. Big Burger maximizes its profit with 6 ads when Best Burger places 8 ads; Best Burger maximizes its profit with 8 ads when Big Burger places 6 ads.

FIGURE 6
Nash Equilibrium: Advertising

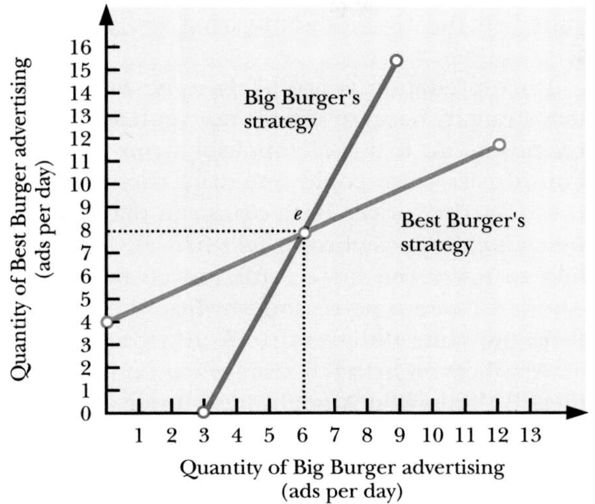

The blue line shows Big Burger's best response to Best Burger's ads. The orange line shows Best Burger's best response to Big Burger's ads. Where the two curves intersect is a Nash equilibrium, where each firm's guess about the other firm's strategy is confirmed. In other words, Big Burger wants 6 ads when Best Burger places 8 ads, and Best Burger wants 8 ads when Big Burger places 6 ads.

At this point, each company is employing its best strategy for dealing with a correct assessment of how many ads the other company will place.

The advertising example is interesting because the firms advertise much more at the Nash equilibrium than they would if they reached an informal agreement to deliberately keep their advertising expenditures to a minimum.

A Credible Threat

Suppose an industry contains one actual monopolist and one *potential* entrant. To discourage entry, the monopolist might let the potential rival know that there would be a costly price war (prices would be set below costs) if the potential rival were to enter the industry. The rival may not believe the monopolist's threat, however, unless the monopolist makes some commitment to make this threat credible. If the potential entrant calculates that the monopolist would also lose from the price war and would eventually have to share the market, the monopolist's threat will be ignored. But the monopolist can make an irreversible commitment. For example, the monopolist might spend $10 million to secure the services of the best advertising agency before the potential rival enters the business. Or the monopolist might accumulate large cash resources to convince the potential rival of its willingness to engage in a price war. A **credible threat** makes it easier for the potential entrant to make a correct assumption about the monopolist's behavior.

> A **credible threat** is the commitment of significant resources by an oligopolist to convince potential entrants to the oligopolistic industry that entry would result in severe losses for the entrant.

A Nash equilibrium results when the monopolist maximizes profits by making a credible threat that succeeds in keeping out the potential entrant (on the correct assumption that the potential rival would actually enter the market in the absence of the credible threat) and when the potential entrant minimizes losses by not entering the market, on the correct assumption that the monopolist would indeed start a price war. (See Example 7.)

The behavior of a wide variety of noncooperative oligopolies can be explained using the concept of a Nash equilibrium. Indeed, the Nash equilibrium concept can even be applied to many social behaviors. Game theorists are hard at work on new concepts of equilibrium that can explain even more complicated oligopolistic strategies—such as setting low prices today and high prices tomorrow.

CONTESTABLE MARKETS: COMPLETE FREEDOM OF ENTRY AND EXIT

Even if an industry has only a few firms, economists William J. Baumol, John Panzer, and Robert Willig argue that potential entrants can cause the industry to act competitively.[14] A monopoly or an oligopolistic

[14]William J. Baumol, "Contestable Markets: An Uprising in the Theory of Industry Structure," *American Economic Review* 72 (March 1982): 1–15.

EXAMPLE 7 Predatory Pricing and the Credible Threat

The theory of predatory pricing is quite simple. An oligopolistic firm drives out all its competitors by setting price below cost. The most famous case is the creation of the Standard Oil Company. In the nineteenth century, John D. Rockefeller supposedly lowered the price of oil, drove the small oil refineries to the brink of bankruptcy, and then bought them out at a bargain price.

The only trouble with the theory of predatory pricing is that in most cases the scenario works out differently. John McGee studied the historical record and found that Rockefeller's rivals were bought out on very favorable terms. Roland Koller examined 26 cases of alleged predatory pricing dating from 1890. Koller found only seven cases in which there was pricing below cost. Of these seven cases, only one resulted in the rival's disappearing without a trace.

Price predation is not likely to be a profitable strategy, because it does not represent a credible threat. If two oligopolistic firms have identical costs, how could one drive the other out by lowering price? Both firms can play the same game. Suppose firm A tells firm B, "I am going to lower the price until you go out of business." There is no reason why firm B could not do the same thing to firm A. Any damage firm A inflicts on firm B it also inflicts on itself. Unless B thinks that A might have lower costs, predation is not likely to work.

Sources: John McGee, "Predatory Price Cutting," *Journal of Law and Economics* 1 (1958): 137–69; Roland Koller, "The Myth of Predatory Pricing," *Antitrust Law and Economics Review* (Summer 1971): 105–23.

market can be contested by those who could compete under the right conditions. A **contestable market** is one in which the potential for competition has the same effect as actual competition on firm behavior. The theory of contestable markets applies to an oligopolistic market or even to a monopoly in which new firms can enter and exit with complete ease.

> A **contestable market** is one in which (1) entry and exit by new firms is completely free, (2) the new firms can produce with the same costs as the established firms, (3) firms can easily dispose of their fixed assets by selling them elsewhere (fixed costs are not sunk but are recoverable), and (4) customers buy from the firm (or firms) that first offers the lowest price.

With complete freedom of entry and exit of potential rivals, firms in contestable markets will behave like competitive firms. Recall that competitive firms earn (in the long run) zero economic profits (they produce at minimum average cost). Any economic profits will draw new firms into the perfectly competitive industry and cause profits to disappear. Even if there are only one or two firms in a contestable market, established firms dare earn only a normal profit. If any firm sells at a price greater than average total cost, rival firms that could earn a temporary profit and then leave the market at will would immediately enter. Any price that would yield an economic profit would invite hit-and-run entry by rival firms and induce losses for established firms. In contestable markets, concentration ratios or the number of firms in the market are not valid measures of the degree of competition. The knowledge that a potential rival is poised in the wings forces the few firms already in the industry to behave like perfect competitors.

A contestable market works much like a perfectly competitive market. The solution is efficient in that it gives the product to consumers at the lowest possible cost. A contestable market does not require many actual firms—only many potential entrants—to achieve this efficient result. When entry is completely free and exit is absolutely costless, the number of potential firms is enormous.

The theory of contestable markets is relatively new. Some economists question whether there are indeed industries in which entry and exit are completely costless. The greater the costs of entry or the sunk costs of exit, the less powerful is the competitive effect of potential entry.[15]

Even though it may be difficult to find a perfect real-world example of a contestable market, the theory sheds light on how markets with easy entry and exit operate.

AN EVALUATION OF OLIGOPOLY

The Diversity of Oligopoly

Oligopoly is too varied to permit general conclusions that apply to all its forms. In less concentrated oligopolies, the number of firms is too large for formal or tacit collusion to occur, and it is difficult to prevent competitive behavior from erupting. According to Scherer, if firms supply a homogeneous product, it generally takes only 10 to 12 evenly matched suppliers for them to ignore one another's influence on price.[16]

When barriers to entry are low, the behavior of the oligopolistic firm should not differ very much from that of monopolistically competitive or even perfectly competitive firms. Large economic profits would not be expected.

Only in highly concentrated oligopolies with high entry barriers is coordinated action possible, but the temptations to cheat are substantial, and collusive agreements often fall apart. In its most successful form, however, a cartel arrangement yields a result that is really no different from monopoly.

A Criticism of Oligopoly

The previous chapter described positive features of perfect competition—efficiency, production at minimum average cost, and lower prices with higher output. It also described the negative features of monopoly—production above minimum average cost, long-term monopoly profits, prices not equal to marginal costs, restricted output with higher prices.

Some oligopolies bear a strong resemblance to competitive markets, whereas other oligopolies, especially in their collusive form, can bear a strong resemblance to monopoly. If the reader was convinced in the previous chapter that monopoly is bad and competition is good, then it is likely that same reader will conclude that less concentrated oligopolies are better than collusive oligopolies.

Do oligopolies earn extraordinary profits? This question is not easy to answer for two reasons. First, it is difficult to measure economic profits (as opposed to accounting profits). Second, there is the problem of accurately measuring the degree of oligopoly. Concentration ratios are imperfect measures, and entry barriers are difficult to measure.

Joe S. Bain and H. Michael Mann have shown that profit rates in the 1930s and 1950s tended to rise with barriers to entry and with concentration, although these results were more pronounced in the 1950s than in the 1930s.[17] More recent studies find that, particularly at high four-firm concentration ratios (50 percent or above), concentration is positively related to profits and barriers to entry have a stronger effect on profits than do concentration ratios. Less concentrated oligopolies (four-firm concentration ratios below 50 percent), however, have profit rates that are not correlated with concentration or barriers to entry.[18]

The theory of contestable markets implies that profit rates are uncorrelated with concentration ratios when the market is contestable. Industry studies that find a relationship between concentration ratios and profits would indicate that those markets are not contestable.

[15]For a critique of the contestable market theory, see William G. Shepherd, " 'Contestability' vs. Competition," *American Economic Review* 74 (September 1984): 572–87. Other critics of the theory include Martin Weitzman, Marius Schwartz, and Robert Reynolds.

[16]Scherer, *Industrial Market Structure,* 199.

[17]Joe S. Bain, *Barriers to New Competition,* 192–200; H. Michael Mann, "Seller Concentration, Barriers to Entry and Rates of Return in Thirty Industries," *Review of Economics and Statistics* (August 1966): 296–307.

[18]Leonard W. Weiss, "Quantitative Studies of Industrial Organization," in *Frontiers of Quantitative Economics,* ed. Michael D. Intriligator (Amsterdam: North Holland, 1971); Leonard W. Weiss, "Concentration/Profits Relationship and Antitrust," in *Industrial Concentration: The New Learning,* ed. Goldschmid et al. (Boston: Little, Brown, 1974), 184–233; Frederick Geithman, Howard Marvel, and Leonard W. Weiss, "Concentration, Price, and Critical Concentration Ratios," *The Review of Economics and Statistics* (August 1981): 346–53.

A Defense of Oligopoly

Some economists defend oligopoly as an efficient form of market. Harold Demsetz sees the positive relationship between profit rates and concentration or barriers to entry as an indicator of the greater efficiency of large firms.[19]

Demsetz maintains that higher profits are the result of the superior cost performance of larger firms in the industry. Even if prices are set competitively so that each firm acts more or less like a price taker (exerting no monopoly power over prices), economic profits will accrue only to those firms that have lower costs, not to all firms in the industry. There is evidence that oligopoly profits are earned only by the largest firms in oligopolistic industries, not by all firms. Demsetz therefore concludes that oligopoly profits are the result not of excessive market power but of the superior efficiency of large oligopolistic firms.

FIGURE 7
The Demsetz Thesis

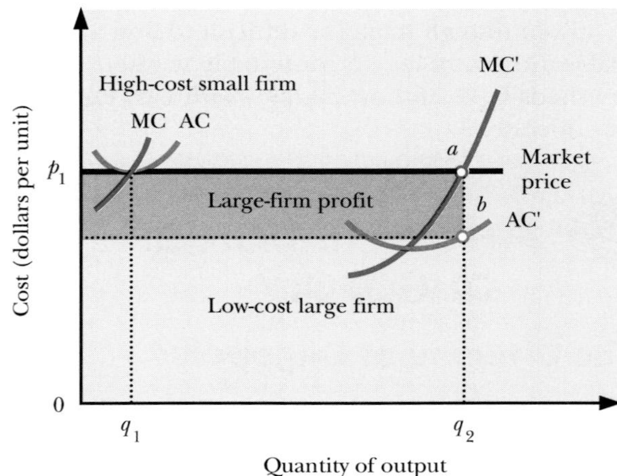

The large, efficient firm produces an output of q_2 units with a per-unit profit of ab. The small, inefficient firm produces an output of q_1 units with a zero economic profit. According to Demsetz, perfect competition can be consistent with the positive association between concentration rates and economic profits.

Figure 7 illustrates the Demsetz argument. It takes the case of a homogeneous product that is being produced by a large low-cost producer and by small high-cost producers. Perfect competition prevails, and each firm equates marginal costs to the price. When these conditions prevail, economic profits are earned only by the large low-cost producer. The small high-cost firms earn only a normal return. Higher profits are associated with higher concentration because large firms can produce at lower costs due to significant economies of scale.[20]

John K. Galbraith agrees with Demsetz that large oligopolies are more efficient than competitive industries. In fact, Galbraith argues that there is a power imbalance between the competitive sector and the oligopoly/monopoly sector.

In Galbraith's view, the competitive sector is being gradually worn down by the technically superior oligopoly sector. Rather than accept the theory that the competitive sector efficiently utilizes resources and monopoly/oligopoly underutilizes resources, Galbraith maintains that the reverse is true. The competitive sector cannot advertise like the large corporations, which can manipulate the demand for their products and produce output in large volumes at low cost.[21]

Joseph Schumpeter argued that large enterprises generate more technological progress, the moving force behind economic progress that temporarily establishes some firms as dominant in their industry. Through the process of "creative destruction," Schumpeter believes that new ideas and new technologies replace the old and that the monopoly power created by technological innovation will prove to be transitory.

It is clear that high concentration can be the natural outcome of the competitive process. One firm

[19]Harold Demsetz, "Industry Structure, Market Rivalry, and Public Policy," *Journal of Law and Economics* 16 (April 1973): 1–10.

[20]Scherer argues that a proper test of Demsetz's oligopoly superiority hypothesis has yet to be undertaken. Such a test must take into account the interdependence between profitability, concentration, market shares, and differentiation. The superiority hypothesis would be easy to test if oligopolies produced a homogeneous good and no other. But in the real world, oligopolies tend to produce many differentiated products that may be reflected in different costs. To assume that higher profits reflect the same price for the same good and thus lower the unit cost remains to be demonstrated. See Scherer, *Industrial Market Structure,* 290–91.

[21]John K. Galbraith, *The Affluent Society* (Boston: Houghton Mifflin, 1957); *American Capitalism* (Boston: Houghton Mifflin, 1956); *Economics and the Public Purpose* (Boston: Houghton Mifflin, 1973); *The New Industrial State* (Boston: Houghton Mifflin, 1967).

may come to dominate an industry because it is more innovative, its management is more efficient, and it has taken more risks. If one or two firms tower over an industry because they have played the game better than others (Schumpeter's "creative destruction"), are not high profits their just reward? We cannot hope to answer the question, Are concentrated oligopolists necessarily bad? This important policy issue will be discussed in the chapter on antitrust policy.

This chapter completes our study of the four basic market models. The next chapter will examine the use of government action in the forms of regulation and antitrust legislation to deal with monopoly power.

SUMMARY

1. An oligopoly is characterized by a small number of firms, barriers to entry, mutual interdependence, and price searching. The number of firms is so small that the actions of one firm have a significant effect on other firms in the industry.
2. The presence of barriers to entry explains the small number of firms in an oligopoly. Types of barriers to entry are economies of scale and scope, product differentiation, control over input supplies, government barriers to entry, technological advantages, and sunk costs.
3. An industry's concentration ratio is the percentage of domestic sales accounted for by the top (four or eight) firms.
4. Oligopolies exercise varying degrees of control over price. Because of mutual interdependence, the oligopolist's demand curve cannot be defined until the reaction pattern of rival firms is specified. The demand curve can vary from the kinked demand curve to the perfectly coordinated demand curve of a cartel arrangement. Methods of oligopoly coordination range from formal agreements (cartels) to informal arrangements, such as price leadership or conscious parallelism. Collusive agreements, if successful, allow the participating firms to earn monopoly profits. Because there are incentives to cheat on the cartel agreement, however, collusive agreements tend to be unstable. Collusion is difficult when there are many sellers, low barriers to entry, heterogeneous products, high rates of innovation, high fixed costs, easy price cheating, or laws against collusion.
5. Game theory analyzes the incentives to cheat on collusive agreements. A *Nash equilibrium* prevails in an oligopolistic market if each firm's profit-maximizing behavior is based on a correct guess about the behavior of rivals. Four ways in which firms can achieve a Nash equilibrium are playing the Cournot oligopoly game, playing the prisoners' dilemma game, advertising, and making a credible threat.
6. A *contestable market* is one in which the potential for competition has the same effect on a firm's behavior as actual competition.
7. At high levels of concentration, there is a positive relationship between economic profits and concentration, and between economic profits and barriers to entry. Some economists argue that the higher profits of concentrated oligopolies are the result of the superior technological and cost performance of large firms (Demsetz, Galbraith, and Schumpeter), but there is substantial disagreement among economists on this point.

KEY TERMS

oligopoly
mutual interdependence
barrier to entry
sunk costs
concentration ratio
kinked demand curve
cartel
price leader
conscious parallelism
noncooperative oligopoly behavior
Nash equilibrium
Cournot oligopoly
prisoners' dilemma game
credible threat
contestable market

QUESTIONS AND PROBLEMS

1. Consider the four-firm concentration ratio for motor vehicles shown in Table 1. Is this figure an accurate measure of the extent of oligopoly? Explain.
2. What is the relationship between the small number of firms and mutual interdependence in oligopoly theory? Why was mutual interdependence not considered in the chapter on monopoly and monopolistic competition?
3. Firm ZYX is one of three equal-sized firms in the widget market. It currently charges $20 per widget and sells 1 million widgets per year. It is

considering raising its price to $22 and needs some estimate of what will happen to its widget sales. Why would it be difficult to make such an estimate?

4. Firm ZYX and the two other widget manufacturers meet in secret and agree to charge a uniform price of $50 and share the market equally (each gets one-third of sales). At the price of $50, each firm's marginal cost is $10. What are the rewards for cheating on the agreement if ZYX does not get caught? What is likely to happen if all three try to cheat?
5. The prisoners' dilemma game is also used to explain how oligopolists devise advertising strategy. Try to apply the prisoners' dilemma game to advertising in highly concentrated oligopolies.
6. Why is nonprice competition frequently encountered in oligopolistic industries?
7. In an oligopolistic industry composed of three large firms and ten small firms, the large firms earn an economic profit while the small firms earn normal profits. What do you know about the sources of economic profit in this industry?
8. How does oligopoly theory explain why there are so many different types of oligopoly behavior—collusion, nonprice competition, conscious parallelism, price leadership?
9. What is a *Nash equilibrium?*
10. Which of the following are examples of a Nash equilibrium?

    a. The prisoners' dilemma game
    b. Cartel pricing
    c. The credible threat
    d. Pricing by focal points

11. What would happen in a contestable market if established firms made economic profits? Would the reaction be different if there were significant sunk costs?
12. William G. Shepherd has written that the theory of contestable markets "treats a specialized, extreme set of conditions, which are probably found in no real markets which have significant internal market power." Evaluate the validity of this statement.
13. What is the difference between *sunk costs* and *fixed costs?* Why is the difference important?
14. Consider an industry that consists of three equal-sized firms. Their marginal cost of production is $2.99 at each level of output. The industry demand schedule is given in Table A. Assume that the three firms divide the market equally.

    a. What is the demand schedule facing each firm?
    b. What will be the cartel price and quantity?
    c. What is the incentive for each firm to cheat on the agreement?

TABLE A

Price (dollars per unit)	Quantity Demanded (units)
15	3
12	6
9	9
6	12
3	15

15. Suppose two Cournot firms face the same marginal costs of $2. They face the market demand curve $P = 8 - Q$. Draw the reaction curves, calculate P, Q, firm profit, and the output of each firm.

SUGGESTED READINGS

Adams, Walter, ed. *The Structure of American Industry,* 8th ed. New York: Macmillan, 1989.

Bain, Joe S. *Barriers to New Competition.* Cambridge, Mass.: Harvard University Press, 1965.

Carlton, Dennis V., and Jeffrey M. Perloff. *Modern Industrial Organization.* New York: HarperCollins, 1990, chaps. 7, 9, and 12.

Caves, Richard. *American Industry: Structure, Conduct, Performance,* 6th ed. Englewood Cliffs, NJ: Prentice Hall, 1987.

Dixit, Avinash, and Barry Nalebuff. *Thinking Strategically.* New York: W.W. Norton, 1991, chaps. 5 and 6.

Galbraith, John K. *American Capitalism,* rev. ed. Cambridge: The Riverside Press, 1956.

Koch, James V. *Industrial Organization and Prices,* 2d ed. Englewood Cliffs, NJ: Prentice Hall, 1980.

Scherer, Frederic M. *Industrial Market Structure and Economic Performance,* 2nd ed. Boston: Houghton Mifflin, 1980.

Williamson, Oliver. *Markets and Hierarchies: Analysis and Antitrust Implications.* New York: The Free Press, 1975.

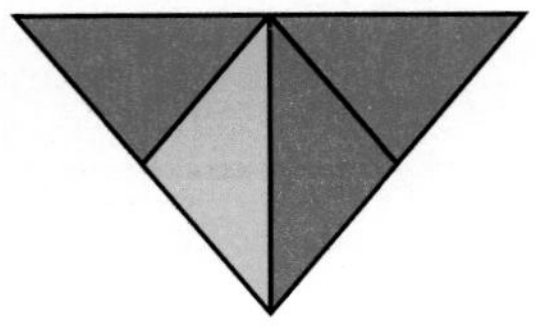

34 Antitrust Law and Regulation

CHAPTER INSIGHT

Every era has its own symbol of greed. In the late nineteenth and early twentieth centuries, John D. Rockefeller was the most prominent "robber baron." His Standard Oil had monopolized the oil industry by gaining control of the refining and transportation of oil. The public clamor against Rockefeller, fueled by the "trust busting" efforts of President Theodore Roosevelt, culminated in a series of court actions against Standard Oil under the Sherman Antitrust Act. In May 1911, a mumbling Chief Justice Edward White announced the dissolution of Standard Oil and issued the "rule of reason": that restraint of trade would be subject to penalty only if it was unreasonable and worked against the public interest. No one at Standard Oil's New York headquarters was prepared for the devastating effect of the Supreme Court judgment. John Archibald, the chief executive of Standard Oil, walked over to the mantle and stated, "Well, gentlemen, life's just one damn thing after another."[1] Today's modern oil companies emerged from the dissolution of Standard Oil. Standard Oil of New Jersey eventually became Exxon, which never lost its leading position in the industry; Standard Oil of California eventually became Chevron; and so on.

This chapter examines government policy toward monopoly and competition. It studies the various ways that public policy can be used to limit monopoly power and enhance competition.

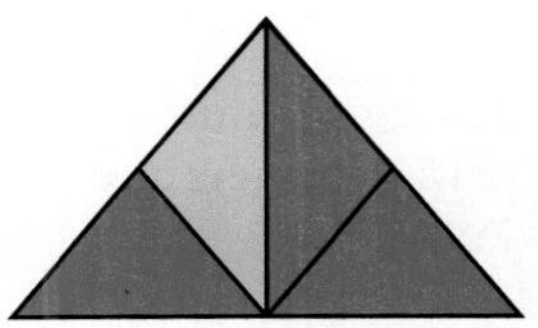

THE NATURAL MONOPOLY

When alternative market structures are possible, government policy can be used to shift from one to another. For example, a large company may be broken up into several smaller companies if it has used its monopoly power in a harmful way. Sometimes, though, such alteration of the market structure is impossible, as in the case of a **natural monopoly.**

> A **natural monopoly** exists when it is cheaper for one firm to produce a product over the relevant range of output than for two or more firms to do so.

Natural monopoly occurs when a single firm can produce the industry level of output at a long-run average cost below that of any firm that produces less than the industry level of output (see Figure 1). Some examples of natural monopolies are electric utilities, natural gas utilities, and local telephone service. For such industries, long-run average cost falls as output is increased.

If the industry is a natural monopoly, industry output will be produced at a lower long-run average cost by one firm than if the industry were made up of more than one producer. Imagine, for example, having three electric utilities operating in the same market with three systems of power lines and underground cables. For natural monopolies, economies of large-scale production are so staggering that there is little choice but to operate as a single-firm industry.

Because a certain amount of monopoly power is unavoidable in some industries, government must decide *whether or not* and *how* to control monopoly power. If a government chooses to control monopoly power, it has three options: government ownership, regulation, and antitrust legislation.

FIGURE 1
The Natural Monopoly

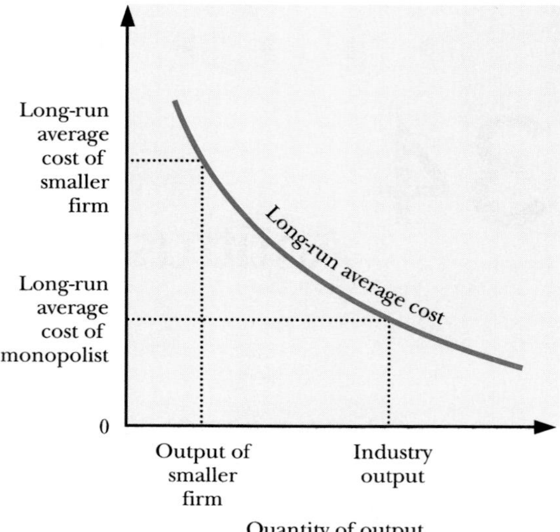

This figure shows the long-run average cost curve of producing a certain product. As the curve shows, the long-run average cost of producing this product is lower at the output level corresponding to total industry output than for any output level less than total industry output. A single producer can, therefore, produce at a much lower average cost than any of the smaller producers who might together try to produce the industry quantity by each producing a portion of total industry output.

GOVERNMENT OWNERSHIP

The government can purchase the monopoly from private owners and operate it "in the public interest." Public ownership of business in the United States is more common at the municipal and state levels than at the federal level and is frequently utilized for such services as local transportation, water, sanitation, gas, and electricity. During the 1990s, about one-quarter of all electrical energy will be generated by government-owned enterprises.

At the federal level, government enterprises are fewer in number. They include, among others, the Tennessee Valley Authority (a giant, government-owned electrical utility), the U.S. Postal Service (now a semigovernmental organization), government home mortgage programs (the Veterans Administration and Federal Housing Authority programs), various weapons-producing arsenals, and the Government Printing Office. These activities may appear substantial, but they account for only 2 percent

[1]Daniel Yergin, *The Prize* (New York: Simon and Schuster, 1991), 109–10.

FIGURE 2
The Dilemma of a Public Enterprise

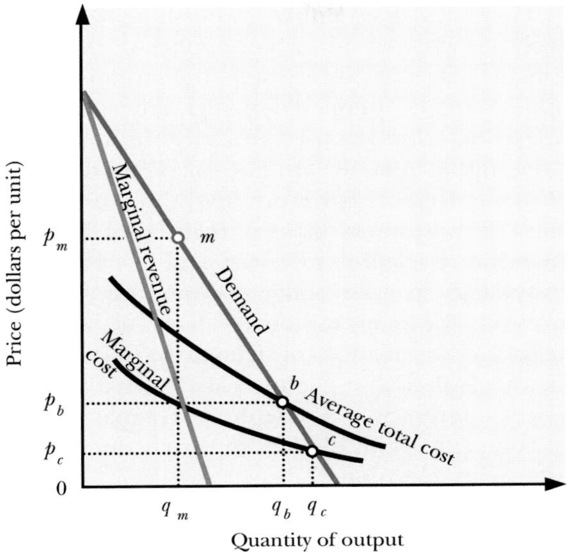

This figure depicts a monopoly that is owned by the public. It is not clear which rules the manager should follow to operate this enterprise "in the public interest." The manager could equate marginal cost and price (point *c*), but the enterprise would be operating at a loss. The manager could attempt to break even (point *b*) by operating where price and average total cost are equal, but the manager would have little incentive to economize on costs because higher costs would translate into higher prices and higher revenues. Finally, the manager could attempt to maximize profits (point *m*), but consumers would receive a relatively small quantity of output and would pay relatively high prices while monopoly profits accrued to the state.

of American national output (or gross national product).[2]

How does the government operate a public enterprise in the public interest? What instructions should be given to the manager of the public enterprise in Figure 2? One option is to produce that quantity of output at which price and marginal cost are equal (point *c*). Point *c* is efficient because the marginal cost (of society's resources) is equated with the marginal benefit (received by society) as reflected in the price. However, the $P = \text{MC}$ rule requires that the enterprise be run at a loss, and taxpayers must make up that loss. Taxpayers who do not use the service will subsidize those who do.

Alternatively, the public enterprise can be instructed to *break even*—to produce where price equals average total cost (at point *b*). At point *b*, price is almost two times greater than marginal cost, and the efficiency rule $P = \text{MC}$ is broken. But the customer is offered a larger quantity of output (q_b) at a lower price (p_b) than if the firm were an unregulated monopoly.

The third option is to allow the public enterprise to operate like a private, unregulated monopoly. This option yields the outcome of point *m* (the enterprise would choose the quantity that equates marginal revenue and marginal cost). Again, the basic efficiency rule is broken: price is more than three times marginal cost in this case. The public is offered a relatively small quantity of output (q_m) for which it must pay a monopoly price (p_m). Moreover, bureaucratic managers may lack the incentive to combine resources efficiently, so public enterprises may operate at higher costs than private enterprises. The only advantage such a government-owned monopoly has over a private monopoly is that the monopoly profit goes to the government and can be used to pay for other government services. (See Example 1.)

REGULATION

Regulation of prices and services is a second means of controlling monopoly. The enterprise remains in private hands, but its activities are regulated by government agencies. The goals of regulation are to ensure the availability of service, establish standards for the quality of service, and guarantee that the public will be charged "reasonable" prices.

In the United States, regulation at the state and local level is largely directed at monopolies—the electric, gas, water, and telephone companies. At the national level, federal regulatory commissions regulate a number of industries, some of which are potentially competitive. The four major federal regulatory commissions are

1. The Interstate Commerce Commission (established in 1887), which regulates railroads, interstate oil pipelines, and interstate motor and water carriers

[2]Paul Gregory and Robert Stuart, *Comparative Economic Systems*, 2nd ed. (Boston: Houghton Mifflin, 1985), 199.

EXAMPLE 1 The German Telephone Monopoly

Germany provides a case study of government ownership of natural monopolies. In addition to providing postal services, the German Postal Service (Deutsche Bundespost) manages German local and long-distance telephone services and television broadcasting. Telephone customers pay their telephone installation and usage bills and television viewers pay monthly usage fees directly to the German Postal Service. Although telephone and television operations tend to be profitable, postal service operations are run at a substantial loss. In effect, German postal authorities subsidize postal service losses with telephone and television profits.

How well does public ownership of the telephone and television monopolies work in Germany? On the positive side, the monopoly profits of the telephone company, rather than taxpayer monies, are used to cover the losses of the postal service. On the negative side, German customers pay more than three times what U.S. customers pay for their local and long-distance telephone service, and television viewers must pay an obligatory monthly fee. Moreover, German customers have to wait longer for installation of telephone service, lack the "call waiting" and "call forwarding" services offered by U.S. telephone companies, and complain about the lack of variety offered by state-run television.

2. The Federal Power Commission (established in 1920), which has jurisdiction over power projects and the interstate transmission of electricity and natural gas
3. The Federal Communications Commission (established in 1934), which regulates interstate telephone and telegraph service and broadcasting
4. The Securities and Exchange Commission (established in 1934), which regulates securities markets

The Civil Aeronautics Board (established in 1938), supervised domestic and international aviation until its dissolution at the end of 1984.

Who Is Regulated?

As previously mentioned, natural monopolies, such as the gas and electric companies and local telephone service, are regulated at the state and local level. However, much state and local regulation is directed at generally *competitive* industries (taxicab licensing, concession franchises in sports stadiums, licensing of barbers and beauticians) and serves to create more monopoly power. Likewise, federal commissions regulate potentially competitive industries such as transportation and broadcasting, often limiting competition. *Government regulation is not consistently enacted;* some is designed to combat monopoly power, but some discourages competition. (See Example 2.)

It is difficult to estimate what proportion of the U.S. economy is regulated because most businesses are regulated in one way or another. On the one hand, regulated industries could include only those industries in which prices are controlled by government agencies (transportation, communications, utilities, banking, and insurance). According to this criterion, as much as 10 percent of national output may be produced by regulated firms. If businesses that are supervised by the government (such as the drug or meat-packing industries) are added, the regulated sector may be as high as one-fifth of national output.[3]

[3]The figures of 20 percent for 1939 and 21.5 percent for 1958 for the "government supervised" sector come from the studies of G. Warren Nutter, *The Extent of Enterprise Monopoly in the United States, 1899–1939* (Chicago: University of Chicago Press, 1951); G. Warren Nutter and Henry A. Einhorn, *Enterprise Monopoly in the United States, 1899–1958* (New York: Columbia University Press, 1969); and George Stigler, *Five Lectures on Economic Problems* (London: Longmans, Green and Company, 1949).

EXAMPLE 2 City Councils and Taxicabs: Who Is Protecting Whom?

City councils often restrict entry into the taxicab business, either by limiting the number of cab licenses (called medallions) or by passing ordinances identifying which cab companies are entitled to pick up passengers at municipal airports or bus terminals. Such licensing and ordinances are justified on the grounds that they ensure safety and quality.

Restrictions on entry raise the price of taxicab services to consumers. By limiting business to a small number of licensed companies, the city council creates a monopoly that permits taxicabs to charge prices well above the competitive price. The attached chart shows that the number of medallions in New York City has remained constant at 11,787 since 1937 and that a medallion cost more than $100,000 in 1990. Similarly, in Houston, Texas, an entrepreneur once attempted to introduce nonlicensed minicabs that charged less than half the normal fare. Outraged public officials, marshalling public sentiment against unlicensed cabs, caused the entrepreneur to be jailed and driven out of the taxicab business. Surprisingly, the public typically does not understand that licensing and ordinances result in higher prices.

The Price of a Taxi Medallion

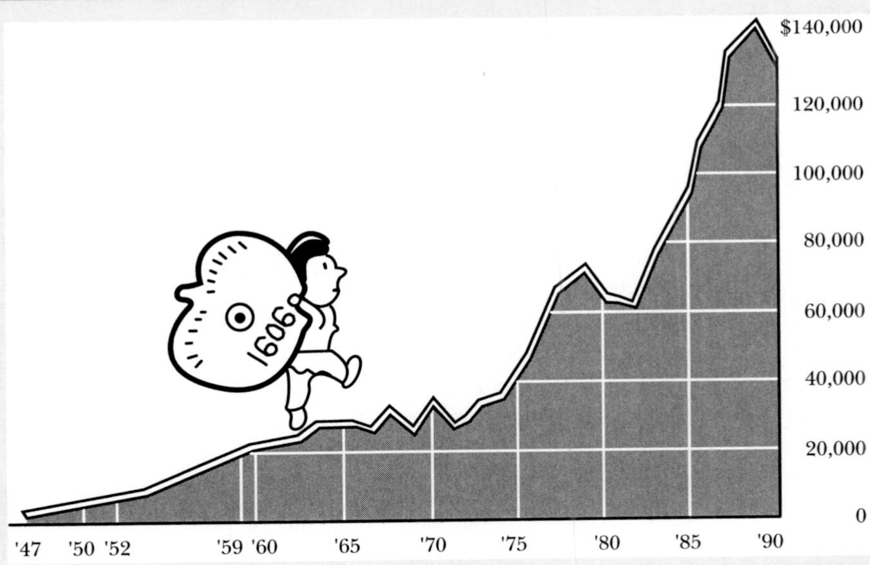

A medallion—the metal stamp in the hood—authorizes a New York City yellow cab to stop for people who hail it on the street. By law, the number of medallion taxis has remained steady at 11,787 since 1937.

Source: *New York Times,* October 6, 1991, E-7. Data from New York City Taxi and Limousine Commission.

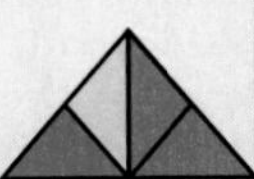

Any single measure of the scope of the regulated sector is misleading because some businesses are more closely supervised than others. (For example, the Food and Drug Administration is stricter in its supervision of the prescription drug industry than the Environmental Protection Agency is in its regulation of the automobile industry.)

Objectives of Regulation

There are three reasons to regulate businesses:[4]

1. To prevent monopoly profits from being earned
2. To encourage the regulated business to operate efficiently and safely
3. To prevent predatory competition that would ultimately decrease competition

Regulators seek to achieve these objectives through rate regulation, or control of the prices (rates) that regulated enterprises are allowed to charge. They also control entry into the industry by issuing licenses and franchises. Regulators can establish rules or standards for the quality of goods or services. Although regulators do more than simply set rates, this chapter will concentrate on rate setting and its effects on the three basic objectives of regulation.

Principles of Rate Regulation

Regulatory commissions are required to set "reasonable" prices, establish standards for minimum quality of service, and guarantee all customers access to the service without discrimination. Regulatory commissions are bound by the private property safeguards of the U.S. Constitution to protect the property rights of the owners of the monopoly. They are not permitted to set rates that do not cover operating costs plus a "fair" rate of return on invested capital. If regulators do not allow regulated monopolies a fair rate of return, the monopoly can appeal to the courts for higher prices.

[4]For a discussion of the objectives of regulation, see William J. Baumol, "Reasonable Rules for Rate Regulation: Plausible Policies in an Imperfect World," in *The Crisis of the Regulatory Commissions*, edited by Paul MacAvoy (New York: W. W. Norton, 1970), 187–206; Robert E. Litan and William D. Nordhaus, *Reforming Federal Regulation* (New Haven, CT: Yale University Press, 1983); and Lawrence J. White, *Reforming Regulation* (Englewood Cliffs, NJ: Prentice Hall, 1981).

The Pricing Formula. The usual regulatory pricing formula is

Price of service = *Average operating cost*
+ *Fair rate of return*
on invested capital

This pricing formula seems simple, but it raises a number of questions. How are operating costs to be established? What constitutes a "fair" rate of return to invested capital? The formula does rule out marginal-cost pricing (point *c* in Figure 2), which typically yields a loss. The fair-rate-of-return pricing formula, however, can result in firms with inefficient operating costs. Because cost increases (whether justified or not) are passed on to the consumer in the form of higher prices, the regulated firm need not be overly concerned with minimizing its costs of production. Regulators typically do not have the information to determine whether reported costs are padded or legitimate, and they are reluctant to substitute their judgment for the information provided by management concerning reasonable costs. (See Example 3.)

The Rate Base. The provision ensuring a fair rate of return on the investment capital of regulated monopolies further promotes inefficiency by encouraging the excessive use of capital.

Suppose regulators have determined that 12 percent is a fair rate of return. The regulated firm will be allowed to earn annual profits equal to 12 percent of invested capital. Thus, the value of invested capital becomes the regulated firm's *rate base*. For example, if a company has a rate base (invested capital) of $10 million and the profit rate ceiling is 12 percent, it will be allowed to earn a maximum profit of $1.2 million per annum.

An unregulated company will add to its invested capital only if the present value of the resulting profits exceeds the cost of acquiring the capital. The regulated monopoly, however, can increase its profits automatically by expanding its rate base. By investing an additional $5 million, the rate base is expanded by $5 million (to $15 million), and the regulated company can now earn $1.8 million profit per annum. Accordingly, regulated firms have a greater incentive to acquire more capital than do unregulated firms. Because regulated firms invest at the margin in projects with lower rates of return than

EXAMPLE 3 What Constitutes "Reasonable" Costs of Utilities?

The regulatory pricing formula (price equals operating costs plus rate of return) requires that regulatory commissions identify the operating costs of public utilities. Typically, regulators simply accept the costs of a utility as reported by its accountants. In some cases, however, regulators conduct "prudency reviews," which often dispute a number of cost items. For example, public utility commissions have challenged the sometimes large public-service advertising budgets of utilities. Why do the utilities need to spend millions of dollars convincing the public that they are concerned corporate citizens? Utility commissions have also challenged the costs of nuclear power plants. In some cases they have even disallowed such expenditures, based on the notion that these billion-dollar investments constitute poor business decisions for which consumers should not be required to pay.

If a public utility commission decides not to allow a utility to pass an expenditure along to consumers by raising prices, the owners of the utility must "pay" in the form of lost dividends and lower stock prices. Utilities have objected to prudency reviews, claiming they second-guess executive decision making and unfairly penalize the incurrence of long-term business risks (as in the case of the development of nuclear power).

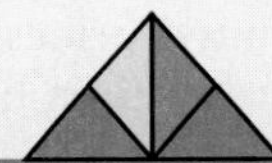

those acceptable to unregulated firms, they operate less efficiently.[5]

Regulatory Lag. Although price regulation appears to eliminate rewards for efficiency and innovation, it does so *only if regulators raise prices immediately when operating costs rise.* In reality, price (rate) increases are not typically granted on a timely basis. Regulated utilities must appeal to regulatory officials to raise rates, and the red tape associated with lengthy hearings can create substantial delays. If rate increases are delayed while operating costs are rising, the regulated firm will not be able to earn its fair rate of return.

Some authorities argue that such **regulatory lag** puts pressure on regulated monopolies to economize on costs. If operating costs rise and if years are required for the approval of higher rates, company earnings fall. By the time higher rates are granted, they are already outdated, and the incentive to hold down costs is still present. Regulatory lag is especially harmful to utility profits during inflationary periods, when costs are increasing faster than rates.

Regulatory lag occurs when government regulators adjust rates some time after operating costs and the rate base have increased.

Regulatory lag reintroduces some incentive for regulated firms to use their resources efficiently, but it is only a partial (and very imperfect) solution to the fundamental problem: How can regulators encourage efficient operation while simultaneously guaranteeing a fair rate of return?

The Effects of Regulation

To evaluate the rate regulation of natural monopolies, one must compare the hypothetical rates, services, and costs that would exist in the absence of regulation to those that actually occur under regulation. No ideal method of comparison exists, but one solution is for researchers to study periods of U.S. history when there were both regulated and unregulated monopolies. In this way, they can determine whether regulated rates were indeed lower.

The most authoritative study of this sort was conducted by the late George Stigler and Claire Friedland. For the period 1912 to 1937, Stigler and

[5]The tendency of regulated monopolies to use too much capital was first analyzed by H. Averch and L. L. Johnson, "Behavior of the Firm under Regulatory Constraint," *American Economic Review* 52 (December 1962).

Friedland compared electric utilities in states with and without regulatory commissions.[6] After 1937, virtually all electric utilities were regulated, so there ceased to be any basis for comparison. Stigler and Friedland found no difference between the rates charged by regulated and unregulated electric utilities holding other factors constant. Studies for more recent periods conclude that utilities "appear to be only moderately restrained by regulation."[7]

Surprisingly, these and other studies indicate that the overall effect of regulation on utilities has been small. Why has regulation not had a greater impact on prices?

First, it is possible that the monopoly power of regulated monopolies may be exaggerated. If effective substitutes are indeed present (natural gas for electricity) or if users (primarily industrial and commercial customers) are prepared to move to another utility region if rates become excessive, then unregulated prices, in fact, would be closer to competitive rather than monopoly prices. If this is true, we should not expect rate regulation to make much difference.

Second, the small, underpaid legal and professional staffs of regulatory agencies cannot compete with the large, well-paid staffs of the regulated firms. Moreover, only the regulated firms know the details of the operation of the company, so they are in a position to circumvent orders from the regulatory commission. Monopoly profits in excess of the fair rate of return, for example, can be concealed by creative accounting.[8]

Third, regulators tend to be captives of, or to have a certain loyalty to, the industry they regulate. They are often recruited from the ranks of the regulated companies and return after leaving the regulatory agency. Thus, many have more in common with the companies they regulate than with the public they are supposed to represent.

[6]George Stigler and Claire Friedland, "What Can Regulators Regulate? The Case of Electricity," reprinted in *The Crisis of the Regulatory Commissions,* edited by Paul MacAvoy (New York: W. W. Norton, 1970), 39–52.

[7]William G. Shepherd, "Causes of Increased Competition in the U.S. Economy, 1939–1980," *Review of Economics and Statistics* (November 1982) 617. This conclusion is based on studies by Alfred Kahn, Almarin Phillips, Stephen Breyer, and Paul MacAvoy.

[8]For a description of how regulated companies are able to evade regulation decrees, see Richard Posner, "Natural Monopoly and Its Regulation," in *The Crisis of the Regulatory Commissions,* edited by Paul MacAvoy (New York: W. W. Norton, 1970), 30–38.

DEREGULATION

Regulation in the United States is not limited to monopolies. It extends to many potentially competitive industries, including radio and television broadcasting, trucking, telecommunications, stock brokerage, passenger and freight airlines, railroads, and banking. Some of these continue to be regulated; others were deregulated in the late 1970s and early 1980s. What was the rationale behind the deregulation movement? What were its consequences?

The Case for and Against Deregulation

Most economists favor deregulation of industries that are potentially competitive. They argue that deregulation allows customers to get what they pay for and eliminates stifling bureaucratic rules.

There are numerous examples of inefficient regulatory rules.[9] During the heyday of interstate trucking regulation, the Interstate Commerce Commission (ICC) forced truckers to travel roundabout routes and to return with empty trucks from long hauls. The ICC also required that prices charged by motor carriers and railroads be the same despite substantial cost differences. The Civil Aeronautics Board (CAB) once required airlines to charge the same fare per passenger mile even if the plane were habitually full on one route and habitually empty on another. Consumers paid for these inefficiencies with higher prices. Proponents of deregulation argue that where the potential for competition exists, it is better for professional managers (as opposed to government bureaucrats) to make decisions about prices and services. The public will likely receive better (and more diversified) service at lower cost. As Alfred Kahn, chairman of the CAB when airline deregulation was initiated, put it: "I have more faith in greed than in regulation."[10]

Economists have attempted to place a price tag on the costs of federal regulation in the United

[9]Case studies of the higher costs of regulated industries are presented in Paul MacAvoy, *The Crisis of the Regulatory Commissions,* parts 3–5.

[10]*New York Times,* October 7, 1980.

States. For 1977, just prior to the start of a broad movement toward deregulation, the estimated price was between $14 billion and $36 billion (between 0.7 percent and 1.8 percent of 1977 total national output). The highest regulation costs were found in the transportation sector.[11]

The case against deregulation rests on three arguments. The first states that without regulation, some consumers may be denied an essential service. A regulated industry is required to provide access to the service to virtually all customers, but firms in a deregulated industry might serve only the most lucrative markets. For example, small communities might find themselves without rail or air service after deregulation. The second argument holds that if deregulation occurs, competition may be eliminated by the emergence of a dominant producer, who will then act like a monopolist. For example, some observers claim that airline deregulation has resulted in the domination of the industry by a few large airlines. The third point is that regulation permits public control of the quality of the service. For example, people worry that public-interest programming would disappear if access to the airwaves were not regulated.[12]

Deregulation Legislation

In October 1978, President Jimmy Carter signed the Airline Deregulation Act, the first of several major deregulation acts. The Airline Deregulation Act allowed the airlines, rather than the Civil Aeronautics Board, to set their own fares (within a broad range set by the CAB) and select their own routes. Service to smaller communities continued for 10 years, financed by government subsidy when necessary. The act phased out the CAB at the end of 1984.

Other federal deregulation legislation followed. The Motor Carrier Act of 1980 curbed the ICC's control over interstate trucking. It allowed truckers greater autonomy in setting rates and changing routes and permitted new firms to enter the business. The Staggers Rail Act of October 1980 gave the railroads more flexibility in setting their own rates, banned the railroad industry's practice of collective rate setting, and allowed railroads to drop unprofitable routes. The year 1980 also saw the passage of the Depository Institutions Deregulation and Monetary Control Act, which eliminated interest-rate ceilings on bank savings deposits and allowed savings and loan associations to offer checking accounts, car loans, and full-service credit cards. In 1982, the Thrift Institutions Restructuring Act enabled savings and loan institutions to operate on a more equal footing with commercial banks. The Bus Deregulatory Reform Act, also of 1982, allowed intercity bus lines to operate in many circumstances without applying for federal licenses.

Other types of deregulation have been introduced by the regulatory commissions themselves. Since 1972, the Federal Communications Commission has been gradually deregulating the television broadcasting industry. (See Example 4.) On May 1, 1975, the Securities and Exchange Commission made the brokerage fees charged by stockbrokers on the New York Stock Exchange freely negotiable. Prior to this change, U.S. brokers were required to charge fixed commissions for stock transactions and were not allowed to compete on price. In the 1960s, the Federal Communications Commission began authorizing competitive long-distance telephone companies to build microwave networks. In a settlement with the Justice Department in 1982, rival long-distance companies were given the right to have the same connection to local telephone networks that AT&T had.

An Evaluation of Deregulation

We can draw some preliminary conclusions about the successes and failures of deregulation, though the movement did not begin until the late 1970s. The early years of deregulation were not tranquil. Airline deregulation was carried out amid two costly recessions and escalating fuel bills. Many smaller airlines were taken over by larger ones. The deregulation of trucking has been fought by unions and by major trucking firms, and much interstate trucking is still subject to some federal regulation. Banking deregulation was undertaken during a period characterized by soaring interest rates; bank failures resulting from problems in farming, real estate, and energy; and an international debt crisis. Rival long-distance

[11] Litan and Nordhaus, *Reforming Federal Regulation,* 23. These figures are based on studies by Murray Weidenbaum and R. DeFina, T. G. Moore, Ann Friedlander, Gerald Jautscher, G. W. Douglas, James C. Miller, and W. Comanor and B. Mitchell.

[12] "Deregulation is Back on Track," *New York Times,* September 7, 1980; "FCC Battleground: Deregulation of TV," *New York Times,* October 20, 1980; "The U.S. Drive for Deregulation," *New York Times,* October 7, 1980.

EXAMPLE 4 Why Monopolies Disappear in the Long Run: The TV Networks

For several decades after its birth in the late 1940s, U.S. television was dominated by three national networks: NBC, ABC, and CBS. In effect, the networks exercised a monopoly over television broadcasting, bolstered by the Federal Communication Commission's restriction on the number of VHF channels. Consequently, they enjoyed monopoly profits from advertising revenues.

Yet, the network monopoly has eroded rapidly since 1972; profitability has fallen, and in recent years, at least one of the networks has operated at a loss. Why? First, the Federal Communications Commission increased the number of broadcast channels and eased restrictions on satellite and cable transmissions. Second, significant technological advances have taken place in cable broadcasting. Now, on any particular evening, less than half of all television viewers watch network broadcasting. The majority watch cable television, the Fox Network (with its popular "Simpsons" and "Married with Children" shows), a sports channel, or a rented movie. Thus, the network monopoly has diminished due to a combination of technological advances and the end of government protection from competition.

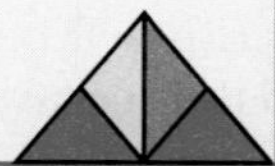

telephone companies did not gain equal access to local telephone exchanges until the mid-1980s.

Deregulation should be judged by examining its effects on prices, costs, and quality of service. Economist Elizabeth Bailey conducted a careful study of the consequences of deregulation as of the mid-1980s.[13] She found that airline fares had fallen considerably (as much as 40 percent) below what they would have been if regulation had continued, with the greatest declines found in large markets (say, Chicago to New York) and on long routes (say, Los Angeles to Boston). The smallest fare declines were on shorter hauls and in smaller markets, and fares actually rose in markets carrying less than 50 passengers per day. Airline costs also fell dramatically after deregulation. Seat patterns were reconfigured, and labor agreements were renegotiated. Labor productivity at the larger airlines rose by 20 percent during the first 5 years of deregulation. Small cities were not left without air service because small commuter airlines expanded their operations and even major carriers increased departures to smaller cities from their main hubs of operation. However, the opening of the passenger airline industry to competition imposed costs as well as benefits. A number of airlines were unable to survive competitive pressures and went bankrupt. Airline employees saw their earnings fall as companies had to cut costs to remain competitive. A number of mergers were negotiated as healthy airlines acquired financially troubled ones. By the early 1990s, mergers and bankruptcies created an airline industry dominated by three strong carriers.

The experience of other industries under deregulation was much like that of the passenger airlines, although less dramatic. Commissions on stock transactions dropped considerably after deregulation, except in the case of small transactions by small traders. An order for 1000 shares cost 20 percent less in 1982 than in 1975, whereas an order for 50 shares cost 12 percent more. Deregulation gave stock purchasers a choice between discount brokers and larger brokers who offer more services at higher prices.

Deregulation encouraged the entry of new firms into trucking, causing rates to decrease. Rates for

[13]Elizabeth E. Bailey, "Price and Productivity Change Following Deregulation: The U.S. Experience," *The Economic Journal* 96 (March 1986): 1–17. See also C. Winston, "Conceptual Developments in the Economics of Transportation," *Journal of Economic Literature* 23 (1985): 57–94; T. Keeler, *Railroads, Freight, and Public Policy* (Washington, D.C.: Brookings, 1983); A. F. Friedlander and R. H. Spady, *Freight Transport Regulation* (Cambridge, MA: MIT Press, 1981).

EXAMPLE 5 The Risks of Deregulation: Rising Concentration and Rising Fares

When the airline industry was deregulated in the late 1970s, fares were pushed down by competition among established firms and from new low-cost airlines. The airline industry went through a series of price wars and energy shocks that caused profits to drop. Marginal airlines either went out of business or were acquired by larger airlines. Antitrust laws were not applied to airline mergers. When the merger movement began in the early 1980s, there were more than 20 airlines. The mergers that took place in the late 1980s typically involved a profitable airline acquiring a failing airline—a practice that antitrust laws permit.

Most industrial organization experts believe that a mistake was made in allowing too many airline mergers. Instead of acting as competitors, rival airline companies began to coordinate their pricing and to operate the industry as an oligopoly. Rival airlines concentrated their operations in different "hubs" (such as TWA in St. Louis, Delta in Atlanta, Continental in Houston, and United in Chicago and Denver), creating markets in which each carrier dominated. After 1987, airlines shifted their strategy from trying to fill empty seats to charging prices that yielded higher profits. Although competitive fares were charged for foreign flights and flights from hubs where no single carrier dominated, airline fares were not as competitive as they had been immediately following deregulation.

Exit from the airline industry accelerated during the recession of the early 1990s. As losses mounted, Eastern, Pan Am, and Midway Airlines ceased operations, and Continental and TWA continued operations under Chapter 11 bankruptcy. Only American, United, Delta, and Southwest were left as healthy airlines.

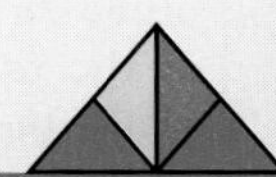

truckload shipments fell by 25 percent (after adjustment for inflation), and rates for less-than-truckload shipments fell by 16 percent.

During regulation, rates for local telephone service were priced below cost, and the loss was covered by profits from long-distance service. As competition in long-distance service drove long-distance rates down, there were no longer substantial profits to cover the losses from local service. Accordingly, although long-distance rates have fallen, there has been upward pressure on monthly rates for local telephone service.

Overall, deregulation led to lower prices for most—but not all—consumers. On the one hand, many consumers benefited from a greater freedom to choose from an increased diversity of services. Moreover, firms that had been protected by regulation lowered their costs substantially, and these lower costs were passed on to their customers. On the other hand, consumers in small, high-cost markets lost their protection and had to pay prices closer to costs. Deregulation had further negative consequences. Firms that could not meet competitive pressures went out of business or were acquired by more successful firms. Employees saw their earnings fall as firms sought ways to lower their costs. (See Example 5.)

ANTITRUST LAW

The major alternative to direct regulation of monopolies is legislation to control market structure and market conduct. Rather than regulating monopolies directly by telling them what prices they can charge and what services they must offer, the government can set the legal rules of the economic game.

Legislation enacted to control market structure and conduct is called *antitrust law.* The cornerstone of U.S. federal antitrust legislation is the Sherman

Antitrust Act of 1890. The Sherman Act was passed in reaction to the public outrage against the **trust** movement in the railroad, steel, tobacco, and oil industries of the late nineteenth century.

> A **trust** is a combination of firms that sets common prices, agrees to restrict output, and punishes member firms who fail to live up to the agreement.

The Sherman Act of 1890

The Sherman Act contains two sections. Section 1 provides that

> every contract, combination in the form of a trust or otherwise, or conspiracy, in restraint of trade or commerce among the several States, or with foreign nations, is hereby declared to be illegal.

Section 2 provides that

> every person who shall monopolize, or attempt to monopolize, or combine or conspire with any other person or persons to monopolize any part of the trade or commerce among the several States, or with foreign nations, shall be guilty of a misdemeanor.[14]

Section 1 prohibits a particular type of market *conduct* (conspiring to restrain trade), whereas Section 2 outlaws a particular market *structure* (monopoly). The vague language of Section 2 has resulted in varying court interpretations over the years. Section 2 prohibits *monopolization,* not *monopolies;* although the act of creating a monopoly is clearly prohibited, the legality of existing monopolies is not addressed.

The Clayton Act and the Federal Trade Commission Act, 1914

The Sherman Act contained a general prohibition on restraints of trade but did not identify specific monopolistic practices that were in violation of the law. Moreover, the Sherman Act did not establish any agency (other than the existing Department of Justice) to enforce its provisions.

The Clayton Act of 1914 declared the following four specific monopolistic practices to be illegal if their "effect was to substantially lessen competition or tend to create a monopoly":

1. Price discrimination (charging different prices to different customers for the same product)
2. Exclusive dealing and *tying contracts* (requiring a buyer to agree not to purchase goods from competitors)
3. Acquisition of competing companies
4. *Interlocking directorates* (in which the directors of one company sit on the board of directors of another company in the same industry)

The Clayton Act gave private parties the right to sue—along with other penalties—for damages for injury to business or property resulting from violations of the antitrust laws.

The Federal Trade Commission Act established the Federal Trade Commission (FTC), whose duty was to secure compliance with the ban on "unfair methods of competition" stated in the FTC Act. It was granted the authority to prosecute unfair competition and to issue cease and desist orders to violators.

Revisions of the Clayton Act

The Robinson-Patman Act of 1936 amended the Clayton Act's prohibition of price discrimination functioning "to substantially lessen competition... or to injure, destroy, or prevent competition with any person who either grants or knowingly receives the benefit of such discrimination, or with customers of either of them." The Robinson-Patman Act—which was passed during Depression times, when the rate of failure for small businesses was high—protected small businesses from the competition of the growing chain stores who were receiving discounts for large purchases. Because the act sought to protect small businesses from large competitors, many authorities regard the Robinson-Patman Act as anticompetitive. Its primary purpose seemed to be protection of *competitors* rather than protection of *competition.*

The Wheeler-Lea Act of 1938 extended the general ban on "unfair methods of competition" to include "unfair or *deceptive*" acts or practices. Under this amendment the FTC was empowered to deal

[14]This discussion is based upon A. D. Neale, *The Antitrust Laws of the United States of America* (Cambridge: The University Press, 1962), 2–5; Eugene Singer, *Antitrust Economics* (Englewood Cliffs, NJ: Prentice Hall, 1968), chap. 2; Marshall C. Howard, *Antitrust and Trade Regulation* (Englewood Cliffs, NJ: Prentice Hall, 1983).

with false and deceptive advertising and the sale of harmful products.

The Celler-Kefauver Act of 1950 broadened the Clayton Act's ban on corporate mergers by limiting the acquisition of one company's assets by another company. This antimerger provision applied if the acquisition served to substantially lessen competition or to create a monopoly. The Hart-Scott-Rodino Antitrust Procedural Improvements Act of 1980 replaced the word *corporations* with the word *persons*, making the antimerger legislation applicable to large unincorporated business firms (such as large accounting partnerships). The act also required that pending mergers be reported in advance to antitrust authorities.

Interpretation of the Sherman Act

American antitrust policy is determined in the courts as well as in Congress. The Sherman Antitrust Act, the mainstay of antitrust legislation, left a basic issue unresolved: Do antitrust laws prohibit only market conduct that leads to monopoly, or does monopoly, by the fact of its existence, constitute a violation?

The Rule of Reason, 1911–45. In early rulings, the courts interpreted the Sherman Act as outlawing specific market *practices* that restrained trade (mergers, price fixing, price slashing to drive out competition), not the existence of monopoly in and of itself. This interpretation became known as the **rule of reason.**[15]

> The **rule of reason** stated that monopolies were in violation of the Sherman Act if they used unfair or illegal business practices. Being a monopoly in and of itself was not a violation of the Sherman Act.

The early landmark tests of the Sherman Act were the Standard Oil and American Tobacco Company cases, both tried in 1911. The Standard Oil case is discussed in the Chapter Insight. In both cases, the Supreme Court ruled that these companies should be broken up into smaller companies. Both Standard Oil and American Tobacco accounted for more than 90 percent of the output in their respective industries. The court's ruling, however, was not based upon their dominant market shares. Standard Oil and American Tobacco were judged in violation of the Sherman Act for engaging in unreasonable restraint of trade, not for being monopolies.

The Standard Oil and American Tobacco rulings implied that a monopoly did not violate the Sherman Act unless it engaged in unfair business practices. This rule of reason was upheld in the U.S. Steel case of 1920. U.S. Steel at the time produced more than half of the industry's output, but it had not treated its competitors unfairly or sought to control steel prices. U.S. Steel was, in effect, a "benevolent" monopolist. In this case, the court stated that the law did not consider mere size or the existence of "unexerted power" to be an offense.

Questioning the Rule of Reason. The rule of reason prevailed until the Aluminum Company of America (Alcoa) case of 1945. The courts ruled that Alcoa violated the Sherman Act because it controlled more than 90 percent of the aluminum ingot market in the United States. Alcoa was also accused of using unfair pricing (setting ingot prices too high relative to aluminum sheet prices). The courts (in a famous decision written by Judge Learned Hand) ruled that size alone was a violation of the Sherman Act.

The Alcoa decision appeared to overturn the rule of reason, removing an important inconsistency in the law. The rule of reason suggested that companies engaging in practices that would ultimately lead to monopoly were in violation of the Sherman Act, but companies that were already monopolies, if they were well behaved, were not. The Alcoa case seemed to replace the older "abuse theory," which required proof of the monopoly's predatory conduct, with a "structure test," in which size was the determining factor. Actual monopolization—rather than the attempt to monopolize—was deemed Alcoa's offense.

Definition of Market. The Alcoa decision raised a fundamental issue: If the existence of monopoly is itself a violation of the Sherman Act, how is the market to be defined?

In the Alcoa case, the definition of the aluminum market was crucial to the courts' decision. Alcoa controlled 90 percent of the virgin aluminum ingot market, but it had to compete in the scrap

[15]This discussion of court rulings is based upon Frederic Scherer, *Industrial Structure and Economic Performance,* 2nd ed. (Boston: Houghton Mifflin, 1980); Oliver Williamson, *Markets and Hierarchies: Analysis and Antitrust Implications* (New York: The Free Press, 1975); and Howard, *Antitrust and Trade Regulation.*

EXAMPLE 6 Cross-Price Elasticities and Antitrust: What Constitutes a Market?

Cross-price elasticities, introduced in an earlier chapter, are an important tool in defining what constitutes a market. The cross-price elasticity measures the response in sales of product A to a change in the price of product B. If an increase in the price of A causes sales of B to increase, then A and B are substitutes. A very elastic cross-price coefficient means that the two goods are close substitutes and form a single market. Economists are often called upon to estimate cross-price elasticities to present as evidence in modern antitrust cases.

In the Du Pont cellophane case (mentioned in the text), the court ruled in favor of Du Pont on the grounds that Du Pont's cellophane faced close substitutes in the marketplace. (This meant that cellophane had a high cross-price elasticity relative to aluminum foil and plastic wraps.) The judge's decision stated, "Market control or lack of market control are ultimate facts. They are determined by fact-finding processes and on the basis of knowledge and analysis of all competitive factors which bear on a seller's power to raise prices, or to exclude competition.... Facts, in large part uncontested, demonstrate Du Pont cellophane is sold under such intense, competitive conditions, acquisition of market control or monopoly power is a practical impossibility."

Source: A. D. Neale, *The Antitrust Laws of the United States of America* (Cambridge: Cambridge University Press, 1962), 123.

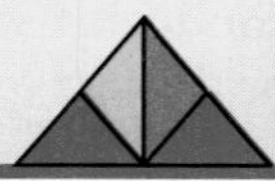

ingot market and faced competition from stainless steel, lead, nickel, tin, zinc, copper, and imported aluminum. The court ruled that substitutes for aluminum should not be included in Alcoa's market; thus, Alcoa was characterized as a monopoly.

The Du Pont cellophane case of 1956 broadened the definition of the market. Du Pont, in 1956, produced almost 75 percent of the *cellophane* sold in the United States but accounted for less than 20 percent of the sales of *flexible wrapping materials.* Du Pont was accused of monopolizing the cellophane market. The Supreme Court ruled in favor of Du Pont, judging that the market should be defined to include products that are "reasonably interchangeable" with cellophane (such as aluminum foil, waxed paper, or vegetable parchment). The court ruled that a 20 percent share was insufficient to establish monopoly power. (See Example 6.)

In 1975, the Justice Department won an antitrust judgment against Xerox Corporation. At the time of the 1975 decision, Xerox produced more than 90 percent of plain-paper copiers and 65 percent of all copying equipment. The courts ruled that Xerox monopolized the copying equipment market and required the company to make some of its patents available to competitors in order to increase competition in the market.

In 1969, the Justice Department filed suit against IBM for monopolizing the "general-purpose computer and peripheral-equipment industry." At that time, IBM controlled about 70 percent of the mainframe computer market but held less than 40 percent of the office equipment market. The specific complaint against IBM was that it combined the price of hardware, software, and support services, thereby preventing competition in the software and support markets. Again, the courts had to decide what constituted IBM's market.

After more than a decade of litigation involving 66 million pages of documents, the Justice Department decided in 1982 to drop the case. In the intervening years, IBM's competition in the computer industry had increased substantially. By 1982, IBM dominated only the mainframe computer industry (with 70 percent of the U.S. market). In its other lines of business, IBM's shares were relatively small: 20 percent of the minicomputer market, 18 percent of the word-processor market, and less than

5 percent of the telecommunications and computer services markets. Based on these developments, the Justice Department decided that IBM did not monopolize the computer industry as broadly defined.

In 1982, a compromise court decision was reached in which American Telephone and Telegraph agreed to divest itself of its local operating companies. AT&T agreed to give up its regional Bell affiliates (which remained subject to rate regulation) in return for permission to enter unregulated telecommunications and computer markets.

In general, court rulings after 1950 moved away from the narrow Alcoa ruling toward a more liberal interpretation of the definition of a market.

Superior Innovation. The Alcoa decision, by declaring size alone to be a violation of the Sherman Act, raised concern among businesses that it would, in the words of a former head of the Justice Department's Antitrust Division, be used "to punish innovative success."[16] The ruling itself cautioned against penalizing the successful competitor.

Some companies gain monopoly positions not through unfair business practices but with superior innovation. Is a company that attains a dominant position through superior foresight, good planning, proper risk taking, and aggressive technological innovation violating the Sherman Act?[17]

The Eastman Kodak case provided an important test case. In 1972, Berkey Photo, Inc. filed an antitrust suit charging that Eastman Kodak's method of introducing its pocket-sized instamatic camera and film gave it an unfair advantage over other film processors. The court ruled in favor of Eastman Kodak, concluding that the company had earned certain advantages by "reaping the competitive rewards attributable to efficient size."[18] In a 1978 complaint, the FTC staff accused Du Pont of illegally using unfair competition to overwhelm smaller rivals in the titanium dioxide market. In a ruling similar to that in the Kodak case, the FTC dismissed antitrust charges against Du Pont:

> The essence of the competitive process is to induce firms to become more efficient and to pass the benefits of the efficiency along to consumers. That process would be ill served by using antitrust to block hard, aggressive competition that is solidly based on efficiencies and growth opportunities, even if monopoly is an inevitable result.[19]

These judgments seem inconsistent with the apparent intent of the Alcoa ruling to declare monopoly illegal, irrespective of its origin. The Du Pont and Eastman Kodak rulings required the courts to weigh how a monopoly came into being—whether through restrictive or unfair business practices or through efficient management and innovation.

MERGERS

Antimerger Legislation

The Clayton Act of 1914 and the Celler-Kefauver Act of 1950 prohibit the acquisition of one company by another if such action reduces competition. Mergers, in which two firms combine to form one, can be of two general types: **horizontal mergers** and **vertical mergers.**

> A **horizontal merger** is a merger of two firms in the same line of business (such as two insurance companies or two shoe manufacturers).
>
> A **vertical merger** is a merger of two firms that are part of the same materials, production, or distribution network (such as a personal-computer manufacturer and a retail computer distribution chain or a machinery manufacturer and a machinery parts supplier).

The courts (especially since 1950) have adopted a virtual prohibition of horizontal mergers if both firms have substantial market shares. In June 1986, the Federal Trade Commission blocked Coca-Cola's

[16] *Wall Street Journal,* November 10, 1980.

[17] The Grinnel case of 1966 noted that if monopoly was the "consequence of a superior product, business acumen, or historic accident," the Sherman Act was not violated. See Williamson, *Markets and Hierarchies,* 209–10.

[18] This case is summarized in "FTC Dismisses Charges against Du Pont in Major Statement of Its Antitrust Policy," *Wall Street Journal,* November 10, 1980.

[19] *Wall Street Journal,* November 10, 1980.

EXAMPLE 7 Contestable Markets and Antitrust Policy

According to contestable markets theory, discussed in the chapter on oligopoly, the structure of a market (as measured by its concentration ratio) is a poor measure of monopoly power. In a contestable market (which is characterized by complete freedom of entry), if a monopoly firm attempted to charge monopoly prices, rival firms would immediately enter the market, undercut prices, and take profits away from the established firm.

Contestable markets theory argues against basing antitrust policy decisions on existing concentration in an industry. The existence of a single dominant producer (such as one airline flying from Pittsburgh to Charlotte) does not necessarily indicate a problem with monopoly power. In a one-producer market that potential competitors can enter quickly and easily, the single producer must behave in a competitive manner. If it attempts to charge a monopoly price, competitors will quickly enter the market and drive the price back to its competitive level.

Contestable markets theory also implies that merger decisions should be based on the speed and ease of entry of potential competitors, not on concentration ratios. For example, mergers in the airline industry have been allowed on the grounds that even though one airline may hold a monopoly on certain routes, potential competitors could enter easily if monopoly profits were being earned.

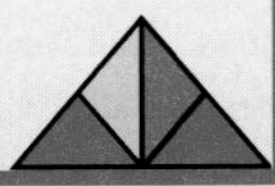

acquisition of Dr. Pepper and Pepsico's acquisition of Seven-Up. If the mergers had been allowed, the combined market share of Coca-Cola and Pepsico would have been 80 percent.

Exceptions are allowed when one firm takes over another firm that is on the verge of bankruptcy. Jones & Laughlin Industries and Youngstown Steel were allowed to merge in 1978 to form the third largest producer of basic steel. The many airline mergers of the 1980s were motivated by the desire to keep the assets of failing companies in the airline business.

Vertical mergers are in violation of the Clayton Act if merging with a supplier enables the buyer to cut out other buyers, or if the vertical merger results in a transfer of significant market power. On these grounds, Du Pont (a major supplier of automotive fabrics and finishes) was required to sell its 23 percent holding of General Motors stock in 1957 because Du Pont's influence over GM gave it a competitive advantage over other automotive suppliers. For similar reasons, Brown Shoe Company was not allowed in 1962 to acquire Kinney (a large retail shoe chain). An exception was made in 1986, when the ban on vertical mergers between moviemakers and movie theaters was eased in response to technological change in the entertainment industry. (See Example 7.)

Conglomerate Mergers

The major exception to the prohibition of mergers between large companies is the **conglomerate merger.** Conglomerate mergers are less likely to be opposed by the Justice Department because they do not involve competing companies. Thus, U.S. Steel was permitted to acquire Marathon Oil, and Du Pont was allowed to acquire Conoco because the merging companies operated in different markets.

> A **conglomerate merger** occurs when one company takes over another company in a different line of business.

Conglomerate mergers have led to a substantial increase over the past 30 years in the share of corporate assets controlled by the largest U.S. corporations. According to FTC statistics, the 451 largest corporations controlled 50 percent of corporate assets in 1960; in the early 1990s, they controlled almost three-quarters of corporate assets.[20]

[20] "Government May Abandon Fight to Stop Conglomerate Takeovers," *Wall Street Journal*, November 24, 1980.

FIGURE 3
Mergers in the United States, 1890–1990

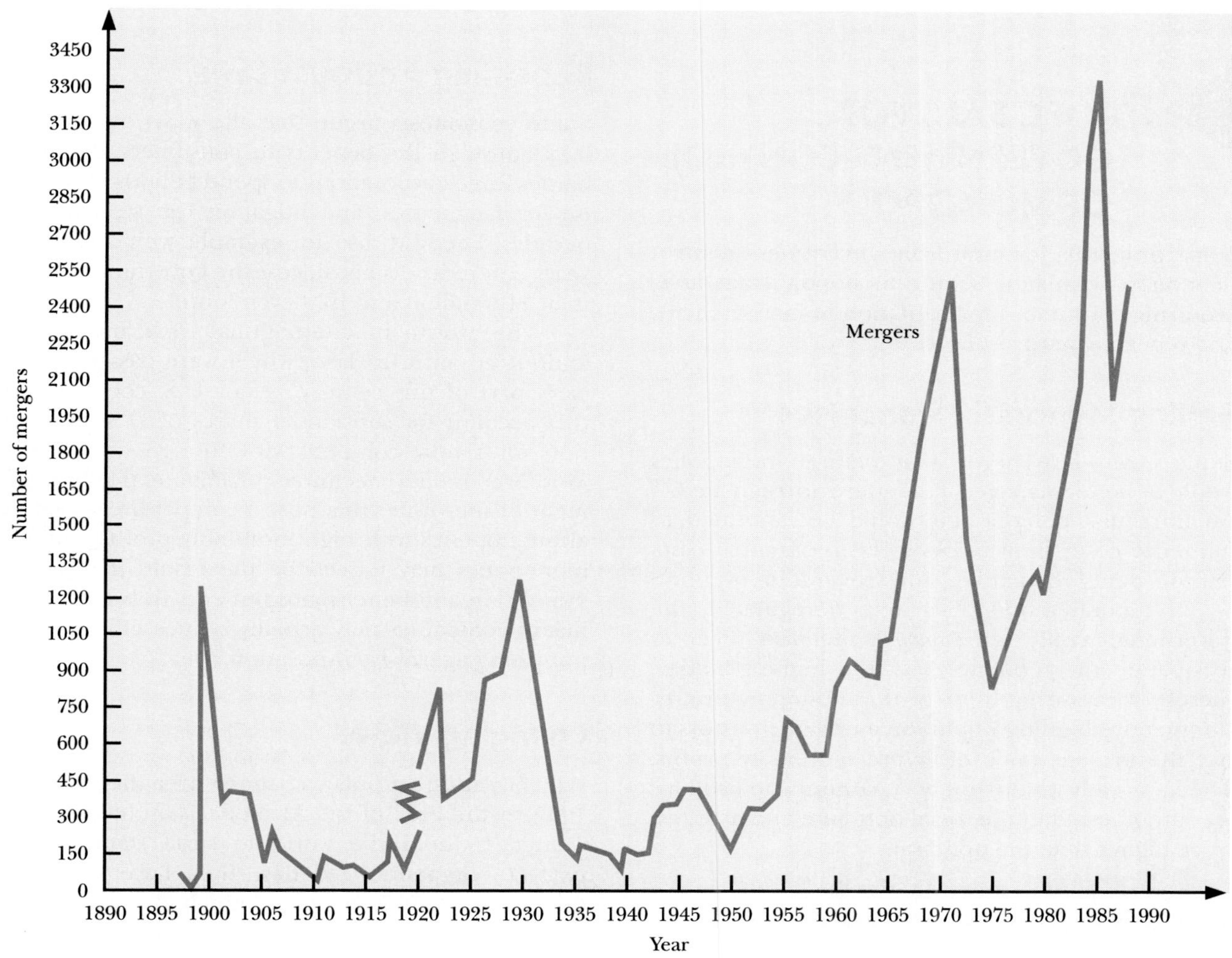

Sources: The National Bureau of Economic Research and the Federal Trade Commission, *Mergers and Acquisitions.* Updated data courtesy of W. T. Grimm & Co.

The pace of mergers has been highly uneven over the years (see Figure 3). In part, this pattern reflects the fact that both antimerger legislation and the rigor of enforcement of such legislation have varied over the years.

The FTC and the Justice Department have led the battle against conglomerate takeovers. In the 1960s, they were able to win about half of the cases brought against conglomerate mergers. Prior to 1973, the government was able to fight proposed mergers on the grounds of a *potential* threat to competition. If a steel company wanted to acquire an aluminum company, this merger could be denied because the aluminum company might eventually compete with the parent company—whether it currently did so or not. For instance, Procter & Gamble was not allowed to acquire Clorox in the mid-1960s because Procter & Gamble was viewed as a potential entrant into the liquid bleach market. Since 1973, however, the government has lost all of its attempts to prevent conglomerate takeovers. The burden of proof has fallen on the government to provide concrete proof that a conglomerate merger will actually (not potentially) reduce competition.

PROPOSALS FOR GOVERNMENT CONTROL OF MONOPOLY

Some proposals for improving government control of monopoly include selling monopoly franchises, requiring consumer representation in management, and repealing antitrust laws.

Selling Monopoly Franchises

Some economists argue that natural monopolies would be better managed if they were not regulated.[21] An unregulated monopoly would be motivated to minimize costs, limit prices to keep potential competitors out of the market, and seek out innovation.

If natural monopolies were deregulated, the government could sell *monopoly franchises* (licenses to operate the monopoly) to the highest bidder, thereby recapturing most of the monopoly profits. Competitive bidding would force private investors to pay the present value of future monopoly profits. The monopoly would, however, continue to produce an output less than the social optimum and charge a price higher than the optimum.

Requiring Consumer Representation in Management

A second proposal is to place consumer representatives on the board of directors of natural monopolies or to grant consumers a voting interest in firms designated as public utilities. Important actions of the board of directors could be referred to consumers by means of municipal elections.

If these measures were undertaken, it is argued, management would identify more closely with the interests of consumers and would refrain from abusing monopoly power.[22]

Repealing Antitrust Laws

Some economists argue that the costs of antitrust laws outweigh the benefits to consumers. Antitrust battles force corporations to spend billions of dollars on legal expenses, and litigation can stretch over decades. The IBM case, for example, which lasted 13 years before its dismissal, cost the government more than $12 million and IBM even more.

The growth in international trade has largely antiquated antitrust laws, which were passed in the early part of this century. Major U.S. corporations that account for substantial shares of U.S. production must now compete with foreign companies. Moreover, modern technology facilitates the development of substitutes that pose a competitive threat to all monopolies with high monopoly profits. Finally, monopolies may indeed be the result of superior innovation and better management. To break up efficient companies may actually reduce efficiency by punishing aggressive innovation.[23]

Changing Views

Why has antitrust policy changed over the years? In 1945, at the time of the Alcoa decision, economists wanted to hold the world to strict standards of perfect competition. Today, they have come to understand that it is not so much the world that is imperfect but the theory of perfect competition. The presence of information and transaction costs precludes the existence of perfect competition in its pure form. The consequent divergence of real-world industries from the assumptions of perfect competition, therefore, need not represent a case for antitrust action. Economists realize that the world is complex, and efficient arrangements may take many forms.

[21]This position is associated with Milton Friedman and George Stigler. See Milton Friedman, "Monopoly and Social Responsibility of Business and Labor," in *Monopoly Power and Economic Performance*, edited by Edwin Mansfield, 3rd ed. (New York: W. W. Norton, 1974), 57–68; George Stigler, "Government of the Economy," in *Readings in Economics,* edited by Paul Samuelson, 7th ed. (New York: McGraw-Hill, 1973), 73–77.

[22]Edward Renshaw, "Possible Alternatives to Direct Regulation," in *The Crisis of the Regulatory Commissions,* edited by Paul MacAvoy (New York: W. W. Norton, 1970), 209–11.

[23]For one view of why antitrust laws should be abolished, see Lester Thurow, "Let's Abolish the Antitrust Laws," *New York Times,* October 19, 1980.

This chapter studied antitrust law and regulation. The next chapter considers the role of information in the economy.

SUMMARY

1. A natural monopoly contains a single producer because economies of scale are experienced over the entire range of the industry's output.

2. It is not clear how to operate government monopolies "in the public interest." Marginal-cost pricing will normally lead to losses. A break-even strategy will provide little incentive to reduce costs or innovate. If the government monopoly tries to maximize profits, the consumer will receive no benefit.

3. Regulation of natural monopolies is aimed at limiting monopoly profits while allowing the monopoly to operate profitably, encouraging efficient operation and preventing predatory competition. Regulated monopolies are normally allowed to charge a price that covers operating costs plus a "fair" rate of return on invested capital. This pricing formula fosters inefficiency because higher costs can be passed on to the consumer and higher investment automatically yields higher profits. Regulatory lag provides some incentive to minimize costs.

4. Regulation of potentially competitive industries creates inefficiencies and poor service. A significant deregulation movement to free competitive industries in the United States from government supervision began in the late 1970s.

5. The goal of antitrust legislation is to control market structure and market conduct by setting legal rules for businesses to follow. The Sherman Act outlaws the restraint of trade and the act of monopolization. The Clayton Act specifies which business practices illegally restrain trade (price discrimination, mergers, tying contracts, and interlocking directorates). The Federal Trade Commission Act established the Federal Trade Commission and banned unfair methods of competition. The Celler-Kefauver Act toughened the antimerger provisions of the Clayton Act. The "rule of reason," which held that only unreasonable restraint of trade violated the Sherman Act, was applied by the courts in antitrust cases until 1945. The rule of reason appeared to be overturned in 1945 with the Alcoa decision, when the courts judged size alone to be a violation of the Sherman Act. In subsequent cases, however, the courts have ruled that monopolies created by superior technological achievement do not violate the Sherman Act.

6. Mergers between firms in the same industry are prohibited if both have substantial market shares. Exceptions are allowed when one firm takes over another that is on the verge of bankruptcy. Conglomerate mergers are usually not opposed because they do not involve competing companies.

7. Some alternative methods of controlling monopoly that have been proposed include deregulating natural monopolies and selling monopoly franchises to the highest bidder, placing consumer representatives on the boards of directors of monopoly corporations, and repealing antitrust laws.

KEY TERMS

natural monopoly	horizontal merger
regulatory lag	vertical merger
trust	conglomerate merger
rule of reason	

QUESTIONS AND PROBLEMS

1. Explain why, in the case of a natural monopoly, the industry functions most efficiently with only one producer.
2. Devise a set of rules that would, in your opinion, allow a government-owned natural monopoly to operate "in the public interest." How would these rules be different if the firm were not a natural monopoly?
3. You are the president of a regulated monopoly. You know that the regulators will allow you to set prices to cover operating costs plus a "fair" rate of return on invested capital. How would you behave? Would you behave differently if you were not regulated?
4. One explanation offered for why regulation of electric utilities has not made much of a difference in utility rates is that electric utilities face competition. What kind of competition can a monopoly like an electric power utility face?
5. You operate a regulated monopoly that sells in both a competitive and a monopolistic market. How would your company's price and output decisions differ in the two markets? What steps would you take to improve your position in the competitive market?
6. Deregulation of the television broadcasting industry has been opposed by the three major

networks. How would deregulation affect their profits?

7. Explain the contradiction raised by the rule of reason.
8. Why would innovative and risk-taking firms such as Boeing and Eastman Kodak oppose the Alcoa decision?
9. Evaluate the proposal to auction off monopoly franchises to the highest bidder. Why would this return most of the monopoly profits to the government?
10. Evaluate the validity of the following statement: "Several ill-informed people have suggested doing away with our antitrust laws. To do so would return us to the days of the nineteenth-century robber barons."
11. Would regulatory lag tend to raise or lower economic efficiency? Why?
12. Which of the following pairs of companies would antitrust authorities be more likely to allow to merge?
    a. General Motors and Chrysler
    b. Prudential Insurance and McDonald's
    c. Hyatt Hotels and the bankrupt Braniff International Corporation
    d. U.S. Foods and Safeway Stores
    e. U.S. Steel and Ford Motor Company
    f. B. F. Goodrich and General Motors
13. Economists who have studied the regulation of electric utilities have found that regulation has had little effect on prices. How do you explain the absence of a change in prices despite the ability of regulators to set prices?
14. Explain why the definition of the market has become a critical issue in antitrust law.

SUGGESTED READINGS

Fisher, Franklyn, John J. McGowan, and Joen E. Greenwood. *Folded, Spindled, and Mutilated: Economic Analysis and* U.S. *v.* IBM. Cambridge, MA: MIT Press, 1985.

Howard, Marshall C. *Antitrust and Trade Regulation: Selected Issues and Case Studies.* Englewood Cliffs, NJ: Prentice Hall, 1983.

Litan, Robert E., and William D. Nordhaus. *Reforming Federal Regulation.* New Haven, CT: Yale University Press, 1983.

Mansfield, Edwin. *Monopoly Power and Economic Performance,* 4th ed. New York: W. W. Norton, 1978.

Reagan, Michael. *Regulation: The Politics of Policy.* Boston: Little, Brown and Company, 1986.

Singer, Eugene. *Antitrust Economics.* Englewood Cliffs, NJ: Prentice Hall, 1968, chap. 2.

Swartz, Thomas R., and Frank J. Bonello, eds. *Taking Sides: Clashing Views on Controversial Economic Issues,* 4th ed. Guilford, CT: Duskin Publishing Group, 1990.

Waldman, Don. *The Economics of Antitrust.* Boston: Little, Brown and Company, 1986.

Weidenbaum, Murray L. *Business, Government and the Public,* 4th ed. Englewood Cliffs, NJ: Prentice Hall, 1990.

Weiss, Leonard, and Michael Klass, eds. *Regulatory Reform: What Really Happened.* Boston: Little, Brown and Company, 1986.

White, Lawrence J. *Reforming Regulation: Processes and Problems.* Englewood Cliffs, NJ: Prentice Hall, 1981.

Williamson, Oliver. *Markets and Hierarchies: Analysis and Antitrust Implications.* New York: The Free Press, 1975.

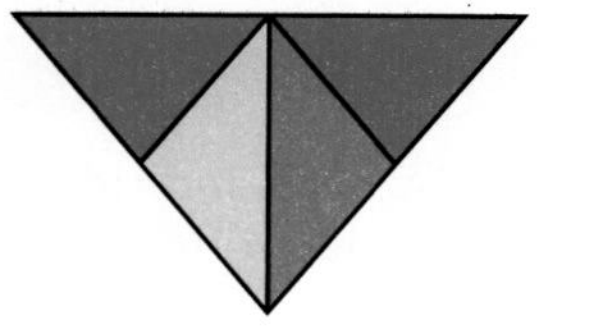

35 The Economics of Information

CHAPTER INSIGHT

"Speculators," "intermediaries" (or "middlemen"), and others in the "information business" are often unpopular people. Farmers complain about the speculators who buy from them when the price is low and resell later at a higher price. Consumers complain about rising grocery prices, which they attribute to greedy middlemen. The family that sells its home for $100,000 complains about the $6,000 fee collected by their realtor. In some socialist economies, buying low and selling high is considered a crime.

This chapter focuses on the role of information in an economy. The information provided by those in the "information business"—speculators, realtors, agents, middlemen, stockbrokers, and others—is a valuable commodity. People and businesses voluntarily pay billions of dollars to acquire information on prices, location, and quality.

This chapter examines why information is a valuable commodity; the role of intermediaries, speculators, and hedgers; the costs of gathering information about markets and products; and the problems of moral hazard and adverse selection.

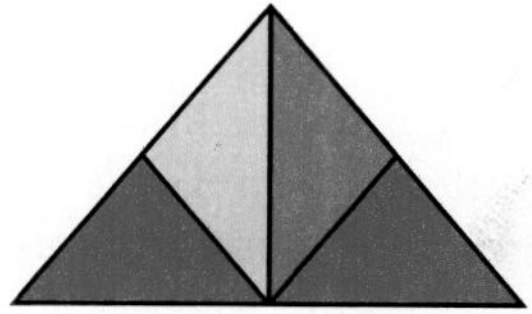

TRANSACTION COSTS AND INFORMATION COSTS

It is costly to bring buyers and sellers together. The costs associated with making exchange possible are **transaction costs.** Some examples are the cost of travel, the cost of negotiation, the cost of property-rights enforcement, and the cost of acquiring information.

> **Transaction costs** are the costs associated with bringing buyers and sellers together.

In real-world markets—even those that are highly competitive—there is considerable uncertainty about current or future prices and even about product qualities. If such information were available instantaneously at no cost of time or money, such uncertainty would evaporate. But acquiring information typically does have its costs, and **information costs** have a substantial effect on real-world markets.

> **Information costs** are the costs of acquiring information on prices, product qualities, and product performance.

Information costs include the costs of telephoning, shopping, checking credentials, inspecting goods, monitoring the honesty of workers or customers, placing ads, and reading ads and consumer reports in order to acquire more economic information.

Information is costly because people have a limited capacity to acquire, process, store, and retrieve facts and figures about prices, qualities, and location of products. Information is distributed over the population in bits and pieces.

Transaction costs are affected by information costs. The buyer and seller must first find each other and then agree on the price and other terms of the contract. Knowledge of the existence and location of a willing buyer is valuable information to the seller, just as knowledge of a willing seller is valuable information to the buyer. Without this information, economic transactions cannot take place.

Because information is costly, each individual accumulates information that is specific to that person's particular circumstances. For example, a farmer has detailed knowledge about local growing conditions, and consumers know a great deal about local food prices. This special information can be valuable. (See Example 1.) To quote the Nobel Prize laureate, Friedrich A. Hayek:

> . . . a little reflection will show that there is beyond question a body of very important but unorganized knowledge which cannot possibly be called scientific in the sense of knowledge of general rules: the knowledge of particular circumstances of time and place. It is with respect to this that every individual has some advantage over all others in that he possesses unique information of which beneficial use might be made.[1]

By allowing people to be paid for their scarce information, the price system economizes on information costs. The auto mechanic does not have to learn nuclear physics, and the physicist does not have to know how to repair a car.

> Information is typically a scarce and valuable commodity.

THE ECONOMICS OF SEARCH

Earlier, a *perfectly competitive market* was described as one in which all buyers paid the same price for the same product. In many real-world markets, the prices of even homogeneous goods (milk, bread, gasoline, etc.) differ from store to store. In these real-world markets, it is more difficult for customers to know the prices charged for the same items in different stores—even if consumers are aware of price differences, the transaction costs of always going to the cheapest store may outweigh the advantages of the lower price. As a consequence, prices of the same good will differ from location to location. Such markets are usually imperfect because different buyers appear to pay different prices for the same prod-

[1] F. A. Hayek, "The Use of Knowledge in Society," *American Economic Review* 35 (1945): 510–30.

EXAMPLE 1 The Value of Good Taste: A Fish Story

Tokyo's Tsukiji fish market may well be the largest wholesale fish market in the world. Fish are everywhere—in bins and forklifts, on bidding floors and tables, on the shoulders of workers. There are live squid and octopus, huge shrimp, big crabs, tuna—about 500 varieties of fish from all over the world. The place is so clean and the fish so fresh that there is no telltale fish odor. In about 90 minutes, the Tsukiji fish market sells 3,000 metric tons of fish.

Perhaps the most interesting part of this fish story is the tuna market. Even though several thousand tuna are sold on a given day, each tuna is auctioned individually. A platoon of tuna experts checks each tuna for the ratio of fat to meat. Tuna buyers use this information to bid on the individual tunas. A high-quality tuna with a high ratio of fat to meat tastes better and, therefore, might sell for as much as $36 per pound, while a tuna with very little fat might only sell for $1.80 per pound. The information regarding fat content can cause the price to vary by as much as 20 times! Without this information—in a world of ignorance—all tuna would sell for the same price. People are willing to pay for better-tasting tuna.

Source: George L. Rosenblatt, "Fish Story," *Houston Chronicle*, April 21, 1991.

uct. From an economic viewpoint, however, the same good in a different location is considered a different product.

Information Gathering and Price Dispersion

A consumer incurs search costs while shopping, reading, or consulting experts in order to acquire pricing or quality information. Search costs explain why homogeneous products sell for different prices in different locations. A 19-inch Zenith color TV set may sell for different prices in stores one block apart; the same brand of milk may sell for different prices in adjacent grocery stores; the same brand of automobile may sell at different prices in two dealerships located in the same part of town.

If information about the prices charged by different retail outlets were free (assuming that no location is more convenient than another), the same commodity would sell for the same price, as predicted by the theory of perfect competition. But information is not free; real resources must be devoted to gathering information. Therefore, in the real world, the prices of homogeneous products sold in different locations will be dispersed.

In gathering costly information, people follow the **optimal-search rule.**

The **optimal-search rule** is that people will continue to acquire economic information as long as the marginal benefits of gathering information exceed the marginal costs.

When a person decides to buy a new car, the more information that person has on prices and on the technical qualities of various automobiles, the better the eventual choice is likely to be. But it is costly to gather such information. It is costly to drive all over town to the various dealers; it is costly to take time off from work or from leisure activities to compare prices; it may be expensive in terms of time and money to acquire and master technical information contained in the various consumer-guide reports on new automobiles. To gather all the available information about new cars would take an inordinate amount of time and money; therefore, the prospective buyer must draw the line at the point where the marginal benefit from acquiring more information is equal to the marginal cost of acquiring more information.

Figure 1 illustrates the optimal-search rule. Suppose a consumer has just moved to a new town and is looking for the best place to buy a particular product. The consumer might visit several stores to collect

FIGURE 1
Optimal-Search Rule

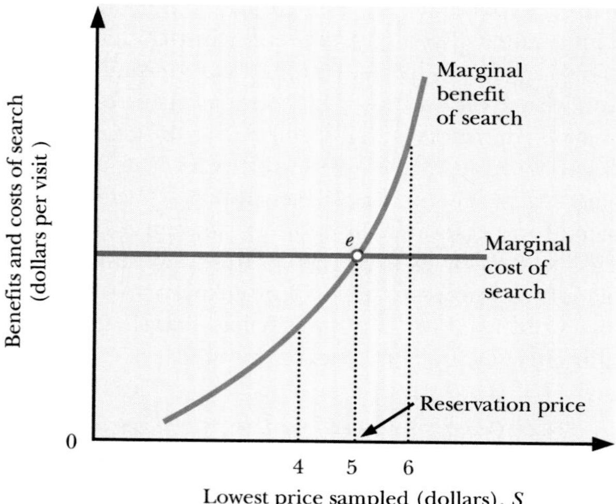

The higher the lowest price sampled, the higher the marginal benefit of search. (The lowest price sampled is the best price quoted to the consumer.) The reservation price is the best price when the marginal benefit of search equals the marginal cost of search, or $5 in the case illustrated. If the lowest price sampled is $6, further search is required.

valid price information. Thus, after some comparison shopping, the consumer will have a sample of the various prices charged. The benefits and costs of search per visit are measured on the vertical axis. The horizontal axis measures the lowest sample price (S) that the consumer has collected through search. If the lowest sample price is very small, the marginal benefit of search for that consumer will be low; if the lowest sample price is very high, the marginal benefit of search will also be high. The upward-sloping curve in Figure 1 shows the marginal benefit of search for different values of the lowest sampled price. The marginal cost of search is assumed to be independent of the lowest price sampled and so will remain unchanged over the range of S values. The price at which the marginal cost of search equals the marginal benefit of search (at point e) is the consumer's **reservation price**—the highest price at which the consumer will actually buy the good.

The **reservation price** is the highest price at which the consumer will buy a good. Although the consumer will buy any good with a price lower than the reservation price, he or she will continue to search for a lower price only if the lowest price found exceeds the reservation price.

The reservation price in Figure 1 is $5. If the lowest price sampled is $6, the consumer should still search because the marginal benefit of search exceeds the marginal cost of search. If the lowest price is below $5—say, $4—the consumer will purchase the good because the marginal cost of search exceeds the marginal benefit of search. If the lowest price sampled is $5, the consumer is indifferent regarding continued search, because $5 is the highest price the consumer will pay for the product.

The reservation price occurs at a sampled price at which the marginal benefit of search equals the marginal cost of search.

The theory that consumers use a search rule where marginal benefits equal marginal costs can be used to predict the extent of price dispersion on different products. Clearly, anything that raises the marginal benefits of search relative to the marginal costs of search will increase the amount of searching. The more resources devoted to searching, the closer the prices of homogeneous products sold at different stores will be (high-priced stores will lose business to low-priced stores). The marginal benefits of search should be greater for more expensive items; therefore, the theory of search suggests that prices of more expensive items will be less widely dispersed than those of less expensive items.

There is considerable evidence to support this proposition. In one such study, the prices of automobiles and washing machines were found to be less widely dispersed for identical makes of automobiles than for identical brands of washing machines.[2]

An interesting paradox is that the greater the number of people who search, the less the individual

[2]George Stigler, *The Theory of Price,* 4th ed. (New York: Macmillan, 1986), 4.

needs to search. If everyone devoted considerable resources to information searching, price dispersion—and the gains to further search—would be reduced because the sellers would be aware of the search behavior.

Search and Unemployment

One of the most important applications of the economics of search is the labor market. Individuals have preferences for particular jobs at particular wages; business firms want to fill particular positions with specific types of individuals. Business firms must search for workers, and workers must search for jobs. People are unemployed because it is difficult to match people to jobs.

If everything else is equal, higher search costs should mean a higher unemployment rate. In a world of zero search costs and perfect information, unemployment would be minimal or nonexistent. For example, if 10 people were shipwrecked on a desert island, everyone would be engaged in some fruitful activity; indeed, it would be easy for people to find their comparative advantages among the limited set of activities, such as fishing, sewing, building, climbing, cutting down trees, and hunting.

INFORMATION PROBLEMS

Economic dealings between individuals are governed by contracts. When a good is purchased, the seller explicitly or implicitly guarantees that the good will work according to an expected performance standard. An insurance contract stipulates that for a certain premium, the insurance company will pay out a certain amount of insurance if one or more specified events (a fire, a theft, or an automobile accident) occur. When information is costly, however, it can become difficult for one party in a contract to monitor the other party's performance, and it can be difficult to check the claims made by economic agents trying to secure favorable contracts.

The Moral-Hazard Problem

It is not possible to buy insurance against poverty. No insurance company will sell you a policy that will pay you in the event of bankruptcy or unemployment. Such insurance does not exist because it could provide an incentive for a person to quit working or seek bankruptcy. Such **moral-hazard problems** are also a reason why every fire insurance policy contains a provision that fires deliberately set by a policy owner (or agent of the owner) are not covered. Indeed, insurance companies spend millions to investigate fires to determine if there was any foul play.

A **moral-hazard problem** exists when one of the parties to a contract has an incentive to alter his or her behavior after the contract is made at the expense of the second party. It arises because it is too costly for the second party to obtain information about the first party's postcontractual behavior.

The basic consequence of the moral-hazard problem is that firms can offer only those contracts that will not be flagrantly abused by their customers. The kinds of contracts offered must be limited to those that will minimize the moral-hazard problem. (See Example 2.)

As an illustration of the moral-hazard problem, suppose the Zantack Sporting Goods Company foolishly issues a guarantee that its ceramic tennis racket will be replaced free of charge if it breaks under normal use within a 2-year period. Such a contract gives opportunistic individuals (who would normally take good care of their sports equipment) an incentive to alter their behavior. Knowing that the racket would be replaced if broken, they would be generally less careful, throw the racket against the fence, or even deliberately break it. These are not normal conditions of use, but the manufacturer cannot afford the information costs of keeping an eye on all users, and it would be very costly to gather information proving that the user had abused the tennis racket.

A moral-hazard problem would also be present if a publishing company were to offer its best-selling author a contract guaranteeing a minimum income of $200,000 per year for 10 years in return for the author's agreement to write one book of the highest possible quality every 2 years. Such a contract gives the author the chance to opportunistically alter behavior. The author would be tempted to take it easy and write shoddy, ill-researched manuscripts with little public appeal. The cost to the publisher of monitoring the author and gathering information to prove that the terms of the contract were not being met would be excessive.

EXAMPLE 2 Moral Hazard and the Baseball World Series

A moral-hazard problem occurs when a contract gives incentives to agents to alter their behavior opportunistically after the contract is made. The moral-hazard problem can be avoided in some cases by writing contracts that remove the incentive to engage in opportunistic behavior. An unusual case is the formula for dividing prize money in the World Series of baseball. The World Series is won by the American or National League team that wins the first four out of seven games of the series. Players in the World Series receive a share of the attendance revenues. The winning team's share is larger than the losing team's, and players have a strong financial incentive to win. Their implicit contract calls for them to play their best and to make each World Series game as enjoyable as possible for the paying spectators.

It might be expected that World Series prize earnings would depend upon total gate revenues from all games played. In reality, they depend only upon gate revenues from the first four games. Why? If the prize money depended upon total gate revenues from all games played, players might have an incentive to alter their playing behavior to make sure that one team did not win in four straight games. The management of professional baseball fears that players might alter their behavior opportunistically to increase their incomes and has come up with this prize formula to prevent such opportunistic behavior. Even in a profession in which the participants play for pride and ego as well as money, contracts must be written to solve the moral-hazard problem.

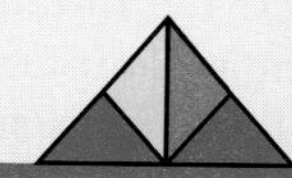

A third example of moral hazard would be an automobile insurance policy that pays all damages if the policyholder is involved in a collision. Although it is unlikely that insured drivers would deliberately have collisions, such an insurance policy might give the driver an incentive to alter driving behavior. The driver might be less cautious in parking lots where most fender-bender accidents occur and might generally drive less defensively than normal. The insurance company cannot write into the contract that the driver must drive defensively because it is not possible to monitor the behavior of individual drivers.

The contracting parties who stand to suffer will adopt measures to minimize or prevent postcontractual opportunistic behavior. Most life insurance policies contain a clause that nullifies the contract in the case of suicide. The tennis racket manufacturer's guarantee may put the burden of proof on the buyer to demonstrate that the racket broke under normal usage, or the manufacturer may insist on a stiff processing charge for returned rackets. The author's publishing contract will call for a percentage of book sales rather than a guaranteed income. The automobile insurer will require that drivers who have had accidents share the costs of losses by paying the first $250 or $500 to repair the damage. If the claim is extremely large, the insurance company may even expend resources to investigate whether careless driving was involved.

In some instances, the moral-hazard problem is so severe that certain contracts cannot be written at all, at least not by private profit-maximizing companies. The poverty insurance mentioned earlier is such an example. In other cases, the moral-hazard problem is threatening enough that contracts must be limited. For example, private insurance companies find it difficult to issue general disability insurance because of opportunistic behavior. Although it is easy to establish disability in the case of lost arms or legs, it is difficult in the case of general back problems or emotional disturbances. Insurance companies expend enormous sums on information costs (maintaining a staff of physicians and investigators) to detect the opportunistic behavior that threatens their profitability.

When private markets cannot provide goods and services because of moral-hazard problems, these

EXAMPLE 3 Moral Hazard and the Savings and Loan Crisis

Deposits in savings and loan institutions (S&Ls) are insured by the Federal Savings and Loan Insurance Corporation (FSLIC). If an S&L fails, the FSLIC (a federally run insurance company) must make good on the deposits from its insurance funds.

In the late 1970s and early 1980s unexpected inflation pushed the interest rates that S&Ls had to pay their depositors. At the same time S&Ls were tied up in long-term, low-interest loans. When interest rates fell in the mid- and late 1980s, only part of the S&L industry recovered.

According to many economists, the moral-hazard problem led to the S&L crisis. The S&Ls that experienced severe losses in the early 1980s were tempted to recoup their losses (and escape the crisis) by making risky, high-interest loans. They knew that if the loans were not repaid, depositors would be reimbursed by FSLIC insurance funds.

The contractual relationship between the S&Ls and the FSLIC encouraged failing S&Ls to engage in opportunistic behavior. The S&Ls made the risky loans knowing that the FSLIC would bail them out. According to the implicit contract between the FSLIC and the S&Ls, the S&L is obliged to act prudently in giving out loans. However, there is nothing in that contract to prevent a failing S&L from changing its postcontractual behavior—that is, acting imprudently in hopes of rescuing itself.

The S&L crisis has left the FSLIC insurance fund bankrupt. It has also threatened to shake up the entire banking industry. This crisis shows the destructive power of the moral-hazard problem.

Source: Edward Kane, "The High Cost of Incompletely Funding the FSLIC Shortage of Explicit Capital," *Journal of Economic Perspectives* 3 (Fall 1989): 31–47.

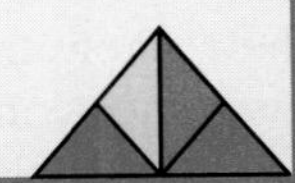

goods and services are sometimes provided by the state. (See Example 3.)

The Adverse-Selection Problem

The moral-hazard problem occurs when one party to a contract engages in opportunistic behavior after the contract is made. The **adverse-selection problem** arises prior to the making of the contract.

> The **adverse-selection problem** occurs when a buyer or seller enters a disadvantageous contract on the basis of incomplete or inaccurate information because the cost of obtaining the relevant information makes it difficult to determine whether the deal is a good one or a bad one.

When a contracting party does not know the real intentions of the other party, the party with the superior information may be able to lure the other party into accepting an unfavorable contract. A contract is unfavorable if one of the contracting parties would not have entered into it if he or she had the same information as the other party.

The adverse-selection problem is faced by those who set automobile insurance rates. Good drivers are less likely than bad drivers to have accidents that lead to costly claims against the insurance company. In an efficient insurance system, good drivers should not have to subsidize bad drivers, so insurance companies should be able to differentiate between good drivers and bad drivers. Smith and Jones are exactly alike except that Smith is a good driver who has never had an accident and Jones is a terrible driver who has been lucky never to have had an accident. Smith knows she is a good driver; Jones knows she is an accident waiting to happen. What about the insurance company? Unless insurance agents were to follow Smith and Jones around town and interview friends and neighbors, the insurance company cannot differentiate between Smith and Jones. Unable to gather such costly information, the insurance company sells automobile insurance to Smith and Jones at the same rate. Jones, who knows she is a terrible driver, will jump at the chance to buy insurance at the same rate as Smith. If the insurance company knew more about Smith and Jones, Jones would have to pay higher insurance rates to compensate for the higher probability of an accident.

In another example, business firms wish to hire high-quality workers, but it is very costly to find out in advance the true characteristics of workers. O'Neill and O'Leary are alike except that O'Neill is diligent and hardworking while O'Leary is lazy and without ambition. There is no reason for O'Leary to inform a potential employer of his laziness, and O'Neill's claims of diligence are likely to be dismissed as boasting. Because O'Leary and O'Neill appear alike to the firm, they are hired at the same wage rate. O'Leary, aware of his bad work skills, jumps at the chance. Armed with better information, the firm would not have entered into this contract.

Health insurance companies must also face the adverse-selection problem. If insurance companies had perfect information on the health of insurance applicants, they would offer health insurance to healthy 70-year-old people at rates that would reflect their likely health claims. However, it is costly for insurance companies to gather extensive health data on individuals, so the insurance company will have to rely on available statistical data on general trends for different age groups. The healthy 70-year-old knows his or her health history and is aware that likely claims would be low for a person of that age with good health, but the insurance company does not have the same information. The healthy 70-year-old must therefore enter into a health insurance contract paying the same premiums as unhealthy 70-year-olds. If both parties had the same information, a more favorable contract would have been written for the healthy 70-year-old.

Markets have developed responses to a variety of information problems. (See Example 4.) Every effort is made by buyers and sellers to devise contracts that will somehow reveal the true character of the parties involved. For example, to deal with adverse selection and moral hazard, insurance companies put in clauses so that they can either cancel a person's insurance or raise the rates as experience dictates. Adverse selection can be countered by changing the relative sizes of the basic insurance rate and the penalties, so that drivers will self-select themselves into good-risk or bad-risk categories. A low insurance rate with a high penalty for an accident will attract good drivers. A high insurance rate with a low penalty will attract bad drivers. The same principle applies to different categories of coverage. If you have *liability insurance,* the insurance company pays for the damage you cause to the other party. If you have *collision insurance,* the insurance company pays for part of the damage to your own car. Good drivers might opt for collision insurance instead of liability insurance.

THE ROLE OF INTERMEDIARIES

Intermediaries, or "middlemen," specialize in information concerning:

1. Exchange opportunities between buyers and sellers
2. The variety and qualities of different products
3. The channels of marketing distribution for produced goods

> **Intermediaries** buy in order to sell again or simply bring together a buyer and a seller.

Real estate brokers, grocery stores, department stores, used-car dealers, auctioneers, stockbrokers, insurance agents, and travel agents are all intermediaries. All these professions "mediate" or stand between ultimate buyers and sellers in return for a profit.

Suppose an individual is willing to sell a private airplane for no less than $20 million, and a potential buyer residing in some distant country is willing to pay $25 million for such an airplane. How will they locate one another? Someone with information about the existence of the potential buyer and seller could act as an intermediary and bring the two together. It would be possible for the seller to get $20 million, for the buyer to pay $25 million, and for the intermediary to charge as much as $5 million for the service of bringing the two together.

Transactions of this sort occur frequently, although most transactions are less spectacular. The buyers and sellers of residential homes are brought together by realtors who charge a fee for this service. Stockbrokers bring together buyers and sellers of a particular stock. Auction houses bring together

EXAMPLE 4 The Health Care Crisis

America's health care system is the most expensive in the world—12 percent of every dollar is spent on health care. Costs are rising at a rate of nearly 20 percent per year. Prices and costs are out of control. The problem has been traced to a simple culprit: information.

When a person buys a television set, he or she decides whether to purchase a 27-inch or 19-inch set. When a person buys medical services, the doctor often suggests certain tests, surgery, or treatments. Patients often buy medical services under a veil of ignorance. If an insurance company is paying the bill, the patient does not have much incentive to keep costs down, and the insurance company cannot negotiate with the doctor because patients have freedom of choice. Insurers try to hold down costs by making it difficult for high-risk individuals to get insurance. As a consequence, some of the neediest people in America have no medical insurance to pay for the escalating costs of health care.

The moral-hazard problem leads patients and doctors to utilize too many medical services. Adverse selection causes insurance companies to limit the insurance that low-risk people can get because high-risk people drive up their costs. Individuals have great difficulty comparing and evaluating policies because the policies are complicated and tailored to attract low-risk individuals. It is difficult to comparison shop for insurance policies.

The solution to the problem is not simple. Two economists, Alan Enthoven of Stanford University and Peter Diamond of MIT, have suggested a managed care system that they think will solve the major problems. They suggest grouping people by geography, regardless of their health needs. A sponsor, either a public agency or large employer, would then organize insurance for the group. The sponsor would determine which doctors and hospitals could be used. This would provide the sponsor with the power to negotiate treatments and fees. The sponsor could offer a limited set of insurance packages that would be easy for the individual member to understand when comparing costs and benefits. The managed care system would leave room for independent doctors and insurance companies, for those people willing to pay the price.

Who decides how these groups are formed? And if the proposed program is so good, why haven't private insurance companies offered such a program? At present, some people can select Health Maintenance Organizations (HMOs) that are similar to the managed care system, but many people do not join them because of the absence of choice. People feel that freedom of choice (of doctors and hospitals) could increase the chances of finding the right diagnosis in difficult cases.

Source: "The Wrong Medicine," *New York Times*, May 26, 1991; "The Right Medicine," *New York Times*, May 27, 1991.

sellers of rare works of art and potential buyers, and they charge a fee for this service. Are such middlemen cheating innocent buyers and sellers, or are they providing a service that is worth the price?

The role of intermediaries in providing information to buyers and sellers is often misunderstood. The export/import agent who brings the airplane buyer and seller together and pockets $5 million may be regarded as criminal by people who think that this "go-between" is trading on the ignorance of others. When food prices rise, many consumers blame the intermediaries. Buyers and sellers of real estate often become upset with the high fees charged by realtors. Implicit in these complaints is the belief that the intermediaries are getting a reward for doing nothing or for doing very little.

The intermediary's share of the price varies substantially from good to good. In real estate, the broker typically receives a 5 to 10 percent fee for bringing together the buyer and seller. This fee depends upon competitive conditions in the market. In stock market transactions the fee varies from about 0.5 percent to about 2 percent of the price of the stock. Supermarkets charge an intermediary fee of perhaps 10 percent to 50 percent of the wholesale price at which they buy.

The fee that intermediaries charge for their services, like other prices, depends on the amount of competition, on the degree of freedom of entry into the business, and on the opportunity costs of bringing goods to the market. If the business is competitive, the fee will reflect a normal profit in the long run. For example, retail grocery stores are in a very competitive business; the typical supermarket earns an accounting profit of about 1 percent on its sales. The markups found in the supermarket are almost entirely used for paying rent, stock clerks, checkout clerks, produce specialists, and butchers. The grocery store, for example, must hire employees to prepare produce and meat for display in quantities convenient for inspection and purchase; the store must maintain inventories of products on which it must pay carrying charges. The grocery store must select a location convenient to its customers and pay substantial rents for a good location. In return for the intermediary fee, consumers receive a convenient location, the convenience of inspecting goods before purchase, and the convenience of finding the quantity and quality of goods they want without packing, sorting, and searching for themselves.

Buyers and sellers could, in most situations, avoid paying the intermediary fee. Consumers could drive to farmers' markets and to wholesale distributors of meats and dairy products. They could even drive to canning factories. The intermediary, by specializing in bringing together buyers and sellers, is able to provide the service at a lower cost than if the individuals involved performed the service themselves.

Another function of intermediaries is to certify the quality of goods. The consumer is confronted with a vast array of goods, some of which are so complicated that the buyer is at an enormous information disadvantage relative to the producer. In short, the consumer faces the adverse-selection problem. The number of producers is larger than the number of actual stores with which the consumer deals. In such circumstances, the intermediary performs the function of certifying the quality of the good for the buyer. The customer is prepared to pay a price for this valuable service; thus, the intermediary is able to charge a higher markup over costs.

Car dealerships are certifiers of quality. These intermediaries are better informed about the quality of cars (because they can hire skilled mechanics) than the typical car buyer, and they will take advantage of profit opportunities by buying used cars (perhaps from their new-car customers) and reselling them on their used-car lots. They may even provide a guarantee (usually with a time limit) that the used car is not a "lemon." Customers will be willing to pay a fee (in the form of a price markup) for this certifier-of-quality service. (See Example 5.)

The same principle applies to the products sold by major grocery chains or major department stores. Customers know that the retailer serves as a certifier of quality and, if the product happens to be defective, that their money will be returned. Manufacturers also certify quality by identifying their products with brand names. If prior to purchase and use consumers could not distinguish the product of one manufacturer from that of all other manufacturers, there would be little incentive for the manufacturer to produce products of reasonable or uniform quality. Brand names such as Sara Lee, Levi's, Maytag, and Xerox serve as certifiers of product quality.

PRODUCT INFORMATION

Advertising

Advertising provides information to potential buyers; therefore, it might be expected to reduce market imperfections by reducing price dispersion. However, when advertising helps to differentiate products, it can erect a barrier to entry that reinforces monopoly power.

There are essentially two views of advertising. According to the procompetitive view, advertising provides information about prices and product qualities to buyers, thereby increasing competition by making consumers aware of substitutes. Supporters of the anticompetitive view of advertising, however, believe that advertising reduces competition by giving large, established firms a competitive advantage over smaller, less established firms. Advertising creates barriers to entry that limit competition and allow established firms to earn long-run profits.

Whether advertising increases or reduces competition in an industry is largely an empirical issue. If advertising's effect is anticompetitive, advertising would be likely to raise profit rates and industry concentration. If advertising is procompetitive,

EXAMPLE 5 The Lemons Principle: Adverse Selection

The certification of quality helps prevent market breakdown resulting from adverse selection. In the case of used cars, the seller knows the value of the product, but the buyer must guess the quality. Most buyers would probably assume that the car is of average quality. If every used-car dealer operated on a disreputable basis, the only used cars that would sell would be the lemons—those of lowest quality. If there were used cars in the market ranging from $1000 to $6000 in true value (a range known, say, to all potential buyers), but potential buyers could not tell the difference among them, would any rational consumer buy a used car priced at $5000? At a price of $5000, cars worth more than $5000 would not be offered for sale; only those worth $5000 or less would be put on the market—so that the average car offered for sale would be worth $3000. Why pay $5000 for a car that is more than likely worth much less than $5000? At a price of $3000, only cars worth $3000 or less would be placed on the market (so the average car offered would be worth only $2000). Why pay $3000 for a car that is likely worth much less than $3000? Indeed, any price above $1000 would bring forth cars worth less than the price. What type of cars would, therefore, be sold in this fly-by-night market? Only those lemons that are worth exactly $1000 because buyers paying more could only expect to be ripped off. In these circumstances, only when established dealers serve as certifiers of quality will nonlemons be placed on the market.

Source: Based upon George Akerlof, "The Market for 'Lemons': Quality, Uncertainty, and the Market Mechanism," *Quarterly Journal of Economics* 84 (August 1970): 488–500.

advertising would be likely to reduce industry concentration and even out profit rates among firms.

Different researchers have reached contradictory conclusions regarding the influence of advertising. Moreover, advertising's impact is not uniform across industries; it appears to depend upon the particular industry.[3]

1. Advertising has different effects on different products. Studies show that advertising has a greater positive effect on the profitability of nondurable goods than on durable goods. Durable goods (TV sets, washing machines, automobiles) are usually more expensive products for which the marginal benefits to search are high. Nondurable goods (groceries, kitchen products, deodorant sprays, mouthwashes) are usually less expensive items for which the marginal benefits of search are small. Advertising appears to have a larger positive effect on profitability in the area of convenience goods, such as paper towels and aspirin.

2. Advertising has a procompetitive effect on retail trade. This suggests that retail advertising conveys information on prices and product qualities to consumers and reduces the cost of search. Empirical studies show that the higher is the advertising intensity the lower are the profit margins of retail and service industries. The opposite result is obtained for industries that manufacture consumer goods, where advertising creates barriers to entry and increases product differentiation.

3. There are significant economies of scale of advertising present in specific industries. In the cigarette industry, for example, the advertising of large firms has a substantially greater sales impact than that of small firms. In this industry the ratio of advertising expenditures to sales declines steeply up to sales of 20 to 30 billion cigarettes, a level of sales that may take years to attain.[4]

[3]The literature on advertising has been developed by numerous economists including Lester Telser, Nicholas Kaldor, Richard Schmalensee, Phillip Nelson, William Comanor, Thomas Wilson, Michael Porter, Randall Brown, and many others. The available evidence is summarized in William Comanor and Thomas Wilson, "The Effect of Advertising on Competition," *Journal of Economic Literature* 17 (June 1979): 453–76.

[4]Randall Brown, "Estimating Advantages to Large-Scale Advertising," *Review of Economics and Statistics* 60 (August 1978): 428–37.

EXAMPLE 6 The Effect of Advertising on Prices

Economist Lee Benham studied the effect of advertising on the prices of eyeglasses in a research report published in 1972. The advertising of eyeglasses is prohibited in some states and is allowed in others. Benham compared the prices of eyeglasses in states that allowed advertising with those where advertising is not allowed.

Benham found that the average price of eyeglasses in states that barred advertising was more than double the average price in states where advertising was allowed. This study shows how advertising can promote competition. Advertising, by providing information on prices and product quality, renders the demands for the products of individual suppliers more elastic and, thus, lowers the prices paid by consumers.

Consumers have comparatively little information about drug prices. Advertising is either prohibited or limited in most states. Some time ago, the Consumers' Union sent shoppers to 60 drugstores and found that the retail prices of tetracycline (a broad-based antibiotic) varied from $0.79 to $7.45. With greater information available about the qualities of generic drugs and more retail advertising, drug prices would probably fall and price dispersion would probably be lessened. Some doctors have concluded that generic and brand name drugs are not significantly different in quality. These examples show how advertising may encourage competition.

Sources: Lee Benham, "The Effect of Advertising on the Price of Eyeglasses." *The Journal of Law and Economics* 15 (October 1972): 337–52; *The Medicine Show*, 5th ed. (Mount Vernon, N.Y.: Consumers' Union, 1983), chap. 25.

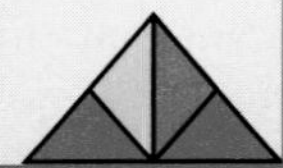

Advertising can lead to lower prices paid by consumers when its function is to provide information on prices and quality. In this regard, consumers benefit from the advertising of retailers because advertising lowers search costs. But if advertising reduces competition, are consumers made worse off by advertising? (See Example 6.)

The higher price the consumer pays for advertised convenience products, such as over-the-counter drugs, children's clothes, or bleaches, may be a price willingly paid for the assurance of product quality. If, however, information were free and the consumer were perfectly informed about prices and product qualities, it is unlikely such price differentials would persist.

Product Quality, Durability, and Safety

Because information is costly to acquire, consumers may be uncertain about a product's quality, durability, and safety. Advertising makes more information available to the consumers. They avoid adverse-selection problems by relying on brand names to certify the quality of the product.

Some firms guarantee that the product will meet the customer's expectations and promise to refund the customer's money or allow the customer to exchange a defective product for another one when the product fails to meet the quality, safety, or durability standards the customer expects. For example, every product sold by Quaker Oats carries a guarantee: Buyers can get their money back by sending in the label with a brief explanation of what was wrong. Firms presumably do not want to be deluged with demands to reimburse buyers for defective products, so they seek to produce a product that meets consumer expectations.

But what about cases where severe damages are inflicted upon unsuspecting buyers, even by brand name products? Teenagers have been killed in automobiles with poorly designed gas tanks (that ignite on impact). Babies have been born deformed when their mothers took a particular drug during pregnancy; fingers have been severed by poorly designed lawnmowers. Who should be liable for the damages caused by products? Two legal doctrines help answer this question: *caveat emptor* (let the buyer beware) and *caveat venditor* (let the seller beware).

Caveat Emptor. There is a big difference between professional buyers employed by large enterprises and the ordinary consumer. The large enterprise employs a purchasing agent who is a specialist in the goods purchased by the firm. Such agents know as much as (or more than) the seller about the products they buy. Centuries ago, the average customer may have been in roughly the same position as this specialized purchasing agent. Goods were simple, and the buyer could assess their quality rather easily. The buyer was not at an information disadvantage relative to the seller. Thus, there was no adverse-selection problem.

Under these circumstances—where the buyer and seller possess the same information—the legal doctrine of *caveat emptor* (let the buyer beware) would be efficient and would work well. However, circumstances are different today. Products are exceedingly complex. When consumers select automobiles, television sets, home furnaces, or electrical wiring, they are at an enormous information disadvantage relative to the seller. For this reason, the legal doctrine of *caveat emptor* has been modified to protect the buyer from fraud, warranty violations, and negligence.

Fraud is an act of deceit or misrepresentation. It occurs when the purchased product is never delivered or when a promised service is not supplied as contracted. A *warranty* is a guarantee of the integrity of a product and of the seller's responsibility for the repair or replacement of defective parts. Warranties may be expressed or implied. A good is supposed to do what it is designed to do (a washing machine is expected to wash clothes, a reclining chair is expected to recline). Whether the warranty is written or not, if the good does not perform its function, the seller has legally violated the warranty. *Negligence* occurs when the seller does not reveal to the buyer a hidden defect that later causes injury.[5]

The rule of *caveat emptor,* even in our modern world of complex products, does have some advantages. First, it provides the customer with an incentive to gain information about product quality, durability, and safety. If the user of the good is not liable for damages incurred while using the product, the consumer may not be as careful in choosing products.

Second, if the seller were liable for all damages caused by the use of a product, even by careless users, the cost of the product to the consumer could become excessive. If, for example, manufacturers of sulfuric acid were liable for all personal injuries associated with the use of the product, there would be little sulfuric acid supplied, and it would sell at a very high price. A moral-hazard problem could arise if sellers were liable for all loss or damage associated with the use of their products because this liability would encourage consumers to be less careful in the use of the products. It is more efficient to require the manufacturer to simply label the product as dangerous. If the user fails to heed this warning, the manufacturer is not liable for damages.

Third, because products are put to different uses by different consumers, it would be prohibitively expensive to design a product that would be safe in all uses. An automobile can be used either for transportation in a quiet suburb or for high-speed stock-car racing. The car manufacturer who is held liable for brake failure when the car is racing at 130 miles per hour would be forced to produce a car that would cost the average buyer much more and would have technical characteristics of little use to the majority of users. As Roland McKean observes:

> The buyer is in a better position than anyone else to know the exact use to which he plans to put a product and what alternative qualities, or degrees of safety, in the product would mean to his costs and gains. The customer, if he is liable, has an extra incentive to acquire and make appropriate use of the information.[6]

Caveat Venditor. The doctrine of *caveat emptor* does not work well when the cost of acquiring information is very high to the consumer. Manufacturers know more than anyone else about their products. When it is very costly for consumers to acquire information, producer responsibility (*caveat venditor*) may be a more efficient system of assigning liability.

[5] For this reason, in court cases involving personal injury resulting from manufacturing defects—such as a case against Ford Motors involving a fireprone gas tank—it is very important for the claimant to establish that the company was aware of the defect.

[6] Roland McKean, "Product Liability: Implications of Some Changing Property Rights," *Quarterly Journal of Economics* 84 (November 1970): 611–26.

Information costs can be kept down for consumers by organizations such as the Consumers' Union, which tests products and sells the results in a monthly magazine. Government can also reduce information costs by establishing minimum standards and carrying out inspections to ensure that these standards are being observed. Municipal governments usually have health inspectors to inspect public dining places and public swimming pools. There are universal standards of weights and measures and inspections to ensure that the butcher's scale is accurate. Without these governmental regulations and inspections, the costs of personal inspection and information gathering would be excessive.

SPECULATION

Although product information is important to consumers, information about changes in the market conditions for any number of goods and services is important to **speculators.** The person who stocks up on peanut butter after hearing of a shortage of peanuts, the frozen-orange-juice distributor who buys oranges in response to a late frost in Florida, and the young couple that buys a house now because they fear home prices will rise beyond reach if they wait another year are all speculators. The professional speculator, however, is more maligned than any other economic agent.

> **Speculators** are those who buy or sell in the hope of profiting from market fluctuations.

Most people do not associate the term *speculator* with the family that stocks up on goods whose prices are expected to shoot up or the family that purchases a home as an inflation hedge. Most people associate the term *speculator* with the person who buys up agricultural land and holds it for future shopping-center development or the person who buys and sells foreign currencies or gold in the hopes of buying low and selling high. Such speculators buy or sell commodities in huge quantities hoping to profit from a frost, war scare, bumper crop, bad news, or good news.

The Role of the Speculator in the Economy

Speculators do, indeed, often profit from the misfortunes of others. They buy from the hard-pressed farmer when prices are low, and they sell later at much higher prices. Has the farm family been robbed by the speculator? Upon hearing of a frost in Florida, speculators buy oranges in large quantities, thereby driving up the prices of orange juice for the consumer. Speculators, at the first sign of international trouble, may buy gold and sell American dollars, thereby weakening the American dollar. The popular view of speculators is that they do only harm; however, speculators often perform a useful economic function—that is, engaging in **arbitrage** *through time.*

> **Arbitrage** is buying in a market where a commodity is cheap and reselling in a market where the commodity is more expensive.

The arbitrageur buys wheat in Chicago at $5 per bushel and resells it for $5.10 the next minute in Kansas City. Arbitrageurs, therefore, serve to keep the prices of wheat in Chicago and Kansas City approximately equal.

Simple arbitrage of this type is not very risky because information about prices in Chicago and Kansas City can be obtained instantly from commodity brokers. Arbitrageurs must act quickly and have sharp pencils and keen minds if they are to prosper. Unlike the arbitrageur, who buys in one location and sells in another, the speculator buys goods *at one time* and resells *at another time.* Speculation is a risky business because tomorrow's prices cannot be known with certainty.

> Arbitrage serves to equalize prices in different markets because, when price differences arise, arbitrageurs buy in the cheap market and resell in the expensive market.

Profitable Speculation

The objective of the speculator is to make a profit by buying low and selling high. When the speculator

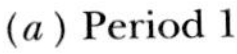

FIGURE 2
Profitable Speculation

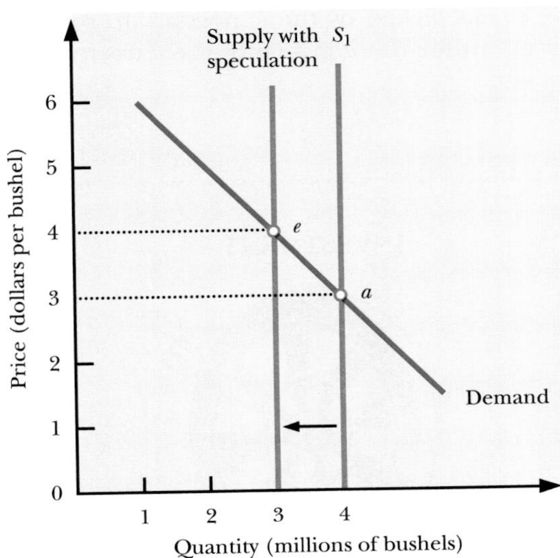

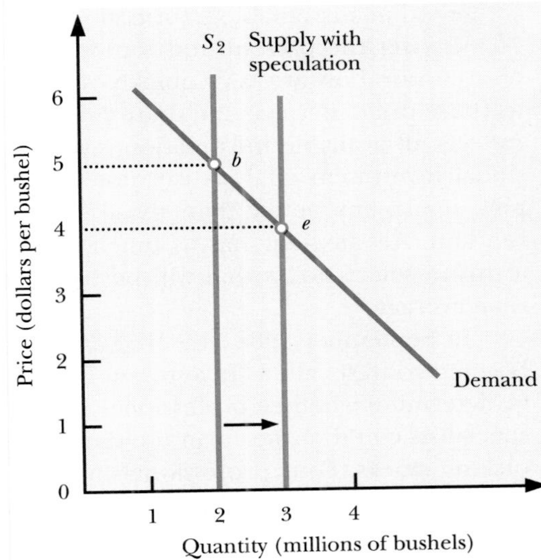

Period 1's wheat harvest is 4 million bushels, while period 2's wheat harvest is only 2 million bushels. If there were no speculation, the price would be \$3 in period 1 and \$5 in period 2. Perfect speculation will cause 1 million bushels of wheat to be purchased and stored by speculators in period 1, to be sold in period 2. As a result, the price is driven up to \$4 in period 1 and driven down to \$4 in period 2. Both price and consumption are stabilized by the speculation in this case.

is making a profit—and when there are enough speculators—low prices will be driven up and high prices will be driven down. When speculators buy at low prices, they add to the demand and drive prices up. When speculators sell when prices are high, they drive prices down by adding to the supply.

> Profitable speculation (that is, speculation that succeeds in buying low and selling high) stabilizes prices and consumption over time by reducing fluctuation in prices and consumption over time.

Profitable speculation is illustrated in Figure 2. Panel *a* shows that the supply of wheat in the first period (say, 1993) is S_1, or 4 million bushels. Panel *b* shows that the supply of wheat in the second period (say, 1994) is S_2, or 2 million bushels. If there were no speculation, the price of wheat would be \$3 in period 1 and \$5 in period 2 (we assume that demand does not change between the two periods). Thus, without speculation, prices and consumption would vary dramatically between the two periods.

If speculators correctly anticipate that next year's wheat crop will be small, they could make handsome profits by buying at \$3 and selling next year at \$5. But what happens as speculators begin to buy this year's wheat? When speculators buy wheat, they withdraw it from the market and place it in storage. As a result, the supply of wheat offered on the market is reduced. This will continue until the profits of the marginal speculator are driven down to zero. When speculators buy 1 million bushels in the first period, the effective supply shifts (left) to 3 million bushels, and the price rises to \$4. When speculators resell this wheat in the second period, the effective supply also shifts (right) to 3 million bushels in year 2. When speculative profits are zero, the price will remain stable at \$4 and the quantity of wheat sold on

EXAMPLE 7 The Pros and the Dartboard after Two Years

The "efficient market theory" maintains that all available information concerning the present and future prospects of a corporation are very quickly reflected in its share price. Because the share price already reflects all available information, even professional investment analysts will not be able to pick stocks any better than those selected at random. An amateur has as much chance as a pro to select stocks that will perform better than average.

In September 1988, the *Wall Street Journal* began a contest called "Investment Dartboard" to determine whether professional investment specialists could outperform the dart board in picking stocks. Four professionals are allowed to pick four stocks, and four stocks are picked at random by throwing darts at a printed list of stocks. The picks of the four pros and the darts are then tracked over a six-month period.

Since the game began, the pros have a 10 to 8 lead over the darts under the current rules. Only three pros have finished "in the money" five or more times since the contest began. One contestant finished first five times but last four times. During the recession of 1990–91, the pros significantly outperformed the darts. The stocks picked by the expert group rose 3 percent, while those picked by the darts fell 23 percent.

Source: "Pro Stock-Pickers Outperform the Darts," *Wall Street Journal*, December 6, 1991.

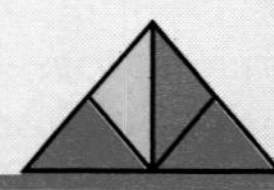

the market will remain stable at 3 million bushels—despite substantial differences in the wheat harvest in the two periods. In this example, we assume that storage costs are zero. Had storage costs been positive, the price of wheat in the second period would have been higher by the cost of storage.

> Profitable speculation shifts supplies from periods when supplies are relatively abundant and prices potentially low to periods when supplies are relatively scarce and prices potentially high. In this sense, profitable speculation provides the valuable economic service of stabilizing prices and consumption over time.

The $4 price of wheat reflects all the available information about the future. In this sense, the market is efficient. (See Example 7.) No one can then make a profit buying wheat and reselling it because the price is the same in both periods. Profits can only be made when information available to some people is not reflected in the current market price. Those individuals can make a profit by exploiting their information advantage.

In the preceding example, speculators accurately predicted the future. Such predictions are not as difficult as one might expect. For example, spring wheat is harvested in September and winter wheat is harvested in June or July. The amount of wheat harvested in other months is negligible. This seasonal pattern of wheat supply is predictable. What if no one

FIGURE 3
Unprofitable Speculation

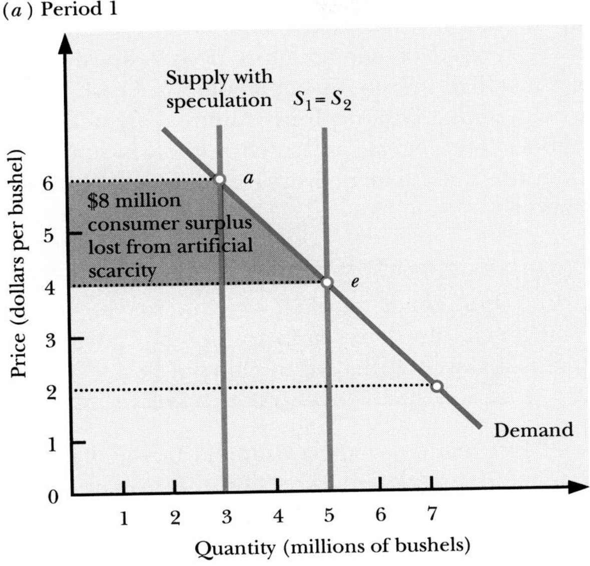

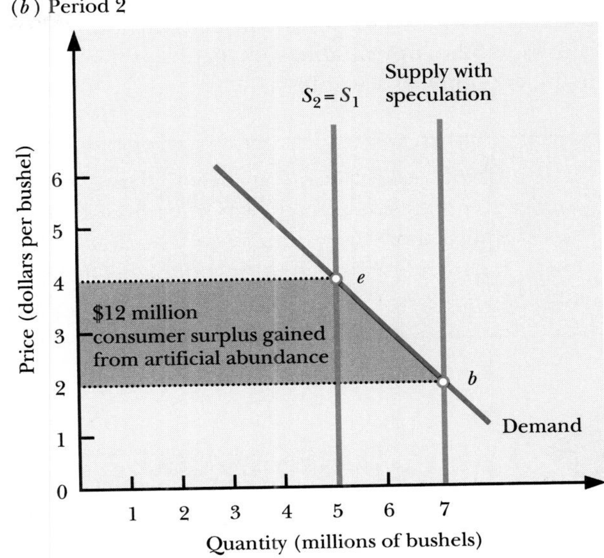

In this example, period 1 and period 2 have the same demand and supply conditions. Without speculation, the price would be $4 in both periods. Speculators guess incorrectly that the supply of corn in period 2 will be less than in period 1. They buy 2 million bushels in period 1 and drive period 1's price up to $6. When they must resell the 2 million bushels in period 2, they drive the price down to $2. In the case of unprofitable speculation, price and consumption are seriously destabilized.

were to speculate in this situation? In harvest months, farmers would harvest and sell their wheat, and wheat prices would be driven down to very low levels. In the months when very little wheat is harvested, wheat prices would be astronomical. Such a situation would not be satisfactory. Because the pattern of wheat harvesting is well known, speculators (who also include the farmers who put their grain into storage rather than sell it immediately) purchase grain at harvest time, put it into storage, and then sell it throughout the rest of the year. This activity assures that society will not lack for wheat during the remainder of the year and that consumers will not have to pay wildly fluctuating prices. Of course, speculators will make some errors in the process; for instance, they may incorrectly predict the size of the upcoming harvest. However, these mistakes are minor compared to the situation that would exist if there were no speculators.

Unprofitable Speculation

Speculation is risky. Speculators cannot always guess correctly. They may buy when they think prices are low only to find that prices sink even lower. They may sell when they think prices are at their peak only to watch the prices rise even further. In such cases, speculation destabilizes prices and consumption over time. When prices would otherwise be high, such speculators are buying and driving prices even higher; when prices would otherwise be low, such speculators are selling and driving prices even lower.

Unprofitable speculation is shown in Figure 3. The supply of corn is 5 million bushels in period 1 and will also be 5 million bushels in period 2. Because demand remains the same in the two periods, the equilibrium price of corn will be $4 in both periods without speculation. Now assume speculators incorrectly guess that the supply of corn will fall in period 2 because of an anticipated poor harvest. Speculators buy 2 million bushels, which they place in storage for later sale, driving up the price to $6 in period 1 (point *a*). The speculators then wait in vain for a decline in supply that never materializes. They must then sell the 2 million bushels in period 2, and they drive the price down to $2 a bushel (point *b*).

Without speculation, the price and consumption of corn would have been the same in both periods (point *e*). With unprofitable speculation, consumption is 3 million bushels in period 1 and 7 million bushels in period 2. Period 1's price is $6 and period 2's price is $2. Unprofitable speculation is inefficient for the economy as a whole.[7]

> Unprofitable speculation is destabilizing because it creates artificial scarcities in some periods and artificial abundance in other periods. In this sense, speculation can be costly to society.

THE FUTURES MARKET

Speculation is so highly specialized that markets have developed that separate the business of storing the commodity being bought and sold from the actual business of speculation. The grain speculator does not have to worry about what the purchased grain looks like, where it is stored, and how much to take out of storage. Those who wish only to speculate can buy and sell in a **futures market.**

> A **futures market** is an organized market in which a buyer and seller agree now on the price of a commodity to be delivered at some specified date in the future.

Many are familiar with futures markets only through sensational press reports, like those about the oil-rich Hunt family seeking unsuccessfully to corner the silver market, about European and Asian speculators driving the price of gold to dizzying heights, or about the increase in coffee prices following a freeze in Brazil that is blamed on speculators.

The type of market most people know best is one in which there is an actual outlay of cash (or the arrangement of credit) for the immediate delivery of a good. The market in which a good is purchased today for immediate delivery is called a **spot** (or **cash**) **market.**

> In a **spot (cash) market,** agreements between buyers and sellers are made now for payment and delivery of the product now.

Most of the goods consumers buy and sell are transacted in spot markets. In the grocery store, consumers pay now for goods that are delivered now. Stocks, foreign exchange, gold, and commodities such as wheat, pork bellies, lumber, and copper are traded in organized spot markets. Unlike the grocery store, however, such commodities are also traded on futures markets.

Futures contracts are bought and sold in futures markets. In a futures contract, the terms (the price and the quantity) of a future transaction are set today. The buyer of a futures contract enters a contract today to purchase a specified quantity of a good at a specified price at some specified date in the future. Both delivery and payment are to be made *in the future.* The seller is obliged to deliver the specified quantity of the good at the specified price at the specified future date. The seller of a futures contract need not even own the commodity at the time of the sale (but will, in many instances).

> The *seller* of a futures contract is in a *short position* because something is being sold that is not owned. The *buyer* of a futures contract is in a *long position* because a claim on a good is being acquired.

When the seller agrees to sell and the buyer agrees to buy at a specified price at a specified date in the future, what guarantees that both parties live up to their ends of the bargain? The buyer and seller must

[7]When considered together, both speculators and nonspeculators (the consumers of corn) are worse off because the economy is worse off. But considered alone, consumers are better off. The consumers of corn do indeed lose consumer surplus of $8 million in period 1 when the price rises from $4 to $6, but they gain it all back and more when consumer surplus rises $12 million above what it would have been had the price remained at $4. The gain to consumers is $4 million worth of consumer surplus. But speculators lose $8 million (the 2 million bushels bought at $6 and sold at $2). Since this loss exceeds the gain of consumers, the economy is worse off.

each put up cash—called a *margin requirement*—equal to a small percentage of the value of the contract.[8]

The Mechanics of Futures Trading

Futures trading is different from the types of transactions with which most people are familiar. Futures trading is a topsy-turvy world. Traders can sell something before they buy it: traders are buying and selling obligations to buy or sell in the future a commodity they will likely never even see.

Most daily newspapers supply futures prices. For example, on July 17, 1991, the futures price of December 1991 corn was about $2.41 per bushel in Chicago. The futures price is the price agreed upon now for a commodity to be paid for and delivered on some future date; yet at any time between now and the future date, the seller or buyer can *close out* the futures contract by engaging in an offsetting transaction. The seller offsets the transaction by simply buying another futures contract with the same delivery date; a buyer closes out by selling another futures contract with the same delivery date. Two examples of futures trading, illustrating a long position and a short position, follow.

A Long Position. George Bull thinks that wheat prices will rise in the future more than other buyers generally expect them to rise. In January, George thinks that the July wheat price of $3.40 is too low; he expects the actual price of wheat in July to be well above $3.40. On January 1, George buys 5000 bushels of July wheat, paying the futures price of $3.40. George is now in a long position in wheat.

On March 1, the price of July wheat rises to $3.50. George has made a profit because he bought the wheat at $3.40 a bushel and can now sell it for $3.50 a bushel. If George closes out his long position by selling a contract for 5000 bushels of July wheat, he will make a profit of $500 (or $0.10 × 5000 bushels). Even if George does not close out his long position, his broker will add $500 to his account.

[8]The actual percentage *margin requirement* varies from commodity to commodity. Wheat usually has a 5 percent requirement. If you are wealthy and an established customer, it would have been possible to deposit some of your assets (stocks, bonds) with your commodity broker to guarantee the contract. The amount of cash put up is negligible; it basically screens out individuals who may run out on the contract if things go badly.

A Short Position. In January, Sue Bear thinks that July wheat will be lower in price than people currently anticipate. She thinks that if she sells July wheat at $3.40 per bushel, the futures prices will fall and she can make a profit. Thus, Sue Bear sells 5000 bushels of July wheat on January 1 at the market futures price of $3.40 a bushel. Sue is now in a short position in wheat (she sold something she doesn't completely own). While this will probably not be the case, it is convenient to think of Sue as the one who sells to George. If the price of July wheat rises above $3.40, Sue loses; if the price falls below $3.40, Sue wins. As we already indicated, on March 1, the futures price of July wheat is $3.50. If Sue closes out her short position, she loses $0.10 per bushel, or $500. Even if Sue does not close out her short position, her broker will deduct $500 from her account. In the futures market, there are no paper losses or paper gains.

Hedging

The person who "hedges a bet" bets both sides in order to minimize the risks of heavy losses. Such a person might bet $5 it will rain tomorrow and $4 it won't rain. **Hedging** also takes place in futures markets.

> **Hedging** is the temporary substitution of a futures market transaction for an intended spot transaction.

Futures markets can provide an opportunity to traders of commodities in both spot and futures markets to reduce the risks of price fluctuations over time as well as to increase their profits. A futures market allows those involved in the distribution, processing, or storage of a good to concentrate on their specialized productive activities by taking advantage of the relationship between spot and futures prices.

Suppose, for example, that on July 1, the operator of a grain elevator buys 5000 bushels of wheat from a farmer for $5 a bushel (the spot price on that date). The grain is put into storage for intended sale at some date in the future. What are the risks to the operator? If the price of wheat were to drop, the operator could incur substantial losses. Through the futures market, the elevator operator hedges by immediately selling a futures contract for 5000 bushels of wheat to be delivered at a price of, say, $5.15 in November.

If the elevator operator holds his wheat until November, the wheat purchased for $5 can be delivered on the futures contract for $5.15. The elevator operator has locked in a profit of $0.15 per bushel to cover his carrying charges.

Now suppose the spot price of wheat drops and, 1 month later, the elevator operator sells this wheat for $4 on the spot market to General Mills. On this spot transaction, he has lost $5000 ($1 per bushel on 5000 bushels). But what about the November futures contract that he previously sold? Because wheat prices are falling, the price of November wheat might drop to $4.10. Because the elevator operator previously sold November wheat for $5.15 per bushel, this operator can close out the position by buying November wheat at $4.10, for a profit per bushel of $1.05. The elevator operator can earn $1.05 × 5000, or $5250, by closing out the position. Through hedging, the elevator operator has not only limited the risks from falling grain prices but has made a profit. The elevator operator lost $5000 from the spot market and gained $5250 in the futures market and, in effect, earned $250—$0.05 per bushel—by holding wheat for 1 month.

Large grain users, such as General Mills, can also hedge against the risks of fluctuating wheat prices by using the futures market. General Mills knows in July that it will require 100,000 bushels of wheat in December. It does not know what the price of wheat will be in December, but it can purchase a December futures contract for 100,000 bushels of wheat at $5 per bushel and, thus, protect itself against the risk that wheat will be selling well above $5 in December.

Hedgers and speculators play highly complementary roles in the economy. Hedgers are interested primarily in storing commodities or in using these commodities in their business; they are interested in their particular business and in minimizing the risks of price fluctuations. The speculator, on the other hand, does not have to be concerned with the details of storing grain or making flour and grain products. The speculator specializes in information about supply and demand in the future. There is division of labor between the hedger and the speculator.

Information and Speculation in the Futures Market

The futures market provides information concerning the future. This information is not always accurate; sometimes it predicts that prices will rise but instead they fall, and vice versa. Prices in futures markets reveal to the economy what speculators *anticipate* will happen to the prices of different commodities in the future. If the futures price of wheat is well above the current spot price, then speculators believe that wheat prices will rise. These futures prices represent the best information available to the economy on the course of prices in the future.

Economic decisions must be made today concerning actions that must be taken in the future. Farmers must plant crops that will not be harvested for many months; mine operators must plan the expansion of mine capacity. If prices in the future were known with certainty, such planning would be grossly simplified; however, the future is always uncertain. Clearly, having a futures market that establishes effective future prices today is of great benefit in an uncertain world. For those who need to know future prices, a futures market provides a summary indicator of market sentiment—a single price reflects much of what people know today about tomorrow.

This chapter completes our study of product markets. The next section will turn to the bottom half of the circular-flow diagram: factor markets. The next chapter will give an introduction to factor markets and how they compare to product markets. Subsequent chapters examine the markets for the different kinds of factors—labor, land, capital, entrepreneurship—individually.

SUMMARY

1. Information is costly because of our limited ability to process, store, and retrieve facts and figures about the economy and because real resources are required to gather information. Individuals acquire information to the point where the marginal cost of acquiring more information equals the marginal benefit of more information.

2. Search costs explain the observed dispersion of prices. When the benefits to further search are great, price dispersion will be limited.

3. Two problems encountered by buyers and sellers because of the cost of information are the moral-hazard problem and the adverse-selection problem. The moral-hazard problem refers to postcontractual opportunistic behavior; the adverse-selection problem refers to precontractual opportunistic behavior. Both arise because one party cannot verify the claims of the other party.

4. Intermediaries bring together buyers and sellers; they often buy in order to sell again and sometimes serve as certifiers of quality.

5. Advertising can have both procompetitive and anticompetitive effects. By providing information, advertising makes markets more competitive; however, it can also erect barriers to entry and thereby create monopoly power. In a complex world where the seller has more information about product quality, durability, and safety, the doctrine of *caveat emptor* (let the buyer beware) has its limitations. But there are still some advantages to *caveat emptor.*

6. Speculators buy now in order to sell later for a profit. If speculators are profitable, they stabilize prices and consumption over time. If they are unprofitable, they destabilize prices and consumption over time.

7. In a futures market, contracts are made now for payment and delivery of commodities in the future. Futures markets provide information about the uncertain future and allow hedging by those who wish to reduce risks.

KEY TERMS

transaction costs	intermediaries
information costs	speculators
optimal-search rule	arbitrage
reservation price	futures market
moral-hazard problem	spot (cash) market
adverse-selection problem	hedging

QUESTIONS AND PROBLEMS

1. Investors can purchase shares of stock through a full-service broker (who provides information and investment advice) or through a discount broker. The commission charged by the full-service broker is much higher than that charged by the discount broker. They both provide the service of buying the shares of stock ordered by the buyer. Explain why most investors use the services of the higher-priced brokers.
2. The market for wheat is highly centralized. In fact, one can say there is a world market for wheat. Why is this market centralized while other markets, such as the automobile market, are decentralized?
3. A consumer has learned that prices of $3, $3.50, and $4 are being charged by various pharmacies for the same generic drug. The marginal benefit of further search is $0.15; marginal cost is $0.10. Should the consumer search for a lower price?
4. A consumer has been quoted the prices of $20, $21, $23, and $24 for a wheel alignment on his car. The marginal benefit for further search is $1, and the marginal cost is also $1. What is the consumer's reservation price? Should the consumer search further?
5. What are the transaction costs of selling a home? What effect do real estate brokers have on these costs?
6. Explain why more is spent on the advertising of deodorants than on the advertising of farm machinery.
7. If search costs in a market are zero and the market is competitively organized, what predictions can you make about prices in this market?
8. Under what conditions does *caveat emptor* work well? Under what conditions would *caveat emptor* not work well?
9. The stock market is highly competitive, with thousands of speculators trying to buy low and sell high. Using the concepts of information and search costs, explain why we all can't get rich with a little study and research by playing the stock market.
10. What is the moral-hazard problem? Give examples.
11. An attendance clause gives a major-league baseball player a season-end bonus if attendance exceeds a target figure. Explain how this is a result from the moral-hazard problem.
12. What is the adverse-selection problem? Give examples.
13. Assume that on January 1, July wheat is selling for $4. How could a speculator profit from the expectation that in July spot wheat will sell for $3.50? How could a speculator profit from the expectation that in July spot wheat will sell for $4.50?
14. Indicate which of the following examples is a potential moral-hazard problem or a potential adverse-selection problem.
    a. "The chair broke when I sat down," complained the customer to the furniture store.
    b. "This chair will last a lifetime," asserted the furniture salesperson.
    c. "I am a safe, married driver," claimed the student buying car insurance.
    d. "We insure all drivers," claims the ad.

V

Factor Markets

Chapter 36 Factor Markets
Chapter 37 Labor Markets
Chapter 38 Labor Unions
Chapter 39 Interest, Rent, and Profit
Chapter 40 Income Distribution and Poverty

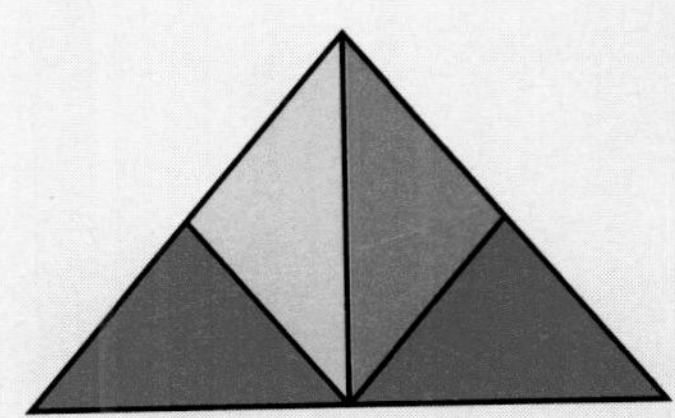

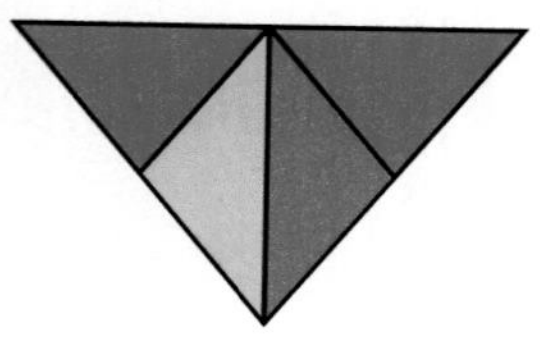

36

Factor Markets

CHAPTER INSIGHT

The firm operates in two distinct markets: the product (or output) market and the factor (or input) market. The preceding chapters focused on the firm's behavior as a seller in the product market. They studied how different degrees of competition in the market affect the firm's pricing and output decisions. Firms also act as buyers of factors or inputs. The prices of labor, land, and capital are determined in factor markets, and these prices determine the incomes of the individuals and agents who own these productive factors.

This chapter identifies the main economic forces in the factor market. Rather than concentrating on one specific factor of production (such as labor) this chapter examines the general rules that govern the behavior of firms in factor markets and explains why the demand for the factors of production depends upon the product market and productivity. Just as firms in the product market are motivated by profit maximization, so are firms in the factor market.

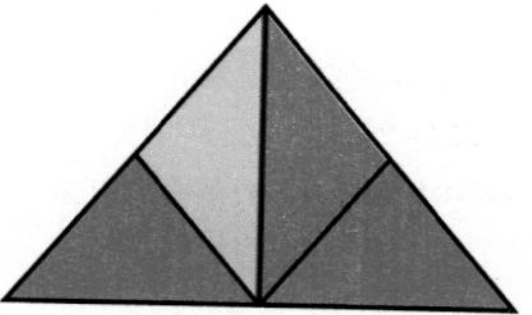

THE TWO FACES OF THE FIRM

The firm displays two faces to the outside world: the face of a *seller of the goods and services it produces* and the face of a *buyer of factor inputs*. In both cases, the firm can be either a price taker or a price searcher (as described in an earlier chapter).

In terms of the circular-flow diagram (see Figure 1), the activities of firms in the product or output market (the upper half of the diagram) determine the solution to the *what* problem of economics. The activities of firms in the factor market (the lower half of the diagram) determine the solutions to the *how* and *for whom* problems.

Price Searching and Price Taking in the Factor Market

The definitions of a **price taker** and **price searcher** in factor markets are the same as those definitions given in the chapters on product markets.

> A **price taker** in a factor market is a buyer of an input whose purchases are not large enough to affect the price of the input. The price-taking firm must accept the market price as given.
>
> A **price searcher** in a factor market is a buyer of inputs whose purchases are large enough to affect the price of the input.

FIGURE 1
The Circular Flow of Economic Activity

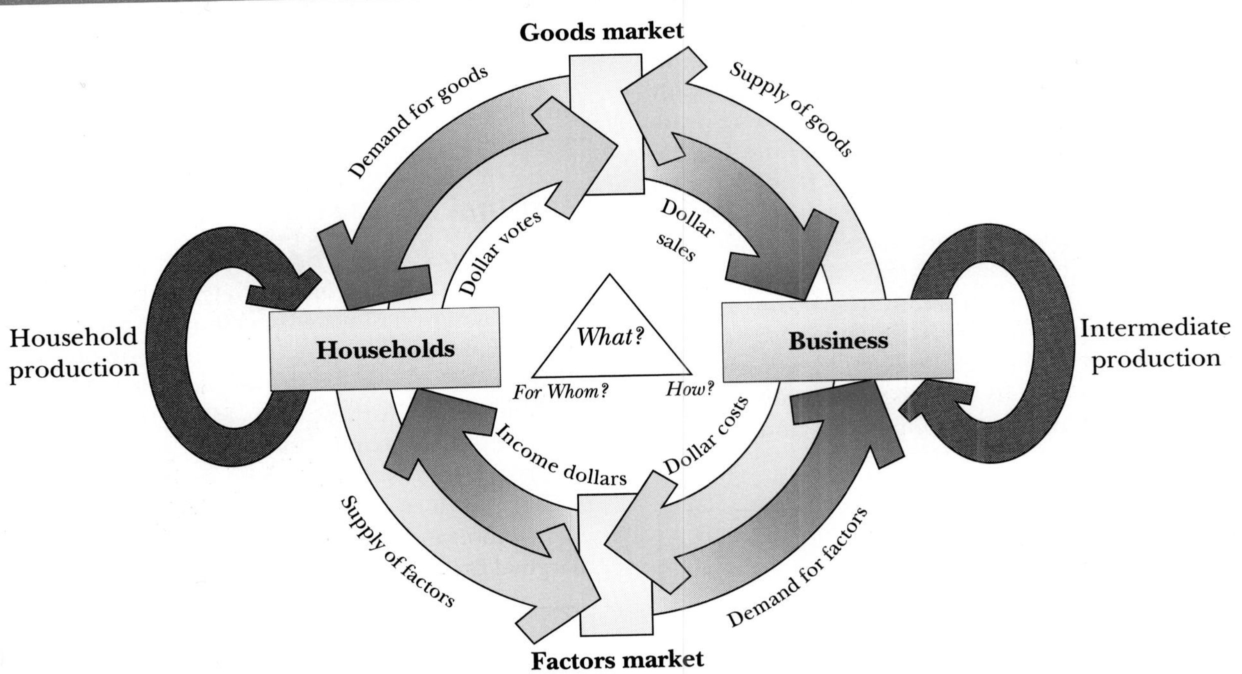

The circular-flow diagram shows that firms operate simultaneously in the product market and in the factor market. The upper half of the circular flow shows the flows of products and purchases between the business and household sectors. The bottom half shows the flows of factors from the households to business firms and the payment of factor income from business firms to households for the factors of production.

Figure 2 shows the four possible market conditions the firm may face in its role as either a seller of products or a buyer of factor inputs and in its role as either a price taker or a price searcher.

1. The firm may be a price taker in both the product and factor markets (see panels *a* and *b*).
2. The firm may be a price searcher in both the product and factor markets (see panels *c* and *d*).
3. The firm may be a price taker in the product market and a price searcher in the factor market (see panels *a* and *d*).
4. The firm may be a price searcher in the product market and a price taker in the factor market (see panels *b* and *c*).

There is no necessary link between the amount of competition a firm faces on one side of the market and the amount it faces on the other side. A monopolist may purchase its land, labor, and capital inputs as a price taker. A perfectly competitive firm may be a price searcher in the factor market. Although there are numerous exceptions, the most likely scenario is that the firm will face more competition on the input (factor) side than on the output (product) side. In selling its products, the firm faces competition only from other firms that produce either the same product or a product that serves as a substitute for the goods it produces. However, in factor markets, all firms compete with one another for labor, capital, and land. The firm, therefore, faces competition for inputs not only from those firms with which it competes in the product market but also from firms in entirely different industries. Oil companies, universities, law offices, and retailers all compete for skilled secretaries. Restaurants, motels, gas stations, retailers, and home builders all compete for land in major cities.

> A firm will usually face more competition from other firms when hiring inputs than when selling outputs.

Of course, not all firms face more competition on the input side than the output side. For example, a textile mill located in a small, isolated town may face little competition from other employers in its hiring of local labor, while its sales on the output side may be in a perfectly (or near perfect) competitive product market. Certain skilled people (professional athletes, for example) are so specialized that they are suited for employment in only one industry. The employer is, therefore, likely to be a price searcher in this factor market. Certain types of capital—such as oil-drilling rigs—are suited to only one use, unlike trucks, lathes, and computers. Firms purchasing such specialized equipment are more likely to be price searchers.

When the firm has the power to influence the price at which it purchases inputs, the firm has **monopsony** power.

> A **monopsony** is a firm that faces an upward-sloping supply curve for one or more factors of production. A *pure monopsony* is the only buyer of some input.

Like pure monopoly, pure monopsony is rare. Few firms are the sole buyer of a factor of production. Even if the isolated textile mill—which appears to have a monopsony over the local labor market as the sole major employer in town—offers wages that are too low, people may move to other cities, or outside firms might be attracted into the market by the prospect of cheap labor, both of which will result in competition for the mill.

Marginal Factor Cost

The concepts of marginal revenue and marginal cost play a decisive role in the theory of product markets described in the preceding chapters. Profit-maximizing firms produce that level of output at which marginal revenue (MR) and marginal costs (MC) are equal. If those firms follow the MC = MR rule, they will maximize profits or minimize losses. Inputs have costs and benefits to the firm, just as production does. In making its input decisions, the most important cost the firm must consider is the **marginal factor cost (MFC)**.

> **Marginal factor cost (MFC)** is the extra cost to the firm per unit increase in the amount of the factor; it is the increase in costs divided by the increase in the amount of the factor.

The price of a factor of production is the wage (in the case of labor) or the rental (in the case of capital or land) that the firm must pay to hire or

FIGURE 2
The Two Faces of the Firm: Product Market and Factor Market

Firm as Seller of Output

(*a*) Product Demand When the Firm Faces Many Competitors for Output

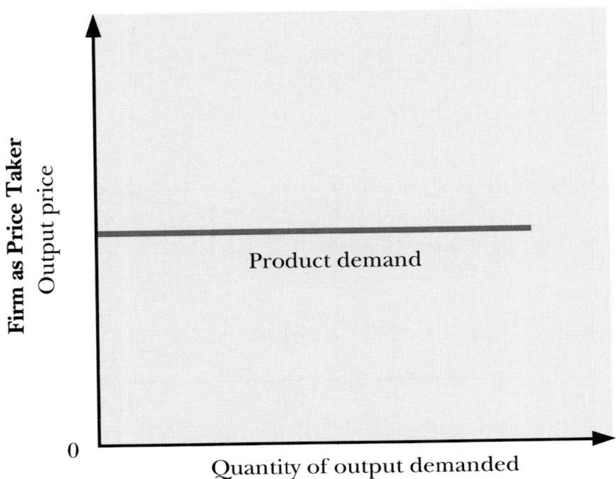

Firm as Buyer of Inputs

(*b*) Factor Supply When the Firm Faces Many Competitors for Inputs

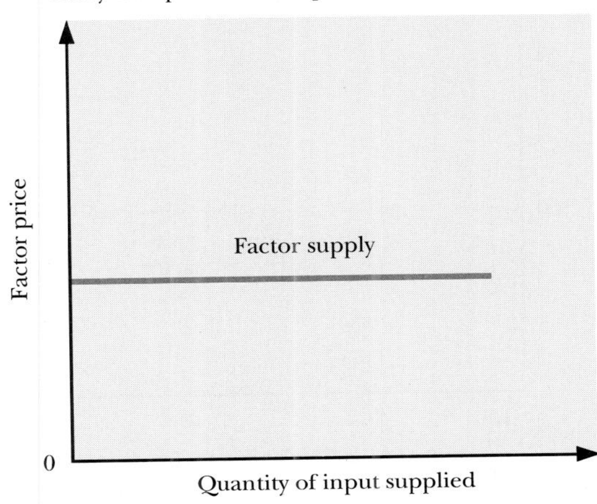

Firm as Seller of Output

(*c*) Product Demand When the Firm Faces Few Competitors for Output

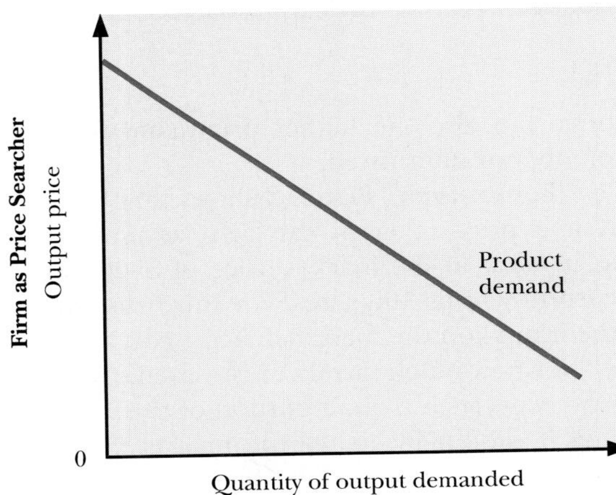

Firm as Buyer of Inputs

(*d*) Factor Supply When the Firm Faces Few Competitors for Inputs

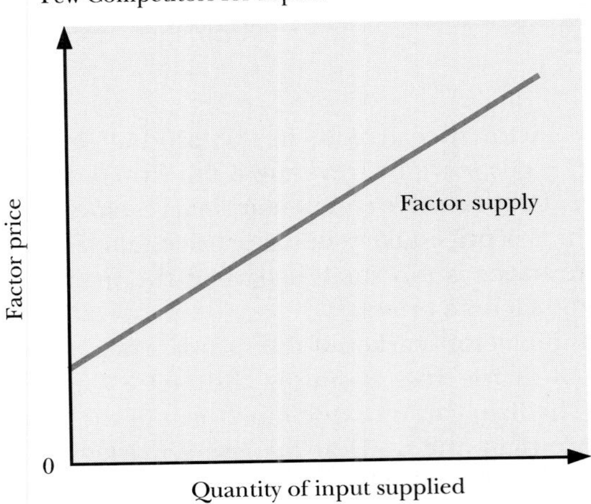

Panels *a* and *b* show a price-taking firm in the product and factor markets, respectively. Price taking on the product side means that the firm can sell all it wants at the existing market price (demand is perfectly elastic). Price taking in the factor market means that the firm can hire all the factors it wants at the prevailing factor price (factor supply is perfectly elastic).

Panels *c* and *d* show price searching in the product and factor markets, respectively. Price searching on the product side means that the firm faces a downward-sloping product demand curve. To sell more, it must lower its price. Price searching on the factor side means that the firm faces an upward-sloping factor supply curve. To hire more factor inputs, the firm must pay a higher factor price.

FIGURE 3
Competition versus Monopsony in the Market for Inputs

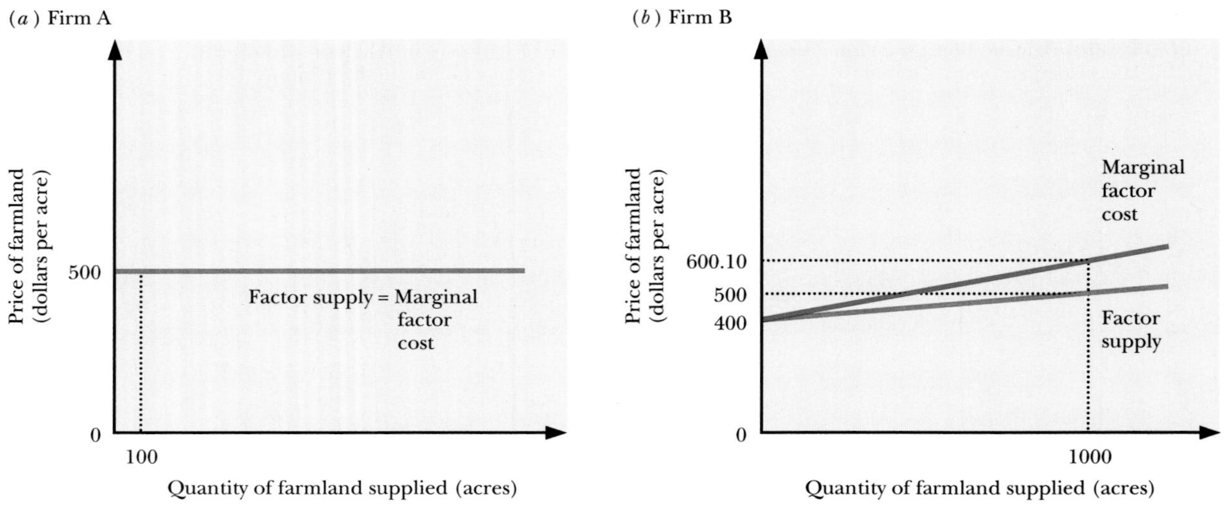

Panel *a* shows a price-taking firm that can hire all the inputs it wants at the going market price. The horizontal supply curve facing the firm is its MFC curve. Panel *b* shows a price-searching firm on the factor side that must pay higher input prices to get larger quantities of the input. To use more input per period requires a higher price for all quantities of the input; therefore, the extra cost of hiring one more unit of the input is the price *plus the increase in the cost of using the smaller input quantity*. Thus, the MFC curve lies above the factor's supply curve.

use the factor. Recall that, in the product market, price exceeds marginal revenue if the firm is a price searcher but that price equals marginal revenue when the firm is a price taker. Being a price taker means that the buyer is too small a part of the market to affect the factor's price.

In the factor market, if the firm is a price taker, marginal factor cost is simply the factor's market price. The firm can hire one more unit of the factor (or more than one unit) at the going market price. The firm's actions have no effect on the input's price.

If the firm is a price searcher in the factor market, the firm's marginal factor cost will exceed the market price of the factor. As a price searcher, the firm is a large enough portion of the particular factor market so that it cannot buy more of the factor without driving up its market price. To use one more unit of the input per period, the firm must pay the same higher price for all units that it would need to pay for the last unit hired. In other words, the extra unit of the factor will cost the firm not only its market price but also the higher price paid for a smaller number of units hired.

For example, Figure 3 shows that because Firm A is a price taker, it can rent as much farmland as it wants at the market price of $500 per acre. It currently rents 100 acres. For this firm, the price of the input and the marginal factor cost are equal. No matter how much farmland is rented, the individual firm rents such a small portion of the available land that it cannot influence the market price. Firm B, which is a price searcher that currently rents 1000 acres at $500 per acre, is large enough to affect the market price. The marginal factor cost of Firm A is the market price of $500. The marginal factor cost of Firm B is the price of the 1001st acre ($500.10) plus the $100 extra ($0.10 × 1000) it must pay for the original 1000 acres. Thus, the marginal factor cost of Firm B at an input level of 1000 acres is $600.10, which is higher than the factor price ($500). Thus, B's MFC curve lies everywhere above the factor's supply curve.

For price searchers in factor markets, marginal factor cost is greater than the factor prices; for price takers in factor markets, marginal factor cost equals the factor's price.

In factor markets, price taking is more likely than price searching (monopsony). The remainder of this chapter will examine the behavior of firms that are price takers in factor markets—firms in which marginal factor cost and factor price are the same. (A later chapter will examine the behavior of price-searching firms in the factor market.)

THE FIRM'S DEMAND FOR FACTORS OF PRODUCTION

The firm's demand for a factor input depends upon the input's physical productivity and the demand for the good the factor is being used to produce. The chapter on costs and productivity defined the production function as the relationship between outputs and inputs. Recall that a factor's marginal physical product (MPP) is the increase in output divided by the increase in the amount of the factor, holding all other factors constant.

As explained earlier, all production functions exhibit the law of diminishing returns, which states that as ever larger quantities of a variable factor are combined with fixed amounts of the firm's other factors, the marginal physical product of the variable factor will eventually decline.

Derived Demand

A consumer buys products because they provide satisfaction. The firm buys factors of production because they produce goods and services that create revenue for the firm. The garment industry buys sewing machines because they help to produce suits, shirts, and dresses that consumers will buy. Automobile workers are hired because they help produce automobiles that people will buy. Farmland is rented because it yields wheat that people will consume. The demand for workers, the demand for farmland, and the demand for tailors are all examples of **derived demand.**

The demand for a factor of production is a **derived demand** because it results (is derived) from the demand for the goods and services the factor of production helps produce.

The principle of derived demand is essential to understanding the workings of factor markets. (See Example 1.) If consumers reduce their demand for lettuce, the demand for workers employed in lettuce growing, the demand for farmland used for lettuce, and even the demand for water used in farm irrigation would also fall. When the demand for automobiles falls, there is unemployment in Detroit. When world demand for Boeing commercial aircraft is booming, employment in Seattle and Wichita (the cities where Boeing is located) rises.

Joint Determination of Factor Demand

The production of a good requires the cooperation of different factors of production. Farm workers can produce no corn without farmland; farmland without farm labor is useless. Both farmland and farm workers require farm implements (ranging from hand tools to sophisticated farm machinery) to produce corn.

In general, the marginal physical product of any factor of production depends upon the quantity and quality of the cooperating factors of production.

The marginal physical product of the farm worker will be higher on 1 acre of farmland than on 1 square yard of land; it will be higher on 1 acre of fertile Iowa land than on 1 acre of rocky New England land; and it will be higher when working with modern heavy farm machinery than with hand implements. The interdependence of the marginal physical products of land, labor, and capital makes the problem of factor pricing in a market setting difficult to analyze.

Marginal Revenue Product

The demand for a factor of production—land, labor, or capital—is a derived demand. The factor is

EXAMPLE 1 Derived Demand: Oil Prices and Drilling Rigs

The demand for a factor of production is a derived demand because the demand for the factor depends upon the demand for the product that the factors help produce. The derived nature of the demand for the factors of production is illustrated by the relationship between crude oil prices and drilling rigs. Drilling rigs are capital goods used (along with labor and materials) to produce crude oil. Changes in crude oil prices reflect changes in the demand for the product that drilling rigs help to produce. As the demand for crude oil falls, its price falls, and the derived demand for drilling rigs falls. The accompanying figures illustrate this principle. As crude oil prices fell from 1982 to 1985, the drilling-rig count fell as well. When crude oil prices plunged in 1986, the drilling-rig count plunged as well.

Sources: Figure A data from *Oil and Gas Journal:* Figure B data from Hughes Tool Company. Reported in *Houston Update,* July 1986.

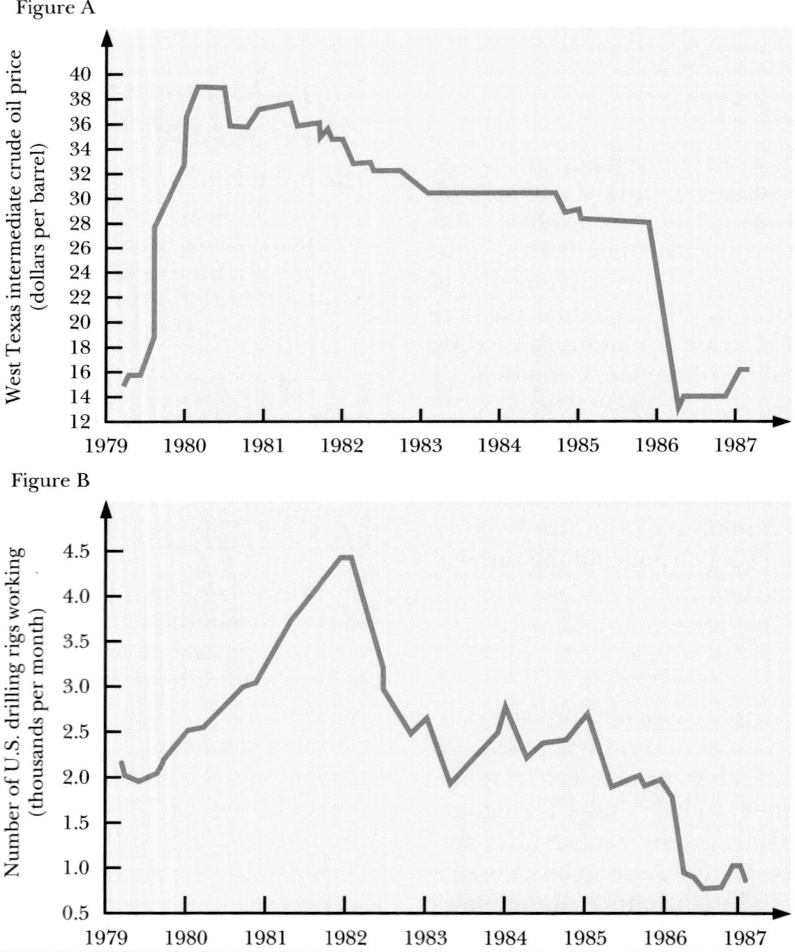

TABLE 1
Marginal Revenue Product

Labor (workers), L (1)	Output (units), Q (2)	Price, P (3)	Total Revenue, TR (4) = (2) × (3)	Marginal Revenue Product, MRP (5) = (6) × (7) = Δ(4) ÷ Δ(1)	Marginal Revenue, MR (6) = Δ(4) ÷ Δ(2)	Marginal Physical Product (units), MPP (7) = Δ(2)
0	0	$24	$ 0			
				$95	$19	5
1	5	19	95			
				40	10	4
2	9	15	135			
				9	3	3
3	12	12	144			

Columns 1 and 2 give the production function (the amount of output produced by 0, 1, 2, and 3 units of labor input). Columns 2 and 3 give the demand schedule facing the firm. MRP is calculated by taking the increase in total revenue associated with one-unit increases in the labor input. It can also be calculated by multiplying MR times MPP. MR in column 6 is calculated by dividing the increase in revenue in column 5 by the difference between rows in column 2. MPP in column 7 is the increase in output for every unit increase in the factor, or the difference between rows in column 2.

valuable because the firm sells the output on the product market. Thus, the dollar value of an extra worker, an extra unit of land, or an extra machine is that factor's **marginal revenue product (MRP)**.

> The **marginal revenue product (MRP)** of any factor of production is the extra revenue generated per unit increase in the amount of the factor.

There are two ways of calculating a factor's marginal revenue product. Both approaches yield the same value.

Method 1. The first method of calculating marginal revenue product is to simply change the quantity of the factor and observe the change in revenue. According to this direct method, marginal revenue product is the change in total revenue (TR) divided by the change (increase or decrease) in the factor.

$$MRP = \frac{\Delta TR}{\Delta Factor}$$

Table 1 demonstrates this method. The different quantities of labor the firm employs are given in column 1, and the resulting output is given in column 2. Columns 1 and 2, therefore, represent the production function. Column 3 shows the market prices that clear the market (equate quantity supplied and demanded) for the various output levels produced. This firm is a price searcher in the product market because the price falls with higher output levels. The firm's total revenue (price times quantity of output) is given in column 4. Because marginal revenue (see column 5) is the difference between the revenues generated at consecutive levels of labor input, it is recorded between the rows corresponding to the input levels. The revenue generated when one worker is employed is $95; the revenue when two workers are employed is $135. The marginal revenue product therefore, is $135 – $95 = $40. In other words, the firm's total revenue would increase by $40 if the firm hired a second worker.

Method 2. A factor's marginal revenue product can be calculated indirectly as well. The marginal physical product MPP is the increase in output associated with a one-unit increase in the factor; the marginal-revenue (MR) indicates the increase in revenue associated with this increase in output of one unit.[1] Therefore:

$$MRP = MPP \times MR$$

This formula works for the price searcher (see Table 1). Because the firm increases its output from five to nine units as a consequence of adding a second unit of labor, marginal physical product equals four units. The four extra units of output add $40 to revenue, or $10 per extra unit ($40/4); therefore, the marginal revenue is $10. The marginal revenue product equals $40($10 × 4). Thus, the indirect method of calculating marginal revenue product yields the same answer as the direct method.

> The marginal revenue product of a factor can be calculated directly, by determining the increase in revenue at different input levels, or indirectly, by multiplying marginal physical product by marginal revenue.

PROFIT MAXIMIZATION

In the product market, the firm maximizes profit by producing that output at which marginal revenue and marginal cost are equal. The firm is also guided by profit maximization in the factor market. Profit-maximizing decisions in the product market are basically the same as profit-maximizing decisions in the factor market because deciding on the quantity of inputs determines the level of output.

The MRP = MFC Rule

To understand how firms choose the profit-maximizing level of factor inputs, consider the case of a firm deciding how much unskilled labor to hire. *The firm will hire one more unit of unskilled labor if the extra revenue (the extra benefit) the firm derives from the sale of the output produced by the extra unit exceeds the marginal factor cost of the extra unit of unskilled labor.* If the firm is a price taker, MFC will be the market wage. As in any other economic activity, a firm will hire inputs to the point where marginal benefits equal marginal costs.

The firm will continue to hire inputs as long as their marginal revenue product exceeds their marginal factor cost. As indicated earlier, it is assumed that the firm is a price taker in the factor market. Thus, the market prices of the inputs the firm uses (wage rates, rental rates, interest rates) are the marginal factor costs of these inputs. The marginal benefit of an additional unit of factor input is its marginal revenue product. As long as the marginal revenue product exceeds the price of the input, it pays the firm to hire the factor. (See Example 2.) If the marginal revenue product of Factor A is $40 and its price is $30, it pays the firm to hire the factor. By hiring an additional unit of the factor, the firm expects to increase its profit by $10 (= MRP − MFC).

The Demand Curve for a Factor

Figure 4 shows the MRP curve of Factor A. The curve is downward sloping because in the short run the greater the amount of Factor A used, the lower its marginal physical product (because of the law of diminishing returns). Also, if the firm is a price searcher in the product market, higher levels of output mean a lower marginal revenue. Thus, as the quantity of Factor A increases, both marginal physical product and marginal revenue tend to decline, so that MRP (which is MR × MPP) declines. The firm will hire Factor A until its price equals marginal revenue product.

> The MRP curve is the firm's demand curve for a factor because the firm hires that factor quantity until the marginal revenue product of the factor equals the price of the factor.

In Figure 4, the supply curve of Factor A to the firm is horizontal at the market price of $14. The price-taking firm in the factor market can hire all it wants at $14. If the firm hired only 60 units of Factor A (point *a*), it would not maximize its profit: at 60 units, A's MRP equals $22 and A's MFC equals $14. The firm's incentive to hire additional factors continues as long as MRP exceeds $14. Thus, the

[1] For a price taker in the product market, $P \times MPP = MR \times MPP$. For a price searcher in the product market, $P \times MPP > MR \times MPP$. In intermediate textbooks, the product $P \times MPP$ is called the *value of the marginal product.*

EXAMPLE 2 Marginal Analysis: The Gretzky Trade

People enter into economic activities as long as the extra benefits from the activity exceed its extra costs. For example, in August 1988 the Los Angeles Kings professional hockey team decided to pay $15 million in cash for Wayne Gretzky, one of the most dominating hockey players of all time. Why were the Los Angeles Kings willing to pay $15 million for a single hockey player? The team's management concluded that the additional revenue that would be brought in by Gretzky fans exceeded Gretzky's $15 million price tag. Within 3 years, the extra revenues from ticket sales and cable television rights would be in the neighborhood of $27 million. For this deal, the estimated marginal revenue far exceeded the marginal cost.

Source: "Gretzky: Deal With Dividends," *New York Times*, August 20, 1988, 30.

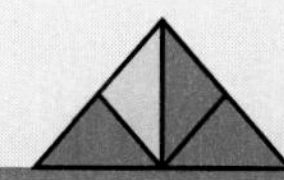

FIGURE 4
Firm Equilibrium: The Hiring of Factor Inputs

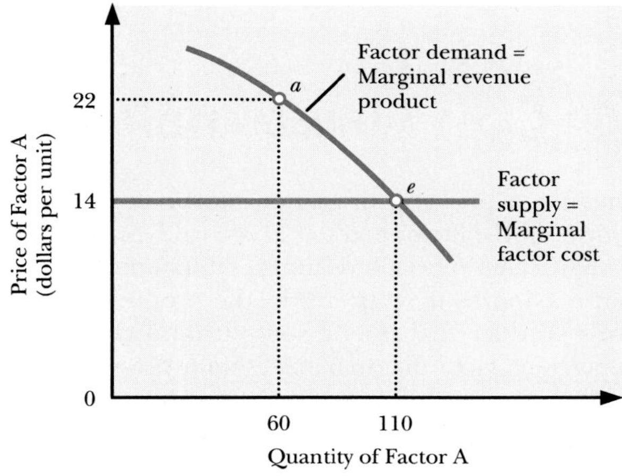

The firm's derived demand for Factor A is the MRP curve. The supply schedule of Factor A as seen by the firm is perfectly horizontal at the market price of $14. Equilibrium *e* will be reached at a price of $14 and a quantity of 110 units of Factor A. At this point, MRP = MFC.

firm will continue to hire to the point where MRP and MFC are equal, which occurs at 110 units of Factor A (point *e*). The firm will be in equilibrium (earning a maximum profit or minimizing its losses) when each factor is employed up to the point where marginal factor cost (which equals the price of the factor when the input market is competitive) equals the marginal revenue product of the factor.

In equilibrium, $MRP_A = MFC_A, MRP_B = MFC_B$, and so on, where *A* and *B* are specific factors.

The Two Sides of the Firm

In the product market, the rule of profit maximization is MR = MC. In the factor market, the rule is MRP = MFC for each factor. These rules are logically the same. Recall that marginal cost is the mirror image of marginal physical product. That is:

$$MC = \frac{W}{MPP_L} \quad (1)$$

where MPP_L is the marginal physical product of labor and *W* is the wage rate.

The rule for profit maximization in the product market is:

$$MR = MC \quad (2)$$

Because MC equals W/MPP_L according to equation (1), equation (2) can be rewritten as:

$$W = MR \times MPP_L \quad (3)$$

TABLE 2
Two Ways of Looking at Profit Maximization

Labor Hours L (1)	Units of Marginal Physical Product, MPP (2)	Price Equals Marginal Revenue, P = MR (3)	Wage Equals Marginal Factor Cost, W = MFC (4)	Marginal Revenue Product, MRP (5) = (2) × (3)	Marginal Cost, MC (6) = (4) ÷ (2)
0					
	5	$10	$20	$50	$ 4
1					
	4	10	20	40	5
2					
	2	10	20	20	10
3					

This firm is a price taker on both sides of the market. Column 5 equals column 2 times column 3 because the additional revenue from 1 more unit of labor is simply the marginal product multiplied by the price (or marginal revenue). Column 6 equals column 4 divided by column 2 because marginal cost equals the wage per unit of marginal physical product. This table shows that profits are maximized at 3 units of labor where MFC = MRP and P = MC.

Because the wage for a factor is equal to the marginal factor cost (when a firm is a price taker in the factor market), and because MR × MPP = MRP, equation (3) can become:

$$\text{MFC} = \text{MRP} \quad (4)$$

which is the profit-maximizing rule in the factor market.

Table 2 provides a numerical example of how profit maximization in the product market is equivalent to profit maximization in the factor market. The firm is a price taker in both markets, so W = MFC and P = MR. The product price is $10 and the wage rate is $20 per day. The MPP schedule is given in columns 1 and 2 of Table 2. Column 3 shows marginal revenue (which equals price in this case), and column 4 shows marginal factor cost (which equals wage in this case). Marginal revenue product is simply column 2 multiplied by column 3 and is shown in column 5. Marginal cost is the wage for an additional unit of labor divided by the change in output resulting from the additional unit, or W ÷ MPP (see column 6). When P = MC (both $10), it is also true that MRP = MFC (both $20). When one rule is satisfied, the other rule is also satisfied.

COST MINIMIZATION

The rules of profit maximization explain the behavior of firms in the factor market. These rules predict that firms will employ that level and combination of inputs that maximizes their profit. In the product market, firms produce that level of output (and charge the associated price) that maximizes their profit.

To maximize profit, it is necessary to minimize the cost of producing a given quantity of output. Thus far, we have explained how a firm selects the optimal level of *one* factor input. But firms produce output with cooperating factors. How will they know when they are combining *all* their inputs in a least-cost fashion? Suppose a firm has decided to produce 200 units of output and currently uses 15 labor hours and 25 machine hours to produce this output. The wage rate (the price of labor) is $5 per hour, and the rental rate on the machinery is $20 per hour. Thus, an extra hour of machine time costs four times as much as an extra hour of labor. The marginal physical product of capital is 30 units of output. The marginal physical product of labor is 10 units of output. Thus, an extra hour of machine time produces three times as much

EXAMPLE 3 One Doctor, Two Offices

The least-cost rule states that the factors of production will be combined so that their marginal physical products per dollar are equal. Physicians, for example, produce medical services by combining their labor with capital. Your doctor practices in an office equipped with scales, lab equipment, and medical supplies. He or she combines labor, capital, and supplies so that medical services can be provided "efficiently."

Until recently, it was most efficient for a physician to practice out of one office. However, in the late 1980s and early 1990s, many physicians began to operate out of two or more offices in order to serve patients in the city as well as the suburbs.

This trend came about as the result of declining office rents, which were associated with the overbuilding of office space during that time. As rents declined, physicians saw that they were not allocating resources efficiently. They could provide "more efficient" medical care if they rented an extra office. This use of more capital relative to labor allowed physicians to reach a new, efficient combination of labor and capital.

as an extra hour of labor. Is the firm using the optimal amount of labor and capital?

In this example, the firm is using too much capital and too little labor. If the firm were to substitute 3 hours of labor for 1 hour of capital, total output would not change, but costs would be reduced by $5. One hour of capital (at the margin) is three times as productive as 1 hour of labor. Adding 3 units of labor increases output by 30, and subtracting 1 machine hour decreases output by 30; there is no net change in output. However, cutting back on 1 machine hour saves $20, while hiring 3 more hours of labor costs $15. Output remains the same, but costs fall by $5.

To determine whether a substitution of this sort will increase profits, the firm will look at marginal physical product *per dollar of cost.* In this example, because an extra hour of labor increases output by 10 units and increases costs by $5, an extra dollar spent on labor produces 2 units (10/$5) of output. Because an extra machine hour increases output by 30 units and increases costs by $20, an extra dollar spent on capital produces 1.5 units of output. In our example, a dollar spent on more labor is more effective than a dollar spent on more capital. (See Example 3.)

The marginal physical product per dollar of a factor is its marginal physical product divided by its price. The price-taking firm takes both the wage rate for labor (W) and the rental rate on capital (R) as given. As the preceding example shows, if the marginal physical product per dollar of labor is greater than the marginal physical product per dollar of capital, the firm is not combining inputs in a least-cost fashion. It can produce the same output at lower cost by substituting labor for capital until:

$$\frac{\text{MPP}_L}{W} = \frac{\text{MPP}_K}{R}$$

where MPP_K is the marginal physical product of capital.

> According to the least-cost rule, the price-taking firm is producing at minimum cost only if the marginal physical products per dollar of the various factors are equal.

THE MARGINAL PRODUCTIVITY THEORY OF INCOME DISTRIBUTION

Economists distinguish between the **functional distribution of income** and the **personal distribution of income,** both of which are determined in the factor market.

The **functional distribution of income** is the distribution of income among the four broad classes of productive factors—land, labor, capital, and entrepreneurship.

The **personal distribution of income** is the distribution of income among households, or how much income one family earns from the factors of production it owns relative to other families.

The profit-maximizing and least-cost rules resolve the *how* problem in economics. They show how firms go about combining inputs to produce output. These same rules also resolve the *for whom* problem. Given the prices of the factors of production, what people earn depends on the resources they own.

FIGURE 5
Determination of the Market Price (Wage) of Truck Drivers in a Competitive Market

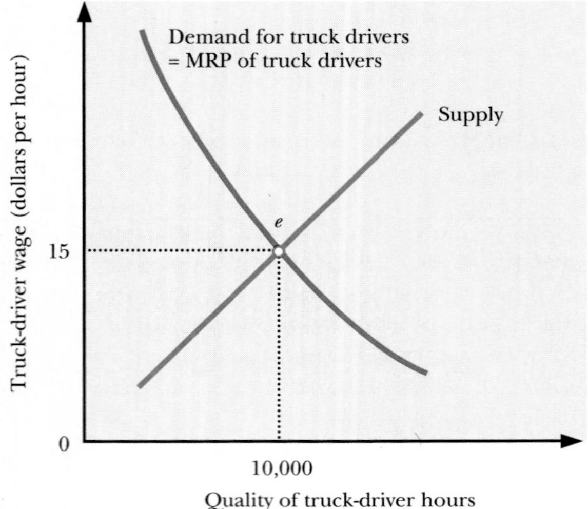

The market supply curve of truck drivers is upward sloping, which indicates that truck drivers are prepared to work more hours at high wages than at low wages. The market demand curve is derived from the MRP curve of truck drivers across several industries. Equilibrium is achieved at point *e*, where the supply of truck drivers equals the quantity demanded. At the equilibrium wage of $15, there are 10,000 labor hours used in the various industries using truck drivers.

Factors of production, unless they are highly specialized (such as 7-foot basketball players), are demanded by many firms and by many industries. For example, the market demand for truck drivers will come from a wide cross section of American industry: The steel industry, retailers, the moving industry, and the local florist will all have a derived demand for truck drivers. The demand for urban land will also come from a broad cross section of American industry: Heavy industry requires land for its plant sites; motel chains require land for their motels; home builders require land to develop subdivisions. Similarly, the demand for capital goods will come from a cross section of American industry.

How the price (wage) of truck drivers is determined is shown in Figure 5. The wage rate of truck drivers reflects two forces: the derived demand for truck drivers as represented by their marginal revenue product and the supply of truck drivers. At equilibrium (point *e*), quantity supplied and quantity demanded will be equal and the wage will equal the marginal revenue product. In other words, truck drivers will be paid their marginal revenue product. The same is true of the other factors of production, as the **marginal productivity theory of income distribution** states.

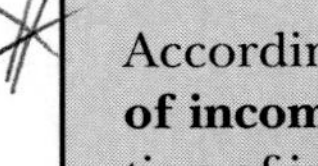

According to the **marginal productivity theory of income distribution,** the functional distribution of income between land, labor, and capital is determined by the relative marginal revenue products of the different factors of production. The price of each factor will equal the marginal revenue product of that factor.

The reasons why some factors have high MRPs and others low MRPs will be discussed later in this chapter.

Marginal Productivity and Efficiency

The preceding chapters on product markets examined the relative efficiency of different market structures, particularly perfect competition and monopoly. It was argued that monopoly is inefficient because it creates contrived scarcity by failing to expand output to the point where price (the measure of the marginal benefit to society) and marginal cost (the measure of the extra cost to society) are equal.

If a firm has monopoly power in the product market, $P >$ MR. Although the monopolistic firm will pay each input its marginal revenue product, which will equal MR × MPP, the factor is actually worth P × MPP to society because each unit of MPP is valued at P. Because MR × MPP is less than P × MPP, the monopolist is paying less for factors than what they are worth to society.

Figure 6 illustrates a monopolist in the product market who is a price taker in the factor market. The curve P × MPP shows the marginal benefits to society of an additional unit of the factor. The MRP curve shows the marginal benefit to the monopolist of hiring an additional unit of the factor. When the monopolist operates at point a rather than at point b, the monopolist stops hiring workers short of their marginal worth to society (or pays them less than they are worth to society, as represented by point c). Society loses the blue area abc.

FIGURE 6
The Monopolist Hires Too Few Inputs

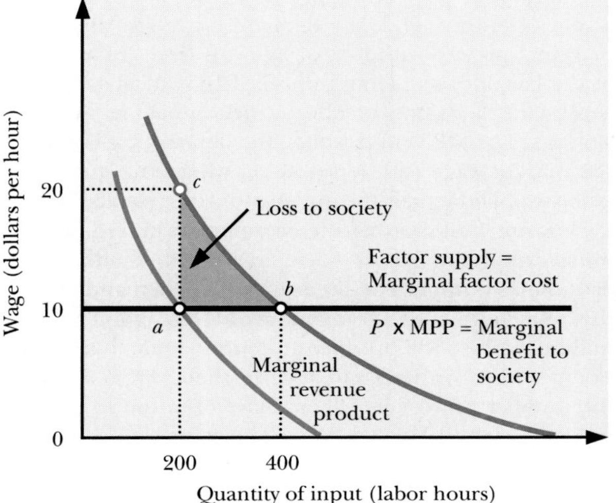

The firm is a monopolist in the product market and a price taker in the factor market. The value of the marginal product to society is P × MPP (the marginal benefit to society), and the marginal benefit to the monopolist is its marginal revenue product. If the wage rate is \$10, the monopolist employs 200 labor hours because at that point marginal revenue product equals the wage.

If the firm is perfectly competitive in the product market, the marginal revenue product of a factor equals the marginal benefit of the factor to society. Because price equals marginal revenue in a competitive firm, the firm will hire factors until the point at which P × MPP equals the factor's price. Each factor adds a net marginal benefit to society equal to the factor's market price. This market price reflects its opportunity cost to society.

Marginal Productivity and Factor Incomes

The marginal productivity theory of income distribution suggests that a productive factor is usually paid its marginal revenue product. The marginal revenue product of one factor depends upon the quantity and quality of cooperating factors. For example, two textile workers, one in the United States and the other in India, may be equally skilled and diligent, but one works with a \$50 sewing machine while the other works with a \$100,000 advanced knitting machine. The New England farmer may be just as skilled as the Kansas farmer but may have a low MRP because of the low quality of the land. Marginal revenue product also depends upon the supplies of factors. The supply of residential land is quite limited in Hawaii but abundant in Iowa. The equilibrium MRP of land is, therefore, higher in Hawaii. If women are limited to employment opportunities in only a few professions, they will overcrowd these professions and drive down the MRP and, thus, wages. Finally, marginal revenue product, as stated earlier, depends upon the demand for the product being produced. If product demand falls, so will the factor's MRP.

The marginal productivity theory of income distribution states that a competitively determined factor price reflects the factor's marginal revenue product. Marginal revenue product is the result of: (1) the relative supplies of the different factors, (2) the quantity and quality of cooperating factors, and (3) the market demands for the goods the factors produce.

The Aggregate Production Function

The marginal productivity theory of income distribution has both wide and narrow applications. In its narrow form, the theory can explain why one person earns more than another or why one plot of land rents for more than another. The aggregate economy is the summation of all the participants in the economy; therefore, it is possible to talk about average wages, average land-rental rates, and average interest rates. The relationship between the total inputs used by an economy and the total amount of goods and services produced by an economy can be expressed by an **aggregate production function.**

> The **aggregate production function** shows the relationship between the total output produced by the economy and the total labor, capital, and land inputs used by the economy.

The aggregate production function is a simplified representation of the economy, but it is a useful tool for investigating the functional distribution of income among the broad factors of production—land, labor, and capital. (See Figure 7.)

To simplify the analysis, assume the economy produces only one product—corn—and that it is perfectly competitive in all markets. The demand curve for labor is then the marginal physical product of labor for the entire economy. If we assume that the price of a bushel of corn is $1, then the demand curve for labor measures both the marginal physical product and marginal revenue product for the entire economy. The supply of labor is assumed to be fixed at 50 million workers. The equilibrium wage rate is w_O, which brings about a quantity of labor demanded of 50 million workers (the quantity supplied).

The total output of the economy is the area under the demand curve in Figure 7, because each point on the curve shows the additional corn produced by the last worker. (The demand curve shows the MPP at each level of labor input. The MPPs for each successive unit of labor can be added together to yield total output. For 50 million workers, total output is the entire orange area in Figure 7.) Of this total output, labor will receive the area of the dark orange rectangle labeled *Wages*. The nonlabor factors, such as capital and land, will receive the area of the light orange triangle labeled *Rents*. Each worker is paid the dollar value of the marginal physical product of the 50-millionth unit rather than the dollar value of earlier units that have larger MPPs (as measured by the height of the demand curve).

FIGURE 7
The Aggregate Production Function and the Functional Distribution of Income

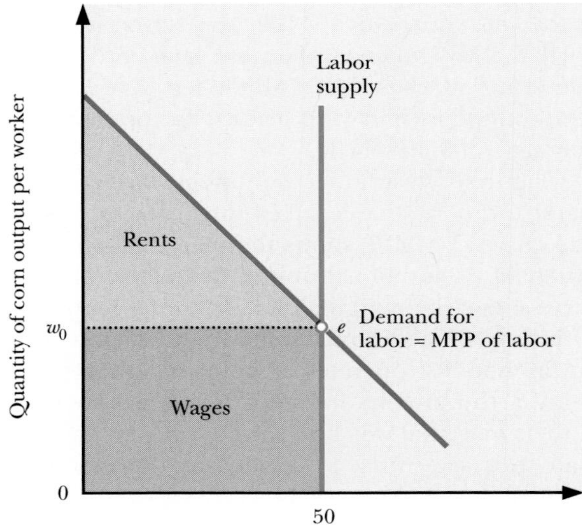

This figure represents the aggregate production function of an entire economy. The economy produces a generalized physical output at a product price of $1. All markets are assumed to be perfectly competitive. Because the price of a unit of output is $1, the demand curve for labor is the marginal physical product of labor; it declines according to the law of diminishing returns. The vertical supply line represents the supply of labor, which is fixed at 50 million workers. The MPP curve will be the demand for labor, and the market wage will be set at w_O where the quantity of labor supplied equals the quantity of labor demanded.

How much output has the economy produced and how much will go to labor? Each unit of labor adds to the economy's output. The area under the demand curve is the total output of the economy at that point. The 50 million workers will produce an output equal to the entire orange area. Workers will receive their wage, w_O, times the number of workers. Their share of output is the dark orange rectangle labeled *Wages*. The cooperating nonlabor factors (land and capital) will get what is left over, or the light orange triangle labeled *Rents*.

The marginal productivity theory states that each factor of production will be paid its marginal revenue product. If the world is sufficiently competitive, the theory suggests that each factor of production will be paid the dollar value of its marginal physical product. (See Example 4.)

EXAMPLE 4 Is the Marginal Productivity Theory Realistic?

The accompanying table shows the actual distribution of earnings between labor and capital in the American private business sector from 1948 to 1990. According to this table, the share of labor has remained fairly constant at around 65 percent of earnings (ranging from a low of 61 percent to a high of about 66 percent), and the share of capital has ranged from 34 percent to 39 percent of total income.

Is the marginal productivity theory consistent with these facts? Why should the labor share be nearly constant over this 42-year period? In fact, labor's share has been nearly constant since 1929. Between 1929 and 1990, the economy's capital stock more than doubled, while the number of hours worked increased only 20 percent. Under these conditions, why didn't the share of capital increase?

The marginal productivity theory of income distribution provides an explanation. Because the cooperating factor to labor—capital—has been increasing relative to labor, we would expect the marginal physical product of labor to rise relative to the marginal physical product of capital. This rise in the MPP of labor, according to marginal productivity theory, would be reflected in an increase in the price of labor relative to the price of capital. Indeed, the price of labor (relative to capital) did rise substantially over this period. The fact that the slower growth of labor was, therefore, offset by the increase in its relative price explains the constant shares of labor and capital.

Percentage Distribution of Earnings in the U.S. Private Business Sector, 1948–1990

Year	Labor	Capital
1948	62.2	37.8
1950	61.3	38.7
1955	63.3	36.7
1960	63.6	36.4
1965	60.9	39.1
1970	65.8	34.2
1975	63.8	36.2
1980	65.5	34.5
1985	63.2	36.8
1990	63.8	37.0

Source: U.S. Department of Labor, Bureau of Labor Statistics, *Trends in Multifactor Productivity, 1948–81,* Bulletin 2178, September 1983, 20. 1982–1990 data estimated by authors.

Source: Edward Denison, *Accounting for Economic Growth in the United States,* 1929–1969 (Washington, D.C.: The Brookings Institution, 1974), 32, 54.

While this chapter presented an overview of how factor markets work, it is important to note that each market has its own unique features. In the labor market, the supply of labor is determined by how individuals choose among market work, work in the home, and leisure. These are choices not faced by the owners of capital and land. Moreover, the labor market is affected by the organization of workers into unions and by the effect of education and training on labor's marginal physical product. In the capital market, buyers of capital receive the benefits of capital over a long period of time; suppliers of capital must choose between consumption today and more consumption tomorrow. The market for land is characterized by the relatively fixed supply of land.

The next three chapters will examine each factor market in detail, building upon the general theoretical framework established in this chapter.

SUMMARY

1. Firms sell their output in the product market, and they buy inputs to produce output in the factor market. Marginal factor cost (MFC) is the extra cost of hiring one more unit of the factor of production. A price-searching firm in the factor market will have a marginal factor cost that is greater than price. A price taker in the input market will have a marginal factor cost equal to the price of the input.

2. The firm's demand for a factor of production will depend upon the demand for the product being produced and upon the factor's productivity. The marginal physical product (MPP) of a factor of production is the increase in output that results from increasing the factor by one unit, other things being equal. The demand for a factor of production is a derived demand because it depends on the demand for the goods and services the factor helps produce. Marginal revenue product (MRP) is the increase in revenue brought about by hiring one more unit of the factor of production.

3. Profit-maximizing firms will observe the following rule in factor markets: Factors of production will be hired to the point where MFC = MRP. The MFC = MRP rule in the factor market is equivalent to the MR = MC rule in the product market. If firms are perfectly competitive in the factor market, they will hire the various factors of production to the point where the MRP of each factor equals its price.

4. The least-cost rule for firms is to hire factors of production so that MPP per dollar of one factor equals the MPP per dollar of any other factor.

5. The marginal productivity theory of income distribution helps to explain the functional distribution of income (among the three classes of production factors) and the personal distribution of income (among households).

KEY TERMS

price taker
price searcher
monopsony
marginal factor cost (MFC)
derived demand
marginal revenue product (MRP)
functional distribution of income
personal distribution of income
marginal productivity theory of income distribution
aggregate production function

QUESTIONS AND PROBLEMS

1. The MPP of a 100th worker is 33 units of output. The marginal revenue of the firm for the corresponding level of output is $2, the price of the product is $3, and the wage rate is $99.
   a. Is the firm maximizing its profit?
   b. What would the wage rate have to be for 100 workers to maximize profit?
2. Explain how workers in Country X could earn $10 per hour while workers in the same industry in Country Y earn only $0.50 per hour. Do the higher wages in Country X mean that workers in this country work harder than those in Country Y?
3. The last unit of land rented by a farmer costs $100 and increases output by 1000 bushels. The last unit of capital costs $1000 to rent and increases output by 20,000 bushels. Is this farmer minimizing costs? If not, what should he or she do?
4. In Russian industry, capital has been growing about 10 times as fast as labor. What would you expect to happen to the marginal physical product of capital?
5. Evaluate the following statement: "Income distribution as explained by the marginal productivity theory is entirely fair. After all, people are simply getting back what they personally have contributed to society."
6. A manufacturing plant in a small town accounts for 85 percent of employment in the town. The plant receives a large contract and decides to expand its work force by 40 percent. What will be the relationship between marginal factor cost and the wage rate in this case? Construct a graph to illustrate your answer.
7. One type of equipment—such as specialized oil-drilling equipment—can be used only in one particular industry. Another type—such as general-purpose lathes—can be used in a wide variety of industries. How would the amount of monopsony differ for these two types of equipment?
8. Complete Table A (top next page) by filling in columns 4 and 5.
   a. Is the firm in Table A a price searcher or a price taker in the product market?
   b. If the wage rate is $55, how many units of labor should the firm hire?
9. Assume that the MPP of a first worker is 20 units of output, that the MPP of a second worker is 30 units, that the MPP of a third worker is 20 units, and that the MPP of a fourth worker is 15 units. If four workers are hired, how many units of output are produced?
10. A Ph.D. engineer costs a firm $100,000 a year; an engineer with a B.A. degree costs a firm only $50,000 a year. What information is required to determine the firm's optimal decision?

TABLE A

Labor (number of workers), L (1)	Units of Output, Q (2)	Price, P (3)	Units of Marginal Physical Product, MPP (4)	Marginal Revenue Product, MRP (5)
0	0	$8		
1	10	8		
2	17	8		
3	23	8		
4	28	8		

SUGGESTED READINGS

Alchien, Armen, and Harold Demsetz. "Production, Information Costs, and Economic Organization." *American Economic Review* 62 (December 1972): 777–95.

Kohler, Heinz. *Intermediate Microeconomics: Theory and Applications,* 3rd ed. New York: HarperCollins, 1990.

North, Douglas C., and Roger LeRoy Miller. *The Economics of Public Issues,* 8th ed. New York: HarperCollins, 1990, chap. 3.

Stigler, George. *The Theory of Price,* 4th ed. New York: Macmillan, 1987, chap. 15.

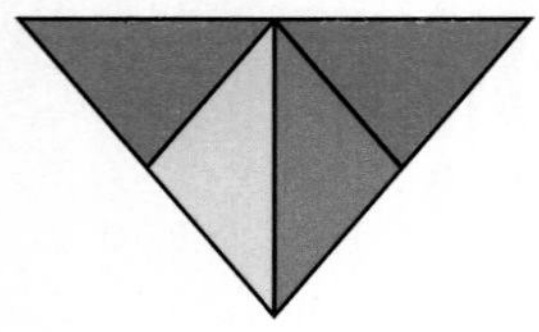

37

Labor Markets

CHAPTER INSIGHT

In 1910, the 7-year-old Ford Motor Company moved into a new plant in Highland Park, Michigan, that boasted the world's first automobile assembly line. This new factory used the "work-in-motion" concept, in which individual workers repeated one or two steps over and over while rope cables towed partly assembled cars from one worker to the next, to improve the rate of production from 15 cars per day to one car every 10 seconds.

On January 5, 1914, Henry Ford announced he would pay his workers the (then) incredible sum of $5 per day. Just a few years before, auto workers had been paid only $0.15 per day. Despite paying workers the outrageous daily wage of $5, Ford was able to sell cars to a mass market and achieve the high levels of profits that made him one of the richest men of his day.

Ford understood how the labor market worked. By investing in productivity, he succeeded where others had failed. This chapter examines the labor market: how wages are determined, why some people earn more than others, why some jobs pay more than others, why wages and productivity are positively related, and why some people remain out of the labor force. It also explains how supply, demand, and market equilibrium are determined in the labor market and examines alternative uses of time for the owners of labor services.

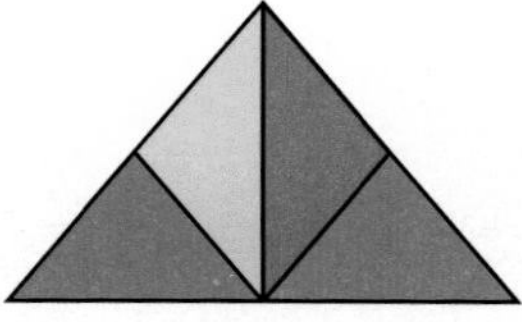

WHY LABOR IS DIFFERENT FROM OTHER FACTORS OF PRODUCTION

The preceding chapter explained how factor markets work. It gave general rules for the hiring of land, labor, and capital inputs. Four special features differentiate the labor market from other factor markets:

1. A person cannot be bought like an acre of land or a piece of equipment; slavery is against the law. Land and capital assets can be bought and sold, but the owner of labor can only rent out his or her services. Professional athletes may be under contract for a number of years; many workers in Japan appear to have lifetime labor contracts. But professional athletes and Japanese workers can be used only for the specific tasks designated in the contract; a slave, a piece of land, or a machine can be used for most anything the owner wants.

2. Owners of labor services can use their resources for useful alternatives to labor service. If land and machines are not put to productive use, they stand idle, and the owners do not normally benefit. When people are not engaged in the labor market, they can spend time in domestic or leisure activities.

3. Land and capital do not care about the use to which they are put. People have preferences for particular types of work in particular locations.

4. Labor unions (to be discussed in the next chapter) also differentiate labor from the other factors of production. By joining a *labor union,* an organization that seeks to affect the conditions of work and pay of the workers it represents, a worker can help to determine the nature of the labor market.

Labor Facts and Trends

A useful economic analysis of the labor market must be able to explain observed trends and patterns, the most important of which include the following:

1. *The average number of hours worked per week have declined over the long run.* In 1914, workers in manufacturing worked an average of 49.4 hours per week (see Table 1). By 1992, this number had fallen to 41 hours per week.

2. *Real wages have risen over the long run.* After adjustment for inflation, the real hourly wage rate of American manufacturing workers increased almost four times between 1914 and 1991 (see Table 1). In other words, an hour of work in 1991 bought nearly four times the quantity of goods and services as an hour of work in 1914.

3. *The participation rate of American women in the labor force has risen dramatically over the long run.* The *female labor-force participation rate* is the ratio of women 16 years or older in the labor force to the total number of woman 16 years or older. Since 1914, the female labor-force participation rate has risen from 23 percent to 58 percent. (See Table 1.)

4. *Some people earn more than others.* Coal miners earn about $14 per hour on average while textile workers earn only about $7 per hour. The president of a large corporation may earn $1 million per year, a surgeon may earn $250,000 per year, a school teacher may earn $20,000 per year, and a roustabout on an offshore drilling rig may earn $45,000 per year.

5. *Despite the rising trend, real wages fall during some periods. Real hourly wages fell from 1975 to 1991.* Table 1 shows that real hourly wages rose by over 400 percent from 1914 to 1975, but then fell by about 9 percent from 1975 to 1991.

The Working of the Labor Market

A market is an arrangement that allows buyers and sellers of a particular good or service to come together for the purpose of making transactions. The **labor market** brings together buyers and sellers of labor. Its distinguishing feature is that labor services, rather than inanimate goods and services, are being bought and sold.

> A **labor market** is an arrangement that brings together buyers and sellers of labor services to agree on pay and working conditions.

Labor markets differ in many ways. They may be national or local in scope. There are national and even international labor markets for the services of some engineers, academics, airline pilots, and upper-level executives, whereas the services of sales clerks, teenage employees, unskilled workers, and sanitation workers are bought and sold only in local markets.

Labor markets can also vary in their formality and structure. Some are highly informal. Job openings are announced by notices posted at the factory

TABLE 1
Facts About the Labor Market, 1914–1991

Year	Average Hours Worked per Week in Manufacturing (1)	Index of Hourly Earnings in Manufacturing, 1914 = 100 (adjusted for inflation) (2)	Female Labor-Force Participation Rate (3)
1914	49.4	100	22.8(1910)
1930	42.1	151	24.8
1940	38.1	214	27.4
1950	40.5	273	31.4
1960	39.7	348	34.8
1970	39.8	396	42.6
1975	39.4	408	45.9
1980	39.7	403	51.5
1991	41.0	372	57.5

Sources: Hours and real wages are from Ronald Ehrenberg and Robert Smith, *Modern Labor Economics: Theory and Public Policy* (New York: HarperCollins, 1991), Table 2.4. The female participation rate data are from *Historical Statistics of the United States: Colonial Times to the Present,* series D29-41, 133; and from *Statistical Abstract of the United States.* Figures are updated using the *Survey of Current Business.*

gate, "help wanted" ads in the local newspaper, or word of mouth. Other labor markets fill positions according to a well-defined set of rules. Civil service jobs are regulated by detailed legislation and rules, and in unionized industries, rules governing hiring and firing are spelled out in considerable detail.

Most labor arrangements are governed by contracts between the employer and employee. Labor contracts, which spell out conditions of work and pay, can be either formal (explicit) or implicit. An explicit contract specifies the wage rate, the term of employment, and the conditions under which the contract can be terminated. A formal union contract, for example, spells out base pay, overtime rates, bonuses, the length of the contract, work rules (which tasks particular employees can and cannot perform), and the order in which employees are to be laid off in the case of cutbacks. Other labor contracts are implicit. Although not formally spelled out in any contract, it may be understood between worker and employer that workers are to receive generous wages when jobs exist but are to be laid off when business is bad. It is also understood that laid-off workers will not seek other jobs during short layoffs in return for the understanding that they will be rehired over other workers when business improves.

The term *labor market* encompasses a wide range of market behavior. Labor markets can be differentiated by the ability of hiring firms to affect wage rates. If the buyer of a labor service must pay the wage rate dictated by the market regardless of how much labor is hired, the buyer is a *price taker.* If the buyer of a labor service is large enough to raise the wage rate by buying more, and lower it by buying less of a labor service, this buyer is a *price searcher* and has monopsonistic power in the labor market. If the seller of a labor service must accept the market wage as given, the seller is a perfectly competitive seller of labor services. If the seller affects wage rates by selling more or less of the labor service, the seller has monopoly power in the labor market.

The discussion in this chapter deals only with perfectly competitive buyers of labor. As the preceding chapter argued, competition in the labor market (and other factor markets) is more common than competition in the product market. (The next chapter on labor unions will analyze the case of labor monopsony.)

Leisure and Household Production

Individuals have options other than work in the labor force. They may also choose **household production** or **leisure.** These other options affect the total supply of labor to the economy.

> **Household production** is work in the home, including such activities as meal preparation, do-it-yourself repair, childrearing, and cleaning.
>
> **Leisure** is time spent in any activity other than work in the labor force or work in the home.

What determines how individuals allocate their time among these three activities? The theory of the allocation of time developed by economists Gary Becker, Jacob Mincer, Yoram Ben Porath, and others is designed to analyze this choice in the framework of rational economic decision making.

FIGURE 1
The Backward-Bending Labor Supply Curve

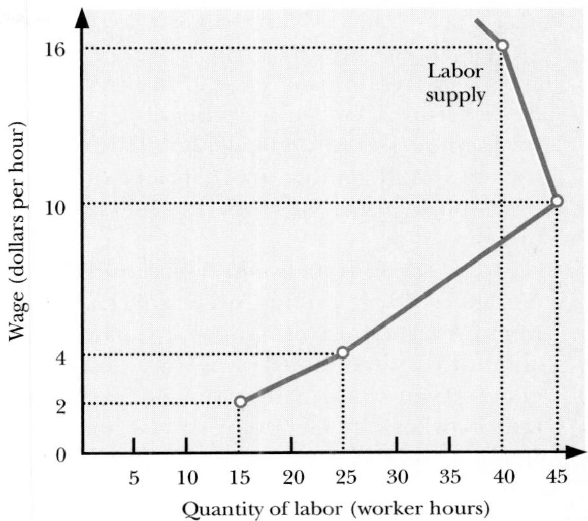

The labor supply curve is upward sloping until a wage of $10 per hour is reached. Below $10, the substitution effect of higher wages dominates the income effect of higher wages. At wage rates above $10, the quantity of labor supplied falls as the wage rate increases because the income effect dominates the substitution effect.

Choosing Labor or Leisure

The opportunity cost of leisure is the income (or household production) that must be given up to enjoy it. The opportunity cost of leisure therefore rises when the price of market work rises. If real wages have risen over time, one would expect the average quantity of market work that each person performs to have increased over time. Table 1, however, shows that since 1914 real wages have in fact risen, while average hours worked per week have declined substantially.

The evidence in Table 1 suggests that the labor supply curve relating wages and hours worked per person is *backward bending* (it has a section with a negative slope), as shown in Figure 1.

The chapter on demand and utility identified two effects of a price change on the consumption of goods: the *income effect* (the impact of the change in real income that results from a price change) and the *substitution effect* (the substitution of cheaper goods for more expensive goods that result from a price change).

The increase in wages (or the "price" of leisure) also results in income and substitution effects. The increase in wages raises the relative price of leisure and motivates individuals to substitute other things—in this case, market work—for leisure, thereby discouraging leisure. On the other hand, the increase in wages increases income (an income effect), making more income available for leisure. Typically, as income rises, more consumption of a good occurs—if the good is a *normal good* (a good whose demand increases as income rises). If the substitution effect of a wage increase discourages leisure and the income effect of a wage increase encourages leisure, the overall effect depends upon which effect is stronger.

In Figure 1, when the wage is a low $2 per hour and only 15 hours are worked per week, a dollar increase in wages adds up to only an additional $15 per week; the income effect is weak. When wages are $4 per hour and 25 hours are worked per week, a dollar increase in wages is like an extra $25 per week; the income effect is stronger. When wages are $10 per hour and 45 hours are worked per week, the income effect is even stronger. In Figure 1, the income effect dominates the substitution effect after wages reach $10 per hour. Further increases in wages cause hours worked per person to decline, as shown

EXAMPLE 1 Labor versus Leisure in Germany and Japan

The more hours you work, the fewer hours you have for leisure. As wages increase, workers can afford to "buy" more leisure. The backward-bending labor supply suggests that affluent workers (and affluent societies) will choose more hours of leisure over more hours of work as their earnings increase.

The choices between labor and leisure are affected by earnings, preferences, and customs. Workers in Germany and Japan receive about the same hourly earnings, but workers in Japan work many more hours per year than workers in Germany. In Germany, for example, a 35-hour work week is common for manufacturing workers; beginning workers receive two weeks or more paid vacation per year; and experienced workers receive one month or more paid vacation per year. Moreover, Germany has more than 20 paid official holidays per year.

In sharp contrast, Japanese manufacturing workers work a standard 40 hours per week and typically work overtime without extra pay. Managers are expected to work 12 or more hours per day. Japan has 13 paid official holidays per year, and beginning Japanese workers receive less than one week paid vacation, while experienced workers receive no more than two weeks per year.

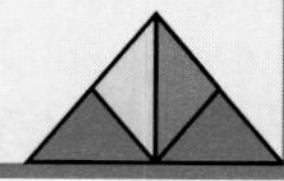

by the backward-bending section of the labor supply curve.

The data presented in Table 1 suggest that in the long run the income effect is stronger than the substitution effect, which explains why average hours worked per week have been dropping despite rising real wages. The data are generally consistent with a backward-bending labor supply curve.

Over the long run, mechanization has raised labor productivity, which translates into higher real wages. Higher real earnings enable people to opt for more leisure and fewer hours worked. The ultimate payoff of mechanization is that it has enabled people to have more leisure while still earning high incomes. Societies choose between labor and leisure in different ways. (See Example 1.)

Wages and Household Production

The social roles of men and women have changed dramatically over the past half-century. High divorce rates, a larger number of one-parent families, an increase in the number of part-time jobs, the growth of service and sales employment, and the enforcement of antidiscrimination legislation help explain the rising female labor-force participation rate reported in Table 1.

Economic theory provides another plausible explanation. Whether people work in the labor force or in household production depends in part upon the value of their household production relative to the wage they could earn in market employment. If work in the home (childrearing, cleaning, food preparation) is worth, say $10 per hour, and the market wage a woman could earn in the labor market is $8 per hour, she would not enter the labor force. If however, the market wages of women rise more rapidly than the value of household production, one would expect women to enter the labor force. The substantial rise in the real wages of women in recent decades is the explanation cited by some economists for the rise in the labor-force participation rates of women.

THE DEMAND FOR A SINGLE GRADE OF LABOR

The wage rate for a particular type of labor is determined in the labor market for that type of labor. The equilibrium wage rate and the quantity of labor exchanged are determined by the forces of demand for and supply of that grade of labor, just as product price and quantity are determined by supply and demand.

The Firm's Demand for Labor

How does a firm decide how much labor of a single grade to hire at different wage rates? According to the preceding chapter, profit-maximizing firms hire factors up to the point where the marginal factor cost (MFC) equals the marginal revenue product (MRP) of the factor. The firm will therefore continue to hire labor as long as the marginal revenue product of the additional worker exceeds that worker's marginal factor cost. The firm in Figure 2 is perfectly competitive in the computer programmer market (it must take the market wage as given), and its marginal factor cost is the market wage rate. This firm can hire all the labor it wants at the prevailing market wage rate. Its labor supply schedule is a horizontal line (perfectly elastic) at the market wage.

FIGURE 2
The Firm's Demand for Computer Programmers

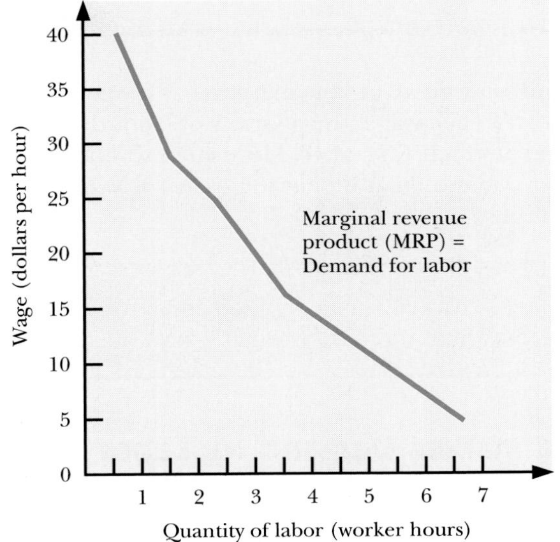

The labor demand curve shows the marginal revenue product of different quantities of labor hours. This firm is competitive in both the labor market and the product market. The firm uses 4 programmer hours when the wage rate is $16 per hour (the marginal revenue product of the fourth hour is equal to the market wage of $16 per hour). If the market wage rate rises to $28 per hour, the $16 marginal revenue product of the fourth worker hour is well below the wage rate. The firm would not wish to employ 4 hours at a wage of $28 but would employ only 2 programmer hours because the marginal revenue product of the second hour equals $28.

TABLE 2
The Demand for Computer Programmers

Labor Input (hours) (1)	Quantity of Output (lines programmed) (2)	Marginal Physical Product (lines), MPP (3)	Marginal Revenue Product, MRP = $P \times$ MPP (4)
0	0		
		20	$40
1	20		
		14	28
2	34		
		12	24
3	46		
		8	16
4	54		
		6	12
5	60		
		4	8
6	64		
		2	4
7	66		

The price of this firm's output is $2 per line. Its capital input is fixed in the short run. Hence, MRP = MPP × $2. The demand schedule is the marginal revenue product schedule in column 4.

Columns 1 and 2 of Table 2 show the amounts of output associated with various amounts of labor input for this firm. Columns 3 and 4 give the marginal physical product and marginal revenue product for each level of input. The firm's product sells for $2 per program line, and the capital input is fixed in the short run. With capital input fixed, the law of diminishing returns applies to the labor input; MPP and MRP decline. Figure 2 graphs the data from columns 1 and 4 of Table 2.

The firm is a price taker in the product market as well as in the factor market; therefore, its marginal revenue product equals its product price, *P*, times

EXAMPLE 2 Marginal Revenue Product and Baseball Players

The proposition that a factor of production will be paid its marginal revenue product is difficult to test empirically but is supported by the behavior of the market for star baseball players. Marginal productivity theory teaches that firms will hire factors of production as long as the extra revenue (the MRP) of the factor is not lower than the wage. The MRP of an extra star player on a team that already has a large number of star players on its roster is likely to be lower than on a team with few star players. If the star player is the first star to be added to a roster, the MRP of that player would be very large, and the team's owners should be willing to pay a high salary to that player. Teams with few star players are therefore likely to win the bidding war for star players. In 1975, a National Labor Relations Board ruling allowed certain players for the first time to sell their services to any team as free agents. Through 1990, of the first 69 free agents signed, 45 were signed by teams that had poorer records than the teams the players left. This pattern is exactly what the marginal productivity theory predicts.

Source: Ronald G. Ehrenberg and Robert S. Smith, *Modern Labor Economics* (New York: HarperCollins, 1991), 69–70.

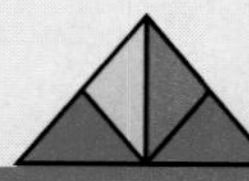

labor's marginal physical product (MPP). As the preceding chapter demonstrated, the firm will demand the quantity of labor at which $W =$ MRP.

When the market wage is $28 per hour, the firm will demand that quantity of labor at which MRP is $28. Table 2 shows that the MRP of the second programmer hour is $28; therefore, the firm will demand 2 programmer hours. If the market wage falls to $16 per hour, the firm will no longer demand only 2 programmer hours because $28 (the MRP of the second hour) is greater than $16 (the wage being paid), and the firm is paying for the last hour a wage that is less than the hour's contribution to the firm's revenue. The situation offers a profit opportunity to the firm; it reacts by hiring more programmer hours. As the firm increases employment, MRP falls because of the law of diminishing returns. The firm continues to increase labor until the last hour's MRP just equals the market wage of $16. At the smaller $16 wage, the firm would use 4 programmer hours because the MRP of the fourth hour is $16. If the market wage had risen (instead of fallen), the firm would have reacted by hiring less labor. The quantity of labor demanded varies inversely with the wage rate, which can be seen by comparing columns 1 and 4 or by observing the downward-sloping shape of the demand curve in Figure 2. The demand curve is nothing more than the marginal revenue product curve. At each wage, the quantity of labor demanded is that at which $W =$ MRP. More labor will be hired at lower wages than at higher wages, *ceteris paribus.* (See Example 2.)

> The individual firm's demand curve for labor is its marginal revenue product curve.

The Market Demand for Labor

If 400 firms are demanding computer programmers, the market demand for computer programmers is the sum of the demand of all 400 firms that purchase labor of that grade. The market demand curve shows how the total quantity of labor demanded varies as the wage changes.

The market demand curve for labor is a *derived demand curve,* reflecting the demand for the product that that particular grade of labor produces.

A typical market demand curve for labor is given in Figure 3. This curve shows the quantities of a single grade of labor demanded by all 400 employers of that type of labor at different wage rates. Because the labor demand curves of individual firms are

FIGURE 3
The Market Demand for Computer Programmers

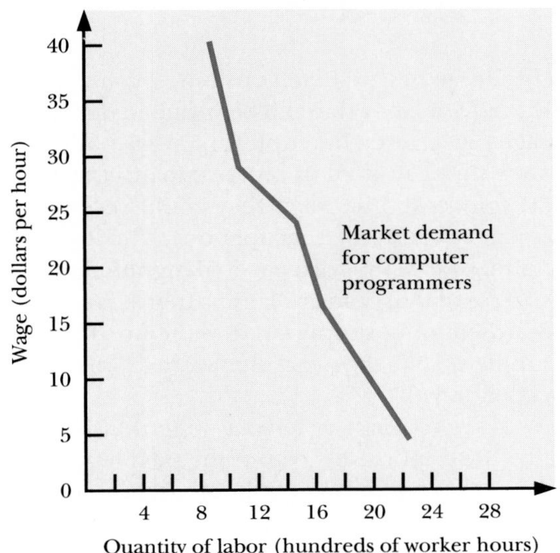

The market labor demand curve for programmers indicates the number of programmer hours that would be demanded by all firms that hire programmers at different wage rates. Because the demand curves of each firm are negatively sloped, the market labor demand curve is also negatively sloped.

negatively sloped, the market demand curve will be negatively sloped as well.[1]

Elasticity of Demand for Labor

Just as the price elasticity of product demand curves reflects the responsiveness of quantity demanded to changes in product prices, so the price elasticity of labor demand curves reflects the responsiveness of the quantity of labor demanded to changes in the wage rate.[2]

Three (major) factors determine the elasticity of demand for labor of a single grade: the price elasticity for the good that labor helps produce, the substitutability of other factors, and the ratio of labor costs to total costs.

1. *The derived demand for labor will be more elastic as the demand for the product that labor produces becomes more price elastic.* When labor costs rise, the cost of producing the product increases. Therefore, an increase in the wage rate is passed on in the form of a higher product price. When price elasticity is high, the quantity of the product demanded drops sharply with each price increase, and hence the quantity demanded of labor and other factors used in its production drops sharply. For example, the price elasticity of demand for meat cutters by one supermarket will be higher than the price elasticity of demand for all meat cutters, simply because the price elasticity of demand for Supermarket A's beef will be higher than for beef in general.
2. *The derived demand for labor will be more elastic as it becomes easier to substitute other productive factors for labor.* The more substitutes there are for anything, the greater the elasticity of demand. If machines that can do the work of people become available, the demand for workers will become more price elastic. For example, retail trade generally has a more elastic demand for labor than manufacturing. A retail store may be able to use fewer sales clerks, but a production plant may still have to have one worker at each station.
3. *The derived demand for labor will be more elastic as the ratio of labor costs to total costs increases.* If costs for labor of a particular grade are a large fraction of total costs, wage increases will be passed on to product buyers in the form of higher prices. The higher prices will cause a larger decline in the quantity demanded of output—and hence of labor—than they would if labor were a small fraction of costs.

[1]The market demand curve is *not* just the horizontal sum of all the individual demand curves for labor. The individual-firm demand curves for labor can hold product prices constant, but, as all the firms expand output, the fall in product prices affects the marginal revenue product of each of the individual firms. It is still true that at any given wage rate, the market demand is the sum of all the individual-firm demands in terms of quantity demanded. In terms of demand schedule, the market demand curve for labor will be steeper than the simple horizontal sum of the individual demand curves because the product price must fall to sell additional industry output.

[2]The *elasticity of demand for labor* is the percentage change in the quantity demanded of labor divided by the percentage change in the wage rate. If this ratio is greater than unity, demand is elastic. If it equals 1, demand is unitary elastic. If it is less than 1, demand is inelastic.

Factors That Shift the Labor Demand Curve

In addition to wages, there are four factors that affect the demand curve for labor. These factors tend to shift the demand curve for labor to the right (that is, to increase demand), *ceteris paribus.*

1. Labor demand increases when the demand for the final product produced by that grade of labor increases, *ceteris paribus.* If the demand for a product increases, the price of the product will also increase, *ceteris paribus.* This price increase will raise the marginal revenue product of labor, shifting the demand curve to the right.
2. Labor demand increases when the price of a substitute factor of production increases, *ceteris paribus.* Automated equipment may be substituted for bank tellers; sophisticated word-processing equipment may be substituted for secretaries; skilled labor may be substituted for unskilled labor; chemical fertilizers may be substituted for farm workers. If the prices of substitute factors increase, firms will increase their demand for labor.
3. Labor demand increases when the price of a complementary factor of production decreases, *ceteris paribus.* Complementary factors are those used in combination with the factor in question. Materials such as steel, aluminum, and plastics are used in combination with labor to make automobiles, for example. If the prices of these materials fall, the demand for labor will rise.
4. Labor demand increases when the productivity of labor increases, *ceteris paribus.* When the marginal physical product of labor rises at each level of labor input, the marginal revenue product of (and therefore the demand for) labor rises. Labor productivity and real wages have a positive relationship because rising labor productivity increases the demand for labor, thereby raising wages. Competitive industries will pay a real wage (W/P) that equals the marginal physical product of labor (competitive firms hire to the point where $W = P \times \text{MPP}$). Accordingly, real wages rise when the marginal physical product of labor rises. The increase in real wages since 1914, noted in Table 1, is explained largely by rising labor productivity. The main causes of these improvements are increases in technological knowledge, increases in the volume of cooperative factors (particularly capital), and investment in human capital.

THE SUPPLY OF A SINGLE GRADE OF LABOR

If all other factors are held constant, the amount of a single grade of labor that will be supplied depends on the wage rate offered by employers. Workers compare the wage they can earn in one occupation with their opportunity cost (the wage they could receive from employment in another occupation). The higher the wage offered for labor of a particular grade, the more the workers of that grade will offer their services. (The backward-bending supply curve in Figure 1 refers to the supply of *all* labor and the average wage across all occupations.)

Workers typically receive a wage that is at least equal to the opportunity cost of the next best alternative that they sacrifice in accepting employment. The employer who fails to pay workers their opportunity costs will have no workers because they will all take the next best alternative—which then becomes their best alternative.

The Labor Supply Curve

Figure 4 gives a hypothetical market supply curve that shows the number of hours computer programmers are willing to work at different wage rates. The supply curve is positively sloped because at higher wages, computer programming employment becomes more attractive relative to employment in other occupations. Computer programmers will therefore shift hours from other occupations for which they are qualified (engineering, accounting, math) into programming work. The market labor supply curve is the sum of the individual labor supply curves of computer programmers.

Factors That Shift the Labor Supply Curve

In addition to wages, two basic factors affect the supply of labor to a particular occupation:

1. The wages that can be earned in other occupations. If engineering wages increase, the supply of computer programmers should fall, for example.

FIGURE 4
The Market Supply of Computer Programmers

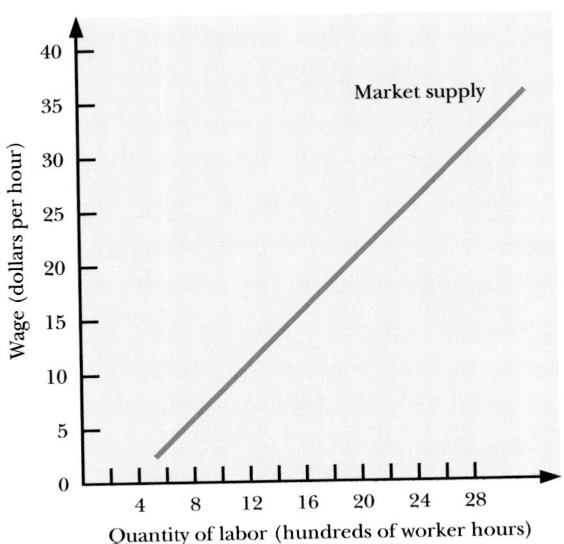

This market labor supply curve shows the number of hours programmers are willing to work at different wage rates, all other things remaining the same. The labor supply curve is positively sloped because at higher wages, programmer employment is more attractive relative to other types of employment.

2. The nonpecuniary aspects of the occupation. People dislike heavy, unpleasant, or dangerous work or work in harsh climates. An increase in the unpleasantness or danger associated with a particular job will decrease the supply of labor.

These factors are discussed later in this chapter. (Unions can also affect labor supply, as will be shown in the next chapter.)

LABOR MARKET EQUILIBRIUM

As we have seen, wage rates are determined in a competitive labor market by supply and demand. The market demand curve for labor of a single grade is negatively sloped; the market supply curve for labor of a single grade is positively sloped.

FIGURE 5
Equilibrium in the Market for Computer Programmers

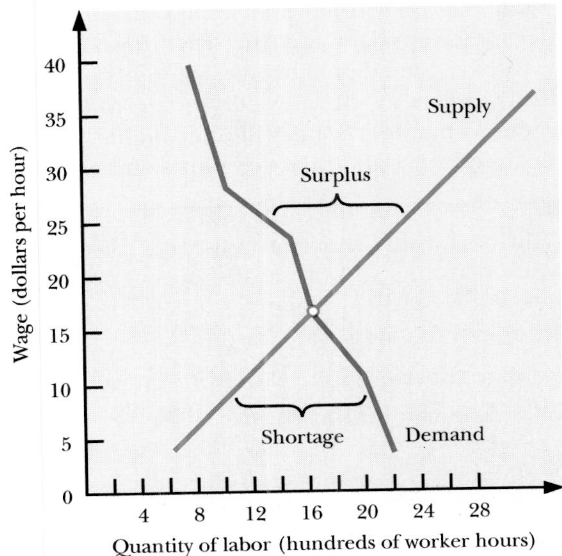

The market supply of programmers (from Figure 4) and the market demand for programmers (from Figure 3) are brought together in this figure. The equilibrium wage rate is $16 per hour. At the $16 wage, the quantity demanded (1600 hours) equals the quantity supplied. At wage rates above $16, there is a surplus (quantity supplied exceeds quantity demanded); at wage rates below $16, there is a shortage of labor (quantity demanded exceeds quantity supplied).

The market supply and demand curves for computer programmers given in Figures 3 and 4 are brought together in Figure 5. The wage rate of $16 equates the quantity of programmer hours supplied with the quantity of programmer hours demanded, or 1600 hours. At any wage above $16, the number of hours programmers wish to work exceeds the number demanded. At any wage below $16, the number of hours firms wish programmers to work exceeds the number programmers are willing to work.

> The equilibrium wage rate in the labor market is the wage rate at which the quantity of labor demanded equals the quantity of labor supplied.

Labor Shortages and Surpluses

In a free labor market, wage rates adjust until they equal the equilibrium wage rate. If there is a **labor surplus,** some workers willing to work at the prevailing wage will be without jobs. Some will offer their services at lower wages and thus drive down the wage rate. If there is a **labor shortage,** some firms wishing to hire workers at the prevailing wage rate will go away empty-handed. Some will offer higher wages to attract employees and thus drive up wage rates.

> A **labor surplus** occurs when the number of workers willing to work at the prevailing wage rate exceeds the number that firms wish to employ at that wage rate.
>
> A **labor shortage** occurs when the number of workers firms wish to hire at the prevailing wage rate exceeds the number willing to work at that wage rate.

In certain cases, wages are not permitted to adjust to equate quantity demanded with quantity supplied. The Fair Labor Standards Act of 1938 required that employers pay a mandated minimum wage to workers covered by minimum-wage legislation. In 1950, the minimum wage was $0.75 per hour. By mid-1991, it was $4.25 per hour.

Any large boost in the minimum wage can be expected to cause unemployment among the very people minimum-wage legislation intends to help—the working poor and teenagers. If the minimum wage is set above the market equilibrium wage rates of the working poor and of teenage workers, there will be an excess supply (unemployment) of these types of labor.

Although minimum wages could cause labor surpluses, the empirical evidence suggests that the minimum wage has not substantially distorted the U.S. labor market. Small firms have been exempted, and the minimum wage has generally been set low enough that it has not reduced employment by a substantial amount.[3]

Shifts in Labor Supply and Demand

Unless something happens to prevent it, the market wage will be the equilibrium wage that equates the quantity of labor demanded with the quantity of labor supplied. If a change occurs in any of the factors that shift a demand or supply curve, the equilibrium is disrupted and a new wage rate is established by the market.

Changes in conditions other than the wage rate can shift the supply or demand curve. The supply curve of labor may shift to the left because of higher wages in other occupations or increased health hazards on the job. As Figure 6 shows, if the supply of labor falls (shifts left) from S to S', there will be a shortage of labor at the initial wage, w. Therefore, the wage will rise (to w'). If the demand for labor falls (shifts left), there will be a surplus of labor at the initial wage, w, and the wage rate will fall to w''. The possible causes of a demand reduction include a decline in labor productivity, a fall in the demand for the product labor produces, or an increase in the prices of other inputs used with labor.

From Baby Boom to Baby Bust

As pointed out earlier, one of the facts that economic theory should explain is the fall in real hourly wages from 1975 to 1991. Journalists, politicians, and pundits often interpret this phenomenon as an indication that the American economy is in decline. But it is, in fact, a response to the dramatic increase in birth rates after World War II. Figure 7 provides population profiles for this "baby boom." The length of each bar shows the percentage of the U.S. population in each age cohort or group (0–4, 5–9, 10–14, 15–19, and so on); for example, in 1970, about 20 percent of the U.S. population was in the 5–9 age cohort. The blue bars show the baby boom cohort. In 1970, the baby boomers were between 25 and 5: They cause a distinctive bulge in the population profile. Notice that the bulge moves upward from 1970 to 1989. In 1989, the baby boomers were the most productive members of the American economy, ranging in age from 25 to 44. In addition, the female labor-force participation rate (analyzed later) increased from about 46 percent to 58 percent. The fall in average hourly wages was the natural outcome of this enormous increase in the labor supply, which overwhelmed the normal increase in the demand for labor arising from increases in productivity.

When the baby boomers hit the job market, employment (as should be expected from economic

[3]Charles Brown, "Minimum Wage Laws: Are They Overrated?" *Journal of Economic Perspectives* 2, 3 (Summer 1988): 113–45.

FIGURE 6
Shifts in Labor Supply and Demand

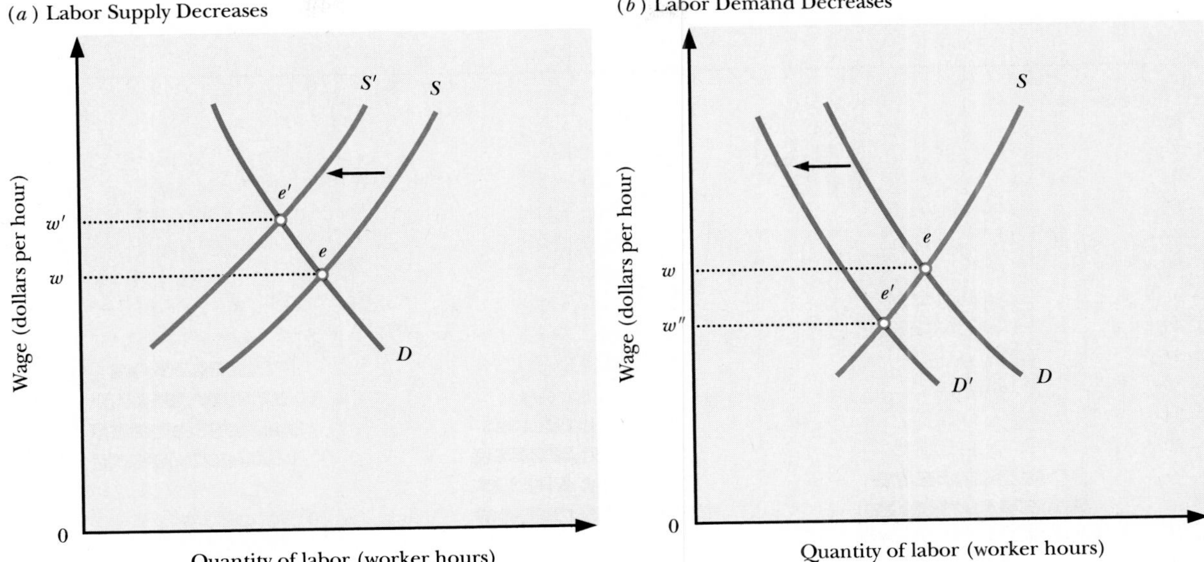

Panel *a* shows the effect of a decrease in the supply of labor. When there is a reduction in supply from S to S', there is a shortage of labor (firms want to use more worker hours than workers are willing to work) at the equilibrium wage, w. The competition for labor among firms will bid the wage up to w'. Panel *b* shows the effect of a decrease in demand. When the demand curve shifts from D to D', there is a surplus of labor (workers wish to work more hours than employers wish to use) at the original equilibrium wage. Competition among workers will drive the wage down to w''.

theory) grew at a higher rate than at any time this century! For example, from 1975 to 1989, employment rose at an annual rate of 2 percent, compared to an annual rate of 1.6 percent from 1929 to 1975. The baby boomers found jobs, and the real hourly wage rate fell to accommodate their demand for work.

After 1965, birth rates dropped. Since then, there has been a baby bust instead of a baby boom. As the baby bust cohort moves through the U.S. population profile, real wage rates should rise faster than normal and employment should grow at slower rates than normal. In the year 2001, the first baby busters will be 35 years old: prime age, productive adults. At the same time, the first baby boomers will be 55 years old and thinking about retirement. As the baby busters begin to push the baby boomers out of the productive segment of the U.S. population profile, journalists, politicians, and pundits will be discussing the historic reversal of U.S. fortunes. In fact, the new conditions will simply be the way that supply and demand reflect changes in the U.S. population profile. (See Example 3.)

WAGE STRUCTURE

We have seen how the wage rate for labor of a single homogeneous grade is determined, but this does not explain why some people earn more than others or why some occupations command a higher wage than others. Very simply, these wage differences occur because *people are different* and because *jobs are different.* Under competitive conditions, if all people were the same and if all jobs were the same, everyone would earn the same wage.

Compensating Wage Differentials

Throughout the world, underground coal miners are paid more than manufacturing workers. In Canada, miners earn 20 percent more than manufacturing workers. In Hungary and the Commonwealth of Independent States (formerly the Soviet Union), the

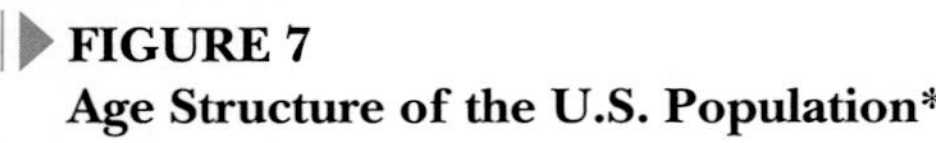

FIGURE 7
Age Structure of the U.S. Population*

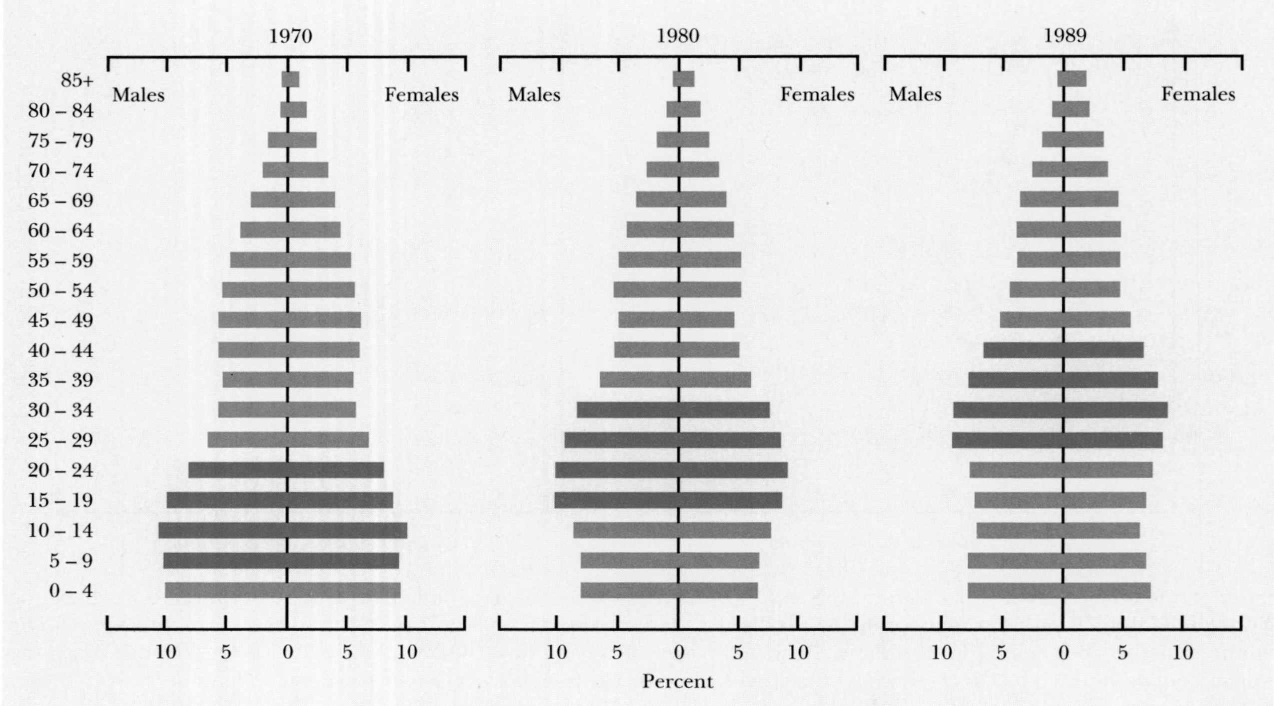

* Blue bars indicate the baby-boom cohort.

Source: U.S. Bureau of the Census and *Federal Reserve Bulletin*, June 1991.

percentages are even higher. In the United States in 1989, workers in coal mining were paid an average wage of $16.25 per hour—compared to the average wage of $9.66 per hour in nonagricultural industries.[4] Yet coal mining does not require highly specialized skills or training; the skills of most manufacturing workers could readily be used in underground coal mining. The reason for the wage difference lies on the supply side of the labor market: Jobs are different.

One of the factors capable of shifting the labor supply curve is the general desirability of the job. People prefer to avoid dirty, monotonous, and dangerous jobs, other things being equal. Coal mining is one of the most dangerous professions, with a fatality rate per work hour 50 percent higher than minerals mining. Accordingly, the hourly wage in minerals mining is 77 percent that of coal mining.[5]

Figure 8 shows the effect on relative wages of differences in the danger of the occupation. For simplicity, the demand curve for coal miners is assumed to be identical to the demand curve for textile workers. Suppose also that that all workers are identical. Even so, the labor supply curves are quite different. The higher placement of the coal miners' supply curve reflects the fact that workers prefer, *ceteris paribus*, less dangerous employment. When workers are identical, to get an equivalent supply of coal miners, coal mine employers must offer higher wages than textile employers.

This model can be used to explain a wide variety of **compensating wage differentials:** why welders

[4]U.S. Department of Labor, *Employment and Earnings*.

[5]*Statistical Abstract of the United States.*

EXAMPLE 3 Generational Crowding, Birth Rates, and Real Wages

The decline in real wages in the 1980s is consistent with the "generational crowding experiences" of earlier generations first noted by economist Richard Easterlin. Easterlin found that real wages drop (or do not rise as fast) during periods when the number of young people in the job market is high. Real wages rise when the number of young people in the job market is low. Because birth rates were low in the 1930s, the 1950s and 1960s were periods of "uncrowded" labor markets. Employers competed for the limited supply of workers and bid up real wages. Birth rates were exceptionally high in the 1950s (the postwar baby boom), which meant that labor markets from 1975 to 1990 were "crowded" and real wages fell.

Labor markets continue to be affected by events that took place in earlier generations. The large number of births in the 1950s was echoed by a large number of births in the 1970s and 1980s, which will be echoed by a large number of births at the turn of the century. Two to three decades after these periods of high birth rate, real wages will be depressed as large numbers of workers crowd the labor market.

Easterlin predicts that the echoes of the birth dearth of the 1930s and the baby boom of the 1950s will dim with successive generations. Baby boomers, whose income expectations were not fulfilled, responded by having fewer children. This means that when their children enter the labor market, there will be less generational crowding and less downward pressure on real wages.

Source: Richard Easterlin, *Population, Labor Force, and Long Swings in Economic Growth* (New York: National Bureau of Economic Research, 1968).

on the Alaskan pipeline have to be paid so much (to compensate for the harsh climate and higher living costs) or why sanitation workers are usually better paid than clerical workers (to compensate for the unpleasantness and social stigma).

Compensating wage differentials are the higher wages or fringe benefits that must be paid to compensate workers for undesirable job characteristics.

Numerous studies by economists have demonstrated that compensating wage differentials are indeed paid to offset undesirable job characteristics. Although individuals differ a great deal (some enjoy heavy outdoor work and would detest office work; others enjoy work in the office but hate being outdoors), almost everyone wishes to avoid injury and disease. Studies from different countries show that wages are positively associated with the risk of being killed or seriously injured on the job. These studies show that workers receive, depending upon the job, between $35 and $500 more per year for every 1 in 10,000 increase in the death rate associated with a job.[6] (See Example 4).

Compensating wage differentials also reflect the costs of training. Clearly, investing in **human capital** through schooling, training, and health care raise workers' income by increasing their productivity.

Human capital is the value of all investments in the capacity of a worker to earn income.

For example, on the average, people with a college education earn about $600,000 more over their lifetimes than people with a high school education. Part of the higher wage earned by engineers, lawyers, physicians, and so forth, can be considered a compensating wage differential that reflects the cost of developing certain specialized skills. These costs even

[6]Ronald Ehrenberg and Robert Smith, *Modern Labor Economics Theory and Public Policy,* 4th ed. (New York: HarperCollins, 1991), 275–76.

FIGURE 8
Wages in Coal Mining and Textiles

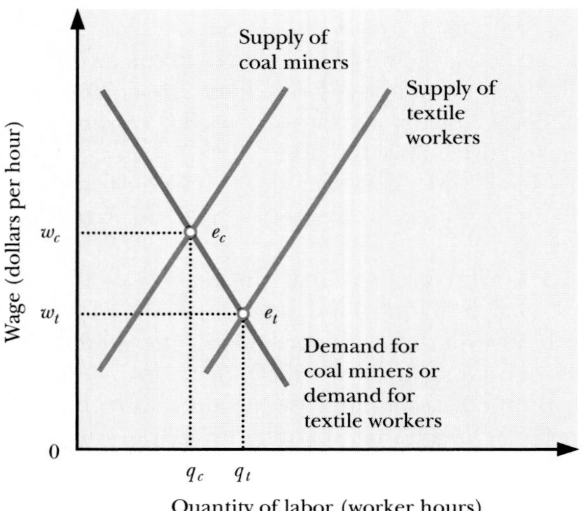

For simplicity, the demand curve for coal miners is assumed to be identical to the demand curve for textile workers. Wages are higher for coal miners because the quantity supplied of coal miners is less than the quantity supplied of textile workers at each wage rate.

differ between people; thus not everybody becomes a doctor, lawyer, or college professor.

Noncompeting Groups

The discussion of the labor market in this chapter has thus far assumed that all labor is the same (homogeneous). The difference in the wages earned by identical workers was attributed to differences in job characteristics. In reality, both jobs *and* people are different. Because people are different, firms must try to distinguish between high-productivity workers and low-productivity workers. Some individuals are qualified by mental and physical skills and training for a wide variety of occupations. Others are qualified for only a few occupations. A limited number of people have the peculiar abilities to become brain surgeons, trial lawyers, or theoretical physicists. Surgeons must have extremely sensitive and sure hands; trial lawyers must be articulate and able to think quickly on their feet; theoretical physicists must have an enormous analytical aptitude. The number of individuals qualified to be professional athletes is limited to those who possess extraordinary physical attributes. On the other hand, the number of individuals qualified to be stock clerks, manage-

EXAMPLE 4 Compensating Wages in Meat Packing

Meat-packing is unpleasant and dangerous work, with an injury rate five times higher than the typical industry. Meat-packing plants use automated conveyor belts carrying about 4000 cattle each day. Plants are noisy and dangerous. Workers wear ear protection gear, mesh armor protection from knives, and helmets. Long chains move a carcass down the production line at 150 to 200 head an hour. The worker makes one or two cuts on a particular type of meat and repeats those motions several thousand times a day. The workers risk being injured by knives and machines and may suffer from carpal tunnel syndrome—a wrist ailment caused by performing repetitive wrist or arm movements.

Before recent technological improvements, meat-cutting was a skilled occupation. Now, meat-packing plants are staffed by unskilled workers, who regularly migrate from Texas, where they are unemployed or earn minimum wages, to Iowa or Nebraska for jobs in meat-packing plants.

The theory of compensating wage differentials suggests that workers of a given skill level will receive higher wages for working in unpleasant and dangerous jobs. The meat-packing industry bears out this theory. An entry-level meat-cutter with no experience can earn about 70 percent more than the minimum wage. Meat-packing plants must offer such a premium to attract unskilled workers.

Source: James Pinkerton, "Hispanics Brave Meatpacking Dangers in Quest of Better Life," *Houston Chronicle*, September 2, 1990,: 1A; and "Industry Giant IBP Recruiting Heavily in Texas," *Houston Chronicle*, September 2, 1990,: 1D.

ment trainees, factory workers, and so on is much greater.

Adam Smith pointed out that the natural differences among people are less than commonly supposed, while training is responsible for the significant differences among people. Although the genetic differences between the philosopher and electrician may not be significant, background, education, and experience differentiate them to the point where it becomes difficult for electricians to compete with philosophers. Labor suppliers are divided into such **noncompeting groups.**

> **Noncompeting groups** are labor suppliers differentiated by natural ability and abilities acquired through education, training, and experience to the extent that one group does not compete with another for jobs.

If all people were the same and they had equal access to all occupations, the remaining wage differences would be the consequence of different job conditions. The brain surgeon would earn as much as the garbage collector if the two jobs were equally desirable.[7] In the absence of differences in people, if brain surgery were regarded as a better job than garbage collection, it is even conceivable that garbage collectors would receive higher wages.

Signaling and the Internal Labor Market

Because people are different, it is often costly for the potential employer to determine the marginal physical product of each worker. Employers typically do not know exactly how productive a potential employee will be in a particular position. The problem of gathering information on the productivity of different workers is similar to the consumer's problem of gathering information on product quality and product prices (discussed in an earlier chapter). Consumers solve the problem of costly information by buying brand names and limiting search time in the case of less expensive items. Employers have similar techniques to distinguish low-productivity workers from high-productivity workers.

Credentials and Screening. Employers must bear the costs of training employees, but they presumably want to minimize these costs by hiring the most able persons for the job. It is costly for firms to launch intensive investigations into the backgrounds of potential employees or to administer comprehensive examinations to determine worker qualifications. When training costs (for example, the costs of teaching new employees how to operate sophisticated equipment) are high, firms will spend more on testing employees and investigating their backgrounds. A recent study by the Carnegie Foundation for the Advancement of Teaching found that corporations spend about $40 billion per year training employees. This expenditure approaches the total annual expenditures of U.S. colleges and universities. Even though training costs may be high, firms cannot afford to gather detailed information on all potential employees. Many firms therefore rely on the **screening** of potential employees.

> **Screening** is the process by which employers select the most qualified workers on the basis of easily observable characteristics.

By selecting employees on the basis of easily observable characteristics (like age, degrees, experience) that are known to be correlated with productivity on that job, firms can select employees at relatively low information costs. This can cause firms to discriminate against people who are more productive than their statistical category would predict.

To hold down screening costs employers rely on worker **signals**. For example, employers may know from experience that math or business graduates are on average more productive in technical occupations than graduates of other disciplines. Such employers therefore specify that a business or math degree is a requirement for the job. Employers may know from experience that, on the average, scholastic grades are an indicator of worker productivity. They may therefore specify that only students with a B average or better can be hired for particular positions.

[7]A person can become a brain surgeon only after years of advanced study, while the garbage collector may begin work immediately after high school. Wage differences attributable to differences in the amount of training and education would still remain, but everyone would have the opportunity to become a brain surgeon.

EXAMPLE 5 Tattoos and Labor Market Signaling

Firms economize on information costs by hiring according to labor market signals, which individuals can acquire. An unusual example of a labor market signal is a tattoo. Surveys of employers find that many are reluctant to hire anyone with a visible tattoo. Tattoos are regarded as negative signals—indicators of potential drug use or gang membership. Although someone with a visible tattoo may have turned out to be the best person for the job, it would be costly for the firm to acquire this information; so it uses a simple signal to make its decisions.

Because tattoos are negative labor market signals, tattooed persons have to spend money to get them removed. Rather than spending money to acquire a signal, such as a college degree, tattooed persons have to spend money to remove a signal.

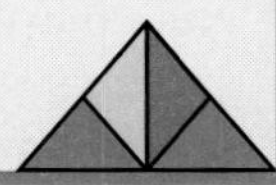

Signals are credentials or qualifications—such as formal schooling—that can be acquired by workers and that employers believe to be indicators of productivity.

Workers can send out signals of high productivity by acquiring credentials or qualifications. Because acquiring a signal (such as a college degree) is costly, workers will weigh the costs and benefits of the signal.

By requiring college degrees or minimum grade-point averages, employers screen out job candidates who, on average, are unqualified. The use of tested credentials allows employers to reduce the costs of distinguishing qualified from unqualified job applicants. Employers know that these techniques will be correct only on average, however. Not every person who holds the desired credentials will actually be suited for the job, while some individuals who do not hold the right credentials may be ideally suited. (See Example 5.)

Internal Labor Markets. Employers can use an **internal labor market** to obtain the most qualified persons with a minimum of hiring costs.

A firm uses an **internal labor market** when it fills its jobs by promoting or transferring workers it already employs.

Workers enter a firm's internal labor market through general entry-level positions such as management trainee, bookkeeper, or apprentice machinist. In internal labor markets, rules and established procedures determine who will be promoted, the role of the union organization, and the manner in which vacancies are filled. Rather than screening potential employees on the basis of credentials, firms that use an internal labor market hire a large number of entry-level people without much testing, interviewing, or screening. A large department store will hire a large number of management trainees; a factory will hire a large number of general laborers. Once on the job, the firm has the opportunity to observe actual job performance. The major benefit of using the internal labor market to fill job vacancies is that the firm can learn a great deal about the person being considered for a job. The major cost of using the internal labor market is that the firm passes up the opportunity to hire more qualified persons from outside by restricting promotions to those it already employs.

Cost Monitoring and the Principal/Agent Problem

The goal of the employer is to maximize the long-run profits of the firm. Employees often have personal objectives that differ from the firm's objectives. One employee may wish to maximize the income from the job. Another may wish to minimize the amount of stress and exertion the job requires while earning a target level of income. Employees are different, and they behave differently. As long as the employer and employee have different objectives, a **principal/agent problem** exists.

> A **principal/agent problem** exists when the firm (the principal) and the employee (its agent) have different goals and objectives for the employee's behavior.

The employer cannot constantly monitor the performance of each employee because the information costs would be prohibitive: The management staff would have to be increased dramatically. When workers are part of a team, it is even more difficult to monitor the productivity of any one member. When it is easy to monitor performance (as in the case of salespersons who work on commissions), the principal/agent problem is less difficult to solve. Firms minimize the principal/agent problem in a number of ways. To prevent assembly-line workers from shirking responsibility, the firm pays bonuses for exceeding production norms. Professional athletes are given performance-based incentive contracts. A baseball player may be given a bonus for every extra base hit over 50 in a season; a football running back may be given a bonus for gaining more than 1000 yards per season. A company gives its employees an annual bonus if the company exceeds a profit target. All these bonus and incentive schemes are designed to improve the work performance of the agent (the worker) without raising the monitoring costs of the principal (the employer).

It is difficult to design incentive pay systems that eliminate the principal/agent problem. Assembly-line workers may exceed production norms by reducing the quality of their work. Professional baseball players may lose games by attempting to get extra base hits when a sacrifice fly is required. When workers feel they are too small a part of the company to affect company profitability, profit-based bonuses do not affect their performance. The more specific the incentive target is, the more likely the employee will be to achieve the target by sacrificing some other worthwhile outcome (for example, sacrificing quality for quantity). The more general the incentive target is—such as a bonus based on company profits—the less likely employees will be to believe that their actions affect the outcome.

Efficiency-Wage Models

If wages were above equilibrium rates, the number of people willing to work at those jobs would exceed the number of jobs available. Employers could still fill jobs and yet offer lower wages. Therefore, equilibrium wages would be expected to prevail. The **efficiency-wage model** explains why firms might want to pay a wage rate that exceeds the equilibrium wage rate. Economists often cite the example of Henry Ford's 1914 policy of paying workers $5 a day (described in the Chapter Insight). Firms realize that workers have some discretion over their performance. Employment contracts cannot specify all aspects of a worker's performance. By paying wages in excess of equilibrium, firms create an incentive for workers to work efficiently without careful monitoring. The costs of shirking and getting caught are high when the worker is receiving the bonus of an above-equilibrium wage.

> The **efficiency-wage model** states that it is rational for certain firms to pay workers a wage rate above equilibrium to improve worker performance and productivity.

Firms also use above-equilibrium wages to reduce turnover and create a stable work force. If all wages were finely balanced at equilibrium, workers could move from one job to another at relatively low cost. With wages set above equilibrium, workers are less inclined to leave high-paying jobs. With a stable work force, training and search costs are reduced, and workers become more specialized and skilled the longer they stay on the job. Firms can use higher wages as a screening device to sort out less desirable job candidates. A higher wage attracts more able job candidates, and workers willing to work for less can be screened out as potential labor market "lemons."

Finally, each worker's effort may depend upon the work norm of the group. If employers offer the work group a reward in the form of an above-equilibrium wage, the work group may give the firm

EXAMPLE 6 Efficiency Wages: To Underpay or Overpay?

Efficiency wages teach that managers get more power over their employees if they overpay them. This concept is contrary to the popular conception that managers exercise power by underpaying workers. If workers are underpaid—or are simply paid their opportunity costs—they have no incentive to be loyal, tolerate difficult and demanding working conditions, and shoulder their share of teamwork. If workers are paid more by one firm than they could get elsewhere, they will tolerate unpleasant job assignments, overtime, and risky assignments from their supervisors before quitting. Overpaid workers have a lot to lose by leaving the firm; they are therefore more anxious to please their bosses.

Source: Adapted from Ronald Ehrenberg and Robert Smith, *Modern Labor Economics*, 4th ed. (New York: HarperCollins, 1991), 435.

an effort above the minimum required by the formal work contract.[8] (See Example 6.)

This chapter examined how labor markets work. The next chapter will take a look at the effect of labor unions on the labor market.

SUMMARY

1. Labor markets operate like other factor markets, but labor is different because workers desire leisure and have preferences concerning different jobs. Labor cannot be bought and sold like the other factors of production. A labor market brings buyers and sellers of labor services together. The buyer who must accept the market wage as given is perfectly competitive in the labor market. The buyer who can affect wage rates has some monopsony power.

2. When wage rates in general rise, the opportunity cost of leisure increases, as does income. Whether or not the aggregate labor-supply curve will be backward bending depends upon the relative strengths of the income and substitution effects. Whether people work in household production or in the market labor force depends upon the value of time in the home compared to their market wage.

3. If firms are price takers, they hire labor to the point where W = MRP. The firm's MRP schedule is its labor demand schedule. The labor demand curve will be negatively sloped both for firms and for the market. The labor demand curve will shift if the demand for the firm's final product changes, if the price of either substitute or complementary factors changes, or if the productivity of labor changes.

4. The labor supply curve for a particular occupation will be positively sloped because workers must be paid their opportunity costs. The labor supply curve will shift if job conditions or wages in other industries change.

5. The market wage rate is typically that wage at which the quantity demanded of labor of a single grade equals the quantity supplied. A shortage exists when the quantity demanded exceeds the quantity supplied at that wage. A surplus exists when the quantity supplied exceeds the quantity demanded at that wage. A new equilibrium wage/quantity combination will result when either the market supply or market demand curve shifts because of changes in productivity, product prices, prices of other factors, or job conditions. The post–World War II baby boom helps explain the recent decline in real wage rates.

[8]For discussion of the efficiency-wage concept, see Janet Yellin, "Efficiency Models of Unemployment," *American Economic Review* (May 1984): 200–205; George Akerlof, "Labor Contracts as Partial Gift Exchanges," *Quarterly Journal of Economics* 9 (November 1982): 543–67; Joseph Stiglitz, "The Efficiency-Wage Hypothesis, Surplus Labor, and the Distribution of Income in LDCs," *Oxford Economic Papers* 28 (July 1976): 185–208. The efficiency-wage theory is relatively new and not yet fully tested. It offers an explanation for observed patterns of unemployment and for wage differentials not explained by the economic factors studied in this chapter. For a critical survey see H. Lorne Carmichael, "Efficiency Wage Models of Unemployment," *Economic Inquiry* 28 (April 1990): 269–95.

6. The theory of compensating wage differentials explains why workers in dangerous occupations are paid more. Noncompeting groups are workers with different abilities who do not compete for the same jobs. It is costly for employers to determine the real productivities of potential employees. They therefore use signals and internal labor markets to distinguish high-productivity workers from low-productivity workers. Employers use incentive-pay schemes to deal with the principal/agent problem.

KEY TERMS

labor market	noncompeting groups
household production	screening
leisure	signals
labor surplus	internal labor market
labor shortage	principal/agent problem
compensating wage differentials	efficiency-wage model
human capital	

QUESTIONS AND PROBLEMS

1. Why do labor's special features cause the labor market to work differently from the other factor markets?
2. What is the information and screening cost strategy of a firm that fills all positions by promoting from within?
3. A price-taking firm in both its product and factor markets is currently employing 25 workers. The twenty-fifth worker's marginal revenue product is $300 per week, and the worker's wage is $200 per week. Is this firm maximizing its profits? If not, what would you advise the company to do?
4. There is a close positive association between labor productivity and wages. Use the theory presented in this chapter to explain this relationship.
5. State law in New Jersey requires that employees in licensed gambling casinos be residents of New Jersey for a specified period of time. What effect does this legislation have upon the elasticity of demand for casino employees in New Jersey?
6. During recessions and periods of falling wages, the number of volunteers for the all-volunteer army rises. Use the theory of this chapter to explain why this supply of labor rises.
7. Explain why a worker in India earns much less than a worker in Germany.
8. Evaluate the validity of the following statement: "If all jobs were the same, everyone would earn the same wage."
9. Evaluate the validity of the following statement: "If all people were the same, everyone would earn the same wage."
10. You are a surgeon earning $200,000 per year. When the demand for your services increases, the charge for each operation increases by 25 percent. What effect will this increase have on the number of operations you perform?
11. Rank each of the following jobs according to the difficulty of devising an incentive pay system that is compatible with the overall objectives of the firm. Explain your ranking.

    a. Janitorial work performed at night in an office building
    b. Assembly-line work in a washing-machine factory
    c. Traveling sales work
    d. The creation of hand-carved figures for a crafts company
    e. Professional basketball playing

12. Evaluate the validity of the following statement: "If there were no monitoring costs, there would be no principal/agent problem between firms and employees."
13. Referring to Table 2, explain what would happen to the wage of computer programmers if the number of program lines produced per hour were to double for each level of labor input. Explain what would happen if the price fell to $1.
14. Draw hypothetical labor supply and labor demand curves for truck drivers. Shift the curves to show what happens when

    a. Truck driving becomes safer.
    b. Truck drivers become more efficient.
    c. Truck drivers must be licensed by a state agency.
    d. The earnings of surgeons increase.
    e. The earnings of moving-equipment operators fall.

15. Explain how the efficiency-wage model justifies paying wages that exceed marginal productivity.

SUGGESTED READINGS

Addison, John T., and W. Stanley Siebert. *The Market for Labor: An Analytical Treatment.* Glenview, IL: Scott, Foresman, 1979.

Becker, Gary. *Human Capital,* 2d ed. New York: National Bureau of Economic Research, 1975.

Doeringer, Peter, and Michael Piore. *Internal Labor Markets and Manpower Analysis.* Lexington, MA: D. C. Heath, 1971.

Dunlop, John T., and Walter Galenson, eds. *Labor in the Twentieth Century.* New York: Academic Press, 1978.

Ehrenberg, Ronald G., and Robert S. Smith. *Modern Labor Economics: Theory and Public Policy,* 4th ed. New York: HarperCollins, 1991.

Federal Reserve Bulletin (June 1991), "Issues in Labor Supply." 375–87.

Reynolds, Lloyd E. and Stanley H. Masters. *Labor Economics and Labor Relations,* 9th ed. Englewood Cliffs, NJ: Prentice Hall, 1986.

Welch, Finis. *Minimum Wages: Issues and Evidence.* Washington, DC: American Enterprise Institute, 1978.

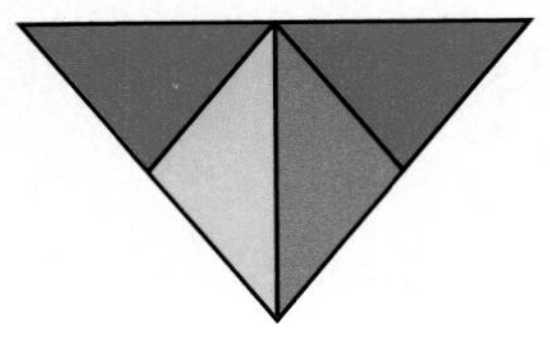

38 Labor Unions

CHAPTER INSIGHT

On August 5, 1981, President Ronald Reagan fired 11,500 of the 15,000 members of the Professional Air Traffic Controllers Organization (PATCO), two days after they had gone on strike. As federal employees, air traffic controllers were prohibited by law from striking. Consequently, two months later, the Federal Labor Relations Authority stripped PATCO of its status as the legal representative of the air traffic controllers. Relations between government and organized labor had reached a new low. Airline traffic collapsed as the nation struggled to rebuild its air traffic control system.

Public opinion was split by the administration's firing of the air traffic controllers. Some Americans viewed Reagan's action as a bold move against a union that demanded excessive benefits for its members at the nation's expense. Others viewed it as part of a sinister effort to destroy a union that served as a positive force for justice, equality, and even economic efficiency. In any case, the breaking of the air traffic controller strike in 1981 was a major setback from which organized American labor has yet to recover.

This chapter will examine the role of labor unions in the labor market and will discuss the history of the American labor movement and the effects of unions on wages, employment, and economic efficiency.

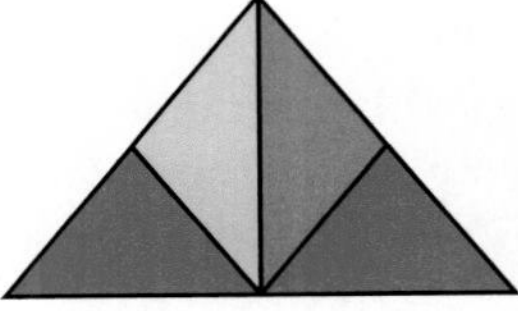

Definitions

Workers in the same industry or occupation may join together to form a **labor union.**

> A **labor union** is a collective organization of workers and employees whose objective is to improve conditions of pay and work.

Three types of labor unions can be distinguished: **craft unions,** such as an electricians' union or a plumbers' union; **industrial unions,** such as the United Automobile Workers (a union that represents automobile workers of all types) and the United Mine Workers (a union that represents all types of workers engaged in mining); and **employee associations,** such as the National Education Association, the American Bar Association, the American Medical Association, and state employee associations. Historically, employee associations were primarily concerned with maintaining professional standards. In recent years, however, they have become increasingly involved in the customary union function of improving the pay and work conditions of members.

> A **craft union** represents workers of a single occupation.
>
> An **industrial union** represents employees of an industry regardless of their specific occupation.
>
> An **employee association** represents employees in a particular profession in order to both maintain professional standards and improve conditions of pay and work.

Unions perform a variety of functions, the most visible of which is to engage in *collective bargaining* with employers. Instead of each employee negotiating individually with the employer concerning wages, fringe benefits (such as vacation time and group health insurance), job security, and work conditions, the union represents all employees in collective negotiations with employers.

Facts and Figures: American Unionism

In the United States, there are fewer than 16 million union members. Figure 1 shows that less than one of every five workers in the labor force belongs to a union. In the 1930s, union members accounted for between 6 percent and 7 percent of the labor force. This proportion rose in the late 1930s and 1940s, peaking at 25 percent in the mid-1950s. Since then, the share of union members has fallen steadily, to less than 14 percent in 1991.

Union membership has declined as a percentage of employment for several reasons. First, the percentage of women in the labor force has been rapidly increasing, and women have historically tended not to join unions. Table 1 shows that in 1990, 22 percent of male workers and 15 percent of female workers belonged to unions. The total employment share of another group that tends not to join unions, white-collar workers, has risen as well. About one-third of blue-collar workers, compared to 11 percent to 15 percent of white-collar workers, belong to unions. Increased employment in the service sector (which is only 6 percent unionized) has also reduced overall unionization figures. Moreover, there has been a shift in population from the northeastern and midwestern states to the southern and southwestern states, where union membership has been weakest. The rapid unionization of public employees represents the sole positive trend. In 1964, only 8 percent of state and local government employees belonged to unions; by 1991, the proportion had risen to over 43 percent. The rise in public-sector unionism, while significant, has not been sufficient to brace the falling share of union members among all employees.

The relative decline of unionism may also be due to a perception of the growing weakness of unions. President Reagan's firing of the striking air traffic controllers in 1981 dealt a severe psychological blow to unions, as did the failure of the UAW strike against Caterpillar in April 1992. (See Example 1.)

Table 2 lists the largest U.S. unions and their membership. The overwhelming majority of American unions are affiliated with the AFL–CIO (American Federation of Labor–Congress of Industrial Organizations).

FIGURE 1
Union and Employee-Association Membership as a Percentage of Labor Force, 1870–1991

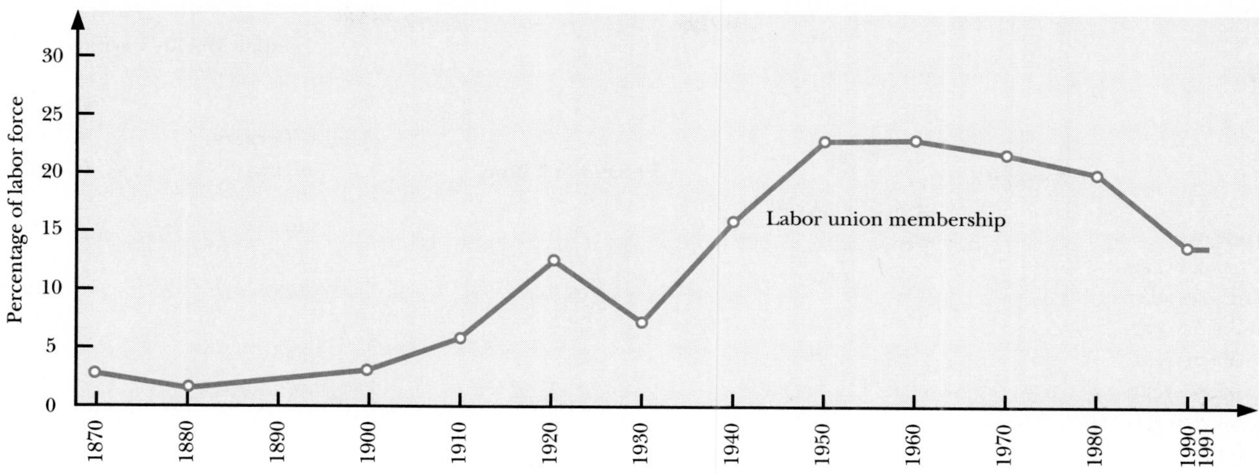

Less than one in five members of the labor force in the United States belongs to a union. Union membership rose from 6.7 percent in the 1930s to a peak of 25 percent in the 1950s before declining to recent levels.

Sources: *Statistical Abstract of the United States; Handbook of Labor Statistics; Historical Statistics of the United States, Colonial Times to 1970, 1976, part 1.*

EXAMPLE 1 Representation Elections and Decertification Polls: The Birth and Death of Union Representation

Under existing legislation, unions can seek the right to represent unorganized workers in a representation election supervised by the National Labor Relations Board. If a majority of workers in XYZ Company agree, the "United Pumpmakers Union" becomes their representative. The National Labor Relations Board also supervises decertification polls. Management can challenge the claim that the union represents a majority of its workers. If a majority of XYZ workers fail to vote for the union, then the union is decertified as their representative.

One indicator of the apparent waning of union influence in the United States has been the declining percentage of representation elections won by unions and the rising share of decertification elections lost by unions. In the early 1970s, unions won more than half of their representation elections and lost less than 70 percent of decertification elections. By the late 1980s and early 1990s, unions were winning only about 40 percent of their representation elections and losing more than three-quarters of their decertification elections.

Source: *Annual Report of the National Labor Relations Board*, various years.

TABLE 1
Characteristics of Union Members: U.S. Labor Force

Category	Percent in Union	Median Weekly Earnings: Union Workers (dollars)	Median Weekly Earnings: Nonunion Workers (dollars)
Total Work Force	18.6	494	372
16–24 years	7.4	335	252
25–34 years	16.5	473	378
35–44 years	23.6	518	438
45–54 years	25.5	523	431
55–64 years	24.4	504	401
65 years and over	10.7	470	306
Men	21.8	524	430
Women	14.9	416	312
White	17.7	503	384
Men	21.2	537	452
Women	13.7	423	317
Black	25.4	423	290
Men	28.0	470	305
Women	22.9	390	276
Hispanic	16.8	417	276
Men	18.5	451	291
Women	14.5	368	255
Full-time workers	20.9	494	372
Managerial and professional specialty	15.2	581	584
Technical, sales, and administrative support	12.1	431	346
Service occupations	15.1	406	226
Precision production, craft, and repair	28.2	568	405
Operators, fabricators, and laborers	29.0	448	287
Farming, forestry, and fishing	4.6	379	239
Private nonagricultural wage and salary workers	13.7	485	368
Mining	19.7	572	561
Construction	22.6	634	393
Manufacturing	23.1	458	400
Transportation and public utilities	34.1	561	458
Wholesale and retail trade, total	7.0	402	298
Finance, insurance, and real estate	3.1	399	407
Services	7.0	402	352
Government	43.6	506	419

Source: U.S. Bureau of Labor Statistics, *Employment and Earnings*, annual. The above data are for 1990.

TABLE 2
Membership in Large Unions, United States

Union	Membership (in thousands)
Teamsters	1161
State, county workers (AFSCME)	1090
Automobile workers (UAW)	917
Service employees (SEIU)	762
Electrical workers (IBEW)	744
Carpenters	613
Teachers (AFT)	544
Machinists	517
Communications workers	492
Steelworkers	481
Laborers (LIUNA)	406
Engineers, operating	330
Hotel and restaurant workers	278
Mine workers	245
Plumbers	220
Postal workers	213
Paper workers	210
Letter carriers	201
Clothing and textile workers	180
Government workers (AFGE)	156
Ladies' garment workers (ILGWU)	153
Firefighters	142
Retail, wholesale department store	137
Painters	128
Graphic communication (IPGCU)	124
Woodworkers	112
Iron workers	111
Bakery, confectionery workers	103
Transit union workers	96
Rubber workers	92
Transport workers	85
Bricklayers	84
Boilermakers	75
Oil, chemical workers	71
Musicians	60

Source: *Statistical Abstract of the United States.* The above data are for 1989.

HISTORY AND LEGISLATION OF AMERICAN UNIONISM

The Growth of the AFL–CIO

As Figure 1 shows, unions were not a powerful force in the American workplace until the late 1930s, even though the first national conventions of labor unions met as early as 1869 to lobby for restrictions on Chinese immigration.[1] Union membership expanded rapidly after 1886, when the traditional craft unions banded together to form the American Federation of Labor (AFL) under the leadership of Samuel Gompers, the "father of the American labor movement." Gompers made a lasting imprint on American unionism through his nonpolitical, nonsocialist approach. Gompers believed that unions should be organized by craft and should not include unskilled workers.

Unskilled and semiskilled workers first joined the Knights of Labor (organized in 1869), which experienced phenomenal growth in the early 1880s. Unlike the AFL, the Knights of Labor was committed as much or more to political goals as to wage increases. When violence in Chicago's Haymarket Square in 1887 stiffened employer resistance and turned public opinion against organized labor, the Knights of Labor suffered a fatal collapse.

One reason for the difficulty in unionizing the American labor force was the unfavorable political climate that prevailed until the 1930s. Antitrust laws (the Sherman Antitrust Act of 1890 in particular) were applied against "monopolistic" labor unions; and companies used private police forces, threats, and intimidation to prevent the formation of labor unions. Management was often able to obtain court orders that prohibited union activity, and employers were allowed to require new employees to sign "yellow dog" contracts, in which the employee had to agree as a condition of employment not to join a union. It was not until 1932 that the government adopted a policy explicitly favoring the organization of unions.

Industrial unionism, which had suffered a severe setback with the collapse of the Knights of Labor, made a comeback in the 1930s under the leadership of John L. Lewis. The failure of the AFL to organize unskilled and semiskilled workers in assembly-line production caused conflicts within the AFL organization. Consequently, the Congress of Industrial Organizations (CIO) was formed in 1936 to organize workers on an industrial rather than a craft basis. In 1955, the AFL and CIO merged to form the AFL–CIO.

The Courts and Legislation

Until the passage of federal legislation in the 1930s, the courts applied common-law principles to union activities. Common law, however, presented the courts with difficult choices. On the one hand, common-law principles hold that intentional harm to private property, as is often undertaken during strikes, picketing, and boycotts, is illegal. On the other hand, the right of people to combine for mutual assistance is also accepted by common law. In the early nineteenth century, the courts typically judged that union efforts to raise wages through strikes, picketing, and boycotts constituted criminal conspiracies. Under such rulings, union leaders were criminally prosecuted and sued for damages. The basic legality of trade unionism was not settled until 1842, when the Supreme Court of Massachusetts ruled that union legality depended upon union objectives. Unions *per se* were not illegal. Following this ruling, peaceful strikes were generally accepted as legal, but violent strikes or sympathy strikes to aid workers in other industries were rejected by the courts.

In the 1880s, employers began using court *injunctions* to prevent strikes, pickets, and boycotts. The injunction was originally designed to prevent threatened damage when regular court processes would be too slow. Employers could go to a sympathetic judge and obtain a restraining order to close down a picket line or head off a strike within a matter of hours. The range of applicability for injunctions was eventually broadened to include safeguarding businesses' "justifiable expectation of profit." The liberal use of injunctions in the late nineteenth and early twentieth centuries made it very difficult for unions to strike. The company only needed to claim that the strike threatened damage to its property. In the early twen-

[1]For a history of the American labor movement, see Lance E. Davis et al., *American Economic Growth* (New York: Harper and Row, 1972), 219–27; Robert F. Flanagan, Robert S. Smith, and Ronald G. Ehrenberg, *Labor Economics and Labor Relations* (Glenview, IL: Scott, Foresman, 1984); Lloyd G. Reynolds and Stanley H. Masters, *Labor Economics and Labor Relations,* 9th ed. (Englewood Cliffs, NJ: Prentice Hall, 1986).

tieth century, court rulings further weakened unions by upholding the validity of "yellow dog" contracts. In effect, the courts ruled that employers could legally require a nonunion pledge as a legitimate condition for employment. A further point of vulnerability was the possibility of applying the restraint-of-trade provisions of the 1890 Sherman Act to unions, a point resolved in 1932.

Two pro-union laws passed during the Great Depression paved the way for the growth of organized labor in the 1930s and 1940s. The Norris-LaGuardia Act of 1932 declared that a worker "has full freedom of association, self-organization, and designation of representatives of his own choosing, to negotiate the terms and conditions of his employment" and that workers should be "free from the interference, restraint, or coercion of employers" in the choice of union representatives. The Norris-LaGuardia Act restricted the use of court orders and injunctions to combat union organizing drives and strikes and prohibited "yellow dog" contracts. The National Labor Relations Act (the Wagner Act) of 1935 defined specific unfair labor practices. Employers were required to bargain in good faith with unions, and it became illegal to interfere with employees' rights to organize into unions. The National Labor Relations Board (NLRB) was authorized to investigate unfair labor practices and conduct elections to determine which union the employees wanted, if any, to represent them.

The Norris-LaGuardia Act of 1932 and the Wagner Act of 1935 encouraged union growth in the 1930s and 1940s. Figure 1 clearly illustrates that before these laws were passed, labor unions were relatively insignificant in size. After World War II, unions lost some of their popular support; the Taft-Hartley and Landrum-Griffin Acts were the result of this renewed antiunion sentiment. The Taft-Hartley Act of 1947 permitted states to pass *right-to-work laws* prohibiting the requirement that union membership be a condition for employment. *Closed-shop agreements* that required firms to hire only union members were outlawed for firms engaged in interstate commerce. Major strikes that threatened to disrupt the economy could be delayed by an 80-day cooling-off period if ordered by the president. The Landrum-Griffin Act of 1959 was designed to protect the rights of union members and to increase union democracy. It included provisions for the periodic reporting of union finances and for regulating union elections.

LABOR UNIONS: AN INTERNATIONAL PERSPECTIVE

There are significant differences between the labor union movements in the United States and in Europe. Although associations of journeymen existed in the form of medieval guilds, labor unions were not organized in Europe until the nineteenth century. The United Kingdom reversed earlier antiunion acts when it passed the Trade Union Act of 1871, which guaranteed legal recognition for labor unions. On the Continent, unions were organized on industrial rather than craft lines, and they engaged in more partisan political activity. In Germany, for example, unions were responsible for much social legislation prior to World War I.

In Europe today, labor organizations tend to be either constituted as or affiliated with political parties, usually from the left wing. In England, the labor unions joined forces with the socialists to form the Labour Party in 1893. In Sweden, there is a close alliance between the two major labor unions and the Social Democratic Party. In Italy, Belgium, and the Netherlands, rival Christian and socialist trade union movements are present. Unlike its European counterparts, the American labor movement has avoided forming a political party, remaining instead within the framework of the two-party system.

The United States is one of the least unionized industrial economies (Table 3). Between 65 percent and 90 percent of workers in Scandinavian countries are unionized. The proportions for Germany, Japan, and the United Kingdom hover around one-third. The United States resembles France, Switzerland, Hong Kong, and Taiwan, where unionization rates are 20 percent or less.

The industrialized countries have developed many types of labor unions. In Germany, unions are organized on an industry basis and are grouped into federations. Collective bargaining usually takes place at industrywide levels, and compulsory arbitration is often used to settle disputes. German enterprise laws require that union representatives sit on management boards in large companies. The German labor movement plays a prominent role in the German Social Democratic Party.

TABLE 3
Union Members as a Percentage of the Labor Force

Country	Percentage	Country	Percentage
Israel	90%	Canada	31%
Sweden	90	Netherlands	29
Finland	80	Japan	29
Belgium	70	France	20
Norway	66	Switzerland	20
Denmark	65	Taiwan	18
Austria	62	Singapore	17
Italy	42	Hong Kong	15
United Kingdom	37	United States	14
Ireland	36	South Korea	10
Germany	34		

Source: *The World Factbook 1990.*

Sweden is dominated by a highly disciplined and comprehensive labor movement. Virtually all blue-collar workers belong to the Confederation of Trade Unions, and white-collar workers belong to one of two other unions. As close allies of the Social Democratic Party, Swedish unions have developed profit-sharing plans and have pushed for social welfare policies to equalize the distribution of income.

The Japanese economy is characterized by company unionism. Each company has its own union that cuts across all craft and class boundaries. Japanese union presidents are key workers who are often promoted to the ranks of management. Japanese unions typically foster cooperation between management and workers and commonly adopt a management perspective. The founding slogan of the Nissan Company labor union is "Those who truly love their union, love their company."[2]

UNION OBJECTIVES

What are the economic objectives of labor unions? Unions desire higher wages, better fringe benefits, and safer working conditions for their members. They also seek to keep their members employed. Are the two objectives of higher wages and lower unemployment compatible, given the fact (demonstrated in the previous chapter) that the firm will hire more labor at low wages than at high wages, *ceteris paribus?*

Assume that two unions, A and B, collectively bargain with management to determine wages. For simplicity, we assume that the average worker in each union is earning the same wage (w_c) and that employment is the same in both cases (at l_c). The derived demand curve for each union's labor force is graphed in Figure 2. The demand in the case of Union A is inelastic. Thus, moving from point c to point a in panel a results in a large percentage increase in the wage (to w_a) compared to the percentage reduction in the quantity of labor demanded (from l_c to l_a). The demand is elastic in the case of Union B. Thus, moving from point c to point b in panel b causes a large percentage decrease in the quantity of labor demanded (from l_c to l_b) compared to the percentage increase in the wage.

The leadership of Union B is faced with a dilemma. If it pushes for wages higher than w_c—such as w_b—the number of union jobs will decline from l_c to l_b. Jobs will be traded for higher wages, and those who lose their jobs will be dissatisfied. (See Example 2.) This **wage/employment trade-off** is less acute in the case of Union A because the same increase in wages loses fewer jobs (due to the difference in elasticity between A and B).

> The **wage/employment trade-off** means that higher wages reduce the number of jobs; lower unemployment requires sacrificing higher wages.

Union Behavior

The wage/employment trade-off concept allows economists to predict which types of industries will be most easily unionized. We would expect unions to be formed first in those industries where the demand for labor is relatively inelastic. Indeed, history shows that skilled crafts such as carpentry, printing, glass-blowing, and shoemaking were the first occupations to be unionized.

The demand for skilled labor is relatively inelastic due to the lack of close substitutes. It is not easy to substitute unskilled for skilled labor or a

[2]Andrew Zimbalist and Howard Sherman, *Comparing Economic Systems* (New York: Academic Press, 1984), 48.

FIGURE 2
The Trade-off between Wages and Employment: The Competitive Case

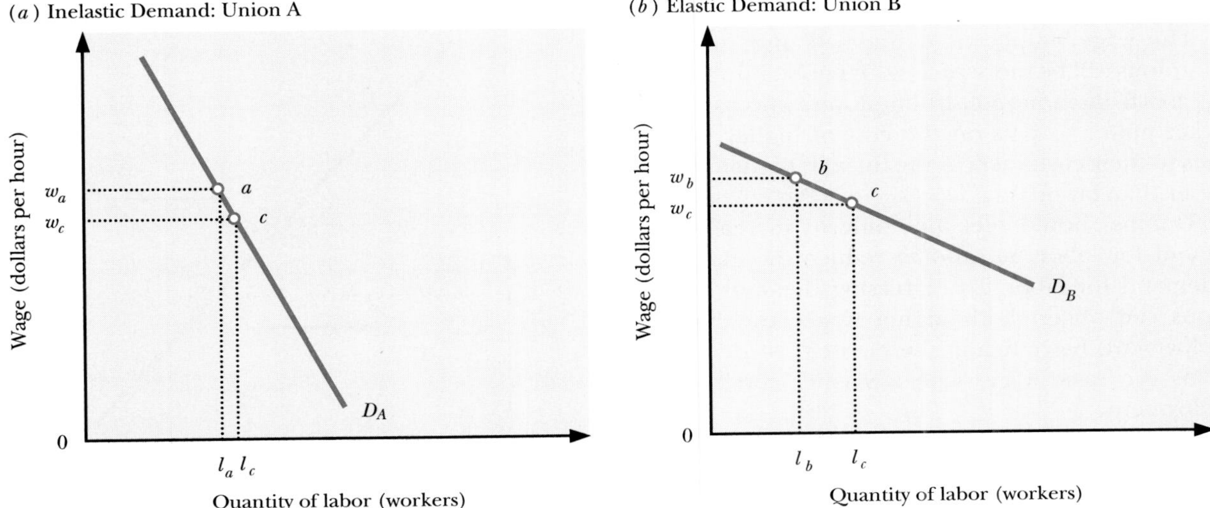

The demand curve for the members of Union A is relatively inelastic, whereas the demand curve for the members of Union B is relatively elastic. If both unions, in the collective bargaining process, push for the same wage increases, more jobs will be lost by workers in Union B (where demand is elastic) than by workers in Union A.

EXAMPLE 2 The Wage/Employment Trade-Off: A Union Strikes for Lower Wages!

One of the most unusual strikes in union history was called in September 1984, by the New Jersey Building and Construction Trades Council of the AFL–CIO on behalf of unionized insulation installers. The goal of the strike, which lasted two days, was to force employers to agree to pay union workers $1.60 an hour less than the employers had offered! Why would a union go on strike to gain lower wages? The union leadership interpreted management's offer as a subtle attempt to price union members out of the market. The higher wage would have provided firms with an excuse to hire more nonunion labor, causing a decline in union membership. In this case, the union members clearly understood the wage/employment trade-off. They were willing to accept lower wages for more jobs.

Source: "Union Asks for Lower Wages to Save Jobs," *Christian Science Monitor*, September 24, 1984.

skilled printer for a skilled glassblower. The last (and presumably most difficult) occupations to organize were the unskilled occupations in which the demand for labor is highly elastic, such as wholesale and retail trade.

The wage/employment trade-off also suggests that unions will be more successful in obtaining wage increases from monopolistic employers who have the market power to pass on the cost of higher union wages to their customers in the form of higher prices (rather than lay-offs).

Unions should seek not only to increase the demand for labor but also to reduce the elasticity of demand for labor. By increasing demand, labor unions can obtain both higher wages and higher employment. By reducing the elasticity of demand, unions can raise wages with a smaller cost in lost employment.

Unions attempt to increase the demand for labor and lower its elasticity of demand in a variety of ways. They lobby for tariffs and quotas on competing foreign products and conduct advertising campaigns telling the public to "look for the union label" or to "buy American." The AFL–CIO has opposed the relaxation of immigration laws and has spoken out against illegal immigration. Unions have traditionally supported raising the minimum wage—an act that makes unskilled labor more expensive relative to the more skilled workers that tend to belong to unions.

Unions have also pushed for minimum staffing requirements. In the 1970s, for example, pilot unions unsuccessfully lobbied for MD-80 aircraft to be staffed by three cockpit personnel (two pilots and a flight engineer) rather than two pilots. Staffing requirements that perpetuate jobs that have become redundant (such as fire stokers on diesel-powered locomotives) are called *featherbedding*. Unions may also bargain for rules that make it difficult to substitute other grades of labor for union labor. In construction contracts, unions specify in detail which jobs can be performed only by electricians and plumbers, and they impose sanctions against builders who hire nonunion employees.

Limitations of Labor Supply

One strategy for raising wages is to limit the supply of union labor. Some unions control who will be allowed to work in a particular occupation by means of certification and qualification requirements. In craft unions, the number of union members can be restricted by long apprenticeships, difficult qualifying exams, state licensing, and ceilings on total membership. In the process of limiting labor supply, the union screens out unqualified workers, but it may also exclude some qualified people who are prepared to work in a particular occupation.

FIGURE 3
Craft Unions and Wages: Limiting Supply

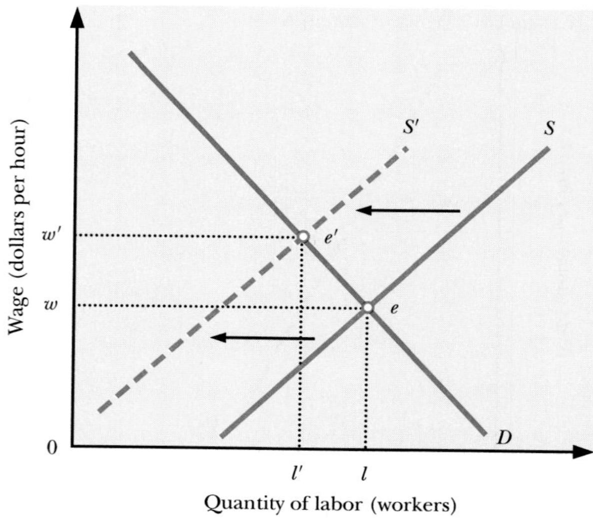

By limiting entry into the profession, a craft union shifts the labor supply curve to the left (from S to S'), and the wage rate of union members is raised above what it would have been without the union.

Figure 3 shows the effect that limiting the labor supply has on wages. The decrease in supply (from S to S') moves the equilibrium wage/employment combination from e to e'; at e', wages are higher but the number of jobs is fewer. If unions are to control wages through limitations on the supply of union labor, it is necessary to prevent employers from substituting nonunion labor. For this reason, craft unions favor rigid certification requirements and rules prohibiting nonunion workers from performing their tasks.

Strikes and Collective Bargaining

Industrial unions that represent all of the workers in a particular industry find it difficult to limit the supply of labor. Such unions wield some influence on overall labor supply conditions through supporting immigration restrictions, mandatory retirement, shorter

FIGURE 4
Collective Bargaining with the Threat of a Strike

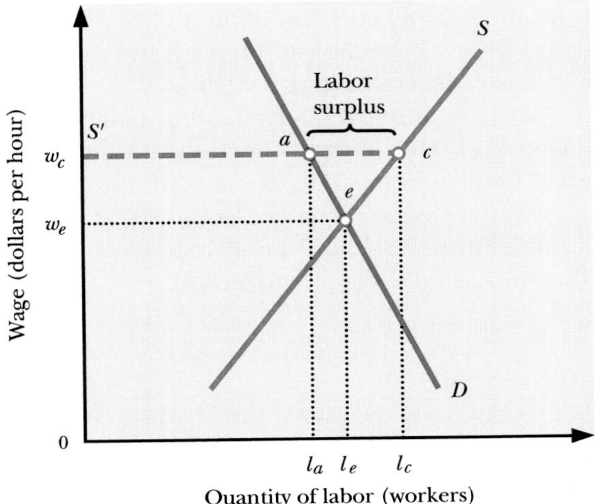

The supply curve S represents the labor supply if each worker were to bargain separately with the employer. The supply curve formed by S' to the left of point c and S above c results from collective bargaining; no union labor will be supplied at a wage below w_c. Point e is the equilibrium wage/employment combination without collective bargaining or the threat of a strike; point a is the equilibrium wage/employment combination with collective bargaining.

work weeks, and laws against teenage employment. Unlike plumbers, electricians, and physicians, industrial unions cannot control the number of union members by licensing, exams, and apprenticeship programs. Industrial unions, therefore, use **collective bargaining** to raise the wages of union members.

> **Collective bargaining** is the process whereby a union bargains with management as the representative of all union employees.

The collective bargaining process gives workers a stronger voice than if each worker negotiated separately with management.

The threat of a **strike** is a union's most potent weapon in collective bargaining. The effect of the collective-bargaining process (with threat of strike) is portrayed in Figure 4. The supply curve S represents the supply of labor to the industry if each individual were to bargain separately with management. When a union threatens to strike, it is, in effect, telling management that at wages less than w_c, no labor will be supplied; at the wage of w_c, management can hire as much labor as it wants up to l_c; as wages increase above w_c, management can hire increasing amounts of labor beyond l_c. Thus, the new labor supply curve incorporating the threat of a strike is the line S' that connects w_c on the vertical axis with point c and then continues along the original supply curve above point c. Without the threat of a strike, the supply curve would be the original curve S, and point e would be the equilibrium wage/employment combination. With the threat of a strike, the demand curve meets the new supply curve at point a, and the firm hires l_a workers at a wage of w_c.

> A **strike** occurs when all unionized employees cease to work until management agrees to specific union demands.

From the standpoint of union members, collective bargaining has both costs and benefits. The benefits are the higher wages that collective bargaining brings (w_c is higher than w_e). However, if the industry is entirely unionized, some union members who are willing to work at the negotiated wage will not be employed. Although l_c workers are willing to work at w_c, only l_a workers will be hired. The unemployment effects of collective bargaining are softened by numerous rules within the union (an internal labor market) governing the order of lay-offs. Typically, union members who have *seniority* (have been in the union the longest time) are laid off last. (See Example 3.)

Collective Bargaining with Monopsony

If employers have monopsony power over their labor market, there is no trade-off between higher wages and union employment. An employer that has monopsony power accounts for a large enough portion of total hiring in the labor market to affect the market wage. The labor supply curve for a monopsonistic firm is not horizontal at the prevailing market wage because the firm cannot hire all the labor it wants at the market wage. Instead, to hire more labor, the monopsonistic firm must offer higher wages to all its employees.

EXAMPLE 3 The *Aussperrung* (Lockout)

In Germany, employers have used the lockout (*Aussperrung*) as both an offensive and defensive weapon against unions in collective bargaining. A lockout occurs when the employer association shuts down the industry until it reaches acceptable agreements with the union. The industry shutdown imposes hardships on the union membership and pressures members to accept the terms offered by employers. The shutdown is also used as a defense against threatened strikes.

Although German unions have challenged the legality of lockouts, the courts have ruled that employers have the right to lock out workers, just as workers have the right to strike. In fact, German employer associations (such as the iron and steel industry or the printing industry) have used lockouts about as frequently as unions have gone on strike. In the 1970s, for example, industries lost as many man days due to lockouts as they lost due to strikes.

Source: Gerhard Brinkmann, *Oekonomik der Arbeit* (Stuttgart: Klett, 1981), 270–74.

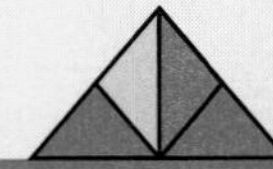

Consider a monopsonist faced with the labor supply schedule given in Table 4. The wage rate is not the marginal factor cost (MFC) in the case of the monopsonist. To hire one more unit of labor, the monopsonist must pay a higher wage not just to the extra worker, but to all workers. The MFC of the second worker is, therefore, the wage paid to the second worker ($7) plus the increase in the wage of the first worker ($2), for a total of $9. The MFC for each additional worker is shown in column 4.

> The marginal factor cost of the monopsonist is greater than the wage rate.

The relationship between MFC and wages is shown in Figure 5. The monopsonist will hire that quantity of labor at which marginal factor cost and marginal revenue product (MRP) are equal (but will pay the wage corresponding to that quantity on the labor supply curve). In the absence of collective bargaining, MFC = MRP at point *e*, so the monopsonist will operate at point *m*, hiring l_m workers at a wage of w_m.

Since MFC exceeds the wage rate (given by *S*) the monopsonist will hire less labor than if the industry were competitive in the labor market and each firm treated the wage rate as its MFC. In Figure 5, the competitive industry will operate at point *c*, where *S* (which equals MFC) equals MRP.

If a union collectively bargains for a wage of w_u in Figure 5, the monopsonist MFC curve becomes a horizontal line at w_u (MFC′). Collective bargaining makes the supply of union labor perfectly elastic

TABLE 4
The Monopsonist's Labor Cost

Labor (workers), *L* (1)	Wage (dollars per hours), *W* (2)	Labor Cost (dollars) (3) = (1) × (2)	Marginal Factor Cost (dollars), MFC (4)
1	5	5	
			9
2	7	14	
			13
3	9	27	
			21
4	12	48	

The monopsonist must pay a higher wage to employ more workers. The marginal factor cost of an extra worker is, therefore, greater than the wage. For example, the wage of the second worker is $7 per hour, but the marginal factor cost is $9 (or $7 plus the $2 difference between the wage necessary to hire one worker and the wage necessary to hire two workers).

FIGURE 5
Monopsony and Collective Bargaining

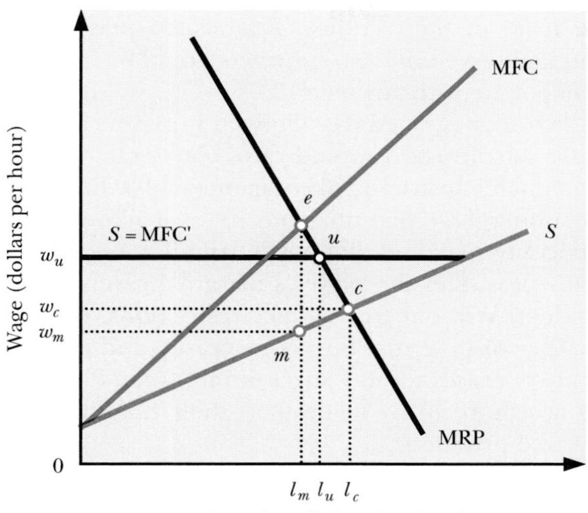

Because this industry is monopsonistic, MFC is greater than the wage of labor at each quantity (given by S). The monopsonist will hire that quantity of labor at which MFC = MRP and pay the wage that corresponds to that labor quantity on the supply curve, or w_m. Without unions, MFC = MRP at point *e;* the monopsonist will hire l_m workers and pay the wage of w_m. Thus, the monopsonistic employer provides less employment and lower wages than would a competitive industry (point c). If a union collectively bargains for a wage of w_u, the monopsonist's MFC curve shifts to MFC′, due to the change in labor supply, and becomes a horizontal line at w_u; MFC′ will now equal MRP at point u. In this case, collective bargaining actually increased both wages (from w_m to w_u) and union employment (from l_m to l_u).

(horizontal) at the union wage. By demanding w_u, the union makes this wage the MFC of the monopsonist. In this case, MRP = MFC′ at point u, where the monopsonist hires l_u of labor. Collective bargaining succeeds in raising both wages and union employment when the firm is a monopsonist.

> The wage/employment trade-off does not exist when the employer is a monopsonist.

In an earlier chapter, it was argued that monopsony in factor markets is less likely than monopoly in product markets. Although important cases of monopsony can be found, the observed behavior of labor unions—their obvious efforts to soften the wage/employment trade-off—suggests that monopsony is not prevalent and that in most cases, unions must trade off jobs for higher wages. (See Example 4.)

THE EFFECT OF UNIONS ON WAGES

Labor economists have sought to estimate the extent to which unions have been able to raise their wages relative to nonunion wages.

Union Effect on Union Wages

Studies of the effect of unions on wages find that unions have indeed succeeded in raising the wages of their members above nonunion wages.[3] Table 1 shows that union members earned $494 per week in 1990, a figure that is more than $100 higher than the $372 nonunion weekly earnings figure. The effects of unions have varied over time by industry, gender, and race. Studies for the 1960s, for example, show that unions raised the wages of laborers by the highest percentages but had little or no effect on managerial and professional wages. Table 5 indicates that from 1967 to 1975, the wage advantage of union members increased from 12 percent to 17 percent. A pioneering researcher in this area, H. Gregg Lewis, found that the average union/nonunion wage gap was 15 percent for the period 1967 to 1979. The most substantial improvements were experienced by white male and black female union members; white female union members scarcely increased their wage advantage

[3]The pioneering study of the effects of unions on wage rates is by H. G. Lewis, *Unionism and Relative Wages in the United States* (Chicago: University of Chicago Press, 1963). Lewis's more recent study is found in his *Union Relative Wage Effects: A Survey* (Chicago: University of Chicago Press, 1986). A survey of this literature is provided by C. J. Paisley, "Labor Union Effects on Wage Gains: A Survey of Recent Literature," *Journal of Economic Literature* 18, 1 (March 1980): 1–31. See also Flanagan, Smith, and Ehrenberg, *Labor Economics and Industrial Relations,* 560–66.

EXAMPLE 4 Monopsony and Free Agency for NBA Athletes

A monopsony exists when there is one buyer of a factor of production. For many years, owners of professional basketball teams maintained a monopsony through "free agency" rules. Under free agency players finished with college had no choice but to sign with the team that drafted them. Veteran players did not have the freedom to switch jobs because owners had the right to first refusal when a player's contract expired. These rules ensured that there would be only one bidder for the professional athlete's services—that a single buyer had a monopsony.

In May 1988, the basketball owners and the players' union agreed to new rules, allowing owners to draft only 50 players. All other college players would be able to negotiate freely with the team of their choice. Established players who had served out two contracts would be free to negotiate with any team.

Owners resisted free choice for players because they feared it would raise player salaries too much. Restrictive free agency rules limit the number of potential buyers of a player's services to one, and that buyer can offer a wage that is less than the player's marginal revenue product. Without free agency restrictions, the number of potential buyers increases, and the industry ceases to be a strict monopsony. Players are more likely to be paid their marginal revenue products.

Source: "Free Agency: The Players and the NBA meet at Half Court," *Business Week* (May 16, 1988): 46.

TABLE 5
Estimated Union Wage Advantage over Nonunion Workers, 1967, 1973, and 1975

	Percentage Union Wage Advantage			Percentage Unionized		
	1967	**1973**	**1975**	**1967**	**1973**	**1975**
All workers	11.6	14.8	16.8	23	26	25
White males	9.6	15.5	16.3	31	33	31
Black males	21.5	22.5	22.5	32	37	37
White females	14.4	12.7	16.6	12	14	14
Black females	5.6	13.2	17.1	13	22	22

Source: Orley Ashenfelter, "Union Relative Wage Effects: New Evidence and a Survey of Their Implications for Wage Inflation," in *Econometric Contributions to Public Policy,* edited by R. Stone and W. Peterson (New York: St. Martin's, 1979), Tables 2.1 and 2.2.

relative to nonunion members. Black males consistently maintained the highest wage advantage from union membership. In 1975, for example, black male union members earned 22.5 percent higher wages than their nonunion counterparts.

Studies show that historically, craft unions in construction and transportation have achieved the largest relative wage effects (20 percent to 25 percent). Industrial unions have had a smaller relative wage effect (10 percent to 15 percent). Unions have made their smallest impact on relative wages in competitive industries such as textiles and apparel.

Union Effect on Nonunion Wages

It is more difficult to establish the effect of unions on the general level of wages or on the wages of nonunion workers. Theory suggests that unions could either depress or increase the wage rates of nonunion workers.

The labor force is made up of both unionized and nonunionized sectors. If unions gain substantial wage increases by giving up jobs, then some union members who are willing to work at the union wage are unemployed, and they "spill over" into the nonunion sector. Young union members with low seniority are the ones most likely to be laid off. When they seek employment in the nonunionized sector, wages in the nonunionized sector are bid down. This *spillover effect,* therefore, depresses the wages of nonunion workers.

A highly simplified view of the spillover effect is shown in Figure 6. Before Industry A is unionized, both industries pay $8 per hour; A uses 50 workers, and B uses 90 workers. When A becomes unionized, employment in A falls to 30 workers and employment

FIGURE 6
The Effect of Unions on Nonunion Wages: The Spillover Effect

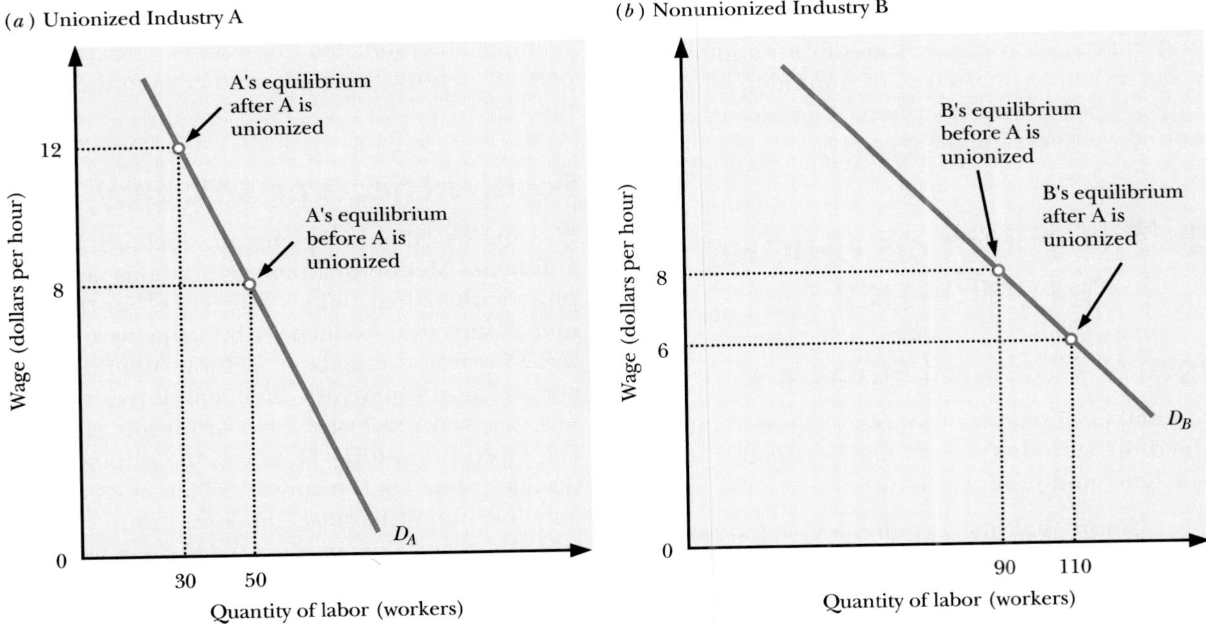

Before Industry A is unionized, wages are $8 per hour in both A and B; 50 workers are employed in A and 90 are employed in B. After A is unionized, workers in A earn a new wage of $12, but 20 workers lose their jobs and must be absorbed into Industry B. A's unionization drives the wage down to $6 in the nonunionized industry by increasing the supply of workers to Industry B. This example assumes that the employer is perfectly competitive, that the workers have perfect information about jobs, and that labor is homogeneous.

in B rises to 110 workers. The wage rate in A rises to $12, and wages in B fall to $6 as a result of A's unionization. This example assumes perfect competition in the firm's product market, perfect information about jobs, and homogeneous labor. Here the 30 original members of Industry A benefit at the expense of the 20 workers who move to Industry B and must take lower wages.

Yet, it may not be the case that union activity decreases wages in the nonunionized sector. Employers of nonunion workers may fear that if they do not match union wage increases, pressure will build to form a union. In addition, unionized workers who are laid off may wait until they are recalled to their jobs rather than spill over into the nonunionized sector. The probability of such *wait unemployment* is greatest when there is a substantial wage differential between nonunion and union jobs, when the likelihood of recall is high, and when the costs of unemployment are low (because unemployment benefits are available). If unemployed union workers do not spill over into nonunionized jobs, the downward pressure on nonunion wages is removed.

The empirical evidence regarding union effects on nonunion wages is not extensive, but it does suggest that unions depress wages in nonunionized jobs. For example, the wages of nonunion workers are typically lower in cities where the percentage of unionized workers is high.[4]

THE EFFECT OF UNIONS ON EFFICIENCY

Negative Effects on Efficiency

For a number of reasons, economists have traditionally held the view that unions have a negative effect on efficiency and productivity.

1. Union staffing requirements (*featherbedding*) prevent employers from using labor and capital in the most efficient manner. If union rules prevent carpenters from turning a screw on any electrical fixture, for example, the economy will operate below its potential.

2. Union strikes cause the economy to produce below its potential. Strikes in major industries, like steel and rail transportation, can disrupt other sectors of the economy and cause losses in real output.

3. Unions drive a wedge between the wages of union and nonunion workers in comparable employment.

If two identical workers are paid different wages because one belongs to a union and the other does not, the economy loses potential output. In both the unionized and nonunionized sectors, workers will be employed to the point where their wage equals their MRP, but the MRPs of union workers will be higher than those of comparable nonunion workers. The economy could increase its output by reallocating workers from the nonunionized sector (where MRP is lower) into the union sector (where MRP is higher). But the task of unions is to raise the wages of their members above what they would have been without the union by limiting the labor supply. Thus, whenever significant spillover effects result, MRPs will be different.

Economists have attempted to estimate the output lost due to unions. Economist Albert Rees, for example, has estimated this loss at approximately 0.8 percent of gross national product from the 1930s to the 1960s.[5]

Positive Effects on Efficiency

Economists Albert Hirschman, Richard Freeman, and James Medoff maintain that unions actually improve rather than reduce efficiency.[6] In their view, unions improve productivity by acting as a collective voice for union members. Without unions, if workers are dissatisfied with their employer, their only recourse is the *exit mechanism*—to revolt against bad employers by quitting. However, the exit mechanism results in heavy job turnover, which costs the economy lost output because employees must learn new jobs and spend time in often lengthy job searches.

Unions offer an alternative to the exit mechanism by enabling workers to have an effective voice in enterprise affairs. Individuals are rarely willing to assume sole responsibility for seeking improved

[4]Lawrence Kahn, "The Effect of Unions on the Earnings of Nonunion Workers," *Industrial and Labor Relations Review* 31 (January 1978): 205–16.

[5]Albert Rees, "The Effects of Unions on Resource Allocation," *Journal of Law and Economics* 6 (October 1963): 69–78.

[6]Richard B. Freeman and James L. Medoff, *What Do Unions Do?* (New York: Basic Books, 1982).

conditions for all workers. Not only is such action time-consuming, it may also be risky; employers may seek to get rid of activists. Collective action through unions, however, spreads the burden of time among many workers and is protected (individual action is not) by the National Labor Relations Act.

Unions can have a positive effect on productivity in three ways. First, because grievances are handled by the union, workers need not leave the firm in order to improve their work conditions. If fewer workers are driven to quit by their complaints, the firm can reduce its hiring and training costs and work groups function more smoothly. Second, the union provides a channel of communication between workers and management improving information flows and thereby increasing the efficiency of the enterprise. Third, the seniority system fostered by unions reduces friction between junior and senior workers. Senior workers (who are most important politically in the union organization) are more likely to provide informal training and assistance and junior workers are more willing to learn, knowing they will move up in the ranks.

Evidence of Union Effects

The characterization of unions as a positive factor in labor productivity is relatively recent. The final word on whether unions raise or lower economic efficiency remains to be written.

What does the empirical evidence suggest about the effect of unions on productivity? First, there is strong evidence that the presence of unions causes a dramatic reduction in employee turnover (see Table 6). Although the quit rates of young workers (who are the first to be laid off in unions) decline only slightly with unionization, those for all other workers are substantially reduced by the presence of unions.

Although the evidence that unions reduce quit rates does not necessarily prove that unions improve labor productivity, other evidence (see Table 7) does suggest that unions have increased output per worker in those industries studied, with the exception of underground bituminous coal mining. The negative effect of unions in coal mining may be due to deteriorating industrial relations in the late 1960s that prevented the United Mine Workers from being an effective union voice.

The productivity advantage of union workers (according to Freeman and Medoff) may be large enough to offset the wage advantage of union workers. If union workers are 20 percent more productive and earn 20 percent more than nonunion workers, average labor costs per unit of output are the same.

TABLE 6
Effect of Unions on Quit Rates

Sample	Percentage by which Quits Are Reduced by Unionism
All workers, 1968–78	45
All workers, 1973–75	86
Men 48–62 in 1969	107
Men 17–27 in 1969	11
Manufacturing workers	34–48

Source: Richard Freeman and James Medoff, "The Two Faces of Unionism," *The Public Interest* 57 (Fall 1979): 79.

TABLE 7
Effect of Unions on Productivity in U.S. Industries

Industry	Percentage Increase in Output per Worker Due to Unions
Manufacturing, 1972	20–25
Wooden furniture, 1972	15
Cement, 1953–76	6–8
Underground coal, 1965	25–30
Underground coal, 1975	(−20)-(−25)
Construction, 1972	29–38
Construction, office buildings, 1973–74	30
Construction, retail stores and shopping centers, 1976–78	51

Sources: Richard Freeman and James Medoff, "The Two Faces of Unionism," *The Public Interest* 57 (Fall 1979): 80; Kim Clark, "The Impact of Unionization on Productivity: A Case Study," *Industrial and Labor Relations Review* (July 1980): 451–69; and Ronald Ehrinberg and Robert Smith, *Modern Labor Economics,* 4th ed. (New York: HarperCollins, 1991), 483.

Richard Ruback and Martin Zimmerman, however, cite evidence to dispute this point. They find that the share price of a company typically falls (by about 4 percent, on average) when that company becomes unionized—which means that the investment community believes that unions reduce long-run profitability.[7]

This chapter continued the discussion of labor markets begun in the preceding chapter by examining how unions affect wages and economic efficiency. The next chapter will turn to the nonlabor factors of production: land, capital, and entrepreneurship.

SUMMARY

1. A union is a collective organization of workers and employees whose objective is to improve pay and work conditions. A craft union represents workers of a particular occupation. An industrial union represents workers of a particular industry. Less than 15 percent of the U.S. labor force belongs to unions—a decline from the high of 25 percent in the 1950s. This decrease is due to the rise of white-collar employment, the rising share of women in the work force, and the shift of industry to the South and Southwest. The most substantial gains in union membership in recent years have been in public employment.

2. During the nineteenth century, the U.S. courts used common-law rulings and injunctions to limit union activity. The formation of unions was aided by prolabor legislation beginning with the Norris-LaGuardia Act of 1932, which facilitated union organizing drives. The National Labor Relations Act of 1935 made it illegal for employers to interfere with the rights of employees to organize. The Taft-Hartley Act of 1947 was a reaction against the pro-union legislation of the 1930s.

3. Union membership in the United States is lower than that of most industrialized countries.

4. Unions must weigh the advantages of higher wages against the disadvantages of less employment. Unions respond to the trade-off between jobs and employment by attempting to increase the demand for union labor and reduce the elasticity of that demand. In collective bargaining, the most potent weapon of the union is the threat of a strike. In the case of monopsony, the trade-off between higher wages and employment does not exist. The attempts of unions to minimize their losses in this trade-off suggest that monopsony is not prevalent.

5. Unions have raised the wages of their members relative to nonunion wages. The size of the raise varies by industry and by union. Unions can have both a positive and a negative effect on nonunion wages. When unions raise wages in the union sector, the workers who lose employment spill over into the nonunion sector. This increase in the labor supply lowers nonunion wages. However, when unions raise wages in the union sector, nonunion employers may raise wages to prevent the formation of a union in their enterprise.

6. There are two views on the effect of unions on productivity. The traditional view maintains that unions adversely affect labor productivity. A more recent view argues that unions serve as a collective voice that raises the labor productivity of union workers.

KEY TERMS

labor union	wage/employment trade-off
craft union	collective bargaining
industrial union	strike
employee association	

QUESTIONS AND PROBLEMS

1. The elasticity of demand for labor (the percentage change in quantity of labor demanded divided by the percentage change in the wage) is 1.5 in the widget industry and 0.5 in the ratchet industry at current wage and employment levels. Which industry would be easier to unionize? In which industry is the trade-off between employment and higher wages more costly?
2. If you were the president of a major industrial union, what would your attitude be toward free immigration? What would your attitude be toward the minimum-wage law? Explain.
3. Explain why the wage/employment trade-off does not exist for a monopsonistic industry.
4. Explain why both the automobile unions and the management of the automobile industry favor import restrictions on foreign-made cars.

[7]Richard S. Ruback and Martin B. Zimmerman, "Unionization and Profitability: Evidence from the Capital Market," *Journal of Political Economy* (December 1984): 1134–57.

5. You belong to a union of bank tellers. What would your attitude be toward automated bank tellers? Explain.
6. Explain why the impact of higher union wages on nonunion wages might depend upon the extent of wait unemployment.
7. Which of the following policies would unions tend to favor? Explain your answer.

   a. Liberal immigration laws
   b. Free trade
   c. Reductions of quotas on foreign goods
   d. A higher minimum wage

8. If unions do succeed in raising productivity, what effect would this increase have on the costs of production of unionized versus nonunionized companies?
9. Explain the contradiction that common-law principles presented to judges who had to rule on the legality of strikes in the eighteenth and nineteenth centuries.
10. A firm is considering employing 100 workers at a wage of $50 per week. In order to hire 105 workers, the employer must raise the wage rate to $55.10. What is the marginal factor cost of hiring one more worker? What is the relationship between marginal factor cost and the wage rate? What kind of firm is this?
11. Explain the connection between lower quit rates and increased productivity under unionization.
12. A firm is currently paying labor $5 per hour. If this firm can double its labor force and still pay $5 per hour, what kind of a firm is it?
13. Describe the legislation of the 1930s and 1940s that is said to have made the growth of unionism possible.
14. The chapter on factor markets said that factor markets are more likely to be competitive than product markets. What does this information imply about the wage/employment trade-off?

SUGGESTED READINGS

Barbash, Jack. "The Labor Movement after World War II." *Monthly Labor Review* (November 1976).

Bowen, William G., and Orley Ashenfelter, eds. *Labor and the National Economy,* rev. ed. New York: W. W. Norton, 1975.

Ehrenberg, Ronald G., and Robert S. Smith. *Modern Labor Economics: Theory and Public Policy,* 4th ed. New York: HarperCollins, 1991.

Freeman, Richard B., and James L. Medoff. "The Two Faces of Unionism." *Public Interest* 57 (Fall 1979): 69–93.

Freeman, Richard B., and James L. Medoff. *What Do Unions Do?* New York: Basic Books, 1982.

Hughes, J. *American Economic History,* 3rd ed. New York: HarperCollins, 1990.

Lewis, H. Gregg. *Union Relative Wage Effects: A Survey.* Chicago: University of Chicago Press, 1986.

Paisley, C. J. "Labor Unions and Wages: A Survey." *Journal of Economic Literature* 18 (March 1980): 1–31.

Reynolds, Lloyd G. and Stanley H. Masters. *Labor Economics and Labor Relations.* 9th ed. Englewood Cliffs, NJ: Prentice Hall, 1986.

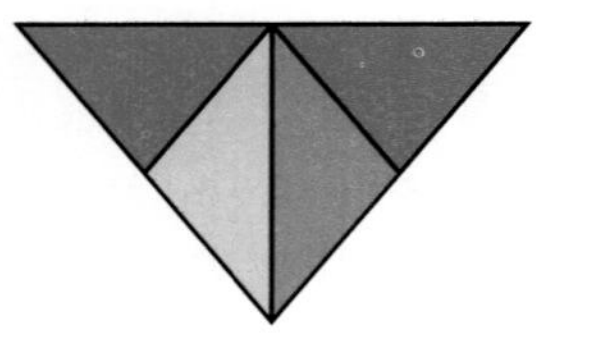

39 Interest, Rent, and Profit

CHAPTER INSIGHT

Historically, interest, rent, and profit account for approximately 25 percent of national income in the United States; wages and salaries constitute the remaining 75 percent. The previous two chapters described wages, or the payments to labor; this chapter will describe the income earned by the remaining factors of production: land, capital, and entrepreneurship. The owner of each of these three factors of production offers the use of the factor in return for payment.

The payment for the use of capital is *interest.* The supply of capital consists of the accumulation of savings by households and firms. The payment for the use of land and other natural resources is *rent.* The supply of land or natural resources is relatively fixed. *Profit* is a more complicated concept, but in some instances it can be regarded as a payment for the use of an entrepreneur's services. The supply of entrepreneurship depends heavily on the detailed social, educational, and economic characteristics of the society from which entrepreneurs are drawn. This chapter will identify the principal forces determining interest, rent, and profit.

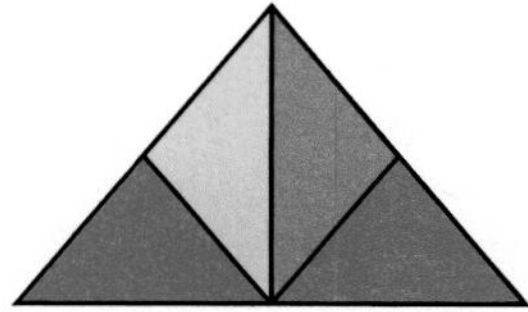

INTEREST

Capital goods are required for the indirect, or roundabout, production of consumer goods. Roundabout production is typically more productive than direct production. Capital goods such as trucks, conveyors, buildings, lathes, cranes, hammers, and computers harness the mechanical, electrical, and chemical powers of nature to expand the production possibilities of society far beyond what could otherwise be accomplished by unaided human hands or minds. Productivity is raised, for example, when a net is used instead of bare hands to catch fish, or when workers assemble cars on an assembly line with sophisticated equipment rather than in a small garage with hand tools.

Saving is necessary if a society is to invest in capital goods. Through saving, resources are diverted from producing consumption goods to producing capital goods. When people save, they buy stocks and bonds or deposit their funds in various bank accounts. Although some of these funds are used to finance the consumption expenditures of ordinary people, the rest are channeled (directly or indirectly) into investments in new buildings, plants, machinery, and so forth.

Interest is the price paid for borrowed funds or credit. People are impatient. To be convinced of the value of saving a dollar today, they must be rewarded with more than a dollar tomorrow. As capital is productive, a dollar invested today in actual capital goods yields more than a dollar tomorrow. Thus, investors are willing to pay the interest that savers demand. Interest coordinates the number of dollars that businesses want to invest with the number that people want to save.

> **Interest** is the price of credit and is determined in credit markets, where the amount businesses wish to invest is balanced with the amount people are prepared to save.

The Stock of Capital

Economists distinguish between *tangible capital* and *intangible capital.* Tangible capital differs from the other factors of production in that in its concrete form (from trucks and computers to fish nets and shovels), it has already been produced. Land that has been improved by irrigation, by the clearing of forests, or by the draining of swamps is also "produced" and as such is a capital good just like machines and factories.

Intangible capital has two forms. *Research and development (R&D) capital* consists of accumulated investments in technology, productive knowledge, and know-how; *human capital* consists of accumulated investments in human beings—investments in training, education, and improved health that increase the productive capacities of people. The stock of intangible capital available to a society at any given point in time can be measured by the cost of the resources that have been devoted to R&D investment and to human-capital investment. Human-capital investments, which are an important determinant of the distribution of income, will be discussed in more detail in the next chapter. Human-capital theory suggests that the human capital embodied in trained labor is "produced" in the same economic sense as a truck or factory.

The inventory, or stock, of capital that exists in an economy at any given moment depends on (1) the accumulated savings and investment decisions that have been made in the past and (2) the extent to which old capital goods have undergone **depreciation** through use or obsolescence.

> **Depreciation** is the decrease in the economic value of capital goods as they are used in the production process.

The amount of new capital goods that are added to the stock of capital during a given period depends on how much consumers are saving and how much firms are investing. Over time, capital goods (broadly defined to include human capital and investments in land improvements) accumulate and depreciate. If the rate of accumulation exceeds the rate of depreciation, the stock of capital will grow.

> The current stock of capital is determined by past savings and investment decisions. The stock of capital grows if the rate of capital accumulation exceeds the rate of depreciation. The stock of capital declines if the rate of accumulation is less than the rate of depreciation.

Credit Markets

Robinson Crusoe, living alone on a deserted island, did not need credit markets to coordinate saving and investing. When he took 3 days off from fishing to weave a net, he was both *saving* (giving up some present consumption) and *investing* (engaging in roundabout production to increase his future consumption). Simultaneous saving and investing was also characteristic of early agricultural societies. Farmers saved and invested in the same act of taking time off from current production to drain a swamp or build an earthen dam (that is, to produce capital goods). In a modern economy, however, financial assets—stocks, bonds, bank credit, and trade credit—are used to finance the accumulation of capital goods. Investors and savers are often separate entities, with their actions coordinated by **credit,** or **capital, markets.**

> **Credit,** or **capital, markets** facilitate the exchange of financial assets in a modern society.

Credit, or capital, markets are necessitated by specialization. Business firms have the ability to take advantage of profitable investment opportunities by expanding production capacities, but, unlike Robinson Crusoe, they must usually find a separate source of funds. Households, meanwhile, specialize in saving because they do not have the information to act on profitable investment opportunities. Therefore, a natural trade can be set up between households and businesses. In credit markets, firms wishing to invest in capital goods borrow from households (and other businesses); similarly, savers (households and businesses) lend to investors.

The growth of the stock of tangible capital is paralleled by the growth of the financial assets of those individuals or firms who accumulate savings. These financial assets (stocks, bonds, and various IOUs) are specific types of claims on the net productivity of real capital. The owners of such capital receive *interest* (or dividend) *income* from investors as payment for the use of their capital.

The Rate of Interest

By convention, an **interest rate** is usually expressed as an annual percentage rate.

> An **interest rate** measures the yearly cost of borrowing as a percentage of the amount loaned.

If $1000 is borrowed on January 1 and $1100 (the $1000 borrowed plus $100 interest) is repaid on December 31 of that same year, the $100 interest represents a 10 percent rate of interest on an annual percentage basis. If the loan is for only 6 months and $1050 is repaid on June 30, the $50 interest still represents a 10 percent annual rate.

The common reference to the rate of interest as the "price of money" is both confusing and misleading. Strictly speaking, in economics the term *money* is the medium of exchange used by an economy; it constitutes the unit of borrowing, rather than the act itself. The "price of credit" is a better definition because the term *credit* incorporates the passage of time between borrowing and repayment.

The rate of interest represents the terms of trade between the present and future. A low interest rate means that future goods are expensive relative to present goods; a high interest rate means future goods are cheap relative to present goods. Suppose, for example, that a college education costs $50,000. A family knows that it may incur this cost in 18 to 20 years. If interest rates are high, the family will not have to save as much as with low interest rates. In other words, high interest rates make future goods and services (i.e., the college education) cheaper in terms of present sacrifices.

Because the interest rate is the price that links the present and the future, it can be used to convert future values into present values. The concept of present value is important because it forms the basis for pricing assets as well as determining such expenses as the monthly car payments. The simplest case of present value is that of a *perpetual income stream* (a fixed amount of income to be received every year forever). As shown in the chapter on business organization, the present value (PV) of a perpetual income stream is

$$\text{PV} = \frac{R}{i} \tag{1}$$

where R is the annual income stream, and i is the rate of interest expressed in decimal form. For example, the present value of $100 per year in perpetuity with an interest rate of 10 percent is $100/0.10 = $1000. An income of $100 per year in perpetuity is worth $1000 today at a 10 percent interest rate because if you deposit $1000 in a bank account paying a 10 percent interest rate and leave it there forever, you will earn $100 per year.

Rather than perpetual income streams, financial assets typically yield payments of specified amounts for a limited number of years. For example, the present value of an IOU that pays $100 per year for 3 years is calculated using the following formula for the present value of a future sum of money, previously given in the business-organization chapter.

$$PV = \frac{R_n}{(1 + i)^n} \qquad (2)$$

where R_n is the sum of money to be paid in the nth year and i is the interest rate in decimal form. At a 10 percent interest rate, the $100 to be received 1 year from now is worth $90.91 (= $100/1.10). In other words, if you deposit $90.91 in a savings account paying 10 percent interest, you will have accumulated $100 at the end of the first year. The $100 to be received 2 years from today is worth $82.65 (= $100/1.21) because if you deposit $82.65 in a 10 percent savings account, you will have accumulated $100 after 2 years. Similarly, the $100 to be received 3 years from now is worth $75.19 (= $100/1.33). Thus, the PV of the IOU that pays $100 per year for 3 years is calculated as follows:

$$PV = \frac{R_1}{1+i} + \frac{R_2}{(1+i)^2} + \frac{R_3}{(1+i)^3}$$

$$= \frac{100}{1.10} + \frac{100}{1.21} + \frac{100}{1.33}$$

$$= \$90.91 + \$82.65 + \$75.19$$

$$= \$248.75$$

Car and mortgage payments are determined in this manner. The amount of the loan equals the present value of the stream of payments.

Present values fall as the interest rate rises and rise as the interest rate falls. At a 15 percent interest rate, the present value of the foregoing 3-year, $100-a-year IOU would be $228.32. At a 5 percent interest rate, the present value of the 3-year, $100-a-year IOU would be $272.32.

Determining the Rate of Interest

The interest rate is determined in a market just like the price of General Motors stock or the price of corn. The market institutions may differ, but the fundamental factors at work are the same.

The Supply of Loanable Funds. The rate of interest is determined in the market for **loanable funds.**

> **Loanable funds** comprise the amount of lending from all households, governments, and businesses, or the bank credit made available to borrowers in credit markets.

For credit markets as a whole, the supply of loanable funds during a given period comes primarily from the net savings of businesses and households during that period. People place their savings in banks, mutual funds, bonds, and even stocks. It will simplify matters if we just think about people purchasing bonds. The supply curve in Figure 1 shows the quantity of loanable funds savers are willing to save (and, thereby, make available to lenders) at each

FIGURE 1
The Market for Loanable Funds

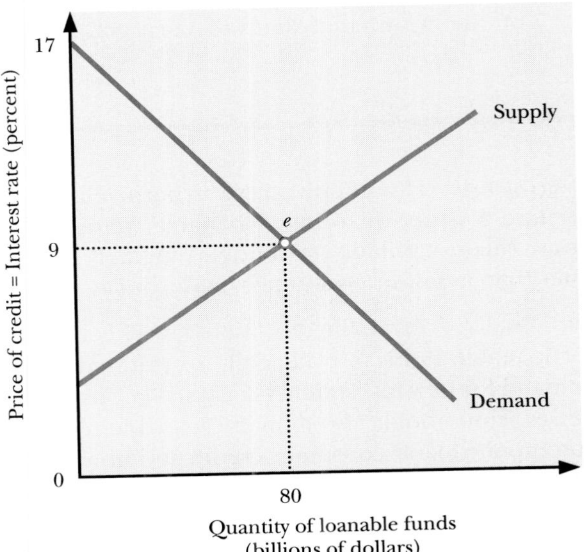

The supply curve shows the quantity of loanable funds offered by lenders at different interest rates; lenders will offer more at high interest rates. The demand curve shows the quantity of loanable funds demanded by borrowers at different interest rates; less will be demanded at high interest rates. The market for loanable funds is in equilibrium at an interest rate of 9 percent, where the quantity demanded equals the quantity supplied.

EXAMPLE 1 The Rate of Return from Cornering the Virginia Lottery

In response to their fiscal crises, many states have instituted state lotteries. In the Virginia lottery, people pay $1 for tickets with combinations of six numbers. The jackpot is won only if someone has a ticket with the exact combination of the six numbers. If no one matches the winning combination, the jackpot is rolled over. It continues to grow until someone eventually wins.

On February 15, 1992, the jackpot of the Virginia lottery had grown to $27 million. When the jackpot becomes big enough, it pays for an individual or group of individuals to buy one lottery ticket for every possible combination of numbers. In the Virginia case, it costs $7 million to buy lottery tickets for all 7 million possible combinations and, hence, to guarantee winning the jackpot. As long as no one else buys a lottery ticket with the jackpot combination, the holder of the winning ticket will earn $27 million from a $7 million investment. The Virginia jackpot is paid out over 20 equal yearly installments of $1.3 million after an initial payment of $2.2 million in the first year.

The rate of return to an investor who pays $7 million and wins the $27 million jackpot is 26 percent per year. Thus, an investor who had put $7 million in a more conventional investment (such as a bond) that paid a guaranteed annual return of 26 percent would have been equally well off receiving the $2.2 million in the first year and $1.3 million for 19 years.

State lottery officials have detected that investor groups from as far away as Australia have begun buying large chunks of lottery tickets, even attempting to buy all possible combinations, in order to win jackpots with high rates of return to investment.

Source: "With Millions Group Seeks Lottery Prize," *New York Times*, February 25, 1992, A9.

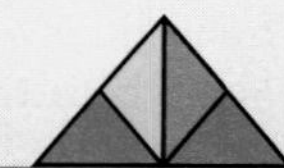

interest rate. This supply curve is positively sloped because a larger quantity of loanable funds will be saved (made available to lenders) at high interest rates than at low interest rates, *ceteris paribus.*

The Demand for Loanable Funds. The demand for loanable funds is principally constituted by the demand for new investments in capital goods of businesses. Households also demand loanable funds for automobile loans, consumer credit, and home mortgages, but this chapter will concentrate on business investment.

What determines the demand for capital goods? New capital raises the output (and, therefore, the revenue) of the firm for a number of years because capital goods are in use for more than 1 year. For example, a machine will be used for 8 years on average, and a plant will be used for 35 years on average. Capital's *marginal revenue product* (the amount an extra unit of capital will contribute to a firm's revenues) must be estimated over each year of the capital's useful life in order to determine the **rate of return of a capital good.**

> The **rate of return of a capital good** is that rate of interest for which the present value of the stream of marginal revenue products for each year of the good's life is equal to the cost of the good.

Example 1 shows how this rate of return is calculated in the case of a state lottery.

The rate of return measures the marginal benefit of capital, and the interest rate measures the marginal cost of capital. Business firms will carry out those investment projects in which the rate of return exceeds the interest rate (or is expected to). Firms will not carry out investment projects with returns below the interest rate.

> The cost of additional capital is usually the interest rate that firms must pay for credit. The marginal benefit of capital is its rate of return.

> The equilibrium amount of capital for the firm will be that amount at which the rate of interest and the rate of return on the last investment project are equal.

The law of diminishing returns applies to capital just as it applies to labor. Additional capital investment projects will yield successively lower rates of return. In making their investment plans, businesses will consider a variety of investment projects. By adding a new wing onto their plant, they may achieve a high rate of return. By acquiring new equipment, they may achieve a substantial but lower rate of return. Successive projects bring lower and lower rates of return due to the law of diminishing returns.

The demand curve for loanable funds in Figure 1 shows the quantity of loanable funds that investors are prepared to borrow at each interest rate. It is negatively sloped because at high interest rates there are fewer investment projects that have a rate of return equal to or greater than the interest rate. At low interest rates, there are more investment projects with rates of return equal to or greater than the interest rate. The demand curve also reflects the rate of return on capital-investment projects; business firms will be willing to add to their capital stock as long as the rate of return of investment projects exceeds the rate of interest.

The Equilibrium Interest Rate. Like any other price, the equilibrium (market) rate of interest established by the credit market is that rate at which the quantity of loanable funds supplied equals the quantity demanded.

In Figure 1, the quantity supplied of loanable funds equals the quantity demanded at point *e*, where the interest rate is 9 percent and there are $80 billion worth of investment projects that yield a rate of return of 9 percent or above. Thus, the equilibrium rate of interest is 9 percent.

> The equilibrium interest rate equates the quantity demanded and quantity supplied for loanable funds. Only those investments yielding the equilibrium (market) interest rate or above are financed.

The Productivity of Capital. The demand for loanable funds reflects the basic productivity of capital. Firms demand loanable funds for investment as long as rates of return are greater than or equal to the rate of interest. Any occurrence that makes capital more productive will shift the demand curve to the right and cause the interest rate to rise. The supply curve of loanable funds reflects the basic thriftiness of the population. Any occurrence that causes the population to be more thrifty (that is, to save more at each interest rate) will shift the supply curve to the right and cause the interest rate to fall.

If an important technological breakthrough raises the productivity of capital, the demand curve will shift to the right, driving up the interest rate, *ceteris paribus,* as in panel *a* of Figure 2. If tax laws are changed to reward those families that save, the supply curve will shift to the right, lowering the market rate of interest, *ceteris paribus,* as in panel *b* of Figure 2.

Real versus Nominal Interest Rates

Inflation occurs when the money prices of goods, on the average, rise over time. How does inflation affect interest rates? Supply-and-demand analysis provides a clear answer. Anticipated inflation affects both the demand and supply of loanable funds. Loans are repaid in dollars over the course of the loan. Inflation causes these dollars to become cheaper over time. Lenders will become less anxious to lend and the borrower more anxious to borrow if the rate of inflation is expected to increase. Clearly, lenders will want to be compensated for the declining value of the dollars in which the loan is repaid, and borrowers will be willing to pay a higher interest rate because they can repay the loan in cheaper dollars.

What matters to borrowers and lenders is not so much the **nominal interest rate** but the **real interest rate.**

> The **nominal interest rate** is the cost of borrowing expressed in terms of current dollars (unadjusted for inflation).
>
> The **real interest rate** equals the nominal interest rate minus the anticipated rate of inflation.[1]

[1]This formula holds approximately. The actual formula is

$$r = i - p - rp$$

where r is the real interest rate, p is the inflation rate, and i is the nominal interest rate. When r and p are small, rp is close to zero. If $r = 0.10$ and $p = 0.05$, then $rp = 0.005$.

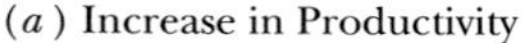

FIGURE 2
Interest Rates, Productivity, and Thriftiness

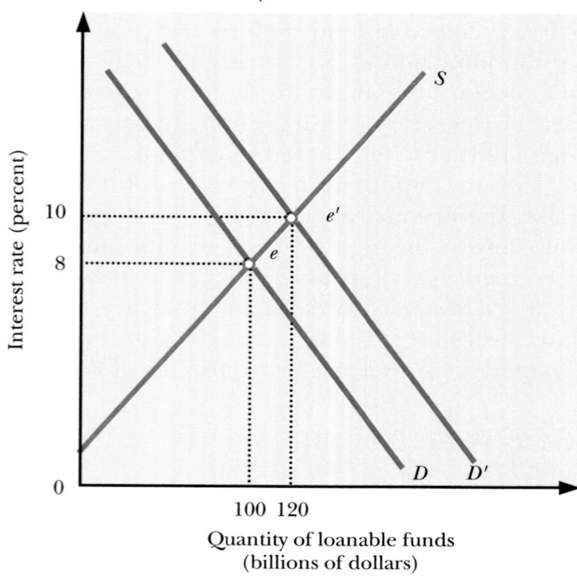

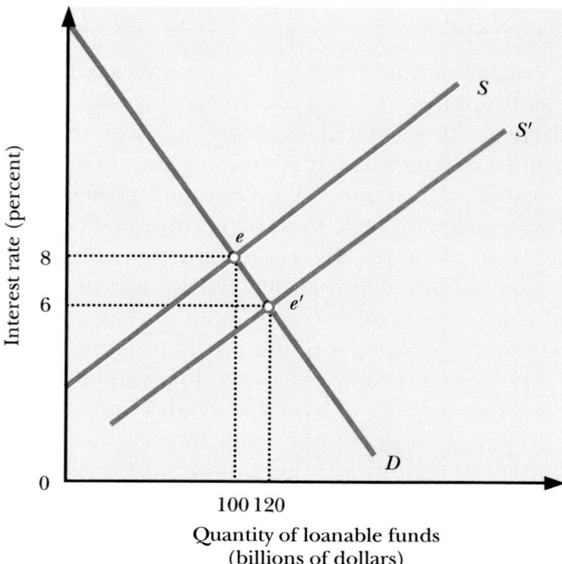

Panel *a* shows that an increase in the productivity of capital raises interest rates, and panel *b* shows that an increase in the thriftiness of the population lowers interest rates.

Anticipated inflation causes the demand curve for loanable funds to shift to the right and the supply curve of loanable funds to shift to the left. In Figure 3, the initial equilibrium interest rate is 9 percent when there is 0 percent inflation. If borrowers and lenders anticipate the same 5 percent rate of inflation, both curves shift upward by the same amount.

The anticipated supply and demand curves for loanable funds at 14 percent nominal interest intersect at the same quantity of loanable funds (in constant dollars) as at 9 percent nominal interest, or $80 billion worth of loanable funds. Example 2 shows that real interest rates in the United States have averaged about 3 percent. A 14 percent nominal rate of interest with a 5 percent rate of inflation yields the same real rate of interest as a 9 percent real interest rate with 0 percent inflation.

The Structure of Interest Rates

Although the interest rate is the price of credit, this price is not the same for all borrowers. Savings and loan associations may pay as little as 4 percent when they borrow from their depositors, whereas individuals who borrow from savings and loan associations may be charged interest rates of 9 percent for automobile and home mortgage loans. The U.S. Treasury may pay 5 percent to purchasers of its 6-month treasury bill and 7 percent on a 3-year Treasury bond, whereas a near-bankrupt company must pay 21 percent on a 6-month bank loan. *Different interest rates are paid on different financial assets.* Interest rates vary with the conditions of *risk, liquidity,* and *maturity* associated with a loan.

Risk. Borrowers with high credit ratings will pay lower interest rates than borrowers with low credit ratings. To be competitive and earn a normal profit, lenders must be compensated for the extra risk associated with lending to borrowers with low credit ratings. If a certain type of borrower fails to repay bank loans 1 percent of the time, banks will require such a borrower to pay an interest rate at least 1 percent above the interest rate charged borrowers with a 0 percent risk of default. The extra 1 percent

EXAMPLE 2 The Timeless Real Rate of Interest

The real interest rate is the nominal interest rate minus the anticipated rate of inflation. The real interest rate balances the thriftiness of the population with the productivity of capital; any fluctuations in the real interest rate reflect changes in these two factors.

Surprisingly, it appears that the real rate of interest has remained about the same for centuries. It is possible to trace the course of real interest rates from Roman times to the present by examining newspapers and other records. In Rome, for a hundred years around the beginning of the common era, the real interest rate was 4 percent. In the United States and England, the real interest rate was around 3 percent from 1867 to 1990.

The long-term stability of real interest rates suggests that the real productivity of capital and thriftiness has been remarkably stable over time.

Source: Julian Simon, "Great and Almost Great Magnitudes in Economics," *Journal of Economic Perspectives* 4 (Winter 1990): 151–52.

FIGURE 3
Anticipated Inflation and Interest Rates

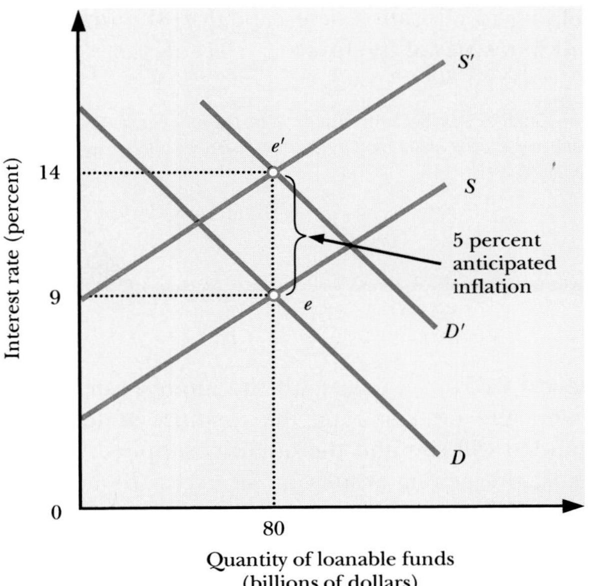

The original equilibrium at a 0 percent rate of inflation is point *e*. When a 5 percent inflation rate is anticipated, borrowers will be willing to pay an interest rate 5 percent higher than before, and lenders must be paid an interest rate 5 percent higher because repayments are in cheaper dollars. Thus, both *S* and *D* shift upward by 5 percent. The new equilibrium is point *e′*, at a 14 percent nominal interest rate. The real interest rate is still 9 percent (equal to the nominal rate minus the anticipated rate of inflation).

is called a *risk premium.* So-called junk bonds have a default rate of about 2 percent. (See Example 3.)

Liquidity. A financial asset that can be turned into cash quickly or with a small penalty is said to be *liquid.* People may be willing to hold savings accounts paying 5 percent interest when 6-month certificates of deposit pay 18 percent simply because the former can be turned into cash (the medium of exchange) quickly and without penalty. The general rule is that interest rates will vary inversely with liquidity, *ceteris paribus.*

Maturity. Interest rates will also vary with the term of maturity. A corporation borrowing $1000 for 1 year may pay a lower rate of interest than if it borrows the same $1000 for 2 years because credit-market conditions during the second year are expected to differ from conditions in the first year. If the credit market expects the interest rate on 1-year loans to be 6 percent during one year and 12 percent during the next, the interest rate on a 2-year loan covering the same period will be 9 percent. If $1000 is invested for 1 year at 6 percent, it will yield $1060; if the $1060 is then reinvested at 12 percent it will yield $1188. Likewise, if $1000 is invested at 9 percent for 2 years, it will yield $1188. Thus, $1000 invested at 6 percent for 1 year with the proceeds invested for 1 more year at 12 percent has the same yield as investing $1000 for 2 years at 9 percent. Roughly speaking, the 2-year interest rate (expressed on an annual basis) will be an average of the 1-year interest rates that the credit market anticipates over the 2 years.

EXAMPLE 3 Are Junk Bonds Good Investments?

Corporations finance their operations by selling stock, issuing bonds, or borrowing from banks. If the corporation goes bankrupt, the owners of debt (bondholders and banks) are paid before stockholders, but all parties risk losing some portion of their investment. In the case of bonds, the major ratings services issue letter grades to measure this risk. The highest grades are given to *investment-grade bonds,* for which the investor need not be overly concerned about default. The lower grades are reserved for *speculative-grade bonds.*

In recent years, speculative bonds have been called *junk bonds* due to their association in the popular press with shady dealings, the bankruptcy of well-known investment-banking firms (that promote and market corporate bonds), and even jail terms for some brokers. According to sophisticated critics, junk bonds helped fuel the merger mania in the 1980s, contributing to a rise in corporation debt and to financial market instability.

Junk bonds are speculative investments that pay a higher rate of return than investment-grade bonds but a lower rate of return than stocks. From 1977 to 1988, one study found that investment-grade bonds paid an annual return of about 8.5 percent; junk bonds, 10.5 percent; and equities (stocks), almost 13.75 percent. Junk bonds suffered a default risk of about 2 percent from 1970 to 1986. This risk accounts for the difference in the rate of return on investment-grade bonds and junk bonds.

The small volume of junk bonds raises doubts as to whether they could have fueled the merger mania of the 1980s. At most, junk bonds could have financed no more than 8 percent of U.S. mergers in any one year. It seems that observers have criticized junk bonds as being intrinsically different from other kinds of investments. In reality, they are simply bonds that must pay a higher rate of return due to the possibility of default. Junk bonds are an important component of corporate financing, helping to allocate scarce capital to the firms and industries of the future.

Source: Sean Becketti, "The Truth about Junk Bonds," *Federal Reserve Bank of Kansas City Economic Review* (July/August 1990): 45–54.

Interest-Rate Ceilings

Usury laws (that place ceilings on interest rates charged by lenders) are in effect in many states and countries. An interest-rate ceiling is said to be effective if the legislated rate is below the market interest rate that would have prevailed without the usury law.

Usury laws have considerable popular support because they claim to protect the poor from excessive interest rates charged by the rich. Insofar as the rich are the large lenders and the poor are the ones who must borrow, usury laws are thought to redistribute wealth from the rich to the poor. However, most economists agree that effective interest-rate ceilings function in the opposite manner.

Wealth Redistributions. If the interest-rate ceiling lowers the interest rate, the quantity of loans demanded will rise and the quantity supplied will fall. Thus, the ceiling results in an excess demand for loans. The interest rate cannot rise sufficiently to ration the scarce supply of loanable funds.

Figure 4 shows how interest-rate ceilings create shortages of loanable funds. The interest-rate ceiling of 7 percent causes the amount of loanable funds demanded by borrowers to exceed what lenders are willing to supply by $50 billion. The excess demand means that some potential borrowers will be unable to get the financing they desire at the interest-rate ceiling (at least those lenders that abide by the law) because they are able to lend fewer funds at lower interest rates. The borrowers who actually obtain

FIGURE 4
Interest-Rate Ceilings and Credit Rationing

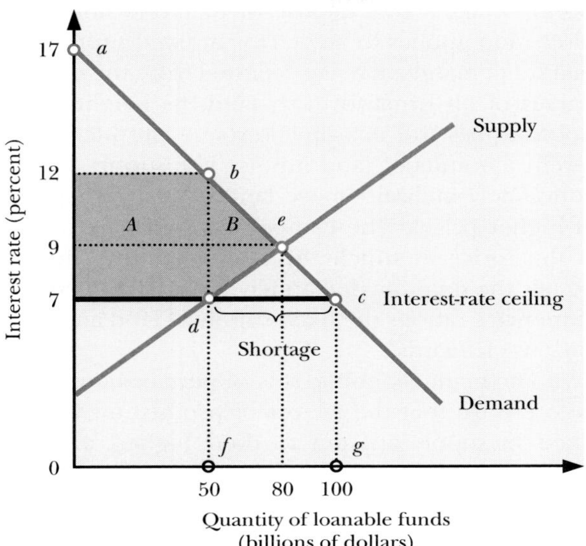

The equilibrium interest rate at point *e* is 9 percent, where \$80 billion worth of loanable funds are borrowed. When an interest-rate ceiling of 7 percent is imposed, \$100 billion worth of investment projects are demanded with returns ranging from 17 percent to 7 percent. At an interest rate of 7 percent, only \$50 billion worth of these projects can be financed (point *d*). Therefore, some credit rationing must occur. If rationing is efficient, the best half of all the desirable projects—those with returns ranging from 17 percent to 12 percent along segment *ab*—will receive financing, and society loses the welfare represented by triangle *B*. If only those projects that earn the lowest rates of return—those represented by segment *bc* of the demand curve, earning 12 to 7 percent rates of return—are financed, society loses area $A + B$, which is the maximum loss from interest-rate ceilings. Switching from the first \$50 billion (along *ab*) to the second \$50 billion (along *bc*) would lower total returns from $0abf$ to $fbcg$.

financing at lower rates are made better off because they will be earning high rates of return on their investment projects but will be paying back their loans at the lower ceiling rate of interest. Those shut out of the loan market lose the returns they could have gained if funds had been available for investment. Ceilings, therefore, redistribute wealth from those who are unable to obtain financing at the ceiling rate to those who are.

Interest-rate ceilings tend to allocate loanable funds to borrowers who can earn higher returns because they are better risks. Unfortunately, many poor people are bad credit risks, and they will be the ones who suffer the major burden of the ceiling. In many cases, the only alternative of poor people driven out of the legal loan markets is to find a loan shark, who will charge them much more than what the interest rate would be in the absence of ceilings. The loan shark is an entrepreneur who must be compensated for taking such risks as breaking the law and dealing with people who, through self-selection, reveal themselves to have inferior credit ratings.[2]

Economic Efficiency. Interest-rate ceilings reduce economic efficiency because society must give up beneficial investment projects. When this happens society incurs a deadweight loss in economic output. Figure 4 explains how to calculate society's loss of output due to credit rationing. It shows that credit rationing causes deadweight losses, even if loans go to those projects with the highest rates of return, due to a lower volume of loans.

RENT

The rent on land is a relatively small proportion—about 2 or 3 percent—of the total of all payments to factors of production in the United States. This figure includes payments based on the natural fertility of the land and its locational advantages but excludes the returns to investments erected on the land or capital improvements in the land (such as irrigation). The crucial feature of land and other natural resources is that they are relatively inelastic in supply. They are nature's bounty, and the quantity supplied is not affected by the price received as a factor payment.

Relative inelasticity of supply can characterize productive factors other than land and natural resources. Because other types of factor payments

[2]It was probably through the usury laws that the early economists such as Adam Smith were alerted to the unfortunate effects of interfering with the market mechanism. Adam Smith realized that the results intended by legislators often differed greatly from the actual impact of laws, as in the case of interest-rate ceilings.

resemble land rents, the study of rents for land and natural resources is much more important than the small percentages of factor payments to land suggest.

"Rents" paid for apartments, cars, tools, or moving trucks should not be confused with the *economic rents* studied in this section. "Rental payments" for the temporary use of a particular piece of property owned by someone else can be returns to land, labor, or capital. Apartment rent is a payment both to land (for the land on which the apartment building sits) and to capital (for the structure itself). Thus, the common term *rent* is simply a price or rental rate rather than a payment to a specific factor of production.

FIGURE 5
Pure Economic Rent

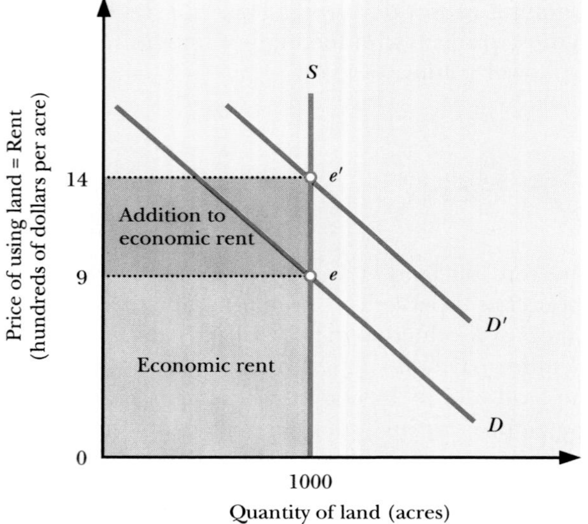

Because the supply of land is fixed at 1000 acres, the supply curve S is perfectly inelastic. The equilibrium rent of $900 per acre at point e gives rise to pure economic rents, since the land has no alternative uses. The entire rental payment is a surplus over opportunity costs. In this case, opportunity costs are zero. If the demand curve for land increases from D to D' due to an increase in the demand for the product the land is used to produce, the economic rent will rise from $900 to $1400 per acre at point e'. Changes in economic rents are determined by demand because supply is fixed.

Pure Economic Rent

Figure 5 shows the determination of the competitive price for a fixed amount of land or some natural resource like a coal deposit or diamond mine. The discussion applies to any factor in fixed supply. The market demand curve is generated from the demand curves of all firms for, say, land; its height at any point equals the marginal revenue product of different amounts of land inputs. The supply curve is completely inelastic; more land is not forthcoming at higher prices. The competitive rent paid to land is that price at which the fixed quantity supplied equals the quantity demanded. As such, the equilibrium price rations the fixed supply of land among its various claimants.

The main economic role of **pure economic rent** is to ensure that the factors of production that are fixed in supply are put to their highest and best use.

> A **pure economic rent** is the price paid to a productive factor that is completely inelastic in supply. Land is the classic example of such a factor.

Figure 5 illustrates the concept of pure economic rent. The same quantity of land would be supplied, no matter what the price per acre (whether $0, $900, or $1400), as shown by the vertical supply curve. The quantity demanded at, say, a zero price would probably be very large. At that zero price, prime agricultural land might be used as a garbage dump or as a junkyard for old cars. (For a different case see Example 4.) A higher price of land will cut off the various demands for the land that have a low MRP. If the price is too high, the land will not be fully used, and there will be an excess supply. If the price is too low, the land may not be put to its best use. Land rents that are below equilibrium levels can allow land to be put to uses that yield relatively low MRPs. Efficiency requires that the price be set where the quantity supplied equals the quantity demanded of land.

Suppose a piece of land is worth $1,000 to Jack and $2,000 to Jill. If both can rent the land for, say, $800, Jack could prevent Jill from using it. But if the price rose to $1001, the land, reserved for its highest and best use, would go to Jill.

EXAMPLE 4 Economic Rents and "Happy Birthday"

There is only one "Happy Birthday" song and, believe it or not, the rights to this song are owned by the copyright holder, Birchtree, Ltd. Written by two sisters in 1893, "Happy Birthday" was copyrighted, and for it to be played at official functions a fee must be paid to the current owners of the copyright. "Happy Birthday" currently brings in about one million dollars per year. The copyright will not expire until 2010, at which time it becomes part of the public domain. Birchtree, Ltd. is prepared to sell the rights to "Happy Birthday," and it expects to receive $12 million for the sale. The copyright fees earned on "Happy Birthday" are economic rents. The supply of "Happy Birthday" is fixed; it is there whether people play it or not.

Source: "Yes, You Did Hear It Right: 'Happy Birthday' Is for Sale." *New York Times*, October 20, 1988.

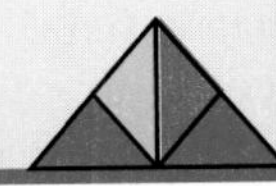

The pure economic rent that is paid to a productive factor does not serve the incentive function of increasing the quantity supplied of the scarce factor because the supply is perfectly inelastic. Pure economic rent in a competitive market serves as a guide to efficient resource use by rationing the available supply to the most efficient use.

When something is perfectly inelastic in supply, price incentives cannot lead to an increase in its supply. This feature has made land an attractive target of taxation. The price of a good or factor that is perfectly inelastic in supply must, therefore, be determined by demand. If the demand curve in Figure 5 shifts from D to D' due to technological advances in the use of the land or increases in the final demands for goods that the land is used to produce, competitive economic rents will be bid up.

From the standpoint of the economy as a whole, rent is not a true opportunity cost to society. The available amount of land and other resources that are fixed in supply is a free gift of nature; the economy has use of the land whether it pays something or nothing. In the case of pure rent, the payment to the factor of production exceeds the payment required to keep the resource available to the economy by the entire amount of the rental payment. Thus, the opportunity cost is zero. From the standpoint of an individual firm using agricultural land, however, economic rent is most certainly a cost of production. In order to bid the land away from other uses, the individual firm must pay the competitive price. In other words, *rents accrue to factor owners, not factor users.*

Quasi Rents

Naturally productive land and land located in prime urban and manufacturing areas is inelastic in supply in the long run. No matter what is done, no matter what economic rents are paid, such land cannot be increased in supply. Payments for such land are *pure economic rents.* Because the opportunity cost to society of this land is zero in both the long and short runs, the entire factor payment is a payment of economic rent. Many factors that are fixed in supply in the short run, however, are more elastic in supply in the long run.

Many factors are fixed in supply in the short run. For example, in a booming Sun Belt city, the amount of space in office buildings is fixed in supply in the short run; when the demand for office space increases, office rental rates rise dramatically. The demand curve shifts upward (or to the right) along a vertical supply curve. In the long run, however, developers will respond to soaring office rents by constructing new office buildings. As these buildings are completed, the supply curve becomes more elastic and office rents are reduced.

The supply of professional tennis players is essentially fixed in the short run, for it takes years of training and practice to develop players of professional caliber. If the demand for professional tennis players increases due to an increase in the popularity of the sport, the earnings of the fixed number of tennis professionals will increase. In the short run, they will be able to earn extraordinary salaries. In the long run, however, new professional-caliber players will enter the profession, attracted by the high earnings. The supply becomes more elastic, and the extraordinary earnings of tennis professionals will be bid down.

As these examples show, the owners of a resource that is fixed in supply in the short run will receive economic rent. But such a payment is a **quasi rent,** not a pure economic rent, because it cannot be maintained in the long run.

> A **quasi rent** is a payment in excess of the short-run opportunity cost necessary to induce the owners of the resources to offer their resources for sale or rent in the short run.

In the long run, quasi rents will disappear as the supply curve becomes more elastic. In the long run, the supply curve will become more and more elastic until quasi rents have been dissipated. At this point, the factor of production receives only economic rents.

Economic Rent and Other Factors of Production

Pure economic rents represent an extreme case of factor payment. At the other extreme is a payment to a factor that just equals its *opportunity cost* (its earnings in its next best alternative use). A factor of production that is perfectly elastic in supply earns no economic rent because the factor is paid its opportunity cost. For example, a small farmer must compete with other farmers and potential users of the land. If the farmer does not pay what the land could earn in its next best use, the land will be used elsewhere.

In between factors of production that are perfectly elastic in supply and those that are perfectly inelastic are numerous factors of production that earn some surplus return over their opportunity costs, or **economic rent.**

> **Economic rent** is the amount by which the payment to a factor exceeds its opportunity cost.

The major distinction between *economic rent* and *pure economic rent* is that a factor earning pure economic rent has an opportunity cost of zero. A factor earning economic rent has an opportunity cost that is positive but smaller than the payment to the factor.

The amount of economic rent earned by a factor depends upon the perspective from which the factor is viewed. The economic rent of John Smith as an *engineer* differs from the economic rent of John Smith as an engineer *for General Motors Corp.* Smith can earn $30,000 per year working for GM, $29,000 working for Ford, and $20,000 working in his best nonengineering job. Smith's economic rent as a GM engineer is $1000 (his earnings in excess of his opportunity cost); his economic rent as an engineer is $10,000 (his greatest potential earnings as an engineer in excess of his salary in his best nonengineering alternative).

The prices paid to an attractive movie star, a late-night talk-show host, the best pitcher in major-league baseball, Iowa farmland, and offices in New York City surprisingly have much in common: a large fraction of each factor's income is economic rent. These factors receive payments in excess of their opportunity cost (their earnings in alternative uses). The factor payment serves the function of ensuring that the factor is employed efficiently in its highest and best use. Boxing great Muhammed Ali's million-dollar contracts served the important economic function of promoting an efficient utilization of his assets; the utility of sports fans would have been reduced if he had been employed as a waiter at a local restaurant. Paying one of the world's most talented tenors $50,000 per performance ensures that he will devote himself to opera rather than work as a plumber.

Although people often resent individuals with inherited talents, rare skills, or good looks who earn substantial salaries, it should be recognized that oil-drilling rigs, Hawaiian real estate, Iowa corn land, and high-speed computers are earning similar rewards; namely, payments in excess of their opportunity costs. Although land is the most obvious, economic rents are paid to a wide variety of economic factors. Actors, professional athletes, musicians,

EXAMPLE 5 Why Professional Football Players Should Not Strike

In 1987, the professional football player's association called a strike that was honored by the vast majority of players. Deprived of their regular players, the National Football League team owners recruited entire teams of new players. The athletes selected were primarily young players who had sought a career in professional football but had not been hired. A sampling of the jobs the new players held provides insights into the opportunity costs of professional football players. Typical jobs were bartender, bouncer, and high-school coach—all comparatively low-paying. The average professional football player earns an annual salary in excess of $100,000, but his next best job (the opportunity cost) would bring in only $20,000.

In effect, professional football players earn economic rents: their earnings exceed their opportunity costs. Not surprisingly, strikes of professional athletes have been less successful than industrial strikes, in which the strikers do not begin with such substantial economic rents.

surgeons, professors, television repair persons, and even nobility can earn economic rents. (See Example 5.)

PROFITS

People are often suspicious of the ethics of those individuals and companies who earn high profits. (In the Middle Ages, high profits were seen as a sure sign that a pact had been made with the devil.)

Profits that are headlined on the business pages are **accounting profits.** From an economist's point of view, accounting profits can be misleading because they do not take into account the firm's *opportunity costs,* which include both actual payments to factors of production and the costs of the next best alternative that the firm has sacrificed. Economists prefer to evaluate a firm's profitability on the basis of **normal profits** and **economic profits.**

> **Accounting profits** are enterprise revenues minus explicit enterprise costs.
>
> **Normal profits** are the profits required to keep resources in that particular business. Normal profits are earned when revenues equal opportunity costs.

> **Economic profits** are revenues in excess of total opportunity costs (which include both actual payments and sacrificed alternatives). Economic profits are profits in excess of normal profits.

As explained in earlier chapters, economic profits regulate entry into and exit from an industry. When they are positive, firms will enter; when they are negative, firms will exit.

Sources of Economic Profits

There are three basic sources of economic profits. The first is the existence of barriers to entry in an industry or business. The resulting economic profits, called *monopoly profits,* form the basis of popular misgivings about profits. The second source of profits is the dynamic and ever-changing nature of the economic system, which renders the success of some activities risky or uncertain. The third source of economic profits is innovation. Economic profits that are not the result of monopoly restrictions are often considered a reward for the *entrepreneurship* of individuals (or groups of individuals) who engage in risk-taking and innovative activities.

Entry Restrictions. As we have shown, monopolies can earn a profit rate in excess of normal profits.

Moreover, unlike the transitory profits of a competitive industry, monopoly profits can persist over a long period of time. In other words, under conditions of monopoly, businesses can earn revenues that exceed the opportunity costs of the factors they employ. In this sense, monopoly profits are like economic rents, and consequently, economists often refer to monopoly profits as *monopoly rents.* Monopoly profits can also be earned in a potentially competitive industry where entry is restricted by government licensing or franchising. As long as monopoly profits cannot be eliminated by the entry of new firms, existing firms can enjoy monopoly rents. The source of these monopoly rents is the ceiling placed on supply by entry restrictions.

Examples of monopoly profits due to entry restrictions are plentiful. Cable-television franchises are granted by municipal authorities, protecting companies by law from the entry of competitors. In many cities, taxicab drivers must be licensed, and entry into the business is controlled by the high cost of the license. Monopoly profits in the prescription-drug industry are protected by patents. Economies of scale similarly limit the entry of competitors into power generation, telecommunications, and parcel delivery services.

Monopoly profits are often not reflected in accounting profits because they are *capitalized* (converted to their present value) when the firm is sold to a new owner. For example, in New York City, when taxicab drivers sell their licenses (called *medallions*) to others, the market price that the license brings is equal to the present value of the cab's monopoly profits. The cab driver who purchases the license earns no economic profit because it has gone to the original owner of the license.

Risk. If there were no entry restrictions, if people could predict the future perfectly, and if there were no costs for obtaining information about current market opportunities, there would be no economic profits. All businesses would earn normal profits. Any opportunity to earn economic profits would be anticipated and the free entry of new firms would serve to keep profits down to a normal return.

However, no one can predict the future. Industry is unprepared for wars, new inventions, and changes in fashion, preferences, and weather. Even with free entry, at any given time some industries will earn economic profits and others will suffer negative economic profits. Unanticipated shifts in demand or costs cause economic profits to rise and fall. The majority of people wish to limit their exposure to the ups and downs of the economy; they want a steady income. Therefore, there must be rewards for those who are willing to risk the ups and downs of economic fortunes. Just as those who lend money to poor credit risks require risk premiums, so those who desire economic profits must be willing to reward risk bearing. In his book, *Risk, Uncertainty, and Profit* (1921), economist Frank Knight emphasized that uncertainty and risk taking are the ultimate source of profit. Knight noted the presence of a large element of luck in the fortunes of different enterprises. Economic profits cannot be assured in an uncertain world; the outcome of the profit game will be, to a large extent, random.

Uncertainty turns the quest for profits into something resembling a game of chance in which there are winners and losers even in the long run. Entrepreneurs are the ones who bear this risk. The winners earn economic profits; the losers incur losses. As in a game of chance, profits average out to a normal return over all firms, but there is a wide range of profit outcomes. Most business firms deviate little from the average return to risk bearing. Some, though, have extreme good luck and experience large returns; others experience large misfortunes. All is not fair in love, war, and . . . business.

Innovation. Blind luck cannot explain all economic profits. The economy is in a constant state of flux. Consumer tastes are changing; new technologies are being developed; new markets are being discovered; resource availabilities are being altered. To be an innovator requires ability and foresight in order to take advantage of these changes.

Austrian-born economist Joseph Schumpeter (1883–1950) maintained that profits, primarily the return to the entrepreneur and innovator, are temporary. Economic progress requires a succession of new innovations. A successful entrepreneur will earn substantial economic profits only until another entrepreneur with a newer and better idea comes along to take customers and profits away.

Business history is replete with success stories of business geniuses—Henry Ford and the Model T, Edwin Land and the Polaroid camera, Richard Sears and Alvah Roebuck and their mass retailing, and Louis Marx and his children's toy empire. (See Example 6.) More was involved than a game of chance with an uncertain outcome; ability and en-

EXAMPLE 6 The Entrepreneurship of Fred Smith

Successful entrepreneurs are those who are able to recognize new profit opportunities. One example is Fred Smith, the founder of Federal Express. Smith began in business by purchasing and selling used jets, but he dreamed of forming a company that could guarantee the delivery of packages overnight from both large and small cities. The air express business was not new. It already had two giant firms—Emery Air Freight and Flying Tiger, but Smith was convinced his company could offer a better product. Smith's entrepreneurial genius recognized opportunities that his competitors failed to see. First, Smith knew that 9 out of 10 commercial airliners were on the ground between 10:00 P.M. and 8:00 A.M., so the air lanes were wide open during these hours. The uncongested airways would make overnight delivery possible. Second, Smith recognized that the bulk of urgent, small package business originated and terminated outside the 25 largest cities. A successful delivery system would need the ability to handle such packages. Third, Smith realized that it would be more efficient to have a single hub system (which he located in Memphis) with a central processing facility through which all packages would flow. A package originating in Los Angeles for San Francisco would be flown to Memphis, processed, and then sent on another plane to San Francisco. Armed with these business insights, Smith committed all of his own capital to starting up Federal Express. The phenomenal success of the company was due to the entrepreneurial genius of its founder.

Source: Robert Sobel and David B. Sicilia, *The Entrepreneurs: An American Adventure* (Boston: Houghton Mifflin Company, 1986), 42–48.

trepreneurial genius were crucial to the success of each of these companies. Yet even ability does not guarantee success. Many able people are trying to become the next Henry Ford, but few succeed.

Armen Alchian has pointed out that it is not even necessary for the entrepreneur to maximize profits:

> [R]ealized positive profits, not *maximum* profits, are the mark of success and viability. It does not matter through what process of reasoning or motivation such success was achieved. The fact of its accomplishment is sufficient. This is the criterion by which the economic system selects survivors: those who realize *positive profits* are survivors; those who suffer losses disappear. The pertinent requirement—positive profits through *relative* efficiency—is weaker than "maximized profits," with which, unfortunately, it has become confused.[3]

Empirical Evidence

According to economic theory, profits arise from monopoly restrictions and barriers, uncertainty and risk, and entrepreneurial innovation. Does the factual record support these propositions? It is very difficult for economists to test the relationship between economic profits and these three factors because it is virtually impossible to measure economic profits. Although it is easier to determine accounting profits—a measure that includes elements of normal returns to land, labor, and capital—accounting profits are less valuable as an economic measure. Nevertheless, empirical studies typically assume that rates of return based on accounting profits are indicative of rates of return based on economic profits.

Barriers to Entry and Profits. The empirical literature supports the theory that economic profits are strongly associated with monopoly barriers to entry. For example, prescription drugs protected by patents sell at 60 to 100 times average costs, and price-fixing conspiracies have been shown to create extraordinary profits. Other examples of the correlation between

[3]Armen A. Alchian, "Uncertainty, Evolution, and Economic Theory," *Journal of Political Economy* 58, 3 (June 1950): 211–21; reprinted in *Economic Forces at Work* (Indianapolis: Liberty Press, 1977), 15–36.

FIGURE 6
Compensation of Employees and Corporate Profits, 1960–1990

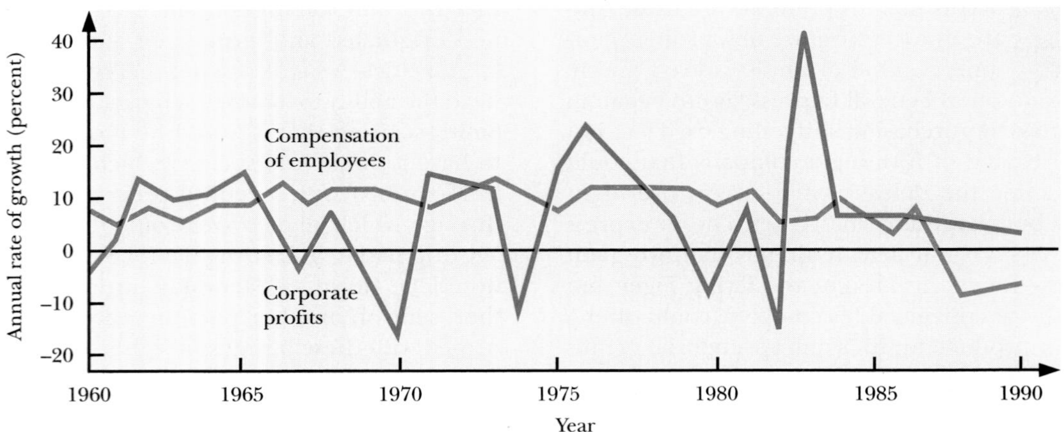

This graph shows that corporate profits are characterized by greater variability than wage income over time—suggesting that it is more risky to be dependent on profits than on wage income.

Source: Survey of Current Business.

barriers to entry and profit rates can be found in the chapter on oligopoly.

Risk and Profits. Determining the relationship between risk and profit rates is problematic due to the difficulty of measuring the amount of risk a firm or an industry faces. In empirical studies, risk is typically measured by the variability of profits. If there are considerable fluctuations in profits over time or among firms in a particular industry, substantial risk is said to be present.

Figure 6 plots annual growth in wage income (employee compensation) and corporate profits over time. The most striking difference between the two series is the much greater variability of profits. Unlike earnings from labor, which tend to rise smoothly from year to year, profits rise and fall—sometimes with very substantial declines from one year to the next. If risk is indeed measured by fluctuations it is definitely more risky to be dependent upon profits than on wages, at least as far as the aggregate economy is concerned. The annual ups and downs of aggregate profits may not be an accurate guide to risk, however, because more serious risk stems from longer-run dangers from new technology and new competition that can cause a permanent decline in the profits earned by individual firms.

Economists who have studied the relationship between the rate of profit and risk (as measured by the variability of profits) find that profit rates are indeed higher in risky industries (although there is some dispute on this matter). Firms and industries that are subject to greater risk earn *risk premiums.* Entrepreneurs and stockholders who bear more risk than others are compensated in the form of higher average profits.[4]

Innovation and Profits. As in the case of risk, the difficulty in measuring the trends in entrepreneurial activity precludes the establishment of an empirical correlation with the fluctuations of profits. Although

[4]Empirical studies of the relationship between risk and profitability have been conducted by I. N. Fisher and G. R. Hall, "Risk and Corporate Rates of Return," *Quarterly Journal of Economics* 83 (February 1969): 79–92; and P. Cootner and D. Holland, "Rate of Return and Business Risk," *Bell Journal of Economics* 1 (Fall 1970): 211–16. Both studies found a positive association between risk and corporate profit rates. A different interpretation of these findings has been suggested by Richard Caves and Basil Yamey, "Risk and Corporate Returns: Comment," *Quarterly Journal of Economics* 85 (August 1971): 513–17; and by W. G. Shepherd, *The Treatment of Market Power* (New York: Columbia University Press, 1975), who argue that these higher rates of return are the result of oligopoly structure rather than greater risk.

statistical tests have yet to be conducted, economic history shows that great fortunes (such as those of the Rockefeller, Carnegie, Mellon, and Ford families) have been amassed by great entrepreneurs. Although good luck may have played a role in the accumulation of these fortunes, a more likely interpretation is that they were the consequence of entrepreneurial innovation.

The last three chapters surveyed how the economy determines wages, rents, interest, and profit—the payments to the productive factors of labor, land, capital, and entrepreneurship. The next chapter will turn from the functional distribution of income to the personal distribution of income, addressing questions such as these: How equally or unequally is income distributed among persons? How has the personal distribution of income changed over time? How does America's income distribution compare to that of other countries? What can be done about poverty?

SUMMARY

1. Interest is payment for the use of capital. The supply of capital is the result of past saving and investment decisions. Interest rates are determined in credit markets, which are necessitated by the specialization of savings and investment decisions in today's modern economy. Interest rates are determined in the market by the demand and supply of loanable funds. The real rate of interest is the nominal interest rate minus the anticipated rate of inflation. The structure of interest rates depends upon risk, liquidity, and maturity.

2. Pure economic rent is the payment to a factor of production that is completely inelastic in supply and for which the price is determined by demand. A quasi rent is payment to a factor of production in excess of short-run opportunity costs. In the long run, quasi rents tend to disappear. Economic rent is the amount by which the payment to a factor exceeds its opportunity cost.

3. Economic profits are revenues in excess of total opportunity costs. The sources of economic profits are restrictions to entry into an industry, uncertainty, and entrepreneurship. Empirical evidence, though limited in the cases of uncertainty and entrepreneurship, generally supports the correlation between profits and each of the three sources.

KEY TERMS

interest
depreciation
credit markets (capital markets)
interest rate
loanable funds
rate of return of a capital good
nominal interest rate
real interest rate
pure economic rent
quasi rent
economic rent
accounting profits
normal profits
economic profits

QUESTIONS AND PROBLEMS

1. Why is it misleading to call interest the price of money?
2. This chapter emphasized that the credit market is another example of specialization in economics. Explain how this specialization works and how it effects economic efficiency.
3. If you borrow \$10,000 from the bank and repay the bank \$12,000 after 1 year, what is the annual rate of interest?
4. A business is expected to earn economic profits of \$1000 per year in perpetuity. The current market interest rate is 10 percent. What is the present value of these economic profits? How is the present value related to the rate of interest?
5. A machine that costs \$1000 will last 2 years, after which it must be scrapped with no salvage value. If the machine is purchased, it will raise profits by \$0 the first year and \$2250 the second. What is the rate of return on this investment? Would the firm invest in the machine if the interest rate were 40 percent?
6. A company is considering four investment projects that yield returns of 20 percent, 15 percent, 10 percent, and 5 percent, respectively. Explain how the company will decide which of these projects to carry out.
7. The interest rate is currently 10 percent and the inflation rate is 5 percent. If people anticipate that the inflation rate will rise to 10 percent, what will happen to interest rates?
8. Distinguish between pure economic rents and quasi rents.
9. Evaluate the validity of the following statement: "Pure economic rents play no useful role in the economy because the supply of the factor in question is fixed. The factor will be supplied no matter what rent is paid."

10. Why should the profit rate be higher for businesses that are risky? How do we measure risk?
11. What is the logic behind taxing economic rents rather than other kinds of factor incomes?
12. Identify the sources of economic profits earned by the following:
    a. Steel companies after the government imposed restrictions on competitive steel imports from foreign countries
    b. The coal industry after the Organization of Petroleum Exporting Countries quadrupled the price of oil in 1974
    c. A firm that developed a surefire method of increasing gas mileage
13. Evaluate the validity of the following statement: "High interest rates make for a better retirement."
14. The great baseball player Babe Ruth earned more than the President of the United States; yet if he had not played baseball, his income might have equaled that of a common laborer. Explain this situation in terms of the concepts of this chapter.

SUGGESTED READINGS

Heyne, Paul, and Thomas Johnson. *Toward Understanding Microeconomics.* Chicago: SRA, 1976, chaps. 2, 13.

Knight, Frank. *Risk, Uncertainty, and Profit.* Chicago: University of Chicago Press, 1985.

Schumpeter, Joseph. *Theory of Economic Development.* Cambridge, MA: Harvard University Press, 1949.

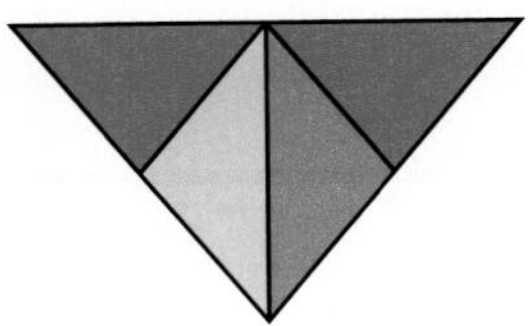

40

Income Distribution and Poverty

CHAPTER INSIGHT

In the former Soviet Union, *leveling* was widely practiced in an attempt to minimize the gap in pay between workers in different positions. Thus, an unskilled worker in an automobile plant might earn 200 rubles per month; a university-educated engineer might earn 300 rubles; and the plant's manager might earn 500 rubles. This leveling of wages was consistent with a socialist philosophy of equality that sought to eliminate large differences between the rich and the poor.

The new leadership of the former Soviet Union has decided that the excessive equality of the old system must be reduced in order to have a sound economy. It understands how leveling exacted costs in the form of less productive workers and lower levels of output. If everyone, no matter what his or her qualifications, effort, and responsibilities are, earns about the same amount, why should anyone work harder, acquire more skills, or take risks?

Each society must determine through its tax system and social policies the degree of inequality that should be present. Although the notion of equality is attractive, there is a trade-off between equality and efficiency. Too much equality can be just as bad for a society as too much inequality.

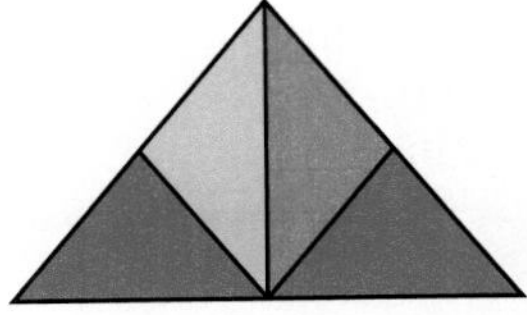

MEASUREMENT OF INCOME INEQUALITY

The Lorenz Curve

The most common measure of the degree of inequality in the distribution of income is the **Lorenz curve.**

> The **Lorenz curve** shows the percentages of total income earned by households at successive income levels. The cumulative percentage of households (ranked from lowest to highest incomes) is plotted on the horizontal axis of the Lorenz curve, and the cumulative share of income earned by each cumulative percentage of households is plotted on the vertical axis.

Typically, Lorenz curves are plotted in *quintiles,* or fifths. A household in the top fifth of the income distribution has greater earnings than at least 80 percent of all households. A household in the bottom fifth has lower earnings than at least 80 percent of all households. Figure 1 shows a hypothetical Lorenz curve, plotting the cumulative percentage of households against their cumulative share of income, which is given in column 3 of Table 1. For example, the cumulative share of income for the first four quintiles is 55 percent. That is, the bottom 80 percent of households accounts for 55 percent of all income. The bottom 20 percent of households earns only 5 percent of all income, and the top 20 percent earns 45 percent of all income.

A 45-degree-line Lorenz curve shows absolute equality. If income were distributed equally, the bottom 20 percent of households would receive 20 percent of all income; the bottom 40 percent of households would receive 40 percent of all income; and so on. When the Lorenz curve deviates from the 45-degree line, or the *line of perfect equality,* the income distribution departs from perfect equality.

FIGURE 1
The Lorenz Curve

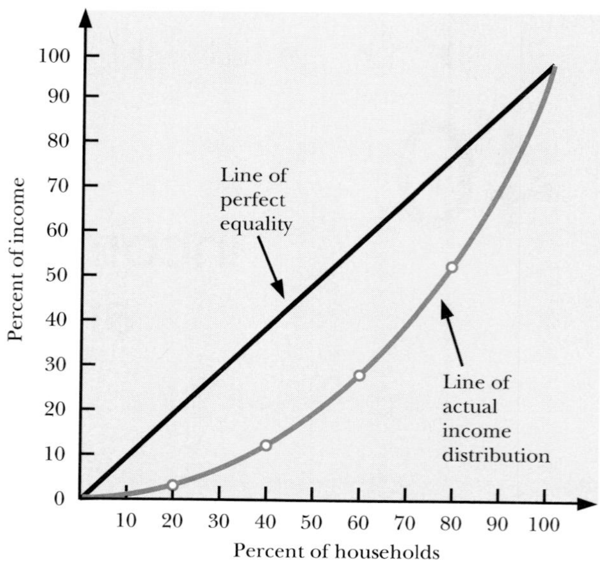

The Lorenz curve measures the cumulative percentage of households (ranked from lowest to highest incomes) on the horizontal axis and the cumulative percentage of income earned by these households on the vertical axis. If all households earned the same income (perfect equality), the Lorenz curve would be a 45-degree line called the *line of perfect equality.* The bowed Lorenz curve shows an unequal distribution of income. The more the Lorenz curve for a society is bowed away from the line of perfect equality, the greater is the inequality in the distribution of income in that society.

TABLE 1
A Hypothetical Lorenz Curve

Quintile (1)	Share of Income (percent) (2)	Cumulative Share of Income (percent) (3)
Lowest fifth	5	5
Second fifth	10	15
Third fifth	15	30
Fourth fifth	25	55
Highest fifth	45	100

TABLE 2
The U.S. Distribution of Income (before taxes), 1929, 1970, and 1991

	1929		1970		1991	
Quintile of Households	**Share of Income (percent)**	**Cumulative Share of Income (percent)**	**Share of Income (percent)**	**Cumulative Share of Income (percent)**	**Share of Income (percent)**	**Cumulative Share of Income (percent)**
Lowest fifth	3.9	3.9	5.5	5.5	4.6	4.6
Second fifth	8.6	12.5	12.2	17.7	10.8	15.4
Third fifth	13.8	26.3	17.6	35.3	16.6	32.0
Fourth fifth	19.3	45.6	23.8	59.1	23.8	55.8
Highest fifth	54.5	100.0	40.9	100.0	44.3	100.0
Top 5 percent	30.0		15.6		17.4	

Source: *Historical Statistics of the United States;* U.S. Bureau of the Census.

The more bowed the Lorenz curve is from the line of perfect equality, the more unequal is the distribution of income.[1]

HOW UNEQUAL IS U.S. INCOME DISTRIBUTION?

Facts and Figures

Table 2 gives some facts about the U.S. distribution of income in 1929, 1970, and 1991. The corresponding Lorenz curves are drawn in Figure 2. Over the past half-century, there has been a noticeable leveling in the distribution of income—a distinct trend toward greater equality. Households in the top fifth accounted for 54.5 percent of all income in 1929

FIGURE 2
Lorenz Curves of the U.S. Income Distribution, 1929, 1970, and 1991

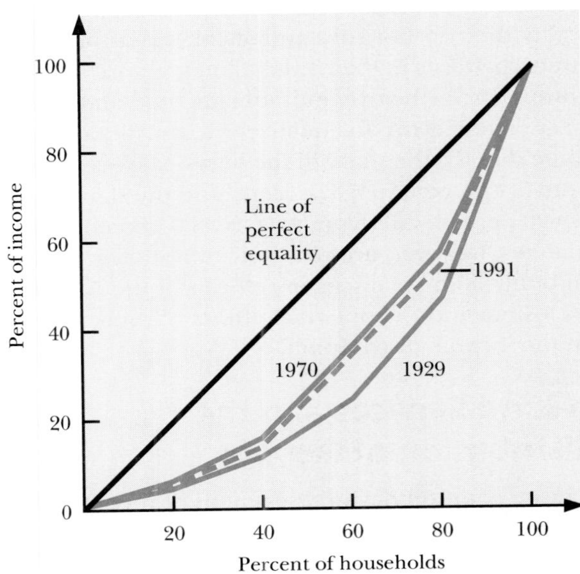

For more than 60 years, there has been a distinct trend toward more equality in the U.S. distribution of income. Since 1970, however, there has been a trend toward greater inequality.

[1]Another measure of the inequality of income distribution is the *Gini coefficient,* a numerical measure of inequality. The Gini coefficient is defined as the area between the 45-degree line and the Lorenz curve, divided by the total area under the 45-degree line. If there is perfect equality, the Lorenz curve and the 45-degree line coincide, and the Gini coefficient is zero. If there is perfect inequality (one household gets all the income), then the difference between the Lorenz curve and the 45-degree line equals the entire area under the 45-degree line, and the Gini coefficient equals 1. In between these two extremes, the Gini coefficient can measure whether one income distribution is more or less unequal than another.

but only 44.3 percent in 1991. The top 5 percent accounted for 30 percent of all income in 1929 but for only 17.4 percent in 1991. The share of the lowest 40 percent of households rose from 12.5 percent in 1929 to 15.4 percent in 1991. The *middle class* (households in the third and fourth quintiles) increased its relative standing most over the past 60 years: its share of income rose from 33.1 percent to 40.4 percent.

Despite the long-term trend toward a more equal distribution of income in the United States, considerable inequality still exists. The top 5 percent of U.S. households accounts for 17.4 percent of all income, whereas the bottom 20 percent accounts for only 4.6 percent. Since the top 20 percent earns 44.3 percent of all income, households in the top 20 percent earn, on average, ten times as much as those in the bottom 20 percent. Moreover, the U.S. income distribution became more unequal during the 1980s. By international standards, it is relatively unequal for an advanced industrialized economy (see Example 1).

FIGURE 3
The Distribution of Income Before and After Taxes and In-Kind Benefits

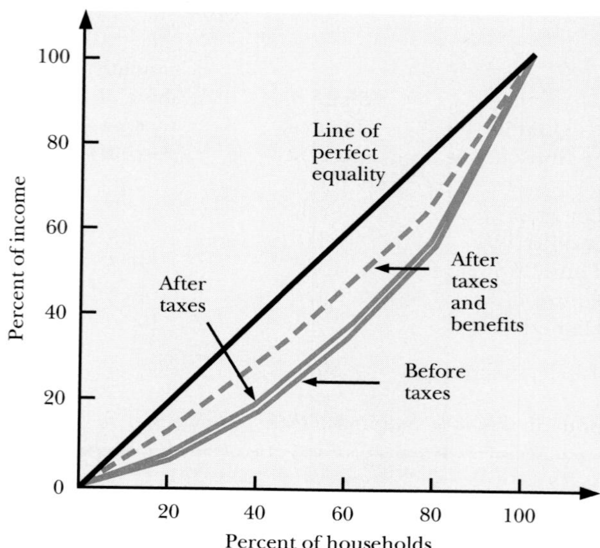

Income and payroll taxes have only a minor equalizing effect on U.S. income distribution. The distribution, however, becomes much more equal when all sources of income and in-kind benefits are included as income. These calculations are inexact because it is difficult to place an appropriate price tag on in-kind benefits. The recipient of a public service that costs $20 to produce (say, public health) may value that service at less than $20 or may even give it a zero value. In-kind benefits are typically valued at cost due to the lack of knowledge concerning the recipient's valuation.

Source: Based on Edgar K. Browning, "The Trend Toward Equality in the Distribution of Net Income," *Southern Economic Journal* 43, 1 (July 1976): 914. The calculations are for 1972.

Taxes and the Distribution of Income

Although income and payroll taxes are intended to redistribute income from the rich to the poor, in reality they do not substantially alter existing distribution patterns in the United States. Figure 3 graphs Lorenz curves before and after income and payroll taxes. These taxes do equalize the distribution of income slightly; the share of the lowest 20 percent rises from 5.4 percent to 6.3 percent, and the share of the top 20 percent falls from 41.4 to 38.0 percent. These changes, however, are relatively minor. The chapter on public finance discusses reforms of the American tax system and the potential effects of those reforms on the income distribution.

In-Kind Services and the Distribution of Income

A more comprehensive assessment of income distribution incorporates both components of household income, money income, and **in-kind income.**

> **In-kind income** consists primarily of benefits—such as free public education, school lunch programs, public housing, or food stamps—for which the recipient is not required to pay.

Figure 3 showed that transfers of income through the tax system (taxing the more fortunate to finance money payments to the less fortunate) do not materially alter the distribution of income. What happens to the distribution of income when in-kind benefits are included? Figure 3 also graphs the Lorenz curve based on Edgar Browning's calculation of the distribution of income after taxes, which includes receipts of public services such as public education, government medical services, and other categories of in-kind income. Browning's calculation shows that the distribution of income becomes much

EXAMPLE 1 International Comparisons of Income Distributions

The accompanying figure shows the income distribution in five countries. The figure illustrates three important facts about the distribution of income. First, income tends to be more unequally distributed in low-income countries than in rich countries. Brazil, with the most unequal income distribution shown, is representative of low-income countries. Second, demographic characteristics and government policy affect the distribution of income. Although it has about the same average income as the United States, Sweden's income distribution is more equal. Sweden's greater equality is explained by the greater homogeneity of its population and by the greater role of the Swedish state in redistributing income. Third, planned socialism appears to equalize the distribution of income. Although Hungary is a relatively poor country, its income distribution is the most equal of the five countries in the figure.

Approximate Lorenz Curves for the Distribution of Income in the United States and Other Countries

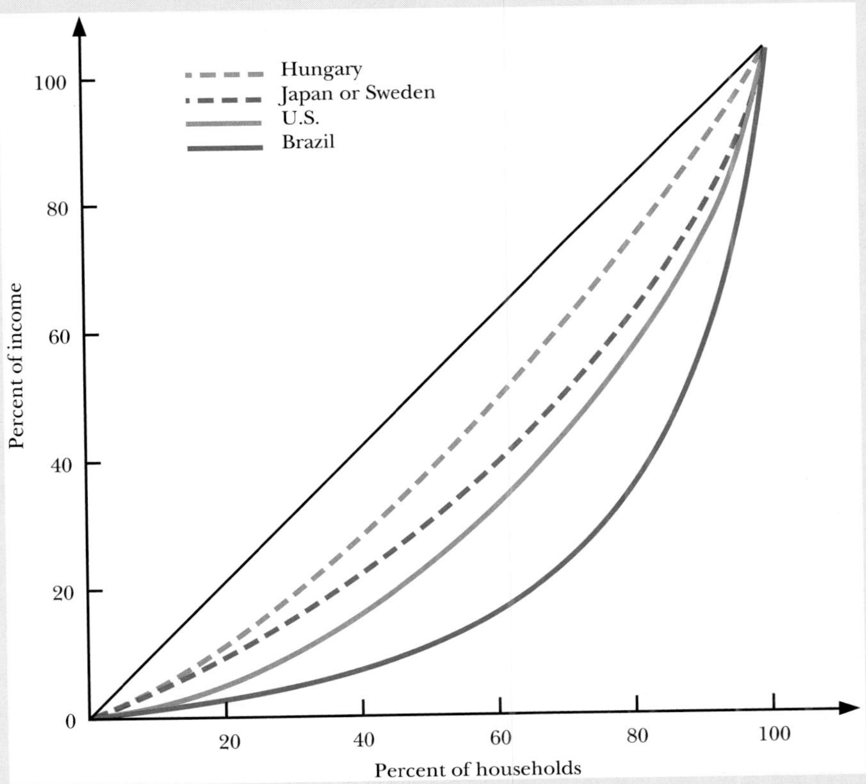

Source: The World Bank, *World Development Report, 1991* (New York: Oxford University Press).

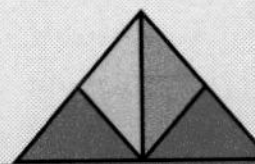

FIGURE 4
Age and Earnings of U.S. Males

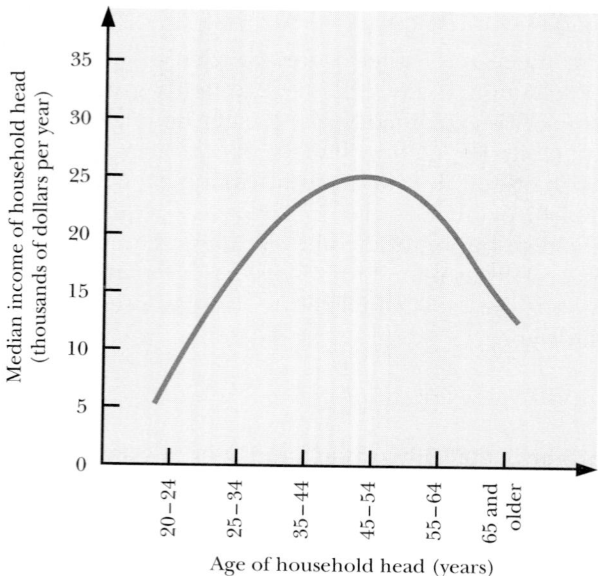

Income tends to be low at the beginning of one's career, rise until one's fifties, and tail off at retirement age. The above data are for 1985.

Source: *Statistical Abstract of the United States.*

more equal when in-kind income is included. This result occurs because the poor receive a larger share of public services than the rich.[2]

Life Cycle and the Distribution of Income

Income varies systematically with the life cycle. Incomes tend to be low at the beginning of a person's career (say, ages 20 to 24); earnings subsequently rise until a person's mid-fifties and then drop off at retirement age. These trends in lifetime earnings are plotted in Figure 4. The appropriate measure of inequality, therefore, is the distribution of the *life-time incomes* of households.

Because incomes vary over the life cycle, standard Lorenz curves overstate the degree of actual inequality at any point in time. Households with wage earners in their twenties or sixties will typically have lower incomes than those with wage earners in their thirties, forties, and fifties, even though their lifetime earnings may actually be identical.

Economist Morton Paglin has estimated that the U.S. lifetime Lorenz curve (the distribution of income adjusted for difference in age) has about 50 percent less inequality than the ordinary Lorenz curve. Critics of this study believe that he overstates the correction for age, but they agree that if age is held constant, the amount of inequality is reduced.[3]

SOURCES OF INCOME INEQUALITY

The causes of income inequality include variations in ability, discrimination, occupation, human-capital investment, chance and luck, inheritance, and screening.

Differences in Ability

People are born with or develop different mental and physical abilities that determine their available choice of occupation. Not everyone has the mental skills and manual dexterity to become a surgeon; few people have the physical endowments to become pro-

[2]Alternate calculations showing a smaller effect of in-kind services have been prepared by Timothy Smeeding, "On the Distribution of Net Income: Comment," *Southern Economic Journal,* 46, 1, (January 1979): 932–44.

[3]Morton Paglin, in "The Measurement and Trend of Inequality: A Basic Revision," *American Economic Review* 65, 4 (September 1975): 598–609, reports that there is a significant trend toward a more equal distribution of income between 1947 and 1972 if the effects of age on the distribution of income are removed. Paglin's findings have been disputed by several authors, in particular by Sheldon Danziger, Robert Haveman, and Eugene Smolensky in "The Measurement and Trend of Inequality: Comment," *American Economic Review* 67, 3 (June 1977): 502–13. For a survey of this literature, see Alan Blinder, "The Level and Distribution of Economic Well-Being," in *The American Economy in Transition,* edited by Martin Feldstein (Chicago: The University of Chicago Press, 1980), 450–53.

fessional athletes or highly paid fashion models. By contrast, many possess the necessary skills to perform unskilled labor, type, or serve as bank tellers.

Because people are different, the labor market segregates them into noncompeting groups, as mentioned in the chapter on labor markets. The few people with superb athletic ability compete among themselves for jobs as professional athletes. Individuals with extroverted personalities and communication skills compete among themselves for jobs as sales representatives, public-relations agents, politicians, and union organizers.

Because people are segregated into noncompeting groups, wage differentials can persist over a long period of time. Workers from a low-wage, noncompeting group will be excluded from the high-wage market because they lack some ability, strength, or other talent. The six-figure earnings of surgeons will not cause ditchdiggers to switch to surgery. The requirement of being able to lift 100 pounds will keep many people from seeking employment on offshore drilling rigs despite its high wage rates.

Discrimination

Discrimination, another factor contributing to income inequality, occurs when qualified individuals are blocked from entering jobs and occupations or when workers with equal skills and qualifications performing the same tasks are treated differently on the grounds of race, sex, or creed. Individuals who are denied equal access to education and training will be limited, through no fault of their own, in their career opportunities. Individuals who are denied access to jobs in craft unions or industrial unions will spill over into the non-unionized sector, creating a wage differential in favor of unionized workers. Individuals who are restricted in their choice of occupation even though they may possess the necessary qualifications will be unable to compete for the higher-paying positions that they may merit.

During the postwar period, the median income of nonwhite households in the United States has averaged about 60 percent that of white households. The postwar trend in the ratio of nonwhite to white incomes has been upward, beginning at 51 percent in 1947 and rising to an average of 61 percent in the mid-1970s. The economic downturns of the late 1970s and early 1980s caused a slight reversal of the upward movement, so that in 1990, the ratio of median nonwhite to white income was 56 percent.

Likewise, substantial differences exist in the average incomes of males and females. (See Figure 5.) Women who work full time have had an average income equal to slightly more than 60 percent of male incomes since the late 1950s. Although the ratio of nonwhite to white earnings has improved since 1947, the female/male income differences remained almost constant until 1980 (the relative female earnings actually worsened during the mid-1950s). However, between 1980 and 1991, women's pay jumped from 60 percent to 70 percent of men's salaries.

Studies of the effects of discrimination on nonwhite/white earning differences conclude that about one-half of observed differences in earnings can be attributed to a disparity in the quantity and quality of schooling received by the different races. More than twice the percentage of whites complete four years of college than do blacks or Hispanics. High-school completion rates are closer, at 37 percent for whites, 34 percent for blacks, and 27 percent for Hispanics. The most effective means of reducing nonwhite/white earning differentials, therefore, is to provide equal access to quality education, irrespective of race.

Notably, the male/female differential in college completion rates is much smaller (23 percent for males to 16 percent for females). A higher percentage of women than men complete high school, and about the same percentage as men have at least some college-level education. The male/female income differential does not result from a disparity in years of schooling. Although women tend to work fewer hours and spend fewer years in the labor force, these factors cannot explain more than half of the female earnings gap.[4] (See Example 2.)

After completion of schooling, individuals may encounter labor market discrimination. Certain

[4]Henry Aaron and Cameron Loughy, *The Comparable Worth Controversy* (Washington, DC: The Brookings Institution, 1986), 12–13; Ronald Ehrenberg and Robert Smith, *Modern Labor Economics*, 4th ed. (New York: HarperCollins, 1991), chap. 14; James Smith and Michael Ward, *Women's Wages and Work in the Twentieth Century*, (New York: Rand Corporation, 1984).

FIGURE 5
Income Differentials by Sex and Race

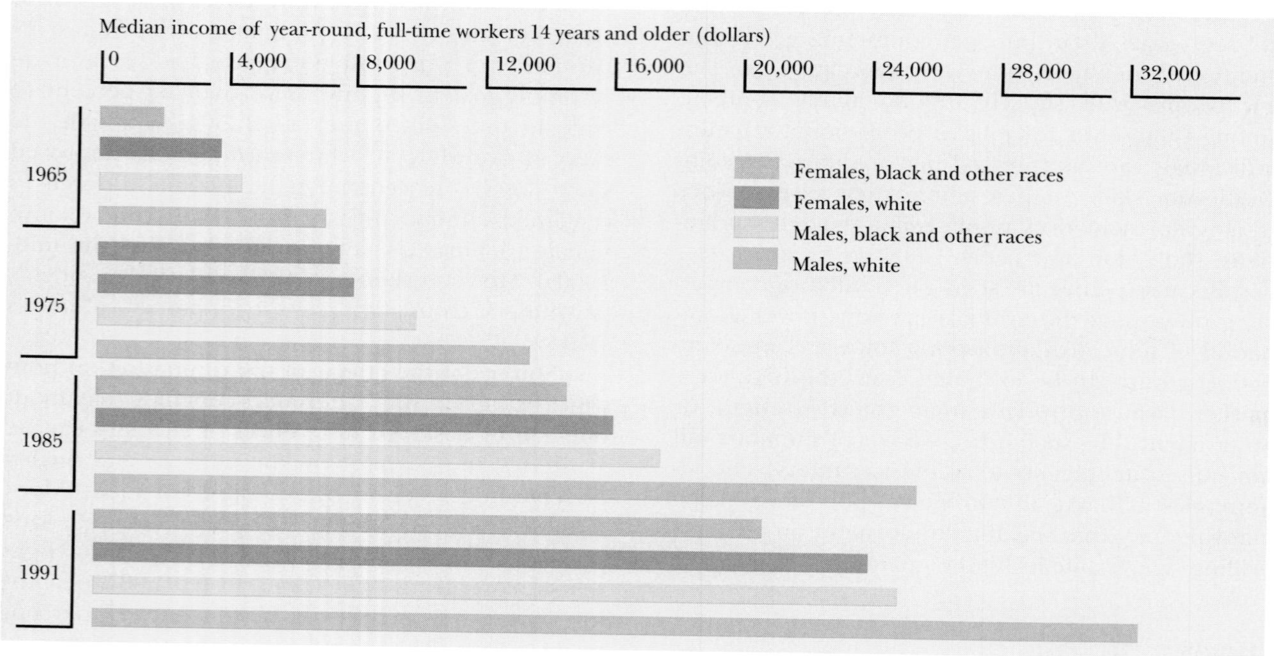

This figure illustrates that substantial differences in the incomes of nonwhites and whites and in the incomes of males and females are still present in the United States.

Source: U.S. Bureau of the Census; U.S. Bureau of Labor Statistics, *Handbook of Labor Statistics.*

unions or professional organizations may not accept blacks, Hispanics, or women. Discrimination may be in the subtle form of certain jobs being set aside for specific races or for women. Moreover, women may receive less on-the-job training on the grounds that they will spend fewer years in the labor force than men.

Labor-market discrimination according to sex and race does not normally entail discrimination between two workers (of different race or sex) performing the same job. In fact, federal laws guarantee equal pay for equal, and even "comparable," work. (See Example 3.) More often, discrimination occurs when nonwhites or women are channeled into occupations regarded as "suitable" for them. This channeling may result from an employee's own preferences (a woman may want to be a schoolteacher) or employer discrimination (an employer may be unwilling to hire women for assembly-line work). The employer may use simple screening rules (such as not hiring women for manual labor) to deny access to certain jobs and professions. As a consequence, "suitable" professions—say, nursing and schoolteaching for women or bus driving for black males—become *crowded,* and the relative earnings of these professions are driven down. Table 3 shows that industries in which women are concentrated have low pay. If there were fewer restrictions on the occupational choices of women and blacks, then public schoolteaching, bus driving, and nursing would be less crowded, and relative earnings in these professions would be less depressed.[5]

[5]Ehrenberg and Smith, 551–52.

EXAMPLE 2 Why Women Earn Less

Empirical studies of male/female earnings differences seek to determine how much of the 30 percent to 35 percent female earning gap is explained by "objective" factors such as less education or less experience. Empirical studies find that the gap is not satisfactorily explained by objective differences among men and women. Researchers agree that a major cause of the female earning gap is the concentration of women into low-paying professions.

One study of the personnel practices of 373 firms found that in 60 percent of them, men and women were perfectly segregated by job title. In other words, there was not a single job type in those establishments to which the employer assigned both sexes. Another study, based upon wage surveys, found extensive segregation in white-collar job titles within firms, despite the availability of women for each job title. If a firm hired men for a particular job title, it hired no women for that title. Since salary is usually set by job title, such segregation allows employers to create different pay scales for men and women. Sometimes, however, the disparity is not so subtle. Research has demonstrated that even within narrowly defined occupations, for which it is relatively certain that the jobs have similar duties, men earn more than women (see table below).

Source: Barbara Bergmann, "Does the Market for Women's Labor Need Fixing?" *Journal of Economic Perspectives* 3 (Winter 1989): 43–60.

Average Weekly Wages for Women and Men in Selected Narrowly Defined Occupations, 1985

Occupation	Women	Men
Secretaries	$278	$365
Stock and inventory clerks	265	326
Bookkeepers, accounting and auditing clerks	263	341
Expediters	257	413
Machinists	257	408
Bus drivers	257	404
General office clerks	255	323
Cost and rate clerks	254	483
Sales workers, furniture and home furnishings	252	307
Grinding, abrading, buffing machine operators	251	330
Production inspectors, checkers, examiners	249	406
Traffic, shipping and receiving clerks	247	305
Electrical and electronic equipment assemblers	243	284
Packaging and filling machine operators	234	286
Printing machine operators	225	363
Molding and casting machine operators	222	347
Painting and paint-spraying machine operators	218	313
Solderers and brazers	216	287
Photographic process machine operators	208	297
Butchers and meat cutters	204	326
Bakers	202	301
Truck drivers, light	200	281
Slicing and cutting machine operators	192	303
Hotel clerks	191	279
Sales workers, apparel	168	281

Note: These figures are estimates of medians of usual weekly earnings of employed wage and salary workers who usually work full-time. They are based on data collected by the Bureau of Labor Statistics, but the medians have been computed on a basis that differs slightly from the method used to produce the official BLS estimates. Moreover, BLS does not officially issue figures on wages for groups of less than 50,000, while some of the wages quoted in the table are for groups of size 19,000–50,000. Wage estimates included in the table have a standard error of estimate less than 10 percent.

EXAMPLE 3 Comparable Worth

The Supreme Court and the federal courts have ruled that employees have a right to equal pay for "comparable" work. This is a significant extension of the law requiring equal pay for equal work. On the basis of the rulings, suits have been filed by persons who claim that they are being paid less than others who perform comparable work. In Oregon and Washington, the courts ordered employers to adjust pay scales so that employees with comparable jobs would receive the same pay.

In the state of Washington, a committee assigned points to each job on the basis of knowledge and skills, mental demands, accountability, and work conditions. Registered nurses won the highest evaluation, well above computer system analysts. Clerical supervisors won a higher rating than chemists; electricians were assigned lower points than beginning secretaries. In all these evaluations, the market had assigned different relative wages than the comparable-worth point system.

A number of economists have argued against the comparable-worth principle. First, a difference between the comparable-worth wage and the market-clearing wage will cause surpluses and shortages in the labor market. Second, if the comparable-worth wage is set high in traditionally female-dominated professions, the incentive for women to break into higher-paying male professions will be reduced. Third, many economists doubt that experts will be able to agree on rational formulas for determining the comparable worth of different jobs.

Source: Henry J. Aaron and Cameron M. Loughy, *The Comparable Worth Controversy* (Washington, DC: The Brookings Institution, 1986); June O'Neill, "The 'Comparable Worth' Trap," *Wall Street Journal*, January 20, 1984; Robert Higgs, "The Economic Consequences of Comparable Worth," *The Collegiate Forum*, Spring 1984.

Occupational Differences

Other things being the same, most people prefer to work in occupations that are safe, offer pleasant surroundings, and do not involve heavy or dirty work. The supply of labor to attractive occupations and jobs will be greater than the supply to unattractive ones, *ceteris paribus*. Even though the coal miner and the garbage collector earn more than many others with the same physical and mental skills, labor does not move automatically into these higher-paying jobs to wipe out the wage differential. Compensating wage differentials exist because people require a reward for working in unpleasant and dangerous jobs.

The existence of compensating wage differentials implies that some inequality is a matter of conscious choice. The terms of this choice may involve a trade-off between pay and leisure. Some people value leisure time more than others. One person may work a 60-hour week, whereas another (who earns the same hourly wage) works a 30-hour week. The first person will have weekly earnings twice those of the second, but the second will have twice as much leisure. This extra leisure has a value to the recipient that is not reflected in his or her monetary income.

Different occupations also involve different degrees of risk. An owner of a small business has a more uncertain income than a tenured university professor. A wheat farmer, whose crops may be destroyed by blights and droughts, has a more uncertain income than a union employee with seniority. A real estate speculator stands to make a fortune if lucky but will go bankrupt if unlucky.

Society is comprised of individuals with differing attitudes toward risk. *Risk seekers* are more willing to incur risks than *risk avoiders*, who are reluctant to take on risks.[6] A predominance of risk avoiders in a society will, in and of itself, cause the distribution of income to be unequal. Some of those willing to incur risks will strike it rich and rise to the top income level.

[6] The theory of individual choice of inequality was formulated by Milton Friedman in the article "Choice, Chance, and the Personal Distribution of Income," *Journal of Political Economy* 61, 4 (August 1953): 277–90.

 **TABLE 3**
Average Hourly Earnings Among Industries, by Proportion of Female Workers

Proportion of Female Workers in Industry (percent)	Average Hourly Earnings in Industry (dollars)
70 and over	5.71
50–69.9	6.08
40–49.9	7.58
30–39.9	8.15
20–29.99	8.34
10–19.9	9.53
0–9.9	11.56

Sources: Cited in Henry J. Aaron and Cameron M. Loughy, *The Comparable Worth Controversy* (Washington, DC: The Brookings Institution, 1986), 9. The authors' calculations are based on Janet L. Norwood, *The Female-Male Earnings Gap: A Review of Employment and Earnings Issues,* U.S. Department of Labor, Bureau of Labor Statistics, Report no. 673 (Washington, DC: U.S. Government Printing Office, September 1982), Table 4; based on July 1982 averages.

Less fortunate risk seekers will sink to the bottom. The vast majority—the risk avoiders—will be in the middle, earning steadier incomes.

Human-Capital Investment

Human-capital theory, pioneered by Theodore W. Schultz, Gary Becker, and Jacob Mincer, is based on the premise that individuals are faced with the choice of different lifetime earnings streams.[7] Individuals will make rational personal optimizing decisions based upon the costs and benefits of the different earnings streams.

Just as businesses invest in plant and equipment to increase the firm's productive capacity, so human beings invest in themselves to raise their own productivity, and, hence, their future earning capacity. They (and their parents) can invest in education. They can pay the costs of migrating to areas with better job opportunities. They can invest in medical care to improve their health. These activities can be classified as investments because they raise the productive capacity of individuals. (See Example 4.)

If human-capital investment translates into higher lifetime earnings, why does not everyone demand equal levels of such investment? Although human-capital investment yields benefits, it also has its costs. In obtaining a college degree, a student must pay not only for tuition and books but also for the loss of current earnings. A person who moves to another city to seek a better job incurs moving costs, the loss of income between jobs, and the personal costs of leaving family and friends behind. Confronted with the costs and benefits of human-capital investment, individuals are presumed to make rational investment decisions. They acquire more human capital as long as the marginal benefit exceeds the marginal cost. Insofar as the benefits from the human-capital investment will be spread out over a number of years in the form of higher earnings in the future, the appropriate measure of these benefits is the present value of the increase in future earnings.

Human-capital theory views inequalities in the distribution of income as partly the result of rational decision making. Individuals must choose between more money now (going to work after high school) and more money later (going to college with no earnings now). This decision will depend upon the anticipated rate of return of the human-capital investment, which in turn will depend upon both the interest rate used to calculate present value and the anticipated increase in future earnings. Individuals who place a high value on having money now (a high implicit interest rate) are less likely to acquire human capital, everything else equal.[8]

[7]The pioneering articles in human-capital theory are: Gary Becker, "Investment in Human Capital: A Theoretical Analysis," *Journal of Political Economy* 70, 5 (October 1962): 9–49: Theodore W. Schultz, "Capital Formation by Education," *Journal of Political Economy* 68, 6 (December 1960): 571–83.

[8]To show how human-capital investment decisions are made, assume an 8-year medical-degree training program costs $100,000. Once the training is complete, it promises to raise annual earnings $15,000 each year above what they would have been without additional training. In making this decision, the present value of the extra income ($15,000 in the ninth year, $15,000 in the tenth year, and so on until retirement from practice) must be calculated by converting each year's earnings to a present value. If the sum of the present values for each year's earnings exceeds the $100,000 cost, this human-capital investment is profitable.

Alternatively, one could calculate the rate of return that equates the cost and the present value. If this rate of return exceeds the rate of interest at which the $100,000 could be borrowed, then the investment is a profitable one.

EXAMPLE 4 Higher Education Pays

A census report published in 1990 confirms that college diplomas are still worth their weight in dollar bills. Consider the following information: In 1987, high school graduates with no college education earned $921 per month. People who went to college but failed to earn a degree earned only slightly more. People with junior college degrees earned $1458 per month, and those with bachelor's degrees earned $1829. People with postgraduate degrees earned even more: M.A.'s earned $2378 and Ph.D.'s earned $3637. Graduates with professional degrees in law and medicine earned the most, at $4003 per month.

These figures confirm the existence of a monetary return to higher education. Calculating the lifetime return from such earnings differentials demonstrates that even an expensive college education yields a positive rate of return.

Source: "Higher Earnings Are a Matter of Degree," *Wall Street Journal*, December 13, 1990.

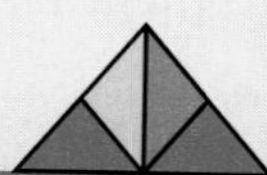

Social policy also affects human capital. Over the years (especially in the 1960s), various government programs have been implemented to increase the human capital of the poor and the young. These government programs (such as the Job Corps, Manpower Training and Development, and Neighborhood Youth Programs) are aimed at training disadvantaged persons at government expense to learn marketable skills.

Chance and Luck

Other sources of income inequality are chance (random occurrences) and luck. Accidents and poor health can unexpectedly destroy one's earning capacity. Choosing to train for a profession in which there is an unexpected decline in demand or in which there is an unexpected increase in demand (such as petroleum engineering in the late 1970s) can have a significant unplanned effect on lifetime earnings. Luck determines whether individuals earn the economic rents discussed in the preceding chapter. Having the good fortune to be in the right place at the right time can yield great rewards. Having the bad fortune to be in the wrong profession or industry during downswings in the business cycle can result in unemployment that reduces not only current earnings but also the amount of work experience and training an individual accumulates.

Typically, chance and luck have a short-term effect on a family's place in the income distribution. Spells of unemployment usually pass; the entrepreneur who has good luck in one period may experience bad luck in the next period. (See Example 5.)

Inheritance

Thus far, this chapter has offered several explanations for inequalities in the distribution of *labor income.* But income from other factors of production—land, capital, and entrepreneurship—is also unequally distributed. In fact, income from the ownership of land, mineral, and capital property is distributed more unequally than income from labor. Most nonlabor income derives from the ownership of **wealth** (stocks, bonds, real estate).

> Personal **wealth** (or net worth) is the value of one's total assets minus one's liabilities.

In 1989 the wealthiest 1 percent of the population in the United States accounted for 37 percent of all wealth (Table 4). The top 10 percent accounted for about 68 percent of all wealth. On the income side, the top 5 percent of households accounted for

EXAMPLE 5 Chance, Luck, and Earnings: The Vietnam Draft Lottery

No one has been drafted into the armed forces since 1972. Congressional authority to conscript expired in July 1973, largely as a consequence of the unpopular drafts of the Vietnam War. There were five draft lotteries during the Vietnam War period. Birth dates were drawn by lottery, and men with birth dates drawn early were the first to be drafted.

Sufficient time has passed to allow economists to determine the effect of being drafted for Vietnam upon earnings after return to civilian life. Earnings information from the Social Security Administration show that white male veterans in the 1980s earned 15 percent less than comparable nonveterans. Vietnam veterans were earning about $4000 less per year than nonveterans in the early 1990s.

Why did service in Vietnam reduce lifetime earnings? One explanation is that people who served in Vietnam lost about two years of experience in the civilian labor market. In addition, some employers may have systematically avoided hiring Vietnam veterans.

Although earnings statistics clearly show that Vietnam veterans earn less, they are less clear on the effects of service in World War II on earnings. In fact, many studies show the effect of World War II service to be positive or at least neutral on lifetime earnings.

Source: Joshua Angrist, "Lifetime Earnings and the Vietnam Era Draft Lottery," *American Economic Review,* 80 (June 1990): 313–36.

17.4 percent of all income in 1991 (see Table 2). Wealth, therefore, is distributed more unequally than income. Yet, like the distribution of income, the distribution of wealth has become more equal over the years. Since 1929, the share of all wealth held by the top 1 percent has fallen by 75 percent.[9]

One important cause of the unequal distribution of wealth is *inheritance,* or the passing of wealth from one generation to the next. The concentration of wealth due to inheritance is intensified by two factors. First, the children of the wealthy, in addition to inheriting personal wealth, typically receive better education and training and develop important social contacts. Second, the children of the wealthy often marry others who are likely to inherit wealth. These advantages are called "fortunes" by Nobel Prize-winning English economist James Meade. Those who inherit these fortunes (wealth, education opportunities, abilities) have the opportunity to earn substantial income not only from wealth but also from labor.

TABLE 4
Distribution of Wealth in the United States

Population Segment	Share of Total Wealth (percent) 1963	1989
Top 0.5 percent	25	29
Top 1 percent	32	37
Top 10 percent	64	68

Sources: *Statistical Abstract of the United States,* 1981, 453; *Federal Reserve Bulletin, Survey of Consumer Finances,* 1992.

Empirical studies of the effects of inheritance on the overall distribution of income fail to delineate a significant role for inherited wealth. The share of income from wealth has been declining, and even for high-income families, income from wealth accounts

[9]These estimates are by Robert Lampman, James D. Smith, and Staunton Calvert and are cited in *Statistical Abstract of the United States,* 1981, 453.

for only 10 percent of total income. One study found that inherited wealth accounted for only 2 percent of the income inequality in the United States.[10]

Screening and Inequality

Most researchers agree that human-capital investments account for a substantial portion of income inequality. Jacob Mincer, for example, has found that human capital accounts for one half of the total inequality. However, if education and training were the sole causes of income inequality, educational achievements would be as unequally distributed as income. Yet, education is distributed much more equally among the adult population than income.[11] Hence, it is clear that factors other than schooling affect the distribution of income.

Ability is also much more equally distributed than income. People with either very high or very low IQ scores are relatively rare; most fall in the middle. In the distribution of income, more families fall in the lower income groups than in the higher ones. Why does ability, as implied by this differential distribution, have only a relatively small independent effect on earnings? Using schooling as an indicator of ability, Michael Spence and Nobel laureate Kenneth Arrow maintain that schooling signals to employers that the individual is likely to possess sought-after traits. Prospective employers filter out individuals who lack educational credentials, assuming that they are likely to be less productive. As long as schooling simply serves to screen employees, the effect of ability on earnings should be modest.

Screening deviates from traditional human-capital theory, which argues that individuals with more schooling and training earn more because they are more productive. Screening suggests that education simply serves as a filter to admit some people to high-paying jobs while excluding others who lack such credentials.[12]

[10]Alan S. Blinder, *Toward an Economic Theory of Income Distribution* (Cambridge, MA: MIT Press, 1974).

[11]Lester C. Thurow, *Poverty and Discrimination* (Washington, DC: Brookings Institution, 1969), 68.

[12]Signaling theory is treated in Michael Spence, "Job Market Signaling," *Quarterly Journal of Economics* 87, 3 (August 1973): 355–74; Kenneth Arrow, "Higher Education as a Filter," *Journal of Public Economics* 2, 3 (July 1973): 193–216.

WHAT IS A JUST DISTRIBUTION OF INCOME?

Philosophers have debated the ethical issue of distributive justice for centuries. Is it fair to have extremes of wealth and poverty? Are unequal rewards required in order to bring out extra effort and talents? In general, economists are in a better position to describe the economic consequences of different distributions of income than to judge whether one is better than another, but we will briefly examine some of the philosophies of distributive justice that have been formulated over the years.

Natural Law and the Leaky Bucket

According to the natural-law philosophers of the seventeenth century, each individual has the right to receive the fruits of his or her labors. This philosophy translates into the modern marginal productivity theory of income distribution. According to marginal productivity theory, the owner of a factor of production receives the equivalent of the factor's marginal revenue product (MRP). Under this system, those who are more productive (those who have high MRPs) will receive more than those with low MRPs.

Critics point out that factor payments based on marginal productivity will lead to inequities. Some individuals will inherit factors with high MRPs; those who are lucky will receive high rewards.

The major advantage of distributing income according to marginal productivities is that the owners of factors of production are encouraged to raise the marginal productivity of their factors. Thus, individuals are prompted to invest in human capital; people are motivated to acquire more physical capital; entrepreneurs are spurred to assume risks. If factors of production were not paid in accordance with marginal productivity, there would be a tendency to reduce effort, to acquire less human and physical capital, and to take fewer risks; the economy would produce less income overall.

Most economists agree that there is a trade-off between equality and income. If income were redistributed away from those who possess high-priced factors of production (by means of a high tax), the efficiency of the economy would decline, and less income would be available for society as a whole. Economist Arthur Okun described the equity/efficiency trade-off using the analogy of a leaky bucket.[13] Redistributing income from the fortunate to the unfortunate is like transferring water from one barrel to another with a leaky bucket. In the process of making the transfer, water (income) is lost forever. If the leak is a slow one, then the costs to society of the redistribution are small. If the leak is fast, then the losses of total income will be substantial. Society must decide whether the costs of greater equality are worth the price.

The Utilitarian Case for Equality

Natural-law philosophy and marginal productivity theory support an unequal distribution of income. Inequality allows individuals to reap the fruits of their efforts and raises economic efficiency. At the other end of the spectrum is the *utilitarian theory,* which holds that equal income distribution will maximize the utility of society.

The law of diminishing marginal utility supplies the underlying rationale of the utilitarian theory. If we assume that people are basically alike (if they have the same tastes, obtain the same satisfaction from the same amount of income, and so on), the total utility of society will be greatest when income is distributed equally because everyone is subject to the law of diminishing marginal utility. If Jones were rich and Smith were poor, Jones would be getting much less utility from his last dollar than Smith. If income were shifted from Jones to Smith, Smith's utility would increase more than Jones's would be reduced. Therefore, the reduction in inequality would increase the total utility of society.

If, indeed, everyone were alike, then the total utility of society would be greatest when income distribution among individuals was perfectly equal. But, people are, in fact, different. Some care little for money and wordly goods; others care a great deal. Therefore, it is not at all certain that the rich get less marginal utility from their last dollar than do the poor. Modern economists agree that because we cannot make interpersonal utility comparisons of this sort, we cannot argue scientifically that the total utility of society is greatest when income is equally distributed.

Rawlsian Equality

Philosopher John Rawls has proposed a different argument concerning equality.[14] Rawls maintains that inequality and injustice result from the fact that people know in advance whether they will be rich or poor. Hence, privileged people will not agree to social arrangements that give away these advantages (such as highly redistributive taxes). The rational self-interest of the privileged will not allow a social consensus for a more equal distribution to emerge.

According to Rawls, if everyone were operating behind a "veil of ignorance" (if people did not know in advance whether they would be rich or poor), rational, self-interested individuals would act as risk avoiders. In his system, there would be widespread social support for an equal distribution of income: Risk-averse individuals would be concerned about the welfare of the poor because no one could be sure of avoiding poorness. For example, if there were three possible income distributions, A, B, and C—where A meant the bottom 20 percent got 1 percent of all income, B meant the bottom 20 percent got 5 percent of all income, and C meant that the bottom 20 percent got 15 percent of all income—people who were ignorant of their future advantages would opt for C to avoid the risks of outcomes A and B since they themselves might end up in the bottom 20 percent.

Rawls's policy implication is that government should push society toward that income distribution that would prevail if people did not know in advance who would be privileged and who would be without privilege.

Critics of Rawls's notion of distributive justice argue that there is no guarantee that individuals placed in Rawls's original position would indeed reach a consensus for an equal income distribution. Even in the original position, there would be some risk seekers who would dissent. Moreover, Rawls ignores the problem of the efficiency/inequality trade-off. If the trade-off is substantial, a scheme that concentrates on protecting the least advantaged could lead to a considerable loss of efficiency.

[13] Arthur Okun, *Equality and Efficiency: The Big Trade-Off* (Washington, DC: The Brookings Institution, 1975).

[14] John Rawls, *A Theory of Justice* (Cambridge, MA: Harvard University Press, 1971); and "Some Reasons for the Maximin Criterion," *American Economic Review* 64, 2 (May 1974): 141–46.

POVERTY

The causes of poverty are the same as the causes of income inequality. The poor are poor because of their limited endowments of ability and skills, their limited amount of human capital, bad luck, discrimination, and (some might even argue) conscious choice. The poor are poor because their capacity to earn a "sufficient" income is, for some reason, impaired.

Defining poverty is not an easy task. Analysts will always disagree over what constitutes a poverty income. Some define poverty in terms of the amount of income necessary to provide a family of a certain size with the minimum essentials of food, clothing, shelter, and education. This approach provides an **absolute poverty standard.**

> An **absolute poverty standard** establishes a specific income level for a household of a given size, below which the household is judged to be living in a state of poverty.

But is an absolute measure of poverty appropriate? Poverty can, after all, be relative. A person's sense of poverty depends upon the incomes of others in the community. Thus, a person whose income is 10 percent of everyone else's may feel poor even if that income is above the level required to purchase the minimum essentials. Similarly, the American conception of poverty does not necessarily match that of other countries. The American poor would be considered wealthy in many Asian and African nations. Yet, they are still categorized as poor because they measure themselves against other Americans, not against the poor in other countries. A second approach to poverty, therefore, is a measurement in relative terms. A **relative poverty standard** might classify a household as poor if the household's income is, say, less than 25 percent of an average household's income.

> A **relative poverty standard** defines the poor in terms of the income of others in some defined group.

The choice of a poverty definition will determine to a great extent the number of poor and the rate at which poverty is being eliminated. If an absolute standard is selected, increasing real living standards will push more and more families above the poverty line. According to a relative standard, poverty can be eliminated only by equalizing the distribution of income. If both the rich and the poor experience equal percentage increases in income, the poor will not have improved their relative position. as economist Alan Blinder writes with regard to relative poverty standards: "Under this definition, the War on Poverty would be unwinnable by definition, and the Bible would be literally correct: ye have the poor always with you."[15] Because trends in relative poverty are implicit in the previous discussion of trends in income distribution, the following discussion of trends in poverty uses the official absolute poverty standards of the U.S. government.

Trends in Poverty

Table 5 lists the official statistics on the number of persons below poverty levels in the United States for the period 1959 to 1991. According to the absolute poverty standards of the U.S. government, the number of persons in households below the poverty level declined from 39.5 million to 34.1 million between 1959 and 1991. As a percent of the U.S. population, the figure has declined from 22.4 percent to 14.1 percent. Progress has been uneven, however. Large percentage declines were experienced in the 1960s; subsequently, the number of people below the poverty level remained roughly the same through the 1970s, rose with the severe recessions of the early 1980s, declined with the recovery of the mid 1980s, and rose with the recession at the outset of the 1990s.

A long-run decline in poverty rates is to be expected in a world of rising living standards. Rising real output pulls up the poor along with the rich. Similarly, as the figures show, the incidence of poverty remains quite sensitive to general economic downturns. (See Example 6.)

Table 5 refers only to money income, which does not include in-kind services received by the poor but does include government cash transfers, such as

[15]Blinder, "The Level and Distribution of Economic Well-Being," 456.

TABLE 5
Persons Living in Households with Money Incomes Below Poverty Levels, 1959–1991

Year	Number of Persons Below Poverty Level (millions)	Percentage of Population	Poverty Income for Household of Four (dollars)
1959	39.5	22.4	2,973
1960	39.9	22.2	3,022
1965	33.2	17.3	3,223
1966	28.5	14.7	3,317
1968	25.4	12.8	3,553
1970	25.4	12.6	3,968
1972	24.5	11.9	4,275
1974	24.3	11.6	5,038
1976	25.0	11.8	5,815
1978	24.5	11.4	6,662
1979	25.3	11.6	7,412
1980	29.3	13.0	8,414
1981	31.8	14.0	9,287
1982	34.4	15.0	9,862
1983	35.3	15.2	10,178
1984	33.7	14.4	10,609
1985	33.1	14.0	10,989
1986	32.4	13.6	11,285
1987	32.2	13.4	11,611
1988	31.7	13.0	12,092
1989	31.5	12.8	12,675
1990	33.6	13.5	13,207
1991	34.1	14.1	13,682

Sources: *Economic Report of the President;* U.S. Bureau of the Census. 1991 figures updated by authors.

welfare payments and unemployment insurance. Yet, government antipoverty programs emphasize in-kind benefits more than cash transfers. The government spends $3 in noncash benefits for every $2 in cash payments.

What effects do government antipoverty program have on the number of persons living below the poverty line? Table 6 shows the number of persons living below poverty levels in 1986 before and after government antipoverty programs are taken into account. The percentage of Americans living below the poverty line would be much higher in the absence of government cash-transfer programs. Cash payments reduce the number of persons below the poverty line by 65 percent. When in-kind transfers are included with cash payments, government programs reduce the number living below poverty by almost one-half. Without cash or in-kind payments, 19 percent of the total U.S. population and more than one-third of the nonwhite U.S. population would be below the poverty line. If both cash payments and in-kind benefits are included in income, the percentage of those living below poverty levels falls to 6.9 percent of the white population, 21.2 percent of the black population, and 19.4 percent of the Hispanic population.

The percentage of elderly persons living below poverty is reduced more than that of other groups by in-kind benefits. Their poverty incidence falls from 15 percent to 4.5 percent. This reduction results almost

EXAMPLE 6 Is There an Underclass in the United States?

A number of writers claim that there is a growing underclass of disadvantaged people living in depressed inner-city areas. Crime, welfare dependency, chronic joblessness, and families headed by women have become pronounced, and this hard core of poverty seemingly cannot be reduced by improving economic conditions elsewhere in the economy. There is no single definition of this underclass but, according to the different estimates (see the accompanying table), it constitutes between 0.8 percent and 5.3 percent of the U.S. population and between 5 percent and 37.5 percent of the poor. Although the underclass does not constitute a large proportion of the U.S. population, it does appear to be growing. Between 1970 and 1980, the overall poverty population grew by 8 percent, and the number of poor people living in concentrated poverty areas (40 percent or more) grew by 36 percent.

Source: Isabel Sawhill, "Poverty in the U.S.: Why Is It So Persistent?" *Journal of Economic Literature* 26, 3 (September 1988): 1073–1119.

Definition	Date	Number	Proportion of U.S Poverty Population	Proportion of U.S. Population
Persistently poor who are neither elderly nor disabled	1985	8 million	23.5	3.5
Poor living in poverty areas[a]	1979	1.8 million	7.1	0.8
Poor at least 5 years between 1967 and 1973	1967	10–11 million	37.5	5.3
Upper bound: all persons living in poverty areas[a]	1979	3.7 million	14.2	1.6
Lower bound: long-term AFDC recipients living in poverty areas[a]	1984	1 million		
Black and Hispanic poor living in poverty areas[b]	1979	4.1 million	15.7	1.8
Total population living in "underclass areas"[c]	1979	2.5 million	5.0	1.0

[a] Poverty areas are defined as census tracts with poverty rates above 40 percent in the 100 largest standard metropolitan areas.

[b] Poverty areas are defined as census tracts with poverty rates above 20 percent in 100 standard metropolitan areas.

[c] Underclass areas are defined as census tracts in which each of four indicators is one standard deviation above the mean for the country as a whole. The indicators are the high-school dropout rate, the female headship rate, the welfare dependency rate, and the proportion of prime-age males not regularly attached to the labor force.

Source: Sawhill, 1108.

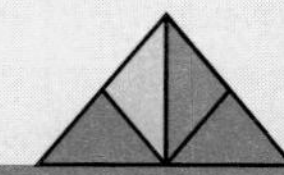

TABLE 6
The Percentage of Persons Below Poverty Before and After Government Antipoverty Programs

Classification	All Households (percent)	White Households (percent)	Black Households (percent)	Hispanic Households (percent)
Income before taxes and cash payments	19.4	16.7	37.3	29.9
Income after cash payments	12.8	10.0	30.7	26.2
Income after cash and in-kind payments	8.9	6.9	21.2	19.4

Source: U.S. Bureau of the Census, *Current Population Reports.* The above data are for 1986.

TABLE 7
Characteristics of Poverty

Category	Percentage of Families Below Poverty Levels
Race	
White	17.8
Black	27.8
Hispanic	23.4
Size of family	
2 persons	8.2
3 persons	9.8
4 persons	10.1
5 persons	13.5
7 or more persons	32.3
Education of family head	
Less than 8 years	25.5
8 years	15.9
1–3 years high school	19.2
4 years high school	8.9
1 or more years college	3.6
Families headed by single mothers	45.0
Age of family head	
15–24 years	30.4
25–34 years	14.9
35–44 years	9.4
45–54 years	6.3
55–64 years	7.4
65 or more years	6.6
Did not work	23.4

Source: *Statistical Abstract of the United States.* These figures are for 1989.

entirely from government Medicare and Medicaid programs that help pay the bills of the elderly.[16]

Who Are the Poor?

Table 7 provides a statistical profile of poor families in the United States. The poor tend to be disproportionately black and of Hispanic origin. They tend to live in large families; the family head tends to have little education, to be young, and to be female. Over 40 percent of the American poor are children under the age of 18. The poor tend to concentrate in central cities and in rural areas. Contrary to popular myth, a majority are working poor. Similarly, only 64 percent of the poor receive some form of cash assistance from government antipoverty programs.

These figures suggest that for the majority of families, poverty results from a limited earning capacity. Employment *per se* does not pull them out of poverty. Only in poor families headed by females do a majority of household heads not hold jobs.

The official poverty income standard does not provide for an attractive standard of living. The 1991 poverty income standard of about $13,500 for a family of four allowed for $3.00 per person each day in food expenditures. A Gallup poll asking Americans what poverty income would be required to make ends meet yielded a figure 50 percent larger than the official poverty standard.[17]

[16] U.S. Bureau of the Census, *Alternative Methods for Valuing Selected In-Kind Benefits and Measuring Their Effect on Poverty* (Washington, DC: U.S. Government Printing Office, 1982).

[17] Bradley R. Schiller, *The Economics of Poverty and Discrimination,* 4th ed. (Englewood Cliffs, NJ: Prentice Hall, 1984), 18–19.

SOLUTIONS TO THE POVERTY PROBLEM

Income Maintenance

One solution to poverty is to raise the incomes of the poor. The two mechanisms used to accomplish this goal—voluntary private charitable contributions and government cash-assistance programs—require a transfer of income from those above the poverty line to those below it. The next chapter, on externalities, explains why private charity alone will not eliminate poverty. The redistribution of income, however, can affect the efficiency of society's resource utilization. First, the redistribution from the rich to the poor may discourage work effort on the part of the rich and, thus, reduce the income available for redistribution. Second, assistance to the poor may discourage their own work effort, further reducing the size of the income pie.

The Welfare System. In the United States, the current welfare system is founded on the principle that public assistance should be granted primarily on the basis of need. For this purpose, the government has established a number of programs—such as Aid to Families with Dependent Children (AFDC), the Food Stamp Program, public housing, and Medicaid—in which the amount of public assistance is based upon family income. Welfare authorities determine what resources the family has (totaling the earnings of the family head, contributions from relatives, and so on) and grant public assistance on the basis of the perceived need. The greater the resources of the family, the less public assistance it receives. The welfare family is, therefore, discouraged from working because additional earnings—if detected by welfare authorities—will cause a reduction in public assistance. Proposals have been made to build better incentives into the existing system. In particular, it has been suggested that welfare recipients be permitted to keep a specified percentage of extra earnings without a reduction in existing public assistance.

A second drawback of the current public-assistance is that an army of welfare workers is required to document needs and resources, making the system very costly. Dollars that could be devoted to public assistance are diverted to pay the bureaucratic costs of operating the system.

The Negative Income Tax. Economists have proposed that the current welfare system can be replaced by a **negative income tax (NIT).**

> A **negative income tax (NIT)** supplements incomes by making payments to recipients who earn less than a specified minimum income. Each payment will be an amount equal to the minimum income minus a given percentage of each dollar the recipient earns.

A negative income tax would function as outlined in Table 8 and Figure 6. First, the government would set a floor below which family incomes would not be allowed to fall. For purposes of illustration, we will set this floor at $6000 for a family of four. Second, the government would set a negative tax rate. In our example, this rate is 50 percent; benefits are reduced from the $6000 minimum income base by $0.50 for every dollar earned.

Families of four would be guaranteed an income of $6000. This figure becomes the base from which tax benefits are calculated. A family that earned no income would receive a negative income tax benefit of $6000. But what about the family that earns between $0 and $6000? If a family that earns $3000 were to receive a negative income tax payment of $3000 to bring it up to the $6000 floor, it would be no better than the family that has zero income. Thus, there would be no incentive to earn income. With

TABLE 8
Hypothetical Negative Income Tax

Earnings (dollars)	Negative Income Tax Benefit (dollars)	Total Disposable Income (dollars)
0	6,000	6,000
3,000	4,500	7,500
6,000	3,000	9,000
9,000	1,500	10,500
12,000	0	12,000

This example assumes a guaranteed income of $6000 and a negative tax rate of 50 percent.

FIGURE 6
Hypothetical Negative Income Tax

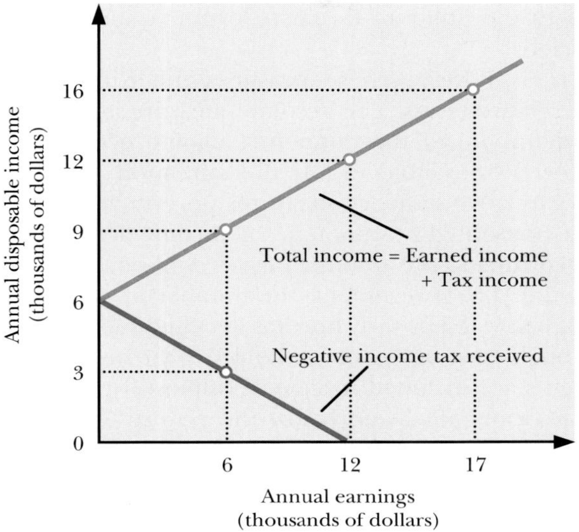

This figure illustrates a hypothetical negative income tax. The negative tax rate is set at 50 percent and a floor income is set at $6000. A family with $0 income would receive $6000 in benefits. Any family that earned more than $0 would have their $6000 benefits reduced by $0.50 for every dollar earned. For example, a family earning $3000 would receive $6000 − (0.50 × $3000), or $4500, in addition to the $3000 they earned. Up to an income of $12,000, families would still receive some benefits in addition to their income (benefits equal to $6000 minus $0.50 times the amount of income earned). At an income of $12,000, however, families would receive no benefits because the $6000 would be reduced by 0.50 × $12, 000, or by $6000 ($6000 − $6000 = $0). Beyond an income of $12,000, families would pay taxes. For example, a family earning $17,000 would pay taxes on the $5000 difference between $17,000 and $12,000. If the tax rate were 20 percent, the family earning $17,000 would pay $1000 in taxes (0.20 × $5000) and would have a disposable income of $16,000.

a 50 percent negative tax rate in effect, the family that earns $3000 still receives benefits, though they are reduced by $1500 (one-half of the $3000 earnings), from $6000 to $4500. The total income is, therefore, $3000 plus $4500, or $7500, so that the family is better off earning the $3000 than not working. The negative income tax payment falls to zero when a family earns $12000 (benefits are reduced from the $6000 base by $0.50 for every dollar earned, or by $6000 for this family). In this example, the $12,000 income is the *break-even income.* At $12,000 and above, a family's total income will equal its own earnings *minus* income taxes.

The negative income tax offers two advantages over the existing welfare system. First, it preserves work incentives by allowing low-income families to keep a prescribed portion of their earnings. Second, it promises to do away with the costly bureaucracy of the existing system. Administration of the negative income tax would be carried out by the same authority—the Internal Revenue Service—that administers the current income tax system.

The main disadvantage is that work incentives depend on the negative tax rate. A 50 percent negative tax rate means that families can keep only one-half of their own earnings below the break-even point. Ensuring strong incentives requires low tax rates, but these have the less desirable consequence of giving negative income tax payments to those who are not poor. Lowering the tax rate to 25 percent, for example, raises the break-even income to $24,000—well above any conceivable poverty level.

The idea of a negative income tax has widespread support among economists. Two U.S. presidents—Nixon and Carter—proposed negative income tax programs, and so far, a modified NIT program called the Earned Income Tax Credit for the Working Poor has been adopted.

Long-Run Solutions

Income maintenance programs—be they a negative income tax or need-based assistance—offer only short-run solutions to the poverty problem. The long-run solution requires an attack on poverty's fundamental sources. Income maintenance programs may assist the children of the poor by providing the money to maintain health and by funding training and education, but they may also perpetuate the poverty problem by discouraging work effort. To provide a long-run solution, government policy should aim to eliminate racial and sexual discrimination in the job market and education, as well as encourage the children of the poor to invest in human-capital resources. The problem is how to devise a policy that does not defeat itself by fostering reverse discrimination or by making the trade-off between equity and efficiency too costly. The intended effects of legislation can often differ dramatically from the actual effects. In the 1960s and 1970s, the government embarked on a series of training programs (called the "Great Society") aimed at providing education and training for the children of the poor. Many of these programs have since been abandoned because of their cost ineffectiveness, but they represented an important social effort to eliminate the root sources of poverty.

This chapter examined the causes of inequality in the distribution of income and directed attention to the role of government in the redistribution of income to the poor. The next three chapters will focus on the role of government and its impact on the environment, public finance, and public choice.

SUMMARY

1. The distribution of income is determined in factor markets. The government may change this distribution of income through taxes and the distribution of public services. The Lorenz curve measures the degree of income inequality. It shows the cumulative percentages of all income earned by households at successive income levels. If the Lorenz curve is a 45-degree line, income distribution is perfectly equal. The more the Lorenz curve bows away from the 45-degree line, the more unequal is the distribution of income.

2. The U.S. distribution of income has become more equal since 1929. It also becomes more equal after it is adjusted for taxes, in-kind services, and life-cycle effects.

3. The sources of income inequality include different abilities, discrimination, occupational differences, different amounts of human-capital investment, chance and luck, and inheritance. Differences in schooling may affect earnings because employers use educational credentials to screen and select job candidates for high-paying careers. Earning differentials, both between whites and nonwhites and between males and females, have been reduced in recent years.

4. There are different views on what constitutes distributive justice. Marginal productivity theory calls for a distribution of income according to the marginal productivity of the resources owned by households. The utilitarian school believes an equal distribution of income maximizes total utility. John Rawls proposes a distribution of income that maximizes the utility of the least fortunate members of society.

5. Poverty can be measured either in absolute or relative terms. The absolute measure is based on a definition of the minimum income necessary to allow a household to buy the minimum essentials. The relative standard measures poverty in terms of the household's location in the income distribution. According to the absolute measures of poverty made by the U.S. government, the number of people living below the poverty line has declined substantially, though unsteadily, since the 1950s. If in-kind payments are included in income, almost 9 percent of Americans are living below the poverty line. Poor Americans tend to be nonwhite, poorly educated members of households headed by females, and either very young or very old.

6. Income maintenance programs provide short-run solutions to the problem of poverty. Many economists favor the negative income tax as an efficient income maintenance program. Long-run solutions involve raising the income-earning capacity of the children of the poor.

KEY TERMS

Lorenz curve
in-kind income
wealth
absolute poverty standard
relative poverty standard
negative income tax (NIT)

QUESTIONS AND PROBLEMS

1. Draw a Lorenz curve for absolute equality. Draw a Lorenz curve for absolute inequality. Explain the situation illustrated by the absolute inequality Lorenz curve.
2. Evaluate the validity of the following statement: "If all people were the same, the Lorenz curve would be a 45-degree line."
3. Evaluate the validity of the following statement: "The fact that a woman earns, on average, two-thirds of what a man earns proves beyond a shadow of a doubt that there is sexual discrimination."

4. There are two views of the causes of poverty. One school says that the poor are poor through no fault of their own. The other says that the poor are poor through choice. Give arguments for each position.
5. How does screening theory explain the apparently poor correlation between ability and inequality?
6. Contrast the utilitarian view of distributive justice with the Rawlsian view.
7. Explain why measured Lorenz curves that use disposable income before and after taxes may not give an accurate picture of the distribution of real income.
8. Would the work incentives be greater with a 25 percent negative income tax (NIT) rate or a 50 percent NIT rate? Rework Table 8 and Figure 6 in the text to illustrate your answer.
9. Assume a society consists of eight risk avoiders and two risk seekers. Contrast that society with one that consists of five risk seekers and five risk avoiders. Which society will have a more equal distribution of income?
10. In society A, 50 percent of the adult population is between 18 and 25 or over 65. In society B, 25 percent of the adult population is between 18 and 25 or over 65. Using Lorenz curves, which society would appear to be more unequal in its distribution of income due to life-cycle effects?
11. Joe wants goods today; Bill is more willing to wait until tomorrow. Which one is more likely to invest in human capital?
12. The official U.S. poverty income standard is adjusted upward each year to account for the general increase in prices. If a family's income just keeps up with the poverty income over the years, what is happening to its relative poverty position?
13. Explain why the market value of in-kind benefits provided to the poor may be a misleading measure of their impact on poverty.
14. Education is distributed among the population more equally than income. What does this tell us about the relationship between education and inequality?

SUGGESTED READINGS

Aaron, Henry J., and Cameron M. Loughy. *The Comparable Worth Controversy.* Washington, DC: The Brookings Institution, 1986.

Blinder, Alan S. *Toward an Economic Theory of Income Distribution.* Cambridge, MA: MIT Press, 1974.

Blinder, Alan S. "The Level and Distribution of Economic Well-Being." In *The American Economy in Transition,* edited by Martin Feldstein, 450–53. Chicago: University of Chicago Press, 1980.

Friedman, Milton. "Choice, Chance, and the Personal Distribution of Income." *Journal of Political Economy* 61, 4 (August 1953): 277–90.

Kohler, Heinz. *Scarcity and Freedom.* Lexington, MA: D.C. Heath, 1977, 339–80.

Lloyd, Cynthia B., ed. *Sex, Discrimination, and the Division of Labor.* New York: Columbia University Press, 1975.

Okun, Arthur. *Equality and Efficiency: The Big Trade-Off.* Washington, DC: The Brookings Institution, 1975.

Paglin, Morton. "The Measurement and Trend of Inequality: A Basic Revision." *American Economic Review* 65, 4 (September 1975): 598–609.

Rawls, John. *A Theory of Justice.* Cambridge, MA: Harvard University Press, 1971.

Rawls, John. "Some Reasons for the Maximin Criterion." *American Economic Review* 64, 2 (May 1974): 141–46.

Schiller, Bradley. *The Economics of Poverty and Discrimination,* 5th ed. Englewood Cliffs, NJ: Prentice Hall, 1989.

VI

Microeconomic Issues

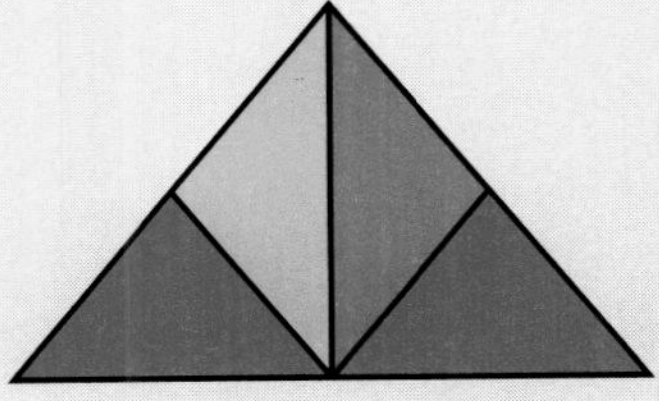

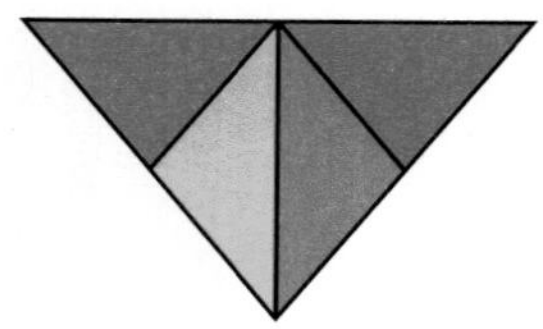

41

Market Failure, the Environment, and Exhaustible Resources

CHAPTER INSIGHT

People have strong views regarding the relationship between the economy and the environment. Many believe that news reports of oil spills, toxic waste dumping, and the killing of whales and dolphins indicate the failure of private economic decision making. A more extreme conclusion, drawn from reports of global warming and a disappearing ozone layer, is that our lives or the lives of future generations are in danger. In both cases, people call for steps to be taken to preserve the environment. Perhaps it is necessary to return to a simpler lifestyle, with less production, fewer automobiles, and no aerosol spray cans.

This chapter examines whether markets and private decision making can solve *externality problems*—that is, situations in which private costs and benefits diverge from social costs and benefits. When is government intervention required, and, if necessary, what form should such intervention take?

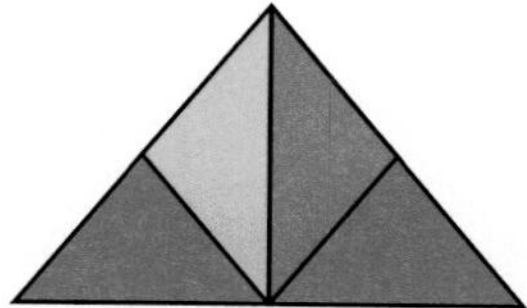

EXTERNALITIES

Externalities plague all economic systems. They are present whenever the actions of one agent have direct economic effects on other agents. The simplest examples would be the external effects of smoking, noisy neighbors, or a neighbor's beautiful rose bushes. (See Example 1.)

> **Externalities** exist when a producer or consumer does not bear the full marginal cost or enjoy the full marginal benefit of an economic action.

When externalities are present, market transactions between two parties will have harmful or beneficial effects on third parties. The effects are "external" to the price system and are not the outcome of mutual agreement between all the interested parties.

Take the case of a factory that pollutes the air, thereby imposing external cleaning or health-care costs on the surrounding community. The unique feature of these external costs is that they are paid not by the factory, but by agents external to the factory; they do not appear in the factory's accounting.

On the other hand, the person who pays for an education is not the only one who reaps its rewards. Society benefits because education provides a common culture and language and encourages scientific progress.

Social Efficiency and Market Failure

When external costs or benefits are present, economists measure social efficiency by comparing **social costs** and **social benefits.**

EXAMPLE 1 Externalities and Creepy Neighbors

Consider the following Ann Landers column:

> Dear Ann Landers: We live on a private road with 10 other families. Except for our next-door neighbors, everyone contributes to maintain the road (paving, snow removal, pruning, etc.).
>
> Whenever we approach the people next door about contributing their fair share, they become extremely unpleasant. So far they have yet to give a dime although they enjoy all the benefits made possible by the rest of us.
>
> The immediate problem involves their Halloween display, which usually stays up until Thanksgiving. Were it only jack-o'-lanterns, scarecrows and witches, we would not mind, but they have assembled a chilling facsimile of a graveyard with tombstones everywhere. A skeleton hangs from a tree and a hand comes out of the ground, giving this area an eerie and frightening appearance. They've recently installed powerful floodlights that turn night into day and make the street look like a tourist attraction.
>
> Is there anything we can do about this? —Victims in New England

The creepy people next door possess two characteristics that make them bad neighbors, economically speaking. First, they are free riders. The other nine families voluntarily contribute their share toward maintaining the common private road. The neighbors in question take advantage of these conscientious families by using the road without paying. Second, the bad neighbors, with their creepy Halloween exhibit, create external costs for the others. Not only is their exhibit in bad taste, but it also turns the neighborhood into a tourist attraction.

Ann Landers' only advice to the frustrated writer was to build a high brick wall. Unfortunately, the free-riding and creepy neighbor family was within its legal rights.

Source: Ann Landers, "Handling Creepy Neighbors," *Houston Chronicle*, October 25, 1991, 2C.

Social costs equal private costs plus external costs.

Social benefits equal private benefits plus external benefits.

Significant external costs indicate that the competitive firm is producing too much output. The firm produces that level of output at which marginal *private* costs and marginal *private* benefits are equal (see Figure 1). When it ignores the *external* costs of its actions, marginal social costs exceed marginal social benefits at the profit-maximizing level of output. Society as a whole will be better off if the competitive firm reduces its output to the level at which marginal social costs and marginal social benefits are equal. Figure 1 shows that the socially optimal level of output of a competitive firm is less than the competitive output when external costs are present.

Social efficiency requires that marginal social benefits and marginal social costs be equal, but private participants equate only marginal private benefits with marginal private costs.

Pollution by industry and private cars are examples of externalities that can impose substantial external costs on the surrounding community. Ocean fishing waters are depleted because commercial fishing businesses do not consider the external costs of overfishing. Modern skyscrapers built with reflective glass raise the air-conditioning costs for neighboring buildings. Any family that allows its house and lawn to deteriorate reduces the pleasure neighbors obtain from their own houses and lawns.

The failure of even competitive firms to produce the socially optimal level of output represents a **market failure.**

Market failure occurs when the price system fails to yield the socially optimal quantity of a good.

As Figure 1 demonstrates, externalities are a potential source of market failure.

FIGURE 1
Perfect Competition with External Costs

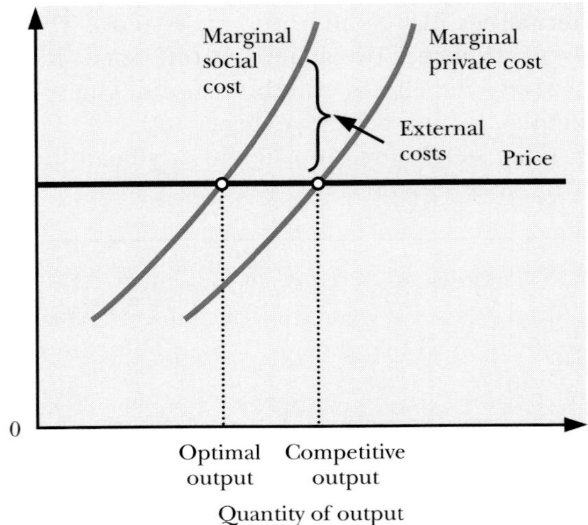

When external costs are present, competitive firms produce too much output because they produce at the level where marginal private costs equal price, not where marginal social costs equal price.

INTERNALIZING EXTERNALITIES

In order to eliminate the externality problem, external costs or benefits must be included in calculations of private gain. The solution is to **internalize,** or put a private price tag on, externalities. This price must be paid by economic agents imposing cost or received by agents bestowing benefits.

To **internalize** an externality involves placing private price tags on external costs (or benefits) so that private and social costs (or benefits) coincide.

If economic agents pay for the costs imposed on others or receive a price for the benefits that others experience they will incorporate such costs and benefits into private cost-benefit calculations. A simple example of internalization is the merger of two factories located on a river. Prior to the merger, the downstream factory has to pay water purification costs because the upstream factory is polluting the water. After the merger, the external costs imposed on the downstream factory become internal costs that the merged firm considers in private cost/benefit calculations.

Redefinition of Property Rights

An externality can be internalized by redefining property rights. Property rights specify who owns a resource and who has the right to use it. Poor definition of these rights is the source of many externalities. Do firms or the community own the property rights to the air? Who owns the property rights to fish in the seas? If the property rights for a resource are held by the community but each person has free access to the resource, the resource will likely be exploited and abused. Fishing businesses will overfish ocean waters; factories will pollute the air.

One method of internalizing externalities is to establish private property rights. The rational private owner of hunting land will set fees high enough to prevent game from being depleted. If someone were somehow given ownership of the community's air, that person could charge a polluting factory for its use of the air. Every month, the factory would get a bill from the owner of the community's air. If one country held the property rights to the ocean's fishing grounds, it could charge fishing businesses from all countries for their use of the ocean.

As these examples imply, it is not easy to eliminate externalities by changing property rights. This strategy will not work when it is very costly to define or enforce property rights. Consider the overkilling of whales. How does one determine who owns the whales and how does one protect the owner's property rights? Pollution results from another case of poorly defined property rights. The ownership rights to clean air are so vague that people harmed by pollution have difficulty suing polluters. In both cases, the amount of information required to enforce property rights is excessive. The external costs each agent imposes must be known in order to redefine the rights. How many whales are there, and how many has each whaler killed? Exactly how much pollution has each car emitted? What is the real marginal cost to society of each whale killed or the pollution from each car?

Voluntary Agreements

Voluntary agreements are a second means of internalizing externalities. The merger of the two factories on a river is an example of a voluntary agreement. The number of individuals involved in a voluntary agreement must be small in order to limit bargaining costs and to prevent other parties from "riding free." When property rights are well defined, voluntary agreements negotiated through the legal system can internalize external costs.

The proposition that voluntary agreements can solve some externality problems is called *the Coase theorem,* after 1991 Nobel laureate Ronald H. Coase. Coase argues that external costs and benefits can be internalized by negotiations among affected parties. He uses the example of a rancher whose cattle occasionally stray onto a neighboring farm and damage the neighbor's crops. If the rancher were legally liable for the crop damage, private bargaining would result in a deal in which the farmer would be paid for the increased cost imposed by the straying cattle. These extra costs would induce the rancher to reduce the size of the herd (or build better fences).

Likewise, efficiency would still result if the rancher's cattle had the legal right to stray onto the farmer's land. The farmer in this case could pay the rancher to reduce the size of the herd or build a fence. Again, when a price tag is placed on the externality, it disappears. Although the social effect—the amounts of crops and cattle produced—is the same in both cases, the income-distribution effects are quite different. In the first case, the rancher transfers income to the farmer. In the second case, the farmer transfers income to the rancher. The distribution of income will depend upon who has the property rights.

Negotiated voluntary agreements are used in the real world to solve externality problems. Nobel laureate James Meade used honey and apples as a classic example of externalities. The production of honey is stimulated by apple blossoms; the pollination of apple blossoms is facilitated by bees. Owners of apple orchards provide a benefit to beekeepers that does not directly enter into their private cost/benefit calculations. Beekeepers provide a benefit to apple growers that does not enter their private cost/benefit calculations.

Steven S. Cheung found that these externalities of the nectar and pollination business are bought and sold in the marketplace.[1] Beekeepers and apple growers have worked out a compensation system that covers external benefits. Apple growers actually pay beekeepers for the pollination activities of their bees. Cheung found, in the state of Washington, that the beekeeper's fee for pollination is smaller the greater is the expected yield of honey because apple tree pollination improves honey production. By reducing the pollination fee, the beekeeper is, in effect, paying the apple grower for the external benefit to honey production that is provided by the apple blossoms. This real-world example shows that markets are sometimes able to place price tags on external costs and benefits.

> The Coase theorem states that if small numbers are involved and bargaining costs are small, the market will internalize the externality. When large numbers are involved and the costs are widely dispersed, voluntary agreements will be difficult to reach.

Government Taxes and Subsidies

A third way for an externality to be internalized is for the government to impose corrective taxes or subsidies. When private activities impose external costs, the volume of transactions will exceed what is efficient because private agents ignore the costs imposed on others (refer again to Figure 1). An appropriate tax on the externality will force the economic agent to take into account the costs imposed on others and will, accordingly, reduce the amount of activity to the efficient level where marginal social costs equal marginal social benefits. When market transactions involve external benefits, the volume of transactions will fall short of the efficient level. In this case, a government subsidy will encourage private firms to increase the activity to the efficient level.

Government internalization is appropriate when private bargaining costs are high and voluntary agreements cannot be reached. If the externality affects many people, collective action is cheaper to implement and likelier to succeed than voluntary agreement among the affected parties. The government, however, must be able to measure the external costs and benefits in order to set the taxes or subsidies at an appropriate level.

When it steps in with corrective taxes or subsidies, the government assumes the bargaining costs of the private parties. Because making collective decisions is costly in and of itself, society must weigh the costs and benefits of government action. Society cannot afford to use collective action to deal with trivial external costs or benefits. On the other hand, activities that create substantial social costs require government action.

Both the market mechanism and government action have strengths and limitations in correcting externalities. Therefore, few hard and fast rules exist for determining whether the government or the market will be more effective. It is necessary to weigh the advantages and disadvantages in each particular instance.

Some examples of externalities that have required government action are automobile pollution, nonlocalized factory pollution, the abuse of scenic beauty, and the killing of whales and fish. In these cases, the costs of negotiating and enforcing private contracts exceed the potential gains. Examples of externalities that do not require government action are honey and apple production or localized pollution. In the case of localized pollution (air or noise), people who feel the external costs are too high can move (vote with their feet). A person who resides near a foul-smelling paper mill may receive a compensatory wage differential for being willing to live and work in that community; residents who buy homes near an airport have lower home costs. Whenever people have the choice of avoiding the external costs by moving or whenever people receive compensatory wage differentials or lower living costs because of external costs, government action may not be necessary.

PUBLIC GOODS

Public goods provide another example of market failure. Because competitive markets undersupply or fail to supply them, public goods—such as public schools, public parks, public roads and bridges, national defense, police protection, or public health services—are generally made available to the public at no explicit charge and are financed by taxes.

[1] Steven S. Cheung, "The Fable of the Bees: An Economic Investigation," *Journal of Law and Economics* (April 1973).

> **Public goods** are characterized by nonrival consumption and nonexclusion.

Nonrival consumption refers to the ability of one consumer to use a public good without detracting from the ability of others to use it. Nonexclusion refers to the inability to keep nonpayers from using a public good.

Nonrival Consumption

If a dam is built to prevent flooding, everyone who lives in the protected area benefits. Moreover, the fact that one person's house is protected by the dam does not reduce the protection any other house receives. In another example, one person can watch a television program without reducing the amount of the program any other viewer enjoys. These situations illustrate **nonrival consumption.**

> A good is characterized by **nonrival consumption** if its consumption by one person does not reduce its consumption by others at a given level of production.

The classic example of nonrival consumption is national defense. If the government builds an antimissile system that reduces the likelihood of nuclear attack, everyone in the protected area benefits. The protection of one person's life and property does not reduce the level available to others.

Nonrival consumption does not mean that everyone benefits to the same degree. A pacifist would not like the national defense effort—nor would an enemy spy. A family with a large estate may benefit more from flood control than one living in a wooden shack because the estate family has more to protect (or lose).

Most goods and services are characterized by **rival consumption.**

> A good is characterized by **rival consumption** if the consumption of the good by one person lowers the consumption available to others, given the level of production.

Food and drink, cars, houses, shoes, dresses, and medical services are rival in consumption. A hamburger eaten by one person cannot be eaten by someone else; a house occupied by one family cannot be occupied by another. Some goods can be either rival or nonrival, depending on the circumstances. An uncrowded movie or sporting event is nonrival; one person can enjoy it without reducing another person's consumption. A sold-out movie or sporting event, however, is rival because each additional spectator displaces another possible spectator. The available supply of rival goods is typically rationed by charging prices; those who consume the rival good place a higher value on it than those who do not.

Nonexclusion

The second characteristic of public goods is **nonexclusion**, which results from the extreme cost required to exclude people from using certain goods (once they have been produced).

> A good is characterized by **nonexclusion** if extreme costs eliminate the possibility (or practicality) of excluding some people from using it.

National defense and flood control provide classic illustrations of nonexclusion. It is virtually impossible to exclude any person in the protected area from enjoying the benefits of the good; **exclusion costs** are prohibitive.

> **Exclusion costs** are the costs of preventing those who do not have property rights from enjoying a good.

Nonrivalry should not be confused with nonexclusion. An uncrowded movie theater is nonrival in consumption, but those who have not purchased tickets can be prevented from viewing a sparsely attended movie.

Nobel laureate Paul Samuelson used a lighthouse as an example of a public good. Samuelson reasoned that any one ship's use of the light does not detract from any other ship's use (nonrivalry), and it is difficult for the lighthouse to exclude nonpaying ships from using the light (nonexclusion). Ronald H. Coase, however, found that English lighthouses were for many years privately owned and operated.[2] From 1700 to 1834, the number of privately operated lighthouses increased, so the business was obviously profitable. Lighthouse owners were paid by the shipowners at the docks according to the tonnage of the ship. Thus, exclusion costs were low in reality, enabling the private market in lighthouses to experience success, rather than failure, in providing this seemingly public good.

Most private goods are rival in consumption and have low costs of excluding nonpayers. Some goods, however, are rival in consumption and also have high exclusion costs. One person's use of a congested road reduces another person's enjoyment of the road, but it is too costly to exclude nonpayers. Goods with high exclusion costs, be they rival or nonrival, are normally provided through the government.

Nonrival Goods with High Exclusion Costs. It is not possible to require people to pay for a public good since they cannot be excluded from its use. A person who enjoys the benefits of a good without paying is a **free rider.**

> A **free rider** enjoys the benefits of a good or service without paying the cost.

When some of the beneficiaries are free riders, the private revenues voluntarily contributed to pay for a public good may be less than its social benefits—in which case, the good will not be produced or will be underproduced by the private market. Noncontributors to public television cannot be prevented from viewing its programming. For this reason, public television stations need government subsidies to maintain their operations.

The free-rider problem confounds the production of public goods. Suppose a dam costing $2000 will protect a community of ten people and that the flood protection of the dam is worth $400 to each person. The total value of the dam is $4000; it is worth building because it costs only $2000. Building the dam by charging $200 to each person would clearly benefit everyone.

However, voluntary agreement among the ten people may be difficult to obtain. People realize that if the other nine build the dam without their contribution, they can still enjoy the benefits. In this example, will the dam be built? If six people behave as free riders, the dam will not be built by voluntary agreement; the contributors can raise only $1600. If only four people behave as free riders, the dam will be built. (Refer to Example 1.)

> Voluntary agreements will work only if the amount of free riding is not excessive.

Examples of cooperative behavior abound. People make voluntary contributions to civic clubs for extra police protection; most people obey the law; volunteers work to improve the community. But if the group is large, if collective decisions are made infrequently, and if the individual gains to cooperation are small, free riding will be more prevalent. (See the discussion of recycling later in this chapter.)

Nonrival Goods with Low Exclusion Costs. For many nonrival goods, however, exclusion costs are not excessive. Pay television is an example of a nonrival good with low exclusion costs. Private markets may not provide the socially optimum level of pay TV. In a world of diverse tastes, any price charged for pay TV will exclude some people from the market. If it costs society nothing to add one more user (because of nonrivalry), it seems wasteful to exclude that user. However, if a public TV monopoly were instituted, all people would pay the costs in taxes, regardless of whether they watched TV or not. Is it fair for people who hate baseball to be forced to pay for those who love baseball? (See Example 2.)

In reality, the private market ingeniously finances network TV through advertising. Thus, viewers can watch as much television as they like at no cost (once they have acquired a receiver). By contrast, toll bridges fall under public jurisdiction. Charging a toll on an uncrowded bridge is, to be sure, economically inefficient because some users are excluded even though they do not keep others from using the bridge. Without the toll, however, nonusers would be forced to pay for the bridge in taxes. Why is it that toll bridges are publicly owned but movies and sporting events are privately produced? The justification for public ownership of bridges is that a private owner

[2]Ronald H. Coase, "The Lighthouse in Economics," *Journal of Law and Economics* (October 1976).

EXAMPLE 2 Championship Fights and Pay-per-View Television

New satellite transmission technology that allows broadcasters to scramble signals to nonpayers (free riders) has created a new approach to sports broadcasting. Cable viewers can subscribe to pay-TV broadcasts of championship boxing events by dialing a telephone number and giving a viewer code. After the pay-per-view event, the subscriber's account is automatically billed by computer. This scrambling technology enables pay-per-view television to exclude the free riders who pose a problem for conventional network television.

Given the commercial success thus far, more major sports events are expected to be broadcast on a pay-per-view basis. It is difficult to conclude whether or not this outcome is desirable. Economic analysis holds that because television broadcasts are nonrival goods, the exclusion of extra viewers is inefficient. On the other hand, without scrambling the signal, an excessive number of free riders may prevent the broadcast of some events.

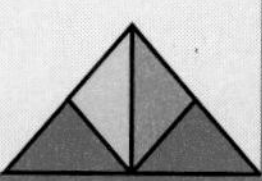

would have a monopoly position and could charge monopoly prices.

Figure 2 ranks selected goods along a continuum from private goods (characterized by low exclusion costs and rival consumption) to public goods (characterized by high exclusion costs and rival consumption).

POLLUTION AND GOVERNMENT ACTION

Pollution results from both production and consumption. Factories discharge waste into the atmosphere and water; consumers produce sewage and garbage. It is in the interest of society to ensure that pollutants are returned to the environment as safely and efficiently as possible.[3]

Some pollutants can be returned naturally to the environment. Carbon dioxide, for example, is absorbed by plant life and by the oceans. Other pollutants, such as nonbiodegradable bottles or lead, cannot be absorbed naturally. When the emission of pollutants exceeds the environment's absorptive capacity, pollutants accumulate and often inflict great damage.

Pollution can be *local, regional,* or even *global.* Local pollution affects the immediate surroundings of the site of emission. The damage from regional pollution is felt at a substantial distance from its source. Global pollution occurs when pollutants are concentrated in the earth's upper atmosphere.

Waste Disposal Costs

Production and consumption impose significant *waste disposal costs* on society. Waste must be disposed of, whether in the ground, in water, or in the air. (Someday, it may be disposed of in outer space.)

Waste disposal costs are real opportunity costs. Public or private resources that are devoted to pollution prevention (scrubbers on smokestacks, for example) are not available for other uses. Individuals who purchase unpolluted water to prevent health damages also incur opportunity costs. If pollution from toxic-waste dumps causes the health of individuals in the community to deteriorate, there are costs to each individual and community—be they explicit cash outlays or less visible opportunity costs.

Optimal Abatement

Modern societies produce vast quantities of waste. Accordingly, decisions must be made about how much

[3]The following discussion is based largely on Joseph Seneca and Michael Taussig, *Environmental Economics,* 3rd ed. (Englewood Cliffs, NJ: Prentice Hall, 1984), and Tom Tietenberg, *Environmental and Natural Resource Economics,* 3rd ed. (New York: HarperCollins, 1992).

FIGURE 2
Classifying Selected Goods as Private Goods or Public Goods

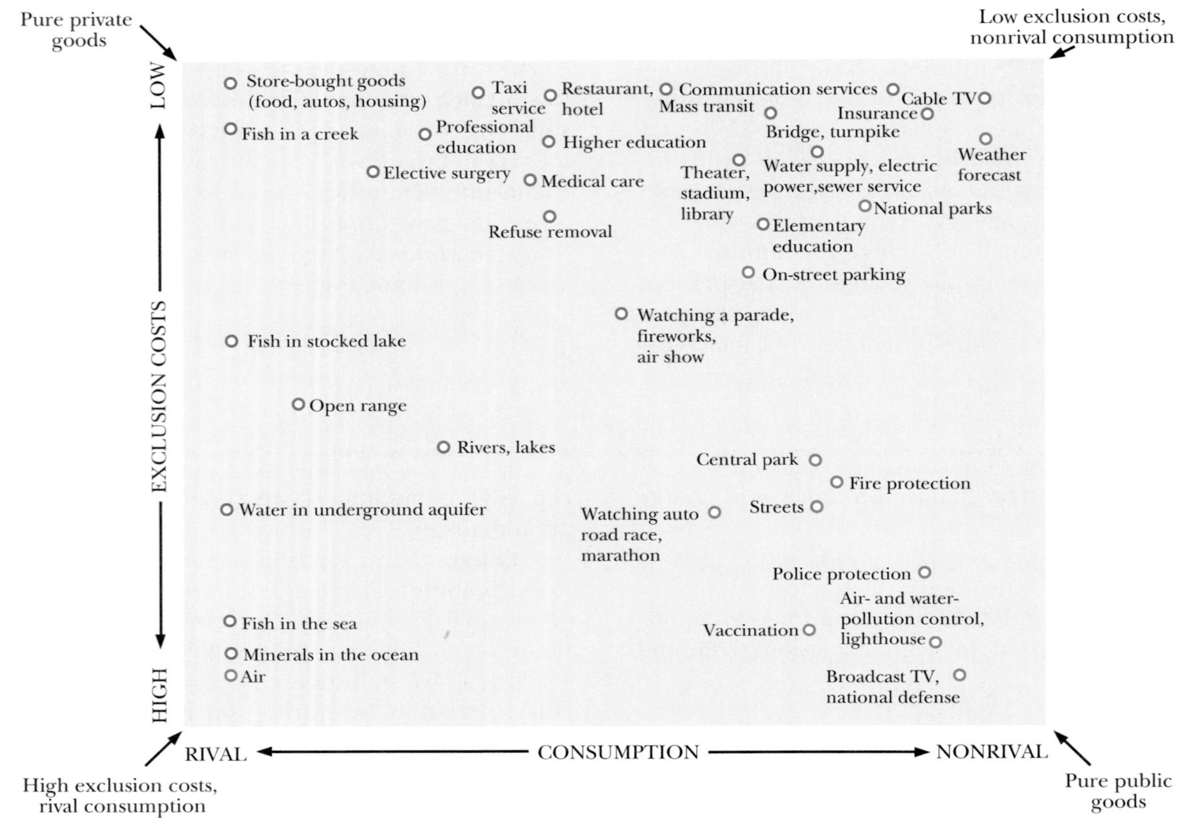

Pure private goods, in the upper left corner, are characterized by low exclusion costs (free riders can be excluded easily) and by rival consumption. Pure public goods, in the lower right corner, are characterized by high exclusion costs (free riding can't be prevented) and by nonrival consumption (one person's consumption of a good does not detract from another's consumption of it). Goods in the other two corners meet only one of the two characteristics of a public good. In the lower left corner, goods are characterized by high exclusion costs but rival consumption. In the upper right corner, goods are characterized by nonrival consumption but low exclusion costs.

Source: E. S. Savas, *Privatizing the Public Sector* (Chatham, NJ: Chatham House Publishers, Inc., 1982), 34.

of society's resources should be devoted to its disposal. Figure 3 shows the marginal social costs and marginal social benefits of different quantities of pollution abatement—in this case, the number of gallons of water purified through filtration. For simplicity, we let the marginal social cost of each successive unit of abatement be constant. Marginal social benefits decline as abatement intensifies because society values the first units of abatement more highly than subsequent units. The *optimal level of abatement* occurs when the marginal social cost of an extra unit of abatement equals the marginal social benefit. If abatement is undertaken beyond this optimal level, the extra benefits fall short of the extra opportunity costs to society. Society should not aim for the total elimination of pollution. To do so, it would have to

FIGURE 3
Optimal Pollution Abatement

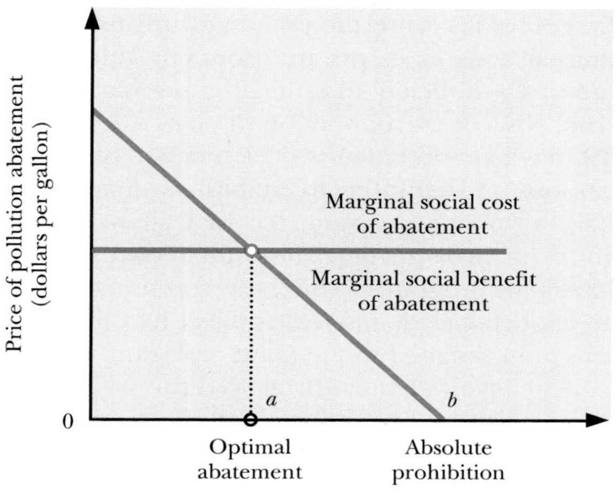

This figure shows how the optimal amount of pollution abatement is determined. The marginal social benefit curve is downward sloping (people place a higher value on the first units of abatement). The marginal social cost of pollution abatement is assumed constant. The optimal amount of abatement is quantity *a* (where marginal social cost equals marginal social benefit). Point *b*, the total prohibition of pollution, is not optimal because the marginal social benefit (zero) is less than the marginal social cost.

devote scarce resources to abatement, driving the marginal social benefits down to zero. The last dollar spent on pollution abatement yields zero benefits but has a positive marginal cost to society.

Although Figure 3 provides a theoretical standard for determining a pollution abatement strategy, the application of such a cost/benefit analysis presents enormous practical problems. First, it is very difficult to calculate the marginal costs and benefits of various pollution abatement activities. Some costs and benefits emerge only over time. Moreover, the measurement of the full costs even at a single point in time is difficult due to the complexity of pollution, which affects large numbers of people and areas to varying degrees. Second, waste disposal involves complicated physical, biological, and chemical interactions. A particular abatement procedure that increases water purity may shift discharges to the atmosphere. Third, society must decide who should receive the benefits and who should bear the costs of pollution abatement. Should private firms pay? Should only affected individuals pay? Should the general public pay? The outcome of this decision will affect the distribution of income in the society.

Government Intervention

As noted earlier in this chapter, environmental pollution is a classic example of an externality; private costs and benefits diverge from social costs and benefits. The person who litters does so at little or no private cost but at a substantial social cost. The factory that pollutes the water or the air does not pay the full social costs of its action.

Environmental pollution is an externality that has required government intervention. Other means of internalization—redefinition of property rights and voluntary agreements—have rarely proved effective. It is difficult, if not impossible, to assign property rights to a river, a lake, air, or outer space. Even if property rights can be established, the legal costs of suing another party for violating a property right can be quite high. Because pollutants cross political boundaries and many parties suffer from pollution problems, an effective private opposition rarely coalesces. It is difficult to enforce those private contracts that are negotiated when polluters are numerous or when monitoring costs are excessive. Moreover, once a community agrees to pay a firm to stop polluting, other firms may issue credible (and costless) threats that they will begin pollution activities. Such agreements, therefore, leave the community open to the threat of extortion.

Figure 3 illustrated a theoretical target for government environmental policy—the achievement of optimal levels of pollution at which the marginal cost and marginal benefit are equal. Assuming government can properly assess these costs, it can apply either a *regulatory* approach or an *incentive-based* approach to attain the optimal pollution level.

In a regulatory approach, the government requires the polluting agents to limit emissions to the optimal level. Factories, for example, are issued licenses putting a ceiling on the amount of pollutants that they are allowed to emit into the atmosphere. Automobile manufacturers must place catalytic converters on their products. A refining process that eliminates lead from gasoline is mandated for oil refiners. An incentive-based approach, meanwhile, uses economic incentives or penalties to induce polluting agents to restrict their emissions to the efficient level. Factories, for example, are charged a fee for every ton of pollutant emitted into the atmosphere. Automobile owners must pay a tax for purchasing automobiles without catalytic converters, and so on.[4]

As United States environmental policy experience shows, both the regulatory and incentive-based approaches are difficult to put into practice.

U.S. Environmental Policy

In the United States, many state, local, and federal agencies are involved in pollution control. The most important is the Environmental Protection Agency (EPA), which, since 1970, has been charged with regulating pollution activities, acting through the states and on its own. The EPA derives its legislative authority from a number of congressional acts (the Clean Air Act, the Water Pollution Control Act, the National Environmental Policy Act, the Toxic Substances Control Act, and other environmental acts).

In enforcing federal environmental laws, the EPA has usually followed the regulatory approach. The EPA specifies the standards to which each individual waste discharger must adhere with respect to air, water, and noise pollution. The EPA issues permits setting ceilings on the amounts of pollutants that can be discharged and requiring that the discharger meet these ceilings by a specified date using the most practical (or best available) technology.

It is difficult to devise regulatory controls that are calibrated to lead to optimal abatement policies. The EPA sets discharge limits without reference to marginal costs and benefits. Yet, environmental policies (which are already costly) require a balancing of costs and benefits. For this reason, the EPA has experimented with incentive-based approaches.

In an ideal incentive-based policy, the government controls the discharge of pollutants by imposing fees—called *effluent charges*—that are equal to the marginal external cost of the pollutant. Such effluent charges would cause the polluting firm to consider external costs in its private economic calculations. Due to the difficulty of estimating the marginal external costs of each pollution discharge activity, the EPA has experimented with a number of "market solutions" in attempting to establish optimal effluent charges. In one program, the EPA allows firms or groups of firms to determine their own pollution abatement programs (which they presumably do at the least cost to themselves) subject to a total emissions limit assigned to the plant or region. If several firms are involved, they are allowed (in certain cases) to trade, or even buy and sell, pollution rights within the group. (See Example 3.) Another EPA program permits new pollution sources to operate if they are able to obtain an equivalent reduction in pollution discharges from existing firms.

The basic notion behind these incentive schemes is that the costs of pollution abatement will be reduced if dischargers are allowed to make their own decisions. Firms that can reduce discharges cheaply will buy pollution rights from firms that can only reduce emissions at high costs. Even if the end result is not optimal, at least the costs of pollution control will be reduced.

U.S. practice has demonstrated that government agencies are ineffective at devising environmental policies that yield optimal pollution abatement. The regulatory approach has been increasingly criticized for its rigidity and its high-cost results. Accordingly, there has been a distinct trend towards incentive-based programs, which use market solutions to place price tags on pollution externalities. Current incentive-based programs, however, do not yield optimal abatement because of the complexity of the pollution problem and the consequent difficulty of setting appropriate price tags.

International Experience

Global pollution transcends national boundaries. The destruction of rain forests in Brazil may cause worldwide *global warming*. The widespread use of chlorofluorocarbons in aerosol sprays in industrialized countries may thin the protective ozone layer over the Arctic. Sulphur emissions in the United

[4]The determination of the optimal level of waste discharges is complicated because the proper emission tax rates cannot be determined without knowing the damage reduction activities undertaken by the victims of pollution. See Richard V. Butler and Michael D. Maher, "The Control of Externalities: Abatement vs. Damage Prevention," *Southern Economic Journal* (April, 1986): 1088–1102.

EXAMPLE 3 Trading Pollution Rights

In December 1990, in an unprecedented arrangement, Metallized Paper Corporation of America bought pollution rights from USX's Clairton Works and from Papercraft Corporation in Allegheny County, Pennsylvania. Metallized Paper paid USX $75,000 for the right to emit 75 tons of pollution per year, purchased 32 tons from Papercraft, and received an additional 500-ton donation from USX. This sale of pollution rights was legal under the Federal Clean Air Act. Both USX and Papercraft Corporation possessed rights to emit a certain number of tons of pollutants into the environment up to a limit determined by the Environmental Protection Agency. By selling these rights, both agreed to cut back on their pollution emissions by the number of tons sold.

The sale was sanctioned by county and state officials, who had spent two years persuading Metallized Paper to locate in Allegheny County. Various environmental groups protested the sale because the company's plant would emit chemicals, known as volatile organic compounds, that contribute to the formation of ozone. State officials, however, defended their action on the grounds that the overall amount of pollution would not increase. Rights to pollute were merely traded from companies that could reduce their emissions cheaply to one that required significant expenditures to limit pollution.

Source: "Trading of Pollution Rights Draws Fire," *Christian Science Monitor*, December 4, 1990.

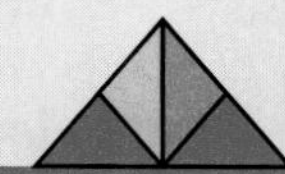

States may cause acid rains as far north as Canada and as far south as Latin America.

Coordinated international action to combat global pollution has not been effective to date. The international cooperation that does exist has focused on narrow effects of global pollution. For example, the United Nations has formed a committee to assess the depletion of the ozone layer on an annual basis. Efforts to coordinate actions on a broader front, as against global warming, have not succeeded due to the diversity of interests and resources among nations. Some areas, such as Canada, the northern United States, and the former Soviet Union could even benefit from global warming. Nations that act on their own (for example, by imposing a tax on fossil-fuel emissions) might contribute to the solution of the problem while free-riding countries benefit without paying any of the cost. (See Example 4.)

Compounding the difficulty of dealing with global pollution is the uncertainty over its causes, costs, and remedies. In the case of the greenhouse effect, Tom Tietenberg writes that "due to the rampant uncertainties in virtually every logical link in the chain from human activities to subsequent consequences, no one at this juncture can state unequivocably how serious the damage will be."[5]

EXHAUSTIBLE RESOURCES

Externalities and public goods are likely to lead to market failure and require government action. Some scientists argue that the problem of allocating **exhaustible resources** represents another potential market failure. Government action may also be necessary to prevent the exhaustion of the earth's nonrenewable resources.

[5]Tom Tietenberg, *Environmental and Natural Resource Economics*, 3rd ed. (New York: HarperCollins, 1992), 445.

EXAMPLE 4 Global Warming

Greenhouse gases (carbon dioxide, chloroflourocarbons, nitrous oxide, methane, and tropospheric ozone) absorb infrared radiation from the earth's surface and raise the earth's temperature. Were it not for these gases, the earth would be too cold for human and animal life. Scientists cannot gauge the long-term effects of substantial increases in the emissions of greenhouse gases (which emanate, it is felt, by the burning of fossil fuels, the leveling of tropical forests, and the greater use of other greenhouse gases) on the world's atmosphere. Some scientists predict a surface air warming of 1.5 to 4.5 degrees centigrade within a century, which would produce the warmest climate in 6000 years. Scientists conclude that a warming of 3 to 4 degrees centigrade would raise the global sea level by 70 centimeters.

Although no one is certain about its long-range effects, there is agreement that global warming is a matter of concern. Because it is a global problem, only a negotiated international agreement would be effective. Experts predict that it would be difficult to reach such an agreement even if all the long-range consequences of global warming were known. First, the effects of climate change would fall unequally on the world's population. Canada and the former Soviet Union would actually benefit because their cold climates would be subject to a warming trend. Brazil would lose revenues from lumber if it were to cease harvesting its timber reserves. Countries that are dependent on the burning of fossil fuels (such as Canada, India, and Russia) would be forced to find alternative energy sources. Moreover, the costs of combating global warming must be borne by the present generation for the benefit of future generations.

Source: Tom Tietenberg, *Environmental and Natural Resource Economics*, 3rd ed. (New York: HarperCollins, 1992) 438–446.

An **exhaustible** (or nonrenewable) **resource** is any resource of which there is a finite amount in the long run because the stock is fixed by nature.

Rational Allocation of Exhaustible Resources

Consider a firm that owns an exhaustible resource. It must decide how to allocate its fixed stock over time. A firm that extracts crude oil from a reservoir must decide how much to supply to the market this year, next year, 5 years from now, and 20 years from now.

A firm producing (extracting) nonrenewable resources faces an opportunity cost not present for other firms. In the case of renewable resources, the decision to supply x units this year does not limit the future supply (another tree can be planted). In the case of nonrenewable resources, every unit supplied this year constitutes 1 unit not available for subsequent years. Accordingly, suppliers of nonrenewable resources must make an *intertemporal* (across time) comparison of the costs and benefits of supplying the resource today versus supplying it tomorrow.

Suppose a firm can extract crude oil from a 1000-barrel reservoir at a zero marginal extraction cost (the oil simply rises by itself to the surface). For simplicity, suppose also that the firm must sell its entire stock of 1000 barrels within a 2-year period. The market rate of interest is 10 percent. How will this firm rationally allocate its stock of crude oil between the 2 years? If the price of crude oil today is $20 per barrel and the price expected next year is $21.50, the firm should sell all 1000 barrels this year. By selling now, the firm gets $20 per barrel that can be invested at 10 percent interest; next year, the firm will receive $22 per barrel ($20 × 1.1), a greater return than the selling price of $21.50. If next year's price is more than $22, the firm should wait to sell all 1000 barrels next year. *If the price rises at the same rate as the market interest rate (in this case, by 10 percent per annum), the firm will be indifferent as to whether it sells its stock of the nonrenewable resource this year or next year.*

The Market for Exhaustible Resources

Turning from the firm to the market for an exhaustible resource, suppose a perfectly competitive market consists of a large number of price-taking firms (see Figure 4). The stock of the exhaustible resource owned by all the firms together is fixed (at 30 units), and firms must sell their entire stock within a 2-year period (either in period 0 or period 1). The market rate of interest is 10 percent.

In Figure 4, the horizontal axis is 30 units long because only 30 units of the resource are available; what is extracted in period 0 will not be available for period 1. The period 0 demand curve is a standard demand curve read from left to right, but the period 1 demand curve must be read from right to left. Both demand curves indicate what quantities will be demanded in each period at various prices. Because only 30 units are available, the quantity remaining after period 0's supply is set, is the quantity available for period 1.

If 20 units are sold in period 0 and 10 units are sold in period 1, Figure 4 shows a period 0 price of \$6 per unit (point *a*) and a period 1 price of \$11 per unit (point *b*). Will the individual firms be content with this outcome? No. Each unit sold in period 0 and invested at 10 percent interest is worth only \$6.60

FIGURE 4
Market Equilibrium for an Exhaustible Resource in Two Periods

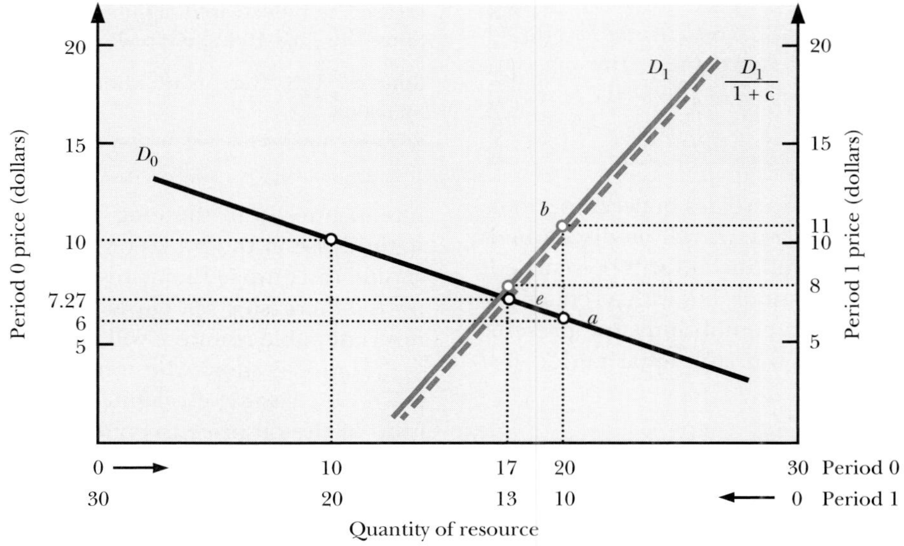

This figure represents a competitive market composed of a large number of perfectly competitive firms. The firms in the market together have a fixed supply of 30 units of the nonrenewable resource, and these 30 units must be used either in period 0 or period 1. The market demand curves are D_0 for period 0 and D_1 for period 1. (Period 1 quantity increases from right to left rather than from left to right.) Firms will contrast the price received in period 0 with the present discounted value of the price received in period 1. If the interest rate is 10 percent, $D_1 \div 1.1$ is the present discounted value of the period 1 demand curve. When the available supply is allocated between periods 0 and 1, the prices in the two periods are established. As long as the period 0 price is less than the present value of the period 1 price (as it is when the period 0 quantity is 20 and the period 1 quantity is 10), firms will reallocate supplies from period 0 to period 1. Equilibrium is attained when quantity is 17 in period 0 and 13 in period 1 and when price is \$8 in period 1 and \$7.27 in period 0. In equilibrium, the ratio of the price in period 1 to the price in period 0 will be 1 plus the interest rate, or 1.1.

in period 1, whereas each unit sold in period 1 yields \$11. Clearly, firms will want to supply less than 20 units in period 0 and more than 10 units in period 1.

An equilibrium is attained when the period 0 price equals the present discounted value of the period 1 price (when the period 0 price equals the period 1 price divided by 1.1). At this point, an incentive no longer exists for firms to switch supplies from one period to the other. The dashed demand curve in Figure 4 shows the period 1 prices divided by 1.1 and represents the present discounted values of the period 1 prices. The quantity where the dashed curve intersects the period 0 demand curve (at point e) is the equilibrium quantity. The quantity corresponding to point e is 17 units in period 0 and 13 units in period 1. In Figure 4, the period 0 price for 17 units is \$7.27, and the period 1 price for 13 units is \$8. These prices reflect the fact that the present discounted value of \$8 is \$7.27 at a 10 percent rate of interest. At these prices, firms no longer have an incentive to shift supplies from one period to the other.

> When marginal extraction costs are zero and the market is perfectly competitive, the price of an exhaustible resource will rise at the same rate as the interest rate.

If period 1's demand increases between periods 0 and 1, D_1 will shift upward, as will its discounted present value. The new equilibrium will be reached at higher prices in both periods, but with a reduction in the period 0 supply. In equilibrium, the present value of period 1's price will still equal period 0's price.

> The anticipation of an increase in demand in some future period will tend to redistribute supplies of exhaustible resources from the present to the future.

The Technology of Resource Extraction

Figure 4 delivers a reassuring message consistent with economic theory: Competitive markets deal automatically with the rising scarcity of exhaustible resources. The theory predicts that the annual growth rate of the prices of exhaustible resources will equal the market rate of interest in the long run. In other words, the natural rise in the prices of nonrenewable resources should discourage their present consumption. Moreover, if increasing scarcity is expected, supplies of the nonrenewable resource will be shifted to the future.

FIGURE 5
Real U.S. Crude Oil Prices, 1880–1991

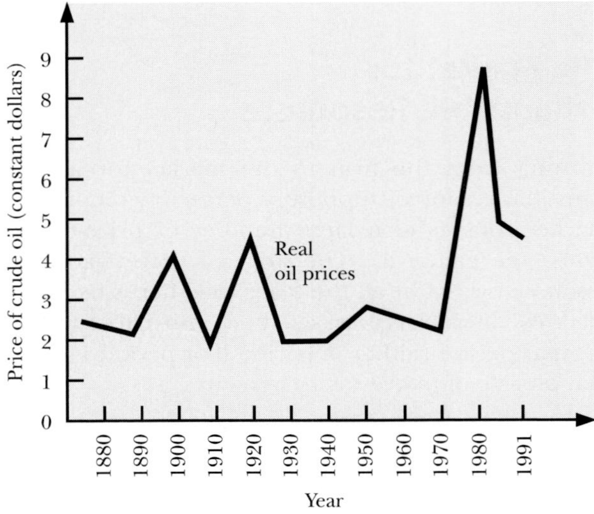

Since 1880, overall *real* U.S. crude oil prices neither increased nor decreased significantly until the late 1970s. Since the early 1980s, the real price has been falling.

Sources: U.S. Bureau of Mines; U.S. Bureau of Labor Statistics.

Figure 5 shows the long-run trend in the real price of a barrel of oil since 1880 by graphing the ratio of the oil price to consumer prices in general. No trend in the real price of oil can be discerned until the late 1970s, at which time the real price rose. In the 1980s and early 1990s, the real price of oil fell. Since 1800 there has been a distinct downward trend in the real price of other exhaustible resources, such as copper, aluminum, and pig iron. Why have the real prices of exhaustible resources not risen steadily as economic theory predicts? Falling extraction costs and technological advances can cause the behavior of prices to differ from that outlined by the theory (which does not take into account marginal extraction costs and technological change). If marginal extraction costs are falling over time, the price of an exhaustible resource may rise more slowly than the rate of interest. (See Example 5.)

EXAMPLE 5 Doomster versus Boomster: Are We Running Out of Natural Resources?

Doomsday forecasters ("Doomsters") predict that the world will run out of natural resources within the lifetime of our children or grandchildren. More optimistic economists ("Boomsters") argue that markets naturally conserve exhaustible resources, as explained in the text.

In 1980, a prominent Boomster, economist Julian Simon, and a prominent Doomster, biologist Paul Ehrlich, entered into a $1000 bet. Simon allowed Ehrlich to select five natural resources that he thought were being exhausted. Supply-and-demand analysis suggests that if a resource is disappearing, its price will increase. Accordingly, the two decided that Ehrlich would win if the prices of the five natural resources had increased faster than inflation at the end of 10 years.

In 1990, Simon received a $1000 check from Ehrlich. The prices of all five natural resources (shown in the figure) declined between 1980 and 1990. More surprisingly, the prices had declined in absolute terms. Their money prices were lower in 1990 than in 1980!

Source: John Tierney, "Betting the Planet," *New York Times Magazine*, December 2, 1990.

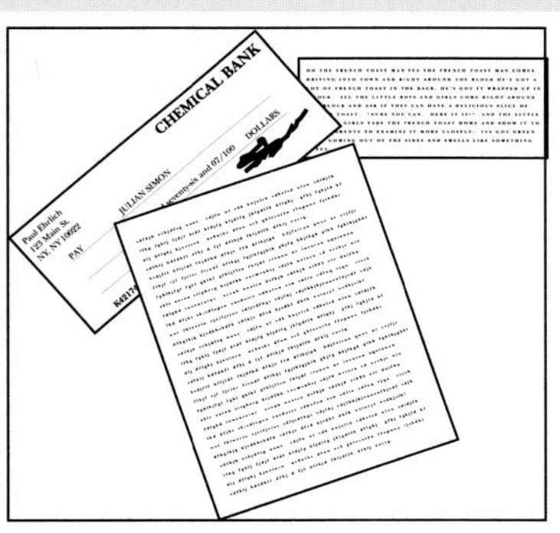

FIVE EASY PIECES

The spoils of victory: a sheet of calculations and, most important, a check from Ehrlich to Simon. The prices of all the wagered metals declined between 1980 and 1990.

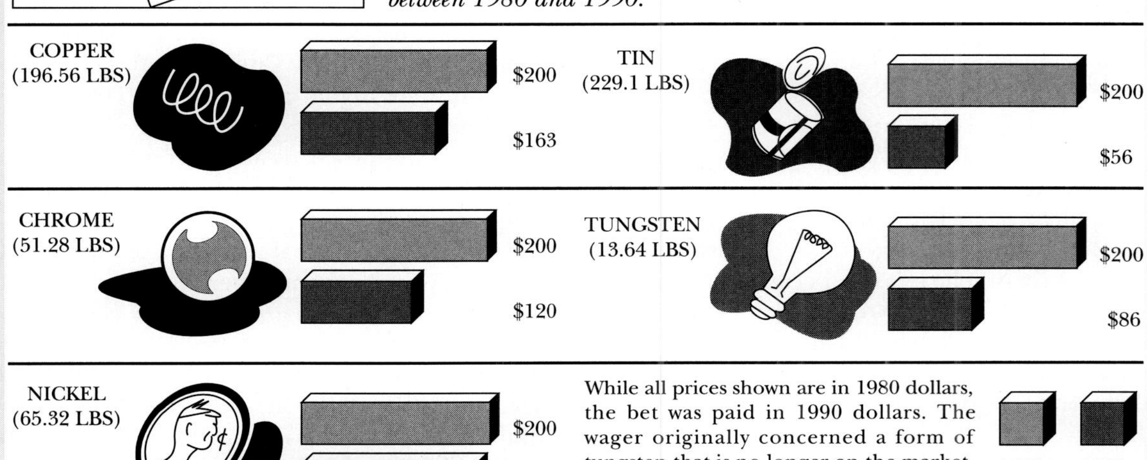

Technological Advances. If technological advances allow producers of exhaustible resources to increase their recovery rates, prices should not be expected to rise at the rate of interest. In fact, if technological advances are large, exhaustible resource prices can fall.

Consider a resource firm that develops a new technology enabling it to recover more of the exhaustible resource in period 1 than in period 0. For example, suppose an oil company has a total of 200 barrels underground and, with existing technology, can recover one out of every two barrels extracted from underground in period 0. A new technology that permits the recovery of 1.5 barrels from every 2 barrels underground is scheduled to be implemented in period 1. Thus, for every barrel sold in period 0, the firm passes up the opportunity to sell 1.5 barrels (with the new technology) in period 1. As a result, more supplies will be shifted to period 1, thereby lowering the period 1 price and raising the period 0 price.

> Technological advances that are scheduled to take place in the future cause supplies of exhaustible resources to be shifted to the future, thereby raising current prices and lowering future prices.

Backstop Resources. A *backstop resource* is a close substitute for an exhaustible resource, available in virtually unlimited supply but at a higher cost. Solar energy is a backstop for conventional energy, and shale oil and tar sands are backstops for conventional crude oil.

What effect does the availability of a backstop fuel—such as shale oil—have on the allocation of crude oil and oil prices over time? Suppose that shale oil is available in virtually unlimited supply at a price of $40 a barrel. This backstop fuel sets a price limit of $40 per barrel on conventional crude oil because consumers will switch to shale oil if the crude oil price rises above $40. The price should increase by the rate of interest until the $40 backstop price is reached. After that point, the price will remain constant.

The existence of a backstop resource allows greater consumption of the nonrenewable resource in the present and at lower prices. Supplies of the nonrenewable resource need cover demands only up to the backstop price. As a result, more of the resource can be consumed now with the knowledge that needs in the distant future will be met by the alternative resource.

Recycling of Exhaustible Resources

The price system encourages producers of exhaustible resources to sell less today in anticipation of growing scarcity tomorrow. **Recycling** offers yet another opportunity for owners and users of exhaustible resources to be assured of a supply of the resource both now and in the future.

> **Recycling** reintroduces used exhaustible resources (such as iron, metals, and petrochemicals) into the system, providing an alternative to production and reducing waste disposal costs.

Recycling of exhaustible resources can occur automatically through the price system or it can be stimulated by government intervention.

Consider the case of mercury, an exhaustible resource in which there is an active market for recycling. Mercury is a resource that is limited in supply but is found in many products, including industrial and control instruments, batteries, and dental amalgams. It has high disposal costs because of its toxic characteristics. Currently, about 47 percent of industrial mercury usage is from recycled mercury. The percentage of recycled mercury depends upon its price and disposal cost. If mercury prices rise, more mercury is recycled. There is also active recycling of aluminum. Currently, about 38 percent of aluminum ingots are produced from recycled aluminum.[6]

Recycling proceeds at an economically efficient level when the marginal cost of recycling equals the marginal social cost of disposal. If it costs society $200 per ton to dispose of aluminum cans and $100 per ton to recycle aluminum, then too little is being recycled. Whenever the marginal private cost of disposal is less than the marginal social cost, the amount of recycling falls short of the optimum. If people do not have to bear the full marginal costs of throwing away aluminum cans, tires, used cars, or old car batteries,

[6]Tietenberg, 195, 201.

EXAMPLE 6 Ecological Economists and Sustainable Growth

Biologists, ecologists and other natural scientists have formed a new branch of economics called *ecological economics.* Ecological economists reject the traditional economic approach to environmental analysis, which recommends balancing costs and benefits in making environmental decisions. The stated goal of the ecological economists is to persuade governments to give the "sustainability of natural life support systems" priority over conventionally measured economic growth. In particular, ecological economists argue that environmental costs should be included in conventional measures of economic growth and that government policy must aim at achieving "sustainable growth." Current and future generations may have to lower their material standards of living to ensure an environment that will sustain human and plant life in the distant future.

Ecological economists offer several reasons why markets cannot successfully deal with environmental problems. First, people naturally tend to value present lives more than future lives. Accordingly, private economic decision making will trade off future lives for a higher standard of living today. Second, markets put price tags on market goods but not on environmental benefits. Hence, market goods will be produced; environmental benefits will not. Third, markets do not take into account the irreversibility of some environmental decisions. A species, once extinct, cannot be resurrected. Fourth, environmental investments may be required today to prevent risks in the distant future. Aerosol sprays could cause environmental disaster a century from now. Finally, the large time gap between the causes and effects of environmental destruction diminishes the motivation for corrective action. Nitrates may take 40 years to seep into and contaminate the water supply.

For all these reasons, ecological economists argue that enlightened government decision making must replace private decision making in the area of environmental protection. Only public policy will have sufficient foresight to prevent environmental disaster in the future.

Source: "Rebel Economists Add Ecological Cost to Price of Progress," *New York Times*, November 27, 1990; "What Price Posterity?" *The Economist* (March 23, 1991): 73.

then recycling levels will be insufficient. It is for this reason that many states and communities have passed mandatory recycling laws.[7]

The Price System and Exhaustible Resources

As demonstrated in this chapter, natural market forces should cause nonrenewable resources to be allocated efficiently over time. (But see Example 6.)

Suppliers must weigh the returns from exploiting the resource now against waiting for the resource to become more scarce (and, thus, to sell for a higher price) tomorrow. Unless rapid technological progress increases the supply of recoverable nonrenewable resources, their prices will tend to rise at the rate of interest.

The major threat to the rational use of nonrenewable resources is interference in the pricing of resources. If prices are controlled—for example, if price ceilings are placed on oil or natural gas—then firms producing these resources will have to make resource allocation decisions on the basis of prices that do not correctly reflect scarcities today and tomorrow. In other words, price controls could result in too little being allocated to present consumption and too much being allocated to future consumption.

[7] "As Recycling Surges, Markets for Materials Slow to Develop," *Wall Street Journal*, January 17, 1992. The National Solid Waste Management Association estimated that there were 3500 curbside collection programs in 1992 (up from 600 in 1989), of which 40 percent were mandatory.

This chapter discussed some of the possible arguments for government intervention in the economic arena. Externalities, particularly the environmental problem of waste disposal, and public goods represent legitimate cases of market failure. The next chapter will examine the patterns of government spending and taxation.

SUMMARY

1. Market failure occurs when the price system fails to produce the socially optimal quantity of a good. Two examples of market failure are externalities and public goods. Externalities occur when marginal social costs (or benefits) do not equal marginal private costs (or benefits). Social efficiency requires that marginal social benefits and marginal social costs be equal, but private market participants equate marginal private benefits with marginal private costs. Externalities can be internalized by redefining property rights, by making voluntary agreements, or by taxing or subsidizing the externality generator.

2. Pure public goods have two characteristics: First, the consumption of the good by one user does not reduce its consumption by others (nonrival consumption). Second, no one can in practice be prevented from using the good (nonexclusion).

3. Waste disposal costs arise because modern production and consumption require disposing of residual wastes such as air pollutants, toxic chemicals, and solid wastes. Pollution problems cannot easily be solved by redefining property rights or by voluntary agreement; government intervention is typically required. In the United States, the Environmental Protection Agency (EPA) is charged with environmental protection. The EPA regulates pollution standards but in recent years has been experimenting with incentive-based market solutions.

4. Firms that produce nonrenewable (exhaustible) resources must determine how to allocate the available fixed supply over time. When marginal extraction costs are zero, when the industry is perfectly competitive, and when there is no technological progress, firms will allocate the resource so that the present discounted values of the prices in each period are the same. Prices will rise at the rate of interest. If increasing scarcity is anticipated, supplies of the nonrenewable resource will be reallocated from the present to the future. The prices of nonrenewable resources in general have not risen in real terms because of declining marginal extraction costs and rapid technological progress. Natural market forces should cause the efficient allocation of nonrenewable resources over time. Recycling is another means of stretching out the supply of exhaustible resources.

KEY TERMS

externalities	rival consumption
social costs	nonexclusion
social benefits	exclusion costs
market failure	free rider
internalize	exhaustible resource
public goods	recycling
nonrival consumption	

QUESTIONS AND PROBLEMS

1. Factory A produces 1000 tons of sulfuric acid at a cost of $10,000 to produce 1000 tons. For the people in the community, the production of 1000 tons of sulfuric acid causes an increase of $5000 in medical payments, a loss of $4000 in wages by being sick, and an increase of $1000 in dry-cleaning bills. What are the private and social costs of the 1000 tons of sulfuric acid?
2. Explain how the external costs calculated in the previous example might be internalized. Will this internalization be handled differently when there are three people hurt by the factory than when 300,000 people are hurt? In which case is government action more likely?
3. Many people think we need national defense. Why is it, therefore, difficult to get people to pay voluntarily their share of national defense costs? Why is there no problem in getting people to pay for shoes?
4. Explain why two people are nonrival consumers of a big-city expressway when driving at 3:00 A.M. but are rival consumers when driving at 5:00 P.M.
5. An oil producer has 100 barrels of oil that must be sold within a 2-year period. The interest rate is 20 percent, and the price of crude oil expected next year is $35 per barrel. At which prices would the oil producer sell all the oil this year? At which prices would the oil producer sell all the oil next year? What will happen if

the oil producer expects an improvement in technology to increase the recovery rate by 10 percent next year?

6. If new cost-efficient technologies that reduced the marginal costs of pollution abatement were developed, what would happen to the optimal level of pollution abatement?
7. Does the pollution-trading concept used in recent years by the EPA solve the problem of determining the optimal level of pollution?
8. Explain why economists do not favor the total elimination of pollution.
9. Discuss the two characteristics of public goods. Give an example of a good that is nonrival in consumption but has low exclusion costs. Give an example of a good that has high exclusion costs but is rival in consumption. Finally, given an example of a good that simultaneously is nonrival and has high exclusion costs.
10. In 1986, it was proposed that a worldwide tax be placed on aerosol sprays to protect the world's ozone layer. At what rate should the tax be set?
11. In which of these three cases would it be easier to establish property rights? First, Farmer Jones wishes to keep stray cattle off his farmlands. Second, Farmer Jones wishes to prevent the commercial jets landing at a nearby airport from disturbing his egg-laying chickens. Third, Farmer Jones wishes to keep Farmer Smith from depleting the stock of fish in a lake that is shared by the two farms.
12. Many agricultural crops are harmed by beetles and other insects. These harmful insects are prey for the praying mantis, a large insect. The praying mantis is not an endangered species, but several agricultural states still impose a fine on anyone caught killing a praying mantis. Is there a good economic reason for such a fine? Explain.
13. For about 4000 years, mariners have been dumping wastes into the ocean. In many places, the ocean floor is covered with plastics, bottles, and other refuse. Explain why the market mechanism does not correct for this waste disposal problem. How might the problem be solved with internalization?

SUGGESTED READINGS

Bromley, Daniel W., ed. *Natural Resource Economics.* Hingham, MA: Kluwer Academic Publishers, 1986.

Cheung, Steven S. "The Fable of the Bees: An Economic Investigation." *Journal of Law and Economics* (April 1973).

Coase, Ronald H. "The Lighthouse in Economics." *Journal of Law and Economics* (October 1976).

Griffin, James A., and Henry B. Steele. *Energy Economics and Policy,* 2d ed. San Diego: Harcourt Brace Jovanovich, 1986.

Heyne, Paul, and Thomas Johnson. *Toward Understanding Microeconomics.* Chicago: SRA, 1976, chap. 14.

Krutilla, John V., and Anthony C. Fisher. *The Economics of Natural Environments,* Rev. ed. Washington, DC: Resources for the Future, 1985.

Tietenberg, Tom. *Environmental and Natural Resource Economics,* 3rd ed. New York: HarperCollins, 1992.

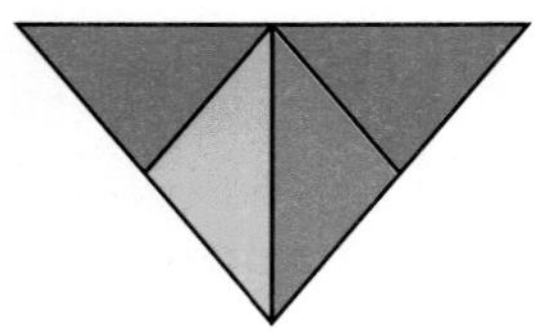

42 Public Finance

CHAPTER INSIGHT

Government affects our lives in many ways. Each year individuals fill out federal income tax returns. Treasurers of corporations repeat this exercise each quarter of the year. When we buy goods in a pharmacy or department store, a percentage sales tax is assessed on many items. Although the government collects taxes, it provides services in return. Without government services, there would be no police, no clerk to issue drivers' licenses, no courts to settle disputes, and no leader to conduct foreign policy.

The relationship between the public and the government is one of give and take. Is the government taking more than it should? Is it giving more than it should? Is everyone paying their fair share, or are some individuals or corporations paying too little? Is the government spending its resources wisely?

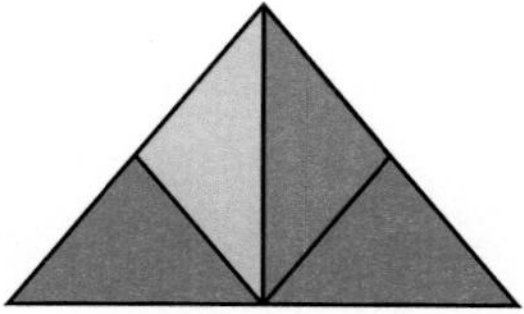

PUBLIC FINANCE

In preceding chapters, the behavior of private markets was examined. In addition to the private sector, a significant amount of economic activity is carried out by the *public sector,* or local, state, and federal governments. Public-sector economics is the study of the resource allocation activities of government. One branch of public-sector economics is **public finance.**

> **Public finance** is the study of government revenues and expenditures at all levels of government—local, state, and federal.

This chapter focuses on how governments raise revenues through taxes and fees and how they spend those revenues on various activities. The next chapter examines public choice, a second branch of public-sector economics, which focuses on how government spending decisions are made.

THE SCOPE OF GOVERNMENT ECONOMIC ACTIVITY

Government expenditures fall into one of two categories: **exhaustive expenditures** or **transfer payments.**

> **Exhaustive expenditures** are government purchases of goods and services that divert resources from the private sector, making them no longer available for private use.
>
> **Transfer payments** transfer income from one individual or organization to another.

In 1991, the government purchased 19 percent of all goods and services (see Table 1). In an economy that produced $5.7 trillion worth of goods and services, government purchases totaled more than $1 trillion.

In 1991, exhaustive expenditures accounted for 57 percent of total government spending. The remaining 43 percent of government expenditures were government transfer payments.

Transfer payments affect the distribution of income among families but do not change the amount of goods and services exhausted (consumed) by government. For example, the Social Security Program transfers income from currently employed workers to retired or disabled workers. The federal government transfers funds to state and local governments.

As Table 1 reports, total government expenditures in 1991 accounted for 33 percent of the total output of the U.S. economy. The ratio of total government expenditures to total output is a common measure of the economic scope of government.

The average citizen's impression of the scope of government is formed from the share of personal

TABLE 1
Exhaustive Expenditures and Transfer Payments of Government in 1991

Government	Purchase of Goods and Services, Including Interest Payments (billions of dollars)	Purchase as Percent of Gross Domestic Product	Transfer Payments (billions of dollars)*	Total Expenditures for Goods and Services and Transfers (billions of dollars)	Total Expenditure as Percent of GDP
Federal government	445	7.8	754	1199	21.0
State and local governments	644	11.3	64	708	12.4
Total government	1089	19.1	818	1907	33.4

*Federal transfers exclude grants to state and local governments.

Source: *Survey of Current Business.*

FIGURE 1
Tax Burden of Workers in Various Countries

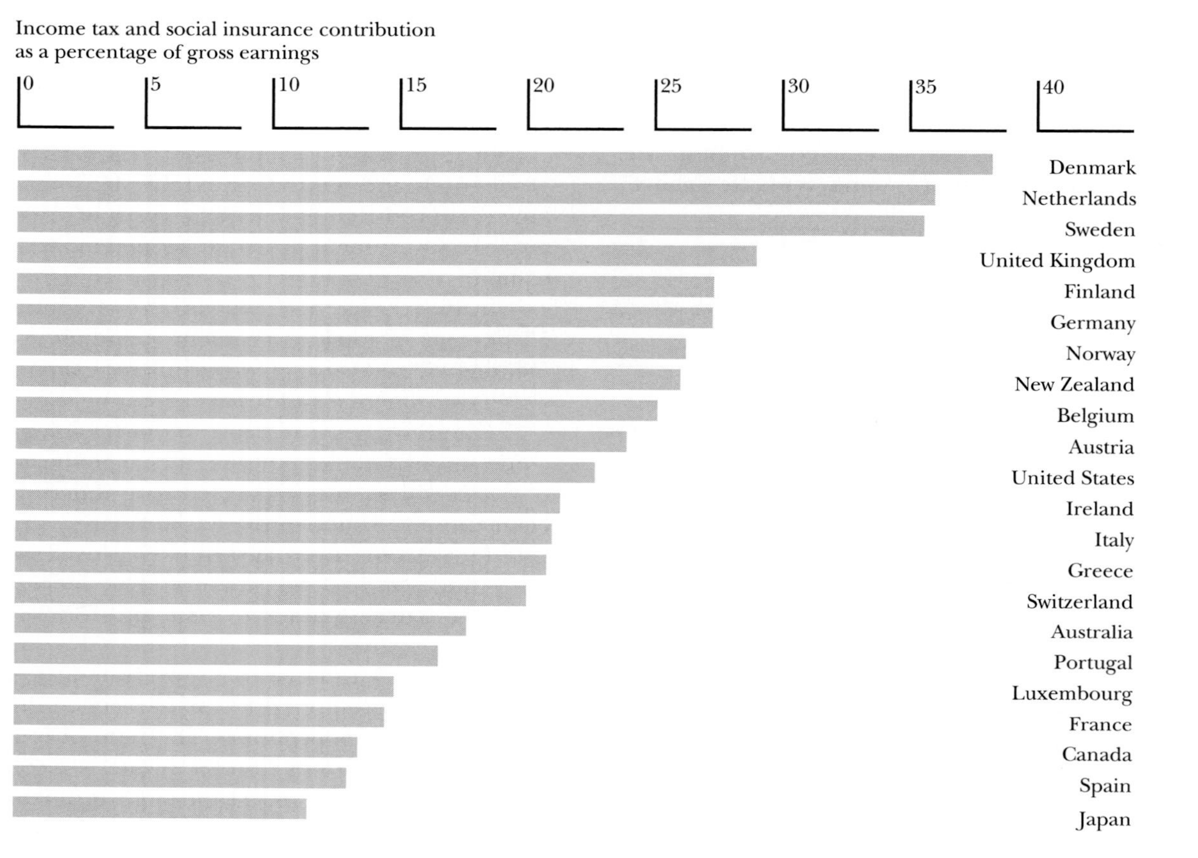

Source: *The 1982 Tax/Benefit Position of a Typical Worker in OECD Member Countries* (Paris: OECD, 1983), 25.

income that he or she must pay to the government in the form of taxes. In 1991, governments collected $725 billion in personal income taxes, which amounted to 17 percent of total personal income. In addition, governments collected $435 billion from sales and excise taxes and $500 billion in Social Security taxes and insurance. Together, these taxes added up to 39 percent of personal income.

Although U.S. tax payments amount to almost $1.5 trillion, taxes as a percentage of earnings are about average or slightly below average for the industrialized countries. As Figure 1 shows, American workers pay a smaller percentage of their earnings in income and Social Security taxes than do most European workers. For its level of economic development, the United States has a relatively low tax burden. (See Example 1.)

Trends in Government

Government revenues and expenditures have increased at a rapid pace. Figure 2 shows the enormous acceleration of government expenditures and transfer payments since 1929. Dollar figures exaggerate the growth of government because of the general rise in prosperity and prices. (Recall the discussion in Appendix 1A of inflation and growth distortion.) We would expect government revenues and expenditures to rise along with the general economy. A more relevant yardstick is the ratio of total government

EXAMPLE 1 The United States as a Tax Haven

Although U.S. federal income tax rates appear high, they have become relatively low when compared to other industrialized countries. In fact, after tax revisions went into effect in 1987, experts call the United States a tax haven. The accompanying table shows the after-tax income and the effective tax rate for a family with two children and one income of $50,000, as well as the top marginal tax rates. By both standards, U.S. federal income tax rates are among the lowest of the industrialized nations. In addition, other countries rely heavily on national sales taxes, such as the value-added tax, which are not used in the United States.

How Much Can We Keep? The After-Tax Income of a Family with a $50,000 Income

Country	After-Tax Income	Effective Tax Rate (percent)	Top Marginal Rates (percent)
Australia	$30,642	38.70%	49
Britain	29,052	29.18	60
Canada	39,575	20.85	34
France	37,900	24.20	58
Japan	42,620	14.76	70
Spain	35,788	28.40	66
U.S.	43,451	13.10	34
West Germany	36,779	26.40	56

Source: "No Joke, U.S. Now a Tax Haven," *Christian Science Monitor*, December 4, 1987: 13.

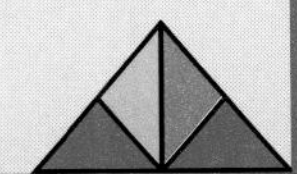

spending to total output (see Figure 3). In 1890, government expenditures accounted for 6.5 percent of total output, but by 1991 this ratio had risen to 33 percent. An increase in the government share has characterized other industrialized countries, as Figure 3 shows.

The economic role of government in the United States, especially of the federal government, has increased dramatically over the past half century for five reasons.

1. The United States, as a military superpower, has devoted an increasing share of its economic resources to national defense. On the eve of World War II, national defense expenditures accounted for 1.3 percent of the GDP. At the peak of the Vietnam conflict, national defense accounted for almost 9 percent of the GDP, falling to 6 percent in 1992. It remains to be seen whether this figure will decline dramatically as a result of the collapse of the Soviet Union in late 1991.

2. Government has increasingly taken responsibility for the health, education, and welfare of the American population. Prior to the Great Depression, it was primarily the responsibility of the individual to provide for family health, income security, and retirement needs. Educational needs were provided for by the local community, and private charitable organizations cared for the needy. This attitude has changed over the years. In 1929, prior to the establishment of the Social Security Program, government social-welfare programs cost a minute fraction of 1 percent of total output. Today, government expenditures for health, education, and welfare account for almost 10 percent of the total output.

3. The more modern and complex an economy becomes, the more government services it requires. In effect, government services represent a luxury good, the demand for which increases at a slightly higher pace than income. Urban societies require more government services—sanitation, traffic control, water supplies—than rural societies. Congested areas require more police protection than sparsely populated communities. Modern industrial societies require a more complex legal system.

4. Unlike manufacturing or agriculture, which have experienced substantial increases in productivity, efficiency gains in the government sector have been slow. It is easier to increase productivity in the private sector than in the public sector where

FIGURE 2
Total Government Expenditures, 1929–1991

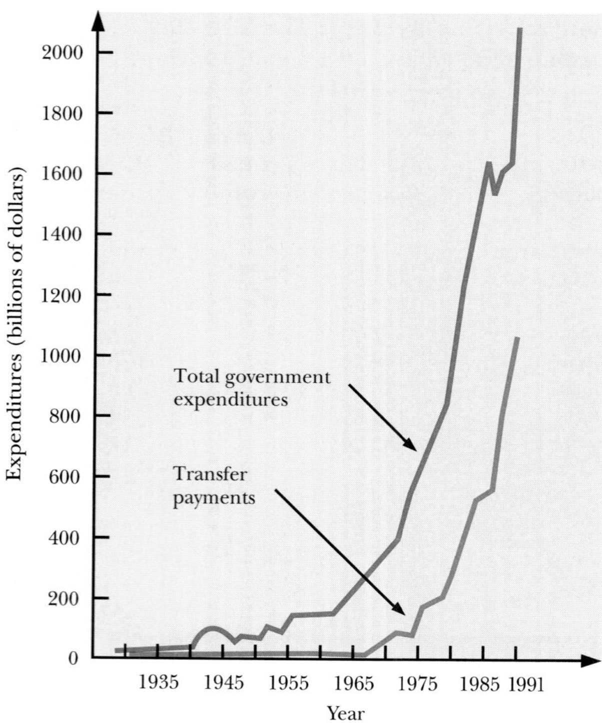

Total government expenditures and transfer payments have increased at an accelerating rate since 1929.

Source: *Survey of Current Business.*

FIGURE 3
Total Government Spending as a Percentage of GDP, U.S. and Other Countries, 1890–1991

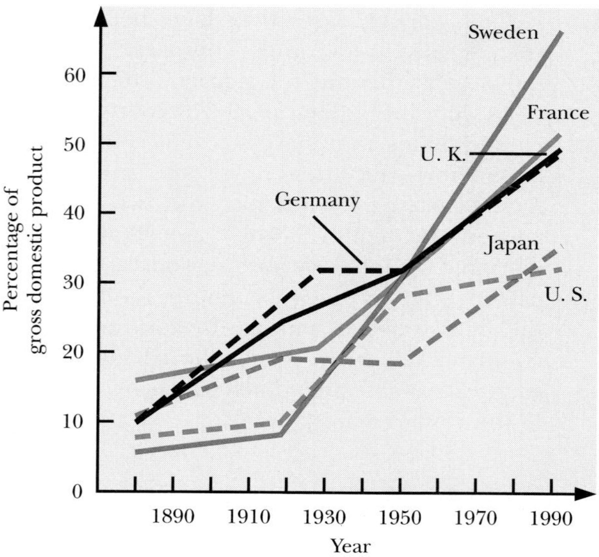

The ratio of total government expenditures to total economic activity (or GDP) is a better measure of the changing role of government than measures of government spending alone.

Source: *World Development Report 1991* (Oxford: Oxford University Press, 1991), 139. Figures updated by authors.

services—such as education, police protection, judicial services, and general record keeping—rather than *goods* are being provided. Because of slow productivity growth, price increases have been more rapid in the public sector than in the private sector. Since 1950, there has been an eightfold increase in the prices paid by government to purchase goods and services compared to a fivefold increase in consumer prices.

5. Because of the power of special-interest groups and lobbyists, democratic societies have been gradually increasing their support of government spending (see the next chapter for further discussion). Special-interest groups, logrolling, and vote trading have made it increasingly difficult for democratic societies to control government spending.

Shares of Federal, State, and Local Governments

Government economic activities are distributed among federal, state, and local governments. Each society must determine at what level of government a given public service should be provided. Should roads be built by federal or local government? Should the municipalities, the states, or the federal government supply public education? There has been intense debate over these issues since the founding of this country. Some citizens fear that the federal government is too remote and too powerful, while the states and localities have too little power. Others consider the federal government to be a more efficient and rational supplier of government services and the best enforcer of national standards and legislation.

In 1991, the federal government (not including grants in aid to state and local governments) accounted for 66 percent of all government expenditures, while state and local government accounted for the remainder. Figure 4 shows that the dominance by federal government is a fairly new phenomenon. In 1932, state and local government accounted for almost 70 percent of government expenditures. As late as 1940, state and local government still accounted for about one-half of all government revenues and expenditures. However, World War II dramatically altered the balance. In 1946, shortly after the war's end, the federal government accounted for more than 80 percent of government spending. From 1955 to the mid-1970s, state and local government grew in importance—from 34 percent to more than 45 percent of total government. Since the mid-1970s, the federal share has again been on the rise.

Government Surpluses and Government Deficits

Governments collect revenue (through taxes and sales of services) and make expenditures (on purchases of goods and services and transfer payments). Governments, like households and businesses, can spend more or less than their income. The **government surplus** or **deficit** shows the relationship between government revenue and outlays.

> A **government surplus** is an excess of government revenues over government outlays.
>
> A **government deficit** is an excess of government outlays over government revenues.

FIGURE 4
State and Local Expenditures versus Federal Expenditures, 1930–1991

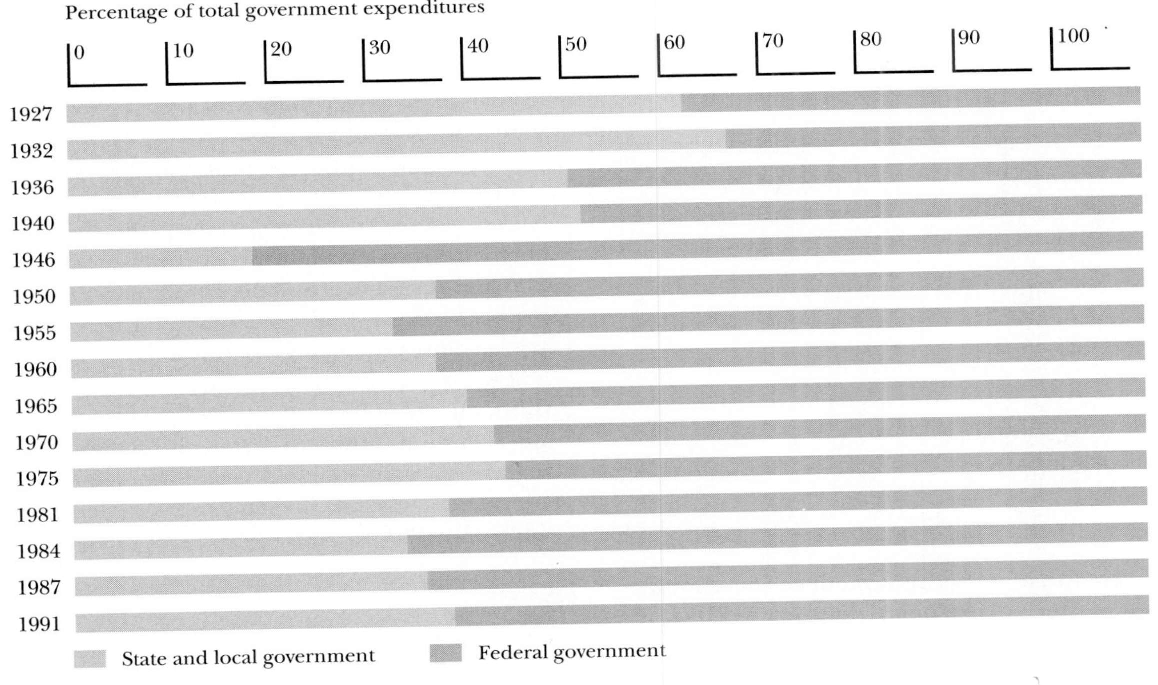

This graph shows that the dominance of federal over state and local spending is a fairly recent phenomenon. *Note:* Federal expenditures do not include grants in aid to state and local governments.

Source: *Survey of Current Business; Historical Statistics of the United States,* vol. 2, 1124–29.

EXAMPLE 2 Boris Yeltsin, the Russian Deficit, and the Printing Press

Although the U.S. federal deficit appears overwhelming (at some $300 billion), it is far less troublesome than the budget deficit that Boris Yeltsin inherited when he took charge of the Russian Republic after the abortive August 1991 coup. While U.S. deficits constitute 3 to 4 percent of total output, the Russian deficit constituted 10 to 15 percent of total output and was rising rapidly.

Unlike the U.S. federal government, which finances its deficits by selling bonds, the Yeltsin government had no one willing or able to buy Russian government bonds. Although the government tried to peddle interest-bearing securities, there were few takers. Russian government revenues were shrinking as the economy collapsed and as the various local governments refused to pay their taxes. On the expenditure side, Yeltsin had to pay the restive armed forces and meet the payrolls of failing state companies. The only apparent choice was to use government printing presses (which he seized from the failing union government of Gorbachev) to print money. One-hundred-ruble notes, which had been banned by the previous government, began to circulate in great numbers in the form of military pay and wage payments to state workers and bureaucrats.

Yeltsin's decision to print money to handle the soaring budget deficit led to more inflation.

Source: International Monetary Fund, *A Study of the Soviet Economy*, vol. 1. (Paris: IMF, 1991).

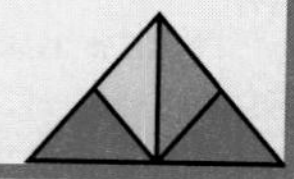

Governments that run a deficit typically use **deficit financing.**

> **Deficit financing** is the borrowing of funds in credit markets to finance a government deficit.

If a government borrows funds over a number of years to finance its deficits, it accumulates a **government debt.**

> The **government debt** is the cumulated sum of outstanding IOUs that a government owes its creditors.

A government debt can be reduced by running a surplus. If the government debt were $100 billion and government ran a $10 billion surplus, the government debt would be reduced by $10 billion.

Government finances differ from household and business finances in one important respect: Governments can make up the difference between expenditures and revenues by printing money. The financing of deficits through the printing press has been used by governments to pay for wars and for costly government programs. (See Example 2.)

Table 2 provides current information on government budgets, surpluses, deficits, and debt in the United States. As the table shows, the total government deficit is less than the federal deficit because state and local governments combined tend to have surpluses. Since 1950, the federal government has run surpluses in only 5 years. In 1950, the federal debt was $257 billion—7 percent of the 1991 figure. Although the federal debt has grown considerably and is large in absolute terms, the federal debt has shrunk as a percentage of total output. In 1950, the federal debt was almost 90 percent of total economic output. In 1991, it was 64 percent of total output.

PRINCIPLES OF TAXATION

To finance its many expenditures, government—whether local, state, or federal—must have revenues. Taxation is the major source of government revenue in all countries.

TABLE 2
Information on U.S. Government Budgets and Debt, 1991

	Receipts (billions of dollars)	Expenditures (billions of dollars)	Surplus or Deficit (−) (billions of dollars)	Total Debt (billions of dollars)	Total Debt as Percent of GDP
Total government*	1738	1909	−171	3860	68
Federal government	1119	1320	−201	3618	64
State and local governments	771	741	30	242	4

*Total government expenditures do not equal the sum of federal, state and local expenditures because federal grants to state and local governments are double counted.

Sources: *Statistical Abstract of the United States; Economic Report of the President.*

Fairness and the Tax System

There has always been debate over what constitutes a fair tax system. If people believe that taxes are unfair, they will seek to evade them and join taxpayer revolts. In some countries, tax evasion is an accepted social practice; in other countries, it is considered immoral. Whether the public voluntarily pays taxes depends upon whether the tax system is perceived as fair.

The Benefit Principle. The **benefit principle** is one approach to fairness.

> The **benefit principle** of taxation states that those who benefit from the public expenditure should pay the tax that finances it.

According to this principle, those who benefit from a new state highway, a new airport, or a flood-control project—all financed from tax revenues—should pay for it. If community members are not willing to pay for a public project (for example, if citizens vote against a flood-control project in their community), they are revealing that they do not consider the project's benefits to outweigh its costs. If all taxes were levied on the principle that the beneficiaries bear the full burden of the tax (and if the beneficiaries were given the opportunity to vote on each public expenditure), benefits of voter-approved projects would exceed costs.

One example of a benefit tax is a tax on gasoline that is used to finance highway construction. In many communities, special taxes are assessed for specific road repairs, street lighting, and sidewalks.

To apply the benefit principle, one must first identify who benefits and by how much—and this is often difficult to do. While automobile drivers benefit from public highways and residents of New York City benefit from the New York subway system, it is often difficult to determine who benefits from national defense, police protection, or the legal system. Do the poor benefit less than the rich?

The Ability-to-Pay Principle. The second approach to fairness is the **ability-to-pay principle.**

> The **ability-to-pay principle** states that those better able to pay should bear the greater burden of taxes, whether or not they benefit more.

According to this principle, the rich may benefit less from public education and public hospitals because they may choose to use private facilities; however, because they are better able to pay than the poor, they should bear a heavier burden.

A tax system that follows the ability-to-pay principle must have both **vertical equity** and **horizontal equity.**

Vertical equity exists when those with a greater ability to pay bear a heavier tax burden.

Horizontal equity exists when those with equal abilities to pay do pay the same amount of tax.

If vertical equity is lacking, then taxes are not being paid on an ability-to-pay basis. If horizontal equity is not present, then the ability-to-pay principle is being violated because taxpayers with equal abilities to pay are being treated differently.

Like the benefit principle, the ability-to-pay principle is difficult to apply universally. How can ability to pay be measured? How can adjustments be made for family size and medical and college expenses?

Incidence of Taxation. Society must decide who should bear the burden of taxes. Once this decision is made, tax authorities must devise a tax system that fulfills its goals. At first glance, it seems simple. If society wants the rich to pay 40 percent of their income and the poor to pay 10 percent, then income tax rates need only be set at 40 percent and 10 percent for these two groups. Or, if society decides that cigarette manufacturers and big oil companies should pay a heavy share of taxes, then it simply levies a tax on each carton of cigarettes and on each barrel of oil.

In reality, the individual or company that is being taxed does not necessarily bear the burden of the tax. In many cases, the **incidence of a tax** can be shifted to someone else.

The **incidence of a tax** is the actual distribution of the burden of tax payments.

Consider what happens when a $1 tax is levied on each carton of cigarettes. Cigarette manufacturers supply fewer cigarettes at established prices, thereby raising the price. When the price of cigarettes rises, the manufacturer has *shifted the tax forward* so that the consumer is paying a part of the tax in the form of a higher price. If the price rises by $0.80 as a consequence of the $1 tax, then 80 percent of the tax has been shifted forward to the consumer. In this example, most of the tax burden is borne not by the manufacturer, but by the final consumer.

A tax is shifted forward to the consumer when the consumer pays a portion of the tax by paying a higher price for the product.

Virtually any tax—an income tax, a sales tax, a payroll tax, a wealth tax, an inheritance tax, or a tariff on foreign goods—can be shifted. An increase in income tax rates may persuade physicians to reduce their patient load. If physicians generally reduce their supply of labor, physicians' fees rise. Who has paid the tax? The patient pays a portion of the tax in the form of higher doctors' bills. If the government places a tax on imported cars, car buyers pay in the form of higher prices on imported cars.

Taxes and Efficiency

The fairness of a tax system is only one measure of how "good" it is. Tax systems can also be judged by how they affect economic efficiency.

Taxes can cause people to change their economic behavior. When the corporate income tax taxes dividends twice, corporations are encouraged not to pay dividends. Increases in income tax rates may cause high-income earners to reduce their supply of effort. High property taxes affect where people and businesses locate. Tax breaks on the restoration costs cause historic buildings to be preserved. Sales taxes cause prices to rise. All these taxes affect private economic decisions; however, a **neutral tax** does not.

A **neutral tax** cannot be altered by any change in private production, consumption, or investment decisions.

Society would like to operate on its production possibilities frontier. If taxes reduce output, then the tax has reduced the efficiency of the economy.

Public-finance specialists agree that it is very difficult, if not impossible, to devise a neutral tax system. Any tax that individuals could reduce as a consequence of their actions is not neutral. A $1000 tax on each adult male between the ages of 20 and 55 would be neutral because there is nothing the taxpayer can do to avoid or reduce the tax (outside of a sex-change operation). But such a tax would violate both the benefit principle and the ability-to-

EXAMPLE 3 The Fall of Margaret Thatcher and the Poll Tax

Public-finance specialists have demonstrated that the most "efficient" tax is a neutral tax because it is not affected by private economic decisions and, therefore, will not change the taxpayer's behavior.

British Prime Minister Margaret Thatcher resigned in 1991 due in part to the unpopularity of her poll tax—a neutral tax sponsored by Thatcher's Conservative government. This levy on all adults was designed to replace property taxes. The poll tax was the same for rich and poor alike.

Thatcher's poll tax was economically efficient, but it had no friends, only enemies. The Labour opposition described the poll tax as "a fox they were delighted to shoot at." When John Major replaced Thatcher as prime minister, his first move was to replace the hated poll tax with a property tax based on the value of the property.

Thatcher's experience with the poll tax shows that economic efficiency criteria are not persuasive when the public regards a tax measure as unfair.

Source: "Britain's Prime Minister Jettisons Poll Tax," *Christian Science Monitor*, April 25, 1991.

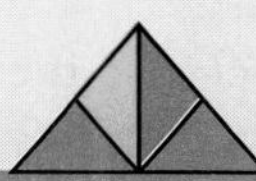

pay principle. A tax that takes 20 percent of income is not neutral because individuals can reduce the tax by earning less income. (See Example 3.)

Marginal Tax Rates and Work Effort. Labor-supply decisions can be affected by the tax system. When deciding whether to work overtime, whether both husband and wife should work, or whether to play golf 1 or 2 days a week, individuals consider their **marginal tax rate.**

> The **marginal tax rate** is the ratio of the increase in tax payments to an increase in income. The marginal tax rate shows how much extra taxes must be paid per dollar of extra earnings.

The marginal tax rate must be distinguished from the **average tax rate.**

> The **average tax rate** is the ratio of the tax payment to taxable income.

Table 3 gives a hypothetical example of average and marginal tax rates. The tax on an income of \$10,000 is \$500, for an average tax rate of 5 percent ($\$500/\$10,000 \times 100$). The tax on an income of \$20,000 is \$1500, for an average tax rate of 7.5 percent ($\$1500/\$20,000 \times 100$). As a consequence of income increasing from \$10,000 to \$20,000 (an increase of \$10,000), the tax payment has increased by \$1000 (from \$500 to \$1500). Hence, the marginal tax rate is 10 percent ($\$1000/\$10,000 \times 100$). When income increases from \$30,000 to \$40,000, the tax increases by \$5000. The marginal tax rate at a \$40,000 income level is 50 percent ($\$5000/\$10,000 \times 100$), while the average rate is 20 percent ($\$8000/\$40,000 \times 100$).

The distinction between average and marginal tax rates is important. Suppose Ann Smith is a physician who earns \$150,000 annually and who pays an average tax rate of 40 percent (or \$60,000 a year). If working a few more hours per week would increase her taxable income by \$50,000 (from \$150,000 to \$200,000), Smith's taxes would rise to \$90,000. The \$50,000 increase in taxable income would cause taxes to rise by \$30,000. Her marginal tax rate is the ratio of the increase in taxes (\$30,000) to the increase in earnings (\$50,000), or 60 percent.

Taxpayers base their economic decisions on marginal tax rates rather than on average tax rates. For example, faced with a marginal tax rate of 60 percent, Smith may decide it is not worth the extra effort to earn an additional \$50,000 of taxable income if she can only keep \$20,000. If she decides not to work the extra hours, economic efficiency has been reduced

TABLE 3
Average and Marginal Tax Rates: A Hypothetical Example

Income (dollars) (1)	Tax Payment (dollars) (2)	Average Tax Rate (percent) (3)	Marginal Tax Rate (percent) (4)
10,000	500	5.0	—
20,000	1500	7.5	10
30,000	3000	10.0	15
40,000	8000	20.0	50

The average tax rate is the ratio of column 2 to column 1. It represents the percentage of income paid in taxes. The marginal tax rate is the ratio of the increase in the tax payment to the increase in income. As income rises from $10,000 to $20,000, the tax payment rises from $500 to $1500, for a marginal tax rate of 10 percent.

because the economy is producing fewer goods and services than it would have without the tax.

Some tax reformers favor lowering marginal tax rates to encourage greater work effort. They argue that lower marginal tax rates would raise the output of goods and services, thereby improving economic efficiency. This type of thinking played an important role in the 1986 tax reforms. (See Example 4.)

Workability. In addition to being fair, a good tax system must be simple and certain and must have reasonable compliance and collection costs. A tax is *simple* if taxpayers can determine their tax liability without incurring substantial costs. The tax system should not force people to bear large accounting and legal costs. A tax is *certain* if taxpayers are able to ascertain the tax consequences of their actions when they make their economic decisions. The rules of the game must be known by all, and changes in those rules should not affect actions that have already been taken. Finally, the tax system should not have high collection costs.

Taxes and Social Goals

Opponents of neutral taxes argue that the tax system should be used as an instrument of social policy. Because people respond to marginal tax rates, the tax system can be engineered to cause people to engage in desirable behavior. For example, society may wish to promote private home ownership, so it offers tax incentives to buy homes. Society may wish to encourage marriage, so it taxes married couples at lower rates. Society may wish to encourage risk taking or innovation, so it gives tax breaks to those who earn income through innovation and risk taking.

Taxes will continue to affect economic decision making. The challenge to politicians and tax authorities is to devise a tax system that minimizes the efficiency losses of nonneutral taxes while moving society in the direction of desirable social goals.

The U.S. tax system consists of a variety of federal, state, and local taxes. The federal government obtains the overwhelming portion of its revenues from individual income taxes and Social Security contributions. (See Table 4.) Corporate income taxes and sales taxes (excises, customs, and duties) account for a small percentage of the total. Over the past quarter century, the structure of federal revenues has changed substantially. The revenue share of the personal income tax has remained fairly steady at around 44 percent, but the shares of the corporate income tax and of sales taxes have dropped considerably. The share of Social Security contributions has risen considerably (from about 12 percent in 1955 to more than 40 percent today).

The structure of financing state and local governments has changed as well over the past quarter

EXAMPLE 4 The U.S. Income Tax: A Brief History

In 1913, the Sixteenth Amendment to the U.S. Constitution authorized the federal government to levy a personal income tax. Prior to World War II, the personal income tax was not a major source of federal government revenue. In the 1930s, it accounted for only about 14 percent of federal revenues. Tax rates were low. In the 1920s and 1930s, the tax rate on the lowest income bracket ranged from 1 to 4 percent and the tax rate on an income of $100,000 (the equivalent of more than $1 million in the early 1990s) was no higher than 25 percent. It was during World War II that the federal personal income tax became the federal government's most important revenue source. Tax rates on the bottom and top income brackets were raised (to over 20 for the bottom income bracket and to a high of 92 percent for the top income bracket). By the end of the war, the 1948 personal income tax accounted for 40 percent of all federal revenue.

The United States entered the postwar era with high personal tax rates. In 1951, for example, the tax rate on the top income bracket ($200,000 and above) was 91 percent. Tax rates of this magnitude were clearly unacceptable; therefore, various tax reforms altered the personal income tax system in three directions between 1951 and 1986. First, tax rates were reduced. By 1970, the tax rate on the lowest income bracket was 20 percent, and the tax rate on the top income bracket was 75 percent. The tax reform of 1981 lowered rates to a range of 11 to 50 percent and indexed tax rates to prevent them from being pushed up by inflation.

The second direction was to allow numerous deductions and exemptions from taxable income. Over the years, interest earned on bonds of state and local governments (so-called *tax-exempt bonds*), contributions to retirement programs (such as Keogh accounts), taxes paid to state and local governments, medical expenditures, charitable contributions, fire and theft losses, and child-care costs for working mothers have been deductible. Capital gains were taxed at a lower rate than other forms of income.

The third direction of tax change was to use the personal income tax to promote economic or social goals. Tax credits for investments in equipment (the investment tax credit) were used to encourage capital formation. The deduction of certain forms of savings (such as in retirement accounts) from taxable income encouraged increased savings. Mortgage-interest deductions encouraged home ownership.

All these changes had made the federal income tax extremely complex. The system's critics felt it gave too many tax loopholes to the rich and that its high marginal tax rates discouraged hard work and risk takings.

In September of 1986, Congress passed, and President Reagan signed, the Tax Reform Act of 1986. The number of tax rates was reduced from the previous fourteen (ranging from 11 percent to 50 percent) to three (15 percent, 28 percent, and 34 percent). The top rate on taxable income was lowered from 50 percent to 34 percent. Tax rates were adjusted for inflation by indexing tax-rate brackets, personal exemptions, and standard deductions to inflation. Many low-income families were removed from the tax rolls.

Deductions, exemptions, and exclusions from income were dramatically restricted to make up for the loss of tax revenue due to lower tax rates. Special tax treatment of certain industries such as oil drilling, cattle raising, and apartment constuction was terminated. Capital gains income was no longer taxed at lower rates than ordinary income. Corporate income taxes were raised.

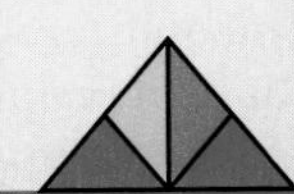

TABLE 4
Sources of Federal Government Revenue, 1955 and 1991

Source of Revenue	1955		1991	
	Percentage of Total Revenue for the Year			
Taxes		87.6		59.6
Individual income	44.6		43.8	
Corporate income	27.5		9.8	
Sales taxes, customs, excises	15.5		6.0	
Social Security contributions		12.4		40.4
Total		**100.0**		**100.0**

Sources: *Historical Statistics of the United States,* Series Y567–89; *Economic Report of the President.*

TABLE 5
Sources of Local and State Government Revenue, 1955 and 1991

Source of Revenue	1955		1991	
	Percentage of Total Revenue for the Year			
Taxes		65.5		55.6
Individual income	4.0		12.4	
Corporate income	2.4		3.3	
Sales taxes	24.5		21.1	
Property taxes	34.6		18.8	
Revenue from federal government		10.0		16.1
All other (other taxes and charges and miscellaneous revenues)		24.5		28.3
Total		**100.0**		**100.0**

Sources: *Historical Statistics of the United States,* Series Y652–70; *Economic Report of the President.*

century. (See Table 5.) The share of sales taxes in total revenues has remained fairly steady, at around one-quarter, but there has been a notable drop in the share of property taxes and a notable rise in the share of state income taxes. Local and state governments have become more dependent upon transfers from the federal government, which accounted for 16 percent of revenue in 1991.

The Federal Individual Income Tax

As Table 4 shows, personal income tax is the most important single source of revenue for the federal government. The current federal income tax system is the result of countless changes, reforms, and revisions. (See Example 4.)

The U.S. federal income tax is administered for the U.S. Treasury by the Internal Revenue Service. In its current form, the personal income tax is levied on **taxable income** according to tax rates set by Congress. Currently, taxable income is taxed at three rates: 15 percent, 28 percent, and 34 percent.

Taxable income is the income that remains after all deductions and exemptions are subtracted. Taxes are levied on taxable income.

Taxpayers are allowed to take itemized deductions (medical and dental expenses, state and local taxes, mortgage interest, and charitable contributions), standard deductions for each family member, and contributions to retirement accounts from their gross income. Because of these various subtractions, taxable income is reduced; on average it is approximately 65 percent of gross income.

Effective tax rates measure the *average* percentage of gross income paid in federal income taxes. The taxpayer's *marginal* tax rate measures by how much the tax increases for each extra dollar of income. Table 6 shows that these marginal rates vary from 0 percent to 34 percent. Both average and marginal tax rates rise with income. For example, low-income families earning $10,000 per year or less pay no income taxes; families earning $25,000 per year pay almost 7 percent of their gross income in income taxes; and families earning $150,000 per year pay 20 percent of their gross income as personal income taxes.

TABLE 6
1990 U.S. Federal Personal Income Tax System (Married Couple, 2 Dependents)

Adjusted Gross Income	Tax Liability (1)	Effective Rate (percent) (2)	Marginal Rate (percent) (3)
$ 10,000	$ −953	—	0
$ 25,000	1,703	6.8	15
$ 50,000	5,960	11.9	28
$ 75,000	12,386	16.5	28
$150,000	30,530	20.4	34

Source: International Revenue Service, *Statistics of Income Bulletin.*

Since 1970, various tax reforms (particularly the 1986 tax reform) have lowered marginal tax rates in the United States. In 1970, the marginal tax rate for a family earning $75,000 per year was 56 percent. In 1991, the marginal tax rate for that same family was 34 percent. These reductions were enacted to increase the incentives to work harder and longer and to take more risks.

The federal income tax serves as an instrument of social policy through deductions and exemptions. By allowing charitable contribution deductions, families are encouraged by the tax system to give to charities. By allowing interest on home mortgages to be deducted, Congress encourages home ownership. By allowing contributions to retirement programs to be deducted, workers are encouraged to save for retirement.

Although some critics believe the current tax system should be more "neutral," the public appears to favor the current system as a method to encourage specific desirable economic activities.

The Federal Corporate Income Tax

U.S. corporations are subject to a federal tax on their profits, called the *federal corporate income tax.* As Table 4 showed, the share of the corporate income tax of total federal tax revenues has been declining over the years, accounting for about 10 percent in the early 1990s.

Prior to 1986, corporations had been allowed to reduce their taxes considerably by a number of methods. The average corporation paid only 15 percent of corporate income in corporate income taxes in the mid-1970s.[1]

The 1986 Tax Reform Act lowered the top tax rate from 46 percent to 34 percent on corporate incomes of $75,000 or more. To compensate for the lower tax rates, various exemptions and deductions were eliminated.

Critics of higher corporate income taxes argue that corporations will pass a fairly large portion of their tax increases forward in the form of higher

[1]George Break and Joseph Pechman, *Federal Tax Reform: The Impossible Dream?* (Washington, DC: The Brookings Institution, 1975), 91.

prices. Although voters may think that the tax burden of corporations is rising, this may be purely illusory.

Corporate profits that are distributed to stockholders as dividends are taxed twice: once as corporate income and again when stockholders pay taxes on their dividends (see the chapter on business organization for a more detailed discussion of double taxation). Many public-finance specialists have argued against the double taxation of corporate profits, and some propose one tax on dividends.

Social Security and Payroll Taxes

Since it was founded in 1935, the Social Security Program has been financed by a payroll tax, half of which is paid by the employer and half by the employee. Unlike the individual income tax, where families below a certain income level do not have to pay the tax, Social Security payroll taxes are paid starting with the first dollar of earnings. By 1996, the payroll tax is scheduled to be 19.7 percent of the first $72,600 of earnings with the employer paying 60 percent of the tax. A worker earning $15,000 per year would pay $1,182 in payroll taxes (and the employer would pay $1,773). Because the tax is imposed only on the first $72,600, a person earning $500,000 would pay the same tax as one earning $72,600.

Social Security payroll taxes finance the Social Security retirement, health, and disability programs. The Medicare program that subsidizes medical care for the elderly is part of the Social Security system. According to existing benefit schedules, a low-income worker retiring at age 65 receives retirement benefits greater than earnings, while the retired worker who had above-average earnings receives about one-half of previous earnings. In the early 1990s, Social Security old-age pensions replaced about two-thirds of the earnings retired couples had earned immediately before retirement.

Is the U.S. Tax System Progressive?

The U.S. tax system consists of different taxes at the local, state, and federal level. The federal tax system relies primarily on individual income and payroll taxes. State and local governments use sales and property taxes to raise their revenues.

The fraction of income paid by taxpayers who earn different amounts of income determines whether the tax system redistributes income. A tax can be either a **proportional tax,** a **progressive tax,** or a **regressive tax.**

> With **proportional tax**, each taxpaying unit pays the same percentage of income as taxes.
>
> With **progressive tax**, the percentage of income paid as taxes increases as income increases.
>
> With **regressive tax**, the percentage of income paid as taxes decreases as income increases.

The federal income tax is a progressive tax, as shown in Table 6. Families with higher incomes, up to a certain level, pay higher effective tax rates.

Sales taxes are regressive because the wealthy spend a smaller portion of their income than do the poor. Suppose a family with $40,000 of taxable income spends $20,000 and saves the rest, while a family with $10,000 taxable income spends the full $10,000. Each pays a 5 percent sales tax; the higher-income ($40,000) family pays sales taxes of $1000, or 1/40 of its income, while the lower-income ($10,000) family pays sales taxes of $500, or 1/20 of its income. Although the poor family spends fewer dollars on sales taxes, it spends a larger percentage of its income.

When progressive income taxes are combined with regressive sales taxes, is the overall U.S. tax system regressive, proportional, or progressive? The answer depends on the incidence of taxation. Economists disagree substantially on how the burden of taxes is distributed among different income groups.

In a study of taxes conducted in 1974, Joseph Pechman and Benjamin Okner concluded that the U.S. tax system was basically proportional. According to their study, only the very poor (those in the bottom 5 percent of the income distribution) and the very rich (those in the top 5 percent) paid a higher proportion of their income in taxes. For other families, the percentage of income paid in taxes was basically uniform. In a 1985 follow-up study, Pechman concluded that the U.S. tax system was still basically proportional (except at the very top and bottom) and that tax changes of the early 1980s disproportionately raised the tax rates of the poor while lowering the rates of the rich because of the rising importance of payroll taxes (see panel *a* of Figure 5).[2]

[2]Joseph Pechman and Benjamin Okner, *Who Bears the Tax Burden?* (Washington, DC: The Brookings Institution, 1974); Joseph A. Pechman, *Who Paid the Taxes, 1966–85?* (Washington, DC: The Brookings Institution, 1985).

FIGURE 5
Two Views of the Tax Burden

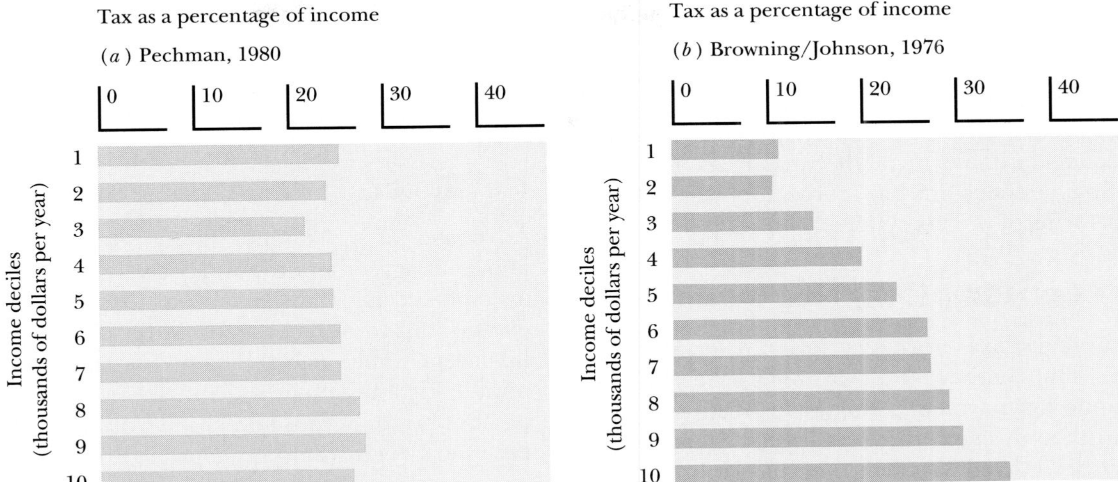

Browning and Johnson's findings for 1976 indicate that the U.S. tax system is more progressive than Pechman's findings for 1980 suggest.

Sources: Joseph Pechman, *Who Paid the Taxes, 1966–85?* (Washington, DC: The Brookings Institution, 1985). Edgar K. Browning and William R. Johnson, *The Distribution of the Tax Burden* (Washington, DC: American Enterprise Institute, 1979).

A 1979 study by Edgar Browning and William Johnson disputes the conclusion of Pechman and Okner.[3] Browning and Johnson found that the overall tax system was, as of 1976, highly progressive, as shown in panel *b* of Figure 5. Families in the bottom 10 percent of the income distribution paid 10.7 percent of their income as taxes, while families in the top 10 percent paid 36.4 percent of their income. These two studies come to different conclusions because they calculate the incidence of sales taxes differently, and they disagree on how much transfer income poor families receive.[4]

The difference of opinion over the burden of the tax system is important. If the tax burden is indeed heavier on the poor than on the rich, tax reformers could argue that the rich should be taxed more heavily. On the other hand, if the current tax system is as progressive as Browning and Johnson find, then society may be content with the existing system.

[3]Edgar K. Browning and William R. Johnson, *The Distribution of the Tax Burden* (Washington, DC: American Enterprise Institute, 1979).

[4]Edgar K. Browning, "Pechman's Tax Incidence Study: A Note on the Data," *American Economic Review*, 76(December 1986): 1214–18. Also see the reply by Pechman in the same issue, 1219–20.

Browning and Johnson argue that the transfer payments received by the poor (Social Security; welfare and so on) are raised almost automatically when prices rise because transfer payments are typically adjusted for inflation. If a sales tax causes prices to rise, the price increase will not be passed on to the poor because the poor's incomes will rise along with the price. Therefore, sales taxes are not regressive, as had been thought, but are actually progressive because they are shifted primarily to the rich.

A second reason for the wide difference between the results of the two studies is disagreement over the shares of labor and transfer income of low-income families. Browning argues that the transfer-income share of low-income families is higher than that calculated by Pechman. If a low-income family has an income of $4000 based entirely on labor earnings, then it pays 7 percent of its income as a Social Security payroll tax. If, however, another low-income family has an income of $4000 based entirely on transfer payments, then it pays no Social Security taxes because Social Security taxes are not paid on transfer payments. Therefore, the greater the share of labor income of the low-income family, the less progressive the overall tax system.

PROPOSALS FOR TAX REFORM

Our system of federal taxation has evolved over the years through a series of tax reforms, legislative amendments, and court interpretations.

Can the tax system be made significantly more efficient or equitable through further tax reform? Public-finance specialists have recommended a number of reforms of the tax system.[5]

Taxing Consumption, Not Income

Personal taxes are normally levied on personal income. The higher the earnings, the higher the income tax payments. Numerous distinguished economists and social thinkers—John Stuart Mill, Irving Fisher, Alfred Marshall, Thomas Hobbes, and Nicholas Kaldor—have favored the taxing of consumption rather than income for two reasons. First, if people are taxed according to what they take out of production (consumption) rather than according to what they put in (saving), society gains a larger stock of capital. Second, expenditures are a more accurate measure of a household's permanent spending power or ability to pay taxes than is income. Taxpayers could reduce consumption tax payments by spending less (and saving more).

Consumption taxes are typically collected as sales taxes. The *value-added tax* (or VAT) that is widely used in Europe is a form of consumption tax. Although sales taxes are regressive, consumption taxes can be made progressive. For example, taxpayers could report their income minus savings (which would equal their consumption), and then government could tax income minus savings using progressive tax rates.

Eliminating Corporate Income Taxes

As explained in an earlier chapter, corporations are useful devices for raising capital in a world of costly information and uncertainty. Many economists argue that taxing corporate income reduces the social gains of the corporation. The double taxation of dividends dams up billions of dollars of investment funds inside corporate treasuries and encourages reinvestment in the corporation itself. Eliminating the tax on corporate dividends would allow these funds to be used for other purposes. The elimination of the corporate income tax would be opposed by many as a pro-business reform, but the *social* loss due to the corporation income tax may be between 0.2 percent and 0.3 percent of total income.[6]

Flat Taxes

Advocates of a flat tax call for everyone earning above an agreed-upon poverty level to pay the same average tax rate (say, 25 percent). No deductions or exemptions from income would be allowed. Wealthy taxpayers would pay the same average tax rate as middle-income taxpayers, but they would lose their tax loopholes. Because everyone would pay the same tax rate (which would be kept low), there would be less unproductive tax-avoidance activity, and people would go about the business of earning money, not avoiding taxes.

Tax Real Capital Gains

When people sell stocks, bonds, or other assets for more than their purchase price, they earn a **capital gain.**

> A **capital gain** occurs whenever assets such as stocks, bonds, or real estate increase in market value over the price paid to acquire the asset.

The capital gain is "realized" when the asset that has risen in price is actually sold, thereby creating the gain. Prior to the 1986 tax reform, capital gains were taxed at lower rates than ordinary income to encourage people to take risks and to innovate. Since 1986, capital gains have been taxed at the same rate as other forms of income.

When a capital gain is realized on the sale of an asset that has been held for a period of time, much of the gain may be eaten up by inflation. If a stock that has been held for 10 years is sold at a price 50

[5]For a collection of studies by public-finance experts on tax reform, see Michael J. Boskin, ed., *Federal Tax Reform: Myths and Realities* (San Francisco: Institute for Contemporary Studies, 1978).

[6]Martin Feldstein and Daniel Frisch, "Corporate Tax Integration: The Estimated Effects on Capital Accumulation and Tax Distribution of Two Integration Proposals," *Discussion Paper 541* (Cambridge, MA: Harvard University Institute of Economic Research, 1980).

percent higher than the purchase price but inflation over that period has also been 50 percent, then there is no real profit after adjustment for inflation. For this reason, some public-finance experts favor taxing only real capital gains—capital gains in excess of the inflation that has occurred over the period during which the asset has been held.

Indexing for Inflation

When individuals whose earnings have been raised by inflation are pushed into higher tax brackets, their real income after taxes can be reduced. **Indexing** prevents inflation from pushing people into higher tax brackets.

> **Indexing** is the tying of tax rates to the rate of inflation. Tax rates are lowered as prices generally increase.

Critics of the current system argue that tax rates should be lowered when inflation occurs. The 1986 tax reform partially indexed the federal personal income tax by tying personal deductions to the inflation rate.

THE U.S. TAX SYSTEM IN INTERNATIONAL PERSPECTIVE

To what degree is the U.S. tax system typical of the tax systems of other industrialized countries? As Table 7 shows, taxes as a percentage of total output are relatively low in the United States, compared to other industrialized countries. With the exception of Japan, other industrialized countries collect relatively more tax revenues out of each dollar of income than the United States does. Payroll tax rates for Social Security are also lower in the United States than in the other industrialized countries (except the United Kingdom and Canada).

The United States also relies less on sales taxes than the other industrialized countries (with the exception of Japan) and more on income and profit taxes. The other countries rely on a combination of Social Security taxes and sales taxes, the most prominent of which is the VAT mentioned earlier.

This chapter examined how government collects revenues and spends income, and the effects of taxes

TABLE 7
The U.S. Tax System in International Perspective

	Tax Revenues as a Percentage of Total Output (1)	Percentage Distribution of Tax Receipts (2)		
		Income Profit Tax (a)	Social Security (b)	Sales Taxes (c)
United States	29.8	43.1	29.7	16.9
Canada	34.0	46.1	13.2	30.1
France	44.4	17.4	43.3	29.4
Italy	37.1	35.7	33.3	28.0
Japan	31.3	47.3	29.0	12.6
Netherlands	48.2	27.9	42.5	25.9
Sweden	55.3	43.9	25.1	24.2
United Kingdom	37.3	37.5	18.5	31.2
Germany	37.4	34.2	37.4	25.2

Source: *Statistical Abstract of the United States, 1991,* Comparative International Statistics.

and government expenditures on private economic activity. The next chapter will explore the question: If government action is needed, how does government work in a world of limited information, majority rule, and self-interest?

SUMMARY

1. Public finance is the study of the effects of government taxes and spending on private economic activity. Government expenditures are either exhaustive expenditures or transfer payments. Exhaustive expenditures divert resources to the public sector. Transfer payments affect the distribution of income in the private sector. Government spending rose from 10 percent of GDP in the late 1920s to 33 percent in the early 1990s. Expenditures shifted away from local government and toward state and federal government.

2. There are two competing principles of fairness in taxation. One is that taxes should be levied according to benefits received. The other is that taxes should be allocated on the basis of ability to pay. If the ability-to-pay principle is used, the tax system should have both vertical and horizontal equity.

3. A neutral tax system is one that does not influence production, consumption, and investment decisions. In reality, neutral taxes are almost impossible to devise. Taxes do affect economic efficiency. The challenge is how to devise a tax system that moves the economy in a socially desired direction without severe losses of efficiency. Taxpayers are presumed to base their economic behavior on marginal tax rates. A tax system should be simple and certain and should not involve large collection costs.

4. The U.S. tax system blends personal income taxes, corporate income taxes, sales and property taxes, and payroll taxes collected by the federal, state, and local governments. The federal tax system has changed over the years from high tax rates combined with liberal exemptions, deductions, and credits to lower effective tax rates for both individual and corporate income taxes. The tax reform of 1986 lowered tax rates for both persons and corporations and eliminated many tax loopholes that had previously eroded the tax base. There is disagreement as to whether the overall U.S. tax system is progressive or proportional.

5. Suggestions to change the current tax system include taxing consumption instead of income, eliminating the corporate income tax, taxing real capital gains, indexing for inflation, and levying a flat tax.

KEY TERMS

public finance
exhaustive expenditures
transfer payments
government surplus
government deficit
deficit financing
government debt
benefit principle
ability-to-pay principle
vertical equity
horizontal equity
incidence of a tax
neutral tax
marginal tax rate
average tax rate
taxable income
proportional tax
progressive tax
regressive tax
capital gain
indexing

QUESTIONS AND PROBLEMS

1. Explain why a tax on Japanese cars (to be paid by Japanese manufacturers) may end up being paid by someone else.
2. Explain the different principles of fairness in taxation. Why can't the benefit principle simply be applied to all taxes?
3. What is meant by vertical and horizontal equity in a tax system?
4. Mr. Jones has a taxable income of $25,000. He pays a tax of $5,000. Ms. Smith has a taxable income of $50,000. How much tax would Smith have to pay for the tax system to be:

   a. Proportional
   b. Progressive
   c. Regressive

5. Evaluate the validity of the following statement: "A tax on shoe sales that requires the dealer to pay a $2 tax on every pair of shoes sold should not be of concern to consumers because the dealer has to pay the tax."
6. Define the *marginal tax rate*.
7. Explain double taxation of corporations.
8. Why is there a trade-off between equity and efficiency in any tax system?

9. When Jones's taxable income increases by $1000, Jones's income tax increases by $200. What is Jones's marginal tax rate?
10. Explain why a consumption tax would likely result in a higher national saving rate rather than a higher income tax.
11. Proponents of flat taxes maintain that flat taxes are more fair than the existing tax system. How can they make this argument when both high-income and low-income taxpayers would pay the same rate under a flat tax?
12. The state of Michigan hires an assistant professor to teach at one of its state universities. The state of Michigan pays an unemployed automobile worker $500 in unemployment compensation out of state funds. Which transaction is an exhaustive expenditure? How will the two transactions differ in their effect on resource allocation?
13. Which of the following taxes satisfies the benefit principle? Which satisfies the ability-to-pay principle?
    a. A gasoline tax
    b. A progressive income tax
    c. A general sales tax
    d. A special levy on a community to build a dam
14. Is the Social Security payroll tax progressive or regressive? Explain your answer.

SUGGESTED READINGS

Aronson, J. Richard, and John L. Hilley. *Financing State and Local Governments*, 4th ed. Washington, DC: The Brookings Institution, 1986.

Boskin, Michael J., ed. *Federal Tax Reform: Myths and Realities.* San Francisco: Institute for Contemporary Studies, 1978.

Break, George, and Joseph Pechman. *Federal Tax Reform: The Impossible Dream?* Washington, DC: The Brookings Institution, 1975.

Browning, Edgar K., and Jacqueline Browning. *Public Finance and the Price System*, 3rd ed. New York: Macmillan, 1987.

Browning, Edgar K., and William R. Johnson. *The Distribution of the Tax Burden.* Washington, DC: American Enterprise Institute, 1979.

Musgrave, Richard A., and Peggy B. Musgrave. *Public Finance Theory and Practice*, 5th ed. New York: McGraw-Hill, 1988.

Pechman, Joseph A. *Who Paid the Taxes, 1966–85?* Washington, DC: The Brookings Institution, 1985.

Pechman, Joseph, and Benjamin Okner. *Who Bears the Tax Burden?* Washington, DC: The Brookings Institution, 1974.

"Tax Reform: A Synposium," *Journal of Economic Perspectives* 1, 1 (Summer 1987): 7–120.

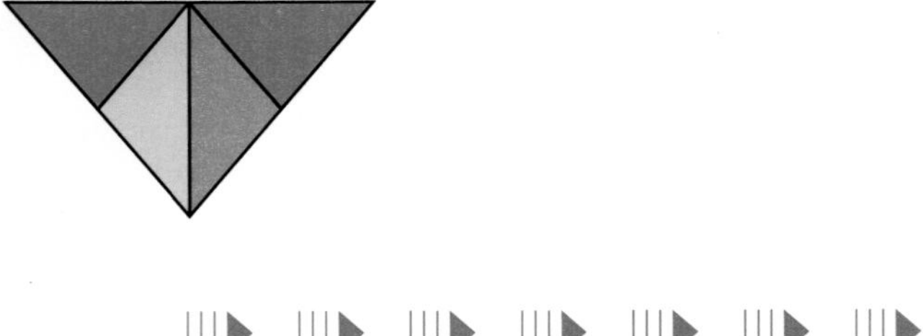

43 Public Choice

CHAPTER INSIGHT

A distinguished politician once described democracy as a flawed system; but he added that society has yet to invent anything better. This chapter describes how public choices are made in democratic societies. The previous chapter showed that government economic action is necessary: We generally agree that government must provide public goods to prevent market failure. Nonetheless, we continue to be disturbed by political decision making. Television and the press provide endless accounts of the corruption of elected and appointed officials, of costly programs that benefit narrow special-interest groups, of logrolling and vote trading in smoke-filled rooms. These instances lead us to question whether public choices are indeed being made in the best interest of the majority.

Public choice economists consider how public decisions contribute to or detract from economic efficiency. Their work has contributed to a greater understanding of the circumstances that determine government successes and failures. Indeed, public choice theory shows that it is entirely possible for government action to make a bad situation even worse.

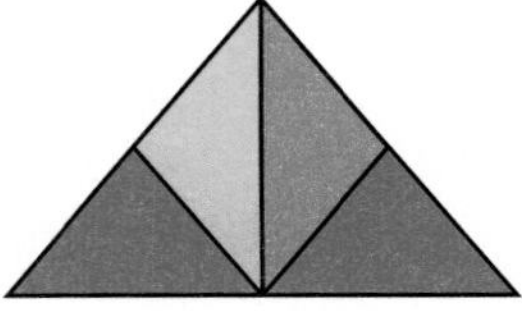

COST/BENEFIT ANALYSIS OF GOVERNMENT ACTIVITY

The rule that guides the private sector's economic decision making has been repeated over and over in this book: *Any economic activity should be carried out as long as its marginal benefit exceeds or equals its marginal cost.* The profit-maximizing firm expands its production to the point where marginal costs and marginal revenues are equal. It carries out investment projects as long as the rate of return exceeds the interest rate.

Private decision making follows the logic of cost/benefit analysis. When a firm is perfectly competitive and no externalities are involved, production is carried out to the point where price and marginal cost are equal—the result required for economic efficiency. In principle, cost/benefit analysis could play the same role in public decision making as it does in private decision making.

The efficiency rule for the public sector is similar to that for the private sector, except that it is based on a comparison between the marginal benefit and marginal cost to *society.* A government project that yields $10 million in benefits while costing $5 million is worth undertaking according to this rule. A project that yields $50 million in benefits while costing $200 million should not be undertaken.

> The optimal amount of government spending is that amount at which the marginal social costs and marginal social benefits of the last public expenditure program are equal.

Even if public officials were determined to base all public expenditure decisions on cost/benefit analysis, they would find the application difficult. The major problem is how to assess the social costs and benefits of different government programs. Consider the proposed building of a dam that will benefit down-river communities with better flood control and cheaper electricity but will displace long-time residents or threaten an endangered species of fish with extinction: What cost/benefit price tags should be placed on the project? The private firm can readily assess its own costs and benefits, but in society at large, there will often be substantial differences of opinion on costs and benefits.

Cost/benefit analysis also ignores questions of income distribution or equity. The benefits of a government program may go to one group, and its costs may be imposed on another group. Unless the people who pay the costs are somehow compensated—which seldom occurs—the government program entails some redistribution of income.

In the private sector, the market provides safeguards to prevent costs from exceeding benefits. If private firms produce a product whose benefit to society (as reflected in its market price) is less than its cost, the firm will incur losses. In the long run, it will either go out of business or switch to producing products that yield a benefit equal to or greater than cost. This process is called the **market test.**

> The **market test** ensures that goods and services in the private sector yield a benefit equal to or greater than their cost.

Goods provided by government are not subject to this market test. There is no guarantee that public expenditures will yield benefits equal to or greater than cost. Politicians make public choices with an eye toward reelection. The rest of this chapter explains how such decisions are made. Cost/benefit analysis provides a framework for evaluating the efficiency of public choices. (See Example 1.)

UNANIMITY: THE IDEAL WORLD

In an ideal world, government would work so well that everyone would unanimously approve its actions. The criterion of a perfect government is similar to that of a perfectly working price system. The price system is *efficient* when it is impossible to make anyone better off without hurting someone else. An efficient economic system makes as large a pie as possible; in an efficient system, to give one person a larger piece is to give someone else a smaller piece. An *inefficient* economic system is one in which the pie could be made larger. In a sense, unanimity is at the base of an evaluation of a good price system. When two people engage in an exchange, they are both made better off; they are unanimous in agreeing to the deal.

EXAMPLE 1 Cost/Benefit Analysis and Zero-Tolerance Drug Enforcement

This chapter teaches that government actions are not efficient if their social cost exceeds their social benefit. In 1988, the U.S. government embarked on a "zero-tolerance" drug enforcement program, whereby arrests were authorized for possession of even very small quantities of illegal drugs. A number of boats were seized in which a fraction of an ounce of marijuana or cocaine were found. Previous enforcement rules set minimum possession limits before arrests and impoundment of property were allowed.

Law enforcement officials have complained that the zero-tolerance program is economically inefficient. Law enforcement resources are limited; they cannot be stretched to apprehend all drug abusers and dealers. Previous rules set minimum possession limits to encourage law enforcement officials to pursue only those drug dealers or large users guilty of major offenses. The marginal social benefits to a big drug bust are much larger than those of apprehending a small consumer of illegal drugs. The marginal social costs of arresting small drug users far exceeds the social benefits. Without rules setting minimum possession limits, law enforcement resources will not be efficiently allocated.

A turn-of-the-century Swedish economist, Knut Wicksell, suggested that the public analogue to the private market is **unanimity.**

Unanimity is the result of a vote in which all voters agree on or consent to a particular government action.

Under certain circumstances, government action can reflect the voluntary and unanimous actions of each individual. Consider a hypothetical community that has no information costs or bargaining costs. Everyone knows everything about everyone else. In such a community, unanimous collective decisions are not difficult. Consider the adoption of a flood-control project. Flood control is a pure public good because it is nonrival in consumption and no one can be excluded from its benefits. The market will fail to provide it; the community must therefore decide how much flood control to produce. In our hypothetical community, each person's demand schedule for flood control is known to everyone else.

Suppose the community consists of individuals A, B, and C. Figure 1 shows their three demand schedules. The demand curve D_A shows person A's marginal valuation of flood control at different amounts. (Assume that the quantity of flood control is measured in terms of the height of a dam. A higher dam provides a larger "quantity" of flood control.) In Figure 1, the hundredth foot of a dam is worth $1 to person A. Because flood control is characterized by nonrival consumption, if the community provides a 100-foot dam, the same amount of flood control is available to A as to B or C. According to the three demand schedules, A's marginal valuation of the hundredth foot of a dam is $1, B's valuation is $5, and C's valuation is $6. The vertical height of each person's demand curve at any quantity of flood control is his or her marginal valuation at that quantity. The community's *total* marginal valuation of the hundredth foot of a dam is thus $12 ($1 + $5 + $6). When consumption is nonrival, the total demand curve is the *vertical sum* of each of the individual demand curves.

The demand curve for a nonrival (public) good differs from the demand curve for a rival (private) good. The market demand curve for a nonrival good is the *vertical* sum of each individual's demand curve. (Recall for contrast that the market demand curve for a rival good is the *horizontal* sum of all the individual demand curves.)

FIGURE 1
Unanimity: Benefit Taxes in an Ideal Community

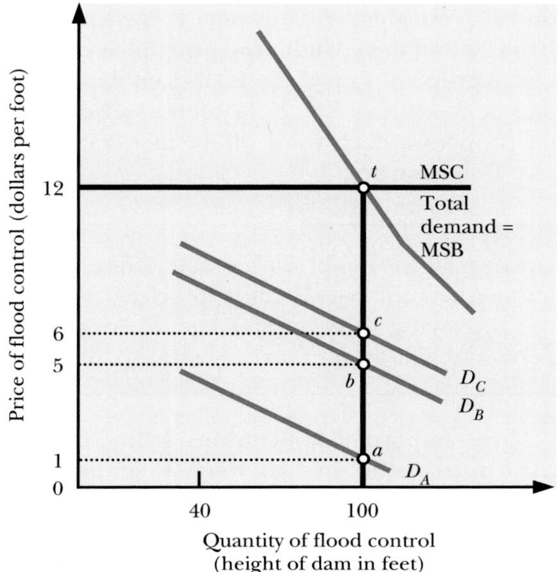

This graph represents an ideal three-person community where the demand curves of persons A, B, and C for a nonrival good—flood control—are known to all. The total demand for flood control is the vertical sum of the three individual demand curves because, with a nonrival good, providing one person with flood control provides all with flood control. The marginal social cost (MSC) of flood control is $12; the height of the demand curve measures the marginal social benefit (MSB) of flood control. The optimal amount of flood control is a 100-foot dam because marginal social cost equals marginal social benefit at 100 units. With the individual demand curves known to all, benefit taxes of $1 (per unit of flood control) imposed on A, $5 per unit imposed on B, and $6 per unit imposed on C would lead to the unanimous choice of 100 units of flood control.

The optimal quantity of flood control in Figure 1 is a 100-foot dam because the $12 marginal social cost (MSC) of this quantity of flood control (which, for simplicity, we assume to be constant) equals marginal social benefits.

In our hypothetical community, an optimal result (unanimity) can easily be attained. The ideal government knows the demand schedules of all its citizens and simply taxes them according to their marginal valuations. Thus A pays $1 per unit of flood control; B and C pay $5 and $6 per unit, respectively. The prices paid by each individual exactly match the benefits they receive. If such taxes were imposed, citizens would vote unanimously for a 100-foot dam's worth of flood control.

In the real world, governments do not have enough information to operate on the basis of unanimity. If the individual demand schedules for a public good are not known, some voting process other than unanimity must be used. The costs of discovering the government expenditure/tax program that would bring about unanimous approval are prohibitive; hence it is necessary to accept some principle of collective action short of unanimity.

MAJORITY RULE

The most popular method of making political decisions is **majority rule.** In the hypothetical three-person community, any proposal for flood control under this system would require only two yes votes to be carried out.

> **Majority rule** is a system of voting in which a government action or decision is approved if more than 50 percent of the voters approve.

For simplicity, assume that the $12 marginal cost per unit of flood control is divided equally among the three persons. The "tax price" of flood control would then be $4 per person per unit of flood control. The total tax liability of each individual would depend on the number of units the community chooses to produce.

Figure 2 illustrates the majority voting process. With a tax price of $4 per person, A prefers a 40-foot dam, B prefers a 120-foot dam, and C prefers a 140-foot dam. If any dam lower than 40 feet is proposed (the dam height desired by the person who desires the least flood control), all three would favor flood control. But B and C would not be happy with such a small dam. At a tax price of $4, B and C want a 120-foot and a 140-foot dam, respectively. To them, a 40-foot dam is far too small for the price. If a 100-foot dam (the optimal height) is proposed, A (who wants only a 40-foot dam) would vote against the proposal, but B and C would favor it over a 40-foot

FIGURE 2
Majority Rule

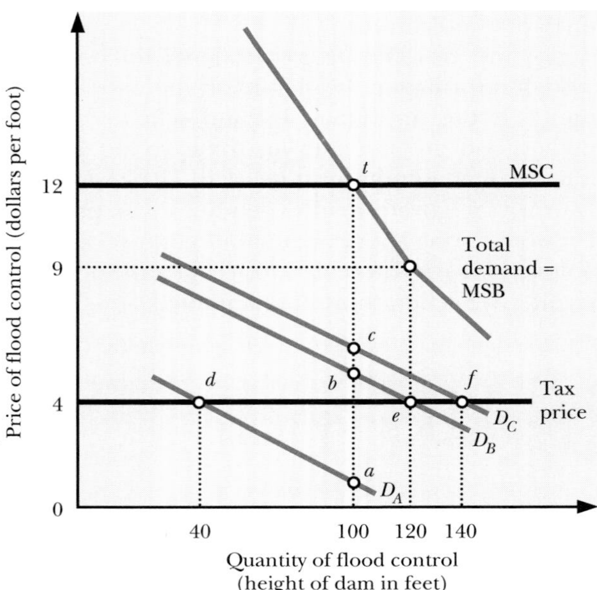

This figure represents the same three-person community portrayed in Figure 1, except that now majority rule reigns and the individual demand curves are not known to all. For simplicity, suppose that the $12-per-unit cost of flood control is shared equally by all so that the tax price is $4 per unit of flood control per person. At this price, A will want 40 units, B will want 120 units, and C will want 140 units of flood control. Voter B is the median voter; under majority rule, the median voter determines the outcome. Thus, 120 units of flood control will be provided. This quantity is inefficient because the marginal social benefit of the 120th unit is only $9 (compared to the marginal social costs of $12).

dam. However, B and C would still realize that a 100-foot dam is not enough flood control for the price. The **median voter,** B, wants a 120-foot dam.

> The **median voter** on a public expenditure program wants more expenditure than half the remaining voters and less expenditure than the other half of the remaining voters.

Voters B and C will press for higher and higher levels of flood control until the median voter is satisfied. If a 120-foot dam is proposed, A will vote against it, but both B and C will vote for it. If a dam higher than 120 feet is proposed, A and B will vote against it. Thus the median voter (B) gets his or her wish: a 120-foot dam. Under the principle of majority rule, the proposal to provide a 120-foot dam costing a total of $1440 (= $12 × 120 feet) will defeat all other proposals. Each voter will be assessed $480 to pay for flood control.

> Under majority rule, the median voter determines the outcome because precisely half of the remaining voters prefer less of the public good and half prefer more.

Three important conclusions follow from the decisive role of the median voter in simple, direct voting under majority rule.

1. *Social choices need not respond to individual wants.* Many people are dissatisfied with the government's reaction to the individual, because the votes of those in the minority (or 49 percent of the voters on some issues) do not count. The most disgruntled members of our society are those whose preferences are almost always in the minority.

2. *Majority voting rules may not reflect the relative intensity of preferences.* Because the median voter determines the outcome, a change in the intensity of anyone else's preferences has no impact. Shifting the demand curve of A downward and C upward in Figure 2 would have no impact on the outcome. The intensity of A's and C's preferences is irrelevant. Only the intensity of the median voter's preference counts. This system contrasts sharply with the market for private goods, where dollar votes for goods duly register the intensity of each person's preferences.

3. *Majority voting need not be optimal.* In Figure 2, majority rule led to a 120-foot dam, which is higher than the 100-foot dam an efficient economy would provide. Although the intensity of preferences of nonmedian voters is irrelevant, as we just saw, the intensity of preferences of nonmedian voters affects marginal social benefits. In Figure 2, too much of the public good is produced. Whether too much or too little is produced depends on the distribution of demands around the median voter. (See Example 2.)

EXAMPLE 2 The Median-Voter Rule and School District Budgets

The median-voter hypothesis states that the preferences of the median voter will dominate in single-issue elections. A number of economists have looked at public school finance referenda to determine if the level of public school expenditure per pupil typically corresponds to the level desired by the median voter. Public school finance referenda tend to be single-issue votes and should conform to the median-voter hypothesis.

Studies of finance referenda in Michigan school districts (by Randall Holcombe), in New York State school districts (by Vincent Munley), and in Long Island school districts (by Robert Inman) find that the actual level of spending per pupil is very close to that preferred by the median voter.

Surprisingly, a study for Oregon school districts fails to support the median-voter hypothesis. Economists Radu Filimon, Thomas Romer, and Howard Rosenthal find that the level of spending tends to exceed that desired by median voters. What is the explanation for these different results? In voting on school funding referenda, voters must consider the alternative to supporting the spending package proposed by the school board. If the alternative is to revert to a very low level of spending (as apparently is the case in Oregon), school boards can propose levels of spending higher than desired by the median voter, yet the median voter will approve because of the undesirable alternative. In other school districts (such as in Michigan and New York state), if the spending package proposed by the school board fails to pass, the school budget reverts to the status quo budget. In this case, the median voter feels freer to vote against school spending programs that are higher than desired.

Sources: Radu Filimon, Thomas Romer, and Howard Rosenthal, "Asymmetric Information and Agenda Control," *Journal of Public Economics* 17 (February 1982); Randall Holcombe, "An Empirical Test of the Median Voter Model," *Economic Inquiry* 18 (April 1980); Robert Inman, "Testing Political Economy's *As If* Proposition: Is the Median Voter Really Decisive?" *Public Choice* 33 (1978).

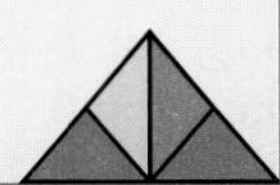

VOTING PROBLEMS

In our example, the flood-control program that was adopted had the support of the majority of voters. When more than one issue is involved, however, **logrolling,** or "pork-barrel politics," can result in the approval of policies that are actually opposed by a majority.

> **Logrolling** is the trading of votes to secure a favorable outcome on decisions of more intense interest to each voter.

Logrolling

On a single issue, differences in preference intensities have no effect on the outcome in majority-rule voting. The vote of a person who is passionately against some measure and the vote of one who is only marginally in favor are given equal weight in deciding the final outcome. But the political process involves not just one decision but a stream of decisions that are both complex and simple. The person who is only mildly in favor of one proposal might trade his or her vote with a person strongly against the proposal in exchange for a similar trade when their positions are reversed.

Consider three farmers, A, B, and C. Suppose B and C could each use a separate access road to the main highway. Farmer B would gain $7 from one

TABLE 1
Building Access Roads for Farmers B and C: Benefits Exceed Costs

Beneficiaries	Net Benefit (+) or Cost (−) of Access Road for B (dollars)	Net Benefit (+) or Cost (−) of Access Road for C (dollars)
A	−2	−2
B	+5	−2
C	−2	+5
Society	+1	+1

In this example, access roads cost \$6; these costs are shared equally by each farmer (\$2 each). But each access road is worth \$7 to the affected farmer. Building both roads is socially efficient in this case because total benefits (\$14) exceed costs (\$12). Under simple majority rule without logrolling, neither road is built, because the *number* of voters benefiting does not exceed the number of voters who do not benefit. But if farmers B and C link their vote (if both vote for both roads), then both roads can be built and society benefits.

access road, and Farmer C would gain \$7 from the other access road; each access road would cost the community \$6. This cost would be equally shared by all three farmers (\$2 each). Table 1 describes the net benefits (+) or costs (−) to each farmer from building these access roads at the public expense.

Because the \$6 cost would be shared equally, building each road has a \$2 cost per farmer. Roads built for B or C do not benefit A at all. But a road built for B gives B a net benefit of \$5, as the gains from the road are worth \$7 and B's share of the cost is only \$2. If a road is built for C, B is in the same position as A, but C gains a net benefit of \$5.

According to majority rule, if an access road for B is proposed, farmers A and C will vote against it; similarly, an access road for C will be defeated by A and B. Majority rule without logrolling causes the defeat of such special-interest legislation.

But farmers B and C will each perceive that they can gain by voting for the other farmer's access road. If farmers B and C link their votes, both roads will be built, and farmer A will have to shell out \$4 in taxes. Farmers B and C each receive a net gain of \$3 (= \$7 − \$4) from building both roads.

Whether logrolling increases or decreases economic efficiency depends on the circumstances. In this example, building both roads has a net social benefit of \$2. Each road costs \$6; each road brings benefits of \$7. Thus, from a purely social point of view, it is worthwhile to build the two roads. Without logrolling in this instance, the roads would not have been built.

But logrolling can also result in inefficiencies (see Table 2). Suppose each road brings in net benefits of only \$5 each to farmers B and C instead of \$7 each. If farmers B and C link their votes, each must pay out \$4 (\$2 for each access road). Because the benefit to B and C (\$5 each) exceeds their cost (\$4 each), it is still worthwhile to them to logroll. But now the net social benefit is −\$2 rather than +\$2.

The example described in Table 2 demonstrates that majority rule with logrolling can result in policies that reduce the size of the total economic pie. This result occurs because the majority is shifting the cost of the public good or project onto the minority. Thus it is highly likely that majority-rule voting will result in more government spending than is optimal. As James Buchanan and Gordon Tullock have stated,

> There is nothing inherent in the operation of [a majority voting] rule that will produce "desirable" collective decisions, considered in terms of individuals' own evaluations of possible social alternatives. Instead, majority rule will result in an overinvestment in the public sector when the investment projects provide differential benefits or are financed from differential taxation.[1]

[1]James Buchanan and Gordon Tullock, *The Calculus of Consent* (Ann Arbor: University of Michigan Press, 1962), 169.

TABLE 2
Building Access Roads for Farmers B and C: Costs Exceed Benefits

Beneficiaries	Net Benefit (+) or Cost (−) of Access Road for B (dollars)	Net Benefit (+) or Cost (−) of Access Road for C (dollars)
A	−2	−2
B	+3	−2
C	−2	+3
Society	−1	−1

In this case, access roads still cost $6 each, and cost is still shared equally by all three farmers. But each access road is worth only $5 to the affected farmer. Building the roads is socially inefficient in this case. Under simple majority rule without logrolling, neither road is built; but when farmers B and C link their votes, both roads are built even though the benefits to the two farmers do not exceed the costs to society.

The Paradox of Voting

Majority-rule voting may lead to paradoxical outcomes. The real world is filled with examples of policy inconsistencies. Governments pass minimum-wage laws that create unemployment and then create job-training programs to put people to work. Governments raise the cost of food to the poor through farm price supports and then give food stamps to the poor. Governments fight inflation and then put a tax on imports of cheap foreign goods.

This inconsistency can be explained by an example. Suppose three voters (A, B, and C) must vote on three policies (Alpha, Beta, and Gamma). The Alpha policy redistributes income to voter A, Beta redistributes income to voter B, and Gamma redistributes income to voter C. Table 3 describes how voters A, B, and C rank these policies. Naturally, the first choice of each voter is the policy that benefits him or her. But each voter also has preferences for the other policies as well. Voter A, for instance, might like voter B more than voter C. Hence the Beta policy is A's second choice, and Gamma policy is A's third choice. Table 3 shows that voter B prefers Gamma to Alpha and that voter C prefers Alpha to Beta.

Notice that every policy in this example is one person's first choice, another's second choice, and a third person's third choice. The table is therefore perfectly symmetrical in this respect. Only two issues are voted on at a time. In a contest between policies Alpha and Beta, voter C determines the outcome because A and B vote for their own policies. Because voter C prefers Alpha to Beta, the Alpha policy wins.

Table 4 shows the three possible contests and outcomes. In each contest, a different policy wins. No one policy wins more than one contest. If someone witnessed only the first two contests and saw that Alpha was preferred to Beta and Beta to Gamma, logic would suggest that Alpha should be preferred

TABLE 3
Policy Rankings

Policy	Voter A	Voter B	Voter C
Alpha	First choice	Third choice	Second choice
Beta	Second choice	First choice	Third choice
Gamma	Third choice	Second choice	First choice

TABLE 4
Possible Contests and Outcomes

Contest	Winning Policy
Alpha versus Beta	Alpha
Beta versus Gamma	Beta
Alpha versus Gamma	Gamma

to Gamma. However, the third row of Table 4 shows that Gamma is preferred to Alpha. Majority rule has resulted in an inconsistent outcome, the **paradox of voting.** If one reverses the second and third choices of just one of the voters, however, the paradox disappears.

The **paradox of voting** is that majority rule can yield inconsistent social choices. Even if each voter is perfectly rational, the majority of voters can choose *a* over *b*, *b* over *c*, and then *c* over *a*.

THE POLITICAL MARKET

The political market consists of voters, politicians, political parties, special-interest groups, and government bureaucracy. How does each group affect the public choices made by democratic governments?

Voters

After an election, journalists and television commentators frequently bemoan the difficulty of motivating people to vote. The decline in voter turnout in the U.S. presidential elections from 1960 to the 1992 election has led observers to conclude that there is considerable voter apathy.

What motivates a person to vote? Objectively, there is a marginal cost (in time and effort) of going to vote. The probability of any single person's vote deciding an election is close to zero. According to one study,[2] most people vote out of a sense of obligation and duty, but an important determinant of voter turnout is the cost of going to the polls and the closeness of the election. If people expect a close election, the chances of voting are larger.

The evidence suggests that people make a cost/benefit calculation when they decide whether or not to vote. The benefit voters enjoy is the knowledge that they have performed their civic duty; this benefit increases with closer elections. Thus, in the 1988 election, the perception that Republican George Bush would easily win over Democrat Michael Dukakis may have contributed to the relatively low 50 percent voter turnout.

Do people make informed decisions when they go to the polls? Anthony Downs calls the lack of information gathering on the part of the voting public **rational ignorance.**[3]

Rational ignorance is a decision not to acquire information because the marginal cost exceeds the marginal benefit of gathering the information.

An earlier chapter on information costs explained that people gather information as long as the extra benefits exceed the extra cost. The cost of acquiring information is greater for public choices than for private choices because public programs are more complicated than most private goods and the link between the act of voting and the benefits received is very uncertain. Hence most people know much more about private choices than public ones. This ignorance is a rational response to the costs of information.

Special-Interest Groups

The major implication of rational ignorance is that voters know much more about legislation that affects them than about legislation that affects someone else. Thus **special-interest groups** emerge.

Special-interest groups are minority groups with intense, narrowly defined preferences about specific government policies.

[2] O. Ashenfelter and S. Kelly, Jr., "Determinants of Participation in Presidential Elections," *Journal of Law and Economics* 18 (December 1975): 695–733.

[3] Anthony Downs, *An Economic Theory of Democracy* (New York: Harper and Row, 1957).

Dairy farmers are very well-informed about milk price supports; many consumers do not even know they exist. The benefits to dairy farmers from higher milk price supports are enormous; the costs to the typical voter are comparatively small. To the individual voter, the cost of finding out about the milk price support program exceeds the increase in the price caused by the program. Thus the dairy farmers have intense preferences for milk price supports and the rest of the public is nearly indifferent. In this type of situation, logrolling and vote trading among politicians can result in special-interest legislation that is economically inefficient. (See Example 3.)

Politicians and Political Parties

President John F. Kennedy was fond of quoting the typical mother who wanted her offspring to grow up to be president but did not want a politician in the family. For reasons imbedded deep in human psychology, people expect politicians to behave on a higher or more altruistic level than the average person. When politicians act just like anyone else, people are disappointed in their low moral character.

The successful politician is a political entrepreneur who determines government policies by voting and logrolling. Like a private entrepreneur who stays in business by offering consumers what they want, the political entrepreneur who earns his or her living by getting reelected, can only stay in office by offering a platform of positions that will attract enough votes at election time. The rewards of reelection are many: popularity, power, prestige, and increased income opportunities. The public choice economist assumes that politicians are more interested in getting votes than in serving the public

EXAMPLE 3 One Man, One Vote, and the Dairy Subsidy

In September of 1984, the U.S. House of Representatives voted on whether to continue the government program of dairy price supports that expert testimony indicated would cost dairy consumers an extra 60 cents a gallon plus their share of the $2.7 billion, 5-year cost of the program as taxpayers. Insofar as millions of dairy consumers would be hurt by the program and only 200,000 dairy farmers would be helped, one would have expected elected representatives to vote against the dairy subsidy. In fact, the dairy subsidy was passed by a 78-vote majority.

The congressional victory of the dairy farmers shows how a relatively small group of persons who stand to gain a great deal from a government program can muster more votes than a much larger, diverse group of people who each stand to lose a relatively small sum of money. The dairy cooperatives collected $3.3 million for political contributions by withholding contributions from the checks sent to dairy farmers for selling their milk. The dairy cooperatives then made sizeable contributions to 327 congressional candidates, including even those running in big cities who had no dairy producers in their districts. One congressman from a large city has the distinction of being the fifteenth highest recipient of dairy money. The statistical evidence shows a strong correlation between dairy money and voting behavior, as shown in the accompanying table.

Dairy Contributions Received from 1979 to 1984	Recipients Voting for Dairy Subsidies in 1985 (percent)
More than $30,000	100
$20,000 to $30,000	97
$10,000 to $20,000	81
$2500 to $10,000	60
$1 to $2500	33
$0	23

Source: Philip M. Stern, *The Best Congress Money Can Buy* (New York: Pantheon Books, 1988), 45–47.

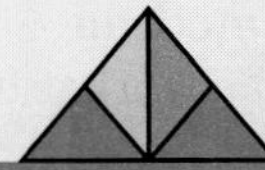

EXAMPLE 4 Special Interest Legislation

A Texas legislator, Representative Sue Schechter (D-Houston), has complained that members of the Texas House of Representatives are overly responsive to the desires of special-interest groups and primarily concerned with securing their own reelection. For example, the House rejected all the amendments in an ethics bill that prohibited gifts from paid lobbyists or required full disclosure. One legislator (a real estate agent) exempted himself from the educational requirements of ordinary real estate agents!

To reform this system, Schechter recommends a term limitation. She feels that if legislators knew they would not be returning year after year, they might vote their consciences. As it stands now, a representative will often vote to pass a bill just to get along with the other House members.

According to Schechter, journalists help perpetuate the system. "Newspapers must identify the people carrying self-interest legislation and reveal who is pushing what to the floor and why. The process is being hidden by reporters who are accustomed to the status quo," she states.

This frank statement by a political insider is consistent with the hypothesis made by public choice theorists that politicians are motivated by the desire to be reelected rather than to promote the public good.

Source: Rep. Sue Schechter, "The Legislature Lacks Integrity, and Process Must Be Changed," *Houston Chronicle*, July 23, 1991.

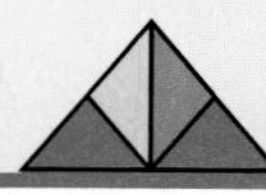

interest. Even if they are completely unselfish, politicians cannot serve society unless they are reelected. (See Example 4.)

Remembering that voters are rationally ignorant about the complex group of policies a particular politician supports, a vote-maximizing politician can put together a package of policies in support of special-interest legislation that benefits a minority but hurts the majority. Each member of each minority will benefit enormously while each member of the majority will be hurt only a trivial amount. The politician can thereby attract enough support from a coalition of minority groups to win. The politician who opposes all the special-interest legislation might be looking for a job after the next election.

> The central problem of public choice is that the benefits of government policies are highly concentrated while the costs are highly diffused.

Restricting Japanese car imports makes the American automobile manufacturer and automobile worker better off in an obvious way. The costs of import restrictions, however, are distributed over the entire population in such a subtle fashion that the public cannot distinguish between the increase in the price caused by the policy and, say, inflation. The French economist, Frederick Bastiat, referred to this as *what is seen* and *what is unseen*. What is seen is the fact that auto firms and workers are better off with import restrictions; what is unseen is that the price of automobiles is higher for everyone. The consumer does not know how much of the price paid for sugar is a result of import restrictions on imported sugar. But American sugar producers and workers are very aware of the protection.

Not all government policies make the public worse off. Yet the same political process that provides valuable pure public goods may result in inefficient levels of public goods (which may be unavoidable) and costly special-interest policies.

Bureaucrats

Aside from assorted lobbyists and pressure groups, the final actor on the political stage is the much-maligned **bureaucrat.**

A **bureaucrat** is a nonelected government official responsible for carrying out a specific, narrowly defined task.

A bureaucracy is needed to run the government programs enacted by politicians. The bureaucrats tend to be the experts (social scientists, lawyers, accountants) who execute the programs.

Many observers have pointed out that bureaucracies tend to produce budgets that are too large. In market firms, profits provide the incentive to minimize costs. If the firm's resources are not allocated efficiently, profits will fall or the firm will go out of business. In bureaucracies, there are few incentives to minimize costs—instead, bureaucrats may maximize "personal profits" in the form of plush offices or European trips.

Because of their rational ignorance, the ultimate beneficiaries of bureaucratic efficiency—the taxpayers—do not even know when bureaucrats succeed in running their offices or agencies more efficiently. Because of *their* rational ignorance, elected politicians cannot monitor the large budgets they must approve. Legislators, who must be concerned with thousands of different programs, get the bulk of their information from the very bureaucracies they are trying to oversee. The bureaucrat has an enormous information advantage over the typical legislator. Because the bureaucrat is interested in expanding the budget and the legislator is not interested in cutting out the program completely (because of the importance of special interests), the budget will tend to be larger than necessary.

Competition among Local Communities

Not all voting occurs at the ballot box. As economist Charles Tiebout points out, voters can "vote with their feet." Households, Tiebout observes, are not frozen in particular localities but can instead shop around for the bundle of public goods and taxes that most closely approximates their demands for local public goods, such as parks, police protection, roads, zoos, and schools.[4] Consumers thus have some discretion over their consumption of public services. The competitive aspects of the provision of public services may stimulate local officials to try to minimize costs and respond to consumer tastes.

Proposals for Government Reform

Economic analysis suggests that some government resource allocations may be carried too far while others are not carried far enough. Many people support the view that government is too large. They criticize the combination of special interests, logrolling, and rational ignorance on the part of both the public and our representatives. Public spending in support of particular groups or industries—such as agriculture or steel—they maintain, is in the public interest.

Anthony Downs has pointed out that rational ignorance is also responsible for government's being too small. According to Downs, the voter will usually underestimate the *benefits* (not just the costs) of fully justifiable government expenditures because they are remote and uncertain. In Downs's view, a fully informed voter would vote for larger budgets, but voters are not so informed because of private information costs. John Kenneth Galbraith has also argued that private advertising makes people more aware of private needs than public needs.

Many public choice economists believe that government has grown too large. The 1986 Nobel Prize winner James Buchanan argues that constitutional limits must be imposed on democratic governments in order to constrain their inherent tendencies to overexpand.

> Modern America confronts a crisis of major proportions in the last decades of the 20th century. In the seven decades from 1900 to 1970, total government spending in real terms increased 40 times over, attaining a share of one third in national product. These basic facts are familiar.... The point of emphasis is that this growth has occurred, almost exclusively, within the predictable workings of orderly democratic procedures.[5]

[4]Wallace E. Oates, "On Local Finance and the Tiebout Model," *American Economic Review* 71 (May 1981): 93–98.

[5]James M. Buchanan, *The Limits of Liberty* (Chicago: The University of Chicago Press, 1975), 162. Chapter 9 of Buchanan's book contains compelling reasons why governments can get too large.

EXAMPLE 5 The Role of Government in Economic Growth

Although it is difficult to determine whether democracy is the most efficient form of government, economists *can* consider the more limited issue of the impact of government spending on economic growth. If democracy is efficient, government spending should *not* lower economic growth.

Government spending can be divided into two categories: consumption spending and investment spending. Government consumption includes education and defense expenditures, but excludes public investment (e.g., roads) and transfers (e.g., social security) from total government spending.

Kevin Grier and Gordon Tullock studied the relationship between government consumption and economic growth in 115 countries. They found that there is a significantly negative relationship between the growth rate of a country and the share of its output devoted to government consumption. In a study of 98 countries, Robert Barro found a similar relationship when defense and education expenditures are excluded from the definition of government consumption. But Barro found that government investment appeared to have a very small positive impact on the rate of economic growth.

Source: Robert J. Barro, "Government Spending in a Simple Model of Endogenous Growth," *Journal of Political Economy* 98 (October 1990): S103–S125.

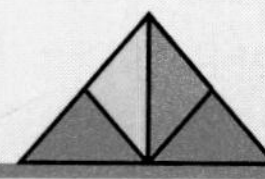

Modern public choice theory suggests that, regardless of the size of government, there are substantial government failures involved in the way public choices are made. The preferences of everyone, from the lowest worker to the captain of industry, should be duly registered when public choices are made. Currently, however, the median voter dominates; logrolling and vote trading allow the passage of special-interest legislation; voters are rationally ignorant about the costs and benefits of government programs. Thus, as Buchanan has argued, there is constant pressure for the government to engage in economically inefficient activities. Public choice economists have proposed a variety of reforms to make government more responsive to individual preferences, including the following:

1. A three-fourths majority should be required for some types of legislation (particularly obvious special-interest legislation, such as tariffs, price supports, minimum-wage laws, and loans to bankruptcy-prone firms).
2. Decisions on major proposals should be made by direct majority voting by the general public.
3. All new expenditure programs should be linked to a visible tax increase.
4. Members of Congress should be determined by a process of random selection from the general public.[6]

These reforms attempt to address the problems of rational ignorance, logrolling, and the overrepresentation of special interests.

DEMOCRACIES AND ECONOMIC EFFICIENCY

The argument that democracies produce inefficient results has been questioned by some economists, who contend that both the private market and the public market are subject to the same forces.[7] In the private market, problems arise when principals have differ-

[6]The proposals are given in E. Browning and J. Browning, *Public Finance and the Price System,* 3rd ed. (New York: Macmillan Publishing Co., 1987).

[7]See Donald Wittman, "Why Democracies Produce Efficient Results," *Journal of Political Economy* 97 (December 1989): 1395–1424.

ent goals than their agents. For example, a firm might want to enter into a long-term contract with an employee with incentives to ensure that the employee works on behalf of the firm. A temporary worker might simply take his or her salary and run. Similarly, politicians may be considered agents with the voters as their principals. Competition from other politicians, the need to maintain their reputations, and monitoring by various organizations could prevent politicians from engaging in excessively opportunistic behavior.

In the private market, a corporation's management is prevented from shirking its duty by the constant threat of a takeover in which the members of the management team could lose their jobs. Similarly, politicians can lose office by engaging in opportunistic behavior. In the political market, elections are a cheap way of carrying out political takeovers.

Despite voter ignorance, lack of competition, and the costs of forming coalitions, then, it is nonetheless possible for the political and private markets to work as well as can be expected on the problems for which each is suited. Many have pointed out that however imperfect democracy may be, we must always consider the alternative. (See Example 5.)

This chapter examined how government works in the political economic system of democratic capitalism. It focused on the manner in which the self-interest of politicians and bureaucrats combined with limited information can often result in poor public policies.

SUMMARY

1. Cost/benefit analysis suggests that government spending should be carried to the point where marginal social benefits and marginal social costs are equal. Cost/benefit analysis could serve as a substitute for the market test that private goods must pass.

2. The government must make resource allocations because the market fails to efficiently allocate public goods. In an ideal world, all government actions would have the unanimous support of all citizens. Unanimous collective decisions, however, require perfect information and zero bargaining costs. Governments would have to price public goods according to each individual's marginal valuation of the good.

3. Unanimity is virtually impossible in the real world. The most popular alternative in democratic societies is majority rule. Under majority rule, the median voter decides on public goods. Social choices therefore do not reflect the relative intensities of preferences of different voters. Majority rule does not guarantee that the socially optimal amount of the public good will be produced.

4. Majority rule makes logrolling possible in situations involving more than one decision. By forming vote-trading coalitions, beneficiaries of public goods can create majorities that would not have been possible otherwise. Majority voting can also lead to the paradox of voting.

5. The political market consists of voters, politicians, political parties, special-interest groups, and the government bureaucracy. Voters use personal cost/benefit analysis in their voting decisions; they vote when the perceived costs are low and the perceived benefits are high. Voting decisions are characterized by *rational ignorance.* The costs to most voters of acquiring information on complex public issues are high, and the benefits are low. For special-interest groups, however, the benefits are high relative to the costs of acquiring information. Politicians must adopt policies that will improve their chances of reelection. The fact that voters are rationally ignorant and do not see the effects of many government policies encourages special-interest legislation.

6. Economic analysis indicates that government undertakes many programs for which the marginal social benefits do not exceed the marginal social costs or that government fails to undertake many programs for which the marginal social benefits exceed the marginal social costs. Public choice economists have offered suggestions on how to improve public choices. These suggestions attempt to solve the problems of rational ignorance, logrolling, and overrepresentation of special interests.

7. From the viewpoint of the principal/agent problem, democracies might be just as efficient in their sphere as the private market is in its sphere.

KEY TERMS

market test
unanimity
majority rule
median voter
logrolling
paradox of voting
rational ignorance
special-interest groups
bureaucrat

QUESTIONS AND PROBLEMS

1. What factors limit unanimity on political decisions?
2. Some politicians have been observed to switch their positions in the course of political contests (for example, between the primary and the general election). Is this fact consistent with the theory of the role of the median voter in majority-rule elections? Why or why not?
3. If people are rational, how can public choice result in government actions with benefits that are less than the costs?
4. Explain why government bureaucrats would be less interested in cost minimization than would managers of private firms.
5. Do you think government is more or less efficient than a competitive enterprise? Is it more or less efficient than private monopoly? Explain.
6. Do you think lobbying promotes or reduces the general welfare? Explain.
7. How would you reform the political process to make majority rule work better?
8. Evaluate the validity of the following statement: "The more localized are public goods, the more likely it is that unanimity can be achieved in public choices."
9. There was much discussion of a balanced-budget amendment in the popular press during the Reagan administration. How would you justify such an amendment in terms of the concepts used in this chapter?
10. How can majority rule be inefficient? Does inefficiency mean majority rule should be avoided?
11. Must logrolling result in economic inefficiency? Explain.
12. Bob prefers apples over bananas and bananas over oranges. Maria prefers oranges to apples and apples to bananas. Sam prefers bananas to apples and apples to oranges. If majority rule is used to choose among these goods, does a voting paradox arise?
13. Would a world with zero information costs have economic inefficiency in the provision of government services?
14. Art, Bob, and Charlie own a lake in Wisconsin that they use for recreational purposes. A mosquito abatement program will benefit all. Art places a value of $1, Bob places a value of $19, and Charlie places a value of $100 on a mosquito-free environment. A firm will spray the lake and charge each owner $35.

    a. What decision would be reached under majority rule? Would the result be efficient?
    b. What decision would be reached if Art, Bob, and Charlie could engage in costless negotiation? Could unanimity be achieved?

SUGGESTED READINGS

Browning, F., and J. Browning. *Public Finance and the Price System,* 3rd ed. New York: Macmillan, 1987.

Buchanan, James M. *The Limits of Liberty.* Chicago: The University of Chicago Press, 1975.

Buchanan, James M., and Gordon Tullock. *The Calculus of Consent.* Ann Arbor: University of Michigan Press, 1962.

Downs, Anthony. *An Economic Theory of Democracy.* New York: Harper and Row, 1957.

Mueller, Dennis C. *Public Choice,* rev. ed. Cambridge: Cambridge University Press, 1989.

Romer, Thomas. "Nobel Laureate: On James Buchanan's Contributions to Public Economics." *Journal of Economic Perspectives* 2 (Fall 1988): 165–79.

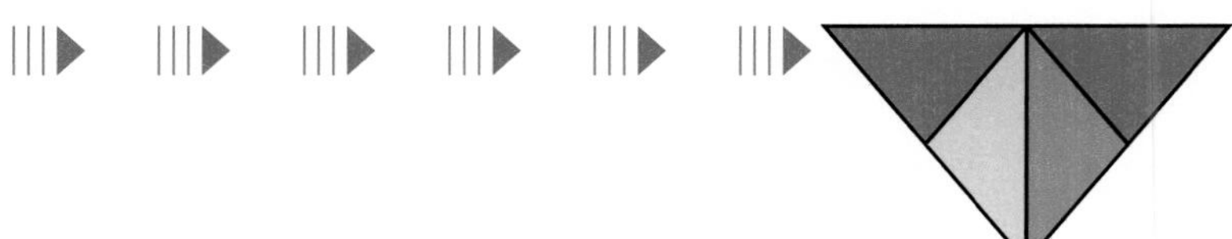

GLOSSARY

ability-to-pay principle states that those better able to pay should bear the greater burden of taxes, whether or not they benefit more **(42)**.

absolute advantage in the production of a good exists for a country if it uses fewer resources to produce a unit of the good than any other country **(23)**.

absolute poverty standard establishes a specific income level for a household of a given size, below which the household is judged to be living in a state of poverty **(40)**.

accounting profits are enterprise revenues minus explicit enterprise costs **(39)**.

activist policy selects monetary and fiscal policy actions on the basis of the economic conditions and changes that are perceived as economic conditions change **(20)**.

adaptive expectations are expectations of the future that people form from past experience and modify only gradually as experience unfolds **(17)**.

administrative-command economy is an economic system in which the Communist party provides overall direction, a state planning apparatus determines the uses of resources, capital is owned by the state, and managerial rewards are based upon fulfillment of output targets **(4)**.

adverse-selection problem occurs when a buyer or seller enters a disadvantageous contract on the basis of incomplete or inaccurate information because the cost of obtaining the relevant information makes it difficult to determine whether the deal is a good one or a bad one **(35)**.

adverse supply shock occurs when the short-run aggregate supply curve shifts to the left, raising the price level and reducing output **(9)**.

agent is a party that acts for, on behalf of, or as a representative of a principal **(28)**.

aggregate demand curve (AD) shows the levels of real GDP that agents (households, businesses, government and foreigners) are prepared to buy at different price levels **(9)**.

aggregate expenditure (AE) schedule shows the relationship between the desired amount of total spending $[C + I + G + (X - M)]$ and income **(11)**.

aggregate production function shows the relationship between the total output produced by the economy and the total labor, capital, and land inputs used by the economy **(36)**.

allocation is the apportionment of scarce resources to specific productive uses or to particular persons or groups **(2)**.

arbitrage is buying in a market where a commodity is cheap and reselling it in a market where the commodity is more expensive **(35)**.

assets are anything of any value that is owned **(15)**.

auction market is a market in which the market price is renegotiated on a regular basis **(20)**.

automatic stabilizers are government spending or taxation actions that take place without any deliberate government control and that tend automatically to dampen the business cycle **(12)**.

autonomous changes in taxes and government spending are independent of changes in income **(12)**.

autonomous expenditure multiplier ($\Delta Y/\Delta I$) is the ratio of the change in output to the change in autonomous investment, government consumption, or net export spending **(11)**.

autonomous expenditures are expenditures that are independent of income changes **(11)**.

average fixed cost (AFC) is fixed cost divided by output: $\text{AFC} = \text{FC} \div Q$ **(29)**.

average propensity to consume (APC) is consumption divided by income, or C/Y **(8)**.

average revenue (AR) equals total revenue (TR) divided by output **(31)**.

average tax rate is the ratio of the tax payment to taxable income **(12, 42)**.

average total cost (ATC) is total cost divided by output, or the sum of average variable cost and average fixed cost:

$$ATC = TC \div Q = AVC + AFC \qquad \textbf{(29)}.$$

average variable cost (AVC) is variable cost divided by output:

$$AVC = VC \div Q \qquad \textbf{(29)}.$$

balance of payments is a summary record of a country's economic transactions with foreign residents over a year or any other period **(25)**.

balance sheet summarizes the current financial position of a firm by comparing the firm's *assets* and *liabilities* **(15)**.

balanced-budget multiplier is the multiplier when there are equal changes in government spending and taxes. It always equals 1 **(11)**.

bank money consists of deposits in checking accounts **(14)**.

bankruptcy occurs when a corporation cannot pay its bills or its interest obligations **(28)**.

barrier to entry is any advantage that existing firms hold over firms that might seek to enter the market **(33)**.

barter is a system of exchange where products are traded for other products rather than for money **(3)**.

beneficial supply shock occurs when the short-run aggregate supply curve shifts to the right, reducing the price level and raising output **(9)**.

benefit principle of taxation states that those who benefit from the public expenditure should pay the tax that finances it **(42)**.

bonds are obligations that bind the issuer to pay a fixed sum of money (the principal) at maturity and also to pay a fixed sum of money annually until the maturity date. This fixed annual payment is called *interest,* or the *coupon payment* **(28)**.

budget line represents all the combinations of goods the consumer is able to buy, given a certain income and set prices. The budget line shows the consumption possibilities available to the consumer **(27A)**.

bureaucrat is a nonelected government official responsible for carrying out a specific, narrowly defined task **(43)**.

business cycle is the pattern of upward and downward movements in the general level of real business activity **(6)**.

capital consists of the equipment, plants, buildings, and inventories that are available to society **(2)**.

capital gain is the increase in the market value of any asset (stocks, bonds, houses, automobiles, art) above the price originally paid. The capital gain is *realized* when the asset is sold **(28, 42)**.

capitalism is an economic system characterized by private ownership of the factors of production, market allocation of resources, and the use of economic incentives **(4)**.

capital productivity measures output per unit of capital input **(22)**.

cartel is an arrangement that allows the participating firms to operate the industry as a shared monopoly **(33)**.

cash leakage occurs when a check is cashed and not deposited in a checking account. This cash remains in circulation outside of the banking system **(15)**.

***ceteris paribus* problem** occurs when the effect of one factor on another is masked by changes in other factors **(1)**.

change in demand is a shift in the entire demand curve because of a change in a factor other than the good's price **(5)**.

change in quantity demanded is a movement along the demand curve because of a change in the good's price **(5)**.

change in quantity supplied is a movement along the supply curve because of a change in the good's price **(5)**.

change in supply is a shift in the entire supply curve because of a change in a factor other than the good's price **(5)**.

check is a directive to the check writer's bank to pay lawful money to the bearer of the check **(14)**.

circular-flow diagram summarizes the flows of goods and services from producers to households and the flows of the factors of production from households to business firms **(3)**.

collective bargaining is the process whereby a union bargains with management as the representative of all union employees **(38)**.

commercial banks are banks that have been chartered either by a state agency or by the U.S. Treasury's Comptroller of the Currency to make loans and receive deposits **(15)**.

commodity money is money whose value as a commodity is as great as its value as money **(14)**.

common stock confers voting privileges but no prior claim on dividends. Common stock dividends are paid only if they are declared by the board of directors in any given year **(28)**.

compensating wage differentials are the higher wages or fringe benefits that must be paid to compensate workers for undesirable job characteristics **(37)**.

competing ends are the different purposes for which resources can be used **(2)**.

complements are two goods related such that the demand for one falls when the price of the other rises (or the demand for one rises when the price of the other falls) **(5)**.

concentration ratio is the percentage of industry sales accounted for by the *x* largest firms; this is called the *x*-firm concentration ratio **(33)**.

conglomerate merger occurs when one company takes over another company in a different line of business **(34)**.

conscious parallelism occurs when rival firms follow the same pricing and output rules without formal agreement but in accordance with customary industry business practices **(33)**.

constant-cost industry is relatively small and, hence, can expand or contract without significantly affecting the terms at which factors of production used in the industry are purchased. Hence, the long-run industry supply curve for a constant-cost industry is horizontal **(30)**.

constant-money-growth rule states that the money supply should increase at a fixed percentage each year **(16)**.

constant returns to scale are present when an increase in output does not change long-run average costs of production **(29)**.

consumer equilibrium occurs when the consumer has spent all income and marginal utilities per dollar for each good purchased are equal ($MU_A/P_A = MU_B/P_B$). At this point, the consumer is not inclined to change purchases unless some other factor (such as prices, income, or preferences) changes **(27)**.

consumers' surplus is the excess of the total consumer benefit that a good provides beyond consumer cost **(27, 30)**.

consumption/income schedule shows the amount of desired consumption at different levels of income **(8)**.

contestable market is one in which: (1) entry and exit by new firms is completely free; (2) the new firms can produce with the same costs as the established firms; (3) firms can easily dispose of their fixed assets by selling them elsewhere (fixed costs are not sunk but are recoverable); (4) customers buy from the firm (or firms) that first offers the lowest price **(33)**.

contractionary fiscal policy lowers aggregate demand by lowering government spending or by raising tax rates **(12)**.

contrived scarcity is the production of less than the economically efficient quantity of a good by a monopoly **(32)**.

convertible stock is a hybrid between a stock and a bond. The owner of convertible stock receives fixed interest payments but has the privilege of converting the convertible stock into common stock at a fixed rate of exchange **(28)**.

corporation is a business enterprise that has the status of a legal person and is authorized by law to act as a single person. The stockholders elect a board of directors that appoints the management of the corporation **(28)**.

countercyclical monetary policy increases aggregate demand when output is falling too much (or when its rate of growth is declining) and reduces aggregate demand when output is rising too rapidly **(16)**.

countervailing duty is a duty imposed on imports subsidized by the governments of the exporting country **(24)**.

Cournot oligopoly exists when (1) the product is homogenous; (2) each firm supposes that its rivals will continue to produce their current outputs independently of that firm's choice of outputs; (3) there is a fixed number of firms **(33)**.

CPI (consumer price index) measures changes in consumer prices paid by households **(6)**.

craft union represents workers of a single occupation **(38)**.

credible threat is the commitment of significant resources by an oligopolist to convince potential entrants to the oligopolistic industry that entry would result in severe losses for the entrant **(33)**.

credit, or capital, markets facilitate the exchange of financial assets in a modern society **(39)**.

credit rationing occurs when interest rates are not allowed to rise to the rate at which the demand for loans equals the supply of loans. In this situation, the demand for investment funds at the prevailing interest rate exceeds the supply **(16)**.

cross-price elasticity of demand (E_{xy}) is the percentage change in demand of the first product (x) divided by the percentage change in the price of the related product (y) **(26)**.

crowding out occurs when an increase in autonomous spending pushes up interest rates and crowds out some of the private investment spending that would otherwise have taken place **(11)**.

current account balance equals exports of goods (merchandise) and services minus imports of goods (merchandise) and services minus net unilateral transfers abroad **(25)**.

cyclical deficit is the part of the deficit caused by movements in the business cycle **(13)**.

cyclical unemployment is unemployment associated with general downturns in the economy **(18)**.

deadweight loss is a loss to society of consumer or producer surplus that is not offset by anyone else's gain **(32)**.

decreasing costs are present when the cost of production per unit decrease as the number of units produced increases **(23)**.

deficit financing is the borrowing of funds in credit markets to finance a government deficit **(42)**.

deflation is a general decline in prices **(6)**.

deflationary gap exists when the equilibrium level of output falls short of the natural level of output **(9)**.

demand for a good or service is the amount people are prepared to buy under specific circumstances during the specified time period **(5)**.

demand deposit is a deposit of funds that can be withdrawn ("demanded") from a depository institution (such as a bank) at any time without restrictions. The funds are usually withdrawn by writing a check **(14)**.

demand shock is an *unanticipated* shift in the aggregate demand schedule **(21)**.

demand-side inflation occurs when aggregate demand increases and pulls prices up **(17)**.

demographic transition is the process by which countries change from rapid population growth to slow population growth as they modernize **(22)**.

dependent variable —denoted by *Y*—changes as a result of a change in the value of another variable **(1A)**.

deposit multiplier is the ratio of the change in total deposits to the change in reserves **(15)**.

depreciation is the decrease in the economic value of capital goods as they are used in the production process **(7, 39)**.

depression is a very severe downturn in economic activity that lasts for several years. Real output declines during this period by a significant amount, and unemployment rises to very high levels **(6)**.

derived demand is the demand for a factor of production that results (is derived) from the demand for the goods and services a factor of production helps to produce **(36)**.

direct crowding out occurs when an increase in government spending substitutes for private spending by providing similar goods **(12)**.

discouraged worker has stopped looking for a job after becoming convinced (after an unsuccessful job search) that it is not possible to find a suitable job **(18)**.

discretionary fiscal policies are government spending and taxation actions that have been deliberately taken to achieve macroeconomic goals **(12)**.

diseconomies of scale are present when an increase in output causes long-run average costs to increase **(29)**.

dissaving means that total saving is negative; that is, consumption spending exceeds disposable income. The economy is either increasing its indebtedness or financing consumption by drawing down its savings **(8)**.

dumping occurs when a country sells a good in another country for less than the price charged in the home country **(24)**.

earnings per share (EPS) is the annual profit of the corporation divided by the number of shares outstanding **(28)**.

economic development is measured by per capita GDP, industrial structure, population dynamics, and the health and education of the population **(20)**.

economic efficiency exists when it is impossible to make everyone better off by reallocating resources—in other words, making one person better off must necessarily be at the expense of someone else **(32)**.

economic growth is the expansion of the real output of the economy, or the increase of the real output of goods and services **(6)**; is an increase in *real GDP* from one period to the next; an increase from one period to the next in *real GDP per capita,* which is real GDP divided by the country's population **(22)**.

economic inefficiency exists when it is possible to make everyone better off by reallocating resources—in other words, when at least one person could be made better off without hurting anyone else **(32)**.

economic profits are revenues in excess of total opportunity costs (which include both actual payments and sacrificed alternatives). They are profits in excess of normal profits **(30, 39)**.

economic rent is the amount by which the payment to a factor exceeds its opportunity cost **(39)**.

economic system is the set of property rights, resource allocation arrangements, and incentives that a society uses to solve the economic problem **(4)**.

economics studies how people choose to use their limited resources (land, labor, and capital goods) to produce, exchange, and consume goods and services **(1)**; the study of how *scarce resources* are *allocated* among *competing ends* **(2)**.

economies of scale are present when large output volumes can be produced at a lower cost per unit than small output volumes **(28)**; are present when an increase in output causes long-run average costs to fall **(29)**.

economies of scope exist when it is cheaper to produce products A and B in the same firm than in two separate firms **(31)**.

effectiveness lag is the time it takes the change in the money supply to affect the economy **(16)**.

efficiency occurs when the economy is using its resources so well that producing more of one good results in less of other goods: resources are neither misallocated nor unemployed **(2)**.

efficiency-wage model states that it is rational for certain firms to pay workers a wage rate above equilibrium to improve worker performance and productivity **(37)**.

employee association represents employees in a particular profession in order to both maintain professional standards and improve conditions of pay and work **(38)**.

entitlement program requires the government to pay benefits to anyone who meets eligibility requirements **(12)**.

entrepreneur one who organizes, manages, and assumes the risks for an enterprise **(2)**.

equilibrium (market-clearing) price is the price at which the quantity demanded by consumers equals the quantity supplied by producers **(5)**.

equilibrium price of a good or service is that price at which the amount of the good people are prepared to buy (demand) equals the amount offered for sale (supply) **(3)**.

excess reserves are reserves in excess of required reserves. Excess reserves equal total reserves minus required reserves **(15)**.

exclusion costs are the costs of preventing those who do not have property rights from enjoying a specific good **(41)**.

exhaustible (or nonrenewable) resource is any resource of which there is a finite amount in the long run because the stock is fixed by nature **(41)**.

exhaustive expenditures are government purchases of goods and services that divert resources from the private sector, making them no longer available for private use **(42)**.

expansionary fiscal policy increases aggregate demand by raising government spending and/or by lowering tax rates **(12)**.

export promotion occurs when a country encourages exports by subsidizing the production of goods for export **(22)**.

extensive growth occurs when the total amount of land, labor, and capital inputs expands **(22)**.

external costs (or benefits) are the costs (or benefits) borne (or enjoyed) by someone other than the agent producing (or consuming) a good **(32)**.

external debt is national debt owned by citizens of other countries **(13)**.

externalities exist when an economic activity results in direct economic costs or benefits for third parties not immediately involved in the activity **(32)**; exist when a producer or consumer does not bear the full marginal cost or enjoy the full marginal benefit of an economic action **(41)**.

factor productivity increases when more output is produced per unit of factor input **(22)**.

factors of production, or resources, are the inputs used to produce goods and services. They can be divided into three categories: land, labor, and capital **(2)**.

fallacy of composition is the assumption that what is true for each part taken separately is also true for the whole or, in reverse, that what is true for the whole is true for each part considered separately **(1)**.

false-cause fallacy is the assumption that because two events occur together, one event has caused the other **(1)**.

feedback rule establishes a feedback relationship between activist policy and the state of the economy **(20)**.

fiat money is a government-created money whose value or cost as a commodity is less than its value as money **(14)**.

final goods are goods that are destined for final use by consumers or firms, such as bread or investment goods **(7)**.

financial intermediaries borrow funds from one group of economic agents (people or firms with savings) and lend to other agents **(15)**.

fine-tuning is the frequent use of discretionary monetary and fiscal policy to counteract even small movements in business activity **(20)**.

fiscal policy is the use of government spending and taxation to pursue macroeconomic goals **(12)**.

fixed costs (FC) are those costs that do not vary with output **(29)**.

fixed exchange rate is a rate set by government decree or intervention within a small range of variation **(25)**.

fixed investment is investment in plant, structures, and equipment **(7)**.

floating exchange rate is freely determined by the interaction of supply and demand **(25)**.

foreign exchange is the national currency of another country that is needed to carry out international transactions **(25)**.

foreign saving equals imports minus exports **(7)**.

foreign-trade effect occurs when a rise in the domestic price level (holding foreign prices and the exchange rate constant) lowers the aggregate quantity demanded by pushing down net exports $(X - M)$ **(9)**.

free good is an item for which there exists an amount available that is greater than the amount people want at a zero price **(2)**.

free rider enjoys the benefits of a good or service without paying the cost **(41)**.

frictional unemployment is associated with the changing of jobs in a dynamic economy **(18)**.

full-employment deficit (or **surplus**) is what the government budget surplus or deficit would have been had the economy been operating at the natural level of output (full employment) **(13)**.

functional distribution of income is the distribution of income among the four broad classes of productive factors—land, labor, capital, and entrepreneurship **(36)**.

futures market is an organized market in which a buyer and seller agree now on the price of a commodity to be delivered at some specified date in the future **(35)**.

GDP deflator measures the change in the prices of all final goods and services (consumer goods, investment goods, and government) produced by the economy **(6)**.

GDP gap is the difference between current GDP and potential GDP (the output the economy would conceivably have produced at full employment) and is a measure of the social cost of unemployed resources **(20)**.

GDP per capita is a country's GDP divided by its population **(7)**.

government allocation occurs when government authorities determine who gets scarce goods **(2)**.

government debt is the cumulated sum of outstanding IOUs that government owes its creditors **(42)**.

government deficit is an excess of total government outlays over total government spending **(13, 42)**.

government surplus is an excess of total government revenues over total government outlays **(13, 42)**.

gradualist policy calls for steady reductions in monetary growth spread over a period of years to combat accelerating inflation **(19)**.

Gresham's law states that *bad money drives out good.* When depreciated, mutilated, or debased currency is circulated along with money of high value, the good money will either disappear from circulation or circulate at a premium **(14)**.

gross domestic income (GDI) is approximately the sum of all income earned by the factors of production **(7)**.

gross domestic product (GDP) is the market value of all final goods and services produced by the factors of production located in the country during a period of one year **(7)**.

gross national product (GNP) is the market value of all final goods and services produced by the factors of production supplied by U.S. residents, whether the residents are located in the U.S. or abroad **(7)**.

growth distortion is the measurement of changes in a variable over time that does not reflect the concurrent change in other relevant variables with which the variable should be compared, such as population size **(1A)**.

halfway rule states that when the demand curve can be represented by a straight line, the marginal revenue curve bisects the horizontal distance between the demand curve and the vertical axis **(31)**.

hedging is a temporary substitution of a futures market transaction for an intended spot transaction **(35)**.

horizontal equity exists when those with equal abilities to pay do pay the same amount of tax **(42)**.

horizontal merger is a merger of two firms in the same line of business (such as two insurance companies or two shoe manufacturers) **(34)**.

household production is work in the home, including such activities as meal preparation, do-it-yourself repair, childrearing, and cleaning **(37)**.

human capital is the accumulation of past investments in schooling, training, and health that raise the productive capacity of people **(2)**; the value of all investments in the capacity of a worker to earn income **(37)**.

human-resource policy is the use of government training programs and unemployment services to lower the natural rate of unemployment **(19)**.

hyperinflation is a very rapid and accelerating rate of inflation. Prices might double every month or even double daily or hourly **(6)**.

hypothesis is a tentative assumption about a particular aspect of the relationship among several events or factors **(1)**.

immediate run is a period of time so short that the quantity supplied cannot be changed at all. In the immediate run—sometimes called the *momentary period* or *market period*—supply curves are perfectly inelastic **(26)**.

implicit contract is an agreement between an employer and employees concerning conditions of pay, employment, and unemployment that is unwritten but understood by both parties **(18)**.

import quota is a quantitative limitation on the amount of imports of a specific product during a given period **(24)**.

import substitution occurs when a country substitutes domestic production for imports by subsidizing domestic production through tariffs, quotas, and other devices **(22)**.

incidence of a tax is the actual distribution of the burden of tax payments **(42)**.

income effect is the change in the quantity of X demanded that is attributable to the welfare change that accompanies the price change **(27, 27A)**.

income elasticity of demand (E_i) is the percentage change in the demand for a product divided by the percentage change in income, holding all prices fixed **(26)**.

incomes policy is a set of government rules, guidelines, or laws that influence wage and price increases **(17)**.

increasing costs are present when opportunity cost per unit increases as the number of units produced increases **(23)**.

increasing-cost industry is one where, as the industry expands, the factor prices of resources used in the industry are bid upward. As industry output contracts, the prices of these factors fall. Hence, the long-run industry supply curve for an increasing-cost industry is upward sloping **(30)**.

independent variable —denoted by X—causes the change in the value of the dependent variable **(1A)**.

indexing is the tying of tax rates to the rate of inflation. Tax rates are lowered as prices generally increase **(42)**.

indifference curve shows all the alternative combinations of two goods that yield the same total satisfaction to a particular consumer and among which the consumer is indifferent **(27A)**.

industrial union represents employees of an industry regardless of their specific occupation **(38)**.

industry or **market supply curve** is, in the short run, the horizontal summation of the supply curves of each firm, which in turn are those portions of the firms' MC curve located above minimum AVC **(30)**.

inferior good is one for which demand falls as income increases, holding all prices constant **(5)**.

inflation is a general increase in prices **(6)**.

inflation distortion is the measurement of the dollar value of a variable over time without adjustment for inflation over that period **(1A)**.

inflationary gap exists when the equilibrium level of output exceeds the natural level of output **(9)**.

information costs are the costs of acquiring information on prices, product qualities, and product performance **(35)**.

in-kind income consists primarily of benefits—such as free public education, school lunch programs, public housing, or food stamps—for which the recipient is not required to pay **(40)**.

intensive growth occurs when available inputs are used more effectively **(22)**.

interest is the price of credit, usually the annual amount as a percentage of the amount borrowed **(3)**; the price of credit determined in credit markets, where the amount businesses wish to invest is balanced with the amount people are prepared to save **(39)**.

interest rate measures the yearly cost of borrowing as a percentage of the amount loaned **(39)**.

interest-rate effect occurs when desired spending decreases as increases in the price level push up interest rates in credit markets **(9)**.

interest-rate target is a rate of interest that the Fed seeks to achieve through its monetary policy **(16)**.

intermediaries buy in order to sell again or simply bring together a buyer and a seller **(35)**.

intermediate goods are goods used to produce other goods, such as wheat for making flour or flour for making bread **(7)**.

internalizing an externality involves placing private price tags on external costs (or benefits) so that private and social costs (or benefits) coincide **(41)**.

internal debt is national debt owned by the citizens of that country **(13)**.

internal labor market is used by a firm when it fills its jobs by promoting or transferring workers it already employs **(37)**.

inventory investment is the increase (or decrease) in the value of the stocks of inventories that businesses have on hand **(7)**.

investment is addition to the stock of capital **(2)**.

investment demand curve shows the amount of investment desired at different interest rates **(8)**.

***IS* curve** shows all the combinations of interest rates and real income that are consistent with goods market equilibrium (in which desired investment equals desired saving) **(11A)**.

isocost line shows all the combinations of labor and capital that have the same total costs **(29A)**.

isoquant shows the various combinations of two inputs (such as labor and capital) that produce the same output **(29A)**.

Keynesian equilibrium occurs when the economy produces an output that equals desired aggregate expenditures; it is attained at that output at which desired investment equals desired saving **(11)**.

kinked demand curve results when other firms match a firm's price decreases but do not match its price increases **(33)**.

labor is the combination of physical and mental talents that human beings contribute to production **(2)**.

labor force equals the number of persons employed plus the number unemployed **(6)**; consists of employed and unemployed persons 16 years of age or older who either have jobs or are looking for and available for jobs **(18)**.

labor market is an arrangement that brings buyers and sellers of labor services together to agree on pay and working conditions **(37)**.

labor productivity measures output per unit (usually per hour) of labor input **(22)**.

labor shortage occurs when the number of workers firms wish to hire at the prevailing wage rate exceeds the number willing to work at that wage rate **(37)**.

labor surplus occurs when the number of workers willing to work at the prevailing wage rate exceeds the number that firms wish to employ at that wage rate **(37)**.

labor union is a collective organization of workers and employees whose objective is to improve conditions of pay and work **(38)**.

laissez-faire means a hands-off government policy towards the economy. Government intervention in macroeconomic affairs should be strictly limited **(10)**.

land is a catchall term that covers all of nature's bounty—minerals, forests, land, water resources, oxygen, and so on **(2)**.

law of comparative advantage states that it is better for people (or countries) to specialize in those activities in which their advantages over other people are greatest or in which their disadvantages compared to others are the smallest **(3, 23)**.

law of demand states that there is a negative (or inverse) relationship between the price of a good and the quantity demanded, holding other factors constant **(5)**.

law of diminishing marginal rate of substitution states that as more of one good (A) is consumed, the amount of another good (B) that the consumer is willing to sacrifice for one unit of good A declines **(27A)**.

law of diminishing marginal utility states that as more of a good or service is consumed during any given time period, its marginal utility declines, if the consumption of everything else is held constant **(27)**.

law of diminishing returns states that when the amount of one input is increased in equal increments, holding all other inputs constant, the result is ever smaller increases in output **(2)**; states that as ever larger amounts of a variable input are combined with fixed inputs, eventually the extra product attributable to each additional amount of the variable input must decline **(29)**.

law of increasing costs states that as more of a particular commodity is produced, its opportunity cost per unit increases **(2)**.

layoff is a suspension of employment, without pay and without prejudice, that lasts 7 days or more. The laid-off worker may be recalled to his or her old job if economic conditions improve **(18)**.

least-cost rule states that the least-cost combination of two factors can be found at the point where a given isoquant is tangent to the lowest isocost line. In other words, the least-cost combination of two factors can be found where

$$\frac{P_L}{MPP_L} = \frac{P_C}{MPP_C} \qquad \textbf{(29A)}.$$

leisure is time spent in any activity other than work in the labor force or work in the home **(37)**.

less developed country (LDC) is a country with a per capita income far below that of a typical advanced country **(22)**.

level of economic development is measured by per capita GDP, industrial structure, population dynamics, and the health and education of the population **(22)**.

liabilities are anything owed to other economic agents **(15)**.

line-item veto authority is presidential authority to veto specific spending appropriations **(12)**.

liquidity is the ease and speed with which an asset can be converted into a medium of exchange without risk of loss **(14)**.

liquidity preference (LP) curve shows the demand for money as the nominal interest rate changes, holding other factors constant **(14)**.

***LM* curve** shows all the combinations of interest rates and real income that bring about equality between the demand for money and the supply of money **(11A)**.

loanable funds comprise the amount of lending from all households, governments, and businesses, or the bank credit made available to borrowers in credit markets **(39)**.

logrolling is the trading of votes to secure a favorable outcome on decisions of more intense interest to each voter **(43)**.

long run is a period of time long enough for new firms to enter the market, for old firms to disappear, and for existing plants to be expanded. In the long run, firms have more flexibility in adjusting to price changes **(26)**; a period of time long enough to vary all inputs **(29)**.

long-run macroeconomic equilibrium is achieved when inflationary or deflationary gaps are no longer present. This occurs when SRAS intersects AD at the natural level of output **(9)**.

long-run average cost (LRAC) consists of the minimum average cost for each level of output when all factor inputs are variable (and when factor prices and the state of technology are fixed) **(29)**.

long-run industry supply curve shows the quantities that the industry is prepared to supply at different prices *after* the entry and exit of firms is completed **(30)**.

Lorenz curve shows the percentages of all income earned by households at successive income levels. The cumulative percentage of households (ranked from lowest to highest incomes) is plotted on the horizontal axis of the Lorenz curve, and the cumulative share of income earned by each cumulative percentage of households is plotted on the vertical axis **(40)**.

luxuries are those products that have an income elasticity of demand greater than 1 **(26)**.

M1 is the sum of currency (paper money and coins), demand deposits at commercial banks held by the nonbanking public, travelers' checks, and other checkable deposits like NOW (negotiable order of withdrawal) accounts and ATS (automatic transfer services) accounts **(14)**.

M2 equals M1 plus savings and small time deposits, money-market mutual-fund shares, and other highly liquid assets **(14)**.

macroeconomics is the study of the economy as a whole, rather than individual markets, consumers, and producers **(1)**.

majority rule is a system of voting in which a government action or decision is approved if more than 50 percent of the voters approve **(43)**.

managerial coordination is the disposition of the firm's resources according to the directives of the firm's manager(s) **(28)**.

marginal analysis aids decision making by examining the consequences of making relatively small changes from the current state of affairs **(1)**.

marginal cost (MC) is the change in total cost (or equivalently in variable cost) divided by the increase in output; or, alternatively, the increase in costs per unit of increase in output:

$$MC = \frac{\Delta TC}{\Delta Q} = \frac{\Delta VC}{\Delta Q} \quad \textbf{(29)}.$$

marginal factor cost (MFC) is the extra cost to the firm per unit increase in the amount of the factor; it is the increase in costs divided by the increase in the amount of the factor **(36)**.

marginal physical product (MPP) of a factor of production is the change in output divided by the change in the quantity of the input, holding all other inputs constant **(29)**.

marginal productivity theory of income distribution states that the functional distribution of income between land, labor, and capital is determined by the relative marginal revenue products of the different factors of production. The price of each factor will equal the marginal revenue product of that factor **(36)**.

marginal propensity to consume (MPC) is the change in desired consumption (C) per $1 change in income ($Y$):

$$MPC = \frac{\Delta C}{\Delta Y} \quad \textbf{(8)}.$$

marginal propensity to save (MPS) is the change in desired saving (S) per $1 change in income ($Y$):

$$MPS = \frac{\Delta S}{\Delta Y} \quad \textbf{(8)}.$$

marginal rate of substitution (MRS) is how much of one good a person is just willing to give up to acquire one unit of another good **(27A)**.

marginal revenue (MR) is the increase in total revenue (TR) that results from each 1-unit increase in the amount of output:

$$MR = \frac{\Delta TR}{\Delta Q} \quad \textbf{(30)};$$

the additional revenue raised per unit increase in quantity sold **(31)**.

marginal revenue product (MRP) of any factor of production is the extra revenue generated per unit increase in the amount of the factor **(36)**.

marginal-revenue schedule shows how marginal revenue changes as the quantity of output changes **(31)**.

marginal tax rate is the ratio of the increase in tax payments to an increase in income. The marginal tax rate shows how much extra taxes must be paid per dollar of extra earnings **(12, 42)**.

marginal utility (MU) of any good or service is the increase in utility that a consumer experiences when consumption of that good or service (and that good or service alone) is increased by 1 unit. In general,

$$MU = \frac{\Delta TU}{\Delta Q},$$

where TU is total utility and Q is the quantity of the good **(27)**.

marginal utility per dollar is the ratio MU/P and indicates the increase in utility from another dollar spent on the good **(27)**.

market is an arrangement that brings buyers and sellers together to exchange particular goods or services **(2, 5)**.

market demand curve is the demand of all persons participating in the market for a particular product **(5)**; shows the total quantities demanded by all consumers in the market at each price. It is the horizontal summation of all individual demand curves in that market **(27)**.

market failure occurs when the price system fails to yield the socially optimal quantity of a good **(41)**.

market test ensures that goods and services in the private sector yield a benefit equal to or greater than their cost **(43)**.

median voter on a public expenditure program wants more expenditure than half the remaining voters and less expenditures than the other half of the remaining voters **(43)**.

merchandise trade balance equals exports of merchandise minus imports of merchandise. If positive, it is the *merchandise trade surplus*. If negative, it is the *merchandise trade deficit* **(25)**.

microeconomics studies the economic decision making of firms and individuals in a market setting; it is the study of the economy on the small scale **(1)**.

midpoints elasticity formula for determining the elasticity of demand (E_d) for a given segment of the demand curve is E_d = the percent change in quantity demanded divided by the percent change in price = (the change in quantity demanded divided by the average of two quantities), divided by (the change in price divided by the average of two prices) **(26)**.

minimum efficient scale (MES) is the lowest level of output at which average costs are minimized **(29)**.

monetarism is the doctrine that monetary policy should follow a constant-money-growth rule **(16)**.

monetary-aggregate target is a particular money supply or growth rate of the money supply that the Fed seeks to achieve through monetary policy **(16)**.

monetary base is the sum of reserves on deposit at the Fed, all vault cash, and the currency in circulation **(15)**.

monetary policy is the deliberate control of the money supply and, in some cases, credit conditions for the purpose of achieving macroeconomic goals such as a certain level of unemployment or inflation **(16)**.

money is anything that is widely accepted in exchange for goods and services **(3)**.

money price is a price expressed in monetary units (such as dollars, francs, etc.) **(3)**.

money supply in an economy is the sum of all bank accounts and cash held by individuals and nonbank firms **(8)**.

monopolistic competition has four essential characteristics: (1) the number of sellers is large enough to enable each seller to act independently of the others; (2) the product is differentiated from seller to seller; (3) there is free entry into and exit from the industry; (4) sellers are price searchers **(31)**.

monopoly rent-seeking behavior is the use of political power and its accompanying resources to achieve or maintain a monopoly in order to gain the monopoly profits, or "rent" **(32)**.

monopsony is a firm that faces an upward-sloping supply curve for one or more factors of production. A *pure monopsony* is the only buyer of some input **(36)**.

moral-hazard problem exists when one of the parties to a contract has an incentive to alter his or her behavior after the contract is made at the expense of the second party. It arises because it is too costly for the second party to obtain information about the first party's postcontractual behavior **(35)**.

multinational corporation engages in foreign economic activities through its own affiliates located abroad, exercises direct control over the policies of these affiliates, and pursues business strategies that transcend national boundaries **(28)**.

multiple expansion of deposits of the money supply occurs when an increase in reserves causes an expansion of the money supply that is greater than the reserve increase **(15)**.

mutual interdependence is the characteristic whereby the actions of one firm invite reactions by other firms in a given industry **(33)**.

Nash equilibrium exists in an oligopolistic industry if each firm's profit-maximizing behavior is based on a correct guess about the behavior of rivals **(33)**.

national debt is the sum of outstanding federal government IOUs upon which interest and principal payments must be made **(13)**.

national income equals net national product minus indirect business taxes. National income equals the sum of all factor payments made to the factors of production in the economy **(7)**.

national income accounting defines and measures the total output of an economy and distinguishes the components of the total output **(7)**.

natural level of real GDP (y_n) is the output produced when the economy is operating at the natural rate of unemployment **(9)**.

natural monopoly exists when it is cheaper for one firm to produce the product over the relevant range of output than for two or more firms to do so **(34)**.

natural rate of unemployment is that unemployment rate at which there is an approximate balance between the number of unfilled jobs and the number of qualified job seekers **(6)**; that rate of unemployment that can be sustained without accelerating or decelerating inflation **(9).**

natural selection theory states that if business firms do not maximize profits, they will be unable to compete with other firms and will be driven out of the market or taken over by outsiders **(28).**

necessities are those products that have an income elasticity of demand less than 1 **(26).**

negative income tax (NIT) supplements incomes by making payments to recipients who earn less than a specified minimum income. Each payment will be an amount equal to the minimum income minus a given percentage of each dollar the recipient earns **(40).**

negative (inverse) relationship exists between two variables if an increase in the value of one variable is associated with a *reduction* in the value of the other variable **(1A).**

net national product (NNP) equals GNP minus depreciation **(7).**

net output or **value added** of an industry (or firm) is the output of that industry (or firm) minus its purchases from other industries (or firms) **(7).**

neutral tax cannot be altered by any change in private production, consumption, or investment decisions **(42).**

nominal GDP or **GDP in current dollars** is the value of final goods and services produced in a given year at that year's prevailing prices **(7).**

nominal interest rate is the interest rate paid on interest-bearing assets expressed in current dollars (unadjusted for inflation) **(14);** is the cost of borrowing expressed in terms of current dollars (unadjusted for inflation) **(39).**

nonactivist policy is independent of prevailing economic conditions and is held steady when economic conditions change **(20).**

noncompeting groups are labor suppliers differentiated by natural ability and abilities acquired through education, training, and experience to the extent that one group does not compete with another for jobs **(37).**

noncooperative oligopoly behavior occurs when mutually interdependent firms do not coordinate their actions but instead engage in strategic decision making **(33).**

nonexclusion characterizes a good if the extreme costs eliminate the possibility (or practicality) of excluding some people from using the good **(41).**

nonmarketed goods are exchanged through barter arrangements or acquired through do-it-yourself activities that would otherwise have been purchased in organized markets **(6).**

nonprice competition is the attempt to attract customers through improvements in product quality or service, thereby shifting the firm's demand curve to the right **(31).**

nonprohibitive tariff is a tariff that does not wipe out all imports of the product **(24).**

nonrival consumption characterizes a good if its consumption by one person does not reduce its consumption by others at a given level of production **(41).**

normal good is one for which demand increases when income increases, holding all prices constant **(5).**

normal profit is the return that the time and capital of an entrepreneur would earn in the best alternative employment. It also equals the return that is earned when total revenues equal total opportunity costs **(30);** normal profits are the profits required to keep resources in a particular business. They are earned when revenues equal opportunity costs **(39).**

normative economics is the study of *what ought to be* in the economy **(1).**

Okun's law states that for every 1 percentage point increase in the unemployment rate, there is a 2.5 percent drop in real GDP **(18).**

oligopoly is an industry characterized by: (1) recognized mutual interdependence; (2) moderate to high entry barriers; (3) relatively few firms; (4) price searching (firms are able to exercise varying degrees of control over price) **(33).**

opportunity cost of a particular action is the loss of the next best alternative **(2, 29).**

optimal-search rule is that people will continue to acquire economic information as long as the marginal benefits of gathering information exceed the marginal costs **(35).**

paradox of voting is that majority rule can yield inconsistent social choices. Even if each voter is perfectly rational, the majority of voters can choose *a* over *b*, *b* over *c*, and then *c* over *a* **(43).**

partnership is a business that is owned by two or more people (called partners) who make all the business decisions, who share the profits, and who bear the financial responsibility for any losses **(28).**

patent is an exclusive right granted to an inventor to make, use, or sell an invention for a term of 17 years in the United States **(32).**

perfect competition in an industry has the characteristics: (1) The market contains a large number of buyers and sellers. (2) Each buyer and seller has perfect information about prices and product. (3) The product being sold is homogeneous; that is, it not possible (or even worthwhile) to distinguish the product of one firm from that of other firms. (4) No barriers obstruct entry into or exit from the market; there is freedom of entry and exit. (5) All firms are price takers; no single seller is large enough to exert any control over the product price, so each seller accepts the market price as given **(30).**

perfectly competitive market is one in which: (1) the product's price is uniform; (2) buyers and sellers have perfect information about price and product quality; (3) there are large numbers of buyers and sellers; (4) no single buyer or seller purchases or sells enough to change the price **(5).**

perfectly elastic demand ($E_d = \infty$) is illustrated by a horizontal demand curve; quantity demanded is most responsive to price **(26).**

perfectly elastic supply ($E_s = \infty$) is illustrated by a horizontal supply curve; quantity supplied is most responsive to price **(26).**

perfectly inelastic demand ($E_d = 0$) is illustrated by a vertical demand curve; quantity demanded is least responsive to price **(26).**

perfectly inelastic supply ($E_s = 0$) is illustrated by a vertical supply curve; quantity supplied is least responsive to price **(26).**

permanent income is an average of the income that an individual anticipates earning over the long run **(12).**

personal disposable income equals personal income minus income tax payments **(7).**

personal distribution of income is the distribution of income among households, or how much income one family earns from the factors of production it owns relative to other families **(36).**

personal income equals national income *minus* retained corporate profits, corporate income taxes, and social insurance contributions *plus* transfer payments and government interest payments **(7).**

personal saving equals personal disposable income minus personal consumption expenditures **(7).**

Phillips curve shows a negative relationship between the unemployment rate and the inflation rate **(19).**

policy activism is the deliberate use of discretionary fiscal or monetary policy to achieve macroeconomic goals **(12).**

policy instruments are variables—such as the money supply, government spending, or tax rates—that affect output, employment, and prices **(20).**

political business cycles occur when the executive branch and Congress select expansionary policies that they believe will increase their chances of reelection **(19).**

positive (direct) relationship exists between two variables if an increase in the value of one variable is associated with an *increase* in the value of the other variable **(1A).**

positive economics is the study of *what is* in the economy **(1).**

preferences are a person's evaluations of goods and services independent of budget and price considerations **(27).**

preferred stock confers a prior claim on dividends but no voting privileges. Dividends on preferred stock must be paid before paying common stock dividends **(28).**

present value (PV) of money is the most anyone would pay today to receive the money in the future. The present value is sometimes called the *discounted value* because it is smaller than the amount to be received in the future **(28).**

price discrimination exists when the same product or service is sold at different prices to different buyers **(31).**

price/earnings (PE) ratio is the price of a share of stock divided by the earnings per share **(28).**

price elasticity of demand (E_d) is the percentage change in the quantity demanded divided by the percentage change in price **(26).**

price elasticity of supply (E_s) is the percentage change in the quantity supplied divided by the percentage change in price **(26).**

price index shows the cost of buying a given market basket of goods as a percentage of the cost of the same market basket in some base year **(6).**

price leader is an oligopolist whose price changes are consistently imitated by other firms in the industry **(33).**

price-level surprise occurs when the actual price level, P, is not equal to the expected price level, P_e **(21).**

price searcher is a firm with some degree of control over the price of the good or service it sells **(31);** in a factor market, a buyer of inputs whose purchases are large enough to affect the price of the input **(36).**

price system coordinates economic decisions by allowing resource owners to trade freely, buying and selling at whatever relative prices emerge in the marketplace **(3).**

price taker in a factor market is a buyer of an input whose purchses are not large enough to affect the price of the input; must accept the market as given.

principal is a party that has controlling authority and that engages an agent to act subject to the principal's control and instruction **(28).**

principal/agent problem exists when the firm (the principal) and the employee (its agent) have different goals and objectives for the employee's behavior **(37).**

principle of substitution states that practically no good is irreplaceable. Users are able to substitute one product for another when relative prices change **(3).**

principle of unintended consequences holds that policies may have ultimate or actual effects that differ from the intended or apparent effects **(1).**

prisoners' dilemma game is a game with two players in which both players benefit from cooperating, but in which each player has an incentive to cheat on the agreement **(33).**

private costs (or **benefits**) are the costs (or benefits) borne (or enjoyed) by the agent producing (or consuming) a good **(32).**

private saving is the sum of personal saving of individuals and of business savings (in the form of retained profits and depreciation) **(7).**

procyclical monetary policy decreases aggregate demand when output is falling and increases aggregate demand when output is rising **(16).**

producers' surplus represents the amount that producers receive in excess of the minimum value the producers would have been willing to accept **(30).**

production function summarizes the relationship between labor, capital, and land inputs and the maximum output these inputs can produce **(29).**

production possibilities frontier (PPF) shows the combination of goods that can be produced when the factors of production are used to their full potential **(2).**

profit maximization is the search by firms for the product quality, output, the price that give the firm the highest possible profits **(28).**

profit-maximization rule states that a firm will maximize profits by producing the level of output at which marginal revenue (MR) equals marginal cost (MC) **(30).**

progressive tax is one where the percentage of income paid as taxes increases as income increases **(42).**

prohibitive tariff is a tariff that is high enough to cut off all imports of the product **(24).**

property rights are the rights of an owner to buy, sell, or use and exchange property (i.e., goods, services, and assets) **(4).**

proportional tax is one where each taxpaying unit pays the same percentage of income as taxes **(42).**

public finance is the study of government revenues and expenditures at all levels of government—local, state, and federal **(42).**

public goods are characterized by nonrival consumption and nonexclusion **(41).**

purchasing-power parity (PPP) is the exchange rate between the currencies of two countries that is necessary in order for those countries to have the same costs of living **(25).**

pure economic rent is the price paid to a productive factor that is completely inelastic in supply. Land is the classic example of such a factor **(39).**

pure monopoly exists when (1) there is one seller in the market for some good or service that has no close substitutes; (2) barriers to entry protect the seller from competition **(31).**

quantity demanded is the amount of a good or service consumers are prepared to buy at a given price (during a specified time period), holding other factors constant **(5).**

quantity supplied of a good or service is the amount offered for sale at a given price, holding other factors constant **(5).**

quasi rent is a payment in excess of the short-run opportunity cost necessary to induce the owners of the resources to offer their resources for sale or rent in the short run **(39).**

rate of return of a capital good is that rate of interest for which the present value of the stream of marginal revenue products for each year of the good's life is equal to the cost of the good **(39).**

ratification of supply-side inflation results if the government increases the money supply to prevent supply-side shocks from raising unemployment **(17).**

rational expectations are expectations that people form by using all available information, relying not only on past experience but also on their predictions about the effects of present and future policy actions **(17);** expectations that people form about the inflation rate and the unemployment rate using their knowledge about current and future monetary and fiscal policy, business and consumer spending plans, and the behavior of the macroeconomy **(21).**

rational ignorance is a decision not to acquire information because the marginal cost exceeds the marginal benefit of gathering the information **(43).**

real interest rate is the nominal interest rate minus the anticipated rate of inflation and is expressed in constant dollars (adjusted for inflation) **(14, 39).**

real GDP or **GDP in constant dollars** measures the volume of real goods and services by removing the effects of rising prices on nominal GDP **(7).**

real-balance effect occurs when desired consumption falls as increases in the price level reduce the purchasing power of money balances, holding other factors constant **(9).**

real business cycle theory supposes that cyclical fluctuations arise from large random shocks to the rate of technological progress **(20).**

recession, as a general rule, occurs when real output declines for a period of 6 months or more **(6).**

recognition lag is the time it takes the Fed to decide to change the supply of money in response to a change in economic conditions **(16).**

recycling reintroduces used exhaustible resources (such as iron, metals, and petrochemicals) into the system, providing an alternative to production and reducing waste disposal costs **(41).**

regressive tax is one where the percentage of income paid as taxes decreases as income increases **(42).**

regulatory lag occurs when government regulators adjust rates some time after operating costs and the rate base have increased **(34).**

relative poverty standard defines the poor in terms of the income of others in some defined group **(40).**

relative price is a price expressed in terms of other related commodities **(3).**

required-reserve ratio is the amount of reserves required for each dollar of deposits **(15).**

reservation wage is the minimum wage offer that a job searcher will accept **(18).**

reservation price is the highest price at which the consumer will buy a good. Although the consumer will buy any good with a price lower than the reservation price, he or she will continue to search for a lower price only if the lowest price found exceeds the reservation price **(35).**

reserve requirements are rules that state the amount of reserves that a bank must keep on hand to back bank deposits **(15).**

reserves are the funds that the bank uses to satisfy the cash demands of its customers **(15).**

resources *See* factors of production.

rival consumption characterizes a good when the consumption of the good by one person lowers the consumption available to others at a given the level of production **(41).**

roundabout production is the production of goods that do not immediately meet consumption needs but may be used to produce more goods **(3).**

rule of reason stated that monopolies were in violation of the Sherman Act if they used unfair or illegal business practices. Being a monopoly in and of itself was not a violation of the Sherman Act **(34).**

saving/income schedule shows the amount of desired saving at different levels of income **(8).**

Say's law states that whatever aggregate output producers decide to supply will be demanded in the aggregate **(10).**

scarce good is an item for which there exists an amount available (offered to users) that is less than the amount people would want if it were given away free of charge **(2).**

scatter diagram consists of a number of separate points, each plotting the value of one variable (measured along the horizontal axis) against a value of another variable (measured along the vertical axis) for a specific time interval **(1A).**

scientific method is the process of formulating theories, collecting data, testing theories, and revising theories **(1).**

screening is the process by which employers select the most qualified workers on the basis of easily observable characteristics **(37).**

shortage results if at the current price the quantity demanded exceeds the quantity supplied; the price is too low to equate the quantity demanded with the quantity supplied **(5).**

short run is a period of time long enough for existing firms to produce more goods but not long enough for existing firms to expand their capacity or for new firms to enter the market. Thus, output can be varied, but only within the limits of existing plant capacity **(26);** a period of time so short that the existing plant and equipment cannot be varied; such inputs are fixed in supply. Additional output can be produced only by expanding the variable inputs of labor and raw materials **(29).**

short-run aggregate supply curve (SRAS) shows the levels of real GDP that firms are prepared to sell at different price levels, holding the anticipated price level and other factors constant **(9).**

short-run macroeconomic equilibrium occurs at that output and price level at which short-run aggregate supply equals aggregate demand **(9).**

short-run Phillips curve shows the negative relationship between inflation and unemployment when inflationary expectations are constant **(19).**

shutdown rule states that if a firm's revenues at all output levels are less than variable costs, it minimizes its losses by shutting down. If there is at least one output level at which revenues exceed variable costs, the firm should not shut down **(30).**

signals are credentials or qualifications—such as formal schooling—that can be acquired by workers and that employers believe to be indicators of productivity **(37).**

simple multiplier shows the impact on income of a change in autonomous spending or taxes when the price level and interest rates are not affected by such changes **(11).**

slope *of a curvilinear relationship* at a particular point is the slope of the straight line tangent to the curve at that point **(1A).**

slope *of a straight line* is the ratio of the rise (or fall) in Y over the run in X (**1A**).

social benefits equal private benefits plus external benefits (**32, 41**).

social costs equal private costs plus external costs (**32, 41**).

socialism is an economic system characterized by state ownership of the factors of production, the use of moral as well as economic incentives, resource allocation by economic plan, and centralized decision making (**4**).

sole proprietorship is owned by one individual who makes all the business decisions, receives the profits that the business earns, and bears the financial responsibility for losses (**28**).

special-interest groups are minority groups with intense, narrowly defined preferences about specific government policies (**43**).

speculators are those who buy or sell in the hope of profiting from market fluctuations (**35**).

spot (cash) market is a market where agreements between buyers and sellers are made now for payment and delivery of the product now (**35**).

stagflation is the combination of high unemployment rates and high inflation over a period of time (**6, 19**).

stock exchange is a market in which shares of stock of corporations are bought and sold and in which the prices of shares of stock are determined (**28**).

stock price index (such as the Dow Jones Industrial Average, the Standard & Poor's Index, and the New York Stock Exchange Index) measures the general movements of stock prices (**28**).

strike occurs when all unionized employees cease to work until management agrees to specific union demands (**38**).

structural unemployment results from the long-term decline of certain industries in response to rising costs, changes in consumer preferences, or technological change (**18**).

structural deficit is the deficit that would occur if there were no business cycle and the economy were operating at the natural level of real GDP (**13**).

substitutes are two goods related such that the demand for one rises when the price of the other rises (or the demand for one falls when the price of the other falls) (**5**).

substitution effect is the change in quantity of X demanded that occurs when the price of X changes and the consumer's utility or welfare is held constant (**27, 27A**).

sunk costs are fixed costs that cannot be recovered even in the long run (**33**).

supply of a good or service is the amount that firms are prepared to sell under specified circumstances during a specified time period (**5**).

supply shock is an unexpected shift in the short-run aggregate supply curve (**17, 21**).

supply-side economics maintains that lower marginal tax rates increase aggregate supply by increasing work effort and by encouraging risk taking and innovation (**12**).

supply-side inflation occurs when aggregate supply declines and pushes prices up (**17**).

surplus results if at the current price the quantity supplied exceeds the quantity demanded; the price is too high to equate the quantity demanded with quantity supplied (**5**).

systemic risk is the additional risk imposed on the economy as a whole arising from the failure of one bank or business unit (**15**).

***T*-accounts** show bank assets and liabilities (**15**).

tangent is a straight line that touches the curve at only one point (**1A**).

tariff is a tax levied on imports (**24**).

taxable income is the income that remains after all deductions and exemptions are subtracted. Taxes are levied on taxable income (**42**).

tax multiplier ($\Delta Y / \Delta T$) is the change in output divided by the change in the tax (**11**).

terms of trade are the rate at which two products can be exchanged for each other between countries (**23**).

theory is an explanation of the relationship among factors that may be crucial determinants of a phenomenon (**1**).

time deposit is a deposit of funds upon which a depository institution (such as a bank) can legally require 30 days notice of withdrawal and on which the financial institution pays the depositor interest (**14**).

total costs (TC) are variable costs plus fixed costs: $TC = VC + FC$ (**29**).

total factor productivity measures output per unit of combined labor and capital input (**22**).

total revenue (TR) of sellers in a market is equal to the price of the commodity times the quantity sold:

$$TR = P \times Q \qquad (26).$$

total revenue test uses the following criteria to determine elasticity:

1. If price and total revenue move in different directions, $E_d > 1$ (demand is elastic).
2. If price and total revenue move in the same direction, $E_d < 1$ (demand is inelastic).
3. If total revenue does not change when price changes, $E_d = 1$ (demand is unitary elastic) (**26**).

trade deficit is an excess of imports over exports (**13**).

transaction costs are the costs associated with bringing buyers and sellers together (**35**).

transfer payments are payments to recipients who have not supplied current goods or services in exchange for these payments (**7**); transfer income from one individual or organization to another (**42**).

trust is a combination of firms that sets common prices, agrees to restrict output, and punishes member firms who fail to live up to the agreement (**34**).

unanimity is the result of a vote in which all voters agree on or consent to a particular government action (**43**).

underground worker is one whose income is unreported or not fully reported to the government (**18**).

unemployment rate is the number of persons unemployed divided by the number in the labor force (**6**).

unintended investment is the difference between desired saving and desired investment at a given level of income (**11**).

utility is a numerical ranking of a consumer's preferences among different commodity bundles (**27**).

value added. *See* net output.

variable costs (VC) are those costs that do vary with output (**29**).

velocity of circulation is the number of times the average dollar is spent on final goods and services in 1 year's time (**10**).

vertical equity exists when those with a greater ability to pay bear a heavier tax burden (**42**).

vertical merger is a merger of two firms that are part of the same materials, production, or distribution network (such as a personal-computer manufacturer and a retail computer distribution chain or a machinery manufacturer and a machinery parts supplier) (**34**).

voluntary export restraint is an agreement between two governments in which the exporting country voluntarily limits the export of a certain product to the importing country (**24**).

wage/employment trade-off means that higher wages reduce the number of jobs; lower unemployment requires sacrificing higher wages (**38**).

wage/price spiral is the phenomenon of higher prices pushing wages higher and then higher wages pushing prices higher, or vice versa. This spiral is sustained when the monetary authorities ratify the resulting supply-side inflation (**17**).

wealth (or net worth) is the value of one's total assets minus one's liabilities (**40**).

X-inefficiency refers to the organizational slack that results from the lack of competition in monopolies. It is characterized by costs that are higher than necessary (**32**).

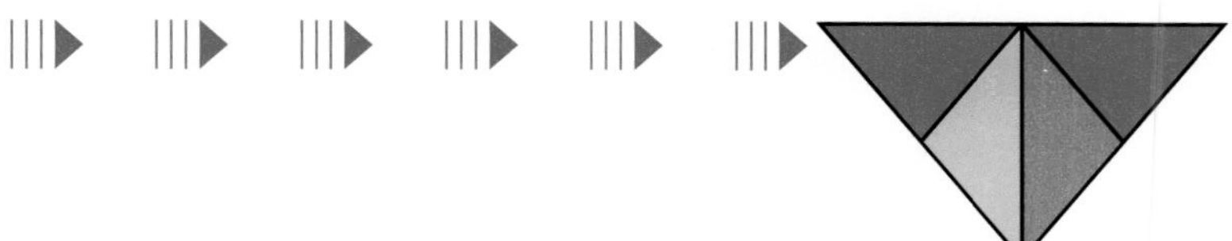

CREDITS

Example 1 figure in Appendix 1A, "The number of damaged O-rings per launch," from *Visual Explanations* by Edward R. Tufte (Cheshire, Connecticut: Graphics Press), Forthcoming. Reprinted by permission.

Example 2 figure in Chapter 6, from figure, "Tracking the Economy" from *The Wall Street Journal*, June 8, 1992. "Reprinted by permission of *The Wall Street Journal*, copyright © 1992 Dow, Jones & Company, Inc. All Rights Reserved Worldwide."

Example 4 figure in Chapter 12 from "How Competing Tax Proposals Compare," from "Proposals Indicate Bush Is Willing to Bend on the Issue of the Deficit," *The Wall Street Journal*, January 30, 1992. Reprinted by permission of *The Wall Street Journal*, copyright © 1992 Dow, Jones & Company, Inc. All Rights Reserved Worldwide.

Example 2 figure in Chapter 20, "200 Years of Booms and Busts," by Geoffrey Moore from *The Wall Street Journal*, August 8, 1991. "Reprinted by permission of *The Wall Street Journal*, Copyright © 1991 Dow, Jones & Company, Inc. All Rights Reserved Worldwide."

Example 5 figure in Chapter 21 from "Why Companies Delay Changing Prices," by Alan S. Blinder from *Scientific American,* March 1991, page 114. Reprinted by permission of the author.

Example 2 figure in Chapter 30 from Oil Price Outlook (constant 1987 dollars per barrel) from "We're Not Going to Freeze in the Dark," by James Cook, *Forbes,* June 27, 1988, p. 107. Reprinted by permission.

Example 2 figure in Chapter 34, "What a taxi medallion sells for" from *The New York Times*, October 6, 1991. "Copyright © 1991 by The New York Times Company. Reprinted by Permission.

Example 7 figure in Chapter 35 from "Investment Dartboard" from "Pro Stock-Pickers Outperform the Darts," *The Wall Street Journal,* December 6, 1991. Reprinted by permission of *The Wall Street Journal,* copyright © 1991 Dow, Jones & Company, Inc. All Rights Reserved Worldwide.

Example 1 figure in Chapter 36 from BASIC ECONOMICS by Roy Ruffin and Paul Gregory, copyright © 1989 HarperCollins*Publishers.*

Example 2 table in Chapter 40 from "Average Weekly Wages for Women and Men in Selected Narrowly Defined Occupations, 1985" from "Does the Market for Women's Labor Need Fixing?" *The Journal of Economic Perspectives,* Vol. 3, Winter 1989. Copyright © 1989 by The American Economic Association. Reprinted by permission.

Example 5 table in Chapter 40 from "Poverty in the U.S.: Why Is It So Persistent?" by Isabell B. Sawhill, *Journal of Economic Literatiure,* Vol. 26, No. 3, Sept. 1988, pp. 1073–1119. Reprinted by permission of the American Economic Association.

Example 1 in Chapter 41 from Ann Landers Column, "Creepy Neighbors." Permission granted by Ann Landers and Creators Syndicate.

Example 5 figure in Chapter 41, "Five Easy Pieces," from "Betting the Planet," *The New York Times*, December 2, 1990. Copyright © 1990 by The New York Times Company. Reprinted by permission. Top illustration adapted from photograph by Dan Borris/Outline.

Example 1 in Chapter 42 from "No Joke, U.S. Now a Tax Haven" by David R. Francis. Reprinted by permission from *The Christian Science Monitor.* Copyright © 1987 The Christian Science Publishing Society. All rights reserved.

NAME INDEX

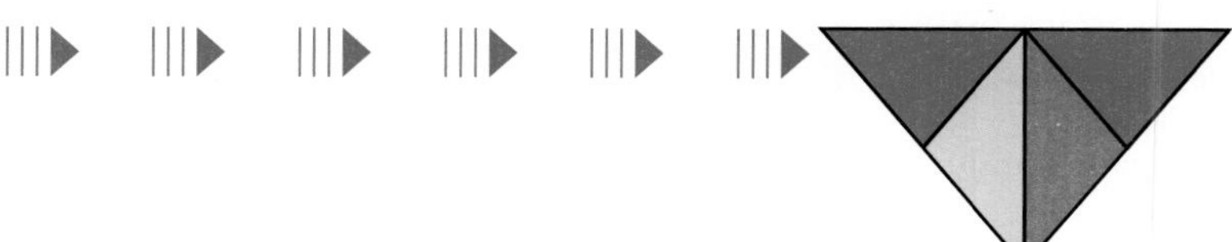

SUBJECT INDEX